Chambers
PHRASE
FILE

a unique crossword reference

Compiled by
Roger Prebble

Chambers

Published 1993 by Chambers Harrap Publishers Ltd
43–45 Annandale Street, Edinburgh EH7 4AZ.

British Library Cataloguing in Publication Data

A catalogue record for this book is
available from the British Library.

ISBN 0 550 19041 4

Typeset by Hewer Text Composition Services, Edinburgh
Printed in England by Clays Ltd, St Ives plc

CONTENTS

INTRODUCTION

In recent years, some crossword compilers have tended to become a little devious by adding a new dimension to their cluing to everyday answers. 'Instead of cluing "on the dot" for PUNCTUALLY,' they have thought, 'why not clue "punctually" for ON THE DOT?' Why not indeed?

One good reason has been that the poor solver had no decent reference book to help combat the use of these many and varied phrases and indeed of any combination of two words or more. Until now, that is.

In *Phrase File* these are exhaustively covered from a solver's and, to be fair, also from a compiler's viewpoint. Here are thousands of phrases, from 3 to 15 letters, selected from Chambers English language database specifically for crosswords. Every entry in the book has been evaluated and assessed on its merits as the likely answer to a clue. The book has two sections, the entries in each arranged differently to serve differing requirements (see How to Use this Book on page v). An aid and an inspiration to both solvers and compilers, *Phrase File* makes a unique contribution to anyone's crossword library.

You can REST ASSURED that everyone, including inveterate browsers, will find no HIDDEN AGENDA, just a TREASURE CHEST of entries that, far from leaving them SICK AS A PARROT, will make them PLEASED AS PUNCH.

HOW TO USE THIS BOOK

Easy access to words is essential in crossword reference books. This has been a high priority for all the volumes in this series, and to this end *Phrase File* has a unique dual listing.

In the first half of the book, entries are arranged in individual word-length order as well as overall 3- to 15- letter word-length order. Thus, if you are looking for a phrase that the clue tells you is split 4,3,7 you can turn to the **14 letters** section and find a further breakdown of all **4,3,7** phrases. These individual listings are in number order from the left-hand number. Therefore, within **14 Letters** for instance, **4,3,7** is followed by **4,4,6** and **4,5,5** etc.

The second half, for compilers and browsers especially, enables the reader to scan all the entries of, say, 12 letters together, regardless of word-breaks within.

All else is self-evident, but the following notes clarify some specific points.

Notes

a) Plurals are in general not listed, but a few appear where they are more common than the singular (eg BAKED BEANS, SALTED PEANUTS).

b) Where relevant, all parts of the verb are listed (eg PASSED THE BUCK, PASSES THE BUCK, and PASSING THE BUCK are listed as well as PASS THE BUCK).

c) Alphabeticization in the Total Length section is by word unit, with ST LEGER coming before STACK UP, LIVE WIRE before LIVED OUT, and QUEEN VICTORIA before QUEENS COUNSEL; abbreviated forms of words (eg ST LEGER, MR RIGHT) are listed in strict alphabetical order.

d) Purists will no doubt spot the lack of hyphens, apostrophes and accents. This has been a conscious decision, especially regarding hyphens and apostrophes. With hyphens being replaced by spaces, a clue, whether indicated as 2-4 or 2,4, can be found in the same place – 2,4. Also, apostrophes have been excluded, as they are not recognized when cluing – ie NEW YEAR'S EVE would be clued as 'December 31st (3,5,3)' *not* '(3,4,1,3); in maintaining uniformity, entries such as DOT THE IS and ILL BET will also appear without apostrophes.

PHRASES BY
INDIVIDUAL WORD-LENGTH

3 LETTERS

1,2
I DO
O ME
O MY

4 LETTERS

1,2,1
C IN C
C OF E

1,3
D DAY
G MAN
I SAY
I SPY
J PEN
M WAY
T BAR
X RAY

2,2
AT IT
DO IN
DO UP
ET AL
GO AT
GO GO
GO IN
GO ON
GO UP
HA HA
HE HE
HI FI
IN IT
IN ON
JU JU
NO GO
NO NO
ON TO
OR SO
RO RO
SO SO
TA TA
TO BE
TO DO
YO YO

3,1
BIG C
NON U
NOT I

5 LETTERS

1,2,2
A GO GO

1,3,1
I AND I

1,4
A BOMB

A DEUX
A ROAD
B SIDE
D MARK
E BOAT
G CLEF
G SUIT
H BOMB
M ROOF
Q BOAT
T BONE
U BEND
U BOAT
U BOLT
U TURN
V BOMB
V NECK
V SIGN
X RAYS

2,3
AD HOC
AD LIB
AD MAN
AD MEN
AS WAS
AS YET
AT ALL
AT ONE
AT SEA
BE OFF
BY FAR
BY LAW
CS GAS
DO OUT
GO APE
GO BAD
GO DRY
GO FAR
GO FOR
GO MAD
GO OFF
GO OUT
HE MAN
HO HUM
ID EST
IN ALL
IN BUD
IN CAR
IN FUN
IN LAW
IN OFF
IN ONE
IN TWO
IN USE
ME TOO
MR BIG
MY EYE
MY GOD
MY HAT

NO END
NO JOY
NO ONE
NO USE
NO WAY
OF OLD
OF USE
OH BOY
ON AIR
ON CUE
ON DIT
ON END
ON ICE
ON OFF
ON TAP
ON TOW
OP ART
OX BOW
OX EYE
PI JAW
SO FAR
TO LET
TO WIT
UH HUH
UP END
UP TOP
VE DAY
VJ DAY
WU SHU

3,2
ACT UP
ADD ON
ADD UP
ALL IN
ALL UP
ATE IN
ATE UP
BID IN
BID UP
BOB UP
BOW IN
BUY IN
BUY UP
CAN DO
CAN IT
COP IT
CRY UP
CUT IN
CUT UP
DIG IN
DIG UP
DIP IN
DRY UP
DUG IN
DUG UP
EAT IN
EAT UP
END ON
END UP

EYE UP
FED UP
FIT IN
FIT UP
FIX IT
FIX ON
FIX UP
FLY BY
FLY IN
FRY UP
GEE UP
GEN UP
GET AT
GET BY
GET IN
GET ON
GET UP
GOT AT
GOT BY
GOT IN
GOT ON
GOT UP
GUM UP
HAD IT
HAD ON
HAD TO
HAD UP
HAS IT
HAS ON
HAS TO
HAS UP
HEM IN
HEN DO
HET UP
HIT IT
HIT ON
HOG IT
HOO HA
HOP IT
HOT UP
HOW SO
INK IN
KEY IN
KUO YU
LAY BY
LAY IN
LAY ON
LAY TO
LAY UP
LED IN
LED ON
LED UP
LET BE
LET GO
LET IN
LET ON
LET UP
LIE BY
LIE IN
LIE ON

LIE TO
LIE UP
LIT UP
LOG IN
LUG IN
MET UP
MID ON
MIX IN
MIX IT
MIX UP
MOP UP
MUG UP
NIP IN
NOT SO
NOT UP
OWN UP
PAY IN
PAY UP
PER SE
PIG IT
PIN UP
POP IN
POP UP
PRO AM
PUT BY
PUT IN
PUT ON
PUT UP
RAN IN
RAN ON
RAN TO
RAN UP
RAT ON
REV UP
RIG UP
RUB ON
RUB UP
RUN IN
RUN ON
RUN TO
RUN UP
SAT BY
SAT IN
SAT ON
SAT UP
SAY SO
SCI FI
SET BY
SET IN
SET ON
SET TO
SET UP
SEW UP
SIT BY
SIT IN
SIT ON
SIT UP
SOL FA
SUM UP
SUN UP

3,2 *contd.*
TEE UP
TIE IN
TIE UP
TIP UP
TOG UP
TON UP
TOP UP
TOT UP
TRY ON
TWO UP
USE UP
WHY SO
ZAP UP
ZIP IN
ZIP ON
ZIP UP

4,1
BAGS I
GOOD O
SAYS I

6 LETTERS

1,3,2
A LEG UP
A RUM DO

1,5
A LEVEL
B MOVIE
E LAYER
G AGENT
I CHING
L PLATE
O LEVEL
Q FEVER
T PLATE
T SHIRT
X RAYED

2,1,3
IN A ROW
IN A RUT
IN A WAY
ON A PAR
TO A MAN
TO A TEE

2,2,2
FA LA LA
LA DI DA
OO LA LA
YO HO HO

2,4
AD MASS
AS SUCH
AS WELL
AT BEST
AT EASE
AT HAND
AT HOME

AT LAST
AT MOST
AT ODDS
AT ONCE
AT REST
AT RISK
AT STUD
AT WILL
AU FAIT
AU FOND
AU PAIR
BO PEEP
BO TREE
BY HAND
BY JOVE
BY LANE
DE LUXE
DE NOVO
DE TROP
DO BIRD
DO DOWN
DO OVER
DO TIME
DO WELL
EN BLOC
ET ALIA
FU YUNG
GO AWAY
GO BACK
GO BUST
GO DOWN
GO EASY
GO INTO
GO KART
GO LIVE
GO OVER
GO PHUT
GO SLOW
GO SOFT
GO WEST
IF ONLY
IN CALF
IN CARE
IN CASE
IN CASH
IN DEBT
IN FACT
IN FOAL
IN FULL
IN HAND
IN HOCK
IN JOKE
IN KIND
IN LAWS
IN LINE
IN LOVE
IN NEED
IN PART
IN PLAY
IN SITU

IN STEP
IN TIME
IN TOTO
IN TRAY
IN TUNE
IN TURN
IN VAIN
IN VIEW
IN WORD
JA WOHL
MR CHAD
MY FOOT
MY LADY
MY LORD
MY WORD
NO BALL
NO DICE
NO FEAR
NO GOOD
NO HOPE
NO JOKE
NO LESS
NO MORE
NO SIDE
OF LATE
OF NOTE
OH DEAR
ON CALL
ON DUTY
ON EDGE
ON FILE
ON FIRE
ON FOOT
ON HAND
ON HIGH
ON HIRE
ON HOLD
ON LINE
ON OATH
ON SPEC
ON TICK
ON TIME
ON VIEW
OR ELSE
OX BIRD
OX EYED
SO LONG
SO MANY
SO MUCH
SO THEN
SO WHAT
TE DEUM
TO BOOT
TO DATE
TO HAND
TV GAME
UP BEAT
UP ENDS
UP LINE
UP TOWN

3,1,2
HAD A GO
HAS A GO

3,3
ACK ACK
ACT ONE
ACT OUT
ACT TWO
ADD ONS
AGE OLD
AIR ARM
AIR BAG
AIR BED
AIR BUS
AIR GAS
AIR GUN
AIR SAC
ALL BUT
ALL DAY
ALL OUT
AND HOW
ASH BIN
ASH CAN
ASH KEY
ASH PAN
ASH PIT
ATE OUT
AYE AYE
BAD LOT
BAG NET
BAY RUM
BED OUT
BED PAN
BEG OFF
BEL AIR
BEL AMI
BEN OIL
BIG BEN
BIG BUG
BIG CAT
BIG END
BIG POT
BIG TOE
BIG TOP
BIN BAG
BOB FLY
BON AMI
BON MOT
BON TON
BOO HOO
BOW LEG
BOW OUT
BOW SAW
BOW TIE
BOX BED
BOX VAN
BUS BAR
BUY OFF
BUY OUT

BYE BYE
BYE LAW
CHA CHA
CHI CHI
CON MAN
CON ROD
COP OUT
CRY OFF
CRY OUT
CUP TIE
CUS CUS
CUT OFF
CUT OUT
DAY BED
DAY GLO
DAY OFF
DAY OLD
DEE JAY
DER TAG
DES RES
DIE OFF
DIE OUT
DIG OUT
DIK DIK
DIM SUM
DIP OUT
DOG EAR
DOG END
DOG LEG
DOG TAG
DRY BOB
DRY FLY
DRY ICE
DRY OUT
DRY ROT
DRY RUN
DRY SKI
DUG OUT
DUN COW
EAT OUT
EEL SET
EGG BOX
END USE
FAG END
FAN JET
FAN OUT
FAN TAN
FAR CRY
FAR OFF
FAR OUT
FAT CAT
FIN RAY
FIT OUT
FLY MAN
FLY OUT
FLY ROD
FOB OFF
FOR ALL
FOR AYE
FOR WHY

3,3 *contd.*

FOX BAT	LAY BYS	ONE OFF	RED DOG	SKI RUN
FUN RUN	LAY LOW	ONE WAY	RED GUM	SKI TOW
GAS BAG	LAY OFF	OPT OUT	RED HAT	SOW BUG
GAS CAP	LAY OUT	PAD OUT	RED HOT	SUB SEA
GAS GUN	LED OFF	PAD SAW	RED MAN	SUN DEW
GAS JAR	LED OUT	PAY BED	RED OUT	SUN GOD
GAS JET	LEG BYE	PAY BOX	RED RAG	TAG END
GAS OIL	LEG MAN	PAY DAY	RED ROT	TAI CHI
GAS TAP	LET FLY	PAY OFF	REX CAT	TAN PIT
GEE GEE	LET OFF	PAY OUT	RIG OUT	TAN VAT
GET OFF	LET OUT	PEA HEN	RIP OFF	TEA BAG
GET OUT	LET RIP	PEG BOX	RIP RAP	TEA SET
GOT OFF	LIE LOW	PEG LEG	RIP SAW	TEA URN
GOT OUT	LOG HUT	PEG OUT	ROW DOW	TEE OFF
GRU GRU	LOG MAN	PEG TOP	RUB OUT	TEX MEX
GUN DOG	LOG OUT	PEN NIB	RUN DRY	THE BOX
GUN SHY	LOG SAW	PEN PAL	RUN LOW	THE END
HAW HAW	LOW KEY	PET SIT	RUN OFF	THE FEW
HEN BIT	LOW TAR	PIG BED	RUN OUT	THE LAW
HEN RUN	MAN DAY	PIG MAN	SAG BAG	THE LOT
HEP CAT	MAP OUT	PIG NUT	SAP ROT	THE MOB
HIT MAN	MAU MAU	PIG RAT	SAT OUT	THE WAY
HIT OFF	MAY BUG	PIN LEG	SAW FIT	TIB CAT
HIT OUT	MAY DEW	PIN MAN	SAW OFF	TIC TAC
HOG PEN	MET MAN	PIT PAT	SAW OUT	TIE PIN
HOG RAT	MID AIR	PIT SAW	SAW RED	TIE ROD
HOP OFF	MID OFF	POO POO	SEA AIR	TIE WIG
HOT AIR	MID SEA	POP ART	SEA APE	TIN CAN
HOT DOG	MID SKY	POP EYE	SEA BOY	TIN GOD
HOT ROD	MOB CAP	POP GUN	SEA CAT	TIN HAT
HOW NOW	MOB LAW	POP OFF	SEA COB	TIP CAT
HUB CAP	MOD CON	POP OUT	SEA COW	TIP OFF
ICE AGE	MOO COW	POT ALE	SEA DOG	TOE RAG
ICE AXE	MUD PIE	POT BOY	SEA EAR	TOM CAT
ICE BAG	MUU MUU	POT HAT	SEA EEL	TOM TOM
ICE CAP	NEM CON	POT LID	SEA FOG	TOO BAD
ICE PAN	NEW AGE	POT MAN	SEA FOX	TOO TOO
ICE RUN	NEW MAN	PRE TAX	SEA GOD	TOP DOG
ILL BET	NID NOD	PRE WAR	SEA ICE	TOP HAT
ILL GOT	NIP OUT	PRO TEM	SEA LAW	TOP OUT
ILL OFF	NOD OFF	PRY OUT	SEA MEW	TOW NET
ILL SAY	NON EGO	PUG DOG	SEA OWL	TOY BOY
ILL USE	NOT OUT	PUT OFF	SEA PAY	TOY DOG
INK BAG	NUT OIL	PUT OUT	SEA PEN	TRY OUT
INK CAP	OAK NUT	PUT PUT	SEA WAY	TUM TUM
INK SAC	OBI MAN	PYE DOG	SEE FIT	TUT TUT
JET LAG	ODD JOB	RAG BAG	SEE OFF	TWO BIT
JET SKI	OFF AIR	RAG DAY	SEE OUT	TWO PLY
JOB LOT	OFF DAY	RAG TAG	SEE RED	TWO WAY
KEY MAN	OFF KEY	RAM JET	SEE YOU	VOX POP
KEY PAD	OIL GAS	RAN DRY	SET OFF	WAR CRY
KEY PIN	OIL MAN	RAN LOW	SET OUT	WAR GOD
KEY WAY	OIL PAN	RAN OFF	SET TOS	WAY OUT
KIA ORA	OIL RIG	RAN OUT	SHE ASS	WET BOB
KIT BAG	OLD AGE	RAT PIT	SIN BIN	WET FLY
KIT CAR	OLD BOY	RAT TAT	SIT OUT	WET ROT
KIT CAT	OLD HAT	RED ANT	SIX DAY	WHY NOT
LAC DYE	OLD MAN	RED BOX	SIX GUN	WIN OUT
LAW DAY	OLD TOM	RED BUD	SKI BOB	WON OUT
	ONE DAY	RED CAP	SKI DOO	WOW WOW

YES MAN
YOM TOB
YOO HOO
YOU ALL
YOU BET
YUM YUM
ZIP OFF

4,2
ACTS UP
ADDS UP
BACK UP
BANG ON
BANG UP
BEAR UP
BEAT IT
BEAT UP
BEEF UP
BEER UP
BELT UP
BIDS IN
BIDS UP
BLEW IN
BLEW UP
BLOW IN
BLOW UP
BONE UP
BOOK IN
BOOK UP
BORE UP
BOWS IN
BREW UP
BUCK UP
BUMP UP
BURN IN
BURN UP
BUST UP
BUTT IN
BUYS IN
BUYS UP
CAGE IN
CALL BY
CALL IN
CALL ON
CALL UP
CAME AT
CAME BY
CAME IN
CAME TO
CAME UP
CASH IN
CASH UP
CAST ON
CAST UP
CAVE IN
CHIN UP
CHIP IN
CHOP UP
CLAM UP

CLIP ON
CLUE IN
COCK UP
COIN IT
COME AT
COME BY
COME IN
COME ON
COME TO
COME UP
COOL IT
COPS IT
CROP UP
CURL UP
CUTS IN
CUTS UP
DEAD ON
DEJA VU
DIGS IN
DIGS UP
DIPS IN
DISH UP
DOES IN
DOES UP
DONE IN
DONE UP
DOSI DO
DRAG ON
DRAG UP
DRAW IN
DRAW ON
DRAW UP
DREW IN
DREW ON
DREW UP
DROP BY
DROP IN
DROP ON
DUFF UP
DUMP ON
DUST UP
EATS IN
EATS UP
ENDS UP
EURO MP
EVEN SO
EVEN UP
EVER SO
EYED UP
EYES UP
FADE IN
FALL IN
FALL ON
FELL IN
FELL ON
FILL IN
FILL UP
FIRE UP
FIRM UP
FITS IN

FITS UP
FLEW BY
FLEW IN
FOLD IN
FOOT IT
FORK UP
FOUL UP
FULL UP
GANG UP
GAVE IN
GAVE UP
GEAR UP
GENS UP
GETS AT
GETS BY
GETS IN
GETS ON
GETS UP
GIVE IN
GIVE UP
GOES AT
GOES IN
GOES ON
GOES UP
GREW IN
GROW UP
GUMS UP
GUNG HO
HAIR DO
HAND IN
HANG IN
HANG ON
HANG UP
HARD BY
HARD UP
HARP ON
HAUL IN
HAUL UP
HAVE IT
HAVE ON
HAVE TO
HAVE UP
HEAD ON
HELD IN
HELD ON
HELD UP
HEMS IN
HIGH UP
HINT AT
HITS UP
HOGS IT
HOLD IN
HOLD IT
HOLD ON
HOLD UP
HOLE UP
HOOK UP
HOOP LA
HOPS IT
HORN IN

HOTS UP
HOVE TO
HUNG IN
HUNG ON
HUNG UP
HUSH UP
HYPE UP
INKS IN
JOIN IN
JOIN UP
JUMP ON
JUST SO
KEEP IN
KEEP ON
KEEP UP
KEPT IN
KEPT ON
KEPT UP
KEYS IN
KICK IN
KISS ME
KUNG FU
LAID BY
LAID IN
LAID ON
LAID UP
LASH UP
LAYS BY
LAYS IN
LAYS ON
LAYS UP
LEAD IN
LEAD ON
LEAD UP
LEAN ON
LEAN TO
LEFT BE
LETS BE
LETS GO
LETS IN
LETS ON
LETS UP
LIES BY
LIES IN
LIES ON
LIES TO
LIES UP
LIFT UP
LINE UP
LINK IN
LINK UP
LIVE IN
LIVE ON
LOCK IN
LOCK ON
LOCK UP
LOFT UP
LOGS IN
LONG ON
LOOK AT

LOOK IN
LOOK ON
LOOK UP
LUGS IN
MADE DO
MADE IT
MADE UP
MAKE DO
MAKE IT
MAKE UP
MARK UP
MASH UP
MEET UP
MESS UP
MIST UP
MOCK UP
MOPS UP
MOVE IN
MUCK IN
MUGS UP
MUSK OX
NEAR BY
NEED BE
NIGH ON
NIPS IN
NOSH UP
ODDS ON
OPEN UP
OWNS UP
PACK UP
PAID IN
PAID UP
PASS BY
PASS ON
PASS UP
PAST IT
PAYS IN
PAYS UP
PENT UP
PERK UP
PICK AT
PICK ON
PICK UP
PIGS IT
PILE UP
PIPE UP
PLAY AT
PLAY ON
PLAY UP
PLUG IN
POPS IN
POPS UP
POST OP
PREY ON
PROP UP
PULL IN
PULL ON
PULL UP
PUMP IN
PUMP UP

4,2 *contd.*
PUTS BY
PUTS IN
PUTS ON
PUTS UP
RACK UP
RAKE IN
RAKE UP
RANG IN
RANG UP
RATS ON
RAVE ON
RAVE UP
READ UP
REIN IN
RELY ON
REVS UP
RIDE UP
RIGS UP
RING IN
RING UP
RISE UP
RISK IT
ROAD UP
RODE UP
ROLL IN
ROLL ON
ROLL UP
ROPE IN
ROSE UP
RUBS UP
RUNS IN
RUNS ON
RUNS TO
RUNS UP
SAIL BY
SANK IN
SAVE UP
SAYS HE
SELL ON
SELL UP
SEND IN
SEND ON
SEND UP
SENT IN
SENT ON
SETS BY
SETS IN
SETS ON
SETS UP
SEWN UP
SEWS UP
SHOT UP
SHOW UP
SHUT IN
SHUT UP
SIDE ON
SIGN IN
SIGN ON
SIGN UP

SINK IN
SITS BY
SITS IN
SITS ON
SITS UP
SIZE UP
SKIP IT
SLIP ON
SLIP UP
SLOW UP
SNAP UP
SOLD ON
SOLD UP
SOUP UP
SPOT ON
STAG DO
STAY IN
STAY ON
STAY UP
STEP IN
STEP UP
STIR UP
STOP GO
STOP IN
SUCH AS
SUCK IN
SUMS UP
SWAN IN
SWAN UP
SWOT UP
TACK ON
TAKE IN
TAKE IT
TAKE ON
TAKE TO
TAKE UP
TALK AT
TALK IN
TALK TO
TALK UP
TART UP
TEAR UP
TEED UP
TEES UP
TELE AD
TELL ON
TIED IN
TIED UP
TIES IN
TIES UP
TOGS UP
TOLD ON
TONE UP
TOOK IN
TOOK IT
TOOK ON
TOOK TO
TOOK UP
TOOL UP
TOPS UP

TORE UP
TORN UP
TOSS UP
TOTS UP
TREK OX
TUCK IN
TUNE IN
TUNE UP
TURN IN
TURN ON
TURN TO
TURN UP
TWIG IT
USED UP
USES UP
VOTE IN
WADE IN
WAIT ON
WAIT UP
WAKE UP
WALK IN
WALK IT
WALK ON
WALL UP
WANT AD
WANT IN
WARM UP
WASH UP
WELL IN
WENT BY
WENT IN
WENT ON
WENT UP
WHAT HO
WHAT IF
WHET ON
WHIP IN
WIND UP
WIPE UP
WIRE IN
WISE UP
WITH IT
WOKE UP
WORK IN
WORK ON
WORK UP
WRAP UP
ZAPS UP
ZERO IN
ZIPS UP

7 LETTERS

1,2,4
A LA MODE

1,3,3
A BAD HAT
A BAD JOB
A FAR CRY
I ASK YOU

1,4,2
I HAVE IT

1,6
A DROITE
A GAUCHE
A PRIORI
D NOTICE
E NUMBER
E REGION
G AGENTS
G STRING
L PLATES
R MONTHS
T SHAPED
T SQUARE
U SHAPED
V NECKED
V SHAPED
X RAYING

2,1,4
AS A RULE
AT A BLOW
AT A LOSS
AT A PUSH
AT A WORD
BY A NOSE
DO A TURN
IN A DAZE
IN A RUSH
IN A SPOT
IN A STEW
IN A WORD
OF A SORT
ON A ROLL
TO A TURN
UP A TREE

2,2,3
AS OF NOW
AT AN END
DO IT NOW
DO OR DIE
GO TO BED
GO TO POT
GO TO SEA
GO TO WAR
IN NO WAY
OF NO USE

2,3,2
AT ONE GO
BY AND BY
BY THE BY
GO FOR IT
GO MAN GO
IN AND IN
IN FOR IT
NO CAN DO
ON AND ON

ON THE GO
ON THE UP
SO AND SO

2,5
AS USUAL
AT FAULT
AT FIRST
AT ISSUE
AT LARGE
AT LEAST
AT PEACE
AT STAKE
AT TABLE
AT TIMES
CB RADIO
DE FACTO
EN EFFET
EN GARDE
EN MASSE
EN PRISE
EN ROUTE
EN SUITE
EX CURIA
EX PARTE
FT INDEX
GO AHEAD
GO DUTCH
GO FORTH
GO ROUND
GO SPARE
GO UNDER
GO WRONG
IN BLOOD
IN BRIEF
IN BUILT
IN CROWD
IN DEPTH
IN DOUBT
IN FOCUS
IN FORCE
IN FRONT
IN HOLES
IN HOUSE
IN LIMBO
IN ORDER
IN PLACE
IN POWER
IN PRINT
IN SHAPE
IN SHORT
IN SPATE
IN STOCK
IN STORE
IN STYLE
IN TEARS
IN THING
IN TOUCH
IN TRAIN
IN TRUST

2,5 *contd.*
IN TRUTH
IN VOICE
JU JITSU
MR RIGHT
NO DOUBT
NO ENTRY
NO HOPER
NO SWEAT
NO TRUMP
OF SORTS
ON APPRO
ON BOARD
ON DRIVE
ON GOING
ON OFFER
ON ORDER
ON PAPER
ON SHORE
ON SIGHT
ON STAGE
ON TERMS
ON TOAST
ON TRIAL
ON TRUST
OX FENCE
PH VALUE
PI MESON
PO FACED
SI UNITS
SO THERE
ST LEGER
TO ORDER
TO SCALE
TO SPARE
UP ENDED
UP FRONT
UP TEMPO
UP TRAIN

3,1,3
BUY A PUP
CAP A PIE
DOS A DOS
HOB A NOB
MAN O WAR
MEN O WAR
PIT A PAT
RAT A TAT
VIS A VIS

3,2,2
AND SO ON
LET IN ON
OUT OF IT
PUT IT ON
PUT ON TO
PUT TO IT
RUB IT IN
SAW TO IT
SEE TO IT

TRY IT ON
WOE IS ME
ZAP IT UP

3,4
ACK EMMA
ACT FOUR
AGA KHAN
AIR BASE
AIR CELL
AIR COOL
AIR CREW
AIR DROP
AIR LANE
AIR LOCK
AIR MISS
AIR PLAY
AIR PUMP
AIR RAID
AIR TRAP
ALI BABA
ALL DONE
ALL HAIL
ALL OVER
ALL STAR
ALL TIME
ALL TOLD
ANT BIRD
ANT HILL
ANT LION
ANY MORE
ARC LAMP
ARM REST
ART DECO
ART FORM
ART SONG
ASH TRAY
ATE AWAY
BAD DEBT
BAD FORM
BAD LUCK
BAD NEWS
BAD SHOT
BAD SHOW
BAD TRIP
BAG LADY
BAR BELL
BAR CODE
BAR IRON
BAR NONE
BAR ROOM
BAY LEAF
BAY SALT
BED DOWN
BED REST
BED ROLL
BED WORK
BEE GLUE
BEE HIVE
BEE KITE

BEE MOTH
BEE SKEP
BID FAIR
BIG BAND
BIG BANG
BIG CATS
BIG DEAL
BIG FISH
BIG GAME
BIG GUNS
BIG HEAD
BIG NAME
BIG SHOT
BIG TIME
BIT PART
BOG DOWN
BOG MOSS
BOW HAND
BOX CALF
BOX COAT
BOX KITE
BOX ROOM
BOX SEAT
BUG EYED
BUM BOAT
BUS FARE
BUS LANE
BUS PASS
BUS STOP
BUY OVER
CAB RANK
CAR COAT
CAR PARK
CAR POOL
CAR SICK
CAR WASH
CAT DOOR
CAT FLAP
CAT LIKE
CAT SHOW
CAT WALK
COB LOAF
COB PIPE
CON BRIO
COP SHOP
COW CALF
CRY BABY
CRY DOWN
CRY WOLF
CUE BALL
CUI BONO
CUP CAKE
CUP GAME
CUP TIED
CUT BACK
CUT DEAD
CUT DOWN
DAY BOOK
DAY CARE
DAY ROOM

DAY TRIP
DAY WORK
DEW DROP
DEW FALL
DEW POND
DID TIME
DIE AWAY
DIE CAST
DIE DOWN
DIE HARD
DIE WORK
DOE EYED
DOE SKIN
DOG ROSE
DOG SHOW
DOG SLED
DON JUAN
DRY CELL
DRY CURE
DRY DOCK
DRY EYED
DRY HOLE
DRY ICED
DRY LAND
DRY SHOD
DRY WASH
DUE EAST
DUE WEST
DUN BIRD
DYE WORK
EAR BONE
EAR HOLE
EAR PLUG
EAR SHOT
EAT AWAY
EGG CASE
EGG COSY
EGG FLIP
EGO TRIP
ELF SHOT
END USER
EWE LAMB
EWE MILK
EWE NECK
EYE BATH
EYE DROP
EYE HOLE
EYE SPOT
EYE WASH
FAN CLUB
FAN MAIL
FAN PALM
FAR EAST
FAR WEST
FAT FACE
FAT HEAD
FEN FIRE
FIG LEAF
FIG TREE
FIR CONE

FIR TREE
FIR WOOD
FLY FISH
FLY FLAP
FLY HALF
FLY HIGH
FLY KICK
FLY LINE
FLY OPEN
FLY PAST
FLY RAIL
FLY SOLO
FLY SWAT
FOG BANK
FOG BELL
FOG LAMP
FOO YUNG
FOR EVER
FOR FREE
FOR GOOD
FOR LIFE
FOR ONCE
FOR REAL
FOR RENT
FOR SALE
FOR SHOW
FOR SURE
FOX EVIL
FOX HUNT
FOX TAIL
FOX TRAP
FOX TROT
FUN FAIR
FUN PARK
FUR BALL
FUR COAT
FUR SEAL
GAS BILL
GAS COAL
GAS COKE
GAS FIRE
GAS LAMP
GAS MAIN
GAS MASK
GAS OVEN
GAS PIPE
GAS RING
GAS TANK
GAS TRAP
GAS WELL
GEE WHIZ
GET BACK
GET DOWN
GET EVEN
GET LOST
GET OVER
GET REAL
GIN FIZZ
GIN TRAP
GOA BEAN

3,4 *contd.*

GOD SLOT	ILL LUCK	LOW LIFE	NUT TREE	PAY LOAD
GOT BACK	ILL USED	LOW PAID	OAK FERN	PAY ROLL
GOT DOWN	ILL WILL	LOW RISE	OAK GALL	PAY SLIP
GOT EVEN	INK FEED	LOW TIDE	OAK LUMP	PEA FOWL
GOT OVER	INK HORN	LOW TOBY	OAK MAST	PEA SOUP
GUM TREE	INN SIGN	MAE WEST	OAK TREE	PEG AWAY
GUN DECK	IVY BUSH	MAN DAYS	OAK WOOD	PEG BACK
GUN LOCK	IVY CLAD	MAN HOUR	OAR FISH	PEG DOWN
GUY ROPE	JAI ALAI	MAN JACK	OAR LOCK	PEG TOPS
GYM SHOE	JAM TART	MAN LIKE	ODD FISH	PEN CASE
GYM SLIP	JET DEAU	MAN MADE	ODD JOBS	PEN NAME
HAG RIDE	JIB BOOM	MAN SIZE	OFF BASE	PEP PILL
HAG SEED	JIB DOOR	MAN WEEK	OFF DUTY	PEP TALK
HAG WEED	JOE SOAP	MAN YEAR	OFF LINE	PER CENT
HAS BEEN	JOY RIDE	MAO SUIT	OFF SITE	PET HATE
HEM LINE	JUG BAND	MAP BOOK	OFF SPIN	PET NAME
HEN COOP	KEG BEER	MAY BIRD	OIL BELT	PEW RENT
HEN TOED	KEY RING	MAY LADY	OIL CAKE	PIE EYED
HEN WIFE	KEY WORD	MAY LILY	OIL DRUM	PIE SHOP
HER NIBS	KID SKIN	MAY LORD	OIL MILL	PIG DEER
HIP BATH	KIP DOWN	MAY TIME	OIL PALM	PIG EYED
HIP BELT	KIT BOAT	MAY TREE	OIL RICH	PIG HERD
HIP BONE	LAW BOOK	MID HOUR	OIL SEED	PIG IRON
HIP LOCK	LAW LIST	MID TERM	OIL WELL	PIN CURL
HIS NIBS	LAW LORD	MID WEEK	OLD BEAN	PIN DOWN
HIT LIST	LAY BACK	MID YEAR	OLD BILL	PIN EYED
HOG DEER	LAY BARE	MOD CONS	OLD BIRD	PIN TUCK
HOG FISH	LAY DOWN	MOT TEST	OLD DEAR	PIP EMMA
HOG MANE	LAY INTO	MRS MOPP	OLD FACE	PIT BROW
HOG NOSE	LAY OPEN	MUD BATH	OLD GANG	PIT BULL
HOG SKIN	LAY OVER	MUD FLAP	OLD GIRL	PIT COAL
HOP HEAD	LEE SIDE	MUD FLAT	OLD GOLD	PIT PONY
HOP POLE	LEE TIDE	MUG SHOT	OLD HAND	PIT PROP
HOP SACK	LEG BAIL	NEO NAZI	OLD LADY	PIT STOP
HOP TREE	LEG IRON	NET CORD	OLD MAID	POE BIRD
HOP VINE	LEG PULL	NET GAME	OLD NICK	POP EYED
HOP YARD	LEG REST	NET PLAY	OLD ROSE	POP SHOP
HOT LINE	LEG SHOW	NEW DEAL	OLD SALT	POP SONG
HOT SEAT	LEG SIDE	NEW LAID	OLD SONG	POT BANK
HOT SPOT	LEG SLIP	NEW LOOK	OLD TIME	POT HEAD
HOT WELL	LEG SPIN	NEW MADE	OLD WIFE	POT HERB
HOW COME	LET DOWN	NEW MOON	ONE EYED	POT LUCK
ICE BLUE	LET DROP	NEW MOWN	ONE SHOT	POT SHOP
ICE BOAT	LET FALL	NEW TOWN	ONE STEP	POT SHOT
ICE COLD	LET SLIP	NEW WAVE	ONE TIME	POY BIRD
ICE CUBE	LIE ABED	NEW YEAR	OUR LADY	PRE EMPT
ICE FALL	LIE BACK	NEW YORK	OUT TAKE	PRE SELL
ICE FERN	LIE DOWN	NIT PICK	OUT TRAY	PRE SOLD
ICE FLOE	LIE HARD	NON DRIP	OWL EYED	PRE WASH
ICE FREE	LIE OVER	NON HERO	OWL MOTH	PRO RATA
ICE HILL	LIP READ	NON SKID	OWN GOAL	PUG MILL
ICE OVER	LOG BOOK	NON SLIP	PAD TREE	PUG MOTH
ICE PICK	LOG FIRE	NON STOP	PAN LOAF	PUG NOSE
ICE RINK	LOG ROLL	NON USER	PAS SEUL	PUP TENT
ICE SHOW	LOW BORN	NOR EAST	PAY BACK	PUT AWAY
ICE SPAR	LOW BRED	NOR WEST	PAY BILL	PUT BACK
ICH DIEN	LOW BROW	NOT HALF	PAY CASH	PUT DOWN
ILL BRED	LOW COST	NOW THEN	PAY DESK	PUT OVER
ILL FAME	LOW DOWN	NUT GALL	PAY DIRT	PUT UPON
	LOW GEAR	NUT HOOK	PAY LIST	QUI VIVE

3,4 *contd.*
QUO JURE
RAG BABY
RAG BOOK
RAG BUSH
RAG DOLL
RAG FAIR
RAG WEEK
RAG WOOL
RAN AMOK
RAN AWAY
RAN DOWN
RAN HARD
RAN INTO
RAN OVER
RAN RIOT
RAN WILD
RAT HOLE
RAT RACE
RAT TRAP
RAW DEAL
RAW SILK
RED BOOK
RED CARD
RED CENT
RED CLAY
RED DEER
RED FACE
RED FLAG
RED GAME
RED HAND
RED HEAD
RED HEAT
RED LANE
RED LEAD
RED MEAT
RED ROOT
RED ROSE
RED SEED
RED SNOW
RED TAPE
RED WINE
RIB BONE
RIP CORD
ROE DEER
ROW PORT
RUB DOWN
RUM BABA
RUM SHOP
RUN AMOK
RUN AWAY
RUN DOWN
RUN HARD
RUN INTO
RUN OVER
RUN RIOT
RUN TIME
RUN WILD
RYE ROLL
RYE WOLF

SAD EYED
SAD IRON
SAT BACK
SAT DOWN
SAW BILL
SAW BUCK
SAW EDGE
SAW FISH
SAW LIFE
SAW MILL
SAW OVER
SAY WHEN
SEA BANK
SEA BASS
SEA BIRD
SEA BLUE
SEA BOAT
SEA CALF
SEA COAL
SEA COOK
SEA CROW
SEA DACE
SEA DOVE
SEA DUCK
SEA FIRE
SEA FISH
SEA FOAM
SEA FOLK
SEA FOWL
SEA FRET
SEA GATE
SEA GIRT
SEA HAAR
SEA HAWK
SEA KALE
SEA KING
SEA LANE
SEA LARK
SEA LEGS
SEA LIKE
SEA LILY
SEA LINE
SEA LION
SEA LOCH
SEA LORD
SEA MAID
SEA MILE
SEA MOSS
SEA PASS
SEA PATH
SEA PIKE
SEA PINK
SEA ROAD
SEA ROOM
SEA SALT
SEA SAND
SEA SLUG
SEA STAR
SEA TANG
SEA TERM

SEA TURN
SEA VIEW
SEA WALL
SEA WARE
SEA WAVE
SEA WIFE
SEA WIND
SEA WING
SEA WOLF
SEA WORM
SEA WORN
SEE HERE
SEE LIFE
SEE OVER
SET BACK
SET DOWN
SET FAIR
SET FOOT
SET FREE
SET LINE
SET SAIL
SET UPON
SEX BOMB
SHE BEAR
SHY COCK
SIT BACK
SIT DOWN
SIT UPON
SIX BITS
SIX FOOT
SIX PACK
SKI LIFT
SKY BLUE
SKY HIGH
SKY SIGN
SKY WAVE
SOW SKIN
SPA WELL
SPY HOLE
SUB HEAD
SUN BIRD
SUN CULT
SUN DECK
SUN DISC
SUN LAMP
SUN ROOF
TAG LINE
TAN BARK
TAP ROOM
TAP SHOE
TAR SAND
TAX DISC
TAX FREE
TEA BAGS
TEA CAKE
TEA COSY
TEA DISH
TEA LADY
TEA LEAF
TEA ROOM

TEA ROSE
TEA SHOP
TEA TIME
TEA TRAY
THE BARD
THE CAPE
THE EAST
THE FLAT
THE LUMP
THE OAKS
THE PILL
THE PITS
THE ROCK
THE ROPE
THE RUMP
THE SAME
THE TOPS
THE WEST
THE WORD
THE YARD
THE YIPS
TIE BEAM
TIE CLIP
TIE DOWN
TIN MINE
TIN TACK
TOC EMMA
TOE HOLD
TOE JUMP
TOE LOOP
TOO MUCH
TOP BOOT
TOP HOLE
TOP LINE
TOP SOIL
TOW PATH
TOW ROPE
TUG BOAT
TWO BITS
TWO DEEP
TWO PART
TWO STEP
TWO TIME
TWO TONE
UVA URSI
VIN ROSE
WAR BABY
WAR DRUM
WAR GAME
WAR HAWK
WAR HEAD
WAR HERO
WAR LOAN
WAR SONG
WAX DOLL
WAX MOTH
WAX TREE
WAY BILL
WAY POST
WEB FOOT

WEB TOED
WEE FREE
WET CELL
WET DOCK
WET FISH
WET LOOK
WET SHOD
WET SUIT
WIN OVER
WON OVER
WRY NECK
YEW TREE
ZIP CODE
ZIP NECK

4,1,2
HALF A MO
HAVE A GO

4,3
ACTS OUT
ALMS FEE
ALMS MAN
ALSO RAN
AMBS ACE
ARMY ANT
AXLE BOX
BABY SIT
BACK END
BACK OFF
BACK OUT
BAIL OUT
BALE OUT
BALL BOY
BAND AID
BAND BOX
BAND SAW
BANG OFF
BANG OUT
BARN OWL
BASE FEE
BASS BAR
BATH BUN
BAWL OUT
BEAM SEA
BEAN BAG
BEAR CAT
BEAR OUT
BEAT OFF
BEAT OUT
BEDS OUT
BEEF TEA
BEER MAT
BEET FLY
BEGS OFF
BELL BOY
BELL JAR
BELT OUT
BEST BOY
BEST END
BEST MAN

4,3 *contd.*	CHOC BAR	DIPS OUT	FISH OUT	GREY HEN
BETH DIN	CHOC ICE	DIRT BED	FITS OUT	GREY LAG
BIRD DOG	CITY MAN	DISH OUT	FIVE BAR	GREY OWL
BLEW OUT	CLAY PIT	DISH RAG	FLAG DAY	GROW BAG
BLOT OUT	COAL BOX	DOES OUT	FLAT CAP	HACK LOG
BLOW DRY	COAL GAS	DOGS EAR	FLAT HAT	HACK SAW
BLOW OUT	COAL PIT	DONE FOR	FLAT OUT	HAIR DOS
BLUE FOX	COAL TAR	DONE OUT	FLEA BAG	HAIR NET
BLUE JAY	COAL TIT	DRAG BAR	FLEA PIT	HAIR OIL
BLUE SKY	COIN BOX	DRAG NET	FLEW OUT	HALF APE
BLUE TIT	COLD WAR	DRAG OUT	FLIP TOP	HALF DAY
BOAT FLY	COMB OUT	DRAW BAR	FOBS OFF	HALF PAY
BOER WAR	COME NOW	DRAW NET	FOLD OUT	HALF WIT
BOGY MAN	COME OFF	DRAW OFF	FOLK ART	HAND GUN
BONE ASH	COME OUT	DRAW OUT	FOOT TON	HAND OUT
BONE BED	CONE OFF	DREW OFF	FORK OUT	HANG OFF
BONE DRY	COOL BAG	DRIP DRY	FOUR ALE	HANG OUT
BONE OIL	COOL BOX	DROP NET	FULL FED	HARD HAT
BOOK END	COOL OFF	DROP OFF	FUSE BOX	HARD HIT
BOOK OUT	COON CAN	DROP OUT	FUSS POT	HARD MAN
BOOT BOY	COPS OUT	DUCK OUT	GALA PIE	HARD PAD
BORE OUT	COPY CAT	DUST BAG	GALL FLY	HARD ROE
BOWL OUT	CORK LEG	DUST PAN	GALL NUT	HARD RUN
BOWS OUT	CORK MAT	EACH WAY	GAME BAG	HARD SET
BRAN TUB	CORK OAK	EASE OFF	GANG SAW	HARD WON
BREN GUN	CORN BIN	EAST END	GATE LEG	HARE LIP
BUCK EYE	CORN FED	EATS OUT	GATE MAN	HAUT TON
BULL ANT	CORN LAW	EDGE OUT	GAVE EAR	HAVE NOT
BULL PEN	CORN OIL	EDIT OUT	GAVE OFF	HAWK EYE
BULL PUP	CORN PIT	EVEN NOW	GAVE OUT	HEAD BOY
BUMP OFF	CRAB NUT	EVEN OUT	GAVE WAY	HEAD OFF
BUNK BED	CRAB OIL	EVIL EYE	GEAR BOX	HEAD OUT
BURN OUT	CREW CUT	FACE OFF	GETS OFF	HEAD SEA
BUSH CAT	CROW BAR	FACE OUT	GETS OUT	HEAL ALL
BUSH FLY	CURE ALL	FADE OUT	GILL NET	HEAR OUT
BUTT END	CUTS OFF	FAIR DAY	GIVE EAR	HEEL TAP
BUYS OFF	CUTS OUT	FAIR DOS	GIVE OFF	HELD OFF
BUYS OUT	DAMN ALL	FALL GUY	GIVE OUT	HELD OUT
BUZZ OFF	DASH OFF	FALL OFF	GIVE WAY	HELL CAT
BUZZ SAW	DASH OUT	FALL OUT	GLAD EYE	HELP OUT
BUZZ WIG	DASH POT	FANS OUT	GLUE EAR	HERB TEA
CALL BOX	DEAD END	FARM OUT	GLUE POT	HIGH DAY
CALL BOY	DEAD EYE	FAST DAY	GOES BAD	HIGH HAT
CALL OFF	DEAD SEA	FAUX PAS	GOES DRY	HIGH KEY
CALL OUT	DEAD SET	FELL OFF	GOES FAR	HIGH SET
CAME OFF	DEAF AID	FELL OUT	GOES FOR	HIGH TEA
CAME OUT	DEAL OUT	FELT HAT	GOES MAD	HIGH TOP
CAMI TOP	DEAR SIR	FERN OWL	GOES OFF	HIND GUT
CAMP BED	DECK OUT	FILE OFF	GOES OUT	HIRE CAR
CAMP OUT	DEEP FRY	FILL OUT	GOLD BUG	HIRE OUT
CART OFF	DEEP SEA	FILM FAN	GOLF BAG	HITS OFF
CASE LAW	DESK TOP	FILM SET	GONE BAD	HITS OUT
CASH COW	DICE BOX	FIND OUT	GONE FOR	HIVE BEE
CAST OFF	DIED OFF	FINE LEG	GONE MAD	HIVE OFF
CAST OUT	DIED OUT	FIRE BAR	GONE OFF	HOCK DAY
CATS EAR	DIES OFF	FIRE BOX	GONE OUT	HOLD ALL
CATS EYE	DIES OUT	FIRE OFF	GOOD AND	HOLD OFF
CATS PAW	DIGS OUT	FISH DAY	GOOD BYE	HOLD OUT
CHIP HAT	DIKA OIL	FISH NET	GOOD DAY	HOLE OUT
CHIP OFF	DINE OUT	FISH OIL	GOOD EGG	HOLM OAK

4,3 *contd.*

HOLY DAY	LEAN TOS	MARL PIT	PALE ALE	PUTT OUT
HOLY JOE	LEAP DAY	MASH TUB	PALM CAT	RACE CUP
HOLY ONE	LEFT OFF	MASH TUN	PALM OIL	RAIL CAR
HOLY SEE	LEFT OUT	MASH VAT	PARA NUT	RAKE OFF
HOLY WAR	LETS FLY	MEAT FLY	PART OFF	RANG OFF
HOME RUN	LETS OFF	MEAT MAN	PASS OFF	RAPE OIL
HOOK PIN	LETS OUT	MEAT PIE	PASS OUT	RARE GAS
HOPS OFF	LETS RIP	MEAT TEA	PAYS OFF	RATE CAP
HORN MAD	LIES LOW	MEAT TUB	PAYS OUT	READ OFF
HORN OWL	LIFT BOY	MENS REA	PEAT BED	READ OUT
HUNG OFF	LIFT MAN	MESS TIN	PEAT BOG	REAL ALE
HUNG OUT	LIFT OFF	MILD ALE	PEEL OFF	REDS OUT
HUNT OUT	LIKE MAD	MILK BAR	PEEP OUT	REED BED
IRON AGE	LILY PAD	MILK CAP	PEEP TOE	REEL OFF
IRON MAN	LINE OUT	MILK COW	PEGS OUT	REIN ARM
IRON ORE	LINK MAN	MILK JUG	PICK OFF	RENT DAY
IRON OUT	LION CUB	MILK RUN	PICK OUT	REST DAY
IRON PAN	LIVE OAK	MILK SOP	PIGS EAR	RIDE OUT
JACK TAR	LIVE OUT	MILL RUN	PILE CAP	RIGS OUT
JAVA MAN	LOCK JAW	MIND OUT	PILL BOX	RING OFF
JAZZ AGE	LOCK NUT	MIND YOU	PINE TAR	RING OUT
JOHN DOE	LOCK OUT	MINI BUS	PINK EYE	RIOT ACT
JUKE BOX	LOGS OUT	MINI CAB	PINK GIN	RIPS OFF
JUMP JET	LONG AGO	MINI CAR	PINT POT	ROAD BED
JUMP OFF	LONG ARM	MINI SUB	PIPE KEY	ROAD HOG
JUNK MAN	LONG HOP	MISS OUT	PITH HAT	ROAD MAP
JURY BOX	LONG LEG	MOCK SUN	PLAY ACT	ROCK COD
JUST NOW	LONG OFF	MOLE OUT	PLAY BOX	ROCK OIL
KEEP FIT	LONG PIG	MONO SKI	PLAY DAY	ROCK TAR
KEEP MUM	LONG TOM	MOON GOD	PLAY OFF	RODE OUT
KEEP OFF	LONG TON	MOVE OUT	PLAY OUT	ROLL BAR
KEPT FIT	LOOK FOR	MUSK RAT	PLAY PEN	ROLL OUT
KEPT MUM	LOOK OUT	NAIL BED	POLE AXE	ROLL TOP
KEPT OFF	LOOK SEE	NAIL GUN	POLL TAX	ROOD DAY
KICK OFF	LOOK YOU	NAME DAY	POOH BAH	ROOF TOP
KICK OUT	LOSE OUT	NEST EGG	POOR BOX	ROOT CAP
KILL OFF	LOST OUT	NINE PIN	POOR LAW	ROOT OUT
KILN DRY	LUMP SUM	NIPS OUT	POPS OFF	ROSE BAY
KING PIN	MADE FOR	NODS OFF	POPS OUT	ROSE BUD
KING ROD	MADE HAY	NOSE JOB	PORK PIE	ROSE BUG
KNEE CAP	MADE OFF	NOSE OUT	POST BAG	ROSE HIP
KNEE PAD	MADE OUT	NOTE PAD	POST BOX	ROSE RED
KNEE PAN	MADE WAR	OHMS LAW	POST BOY	RUBS OUT
KNOW ALL	MADE WAY	OPEN AIR	POST BUS	RUBY RED
KNOW HOW	MAIL BAG	OPEN DAY	POST DAY	RULE OUT
LACE UPS	MAIL BOX	OPEN END	POST WAR	RUMP END
LADY DAY	MAIL CAR	OPEN OUT	POUR OUT	RUNS DRY
LAID OFF	MAIL GIG	OPEN SEA	PROP JET	RUNS LOW
LAID OUT	MAIL VAN	OPEN TOP	PUFF BOX	RUNS OFF
LAND RAT	MAKE FOR	OPTS OUT	PULL OFF	RUNS OUT
LAND TAX	MAKE HAY	OPUS DEI	PULL OUT	RUSH MAT
LASH OUT	MAKE OFF	OVER AGE	PUMP GUN	SAGE TEA
LAST OUT	MAKE OUT	OVER ALL	PUMP OUT	SAIL ARM
LAYS OFF	MAKE WAR	PACK ICE	PUNT GUN	SALT BOX
LAYS OUT	MAKE WAY	PADS OUT	PUSH OFF	SALT EEL
LAZY EYE	MALT TEA	PAGE BOY	PUSH OUT	SALT FAT
LEAD OFF	MANX CAT	PAID OFF	PUSH PIN	SALT PAN
LEAD OUT	MAPS OUT	PAID OUT	PUSH TUG	SALT PIT
LEAK OUT	MARK OFF	PAIR OAR	PUTS OFF	SAND BAR
	MARK OUT	PAIR OFF	PUTS OUT	SAND BED

4,3 *contd.*	SNOW FLY	TILE HAT	WHAT NOT	BOOKS UP
SAND BOX	SNOW ICE	TILE RED	WHEY TUB	BOOZE UP
SAND BOY	SOAP BOX	TIME GUN	WHIP SAW	BOWED IN
SAND EEL	SODA POP	TIME LAG	WHIZ KID	BREAK IN
SAND FLY	SOFA BED	TIME OUT	WHOS WHO	BREAK UP
SAND PIT	SOFT ROE	TIPS OFF	WIDE BOY	BREWS UP
SANG OUT	SOLD OFF	TIRE OUT	WILD ASS	BRING IN
SAVE ALL	SOLD OUT	TOBY JUG	WILD CAT	BRING ON
SAWN OFF	SORT OUT	TOLD OFF	WILD DOG	BRING UP
SAYS SHE	SOUR SOP	TOLL BAR	WILD MAN	BROKE IN
SAYS YOU	SPIN DRY	TOOK AIM	WIND BAG	BRUSH UP
SEAL OFF	SPIN OFF	TOOK OFF	WINE BAG	BUCKS UP
SEAL WAX	SPIN OUT	TOOK OUT	WINE BAR	BUILD IN
SEED OIL	SPUN OUT	TOPS OUT	WINE SAP	BUILD UP
SEEK OUT	STAR LED	TORE OFF	WINE VAT	BUILT IN
SEES FIT	STAR MAP	TOTE BAG	WING NUT	BUILT UP
SEES OFF	STAY OUT	TOWN END	WINS OUT	BUMPS UP
SEES OUT	STAY PUT	TRAM CAR	WIPE OUT	BURNS IN
SEES RED	STEN GUN	TROT OUT	WIRE BAR	BURNT IN
SELL OFF	STEP CUT	TRUE RIB	WIRE MAN	BURNT UP
SELL OUT	STEP OUT	TUCK BOX	WIRE WAY	BUTTS IN
SEND OFF	STEP SON	TURF OUT	WISE GUY	CAGED IN
SEND OUT	STEW CAN	TURN OFF	WOLF CUB	CAGES IN
SENT OFF	STIR FRY	TURN OUT	WOLF DOG	CALLS BY
SENT OUT	STOP GAP	TWIN BED	WOOD OIL	CALLS IN
SETS OFF	STOP OFF	TWIN SET	WOOD OWL	CALLS ON
SETS OUT	STUN GUN	TWIN TUB	WOOD TAR	CARRY ON
SHIH TZU	SUSS OUT	TYPE BAR	WOOL OIL	CARVE UP
SHIP BOY	TAIL END	VENT PEG	WORE OFF	CASTS UP
SHIP WAY	TAIL FLY	VINE ROD	WORK BAG	CATCH IT
SHOE TIE	TAIL OFF	WAGE WAR	WORK BOX	CATCH ON
SHOP BOY	TAKE AIM	WALK OFF	WORK DAY	CATCH UP
SHOT GUN	TAKE OFF	WALK OUT	WORK FOR	CAVED IN
SHOT OFF	TAKE OUT	WALL EYE	WORK OFF	CAVES IN
SHOT PUT	TALK BIG	WANT OUT	WORK OUT	CHAIN UP
SHOW BIZ	TALK OUT	WANT WIT	WORK SHY	CHALK UP
SHOW BOX	TALL HAT	WARD OFF	WORN OUT	CHEAT ON
SHOW OFF	TANK CAR	WART HOG	WYCH ELM	CHECK IN
SHUT EYE	TANK TOP	WASH DAY	YARD ARM	CHECK UP
SHUT OFF	TANT PIS	WASH OUT	YEAR END	CHEER UP
SHUT OUT	TEAR GAS	WASH POT	YOLK SAC	CHIME IN
SICK BAY	TEAR OFF	WASH TUB	YULE LOG	CHIPS IN
SICK BED	TEAR PIT	WEAK TEA		CHOKE UP
SICK DAY	TEED OFF	WEAR OFF	**5,2**	CHOPS UP
SIDE BOX	TEES OFF	WEAR OUT	ACTED UP	CHUCK UP
SIGN OFF	TELE ADS	WEEK END	ADDED UP	CHURN UP
SIGN OUT	TELL OFF	WELL FED	BACKS UP	CLAMS UP
SILK HAT	TENT BED	WELL MET	BANGS UP	CLEAN UP
SINE DIE	TENT FLY	WELL NOW	BARGE IN	CLEAR UP
SING OUT	TENT GUY	WELL OFF	BEARS UP	CLOCK IN
SITS OUT	TENT PEG	WELL SET	BEATS IT	CLOCK ON
SKID LID	TEST BAN	WELL WON	BEATS UP	CLOCK UP
SKID PAD	TEST BED	WENT BAD	BEEFS UP	CLOSE IN
SKID PAN	THAW OUT	WENT DRY	BELTS UP	CLOSE ON
SKID ROW	THIN OUT	WENT FAR	BLAZE UP	CLOSE UP
SLIP OFF	THUS FAR	WENT MAD	BLOWS IN	CLUED IN
SLIP ONS	TICK OFF	WENT OFF	BLOWS UP	CLUED UP
SLOE GIN	TIDE RIP	WENT OUT	BONED UP	CLUES IN
SLOP OUT	TIDE WAY	WEST END	BONES UP	COINS IT
SNOW BOX	TIDY SUM	WHAT FOR	BOOKS IN	COMES AT

5,2 *contd.*

COMES BY	FOOTS IT	LEAVE GO	PLUGS IN	SIZES UP
COMES IN	FORKS UP	LIFTS UP	POINT UP	SKIPS IT
COMES TO	FOULS UP	LIGHT UP	PRESS ON	SLEEP IN
COMES UP	FRAME UP	LINED UP	PRESS UP	SLEEP ON
COUGH UP	FROWN ON	LINES UP	PREYS ON	SLEPT IN
COVER IN	GANGS UP	LINKS IN	PROPS UP	SLEPT ON
COVER UP	GEARS UP	LINKS UP	PSYCH UP	SLICE UP
CRACK UP	GIVES IN	LIVED IN	PULLS IN	SLIPS ON
CRIED UP	GIVES UP	LIVED ON	PULLS UP	SLIPS UP
CRIES UP	GLORY BE	LIVES IN	PUMPS IN	SLOWS UP
CROPS UP	GOING AT	LIVES ON	PUMPS UP	SMASH UP
CURLS UP	GOING IN	LOCKS IN	PUNCH UP	SNAPS UP
DEARY ME	GOING ON	LOCKS ON	QUEUE UP	SNARL UP
DOING IN	GOING UP	LOCKS UP	QUIDS IN	SNEAK UP
DOING UP	GREAT GO	LOFTS UP	QUITE SO	SNUFF IT
DRAFT OX	GROSS UP	LOOKS AT	RACKS UP	SOBER UP
DRAGS ON	GROWN UP	LOOKS IN	RAKED IN	SOUPS UP
DRAGS UP	GROWS UP	LOOKS ON	RAKED UP	SPEAK UP
DRANK IN	HANDS UP	LOOKS UP	RAKES IN	SPEED UP
DRANK UP	HANGS IN	LYING BY	RAKES UP	SPOKE UP
DRAWS IN	HANGS ON	LYING IN	READS UP	SPRAY ON
DRAWS ON	HANGS UP	LYING ON	REINS IN	STACK UP
DRAWS UP	HARPS ON	LYING TO	RIDES UP	STAND BY
DREAM UP	HAULS IN	LYING UP	RIGHT ON	STAND IN
DRESS UP	HAULS UP	MAKES DO	RINGS IN	STAND ON
DRIED UP	HEAVE HO	MAKES IT	RINGS UP	STAND TO
DRIES UP	HEAVE TO	MAKES UP	RISES UP	STAND UP
DRINK IN	HEIGH HO	MARKS UP	RISKS IT	START IN
DRINK UP	HINTS AT	MEETS UP	ROLLS IN	START UP
DRIVE IN	HITCH UP	MISTS UP	ROLLS UP	STAVE IN
DROPS BY	HOLDS IN	MIXED IN	ROPED IN	STAYS IN
DROPS IN	HOLDS ON	MIXED IT	ROPES IN	STAYS ON
DROPS ON	HOLDS UP	MIXED UP	ROUGH IN	STAYS UP
DUFFS UP	HOLED UP	MIXES IN	ROUGH IT	STEAM UP
DUMPS ON	HOLES UP	MIXES IT	ROUND ON	STEPS IN
EARLY ON	HORNS IN	MIXES UP	ROUND UP	STEPS UP
ENDED UP	HOWDY DO	MOVED IN	ROYAL WE	STICK BY
EVENS UP	HURRY UP	MOVES IN	SAILS BY	STICK IN
EYING UP	HYPED UP	MUCKS IN	SAVED UP	STICK TO
FADED IN	HYPES UP	OFFER UP	SAVES UP	STICK UP
FADES IN	INKED IN	OPENS UP	SCARE UP	STIRS UP
FALLS IN	JOINS IN	OWNED UP	SCRUB UP	STOCK UP
FALLS ON	JOINS UP	PACKS UP	SEIZE UP	STOKE UP
FETCH UP	JUMPS ON	PASTE UP	SELLS ON	STONE ME
FILLS IN	KEEPS IN	PATCH UP	SELLS UP	STOOD IN
FILLS UP	KEEPS ON	PERKS UP	SENDS IN	STOOD ON
FIRED UP	KEEPS UP	PHASE IN	SENDS ON	STOOD TO
FIRES UP	KEYED IN	PHONE IN	SENDS UP	STOOD UP
FIRMS UP	KEYED UP	PICKS AT	SERVE UP	STOPS IN
FIXED IT	KICKS IN	PICKS ON	SHAKE UP	STOVE IN
FIXED ON	KNEES UP	PICKS UP	SHAPE UP	STUCK BY
FIXED UP	KNOCK ON	PIECE UP	SHOOK UP	STUCK IN
FIXES IT	KNOCK UP	PILED UP	SHOOT UP	STUCK ON
FIXES ON	LATCH ON	PILES UP	SHOWS UP	STUCK TO
FIXES UP	LEADS IN	PIPED UP	SHUTS IN	STUCK UP
FLARE UP	LEADS ON	PIPES UP	SHUTS UP	STUMP UP
FLIES BY	LEADS UP	PITCH IN	SIGNS IN	SUCKS IN
FLIES IN	LEANS ON	PLAYS AT	SIGNS UP	SWEAR IN
FOLDS IN	LEANT ON	PLAYS ON	SINKS IN	SWEEP UP
	LEAVE BE	PLAYS UP	SIZED UP	SWEPT UP

5,2 *contd.*
SWORN IN
SWOTS UP
TACKS ON
TAKEN IN
TAKEN ON
TAKEN UP
TAKES IN
TAKES IT
TAKES ON
TAKES TO
TAKES UP
TALKS IN
TALKS TO
TALLY HO
TARTS UP
TEACH IN
TEARS UP
TELLS ON
THINK UP
THREW IN
THREW ON
THREW UP
THROW IN
THROW ON
THROW UP
TONED UP
TONES UP
TOOLS UP
TOUCH UP
TRADE IN
TRADE UP
TRIED ON
TRIES ON
TUCKS IN
TUNED IN
TUNED UP
TUNES IN
TUNES UP
TURNS IN
TURNS ON
TURNS TO
TURNS UP
TWIGS IT
TYING IN
TYING UP
USING UP
VOTED IN
VOTES IN
WADED IN
WADES IN
WAITS ON
WAITS UP
WALKS IT
WALKS ON
WALLS UP
WANTS IN
WARMS UP
WATCH IT
WEIGH IN

WEIGH UP
WHATS UP
WHIPS IN
WINDS UP
WIPED UP
WIPES UP
WIRED IN
WIRES IN
WORKS IN
WORKS ON
WORKS UP
WORTH IT
WOULD BE
WOUND UP
WRAPS UP
WRITE UP
WRONG UN
WROTE UP
ZEROS IN

6,1
LINEAR A
LINEAR B
MIDDLE C
RADIUM A
RADIUM B

8 LETTERS

1,2,5
A LA CARTE

1,3,4
A BIT MUCH
A DAB HAND
A DIM VIEW
A RAW DEAL
X RAY TUBE

1,4,3
A FAIR COP
A GOOD JOB
A GOOD RUN
I DARE SAY

1,7
A BIENTOT
E NUMBERS
I DECLARE

2,1,5
AT A PINCH
AT A PRICE
BE A SPORT
IN A FLASH
IN A HURRY
IN A JIFFY
IN A PADDY
IN A SENSE
IN A TRICE
IN A WHILE
TO A FAULT

2,2,4
AS IT WERE
GO GO GIRL
GO TO SEED
GO TO TOWN
IT IS SAID
NO GO AREA
TO BE SURE
UP IN ARMS
UP TO DATE

2,3,3
AS ONE MAN
AT THE BAR
BY THE BYE
BY THE WAY
GO TOO FAR
IN AND OUT
IN MID AIR
IN THE AIR
IN THE BAG
IN THE CAN
IN THE END
IN THE RAW
IN THE RED
IN THE WAY
ON AND OFF
ON THE AIR
ON THE DOT
ON THE HOP
ON THE JOB
ON THE MAP
ON THE MAT
ON THE NOD
ON THE RUN
ON THE SLY
ON THE WAY
TO AND FRO

2,4,2
SO HELP ME
SO MUCH SO

2,6
AD LIBBED
AD LIBBER
AT ANCHOR
AT BOTTOM
AT DINNER
AT LENGTH
AU GRATIN
AU REVOIR
BE MOTHER
BI WEEKLY
BI YEARLY
BY CHANCE
BY CHOICE
BY DESIGN
BY ITSELF
BY RETURN
BY RIGHTS
CI DEVANT

DO BATTLE
DO GOODER
EL DORADO
EN CROUTE
ET CETERA
EX GRATIA
EX LIBRIS
GO ABROAD
GO GETTER
GO HALVES
GO HUNGRY
GO METRIC
GO NATIVE
GO PLACES
GO PUBLIC
GO STEADY
IN CAMERA
IN CHARGE
IN CLOVER
IN COMMON
IN CREDIT
IN DANGER
IN DEMAND
IN DETAIL
IN EFFECT
IN FAVOUR
IN FLIGHT
IN FUTURE
IN PERSON
IN PIECES
IN POCKET
IN PRISON
IN PUBLIC
IN QUOTES
IN SEASON
IN SECRET
IN SHTOOK
IN SPADES
IN TANDEM
IN UNISON
NO LONGER
NO MATTER
NO THANKS
NO TRUMPS
NO WONDER
OF COURSE
ON CAMERA
ON CREDIT
ON DEMAND
ON PARADE
ON PATROL
ON RECORD
ON REMAND
ON SAFARI
ON STREAM
ON STRIKE
ON TARGET
ON TIPTOE
ON VELVET
OX PECKER

OX TONGUE
OX WARBLE
RH FACTOR
SE TENANT
SO CALLED
ST JULIEN
TE IGITUR
TV DINNER
UP ANCHOR
UP ENDING
UP MARKET

3,1,4
CUT A DASH
DID A TURN
FLY A KITE
FOR A TIME
HAD A BALL
HAD A BASH
HAD A STAB
HAS A BALL
HAS A BASH
HAS A STAB
NOT A HOPE
NOT A PEEP
PAY A CALL
RAN A RISK
RUN A RISK
SAW A WOLF
SEE A WOLF
SET A TRAP

3,2,3
ACT OF GOD
ACT OF WAR
AIR TO AIR
ALL AT SEA
ALL IN ALL
ALL IN ONE
ALL MY EYE
ARM IN ARM
BIT BY BIT
CAP IT ALL
COQ AU VIN
CUL DE SAC
CUP OF TEA
CUT IT OUT
CUT NO ICE
DAY BY DAY
DAY TO DAY
EAU DE NIL
EAU DE VIE
END TO END
HAD IT OUT
HAS IT OUT
HIT IT OFF
LAY AN EGG
LET IT RIP
LET ME SEE
MAL DE MER
MAN OF GOD

3,2,3 *contd.*
MAN OF LAW
MAN OF WAR
MAN TO MAN
MEN OF WAR
ONE BY ONE
ONE OR TWO
ONE TO ONE
OUT OF BED
OUT OF USE
POT AU FEU
PUT ON ICE
PUT TO BED
PUT TO SEA
PUT UP JOB
RUM TI TUM
SON IN LAW
SON OF MAN
TAC AU TAC
TOE TO TOE
TUG OF WAR

3,3,2
ALL THE GO
ASK FOR IT
DOT THE IS
GIN AND IT
OFF AND ON
RAN OUT ON
RUB OFF ON
RUN FOR IT
RUN OUT ON
WHO DUN IT

3,5
ACT THREE
AGE GROUP
AIR BENDS
AIR BRAKE
AIR BRICK
AIR BRUSH
AIR COOLS
AIR COVER
AIR FORCE
AIR POWER
AIR RIFLE
AIR SCOUT
ALE HOUSE
ALL ALONE
ALL ALONG
ALL CLEAR
ALL FOUND
ALL FOURS
ALL RIGHT
ALL ROUND
ALL STARS
ALL THERE
ANT EATER
ARC LIGHT
ARK ROYAL

ART CLASS
ART PAPER
ART UNION
ASH BLOND
ASH LEACH
ASH PLANT
ASH STAND
ASK AFTER
AVE MARIA
BAD BLOOD
BAD DREAM
BAD FAITH
BAD LOSER
BAD PATCH
BAR CHART
BAR CODED
BAR GRAPH
BAR LUNCH
BAR STOOL
BAY HORSE
BED LINEN
BED PLATE
BEE BREAD
BEE EATER
BEE HOUSE
BEL CANTO
BEL PAESE
BEN NEVIS
BIG APPLE
BIG BREAK
BIG CHIEF
BIG DADDY
BIG HOUSE
BIG MONEY
BIG MOUTH
BIG NOISE
BIG STICK
BIG WHEEL
BIN LINER
BOB MAJOR
BOB MINOR
BOB ROYAL
BOG LATIN
BOW BELLS
BOX CLOTH
BOX FRAME
BOX PLEAT
BOX WAGON
BOY SCOUT
BUN FIGHT
CAB STAND
CAM WHEEL
CAR CRASH
CAR FERRY
CAR PHONE
CLY FAKER
COD PIECE
COG WHEEL
CON AMORE

CON TRICK
COT DEATH
COW WHALE
CUB SCOUT
CUP FINAL
CUP MATCH
CUT GLASS
CUT LOOSE
CUT PRICE
CUT SHORT
DAY SHIFT
DAY SIGHT
DAY WOMAN
DEW BERRY
DIE HAPPY
DIE STOCK
DIP STICK
DOG DAISY
DOG EARED
DOG HOUSE
DOG LATIN
DOG TIRED
DOG TRICK
DOG WATCH
DOG WEARY
DOG WHEAT
DRY CLEAN
DRY STEAM
DRY STONE
DUE NORTH
DUE SOUTH
DYE HOUSE
DYE WORKS
EAR PLUGS
EAR SHELL
EGG BOUND
EGG FRUIT
EGG PLANT
EGG SLICE
EGG SPOON
EGG TIMER
EGG WHISK
ELF CHILD
END PAPER
EYE DROPS
EYE LEVEL
EYE PIECE
EYE SALVE
EYE TEETH
EYE TOOTH
EYE WATER
FAN DANCE
FAN WHEEL
FAR FLUNG
FAR NORTH
FAR SOUTH
FAT FACED
FAT STOCK
FEN BERRY

FIN WHALE
FLY BLOWN
FLY PAPER
FLY SHEET
FLY SPRAY
FLY TYING
FOB WATCH
FOG LIGHT
FOR KEEPS
FOR KICKS
FOR MERCY
FOR SHAME
FOR SHORT
FOX BRUSH
FOX EARTH
FOX GRAPE
FUR TRADE
GAD ABOUT
GAS BLACK
GAS BOARD
GAS FIRED
GAS GLOBE
GAS METER
GAS MOTOR
GAS PLANT
GAS POKER
GAS STOVE
GAS TIGHT
GAS WORKS
GET ABOUT
GET AHEAD
GET ALONG
GET IDEAS
GET READY
GET ROUND
GET THERE
GET TOUGH
GIG LAMPS
GIN RUMMY
GIN SLING
GOD AWFUL
GOD BLESS
GOD GIVEN
GOD KNOWS
GOT ABOUT
GOT AHEAD
GOT ALONG
GOT IDEAS
GOT READY
GOT ROUND
GOT THERE
GOT TOUGH
GUM RESIN
GYM TUNIC
HAD IDEAS
HAD WORDS
HAS BEENS
HAS IDEAS
HAS WORDS

HAT TRICK
HAY FEVER
HEN COURT
HEN FLESH
HEN HOUSE
HEN NIGHT
HEN PARTY
HEN ROOST
HIC JACET
HIP FLASK
HIP JOINT
HOG MANED
HOT METAL
HOT MONEY
HOT PANTS
HOT PLATE
HOT STUFF
HOT TODDY
HOT WATER
HUB BRAKE
ICE BOUND
ICE CRAFT
ICE CREAM
ICE CUBES
ICE DANCE
ICE FIELD
ICE HOUSE
ICE LOLLY
ICE SHEET
ICE SKATE
ICE WATER
ICE YACHT
ILL BEING
ILL BLOOD
ILL FATED
ILL SPENT
ILL TIMED
ILL TREAT
ILL USAGE
JAW LEVER
JET BLACK
JET PLANE
JET SKIER
JIB CRANE
JIG BORER
JOG ALONG
JOY RIDER
JOY STICK
KEY FRUIT
KEY PLATE
KEY PUNCH
KID GLOVE
LAP BOARD
LAW AGENT
LAW COURT
LAW GIVER
LAW MAKER
LAY ASIDE
LAY AWAKE

3,5 *contd.*	NEW RISEN	PER ANNUM	RIB ROAST _	SEA SHRUB
LAY CLAIM	NEW STYLE	PEW CHAIR	ROW BARGE	SEA SNAIL
LAY SHAFT	NEW WOMAN	PIA MATER	ROW HOUSE	SEA SNAKE
LAY UNDER	NEW WORLD	PIE CHART	RUB ALONG	SEA SNIPE
LAY VICAR	NIT PICKS	PIE GRAPH	RUM PUNCH	SEA STORM
LAY WASTE	NON EVENT	PIG FACED	RUM SHRUB	SEA TROUT
LED HORSE	NON METAL	PIG SWILL	RUN AFTER	SEA WATER
LEE BOARD	NON STICK	PIG WOMAN	RUN ALONG	SEA WOMAN
LEE GAUGE	NON UNION	PIN MAKER	RUN CLOSE	SEA WRACK
LEE SHORE	NUT BROWN	PIN MONEY	RUN SHORT	SEE ROUND
LEG BREAK	OAK APPLE	PIN POINT	RYE BREAD	SEE STARS
LEG GUARD	OAK CHEST	PIN PRICK	RYE FLOUR	SET ABOUT
LEG WOMAN	OAT GRASS	PIN WHEEL	RYE GRASS	SET APART
LET ALONE	OBI WOMAN	PIS ALLER	RYE STRAW	SET ASIDE
LET BLOOD	OFF BOARD	PIT VIPER	SAD FACED	SET FORTH
LET DRIVE	OFF BREAK	POP GROUP	SAP GREEN	SET PIECE
LET LOOSE	OFF DRIVE	POT BELLY	SAT STILL	SET SCREW
LET SLIDE	OFF SALES	POT BOUND	SAT TIGHT	SET TERMS
LIE AWAKE	OFF STAGE	POT METAL	SAW BLADE	SHE DEVIL
LIE DOGGO	OFF WHITE	POT PLANT	SAW BONES	SIN EATER
LIE UNDER	OIL FIELD	POT ROAST	SAW EDGED	SIT STILL
LIP SALVE	OIL FIRED	POT SHARD	SAW FRAME	SIT TIGHT
LOG CABIN	OIL GAUGE	POT STICK	SAW ROUND	SKI SLOPE
LOG CANOE	OIL PAINT	POT STILL	SAW STARS	SKI STICK
LOG HOUSE	OIL PAPER	PRE ELECT	SAW TOOTH	SKY DIVER
LOK SABHA	OIL PRESS	PRE EMPTS	SEA BEACH	SKY PILOT
LOP EARED	OIL SHALE	PRE EXIST	SEA BEAST	SOB STORY
LOP SIDED	OIL SLICK	PRE PRINT	SEA BOOTS	SOB STUFF
LOW DUTCH	OLD FOGEY	PRE SELLS	SEA BORNE	SOW BREAD
LOW LATIN	OLD GLORY	PRO FORMA	SEA BREAM	SPY MONEY
LOW LIVED	OLD GUARD	PUB CRAWL	SEA CHART	SPY PLANE
LOW SLUNG	OLD HARRY	PUG FACED	SEA CLIFF	SRI LANKA
LOW WATER	OLD STORY	PUG NOSED	SEA DEVIL	SUI JURIS
MAD APPLE	OLD STYLE	PUT ABOUT	SEA EAGLE	SUM TOTAL
MAH JONGG	OLD TIMER	QUO VADIS	SEA FIGHT	SUN BAKED
MAN ALIVE	OLD WOMAN	RAG PAPER	SEA FLOOR	SUN BLIND
MAN CHILD	OLD WORLD	RAG TRADE	SEA FRONT	SUN BLINK
MAN EATER	ONE HORSE	RAG WOMAN	SEA FROTH	SUN CURED
MAN HOURS	ONE LINER	RAN AFTER	SEA GOING	SUN DRESS
MAN POWER	ONE PIECE	RAN ALONG	SEA GRAPE	SUN DRIED
MAN SIZED	ONE SIDED	RAN CLOSE	SEA GRASS	SUN DROPS
MAN WEEKS	OUT HEROD	RAN SHORT	SEA GREEN	SUN SHADE
MAN YEARS	OWL GLASS	RAW STEAK	SEA HORSE	SUN VISOR
MAY APPLE	OWL LIGHT	RAW UMBER	SEA HOUND	TAG ALONG
MAY BLOOM	OWN BRAND	RED ALERT	SEA JELLY	TAJ MAHAL
MAY QUEEN	OWN LABEL	RED ALGAE	SEA LEMON	TAN BALLS
MEA CULPA	PAD CLOTH	RED BELLY	SEA LEVEL	TAP DANCE
MEM SAHIB	PAD HORSE	RED BIDDY	SEA LOACH	TAP HOUSE
MID OCEAN	PAN PIPES	RED BRICK	SEA LUNGS	TAP SHOES
MID POINT	PAR AVION	RED CEDAR	SEA MOUNT	TAP WATER
MOT JUSTE	PAR VALUE	RED CROSS	SEA NYMPH	TAR BRUSH
MUD FLATS	PAY PHONE	RED DWARF	SEA ONION	TAR PAPER
MUD GUARD	PAY ROUND	RED FACED	SEA ORACH	TAU CROSS
NEW BLOOD	PAY SHEET	RED GIANT	SEA OTTER	TAU STAFF
NEW BLOWN	PEA CHICK	RED GUARD	SEA PERCH	TAX EXILE
NEW BROOM	PEA GREEN	RED LIGHT	SEA POWER	TAX HAVEN
NEW FOUND	PEA VINER	RED SHANK	SEA ROBIN	TAX PAYER
NEW LIGHT	PEN WIPER	RED SHIFT	SEA ROVER	TAX POINT
NEW MATHS	PEP PILLS	RED SHIRT	SEA SCOUT	TEA BREAK

3,5 *contd.*
TEA CADDY
TEA CHEST
TEA CLOTH
TEA DANCE
TEA HOUSE
TEA PARTY
TEA PLANT
TEA TABLE
TEA TOWEL
TEE SHIRT
TEN PENCE
TEN SCORE
THE ASHES
THE BENDS
THE BLITZ
THE BLUES
THE BRINY
THE BUFFS
THE CHAIR
THE CLOTH
THE DERBY
THE DEVIL
THE DOWNS
THE DRINK
THE ENEMY
THE FANCY
THE FLOOD
THE GOODS
THE GREYS
THE HALLS
THE HOUSE
THE LIONS
THE MAFIA
THE PRESS
THE SKIDS
THE SMOKE
THE THING
THE TWIST
THE UNION
THE USUAL
THE WEALD
THE WORKS
TIE BREAK
TIN MINER
TIN PLATE
TOE PIECE
TOG VALUE
TOM NODDY
TOM THUMB
TOO RIGHT
TOP BRASS
TOP DRESS
TOP HEAVY
TOP LEVEL
TOP LINER
TOP NOTCH
TOP STONE
TOP TABLE

TOW PLANE
TUB THUMP
TWO EDGED
TWO FACED
TWO PIECE
TWO SCORE
TWO SIDED
TWO TICKS
TWO TIMED
TWO TIMER
TWO TIMES
USE FORCE
VEE JOINT
VIN BLANC
VIN ROUGE
WAR BRIDE
WAR CLOUD
WAR CRIME
WAR DANCE
WAR GAMER
WAR HORSE
WAR PAINT
WAR TRIAL
WAR WEARY
WAR WHOOP
WAR WIDOW
WAX CLOTH
WAX LIGHT
WAX MATCH
WAX PAPER
WAY BOARD
WAY GOING
WAY MAKER
WAY POINT
WAY TRAIN
WEE FREES
WET NURSE
WET PAINT
WIG BLOCK
WIG MAKER
WRY SMILE
YET AGAIN
ZIP FRONT

4,1,2,1
FROM A TO B
FROM A TO Z

4,1,3
BUYS A PUP
CAST A NET
LIVE A LIE
MADE A BED
MAKE A BED
PICK N MIX
RENT A MOB
SELL A PUP
SHOW A LEG
SOLD A PUP
TAKE A BOW

TELL A LIE
TOOK A BOW

4,2,2
AUTO DA FE
BEAT TO IT
CAMP IT UP
FELO DE SE
HARD AT IT
JUMP TO IT
KEEP AT IT
KEEP IT UP
KEPT AT IT
LETS IN ON
LIVE IT UP
LOOK UP TO
MADE IT UP
MAKE IT UP
PACK IT IN
PACK IT UP
PICK ME UP
PILE IT ON
PUTS IT ON
PUTS ON TO
PUTS TO IT
RUBS IT ON
SEES TO IT
STEP ON IT
TURN IT IN
TURN IT UP
WAKE UP TO
WELL TO DO
WHAT OF IT
WOKE UP TO
WORK AT IT
ZAPS IT UP
ZERO IN ON

4,4
ACES HIGH
ACES WILD
ACID BATH
ACID DROP
ACID HEAD
ACID RAIN
ACID TEST
AGAR AGAR
ALMS FOLK
ALOE VERA
ANTE POST
ANTI HERO
ANTS EGGS
ANTS NEST
AREA CODE
ARMS RACE
ARMY CAMP
ARMY LIST
ARUM LILY
ATOM BOMB
AWAY GAME

BABY BOOM
BABY DOLL
BABY SITS
BABY TALK
BACK AXLE
BACK COMB
BACK DATE
BACK DOOR
BACK DOWN
BACK HEEL
BACK LANE
BAIL BALL
BAIL DOCK
BALD COOT
BALD HEAD
BALE DOCK
BALE FIRE
BALL BOYS
BALL GAME
BALL GIRL
BALL GOWN
BALL PARK
BALL ROOM
BAND FISH
BANG TAIL
BANK BILL
BANK BOOK
BANK LOAN
BANK NOTE
BANK RATE
BARN DOOR
BASE BORN
BASE COIN
BASE LINE
BASE RATE
BASE RING
BASS CLEF
BASS DRUM
BASS HORN
BASS TUBA
BASS VIOL
BEAD ROLL
BEAM ENDS
BEAM TREE
BEAN KING
BEAN TREE
BEAR ARMS
BEAR AWAY
BEAR DOWN
BEAT DOWN
BEAT TIME
BEAU JOUR
BEAU PERE
BEDS DOWN
BEER PUMP
BELL BIRD
BELL BUOY
BELL PULL
BELL ROPE

BELL TENT
BEND OVER
BENT OVER
BERG WIND
BEST GIRL
BEST MAID
BEST PART
BETA RAYS
BILE DUCT
BIND OVER
BIRD CALL
BIRD EYED
BIRD LIME
BLEW AWAY
BLEW OVER
BLOW AWAY
BLOW LAMP
BLOW OVER
BLUE BABY
BLUE BOOK
BLUE CHIP
BLUE FILM
BLUE FUNK
BLUE GREY
BLUE HARE
BLUE MOON
BLUE NOTE
BOAT DECK
BOAT HOOK
BOAT LOAD
BOAT SONG
BODY BLOW
BODY SHOP
BOGS DOWN
BOIL OVER
BOMB SITE
BONA FIDE
BONE ACHE
BONE DUST
BONE IDLE
BONE LACE
BONE MEAL
BONE MILL
BONY PIKE
BOOB TUBE
BOOK CLUB
BOOK ENDS
BOOK MATE
BOOM IRON
BOOM TOWN
BOOT HOOK
BOOT JACK
BOOT SALE
BORE ARMS
BORE AWAY
BORE DOWN
BORN FOOL
BOSS EYED
BOWL OVER

4,4 contd.
BOYS CLUB
BRAN MASH
BRAT PACK
BRIM FULL
BUFF COAT
BULL BEEF
BULL CALF
BULL HOOF
BULL HORN
BULL RING
BUMP INTO
BUNG HOLE
BUNG VENT
BUNK BEDS
BURN DOWN
BUSH BABY
BUSH BUCK
BUYS OVER
BUZZ BOMB
BUZZ WORD
CAFE NOIR
CAKE HOLE
CALF LOVE
CALF TIME
CALL AWAY
CALL BACK
CALL BIRD
CALL GIRL
CALL NOTE
CALL OVER
CALL SIGN
CALM DOWN
CAME AWAY
CAME BACK
CAME DOWN
CAME HOME
CAME OVER
CAMP FIRE
CAMP SITE
CANE MILL
CANT HOOK
CANT RAIL
CAPE CART
CAPE HORN
CAPE TOWN
CARD CASE
CARD FILE
CARD GAME
CARD PLAY
CARD VOTE
CARE WORN
CASE BOOK
CASE LOAD
CASE WORK
CASH BOOK
CASH CARD
CASH CROP
CASH DESK
CASH DOWN

CASH FLOW
CASH SALE
CAST AWAY
CAST IRON
CAST LOTS
CATS FOOT
CATS MEAT
CATS TAIL
CAVE BEAR
CELL MATE
CHAT SHOW
CHEE CHEE
CHEW OVER
CHEZ NOUS
CHIN CHIN
CHIP SHOP
CHIP SHOT
CHOO CHOO
CHOP CHOP
CHOP SUEY
CHOW CHOW
CHOW MEIN
CINE FILM
CITY DESK
CITY HALL
CLAW BACK
CLAY MILL
CLAY PIPE
CLIP CLOP
CLIP HOOK
CLUB FACE
CLUB FOOT
CLUB HEAD
CLUB SODA
COAL DUST
COAL FACE
COAL FLAP
COAL HOLE
COAL MINE
COAL SACK
COCA COLA
COCK CROW
COCK EYED
COCO WOOD
CODE BOOK
CODE NAME
COLD FEET
COLD FISH
COLD SNAP
COLD SORE
COLE SLAW
COME AWAY
COME BACK
COME COME
COME DOWN
COME HOME
COME OVER
CONY WOOL
CORE TIME
CORK HEEL

CORK SOLE
CORK TREE
CORN BALL
CORN CURE
CORN FLAG
CORN LAWS
CORN MILL
CORN MOTH
CORN RENT
COWS LICK
CRAB TREE
CRAM FULL
CREW NECK
CUBE ROOT
CUFF LINK
CUSS WORD
CUTS BACK
CUTS DEAD
CUTS DOWN
DAMP DOWN
DARK AGES
DARK ROOM
DASH AWAY
DATE LINE
DATE PALM
DATE TREE
DAVY LAMP
DAWN RAID
DEAD BEAT
DEAD CART
DEAD CERT
DEAD DUCK
DEAD HAND
DEAD HEAD
DEAD HEAT
DEAD LOCK
DEAD LOSS
DEAD SHOT
DEAD SPIT
DEAD WOOD
DEAF MUTE
DECK GAME
DECK HAND
DECK LOAD
DEED POLL
DEEP DOWN
DEEP DYED
DEER HORN
DEER PARK
DEMI JOUR
DEMI LUNE
DEMI VOLT
DEMI WOLF
DENE HOLE
DESK WORK
DEWY EYED
DICE GAME
DICE PLAY
DIED AWAY
DIED DOWN

DIED HARD
DIES AWAY
DIES DOWN
DIES HARD
DIES IRAE
DING DONG
DIRT ROAD
DISC FILE
DIVE BOMB
DOCK DUES
DOES DOWN
DOES OVER
DOES TIME
DOES WELL
DOGS BODY
DOGS HOME
DOGS LIFE
DOGS MEAT
DOGS NOSE
DONE DOWN
DONE OVER
DONE WELL
DONT KNOW
DOOR BELL
DOOR CASE
DOOR KNOB
DOOR SILL
DOSS DOWN
DOUM PALM
DOVE COTE
DOVE EYED
DOVE LIKE
DOWN HOME
DOWN LINE
DOWN TOWN
DOWN TROD
DRAG RACE
DRAM SHOP
DRAW BACK
DRAW GEAR
DRAW LOTS
DRAW NEAR
DREW BACK
DREW LOTS
DREW NEAR
DRIP FEED
DROP AWAY
DROP DEAD
DROP DOWN
DROP GOAL
DROP KICK
DROP SHOT
DUCK DOWN
DUCK HAWK
DUCK POND
DUCK SHOT
DUCK SOUP
DUCK TAIL
DULL EYED
DULL THUD

DUMB BELL
DUMB SHOW
DUNG HEAP
DUNG HILL
DUST BALL
DUST BATH
DUST BOWL
DUST CART
DUST COAT
DUST HOLE
DUST TRAP
DUTY FREE
DUTY PAID
EAST SIDE
EATS AWAY
ECCE HOMO
EDGE RAIL
EDGE TOOL
EPIC POEM
ETON CROP
ETON SUIT
EVIL DEED
EVIL DOER
EXIT POLL
EYES DOWN
FACE ACHE
FACE DOWN
FACE LIFT
FACE MASK
FACE PACK
FADE AWAY
FAIL SAFE
FAIR COPY
FAIR DEAL
FAIR GAME
FAIR ISLE
FAIR PLAY
FALL AWAY
FALL BACK
FALL DOWN
FALL OVER
FARM HAND
FAST FOOD
FAST TALK
FEED LINE
FEED PIPE
FEED PUMP
FEEL FREE
FELL BACK
FELL DOWN
FELL OVER
FEME SOLE
FERN SEED
FETE DIEU
FILE COPY
FILE PAST
FILM NOIR
FILM STAR
FINE ARTS
FINE GAEL

4,4 *contd.*

FINE LADY	FOOT RACE	GAOL BIRD	GOOD LADY	HARD CASE
FINE SPUN	FOOT ROPE	GATE FINE	GOOD SHOW	HARD CASH
FINE TUNE	FORE BODY	GATE POST	GOOD TURN	HARD COPY
FIRE AWAY	FORE RANK	GAVE AWAY	GOOD WORK	HARD CORE
FIRE BACK	FORK OVER	GAVE ODDS	GOON SHOW	HARD DISC
FIRE BIRD	FORM ROOM	GAVE REIN	GREY AREA	HARD DISK
FIRE BOMB	FORT KNOX	GEAR CASE	GREY COAT	HARD EDGE
FIRE DOOR	FOUL FISH	GEAR DOWN	GREY EYED	HARD LUCK
FIRE FLAG	FOUL PLAY	GERM CELL	GREY FISH	HARD ROCK
FIRE HOSE	FOUR BALL	GETS BACK	GREY MARE	HARD SELL
FIRE OPAL	FOUR BITS	GETS DOWN	GREY WOLF	HARD WORK
FIRE RISK	FOUR EYES	GETS EVEN	GROG SHOP	HARE FOOT
FIRE TRAP	FOUR PACK	GETS OVER	GROO GROO	HARK BACK
FIRE TUBE	FOUR PART	GIFT BOOK	GRUB SHOP	HARP SEAL
FIRE WALK	FOWL PEST	GIFT SHOP	GULL WING	HAVE NOTS
FIRM DOWN	FREE ATOM	GIFT WRAP	HACK WORK	HAWK EYED
FISH BONE	FREE CITY	GIVE AWAY	HAIL MARY	HAWK MOTH
FISH CAKE	FREE FALL	GIVE ODDS	HAIR BALL	HEAD BOOM
FISH FARM	FREE GIFT	GIVE OVER	HAIR BAND	HEAD COLD
FISH GLUE	FREE HAND	GIVE REIN	HAIR GRIP	HEAD GIRL
FISH GUTS	FREE KICK	GLAD HAND	HAIR TAIL	HEAD RENT
FISH HOOK	FREE LIST	GLAD RAGS	HAIR WAVE	HEAD WIND
FISH MEAL	FREE LOVE	GLAM ROCK	HAIR WORK	HEAR HEAR
FISH POND	FREE PORT	GLEE CLUB	HAIR WORM	HEAR TELL
FISH STEW	FREE SHOT	GLOW WORM	HALF BACK	HEAT PUMP
FISH TAIL	FREE VOTE	GNAW AWAY	HALF BRED	HEAT SINK
FISH TANK	FREE WILL	GOAL KICK	HALF COCK	HEAT UNIT
FISH WEIR	FROG FISH	GOAL LINE	HALF DEAD	HEAT WAVE
FLAG DOWN	FROU FROU	GOAT MOTH	HALF DONE	HEEL BALL
FLAT FOOT	FUEL CELL	GODS ACRE	HALF FACE	HELD BACK
FLAT RACE	FUEL PIPE	GOES AWAY	HALF HOUR	HELD DOWN
FLAT RATE	FUEL TANK	GOES BACK	HALF INCH	HELD GOOD
FLAT SPIN	FULL BACK	GOES BUST	HALF LIFE	HELD OVER
FLAT TYRE	FULL BORE	GOES DOWN	HALF LOAF	HELD SWAY
FLAX BUSH	FULL COCK	GOES INTO	HALF MAST	HELL BENT
FLAX COMB	FULL EYED	GOES LIVE	HALF MOON	HELL FIRE
FLAX LILY	FULL FACE	GOES OVER	HALF NOTE	HELL GATE
FLAX MILL	FULL HAND	GOES SOFT	HALF PINT	HELL HOLE
FLAX SEED	FULL MOON	GOES WEST	HALF TERM	HEMP PALM
FLEA BANE	FULL PAGE	GOLD COIN	HALF TIDE	HEMP SEED
FLEA BITE	FULL PELT	GOLD DISC	HALF TIME	HERB BEER
FLEW HIGH	FULL SAIL	GOLD DUST	HALF TINT	HERE GOES
FLEW OPEN	FULL STOP	GOLD FOIL	HALF TONE	HIDE AWAY
FLEW SOLO	FULL TILT	GOLD LACE	HALF YEAR	HIDY HOLE
FLIM FLAM	FULL TIME	GOLD LEAF	HALL DOOR	HIGH BORN
FLIP FLAP	FULL TOSS	GOLD MINE	HALL MOOT	HIGH BRED
FLIP FLOP	FUSE WIRE	GOLD RING	HAND BALL	HIGH CAMP
FLIP SIDE	FUZZ BALL	GOLD RUSH	HAND CART	HIGH GEAR
FLUE PIPE	GAFF SAIL	GOLD WIRE	HAND DOWN	HIGH HAND
FOAM BATH	GAIN TIME	GOLF BALL	HAND KNIT	HIGH JUMP
FOIE GRAS	GALL DUCT	GOLF CLUB	HAND LINE	HIGH KICK
FOLK HERO	GAME BALL	GONE AWAY	HAND LOOM	HIGH LIFE
FOLK SONG	GAME BIRD	GONE BACK	HAND MILL	HIGH MASS
FOLK TALE	GAME CALL	GONE BUST	HAND OVER	HIGH NOON
FOLK TUNE	GAME COCK	GONE DOWN	HAND PICK	HIGH RISE
FOOD CARD	GAME FISH	GONE INTO	HAND POST	HIGH RISK
FOOD FISH	GAME LAWS	GONE OVER	HANG BACK	HIGH ROAD
FOOT BATH	GAME PLAN	GONE SOFT	HANG FIRE	HIGH SEAS
FOOT PUMP	GANG MILL	GONE WEST	HANG OVER	HIGH SPOT
	GANG SHOW	GOOD FORM	HARA KIRI	HIGH TECH

4,4 *contd.*
HIGH TIDE
HIGH TIME
HIGH TOBY
HIGH WIRE
HILL FORT
HIND WING
HIVE NEST
HOCK CART
HOCK TIDE
HOGS BACK
HOKY POKY
HOLD BACK
HOLD DOWN
HOLD GOOD
HOLD HARD
HOLD OVER
HOLD SWAY
HOLY CITY
HOLY LAND
HOLY ROOD
HOLY WEEK
HOLY WRIT
HOLY YEAR
HOME BASE
HOME BIRD
HOME FARM
HOME FIRE
HOME GAME
HOME HELP
HOME LIFE
HOME LOAN
HOME MADE
HOME PORT
HOME RULE
HOME TOWN
HONG KONG
HOOF MARK
HOOK WORM
HORN RIMS
HOSE REEL
HOUR HAND
HOWL DOWN
HOWS THAT
HULA HOOP
HULA HULA
HUMP BACK
HUNG BACK
HUNG BEEF
HUNG FIRE
HUNG JURY
HUNG MEAT
HUNG OVER
HUNT BALL
HUNT DOWN
HUSH HUSH
HYDE PARK
HYMN BOOK
ICED OVER
ICES OVER

IDEE FIXE
IDLE TIME
INCH TAPE
INCH WORM
IRON CLAD
IRON GREY
IRON HAND
IRON LUNG
IRON MINE
ITCH MITE
JACK BOOT
JACK FOOL
JACK HIGH
JACK PLUG
JAIL BAIT
JAIL BIRD
JAZZ BAND
JEWS HARP
JOHN BULL
JOHN DORY
JOKE BOOK
JUMP BAIL
JUMP SHIP
JUMP SUIT
JUNK BOND
JUNK FOOD
JUNK MAIL
JUNK SHOP
JUNK YARD
JURY LIST
JURY MAST
KAKA BEAK
KAKA BILL
KALA AZAR
KEEL OVER
KEEP BACK
KEEP BUSY
KEEP DOWN
KEEP TIME
KEPT BACK
KEPT BUSY
KEPT DOWN
KEPT TIME
KILL TIME
KING BIRD
KING CRAB
KING CROW
KING JOHN
KING LIKE
KING SIZE
KIPS DOWN
KIRK TOWN
KISS CURL
KITE MARK
KNEE DEEP
KNEE HIGH
KNEE JERK
KNEE SOCK
KNOT HOLE
LACE BOOT

LACE WING
LADY FERN
LADY LOVE
LADY LUCK
LAID BACK
LAID BARE
LAID DOWN
LAID INTO
LAID OPEN
LAID WORK
LAKE ERIE
LAMB LIKE
LAME DUCK
LAND AHOY
LAND ARMY
LAND BANK
LAND CRAB
LAND FISH
LAND GIRL
LAND HAUL
LAND LINE
LAND MINE
LAND ROLL
LAST GASP
LAST HEIR
LAST POST
LAST WORD
LATE CALL
LAYS BARE
LAYS DOWN
LAYS INTO
LAYS OPEN
LAZY DAYS
LAZY JACK
LEAD FREE
LEAD LINE
LEAD MINE
LEAD TIME
LEAF BASE
LEAF CURL
LEAF FALL
LEAF SCAR
LEAP FROG
LEAP YEAR
LEFT BANK
LEFT HAND
LEFT HOOK
LEFT OVER
LEFT SIDE
LEFT WING
LENT LILY
LETS DOWN
LETS DROP
LETS FALL
LETS SLIP
LIAR DICE
LIES BACK
LIES DOWN
LIES OVER
LIFE BUOY

LIFE LINE
LIFE PEER
LIFE RAFT
LIFE RENT
LIFE SIZE
LIFE WORK
LIFT GIRL
LIFT PUMP
LIKE FURY
LILY POND
LIMA WOOD
LIME TREE
LIME TWIG
LIME WOOD
LINE FISH
LINO TILE
LION LIKE
LIVE BAIT
LIVE BORN
LIVE DOWN
LIVE LOAD
LIVE RAIL
LIVE WELL
LIVE WIRE
LOAD LINE
LOAF CAKE
LOAN WORD
LOCH NESS
LOCK AWAY
LOCK GATE
LONE WOLF
LONG FACE
LONG HAIR
LONG HAUL
LONG JUMP
LONG LIFE
LONG MARK
LONG ODDS
LONG ROBE
LONG SHOT
LONG SLIP
LONG SPUN
LONG STAY
LONG STOP
LONG SUIT
LONG TERM
LONG TIME
LONG TOGS
LONG VIEW
LONG WAIT
LONG WAVE
LOOK AWRY
LOOK BACK
LOOK DOWN
LOOK HERE
LOOK INTO
LOOK LIKE
LOOK OVER
LOOP LINE
LOSE FACE

LOSE TIME
LOST FACE
LOST SOUL
LOST TIME
LOVE DRUG
LOVE GAME
LOVE KNOT
LOVE NEST
LOVE SEAT
LOVE SONG
LOVE SUIT
LUNG FISH
LYNX EYED
LYRE BIRD
MADE AWAY
MADE GOOD
MADE LOVE
MADE OVER
MADE PLAY
MADE ROAD
MADE ROOM
MADE SAIL
MADE SURE
MADE TIME
MAIL BOAT
MAIL CART
MAIL SHOT
MAIN DECK
MAIN DRAG
MAIN LINE
MAIN ROAD
MAKE AWAY
MAKE GOOD
MAKE LOVE
MAKE OVER
MAKE PLAY
MAKE ROOM
MAKE SAIL
MAKE SURE
MAKE TIME
MALA FIDE
MALT KILN
MALT MILL
MANY EYED
MANY ROOT
MARK DOWN
MARK TIME
MASS BELL
MASS BOOK
MAXI COAT
MEAL TIME
MEAN BORN
MEAN WELL
MEAT BALL
MEAT LOAF
MEAT RACK
MEAT SAFE
MELT AWAY
MELT DOWN
MESH WORK

4,4 *contd.*

MESS DECK	NEXT DOOR	PINE CONE	POST TIME	REAR RANK
MESS ROOM	NICE WORK	PINE TREE	POST TOWN	REED BAND
MILK LOAF	NINE PINS	PINE WOOD	PRIE DIEU	REED BIRD
MILK WARM	NOSE BAND	PINE WOOL	PRIX FIXE	REED MACE
MILK WEED	NOSE CONE	PING PONG	PUFF BIRD	REED PIPE
MILL GIRL	NOSE DIVE	PINK EYED	PUFF PUFF	REEF BAND
MILL HAND	NOSE RING	PINK LADY	PULL AWAY	REEF KNOT
MILL WORK	NOTA BENE	PINT SIZE	PULL BACK	REIN HAND
MIND CURE	NOTE CASE	PIOU PIOU	PULL DOWN	RENT FREE
MINE HOST	ONCE OVER	PIPE CASE	PULL OVER	RENT ROLL
MINI SKIS	OPEN BOOK	PIPE DOWN	PULL RANK	REST CURE
MIST OVER	OPEN CAST	PIPE LINE	PUMP HEAD	REST HOME
MOBY DICK	OPEN DOOR	PIPE RACK	PUMP HOOD	REST ROOM
MOCK MOON	OPEN FIRE	PIPE ROLL	PUMP IRON	RICE BEER
MOLE EYED	OPEN MIND	PIPE STEM	PUMP ROOM	RICE GLUE
MONA LISA	OPEN PLAN	PIRI PIRI	PUMP WELL	RICE MILK
MOON BOOT	OPEN ROAD	PITH TREE	PUNK ROCK	RICE SOUP
MOON EYED	OPEN SHOP	PIXY RING	PUNT POLE	RICK RACK
MOON FISH	OPEN TOWN	PLAY ACTS	PUPA CASE	RIDE DOWN
MOON POOL	OPEN WORK	PLAY BACK	PURE GOLD	RIFF RAFF
MOOT CASE	ORAL EXAM	PLAY BALL	PUSH BALL	RING BACK
MOOT HALL	OVEN BIRD	PLAY DOWN	PUSH BIKE	RING BARK
MOSS ROSE	OVEN DOOR	PLAY FAIR	PUSH CART	RING BOLT
MOTH BALL	OVER SHOE	PLAY GOER	PUSH OVER	RING DIAL
MOVE AWAY	PACK LOAD	PLAY HOST	PUSH PAST	RING DOVE
MOVE BACK	PACK MULE	PLAY SAFE	PUSH PULL	RING DOWN
MOVE OVER	PAID BACK	PLUG AWAY	PUSS MOTH	RING DYKE
MOWN DOWN	PAID CASH	PLUG UGLY	PUTS AWAY	RING FORT
MUCH LESS	PAIR BOND	PLUM CAKE	PUTS BACK	RING MAIN
MUCK HEAP	PAIR CASE	PLUM DUFF	PUTS DOWN	RING PULL
MUCK RAKE	PALE EYED	PLUS SIGN	PUTS OVER	RING ROAD
MULE DEER	PALL MALL	POLE AXED	PUTS UPON	RING TAIL
MUSK BALL	PALM TREE	POLE AXES	QUAE VIDE	RING TIME
MUSK DEER	PALM WINE	POLE STAR	QUIT RENT	RING TRUE
MUSK PEAR	PART SONG	POLO NECK	QUIZ BOOK	RING WALK
MUSK ROSE	PART TIME	POND LIFE	QUIZ GAME	RING WALL
MUTE SWAN	PASS AWAY	POND LILY	QUIZ SHOW	ROAD BOOK
NAIL BOMB	PASS BAND	PONY CLUB	RACE CARD	ROAD HUMP
NAIL DOWN	PASS BOOK	PONY SKIN	RACE PATH	ROAD SHOW
NAIL FILE	PASS LAWS	PONY TAIL	RACE RIOT	ROAD SIGN
NAIL HEAD	PASS OVER	POOH POOH	RACK RAIL	ROAD TEST
NAIL HOLE	PAYS BACK	POOL ROOM	RACK RENT	ROCK BAND
NAME DROP	PAYS CASH	POOR HAND	RAFT PORT	ROCK BIRD
NAME PART	PEAK LOAD	POOR JACK	RAFT ROPE	ROCK CAKE
NAVY BLUE	PEAK TIME	POOR LAWS	RAIL HEAD	ROCK DOVE
NAVY LIST	PEAR DROP	POOR RATE	RAIN BIRD	ROCK FALL
NAVY YARD	PEAR TREE	POOR SHOW	RAMS HORN	ROCK FISH
NEAP TIDE	PEAT BANK	POOR SOUL	RANG BACK	ROCK HEWN
NEAR BEER	PEAT MOOR	POPE JOAN	RANG DOWN	ROCK SALT
NEAR EAST	PEAT MOSS	PORK CHOP	RANG TRUE	ROCK WOOD
NEAR HAND	PEEP HOLE	PORT WINE	RAPE SEED	ROCK WOOL
NEAR MISS	PEEP SHOW	POST CODE	RARA AVIS	RODE DOWN
NEAT HERD	PEGS AWAY	POST DATE	RARE BIRD	ROLE PLAY
NECK BAND	PEGS BACK	POST FREE	RATE CAPS	ROLL CALL
NECK BONE	PEGS DOWN	POST GIRL	RATS TAIL	ROLL NECK
NEED FIRE	PELL MELL	POST HOLE	REAL BEER	ROLL OVER
NEON LAMP	PICK OVER	POST HORN	REAL LIFE	ROLY POLY
NEWS ROOM	PIED NOIR	POST MILL	REAL TIME	ROMP HOME
NEXT BEST	PIER HEAD	POST PAID	REAR ARCH	ROOD BEAM
	PIKE HEAD	POST ROAD	REAR LAMP	ROOD LOFT

4,4 contd.	SAND LARK	SHOT HOLE	SOAP SUDS	TAIL COAT
ROOF RACK	SAND MOLE	SHOW BILL	SODA JERK	TAIL GATE
ROOM MATE	SAND SHOE	SHOW BOAT	SODA LIME	TAIL PIPE
ROOT BEER	SAND STAR	SHOW DOWN	SOFT LINE	TAIL ROPE
ROOT CROP	SAND TRAP	SHUT AWAY	SOFT LOAN	TAIL SPIN
ROPE WALK	SAND WASP	SHUT DOWN	SOFT MARK	TAIL WIND
ROPE YARN	SAND WORM	SICK JOKE	SOFT MEAT	TAKE ARMS
ROSE BOWL	SAPI UTAN	SICK LIST	SOFT ROCK	TAKE AWAY
ROSE BUSH	SASH CORD	SICK ROOM	SOFT SELL	TAKE BACK
ROSE COMB	SASH DOOR	SIDE DISH	SOFT SHOE	TAKE BETS
ROSE DROP	SAVE FACE	SIDE DOOR	SOFT SOAP	TAKE CARE
ROSE HUED	SAVE TIME	SIDE DRUM	SOFT SPOT	TAKE DOWN
ROSE KNOT	SAXE BLUE	SIDE FACE	SOIL PIPE	TAKE FIVE
ROSE LEAF	SCOT FREE	SIDE KICK	SOLO STOP	TAKE HEED
ROSE PINK	SEAL PIPE	SIDE LAMP	SOME HOPE	TAKE NOTE
ROSE ROOT	SEAL RING	SIDE LINE	SONG FORM	TAKE OVER
ROSE TREE	SEAT BELT	SIDE PATH	SONG LIKE	TAKE PART
RUBS DOWN	SEED CAKE	SIDE POST	SOUL FOOD	TAKE ROOT
RUMP BONE	SEED CORN	SIDE ROAD	SOUL MATE	TAKE SILK
RUNS AMOK	SEED FISH	SIDE SHOW	SOUR EYED	TAKE WING
RUNS AWAY	SEED LEAF	SIDE SLIP	SOUR MASH	TALK BACK
RUNS DOWN	SEED LIKE	SIDE STEP	SOYA BEAN	TALK DOWN
RUNS HARD	SEED PLOT	SIDE VIEW	SPAN ROOF	TALK INTO
RUNS INTO	SEED SHOP	SIDE WIND	SPAR DECK	TALK OVER
RUNS OVER	SEED TIME	SIGN AWAY	SPIT CURL	TALK SHOP
RUNS RIOT	SEES LIFE	SINE WAVE	SPOT CASH	TALK SHOW
RUNS WILD	SEES OVER	SING SONG	SPOT KICK	TALL COPY
RUSH HOUR	SELF HEAL	SINK HOLE	SPOT WELD	TALL SHIP
RUSH LIKE	SELF HELP	SINK UNIT	SPUN SILK	TALL TALE
RUSH RING	SELF LOVE	SINN FEIN	SPUN YARN	TANK TRAP
SACK COAT	SELF MADE	SITS BACK	SPUR GEAR	TAPE DECK
SACK RACE	SELF PITY	SITS DOWN	STAG HUNT	TASK WORK
SACK TREE	SELF RULE	SITZ BATH	STAR DUST	TAXI RANK
SAFE SEAT	SELF SAME	SKIN DEEP	STAR GAZE	TEAM MATE
SAGE COCK	SELF WILL	SKIN GAME	STAR SIGN	TEAM WORK
SAGO PALM	SEMI AXIS	SKIN TEST	STAR TRAP	TEAR AWAY
SAIL BOAT	SEMI DOME	SKUA GULL	STAR TURN	TEAR DOWN
SAIL FISH	SEMI MUTE	SLAG HEAP	STAR WARS	TEAR DROP
SAIL LOFT	SEMI NUDE	SLAP BANG	STAY BOLT	TEAR DUCT
SAIL ROOM	SEND DOWN	SLAP DASH	STAY LACE	TEAR INTO
SAIL YARD	SEND WORD	SLIP AWAY	STAY OVER	TEAR OPEN
SALE ROOM	SENT DOWN	SLIP CASE	STAY TAPE	TELL TALE
SALT AWAY	SENT WORD	SLIP DOCK	STEP DOWN	TENT COAT
SALT BEEF	SETS BACK	SLIP KNOT	STOP COCK	TENT POLE
SALT CAKE	SETS DOWN	SLIP ROAD	STOP DEAD	TENT ROPE
SALT DOME	SETS FOOT	SLIP SHOE	STOP OVER	TENT WORK
SALT DOWN	SETS FREE	SLOP BOWL	STUD BOLT	TERM TIME
SALT FLAT	SETS SAIL	SLOP PAIL	STUD BOOK	TEST ACTS
SALT LAKE	SETS UPON	SLOP SHOP	STUD FARM	TEST CASE
SALT LICK	SHIN BONE	SLOW BURN	SUCH LIKE	TEST TUBE
SALT MINE	SHIP LOAD	SLOW DOWN	SUIT CASE	TEXT BOOK
SALT PLUG	SHIP WORM	SLOW WORM	SURE CARD	TICK AWAY
SAME HERE	SHOE LACE	SNAP LINK	SURE FIRE	TICK OVER
SAND BATH	SHOE SHOP	SNIP SNAP	SURF BOAT	TICK SHOP
SAND DART	SHOE TREE	SNOW BOOT	SWAN LAKE	TICK TACK
SAND DUNE	SHOP BELL	SNOW EYES	SWAN MARK	TICK TICK
SAND FLAG	SHOP DOOR	SNOW HOLE	SWAN NECK	TICK TOCK
SAND HEAP	SHOP GIRL	SNOW SHOE	SWAN SONG	TIDE GATE
SAND HILL	SHOP SIGN	SNUB NOSE	SWAP LINE	TIDE OVER
SAND HOLE	SHOT DOWN	SOAP DISH	SWAP SHOP	TIDE RACE

4,4 *contd.*	TRUE TIME	WELL DOER	WINS OVER	AGNUS DEI
TIED DOWN	TUBE WORM	WELL DONE	WIRE HAIR	ALLEN KEY
TIES DOWN	TUCK SHOP	WELL HEAD	WIRE MESH	ALLEY CAT
TILE HUNG	TURN AWAY	WELL HOLE	WIRE NAIL	ALTER EGO
TILT BOAT	TURN BACK	WELL MADE	WIRE ROPE	ANZAC DAY
TIME BOMB	TURN DOWN	WELL NIGH	WIRE WOOL	APPLE PIE
TIME CARD	TURN INTO	WELL READ	WITH CALF	APRES SKI
TIME CODE	TURN OVER	WELL ROOM	WITH FOAL	ARBOR DAY
TIME FUSE	TURN TAIL	WELL SEEN	WITH THAT	ARECA NUT
TIME SLOT	TURN TURK	WELL THEN	WOLF PACK	ATTIC WIT
TIME UNIT	TURN UPON	WELL WELL	WOOD CHAT	AUGER BIT
TIME WARP	TWIN BEDS	WELL WISH	WOOD COAL	BACKS OFF
TIME WORN	TWIN BORN	WELL WORN	WOOD IBIS	BADLY OFF
TIME ZONE	TWIN TOWN	WENT AWAY	WOOD LARK	BAILS OUT
TINT TOOL	TYPE BODY	WENT BUST	WOOD MITE	BAKER DAY
TINY TOTS	TYPE CASE	WENT DOWN	WOOD PILE	BALED OUT
TOIL WORN	TYPE FACE	WENT INTO	WOOD PULP	BALES OUT
TOLL CALL	TYPE HIGH	WENT LIVE	WOOD RUSH	BANGS OUT
TOLL FREE	UPAS TREE	WENT SOFT	WOOD SAGE	BATON GUN
TOLL GATE	UPON OATH	WEST BANK	WOOD TICK	BAWLS OUT
TONE DEAF	USED CARS	WHAT ELSE	WOOD WASP	BEACH HUT
TONE DOWN	VENA CAVA	WHAT NEXT	WOOD WOOL	BEARS EAR
TONE POEM	VENT HOLE	WHAT THEN	WOOD WREN	BEARS OUT
TOOK ARMS	VENT PIPE	WHEY FACE	WOOL BALL	BEATS OFF
TOOK BACK	VENT PLUG	WHIM WHAM	WOOL CARD	BEATS OUT
TOOK BETS	VERY WELL	WHIP HAND	WOOL COMB	BEDDY BYE
TOOK CARE	VICE DEAN	WHIP TAIL	WOOL DYED	BELLE VUE
TOOK DOWN	VINE CLAD	WHIT WEEK	WOOL MILL	BELOW PAR
TOOK FIVE	VINE GALL	WIDE EYED	WOOL PACK	BELTS OUT
TOOK HEED	VIVA VOCE	WIDE OPEN	WORD PLAY	BERRY BUG
TOOK NOTE	VOTE DOWN	WILD BIRD	WORE AWAY	BETEL NUT
TOOK OVER	WAIT UPON	WILD BOAR	WORE DOWN	BEVIN BOY
TOOK PART	WALK AWAY	WILD BORN	WORE THIN	BILLY CAN
TOOK ROOT	WALK AWRY	WILD CARD	WORK MATE	BIRCH FLY
TOOK SILK	WALK INTO	WILD DUCK	WORK OVER	BIRCH ROD
TOOK WING	WALK OVER	WILD FOWL	WORK UPON	BLACK ART
TOOL SHED	WALK TALL	WILD HUNT	WORM CAST	BLACK BOX
TORE AWAY	WALL BARS	WILD LAND	WORM GEAR	BLACK CAP
TORE DOWN	WALL EYED	WILD MARE	WORM HOLE	BLACK CAT
TORE INTO	WALL GAME	WILD OATS	WORN AWAY	BLACK EYE
TORE OPEN	WALL PASS	WILD RICE	WORN DOWN	BLACK FLY
TORN DOWN	WALL UNIT	WILD SILK	XMAS TREE	BLACK FOX
TOWN HALL	WARD ROOM	WILD WEST	YALE LOCK	BLACK ICE
TRAD JAZZ	WASH AWAY	WILD WOOD	YEAR BOOK	BLACK OUT
TRAM LINE	WASH BOWL	WIND BAND	YOGI BEAR	BLACK RAT
TRAM ROAD	WASH DOWN	WIND CONE	YOKE MATE	BLACK ROD
TRAM STOP	WATT HOUR	WIND DOWN	ZERO HOUR	BLACK SEA
TRAP DOOR	WAVE DOWN	WIND SAIL	ZERO RATE	BLACK TEA
TRAP FALL	WAVY NAVY	WIND SIDE	ZONE AXIS	BLACK TIE
TREE FERN	WEAK EYED	WIND SOCK	ZOOM LENS	BLAST OFF
TREE FROG	WEAK LINK	WIND SURF	ZOOT SUIT	BLESS YOU
TREE LILY	WEAK SPOT	WINE CASK		BLIND GUT
TREE MOSS	WEAR AWAY	WINE GUMS	**5,3**	BLOOD RED
TRIC TRAC	WEAR DOWN	WINE LAKE	ABOVE ALL	BLOTS OUT
TRIP WIRE	WEAR IRON	WINE LIST	ABOVE PAR	BLOWS OUT
TRUE BILL	WEAR THIN	WINE SHOP	ACORN CUP	BLURT OUT
TRUE BLUE	WELL AWAY	WINE SKIN	ACTED OUT	BOARD OUT
TRUE BORN	WELL BORN	WING CASE	ADAMS ALE	BOBBY PIN
TRUE BRED	WELL BRED	WING HALF	ADAMS RIB	BODES LAW
TRUE LOVE	WELL DECK	WING SHOT	AFTER ALL	BOGEY MAN

5,3 contd.	CHILL OUT	DECKS OUT	FARMS OUT	GOING OFF
BOOKS OUT	CHINA INK	DERBY DAY	FEAST DAY	GOING OUT
BORNE OUT	CHINA TEA	DERBY HAT	FETCH OUT	GOOSE EGG
BOWED OUT	CHIPS OFF	DILLY BAG	FIELD BED	GOUGE OUT
BOWLS OUT	CHOKE OFF	DINED OUT	FIELD DAY	GRACE CUP
BRAIN FAG	CHOTA PEG	DINER OUT	FIELD GUN	GRAND CRU
BRAKE PAD	CHOUX BUN	DINES OUT	FIGHT OFF	GRAND MAL
BRAKE VAN	CHUCK OUT	DIRTY DOG	FILED OFF	GRASS BOX
BRAND NEW	CHURN OUT	DITTY BAG	FILES OFF	GREAT APE
BRASS HAT	CHURN OWL	DIVAN BED	FILLS OUT	GREAT AUK
BREAD BIN	CIDER CUP	DOGGY BAG	FINDS OUT	GREAT GUN
BREAK JAW	CIGAR BOX	DOING OUT	FIRED OFF	GREAT MAN
BREAK OFF	CIVIL DAY	DOLLY TUB	FIRES OFF	GREAT TIT
BREAK OUT	CIVIL LAW	DOUGH BOY	FIRST AID	GREAT TOE
BREAK VOW	CIVIL WAR	DOWEL PIN	FIRST DAY	GREAT WAR
BRICK RED	CLASS WAR	DOWEL ROD	FLAKE OUT	GREEK GOD
BRIDE BED	CLEAN CUT	DRAGS OUT	FLASH GUN	GREEN BAG
BRIEF BAG	CLEAN OUT	DRAWS OFF	FLESH FLY	GREEN EYE
BRING OFF	CLEAR CUT	DRAWS OUT	FLESH OUT	GREEN TEA
BRING OUT	CLEAR OFF	DRIED OUT	FLESH POT	GUARD DOG
BROKE OFF	CLEAR OUT	DRIES OUT	FLIES OUT	GUIDE DOG
BROKE OUT	CLOCK OFF	DRIFT ICE	FLING OUT	HANDS OFF
BROOD SAC	CLOCK OUT	DRIFT NET	FLOCK BED	HANDS OUT
BROWN ALE	CLOTH CAP	DRIFT WAY	FLUNG OUT	HANGS OFF
BROWN OWL	COACH BOX	DRIVE OUT	FLUSH BOX	HANGS OUT
BROWN RAT	COACH WAY	DROPS OFF	FOLDS OUT	HARES EAR
BRUSH OFF	COCOA FAT	DROPS OUT	FOOLS CAP	HAZEL NUT
BULLS EYE	COMBS OUT	DROVE OUT	FORCE FED	HEADS OFF
BULLY BOY	COMES OFF	DROWN OUT	FORKS OUT	HEADS OUT
BULLY OFF	COMES OUT	DUCKS EGG	FOSSE WAY	HEARD OUT
BUMPS OFF	CONED OFF	DUCKS OUT	FOUND OUT	HEARS OUT
BUNNY HOP	CONES OFF	DUMMY RUN	FRAME SAW	HEATH HEN
BUNNY HUG	COOLS OFF	DUTCH HOE	FRANK FEE	HEAVY SEA
BURNT OUT	COUNT OUT	DYING OFF	FREAK OUT	HEAVY WET
CABIN BOY	COURT DAY	DYING OUT	FRESH AIR	HEDGE HOP
CABLE CAR	CRANE FLY	EAGLE OWL	FRESH RUN	HELPS OUT
CACHE POT	CRASH OUT	EAGLE RAY	FRIED EGG	HIRED OUT
CALLS OFF	CREAM BUN	EARTH FED	FRONT MAN	HIRES OUT
CALLS OUT	CREAM NUT	EARTH HOG	FROTH FLY	HIVED OFF
CALOR GAS	CREAM TEA	EARTH NUT	FRUIT BAT	HIVES OFF
CAMPS OUT	CRIED OFF	EASED OFF	FRUIT BUD	HOLDS OFF
CANON LAW	CRIED OUT	EASES OFF	FRUIT FLY	HOLDS OUT
CAPER TEA	CRIES OFF	EDGED OUT	FRUIT PIE	HOLED OUT
CARRY ALL	CRIES OUT	EDGES OUT	FUMED OAK	HOLES OUT
CARRY OFF	CROSS EYE	EDITS OUT	FUNNY MAN	HOLLY OAK
CARRY OUT	CROSS PLY	ENTRY FEE	GABLE END	HONEY ANT
CARTS OFF	CROSS RIB	ESSEX MAN	GAMMY LEG	HONEY BEE
CARVE OUT	CROWN CAP	EVENS OUT	GAUDY DAY	HONEY DEW
CASTS OFF	CROWN SAW	FACED OUT	GIVES EAR	HONEY SAC
CASTS OUT	CRUDE OIL	FACES OUT	GIVES OFF	HORSE BOX
CATCH ALL	CRUSH BAR	FADED OUT	GIVES OUT	HORSE BOY
CATCH OUT	CRUSH HAT	FADES OUT	GIVES WAY	HORSE HOE
CEDAR NUT	CYCLE CAR	FALLS OFF	GLASS EYE	HOUSE DOG
CHAIR BED	DAVIS CUP	FALLS OUT	GLASS JAW	HOUSE TAX
CHALK OUT	DEALS OUT	FALSE GOD	GLOVE BOX	HOVER BED
CHECK KEY	DEALT OUT	FALSE HEM	GOING BAD	HOVER BUS
CHECK OFF	DEATH BED	FALSE LEG	GOING DRY	HOVER FLY
CHECK OUT	DEATH CAP	FALSE RIB	GOING FAR	HUNTS OUT
CHESS SET	DEATH RAY	FANCY MAN	GOING FOR	HYENA DOG
CHICK PEA	DEATH ROW	FARCY BUD	GOING MAD	IDEAS MAN

5,3 contd.
IDIOT BOX
INERT GAS
INFRA DIG
INFRA RED
INNER BAR
INNER MAN
INTER NOS
IRISH CAR
IRISH ELK
IRISH SEA
IRONS OUT
IVORY NUT
JAPAN WAX
JELLY BAG
JUMBO JET
JUMPS OFF
KEEPS FIT
KEEPS MUM
KEEPS OFF
KICKS OFF
KICKS OUT
KILLS OFF
KINGS MAN
KNIFE BOX
KNOCK OFF
KNOCK OUT
LABOR DAY
LADLE OUT
LANDS END
LAUGH OFF
LEACH TUB
LEADS OFF
LEADS OUT
LEAKS OUT
LEAVE OFF
LEAVE OUT
LEGAL AID
LEMON DAB
LEVEL OFF
LEWIS GUN
LIFTS OFF
LIGHT ALE
LIGHT PEN
LIVED OUT
LIVES OUT
LOCKS OUT
LOOKS FOR
LOOKS OUT
LOONY BIN
LOOSE BOX
LOOSE CUT
LOOSE END
LORDS DAY
LORRY HOP
LOSES OUT
LOUIS DOR
LUCKY BAG
LUCKY DIP
LUCKY JIM

LUMPY JAW
LUNCH BOX
LYING LOW
LYNCH LAW
LYNCH MOB
MAGIC BOX
MAGIC EYE
MAJOR KEY
MAKES FOR
MAKES HAY
MAKES OFF
MAKES OUT
MAKES WAR
MAKES WAY
MAORI HEN
MARKS OFF
MARKS OUT
MARRY OFF
MARSH GAS
MARSH TIT
MERRY MEN
METER MAN
MILCH COW
MILKY WAY
MINCE PIE
MINDS EYE
MINOR KEY
MIXED BAG
MIXER TAP
MOLED OUT
MOLES OUT
MONEY BAG
MONEY BOX
MORAL LAW
MORAY EEL
MOTOR BUS
MOTOR CAR
MOTOR JET
MOUSE DUN
MOUSE EAR
MOVED OUT
MOVES OUT
MULTI PLY
MUSIC BOX
MUSIC PEN
NAKED EYE
NERVE END
NERVE GAS
NEVER WAS
NEWLY WED
NIGHT AIR
NIGHT APE
NIGHT FLY
NIGHT OUT
NIGHT OWL
NOAHS ARK
NOBLE ART
NOBLE GAS
NORTH SEA
NOSED OUT

NOSES OUT
OCEAN BED
OLIVE OIL
OLIVE OYL
OPENS OUT
OPERA HAT
OPIUM DEN
OPTED OUT
OSIER BED
OUTER BAR
OVERT ACT
PAINT BOX
PANDA CAR
PANEL PIN
PANEL SAW
PAPER BAG
PAPER BOY
PAPER DAY
PARMA HAM
PARTY HAT
PARTY MAN
PATCH BOX
PATTY PAN
PEARL EYE
PEASE COD
PEELS OFF
PEEPS OUT
PETER MAN
PETER PAN
PETIT MAL
PHASE OUT
PHOTO FIT
PIANO KEY
PICKS OFF
PICKS OUT
PIECE OUT
PILOT JET
PINCE NEZ
PINCH HIT
PIVOT MAN
PLACE MAT
PLAIN BOB
PLANK BED
PLANT OUT
PLANT POT
PLAYS OFF
PLAYS OUT
PLEIN AIR
PLUMB BOB
POINT OUT
POINT SET
POLKA DOT
POPES EYE
POPPY DAY
POPPY OIL
POUND DAY
POURS OUT
POWER CUT
PRESS BED
PRESS BOX

PRESS UPS
PRICE TAG
PRICE WAR
PRIED OUT
PRIES OUT
PRINT OUT
PRINT RUN
PRIZE MAN
PRONG HOE
PROSE MAN
PULLS OFF
PULLS OUT
PULZA OIL
PUMPS OUT
PUNCH BAG
PUPIL AGE
PUPPY DOG
PUPPY FAT
PURSE NET
PUSSY CAT
PUTTS OUT
QUART POT
QUEEN BEE
QUILL NIB
QUILL PEN
RADAR GUN
RADIO HAM
RAZOR CUT
REACH OUT
READS OFF
READS OUT
READY WIT
REELS OFF
RIDES OUT
RIFLE PIT
RIGHT ARM
RIGHT OFF
RINGS OFF
RINSE OUT
RIVER BED
RIVER RAT
ROMAN LAW
ROOTS OUT
ROPES END
ROSIN OIL
ROUGH CUT
ROUGH DRY
ROUGH HEW
ROUGH OUT
ROUND ARM
ROUND OFF
ROUND OUT
ROUND TOP
ROWDY DOW
ROYAL BOX
RULED OUT
RULES OUT
RYDER CUP
SABRE CUT
SALAD OIL

SALES TAX
SALIC LAW
SAUCE BOX
SCALY LEG
SCARF PIN
SCENE BAY
SCENE MAN
SCENE ONE
SCENE TWO
SCENT BAG
SCENT BOX
SCOOP NET
SCOOP OUT
SCORE OFF
SCOUT CAR
SCOUT LAW
SCRAG END
SCRAP MAN
SCREW CAP
SEALS OFF
SEDGE FLY
SEEDY TOE
SEEKS OUT
SEINE NET
SELLS OFF
SELLS OUT
SENDS OFF
SENDS OUT
SENNA POD
SENNA TEA
SERVE OUT
SEWER GAS
SEWER RAT
SHAKE OFF
SHAKE OUT
SHALE OIL
SHARE OUT
SHARK OIL
SHARP SET
SHEEP DIP
SHEEP KED
SHEEP PEN
SHEEP POX
SHEEP RUN
SHEER OFF
SHEET FED
SHEET TIN
SHELL OUT
SHIFT KEY
SHIPS LOG
SHIRT PIN
SHOOK OFF
SHOOK OUT
SHOOT OFF
SHOOT OUT
SHORT CUT
SHORT LEG
SHORT SEA
SHOVE OFF
SHOWS OFF

5,3 *contd.*	SPINS OUT	SWORD ARM	TROUT ROD	WIPES OUT
SHRUG OFF	SPLIT PEA	SWORD CUT	TURBO CAR	WITCH ELM
SHUTS OFF	SPLIT PIN	TABBY CAT	TURBO JET	WORKS FOR
SHUTS OUT	SPOKE OUT	TABLE MAT	TURFS OUT	WORKS OFF
SIEGE GUN	SPOON FED	TABLE TOP	TURKS CAP	WORKS OUT
SIGNS OFF	SPRAY GUN	TAILS OFF	TURNS OFF	WORLD WAR
SIGNS OUT	SQUAB PIE	TAKEN OUT	TURNS OUT	WORRY OUT
SILLY ASS	SQUAD CAR	TAKES AIM	UNCLE SAM	WORSE OFF
SINGS OUT	STAFF CAR	TAKES OFF	UNCLE TOM	WRING OUT
SKENE DHU	STAGE BOX	TAKES OUT	UNDER AGE	WRIST PIN
SLACK JAW	STAIR ROD	TALKS BIG	UNDER WAY	WRITE OFF
SLATE AXE	STAKE NET	TALKS OUT	UPPER CUT	WRITE OUT
SLEEP OFF	STAKE OUT	TALLY HOS	VOICE BOX	WROTE OFF
SLEPT OFF	STALL FED	TAPER OFF	WAGON BED	WROTE OUT
SLIME PIT	STAMP ACT	TASTE BUD	WAGON BOX	WRUNG OUT
SLING INK	STAMP OUT	TAWNY OWL	WAGON LIT	YOUNG MAN
SLINK OFF	STAND OFF	TEARS OFF	WALKS OFF	
SLIPS OUT	STAND OUT	TEDDY BOY	WALKS OUT	**6,2**
SLOPE OFF	STAND PAT	TELLS OFF	WANTS OUT	ACTING UP
SLOPS OUT	STANK OUT	TENON SAW	WARDS OFF	ADDING UP
SLUNG INK	START OUT	THANK YOU	WATCH BOX	BACKED UP
SLUNK OFF	STAYS OUT	THAWS OUT	WATCH CAP	BANGED UP
SMALL ADS	STAYS PUT	THICK EAR	WATCH DOG	BARGED IN
SMALL ALE	STEAM CAR	THINK OUT	WATCH KEY	BARGES IN
SMALL ARM	STEEL PEN	THINS OUT	WATCH OUT	BATTLE ON
SMALL FRY	STEPS OUT	THIRD MAN	WATER BAG	BEATEN UP
SMASH HIT	STICK LAC	THOLE PIN	WATER BED	BEEFED UP
SMELL OUT	STICK OUT	THREE MAN	WATER BOX	BELTED UP
SMELT OUT	STING RAY	THREE PLY	WATER BUG	BONING UP
SMOKE BOX	STINK OUT	THREE WAY	WATER BUS	BOOKED IN
SMOKE DRY	STOCK POT	THREW OFF	WATER DOG	BOOKED UP
SMOKE OUT	STONE AGE	THREW OUT	WATER FLY	BOTTLE UP
SNACK BAR	STONE AXE	THROW OFF	WATER GOD	BOUGHT IN
SNAKE OIL	STONE FLY	THROW OUT	WATER ICE	BOUGHT UP
SNAKE PIT	STONE OIL	THRUM CAP	WATER JET	BOWING IN
SNIFF OUT	STONE PIT	TICKS OFF	WATER JUG	BREAKS IN
SNOWY OWL	STONE SAW	TIGER CAT	WATER KEY	BREAKS UP
SNUFF OUT	STOOD OFF	TIGER NUT	WATER RAM	BREWED UP
SOLAR DAY	STOOD OUT	TIGHT FIT	WATER RAT	BRINGS IN
SORTS OUT	STOOD PAT	TIPSY KEY	WATER SKI	BRINGS ON
SOUND BAR	STOPS OFF	TIRED OUT	WATER TAP	BRINGS UP
SOUND BOX	STRAW HAT	TIRES OUT	WATER YAM	BROKEN IN
SOUND OFF	STRAW MAN	TODDY CAT	WEARS OFF	BUBBLE UP
SOUND OUT	STRAY CAT	TOMMY BAR	WEARS OUT	BUCKED UP
SOUSE TUB	STRAY DOG	TOMMY GUN	WEIGH OUT	BUILDS IN
SOUTH SEA	STRIP MAP	TOMMY ROT	WHALE OIL	BUILDS UP
SPACE AGE	STRIP OFF	TOTAL WAR	WHARF RAT	BUMPED UP
SPACE BAR	STRIP OUT	TOUCH OFF	WHATS NEW	BUNGED UP
SPACE OUT	STUCK OUT	TRADE GAP	WHEAT EAR	BUOYED UP
SPARE RIB	STUNT MAN	TRADE OFF	WHITE ANT	BURNED UP
SPARK GAP	SUGAR GUM	TRADE WAR	WHITE EYE	BUTTED IN
SPARK OFF	SUNNY JIM	TRAIL NET	WHITE HOT	BUTTER UP
SPARK OUT	SUPER EGO	TRAIL OFF	WHITE LIE	BUTTON UP
SPEAK OUT	SUPER JET	TRASH CAN	WHITE MAN	BUYING IN
SPEAR GUN	SWAMP OAK	TRAWL NET	WHITE OUT	BUYING UP
SPEED COP	SWEEP NET	TRIAL DAY	WHITE RAT	CAGING IN
SPELL OUT	SWEEP SAW	TRIAL RUN	WHITE TIE	CALLED BY
SPELT OUT	SWEET BAY	TRIED OUT	WHIZZ KID	CALLED IN
SPICE BOX	SWELL BOX	TRIES OUT	WHOLE HOG	CALLED ON
SPIKE OIL	SWILL TUB	TROTS OUT	WIPED OUT	CARVED UP

6,2 *contd.*
CARVES UP
CASHED IN
CASHED UP
CASHES IN
CASHES UP
CAUGHT ON
CAUGHT UP
CAVING IN
CHAINS UP
CHALKS UP
CHANCE IT
CHANGE UP
CHEATS ON
CHECKS IN
CHECKS UP
CHEERS UP
CHIMED IN
CHIMES IN
CHOKED UP
CHOKES UP
CHUCKS UP
CHURNS UP
CLEANS UP
CLEARS UP
CLOCKS IN
CLOCKS UP
CLOSED IN
CLOSED UP
CLOSES IN
CLOSES UP
CLUING IN
COINED IT
COLOUR IN
COLOUR UP
COMING AT
COMING BY
COMING IN
COMING TO
COMING UP
COOPED UP
COPPED IT
COTTON ON
COUGHS UP
COVERS IN
COVERS UP
CRACKS UP
CRYING UP
DIPPED IN
DISHED UP
DISHES UP
DOUBLE UP
DREAMS UP
DREAMT UP
DRINKS IN
DRINKS UP
DRYING UP
DUFFED UP
DUMPED ON
EATING IN

EATING UP
ENDING UP
EVENED UP
EXCUSE ME
FADING IN
FASTEN ON
FATTEN UP
FILLED IN
FILLED UP
FINISH UP
FIRING UP
FIRMED UP
FITTED IN
FITTED UP
FIXING IT
FIXING ON
FIXING UP
FLARED UP
FLARES UP
FLYING BY
FLYING IN
FOLDED IN
FOLLOW ON
FOLLOW UP
FOOTED IT
FORGET IT
FORKED UP
FOULED UP
FREEZE UP
FROWNS ON
GANGED UP
GATHER UP
GEARED UP
GENNED UP
GIVING IN
GIVING UP
GOBBLE UP
GOINGS ON
GUMMED UP
HANGER ON
HARPED ON
HAULED IN
HAULED UP
HAVING IT
HAVING ON
HAVING TO
HAVING UP
HEAVES TO
HEMMED IN
HIGHER UP
HINTED AT
HOGGED IT
HOLING UP
HOPPED IT
HORNED IN
HOTTED UP
HUSHED UP
HUSHES UP
HYPING UP
INKING IN

JOINED IN
JOINED UP
JUMPED ON
JUMPED UP
KEYING IN
KICKED IN
KNOCKS ON
KNOCKS UP
LAYING BY
LAYING IN
LAYING ON
LAYING UP
LEANED ON
LEAVES BE
LIFTED UP
LIGHTS UP
LIMBER UP
LINING UP
LINKED IN
LINKED UP
LISTEN IN
LITTLE GO
LIVING IN
LIVING ON
LOCKED IN
LOCKED ON
LOCKED UP
LOFTED UP
LOGGED IN
LOOKED AT
LOOKED IN
LOOKED ON
LOOKED UP
LOOKER ON
LOOSEN UP
LUGGED IN
MAKING DO
MAKING IT
MAKING UP
MARKED UP
MASHED UP
MASHES UP
MESSED UP
MESSES UP
MISTED UP
MIXING IN
MIXING IT
MIXING UP
MOPPED UP
MOVING IN
MUCKED IN
MUDDLE UP
MUGGED UP
MUSCLE IN
NIPPED IN
OFFERS UP
OPENED UP
OVERDO IT
OWNING UP
PACKED UP

PARDON ME
PASSED BY
PASSED ON
PASSED UP
PASSER BY
PASSES BY
PASSES ON
PASSES UP
PAYING IN
PAYING UP
PERKED UP
PHASED IN
PHASES IN
PHONER IN
PICKED AT
PICKED UP
PICKER UP
PIECED UP
PIECES UP
PIGGED IT
PILING UP
PIPING UP
PLAYED AT
PLAYED ON
PLAYED UP
PLOUGH IN
POINTS UP
POLISH UP
POPPED IN
POPPED UP
POUNCE ON
PREACH AT
PREACH UP
PREYED ON
PSYCHE UP
PUCKER UP
PUFFED UP
PULLED IN
PULLED UP
PUMPED IN
PUMPED UP
PUTTER ON
QUEUED UP
QUEUES UP
RACKED UP
RAKING IN
RAKING UP
RATTED ON
RATTLE ON
RECKON ON
RECKON UP
REINED IN
RELIED ON
RELIES ON
REVVED UP
RIDING UP
RIGGED UP
RISING UP
RISKED IT
ROLLED IN

ROLLED UP
ROPING IN
ROUGHS IN
ROUGHS IT
ROUNDS ON
ROUNDS UP
RUNNER UP
RUSTLE UP
SADDLE UP
SAILED BY
SAVING UP
SCARED UP
SCARES UP
SCRUBS UP
SEARCH ME
SEIZED UP
SEIZES UP
SENTRY GO
SERVED UP
SERVES UP
SETTER UP
SETTLE IN
SETTLE UP
SEWING UP
SHAKES UP
SHAPED UP
SHAPES UP
SHOOTS UP
SHOWED UP
SIGNED IN
SIGNED ON
SIGNED UP
SITTER IN
SIZING UP
SLEEPS IN
SLEEPS ON
SLICED UP
SLICES UP
SLOWED UP
SNEAKS UP
SNOWED IN
SNOWED UP
SNUFFS IT
SOBERS UP
SOFTEN UP
SOUPED UP
SPEAKS UP
SPEEDS UP
SQUARE UP
STACKS UP
STANDS BY
STANDS IN
STANDS ON
STANDS TO
STANDS UP
STARTS IN
STARTS UP
STAVES IN
STAYED IN
STAYED ON

6,2 *contd.*
STAYED UP
STEADY ON
STEAMS UP
STICKS BY
STICKS IN
STICKS TO
STITCH UP
STOCKS UP
STOKED UP
STOKES UP
STRIKE UP
STRING UP
STROLL ON
STRUCK ON
STRUCK UP
STRUNG UP
STUMPS UP
SUCKED IN
SUMMED UP
SUMMON UP
SWEARS IN
SWEEPS UP
SWITCH ON
TACKED ON
TAKING IN
TAKING IT
TAKING ON
TAKING TO
TAKING UP
TALKED AT
TALKED TO
TARTED UP
TEEING UP
THANKS BE
THINKS UP
THROWN IN
THROWN ON
THROWN UP
THROWS IN
THROWS ON
THROWS UP
THUMBS UP
TOGGED UP
TONING UP
TOODLE OO
TOOLED UP
TOPPED UP
TOSSED UP
TOSSES UP
TOTTED UP
TRADED IN
TRADED UP
TRADES IN
TRADES UP
TRYING ON
TUCKED IN
TUNING IN
TUNING UP
TURNED IN

TURNED ON
TURNED TO
TURNED UP
VOTING IN
WADING IN
WAITED ON
WAITED UP
WALKED IT
WALKED ON
WALKER ON
WALLED UP
WANTED AD
WANTED IN
WARMED UP
WASHED UP
WEIGHS IN
WEIGHS UP
WIPING UP
WIRING IN
WORKED IN
WORKED ON
WORKED UP
WRITES UP
ZAPPED UP
ZEROED IN
ZEROES IN
ZIPPED UP

7,1
VITAMIN A
VITAMIN B
VITAMIN C
VITAMIN D
VITAMIN E
VITAMIN H
VITAMIN K
VITAMIN L

9 LETTERS

1,3,5
A BIG NOISE
A BIT THICK
A CUT ABOVE

1,4,4
A DOGS LIFE
A FAST BUCK
A GOOD SORT
A GOOD TURN
A GOOD WORD
A MUGS GAME
A THIN TIME
A VAST MANY

1,5,3
A QUICK ONE
A RAINY DAY
A THICK EAR

1,8
A CAPPELLA
T JUNCTION

X PARTICLE

2,1,3,3
AT A LOW EBB
IN A BAD WAY
IN A BIG WAY

2,1,6
AT A GLANCE
IN A CORNER
IN A PICKLE
ON A STRING
TO A DEGREE

2,2,3,2
IT IS ALL UP

2,2,5
BE MY GUEST
BY NO MEANS
DO TO DEATH
ET TU BRUTE
GO IT ALONE
GO TO COURT
GO TO EARTH
GO TO GRASS
GO TO PRESS
GO TO SLEEP
GO TO WASTE
RA RA SKIRT
SO TO SPEAK
UP TO SNUFF

2,3,4
AS YOU WERE
AT ANY RATE
AT ONE TIME
AT THE HELM
AT THE MOST
AT THE TIME
DO YOU MIND
GO FOR GOLD
IN ANY CASE
IN THE BATH
IN THE BUFF
IN THE CART
IN THE CLUB
IN THE DARK
IN THE DOCK
IN THE KNOW
IN THE MAIN
IN THE NEWS
IN THE NICK
IN THE NUDE
IN THE PINK
IN THE ROAD
IN THE SOUP
IN THE SWIM
IN THE WARS
IN THE WIND
IN TOP FORM
ON THE BALL
ON THE BOIL

ON THE CLUB
ON THE DOLE
ON THE HOOF
ON THE HOUR
ON THE LINE
ON THE MAKE
ON THE MEND
ON THE MOVE
ON THE NAIL
ON THE NOSE
ON THE RACK
ON THE RISE
ON THE ROAD
ON THE SIDE
ON THE SPOT
ON THE TOWN
ON THE TROT
ON THE TURN
ON THE WING
OX BOW LAKE
TO THE BONE
TO THE CORE
TO THE FORE
TO THE FULL
TO THE LAST
UP AND DOWN
UP AND OVER
UP THE POLE
UP THE WALL

2,4,3
AN EVEN BET
AT FULL SEA
DO ONES BIT
DO ONES NUT
EN TOUT CAS
GO ONES WAY
IN FULL CRY
OF THAT ILK
ON ONES OWN
ON ONES TOD
ON ONES WAY
ON THIN ICE

2,5,2
ON STAND BY
YO HEAVE HO

2,7
AD LIBBING
AD NAUSEAM
AD VALOREM
AS REGARDS
AT COMMAND
AT LEISURE
AT LIBERTY
AT PRESENT
AU COURANT
AU FROMAGE
AU NATUREL
AU SECOURS

BE ONESELF
BY DEGREES
BY NUMBERS
BY ONESELF
BY PRODUCT
CT SCANNER
DE RIGUEUR
EN FAMILLE
EN PASSANT
EX LIBRISM
EX LIBRIST
EX OFFICIO
EX SERVICE
GO AGAINST
GO BANANAS
GO BERSERK
GO BETWEEN
GO FORWARD
GO GETTING
GO HAYWIRE
GO MISSING
GO THROUGH
GO WHISTLE
GO WITHOUT
IN ARREARS
IN BETWEEN
IN CAHOOTS
IN COMPANY
IN CONCERT
IN CONTROL
IN COUNCIL
IN DEFAULT
IN DISGUST
IN EARNEST
IN ESSENCE
IN FASHION
IN GENERAL
IN HARNESS
IN KEEPING
IN PASSING
IN PATIENT
IN PRIVATE
IN RESERVE
IN SERVICE
IN TATTERS
IN TRANSIT
IN TROUBLE
MR SPEAKER
NO COMMENT
NO KIDDING
NO PROBLEM
NO SMOKING
ON ACCOUNT
ON BALANCE
ON COMMAND
ON DRAUGHT
ON HOLIDAY
ON IMPULSE
ON LICENCE
ON REQUEST

2,7 *contd.*
SE BAPTIST
ST BERNARD
ST TRINIAN
UP COUNTRY
UP CURRENT
UP DRAUGHT

3,1,5
CUT A CAPER
CUT A TOOTH
FOR A START
HAD A LAUGH
HAS A LAUGH
NOT A THING
PAY A VISIT
TEN A PENNY
TWO A PENNY
UPS A DAISY

3,2,1,3
SLY AS A FOX
SON OF A GUN

3,2,4
ALL AT ONCE
ALL IS LOST
BAR OF SOAP
CAP IN HAND
CUT IT FINE
DAY OF REST
DEN OF VICE
FIT TO BUST
FOR MY PART
GET AT ABLE
HAD NO IDEA
HAS NO IDEA
HIT OR MISS
ILL AT EASE
JEU DE MOTS
JOB OF WORK
JUG OF MILK
LAY IN WAIT
LAY TO REST
LEG OF LAMB
LEG OF PORK
LET IT RIDE
LIE IN WAIT
MAL DU PAYS
MAN AT ARMS
MEN AT ARMS
MEN AT WORK
NOT AT HOME
OUT AT HEEL
OUT OF CASH
OUT OF DATE
OUT OF FORM
OUT OF HAND
OUT OF MIND
OUT OF PLAY
OUT OF STEP

OUT OF SYNC
OUT OF TIME
OUT OF TOWN
OUT OF TRUE
OUT OF TUNE
OUT OF WORK
PAS DE CHAT
PAS DE DEUX
PAY IN FULL
PAY IN KIND
PIN UP GIRL
PRO RE NATA
PUT ON AIRS
PUT UP WITH
RAN TO SEED
RAY OF HOPE
RUN OF LUCK
RUN TO SEED
SEE NO EVIL
SET IN HAND
SET ON EDGE
SET ON FIRE
SET TO WORK
SET UP SHOP
TUG OF LOVE
TWO BY FOUR
VIN DU PAYS
VOL AU VENT

3,3,3
ALL THE WAY
ANY DAY NOW
ANY OLD HOW
BOX AND COX
BUT AND BEN
CHA CHA CHA
CUT AND RUN
DOG EAT DOG
FEE FAW FUM
HIT AND RUN
HIT FOR SIX
HIT THE HAY
HOT AND HOT
HOW ARE YOU
HUE AND CRY
HUM AND HAW
ILL SEE YOU
LED THE WAY
MOP AND MOW
ODD MAN OUT
ODD ONE OUT
OFF THE AIR
OFF THE MAP
OFF THE PEG
ONE AND ALL
OUT AND OUT
PEN AND INK
PRO AND CON
RUE THE DAY

SIX DAY WAR
THE BIG TOP
THE JET SET
TIC TAC TOE
TIP AND RUN
TIT FOR TAT
WIN THE CUP
WIN THE DAY
WON THE CUP
WON THE DAY

3,4,2
ALL ENDS UP
GOD HELP US
LAY EYES ON
OUT WITH IT
PUT PAID TO
SET EYES ON
SET FIRE TO
YOU NAME IT

3,6
ADI GRANTH
AIR BRAKES
AIR BUBBLE
AIR COOLED
AIR ENGINE
AIR JACKET
AIR LETTER
AIR MINDED
AIR PIRACY
AIR POCKET
AIR STRIKE
AIR TRAVEL
ALE CONNER
ALL ABOARD
ALL BLACKS
ALL COMERS
ALL RULING
ALL SEEING
ALL SQUARE
ANY AMOUNT
ANY OFFERS
ART DEALER
ART MASTER
ASH BLONDE
ASH BUCKET
AWE STRUCK
BAD TEMPER
BAL MASQUE
BAR CODING
BAR MAGNET
BAS RELIEF
BAY WINDOW
BED CLOSET
BED JACKET
BEE FLOWER
BEE KEEPER
BEL ESPRIT
BEN VENUTO
BIG BERTHA

BIG CHEESE
BIG DIPPER
BIG ENDIAN
BIG HEADED
BIT PLAYER
BOB CHERRY
BOG MYRTLE
BON MARCHE
BON VIVANT
BON VIVEUR
BON VOYAGE
BOW BACKED
BOW LEGGED
BOW WINDOW
BOX CAMERA
BOX CLEVER
BOX GIRDER
BOX NUMBER
BOX OFFICE
BOY BISHOP
BUG HUNTER
BUS DRIVER
CAB DRIVER
CAN OPENER
CAP PISTOL
CAT FAMILY
CAT LITTER
CAT RIGGED
CAT WITTED
CEE SPRING
CLY FAKING
COD FISHER
CON DOLORE
COR BLIMEY
CRO MAGNON
CUP WINNER
CUT ACROSS
CUT THROAT
DAY CENTRE
DAY LABOUR
DAY RETURN
DAY SCHOOL
DEI GRATIA
DIB STONES
DIE SINKER
DIP SWITCH
DOC MARTEN
DOG COLLAR
DOG KENNEL
DOG RACING
DOG SALMON
DOG VIOLET
DOT MATRIX
DRY CLEANS
DRY SHERRY
DRY SKIING
DRY WALLER
EAR COCKLE
EEL BASKET
EGG BEATER

EGG POWDER
END READER
EWE CHEESE
EWE NECKED
EYE LOTION
EYE MUSCLE
EYE OPENER
EYE SHADOW
EYE SOCKET
EYE STRAIN
FAN SHAPED
FAR AFIELD
FAR SEEING
FAT CHANCE
FAT HEADED
FEE SIMPLE
FIG LEAVES
FLY BITTEN
FLY FISHER
FLY ORCHIS
FLY POWDER
FOG SIGNAL
FOR CHOICE
FOR EFFECT
FOX HUNTER
FUR COLLAR
FUR LINING
GAS BOTTLE
GAS BURNER
GAS COOKER
GAS COOLED
GAS ENGINE
GAS ESCAPE
GAS FILLED
GAS FITTER
GAS HEATER
GAS HELMET
GAS HOLDER
GAS MANTLE
GET ACROSS
GET AROUND
GIN PALACE
GOA BUTTER
GOA POWDER
GOD FORBID
GOT ACROSS
GOT AROUND
GUM ARABIC
GUN BARREL
GUN TURRET
GUY FAWKES
HAG RIDDEN
HAM FISTED
HEM STITCH
HEN WITTED
HEY PRESTO
HIP GIRDLE
HIP POCKET
HIT PARADE
HIT WICKET

3,6 *contd.*	LOG ROLLER	OLD FOSSIL	RAT POISON	SEA WALLED
HOI POLLOI	LOG TABLES	OLD MASTER	RED BERETS	SEE THINGS
HOP GARDEN	LOW CHURCH	OLD SCHOOL	RED CARPET	SET ALIGHT
HOP PICKER	LOW COMEDY	OLD STAGER	RED DEVILS	SET SPEECH
HOP PILLOW	LOW DOWNER	ONE ACROSS	RED DRAGON	SET SQUARE
HOP SCOTCH	LOW GERMAN	ONE HANDED	RED ENSIGN	SEX APPEAL
HOT POTATO	LOW LOADER	ONE LEGGED	RED HAIRED	SEX KITTEN
HOT RODDER	LOW MINDED	ONE OCLOCK	RED HEADED	SEX SYMBOL
HUT CIRCLE	LOW NECKED	OUR FATHER	RED HEELED	SIN EATING
ICE ANCHOR	LOW RELIEF	OUT PARISH	RED INDIAN	SIX FOOTER
ICE BUCKET	LOW SUNDAY	OUT PORTER	RED LEGGED	SIX OCLOCK
ICE HOCKEY	MAD DOCTOR	OUT SENTRY	RED LETTER	SKI FLYING
ICE SKATED	MAD HATTER	PAD SADDLE	RED MULLET	SKI JORING
ICE SKATER	MAN FRIDAY	PAN ARABIC	RED PEPPER	SKI KITING
ICE SKATES	MAO JACKET	PAN SLAVIC	RED PLAGUE	SKI SCHOOL
ILL BODING	MAY BEETLE	PAS DARMES	RED PLANET	SKY DIVING
ILL GOTTEN	MET OFFICE	PAY HOMAGE	RED POLLED	SKY TROOPS
ILL HEALTH	MID SEASON	PAY OFFICE	RED RIBAND	SOB SISTER
ILL HUMOUR	MID WICKET	PAY PACKET	RED RIBBON	SOI DISANT
ILL JUDGED	MID WINTER	PEA JACKET	RED SALMON	SOU WESTER
ILL NATURE	MOB HANDED	PEA SOUPER	RED SPIDER	SRI LANKAN
ILL OMENED	MOP HEADED	PEN DRIVER	RED SQUARE	SUB JUDICE
ILL TEMPER	MRS GRUNDY	PEN FRIEND	RED TAPISM	SUN BONNET
ILL VERSED	MUG HUNTER	PEN PUSHER	RED TAPIST	SUN DOWNER
ILL WISHER	NEO GOTHIC	PER CAPITA	RES GESTAE	SUN LOUNGE
INK BOTTLE	NEO NAZISM	PER CONTRA	REX RABBIT	SUN SPURGE
INK ERASER	NET PLAYER	PER SALTUM	RIX DOLLAR	TAP DANCED
INK PENCIL	NEW GUINEA	PET SITTER	ROD PUPPET	TAP DANCER
IVY LEAGUE	NEW JERSEY	PET THEORY	RUM BUTTER	TAP DANCES
IVY LEAVED	NEW MEXICO	PEW FELLOW	RUM RUNNER	TAX EXEMPT
JAM PACKED	NIP CHEESE	PEW HOLDER	RUN ACROSS	TAX PAYING
JAY WALKER	NIT PICKED	PEW OPENER	RUN RESIST	TAX REBATE
JET DRIVEN	NIT PICKER	PIN MAKING	RUN SCARED	TAX RELIEF
JET LAGGED	NON MEMBER	PIN STRIPE	RYE WHISKY	TAX RETURN
JET SETTER	NON PERSON	PIT SAWYER	SAM BROWNE	TEA DEALER
JET SKIING	NON SMOKER	POP ARTIST	SAW THINGS	TEA GARDEN
JET STREAM	NOR EASTER	POP RECORD	SAY CHEESE	TEA KETTLE
JOB CENTRE	NOR WESTER	POP SINGER	SEA ANCHOR	TEA LEAVES
JOB MASTER	NOT GUILTY	POT BARLEY	SEA BATHER	TEA TASTER
JOE BLOGGS	NOT LIKELY	POT BOILER	SEA BOTTOM	TEA THINGS
JOE MILLER	NOT PROVEN	POT HANGER	SEA BREACH	TEE SQUARE
JOE PUBLIC	NUT BUTTER	POT HUNTER	SEA BREEZE	TEN OCLOCK
JOY RIDING	NUT CUTLET	POT LIQUOR	SEA CHANGE	THE ABDABS
KEG BITTER	NUT WRENCH	POT POURRI	SEA DRAGON	THE ARMADA
KID SISTER	NUX VOMICA	PRE ELECTS	SEA FISHER	THE BOWERY
LAG BEHIND	ODD JOBBER	PRE EMPTED	SEA GINGER	THE CREEPS
LAP ROLLER	ODD JOBMAN	PRE EMPTOR	SEA GIRDLE	THE DAMNED
LAW CENTRE	OFF CENTRE	PRE EXISTS	SEA ISLAND	THE EIGHTS
LAW GIVING	OFF CHANCE	PRE SHRANK	SEA LAWYER	THE OCCULT
LAW WRITER	OFF COLOUR	PRE SHRINK	SEA NETTLE	THE POLICE
LAY FALLOW	OFF LIMITS	PRE SHRUNK	SEA ORANGE	THE PURPLE
LAY FIGURE	OFF PUTTER	PRE VERNAL	SEA RANGER	THE ROYALS
LAY READER	OFF STREAM	PRE WASHED	SEA ROBBER	THE SCRUBS
LAY RECTOR	OFF STREET	PRE WASHES	SEA ROCKET	THE SHIRES
LAY SISTER	OIL BURNER	PRO PATRIA	SEA ROVING	THE SPHINX
LED ASTRAY	OIL COLOUR	PUG ENGINE	SEA SALMON	THE STATES
LEG PULLER	OIL ENGINE	PUT ACROSS	SEA SHANTY	THE STICKS
LEG THEORY	OIL FILTER	RAG PICKER	SEA STRAND	THE UNIONS
LIE FALLOW	OIL TANKER	RAN ACROSS	SEA TURTLE	TIE DYEING
LIP READER	OLD BAILEY	RAN SCARED	SEA URCHIN	TIM WHISKY

3,6 contd.
TIN LIZZIE
TIN MINING
TIN OPENER
TOG RATING
TOP BOOTED
TOP DRAWER
TOP FLIGHT
TOP SAWYER
TOP SECRET
TOY POODLE
TRI WEEKLY
TUB THUMPS
TWO DECKER
TWO FISTED
TWO FOOTED
TWO HANDED
TWO HANDER
TWO HEADED
TWO LEGGED
TWO MASTED
TWO MASTER
TWO OCLOCK
TWO ROOMED
TWO SHAKES
TWO TIMING
URN SHAPED
VEE GUTTER
VIA CRUCIS
VIA LACTEA
VOX POPULI
WAR BONNET
WAR CRIMES
WAR GAMING
WAR MUSEUM
WAR OFFICE
WAX JACKET
WAY WARDEN
WEB FOOTED
WEB OFFSET
WRY NECKED
YES PLEASE
YOM KIPPUR

4,1,4
BLEW A FUSE
BLOW A FUSE
BRIC A BRAC
CALL A HALT
CAST A VOTE
CEST A DIRE
CHAR A BANC
COCK A HOOP
CUTS A DASH
DEAL A BLOW
DIAL A RIDE
DOES A TURN
DROP A LINE
FEEL A FOOL
FELT A FOOL

FIVE A SIDE
FLEW A KITE
HAIL A TAXI
HALF A TICK
HAVE A BALL
HAVE A BASH
HAVE A CARE
HAVE A STAB
JUST A TICK
LEND A HAND
LENT A HAND
LIKE A BIRD
LIKE A SHOT
LOOK A FOOL
MADE A BOMB
MADE A FACE
MADE A MOVE
MAKE A BOMB
MAKE A FACE
MAKE A MOVE
PAID A CALL
PAYS A CALL
PICK A LOCK
PLAY A PART
PULL A FACE
RANG A BELL
RING A BELL
ROCK N ROLL
RUNS A RISK
SEES A WOLF
SETS A TRAP
SHED A TEAR
SHOT A LINE
SPIN A YARN
SPUN A YARN
TAKE A SEAT
TAKE A TURN
TETE A TETE
TING A LING
TOOK A SEAT
TOOK A TURN
WAVE A WAND
WHAT A HOPE
WITH A BUMP
WITH A WILL

4,2,1,2
GAVE IT A GO
GIVE IT A GO

4,2,3
CAST AN EYE
CEST LA VIE
COCO DE MER
COME OF AGE
DOGS OF WAR
FOUR BY TWO
FULL OF WOE
GENS DE LOI
GOES TO BED
GOES TO POT

GOES TO SEA
GOES TO WAR
GONE TO BED
GONE TO POT
GONE TO SEA
GOOD TO SEE
HAND OF GOD
HAVE AT HIM
HAVE IT OUT
HEIR AT LAW
HELL TO PAY
HERE WE ARE
HITS IT OFF
HOLE IN ONE
ISLE OF ELY
ISLE OF MAN
KEEP AT BAY
KEPT AT BAY
LAID AN EGG
LAMB OF GOD
LAND OF NOD
LAYS AN EGG
LEND AN EAR
LENT AN EAR
LETS IT RIP
LIKE AS NOT
LIVE IN SIN
LIVE ON AIR
MAKE MY DAY
MAKE OR MAR
NEXT OF KIN
PEEP OF DAY
PLAY TO WIN
PUTS ON ICE
PUTS TO BED
PUTS TO SEA
SHOT IT OUT
SONS IN LAW
SPIT IT OUT
TAKE IN TOW
THIN ON TOP
TIME OF DAY
TOOK IN TOW
UGLY AS SIN
WALK ON AIR
WENT TO BED
WENT TO POT
WENT TO SEA
WENT TO WAR
WORK IT OUT
WORK OF ART
YARD OF ALE

4,3,2
COME AND GO
COME OFF IT
DOTS THE IS
LAST MAN IN
MADE FUN OF
MADE USE OF

MAKE FUN OF
MAKE USE OF
POKE FUN AT
RUNS OUT ON
THEM AND US
THIS WAY UP
WAIT FOR IT
WALK OUT ON
WELL SET UP

4,5
ACID DROPS
ACID HOUSE
AFRO ASIAN
AIRY FAIRY
ALLA BREVE
ALMA MATER
ALMS HOUSE
ALMS WOMAN
ANDY PANDY
ANTI NOVEL
AQUA REGIA
AQUA VITAE
ARCH ENEMY
ARGY BARGY
ARMY CORPS
AUNT SALLY
AWAY MATCH
BABY BUGGY
BABY GRAND
BABY HOUSE
BACK BENCH
BACK BLOCK
BACK BOARD
BACK CHAIN
BACK CLOTH
BACK COMBS
BACK CRAWL
BACK CROSS
BACK DATED
BACK DATES
BACK HEELS
BACK PEDAL
BACK PLATE
BACK SHIFT
BACK SLANG
BACK WATER
BAIN MARIE
BALD EAGLE
BALD FACED
BALD TRUTH
BALL DRESS
BALL GIRLS
BALL POINT
BAND WHEEL
BANK AGENT
BANK CLERK
BANK PAPER
BANK STOCK
BARD CRAFT

BARE BONES
BARM CLOTH
BARN DANCE
BASE METAL
BATH BRICK
BATH CHAIR
BATH SALTS
BATH STONE
BATH TOWEL
BEAD HOUSE
BEAM TRAWL
BEAN CAPER
BEAR BERRY
BEAT MUSIC
BEAU GESTE
BEAU IDEAL
BEAU MONDE
BEEF CURRY
BEER HOUSE
BEER MONEY
BEET SUGAR
BELL CRANK
BELL GLASS
BELL METAL
BELL PUNCH
BELL TOWER
BERG ADDER
BERG CEDAR
BETE NOIRE
BILE DUCTS
BIRD BRAIN
BIRD TABLE
BLOW DRIED
BLOW DRIES
BLOW TORCH
BLOW VALVE
BLUE BLOOD
BLUE GREEN
BLUE MOULD
BLUE MOVIE
BLUE PETER
BLUE RINSE
BLUE SKIES
BLUE WATER
BLUE WHALE
BOAR HOUND
BOAR SPEAR
BOAT TRAIN
BODY CHECK
BODY CLOCK
BOLD FACED
BOMB ALLEY
BOMB HAPPY
BOMB PROOF
BONA FIDES
BOND PAPER
BOND SLAVE
BOND WOMAN
BONE BLACK
BONE CHINA

4,5 *contd.*
BONE EARTH
BONE WEARY
BOOK TALLY
BOOK TOKEN
BOOK TRADE
BOOK VALUE
BORN AGAIN
BORN MIMIC
BUCK TEETH
BUFF STICK
BUFF WHEEL
BULL NOSED
BULL TROUT
BULL WHALE
BUMP START
BUSH METAL
BUSH PILOT
BUTT SHAFT
CALF BOUND
CALL NAMES
CAME ABOUT
CAME CLEAN
CAME ROUND
CAMP CHAIR
CAMP FEVER
CAMP STOOL
CANE BRAKE
CANE CHAIR
CANE SUGAR
CANT BOARD
CAPE DUTCH
CARD INDEX
CARD SHARP
CARD TABLE
CARD TRICK
CARE LABEL
CARE ORDER
CART HORSE
CART TRACK
CASE BOUND
CASE KNIFE
CASE STUDY
CASH LIMIT
CASH POINT
CASH PRIZE
CASK STAND
CAST ASIDE
CAST DOUBT
CAST LOOSE
CAST STEEL
CAVE CANEM
CELL BLOCK
CERE CLOTH
CHAW BACON
CHOP HOUSE
CHOP LOGIC
CHOP STICK
CITY STATE
CLAM SHELL

CLAP HANDS
CLAY COURT
CLAY SLATE
CLEW LINES
CLIP JOINT
CLOG DANCE
CLUB CLASS
CLUB MONEY
COAL BOARD
COAL FIELD
COAL FIRED
COAL HOUSE
COAL MINER
COAL OWNER
COAT FROCK
COAT TAILS
COCK HORSE
COCK ROBIN
CODE NAMED
COLD CREAM
COLD DRAWN
COLD FRAME
COLD FRONT
COLD HOUSE
COLD STEEL
COLD WATER
COME ABOUT
COME AGAIN
COME CLEAN
COME ROUND
CONE SHELL
CONY CATCH
COOL HOUSE
COPE STONE
CORK SCREW
CORN BORER
CORN BRAKE
CORN BREAD
CORN DOLLY
COST PRICE
COTE DAZUR
COUP DETAT
CRAB APPLE
CRAB EATER
CRAB FACED
CRAB SALAD
CROW BERRY
CUFF LINKS
CUTS LOOSE
CUTS SHORT
DAMP PATCH
DAMP PROOF
DAMP SQUIB
DARE DEVIL
DARK DEEDS
DARK HORSE
DART BOARD
DATE STAMP
DAVY JONES
DEAD DRUNK

DEAD HEADS
DEAD LEVEL
DEAD MARCH
DEAR MADAM
DECK CARGO
DECK CHAIR
DECK HOUSE
DEEP DRAWN
DEEP FRIED
DEEP FRIES
DEEP SOUTH
DEEP TONED
DEEP VOICE
DEEP WATER
DEER HOUND
DEER MOUSE
DEMI DEVIL
DEMI GORGE
DEMI LANCE
DEMI MONDE
DESK BOUND
DESK DIARY
DIED HAPPY
DIES HAPPY
DIET BREAD
DIET SHEET
DIKA BREAD
DILL WATER
DIME NOVEL
DIME STORE
DIRT CHEAP
DIRT TRACK
DISC BRAKE
DISC DRIVE
DISC STORE
DISC WHEEL
DISH CLOTH
DISH WATER
DOGS TOOTH
DOOR CHEEK
DOOR PLATE
DOPE FIEND
DOSS HOUSE
DOVE HOUSE
DOWN LYING
DOWN QUILT
DOWN SOUTH
DOWN TOOLS
DOWN TRAIN
DOWN UNDER
DRAG QUEEN
DRAW BLOOD
DRAW SHEET
DRAW TABLE
DRAW TEETH
DRAY HORSE
DREW BLOOD
DREW TEETH
DRIP STONE
DROP DRILL

DROP SCONE
DRUG FIEND
DRUG STORE
DRUM BRAKE
DRUM MAJOR
DUCK BOARD
DUDE RANCH
DUMB CLUCK
DUMB PIANO
DURA MATER
DUST BRUSH
DUST COVER
DUST DEVIL
DUST SHEET
DUST STORM
DUTY BOUND
EACH OTHER
EAST ENDER
EASY CHAIR
EASY GOING
EASY MONEY
EASY RIDER
EASY TERMS
EASY TOUCH
EVEN MONEY
FACE CLOTH
FACE CREAM
FACE FACTS
FACE GUARD
FACE PLATE
FACE SAVER
FACE VALUE
FACT SHEET
FAIR FACED
FAIR TRIAL
FALL ABOUT
FALL APART
FALL SHORT
FARM PLACE
FARM STEAD
FAST FOODS
FEEL CHEAP
FEEL FAINT
FEEL SMALL
FELL ABOUT
FELL APART
FELL SHORT
FELT CHEAP
FELT FAINT
FELT SMALL
FIFE MAJOR
FILM ACTOR
FILM EXTRA
FILM STRIP
FIND FAULT
FINE DRAWN
FINE SPRAY
FINE TUNED
FIRE ALARM
FIRE ARROW

FIRE BLAST
FIRE BREAK
FIRE DRILL
FIRE EATER
FIRE GRATE
FIRE IRONS
FIRE POWER
FIRE STICK
FIRE STORM
FIRE WATER
FISH CREEL
FISH EATER
FISH JOINT
FISH KNIFE
FISH PLATE
FISH SAUCE
FISH SLICE
FISH SPEAR
FIVE PENCE
FLAG WAVER
FLAP EARED
FLAT BROKE
FLOW CHART
FLOW SHEET
FOAM GLASS
FOLK CRAFT
FOLK DANCE
FOLK MUSIC
FOLK RIGHT
FOLK WEAVE
FOOD CANAL
FOOD CHAIN
FOOL HAPPY
FOOT BRAKE
FOOT FAULT
FOOT POUND
FOOT STALL
FORE BRACE
FORE BRAIN
FORE CITED
FORE WHEEL
FORK CHUCK
FORK LUNCH
FORM CLASS
FORM GENUS
FORM HORSE
FOUR FLUSH
FOUR HORSE
FOUR WHEEL
FREE AGENT
FREE BOARD
FREE DIVER
FREE FIGHT
FREE HOUSE
FREE LANCE
FREE LIVER
FREE LOVER
FREE LUNCH
FREE RANGE
FREE RIDER

4,5 *contd.*	GIRL GUIDE	HALF BAKED	HIGH COURT	JACK BLOCK
FREE SPACE	GIRL SCOUT	HALF BOARD	HIGH CROSS	JACK BOOTS
FREE TRADE	GIVE BIRTH	HALF BREED	HIGH DUTCH	JACK FROST
FREE VERSE	GIVE CHASE	HALF CASTE	HIGH FLIER	JACK KETCH
FREE WHEEL	GIVE FORTH	HALF CROWN	HIGH FLOWN	JACK KNIFE
FREE WORLD	GIVE VOICE	HALF DOZEN	HIGH FLYER	JACK NASTY
FROG EATER	GODS TRUTH	HALF FACED	HIGH GRADE	JACK SNIPE
FROG MARCH	GOES AHEAD	HALF LIGHT	HIGH GROWN	JACK SPRAT
FUEL GAUGE	GOES DUTCH	HALF MILER	HIGH HORSE	JACK STRAW
FULL BLAST	GOES FORTH	HALF POUND	HIGH JINKS	JADE GREEN
FULL BLOOD	GOES ROUND	HALF PRICE	HIGH LEVEL	JAIL BREAK
FULL BLOWN	GOES UNDER	HALF SWORD	HIGH POINT	JAIL FEVER
FULL CREAM	GOES WRONG	HALF TITLE	HIGH SPEED	JENA GLASS
FULL DRESS	GOLD BRICK	HALF TRUTH	HIGH TABLE	JOBS TEARS
FULL FACED	GOLD CHAIN	HALL TABLE	HIGH TONED	JOCK SCOTT
FULL FLING	GOLD CLOTH	HAND BRAKE	HIGH WATER	JOCK STRAP
FULL GROWN	GOLD COAST	HAND GLASS	HILL BILLY	JOGS ALONG
FULL HOUSE	GOLD CREST	HAND ORGAN	HIND BRAIN	JOIN HANDS
FULL MARKS	GOLD FEVER	HAND PAPER	HIND WHEEL	JOSS HOUSE
FULL ORGAN	GOLD LACED	HAND PRESS	HIVE HONEY	JOSS STICK
FULL PITCH	GOLD MEDAL	HAND PUNCH	HOAR FROST	JUKE JOINT
FULL QUOTA	GOLD MINER	HAND SCREW	HOLD COURT	JUMP LEADS
FULL SCALE	GOLD PAINT	HAND TOWEL	HOLD FORTH	JUMP START
FULL SCORE	GOLD PLATE	HANG ABOUT	HOLD HANDS	JUNE BRIDE
FULL SPLIT	GOLD POINT	HANG LOOSE	HOLD WATER	JUST ABOUT
GADS ABOUT	GOLF LINKS	HARD APORT	HOLY BIBLE	JUST CAUSE
GALL MIDGE	GOLF WIDOW	HARD COURT	HOLY GHOST	JUST FANCY
GALL STONE	GONE AHEAD	HARD CURED	HOLY GRAIL	JUST RIGHT
GAME CHIPS	GONE GOOSE	HARD DRAWN	HOLY WATER	KEEP CLEAR
GAME POINT	GONE UNDER	HARD FACTS	HOME COMER	KEEP COUNT
GAOL BREAK	GONE WRONG	HARD LINES	HOME CROFT	KEEP FAITH
GAOL FEVER	GONG STICK	HARD METAL	HOME GROWN	KEEP HOUSE
GATE HOUSE	GOOD CAUSE	HARD PASTE	HOME GUARD	KEEP QUIET
GATE MONEY	GOOD GOING	HARD STUFF	HOME MATCH	KEEP STILL
GATE TOWER	GOOD GRIEF	HARD TIMES	HOME MOVIE	KEEP TRACK
GAVE BIRTH	GOOD HANDS	HARD WORDS	HOME NURSE	KEEP WATCH
GAVE CHASE	GOOD LOOKS	HASH BROWN	HOME RULER	KEPT CLEAR
GAVE FORTH	GOOD ORDER	HAUL ROUND	HOME TRUTH	KEPT FAITH
GAVE VOICE	GOOD SENSE	HAUT MONDE	HOOF PRINT	KEPT HOUSE
GAZE HOUND	GOOD SIZED	HAVE IDEAS	HOOK NOSED	KEPT QUIET
GEAR LEVER	GOOD SPORT	HAVE WORDS	HORN MAKER	KEPT STILL
GEAR RATIO	GOOD STUFF	HAWK NOSED	HORN SPOON	KEPT TRACK
GEAR SHIFT	GOOD TASTE	HEAD COUNT	HORS SERIE	KEPT WATCH
GEAR STICK	GOOD VALUE	HEAD DRESS	HORS TEXTE	KEPT WOMAN
GEAR WHEEL	GOOD WORKS	HEAD FIRST	HOUR GLASS	KERB DRILL
GERM LAYER	GREW APART	HEAD MONEY	HUNG ABOUT	KICK ABOUT
GERM PLASM	GREY FRIAR	HEAD RHYME	HUNG LOOSE	KICK PLEAT
GETS ABOUT	GREY GOOSE	HEAD START	HUNG TILES	KICK START
GETS AHEAD	GROS POINT	HEAD WATER	HUSH MONEY	KIDS STUFF
GETS ALONG	GROW APART	HEEL PIECE	HUSH PUPPY	KILN DRIED
GETS IDEAS	GRUB SCREW	HELD COURT	ICED WATER	KING APPLE
GETS READY	HAIL STORM	HELD FORTH	IDEE RECUE	KING COBRA
GETS ROUND	HAIR BRUSH	HELD HANDS	IDLE WHEEL	KING HENRY
GETS THERE	HAIR DRIER	HELD WATER	IPSE DIXIT	KING JAMES
GETS TOUGH	HAIR DRYER	HERB PETER	IPSO FACTO	KING MIDAS
GIFT HORSE	HAIR PIECE	HIDE BOUND	IRON CROSS	KING PRAWN
GIFT TOKEN	HAIR SHIRT	HIGH ALTAR	IRON CROWN	KING SIZED
GILL HOUSE	HAIR SLIDE	HIGH BLOWN	IRON HORSE	KIWI FRUIT
GILT EDGED	HAIR SPRAY	HIGH CHAIR	IRON MINER	KNEE CORDS
GILT SPURS	HAIR WAVER	HIGH CLASS	ITSY BITSY	KNEE JOINT

4,5 *contd.*	LIFE CLASS	LOUD MOUTH	MILL OWNER	NUNS FLESH
KNOB STICK	LIFE CYCLE	LOVE APPLE	MILL TOOTH	OAST HOUSE
KNOT HOLES	LIFE FORCE	LOVE ARROW	MILL WHEEL	OKEY DOKEY
LACE FRAME	LIFE SAVER	LOVE CHARM	MIND CURER	OPEN ARMED
LACE PAPER	LIFE SIZED	LOVE CHILD	MINE FIELD	OPEN COURT
LACK BRAIN	LIFE STYLE	LOVE MATCH	MINE LAYER	OPEN ENDED
LADY SMOCK	LIFE WEARY	LOVE STORY	MINE OWNER	OPEN HOUSE
LAID ASIDE	LIKE STINK	LOVE TOKEN	MINE SHAFT	OPEN ORDER
LAID CLAIM	LILY WHITE	LUCK PENNY	MINI DRESS	OPEN SKIES
LAID PAPER	LIME GREEN	LUMP SUGAR	MINI SKIRT	OPEN SPACE
LAID WASTE	LIME JUICE	LYAM HOUND	MINT JULEP	OVEN GLOVE
LAKE BASIN	LINE BLOCK	LYME HOUND	MINT SAUCE	OVEN READY
LAKE HURON	LINE FENCE	LYON COURT	MINT STATE	OVER AGAIN
LAKE POETS	LION HEART	MADE AFTER	MIRE SNIPE	OVER SHOES
LAMP BLACK	LION TAMER	MADE HASTE	MISS WORLD	OVER THERE
LAMP GLASS	LIST PRICE	MADE MERRY	MOHS SCALE	PACK CLOTH
LAMP SHADE	LIVE BIRTH	MADE MONEY	MOLE DRAIN	PACK DRILL
LAND AGENT	LIVE SHELL	MADE PEACE	MOLE SPADE	PACK HORSE
LAND FLOOD	LOAF BREAD	MADE READY	MONO SKIER	PACK TRAIN
LAND GRANT	LOAF SUGAR	MADE SENSE	MONT BLANC	PAGE PROOF
LAND ROVER	LOAN SHARK	MADE WAVES	MOON BOOTS	PAIR HORSE
LAND VALUE	LOCK COACH	MAIL COACH	MOON DAISY	PAIR ROYAL
LAND YACHT	LOCK GATES	MAIL ORDER	MOON FACED	PALM BEACH
LARK ABOUT	LOCK HORNS	MAIL PLANE	MOOT COURT	PALM CIVET
LAST DITCH	LOIN CLOTH	MAIL TRAIN	MOOT HOUSE	PALM COURT
LAST RITES	LONG CHAIN	MAIN STORE	MOOT POINT	PALM SUGAR
LAST STRAW	LONG DATED	MAKE AFTER	MOSS AGATE	PANS PIPES
LAST THING	LONG DOZEN	MAKE HASTE	MOSS GREEN	PARA GRASS
LAST WALTZ	LONG DRAWN	MAKE MERRY	MOST NOBLE	PARK BENCH
LATE COMER	LONG DRINK	MAKE MONEY	MOTH BALLS	PART OWNER
LATE SHIFT	LONG EARED	MAKE PEACE	MOTH EATEN	PART TIMER
LATE START	LONG FACED	MAKE READY	MOTH PROOF	PASO DOBLE
LAWN MOWER	LONG JOHNS	MAKE SENSE	MOVE HOUSE	PASS CHECK
LAWN PARTY	LONG LIVED	MAKE WAVES	MUCK RAKER	PAST GLORY
LAYS ASIDE	LONG MARCH	MALT FLOOR	MUCK SWEAT	PAST TENSE
LAYS CLAIM	LONG METRE	MALT HORSE	MUSK MELON	PAUL JONES
LAYS WASTE	LONG RANGE	MALT HOUSE	MUSK PLANT	PEAK HOURS
LAZY BONES	LONG SHEEP	MANY SIDED	MUSK SHREW	PEAT CHEEL
LAZY SUSAN	LONG SKIRT	MASS GRAVE	NAIL BRUSH	PEAT SMOKE
LAZY TONGS	LONG WHIST	MASS MEDIA	NAME BRAND	PEAT SPADE
LEAD COLIC	LOOK AFTER	MAXI DRESS	NAME CHILD	PEAT STACK
LEAD OXIDE	LOOK ALIKE	MAXI SKIRT	NAME NAMES	PEEL HOUSE
LEAD PAINT	LOOK ROUND	MEAT EATER	NAME PLATE	PEEL TOWER
LEAF GREEN	LOOK SHARP	MEAT JELLY	NEAT STALL	PEEP SIGHT
LEAF METAL	LOOK SMALL	MEAT PASTE	NECK CLOTH	PEER GROUP
LEAF MOULD	LOOK SMART	MEAT WAGON	NECK PIECE	PELE HOUSE
LEAF STALK	LOOM LARGE	MESS ABOUT	NEON LIGHT	PELE TOWER
LEAN FACED	LOON PANTS	MILD STEEL	NEWS FLASH	PICK HOLES
LEFT ALONE	LORD KNOWS	MILK CHURN	NEWS PRINT	PICK PURSE
LEFT OVERS	LORD MAYOR	MILK FEVER	NEWS SHEET	PICK THANK
LEFT WHEEL	LOSE COUNT	MILK FLOAT	NEWS STAND	PICK TOOTH
LEND LEASE	LOSE HEART	MILK GLAND	NEWS VALUE	PIED PIPER
LETS ALONE	LOSE TOUCH	MILK HOUSE	NEXT WORLD	PIER GLASS
LETS BLOOD	LOSE TRACK	MILK ROUND	NILE GREEN	PIER TABLE
LETS DRIVE	LOST CAUSE	MILK SHAKE	NINE LIVES	PIKE PERCH
LETS LOOSE	LOST CHORD	MILK STOUT	NONE OTHER	PINE FINCH
LETS SLIDE	LOST COUNT	MILK SUGAR	NOSE BLEED	PINE RESIN
LIES AWAKE	LOST HEART	MILK TEETH	NOSE FLUTE	PINT SIZED
LIES UNDER	LOST TOUCH	MILK TOOTH	NOSE PIECE	PINT STOUP
LIFE BLOOD	LOST TRACK	MILL HORSE	NOSE WHEEL	PIPE DREAM

4,5 *contd.*	REED GRASS	ROSE NOBLE	SEEK AFTER	SNOW BERRY
PIPE LAYER	REED KNIFE	ROSE TOPAZ	SEES ROUND	SNOW BLIND
PIPE LIGHT	REED ORGAN	ROSE WATER	SEES STARS	SNOW BLINK
PIPE MAJOR	REEF POINT	ROSY CROSS	SELF AWARE	SNOW BOOTS
PIPE ORGAN	REST HOUSE	RUBS ALONG	SELF BUILD	SNOW BOUND
PIXY STOOL	RICE FIELD	RUIN AGATE	SELF DOUBT	SNOW BREAK
PLAN AHEAD	RICE FLOUR	RUMP STEAK	SELF DRIVE	SNOW FIELD
PLAY ABOUT	RICE GRAIN	RUNE CRAFT	SELF IMAGE	SNOW GOOSE
PLAY ACTED	RICE GRASS	RUNE STAVE	SELF PRIDE	SNOW GUARD
PLAY ACTOR	RICE PAPER	RUNS AFTER	SELL SHORT	SNOW PLANT
PLAY ALONG	RICE WATER	RUNS ALONG	SEMI GRAND	SNOW SHOES
PLAY FALSE	RICH RHYME	RUNS CLOSE	SEMI LUNAR	SNOW WATER
PLAY GOING	RING CANAL	RUNS SHORT	SEMI METAL	SNOW WHITE
PLAY HAVOC	RING CROSS	RUSH LIGHT	SEMI RIGID	SNUB NOSED
PLAY WORLD	RING DANCE	RUST PROOF	SETS ABOUT	SOAP OPERA
PLUM STONE	RING FENCE	SAFE HOUSE	SETS APART	SOAP WORKS
PLUS FOURS	RING GAUGE	SAGA NOVEL	SETS ASIDE	SOAR EAGLE
POGO STICK	RING MONEY	SAGE APPLE	SETS FORTH	SOAY SHEEP
POLE AXING	RING OUSEL	SAGE DERBY	SHIP CANAL	SODA WATER
POLE VAULT	RING OUZEL	SAGE GREEN	SHIP FEVER	SOFA TABLE
POLL MONEY	RING SNAKE	SAIL ALONG	SHIP MONEY	SOFT DRINK
POND SNAIL	RIOT AGENT	SAIL BORNE	SHIP OWNER	SOFT FRUIT
POOP SCOOP	RIOT SQUAD	SAIL CLOTH	SHIP WATER	SOFT GOODS
POOR CLARE	RISK MONEY	SAIL FLUKE	SHOE BRUSH	SOFT GRASS
PORN SQUAD	ROAD BLOCK	SAIL MAKER	SHOE LACES	SOFT PEDAL
PORT SALUT	ROAD BORNE	SALE PRICE	SHOP FLOOR	SOFT SHELL
POST DATED	ROAD CRAFT	SALT GLAZE	SHOP FRONT	SOFT SOAPS
POST ENTRY	ROAD MAKER	SALT MARSH	SHOT CRAPS	SOFT TOUCH
POST NATAL	ROAD METAL	SALT MONEY	SHOT TOWER	SOLD SHORT
POUR FORTH	ROAD SENSE	SALT SPOON	SHOW FIGHT	SOLO WHIST
PROP SHAFT	ROAD TESTS	SALT WATER	SHOW FORTH	SOME HOPES
PUFF ADDER	ROAD TRAIN	SALT WORKS	SHOW HOUSE	SONG CYCLE
PUFF PASTE	ROAD WORKS	SAME AGAIN	SHOW TRIAL	SONG TITLE
PULL AHEAD	ROBE MAKER	SAND BLAST	SICK HOUSE	SORE POINT
PULL APART	ROCK BASIN	SAND BLIND	SICK LEAVE	SOUL MUSIC
PULL ROUND	ROCK BORER	SAND BREAK	SIDE ISSUE	SOUP PLATE
PULP NOVEL	ROCK CANDY	SAND DANCE	SIDE LIGHT	SOUP SPOON
PUMP WATER	ROCK DRILL	SAND DEVIL	SIDE TABLE	SOUR GOURD
PURE BLOOD	ROCK GROUP	SAND GLASS	SIDE TRACK	SOYA SAUCE
PUSH ALONG	ROCK MUSIC	SAND GRAIN	SIDE WHEEL	SPIN DRIED
PUSH ASIDE	ROCK PERCH	SAND GRASS	SILK GLAND	SPIN DRIER
PUSH CHAIR	ROCK PIPIT	SAND MASON	SILK GRASS	SPIN DRIES
PUSH START	ROCK PLANT	SAND PRIDE	SINE CURVE	SPIN DRYER
PUTS ABOUT	ROCK SNAKE	SAND SNAKE	SING ALONG	SPOT CHECK
QUIT CLAIM	ROCK SOLID	SAND SPOUT	SITS STILL	SPOT DANCE
RACE TRACK	ROLL ALONG	SAND STORM	SITS TIGHT	SPOT WELDS
RAIL BORNE	ROOF BOARD	SAND TABLE	SKEW WHIFF	SPUN SUGAR
RAIL FENCE	ROOF GUARD	SAND WEDGE	SKIN ALIVE	SPUR ROWEL
RAIL MOTOR	ROOF PLATE	SAND YACHT	SKIN DIVER	SPUR WHEEL
RAIN BOUND	ROOT CANAL	SANG ALONG	SKIN GRAFT	STAG DANCE
RAIN CLOUD	ROOT CAUSE	SANS SOUCI	SKIN TIGHT	STAG NIGHT
RAIN GAUGE	ROOT HOUSE	SASH FRAME	SLAP HAPPY	STAG PARTY
RAIN MAKER	ROOT PRUNE	SEAL POINT	SLIP ANGLE	STAR BURST
RAIN WATER	ROPE DANCE	SEAT STICK	SLIP BOARD	STAR DRIFT
RANK RIDER	ROPE HOUSE	SEED DRILL	SLOP BASIN	STAR GAZED
RARE EARTH	ROPE MAKER	SEED FIELD	SLOW HOUND	STAR GAZER
READ ALOUD	ROPE SOLED	SEED MONEY	SLOW MARCH	STAR GAZES
REAL IMAGE	ROPE TRICK	SEED PEARL	SLOW MATCH	STAR GRASS
REAR GUARD	ROSE APPLE	SEED PLANT	SLOW PACED	STAR JELLY
REAR LIGHT	ROSE ELDER	SEED STALK	SMUG FACED	STAR PUPIL

4,5 *contd.*
STAR SHELL
STAR SIGNS
STAR STONE
STAR WHEEL
STAY MAKER
STAY STILL
STEP ASIDE
STEP CHILD
STEP DANCE
STEP STONE
STIR CRAZY
STOP PRESS
STOP SHORT
STOP THIEF
STOP WATCH
STUD GROOM
STUD HORSE
STUD POKER
SUEZ CANAL
SURE THING
SURF CANOE
SURF RIDER
SWAN ABOUT
SWAN GOOSE
TAGS ALONG
TAIL BOARD
TAIL ENDER
TAIL LIGHT
TAIL RHYME
TAKE AFTER
TAKE AMISS
TAKE APART
TAKE COVER
TAKE HEART
TAKE ISSUE
TAKE LEAVE
TAKE PAINS
TAKE PLACE
TAKE SHAPE
TAKE SIDES
TAKE STEPS
TAKE STOCK
TAKE TURNS
TALK ROUND
TALL ORDER
TALL STORY
TANK WAGON
TANT MIEUX
TAPE DRIVE
TAPE PUNCH
TASK FORCE
TASK GROUP
TEAR DROPS
TEAR GLAND
TEAR SHEET
TELL TALES
TENT CLOTH
TENT DRESS
TENT MAKER

TEST DRIVE
TEST MATCH
TEST PAPER
TEST PILOT
THIN FACED
TIDE GAUGE
TIDE TABLE
TIDE WATER
TIED HOUSE
TILE STONE
TIME CLOCK
TIME FLIES
TIME LAPSE
TIME LIMIT
TIME SHARE
TIME SHEET
TIME TRIAL
TINT BLOCK
TOAD EATER
TOLD TALES
TOLL HOUSE
TOOK AFTER
TOOK AMISS
TOOK APART
TOOK COVER
TOOK HEART
TOOK ISSUE
TOOK LEAVE
TOOK PAINS
TOOK PLACE
TOOK SHAPE
TOOK SIDES
TOOK STEPS
TOOK STOCK
TOOK TURNS
TOWN CLERK
TOWN CRIER
TOWN HOUSE
TRAY CLOTH
TREE LINED
TREE RINGS
TREE SHREW
TREE SNAKE
TREE STUMP
TREE TRUNK
TROD WATER
TUBE SKIRT
TURF SPADE
TURN ABOUT
TURN ASIDE
TURN LOOSE
TURN NASTY
TURN ROUND
TWIN BIRTH
TYPE METAL
TYRE CHAIN
TYRE GAUGE
UNIT PRICE
UNIT TRUST
URSA MAJOR

URSA MINOR
USED FORCE
USES FORCE
VADE MECUM
VERS LIBRE
VERY LIGHT
VICE CHAIR
VICE REGAL
VICE SQUAD
VICE VERSA
VIDE INFRA
VIDE SUPRA
VINE FRUIT
VINE STOCK
VITA GLASS
WAGE SLAVE
WAIT ABOUT
WAKE ROBIN
WALK ABOUT
WALL BOARD
WALL PLATE
WALL SPACE
WARM FRONT
WASH BASIN
WASH BOARD
WASH CLOTH
WASH HOUSE
WASH STAND
WASP STING
WASP STUNG
WAVE ASIDE
WAVE POWER
WEAK KNEED
WEAK POINT
WEEK ABOUT
WEEK ENDER
WELL BEING
WELL BORER
WELL BUILT
WELL DOING
WELL HOUSE
WELL KNOWN
WELL LINED
WELL MEANT
WELL OILED
WELL SPENT
WELL TIMED
WENT AHEAD
WENT DUTCH
WENT FORTH
WENT ROUND
WENT UNDER
WENT WRONG
WEST NORTH
WHAT GIVES
WHAT PRICE
WHEY FACED
WHIP ROUND
WHIP SNAKE
WHIP STOCK

WIDE ANGLE
WIDE AWAKE
WILD BIRDS
WILD GEESE
WILD GOOSE
WILD GRAPE
WILD HONEY
WILD MANGO
WILD PARTY
WILD THYME
WILD WATER
WILL POWER
WIND BREAK
WIND CHART
WIND GAUGE
WIND HOVER
WIND POWER
WIND SURFS
WINE GLASS
WINE PARTY
WINE PRESS
WINE VAULT
WING SHELL
WING SNAIL
WIRE BRUSH
WIRE GAUGE
WIRE GAUZE
WIRE GRASS
WIRE WHEEL
WISE WOMAN
WITH CHILD
WITH YOUNG
WOLF HOUND
WOOD BORER
WOOD HOUSE
WOOD NYMPH
WOOD PAPER
WOOD SCREW
WOOD SUGAR
WORD BLIND
WORD SALAD
WORK BENCH
WORK ETHIC
WORK STUDY
WORK TABLE
WORM EATEN
WORM FENCE
WORM WHEEL
WRAP ROUND
WYCH HAZEL
YEAR ROUND
ZERO RATED
ZERO RATES
ZINC COLIC
ZINC OXIDE
ZINC WHITE

5,1,3
BREAK A LEG
CASTS A NET

FLUTE A BEC
LIVED A LIE
LIVES A LIE
MAKES A BED
PLACE A BET
QUITE A FEW
ROMAN A CLE
SELLS A PUP
SHAKE A LEG
SHOOK A LEG
SHOWS A LEG
SMELL A RAT
SMELT A RAT
TAKES A BOW
THREW A FIT
THROW A FIT

5,2,2
AUTOS DA FE
BEATS TO IT
BREAK IT UP
CAMPS IT UP
CEASE TO BE
CHUCK IT IN
FUNNY HA HA
KEEPS AT IT
LIVED IT UP
LIVES IT UP
LOOKS UP TO
MAKES IT UP
PACKS IT IN
PACKS IT UP
PILED IT ON
PILES IT ON
STICK AT IT
STICK EM UP
STUCK AT IT
TRIED IT ON
TRIES IT ON
VINGT ET UN
WHATS TO DO
WHOOP IT UP
WORKS AT IT

5,4
ABOUT FACE
ABOUT TURN
AFTER CROP
AFTER LIFE
AGONY AUNT
AITCH BONE
ALARM BELL
ALARM CALL
ALDIS LAMP
ALICE BAND
ALLEZ VOUS
ALPHA PLUS
ALPHA RAYS
ALTER EGOS
AMBER FISH
AMINO ACID

5,4 *contd.*	BIRDS FOOT	BRAIN WAVE	CAMEO PART	CLOCK GOLF
ANGEL CAKE	BIRDS NEST	BRAKE DRUM	CAMEO ROLE	CLOSE CALL
ANGEL DUST	BIRTH MARK	BRAKE PADS	CAMEO WARE	CLOSE DOWN
ANGEL FISH	BIRTH PILL	BRAKE SHOE	CANAL BANK	CLOSE KNIT
ANGEL FOOD	BIRTH RATE	BRAND IRON	CANAL BOAT	CLOTH EARS
ANGLE IRON	BIRTH SIGN	BRAND NAME	CAPER BUSH	CLOTH HALL
ANGLE SHOT	BLACK ARTS	BRASS BAND	CARRY AWAY	CLOTH YARD
ANGLE WORM	BLACK BASS	BRASS NECK	CARRY BACK	CLOUD BASE
ANKLE BOOT	BLACK BEAR	BREAD CORN	CARRY OVER	CLOUD OVER
ANKLE SOCK	BLACK BELT	BREAD LINE	CASTE MARK	CLOUT NAIL
APPLE CART	BLACK BESS	BREAD ROLL	CASTS AWAY	CLOUT SHOE
APPLE JACK	BLACK BOOK	BREAD TREE	CASTS LOTS	CLOVE HOOK
APPLE JOHN	BLACK FLAG	BREAK AWAY	CATCH COLD	CLOVE PINK
APPLE TART	BLACK GOLD	BREAK CAMP	CATCH CROP	COACH BOLT
APPLE TREE	BLACK HAND	BREAK DOWN	CATCH FIRE	COACH HIRE
APPLE WIFE	BLACK HOLE	BREAK EVEN	CEASE FIRE	COACH HORN
APRES GOUT	BLACK LOOK	BREAK WIND	CEDAR TREE	COACH LINE
APRIL FOOL	BLACK MARK	BRICK DUST	CHAIN BOLT	COACH ROAD
ARGUS EYED	BLACK MASS	BRICK KILN	CHAIN GANG	COACH TOUR
ARROW HEAD	BLACK MONK	BRICK WALL	CHAIN GEAR	COACH TRIP
ARROW SHOT	BLACK POPE	BRIEF CASE	CHAIN MAIL	COAST ROAD
ASHEN GREY	BLACK SPOT	BRIER ROOT	CHAIN PIER	COCKS COMB
ATTIC SALT	BLACK SWAN	BRIER WOOD	CHAIN PUMP	COCOA WOOD
AUGER HOLE	BLADE BONE	BRING DOWN	CHART ROOM	COMES AWAY
AUGER WORM	BLANK DOOR	BRING HOME	CHASE PORT	COMES BACK
AUGUR WELL	BLANK PAGE	BRING OVER	CHEAP JACK	COMES DOWN
AURIC ACID	BLAST HOLE	BROAD BEAN	CHECK BOOK	COMES HOME
BACKS DOWN	BLAST PIPE	BROAD BRIM	CHECK REIN	COMES OVER
BALDI COOT	BLAZE AWAY	BROAD LEAF	CHECK TILL	CONGA DRUM
BALSA WOOD	BLIND DATE	BROKE AWAY	CHEEK BONE	CORAL FISH
BASIC SALT	BLIND ROAD	BROKE CAMP	CHESS CLUB	CORAL REEF
BEACH BALL	BLIND SIDE	BROKE DOWN	CHEWS OVER	CORAL ROCK
BEARS ARMS	BLIND SPOT	BROKE EVEN	CHIEF WHIP	CORAL ROOT
BEARS AWAY	BLOCK BOOK	BROWN BEAR	CHILD CARE	CORAL WORT
BEARS DOWN	BLOCK SHIP	BROWN BESS	CHILD STAR	COSTA RICA
BEARS FOOT	BLOCK TYPE	BROWN COAL	CHILD WIFE	COUGH DROP
BEATS DOWN	BLOCK VOTE	BROWN RICE	CHINA CLAY	COUNT DOWN
BEATS TIME	BLOOD BANK	BRUSH FIRE	CHINA JUTE	COURT CARD
BEAUX ARTS	BLOOD BATH	BUCKS FIZZ	CHINA ROSE	COURT FOOL
BEDDY BYES	BLOOD CLOT	BUCKS HORN	CHINA WARE	COURT HAND
BEECH FERN	BLOOD FEUD	BUGLE DOWN	CHOIR GIRL	COURT ROLL
BEECH MAST	BLOOD LINE	BUGLE CALL	CHOKE BACK	COURT SHOE
BEECH WOOD	BLOOD TEST	BULLY BEEF	CHOKE COIL	COVER GIRL
BELLE AMIE	BLOOD TYPE	BULLY ROOK	CHUBB LOCK	COVER NOTE
BELLE MERE	BLOOD WORM	BUMPS INTO	CHUMP CHOP	COWES WEEK
BELLY ACHE	BLOWS AWAY	BUNNY GIRL	CHURN MILK	CRABS EYES
BELLY BAND	BLOWS OVER	BUONA SERA	CIGAR TREE	CRACK DOWN
BELLY FLOP	BLUSH ROSE	BURMA ROAD	CIVIL LIST	CRAFT SHOP
BENCH HOLE	BOARD GAME	BURMA STAR	CIVIL TIME	CRAMP IRON
BENCH MARK	BOARD ROOM	BURNS DOWN	CIVIL YEAR	CRAMP RING
BENDS OVER	BOARS HEAD	BURNT CORK	CLAMP DOWN	CRASH DIVE
BESOM HEAD	BOILS OVER	BURNT DOWN	CLASS BOOK	CRASH LAND
BEVIN BOYS	BONGO DRUM	BURNT SACK	CLAWS BACK	CRAZY GOLF
BIBLE BELT	BOOBY TRAP	CABIN CREW	CLEAR EYED	CREAM CAKE
BILGE KEEL	BORNE AWAY	CABIN SHIP	CLEAR SOUP	CREAM HORN
BILGE PUMP	BOSSA NOVA	CALFS FOOT	CLERK LIKE	CREAM PUFF
BILLY GOAT	BOUND OVER	CALLS AWAY	CLIFF FACE	CREAM SODA
BILLY LIAR	BOWER BIRD	CALLS BACK	CLIMB DOWN	CRIED DOWN
BINDS OVER	BOWLS OVER	CALLS OVER	CLING FILM	CRIED WOLF
BINGO HALL	BRAIN DEAD	CALMS DOWN	CLOCK CARD	CRIES DOWN

5,4 *contd.*

CRIES WOLF	DOLLY SHOT	FALLS OVER	FLUNG OPEN	GOOSE NECK
CRIME WAVE	DONOR CARD	FALSE DAWN	FLUTE BIRD	GOOSE SKIN
CROSS EYED	DOVER SOLE	FALSE GODS	FOLIC ACID	GOOSE STEP
CROSS KICK	DOVES FOOT	FALSE NOSE	FOOLS GOLD	GOOSE WING
CROSS OVER	DRAIN AWAY	FANCY CAKE	FOOLS MATE	GRACE NOTE
CROSS TALK	DRAIN PIPE	FANCY FAIR	FORCE FEED	GRADE RISE
CROWN BARK	DRAIN TILE	FANCY FREE	FORCE LAND	GRAND AUNT
CROWN LAND	DRAIN TRAP	FEAST RITE	FORCE PUMP	GRAND DUKE
CROWS BILL	DRAWS BACK	FERRY BOAT	FORKS OVER	GRAND PRIX
CROWS FEET	DRAWS LOTS	FEVER HEAT	FRIAR TUCK	GRAND SLAM
CROWS FOOT	DRAWS NEAR	FIELD BOOK	FRIED EGGS	GRAND TOUR
CROWS NEST	DREAM LAND	FIELD GREY	FRIED RICE	GRASS PLOT
CRUEL BLOW	DRESS COAT	FIELD LARK	FROCK COAT	GRAVY BOAT
CUBAN HEEL	DRESS DOWN	FIELD TRIP	FRONT AXLE	GRAVY SOUP
CUBBY HOLE	DRESS SUIT	FIEND LIKE	FRONT DOOR	GREAT AUNT
CUBIC FOOT	DRIED EGGS	FIGHT BACK	FRONT LINE	GREAT DANE
CUBIC INCH	DRIED MILK	FILED PAST	FRONT PAGE	GREAT HALL
CUBIC YARD	DRIFT LAND	FIRED AWAY	FRONT RANK	GREAT SEAL
CURLY KALE	DRIFT SAIL	FIRED BACK	FRONT ROOM	GREEK FIRE
CURRY COMB	DRIFT WEED	FIRES AWAY	FROST BITE	GREEK GIFT
CUTTY SARK	DRIFT WOOD	FIRES BACK	FRUIT CAKE	GREEK GODS
DAIRY FARM	DRILL HALL	FIRMS DOWN	FRUIT TREE	GREEK NOSE
DAISY BELL	DRILL HOLE	FIRST BASE	FUNNY BONE	GREEN BELT
DALAI LAMA	DRIVE HOME	FIRST BORN	FUNNY FARM	GREEN CARD
DAMPS DOWN	DROPS AWAY	FIRST FOOT	GAINS TIME	GREEN CORN
DANCE BAND	DROPS DOWN	FIRST GEAR	GAMES ROOM	GREEN CROP
DANCE HALL	DROVE HOME	FIRST HAND	GAMMA RAYS	GREEN EYED
DANCE STEP	DROVE ROAD	FIRST LADY	GEARS DOWN	GREEN ROOM
DANCE TUNE	DRURY LANE	FIRST MATE	GENOA CAKE	GRILL ROOM
DANDY CART	DUCKS DOWN	FIRST NAME	GHOST LIKE	GRIND DOWN
DANDY ROLL	DUCKS FOOT	FIRST RATE	GHOST MOTH	GRIST MILL
DATUM LINE	DUTCH BARN	FIRST SLIP	GHOST TOWN	GUARD RAIL
DEATH BELL	DUTCH DOLL	FIXED IDEA	GIANT STAR	GUARD ROOM
DEATH CELL	DUTCH LEAF	FIXED ODDS	GIPSY MOTH	GUARD SHIP
DEATH DUTY	DUTCH OVEN	FIXED STAR	GIVEN AWAY	GUESS WORK
DEATH MASK	DUTCH WIFE	FLAGS DOWN	GIVEN NAME	GUEST ROOM
DEATH RATE	DYERS WOAD	FLAME LEAF	GIVES AWAY	GUIDE BOOK
DEATH ROLL	DYING AWAY	FLAME TREE	GIVES ODDS	GUIDE POST
DEATH TRAP	DYING DOWN	FLARE PATH	GIVES REIN	GUIDE RAIL
DEATH WISH	DYING HARD	FLARE STAR	GLASS CHIN	GUIDE ROPE
DEBIT CARD	DYING SWAN	FLASH BACK	GLASS SOAP	GULLY HOLE
DECOY DUCK	EAGLE EYED	FLASH BULB	GLASS WOOL	GYPSY MOTH
DELTA WING	EAGLE HAWK	FLASH BURN	GLIDE PATH	HANDS DOWN
DEMON KING	EARLY BIRD	FLASH CARD	GLOBE FISH	HANDS OVER
DEPTH BOMB	EARLY DAYS	FLASH FIRE	GLORY HOLE	HANDS TURN
DEVIL CRAB	EDGED TOOL	FLASH OVER	GLOSS OVER	HANGS BACK
DEVIL FISH	ELBOW ROOM	FLESH MEAT	GNAWS AWAY	HANGS FIRE
DICKY BIRD	EMBER DAYS	FLESH TINT	GOATS HAIR	HAPPY DAYS
DIRTY LOOK	EMBER WEEK	FLIES HIGH	GOING AWAY	HAPPY HOUR
DIRTY WORD	ENTRE NOUS	FLIES OPEN	GOING BACK	HARES FOOT
DIRTY WORK	ENTRY FORM	FLIES SOLO	GOING BUST	HARKS BACK
DIXIE LAND	ESSEX GIRL	FLING DOWN	GOING DOWN	HATHA YOGA
DOING DOWN	EVERY INCH	FLING OPEN	GOING INTO	HEARD TELL
DOING OVER	EXTRA TIME	FLOAT TANK	GOING OVER	HEARS TELL
DOING TIME	FAIRS FAIR	FLOOD LAMP	GOING SLOW	HEART BEAT
DOING WELL	FAIRY KING	FLOOR PLAN	GOING SOFT	HEART SICK
DOLCE VITA	FAIRY RING	FLOOR SHOW	GOING WEST	HEATH FOWL
DOLLY BIRD	FAIRY TALE	FLOSS SILK	GOOSE FAIR	HEAVY DUTY
DOLLY SHOP	FALLS BACK	FLOUR MILL	GOOSE FISH	HEAVY ROCK
	FALLS DOWN	FLUNG DOWN	GOOSE GIRL	HEAVY SPAR

5,4 *contd.*
HEDGE HOPS
HIDEY HOLE
HIRED HELP
HITCH HIKE
HOLDS BACK
HOLDS DOWN
HOLDS GOOD
HOLDS OVER
HOLDS SWAY
HOLLY FERN
HONEY BEAR
HONEY BIRD
HONEY CART
HONKY TONK
HORSE FAIR
HORSE FOOT
HORSE RACE
HORSE SHOE
HOTEL DIEU
HOUND FISH
HOUSE BOAT
HOUSE CALL
HOUSE COAT
HOUSE DUTY
HOUSE HUNT
HOUSE MATE
HOUSE ROOM
HOWLS DOWN
HUNKY DORY
HUNTS DOWN
ICING OVER
IDEAL HOME
IDIOT CARD
INDEX LINK
INGLE NOOK
INGLE SIDE
INNER CITY
INNER PART
INNER TUBE
INNER WARD
INTER ALIA
INTER ARTS
IRISH MOSS
IRISH STEW
IVORY GATE
IVORY PALM
JELLY BABY
JENNY WREN
JERRY SHOP
JEWEL CASE
JOINT HEIR
JOINT WILL
JOINT WORM
JOLLY GOOD
JUDAS HOLE
JUDAS KISS
JUDAS TREE
JUMPS BAIL
JUMPS SHIP

KAURI PINE
KEELS OVER
KEEPS BACK
KEEPS BUSY
KEEPS DOWN
KEEPS TIME
KILLS TIME
KINGS EVIL
KIRBY GRIP
KLIEG EYES
KNIFE EDGE
KNIFE REST
KNOCK BACK
KNOCK COLD
KNOCK DOWN
KNOCK KNEE
KOALA BEAR
LADYS MAID
LAGER BEER
LAGER LOUT
LAMBS EARS
LAMBS WOOL
LANCE JACK
LANCE WOOD
LAPSE RATE
LARDY CAKE
LARKS HEEL
LASER BEAM
LASER DISC
LAYER CAKE
LEASE LEND
LEGAL MIND
LEGAL YEAR
LEMON CURD
LEMON DROP
LEMON PEEL
LEMON SOLE
LEVEL BEST
LEVEL COIL
LHASA APSO
LIBEL SUIT
LIGHT BULB
LIGHT FOOT
LIGHT WORK
LIGHT YEAR
LINEN FOLD
LIVED DOWN
LIVED WELL
LIVER SPOT
LIVES DOWN
LIVES WELL
LOCAL CALL
LOCAL TIME
LOCKS AWAY
LODGE GATE
LOOKS AWRY
LOOKS BACK
LOOKS DOWN
LOOKS INTO
LOOKS OVER

LOOSE LEAF
LOSES FACE
LOSES TIME
LOUSE WORT
LOWER CASE
LOWER DECK
LUNAR YEAR
LUNCH HOUR
LUNCH TIME
LYING BACK
LYING DOWN
LYING OVER
LYMPH NODE
MAGIC CUBE
MAGIC WAND
MAJOR AXIS
MAJOR DOMO
MAJOR MODE
MAJOR SUIT
MAJOR TERM
MAJOR TONE
MAKES AWAY
MAKES GOOD
MAKES LOVE
MAKES OVER
MAKES PLAY
MAKES ROOM
MAKES SAIL
MAKES SURE
MAKES TIME
MANOR SEAT
MAPLE LEAF
MARCH HARE
MARCH PAST
MARDI GRAS
MARES NEST
MARES TAIL
MARKS DOWN
MARKS TIME
MARSH HAWK
MATCH PLAY
MEANS TEST
MEANS WELL
MEANT WELL
MEDAL PLAY
MELTS AWAY
MELTS DOWN
MERRY MAKE
METAL WORK
METER MAID
MEZZA VOCE
MILLS BOMB
MINOR AXIS
MINOR MODE
MINOR POET
MINOR SUIT
MINOR TERM
MINOR TONE
MINUS SIGN
MISTS OVER

MONEY BAGS
MONEY BELT
MONEY BILL
MONEY DOWN
MONKS HOOD
MORAL CODE
MOTOR BIKE
MOTOR BOAT
MOTOR SHOW
MOUND BIRD
MOUNT ETNA
MOUSE DEER
MOUSE HOLE
MOUSE HUNT
MOUSE TAIL
MOUSE TRAP
MOUTH HARP
MOVED AWAY
MOVED BACK
MOVED OVER
MOVES AWAY
MOVES BACK
MOVES OVER
MULTI WALL
MUMMY CASE
MUSIC CASE
MUSIC HALL
MUSIC RACK
MUSIC ROLL
MUSIC ROOM
NAILS DOWN
NANDI BEAR
NANNY GOAT
NEEDS MUST
NERVE CELL
NERVE ENDS
NEVER MIND
NIGHT BELL
NIGHT BIRD
NIGHT CLUB
NIGHT DUTY
NIGHT GOWN
NIGHT LIFE
NIGHT REST
NIGHT ROBE
NIGHT SPOT
NIGHT TIDE
NIGHT TIME
NIGHT WORK
NONCE WORD
NORTH EAST
NORTH POLE
NORTH STAR
NORTH WEST
NOTRE DAME
NOVUS HOMO
NURSE MAID
NYMPH LIKE
OBJET DART
OLIVE BACK

ONION EYED
ONION SKIN
OPTIC LOBE
OPTIC TUBE
ORANG UTAN
ORDER BOOK
ORDER FORM
ORGAN LOFT
ORGAN PIPE
ORGAN STOP
ORLOP DECK
ORRIS ROOT
OUTER TUBE
PAINT TRAY
PANEL GAME
PANTS SUIT
PAPAL BULL
PAPER CLIP
PAPER FILE
PAPER GIRL
PAPER MILL
PAPER OVER
PAPER PULP
PAPER REED
PAPER TAPE
PARGE WORK
PARTY CALL
PARTY GOER
PARTY JURY
PARTY LINE
PARTY WALL
PASTE DOWN
PATCH TEST
PATNA RICE
PEACE DRUG
PEACE PILL
PEACE PIPE
PEACH PALM
PEACH TREE
PEACH WOOD
PEARL EDGE
PEARL EYED
PEARL GREY
PEASE MEAL
PEDAL BONE
PENAL CODE
PENAL LAWS
PENNY GAFF
PENNY MAIL
PENNY POST
PENNY RENT
PENNY WISE
PENNY WORT
PETER BOAT
PETIT FOUR
PETIT PAIN
PETRI DISH
PETTY CASH
PHONE CALL
PHOTO CALL

5,4 *contd.*	PRESS GANG	RAREE SHOW	ROYAL BLUE	SENNA PODS
PIANO KEYS	PRESS HOME	RAZOR BACK	ROYAL LINE	SERVE TIME
PIANO ROLL	PRESS MARK	RAZOR BILL	ROYAL MAIL	SEVEN SEAS
PIANO WIRE	PRESS ROOM	RAZOR CLAM	ROYAL MAST	SHADE TREE
PICKS OVER	PRESS STUD	RAZOR EDGE	ROYAL MILE	SHAKE DOWN
PIECE RATE	PRESS WORK	RAZOR FISH	ROYAL ROAD	SHALE MINE
PIECE WORK	PRICE CODE	READY MADE	RUGBY BALL	SHANK BONE
PIGGY BANK	PRICE LIST	RELAY RACE	RURAL DEAN	SHARP EYED
PILAU RICE	PRICE RING	REVEL ROUT	SABRE WING	SHEEP HOOK
PILOT BOAT	PRIME COST	RHINE WINE	SAINT JOHN	SHEEP LICE
PILOT FISH	PRIME TIME	RHUMB LINE	SAINT LUKE	SHEEP SCAB
PILOT LAMP	PRINT SHOP	RHYME WORD	SAINT MARK	SHEEP TICK
PINCH HITS	PRIVY SEAL	RIDES DOWN	SAINT PAUL	SHEEP WASH
PIPED DOWN	PRIZE BULL	RIDGE BONE	SALAD BOWL	SHEET FILM
PIPES DOWN	PRIZE CREW	RIDGE POLE	SALAD DAYS	SHEET IRON
PIQUE WORK	PRIZE LIST	RIDGE ROPE	SALAD HERB	SHEET LEAD
PITCH DARK	PRIZE RING	RIDGE TILE	SALES TALK	SHELF LIFE
PIXIE RING	PROOF MARK	RIFLE BIRD	SALLY ARMY	SHELF MARK
PLACE CARD	PROOF READ	RIFLE SHOT	SALLY LUNN	SHELL HOLE
PLACE KICK	PROOF TEXT	RIGHT AWAY	SALTS AWAY	SHELL LIKE
PLACE NAME	PROSE POEM	RIGHT BANK	SALTS DOWN	SHELL PINK
PLAIN COOK	PSALM BOOK	RIGHT HAND	SAUCE BOAT	SHELL SAND
PLAIN DARN	PSALM TUNE	RIGHT HOOK	SAVED FACE	SHELL SUIT
PLAIN JANE	PULLS AWAY	RIGHT SIDE	SAVED TIME	SHIFT WORK
PLANE TREE	PULLS BACK	RIGHT WING	SAVES FACE	SHIRE MOOT
PLANT LICE	PULLS DOWN	RINGS BACK	SAVES TIME	SHIRT BAND
PLANT LIKE	PULLS OVER	RINGS DOWN	SCALE BEAM	SHIRT STUD
PLANT LORE	PULLS RANK	RINGS TRUE	SCALE FERN	SHIRT TAIL
PLATE RACK	PULSE RATE	RINKY DINK	SCALE FISH	SHOCK HEAD
PLATE RAIL	PULSE WAVE	RIVER BANK	SCALE LEAF	SHOCK WAVE
PLATE ROOM	PUMPS IRON	RIVER BOAT	SCALE MOSS	SHOOK DOWN
PLAYS BACK	PUNCH BALL	RIVER HEAD	SCALE WORK	SHOOT DOWN
PLAYS BALL	PUNCH BOWL	RIVER SAND	SCALY BARK	SHOOT HOME
PLAYS DOWN	PUNCH CARD	RIVER TIDE	SCAMP WORK	SHORE BOAT
PLAYS FAIR	PUNCH LINE	RIVER WALL	SCARE LINE	SHORE CRAB
PLAYS HOST	PUPPY LOVE	RIVET HEAD	SCARF RING	SHORE SIDE
PLAYS SAFE	QUAIL PIPE	RIVET HOLE	SCENE DOCK	SHORT COAT
PLUGS AWAY	QUEEN ANNE	ROAST BEEF	SCENE FOUR	SHORT GAME
PLUMB LINE	QUEEN CAKE	ROAST DUCK	SCOOP NECK	SHORT HAUL
PLUMB RULE	QUEEN JANE	ROAST LAMB	SCORE CARD	SHORT HORN
PLUME BIRD	QUEEN LIKE	ROAST PORK	SCORE DRAW	SHORT LIFE
PLUME MOTH	QUEEN MARY	ROBIN HOOD	SCOTS PINE	SHORT LIST
POINT DUTY	QUEEN POST	ROLLS OVER	SCRAP BOOK	SHORT ODDS
POINT LACE	QUEEN SIZE	ROMAN NOSE	SCRAP HEAP	SHORT SALE
POKER DICE	QUEER COVE	ROMAN ROAD	SCRAP IRON	SHORT SLIP
POKER FACE	QUEER FISH	ROMPS HOME	SCRAP YARD	SHORT STOP
POKER WORK	QUEUE JUMP	ROTOR SHIP	SCREW BOLT	SHORT TERM
POLAR AXIS	QUICK BORN	ROUGH DRAW	SCREW DOWN	SHORT TIME
POLAR BEAR	QUICK EYED	ROUGH HEWN	SCREW JACK	SHORT WAVE
POLAR BODY	QUICK FIRE	ROUGH SHOD	SCREW NAIL	SHOUT DOWN
POPES NOSE	QUICK TIME	ROUND DOWN	SCREW PILE	SHUTS AWAY
POPPY HEAD	RADAR TRAP	ROUND EYED	SCREW PINE	SHUTS DOWN
POPPY SEED	RADIO MAST	ROUND FISH	SCREW WORM	SIGHT HOLE
POUND CAKE	RADIO PILL	ROUND GAME	SCRUB BIRD	SIGHT LINE
POWER DIVE	RADIO STAR	ROUND TRIP	SCRUB FOWL	SIGHT READ
POWER LOOM	RADIO WAVE	ROUND WORM	SCRUM HALF	SIGHT SING
POWER PACK	RAISE CAIN	ROUTE STEP	SEAMY SIDE	SIGNS AWAY
POWER UNIT	RAISE HELL	ROWAN TREE	SEINE BOAT	SIMON PURE
PRESS BOOK	RAPID FIRE	ROWEL HEAD	SENDS DOWN	SIREN SUIT
PRESS CLUB	RARAE AVES	ROWEL SPUR	SENDS WORD	SISAL HEMP

5,4 *contd.*	SOUTH WEST	STIFF NECK	SUGAR SOAP	TEARS DOWN
SIXTH FORM	SPACE RACE	STILL BORN	SUNNY SIDE	TEARS INTO
SKATE OVER	SPACE SUIT	STILL LIFE	SWAMP BOAT	TEARS OPEN
SKUNK BIRD	SPACE TIME	STILL ROOM	SWANS DOWN	TEDDY BEAR
SLACK ROPE	SPACE WALK	STINK BOMB	SWARM CELL	TEDDY GIRL
SLANT EYED	SPADE BONE	STINK WOOD	SWART BACK	TEDDY SUIT
SLATE CLUB	SPARE PART	STOCK CUBE	SWEAR WORD	TEMPT FATE
SLATE GREY	SPARE ROOM	STOCK FARM	SWEAT BAND	TENOR CLEF
SLAVE SHIP	SPARE TIME	STOCK LIST	SWEAT SHOP	TESLA COIL
SLIDE RULE	SPARE TYRE	STOCK ROOM	SWEAT SUIT	THATS FLAT
SLING BACK	SPARK COIL	STOCK WHIP	SWEET CORN	THATS THAT
SLIPS AWAY	SPARK PLUG	STOKE HOLE	SWEET FLAG	THEME PARK
SLOPE ARMS	SPEAK EASY	STONE BASS	SWEET SHOP	THEME SONG
SLOTH BEAR	SPEED BOAT	STONE CAST	SWEET TALK	THEME TUNE
SLOWS DOWN	SPEED TRAP	STONE COAL	SWINE FISH	THIGH BONE
SLUSH FUND	SPICE BUSH	STONE COLD	SWING BACK	THIGH BOOT
SMALL ARMS	SPICE CAKE	STONE DEAF	SWING DOOR	THINK BACK
SMALL BEER	SPIKE FISH	STONE HARD	SWING WING	THINK OVER
SMALL BORE	SPILL OVER	STONE HAWK	SWISS ROLL	THINK TANK
SMALL COAL	SPILT OVER	STONE LILY	SWORD BELT	THIRD HAND
SMALL HAND	SPLAY FOOT	STONE MILL	SWORD BILL	THIRD RATE
SMALL PICA	SPLIT MIND	STONE PINE	SWORD CANE	THORN BUSH
SMALL TALK	SPLIT PEAS	STOOD DOWN	SWORD HAND	THREE CARD
SMALL TIME	SPLIT RING	STOOD FAST	SWORD KNOT	THREE DECK
SMALL TOWN	SPOIL BARK	STOOD FIRE	SWORD LIKE	THREE FOOT
SMART ALEC	SPOON FEED	STOOD OVER	SWORD RACK	THREE FOUR
SMART CARD	SPOUT HOLE	STOPS DEAD	SWORD TAIL	THREW AWAY
SMEAR TEST	STACK ROOM	STOPS OVER	SYLPH LIKE	THREW DOWN
SMOCK MILL	STAFF DUTY	STORE ROOM	TABLE BOOK	THREW OPEN
SMOKE BALL	STAFF ROOM	STORE SHIP	TABLE GAME	THREW OVER
SMOKE BOMB	STAGE DOOR	STORM BIRD	TABLE LEAF	THROW AWAY
SMOKE HOLE	STAGE HAND	STORM COCK	TABLE MAID	THROW BACK
SMOKE RING	STAGE LEFT	STORM CONE	TABLE SALT	THROW DOWN
SNAIL FISH	STAGE NAME	STORM DRUM	TABLE TALK	THROW OPEN
SNAIL LIKE	STAGE PLAY	STORM SAIL	TABLE WARE	THROW OVER
SNAKE BELT	STAIR WELL	STORM WIND	TABLE WINE	THUMB HOLE
SNAKE BITE	STAKE BOAT	STORY BOOK	TAKEN BACK	THUMB MARK
SNAKE CULT	STALK EYED	STORY LINE	TAKEN DOWN	THUMB TACK
SNARE DRUM	STALL FEED	STRAP HANG	TAKEN OVER	TICKS AWAY
SNEAK RAID	STAMP DUTY	STRAP WORK	TAKES ARMS	TICKS OVER
SNIPE FISH	STAND DOWN	STRAW POLL	TAKES BACK	TIDAL WAVE
SNUFF FILM	STAND EASY	STRAW ROPE	TAKES BETS	TIDED OVER
SNUFF MILL	STAND FAST	STRAW STEM	TAKES CARE	TIDES OVER
SOLAR CELL	STAND FIRE	STRAW WORK	TAKES DOWN	TIGER LILY
SOLAR TIME	STAND OVER	STRIP CLUB	TAKES FIVE	TIGER MOTH
SOLAR WIND	STAND PIPE	STRIP DOWN	TAKES HEED	TIGER TAIL
SOLAR YEAR	STATE BANK	STRIP LEAF	TAKES NOTE	TIGER WOLF
SOLID FUEL	STAYS OVER	STRIP MILL	TAKES OVER	TIGER WOOD
SONIC BANG	STEAM BATH	STRIP MINE	TAKES PART	TIGHT KNIT
SONIC BOOM	STEAM IRON	STYLE BOOK	TAKES ROOT	TIGHT ROPE
SOTTO VOCE	STEAM OPEN	SUGAR BEAN	TAKES SILK	TIGHT SPOT
SOUND FILM	STEAM PIPE	SUGAR BEET	TAKES WING	TIPSY CAKE
SOUND HOLE	STEEL BAND	SUGAR BOWL	TALKS BACK	TITHE BARN
SOUND POEM	STEEL BLUE	SUGAR CANE	TALKS DOWN	TITHE FREE
SOUND POET	STEEL CLAD	SUGAR CUBE	TALKS INTO	TITLE DEED
SOUND WAVE	STEEL DRUM	SUGAR LOAF	TALKS OVER	TITLE LEAF
SOUTH BANK	STEEL GREY	SUGAR LUMP	TALKS SHOP	TITLE PAGE
SOUTH EAST	STEEL WARE	SUGAR MILL	TAROT CARD	TITLE ROLE
SOUTH POLE	STEEL WOOL	SUGAR PALM	TASTE BUDS	TOAST RACK
SOUTH SEAS	STEPS DOWN	SUGAR PLUM	TEARS AWAY	TONED DOWN

5,4 *contd.*

TONES DOWN	TURNS UPON	WATER POLO	WOUND DOWN	BOTTOM END
TONKA BEAN	TWICE OVER	WATER PUMP	WRIST SHOT	BOTTOM OUT
TOOTH PICK	TYING DOWN	WATER RAIL	WRITE DOWN	BOUGHT OFF
TORCH LILY	UNDER ARMS	WATER RATE	WRITE HOME	BOUGHT OUT
TORCH RACE	UNDER FIRE	WATER RICE	WRONG DOER	BOVVER BOY
TORCH SONG	UNDER OATH	WATER SEAL	WRONG FOOT	BOWING OUT
TOTEM POLE	UNDER RIPE	WATER VOLE	WRONG SIDE	BOWLED OUT
TOUCH DOWN	UNDER SAIL	WATER WORN	WROTE DOWN	BOWLER HAT
TOUCH LINE	UNION FLAG	WAVED DOWN	WROTE HOME	BOXING DAY
TOUCH MARK	UNION JACK	WAVES DOWN	XENON LAMP	BOYLES LAW
TOUCH TYPE	UPPER CASE	WEARS AWAY	YACHT CLUB	BRAZIL NUT
TOUCH WOOD	UPPER DECK	WEARS DOWN	YACHT RACE	BREAKS OFF
TOUGH LUCK	UPPER HAND	WEARS THIN	YOUNG FOGY	BREAKS OUT
TOWEL RACK	VIDEO GAME	WEIGH DOWN	YOUNG LADY	BREAST FED
TOWEL RAIL	VIDEO TUBE	WELSH HARP	YOUNG TURK	BRIDES MAN
TOWER MILL	VISOR MASK	WHALE BACK	YOUTH CLUB	BRINGS OFF
TOWER OVER	VOGUE WORD	WHALE BOAT	ZONAL AXIS	BRINGS OUT
TRACK DOWN	VOICE OVER	WHALE BONE		BROKEN MAN
TRACK SHOE	VOICE VOTE	WHALE CALF	**6,1,2**	BRONZE AGE
TRACK SUIT	VOLTE FACE	WHALE LINE	HAVING A GO	BUBBLE CAR
TRADE DOWN	VOTED DOWN	WHATS WHAT		BUBBLE GUM
TRADE MARK	VOTES DOWN	WHEAT CORN	**6,3**	BUDGET DAY
TRADE NAME	WAFER CAKE	WHEAT CROP	AARONS ROD	BUFFET CAR
TRADE SALE	WAGES SLIP	WHEAT GERM	ACTING OUT	BUMBLE BEE
TRADE WIND	WAGON LOAD	WHEAT MEAL	ALMOND OIL	BUMPED OFF
TRAIL AWAY	WAIST DEEP	WHEAT MOTH	ANCHOR LEG	BURNED OUT
TRAIN BAND	WAIST HIGH	WHEEL LOCK	ANCHOR MAN	BUTTER BOX
TRAIN MILE	WAITS UPON	WHEEL RACE	ANGORA CAT	BUTTER FAT
TRANS SHIP	WAKES WEEK	WHEEL SPIN	APPIAN WAY	BUTTER OIL
TRAWL FISH	WALKS AWAY	WHISK AWAY	ARCTIC FOX	BUTTER PAT
TRAWL LINE	WALKS INTO	WHITE BEAR	BACKED OFF	BUYING OFF
TRIPE SHOP	WALKS TALL	WHITE FLAG	BAILED OUT	BUYING OUT
TROOP SHIP	WASPS NEST	WHITE GOLD	BALING OUT	CADDIE CAR
TROTH RING	WASTE AWAY	WHITE HART	BALLOT BOX	CALLED OFF
TROUT FARM	WASTE PIPE	WHITE HEAT	BALSAM FIR	CALLED OUT
TRUCK LOAD	WATCH BILL	WHITE HOLE	BANANA OIL	CAMERA SHY
TRUCK SHOP	WATCH FIRE	WHITE HOPE	BANGED OUT	CAMPED OUT
TRUMP CARD	WATCH OVER	WHITE LADY	BARRET CAP	CAMPER VAN
TRUMP SUIT	WATER BATH	WHITE LEAD	BARROW BOY	CANADA DAY
TRUNK CALL	WATER BUCK	WHITE LIME	BATTLE AXE	CANCEL OUT
TRUNK LINE	WATER BULL	WHITE LINE	BATTLE CRY	CANDLE END
TRUNK MAIL	WATER BUTT	WHITE ROSE	BAWLED OUT	CANDLE NUT
TRUNK ROAD	WATER CART	WHITE SALE	BEAVER RAT	CANDLE WAX
TRUSS BEAM	WATER CASK	WHITE SALT	BEDDED OUT	CANNON BIT
TRUST DEED	WATER COCK	WHITE TEAK	BEETLE OFF	CAPSID BUG
TRUST FUND	WATER COOL	WHITE WINE	BEGGAR MAN	CARPET BAG
TRUTH DRUG	WATER CURE	WHIZZ BANG	BEGGED OFF	CARPET ROD
TUDOR ROSE	WATER DECK	WHOLE NOTE	BELTED OUT	CARTED OFF
TULIP ROOT	WATER DOWN	WHOLE TONE	BETTER OFF	CARVED OUT
TULIP TREE	WATER FERN	WIDOW BIRD	BLACKS OUT	CARVES OUT
TULIP WOOD	WATER FLOW	WINDS DOWN	BLASTS OFF	CASHEW NUT
TURKS HEAD	WATER FOWL	WITCH HUNT	BLURTS OUT	CASTOR OIL
TURNS AWAY	WATER GATE	WITCH WIFE	BOARDS OUT	CAUDLE CUP
TURNS BACK	WATER HEAD	WOLFS BANE	BOBBLE HAT	CAUGHT OUT
TURNS DOWN	WATER HOLE	WOLFS CLAW	BOFORS GUN	CELTIC SEA
TURNS INTO	WATER JUMP	WOLFS FOOT	BOILED EGG	CENTRE BIT
TURNS OVER	WATER LINE	WORKS OVER	BOOKED OUT	CHALKS OUT
TURNS TAIL	WATER MAIN	WORKS UPON	BOTANY BAY	CHARGE MAN
TURNS TURK	WATER MILL	WORLD BANK	BOTTLE GAS	CHECKS OFF
	WATER PIPE	WORSE LUCK	BOTTLE OFF	CHECKS OUT
			BOTTLE OUT	

6,3 *contd.*

CHEESE VAT	DESERT RAT	FISHES OUT	HANSOM CAB	LITTLE END
CHEONG SAM	DEVILS OWN	FITTED OUT	HARDEN OFF	LITTLE MAN
CHERRY BOB	DIESEL OIL	FLAKED OUT	HEADED OFF	LITTLE TOE
CHERRY PIE	DINING CAR	FLAKES OUT	HEADED OUT	LIVING OUT
CHERRY PIT	DINING OUT	FLINGS OUT	HEARTH RUG	LOCKED OUT
CHILLS OUT	DINNER SET	FLOWER BED	HEARTH TAX	LOGGED OUT
CHOKED OFF	DIPPED OUT	FLOWER BUD	HELPED OUT	LONDON IVY
CHOKES OFF	DIRECT HIT	FLYING FOX	HERBAL TEA	LOOKED FOR
CHUCKS OUT	DIRECT TAX	FLYING JIB	HEROIC AGE	LOOKED OUT
CHURNS OUT	DISHED OUT	FLYING OUT	HINDER END	LOSING OUT
CIPHER KEY	DISHES OUT	FOBBED OFF	HIRING OUT	LOUNGE BAR
CLARET CUP	DOCTOR WHO	FOLDED OUT	HIVING OFF	LOVING CUP
CLARET JUG	DOLLAR GAP	FOLLOW OUT	HOLING OUT	MAKING FOR
CLEANS OUT	DOUBLE ACT	FONDUE SET	HOLLOW OUT	MAKING HAY
CLEARS OUT	DOUBLE BAR	FORAGE CAP	HOPPED OFF	MAKING OFF
CLOCHE HAT	DOUBLE BED	FOREST FLY	HORNED OWL	MAKING OUT
CLOCKS OFF	DOUBLE TOP	FOREST LAW	HUMBLE PIE	MAKING WAR
CLOCKS OUT	DREDGE BOX	FOREST OAK	HUNTED OUT	MAKING WAY
CLUTCH BAG	DRIVES OUT	FORKED OUT	INCOME TAX	MALLEE HEN
COCKED HAT	DROWNS OUT	FOSTER SON	INDIAN FIG	MAPPED OUT
COFFEE BAR	DRYING OUT	FOUGHT OFF	INDIAN INK	MARKED MAN
COFFEE BUG	DUCKED OUT	FREAKS OUT	INDIAN RED	MARKED OFF
COFFEE CUP	DUFFEL BAG	FREEZE DRY	INSECT NET	MARKED OUT
COFFEE POT	DUNCES CAP	FREEZE OUT	INSIDE JOB	MARKET DAY
COFFEE SET	EASILY LED	FRENCH FRY	INSIDE OUT	MARKET MAN
COFFER DAM	EASING OFF	FRIARS CAP	IRONED OUT	MASTER KEY
COLLIE DOG	EASTER DAY	FROZEN OUT	JERSEY COW	MEADOW RUE
COLOUR BAR	EASTER EGG	FRYING PAN	JULIET CAP	MELLOW OUT
COMBED OUT	EATING OUT	FUNNEL NET	JUMPED OFF	MENTAL AGE
COMING OFF	EDGING OUT	FUNNEL WEB	KENNEL MAN	METRIC TON
COMING OUT	EDITED OUT	GALLOP OFF	KICKED OFF	MIDDLE AGE
COMMON ERA	EMBRYO SAC	GALWAY BAY	KICKED OUT	MIDDLE EAR
COMMON LAW	EMPIRE DAY	GATHER WAY	KILLED OFF	MINUTE GUN
CONGER EEL	ENERGY GAP	GINGER ALE	KILNER JAR	MISSED OUT
CONING OFF	ERRAND BOY	GINGER NUT	KNOCKS OFF	MISSES OUT
COOLED OFF	ESKIMO DOG	GINGER POP	KNOCKS OUT	MODERN ART
COPING SAW	ESTATE CAR	GINGER TOM	LABOUR DAY	MOLING OUT
COPPED OUT	EVENED OUT	GIVING EAR	LADIES MAN	MONKEY BAG
COPPER AGE	EXCISE LAW	GIVING OFF	LADLED OUT	MONKEY JAR
CORDON OFF	FACING OUT	GIVING OUT	LADLES OUT	MONKEY NUT
CORNER BOY	FADING OUT	GIVING WAY	LANGUE DOC	MONKEY RUN
COTTER PIN	FAGGED OUT	GOGGLE BOX	LASHED OUT	MORTAL SIN
COTTON GIN	FAMILY MAN	GOLDEN AGE	LASHES OUT	MOSAIC LAW
COUNTS OUT	FANNED OUT	GOLDEN BOY	LATTER DAY	MOSAIC MAP
CRADLE CAP	FARDEL BAG	GOLDEN EYE	LATTER END	MOTHER WIT
CRESTA RUN	FARMED OUT	GOUGED OUT	LAUGHS OFF	MOVING OUT
CRYING OFF	FELLOW MAN	GOUGES OUT	LAUNCH PAD	MUFFIN CAP
CRYING OUT	FIDDLE BOW	GRAVEL PIT	LAYING OFF	MUFFIN MAN
CUPIDS BOW	FIGHTS OFF	GREASE GUN	LAYING OUT	MUMMYS BOY
DAMSON JAM	FILING OFF	GRIMMS LAW	LEAKED OUT	MUSCLE MAN
DAPPLE BAY	FILLED OUT	GROUND ASH	LEAVES OFF	MYRTLE WAX
DASHED OFF	FILLER CAP	GROUND HOG	LEAVES OUT	NEEDLE GUN
DASHED OUT	FILTER BED	GROUND ICE	LETTER BOX	NIPPED OUT
DASHES OFF	FILTER TIP	GROUND NUT	LEVELS OFF	NISSEN HUT
DASHES OUT	FINGER TIP	GROUND OAK	LEYDEN JAR	NODDED OFF
DEADLY SIN	FINING POT	GUARDS VAN	LIFTED OFF	NOISES OFF
DECKED OUT	FINISH OFF	GUINEA HEN	LIGHTS OUT	NOSING OUT
DEGREE DAY	FIRING OFF	GUINEA PIG	LITTER BIN	NUMBER ONE
DESERT PEA	FIRING PIN	HAMMER TOE	LITTER BUG	NUMBER TEN
	FISHED OUT	HANDED OUT	LITTLE AUK	NUMBER TWO

6,3 contd.

OFFICE BOY	POLLEN SAC	SACRED APE	SHOWED OFF	STAKED OUT
OPENED OUT	POMACE FLY	SACRED CAT	SHRIMP NET	STAKES OUT
OPTING OUT	POODLE DOG	SACRED COW	SHRUGS OFF	STAMPS OUT
ORANGE TIP	POPPED OFF	SADDLE BAG	SIGNAL BOX	STANDS OFF
OYSTER BED	POPPED OUT	SADDLE BAR	SIGNED OFF	STANDS OUT
PACKED OUT	POSSET CUP	SADDLE BOW	SIGNED OUT	STANDS PAT
PADDED OUT	POTATO ROT	SAFETY NET	SILVER AGE	STARTS OUT
PADDLE BOX	POUNCE BAG	SAFETY PIN	SILVER FIR	STARVE OUT
PAIRED OFF	POUNCE BOX	SAILOR HAT	SILVER FOX	STATUS QUO
PALACE CAR	POURED OUT	SAILOR MAN	SIMPLE VOW	STAYED OUT
PANAMA HAT	POWDER BOX	SAINTS DAY	SINGED CAT	STAYED PUT
PARIAH DOG	POWDER KEG	SALLEE MAN	SINGLE TAX	STICKS OUT
PARISH TOP	PRAYER MAT	SALMON FLY	SKETCH OUT	STICKY END
PARITY LAW	PRAYER RUG	SALMON FRY	SKINNY DIP	STINKS OUT
PARKED CAR	PRINTS OUT	SALOON BAR	SLEEPS OFF	STOKES LAW
PARROT CRY	PRISON VAN	SALOON CAR	SLEEVE NUT	STREAM ICE
PARROT JAW	PROMPT BOX	SAUCER EYE	SLINGS INK	STREET CAR
PASSED OFF	PRYING OUT	SAVILE ROW	SLINKS OFF	STREET MAP
PASSED OUT	PUBLIC ACT	SCHOOL AGE	SLOPED OFF	STRIKE OFF
PASSES OFF	PUBLIC BAR	SCHOOL DAY	SLOPES OFF	STRIKE OIL
PASSES OUT	PUBLIC KEY	SCHOOL TIE	SLOPPY JOE	STRIKE OUT
PATROL CAR	PUBLIC LAW	SCOOPS OUT	SLOUCH HAT	STRIKE PAY
PAYING OFF	PUFFED OUT	SCORED OFF	SMELLS OUT	STRING BAG
PAYING OUT	PULLED OFF	SCORES OFF	SMOKED HAM	STRING OUT
PEAKED CAP	PULLED OUT	SCOTCH EGG	SMOKED OUT	STRING PEA
PEANUT OIL	PUMPED OUT	SCOTCH ELM	SMOKES OUT	STRING TIE
PEELED OFF	PUSHED OFF	SCOTCH FIR	SMOOTH DAB	STRIPS OFF
PEEPED OUT	PUSHED OUT	SCOTTY DOG	SNEEZE BOX	STRIPS OUT
PEGGED OUT	PUSHES OFF	SCRAPE GUT	SNELLS LAW	STROKE OAR
PEKING MAN	PUSHES OUT	SCRAPE OFF	SNIFFS OUT	STRONG BOX
PELVIC FIN	PUTTED OUT	SCREEN OFF	SNUFFS OUT	STRONG TEA
PENCIL ORE	PUTTER OUT	SCROLL SAW	SOCIAL WAR	STRUCK OFF
PEPPER BOX	PUZZLE PEG	SEALED OFF	SOLEMN VOW	STRUCK OIL
PEPPER POT	RABBIT PIE	SEARCH FEE	SORTED OUT	STRUCK OUT
PETROL CAN	RACING CAR	SECOND MAN	SOUGHT OUT	STRUNG OUT
PEWTER POT	RAINED OFF	SEEING FIT	SOUNDS OFF	SUSSED OUT
PHASED OUT	RAISED PIE	SEEING OFF	SOUNDS OUT	SUSSES OUT
PHASES OUT	RAVING MAD	SEEING OUT	SPACED OUT	SWITCH OFF
PHYSIC NUT	REELED OFF	SEEING RED	SPACES OUT	SWIVEL EYE
PICKED OFF	REFLEX ARC	SENECA OIL	SPARKS OFF	SWIVEL GUN
PICKED OUT	RELIEF MAP	SENTRY BOX	SPARKS OUT	TAILED OFF
PICKET OUT	RENNET BAG	SERVED OUT	SPEAKS OUT	TAKING AIM
PIECED OUT	RESCUE BID	SERVES OUT	SPEECH DAY	TAKING OFF
PIECES OUT	RIDING OUT	SETTER OFF	SPELLS OUT	TAKING OUT
PILLAR BOX	RIDING ROD	SETTER OUT	SPIDER LEG	TALKED BIG
PINEAL EYE	RIGGED OUT	SETTLE BED	SPIDER MAN	TALKED OUT
PIPING HOT	RINSED OUT	SHADOW BOX	SPIDER WEB	TAPERS OFF
PISTON ROD	RINSES OUT	SHAGGY CAP	SPIRAL ARM	TAPPET ROD
PLAGUE PIT	RIPPED OFF	SHAGGY DOG	SPIRIT GUM	TAPPIT HEN
PLANTS OUT	RISING SUN	SHAKES OFF	SPLASH OUT	TARGET MAN
PLAYED OFF	ROBBER FLY	SHAKES OUT	SPOKEN FOR	TEEING OFF
PLAYED OUT	ROMANY RYE	SHARED OUT	SPONGE BAG	THAWED OUT
POINTS OUT	ROOTED OUT	SHARES OUT	SPORTS CAR	THEYRE OFF
POISON GAS	ROTTEN EGG	SHEEPS EYE	SPRING BED	THINKS OUT
POISON IVY	ROTTEN ROW	SHEERS OFF	SPRING GUN	THRASH OUT
POISON PEN	ROUGHS OUT	SHELLS OUT	SPRUCE FIR	THROWN OFF
POLICE BOX	ROUNDS OFF	SHOOTS OFF	SQUARE LEG	THROWN OUT
POLICE DOG	ROUNDS OUT	SHOVED OFF	SQUINT EYE	THROWS OFF
POLISH OFF	RUBBED OUT	SHOVEL HAT	STABLE BOY	THROWS OUT
	RULING OUT	SHOVES OFF	STABLE MAN	THRUST HOE

6,3 contd.	WRINGS OUT	CHECKED IN	FILLING UP	KNOCKER UP
TICKED OFF	WRITES OFF	CHECKED UP	FIRMING UP	LATCHED ON
TICKET DAY	WRITES OUT	CHEERED UP	FITTING IN	LATCHES ON
TINDER BOX	YAKETY YAK	CHIMING IN	FITTING UP	LEADING IN
TIPPED OFF	YANKEE BET	CHIPPED IN	FLARING UP	LEADING ON
TIRING OUT	YELLOW DOG	CHOKING UP	FOLDING IN	LEADING UP
TOILET SET		CHOPPED UP	FOLLOWS ON	LEANING ON
TOODLE PIP	**7,2**	CHUCKED UP	FOLLOWS UP	LEAVING BE
TOPPED OUT	BACKING UP	CHURNED UP	FOOTING IT	LETTING BE
TOWING NET	BANGING UP	CLAMMED UP	FORKING UP	LETTING GO
TRADED OFF	BARGING IN	CLEANED UP	FOULING UP	LETTING IN
TRADES OFF	BATTLED ON	CLEARED UP	FRESHEN UP	LETTING ON
TRAILS OFF	BATTLES ON	CLOCKED IN	FROWNED ON	LETTING UP
TRILBY HAT	BEARING UP	CLOCKED UP	FURTHER ON	LIFTING UP
TRYING OUT	BEATING IT	CLOSING IN	GANGING UP	LIGHTEN UP
TSETSE FLY	BEATING UP	CLOSING UP	GATHERS UP	LIMBERS UP
TUMBLE CAR	BEEFING UP	COINING IT	GEARING UP	LINKING IN
TUNING KEY	BELTING UP	COLOURS IN	GENNING UP	LINKING UP
TUNING PEG	BIDDING IN	COLOURS UP	GETTING AT	LISTENS IN
TUNING PIN	BIDDING UP	CONJURE UP	GETTING BY	LOCKING IN
TURFED OUT	BLOWING IN	COPPING IT	GETTING IN	LOCKING ON
TURKEY HEN	BLOWING UP	COTTONS ON	GETTING ON	LOCKING UO
TURKEY OAK	BOOKING IN	COUGHED UP	GETTING UP	LOFTING UP
TURKEY RED	BOOKING UP	COVERED IN	GOBBLED UP	LOGGING IN
TURNED OFF	BOTTLED UP	COVERED UP	GOBBLES UP	LOOKERS ON
TURNED OUT	BOTTLES UP	CRACKED UP	GROSSED UP	LOOKING AT
TURNIP TOP	BOTTOMS UP	CROPPED UP	GROSSES UP	LOOKING IN
TURRET GUN	BREWING UP	CURLING UP	GROWING UP	LOOKING ON
UNHOLY ROW	BROUGHT IN	CURTAIN UP	GUMMING UP	LOOKING UP
VACANT LOT	BROUGHT ON	CUTTING IN	HANGING IN	LOOSENS UP
VANITY BAG	BROUGHT UP	CUTTING UP	HANGING ON	LUGGING IN
VANITY BOX	BRUSHED UP	DERRING DO	HANGING UP	MARKING UP
VENIAL SIN	BRUSHES UP	DIGGING IN	HARPING ON	MASHING UP
VIOLIN BOW	BUBBLED UP	DIGGING UP	HAULING IN	MEASURE UP
VISION MIX	BUBBLES UP	DIPPING IN	HAULING UP	MEETING UP
VISUAL AID	BUCKING UP	DISHING UP	HEAVING TO	MESSING UP
WALKED OFF	BUMPING UP	DOUBLED UP	HEMMING IN	MISTING UP
WALKED OUT	BURNING IN	DOUBLES UP	HINTING AT	MOPPING UP
WANDER OFF	BURNING UP	DRAGGED ON	HITCHED UP	MUCKING IN
WANTED OUT	BUTTERS UP	DRAGGED UP	HITCHES UP	MUDDLED UP
WARDED OFF	BUTTING IN	DRAUGHT OX	HITTING ON	MUDDLES UP
WARDEN PIE	BUTTONS UP	DRAWING IN	HOGGING IT	MUGGING UP
WASHED OUT	CALLING BY	DRAWING UP	HOLDING IN	MUSCLED IN
WEAKER SEX	CALLING IN	DREAMED UP	HOLDING ON	MUSCLES IN
WEALTH TAX	CALLING ON	DRESSED UP	HOLDING UP	NIPPING IN
WEASEL CAT	CARRIED ON	DRESSES UP	HOPPING IT	NOTHING ON
WEASEL OUT	CARRIES ON	DROPPED BY	HORNING IN	OFFERED UP
WEIGHS OUT	CARVING UP	DROPPED IN	HOTTING UP	OPENING UP
WHISKY MAC	CASHING IN	DROPPED ON	HURRIED UP	OUTSIDE IN
WHITED OUT	CASHING UP	DUFFING UP	HURRIES UP	OVERDID IT
WHITES OUT	CASTING UP	DUMPING ON	HUSHING UP	PACKING UP
WINDOW BAR	CATCHES ON	EARLIER ON	JOINING IN	PASSERS BY
WINDOW BOX	CATCHES UP	EVENING UP	JOINING UP	PASSING BY
WINDOW TAX	CHAINED UP	FALLING IN	JUMPING ON	PASSING ON
WINKLE OUT	CHALKED UP	FALLING ON	KEEPING IN	PASSING UP
WIPING OUT	CHANCED IT	FASTENS ON	KEEPING ON	PATCHED UP
WOODEN LEG	CHANCES IT	FATTENS UP	KEEPING UP	PATCHES UP
WORKED FOR	CHANGED UP	FETCHED UP	KICKING IN	PERKING UP
WORKED OFF	CHANGES UP	FETCHES UP	KNOCKED ON	PHASING IN
WORKED OUT	CHEATED ON	FILLING IN	KNOCKED UP	PICKING AT

7,2 *contd.*
PICKING ON
PICKING UP
PIECING UP
PIGGING IT
PITCHED IN
PITCHES IN
PLAYING AT
PLAYING ON
PLAYING UP
PLOUGHS IN
PLUGGED IN
POINTED UP
POPPING IN
POPPING UP
POUNCED ON
POUNCES ON
PRESSED ON
PRESSES ON
PREYING ON
PROPPED UP
PSYCHED UP
PSYCHES UP
PUCKERS UP
PULLING IN
PULLING UP
PUMPING IN
PUMPING UP
PUTTING BY
PUTTING IN
PUTTING ON
PUTTING UP
QUARTER TO
QUEUING UP
QUICKEN UP
RACKING UP
RATTING ON
RATTLED ON
RATTLES ON
READING UP
RECKONS ON
RECKONS UP
REDDING UP
REINING IN
REJOICE IN
RELYING ON
REVVING UP
RIGGING UP
RINGING IN
RINGING UP
RISKING IT
ROLLING IN
ROLLING UP
ROUGHED IN
ROUGHED IT
ROUNDED ON
ROUNDED UP
RUBBING UP
RUNNERS UP
RUNNING IN

RUNNING ON
RUNNING TO
RUNNING UP
RUSTLED UP
RUSTLES UP
SADDLED UP
SADDLES UP
SAILING BY
SCARING UP
SEIZING UP
SELLING ON
SELLING UP
SENDING IN
SENDING ON
SERVING UP
SETTING BY
SETTING IN
SETTING ON
SETTING UP
SETTLED IN
SETTLED UP
SETTLES IN
SETTLES UP
SHAKING UP
SHANGRI LA
SHAPING UP
SHOWING UP
SHRIVEL UP
SIGNING IN
SIGNING ON
SIGNING UP
SINKING IN
SITTING BY
SITTING IN
SITTING ON
SITTING UP
SKIPPED IT
SLACKEN UP
SLICING UP
SLIPPED ON
SLIPPED UP
SLOWING UP
SNAPPED UP
SNEAKED UP
SNUFFED IT
SNUGGLE UP
SOBERED UP
SOFTENS UP
SOLDIER ON
SOUPING UP
SPEEDED UP
SQUARED UP
SQUARES UP
STACKED UP
STANDER BY
STARTED IN
STARTED UP
STAVING IN
STAYING IN
STAYING ON

STAYING UP
STEAMED UP
STEPPED IN
STEPPED UP
STIRRED UP
STOCKED UP
STOKING UP
STOPPED IN
STRIKES UP
STRINGS UP
STUMPED UP
SUCKING IN
SUMMING UP
SUMMONS UP
SWALLOW UP
SWOTTED UP
TACKING ON
TALKING AT
TALKING TO
TARTING UP
TEARING UP
TELLING ON
THOUGHT UP
TOGGING UP
TOOLING UP
TOPPING UP
TOSSING UP
TOTTING UP
TOUCHED UP
TOUCHES UP
TOUGHEN UP
TRADING IN
TRADING UP
TRUMPED UP
TUCKING IN
TURNING IN
TURNING ON
TURNING TO
TWIGGED IT
UNHEARD OF
UNLIVED IN
WAITING ON
WAITING UP
WALKING IT
WALKING ON
WALLING UP
WANTING IN
WARMING UP
WASHING UP
WEIGHED IN
WEIGHED UP
WHIPPED IN
WHIPPER IN
WINDING UP
WORKING IN
WORKING ON
WORKING UP
WRAPPED UP
WRITING UP

WRITTEN UP
WROUGHT UP
ZAPPING UP
ZEROING IN
ZIPPING UP

10 LETTERS

1,3,3,3
I KID YOU NOT

1,3,6
A FAT CHANCE

1,4,5
A GOOD THING
A NEAR THING
A SOFT TOUCH
A SORE THUMB
T BONE STEAK

1,5,4
A TIGHT SPOT

1,6,3
A BETTER BET

1,7,2
A QUARTER TO
I BELIEVE SO

2,1,3,4
IN A BAD MOOD
UP A GUM TREE

2,1,7
AT A PREMIUM
AT A STRETCH
AT A TANGENT
AT A VENTURE

2,2,1,5
UP TO A POINT

2,2,2,4
UP TO NO GOOD

2,2,3,3
GO TO THE BAD
UP IN THE AIR

2,2,6
GO GO DANCER
GO TO BLAZES
GO TO GROUND
GO TO MARKET
GO TO PIECES
UP TO TRICKS

2,3,2,3
TO CAP IT ALL

2,3,3,2
ON THE WAY UP

2,3,5
AS PER USUAL
AT ALL COSTS
AT ALL HOURS

AT THE READY
AT THE WHEEL
BY ALL MEANS
BY AND LARGE
BY ANY MEANS
DO THE TRICK
DO THE TWIST
GO FOR BROKE
IN ANY EVENT
IN BAD ODOUR
IN HOT WATER
IN THE BLACK
IN THE CHAIR
IN THE CLEAR
IN THE DRINK
IN THE EVENT
IN THE FLESH
IN THE MONEY
IN THE RIGHT
IN THE ROUGH
IN THE ROUND
IN THE SHADE
IN THE WINGS
IN THE WRONG
IN TWO MINDS
IN TWO TICKS
LE MOT JUSTE
MY OLD DUTCH
ON ALL FOURS
ON THE BENCH
ON THE BLINK
ON THE BLOCK
ON THE BRAIN
ON THE BRINK
ON THE CARDS
ON THE CHEAP
ON THE CROSS
ON THE FENCE
ON THE FRITZ
ON THE HOUSE
ON THE LATCH
ON THE LEVEL
ON THE LOOSE
ON THE MARCH
ON THE PROWL
ON THE QUIET
ON THE ROCKS
ON THE ROPES
ON THE SHELF
ON THE SLATE
ON THE STUMP
ON THE TILES
ON THE VERGE
ON THE WAGON
ON THE WATCH
ON THE WHOLE
OX EYE DAISY
TO THE DEATH
TO THE POINT
UP AND ABOUT

2,3,5 *contd.*
UP AND DOING
UP AND UNDER
UP FOR GRABS
UP THE CREEK

2,4,4
AS THEY COME
AT FULL PELT
AT HALF COCK
AT LONG LAST
IN GOOD NICK
IN GOOD PART
IN GOOD TIME
IN NAME ONLY
IN ONES CUPS
IN ONES TURN
KU KLUX KLAN
MY FAIR LADY
NO MANS LAND
NO SUCH LUCK
ON ONES MIND
ON ONES TOES
ON YOUR BIKE
TO ONES FACE

2,5,3
NO THANK YOU
ST JOHNS DAY
ST TIBBS EVE

2,8
AD ABSURDUM
AT GUNPOINT
AT VARIANCE
BE PREPARED
BY CONTRAST
BY ELECTION
DO PORRIDGE
EX CATHEDRA
GO DOWNHILL
GO STRAIGHT
IN ABSENTIA
IN ADDITION
IN BUSINESS
IN CHANCERY
IN CONFLICT
IN DISARRAY
IN DISGRACE
IN DISGUISE
IN DISTRESS
IN EXCELSIS
IN EXTREMIS
IN FIGHTING
IN JEOPARDY
IN MEMORIAM
IN MOURNING
IN POSITION
IN PROGRESS
IN SEQUENCE
IN STITCHES

IN TRACTION
IN TRAINING
MR UNIVERSE
NO NONSENSE
ON APPROVAL
ON FURLOUGH
ON LOCATION
ON OCCASION
ON SCHEDULE
OX ANTELOPE
RH NEGATIVE
RH POSITIVE
ST STEPHENS
ST TRINIANS

3,1,3,3
RUB A DUB DUB

3,1,4,2
GET A LINE ON
GET A MOVE ON
GOT A LINE ON
PUT A STOP TO

3,1,6
CUT A FIGURE
GET A WICKET
GOT A WICKET
LAY A COURSE
SAY A PRAYER
TOM O BEDLAM

3,2,1,4
OUT ON A LIMB
PIG IN A POKE
TWO OF A KIND
WIN BY A HEAD
WIN BY A NECK
WON BY A HEAD
WON BY A NECK

3,2,2,3
AND SO TO BED
FEE FI FO FUM
PUT ON AN ACT

3,2,3,2
GET UP AND GO
HOW DO YOU DO
PUT AN END TO
THE UP AND UP

3,2,5
ACT OF UNION
AND SO FORTH
BAG OF BONES
BED OF NAILS
BED OF ROSES
BIT OF STUFF
CAN OF WORMS
CRI DE COEUR
CUP OF COCOA
CUT UP ROUGH
EGG ON TOAST

END IN TEARS
FER DE LANCE
FLY BY NIGHT
FOR MY MONEY
GET TO GRIPS
GET TO SLEEP
GET UP STEAM
GOT TO GRIPS
GOT TO SLEEP
GOT UP STEAM
HUG ME TIGHT
JAR OF HONEY
JEU DE PAUME
LAY IN STATE
LIE IN STATE
MAN OF STRAW
NOM DE PLUME
NOT TO WORRY
OIL OF THYME
OUT AT ELBOW
OUT OF COURT
OUT OF DOORS
OUT OF FOCUS
OUT OF JOINT
OUT OF ORDER
OUT OF PLACE
OUT OF PRINT
OUT OF REACH
OUT OF SHAPE
OUT OF SIGHT
OUT OF SORTS
OUT OF STOCK
OUT OF SYNCH
OUT OF TOUCH
PAS DE TROIS
POT OF MONEY
PUT ON TRIAL
PUT TO DEATH
PUT TO SHAME
PUT TO SLEEP
RAN TO EARTH
RUN TO EARTH
SET IN ORDER
SET TO MUSIC
SET UP HOUSE
TIP UP TRUCK
VOL AU VENTS

3,3,2,2
RUB OFF ON TO

3,3,4
ACT THE FOOL
ACT THE GOAT
AID AND ABET
ALL MOD CONS
ALL THE BEST
ALL THE RAGE
ALL THE SAME
AND ALL THAT
ANY OLD IRON

BAN THE BOMB
BIG BAD WOLF
BIT THE DUST
BUY AND SELL
CAP AND GOWN
CUP AND BALL
CUP AND RING
DIP THE FLAG
EBB AND FLOW
EGG AND DART
FAR AND AWAY
FAR AND NEAR
FAR AND WIDE
FLY THE FLAG
FOR ALL THAT
FOR THE BEST
FOR THE CHOP
FOR THE REST
FOR TWO PINS
GET THE BIRD
GET THE BOOT
GET THE CHOP
GET THE PUSH
GET THE SACK
GOT THE BIRD
GOT THE BOOT
GOT THE CHOP
GOT THE PUSH
HIT AND MISS
HIT THE DECK
HIT THE ROAD
HIT THE ROOF
HIT THE SACK
HOP THE TWIG
IFS AND BUTS
ILL BUY THAT
INS AND OUTS
MAN AND WIFE
NIP AND TUCK
NOT FOR SALE
NOW AND THEN
OFF THE CUFF
OFF THE FACE
OFF THE HOOK
OFF THE MARK
OFF THE REEL
OFF THE WALL
ONE ACT PLAY
ONE MAN BAND
ONE MAN SHOW
PAD THE HOOF
PUT AND TAKE
PUT THE SHOT
RAN THE SHOW
RUN THE SHOW
SET THE PACE
SON AND HEIR
SOW THE SEED
THE RED ARMY
TIE THE KNOT

3,3,4 *contd.*
TIP THE WINK
TOE THE LINE
TOP THE BILL
TWO ACT PLAY
TWO PIN PLUG

3,4,3
ACT YOUR AGE
BIT ONES LIP
DID ONES BIT
GET ONES WAY
GOT ONES WAY
HAD ONES WAY
HAS ONES WAY
HOW DARE YOU
NEW MOWN HAY
OFF ONES NUT
ONE YEAR OLD
PAY ONES WAY
THE EVIL ONE
THE FAIR SEX
THE HARD WAY
THE WISE MEN
THE YEAR DOT
TIP ONES HAT
TWO YEAR OLD
YOU DONT SAY
YOU KNOW WHO

3,5,2
GET STUCK IN
LAY HANDS ON
SET LIGHT TO
THE THREE RS

3,7
AGE BRACKET
AIR BLADDER
AIR BRUSHED
AIR COOLING
AIR CURTAIN
AIR CUSHION
AIR FREIGHT
AIR HOSTESS
AIR MARSHAL
AIR OFFICER
AIR PASSAGE
AIR SUPPORT
ALL HALLOWS
ALL PURPOSE
ALL ROUNDER
ALL WEATHER
ARC WELDING
ART GALLERY
ART NOUVEAU
ART STUDENT
BAD COMPANY
BAD FEELING
BAD GRAMMAR
BAR COUNCIL

BAR MITZVAH
BAR PARLOUR
BED SWERVER
BED WETTING
BEE KEEPING
BIG BROTHER
BIG MOUTHED
BOB MAXIMUS
BOG TROTTER
BON APPETIT
BOW FRONTED
BUS SHELTER
BUS STATION
CAT BURGLAR
CAT SCANNER
COD FISHERY
COD FISHING
CON SPIRITO
COR ANGLAIS
COW PARSLEY
CUB HUNTING
CUP WINNERS
CUT CORNERS
CUT FLOWERS
DAY BOARDER
DAY NURSERY
DAY RELEASE
DAY SCHOLAR
DAY TRIPPER
DEO GRATIAS
DEO VOLENTE
DIE CASTING
DIE SINKING
DOC MARTENS
DOG BISCUIT
DOG FANCIER
DOG HANDLER
DOG LICENCE
DOG PARSLEY
DRY BATTERY
DRY CANTEEN
DRY CLEANED
DRY FARMING
DRY MEASURE
EAR BASHING
EAR TRUMPET
EAR WITNESS
EGG CUSTARD
EGO TRIPPER
EMI SCANNER
END PRODUCT
EYE CONTACT
EYE WITNESS
FAN TRACERY
FAR FETCHED
FAR SIGHTED
FEN CRICKET
FLY FISHING
FLY FLAPPER
FOR CERTAIN

FOR EXAMPLE
FOR NOTHING
FOX HUNTING
FOX TERRIER
GAP TOOTHED
GAS BRACKET
GAS CHAMBER
GAS FURNACE
GAS GUZZLER
GAS TURBINE
GAY GORDONS
GEM CUTTING
GET DRESSED
GET HITCHED
GET KNOTTED
GET STUFFED
GET THROUGH
GET WEAVING
GOB STOPPER
GOD FEARING
GOD WILLING
GOT DRESSED
GOT HITCHED
GOT THROUGH
GUT SCRAPER
HAD KITTENS
HAS KITTENS
HEN HARRIER
HER MAJESTY
HIP HUGGERS
HIS MAJESTY
HIS WORSHIP
HOD CARRIER
HOP BITTERS
HOP PICKING
HOP SACKING
HOT BLOODED
HUG ONESELF
ICE BREAKER
ICE DANCING
ICE HILLING
ICE MACHINE
ICE SKATING
ILL ADVISED
ILL BEHAVED
ILL DEFINED
ILL FEELING
ILL FORTUNE
ILL FOUNDED
ILL LOOKING
ILL MATCHED
ILL NATURED
ILL STARRED
INK SLINGER
INK STAINED
IVY MANTLED
JAM SESSION
JAW BREAKER
JAY WALKING
JET SETTING

JEU DESPRIT
KEW GARDENS
KID BROTHER
KID ONESELF
LAP JOINTED
LAW ABIDING
LAW BREAKER
LAW OFFICER
LAY BAPTISM
LAY BROTHER
LED CAPTAIN
LEE ENFIELD
LEG PULLING
LEG SPINNER
LEG WARMERS
LEY FARMING
LIP READING
LIP SERVICE
LOG ROLLING
LOW CEILING
LOW COUNTRY
LOW PITCHED
LOW PROFILE
LOW TENSION
MAN SERVANT
MAP MOUNTER
MAP READING
MAY BLOSSOM
MET HALFWAY
MID MORNING
MUD SLINGER
MUD VOLCANO
NET FISHING
NEW EDITION
NEW ENGLAND
NEW ORLEANS
NEW ZEALAND
NIT PICKING
NOD THROUGH
NON ALIGNED
NON CONTENT
NON FERROUS
NON FICTION
NON MEMBERS
NON PAYMENT
NON PLAYING
NON SMOKING
NON STARTER
NON SWIMMER
NON VIOLENT
NOT EXACTLY
ODD LOOKING
OFF BALANCE
OFF LICENCE
OFF PUTTING
OFF SPINNER
OIL COLOURS
OIL PAINTER
OLD COUNTRY
OLD ENGLISH

3,7 *contd.*
OLD HUNDRED
OLD MASTERS
OLD SOLDIER
ONE ANOTHER
ONE NIGHTER
ONE SIDEDLY
OUT DWELLER
OUT PATIENT
OUT PENSION
PAN AFRICAN
PAN ARABISM
PAN SLAVISM
PAR EXEMPLE
PAY STATION
PEA TRAINER
PEG TANKARD
PEN FEATHER
PEN PUSHING
PET SITTING
PIE COUNTER
PIE DIAGRAM
PIG STICKER
PIN CUSHION
PIN FEATHER
PIN STRIPED
PIT VILLAGE
POP CONCERT
POT BELLIED
POT BOILING
POT HUNTING
PRE ELECTED
PRE EMINENT
PRE EMPTING
PRE EMPTION
PRE EMPTIVE
PRE EXISTED
PRE GLACIAL
PRE QUALIFY
PRE SELLING
PRE SHRINKS
PRE TENSION
PRE WASHING
PRO TEMPORE
PUT FORWARD
PUT PUTTING
PUT THROUGH
RAN ERRANDS
RAN THROUGH
RAP SESSION
RAT CATCHER
RAT HUNTING
RAW RECRUIT
RED ADMIRAL
RED BLOODED
RED BRIGADE
RED CABBAGE
RED FIGURED
RED HERRING
RED JASMINE

RED MURRAIN
RED SANDERS
RED SEAWEED
RED SNAPPER
RIB ROASTER
RIB TICKLER
RIP ROARING
RUE BARGAIN
RUM RUNNING
RUN ERRANDS
RUN THROUGH
SAD HEARTED
SAL ATTICUM
SAW TOOTHED
SEA ANEMONE
SEA BATHING
SEA BISCUIT
SEA CABBAGE
SEA CAPTAIN
SEA FISHING
SEA GODDESS
SEA KEEPING
SEA LEOPARD
SEA MONSTER
SEA PASSAGE
SEA POACHER
SEA SERPENT
SEA SERVICE
SEA SOLDIER
SEA SURGEON
SEA UNICORN
SEA WHISTLE
SEE THROUGH
SET AGAINST
SIX SHOOTER
SKI BOBBING
SKI JUMPING
SKI RUNNING
SKY JUMPING
SKY MARSHAL
SKY WRITING
SOW THISTLE
SUB HEADING
SUI GENERIS
SUN LOUNGER
SUN WORSHIP
TAP DANCING
TAX BRACKET
TAX EVASION
TAX SHELTER
TEA BISCUIT
TEA CLIPPER
TEA DRINKER
TEA PLANTER
TEA SERVICE
TEA TASTING
TEA TROLLEY
THE ARCHERS
THE CHANNEL
THE COMMONS

THE COUNTRY
THE CREATOR
THE DANSANT
THE HEAVIES
THE HORRORS
THE NEEDLES
THE ROCKIES
THE SHIVERS
THE TWELFTH
THE UNKNOWN
TIE BREAKER
TIM WHISKEY
TIN SOLDIER
TIN WHISTLE
TOM COLLINS
TOP BILLING
TOP DRESSED
TOP DRESSES
TOP GALLANT
TOP SOILING
TOY SPANIEL
TUB THUMPED
TUB THUMPER
TWO WHEELED
TWO WHEELER
WAR GODDESS
WAR MACHINE
WAX LYRICAL
WAY BAGGAGE
WAY FREIGHT
WAY STATION
WAY TRAFFIC
WET BLANKET
WET THROUGH
WIN THROUGH
WON THROUGH
WRY MOUTHED

4,1,5

CAST A SPELL
CHAR A BANCS
COCK A SNOOK
CUTS A CAPER
CUTS A TOOTH
DRAW A BLANK
DREW A BLANK
DROP A BRICK
HALF A CROWN
HALF A DOZEN
HAVE A DEKKO
HAVE A HEART
HAVE A LAUGH
JACK A DANDY
MADE A POINT
MADE A STAND
MAKE A POINT
MAKE A STAND
PACK A PUNCH
PAID A VISIT
PAYS A VISIT

PICK A FIGHT
PIED A TERRE
RENT A CROWD
RIDE A HOBBY
TAKE A BRIEF
TAKE A CLASS
TAKE A DEKKO
TOOK A BRIEF
TOOK A CLASS
TOOK A DEKKO
WELL I NEVER

4,2,1,3
BUSY AS A BEE
CALL IT A DAY
SICK AS A DOG

4,2,2,2
FACE UP TO IT
SOCK IT TO ME
SUCH AS IT IS

4,2,4
AIDE DE CAMP
BABA AU RHUM
BABE IN ARMS
BACK TO BACK
BALL OF FIRE
BAND OF HOPE
BEAR IN MIND
BILL OF FARE
BILL OF SALE
BIRD OF PREY
BLOW BY BLOW
BLOW ME DOWN
BORE IN MIND
BOYS IN BLUE
CAFE AU LAIT
CALL TO MIND
CAME TO LIFE
CAME TO PASS
CAME TO REST
CASH IN HAND
COAT OF ARMS
COAT OF MAIL
COME AT ABLE
COME ON DOWN
COME TO LIFE
COME TO PASS
COME TO REST
COUP DE MAIN
CUTS IT FINE
DAYS OF YORE
DOOR TO DOOR
DOWN AT HEEL
FACE TO FACE
FALL IN LOVE
FEEL AT HOME
FEET OF CLAY
FELL IN LOVE
FELT AT HOME

4,2,4 *contd.*
FOUR IN HAND
FROM ON HIGH
FULL OF LIFE
GANG OF FOUR
GOES TO SEED
GOES TO TOWN
GONE TO SEED
HALF AN HOUR
HAND IN HAND
HAND ME DOWN
HAND TO HAND
HAVE NO IDEA
HEAR NO EVIL
INCH BY INCH
ISLE OF DOGS
ISLE OF SKYE
JOUR DE FETE
KEEP IN MIND
KEEP IT DARK
KEPT IN MIND
KEPT IT DARK
KILL OR CURE
KING OF ARMS
KISS OF LIFE
LAID TO REST
LAYS TO REST
LETS IT RIDE
LIES IN WAIT
LINE OF LIFE
LOSS OF FACE
LOSS OF LIFE
MILK OF LIME
MORE OR LESS
NECK OF LAMB
NECK OF LAND
NEER DO WELL
NEXT IN LINE
NOSE TO TAIL
NOTE OF HAND
PAID IN FULL
PAID IN KIND
PAYS IN FULL
PAYS IN KIND
PEAU DE SOIE
PINT OF BEER
PINT OF MILK
PLAT DU JOUR
PLAY IT COOL
PORT DE BRAS
PORT OF CALL
PUTS ON AIRS
PUTS UP WITH
READ MY LIPS
RENT AN ARMY
ROAD TO RUIN
ROCK OF AGES
RUNS TO SEED
SACK OF COAL
SALE OF WORK

SELL BY DATE
SELL IN BULK
SETS IN HAND
SETS ON EDGE
SETS ON FIRE
SETS TO WORK
SETS UP SHOP
SHIN OF BEEF
SHUT UP SHOP
SIDE BY SIDE
SIDE OF BEEF
SINK OR SWIM
SLAP UP MEAL
SOLD IN BULK
STAY AT HOME
STEP BY STEP
SUCH IS LIFE
TAKE AN OATH
TAKE AS READ
TAKE IN HAND
TAKE IN VAIN
TAKE IT EASY
TAKE TO TASK
TAKE UP ARMS
TALK IT OVER
TEAM UP WITH
TOOK AN OATH
TOOK IN HAND
TOOK IN VAIN
TOOK IT EASY
TOOK TO TASK
TOOK UP ARMS
TOUR OF DUTY
TOUT DE MEME
TREE OF LIFE
TROU DE LOUP
TRUE TO LIFE
UPON MY SOUL
UPON MY WORD
WALK OF LIFE
WALK ON PART
WALK TO HEEL
WALL TO WALL
WENT TO SEED
WENT TO TOWN
WHEN IN ROME
WORK TO RULE
YARD OF LAND
YEAR ON YEAR

4,3,3
ADAM AND EVE
BEAT THE AIR
BEAT THE GUN
BELL THE CAT
BILL AND COO
CHEW THE CUD
CHEW THE FAT
DOWN AND OUT
EACH WAY BET

FORE AND AFT
FREE FOR ALL
GOES TOO FAR
GOOD FOR YOU
HEEL AND TOE
HERE YOU ARE
HIGH AND DRY
HIGH AND LOW
HITS FOR SIX
HITS THE HAY
HOME AND DRY
HOOK AND EYE
JACK THE LAD
JUMP FOR JOY
JUMP THE GUN
JUST THE JOB
KITH AND KIN
LAST MAN OUT
LEAD THE WAY
LOOK OUT MAN
MISS THE BUS
NAME THE DAY
OVER AND OUT
OVER THE TOP
PAVE THE WAY
PEEL AND EAT
PICK AND MIX
PORK PIE HAT
QUID PRO QUO
RIDE AND TIE
SCOT AND LOT
SHOW THE WAY
SINE QUA NON
STOP THE ROT
TAKE THE AIR
TAKE THE RAP
TAKE THE SUN
TOOK THE AIR
TOOK THE RAP
TOOK THE SUN
WAIT AND SEE
WALK THE DOG
WENT TOO FAR
WHIP THE CAT
WINS THE CUP
WINS THE DAY
WISE OLD OWL

4,4,2
CLAP EYES ON
EASY DOES IT
HARD DONE BY
HIGH TAIL IT
KEEP TABS ON
KEPT TABS ON
LAID EYES ON
LAYS EYES ON
LETS FACE IT
LORD HELP US
MADE EYES AT

MAKE EYES AT
PUTS PAID TO
SETS EYES ON
SETS FIRE TO

4,5,1
LIKE BILLY O

4,6
ABLE BODIED
ABLE SEAMAN
ACOL SYSTEM
AERO ENGINE
ANNO DOMINI
ANTE BELLUM
ANTI RACIST
ANTI SEMITE
AQUA FORTIS
ARCH PRIEST
ARMS LENGTH
ARTY CRAFTY
AULD REEKIE
AXLE GREASE
BABY BOOMER
BABY JUMPER
BABY MINDER
BABY SITTER
BABY WALKER
BACK BLOCKS
BACK BURNER
BACK COMBED
BACK DATING
BACK GARDEN
BACK HANDED
BACK HANDER
BACK HEELED
BACK MARKER
BACK NUMBER
BACK PEDALS
BACK STREET
BACK STROKE
BALD HEADED
BALL FLOWER
BALL PLAYER
BAND STRING
BANK CHEQUE
BARK BEETLE
BASE MINDED
BASS FIDDLE
BASS GUITAR
BATH OLIVER
BEAM ENGINE
BEAM SYSTEM
BEAM WEAPON
BEAN SPROUT
BEAR GARDEN
BEAR LEADER
BEAU GARCON
BEER BARREL
BEER BOTTLE
BEER ENGINE

4,6 *contd.*
BEER GARDEN
BEER PARLOR
BELL BEAKER
BELL FLOWER
BELL RINGER
BELL SHAPED
BELL TURRET
BELL WETHER
BEST SELLER
BILL BROKER
BIRD PEPPER
BIRD SKIING
BIRD SPIDER
BIRD STRIKE
BIRD WITTED
BLOW DRYING
BLUE BONNET
BLUE CHEESE
BLUE COLLAR
BLUE ENSIGN
BLUE MURDER
BLUE PENCIL
BLUE RIBAND
BLUE RIBBON
BOAT PEOPLE
BOAT RACING
BODY CAVITY
BODY COLOUR
BODY POPPER
BODY WARMER
BOLL WEEVIL
BOND HOLDER
BONY FISHES
BOOK HOLDER
BOOK HUNTER
BOOM CARPET
BOOT CLOSER
BOOT POLISH
BUCK RABBIT
BUFF JERKIN
BULK BUYING
BULL HEADED
BULL NECKED
BULL ROARER
BUMP STARTS
BUON GIORNO
BUSH JACKET
BUSH SHRIKE
BUSY LIZZIE
CACK HANDED
CALL OPTION
CALL TRUMPS
CAME ACROSS
CAME ASHORE
CAME UNDONE
CAPE DOCTOR
CAPE PIGEON
CARD HOLDER
CARD PLAYER

CARD READER
CASE BOTTLE
CASE HARDEN
CASE WORKER
CASH CREDIT
CAST ANCHOR
CATS CRADLE
CHIP BASKET
CINE CAMERA
CINE VERITE
CITY CENTRE
CITY EDITOR
CITY LIGHTS
CITY LIMITS
CLAW HAMMER
CLAY PIGEON
CLEW GARNET
CLOG DANCER
CLUB FOOTED
COAL BUNKER
COAL CELLAR
COAL CUTTER
COAL MINING
COAL PORTER
COAT ARMOUR
COAT HANGER
CODE NUMBER
CODS WALLOP
COLD CHISEL
COLD SHOWER
COLD TURKEY
COME ACROSS
COME ASHORE
COME HITHER
COME UNDONE
CONY BURROW
COPY TYPING
COPY TYPIST
CORK CARPET
CORK CUTTER
CORK HEELED
CORK TIPPED
CORN CIRCLE
CORN CUTTER
CORN DEALER
CORN DOLLIE
CORN FACTOR
CORN MILLER
CORN WEEVIL
COSA NOSTRA
COST CENTRE
COUP DESSAI
CRAB NEBULA
CROP CIRCLE
CROP DUSTER
CROW SHRIKE
CURD CHEESE
CUTS ACROSS
DAMP COURSE
DARK SECRET

DART PLAYER
DATA LOGGER
DATE CODING
DAWN CHORUS
DAWN PATROL
DEAD CENTRE
DEAD GROUND
DEAD HEADED
DEAD LETTER
DEAD RINGER
DEAD WEIGHT
DEAF MUTISM
DECK BRIDGE
DECK QUOITS
DECK TENNIS
DEEP FREEZE
DEEP FRYING
DEEP PURPLE
DEEP ROOTED
DEEP SEATED
DEER FOREST
DICE PLAYER
DIKA BUTTER
DILL PICKLE
DISC BRAKES
DISC JOCKEY
DISC PLAYER
DISH WASHER
DIVE BOMBER
DOCK MASTER
DOCK STRIKE
DOGS CHANCE
DOGS DINNER
DOGS FENNEL
DOGS TONGUE
DOOR HANDLE
DOOR KEEPER
DOWN MARKET
DRAG RACING
DRAW STRING
DRAW STUMPS
DREW STUMPS
DROP ANCHOR
DROP HAMMER
DRUG ADDICT
DRUG PUSHER
DRUM BRAKES
DUAL SCHOOL
DUCK BILLED
DUCK LEGGED
DULL WITTED
DUMB BLONDE
DUMB WAITER
DUNG BEETLE
DUST JACKET
EAST ANGLIA
EAST INDIAN
EAST INDIES
EASY STREET
ETON COLLAR

ETON JACKET
EVEN CHANCE
EVEN HANDED
EVIL MINDED
EVIL WORKER
FACE FUNGUS
FACE POWDER
FACE SAVING
FAIR DINKUM
FAIR ENOUGH
FAIR GROUND
FAIR HAIRED
FAIR HEADED
FAIR MINDED
FALL BEHIND
FAST ASLEEP
FAST BOWLER
FAST TALKER
FAST WORKER
FELL BEHIND
FELL WALKER
FEME COVERT
FILE CUTTER
FILE LEADER
FILM CENSOR
FILM CRITIC
FILM REVIEW
FILM STUDIO
FINE TUNING
FIRE BLIGHT
FIRE BUCKET
FIRE EATING
FIRE ENGINE
FIRE ESCAPE
FIRE HAZARD
FIRE OFFICE
FIRE POLICY
FIRE RAISER
FIRE SHOVEL
FIRE WALKER
FIRE WARDEN
FISH CARVER
FISH DINNER
FISH EATERS
FISH FARMER
FISH FINGER
FISH GUTTER
FISH KETTLE
FIVE FINGER
FIVE OCLOCK
FIVE POINTS
FIVE SENSES
FIVE STONES
FLAG WAVING
FLAK JACKET
FLAT FOOTED
FLAT RACING
FLEA BEETLE
FLEA BITTEN
FLEA CIRCUS

4,6 *contd.*

FLEA MARKET	FULL COCKED	HAIR PENCIL	HIGH MINDED
FOAM RUBBER	FULL COUSIN	HAIR POWDER	HIGH NECKED
FOLK MEMORY	FULL HANDED	HAIR RAISER	HIGH OCTANE
FOLK SINGER	FULL LENGTH	HAIR STROKE	HIGH PLACED
FOLK SPEECH	FULL NELSON	HAIR WAVING	HIGH PLACES
FOOD VALUES	FULL ORDERS	HALF COCKED	HIGH PRICED
FOOL AROUND	FULL RIGGED	HALF DOLLAR	HIGH PRIEST
FOOT CANDLE	FULL SAILED	HALF HOURLY	HIGH RANKER
FOOT LICKER	FULL SISTER	HALF HUNTER	HIGH RELIEF
FOOT RACING	FULL VOICED	HALF INCHED	HIGH ROLLER
FOOT WARMER	FUND HOLDER	HALF LENGTH	HIGH SCHOOL
FORE DAMNED	FUND RAISER	HALF NELSON	HIGH SEASON
FORE HAMMER	GAFF RIGGED	HALF SISTER	HIGH STREET
FORE NOTICE	GAIN GROUND	HALF VOLLEY	HILL DIGGER
FORE QUOTED	GALL STONES	HALF WITTED	HOCK MONDAY
FORK TAILED	GAME DEALER	HALF YEARLY	HOLY FATHER
FORM CRITIC	GAME WARDEN	HALL PORTER	HOLY ISLAND
FORM LETTER	GATE KEEPER	HALO EFFECT	HOLY OFFICE
FORM MASTER	GATE LEGGED	HAND BARROW	HOLY ORDERS
FOUL SPOKEN	GAVE GROUND	HAND BASKET	HOLY SPIRIT
FOUR COLOUR	GAVE NOTICE	HAND GALLOP	HOLY TERROR
FOUR FIGURE	GEAR CHANGE	HAND LOTION	HOME BREWED
FOUR FOOTED	GERM THEORY	HAND PICKED	HOME COMING
FOUR HANDED	GETS ACROSS	HAND SIGNAL	HOME GROUND
FOUR LEAFED	GETS AROUND	HANG AROUND	HOME MARKET
FOUR LEAVED	GIRL FRIDAY	HANG GLIDER	HOME MOVIES
FOUR LEGGED	GIRL FRIEND	HARD BITTEN	HORN RIMMED
FOUR OCLOCK	GIVE GROUND	HARD BOILED	HORN SILVER
FOUR POSTER	GIVE NOTICE	HARD CHEESE	HOWS TRICKS
FOUR SEATER	GOAL TENDER	HARD EARNED	HUMP BACKED
FOUR SQUARE	GOBI DESERT	HARD FOUGHT	HUNG AROUND
FREE AGENCY	GOES ABROAD	HARD HEADED	IDLE HEADED
FREE CHURCH	GOES METRIC	HARD LABOUR	IDLE PULLEY
FREE DIVING	GOES NATIVE	HARD PUSHED	IRON FISTED
FREE FISHER	GOLD BEATER	HARD RIDING	IRON HANDED
FREE FLIGHT	GOLD DIGGER	HARD WORKER	IRON MAIDEN
FREE FOODER	GOLD MINING	HARE LIPPED	IRON MINING
FREE FOOTED	GOLD NUGGET	HASH BROWNS	IRON RATION
FREE HANDED	GOLD PLATED	HAWK BEAKED	IRON WILLED
FREE LABOUR	GOLD RECORD	HAWK BILLED	JACK KNIFED
FREE MARKET	GOLD THREAD	HEAD BANGER	JACK KNIFES
FREE MINDED	GOLD WASHER	HEAD HUGGER	JACK PRIEST
FREE PARDON	GOLF COURSE	HEAD OFFICE	JACK RABBIT
FREE SAMPLE	GONE METRIC	HEAD STREAM	JACK STRAWS
FREE SCHOOL	GOOD FRIDAY	HEAD WAITER	JEWS HOUSES
FREE SKATER	GOOD HEALTH	HEAR THINGS	JOIN FORCES
FREE SPEECH	GOOD LOOKER	HEAT SHIELD	JUMP STARTS
FREE SPIRIT	GOOD PEOPLE	HEAT STROKE	JUNK DEALER
FREE SPOKEN	GOOD TEMPER	HEMP NETTLE	JURY RIGGED
FREE STATES	GOOD TIMING	HERB BENNET	JURY RUDDER
FREE STROKE	GREY COATED	HERB GARDEN	JURY SYSTEM
FREE TRADER	GREY HAIRED	HERB ROBERT	KACK HANDED
FREE VERSER	GREY HEADED	HIGH CHURCH	KEEN PRICES
FREE WHEELS	GREY MARKET	HIGH COLOUR	KEEP WICKET
FROG HOPPER	GREY MATTER	HIGH COMEDY	KEPT WICKET
FROM CHOICE	GREY PARROT	HIGH FLYING	KERB MARKET
FULL BODIED	GRUB STREET	HIGH GERMAN	KERB TRADER
FULL BOTTOM	GULF STATES	HIGH HANDED	KERB VENDOR
FULL CIRCLE	GULF STREAM	HIGH HEELED	KICK AROUND
	HAIL FELLOW	HIGH LIVING	KING ALFRED

4,6 *contd.*

KING ARTHUR	LINE FISHER	MILL STREAM	PALM KERNEL
KING CANUTE	LINK MOTION	MIME ARTIST	PALM SUNDAY
KING EDWARD	LION HUNTER	MIND BENDER	PARA RUBBER
KING GEORGE	LOAN HOLDER	MIND HEALER	PARI MUTUEL
KING HAROLD	LOAN OFFICE	MIND READER	PARK KEEPER
KING SALMON	LOCH LOMOND	MINE HUNTER	PASS MUSTER
KITE FLYING	LOCK KEEPER	MINE LAYING	PAST MASTER
KNEE LENGTH	LONG HAIRED	MINE WORKER	PAYS HOMAGE
KNEW BETTER	LONG HEADED	MINI BUDGET	PEAK PERIOD
KNOW BETTER	LONG ISLAND	MINI BUFFET	PEAR SHAPED
LACE PILLOW	LONG LEGGED	MINI SERIES	PEAT CASTER
LACK LUSTRE	LONG PLAYER	MOCK HEROIC	PICK CHEESE
LADY CHAPEL	LONG TAILED	MOCK MODEST	PICK POCKET
LADY GODIVA	LONG WINDED	MOCK ORANGE	PILE DRIVER
LADY KILLER	LOOK AGHAST	MOCK PRIVET	PINA COLADA
LAGS BEHIND	LOOK LIVELY	MOCK TURTLE	PINE BARREN
LAKE SCHOOL	LOSE COLOUR	MOON FLOWER	PINE BEAUTY
LAMP BURNER	LOSE GROUND	MOSS STITCH	PINE BEETLE
LAND BREEZE	LOSE WEIGHT	MOTH FLOWER	PINE FOREST
LAND BRIDGE	LOSS LEADER	MUCK RAKING	PINE KERNEL
LAND JOBBER	LOST COLOUR	MUSK BEETLE	PINE MARTEN
LAND LOCKED	LOST GROUND	MUSK ORCHID	PINE NEEDLE
LAND LUBBER	LOST TRIBES	MUSK TURTLE	PIPE FITTER
LAND MINING	LOST WEIGHT	NAIL BITING	PIPE LAYING
LAND OFFICE	LOUD VOICED	NAIL POLISH	PIPE OPENER
LAND OWNING	LOVE AFFAIR	NEWS AGENCY	PIPE WRENCH
LAND PIRATE	LOVE BROKER	NEWS VENDOR	PITH HELMET
LAST CHANCE	LOVE LETTER	NEWS WRITER	PLAY ACTING
LAST MINUTE	LOVE POTION	NEXT FRIEND	PLAY AROUND
LAST ORDERS	LUCY STONER	NINE OCLOCK	PLAY HOOKEY
LAST RESORT	MACE BEARER	NOUN CLAUSE	PLAY POSSUM
LAST SUPPER	MACH NUMBER	OATH TAKING	PLAY TRICKS
LAWN TENNIS	MADE AMENDS	OBOE DAMORE	PLAY TRUANT
LEAD ASTRAY	MADE GROUND	OLDE WORLDE	PLAY WRITER
LEAD GLANCE	MADE TRACKS	ONYX MARBLE	PLUG SOCKET
LEAD PENCIL	MAID MARIAN	OPEN ACCESS	PLUS STRAIN
LEAD PIPING	MAIN ARTERY	OPEN HANDED	POKE BONNET
LEAF CUTTER	MAIN CHANCE	OPEN LETTER	POLL PARROT
LEAF HOPPER	MAIN CLAUSE	OPEN MARKET	POLO PLAYER
LEAF INSECT	MAIN COURSE	OPEN MINDED	POME CITRON
LEAF MOSAIC	MAIN STREAM	OPEN PRISON	PONY ENGINE
LEAN WITTED	MAIN STREET	OPEN SEASON	POOR RELIEF
LEAP SECOND	MAKE AMENDS	OPEN SECRET	PORK BARREL
LEFT BEHIND	MAKE TRACKS	OPEN SESAME	POST BELLUM
LEFT FOOTED	MAKE WEIGHT	OPEN SPACES	POST CHAISE
LEFT HANDED	MALE RHYMES	OPEN STITCH	POST MODERN
LEFT HANDER	MALT LIQUOR	OPEN TOPPED	POST MORTEM
LEFT UNSAID	MALT WHISKY	OVEN GLOVES	POST OFFICE
LEFT WINGER	MANY HEADED	PACE BOWLER	PREP SCHOOL
LIES FALLOW	MANY THANKS	PACE SETTER	PUFF PASTRY
LIFE GIVING	MARC BRANDY	PACK ANIMAL	PULP CAVITY
LIFE GUARDS	MASS MEDIUM	PACK SADDLE	PULP ENGINE
LIFE JACKET	MASS MURDER	PAGE PROOFS	PUMP ACTION
LIFE MEMBER	MASS NUMBER	PAGE TURNER	PUMP HANDLE
LIFE ROCKET	MEAL TICKET	PAID HOMAGE	PUNK ROCKER
LIFE SAVING	MEAN STREAK	PAIN KILLER	PURE REASON
LIFE SCHOOL	MEAT MARKET	PALL BEARER	PURE SILVER
LIFE TENANT	MENU DRIVEN	PALM BRANCH	PUSH AROUND
LIKE MINDED	MILD SPOKEN	PALM BUTTER	PUSH BUTTON
	MILK BOTTLE	PALM GREASE	PUSH STARTS

4,6 *contd.*
PUSH STROKE
PUTS ACROSS
QUAI DORSAY
QUIZ MASTER
RACE COURSE
RACE MEMORY
RACE WALKER
RACK RENTER
RAFT BRIDGE
RAIN DOCTOR
RAIN FOREST
RAIN MAKING
RAIN PLOVER
RAIN SHOWER
RANK RIDING
RATE CAPPED
REAL ESTATE
REAL NUMBER
REAL SCHOOL
REAL TENNIS
REED THRUSH
REST CENTRE
RICK BARTON
RICK LIFTER
RIFT VALLEY
RING BINDER
RING FINGER
RING MASTER
RING NECKED
RING PLOVER
RING ROLLER
RING TAILED
RIOT POLICE
ROAD BRIDGE
ROAD MAKING
ROAD MENDER
ROAD ROLLER
ROAD RUNNER
ROAD SAFETY
ROAD TESTED
ROCK BADGER
ROCK BOTTOM
ROCK GARDEN
ROCK HOPPER
ROCK LIZARD
ROCK PIGEON
ROCK SALMON
ROCK STEADY
ROCK TURBOT
ROCK VIOLET
ROOD SCREEN
ROOF GARDEN
ROOM FELLOW
ROOT PRUNED
ROOT PRUNES
ROOT RUBBER
ROOT SYSTEM
ROPE DANCER
ROPE LADDER

ROPE MAKING
ROPE STITCH
ROPE WALKER
ROSE BEETLE
ROSE COMBED
ROSE GARDEN
ROSE LAUREL
ROSE LIPPED
ROSE MALLOW
ROSE QUARTZ
ROSE TINTED
ROSE WINDOW
RUBY SILVER
RUIN MARBLE
RUNS ACROSS
RUNS SCARED
RUSH CANDLE
RUSH HOLDER
RUST BUCKET
RUST FUNGUS
SAFE BLOWER
SAGE CHEESE
SAGE GROUSE
SAGE RABBIT
SAIL FLYING
SAIL MAKING
SALT BUTTER
SALT CELLAR
SAND BINDER
SAND BUNKER
SAND CASTLE
SAND GROUSE
SAND HOPPER
SAND LIZARD
SAND MARTIN
SAND PLOUGH
SAND SUCKER
SASH WINDOW
SEAL FISHER
SEAM BOWLER
SEED OYSTER
SEED POTATO
SEED VESSEL
SEES THINGS
SELF ACTION
SELF DECEIT
SELF DENIAL
SELF DRIVEN
SELF ESTEEM
SELF HATRED
SELF PARODY
SELF PRAISE
SELF REGARD
SELF ROLLED
SELF RULING
SELF SEEKER
SELF STYLED
SELF TAUGHT
SELF WILLED
SEMI ANNUAL

SEMI DIVINE
SEMI LIQUID
SEMI LUNATE
SEMI OPAQUE
SEMI WEEKLY
SETS ALIGHT
SHIN BARKER
SHIP LETTER
SHIP MASTER
SHIP RIGGED
SHOE BUCKLE
SHOE POLISH
SHOP AROUND
SHOP LIFTER
SHOP SOILED
SHOP WALKER
SHOP WINDOW
SHOT PUTTER
SICK LISTED
SICK MAKING
SIDE EFFECT
SIDE SADDLE
SIDE STREET
SIDE STROKE
SIDE TRACKS
SIGN MANUAL
SIGN WRITER
SILK COTTON
SILK SCREEN
SINN FEINER
SKIN DIVING
SLIP STITCH
SLIP STREAM
SLIP STRING
SLIT POCKET
SLIT TRENCH
SLOW FOOTED
SLOW MOTION
SLOW MOVING
SLOW WINGED
SNOW CAPPED
SNOW PLOUGH
SOAP BOILER
SOAP BUBBLE
SOAP FLAKES
SOAP POWDER
SODA JERKER
SODA SIPHON
SOFT BOILED
SOFT FRUITS
SOFT HEADED
SOFT OPTION
SOFT PALATE
SOFT PEDALS
SOFT SOAPED
SOFT SPOKEN
SOKA GAKKAI
SONG THRUSH
SORE THROAT
SOUL SISTER

SOUP TICKET
SOUP TUREEN
SOUR GRAPES
SOUR ORANGE
SPIN BOWLER
SPIN DRYING
SPOT HEIGHT
SPOT WELDED
SPOT WELDER
SPUR HEELED
STAG BEETLE
STAR BRIGHT
STAR GAZING
STAR SHAPED
STEM STITCH
STEP DANCER
STEP LADDER
STEP PARENT
STEP ROCKET
STIR ABROAD
SURE ENOUGH
SURF BATHER
SURF RIDING
SWAN AROUND
SWAN MAIDEN
SWAN NECKED
SWAN UPPING
TACK HAMMER
TAKE CHARGE
TAKE EFFECT
TAKE FLIGHT
TAKE FRIGHT
TAKE NOTICE
TAKE ORDERS
TALE TELLER
TALK TURKEY
TANK ENGINE
TAPE READER
TAPE RECORD
TAXI DANCER
TAXI DRIVER
TEAM SPIRIT
TEAR JERKER
TENT STITCH
TEST FLIGHT
THAI BOXING
TILT HAMMER
TIME KEEPER
TIME KILLER
TIME SAVING
TIME SERVER
TIME SHARER
TIME SIGNAL
TIME SWITCH
TOAD EATING
TOOK CHARGE
TOOK EFFECT
TOOK FLIGHT
TOOK FRIGHT
TOOK NOTICE

4,6 *contd.*
TOOK ORDERS
TOPI WALLAH
TOWN CENTRE
TREE HOPPER
TREE MALLOW
TRIP HAMMER
TROY WEIGHT
TURN AROUND
TURN TURTLE
TWIN SISTER
TYPE CUTTER
TYPE HOLDER
UGRO FINNIC
VICE CONSUL
VINE BRANCH
WAGE EARNER
WAGE FREEZE
WAGE PACKET
WAIT AWHILE
WALK AROUND
WALL FACING
WALL LIZARD
WALL STREET
WARD SISTER
WASH BOTTLE
WAVE ENERGY
WAVE MOTION
WEAK HEADED
WEAK MINDED
WEAK MOMENT
WEAK WILLED
WEED KILLER
WEEK ENDING
WELL BORING
WELL CHOSEN
WELL EARNED
WELL ENOUGH
WELL FORMED
WELL HEELED
WELL JUDGED
WELL MINDED
WELL PLACED
WELL SINKER
WELL SPOKEN
WELL SPRING
WELL WISHED
WELL WISHER
WENT ABROAD
WENT HALVES
WENT HUNGRY
WENT NATIVE
WENT PLACES
WEST INDIAN
WEST INDIES
WHIP TAILED
WHIT MONDAY
WIDE BODIED
WIDE SCREEN
WILD ANIMAL

WILD CHERRY
WILD FLOWER
WILD FOWLER
WILD GARLIC
WIND CHANGE
WIND FLOWER
WIND SLEEVE
WIND SURFED
WIND SURFER
WIND TUNNEL
WINE BIBBER
WINE BOTTLE
WINE CELLAR
WINE COOLER
WINE FUNNEL
WINE GROWER
WINE REGION
WINE TASTER
WINE WAITER
WING COLLAR
WING FOOTED
WING MIRROR
WING SPREAD
WING WALKER
WIRE BRIDGE
WIRE DANCER
WIRE HAIRED
WIRE PULLER
WIRE WALKER
WITH WEIGHT
WOLF SPIDER
WOOD BORING
WOOD CARVER
WOOD CUTTER
WOOD GROUSE
WOOD PIGEON
WOOD SORREL
WOOD SPIRIT
WOOL CARDER
WOOL CHURCH
WOOL COMBER
WOOL DRIVER
WOOL GROWER
WOOL PACKER
WOOL PICKER
WOOL SHEARS
WOOL STAPLE
WOOL WINDER
WORD FINDER
WORD MEMORY
WORD SQUARE
WORK BASKET
WORK FELLOW
WORK PEOPLE
WORM POWDER
YARD MASTER
YOKE FELLOW
YOUR HONOUR
ZEND AVESTA
ZERO OPTION

ZERO RATING
ZERO VALENT
ZINC WORKER
ZONE TICKET

5,1,4
BLOWS A FUSE
CALLS A HALT
CASTS A VOTE
CATCH A CRAB
CAUSE A STIR
CRACK A CRIB
CRACK A JOKE
DEALS A BLOW
DEALT A BLOW
DOING A TURN
DROPS A LINE
FEELS A FOOL
FLIES A KITE
GRACE A DIEU
HAILS A TAXI
LENDS A HAND
LOOKS A FOOL
MAKES A BOMB
MAKES A FACE
MAKES A MOVE
PENNY A LINE
PICKS A LOCK
PITCH A TENT
PLAYS A PART
PULLS A FACE
RINGS A BELL
ROMAN A CLEF
SCORE A GOAL
SEVEN A SIDE
SHEDS A TEAR
SHOOT A LINE
SPINS A YARN
START A HARE
STEAL A KISS
STOLE A KISS
TAKES A SEAT
TAKES A TURN
THUMB A LIFT
THUMB A RIDE
WAVED A WAND
WAVES A WAND

5,2,1,2
GIVES IT A GO

5,2,3
BECHE DE MER
BREAK OF DAY
CARRY IT OFF
CASTS AN EYE
CLEAR AS MUD
FIGHT IT OUT
FLEUR DE LIS
FLEUR DE LYS
FLOAT ON AIR

GOING TO BED
GOING TO POT
GOING TO SEA
GOING TO WAR
GRANT IN AID
HEART OF OAK
HERES TO YOU
HOUSE OF GOD
KEEPS AT BAY
KNOCK IT OFF
LAUGH IT OFF
LENDS AN EAR
LIVED IN SIN
LIVED ON AIR
LIVES IN SIN
LIVES ON AIR
NIHIL AD REM
PEACE OF GOD
PLAYS TO WIN
READY TO EAT
READY TO SEW
RIGHT OF WAY
ROLLS OF FAT
SHAME ON YOU
SHEET OF ICE
SHOOT IT OUT
SLOOP OF WAR
SPELL IT OUT
SPELT IT OUT
STAND AT BAY
STAND TO WIN
STATE OF WAR
STICK IT OUT
STOOD AT BAY
STOOD TO WIN
STUCK IT OUT
SUCKS TO YOU
SWEAT IT OUT
TAKEN IN TOW
TAKES IN TOW
TOUCH ME NOT
WALKS ON AIR
WHATS UP DOC
WORKS IT OUT

5,3,2
CROSS THE TS
MAKES FUN OF
MAKES USE OF
PETER SEE ME
POKED FUN AT
POKES FUN AT
SILLY MID ON
TONIC SOL FA
TOUCH AND GO
WALKS OUT ON
WHERE ITS AT

5,5
ABOVE BOARD
ABOVE NAMED

5,5 *contd.*
ABOVE PRICE
ABOVE WATER
ACUTE ANGLE
ADAMS APPLE
ADDLE PATED
AFTER GUARD
AFTER IMAGE
AFTER LIGHT
AGONY UNCLE
ALARM CLOCK
ALARM RADIO
ALLEN SCREW
ALTAR CLOTH
ALTAR RAILS
ALTAR STONE
AMINO ACIDS
AMINO GROUP
ANGEL FALLS
ANGEL WATER
ANGLO IRISH
ANGLO SAXON
ANKLE CHAIN
ANKLE STRAP
APPLE SAUCE
APPLE WOMAN
APRON STAGE
ARROW GRASS
ASSAY PIECE
AUGER SHELL
AVANT GARDE
BAKED APPLE
BAKED BEANS
BANDY WORDS
BARGE BOARD
BASIL THYME
BAWDY HOUSE
BEACH BUGGY
BEARD GRASS
BEAST FABLE
BELLY DANCE
BELLY LAUGH
BESOM RIDER
BIBLE CLASS
BILGE WATER
BLACK BREAD
BLACK CLOUD
BLACK DEATH
BLACK EARTH
BLACK FACED
BLACK FRIAR
BLACK FROST
BLACK LIGHT
BLACK LOOKS
BLACK MAGIC
BLACK MARIA
BLACK MONEY
BLACK PAPER
BLACK PATCH
BLACK POWER

BLACK SHEEP
BLACK SHIRT
BLACK SNAKE
BLACK STONE
BLACK WATCH
BLACK WIDOW
BLANK VERSE
BLIND ALLEY
BLIND DRUNK
BLOCK GRANT
BLOOD COUNT
BLOOD DONOR
BLOOD GROUP
BLOOD MONEY
BLOOD PLATE
BLOOD PURGE
BLOOD ROYAL
BLOOD WAGON
BOARD WAGES
BONDI BEACH
BONGO DRUMS
BONUS ISSUE
BOOBY PRIZE
BORED STIFF
BOSOM BUDDY
BOUTS RIMES
BOWIE KNIFE
BRAIN DEATH
BRAIN DRAIN
BRAKE BLOCK
BRAKE LIGHT
BRAKE WHEEL
BRAND IMAGE
BRASS FACED
BRASS PLATE
BRASS TACKS
BREAD BOARD
BREAD FRUIT
BREAD KNIFE
BREAD SAUCE
BREAD STICK
BREAK COVER
BREAK FORTH
BREAK LOOSE
BREAK POINT
BREAK RANKS
BRENT GOOSE
BRICK EARTH
BRING ABOUT
BRING FORTH
BRING ROUND
BROAD ARROW
BROAD BASED
BROAD BEANS
BROAD GAUGE
BROAD SCOTS
BROKE COVER
BROKE FORTH
BROKE LOOSE
BROKE RANKS

BROME GRASS
BRONX CHEER
BROOD POUCH
BROWN ALGAE
BROWN BREAD
BROWN DWARF
BROWN PAPER
BROWN SAUCE
BROWN SHIRT
BROWN STOUT
BROWN STUDY
BROWN SUGAR
BROWN TROUT
BRUSH ASIDE
BRUTE FORCE
BUCKS PARTY
BUNCH GRASS
BURNT CREAM
BURNT UMBER
CABIN CLASS
CADET CORPS
CADET FORCE
CALLS NAMES
CAMEL CORPS
CAMEO SHELL
CAMPO SANTO
CANDY FLOSS
CANIS MAJOR
CANIS MINOR
CAPER SAUCE
CASTS ASIDE
CASTS LOOSE
CASUS BELLI
CATCH BASIN
CHAIN CABLE
CHAIN DRIVE
CHAIN SMOKE
CHAIN STORE
CHANK SHELL
CHAUD FROID
CHECK CLERK
CHEEK PIECE
CHEEK POUCH
CHIEF BARON
CHIFF CHAFF
CHILD BRIDE
CHILD PROOF
CHINA ASTER
CHINA GOOSE
CHINA GRASS
CHINA STONE
CHINA WHITE
CHOIR ORGAN
CHOKE CHAIN
CHOPS LOGIC
CHOTA HAZRI
CHUCK WAGON
CHURN DRILL
CHURN STAFF
CIDER PRESS

CIVIC CROWN
CIVIL DEATH
CLASP KNIFE
CLEAN BREAK
CLEAN HANDS
CLEAN SLATE
CLEAN SWEEP
CLICK CLACK
CLISH CLASH
CLOCK RADIO
CLOCK TOWER
CLOSE ORDER
CLOSE RANKS
CLOSE SHAVE
CLOSE THING
CLOTH EARED
CLOVE HITCH
COACH BUILT
COACH HORSE
COACH HOUSE
COACH STAND
COACH WHEEL
COCOA BEANS
COLTS TOOTH
COMES ABOUT
COMES CLEAN
COMES ROUND
COMIC OPERA
COMIC STRIP
CORAL BERRY
COSTA BRAVA
COUCH GRASS
COUNT SHEEP
COUNT WHEEL
COURT DRESS
COURT HOUSE
COURT ORDER
COVER DRIVE
COVER POINT
CRAFT GUILD
CRAKE BERRY
CRASH PROOF
CRAZY QUILT
CREAM SLICE
CREPE PAPER
CREPE SOLED
CRIME SHEET
CRISS CROSS
CROSS CHECK
CROSS CLAIM
CROSS GUARD
CROSS PARTY
CROSS REFER
CROWN AGENT
CROWN COURT
CROWN DERBY
CROWN GREEN
CROWN WHEEL
CRUET STAND
CYCLO CROSS

5,5 *contd.*

DAILY BREAD	FACES FACTS	FLOCK PAPER	GOOSE BUMPS
DAILY DOZEN	FAINT HEART	FLOOD GATES	GOOSE GRASS
DAILY PAPER	FAIRY LIGHT	FLOOD LEVEL	GOOSE QUILL
DAIRY CREAM	FAIRY QUEEN	FLOOD PLAIN	GRAND HOTEL
DAISY CHAIN	FAIRY STORY	FLOOR SPACE	GRAND JESUS
DAISY WHEEL	FALLS ABOUT	FLOWN COVER	GRAND JUROR
DANCE MUSIC	FALLS APART	FLUID DRIVE	GRAND MARCH
DANDY BRUSH	FALLS SHORT	FLUID OUNCE	GRAND NIECE
DANKE SCHON	FALSE ALARM	FOCAL POINT	GRAND OPERA
DEATH KNELL	FALSE SHAME	FORTY NINER	GRAND PIANO
DEATH SQUAD	FALSE START	FORTY WINKS	GRAND STYLE
DEATH WATCH	FALSE TEETH	FOUND FAULT	GRAND TOTAL
DELFT CHINA	FANCY DRESS	FOUND MONEY	GRAND UNCLE
DEWAR FLASK	FANCY GOODS	FRAME HOUSE	GRAPE LOUSE
DILLY DALLY	FANCY WOMAN	FRAME MAKER	GRAPE SUGAR
DIRTY MONEY	FATTY ACIDS	FRESH BLOWN	GRAPH PAPER
DIRTY TRICK	FATTY HEART	FRESH FRUIT	GRASS COURT
DITCH WATER	FAULT PLANE	FRIED BREAD	GRASS GREEN
DIZZY SPELL	FEELS CHEAP	FROGS MOUTH	GRASS GROWN
DOLLS HOUSE	FEELS FAINT	FRONT BENCH	GRASS ROOTS
DONER KEBAB	FEELS SMALL	FRONT TEETH	GRASS SKIRT
DOUGH BAKED	FERRO ALLOY	FRONT TOOTH	GRASS SNAKE
DOWEL JOINT	FERRY HOUSE	FRUIT JUICE	GRASS VERGE
DOWER HOUSE	FEVER PITCH	FRUIT KNIFE	GRASS WIDOW
DOWNS TOOLS	FIBRE GLASS	FRUIT SALAD	GRAVE MAKER
DRAFT HORSE	FIELD EVENT	FUDDY DUDDY	GRAVY TRAIN
DRAWS BLOOD	FIELD GLASS	FUNNY MONEY	GREAT GROSS
DRAWS TEETH	FIELD NOTES	FUNNY PAPER	GREAT LAKES
DREAD LOCKS	FIELD TRAIN	FUNNY STUFF	GREAT NIECE
DREAM WORLD	FIFTY FIFTY	FUZZY WUZZY	GREAT SCOTT
DRESS SENSE	FIFTY PENCE	GAUDY NIGHT	GREAT UNCLE
DRESS SHIRT	FINAL SCORE	GAUGE GLASS	GRECO ROMAN
DRIFT APART	FINDS FAULT	GHOST STORY	GREEK CROSS
DRINK MONEY	FINNO UGRIC	GHOST WRITE	GREEK MODES
DRIVE SHAFT	FIRST AIDER	GIANT PANDA	GREEK MYTHS
DUCHY COURT	FIRST CLASS	GIDDY PACED	GREEN ALGAE
DUMMY WHIST	FIRST FLOOR	GIVES BIRTH	GREEN BERET
DUMPY LEVEL	FIRST FRUIT	GIVES CHASE	GREEN EARTH
DUTCH CLOCK	FIRST LIGHT	GIVES FORTH	GREEN GOOSE
DUTCH TREAT	FIRST NIGHT	GIVES VOICE	GREEN LIGHT
DUTCH UNCLE	FIRST PRIZE	GLASS CLOTH	GREEN PAPER
DYING HAPPY	FIRST THING	GLASS COACH	GREEN PARTY
DYING WORDS	FIXED COSTS	GLASS FACED	GREEN POUND
EARLS COURT	FIXED LIGHT	GLASS FIBRE	GREEN SALAD
EARLY START	FIXED STARS	GLASS PAPER	GREEN SNAKE
EARTH HOUSE	FLAKE WHITE	GLEBE HOUSE	GRIPE WATER
EARTH LIGHT	FLASH BOARD	GLIDE SLOPE	GRUFF VOICE
EARTH SHINE	FLASH FLOOD	GLOSS PAINT	GUARD HOUSE
EARTH TABLE	FLASH POINT	GLOVE FIGHT	GUEST HOUSE
EMBER GOOSE	FLESH BROTH	GLOVE MONEY	GUEST NIGHT
EMERY BOARD	FLESH BRUSH	GOATS BEARD	HANDY DANDY
EMERY CLOTH	FLESH EATER	GOING AHEAD	HANGS ABOUT
EMERY PAPER	FLESH WOUND	GOING DUTCH	HANGS LOOSE
EMERY WHEEL	FLICK KNIFE	GOING FORTH	HANKY PANKY
EPSOM DOWNS	FLINT GLASS	GOING ROUND	HAPPY EVENT
EPSOM SALTS	FLINT HEART	GOING UNDER	HAREM SKIRT
EXTRA COVER	FLOAT BOARD	GOING WRONG	HASTA LUEGO
EXTRA SOLAR	FLOAT GLASS	GOODS TRAIN	HAULS ROUND
FACED FACTS	FLOAT PLANE	GOODS WAGON	HAUTE ECOLE
	FLOAT STONE	GOODY GOODY	HEART BLOCK

5,5 contd.
HEART GRIEF
HEART SHELL
HEART SPOON
HEART THROB
HEAVY ARMED
HEAVY GOING
HEAVY METAL
HEAVY SUGAR
HEAVY WATER
HELLO DOLLY
HELLS ANGEL
HELLS BELLS
HELLS TEETH
HINGE JOINT
HIRDY GIRDY
HITCH HIKED
HITCH HIKER
HITCH HIKES
HITTY MISSY
HOBBY HORSE
HOCUS POCUS
HODGE PODGE
HOITY TOITY
HOKEY COKEY
HOLDS COURT
HOLDS FORTH
HOLDS WATER
HOLUS BOLUS
HONEY CROCK
HONEY EATER
HONEY GUIDE
HONEY STALK
HONEY SWEET
HONEY WAGON
HORSE BRASS
HORSE CLOTH
HORSE COPER
HORSE FACED
HORSE RIDER
HORSE SENSE
HORSE TAMER
HORSE THIEF
HOUSE AGENT
HOUSE GUEST
HOUSE PARTY
HOUSE PLANT
HOUSE PROUD
HOUSE RULES
HOVER MOWER
HOVER TRAIN
HUBBA HUBBA
HUMAN BEING
HUMAN ERROR
HURDY GURDY
HURLY BURLY
ICING SUGAR
IDIOT BOARD
IDIOT PROOF
IGNES FATUI

INDIA PAPER
INERT GASES
INGLE CHEEK
INLET VALVE
INNER HOUSE
INNER LIGHT
INNER SPACE
INNER VOICE
IRISH LINEN
ISSUE FORTH
IVORY BLACK
IVORY COAST
IVORY TOWER
JANUS FACED
JAPAN EARTH
JERRY BUILT
JEUNE FILLE
JEWEL HOUSE
JOINT STOCK
JOLIE LAIDE
JOLLY ALONG
JOLLY ROGER
KEEPS CLEAR
KEEPS FAITH
KEEPS HOUSE
KEEPS QUIET
KEEPS STILL
KEEPS TRACK
KEEPS WATCH
KHMER ROUGE
KICKS ABOUT
KINGS BENCH
KINGS CHAIR
KINGS SCOUT
KLIEG LIGHT
KNICK KNACK
KNIFE BOARD
KNIFE PLEAT
KNIFE POINT
KNOCK ABOUT
KNOCK KNEED
LADYS SMOCK
LAMBS TAILS
LARGE ORDER
LARGE SCALE
LARKS ABOUT
LASSA FEVER
LATIN CROSS
LAVER BREAD
LAZAR HOUSE
LEAVE ALONE
LEGAL EAGLE
LEMON DROPS
LEMON JUICE
LEMON THYME
LEVER WATCH
LIGHT ARMED
LIGHT HORSE
LIGHT METER
LIGHT MUSIC

LIGHT OPERA
LIGHT ORGAN
LIGHT PROOF
LIGHT TABLE
LIGHT TOWER
LIGHT WATER
LINEN PAPER
LIONS MOUTH
LIONS SHARE
LIVER SALTS
LOCAL RADIO
LOGAN STONE
LOOKS AFTER
LOOKS SMALL
LOOMS LARGE
LOOSE COVER
LOSES COUNT
LOSES HEART
LOSES TOUCH
LOSES TRACK
LOTUS EATER
LOUIS SEIZE
LOVEY DOVEY
LOWER CLASS
LOWER HOUSE
LUCKY BREAK
LUCKY CHARM
LUCKY PIECE
LUCKY STARS
LUCKY STONE
LUNAR CYCLE
LUNAR MONTH
LUNCH BREAK
LYING AWAKE
LYING UNDER
LYMPH GLAND
MAGIC CUBES
MAGIC SPELL
MAGNA CARTA
MAJOR SCALE
MAJOR THIRD
MAKES AFTER
MAKES HASTE
MAKES MERRY
MAKES MONEY
MAKES PEACE
MAKES READY
MAKES SENSE
MAKES WAVES
MALTA FEVER
MAMMY WAGON
MANNA GRASS
MANOR HOUSE
MAPLE SUGAR
MAPLE SYRUP
MARCH WINDS
MARSH FEVER
MARSH ROBIN
MATCH MAKER
MATCH POINT

MELBA SAUCE
MELBA TOAST
MERRY WIDOW
MEZZO FORTE
MEZZO PIANO
MIDAS TOUCH
MILKY WHITE
MINCE WORDS
MINOR CANON
MINOR SCALE
MINOR THIRD
MITRE SHELL
MIXED GRILL
MIXED TRAIN
MOCHA STONE
MONEY MAKER
MONEY ORDER
MONEY TAKER
MONEY TALKS
MONKS CLOTH
MONTE CARLO
MORAL SENSE
MOTOR COACH
MOTOR CYCLE
MOTOR LORRY
MOUNT GUARD
MOUNT OLIVE
MOUNT SINAI
MOUTH ORGAN
MOVED HOUSE
MOVES HOUSE
MULTI STAGE
MULTI TRACK
MUMBO JUMBO
MUMMY CLOTH
MUNTZ METAL
MUSIC HOUSE
MUSIC PAPER
MUSIC STAND
MUSIC STOOL
NAKED FLAME
NAKED TRUTH
NAMBY PAMBY
NAMED NAMES
NAMES NAMES
NAVAL CROWN
NERVE AGENT
NERVE FIBRE
NEVER NEVER
NIGHT CLOUD
NIGHT GLASS
NIGHT LIGHT
NIGHT NURSE
NIGHT RIDER
NIGHT SHIFT
NIGHT SIGHT
NIGHT TRAIN
NIGHT WATCH
NOBEL PRIZE
NOBLE GASES

5,5 *contd.*
NOBLE HOUSE
NOBLE METAL
NORTH BOUND
NORTH POLAR
NUDGE NUDGE
NURSE CHILD
NURSE SHARK
OCEAN BASIN
OCEAN GOING
OCEAN PERCH
OLIVE GREEN
OPERA BUFFA
OPERA CLOAK
OPERA GLASS
OPERA HOUSE
OPERA SERIA
OPIUM EATER
OPIUM POPPY
OPTIC NERVE
ORDER ABOUT
ORDER PAPER
OTHER RANKS
OTTER HOUND
OTTER SHREW
OUIJA BOARD
OUTER SPACE
OZONE LAYER
PADDY FIELD
PADDY WHACK
PAINT BRUSH
PALSY WALSY
PANEL TRUCK
PAPAL BRIEF
PAPAL CROSS
PAPER CHAIN
PAPER CHASE
PAPER CLIPS
PAPER CLOTH
PAPER GAUGE
PAPER KNIFE
PAPER MAKER
PAPER MONEY
PAPER ROUND
PAPER TIGER
PARIS GREEN
PARTY FUNDS
PARTY GOING
PARTY TRICK
PARVO VIRUS
PASTE GRAIN
PASTY FACED
PEACE CORPS
PEACE ENVOY
PEACE PARTY
PEACH BLOOM
PEACH MELBA
PEACH STONE
PEACH WATER
PEARL DIVER

PEARL SHELL
PEARL STONE
PEARL WHITE
PEASE BROSE
PEDAL BOARD
PEDAL CYCLE
PEDAL ORGAN
PEDAL POINT
PENNY BLACK
PENNY PIECE
PENNY PINCH
PENNY PLAIN
PENNY SHARE
PENNY STONE
PETIT POINT
PETRI PLATE
PIANO ORGAN
PIANO STOOL
PICKS HOLES
PIECE GOODS
PIEDS NOIRS
PILOT CLOTH
PILOT HOUSE
PILOT LIGHT
PILOT WHALE
PINCE NEZED
PIOUS FRAUD
PIPED MUSIC
PITCH BLACK
PITCH WHEEL
PITTA BREAD
PIXIE STOOL
PLAID CYMRU
PLAIN CHANT
PLAIN TRUTH
PLANE CHART
PLANE CRASH
PLANE TABLE
PLANS AHEAD
PLANT HOUSE
PLANT LOUSE
PLATE GLASS
PLATE LAYER
PLATE PROOF
PLAYS ABOUT
PLAYS FALSE
PLAYS HAVOC
PLUME GRASS
POINT BLANK
POINT TAKEN
POKER FACED
POLES APART
POPPY WATER
POTTY CHAIR
POUND FORCE
POURS FORTH
POWER BLOCK
POWER DRILL
POWER HOUSE
POWER LATHE

POWER PLANT
POWER POINT
PREEN GLAND
PRESS AGENT
PRESS AHEAD
PRESS GANGS
PRESS MONEY
PRESS PROOF
PRICE INDEX
PRICE LEVEL
PRICK EARED
PRICK LOUSE
PRIMA DONNA
PRIMA FACIE
PRIME MOVER
PRINT WORKS
PRIVY PURSE
PRIZE COURT
PRIZE FIGHT
PRIZE MONEY
PROOF HOUSE
PROOF READS
PROOF SHEET
PROUD FLESH
PUCKA SAHIB
PULLS AHEAD
PULLS APART
PUNCH DRUNK
PUNCH LADLE
PUNTO BANCO
PURSE SEINE
PUTTY FACED
PUTTY KNIFE
QUEEN SIZED
QUEUE JUMPS
QUICK FIRER
QUICK MARCH
QUICK MATCH
QUICK STICK
QUICK TRICK
QUINK GOOSE
QUINT MAJOR
QUINT MINOR
QUITE RIGHT
RADIO TIMES
RADIO WAVES
RAISE ALOFT
RAISE MONEY
RAJYA SABHA
RALLY CROSS
RALLY ROUND
RAZOR BLADE
RAZOR SHARP
RAZOR SHELL
RAZOR STROP
READS ALOUD
READY MONEY
REPRO PROOF
RHYME ROYAL
RIDGE PIECE

RIFLE CORPS
RIFLE GREEN
RIFLE RANGE
RIGHT ABOUT
RIGHT DRAWN
RIGHT WHALE
RIGHT WHEEL
RIVER BASIN
RIVER CRAFT
RIVER DRIFT
RIVER HORSE
RIVER MOUTH
RIVER WATER
ROGUE MONEY
ROLLS ALONG
ROLLS ROYCE
ROMAN BATHS
ROMAN SNAIL
ROMAN VILLA
ROSIN PLANT
ROTOR PLANE
ROUEN CROSS
ROUGE CROIX
ROUGH CIDER
ROUGH DRAFT
ROUGH DRIED
ROUGH DRIES
ROUGH GUESS
ROUGH GUIDE
ROUGH HEWER
ROUGH HOUND
ROUGH HOUSE
ROUGH RIDER
ROUGH STUFF
ROUGH TRADE
ROUND ABOUT
ROUND DANCE
ROUND DOZEN
ROUND EARED
ROUND FACED
ROUND HOUSE
ROUND NOSED
ROUND ROBIN
ROUND TABLE
ROUND TOWER
ROUTE MARCH
ROVER SCOUT
ROWAN BERRY
ROWDY DOWDY
ROYAL ASCOT
ROYAL BARGE
ROYAL BURGH
ROYAL FLUSH
ROYAL HOUSE
ROYAL ICING
ROYAL JELLY
ROYAL VISIT
ROYAL YACHT
RUGBY UNION
SABRE TOOTH

5,5 *contd.*
SAILS ALONG
SAINT DAVID
SAINT PETER
SALAD CREAM
SALAD PLANT
SALAD PLATE
SALES CLERK
SALES DRIVE
SANTA CLAUS
SATIN PAPER
SAXON SHORE
SCALE BOARD
SCALE MODEL
SCARF JOINT
SCENE THREE
SCENT GLAND
SCENT ORGAN
SCENT SPRAY
SCORE BOARD
SCOTS GREYS
SCOUT ROUND
SCRAP METAL
SCREW PLATE
SCREW PRESS
SCRIP ISSUE
SCRUB ROUND
SCUBA DIVER
SEDAN CHAIR
SEEKS AFTER
SELLS SHORT
SENSE DATUM
SENSE ORGAN
SERBO CROAT
SERVO MOTOR
SEVEN SAGES
SEVEN STARS
SHADE PLANT
SHAFT HORSE
SHAKE HANDS
SHALE MINER
SHARE PRICE
SHARP EDGED
SHARP NOSED
SHEAR STEEL
SHEEP FACED
SHEEP LOUSE
SHEEP TRACK
SHEET GLASS
SHEET METAL
SHEET MUSIC
SHELL MONEY
SHIFT ABOUT
SHIPS WATER
SHIRE HORSE
SHIRE REEVE
SHIRT FRILL
SHIRT FRONT
SHISH KEBAB
SHOCK PROOF

SHOCK STALL
SHOOK HANDS
SHOOT CRAPS
SHORE GOING
SHORE LEAVE
SHORT COATS
SHORT LISTS
SHORT LIVED
SHORT METRE
SHORT RANGE
SHORT TRACK
SHORT WHIST
SHOWS FIGHT
SHOWS FORTH
SIEGE PIECE
SIEGE TRAIN
SIEGE WORKS
SIGHT READS
SIGHT SINGS
SILLY BILLY
SILLY GOOSE
SILLY POINT
SINGS ALONG
SISAL GRASS
SIXTH SENSE
SKATE ROUND
SKENE OCCLE
SKINS ALIVE
SKIRT ROUND
SLACK WATER
SLANG WHANG
SLAVE OWNER
SLAVE TRADE
SLEEP ROUGH
SLEEP TIGHT
SLEPT ROUGH
SLIDE VALVE
SLIME MOULD
SLING BACKS
SLING FRUIT
SLUSH MONEY
SMALL CRAFT
SMALL HOURS
SMALL PRINT
SMALL SWORD
SMALL WARES
SMART ALICK
SMART MONEY
SMOCK FROCK
SMOKE ALARM
SMOKE BOARD
SMOKE DRIED
SMOKE DRIES
SMOKE STACK
SNAIL PACED
SNAIL SHELL
SNAIL WHEEL
SNAKE DANCE
SNAKE HOUSE
SNEAK THIEF

SNUFF BROWN
SNUFF MOVIE
SNUFF SPOON
SNUFF TAKER
SOLAR FLARE
SOLAR MONTH
SOLAR PANEL
SOLAR POWER
SOLID STATE
SOUND BOARD
SOUND MIXER
SOUND RADIO
SOUND SHIFT
SOUND TRACK
SOUTH BOUND
SOUTH POLAR
SPACE PROBE
SPADE BEARD
SPARE PARTS
SPARK PLUGS
SPEAR POINT
SPEAR SHAFT
SPEED LIMIT
SPENT FORCE
SPERM WHALE
SPIKE GRASS
SPLIT HAIRS
SPLIT IMAGE
SPLIT LEVEL
SPLIT SHIFT
SPODE CHINA
SPOIL SPORT
SPOON FEEDS
SPRAY DRIED
SPRAY DRIFT
SPRAY PAINT
STAFF CORPS
STAFF NURSE
STAGE CRAFT
STAGE FEVER
STAGE HORSE
STAGE RIGHT
STAGE WAGON
STAIR TOWER
STAKE MONEY
STALL FEEDS
STAMP ALBUM
STAMP HINGE
STAMP PAPER
STAND ALONE
STAND GUARD
STAND TREAT
STAND TRIAL
STARK NAKED
STATE COACH
STATE HOUSE
STATE PAPER
STATE TRIAL
STAYS STILL
STEAK HOUSE

STEAM CRANE
STEAM GAUGE
STEAM NAVVY
STEAM POWER
STEAM RADIO
STEAM TRAIN
STEAM YACHT
STEEL PLATE
STEER CLEAR
STEPS ASIDE
STERN CHASE
STERN FRAME
STERN SHEET
STILL BIRTH
STILL HOUSE
STILL STAND
STINK BRAND
STOCK AGENT
STOCK STILL
STONE BORER
STONE BREAK
STONE FRUIT
STONE MASON
STONE SNIPE
STONE STILL
STONY BROKE
STOOD ALONE
STOOD GUARD
STOOD TREAT
STOOD TRIAL
STOPS SHORT
STORM CLOUD
STORM GLASS
STORM TRACK
STORM WATER
STRAW PLAIT
STRIP POKER
STRIP TEASE
STUDY GROUP
SUGAR APPLE
SUGAR BASIN
SUGAR CANDY
SUGAR DADDY
SUGAR GRASS
SUGAR MAPLE
SUGAR TONGS
SUPER DUPER
SUPER ROYAL
SWAMP FEVER
SWEAT BLOOD
SWEAT GLAND
SWEAT SHIRT
SWEEP SEINE
SWEET BRIAR
SWEET BRIER
SWEET TALKS
SWELL ORGAN
SWINE FEVER
SWING MUSIC
SWING SHELF

5,5 *contd.*
SWING STOCK
SWING SWANG
SWING WHEEL
SWISS FRANC
SWISS GUARD
SWISS WATCH
SWORD BLADE
SWORD DANCE
SWORD GRASS
SWORD STICK
TABLE CLOTH
TABLE COVER
TABLE DHOTE
TABLE KNIFE
TABLE LINEN
TABLE MONEY
TABLE SPOON
TABLE WATER
TAKEN ABACK
TAKEN APART
TAKES AFTER
TAKES AMISS
TAKES APART
TAKES COVER
TAKES HEART
TAKES ISSUE
TAKES LEAVE
TAKES PAINS
TAKES PLACE
TAKES SHAPE
TAKES SIDES
TAKES STEPS
TAKES STOCK
TAKES TURNS
TALKS ROUND
TALLY CLERK
TALLY TRADE
TAROT CARDS
TAWNY EAGLE
TEENY WEENY
TELLS TALES
TERRA FIRMA
TEXAS TOWER
THERE THERE
THIGH BOOTS
THILL HORSE
THINK AGAIN
THINK ALIKE
THINK ALOUD
THINK TWICE
THIRD CLASS
THIRD FORCE
THIRD PARTY
THIRD REICH
THIRD WORLD
THORN APPLE
THORN HEDGE
THREE BALLS
THREE PARTS

THREE PIECE
THREE SIDED
THROW STICK
THUMB INDEX
THUMB STALL
TIGER BADGE
TIGER SHARK
TIGER SNAKE
TIGHT LACED
TITLE FIGHT
TITLE SHEET
TODDY LADLE
TODDY STICK
TOKEN MONEY
TONIC WATER
TOOTH PASTE
TORCH DANCE
TOTAL WRECK
TOUCH JUDGE
TOUCH PAPER
TOUCH TYPED
TOUCH TYPES
TOWER BLOCK
TOXIC WASTE
TRACE HORSE
TRACK EVENT
TRACK SCOUT
TRACK SHOES
TRADE BOARD
TRADE CYCLE
TRADE PLATE
TRADE PRICE
TRADE ROUTE
TRADE UNION
TRADE WINDS
TRAGI COMIC
TRAIN CRASH
TRAIN FERRY
TRANS SONIC
TREAD WATER
TREAD WHEEL
TRICK TRACK
TROOP HORSE
TROUT SPOON
TRUNK MAKER
TRUST HOUSE
TRUST STOCK
TRUTH SERUM
TRUTH TABLE
TRUTH VALUE
TULIP EARED
TURNS ABOUT
TURNS ASIDE
TURNS LOOSE
TURNS NASTY
TURNS ROUND
TWEET TWEET
TWIST DRILL
ULTRA VIRES
UNDER CLERK

UNDER COVER
UNDER TRICK
UNDER WATER
UNDUE HASTE
UPPER CLASS
UPPER CRUST
UPPER HOUSE
USING FORCE
VALUE ADDED
VENUS SHELL
VEREY LIGHT
VERSE MAKER
VERSE SMITH
VICHY WATER
VIDEO NASTY
VINHO VERDE
VITAL FLAME
VITAL FORCE
VITAL SIGNS
VITAL SPARK
VOCAL CORDS
VOCAL MUSIC
VOCAL SCORE
VOICE PRINT
VOWEL POINT
VOWEL RHYME
WAGON TRAIN
WAGON WHEEL
WAITS ABOUT
WAKEY WAKEY
WALKY TALKY
WASTE PAPER
WATCH CHAIN
WATCH GLASS
WATCH GUARD
WATCH HOUSE
WATCH LIGHT
WATCH NIGHT
WATCH STRAP
WATCH TOWER
WATER BLOOM
WATER BORNE
WATER BOUND
WATER BREAK
WATER CHUTE
WATER CLOCK
WATER COOLS
WATER CRAFT
WATER CRANE
WATER CYCLE
WATER FRAME
WATER GAUGE
WATER GLASS
WATER GUARD
WATER HORSE
WATER JOINT
WATER LEMON
WATER LEVEL
WATER MAIZE
WATER MELON

WATER METER
WATER MOUSE
WATER MUSIC
WATER NYMPH
WATER OUZEL
WATER PIPES
WATER PLANT
WATER PLATE
WATER POWER
WATER SKIED
WATER SKIER
WATER SKIES
WATER SNAKE
WATER SPOUT
WATER TABLE
WATER THYME
WATER TOWER
WATER WHEEL
WATER WINGS
WAVED ASIDE
WAVES ASIDE
WEIGH HOUSE
WELLS FARGO
WELSH ONION
WENDY HOUSE
WHALE SHARK
WHEAT FIELD
WHEAT MIDGE
WHEEL CHAIR
WHEEL CLAMP
WHEEL HOUSE
WHIRL ABOUT
WHIST DRIVE
WHITE BEARD
WHITE BRASS
WHITE BREAD
WHITE DWARF
WHITE FACED
WHITE FLOUR
WHITE FRIAR
WHITE FROST
WHITE GOODS
WHITE HORSE
WHITE HOUSE
WHITE LIGHT
WHITE MAGIC
WHITE METAL
WHITE NIGHT
WHITE NOISE
WHITE PAPER
WHITE SAUCE
WHITE SUGAR
WHITE WATER
WHITE WHALE
WHITE WITCH
WHOLE WHEAT
WILLY NILLY
WIRED GLASS
WISHY WASHY
WITCH ALDER

5,5 *contd.*
WITCH HAZEL
WIZEN FACED
WOMAN HATER
WONGA WONGA
WORLD POWER
WORLD WEARY
WORRY BEADS
WREAK HAVOC
WRIST WATCH
WRONG DOING
WRONG FOOTS
WRONG TIMED
YIELD POINT
YLANG YLANG
YOUNG BLOOD
YOUNG FOGEY
YOURS TRULY
ZEBRA FINCH
ZENER CARDS
ZENER DIODE
ZONAL INDEX

6,1,3
BOUGHT A PUP
BUYING A PUP
LIVING A LIE
MAKING A BED
PLACED A BET
PLACES A BET
SHAKES A LEG
SHOWED A LEG
SMELLS A RAT
TAKING A BOW
THROWS A FIT

6,2,2
BEATEN TO IT
CAMPED IT UP
CEASED TO BE
CHUCKS IT IN
LIVING IT UP
LOOKED UP TO
MAKING IT UP
MOTHER TO BE
PACKED IT IN
PACKED IT UP
PILING IT ON
RARING TO GO
RUBBED IT IN
SEEING TO IT
STICKS AT IT
TRYING IT ON
WHOOPS IT UP
WORKED AT IT
ZAPPED IT UP
ZEROED IN ON
ZEROES IN ON

6,4
ACCESS CARD

ACCESS ROAD
ACCESS TIME
ACTION PLAN
ACTIVE LIFE
ACTIVE LIST
ADVICE NOTE
AERIAL VIEW
AGENCY SHOP
ALMOND CAKE
ALMOND EYED
ALMOND TREE
ALPINE RACE
ANCHOR HOLD
ANSWER BACK
ANYONE ELSE
ARCHER FISH
ARMOUR CLAD
ASTRAL BODY
ATOMIC BOMB
ATOMIC PILE
ATOMIC TIME
BACKED DOWN
BAKING SODA
BALLET GIRL
BALLET SHOE
BANANA BOAT
BANANA SKIN
BARBED WIRE
BARBIE DOLL
BARIUM MEAL
BARLEY WINE
BARREL ROLL
BARROW TRAM
BASSET HORN
BEAKER FOLK
BEARER BOND
BEATEN DOWN
BEAUTY SPOT
BEAVER AWAY
BEAVER TREE
BEAVER WOOD
BEDDED DOWN
BEETLE EYED
BEFORE LONG
BEHIND BARS
BEHIND HAND
BEHIND TIME
BELTED EARL
BENGAL FIRE
BERLIN BLUE
BERLIN WALL
BERLIN WOOL
BETTER HALF
BILLET DOUX
BINARY STAR
BISHOP BIRD
BITTER ROOT
BLEARY EYED
BLOODY EYED
BLOODY MARY

BOBBIN LACE
BOGGED DOWN
BOILED OVER
BOILER SUIT
BOMBAY DUCK
BONDED DEBT
BOTTLE BANK
BOTTLE FEED
BOTTLE FISH
BOTTLE HEAD
BOTTLE NECK
BOTTLE NOSE
BOTTLE TREE
BOTTOM LINE
BOUGHT OVER
BOUNCE BACK
BOWLED OVER
BOXING RING
BRANCH LINE
BRANCH WORK
BRANDY BALL
BRANDY SNAP
BRAZEN FACE
BREAKS AWAY
BREAKS CAMP
BREAKS DOWN
BREAKS EVEN
BREAST FEED
BREAST HIGH
BREAST KNOT
BREAST WALL
BREATH TEST
BRIDES CAKE
BRIDES MAID
BRIDGE CLUB
BRIDGE ROLL
BRIDGE WORK
BRIDLE HAND
BRIDLE PATH
BRIDLE REIN
BRIDLE ROAD
BRINGS DOWN
BRINGS HOME
BRINGS OVER
BROKEN DOWN
BROKEN HOME
BROKEN REED
BROMIC ACID
BRONZE WING
BUBBLE BATH
BUBBLE OVER
BUBBLE PACK
BUBBLY JOCK
BUCKET SEAT
BUCKET SHOP
BUCKLE DOWN
BUENOS DIAS
BUFFER ZONE
BULLET HEAD
BULLET TREE

BUMBLE FOOT
BUMPED INTO
BUNGEE JUMP
BURNET MOTH
BURROW DUCK
BUTTER BALL
BUTTER BEAN
BUTTER BIRD
BUTTER DISH
BUTTER FISH
BUTTER MILK
BUTTER WIFE
BUTTON BUSH
BUTTON HOLE
BUTTON HOOK
BUTTON WOOD
BUYING OVER
CALICO BUSH
CALICO TREE
CALICO WOOD
CALLED AWAY
CALLED BACK
CALLED OVER
CALMED DOWN
CAMELS HAIR
CAMINO REAL
CANARY BIRD
CANARY WOOD
CANDLE COAL
CANDLE FISH
CANDLE TREE
CANDLE WOOD
CANNED BEER
CANNON BONE
CANNON GAME
CANNON SHOT
CANVAS BACK
CANVAS WORK
CARBON COPY
CAREER GIRL
CAREER PATH
CARPET MOTH
CATTLE CAKE
CATTLE GRID
CATTLE SHOW
CAUGHT FIRE
CAVITY WALL
CAXTON HALL
CELLAR BOOK
CELLAR FLAP
CENTRE HALF
CENTRE RAIL
CHAISE CART
CHANGE DOWN
CHANGE ENDS
CHANGE GEAR
CHANGE OVER
CHAPEL CART
CHARGE DOWN
CHARGE HAND

6,4 *contd.*

CHEESE MITE	COMING HOME	DONALD DUCK	FIRING BACK
CHEQUE BOOK	COMING OVER	DONKEY PUMP	FIRING LINE
CHEQUE CARD	COMMON COLD	DONKEY WORK	FIRMED DOWN
CHERRY BEAN	COMMON NOUN	DORIAN MODE	FISCAL YEAR
CHERRY PLUM	COMMON ROOM	DORSAL FINS	FLIGHT CREW
CHERRY TREE	COMMON TIME	DOSSED DOWN	FLIGHT DECK
CHEWED OVER	COOKER HOOD	DOSSES DOWN	FLIGHT PATH
CHILDS PLAY	COPPER NOSE	DOTTED LINE	FLIGHT PLAN
CHOKED BACK	COPPER WIRE	DOTTED NOTE	FLINGS DOWN
CHOKES BACK	COPPER WORK	DOUBLE AXEL	FLINGS OPEN
CHORUS GIRL	CORDON BLEU	DOUBLE BACK	FLOPPY DISC
CHORUS LINE	CORNED BEEF	DOUBLE BASS	FLOPPY DISK
CHURCH ARMY	CORNER FLAG	DOUBLE BILL	FLOWER BELL
CHURCH GOER	CORNER SHOP	DOUBLE CHIN	FLOWER GIRL
CINDER CONE	COSMIC RAYS	DOUBLE DOOR	FLOWER HEAD
CINDER PATH	COTTON BELT	DOUBLE DYED	FLOWER SHOW
CINEMA GOER	COTTON BOLL	DOUBLE FLAT	FLYING BOAT
CINQUE FOIL	COTTON MILL	DOUBLE PARK	FLYING BOMB
CINQUE PORT	COTTON REEL	DOUBLE SALT	FLYING FISH
CIRCLE LINE	COTTON WOOL	DOUBLE STAR	FLYING HIGH
CIRCUS RING	COTTON WORM	DOUBLE TAKE	FLYING LEAP
CITRIC ACID	COUNTY TOWN	DOUBLE TALK	FLYING OPEN
CITRON TREE	CRACKS DOWN	DOUBLE TIME	FLYING SHOT
CITRON WOOD	CRADLE SONG	DRAGON FISH	FLYING SOLO
CITRUS WOOD	CRANES BILL	DRAGON TREE	FLYING SUIT
CLAMPS DOWN	CRATER LAKE	DRAINS AWAY	FLYING WING
CLAWED BACK	CREDIT CARD	DRIVES HOME	FOLLOW HOME
CLEVER DICK	CRYING DOWN	DUCKED DOWN	FOLLOW SUIT
CLIMBS DOWN	CRYING WOLF	DUFFEL COAT	FORCED SALE
CLOSED BOOK	CUCKOO PINT	DUNDEE CAKE	FOREST TREE
CLOSED DOOR	CUCKOO SPIT	EAGLES NEST	FORKED OVER
CLOSED DOWN	CURFEW BELL	EASTER LILY	FORMIC ACID
CLOSED MIND	CUTTLE BONE	EATING AWAY	FOSSIL FUEL
CLOSED SHOP	CYANIC ACID	ECCLES CAKE	FOSTER HOME
CLOSES DOWN	DAMASK PLUM	EIGHTH ARMY	FOUGHT BACK
CLOSET PLAY	DAMASK ROSE	ELEVEN PLUS	FOURTH RATE
CLOUDS OVER	DAMPEN DOWN	EMPIRE GOWN	FOURTH WALL
CLOVEN HOOF	DANGER LINE	ENGINE ROOM	FREEZE DOWN
COARSE FISH	DANISH BLUE	ENTREE DISH	FREEZE OVER
COBALT BLUE	DAPPLE GREY	EQUALS SIGN	FRENCH ALPS
CODLIN MOTH	DASHED AWAY	ERRAND GIRL	FRENCH BEAN
COFFEE BEAN	DASHES AWAY	ESCAPE ROAD	FRENCH HEEL
COFFEE MILL	DEADLY SINS	ESKIMO ROLL	FRENCH HORN
COFFEE ROOM	DEATHS HEAD	ESTATE DUTY	FRENCH KISS
COFFEE SHOP	DECKLE EDGE	EXCESS FARE	FRENCH LOAF
COFFEE TREE	DECREE NISI	FALCON EYED	FRENCH ROLL
COFFER FISH	DENVER BOOT	FALLEN ARCH	FRENCH SASH
COFFIN BONE	DESERT BOOT	FALLEN STAR	FRENCH SEAM
COFFIN NAIL	DINING HALL	FALLOW DEER	FRIARS COWL
COKING COAL	DINING ROOM	FAMILY NAME	FRINGE TREE
COLLAR BONE	DINNER GOWN	FAMILY TREE	FROZEN DOWN
COLLAR STUD	DINNER HOUR	FATHOM LINE	FROZEN OVER
COLOUR CODE	DINNER LADY	FATTED CALF	FUNGUS GALL
COLOUR FAST	DINNER TIME	FELLOW HEIR	FUSION BOMB
COLOUR FILM	DIRECT LINE	FERRIC ACID	GAINED TIME
COLOUR WASH	DIVING BELL	FIANNA FAIL	GALLIC ACID
COMING AWAY	DIVING BIRD	FIGHTS BACK	GALLUP POLL
COMING BACK	DIVING SUIT	FILING PAST	GAMBIT PAWN
COMING DOWN	DOGGER BANK	FINITE VERB	GAMING LAWS
	DOLLAR AREA	FIRING AWAY	GANDER MOON

6,4 contd.
GARAGE SALE
GARDEN CITY
GARDEN GATE
GARDEN PATH
GARDEN PEAS
GARDEN WALL
GEARED DOWN
GEISHA GIRL
GELDER ROSE
GENEVA GOWN
GIMBAL RING
GIMLET EYED
GINGER BEER
GINGER WINE
GIVING AWAY
GIVING ODDS
GIVING REIN
GLANCE COAL
GLASSY EYED
GNAMMA HOLE
GNAWED AWAY
GOGGLE EYED
GOLDEN BULL
GOLDEN CALF
GOLDEN DISC
GOLDEN GATE
GOLDEN GIRL
GOLDEN MEAN
GOLDEN ROSE
GOLDEN RULE
GOLDEN SEAL
GOONEY BIRD
GOSPEL SIDE
GOTHIC ARCH
GRANDE DAME
GRANDS PRIX
GRANNY FLAT
GRANNY KNOT
GRAVEL WALK
GREASY POLE
GREEDY GUTS
GRINDS DOWN
GROUND BASS
GROUND CREW
GROUND DOWN
GROUND GAME
GROUND MAIL
GROUND PLAN
GROUND RENT
GROUND RULE
GROUSE MOOR
GUINEA CORN
GUINEA FOWL
GUINEA WORM
HALTER NECK
HAMMER BEAM
HAMMER HOME
HAMMER TOED
HANDED DOWN

HANDED OVER
HAPPEN UPON
HARKED BACK
HARMAN BECK
HAUNCH BONE
HAWSER LAID
HEALTH CAMP
HEALTH FARM
HEALTH FOOD
HEARTS EASE
HEAVEN SENT
HEBREW YEAR
HERMIT CRAB
HEROIC POEM
HOCKEY LINE
HOLLOW EYED
HOLLOW WARE
HORNED TOAD
HORROR FILM
HOUNDS FOOT
HOWLED DOWN
HUCKLE BONE
HUNTED DOWN
HURDLE RACE
HYBRID BILL
IAMBIC FOOT
IDAEAN VINE
IMMUNE BODY
INDIAN CLUB
INDIAN CORN
INDIAN FILE
INDIAN FIRE
INDIAN HEMP
INDIAN MEAL
INDIAN PIPE
INDIAN RICE
INDIGO BIRD
INDOOR GAME
INJURY TIME
INLAND BILL
INSIDE EDGE
INSIDE LEFT
ITALIC TYPE
JOCKEY CLUB
JUGGED HARE
JULIAN YEAR
JUMBLE SALE
JUMPED BAIL
JUMPED SHIP
JUNGLE FOWL
JUNIOR MISS
KAFFIR CORN
KARATE CHOP
KEELED OVER
KENNEL CLUB
KENNEL MAID
KETTLE PINS
KEWPIE DOLL
KIDNEY BEAN
KILLED TIME

KIPPED DOWN
KITTEN MOTH
KNOCKS BACK
KNOCKS COLD
KNOCKS DOWN
KODIAK BEAR
LABOUR CAMP
LABOUR CLUB
LACTIC ACID
LADDER BACK
LAMMAS TIDE
LANCET ARCH
LANGUE DOIL
LAPPET MOTH
LATENT HEAT
LATTER BORN
LAURIC ACID
LAYING BARE
LAYING DOWN
LAYING INTO
LAYING OPEN
LEAGUE GAME
LEDGER BAIT
LEDGER LINE
LEGACY DUTY
LENTIL SOUP
LETTER BOMB
LETTER BOOK
LETTER CARD
LETTER CLIP
LETTER FILE
LIMBER NECK
LIMPET MINE
LIQUOR LAWS
LITANY DESK
LITMUS TEST
LITTER LOUT
LITTLE BEAR
LITTLE JOHN
LIVING DOWN
LIVING ROOM
LIVING WAGE
LIVING WELL
LIVING WILL
LOADED DICE
LOCKED AWAY
LOCKER ROOM
LOCUST BEAN
LOOKED AWRY
LOOKED BACK
LOOKED DOWN
LOOKED INTO
LOOKED OVER
LOSING FACE
LOSING GAME
LOSING TIME
LOUNGE SUIT
LOUVRE DOOR
LOVERS KNOT
LOVERS LANE

LOVERS LEAP
LOVING CARE
LUMBER MILL
LUMBER ROOM
LUMBER YARD
LUTINE BELL
LYDIAN MODE
MADDER LAKE
MAGNUM OPUS
MAIDEN AUNT
MAIDEN NAME
MAIDEN OVER
MAIDEN PINK
MAIDEN RACE
MAILED FIST
MAKING AWAY
MAKING GOOD
MAKING LOVE
MAKING OVER
MAKING PLAY
MAKING ROOM
MAKING SAIL
MAKING SURE
MAKING TIME
MALLEE BIRD
MALLEE FOWL
MANILA HEMP
MARBLE ARCH
MARCEL WAVE
MARINE GLUE
MARINE SOAP
MARKED DOWN
MARKED TIME
MARKER BOMB
MARKER FLAG
MARKET BELL
MARKET HALL
MARKET TOWN
MARROW BONE
MASKED BALL
MASTER CARD
MASTER HAND
MASTER RACE
MASTER WORK
MATRON LIKE
MEADOW LARK
MEDIUM TERM
MEDIUM WAVE
MELTED AWAY
MELTED DOWN
MEMORY BANK
MENTAL HOME
MERSEY BEAT
MICKEY FINN
MIDDLE AGED
MIDDLE AGES
MIDDLE EAST
MIDDLE GAME
MIDDLE NAME
MIDDLE TERM

6,4 *contd.*

MIDDLE WEST	ORANGE TREE	PIGEON HOLE	PRIEST KING
MILLET SEED	ORANGE WOOD	PIGEON PAIR	PRIEST LIKE
MINERS LAMP	ORIONS BELT	PIGEON POST	PRISON BARS
MINUTE BELL	OWNERS RISK	PIGEON TOED	PRISON CAMP
MINUTE HAND	OXFORD BAGS	PIGEON WING	PRISON CELL
MISSEL TREE	OXFORD BLUE	PILLAR ROOT	PRISON DOOR
MISTED OVER	OXFORD SHOE	PILLOW BERE	PRISON SHIP
MIZZEN MAST	OXTAIL SOUP	PILLOW LACE	PRISON YARD
MIZZEN SAIL	OXYGEN MAST	PILLOW TALK	PROMPT BOOK
MOBILE HOME	OXYGEN TENT	PINEAL BODY	PROMPT COPY
MOBILE SHOP	OYSTER BANK	PIPING CROW	PROMPT NOTE
MODERN JAZZ	PACKET BOAT	PIPING DOWN	PROMPT SIDE
MONDAY CLUB	PACKET SHIP	PIPING HARE	PROPER NAME
MONKEY BOAT	PADDED CELL	PIRATE SHIP	PROPER NOUN
MONKEY NUTS	PADDLE BOAT	PISTOL SHOT	PROTON BEAM
MONKEY PUMP	PADDLE WOOD	PISTOL WHIP	PUBLIC BILL
MONKEY ROPE	PAGODA TREE	PISTON RING	PUBLIC SALE
MONKEY SUIT	PANTON SHOE	PLAGUE SORE	PULLED AWAY
MONKEY TAIL	PAPERS OVER	PLAGUE SPOT	PULLED BACK
MORTAL COIL	PARANA PINE	PLAYED BACK	PULLED DOWN
MOTHER CELL	PARCEL BOMB	PLAYED BALL	PULLED OVER
MOTHER CITY	PARCEL POST	PLAYED DOWN	PULLED RANK
MOTHER LAND	PARISH PUMP	PLAYED FAIR	PUMPED IRON
MOTHER SHIP	PARPEN WALL	PLAYED HOST	PUPPET PLAY
MOVING AWAY	PARROT BEAK	PLAYED SAFE	PUPPET SHOW
MOVING BACK	PARROT BILL	PLOUGH BACK	PURPLE BORN
MOVING OVER	PARROT FISH	PLOUGH IRON	PURPLE FISH
MUFFIN BELL	PARSON BIRD	PLOUGH TAIL	PURPLE HUED
MUSKET SHOT	PASSED AWAY	PLOUGH TEAM	PUSHED PAST
MUSSEL PLUM	PASSED OVER	PLOUGH TREE	PUSHES PAST
MUSTER BOOK	PASSED PAWN	PLUNGE BATH	PUZZLE BOOK
MUSTER FILE	PASSES AWAY	PLURAL VOTE	PUZZLE HEAD
MUTTON CHOP	PASSES OVER	POCKET BOOK	QUAKER BIRD
MUTTON FIST	PASTRY COOK	POCKET COMB	QUARRY TILE
MUTTON HEAD	PATTER SONG	POCKET HOLE	QUARTZ MILL
MUTUAL WALL	PAYING BACK	POISON FANG	QUARTZ ROCK
NAILED DOWN	PAYING CASH	POISON PILL	QUEENS WARE
NAPKIN RING	PEARLY KING	POLLEN TUBE	QUINIC ACID
NARROW BOAT	PEBBLE DASH	POPLAR TREE	QUINSY WORT
NARROW SEAS	PEBBLE WARE	PORTAL VEIN	RABBIT HOLE
NATIVE BORN	PECTIC ACID	POSTAL CARD	RABBIT SKIN
NATIVE LAND	PEGGED AWAY	POSTAL CODE	RACKET TAIL
NATURE CURE	PEGGED BACK	POSTAL NOTE	RADIAL TYRE
NATURE MYTH	PEGGED DOWN	POSTAL TUBE	RADIUM BOMB
NAUTCH GIRL	PENCIL CASE	POSTAL VOTE	RAFTER BIRD
NEEDLE CASE	PENCIL LEAD	POTATO PEEL	RAGGED LADY
NEEDLE FISH	PEPPER CAKE	POTATO RING	RAISED CAIN
NETTLE FISH	PEPPER TREE	POUSSE CAFE	RAISED HELL
NETTLE RASH	PERIOD PLAY	POWDER BLUE	RAISES CAIN
NITRIC ACID	PETITS POIS	POWDER DOWN	RAISES HELL
NORWAY PINE	PETROL BLUE	POWDER MILL	RASCAL LIKE
NUDIST CAMP	PETROL BOMB	POWDER PUFF	RATION BOOK
NUMBER NINE	PETROL PUMP	POWDER ROOM	RATION CARD
OBJECT BALL	PETROL TANK	PRAYER BEAD	RATTLE HEAD
OBJETS DART	PEWTER MILL	PRAYER BOOK	RATTLE PATE
OFFICE GIRL	PHRASE BOOK	PREACH DOWN	RAVENS BONE
ORANGE LILY	PICKED OVER	PRETTY MUCH	RAVENS DUCK
ORANGE PEEL	PICKET DUTY	PRETTY PASS	REFORM BILL
ORANGE ROOT	PICKET LINE	PRETTY WELL	REGENT BIRD
	PIETRA DURA	PRIEST HOLE	REMAND HOME

6,4 *contd.*

REPAIR SHOP	SAILOR SUIT	SHAKES DOWN	SPONGE DOWN
REPORT BACK	SALMON LEAP	SHANTY TOWN	SPREAD OVER
REVIEW BODY	SALMON PINK	SHEATH BILL	SPRING CART
REVIEW COPY	SALOON DECK	SHEATH FISH	SPRING CLIP
RIBBON FISH	SALTED AWAY	SHEEPS HEAD	SPRING HARE
RIBBON SEAL	SALTED DOWN	SHIELD HAND	SPRING LOCK
RIDING BOOT	SAMIAN WARE	SHIELD MAID	SPRING ROLL
RIDING COAT	SAUCER EYED	SHOOTS DOWN	SPRING TIDE
RIDING CROP	SAVAGE BLOW	SHOOTS HOME	SPRUCE PINE
RIDING DOWN	SAVING FACE	SHOUTS DOWN	SQUARE DEAL
RIDING HIGH	SAVING GAME	SHOVEL HEAD	SQUARE FOOT
RIDING HOOD	SAVING TIME	SHOWER BATH	SQUARE INCH
RIDING ROBE	SAXONY BLUE	SHRIMP GIRL	SQUARE KNOT
RIDING SUIT	SCHICK TEST	SIGNED AWAY	SQUARE MEAL
RIDING WHIP	SCHISM SHOP	SIGNED COPY	SQUARE MILE
RIPPLE MARK	SCHOOL BELL	SIGNET RING	SQUARE ROOT
RISING TIDE	SCHOOL BOOK	SILVER COIN	SQUARE SAIL
ROBBER CRAB	SCHOOL DAME	SILVER FISH	SQUARE TOED
ROBING ROOM	SCHOOL FEES	SILVER FOIL	SQUARE TOES
ROLLED GOLD	SCHOOL MAAM	SILVER LEAF	SQUARE YARD
ROLLED OVER	SCHOOL MARM	SILVER TRAY	SQUINT EYED
ROMPED HOME	SCHOOL MATE	SILVER TREE	SQUINT EYES
ROMPER SUIT	SCHOOL MISS	SIMMER DOWN	SQUIRE LIKE
ROTARY CLUB	SCHOOL SONG	SIMNEL CAKE	STABLE GIRL
ROUNDS DOWN	SCHOOL TERM	SINGLE EYED	STABLE ROOM
ROWING BOAT	SCHOOL TIME	SINGLE FILE	STANDS DOWN
ROWING CLUB	SCHOOL WORK	SKATED OVER	STANDS FAST
RUBBED DOWN	SCHOOL YEAR	SKATES OVER	STANDS FIRE
RUBBER BAND	SCOTCH HAND	SKETCH BOOK	STANDS OVER
RUBBER NECK	SCOTCH KALE	SLEEPY HEAD	STAPLE DIET
RUBBER SOLE	SCOTCH MIST	SLEEVE LINK	STARRY EYED
RUBBER SUIT	SCOTCH PINE	SLEIGH BELL	STATIC LINE
RUBBER TREE	SCOTCH ROSE	SLEIGH RIDE	STAYED OVER
RUBBLE WORK	SCOTCH SNAP	SLOPED ARMS	STEAMS OPEN
RUBIKS CUBE	SCOTCH TAPE	SLOPES ARMS	STICKY BACK
RUDDER FISH	SCOUTS PACE	SLOWED DOWN	STIFLE BONE
RUMPUS ROOM	SCREEN TEST	SLUICE GATE	STORKS BILL
RUNNER BEAN	SEALED BEAM	SMOOTH BORE	STREAM GOLD
RUSTIC SEAT	SEALED BOOK	SNAILS PACE	STREET ARAB
RUSTIC WARE	SECOND BEST	SNAKES HEAD	STREET CRED
RUSTIC WORK	SECOND HAND	SOCIAL EVIL	STREET DOOR
SACRED FISH	SECOND HOME	SOCIAL WORK	STREET WARD
SADDLE ROOF	SECOND MARK	SODIUM LAMP	STRICT DIET
SADDLE ROOM	SECOND RATE	SOLEMN MASS	STRIFE TORN
SADDLE SOAP	SECOND SELF	SONATA FORM	STRIKE BACK
SADDLE SORE	SECOND WIND	SORBIC ACID	STRIKE DOWN
SADDLE TREE	SECURE UNIT	SOURCE BOOK	STRIKE DUMB
SAFARI PARK	SEEING LIFE	SPHINX MOTH	STRIKE HOME
SAFARI SUIT	SEEING OVER	SPIDER CRAB	STRING BAND
SAFETY BELT	SEMPER IDEM	SPILLS OVER	STRING BASS
SAFETY BOLT	SEPTIC TANK	SPINAL CORD	STRING BEAN
SAFETY CAGE	SERIAL TIME	SPINEL RUBY	STRING VEST
SAFETY FILM	SERVED TIME	SPIRIT BLUE	STRIPS DOWN
SAFETY FUSE	SERVES TIME	SPIRIT LAMP	STROKE PLAY
SAFETY LAMP	SESAME SEED	SPLASH BACK	STRONG HEAD
SAFETY LOCK	SETTLE DOWN	SPLASH DOWN	STRONG MEAT
SAFETY PLUG	SEWAGE FARM	SPLINT BONE	STRONG SUIT
SAFETY WEAR	SHADOW MARK	SPLINT COAL	STRUCK BACK
SAILOR LIKE	SHADOW PLAY	SPONGE BATH	STRUCK DOWN
	SHAGGY MANE	SPONGE CAKE	STRUCK DUMB

6,4 *contd.*
STRUCK HOME
STUDIO FLAT
SUMMER CAMP
SUMMER TERM
SUMMER TIME
SUNDAY BEST
SUPPLY SIDE
SWITCH OVER
SWIVEL HOOK
TABULA RASA
TAGGED ATOM
TAILOR BIRD
TAILOR MADE
TAKING ARMS
TAKING BACK
TAKING BETS
TAKING CARE
TAKING DOWN
TAKING FIVE
TAKING HEED
TAKING NOTE
TAKING OVER
TAKING PART
TAKING ROOT
TAKING SILK
TAKING WING
TALKED BACK
TALKED DOWN
TALKED INTO
TALKED OVER
TALKED SHOP
TAPPET RING
TARGET AREA
TARIFF WALL
TEMPTS FATE
TENDER LOIN
TENNIS BALL
TENNIS CLUB
TENNIS SHOE
TENTER HOOK
THINKS BACK
THINKS OVER
THREAD LACE
THREAD WORM
THRIFT SHOP
THROAT BAND
THRONE ROOM
THROWN AWAY
THROWN DOWN
THROWN OPEN
THROWN OVER
THROWN SILK
THROWS AWAY
THROWS DOWN
THROWS OPEN
THROWS OVER
THUMBS DOWN
TICKED AWAY
TICKED OVER

TICKER TAPE
TICKLE PINK
TIDING OVER
TIMBER LINE
TIMBER TOES
TIMBER TREE
TIMBER WOLF
TIMBER YARD
TOGGLE IRON
TOILET ROLL
TOILET SOAP
TOMATO SOUP
TONGUE TIED
TONGUE WORK
TOPPLE OVER
TORRID ZONE
TOWERS OVER
TOWING PATH
TRACKS DOWN
TRADED DOWN
TRADES DOWN
TRADES FOLK
TRAILS AWAY
TRAVEL SICK
TREATY PORT
TREBLE CLEF
TRENCH COAT
TRENCH FEET
TRENCH FOOT
TRIPLE BILL
TRIPLE JUMP
TRIPLE TIME
TUMBLE CART
TUMBLE OVER
TUMBLE WEED
TUNING FORK
TURKEY COCK
TURKEY TROT
TURNED AWAY
TURNED BACK
TURNED DOWN
TURNED INTO
TURNED OVER
TURNED TAIL
TURNED TURK
TURNED UPON
TURRET SHIP
TURTLE DOVE
TURTLE NECK
TURTLE SOUP
TYBURN TREE
TYPING POOL
UPHILL TASK
UPSIDE DOWN
VACUUM PUMP
VACUUM TUBE
VANITY CASE
VANITY FAIR
VAPOUR BATH
VELVET CRAB

VELVET DUCK
VELVET PILE
VENUSS COMB
VERBAL NOTE
VERBAL NOUN
VESPER BELL
VESTRY ROOM
VIRGIN GOLD
VIRGIN KNOT
VIRGIN SOIL
VISUAL AIDS
VISUAL ARTS
VISUAL AXIS
VOLLEY BALL
VOTING DOWN
WAITED UPON
WALKED AWAY
WALKED INTO
WALKED TALL
WALNUT TREE
WAMPUM BELT
WANDER PLUG
WARSAW PACT
WASHED AWAY
WASHED DOWN
WASTED AWAY
WASTES AWAY
WATERS DOWN
WATTLE BIRD
WAVING DOWN
WEASEL COOT
WEASEL WORD
WEAVER BIRD
WEIGHS DOWN
WELTER RACE
WHISKS AWAY
WHISKY SOUR
WHYDAH BIRD
WICKET DOOR
WICKET GATE
WIDOWS MITE
WIDOWS PEAK
WILLOW HERB
WILLOW WREN
WINDOW PANE
WINDOW SASH
WINDOW SEAT
WINDOW SHOP
WINDOW SILL
WINTER CLAD
WINTER CROP
WONDER DRUG
WONDER WORK
WOODEN HEAD
WOODEN SHOE
WOODEN TYPE
WOOLLY BEAR
WORKED OVER
WORKED UPON
WRITES DOWN

WRITES HOME
YELLOW CARD
YELLOW FLAG
YELLOW JACK
YELLOW LINE
YELLOW SNOW
YELLOW SOAP
YELLOW SPOT
YELLOW WOOD
ZODIAC SIGN

7,3
ACCOUNT DAY
ANILINE DYE
BACKING OFF
BAGGAGE CAR
BAILING OUT
BANGING OUT
BARBARY APE
BARKING MAD
BARNABY DAY
BARRIER ACT
BASTARD BAR
BATHING BOX
BATHING HUT
BATTERY HEN
BAWLING OUT
BEARING OUT
BEATING OFF
BEATING OUT
BEDDING OUT
BEETLED OFF
BEETLES OFF
BEGGING OFF
BELTING OUT
BERMUDA RIG
BETTING MAN
BISCUIT TIN
BISHOPS CAP
BLACKED OUT
BLASTED OAK
BLASTED OFF
BLOTTED OUT
BLOWING OUT
BLURTED OUT
BOARDED OUT
BOOKING OUT
BOTTLED OFF
BOTTLED OUT
BOTTLES OFF
BOTTLES OUT
BOTTOMS OUT
BOWLING OUT
BRASSED OFF
BROUGHT OFF
BROUGHT OUT
BROWNED OFF
BRUSHED OFF
BRUSHES OFF
BUFFALO NUT

7,3 *contd.*
BULLDOG ANT
BULLIED OFF
BULLIES OFF
BUMPING OFF
BURMESE CAT
BURNING OUT
BUTTERY BAR
CABBAGE FLY
CALLING OFF
CALLING OUT
CAMBRIC TEA
CAMPING OUT
CANCELS OUT
CAPITAL SIN
CAPITAL SUM
CARRIED OFF
CARRIED OUT
CARRIER BAG
CARRIES OFF
CARRIES OUT
CARTING OFF
CARVING OUT
CASPIAN SEA
CASTING NET
CASTING OFF
CASTING OUT
CATCHES OUT
CAUSTIC WIT
CHALKED OUT
CHARITY BOY
CHECKED OFF
CHECKED OUT
CHEESED OFF
CHELSEA BUN
CHEWING GUM
CHICKEN OUT
CHICKEN POX
CHICKEN RUN
CHILLED OUT
CHIMNEY POT
CHIMNEY TOP
CHIPPED OFF
CHOKING OFF
CHUCKED OUT
CHUCKER OUT
CHURNED OUT
CLAPPED OUT
CLASSIC CAR
CLEANED OUT
CLEARED OUT
CLOCKED OFF
CLOCKED OUT
CLOTHES PEG
CLOTHES PIN
CLUSTER CUP
COCONUT OIL
COCONUT SHY
COLLEGE CAP
COMBING OUT

COMPANY CAR
COMPASS SAW
CONTACT MAN
CONTOUR MAP
COOLING OFF
COPPING OUT
COPYING INK
CORDONS OFF
CORKING PIN
COSSACK HAT
COTTAGE PIE
COUNCIL TAX
COUNTED OUT
COUNTER BID
COUNTER SPY
COUNTRY BOX
COUNTRY PUB
COVERED WAY
CRASHED OUT
CRASHES OUT
CRICKET BAT
CRIMEAN WAR
CRYSTAL SET
CURATES EGG
CURRANT BUN
CUSTARD PIE
CUTTING OFF
CUTTING OUT
DAMPING OFF
DASHING OFF
DASHING OUT
DEALING OUT
DECKING OUT
DECLARE WAR
DERNIER CRI
DIGGING OUT
DIPPING OUT
DISHING OUT
DOROTHY BAG
DOUGLAS FIR
DRAGGED OUT
DRAUGHT BAR
DRAWING OFF
DRAWING OUT
DRAWING PEN
DRAWING PIN
DRIVING OUT
DROPPED OFF
DROPPED OUT
DROWNED OUT
DROWNED RAT
DUCKING OUT
EDITING OUT
EMERALD CUT
EVENING OUT
EXHAUST GAS
FALLING OFF
FALLING OUT
FANNING OUT
FARMING OUT

FATHERS DAY
FEATHER BED
FETCHED OUT
FETCHES OUT
FILLING OUT
FINDING OUT
FINGERS END
FISHING OUT
FISHING ROD
FITTING OUT
FLAKING OUT
FLATTEN OUT
FLESHED OUT
FLESHES OUT
FOBBING OFF
FOLDING OUT
FOLLOWS OUT
FORCING PIT
FOREIGN AID
FORKING OUT
FORMULA ONE
FORMULA TWO
FOWLING NET
FREAKED OUT
FREEZES OUT
FREIGHT CAR
GALLOPS OFF
GARBAGE CAN
GATHERS WAY
GATLING GUN
GAUGING ROD
GETTING OFF
GETTING OUT
GLAMOUR BOY
GOMBEEN MAN
GOUGING OUT
GRAVELY ILL
GRECIAN URN
GRIDDLE CAR
GROWING BAG
HACKNEY CAB
HANDING OUT
HANGING OFF
HANGING OUT
HARBOUR BAR
HARDENS OFF
HARPOON GUN
HARVEST BUG
HARVEST FLY
HATCHET JOB
HATCHET MAN
HEADING OFF
HEADING OUT
HEARING AID
HEARING OUT
HEATHER ALE
HELPING OUT
HIPPETY HOP
HITTING OFF
HITTING OUT

HOLDING OFF
HOLDING OUT
HOLLOWS OUT
HOMBURG HAT
HONOURS MAN
HOPPING MAD
HOPPING OFF
HUBBLES LAW
HUMMING TOP
HUNTING BOX
HUNTING CAP
HUNTING OUT
ICELAND DOG
IRONING OUT
JAMAICA RUM
JOCKEYS CAP
JOURNAL BOX
JUMPING OFF
KEEPING FIT
KEEPING MUM
KEEPING OFF
KENTISH COB
KENTISH MAN
KENTISH RAG
KEYHOLE SAW
KICKING OFF
KICKING OUT
KILLING OFF
KINCHIN LAY
KINETIC ART
KNIGHTS FEE
KNOCKED OFF
KNOCKED OUT
KNUCKLE BOW
LADLING OUT
LANTERN JAW
LASHING OUT
LAUGHED OFF
LAUNDRY MAN
LEADING MAN
LEADING OFF
LEADING OUT
LEAKING OUT
LEAVING OFF
LEAVING OUT
LEOPARD CAT
LETTING FLY
LETTING OFF
LETTING OUT
LETTING RIP
LIBERTY CAP
LIFTING OFF
LINSEED OIL
LOADING BAY
LOBSTER POT
LOCKING NUT
LOCKING OUT
LOGGING OUT
LOOKING FOR
LOOKING OUT

7,3 *contd.*

LUGGAGE VAN	PICKLED EGG	RIPPING SAW	SITTING OUT
LYDFORD LAW	PICTURE ROD	ROLLING PIN	SKITTLE OUT
MACHINE GUN	PIECING OUT	ROOTING OUT	SLACKEN OFF
MALTESE DOG	PLANTED OUT	ROUGHED OUT	SLIPPED OFF
MAPPING OUT	PLASTIC ART	ROUNDED OFF	SLOPING OFF
MARKING INK	PLASTIC BAG	ROUNDED OUT	SLOPPED OUT
MARKING OFF	PLASTIC MAC	RUBBING OUT	SMOKING CAP
MARKING OUT	PLAYING OFF	RUNNING DOG	SMOKING OUT
MARRIED OFF	PLAYING OUT	RUNNING DRY	SNAFFLE BIT
MARRIES OFF	PLOVERS EGG	RUNNING GAG	SNIFFED OUT
MARTIAL ART	POACHED EGG	RUNNING LOW	SNIFFER DOG
MARTIAL LAW	POINTED OUT	RUNNING OFF	SNUFFED OUT
MELLOWS OUT	POLLING DAY	RUNNING OUT	SOAKING WET
MELTING POT	POMPOUS ASS	RUSSIAN TEA	SORTING OUT
MESSAGE BOY	POPPING OFF	SABBATH DAY	SOUNDED OFF
MEXICAN TEA	POPPING OUT	SAUSAGE DOG	SOUNDED OUT
MINERAL OIL	POUCHED RAT	SCALDED CAT	SPACING OUT
MINIMAL ART	POUNCET BOX	SCARLET HAT	SPANISH FLY
MISSING OUT	POURING OUT	SCATTER GUN	SPARKED OFF
MONTERO CAP	PRAIRIE DOG	SCISSOR CUT	SPARKED OUT
MOTHERS DAY	PREMIER CRU	SCISSOR LEG	SPECTRE BAT
MURPHYS LAW	PRESENT DAY	SCOOPED OUT	SPIDERS WEB
MUSICAL BOX	PRINTED OUT	SCORING OFF	SPINDLE OIL
MUSTARD GAS	PRIVATE ACT	SCOTTIE DOG	SPOTTED DOG
MYSTERY MAN	PRIVATE BUS	SCRAPED OFF	SQUEEZE BOX
NATURAL GAS	PRIVATE EYE	SCRAPES OFF	STAKING OUT
NATURAL LAW	PRIVATE LAW	SCRATCH PAD	STAMPED OUT
NESTING BOX	PRIVATE WAR	SCRATCH WIG	STARTED OUT
NIPPING OUT	PSYCHIC BID	SCREECH OWL	STARVED OUT
NODDING OFF	PUDDING BAG	SCREENS OFF	STARVES OUT
NOMINAL PAR	PUDDING PIE	SEALING DAY	STATUTE LAW
NOMINAL SUM	PULLING OFF	SEALING OFF	STAYING OUT
NOTHING BUT	PULLING OUT	SEALING WAX	STAYING PUT
NUCLEAR WAR	PULLMAN CAR	SECONDS OUT	STEEPLE HAT
OMNIBUS BOX	PUMPING OUT	SECULAR ARM	STEPPED OUT
OPENING OUT	PUSHING OFF	SEEKING OUT	STIRRUP CUP
OSTRICH EGG	PUSHING OUT	SELLING OFF	STOPPED OFF
PACIFIC RIM	PUTTING OFF	SELLING OUT	STRETCH OUT
PACKING BOX	PUTTING OUT	SENDING OFF	STRIKES OFF
PADDING OUT	QUAKING ASH	SENDING OUT	STRIKES OIL
PAIRING OFF	QUARTER BOY	SERPENT GOD	STRIKES OUT
PANCAKE DAY	QUARTER DAY	SERVANT MAN	STRINGS OUT
PARENTS DAY	QUARTER ILL	SERVING OUT	STUBBLE FED
PARKING BAY	QUONSET HUT	SETTING OFF	SUCKING CUP
PARKING LOT	RACCOON DOG	SETTING OUT	SUCKING PIG
PARLOUR CAR	RANGING ROD	SEVENTH DAY	SUSSING OUT
PARTING CUP	REACHED OUT	SHAKING OFF	SWEETIE PIE
PASSING OFF	REACHES OUT	SHAKING OUT	TAILING OFF
PASSING OUT	READING AGE	SHARING OUT	TALKING BIG
PEELING OFF	READING OFF	SHEERED OFF	TALKING OUT
PEEPING OUT	READING OUT	SHELLED OUT	TAPERED OFF
PEEPING TOM	REAMING BIT	SHOVING OFF	TEARING OFF
PEGGING OUT	REDDING OUT	SHOWING OFF	TELLING OFF
PENALTY BOX	REELING OFF	SHUFFLE CAP	THAWING OUT
PENSION OFF	REMOVAL VAN	SHUFFLE OFF	THIEVES DEN
PERSIAN CAT	RETIRED PAY	SIAMESE CAT	THIMBLE RIG
PHASING OUT	RIGGING OUT	SIGNING OFF	THINNED OUT
PICKING OFF	RINGING OFF	SIGNING OUT	THOUGHT OUT
PICKING OUT	RINSING OUT	SINGING OUT	THROUGH PUT
	RIPPING OFF	SINGLES BAR	THUNDER BOX

7,3 *contd.*

THUNDER GOD	WEDDING DAY	CLOCKING UP	POUNCING ON
TICKETY BOO	WEEDING HOE	COLOURED IN	PREACHED AT
TICKING OFF	WEEPING ASH	COLOURED UP	PREACHED UP
TIPPING OFF	WEEPING ELM	CONJURED UP	PREACHES AT
TOPPING OUT	WEIGHED OUT	CONJURES UP	PREACHES UP
TORPEDO NET	WELCOME MAT	CONTRACT IN	PRESSING ON
TORSION BAR	WHALING GUN	COTTONED ON	PROPPING UP
TOUCHED OFF	WHISTLE OFF	COUGHING UP	PSYCHING UP
TOUCHES OFF	WHITING OUT	COVERING IN	PUCKERED UP
TOURING CAR	WHITSUN ALE	COVERING UP	QUICKENS UP
TRACKER DOG	WINKLED OUT	CRACKING UP	RATTLING ON
TRADING OFF	WINKLES OUT	CROPPING UP	RECKONED ON
TRAFFIC COP	WINNING OUT	DOUBLING UP	RECKONED UP
TRAFFIC JAM	WISHING CAP	DRAGGING ON	REJOICED IN
TRAILED OFF	WITNESS BOX	DRAGGING UP	REJOICES IN
TRAMMEL NET	WORKING DAY	DREAMING UP	ROUGHING IN
TRAMWAY CAR	WORKING FOR	DRESSING UP	ROUGHING IT
TRIGGER OFF	WORKING MAN	DRINKING IN	ROUNDING ON
TROLLEY BUS	WORKING OUT	DRINKING UP	ROUNDING UP
TROLLEY CAR	WORRIED OUT	DROPPING BY	RUSTLING UP
TROLLEY MAN	WORRIES OUT	DROPPING IN	SADDLING UP
TROTTED OUT	WRIGGLE OUT	DROPPING ON	SCRUBBED UP
TROUSER LEG	WRITING INK	FASTENED ON	SETTLING IN
TRUCKLE BED	WRITING OFF	FATTENED UP	SETTLING UP
TRUFFLE DOG	WRITING OUT	FETCHING UP	SHOOTING UP
TRUFFLE PIG	WRITTEN LAW	FINISHED UP	SHRIVELS UP
TRUNDLE BED	WRITTEN OFF	FINISHES UP	SHUTTING IN
TURFING OUT		FOLLOWED ON	SHUTTING UP
TURNING OFF	**8,2**	FOLLOWED UP	SKIPPING IT
TURNING OUT	BATTLING ON	FRESHENS UP	SLACKENS UP
TURNING SAW	BOTTLING UP	FROWNING ON	SLEEPING IN
TWELFTH MAN	BREAKING IN	GATHERED UP	SLEEPING ON
UNCARED FOR	BREAKING UP	GOBBLING UP	SLIPPING ON
UNHOPED FOR	BRINGING IN	GOODNESS ME	SLIPPING UP
UTILITY MAN	BRINGING ON	GRACIOUS ME	SNAPPING UP
VAMPIRE BAT	BRINGING UP	GROSSING UP	SNEAKING UP
VENTURE OUT	BRUSHING UP	HITCHING UP	SNUFFING IT
VERNERS LAW	BUBBLING UP	HURRYING UP	SNUGGLED UP
VETERAN CAR	BUILDING IN	KNOCKING ON	SNUGGLES UP
VIETNAM WAR	BUILDING UP	KNOCKING UP	SOBERING UP
VINTAGE CAR	BUTTERED UP	LATCHING ON	SOFTENED UP
VOLENTE DEO	BUTTONED UP	LIGHTENS UP	SOLDIERS ON
WALKING OFF	CARRYING ON	LIGHTING UP	SPEAKING UP
WALKING OUT	CATCHING ON	LIMBERED UP	SPEEDING UP
WANDERS OFF	CATCHING UP	LISTENED IN	SQUARING UP
WANTING OUT	CHAINING UP	LISTENER IN	STACKING UP
WARDING OFF	CHALKING UP	LOOSENED UP	STANDERS BY
WARMING PAN	CHANCING IT	MEASURED UP	STANDING BY
WASHING OUT	CHANGING UP	MEASURES UP	STANDING IN
WASSAIL CUP	CHEATING ON	MUDDLING UP	STANDING ON
WAYSIDE INN	CHECKING IN	MUSCLING IN	STANDING TO
WEARING OFF	CHECKING UP	OFFERING UP	STANDING UP
WEARING OUT	CHEERING UP	OVERDOES IT	STARTING IN
WEASELS OUT	CHIPPING IN	PATCHING UP	STARTING UP
WEATHER BOX	CHOPPING UP	PITCHING IN	STEAMING UP
WEATHER EYE	CHURNING UP	PLOUGHED IN	STEPPING IN
WEATHER MAP	CLAMMING UP	PLUGGING IN	STEPPING UP
WEATHER OUT	CLEANING UP	POINTING UP	STICKING BY
WEDDING BED	CLEARING UP	POLISHED UP	STICKING IN
	CLOCKING IN	POLISHES UP	STICKING TO

8,2 *contd.*
STICKING UP
STIRRING UP
STITCHED UP
STITCHES UP
STOCKING UP
STOPPING IN
STRAIGHT UP
STRIKING UP
STRUGGLE ON
STUMPING UP
SUMMONED UP
SWALLOWS UP
SWEARING IN
SWEEPING UP
SWITCHED ON
SWITCHES ON
SWOTTING UP
THINKING UP
THROWING IN
THROWING ON
THROWING UP
TOUCHING UP
TOUGHENS UP
TWIGGING IT
WEIGHING IN
WEIGHING UP
WESTWARD HO
WHIPPING IN
WRAPPING UP

11 LETTERS

1,3,2,1,4
A PIG IN A POKE

1,3,2,5
A BAG OF BONES
A BIT OF FLUFF

1,3,7
V FOR VICTORY
X RAY THERAPY

1,4,1,5
A DIME A DOZEN

1,4,2,4
A BONE TO PICK

1,4,3,3
A RIPE OLD AGE

1,4,6
A LONE FIGURE

1,5,5
A CLEAN SHEET
A CLEAN SLATE
A CLEAN SWEEP
A SCREW LOOSE
A SLATE LOOSE
A SWEET TOOTH
A VOTRE SANTE

1,10
X CHROMOSOME
Y CHROMOSOME

2,1,3,5
IN A BAD LIGHT

2,1,4,4
IN A FLAT SPIN
IN A GOOD MOOD

2,1,5,3
AT A LOOSE END
IN A LARGE WAY
IN A SMALL WAY

2,1,6,2
GO A BUNDLE ON

2,1,8
AT A DISCOUNT
IN A MINORITY
IN A NUTSHELL
IN A QUANDARY
ON A PEDESTAL

2,2,1,6
DO ME A FAVOUR
UP ON A CHARGE

2,2,2,5
GO UP IN SMOKE

2,2,3,4
GO BY THE BOOK
GO TO THE DOGS
GO TO THE WALL
GO TO THE WARS
UP ON THE SHOT
UP TO THE EYES
UP TO THE HILT
UP TO THE MARK

2,2,7
IN AN INSTANT
ON NO ACCOUNT
UP TO SCRATCH

2,3,2,4
AS DRY AS DUST
SO FAR SO GOOD

2,3,3,3
ON THE WAY OUT
UP FOR THE CUP

2,3,6
AT ALL EVENTS
AT ALL POINTS
AT THE DOUBLE
AT THE LATEST
AT THE MOMENT
GO ONE BETTER
GO THE ROUNDS
IF YOU PLEASE
IN DUE COURSE
IN THE CHORUS

IN THE MAKING
IN THE MIDDLE
IN THE OFFING
IN THE SADDLE
IN THE THROES
IN TWO SHAKES
LO AND BEHOLD
ON THE CARPET
ON THE FIDDLE
ON THE MARKET
ON THE RAZZLE
ON THE STREET
TO THE LETTER
UP AND COMING

2,4,1,4
GO LIKE A BOMB
GO WITH A BANG

2,4,2,3
AS GOOD AS NEW
AS UGLY AS SIN
NO TIME AT ALL
SO HELP ME GOD

2,4,5
AN EASY TOUCH
AT FULL BLAST
AT ONES ELBOW
DO ONES STUFF
DO ONES WORST
IN ARMS REACH
IN COLD BLOOD
IN DEEP WATER
IN FULL BLAST
IN FULL SWING
IN GOOD FAITH
IN GOOD HEART
IN GOOD ODOUR
IN GOOD SHAPE
IN ONES POWER
IN ONES SLEEP
NE PLUS ULTRA
NO SUCH THING
ON EASY TERMS
ON ONES GUARD
ON ONES PLATE
ON THAT SCORE
ON YOUR MARKS
TO ONES TASTE

2,5,4
AT EVERY TURN
AT FIRST HAND
ON CLOUD NINE
ST ELMOS FIRE
ST JOHNS WORT

2,6,3
ST AGNESS EVE
ST DAVIDS DAY

2,7,2
UP AGAINST IT

2,9
AD INFINITUM
AU CONTRAIRE
DE PROFUNDIS
EX DIRECTORY
GO OVERBOARD
IN ABSTRACTO
IN CHARACTER
IN COMMITTEE
IN DREAMLAND
IN DUPLICATE
IN HYSTERICS
IN MICROCOSM
IN MINIATURE
IN MOTHBALLS
IN PRINCIPLE
IN SUBSTANCE
NO ADMISSION
NO VACANCIES
OF NECESSITY
ON HORSEBACK
ON PRINCIPLE
TO ADVANTAGE

3,1,2,5
HOP O MY THUMB

3,1,3,2,2
NOT A BIT OF IT

3,1,5,2
NOT A PATCH ON

3,1,7
NOT A SAUSAGE
TAM O SHANTER

3,2,1,5
EYE OF A STORM
PUT UP A FIGHT
SON OF A BITCH

3,2,2,4
NOT UP TO MUCH

3,2,3,3
DAY IN DAY OUT
GET IN THE WAY
GOT IN THE WAY
LAY IN THE WAY
LIE IN THE WAY
NIP IN THE AIR
NIP IN THE BUD
ONE IN THE EYE
OUT OF THE ARK
OUT OF THE WAY
PIE IN THE SKY
PUT ON THE MAP
TIP IT AND RUN

3,2,6
AGE OF REASON

3,2,6 *contd.*
BAG OF CRISPS
BAG OF NERVES
BAG OF TRICKS
BED OF HONOUR
CUP OF COFFEE
FIN DE SIECLE
HAD IT COMING
HAS IT COMING
HIC ET UBIQUE
LAP OF HONOUR
LAP OF LUXURY
LAW OF NATURE
LAY AT ANCHOR
LEG OF MUTTON
LIE AT ANCHOR
NOM DE GUERRE
OIL OF CLOVES
OUT OF ACTION
OUT OF BOUNDS
OUT OF BREATH
OUT OF COURSE
OUT OF FAVOUR
OUT OF HUMOUR
OUT OF KILTER
OUT OF POCKET
OUT OF SEASON
OUT ON STRIKE
PAS DE QUATRE
PAT OF BUTTER
PAY BY CHEQUE
PUT IT MILDLY
PUT ON RECORD
PUT TO RIGHTS
RAN TO GROUND
RUN TO GROUND
SET AT NOUGHT
SET TO RIGHTS
SUM OF THINGS
TOP TO BOTTOM
WAR OF NERVES
WIN ON POINTS
WON ON POINTS

3,3,1,4
FOR ALL I CARE
OUT FOR A DUCK

3,3,2,3
SAW EYE TO EYE
SEE EYE TO EYE

3,3,5
ALL THE WHILE
ANY OLD THING
BED AND BOARD
CAP AND BELLS
CAT AND MOUSE
CUT AND DRIED
CUT OFF POINT
CUT THE CARDS

DID THE TRICK
DID THE TWIST
DIE THE DEATH
DOS AND DONTS
DOT AND CARRY
FOR THE BIRDS
FOX AND GEESE
GIN AND TONIC
GOG AND MAGOG
HUG THE COAST
LAW AND ORDER
LAY THE TABLE
LET OFF STEAM
NOW AND AGAIN
OFF THE LEASE
OFF THE RAILS
OFF THE TRACK
OFF THE WAGON
ONE WAY GLASS
OUT AND ABOUT
OUT AND OUTER
OUT FOR BLOOD
PAY THE PIPER
PAY THE PRICE
RED HOT POKER
SAW THE LIGHT
SEE THE LIGHT
SEE YOU LATER
SET THE SCENE
TAI CHI CHUAN
THE BIG APPLE
THE BIG SMOKE
THE NEW WORLD
THE OLD ENEMY
THE OLD WORLD
THE RED CROSS
TIN PAN ALLEY
TIP THE SCALE
TOM AND JERRY
UPS AND DOWNS
WIN THE POOLS
WON THE POOLS
YOU AND YOURS

3,4,2,2
THE GAME IS UP
THE SIZE OF IT

3,4,4
ALL TIME HIGH
ALL VERY WELL
AND THEN SOME
CAR BOOT SALE
CUT BOTH WAYS
FED ONES FACE
FOR GODS SAKE
GET ONES GOAT
GET WELL SOON
GOT ONES GOAT
HID ONES HEAD
INK BLOT TEST

NEW BORN BABE
OFF ONES FEED
OFF ONES FOOD
OFF ONES GAME
OFF ONES HEAD
OFF ONES OATS
OLD KING COLE
PUT ONES CASE
RAN INTO DEBT
RUN INTO DEBT
SIT DOWN MEAL
THE FINE ARTS
THE GOOD BOOK
THE LAST GASP
THE LAST WORD
TRY ONES LUCK
TWO LINE WHIP
USE ONES LOAF
YOU KNOW WHAT

3,5,3
ALL FOOLS DAY
ALL SOULS DAY
COD LIVER OIL
GOD BLESS YOU
HOT CROSS BUN
NEW YEARS DAY
NEW YEARS EVE
OAK APPLE DAY
THE BITER BIT
THE NAKED EYE
THE NOBLE ART
THE OTHER DAY
THE WHOLE HOG
YOU DIRTY RAT

3,8
AIR CORRIDOR
AIR LAYERING
AIR MECHANIC
AIR MINISTRY
AIR SICKNESS
AIR TERMINAL
AIR UMBRELLA
ALL AMERICAN
ALL CHEERING
ALL ELECTRIC
ALL POWERFUL
ALL STANDING
ART MISTRESS
AWE STRICKEN
BAD LANGUAGE
BAD TEMPERED
BAR SINISTER
BAT PRINTING
BAY WINDOWED
BIG BUSINESS
BOG ASPHODEL
BOG TROTTERS
BOW WINDOWED
BOX JUNCTION

CAR SICKNESS
CUB REPORTER
CUP FINALIST
DAK BUNGALOW
DAY LABOURER
DRY CLEANERS
DRY CLEANING
EAR PIERCING
EYE CATCHING
FAN VAULTING
FAR REACHING
FLY DRESSING
FOR INSTANCE
FOR STARTERS
GAS FITTINGS
GAS GUZZLING
GAY DECEIVER
GAY LOTHARIO
GET CRACKING
GET TOGETHER
GOD BOTHERER
GOD FORSAKEN
GOT CRACKING
GOT TOGETHER
GUN CARRIAGE
HER LADYSHIP
HIS HOLINESS
HIS LORDSHIP
HOT SPIRITED
HOT TEMPERED
ICE YACHTING
ILL AFFECTED
ILL ASSORTED
ILL BREEDING
ILL DISPOSED
ILL FAVOURED
ILL HUMOURED
ILL INFORMED
ILL MANNERED
ILL TEMPERED
ION EXCHANGE
JAM DOUGHNUT
JAM TOMORROW
KEY INDUSTRY
LAW BREAKING
LAW MERCHANT
LIE DETECTOR
LIP ROUNDING
LIP SMACKING
LOW PRESSURE
LOW SPIRITED
MAD SCRAMBLE
MAD STAGGERS
MAN WATCHING
MAP MEASURER
MEN SERVANTS
MID ATLANTIC
MRS MALAPROP
MUD SLINGING
MUD WRESTLER

3,8 *contd.*
NET CURTAINS
NET PRACTICE
NEW POTATOES
NON BELIEVER
NON DELIVERY
NON ELECTRIC
NON EXISTENT
NON METALLIC
NON PARTISAN
NON RESIDENT
NON SEQUITUR
NON SPECIFIC
NON UNIONIST
NON VIOLENCE
OFF COLOURED
OIL PAINTING
OIL PLATFORM
OIL REFINERY
OLD BACHELOR
OLD DOMINION
OLD FOGEYISH
OLD TRAFFORD
OUT PATIENTS
PAN AMERICAN
PAN SLAVONIC
PAS REDOUBLE
PAX VOBISCUM
PET AVERSION
PIG IGNORANT
PIG STICKING
PIT DWELLING
POP FASTENER
POP FESTIVAL
PRE CAMBRIAN
PRE CONQUEST
PRE ELECTING
PRE ELECTION
PRE EMINENCE
PRE EMPTIBLE
PRE EXISTENT
PRE EXISTING
PRE IGNITION
PRE STRESSED
PSI PARTICLE
PUT STRAIGHT
QUO WARRANTO
RAN SMOOTHLY
RAS TAFARIAN
RAT CATCHING
RAT KANGAROO
RAW MATERIAL
RED CRESCENT
RED SQUIRREL
RES JUDICATA
RIB ROASTING
RIB TICKLING
RIB VAULTING
ROI FAINEANT
RUN SMOOTHLY

SAL AMMONIAC
SAL VOLATILE
SAT SAPIENTI
SAW DAYLIGHT
SEA CRAYFISH
SEA CUCUMBER
SEA DOTTEREL
SEA ELEPHANT
SEA LAVENDER
SEA PURSLANE
SEA ROSEMARY
SEA SCORPION
SEA SCOUTING
SEE DAYLIGHT
SIN OFFERING
SKY COLOURED
TAN COLOURED
TAP DRESSING
TEA CANISTER
TEA CEREMONY
TEA STRAINER
THE ALMIGHTY
THE CENOTAPH
THE CONQUEST
THE CRUSADES
THE DEPARTED
THE DUKERIES
THE FAITHFUL
THE GREATEST
THE PROPHETS
THE PYRAMIDS
THE REDEEMER
TIN SOLDIERS
TIN STREAMER
TOP DRESSING
TOP PRIORITY
TUB THUMPING
TWO PENNORTH
TWO STOREYED
VIA DOLOROSA
WAR CRIMINAL
WAR MEMORIAL
WAR NEUROSIS
WAX CHANDLER
WAX PAINTING
WEB FINGERED
ZIP FASTENER

4,1,4,2
GETS A LINE ON
MADE A FUSS OF
MADE A PASS AT
MAKE A FUSS OF
MAKE A PASS AT
PUTS A STOP TO

4,1,6
CAST A GLANCE
COCK A LEEKIE
COIN A PHRASE
GETS A WICKET

JUST A MINUTE
KEEP A SECRET
KEPT A SECRET
LAID A COURSE
LAYS A COURSE
LIFT A FINGER
MISS A SITTER
PLOT A COURSE
SAID A PRAYER
SAYS A PRAYER
TAKE A TUMBLE
TAKE A WICKET
TOOK A TUMBLE
TOOK A WICKET

4,2,1,4
BALD AS A COOT
CAME TO A HEAD
COME TO A HEAD
DEAD AS A DODO
DEAF AS A POST
DONE TO A TURN
FREE AS A BIRD
HIGH AS A KITE
KICK UP A FUSS
LOVE IN A MIST
THIN AS A RAKE
WINS BY A HEAD
WINS BY A NECK

4,2,2,3
PLAY IT BY EAR
PUTS ON AN ACT
THAT IS TO SAY

4,2,3,2
KEEP AN EYE ON
KEPT AN EYE ON
PUTS AN END TO
TAKE IT OUT ON
TOOK IT OUT ON

4,2,5
BACK TO EARTH
BACK TO FRONT
BANK OF ISSUE
BILL OF COSTS
BOLD AS BRASS
BOOK OF HOURS
BOOK OF WORDS
CALL IT QUITS
CALL TO ORDER
CAME TO BLOWS
CAME TO GRIEF
CAME TO LIGHT
CARD OF ENTRY
CASE IN POINT
CLUB TO DEATH
COAT OF PAINT
COME TO BLOWS
COME TO GRIEF
COME TO LIGHT

CORN IN EGYPT
COUP DE GRACE
CUTS UP ROUGH
DATE OF BIRTH
DAYS OF GRACE
DEAD OF NIGHT
DECK OF CARDS
DOES TO DEATH
DONE TO DEATH
DOWN TO EARTH
EAST BY NORTH
ENDS IN TEARS
FLAG OF TRUCE
FULL OF BEANS
GAME OF SKILL
GENS DU MONDE
GETS TO GRIPS
GETS TO SLEEP
GETS UP STEAM
GOES IT ALONE
GOES TO COURT
GOES TO EARTH
GOES TO PRESS
GOES TO SLEEP
GOES TO WASTE
GONE TO EARTH
GONE TO GRASS
GONE TO LUNCH
GONE TO SLEEP
GONE TO WASTE
HAND ME DOWNS
HAND OF GLORY
HAND ON HEART
HAND TO MOUTH
HANG IN THERE
HARD AS NAILS
HELD IN CHECK
HELL ON EARTH
HOLD IN CHECK
HUNG IN THERE
INNS OF COURT
ISLE OF WIGHT
JOIE DE VIVRE
KEEP IN CHECK
KEEP IN TOUCH
KEPT IN CHECK
KEPT IN TOUCH
KING OF BIRDS
KING OF KINGS
KISS ME QUICK
KISS OF DEATH
LICK OF PAINT
LIES IN STATE
LIFE IS SWEET
LINE OF SIGHT
LOAF OF BREAD
LOVE IS BLIND
MADE TO ORDER
MAKE OR BREAK
MARK MY WORDS

4,2,5 *contd.*
MISE EN SCENE
MOVE TO TEARS
OEIL DE BOEUF
ONCE OR TWICE
PACK OF CARDS
PAIR OF BOOTS
PAIR OF SHOES
PAIR OF SOCKS
PAIR OF STAYS
PAIR OF STEPS
PEAL OF BELLS
PICK UP SPEED
PICK UP TRUCK
PINT OF LAGER
PIPE OF PEACE
PLAY ON WORDS
PORT OF ENTRY
POTS OF MONEY
PUSS IN BOOTS
PUTS ON TRIAL
PUTS TO DEATH
PUTS TO SHAME
PUTS TO SLEEP
REST IN PEACE
RULE OF FAITH
RULE OF THREE
RULE OF THUMB
RUNS TO EARTH
SANG DE BOEUF
SETS IN ORDER
SETS TO MUSIC
SETS UP HOUSE
SHOW OF HANDS
SICK TO DEATH
SIDE OF BACON
STAR OF DAVID
STEM TO STERN
TAKE BY STORM
TAKE ON BOARD
TAKE ON TRUST
TAKE TO COURT
TAKE TO HEART
TERM OF YEARS
TOOK BY STORM
TOOK ON BOARD
TOOK TO COURT
TOOK TO HEART
TOUR DE FORCE
TOUT DE SUITE
TOUT LE MONDE
TURN OF SPEED
WAIT AT TABLE
WARD OF COURT
WARM AS TOAST
WENT TO COURT
WENT TO EARTH
WENT TO PRESS
WENT TO SLEEP
WENT TO WASTE

WEST BY NORTH
WORD OF MOUTH

4,3,2,2
HARD PUT TO IT
SNAP OUT OF IT
WANT JAM ON IT

4,3,4
ACTS THE FOOL
ACTS THE GOAT
BALL AND CLAW
BANG THE DRUM
BEAT THE BAND
BEAT THE DRUM
BITE THE DUST
BITS AND BOBS
BLEW THE GAFF
BLOW THE GAFF
BODY AND SOUL
BOOM AND BUST
CALL THE TUNE
CAME AND WENT
CLAW AND BALL
COAL TAR SOAP
COCK AND BULL
CUTS AND RUNS
DEAF AND DUMB
DIPS THE FLAG
DISH THE DIRT
DOWN THE LINE
DOWN THE WIND
DRAW THE LINE
DREW THE LINE
EVER AND ANON
FILL THE BILL
FIND THE LADY
FISH EYE LENS
FIVE DAY WEEK
FLEW THE FLAG
FLIP TOP PACK
FOOT THE BILL
FOUR ACT PLAY
FREE AND EASY
FROM WAY BACK
GETS THE BIRD
GETS THE BOOT
GETS THE CHOP
GETS THE PUSH
GETS THE SACK
GILD THE LILY
GILD THE PILL
GIVE AND TAKE
GOES FOR GOLD
HALF AND HALF
HALF THE TIME
HAND AND FOOT
HARD AND FAST
HAVE YOU DONE
HELD THE FORT
HELD THE LINE

HELD THE ROAD
HIDE AND SEEK
HIGH OLD TIME
HITS THE DECK
HITS THE ROAD
HITS THE ROOF
HITS THE SACK
HOLD THE FORT
HOLD THE LINE
HOLD THE ROAD
HOME AND AWAY
HOPS THE TWIG
HOVE THE LEAD
JACK AND JILL
JOIN THE CLUB
KISS AND TELL
KISS THE BOOK
LEFT FOR DEAD
LEFT ONE COLD
LEFT THE ROOM
LIKE FOR LIKE
LIKE THE WIND
LOOP THE LOOP
MADE THE PACE
MAKE THE PACE
MEEK AND MILD
MISS THE BOAT
MISS THE MARK
MISS THE POST
MOPS AND MOWS
MORE AND MORE
MUMS THE WORD
MUTT AND JEFF
NEAR THE BONE
NECK AND NECK
NICE AND EASY
NONE THE LESS
NULL AND VOID
ODDS AND ENDS
OPEN THE DOOR
OVER AND OVER
OVER THE HILL
OVER THE HUMP
OVER THE MOON
OVER THE ODDS
PADS THE HOOF
PARK AND RIDE
PASS THE BUCK
PASS THE TIME
PLAY FOR TIME
PLAY THE FOOL
PLAY THE GAME
PLAY THE LEAD
PONY AND TRAP
POST AND PAIR
POTS AND PANS
PRAY FOR RAIN
PROS AND CONS
PUTS THE SHOT
RACK AND RUIN

RANG THE BELL
RANK AND FILE
RANT AND RAVE
RING THE BELL
ROCK AND ROLL
ROCK THE BOAT
ROLL TOP DESK
RUNS THE SHOW
SETS THE PACE
SHIP THE OARS
SHOW THE FLAG
SKIN AND BONE
SLOW BUT SURE
SOWS THE SEED
SPOT THE BALL
STAY THE PACE
STEM THE TIDE
STOP THE SHOW
SUCH AND SUCH
TAKE POT LUCK
TAKE THE BAIT
TAKE THE CAKE
TAKE THE LEAD
TAKE THE MICK
TAKE THE VEIL
TALK YOU DOWN
THIN RED LINE
THIS AND THAT
TIED THE KNOT
TIES THE KNOT
TIPS THE WINK
TOED THE LINE
TOES THE LINE
TOOK POT LUCK
TOOK THE BAIT
TOOK THE CAKE
TOOK THE LEAD
TOOK THE MICK
TOOK THE VEIL
TOPS THE BILL
TOWN AND GOWN
TURN THE TIDE
WARP AND WEFT
WASH AND WEAR
WEAR AND TEAR
WELL AND GOOD
WENT FOR GOLD
WHAT THE HELL
WINE AND DINE
WORD FOR WORD

4,4,3
BITE ONES LIP
BLEW ONES TOP
BLOW ONES TOP
BLUE EYED BOY
DOES ONES BIT
FELT FELT PEN
FLIP ONES LID
FULL TIME JOB

4,4,3 *contd.*
GETS ONES WAY
GOES ONES WAY
HAVE ONES WAY
HELD ONES OWN
HIGH WIRE ACT
HOLD ONES OWN
HOME MADE JAM
LOSE ONES RAG
LOSE ONES WAY
LOST ONES RAG
LOST ONES WAY
MADE ONES DAY
MADE ONES WAY
MAKE ONES DAY
MAKE ONES WAY
MORE FOOL YOU
PAID ONES WAY
PART TIME JOB
PAYS ONES WAY
PICK ONES WAY
PICK YOUR OWN
PLAY ONES ACE
RING PULL CAN
SELF MADE MAN
SHOW ONES AGE
STUB ONES TOE
TAKE HOME PAY
TAKE ONES CUE
TAKE TIME OFF
TICK TACK MAN
TIPS ONES HAT
TOOK ONES CUE
TOOK TIME OFF
WEND ONES WAY
WENT ONES WAY
WHAT AILS HER
WHAT AILS HIM
WHAT AILS YOU
WHAT HAVE YOU
WHEN PIGS FLY
WING ONES WAY

4,5,2
HIGH TAILS IT
LAID HANDS ON
LAYS HANDS ON
MADE LIGHT OF
MAKE LIGHT OF
POUR SCORN ON
SETS LIGHT TO
SHED LIGHT ON
WITH KNOBS ON

4,7
AIDE MEMOIRE
ALTO RELIEVO
ALTO RILIEVO
ANTI FEDERAL
ANTI HEROINE
ANTI JACOBIN

ANTI SEMITIC
ANTI VITAMIN
ARCH PRELATE
ARCH VILLAIN
ARTS COUNCIL
ARTS STUDENT
ATOM SMASHER
AVEC PLAISIR
BABY BOUNCER
BABY SITTING
BACK BENCHER
BACK BENCHES
BACK BLOCKER
BACK COMBING
BACK COUNTRY
BACK DRAUGHT
BACK HEELING
BACK STREETS
BALL BEARING
BANK ACCOUNT
BANK BALANCE
BANK HOLIDAY
BANK MANAGER
BARE KNUCKLE
BARN STORMER
BATH MITZVAH
BEAM TRAWLER
BEAR BAITING
BEAR WITNESS
BEEF BRAINED
BEER PARLOUR
BEER SHAMPOO
BELL FOUNDER
BELL FOUNDRY
BELL HOUSING
BELL RINGING
BETA BLOCKER
BIAS BINDING
BIAS DRAWING
BIEN ENTENDU
BILL CHAMBER
BIRD BRAINED
BIRD CATCHER
BIRD FANCIER
BIRD WATCHER
BLUE POINTER
BLUE WHITING
BOAT BUILDER
BODY BUILDER
BODY POLITIC
BODY POPPING
BOLT UPRIGHT
BOND SERVICE
BOOK ACCOUNT
BOOK LEARNED
BOOK THROUGH
BOOT TOPPING
BOYS BRIGADE
BUCK PASSING
BUFF LEATHER

BULK CARRIER
BULL BAITING
BULL MASTIFF
BULL TERRIER
BUMP STARTED
BUTT WELDING
CAFE SOCIETY
CAME BETWEEN
CAME FORWARD
CAME UNSTUCK
CAMP MEETING
CAPE SPARROW
CARD SHARPER
CASE HISTORY
CASH ACCOUNT
CASH MACHINE
CASH PAYMENT
CASH RAILWAY
CATS WHISKER
CAVE DWELLER
CAVO RILIEVO
CHEF DOEUVRE
CHIP CARVING
CINE BIOLOGY
CITY COMPANY
CITY FATHERS
CITY MISSION
CITY SLICKER
CLAM CHOWDER
CLOG DANCING
CLUB STEWARD
COAL SCUTTLE
COAL WHIPPER
COCK SPARROW
CODE BREAKER
COLD BLOODED
COLD CALLING
COLD CASTING
COLD COMFORT
COLD FORGING
COLD HARBOUR
COLD HEARTED
COLD STORAGE
COLD WELDING
COME BETWEEN
COME FORWARD
COME UNSTUCK
COME UPPANCE
CONY CATCHER
COOK GENERAL
CORN PLASTER
CORS ANGLAIS
CROP SPRAYER
CUTS CORNERS
DAIL EIREANN
DARE DEVILRY
DARK GLASSES
DAWN CYPRESS
DEAD HEADING
DECK OFFICER

DECK PASSAGE
DENY ONESELF
DICE PLAYING
DIRE STRAITS
DISC PARKING
DIVE BOMBING
DOCK WARRANT
DOGS MERCURY
DOOR KNOCKER
DOWN DRAUGHT
DOWN HEARTED
DOWN PAYMENT
DOWN TRODDEN
DRAM DRINKER
DROP FORGING
DUAL CONTROL
DUAL PURPOSE
DULL BRAINED
DUTY OFFICER
DAIL EIREANN
EARL MARSHAL
ECHO CHAMBER
ECHO SOUNDER
ETON COLLEGE
EURO DOLLARS
EURO SCEPTIC
EVIL STARRED
FACE FLANNEL
FACE LIFTING
FACT FINDING
FAIR DEALING
FAIR WEATHER
FALL THROUGH
FARM OFFICES
FAST BOWLING
FAST FORWARD
FAST NEUTRON
FAST REACTOR
FATA MORGANA
FELL THROUGH
FELL WALKING
FETE GALANTE
FILM ACTRESS
FINE WRITING
FIRE BLANKET
FIRE BOMBING
FIRE BRIGADE
FIRE CONTROL
FIRE CRACKER
FIRE CURTAIN
FIRE FIGHTER
FIRE MARSHAL
FIRE OFFICER
FIRE RAISING
FIRE STATION
FIRE WALKING
FIRE WATCHER
FIRE WORSHIP
FISH BELLIED
FISH FARMING

4,7 _contd._
FISH FINGERS
FISH GUTTING
FISH PACKING
FISH TORPEDO
FIVE EIGHTHS
FLAG CAPTAIN
FLAG OFFICER
FLAG WAGGING
FLAP MOUTHED
FLAT EARTHER
FLAX DRESSER
FLUX DENSITY
FOLK DANCING
FOLK SINGING
FOOT FAULTED
FOOT SLOGGER
FOOT SOLDIER
FORE RECITED
FORM TEACHER
FORT WILLIAM
FOUL MOUTHED
FOUR FLUSHER
FOUR POUNDER
FOUR WHEELED
FOUR WHEELER
FREE COUNTRY
FREE FALLING
FREE HEARTED
FREE PARKING
FREE RADICAL
FREE SKATING
FREE THOUGHT
FREE WHEELED
FROG MARCHED
FROG MARCHES
FROM SCRATCH
FULL BLOODED
FULL BROTHER
FULL CHARGED
FULL FRONTAL
FULL HEARTED
FULL MOUTHED
FUME CHAMBER
FUND RAISING
GAFF TOPSAIL
GAIN CONTROL
GALL BLADDER
GAME FISHING
GAME LICENCE
GANG WARFARE
GAVE OFFENCE
GENS DEGLISE
GERM WARFARE
GETS DRESSED
GETS HITCHED
GETS THROUGH
GIFT VOUCHER
GIFT WRAPPED
GILA MONSTER

GIRD ONESELF
GIVE OFFENCE
GLAD TIDINGS
GLEE SINGERS
GLUE SNIFFER
GOAL TENDING
GODS COUNTRY
GOES AGAINST
GOES FORWARD
GOES MISSING
GOES THROUGH
GOES WITHOUT
GOLD BEATING
GOLD BULLION
GOLD CRESTED
GOLD DIGGING
GOLD RESERVE
GONE FISHING
GONE GOSLING
GONE MISSING
GONE THROUGH
GOOD COMPANY
GOOD EVENING
GOOD FORTUNE
GOOD HEAVENS
GOOD HUNTING
GOOD LOOKING
GOOD MORNING
GOOD NATURED
GOOD OFFICES
GRAN TURISMO
HAIR BRAINED
HAIR RAISING
HAIR TRIGGER
HALF BROTHER
HALF HEARTED
HALF HOLIDAY
HALF MEASURE
HALF POUNDER
HALF STARVED
HALL BEDROOM
HAND FEEDING
HAND GRENADE
HAND KNITTED
HAND SIGNALS
HANG GLIDING
HARD DRINKER
HARD GRAINED
HARD HEARTED
HARD HITTING
HARD PRESSED
HARD WEARING
HARE BRAINED
HARE KRISHNA
HAVE KITTENS
HEAD BANGING
HEAD TEACHER
HEAT BARRIER
HELP ONESELF
HERB TRINITY

HERO WORSHIP
HIGH ADMIRAL
HIGH BAILIFF
HIGH COMMAND
HIGH DENSITY
HIGH FALUTIN
HIGH FINANCE
HIGH HEARTED
HIGH PITCHED
HIGH POWERED
HIGH PROFILE
HIGH RANKING
HIGH ROLLING
HIGH SHERIFF
HIGH SIGHTED
HIGH SOCIETY
HIGH SPIRITS
HIGH STEPPER
HIGH TENSION
HIGH TREASON
HIGH VOLTAGE
HILL PASTURE
HILL STATION
HOME CIRCUIT
HOME COOKING
HOME CROFTER
HOME DEFENCE
HOME KEEPING
HOME STRETCH
HOMO ERECTUS
HOMO HABILIS
HOMO SAPIENS
HORN MADNESS
HORN MERCURY
HORS DOEUVRE
HUGS ONESELF
HUSH PUPPIES
INDO CHINESE
IRON CURTAIN
IRON FILINGS
IRON FOUNDER
IRON FOUNDRY
IRON HEARTED
IRON PYRITES
JACK KNIFING
JACK RUSSELL
JOHN COLLINS
JUMP STARTED
JURY PROCESS
JURY SERVICE
JUST DESERTS
JUST MARRIED
KEEP COUNSEL
KEEP SMILING
KEPT COUNSEL
KERB CRAWLER
KICK ONESELF
KIDS ONESELF
KIND HEARTED
KIND NATURED

KIND REGARDS
KING CHARLES
KING PENGUIN
KING RICHARD
KING STEPHEN
KING WILLIAM
KIRK SESSION
KITE BALLOON
KNEE CAPPING
KNEE TRIBUTE
KNOW NOTHING
KNOW THYSELF
LADY PROVOST
LAKE DWELLER
LAKE ONTARIO
LAND GRABBER
LAND JOBBING
LAND MEASURE
LAND STEWARD
LAST HONOURS
LAST OFFICES
LEAF CUTTING
LESE MAJESTY
LICK PLATTER
LICK SPITTLE
LIFE ANNUITY
LIFE HISTORY
LIFE PEERAGE
LIFE PEERESS
LIFE SAVINGS
LILY LIVERED
LINE DRAWING
LINE FISHING
LINE PRINTER
LINE SHOOTER
LION HEARTED
LIVE CIRCUIT
LIVE CONCERT
LOAD BEARING
LOAN SOCIETY
LONG CLOTHES
LONG HUNDRED
LONG MEASURE
LONG PLAYING
LONG SIGHTED
LONG WAISTED
LOOK ASKANCE
LOOK DAGGERS
LOOK FORWARD
LORD PROVOST
LOSE CONTROL
LOSE ONESELF
LOST CONTROL
LOST HORIZON
LOST ONESELF
LOUD MOUTHED
LOVE LETTERS
MADE BELIEVE
MADE CERTAIN
MADE CHANGES

4,7 *contd.*
MADE FRIENDS
MADE HISTORY
MADE INROADS
MADE WHOOPEE
MAID SERVANT
MAIL CARRIER
MAIL CATCHER
MAKE BELIEVE
MAKE CERTAIN
MAKE CHANGES
MAKE FRIENDS
MAKE HISTORY
MAKE INROADS
MAKE WHOOPEE
MALT EXTRACT
MALT VINEGAR
MANY TONGUED
MASS MEETING
MASS PRODUCE
MEET HALFWAY
MILK PUDDING
MIND BENDING
MIND BLOWING
MIND HEALING
MIND READING
MINE SWEEPER
MINE THROWER
MOCK MODESTY
MOLE DRAINER
MOON GODDESS
MOON MADNESS
MOSS TROOPER
MUCH OBLIGED
NAIL VARNISH
NAME CALLING
NAME DROPPER
NEAR SIGHTED
NODS THROUGH
NOSE NIPPERS
NUEE ARDENTE
NUNS VEILING
OPEN CIRCUIT
OPEN HARMONY
OPEN HEARTED
OPEN MOUTHED
OPEN VERDICT
ORAL HISTORY
PACE BOWLING
PAIN BARRIER
PAIR BONDING
PALM CABBAGE
PARK OFFICER
PART COMPANY
PART PAYMENT
PART SINGING
PART WRITING
PASS CURRENT
PASS THROUGH
PEAK VIEWING

PEAT CASTING
PEEP THROUGH
PIGS WHISPER
PILE DRIVING
PIPE CLEANER
PIPE DREAMER
PIPE FITTING
PIPE LIGHTER
PIPE STOPPLE
PIPE TOBACCO
PLAY ACTRESS
PLAY FOOTSIE
PLEA BARGAIN
PLUM BLOSSOM
PLUM PUDDING
POLE VAULTER
PONT LEVEQUE
PONY EXPRESS
POOR LOOKOUT
PORK BUTCHER
PORT ADMIRAL
PORT CHARGES
POST CAPTAIN
POST GLACIAL
POST NUPTIAL
POST VILLAGE
PROP FORWARD
PULL STRINGS
PULL THROUGH
PUMP PRIMING
PUNT FISHING
PURE BLOODED
PURE CULTURE
PURE SCIENCE
PUSH BICYCLE
PUSH STARTED
PUSH THROUGH
PUTS FORWARD
PUTS THROUGH
RACE MEETING
RACE WALKING
RACK RAILWAY
RAIN CHAMBER
RATE CAPPING
RATE CUTTING
REAR ADMIRAL
REED BUNTING
REED DRAWING
REED SPARROW
REED WARBLER
REEF BUILDER
REST ASSURED
RICE BISCUIT
RICE PUDDING
RING CIRCUIT
RING STOPPER
RISK CAPITAL
ROAD HAULAGE
ROAD MANAGER
ROAD MENDING

ROAD SWEEPER
ROAD TESTING
ROAD TRAFFIC
ROCK CLIMBER
ROCK CRYSTAL
ROCK FORMING
ROCK SPARROW
ROLE PLAYING
ROMP THROUGH
ROOM DIVIDER
ROOM SERVICE
ROOT CLIMBER
ROOT PRUNING
ROSE CAMPION
ROSY CHEEKED
RUBY WEDDING
RUNS ERRANDS
RUNS THROUGH
RUSH BEARING
SAFE BLOWING
SAFE BREAKER
SAFE CONDUCT
SAFE CRACKER
SAFE DEPOSIT
SAFE KEEPING
SALK VACCINE
SALT GLAZING
SAND SKIPPER
SEAL FISHING
SEAL ROOKERY
SEAM BOWLING
SEAM WELDING
SELF ASSUMED
SELF ASSURED
SELF CENTRED
SELF CONCEIT
SELF CONCERN
SELF CONTROL
SELF CREATED
SELF DEFENCE
SELF DESPAIR
SELF DEVOTED
SELF EVIDENT
SELF EXAMPLE
SELF HEALING
SELF IMPOSED
SELF INDUCED
SELF LOADING
SELF LOCKING
SELF NEGLECT
SELF RAISING
SELF RELIANT
SELF RESPECT
SELF SEEKING
SELF SERVICE
SELF SERVING
SELF STARTER
SELF SUPPORT
SELF TORTURE
SELF TRAINED

SELF WORSHIP
SEMI DIURNAL
SEMI ELLIPSE
SEMI MONTHLY
SEMI SKILLED
SEND PACKING
SENT PACKING
SHAM ABRAHAM
SHIP BISCUIT
SHIP CAPTAIN
SHIP RAILWAY
SHOE LEATHER
SHOP LIFTING
SHOP STEWARD
SHOT PUTTING
SHOW PROMISE
SHOW STOPPER
SHOW WILLING
SICK BENEFIT
SIDE EFFECTS
SIDE TRACKED
SIGN PAINTER
SIGN WRITING
SILK THROWER
SINN FEINISM
SKYE TERRIER
SLOT MACHINE
SLOW RELEASE
SLOW SIGHTED
SLUM DWELLER
SNOW GOGGLES
SNOW LEOPARD
SOAP BOILING
SOFT CENTRED
SOFT HEARTED
SOFT SHELLED
SOFT SOAPING
SOIL SCIENCE
SONG SPARROW
SOUL BROTHER
SOUP KITCHEN
SPIN BOWLING
SPOT WELDING
SPUD BASHING
SPUR GEARING
SPUR LEATHER
STAR BILLING
STAR CHAMBER
STAR CROSSED
STAR QUALITY
STAR STUDDED
STAR THISTLE
STEP DANCING
STUN GRENADE
SUET PUDDING
SUIT ONESELF
SURF BATHING
TAIL FEATHER
TAKE COMMAND
TAKE OFFENCE

4,7 *contd.*

TAKE UMBRAGE	WELL MEANING	COCKS A SNOOK	FACTS OF LIFE
TAPE MACHINE	WELL ORDERED	DRAWS A BLANK	FALLS IN LOVE
TAPE RECORDS	WELL ROUNDED	DROPS A BRICK	FEAST OF LOTS
TEAR JERKING	WELL SINKING	MAKES A POINT	FEELS AT HOME
TEAR STAINED	WELL THUMBED	MAKES A STAND	FIELD OF VIEW
TENT PEGGING	WELL TRODDEN	PACKS A PUNCH	FLEET OF CARS
TEST CRICKET	WELL WISHING	PENNY A LINER	FLEET OF FOOT
THAT FIGURES	WENT AGAINST	PICKS A FIGHT	FRAME OF MIND
THIN SKINNED	WENT FORWARD	PIEDS A TERRE	GLASS OF BEER
THIS INSTANT	WENT MISSING	QUITE A CATCH	GLASS OF MILK
TIED COTTAGE	WENT THROUGH	RAISE A SIEGE	GLASS OF WINE
TIME CAPSULE	WENT WITHOUT	RAISE A STINK	GOING TO SEED
TIME DEPOSIT	WEST COUNTRY	ROMAN A THESE	GOING TO TOWN
TIME KEEPING	WIDE RANGING	SCENE A FAIRE	GRAIN OF SAND
TIME KILLING	WILD ANIMALS	SPEND A PENNY	GRANT OF ARMS
TIME MACHINE	WILD FLOWERS	SPENT A PENNY	HOUSE OF KEYS
TIME SERVING	WILD FOWLING	STAKE A CLAIM	KEEPS IN MIND
TIME SHARING	WILD MUSTARD	TAKES A BRIEF	KEEPS IT DARK
TONE CONTROL	WIND FURNACE	TAKES A CLASS	KNOCK ON WOOD
TONE PICTURE	WIND MACHINE	TAKES A DEKKO	LYING IN WAIT
TOOK COMMAND	WIND SURFING	THREW A PARTY	MONEY TO BURN
TOOK OFFENCE	WINE BIBBING	THREW A PUNCH	PEACE OF MIND
TOOK UMBRAGE	WINE GROWING	THROW A PARTY	PIECE OF CAKE
TOWN COUNCIL	WINE HARVEST	THROW A PUNCH	PIECE OF LUCK
TOWN DWELLER	WINE TASTING	UNDER A CLOUD	PIECE OF WORK
TREE BICYCLE	WING FORWARD		PINCH OF SALT
TREE CREEPER	WING WALKING	**5,2,1,3**	PLACE OF WORK
TREE SURGEON	WINS THROUGH	BLIND AS A BAT	PLAYS IT COOL
TREE SURGERY	WIRE DANCING	CALLS IT A DAY	POINT OF SALE
TREE WORSHIP	WIRE NETTING	SWEET AS A NUT	POINT OF VIEW
TRUE HEARTED	WIRE PULLING		REACH ME DOWN
TRUE SEEMING	WIRE WALKING	**5,2,2,2**	READY TO WEAR
TUBE STATION	WIRE WHEELED	FACED UP TO IT	RIGHT AS RAIN
TURN AGAINST	WOLF WHISTLE	FACES UP TO IT	RIGHT OF WAYS
TWIN BROTHER	WOOD ANEMONE		ROUGE ET NOIR
TWOS COMPANY	WOOD CARVING	**5,2,4**	ROUND OF GOLF
TYPE FOUNDER	WOOD CUTTING	AHEAD OF TIME	SANDS OF TIME
TYPE FOUNDRY	WOOD SWALLOW	AIDES DE CAMP	SELLS IN BULK
UNIT PRICING	WOOD WARBLER	BARON OF BEEF	SHUTS UP SHOP
VENN DIAGRAM	WOOL CARDING	BEARS IN MIND	SIGNS OF LIFE
VICE ADMIRAL	WOOL COMBING	BEAST OF PREY	SLICE OF LIFE
VICE MARSHAL	WOOL GROWING	BELLE DE NUIT	SLICE OF LUCK
VINE DISEASE	WOOL PACKING	BLESS MY SOUL	SOUTH BY EAST
VINE DRESSER	WOOL STAPLER	BORNE IN MIND	SOUTH BY WEST
VOIX CELESTE	WORD PAINTER	BRING TO BEAR	SPEAK NO EVIL
WAGE EARNING	WORD PERFECT	BRING TO BOOK	SPECK OF DUST
WARM BLOODED	WORD PICTURE	BRING TO HEEL	STAFF OF LIFE
WARM HEARTED	WORD PUZZLER	BRING TO LIFE	STAND AT EASE
WASP TONGUED	WORK AGAINST	CALLS TO MIND	STAND TO GAIN
WASP WAISTED	WORK STATION	CARTE DU JOUR	STAND TO LOSE
WEAK HEARTED	WORM GEARING	CHEEK BY JOWL	STATE OF FLUX
WEAK SIGHTED	YOUR FUNERAL	CLOSE AT HAND	STATE OF PLAY
WELL BEHAVED	YOUR MAJESTY	CLOTH OF GOLD	STICK OF ROCK
WELL BELOVED	YOUR WORSHIP	CLOUD OF DUST	STOOD TO GAIN
WELL DEFINED		COMES TO LIFE	STOOD TO LOSE
WELL DRESSED	**5,1,5**	COMES TO PASS	SUGAR OF LEAD
WELL ENTERED	BLAZE A TRAIL	COMES TO REST	SWARM OF BEES
WELL FOUNDED	CASTS A SPELL	COMME IL FAUT	SYRUP OF FIGS
WELL GROOMED	CHICK A BIDDY	CRACK OF DAWN	TAKEN AS READ
	CHOCK A BLOCK	CRACK OF DOOM	TAKEN IN HAND
		CROCK OF GOLD	

5,2,4 *contd.*
TAKEN IN VAIN
TAKEN TO TASK
TAKES AN OATH
TAKES AS READ
TAKES IN HAND
TAKES IN VAIN
TAKES IT EASY
TAKES TO TASK
TAKES UP ARMS
TALKS IT OVER
TEAMS UP WITH
TOUCH IN GOAL
TRIAL BY JURY
TRUTH TO TELL
VENUS DE MILO
VICAR OF BRAY
WALKS TO HEEL
WHEEL OF LIFE
WORKS TO RULE

5,3,3
BEATS THE AIR
BEATS THE GUN
BELLS THE CAT
BILLY THE KID
BLACK AND TAN
BRACE AND BIT
BREAK THE ICE
BROKE THE ICE
BULLY FOR HER
BULLY FOR HIM
BULLY FOR YOU
CAKES AND ALE
CARRY THE CAN
CARRY THE DAY
CARRY TOO FAR
CATCH THE SUN
CATCH THE TEN
CHEWS THE CUD
CHEWS THE FAT
CLEAR THE AIR
CLEAR THE WAY
CLOSE THE GAP
COSTA DEL SOL
DIRTY OLD MAN
FELIX THE CAT
FLEET AIR ARM
GOING TOO FAR
GRAND OLD MAN
JUMPS FOR JOY
JUMPS THE GUN
KNOCK FOR SIX
LEADS THE WAY
MONEY FOR JAM
NEVER SAY DIE
PAVED THE WAY
PAVES THE WAY
SHOWN THE WAY
SHOWS THE WAY

SILLY MID OFF
SILLY OLD MOO
SLING THE BAT
STOPS THE ROT
TABLE FOR TWO
TAKES THE AIR
TAKES THE RAP
TAKES THE SUN
THERE YOU ARE
TURBO RAM JET
UNDER THE SUN
WALKS THE DOG
WARTS AND ALL
WHIPS THE CAT
WIDEN THE GAP
WORLD WAR ONE
WORLD WAR TWO

5,4,2
ABIDE WITH ME
FOOLS RUSH IN
KEEPS TABS ON
MAKES EYES AT
SUNNY SIDE UP
THATS DONE IT
THATS TORN IT
WORDS FAIL ME

5,6
ABOVE GROUND
ACUTE ACCENT
ADDLE HEADED
AFTER DINNER
AFTER EFFECT
AGENT ORANGE
AGONY COLUMN
ALBUM SLEEVE
AMOUR PROPRE
ANGLO FRENCH
ANGLO INDIAN
ANGLO NORMAN
ANGST RIDDEN
APPLE BLIGHT
APRON STRING
ARGIE BARGIE
ARMED COMBAT
ARMED ESCORT
ARMED FORCES
ARROW HEADED
ARROW POISON
ASSAY MASTER
ASSAY OFFICE
ASSES BRIDGE
AUDIO VISUAL
BAKED ALASKA
BANDY LEGGED
BARGE COUPLE
BARGE STONES
BARON BAILIE
BASHI BAZOUK
BATON CHARGE

BATON ROUNDS
BEACH MASTER
BEACH RESCUE
BEARS BREECH
BEECH MARTEN
BELLY BUTTON
BELLY DANCER
BELOW STAIRS
BETTY MARTIN
BILLY BUNTER
BLACK BEAUTY
BLACK BEETLE
BLACK BOTTOM
BLACK BROWED
BLACK BRYONY
BLACK CATTLE
BLACK COATED
BLACK COFFEE
BLACK COMEDY
BLACK FISHER
BLACK FOREST
BLACK FRIARS
BLACK FRIDAY
BLACK HUMOUR
BLACK LETTER
BLACK MARKET
BLACK MONDAY
BLACK VELVET
BLANK CHEQUE
BLANK WINDOW
BLIND STOREY
BLOCK LETTER
BLOCK SYSTEM
BLOOD FLOWER
BLOOD ORANGE
BLOOD SPORTS
BLOOD STREAM
BLOOD VESSEL
BLUNT WITTED
BOARD SCHOOL
BONNE CHANCE
BOSOM FRIEND
BOTHY BALLAD
BOXER SHORTS
BRAIN DAMAGE
BRAIN TEASER
BRAKE LINING
BRAND LEADER
BRASS RUBBER
BREAD BASKET
BREAK GROUND
BROAD CHURCH
BROAD LEAVED
BROAD MINDED
BROKE GROUND
BRUSH TURKEY
BUNNY RABBIT
BURNT SIENNA
CABLE LENGTH
CABLE STITCH

CAMEL BACKED
CANDY STRIPE
CAPER SPURGE
CAREY STREET
CARRY WEIGHT
CASTS ANCHOR
CATCH PHRASE
CHAFF CUTTER
CHAIN ARMOUR
CHAIN BRIDGE
CHAIN DRIVEN
CHAIN LETTER
CHAIN PLATES
CHAIN SMOKER
CHAOS THEORY
CHARM SCHOOL
CHART BUSTER
CHEAP LABOUR
CHECK ACTION
CHECK STRING
CHEER LEADER
CHESS PLAYER
CHIEF BARKER
CHILL FACTOR
CHOIR MASTER
CHOIR SCHOOL
CHOIR SCREEN
CHOIR STALLS
CHOUX PASTRY
CIGAR SHAPED
CIVIC CENTRE
CIVIL RIGHTS
CIVVY STREET
CLASS ACTION
CLASS FELLOW
CLASS LEADER
CLEAN BOWLED
CLEAN LIMBED
CLEAN LIVING
CLEAN SHAVEN
CLEAR HEADED
CLEFT PALATE
CLICK BEETLE
CLIFF HANGER
CLOSE FINISH
CLOSE FISTED
CLOSE LIPPED
CLOSE SEASON
CLOSE SECOND
CLOSE TENNIS
COACH OFFICE
COCOA BUTTER
COMES ACROSS
COMES ASHORE
COMES UNDONE
COMET FINDER
COMIC RELIEF
CORAL ISLAND
CORPS DELITE
COSTA BLANCA

5,6 *contd.*

COUCH POTATO	DUSTY MILLER	GABLE WINDOW	HAPPY ENDING
COURT TENNIS	DUTCH CHEESE	GAINS GROUND	HAPPY MEDIUM
COVER CHARGE	DYERS ROCKET	GALAM BUTTER	HARDY ANNUAL
CRACK TROOPS	EAGER BEAVER	GAMES MASTER	HARTS TONGUE
CRANE NECKED	EARTH MOTHER	GAMES THEORY	HARUM SCARUM
CRASH COURSE	EARTH TREMOR	GARAM MASALA	HASTA MANANA
CRASH HELMET	EIGHT OCLOCK	GAUZE WINGED	HEARD THINGS
CRAZY PAVING	ELBOW GREASE	GHOST WRITER	HEARS THINGS
CREAM CHEESE	EMERY POWDER	GIANT FENNEL	HEART ATTACK
CREME BRULEE	EMPTY HANDED	GIANT KILLER	HEART EASING
CREPE RUBBER	EMPTY HEADED	GIDDY HEADED	HEART MURMUR
CROSS LEGGED	EPOCH MAKING	GIVES GROUND	HEART SHAPED
CROSS REFERS	EQUAL RIGHTS	GIVES NOTICE	HEART STRING
CROSS STITCH	FAITH HEALER	GLASS BLOWER	HEAVY HANDED
CROSS SWORDS	FALLS BEHIND	GLASS CUTTER	HEAVY HEADED
CROWD PULLER	FALSE ACACIA	GLASS GAZING	HEAVY SMOKER
CROWN ANTLER	FALSE BOTTOM	GLOVE PUPPET	HEDGE HOPPED
CROWN COLONY	FALSI CRIMEN	GLOVE SHIELD	HEDGE HOPPER
CROWN COURTS	FANCY STITCH	GOING ABROAD	HEDGE PARSON
CROWN JEWELS	FARES PLEASE	GOING HALVES	HEDGE SCHOOL
CROWN LAWYER	FAULT FINDER	GOING HUNGRY	HELLO SAILOR
CROWN LIVING	FEMME FATALE	GOING METRIC	HELVE HAMMER
CROWN OCTAVO	FIBRE OPTICS	GOING NATIVE	HITCH HIKING
CROWN OFFICE	FIELD MADDER	GOING PLACES	HONEY BADGER
CROWN PRINCE	FIELD SPORTS	GOING STEADY	HONEY LOCUST
CUPRO NICKEL	FIFTH AVENUE	GOING STRONG	HONEY SUCKLE
CURLY GREENS	FIFTH COLUMN	GOLGI BODIES	HORSE AROUND
CURLY HEADED	FILET MIGNON	GOODS ENGINE	HORSE COLLAR
CURRY FAVOUR	FINAL DEMAND	GOOSE FLOWER	HORSE DEALER
CURRY POWDER	FINES HERBES	GOOSE WINGED	HORSE DOCTOR
DAIRY CATTLE	FINNO UGRIAN	GRADE SCHOOL	HORSE DRENCH
DAISY CUTTER	FIRST COUSIN	GRAND CANYON	HORSE GUARDS
DEATH RATTLE	FIRST ELEVEN	GRAND FINALE	HORSE MARINE
DEATH THROES	FIRST FOOTER	GRAND MASTER	HORSE PISTOL
DELLA ROBBIA	FIRST FRUITS	GRAND NEPHEW	HORSE RACING
DELTA WINGED	FIRST SCHOOL	GRAND SIECLE	HORSE RIDING
DEMON BARBER	FIRST STOREY	GRASS CUTTER	HOTEL KEEPER
DEMON BOWLER	FIRST STRIKE	GRAVE ACCENT	HOUSE ARREST
DEPTH CHARGE	FIXED ASSETS	GRAVE DIGGER	HOUSE FATHER
DERBY WINNER	FIXED INCOME	GREAT CIRCLE	HOUSE HUNTER
DIANA MONKEY	FLAKY PASTRY	GREAT NEPHEW	HOUSE LIGHTS
DOGGY PADDLE	FLEET FOOTED	GREAT OCTAVE	HOUSE MARTIN
DOLLY CAMERA	FLEET PRISON	GREAT PLAGUE	HOUSE MOTHER
DOLLY SWITCH	FLEET STREET	GREAT SCHISM	HUMAN DYNAMO
DOLLY VARDEN	FLESH COLOUR	GREEK CHURCH	HUMAN NATURE
DRAFT DODGER	FLESH MARKET	GREEN BERETS	HUMAN RIGHTS
DRAMA SCHOOL	FLOCK MASTER	GREEN CHEESE	HURRY SCURRY
DRAWS STUMPS	FLOOR TIMBER	GREEN DRAGON	HYDRA HEADED
DREAM TICKET	FOOLS AROUND	GREEN KEEPER	IGNIS FATUUS
DRESS CIRCLE	FOOLS ERRAND	GREEN LINNET	INDEX FINGER
DRESS LENGTH	FORTH BRIDGE	GREEN MONKEY	INDEX LINKED
DRESS SHIELD	FRANC TIREUR	GREEN PEPPER	INDEX NUMBER
DRIFT ANCHOR	FRANK PLEDGE	GREEN PLOVER	INDIA RUBBER
DRIFT MINING	FRESH FIELDS	GREEN TURTLE	INTER PARTES
DRILL HARROW	FRONT LOADER	GROSS INCOME	IONIC SCHOOL
DRILL MASTER	FRONT RANKER	GROUP THEORY	IRISH COFFEE
DRILL PLOUGH	FRONT RUNNER	GRUFF VOICED	IRISH GUARDS
DRINK DRIVER	FROST BITTEN	GUTTA PERCHA	IRISH SETTER
DROPS ANCHOR	FROTH BLOWER	HAGIA SOPHIA	ITCHY PALMED
	FUZZY HAIRED	HANGS AROUND	JAFFA ORANGE

5,6 *contd.*
JAPAN LAUREL
JAPAN TALLOW
JELLY BABIES
JENNY DONKEY
JESSE WINDOW
JESUS CHRIST
JOINT TENANT
KEEPS WICKET
KHAKI SHORTS
KICKS AROUND
KINGS BOUNTY
KINGS SPEECH
KINGS YELLOW
KLEIN BOTTLE
KNIFE SWITCH
KNOCK AROUND
KNOCK RATING
KNOWS BETTER
KOKUM BUTTER
LADYS FINGER
LADYS MANTLE
LAMBS TONGUE
LANCE KNIGHT
LAPIS LAZULI
LARGE HANDED
LARGE MINDED
LATCH STRING
LEACH TROUGH
LEADS ASTRAY
LEAVE BEHIND
LEAVE TAKING
LEAVE UNSAID
LEGAL TENDER
LEMON BARLEY
LEMON CHEESE
LEMON SQUASH
LEMON YELLOW
LEVEL HEADED
LIBEL ACTION
LIGHT ENGINE
LIGHT FOOTED
LIGHT HANDED
LIGHT HEADED
LIGHT MINDED
LIGHT WINGED
LINEN DRAPER
LOBBY SYSTEM
LOCAL ACTION
LOCAL COLOUR
LOCAL OPTION
LOCUM TENENS
LODGE KEEPER
LOOKS AGHAST
LOOSE BODIED
LOOSE CHANGE
LOOSE LIMBED
LORDS PRAYER
LORRY DRIVER
LOSES COLOUR

LOSES GROUND
LOSES WEIGHT
LOTUS EATERS
LOUIS QUINZE
LOUIS TREIZE
LUCKY NUMBER
LUCKY STRIKE
LUING CATTLE
LUNAR THEORY
LYING FALLOW
MAGIC BULLET
MAGIC CARPET
MAGIC CIRCLE
MAGIC MARKER
MAGIC SPHERE
MAGIC SQUARE
MAKES AMENDS
MAKES TRACKS
MARSH MALLOW
MERRY ANDREW
MERRY MAKERS
MERRY MAKING
MILLE FLEURS
MINOD DETAIL
MINOR ORDERS
MINOR PLANET
MIXED NUMBER
MONEY BROKER
MONEY LENDER
MONEY MAKING
MONEY MARKET
MONEY SPIDER
MONEY SUPPLY
MORAL DEFEAT
MOSES BASKET
MOTOR DRIVEN
MOTOR LAUNCH
MOUNT ARARAT
MOUSE COLOUR
MULTI ACCESS
MUSIC CENTRE
MUSIC HOLDER
MUSIC MASTER
MUSIC SELLER
NAVEL ORANGE
NERVE CENTRE
NERVE ENDING
NEVER ENDING
NEVER FADING
NIGHT ATTIRE
NIGHT FLIGHT
NIGHT FLOWER
NIGHT FLYING
NIGHT HUNTER
NIGHT PORTER
NIGHT SCHOOL
NIGHT WAKING
NIGHT WORKER
NINNY HAMMER
NITTY GRITTY

NOBLE MINDED
NOBLE SAVAGE
NORTH EASTER
NOSEY PARKER
OBJET TROUVE
OCEAN STREAM
OLIVE BRANCH
OPERA DANCER
OPERA SINGER
OPIUM SMOKER
ORDER AROUND
ORGAN SCREEN
ORIEL WINDOW
OWNER DRIVER
PAINT BRIDGE
PAINT ROLLER
PANEL BEATER
PANEL DOCTOR
PANEL SYSTEM
PANIC ATTACK
PANIC BUYING
PANIC MONGER
PANIC STRUCK
PANTY GIRDLE
PAPAL STATES
PAPER CUTTER
PAPER FEEDER
PAPER FOLDER
PAPER HANGER
PAPER MAKING
PAPER OFFICE
PAPER WEIGHT
PARMA VIOLET
PARTI COATED
PARTY POOPER
PARTY POPPER
PARTY SPIRIT
PATCH POCKET
PEACE KEEPER
PEACE MONGER
PEACH BRANDY
PEARL BARLEY
PEARL BUTTON
PEARL DIVING
PEARL FISHER
PEARL HARBOR
PEARL MILLET
PEARL MUSSEL
PEARL OYSTER
PEARL POWDER
PEDAL ACTION
PENAL COLONY
PENAL REFORM
PENAL SYSTEM
PENNY ARCADE
PHONE NUMBER
PHOTO FINISH
PHOTO RELIEF
PIANO NOBILE
PIANO PLAYER

PIANO SCHOOL
PILOT BURNER
PILOT ENGINE
PILOT JACKET
PILOT SCHEME
PINCH HITTER
PITCH ROOFED
PIVOT BRIDGE
PLACE HUNTER
PLAIN DEALER
PLAIN SPOKEN
PLANO CONVEX
PLATE ARMOUR
PLATE BASKET
PLATE LAYING
PLATE WARMER
PLAYS AROUND
PLAYS HOOKEY
PLAYS POSSUM
PLAYS TRICKS
PLAYS TRUANT
PLEAD GUILTY
PLEIN AIRIST
POINT DAPPUI
POINT SOURCE
POLAR CIRCLE
POLAR FORCES
POLAR LIGHTS
POOLS COUPON
POUND KEEPER
POUND WEIGHT
POWER DIVING
POWER DRIVEN
PRESS BUTTON
PRESS GANGED
PRESS OFFICE
PRICE FIXING
PRIME NUMBER
PRINT SELLER
PRIZE WINNER
PRONG HORNED
PROOF CHARGE
PROOF PULLER
PROOF READER
PROOF SPIRIT
PROSE WRITER
PROUD MINDED
PROXY WEDDED
PUPPY WALKER
PURSE BEARER
PURSE SEINER
PURSE TAKING
PUSSY WILLOW
PUTTY POWDER
QUEEN MOTHER
QUEEN REGENT
QUEEN STITCH
QUEER STREET
QUEUE JUMPED
QUEUE JUMPER

5,6 *contd.*

QUICK CHANGE	SCRUB TURKEY	SMOKE SCREEN	STIFF NECKED
QUICK FIRING	SCRUB TYPHUS	SMOKE SIGNAL	STILT WALKER
QUICK FREEZE	SCUBA DIVING	SMOKE TUNNEL	STIRS ABROAD
QUICK FROZEN	SEVEN OCLOCK	SMOKY QUARTZ	STOCK FARMER
QUICK STICKS	SHARD BEETLE	SNAIL DARTER	STOCK FEEDER
QUICK WITTED	SHARE PUSHER	SNUFF DIPPER	STOCK JOBBER
QUIET PLEASE	SHARP WITTED	SNUFF TAKING	STOCK MARKET
QUILL DRIVER	SHAWL COLLAR	SOBER MINDED	STOCK PHRASE
QUOTA SYSTEM	SHEEP FARMER	SOBER SUITED	STOCK SADDLE
RADAR BEACON	SHEET ANCHOR	SOLAR ENERGY	STONE CIRCLE
RADIO BEACON	SHEET COPPER	SOLAR PLEXUS	STONE CURLEW
RADIO GALAXY	SHEET RUBBER	SOLAR SYSTEM	STONE CUTTER
RAMAN EFFECT	SHELL CRATER	SOLID COLOUR	STONE FALCON
READY WITTED	SHELL JACKET	SOLID MATTER	STONE HAMMER
REILS ISLAND	SHELL PARROT	SORBO RUBBER	STONE PLOVER
RETRO ROCKET	SHIFT WORKER	SOUND ADVICE	STOOL PIGEON
RHODE ISLAND	SHIPS PAPERS	SOUND SYSTEM	STORM BEATEN
RHUMB COURSE	SHIRT BUTTON	SOUTH EASTER	STORM CELLAR
RHYME LETTER	SHIRT SLEEVE	SPACE HEATER	STORM CENTRE
RHYME SCHEME	SHOCK HEADED	SPACE TRAVEL	STORM PETREL
RIGHT ANGLED	SHOCK HORROR	SPACE WRITER	STORM SIGNAL
RIGHT HANDED	SHOCK TROOPS	SPADE GUINEA	STORM TOSSED
RIGHT HANDER	SHOPS AROUND	SPANG COCKLE	STORM TROOPS
RIGHT MINDED	SHORT CHANGE	SPILL STREAM	STORM WINDOW
RIGHT WINGER	SHORT HANDED	SPINA BIFIDA	STORY TELLER
RIGHT WRONGS	SHORT LISTED	SPLAY FOOTED	STOUT FELLOW
RIGOR MORTIS	SHORT PRICED	SPLIT SCREEN	STOVE ENAMEL
RIVER BOTTOM	SHORT SHRIFT	SPLIT SECOND	STRAP HANGER
ROMAN CANDLE	SHORT SPOKEN	SPRAY DRYING	STRAW CUTTER
ROMAN EMPIRE	SHORT TENNIS	STAFF SYSTEM	STRIP SEARCH
ROMAN FLEUVE	SHORT TERMER	STAGE DRIVER	STUCK AROUND
ROUGE DRAGON	SHORT WINDED	STAGE EFFECT	STUMP ORATOR
ROUGH COATED	SIEGE BASKET	STAGE FRIGHT	SUGAR COATED
ROUGH DRYING	SIGHT PLAYER	STAGE MANAGE	SUGAR SIFTER
ROUGH LEGGED	SIGHT READER	STAGE PLAYER	SWEEP WASHER
ROUGH SPOKEN	SIGHT SCREEN	STAGE STRUCK	SWEET CICELY
ROUND BACKED	SIGHT SINGER	STAIR CARPET	SWEET FENNEL
ROUND HEADED	SIGHT UNSEEN	STAIR TURRET	SWEET POTATO
ROYAL ASSENT	SILLY SEASON	STALL READER	SWEET SHERRY
ROYAL FAMILY	SLACK HANDED	STAMP OFFICE	SWEET TALKED
ROYAL OCTAVO	SLATE PENCIL	STAND OFFISH	SWEET WILLOW
ROYAL PARDON	SLATE WRITER	STATE PRISON	SWIFT FOOTED
ROYAL TENNIS	SLAVE DRIVER	STATE SCHOOL	SWIFT WINGED
RUGBY LEAGUE	SLAVE HOLDER	STATE SECRET	SWING BRIDGE
SABRE RATTLE	SLAVE LABOUR	STAVE CHURCH	SWING HANDLE
SAINT ANDREW	SLAVE STATES	STEAM BOILER	SWING PLOUGH
SAINT GEORGE	SLAVE TRADER	STEAM DIGGER	SWISS CHEESE
SATAN MONKEY	SLEEP WALKER	STEAM DRIVEN	SWISS GUARDS
SATIN FINISH	SLIME FUNGUS	STEAM ENGINE	SWORD BEARER
SATIN STITCH	SMALL CHANGE	STEAM HAMMER	SWORD SHAPED
SAUCE BOTTLE	SMALL LETTER	STEAM JACKET	TABLE NAPKIN
SCALE ARMOUR	SMALL MINDED	STEAM PACKET	TABLE TENNIS
SCALE INSECT	SMALL OCTAVE	STEAM ROLLER	TAKES CHARGE
SCENT BOTTLE	SMALL QUARTO	STEAM SHOVEL	TAKES EFFECT
SCORE POINTS	SMALL SCREEN	STEAM VESSEL	TAKES FLIGHT
SCOTS GUARDS	SMALL WONDER	STEEL HEADED	TAKES FRIGHT
SCOUT MASTER	SMART TICKET	STEEL PLATED	TAKES NOTICE
SCREW THREAD	SMILE PLEASE	STERN CHASER	TAKES ORDERS
SCREW WRENCH	SMOKE DRYING	STICK AROUND	TALKS TURKEY
	SMOKE HELMET	STICK INSECT	TALLY SYSTEM

5,6 *contd.*
TEENY BOPPER
THICK HEADED
THICK LIPPED
THICK WITTED
THIRD DEGREE
THIRD ESTATE
THREE CHEERS
THREE COLOUR
THREE DECKER
THREE HANDED
THREE LEAVED
THREE LEGGED
THREE MASTED
THREE MASTER
THREE OCLOCK
TIGHT FISTED
TIGHT LACING
TIGHT LIPPED
TITHE PAYING
TITLE HOLDER
TOMMY ATKINS
TOOTH DRAWER
TOOTH PICKER
TOOTH POWDER
TORCH BEARER
TORCH SINGER
TOTAL RECALL
TOUCH BOTTOM
TOUCH SCREEN
TOUCH TYPING
TOUCH TYPIST
TOUGH MINDED
TOWER BRIDGE
TRACK LAYING
TRACK RECORD
TRADE SECRET
TRAGI COMEDY
TRAIL BLAZER
TRAIN BEARER
TRANS SONICS
TROTH PLIGHT
TROUT BASKET
TROUT STREAM
TRUCK DRIVER
TRUCK SYSTEM
TRUST ESTATE
TRUTH TELLER
TUDOR FLOWER
TUMMY BUTTON
TURNS AROUND
TURNS TURTLE
TUTTI FRUTTI
UNDER ARREST
UNDER CANVAS
UNDER DRIVEN
UNDER DURESS
UNDER REVIEW
UNDER SCHOOL
UNDER STRESS

UNION LEADER
UPPER STOREY
VERSE MAKING
VERSE MONGER
VICAR CHORAL
VICAR FORANE
VIDEO CAMERA
VIDEO SIGNAL
VINYL RESINS
VIOLA DAMORE
VOCAL CHORDS
WAITS AWHILE
WASTE BASKET
WATCH POCKET
WATCH SPRING
WATER BARREL
WATER BEARER
WATER BEETLE
WATER BOTTLE
WATER CANNON
WATER CEMENT
WATER CLOSET
WATER COLOUR
WATER COOLED
WATER COOLER
WATER DOCTOR
WATER ENGINE
WATER FINDER
WATER HAMMER
WATER JACKET
WATER MEADOW
WATER MONKEY
WATER PISTOL
WATER SKIING
WATER SPIDER
WATER SPIRIT
WATER SPRING
WATER SPRITE
WATER SUPPLY
WATER THRUSH
WATER VAPOUR
WATER VIOLET
WEARY WILLIE
WEDGE SHAPED
WEIGH ANCHOR
WELSH COLLIE
WELSH GUARDS
WELSH RABBIT
WHALE FISHER
WHEEL CLAMPS
WHEEL PLOUGH
WHIST PLAYER
WHITE BOTTLE
WHITE COFFEE
WHITE COLLAR
WHITE ENSIGN
WHITE FRIARS
WHITE HEADED
WHITE KNIGHT
WHITE LISTED

WHITE RABBIT
WHITE SPIRIT
WHITE WINGED
WHOLE HOGGER
WHOLE NUMBER
WHOLE STITCH
WITCH DOCTOR
WITCH RIDDEN
WORLD BEATER
WORLD CRUISE
WORLD SERIES
WRECK MASTER
WRONG FOOTED
WRONG HEADED
WRONG NUMBER
YEAST POWDER
YOUNG PERSON
YOUTH HOSTEL
YOUTH LEADER

6,1,4
BEYOND A JOKE
CALLED A HALT
CAUGHT A COLD
CAUGHT A CRAB
CAUSED A STIR
CAUSES A STIR
CRACKS A CRIB
CRACKS A JOKE
FLYING A KITE
HAILED A TAXI
HAVING A BALL
HAVING A BASH
HAVING A STAB
LOOKED A FOOL
MAKING A BOMB
MAKING A FACE
MAKING A MOVE
PAYING A CALL
PICKED A LOCK
PLAYED A PART
PULLED A FACE
SCORED A GOAL
SCORES A GOAL
SEEING A WOLF
SHOOTS A LINE
SPRANG A LEAK
SPRING A LEAK
STARTS A HARE
STEALS A KISS
STRIKE A POSE
STRUCK A POSE
TAKING A SEAT
TAKING A TURN
THUMBS A LIFT
THUMBS A RIDE
WAVING A WAND

6,2,1,2
GIVING IT A GO

6,2,3
BUNDLE OF FUN
CHEMIN DE FER
COMING OF AGE
FATHER IN LAW
FIDDLE DE DEE
FIGHTS IT OUT
FIGURE IT OUT
FLEURS DE LIS
FLEURS DE LYS
FLOATS ON AIR
FORGET ME NOT
FOUGHT IT OUT
FRIEND OR FOE
GROUND TO AIR
HAVING IT OUT
HONEST TO GOD
LAUGHS IT OFF
LAYING AN EGG
LIVING IN SIN
LIVING ON AIR
MOTHER IN LAW
PLAYED TO WIN
PROJET DE LOI
RIDDLE ME REE
SHOOTS IT OUT
SINEWS OF WAR
SISTER IN LAW
SPELLS IT OUT
STANDS AT BAY
STANDS TO WIN
STICKS IT OUT
SWEATS IT OUT
TAKING IN TOW
WALKED ON AIR

6,3,2
DOTTED THE IS
MAKING FUN OF
MAKING USE OF
POKING FUN AT
RUMOUR HAS IT
WALKED OUT ON

6,5
AFGHAN HOUND
ANNUAL RINGS
APPEAL COURT
ARCTIC OCEAN
ARMOUR PLATE
ASKING PRICE
ASTRAL PLANE
ATOMIC CLOCK
ATOMIC POWER
AUBREY HOLES
BAILYS BEADS
BAKERS DOZEN
BALLAD OPERA
BALLET SHOES
BALLOT PAPER
BANANA SPLIT

6,5 *contd.*
BANNER CLOUD
BARLEY BRAKE
BARLEY BROTH
BARLEY SUGAR
BARLEY WATER
BARREL HOUSE
BARREL ORGAN
BARREL VAULT
BARYTA PAPER
BASKET CHAIR
BASKET MAKER
BASKET WEAVE
BASSET HOUND
BASTEL HOUSE
BATTLE PIECE
BATTLE ROYAL
BEAUTY QUEEN
BEAUTY SLEEP
BEETLE DRIVE
BENGAL LIGHT
BENGAL TIGER
BEYOND DOUBT
BEYOND PRICE
BINARY SCALE
BITTER APPLE
BITTER LEMON
BITTER SWEET
BLOODY SWEAT
BOILED SHIRT
BOILED SWEET
BOILER MAKER
BOOKER PRIZE
BOTTLE BRUSH
BOTTLE GLASS
BOTTLE GREEN
BOTTLE NOSED
BOTTLE PARTY
BOTTOM HEAVY
BOVVER BOOTS
BOXING GLOVE
BRAINS TRUST
BRAMAH PRESS
BRANCH PILOT
BRANDY GLASS
BRAZEN FACED
BREAKS COVER
BREAKS FORTH
BREAKS LOOSE
BREAKS RANKS
BREECH BIRTH
BREEZE BLOCK
BRIDAL SUITE
BRIDGE HOUSE
BRINGS ABOUT
BRINGS FORTH
BRINGS ROUND
BRONZE MEDAL
BUCKET WHEEL
BUCKLE UNDER

BUFFER STATE
BUFFER STOCK
BULLET PROOF
BUMBLE PUPPY
BURIAL PLACE
BUSTED FLUSH
BUTTED JOINT
BUTTER BEANS
BUTTER CLOTH
BUTTER KNIFE
BUTTER PAPER
BUTTER PLATE
CAAING WHALE
CALLED NAMES
CALLOW YOUTH
CAMELS THORN
CANADA GOOSE
CANARY GRASS
CANDLE LIGHT
CANDLE POWER
CANINE TOOTH
CANNED MUSIC
CANNON METAL
CANNON PROOF
CARBON PAPER
CARBON STEEL
CAREER WOMAN
CARNOT CYCLE
CARPET SNAKE
CARPET TILES
CARVEL BUILT
CASTER SUGAR
CASTLE GUARD
CASTOR SUGAR
CATTLE THIEF
CAUGHT SHORT
CAVEAT ACTOR
CELTIC CROSS
CEMENT MIXER
CEMENT STONE
CEMENT WATER
CENTRE BOARD
CENTRE COURT
CENTRE PARTY
CENTRE PIECE
CHANCE COMER
CHANGE HANDS
CHANGE HOUSE
CHAPEL ROYAL
CHARGE HOUSE
CHARGE NURSE
CHARGE SHEET
CHEESE BOARD
CHEESE PRESS
CHEESE STRAW
CHEESE WRING
CHERRY STONE
CHEVAL GLASS
CHOOSE SIDES
CHURCH BELLS

CHURCH BENCH
CHURCH COURT
CHURCH GOING
CHURCH MOUSE
CHURCH ORGAN
CHURCH TOWER
CINDER TRACK
CINEMA ORGAN
CINQUE PORTS
CIRCLE RIDER
CITRUS FRUIT
CLIENT STATE
CLOSED CHAIN
CLOSED RANKS
CLOSET DRAMA
CLOVER GRASS
COBBLE STONE
COFFEE BERRY
COFFEE BREAK
COFFEE HOUSE
COFFEE MAKER
COFFEE STALL
COFFEE TABLE
COLOUR BLIND
COLOUR CODED
COMING ABOUT
COMING CLEAN
COMING ROUND
COMMON CHORD
COMMON FORMS
COMMON METRE
COMMON SENSE
COMMON THIEF
COMMON TOUCH
CONTRA DANCE
CONTRA TENOR
COPING STONE
COPPER BEECH
COPPER FACED
CORNER STONE
COTTON CANDY
COTTON PLANT
COTTON PRESS
COUNTS SHEEP
COUNTY COURT
COWBOY BOOTS
CRIMEN FALSI
CUCKOO CLOCK
CUSTOM BUILT
CUSTOM HOUSE
DAMASK STEEL
DANGER MONEY
DANGER POINT
DANISH BACON
DECKLE EDGED
DENTAL FLOSS
DESERT BOOTS
DEVILS BONES
DEVILS BOOKS
DICKIN MEDAL

DIESEL TRAIN
DINING TABLE
DINNER DANCE
DINNER PARTY
DINNER TABLE
DINNER WAGON
DIRECT DEBIT
DISMAL JIMMY
DIVINE RIGHT
DIVING BOARD
DIVING DRESS
DONKEY DERBY
DOUBLE AGENT
DOUBLE BLANK
DOUBLE BLIND
DOUBLE BLUFF
DOUBLE CHECK
DOUBLE CREAM
DOUBLE CROSS
DOUBLE DOORS
DOUBLE DUTCH
DOUBLE EAGLE
DOUBLE EDGED
DOUBLE ENTRY
DOUBLE FAULT
DOUBLE FIRST
DOUBLE HELIX
DOUBLE PARKS
DOUBLE QUICK
DOUBLE SHARP
DOUBLE SPACE
DOUBLE SPEAK
DOUBLE THINK
DOWNED TOOLS
DUMDUM FEVER
DUMPER TRUCK
DUPLEX HOUSE
EARTHS CRUST
EATING APPLE
EATING HOUSE
EATING IRONS
EIFFEL TOWER
ESCAPE HATCH
ESCAPE ROUTE
ESCAPE VALVE
ESCAPE WHEEL
ESTATE AGENT
EXEUNT OMNES
EXPORT DRIVE
FACING FACTS
FADING LIGHT
FAMILY BAKER
FAMILY BIBLE
FAMILY CREST
FARMER GILES
FASCIA BOARD
FERRIS WHEEL
FILING CLERK
FILLET STEAK
FILTER PAPER

6,5 *contd.*
FILTHY LUCRE
FINGER FOODS
FIPPLE FLUTE
FIRING ORDER
FIRING PARTY
FIRING POINT
FIRING SQUAD
FLORAL DANCE
FLOWER CHILD
FLOWER CLOCK
FLOWER POWER
FLOWER STALK
FLYING CORPS
FLYING LEMUR
FLYING PARTY
FLYING SQUAD
FLYING START
FLYING VISIT
FOILED AGAIN
FORCED MARCH
FORMAL CAUSE
FORMAL LOGIC
FOSSIL FIRED
FOSTER CHILD
FOSTER NURSE
FOURTH WORLD
FREEZE DRIED
FREEZE DRIES
FREEZE FRAME
FRENCH BERRY
FRENCH BREAD
FRENCH CHALK
FRENCH FRANC
FRENCH FRIES
FRENCH LEAVE
FRENCH PLEAT
FRENCH STICK
FRENCH TOAST
FRENCH WHITE
FRIGID ZONES
FROZEN NORTH
FROZEN PIPES
FROZEN STIFF
FUTURE TENSE
GADDED ABOUT
GALLEY PROOF
GALLEY SLAVE
GAMBIT PIECE
GAMING HOUSE
GAMING TABLE
GAMMON STEAK
GANDER MONTH
GANTRY CRANE
GARAND RIFLE
GARDEN GLASS
GARDEN HOUSE
GARDEN PARTY
GARDEN PATCH
GATHER ROUND

GATHER SPEED
GAZING STOCK
GENEVA BANDS
GENEVA BIBLE
GENEVA CROSS
GENTLE CRAFT
GENTLE GIANT
GENTLE TOUCH
GEORGE CROSS
GEORGE MEDAL
GERMAN FLUTE
GIDEON BIBLE
GILDED SPURS
GILDED YOUTH
GINGER GROUP
GIVING BIRTH
GIVING CHASE
GIVING FORTH
GIVING VOICE
GLIDER PILOT
GLORIA PATRI
GOLDEN ARROW
GOLDEN BOUGH
GOLDEN CHAIN
GOLDEN EAGLE
GOLDEN GOOSE
GOLDEN HELLO
GOLDEN HORDE
GOLDEN OLDIE
GOLDEN SYRUP
GOSPEL TRUTH
GRAECO ROMAN
GRAHAM BREAD
GRAHAM FLOUR
GRANDE ARMEE
GRANDE ECOLE
GRANNY BONDS
GRANNY SMITH
GRANTH SAHIB
GRAVEN IMAGE
GREASE PAINT
GREASE PROOF
GREASY SPOON
GRETNA GREEN
GROUND COVER
GROUND FLOOR
GROUND FROST
GROUND GLASS
GROUND RULES
GROUND SLOTH
GROUND SPEED
GROUND STAFF
GROUND SWELL
GUILTY PARTY
GUINEA GRASS
GUTTER PRESS
GUTTER SNIPE
GYPSUM BLOCK
HAMMER BRACE
HAMMER DRILL

HAMMER THROW
HARRIS TWEED
HARVEY SMITH
HAULED ROUND
HAVING IDEAS
HAVING WORDS
HEALTH STAMP
HEARSE CLOTH
HEARTH BRUSH
HEARTH STONE
HEARTS BLOOD
HEAVEN KNOWS
HECTIC FEVER
HELMET SHELL
HEMPEN WIDOW
HEROIC VERSE
HIDING PLACE
HIGHER GRADE
HOBBLE SKIRT
HOCKEY PITCH
HOCKEY STICK
HOLLOW TOOTH
HONEST INJUN
HONOUR BOUND
HOORAH HENRY
HORNED POPPY
HORNED VIPER
HORROR STORY
HOUNDS TOOTH
HUNGER MARCH
HUNGER PANGS
HURDLE RACER
INDIAN BREAD
INDIAN CRESS
INDIAN CURRY
INDIAN OCEAN
INDOOR GAMES
INKING TABLE
INSIDE RIGHT
INSIDE STORY
INSIDE TRACK
ISSUED FORTH
ISSUES FORTH
JACOBS SHEEP
JACOBS STAFF
JINGLE BELLS
JOGGED ALONG
JOINED HANDS
JOKING APART
JUNGLE FEVER
JUNGLE JUICE
KAFFIR BREAD
KENDAL GREEN
KICKED ABOUT
KIDNEY STONE
KILLER WHALE
KNOCKS ABOUT
LABOUR FORCE
LABOUR PARTY
LABOUR UNION

LARKED ABOUT
LATENT IMAGE
LAUREL WATER
LAYING ASIDE
LAYING CLAIM
LAYING WASTE
LEADER CABLE
LEAGUE MATCH
LEAGUE TABLE
LEAVES ALONE
LECHER WIRES
LETTER BOARD
LETTER STAMP
LIGNUM SCRUB
LIGNUM SWAMP
LINEAR MOTOR
LINKED VERSE
LITANY STOOL
LITMUS PAPER
LITTLE DEVIL
LITTLE WOMAN
LIVING DEATH
LOCKED HORNS
LONDON PRIDE
LONELY HEART
LOOKED AFTER
LOOKED SMALL
LOOMED LARGE
LOSING COUNT
LOSING HEART
LOSING TOUCH
LOSING TRACK
LOUNGE ABOUT
LOUNGE CHAIR
LOUVRE BOARD
LUXURY GOODS
MAGNUM BONUM
MAKING AFTER
MAKING HASTE
MAKING MERRY
MAKING MONEY
MAKING PEACE
MAKING READY
MAKING SENSE
MAKING WAVES
MALIBU BOARD
MANILA PAPER
MARBLE EDGED
MARBLE PAPER
MARINE STORE
MARKED CARDS
MARKET CROSS
MARKET PLACE
MARKET PRICE
MARKET SHARE
MARKET WOMAN
MARLIN SPIKE
MASTER CLASS
MASTER CLOCK
MASTER MASON

6,5 *contd.*

MASTER WHEEL	NARROW GAUGE	PEOPLE MOVER	PUBLIC HOUSE
MAUNDY MONEY	NATURE TRAIL	PEPPER GRASS	PUBLIC IMAGE
MEADOW BROWN	NECTAR GUIDE	PEPTIC ULCER	PUBLIC LANDS
MEADOW GRASS	NEEDLE CRAFT	PERIOD DRESS	PUBLIC PURSE
MEADOW SWEET	NEEDLE PAPER	PERIOD PIECE	PUBLIC WORKS
MEDIUM WAVES	NEEDLE POINT	PETERS PENCE	PULLED AHEAD
MEDLEY RELAY	NICENE CREED	PETITS FOURS	PULLED APART
MEMORY TRACE	NICKEL STEEL	PICKED HOLES	PULLED ROUND
MERSEY SOUND	NIKKEI INDEX	PICKET FENCE	PUMICE STONE
MESSED ABOUT	NITRIC OXIDE	PICKET GUARD	PURPLE FINCH
MESSES ABOUT	NORMAN CROSS	PIGEON FLIER	PURPLE HEART
METHOD ACTOR	NOTICE BOARD	PIGEON FLYER	PURPLE PATCH
MICKEY MOUSE	NUMBER PLATE	PIGEON HOUSE	PUSHED ALONG
MIDDLE CLASS	OBJECT GLASS	PILLAR SAINT	PUSHED ASIDE
MIDDLE EARTH	OBTUSE ANGLE	PILLOW FIGHT	PUSHES ALONG
MIDDLE EIGHT	OCCAMS RAZOR	PIRATE RADIO	PUSHES ASIDE
MIDDLE SIZED	OCTAVE FLUTE	PISTOL WHIPS	PUTRID FEVER
MIDDLE STUMP	OFFICE BLOCK	PLANAR DIODE	QUARTZ GLASS
MIDDLE WATCH	OFFICE HOURS	PLAYED ABOUT	QUEENS BENCH
MIDDLE WORLD	OFFICE PARTY	PLAYED FALSE	QUEENS GUIDE
MILLET GRASS	OLIVER TWIST	PLAYED HAVOC	QUINSY BERRY
MINCED WORDS	ORANGE JUICE	PLAYER PIANO	QUITCH GRASS
MINCES WORDS	ORANGE STICK	PLOUGH STAFF	RABBET JOINT
MINUTE GLASS	ORCHID HOUSE	PLOUGH STILT	RABBIT HUTCH
MINUTE STEAK	ORDERS ABOUT	POCKET GLASS	RABBIT PUNCH
MINUTE WALTZ	OREGON TRAIL	POCKET GUIDE	RABBLE ROUSE
MINUTE WATCH	OXFORD UNION	POCKET HANKY	RACKET COURT
MIRROR IMAGE	OYSTER KNIFE	POCKET KNIFE	RACKET PRESS
MITRAL VALVE	OYSTER PATTY	POCKET MONEY	RAGGED ROBIN
MIXING VALVE	OYSTER PLANT	POCKET MOUSE	RAISED ALOFT
MOBIUS STRIP	OYSTER SHELL	POCKET PIECE	RAISED BEACH
MODERN DANCE	OYSTER TONGS	POCKET SIZED	RAISED MONEY
MONEYS WORTH	PACKED LUNCH	POCKET VENUS	RAISES ALOFT
MONKEY BLOCK	PADDLE BOARD	POISON GLAND	RAISES MONEY
MONKEY BOARD	PADDLE SHAFT	POKING STICK	RAISON DETRE
MONKEY BREAD	PADDLE WHEEL	POLICE COURT	RATION MONEY
MONKEY GLAND	PALACE GUARD	POLICE FORCE	RATTLE BRAIN
MONKEY SHINE	PALAIS GLIDE	POLICE STATE	RATTLE PATED
MONKEY WHEEL	PAMPAS GRASS	POLLEN COUNT	RATTLE SNAKE
MORNAY SAUCE	PANAMA CANAL	POLLEN GRAIN	RECORD TOKEN
MORRIS CHAIR	PAPIER COLLE	POODLE FAKER	REFLEX LIGHT
MORRIS DANCE	PAPIER MACHE	PORTER HOUSE	REPORT STAGE
MORTAR BOARD	PARENT CRAFT	POSTAL ORDER	RESCUE GRASS
MOTHER GOOSE	PARISH CLERK	POSTAL UNION	RESCUE PARTY
MOTIVE POWER	PARITY CHECK	POTASH WATER	RETURN MATCH
MOTTLE FACED	PARPEN STONE	POTATO APPLE	RETURN SHOCK
MOULIN ROUGE	PATENT RIGHT	POTATO CHIPS	RIBBON GRASS
MOUNTS GUARD	PATENT ROLLS	POTATO CRISP	RIDING CLOAK
MOVING HOUSE	PATENT STILL	POTATO SALAD	RIDING GLOVE
MUFFIN FIGHT	PATROL WAGON	POURED FORTH	RIDING HABIT
MURDER PARTY	PATRON SAINT	POWDER FLASK	RIDING HORSE
MUSCLE BOUND	PAVING STONE	PRANCE ABOUT	RIDING SKIRT
MUSEUM PIECE	PAYING GUEST	PRAYER BEADS	RIGHTS ISSUE
MUSSEL SCALP	PEARLY GATES	PRAYER WHEEL	RITUAL CHOIR
MUSSEL SCAUP	PEARLY QUEEN	PRETTY PENNY	ROCKER PANEL
MUSSEL SHELL	PEBBLE STONE	PRIMUS STOVE	ROCKET MOTOR
MUTTON CLOTH	PELTON WHEEL	PRISON HOUSE	ROCKET PLANE
MUTUAL FUNDS	PENCIL CEDAR	PUBLIC BATHS	ROCKET RANGE
NAMING NAMES	PENCIL SKIRT	PUBLIC ENEMY	ROGUES LATIN
	PENCIL STONE	PUBLIC FUNDS	ROGUES MARCH

6,5 *contd.*

ROLLED ALONG
ROLLER BLIND
ROLLER SKATE
ROLLER TOWEL
ROTTEN APPLE
RUBBED ALONG
RUBBER CORED
RUBBER NECKS
RUBBER PLANT
RUBBER SOLED
RUBBER STAMP
RUBBLE STONE
RUMBLE STRIP
SACRED HEART
SADDLE CLOTH
SADDLE GIRTH
SADDLE HORSE
SAFETY CATCH
SAFETY FIRST
SAFETY GLASS
SAFETY LIGHT
SAFETY MATCH
SAFETY PAPER
SAFETY RAZOR
SAFETY VALVE
SAILED ALONG
SALLEE ROVER
SALMON BERRY
SALMON COBLE
SALMON SPEAR
SALMON TROUT
SALOON RIFLE
SAMIAN EARTH
SAMIAN STONE
SANCHO PEDRO
SAVING GRACE
SAVOIR FAIRE
SCARED STIFF
SCHISM HOUSE
SCHOOL BOARD
SCHOOL CHILD
SCHOOL HOUSE
SCHOOL NURSE
SCOTCH BROTH
SCOTCH CATCH
SCOTCH IRISH
SCOUTS ROUND
SCRAPE PENNY
SCREEN WIPER
SCRIVE BOARD
SCRUBS ROUND
SCURVY GRASS
SCUTCH BLADE
SCYTHE STONE
SEARCH PARTY
SECOND CLASS
SECOND FLOOR
SECOND GUESS
SECOND JOINT

SECOND RATER
SECOND REICH
SECOND SIGHT
SECOND TEETH
SECRET AGENT
SEEING ROUND
SEEING STARS
SEEING STONE
SELDOM TIMES
SENATE HOUSE
SESAME GRASS
SESAME SEEDS
SEWAGE WORKS
SHADOW BOXED
SHADOW BOXES
SHADOW FIGHT
SHAKES HANDS
SHEATH KNIFE
SHERRY PARTY
SHIFTS ABOUT
SHINTY STICK
SHODDY GOODS
SHOOTS CRAPS
SHOVEL BOARD
SHOWED FIGHT
SHOWED FORTH
SHRINK PROOF
SIERRA LEONE
SILENT NIGHT
SILVER BIRCH
SILVER MEDAL
SILVER PAPER
SILVER PLATE
SILVER POINT
SILVER SPOON
SILVER WHITE
SIMPLE SIMON
SINGLE CREAM
SINGLE ENTRY
SINGLE HOUSE
SINGLE TRACK
SKATED ROUND
SKATES ROUND
SKIRTS ROUND
SLEDGE CHAIR
SLEEPS ROUGH
SLEEVE BOARD
SLEEVE NOTES
SLEIGH BELLS
SLEUTH HOUND
SMARTY BOOTS
SMARTY PANTS
SMOKED GLASS
SMOKED TROUT
SMOOTH FACED
SMOOTH PACED
SNAKES ALIVE
SNATCH PURSE
SNATCH SQUAD
SNATCH THIEF

SNOWED UNDER
SOCIAL WHALE
SOUGHT AFTER
SPACER PLATE
SPEECH MAKER
SPIDER PLANT
SPIDER WHEEL
SPINAL CANAL
SPINAL CHORD
SPIRIT LEVEL
SPIRIT WORLD
SPLASH BOARD
SPLITS HAIRS
SPOILT PAPER
SPONGE CLOTH
SPONGE DIVER
SPORTS SHIRT
SPREAD EAGLE
SPREAD SHEET
SPRING CLEAN
SPRING FEVER
SPRING ONION
SPRING WATER
SPRING WHEAT
SPROUT WINGS
SQUARE DANCE
SQUARE FACED
SQUASH COURT
STANDS ALONE
STANDS GUARD
STANDS TREAT
STANDS TRIAL
STARCH PAPER
STAYED STILL
STEADY GOING
STEADY STATE
STEERS CLEAR
STEWED FRUIT
STIFLE JOINT
STONES THROW
STRAIT LACED
STRAIT LACER
STREET CRIES
STREET LEVEL
STREET SMART
STREET VALUE
STRIDE PIANO
STRIKE BOUND
STRIKE FORCE
STRIKE HANDS
STRING ALONG
STRONG DRINK
STRONG POINT
STRUNG ALONG
STUDIO COUCH
SUDDEN DEATH
SUMMER HOUSE
SUMMER STOCK
SUMMIT LEVEL
SUMMIT TALKS

SUMMUM BONUM
SUPPER CLOTH
SUPPLY SIDER
SWIVEL CHAIR
SWIVEL JOINT
SYSTEM BUILT
SYSTEM MAKER
TAGGED ALONG
TAILED RHYME
TAKING AFTER
TAKING AMISS
TAKING APART
TAKING COVER
TAKING HEART
TAKING ISSUE
TAKING LEAVE
TAKING PAINS
TAKING PLACE
TAKING SHAPE
TAKING SIDES
TAKING STEPS
TAKING STOCK
TAKING TURNS
TALENT SCOUT
TALKED ROUND
TAMMIE NORIE
TARTAR SAUCE
TATTIE BOGLE
TEETER BOARD
TEMPUS FUGIT
TENNIS COURT
TENNIS ELBOW
TENNIS MATCH
TENTER HOOKS
THATCH BOARD
THESIS NOVEL
THINKS AGAIN
THINKS ALOUD
THINKS TWICE
THROAT STRAP
THRUST STAGE
TICKET AGENT
TICKET PUNCH
TIMBER HITCH
TISSUE PAPER
TOFFEE APPLE
TOFFEE NOSED
TOGGLE JOINT
TOILET CLOTH
TOILET COVER
TOILET GLASS
TOILET PAPER
TOILET TABLE
TOILET WATER
TORQUE METER
TOWING BITTS
TRACER SHELL
TRADES UNION
TRAVEL AGENT
TREADS WATER

6,5 *contd.*
TRENCH FEVER
TRIPLE CROWN
TRIPLE EVENT
TRIPLE POINT
TROJAN HORSE
TROMPE LOEIL
TUMBLE DRIER
TURNED ABOUT
TURNED ASIDE
TURNED LOOSE
TURNED NASTY
TURNED ROUND
TURRET CLOCK
TURRET LATHE
TURTLE SHELL
TWENTY PENCE
ULTIMA THULE
UPCAST SHAFT
VACUUM BRAKE
VACUUM FLASK
VAPOUR TRAIL
VELVET PAPER
VENICE GLASS
VERNAL GRASS
VESTRY CLERK
VIENNA STEAK
VIPERS GRASS
VIRGIN BIRTH
VISION MIXER
VOTING PAPER
VULGAR LATIN
WAITED ABOUT
WAKING HOURS
WALTER MITTY
WATERY GRAVE
WAVING ASIDE
WEASEL FACED
WEAVER FINCH
WHISKY TODDY
WHOLLY OWNED
WIDOWS WEEDS
WINDOW BLIND
WINDOW FRAME
WINDOW GLASS
WINDOW LEDGE
WINDOW SHOPS
WINTER APPLE
WINTER SWEET
WINTER WHEAT
WISDOM TOOTH
WITCHS BROOM
WITHIN REACH
WOBBLE BOARD
WOODEN HORSE
WOODEN SPOON
WREAKS HAVOC
YELLOW BELLY
YELLOW FEVER
YELLOW METAL

YELLOW PAGES
YELLOW PERIL
YELLOW PRESS

7,1,3
CASTING A NET
PLACING A BET
SELLING A PUP
SHAKING A LEG
SHOWING A LEG

7,2,2
BEATING TO IT
CAMPING IT UP
CHUCKED IT IN
KEEPING AT IT
LETTING IN ON
LOOKING UP TO
NOTHING IN IT
NOTHING TO IT
PACKING IT IN
PACKING IT UP
PUTTING IT ON
PUTTING ON TO
PUTTING TO IT
RUBBING IT IN
WHETHER OR NO
WHOOPED IT UP
WORKING AT IT
ZAPPING IT UP
ZEROING IN ON

7,4
ABANDON SHIP
ACCOUNT BOOK
ACETATE FILM
ADDRESS BOOK
ADVANCE COPY
AEOLIAN HARP
AFRICAN TEAK
AGAINST TIME
ANISEED BALL
ANSWERS BACK
ASSAULT BOAT
ATTACHE CASE
AUCTION ROOM
AVOCADO PEAR
BACKING DOWN
BAGGING HOOK
BALLOON BACK
BALLOON TYRE
BANBURY CAKE
BANKERS CARD
BARBERS POLE
BARBERS SHOP
BARBOLA WORK
BARKERS MILL
BARKING DEER
BARRACK ROOM
BARRAGE FIRE

BARRIER REEF
BASTARD FILE
BASTARD TEAK
BATHING SUIT
BEARDED LADY
BEARING ARMS
BEARING AWAY
BEARING DOWN
BEARING REIN
BEATING DOWN
BEATING TIME
BEAVERS AWAY
BEDDING DOWN
BEDSIDE BOOK
BEDSIDE LAMP
BEGGING BOWL
BELGIAN HARE
BELLOWS FISH
BENDING OVER
BERTHON BOAT
BETTING SHOP
BETTING SLIP
BETWEEN MAID
BEWICKS SWAN
BICYCLE BELL
BICYCLE CLIP
BICYCLE POLO
BICYCLE PUMP
BILLETS DOUX
BINDING OVER
BLADDER WORM
BLANKET BATH
BLISTER CARD
BLISTER PACK
BLOWING AWAY
BLOWING OVER
BOGGING DOWN
BOILING OVER
BOOKING HALL
BOULDER CLAY
BOUNCED BACK
BOUNCES BACK
BOWLINE KNOT
BOWLING OVER
BRAMBLE BUSH
BRISTLE FERN
BRISTLE TAIL
BRISTOL MILK
BRITISH RAIL
BRITISH WARM
BRITTLE STAR
BRONZED SKIN
BROUGHT DOWN
BROUGHT HOME
BROUGHT OVER
BUBBLED OVER
BUBBLES OVER
BUCKLED DOWN
BUCKLES DOWN
BUFFALO BILL

BUFFALO BIRD
BULLDOG CLIP
BUMPING INTO
BUMPING RACE
BURLING IRON
BURNING BUSH
BURNING DOWN
BUTCHER BIRD
CABBAGE MOTH
CABBAGE PALM
CABBAGE ROSE
CALABAR BEAN
CALLING AWAY
CALLING BACK
CALLING CARD
CALLING OVER
CALMING DOWN
CANDIED PEEL
CANTING COIN
CAPITAL LEVY
CAPITAL SHIP
CARAVAN PARK
CARAVAN SITE
CARAWAY SEED
CARDING WOOL
CARRICK BEND
CARRIED AWAY
CARRIED BACK
CARRIED OVER
CARRIES AWAY
CARRIES BACK
CARRIES OVER
CARRION CROW
CASTILE SOAP
CASTING AWAY
CASTING LOTS
CASTING VOTE
CATCHES FIRE
CATHODE RAYS
CAUSTIC LIME
CAUSTIC SODA
CENTRAL BANK
CENTRAL FIRE
CENTRAL LINE
CENTRAL PARK
CHANGED DOWN
CHANGED ENDS
CHANGED GEAR
CHANGES DOWN
CHANGES ENDS
CHANGES GEAR
CHANNEL SEAM
CHARGED DOWN
CHARGES DOWN
CHARITY GIRL
CHARITY WALK
CHEDDAR PINK
CHELSEA WARE
CHEQUER WORK
CHEWING OVER

7,4 *contd.*
CHICKEN COOP
CHICKEN FEED
CHICKEN WIRE
CHILEAN PINE
CHIMNEY NOOK
CHINESE BURN
CHLORIC ACID
CHOKING BACK
CHOKING COIL
CHOLERA BELT
CHROMIC ACID
CHUCKLE HEAD
CITIZEN KANE
CLAMPED DOWN
CLARION CALL
CLAWING BACK
CLIMBED DOWN
CLOSING DOWN
CLOSING TIME
CLOTHES LINE
CLOTHES MOTH
CLOTHES POLE
CLOTHES PROP
CLOUDED OVER
CLUSTER BOMB
COCONUT PALM
COMMAND POST
COMPACT DISC
COMPASS CARD
COMPASS ROSE
COMPOST HEAP
CONCERT GOER
CONCERT HALL
CONTACT LENS
CONTOUR LINE
CONTROL ROOM
CONTROL UNIT
COOKERY BOOK
COPPERS NARK
CORNEAL LENS
CORNICE HOOK
CORNICE POLE
CORNICE RAIL
CORNICE RING
CORNISH CLAY
COSTUME PLAY
COTTAGE LOAF
COUNTER BORE
COUNTER MOVE
COUNTER PLOT
COUNTER ROLL
COUNTER TURN
COUNTER VIEW
COUNTER VOTE
COUNTER WORK
COUNTRY CLUB
COUNTRY FOLK
COUNTRY LANE
COUNTRY ROCK

COUNTRY SEAT
COURTLY LOVE
CRACKED DOWN
CRAWLER LANE
CRICKET BALL
CROOKES TUBE
CROQUET LAWN
CROSSED LINE
CROSSED OVER
CROSSES OVER
CROWNED HEAD
CRYPTIC CLUE
CRYSTAL BALL
CULVERS ROOT
CURLING POND
CURRANT CAKE
CURRANT WINE
CURTAIN CALL
CURTAIN WALL
CUSTARD TART
CUTTING BACK
CUTTING DEAD
CUTTING DOWN
CUTTING EDGE
CYCLING CLUB
CYPRESS TREE
DAMPING DOWN
DANCING BEAR
DANCING GIRL
DASHING AWAY
DELAYED DROP
DIAMOND BACK
DIAMOND DUST
DIAMOND MINE
DIAMOND RING
DIGITAL FACE
DISTAFF SIDE
DIVORCE SUIT
DOSSING DOWN
DOUBLED BACK
DOUBLES BACK
DRAGOON BIRD
DRAINED AWAY
DRAWING BACK
DRAWING LOTS
DRAWING NEAR
DRAWING ROOM
DRESDEN WARE
DRESSED CRAB
DRESSED DOWN
DRESSES DOWN
DRIVING GEAR
DRIVING HOME
DRIVING RAIN
DRIVING TEST
DROPPED AWAY
DROPPED DOWN
DUCKING DOWN
DUCKING POND
DWARFED TREE

ECONOMY SIZE
EJECTOR SEAT
ELASTIC BAND
ELKHORN FERN
EMERALD ISLE
EMERALD TYPE
EMPEROR MOTH
ENDLESS WORM
ENGLISH HORN
ETERNAL CITY
ETHMOID BONE
EVENING MEAL
EVENING STAR
EVEREST PACK
EXHAUST PIPE
EXPLAIN AWAY
FACTORY ACTS
FACTORY FARM
FACTORY SHIP
FALLING BACK
FALLING DOWN
FALLING OVER
FALLING STAR
FAMILLE ROSE
FARMERS LUNG
FASHION SHOW
FATIGUE DUTY
FATUOUS FIRE
FEATHER PALM
FEATURE FILM
FIDDLER CRAB
FIRMING DOWN
FISHING BOAT
FISHING LINE
FISSION BOMB
FITTING ROOM
FITTING SHOP
FLAGGED DOWN
FLEMISH BOND
FOLDING DOOR
FOLIAGE LEAF
FOLLOWS HOME
FOLLOWS SUIT
FOREIGN BILL
FOREIGN BODY
FORKING OVER
FORLORN HOPE
FORTUNE BOOK
FORWARD PASS
FOSBURY FLOP
FREEZES DOWN
FREEZES OVER
FRIGATE BIRD
FRITTER AWAY
FULLERS HERB
FULLING MILL
FUNERAL HOME
FUNERAL PYRE
FUSIDIC ACID
GAINING TIME

GALLOWS BIRD
GALLOWS FREE
GALLOWS TREE
GAMBREL ROOF
GASTRIC MILL
GEARING DOWN
GEFILTE FISH
GENERAL LINE
GENERAL POST
GENERIC NAME
GENETIC CODE
GETTING BACK
GETTING DOWN
GETTING EVEN
GETTING OVER
GLAMOUR GIRL
GLOTTAL STOP
GNAWING AWAY
GOLIATH FROG
GORDIAN KNOT
GRAPHIC ARTS
GRAVITY WAVE
GRECIAN BEND
GRECIAN NOSE
GRIZZLY BEAR
GUELDER ROSE
GUIDING STAR
HACKING COAT
HAIRPIN BEND
HALCYON DAYS
HAMMERS HOME
HANDING DOWN
HANDING OVER
HANGDOG LOOK
HANGING BACK
HANGING FIRE
HAPPENS UPON
HARBOUR DUES
HARICOT BEAN
HARKING BACK
HARNESS ROOM
HARVEST HOME
HARVEST LADY
HARVEST LORD
HARVEST MITE
HARVEST MOON
HARVEST TICK
HEARING TELL
HEATHER BELL
HELPING HAND
HERRING BONE
HERRING GULL
HERRING POND
HESSIAN BOOT
HIGHWAY CODE
HISTORY BOOK
HOLDING BACK
HOLDING DOWN
HOLDING GOOD
HOLDING OVER

7,4 *contd.*
HOLDING SWAY
HOLIDAY CAMP
HONITON LACE
HONOURS EASY
HONOURS LIST
HORNETS NEST
HOWLING DOWN
HUMMING BIRD
HUNTERS MOON
HUNTING CROP
HUNTING DOWN
HUNTING HORN
HUNTING SEAT
HUNTING SONG
HUNTING WHIP
ICELAND MOSS
IGNEOUS ROCK
INCENSE BOAT
INERTIA REEL
INITIAL CELL
JAMAICA BARK
JAMAICA PLUM
JELLIED EELS
JESUITS BARK
JOURNEY WORK
JUBILEE CLIP
JUBILEE LINE
JUMPING BAIL
JUMPING BEAN
JUMPING DEER
JUMPING HARE
JUMPING JACK
JUMPING SHIP
JUNIPER TREE
KEELING OVER
KEEPING BACK
KEEPING BUSY
KEEPING DOWN
KEEPING ROOM
KEEPING TIME
KENTISH FIRE
KEPLERS LAWS
KILLING TIME
KINGDOM COME
KIPPING DOWN
KISSING GATE
KITCHEN MAID
KITCHEN SINK
KITCHEN UNIT
KNOCKED BACK
KNOCKED COLD
KNOCKED DOWN
KNUCKLE BONE
KNUCKLE DOWN
KNUCKLE HEAD
LACQUER TREE
LAMBETH WALK
LANDING GEAR
LANDING SHIP

LATTICE LEAF
LAUNDRY LIST
LAUNDRY MAID
LEADING CARD
LEADING CASE
LEADING EDGE
LEADING LADY
LEATHER BACK
LEATHER BELT
LEATHER COAT
LEATHER HEAD
LEATHER NECK
LEAVING SHOP
LECTURE HALL
LECTURE TOUR
LEISURE SUIT
LEISURE WEAR
LEOPARD MOTH
LEOPARD SKIN
LETTING DOWN
LETTING DROP
LETTING FALL
LETTING SLIP
LIBERAL ARTS
LIBERTY BOAT
LIBERTY HALL
LIBERTY SHIP
LIBRARY BOOK
LIBRARY LIST
LIGHTER FUEL
LOCKING AWAY
LOOKING AWRY
LOOKING BACK
LOOKING DOWN
LOOKING INTO
LOOKING OVER
LUGGAGE RACK
MACHINE CODE
MACHINE MADE
MACHINE SHOP
MACHINE TOOL
MACHINE WORK
MADEIRA CAKE
MADEIRA WINE
MADONNA LILY
MAGINOT LINE
MAILING LIST
MALACCA CANE
MARKING DOWN
MARKING TIME
MARTIAL ARTS
MASONIC HALL
MATINEE COAT
MATINEE IDOL
MEANING WELL
MECHLIN LACE
MEGATON BOMB
MEISSEN WARE
MELTING AWAY
MELTING DOWN

MEMBERS ONLY
MEMENTO MORI
MESONIC ATOM
MESSAGE GIRL
MEXICAN WAVE
MIDWIFE TOAD
MILKING TIME
MINERAL WELL
MINIMUM WAGE
MIRACLE DRUG
MIRACLE PLAY
MISSING LINK
MISTING OVER
MOCKING BIRD
MOLUCCA BEAN
MORNING CALL
MORNING COAT
MORNING GOWN
MORNING ROOM
MORNING STAR
MORNING TIDE
MORTISE LOCK
MORTONS FORK
MOTHERS HELP
MOTHERS RUIN
MURPHYS GAME
MUSCOVY DUCK
MUSICAL SAND
MUSTARD BATH
MYSTERY SHIP
MYSTERY TOUR
NAILING DOWN
NAPIERS RODS
NATTIER BLUE
NATURAL BORN
NETBALL TEAM
NEUTRON BOMB
NEUTRON STAR
NITROUS ACID
NOBODYS FOOL
NOTHING LESS
NOWHERE NEAR
NUBBING COVE
NUCLEIC ACID
NURSING HOME
OBLIQUE CASE
OFFSIDE RULE
OMNIBUS BOOK
OPENING TIME
OPINION POLL
ORBITAL ROAD
ORDERLY ROOM
OSTRICH FARM
OSTRICH LIKE
OUTSIDE EDGE
OUTSIDE HALF
OUTSIDE LEFT
PACKAGE DEAL
PACKAGE TOUR
PACKING CASE

PAINTED LADY
PAINTED VEIL
PAIRING TIME
PALMYRA WOOD
PANCAKE BELL
PANCAKE RACE
PANCHEN LAMA
PAPERED OVER
PARLOUR GAME
PARLOUR MAID
PARLOUR PINK
PARSLEY FERN
PARSONS NOSE
PASCHAL LAMB
PASCHAL MOON
PASSAGE BOAT
PASSAGE RITE
PASSING AWAY
PASSING BELL
PASSING NOTE
PASSING OVER
PASSING RICH
PASSING SHOT
PASSION PLAY
PASSION TIDE
PASSION WEEK
PASTURE LAND
PATTERN RACE
PATTERN SHOP
PEACOCK BLUE
PEACOCK FISH
PEACOCK LIKE
PEGGING AWAY
PEGGING BACK
PEGGING DOWN
PENALTY AREA
PENALTY GOAL
PENALTY KICK
PENALTY LINE
PENALTY SHOT
PENALTY SPOT
PENDANT POST
PEREIRA BARK
PERSIAN GULF
PERSIAN LAMB
PERSONA MUTA
PHANTOM LIMB
PHANTOM PAIN
PHRASAL VERB
PICKING OVER
PICKLED EGGS
PICTURE BOOK
PICTURE CARD
PICTURE CORD
PICTURE GOER
PICTURE PLAY
PICTURE RAIL
PICTURE WIRE
PIERCED EARS
PIGEONS MILK

7,4 *contd.*

PILLION SEAT
PINKING IRON
PITCHED ROOF
PLACKET HOLE
PLASTER CAST
PLASTER WORK
PLASTIC BOMB
PLASTIC CLAY
PLAYING BACK
PLAYING BALL
PLAYING CARD
PLAYING DOWN
PLAYING FAIR
PLAYING HOST
PLAYING SAFE
PLOUGHS BACK
PLUGGED AWAY
PLUMBIC ACID
POPULAR SONG
POSTERN GATE
POTTING SHED
POULTRY FARM
POULTRY YARD
POURING RAIN
POVERTY LINE
POVERTY TRAP
PRAIRIE WOLF
PREMIUM BOND
PRESENT ARMS
PRESSED HOME
PRESSES HOME
PRESTER JOHN
PRICKLE BACK
PRICKLY HEAT
PRICKLY PEAR
PRIESTS HOLE
PRIMARY CELL
PRIMARY COIL
PRIMING IRON
PRIMING WIRE
PRIVATE BANK
PRIVATE BILL
PRIVATE LIFE
PRIVATE VIEW
PRIVATE WARD
PROBATE DUTY
PROBLEM PAGE
PROBLEM PLAY
PRUNING BILL
PRUNING HOOK
PRUSSIC ACID
PUDDING PIPE
PULLING AWAY
PULLING BACK
PULLING DOWN
PULLING OVER
PULLING RANK
PUMPING IRON
PUNCHED TAPE

PUSHING PAST
PUTTING AWAY
PUTTING BACK
PUTTING DOWN
PUTTING OVER
PUTTING UPON
QUANTUM JUMP
QUANTUM LEAP
QUARREL PANE
QUARTER BACK
QUARTER DECK
QUARTER HOUR
QUARTER JACK
QUARTER NOTE
QUARTER PAST
QUARTER RAIL
QUARTER SEAL
QUARTER TONE
QUARTER WIND
RACQUET BALL
RADIANT HEAT
RADICAL AXIS
RADICAL SIGN
RAGTIME BAND
RAILWAY LINE
RAISING CAIN
RAISING HELL
RANGING POLE
READING BOOK
READING DESK
READING LAMP
READING ROOM
REAPING HOOK
REDDING COMB
REFUGEE CAMP
REGENCY BUCK
REPORTS BACK
REQUEST NOTE
REQUEST STOP
REQUIEM MASS
RESERVE BANK
RESERVE FUND
RETIRED LIST
REVERSE GEAR
REVERSE PASS
RHENISH WINE
RHODIAN LAWS
RIGGING LOFT
RIGGING TREE
RINGING BACK
RINGING DOWN
RINGING TRUE
ROCKING TOOL
ROLLING MILL
ROLLING OVER
ROMPING HOME
RONTGEN UNIT
ROUNDED DOWN
ROUPING WIFE
ROYSTON CROW

RUBBING DOWN
RUBBING POST
RUBBISH HEAP
RUMMAGE SALE
RUNNING AMOK
RUNNING AWAY
RUNNING COST
RUNNING DOWN
RUNNING FIRE
RUNNING GEAR
RUNNING HARD
RUNNING HEAD
RUNNING INTO
RUNNING KNOT
RUNNING MATE
RUNNING OVER
RUNNING RIOT
RUNNING SORE
RUNNING WILD
RUPERTS DROP
SAFFRON CAKE
SAILING BOAT
SAILING CLUB
SAILING SHIP
SALTING AWAY
SALTING DOWN
SALVAGE CREW
SAMPLER WORK
SANCTUS BELL
SATSUMA WARE
SAUSAGE MEAT
SAUSAGE ROLL
SAVINGS BANK
SCARLET BEAN
SCATTER RUGS
SCHICKS TEST
SCHOLAR LIKE
SCIENCE PARK
SCISSOR BILL
SCISSOR CASE
SCISSOR TAIL
SCRATCH COAT
SCRATCH TEST
SCRATCH WORK
SCREECH HAWK
SCUTTLE BUTT
SEAMING LACE
SEASIDE TOWN
SECONDS HAND
SECTION MARK
SECULAR HYMN
SELENIC ACID
SELLING RACE
SENDING DOWN
SENDING WORD
SERPENT STAR
SERVANT GIRL
SERVICE BOOK
SERVICE FLAT
SERVICE LINE

SERVICE ROAD
SERVICE ROOM
SERVICE TREE
SERVING TIME
SETTING BACK
SETTING DOWN
SETTING FOOT
SETTING FREE
SETTING SAIL
SETTING UPON
SETTLED DOWN
SETTLES DOWN
SHACKLE BOLT
SHACKLE BONE
SHAKING DOWN
SHAVING FOAM
SHAVING SOAP
SHOEING HORN
SHORTEN SAIL
SHOUTED DOWN
SILICON CHIP
SIMMERS DOWN
SINGING AWAY
SINGING SAND
SINGLES CLUB
SINKING FUND
SITTING BACK
SITTING DOWN
SITTING DUCK
SITTING ROOM
SKATING OVER
SKATING RINK
SKIMMED MILK
SKITTLE BALL
SLIDING KEEL
SLIDING SEAT
SLIPPED AWAY
SLIPPED DISC
SLIPPER BATH
SLOPING ARMS
SLOWING DOWN
SMOKING ROOM
SNAFFLE REIN
SOLDIER CRAB
SOLDIER LIKE
SOMEONE ELSE
SPANISH FOWL
SPANISH MAIN
SPANISH MOSS
SPANISH SOAP
SPANISH WALK
SPARROW BILL
SPARROW HAWK
SPATTER WORK
SPECTRE CRAB
SPINACH BEET
SPINDLE LEGS
SPINDLE TREE
SPONGED DOWN
SPONGES DOWN

7,4 *contd.*

SPOTTED DICK	THIMBLE CASE	UTILITY ROOM	WHISTLE AWAY
SQUEEZE HOME	THIMBLE RIGS	VARIETY SHOW	WHISTLE STOP
SQUEEZE PLAY	THIRSTY WORK	VATICAN CITY	WHITING POUT
STAGING AREA	THISTLE DOWN	VEDETTE BOAT	WHITSUN WEEK
STAGING BASE	THOUGHT BACK	VENTRAL FINS	WHITTLE AWAY
STAGING POST	THOUGHT OVER	VENTURI TUBE	WINDING DOWN
STANNIC ACID	THOUGHT WAVE	VICTORY SHIP	WINDSOR KNOT
STARTER HOME	THROUGH BALL	VILLAGE CART	WINDSOR SOAP
STATELY HOME	THROUGH BOLT	VILLAGE HALL	WINNING OVER
STATUTE BOOK	THROUGH PASS	VILLAGE POND	WINNING POST
STATUTE MILE	THUNDER CLAP	VILLAGE PUMP	WISHING BONE
STAYING OVER	THUNDER DART	VINTAGE PORT	WISHING WELL
STEAMED OPEN	THUNDER PEAL	VINTAGE YEAR	WITCHES BREW
STEPPED DOWN	TIBETAN APSO	VITAMIN PILL	WITHOUT FAIL
STIRRUP BONE	TICKING AWAY	VOLTAIC CELL	WOOLLEN MILL
STIRRUP IRON	TICKING OVER	WAILING WALL	WORKING BEAM
STIRRUP PUMP	TICKLED PINK	WAITING LIST	WORKING EDGE
STOMACH ACHE	TICKLES PINK	WAITING MAID	WORKING GIRL
STOMACH PUMP	TIFFANY LAMP	WAITING ROOM	WORKING OVER
STOPPED DEAD	TOBACCO PIPE	WAITING UPON	WORKING UPON
STOPPED OVER	TOPPLED OVER	WALKING AWAY	WORKING WEEK
STRIKES BACK	TOPPLES OVER	WALKING CANE	WORKMAN LIKE
STRIKES DOWN	TORCHON LACE	WALKING CASE	WORLDLY WISE
STRIKES DUMB	TORPEDO BOAT	WALKING INTO	WRITING BOOK
STRIKES HOME	TORPEDO BOOM	WALKING PART	WRITING CASE
STRINGY BARK	TORPEDO TUBE	WALKING RACE	WRITING DESK
STUBBLE RAKE	TOUCHED DOWN	WALKING TALL	WRITING DOWN
SUCKING FISH	TOUCHED WOOD	WALKING TOAD	WRITING HOME
SUCTION PUMP	TOUCHES DOWN	WASHING AWAY	WRITTEN DOWN
SUICIDE PACT	TOUCHES WOOD	WASHING DOWN	WROUGHT IRON
SULPHUR ROOT	TOWERED OVER	WASHING LINE	
SUPPORT AREA	TRACKED DOWN	WASHING SODA	**8,3**
SUPPORT HOSE	TRADING DOWN	WASSAIL BOUT	ABSTRACT ART
SURFACE MAIL	TRADING POST	WASTING AWAY	ALMIGHTY GOD
SURGEON FISH	TRAILED AWAY	WATCHED OVER	ANYTHING BUT
SURINAM TOAD	TRANSIT CAMP	WATCHES OVER	ARMOURED CAR
SWAGGER CANE	TRANSIT DUTY	WATERED DOWN	BARBADOS LEG
SWAGGER COAT	TRELLIS WORK	WEARING AWAY	BASTILLE DAY
SWALLOW DIVE	TRIATIC STAY	WEARING DOWN	BATTALIA PIE
SWALLOW TAIL	TRINITY TERM	WEARING THIN	BEETLING OFF
SWEATER GIRL	TROUBLE SPOT	WEATHER ROLL	BELAYING PIN
SWEENEY TODD	TROUSER CLIP	WEATHER SHIP	BESSEMER PIG
SWELLED HEAD	TROUSER SUIT	WEATHER SIGN	BILLIARD CUE
TALKING BACK	TRUMPET CALL	WEATHER VANE	BLACKING OUT
TALKING BOOK	TRUMPET TONE	WEATHER WISE	BLASTING OFF
TALKING DOWN	TUCKING MILL	WEATHER WORN	BLOTTING OUT
TALKING HEAD	TUMBLED OVER	WEAVERS KNOT	BLOTTING PAD
TALKING INTO	TUMBLES OVER	WEDDING CAKE	BLURTING OUT
TALKING OVER	TURBINE PUMP	WEDDING RING	BOARDING OUT
TALKING SHOP	TURKISH BATH	WEDDING VOWS	BOOTLACE TIE
TAMMANY HALL	TURNING AWAY	WEEDING FORK	BOTTLING OFF
TEARING AWAY	TURNING BACK	WEEDING HOOK	BOTTLING OUT
TEARING DOWN	TURNING DOWN	WEEPING ROCK	BOTTOMED OUT
TEARING INTO	TURNING INTO	WEEPING TREE	BREAKING OFF
TEARING OPEN	TURNING OVER	WEIGHED DOWN	BREAKING OUT
TELPHER LINE	TURNING TAIL	WESTERN ROLL	BRINGING OFF
TEMPTED FATE	TURNING TURK	WESTERN WALL	BRINGING OUT
TERTIUM QUID	TURNING UPON	WHALING PORT	BRUSHING OFF
THEATRE GOER	TUSSOCK MOTH	WHISKED AWAY	BULLYING OFF
	TWEEZER CASE	WHISKEY SOUR	BURIDANS ASS

8,3 *contd.*
CAMOMILE TEA
CARDINAL SIN
CARRIAGE DOG
CARRYING OFF
CARRYING OUT
CATCHING OUT
CHALKING OUT
CHARLESS LAW
CHECKING OFF
CHECKING OUT
CHESHIRE CAT
CHICKENS OUT
CHILLING OUT
CHIPPING OFF
CHURNING OUT
CIRCULAR SAW
CLEANING OUT
CLEARING OUT
CLOCKING OFF
CLOCKING OUT
COACHING INN
COCKTAIL BAR
COMPOUND EYE
CONFOUND YOU
CONTANGO DAY
CONTRACT OUT
CORDONED OFF
COUNTING OUT
COUPLING BOX
CRASHING OUT
CULINARY ART
DECLARED WAR
DECLARES WAR
DEFERRED PAY
DELIVERY MAN
DELIVERY VAN
DISPATCH BOX
DIVINING ROD
DOMESTIC PET
DOMINION DAY
DRAGGING OUT
DREDGING BOX
DRIPPING PAN
DROPPING OFF
DROPPING OUT
DROWNING OUT
DUCHESSE SET
ELECTRIC ARC
ELECTRIC EEL
ELECTRIC EYE
ELECTRIC RAY
ELECTRON GUN
ELEPHANT BOY
ELEPHANT GUN
ENABLING ACT
ENLISTED MAN
ENTRANCE FEE
FETCHING OUT
FIGHTING FIT

FIGHTING OFF
FINISHED OFF
FINISHES OFF
FLATTENS OUT
FLESHING OUT
FLINGING OUT
FLOATING RIB
FLOORING SAW
FOLLOWED OUT
FOUNDERS DAY
FOUNTAIN PEN
FREAKING OUT
FREEZING OUT
FRIGHTEN OFF
GALLOPED OFF
GAMBLING DEN
GATHERED WAY
GRESHAMS LAW
HARDENED OFF
HOLLOWED OUT
HOSPITAL BED
HYDROGEN ION
IGNITION KEY
INDIRECT TAX
JAUNTING CAR
JUDGMENT DAY
JUNCTION BOX
KANGAROO RAT
KNOCKING OFF
KNOCKING OUT
LABRADOR DOG
LABRADOR TEA
LAUGHING GAS
LAUGHING OFF
LEVELLED OFF
LOCHABER AXE
LOLLIPOP MAN
LUNCHEON BAR
MACASSAR OIL
MACKEREL SKY
MAGAZINE GUN
MARRIAGE BED
MARRYING OFF
MEDICINE MAN
MELLOWED OUT
MEMORIAL DAY
MIDNIGHT SUN
MOSQUITO NET
MOUNTAIN AIR
MOUNTAIN ASH
MOUNTAIN CAT
MOUNTAIN DEW
MOUNTAIN TOP
MULBERRY FIG
ORIGINAL SIN
PANDORAS BOX
PARAFFIN OIL
PARAFFIN WAX
PARAGUAY TEA
PEASANTS WAR

PENSIONS OFF
PERIGORD PIE
PHARAOHS ANT
PHRYGIAN CAP
PILTDOWN MAN
PLANTING OUT
PLYMOUTH HOE
POINTING OUT
POLISHED OFF
POLISHES OFF
POMPEIAN RED
PRECIOUS FEW
PRIMROSE WAY
PRINTERS INK
PRINTING INK
PRINTING OUT
PROCHAIN AMI
PRODIGAL SON
PRODUCER GAS
PROPERTY MAN
PROPERTY TAX
PURCHASE TAX
QUILTING BEE
RAILROAD CAR
RALLYING CRY
REACHING OUT
ROSEWOOD OIL
ROUGHING OUT
ROUNDING OFF
ROUNDING OUT
SANDWICH MAN
SARGASSO SEA
SAUCEPAN LID
SCOOPING OUT
SCORPION FLY
SCRAPING OFF
SCREENED OFF
SEMBLING BOX
SETTLING DAY
SHEERING OFF
SHELLING OUT
SHOOTING BOX
SHOOTING OFF
SHOOTING WAR
SHOPPING BAG
SHOULDER BAG
SHOULDER PAD
SHRUGGED OFF
SHUFFLED OFF
SHUFFLES OFF
SHUTTING OFF
SHUTTING OUT
SIDEREAL DAY
SKELETON KEY
SKETCHED OUT
SKETCHES OUT
SKITTLED OUT
SKITTLES OUT
SLACKENS OFF
SLEEPING BAG

SLEEPING CAR
SLEEPING OFF
SLINGING INK
SLINKING OFF
SLIPPERY ELM
SLIPPING OFF
SLOPPING OUT
SMELLING OUT
SNIFFING OUT
SNUFFING OUT
SOUNDING OFF
SOUNDING OUT
SOUNDING ROD
SPARKING OFF
SPARKING OUT
SPAWNING BED
SPEAKING OUT
SPELLING BEE
SPELLING OUT
SPINNING OUT
SPINNING TOP
SPLASHED OUT
SPLASHES OUT
SPLINTER BAR
STAMPING OUT
STANDING OFF
STANDING OUT
STANDING PAT
STARTERS GUN
STARTING OUT
STARVING OUT
STEERAGE WAY
STEPPING OUT
STICKING OUT
STINKING OUT
STOPPING OFF
STRAIGHT ARM
STRAIGHT CUT
STRAIGHT MAN
STRAIGHT OFF
STRAIGHT OUT
STRIKING OFF
STRIKING OIL
STRIKING OUT
STRIPPED OFF
STRIPPED OUT
SWITCHED OFF
SWITCHES OFF
TAKEOVER BID
TANTALUS CUP
TAPERING OFF
TEACHERS PET
TEACHING AID
THINKING OUT
THINNING OUT
THOMPSON GUN
THRASHED OUT
THRASHES OUT
THROWING OFF
THROWING OUT

8,3 *contd.*
TOUCHING OFF
TRAILING OFF
TRANSFER DAY
TRANSFER FEE
TRENCHER CAP
TRENCHER FED
TRENCHER MAN
TRIGGERS OFF
TROTTING OUT
TURNOVER TAX
TURNPIKE MAN
UNCALLED FOR
UNLOOKED FOR
UNWISHED FOR
VAGRANCY ACT
VENETIAN RED
VENTURED OUT
VENTURES OUT
VICTORIA DAY
VISITING DAY
VOLCANIC ASH
VOLCANIC MUD
WANDERED OFF
WATERING CAN
WEASELED OUT
WEATHERS OUT
WEIGHING OUT
WHIPPING BOY
WHIPPING TOP
WHISTLED OFF
WHISTLES OFF
WINDFALL TAX
WINKLING OUT
WORRYING OUT
WRIGGLED OUT
WRIGGLES OUT
WRINGING OUT
WRINGING WET

9,2
BREAKFAST TV
BUTTERING UP
BUTTONING UP
COLOURING IN
COLOURING UP
CONJURING UP
CONTRACTS IN
COTTONING ON
FASTENING ON
FATTENING UP
FINISHING UP
FOLLOWING ON
FOLLOWING UP
FRESHENED UP
GATHERING UP
LIGHTENED UP
LIMBERING UP
LISTENING IN
LOOSENING UP

MEASURING UP
OVERDOING IT
PLOUGHING IN
POLISHING UP
PREACHING AT
PREACHING UP
PUCKERING UP
QUICKENED UP
RECKONING ON
RECKONING UP
REJOICING IN
SCRUBBING UP
SLACKENED UP
SNUGGLING UP
SOFTENING UP
SOLDIERED ON
STITCHING UP
STRINGING UP
STRUGGLED ON
STRUGGLES ON
SUMMONING UP
SWALLOWED UP
SWITCHING ON
TOUGHENED UP
UNTHOUGHT OF

12 LETTERS

1,3,2,6
A BAG OF NERVES

1,3,8
X RAY SPECTRUM

1,4,5,2
I DONT THINK SO

1,4,7
A FINE ROMANCE
A GOOD INNINGS

1,5,2,4
A PIECE OF CAKE

1,5,6
A FOOLS ERRAND
A KINGS RANSOM
A TIGHT CORNER

1,6,5
A CRYING SHAME
A LIKELY STORY
A PRETTY PENNY
I SHOULD WORRY

1,7,4
A QUARTER PAST
I WOULDNT KNOW

2,1,4,5
BY A LONG CHALK
IN A COLD SWEAT
IN A GOOD LIGHT

2,1,5,4
BY A SHORT HEAD
ON A KNIFE EDGE

2,2,2,3,3
GO UP IN THE AIR

2,2,3,5
GO BY THE BOARD
GO ON ALL FOURS
IN AT THE DEATH

2,2,4,4
GO TO ONES HEAD
JE NE SAIS QUOI
ON AN EVEN KEEL
UP TO ONES NECK

2,2,8
DO IT YOURSELF
GO TO EXTREMES

2,3,2,3,2
ON AND ON AND ON
ON THE UP AND UP

2,3,2,5
AN AXE TO GRIND
NO BED OF ROSES
TO ERR IS HUMAN

2,3,3,4
IF THE CAP FITS
IN THE BOX SEAT
ON THE QUI VIVE
ON THE WAY DOWN

2,3,4,3
AN ALL TIME LOW
BE OFF WITH YOU
IN THE LONG RUN

2,3,7
DO NOT DISTURB
DO THE HONOURS
GO FOR NOTHING
IN ALL HONESTY
IN HOT PURSUIT
IN THE BALANCE
IN THE EXTREME
IN THE FASHION
IN THE PICTURE
IN THE RUNNING
OF THE ESSENCE
ON THE DECLINE
ON THE HORIZON
ON THE INSTANT
ON THE PAYROLL
ON THE RAMPAGE
ON THE REBOUND
ON THE STREETS
ON THE WARPATH
TO ALL INTENTS

2,4,1,5
GO LIKE A DREAM

2,4,2,1,3
AS SURE AS A GUN

2,4,2,4
AS GOOD AS GOLD
TU WHIT TU WHOO

2,4,3,3
GO ONES OWN WAY
GO OVER THE TOP
OF MICE AND MEN

2,4,4,2
TO HELL WITH IT

2,4,6
AT ARMS LENGTH
GO INTO DETAIL
GO INTO HIDING
IN FINE FETTLE
IN GOOD HEALTH
IN ONES POCKET
IN POOR HEALTH
IN THIS REGARD
ON ONES UPPERS
UP ONES STREET

2,5,2,3
AS BLACK AS INK
AS CLEAR AS MUD
AS OFTEN AS NOT
NO FLIES ON HER
NO FLIES ON HIM

2,5,5
AT FIRST BLUSH
AT FIRST LIGHT
AT KNIFE POINT
IN OTHER WORDS
IN SHORT ORDER
NO FIXED ABODE

2,6,4
AT DEATHS DOOR
ON BENDED KNEE
ST PETERS FISH
ST PETERS WORT

2,7,3
ST ANDREWS DAY
ST GEORGES DAY

2,10
AD REFERENDUM
EX SERVICEMAN
EX SERVICEMEN
IN CONCLUSION
IN CONFERENCE
IN PARTICULAR
IN PROPORTION
IN QUARANTINE
IN SUCCESSION
TO PERFECTION

3,1,3,5
HIT A BAD PATCH

3,1,4,2,2
HAD A TIME OF IT
HAS A TIME OF IT
PUT A SOCK IN IT

3,1,4,4
HAD A GOOD TIME
HAS A GOOD TIME

3,1,8
CAT O MOUNTAIN
HAD A BASINFUL
HAS A BASINFUL

3,2,1,6
ALL OF A DITHER
ALL OF A DOODAH
ALL OF A SUDDEN
EYE OF A NEEDLE
FIT AS A FIDDLE
MAD AS A HATTER
WIN IN A CANTER
WON IN A CANTER

3,2,2,5
LAY IT ON THICK
TIE UP IN KNOTS

3,2,3,4
ALL OF THE TIME
BAY AT THE MOON
END OF THE LINE
ITS AN ILL WIND
KEY OF THE DOOR
LAW OF THE LAND
LAY ON THE LINE
LAY ON THE OARS
LED BY THE NOSE
LIE OF THE LAND
LIE ON THE OARS
MAN IN THE MOON
ONE OF THE LADS
OUT IN THE OPEN
OUT OF THE BLUE
OUT OF THE BODY
OUT OF THE ROAD
OUT OF THE WOOD
PAT ON THE BACK
PAY AS YOU EARN
PUT ON ONE SIDE
PUT ON THE LINE
RUN OF THE MILL
SET BY THE EARS
SIX OF THE BEST
TAP ON THE HEAD
TOP OF THE FORM
TOP OF THE POPS
TWO UP TWO DOWN
WAG AT THE WALL
WAG BY THE WALL

3,2,4,3
GOD BE WITH YOU

MUD IN YOUR EYE
OUT OF THIN AIR
OUT ON ONES EAR

3,2,7
AGE OF CONSENT
ALL OR NOTHING
AND NO MISTAKE
ASK ME ANOTHER
BOX OF MATCHES
CAP OF LIBERTY
CUT TO RIBBONS
DEN OF THIEVES
EAU DE COLOGNE
EAU DE JAVELLE
LAW OF NATIONS
LAW OF OCTAVES
MAN OF DESTINY
MAN OF LETTERS
OIL OF VITRIOL
OUT OF CONTEXT
OUT OF CONTROL
OUT OF FASHION
OUT OF SPIRITS
OUT OF TROUBLE
PAS DE BOURREE
PAY IN ADVANCE
POP UP TOASTER
SET AN EXAMPLE
SON ET LUMIERE

3,3,2,4
THE DIE IS CAST

3,3,3,3
ONE FOR HIS NOB
PUT THE CAT OUT

3,3,4,2
GET THE WIND UP
GOT THE WIND UP
PUT THE BOOT IN

3,3,6
AIR SEA RESCUE
ALL AND SUNDRY
BIT THE BULLET
BOW AND SCRAPE
CAT AND FIDDLE
CUP AND SAUCER
CUT AND THRUST
CUT THE CACKLE
EGG AND ANCHOR
FOR THE RECORD
FOX AND HOUNDS
GET THE NEEDLE
GOT THE NEEDLE
HIP HIP HOORAY
HIP HIP HURRAH
HIT THE BOTTLE
OFF THE GROUND
OFF THE HINGES
OFF THE RECORD

OIL THE WHEELS
ONE WAY MIRROR
ONE WAY STREET
RIP VAN WINKLE
SAW THE SIGHTS
SEE THE SIGHTS
THE OLD BAILEY
THE RED PLANET
TIP THE SCALES
VIM AND VIGOUR

3,4,2,3
HER NAME IS MUD
HIS NAME IS MUD
THE LAMB OF GOD
THE TIME OF DAY

3,4,3,2
GET ONES EYE IN
GOT ONES EYE IN
PUT ONES OAR IN
SET ONES CAP AT

3,4,5
ATE ONES WORDS
BET ONES BOOTS
BIT ONES THUMB
DID ONES STUFF
DID ONES WORST
EAT ONES WORDS
GET ONES CARDS
GET RICH QUICK
GOT ONES CARDS
LET WELL ALONE
ODD COME SHORT
OFF ONES CHEST
OFF ONES CHUMP
OFF ONES GUARD
OFF ONES HANDS
OLD MANS BEARD
ONE FELL SWOOP
ONE JUMP AHEAD
PHI BETA KAPPA
POP ONES CLOGS
PUT INTO WORDS
RUB ONES HANDS
SIX FEET UNDER
THE BEES KNEES
THE DONE THING
THE HARD STUFF
THE LAST ENEMY
THE LAST STRAW
THE REAL MCCOY
THE REAL THING
THE VERY THING
THE WORM TURNS
WIN ONES SPURS
WON ONES SPURS

3,5,4
AIR FORCE BLUE
AND THATS THAT

BOY MEETS GIRL
FOR PETES SAKE
FOR PITYS SAKE
ICE CREAM SODA
MAN ABOUT TOWN
NEW MODEL ARMY
OLD FOLKS HOME
OLD WIVES TALE
ONE HORSE RACE
ONE HORSE TOWN
ONE TRACK MIND
RED BLOOD CELL
TEN POUND NOTE
THE OTHER SIDE
THE STORY GOES
THE UPPER HAND
TWO HORSE RACE
TWO SPEED GEAR
WHO DARES WINS
WIN HANDS DOWN
WON HANDS DOWN
YOU NEVER KNOW

3,6,3
ALL SAINTS DAY
ATE HUMBLE PIE
EAT HUMBLE PIE
NEW JERSEY TEA
NOT CALLED FOR
OLD SCHOOL TIE
RED LETTER DAY
TEN GALLON HAT
THE BITTER END
THE WICKED ONE
THE WORLDS END
WOE BETIDE HER
WOE BETIDE HIM
WOE BETIDE YOU

3,7,2
ALL SYSTEMS GO
LET ONESELF GO

3,9
AIR AMBULANCE
AIR COMMODORE
AIR CONDITION
ALL IMPORTANT
ALL INCLUSIVE
ANY QUESTIONS
ASH WEDNESDAY
AWE INSPIRING
BAR BILLIARDS
BOG PIMPERNEL
BOW COMPASSES
BUS CONDUCTOR
CUP FINALISTS
DAY BLINDNESS
EAR SPLITTING
GAS CONDENSER
GEM ENGRAVING

3,9 *contd.*
GET UNDRESSED
GOT UNDRESSED
HAD HYSTERICS
HAS HYSTERICS
HIS REVERENCE
HOT CHESTNUTS
HOT FAVOURITE
HOT GOSPELLER
ILL TREATMENT
JET PROPELLED
KEY SIGNATURE
LAW STATIONER
LAY COMMUNION
LOW CHURCHISM
LOW CHURCHMAN
LOW FREQUENCY
LOW WATERMARK
MAN OVERBOARD
MID VICTORIAN
MUD WRESTLING
NEO DARWINIAN
NEO DARWINISM
NEO DARWINIST
NEW DIMENSION
NEW ENGLANDER
NEW FASHIONED
NEW TESTAMENT
NON ADMISSION
NON ALCOHOLIC
NON ALIGNMENT
NON ATTENTION
NON CHRISTIAN
NON COMBATANT
NON COMMITTAL
NON COMMUNION
NON CONDUCTOR
NON EFFECTIVE
NON EFFICIENT
NON ESSENTIAL
NON EXECUTIVE
NON EXISTENCE
NON FICTIONAL
NON FLAMMABLE
NON RESIDENCE
NON RESIDENTS
OLD FASHIONED
OLD PRETENDER
OLD TESTAMENT
ONE SIDEDNESS
ONE UPMANSHIP
OUT PENSIONER
OXY ACETYLENE
PAY ATTENTION
PEN FEATHERED
PIN FEATHERED
POT COMPANION
PRE DRAVIDIAN
PRE ECLAMPSIA
PRE EMINENTLY

PRE ESTABLISH
PRE EXISTENCE
PRE QUALIFIED
PRE QUALIFIES
PRE SHRINKING
PRE TENSIONED
PSI PHENOMENA
RAW MATERIALS
RED CORPUSCLE
RUB SHOULDERS
SEA PORCUPINE
TAX ALLOWANCE
TAX AVOIDANCE
TAX COLLECTOR
TAX THRESHOLD
THE ACROPOLIS
THE TREATMENT
TIN STREAMING
VIN ORDINAIRE
WAY PASSENGER

4,1,3,4
LAND O THE LEAL
WILL O THE WISP

4,1,4,3
HAVE A NICE DAY
PULL A FAST ONE
TURN A DEAF EAR

4,1,5,2
TAKE A PRIDE IN
TAKE A SHINE TO
TOOK A PRIDE IN
TOOK A SHINE TO

4,1,7
BEAT A RETREAT
CAME A CROPPER
COME A CROPPER
DROP A CLANGER
JACK A LANTERN
JACK O LANTERN
MADE A BEELINE
MADE A KILLING
MAKE A BEELINE
MAKE A KILLING
POSE A PROBLEM
PULL A FLANKER
TAKE A BEATING
TOOK A BEATING
TROD A MEASURE
WELL I DECLARE

4,2,1,5
DAFT AS A BRUSH
DRAW TO A CLOSE
DREW TO A CLOSE
GIVE ON A PLATE
KICK UP A STINK
ONCE IN A WHILE
PUTS UP A FIGHT

4,2,2,4
BANG UP TO DATE
LEFT IT AT THAT

4,2,3,3
CORN ON THE COB
CURL UP AND DIE
EACH TO HIS OWN
EASY ON THE EYE
FREE AS THE AIR
GETS IN THE WAY
GIFT OF THE GAB
JACK IN THE BOX
LATE IN THE DAY
LEFT IN THE AIR
LIES IN THE WAY
NIPS IN THE BUD
PICK UP THE TAB
POKE IN THE EYE
PUTS ON THE MAP
ROOM AT THE TOP
SHOT IN THE ARM
STEP ON THE GAS
SUCK IT AND SEE

4,2,6
BACK OF BEYOND
BALL OF STRING
BANG TO RIGHTS
BILL OF LADING
BILL OF RIGHTS
BIRD OF WONDER
CALL OF NATURE
CAME UP TRUMPS
CEST LA GUERRE
CODE OF HONOUR
COME UP TRUMPS
COST OF LIVING
COUP DE FOUDRE
COUP DE MAITRE
CZAR OF RUSSIA
DEAD AS MUTTON
DEBT OF HONOUR
DEBT OF NATURE
FIRE OF LONDON
FREE OF CHARGE
GENS DE GUERRE
GOES TO GROUND
GOES TO PIECES
GONE TO PIECES
HAVE IT COMING
HEIR BY CUSTOM
HELD TO RANSOM
HOLD TO RANSOM
HOLY OF HOLIES
HORN OF PLENTY
HORS DE COMBAT
HORS DE SAISON
HYMN OF PRAISE
JACK IN OFFICE
KING OF BEASTS

LAWS OF HONOUR
LAWS OF MOTION
LIES AT ANCHOR
LINE OF BATTLE
LINE OF BEAUTY
LINE OF VISION
LOCK UP GARAGE
LOSS OF MEMORY
MAID OF HONOUR
MAKE IT SNAPPY
MAKE UP ARTIST
NEAR AS DAMMIT
NECK OF MUTTON
NEST OF TABLES
NONE SO PRETTY
OBOE DI CACCIA
PACK OF HOUNDS
PACK OF WOLVES
PAID BY CHEQUE
PAID UP MEMBER
PAIR OF GLOVES
PAIR OF PLIERS
PAIR OF SHORTS
PAIR OF TIGHTS
PART OF SPEECH
PAYS BY CHEQUE
PICK TO PIECES
PINT OF BITTER
PULL TO PIECES
PUTS IT MILDLY
PUTS ON RECORD
PUTS TO RIGHTS
RAGS TO RICHES
RIDE TO HOUNDS
RIOT OF COLOUR
RODE TO HOUNDS
ROLL OF HONOUR
ROSE OF SHARON
RUNS TO GROUND
SAFE AS HOUSES
SALE OR RETURN
SALT OF SORREL
SALT OF TARTAR
SETS AT NOUGHT
SETS TO RIGHTS
SIDE OF MUTTON
SNOW IN SUMMER
SPOT OF BOTHER
STOP GO POLICY
TAKE TO PIECES
TOOK TO PIECES
TOUR DE FRANCE
TSAR OF RUSSIA
TURN OF PHRASE
TURN UP TRUMPS
UPON MY HONOUR
WALK ON TIPTOE
WENT TO GROUND
WENT TO MARKET
WENT TO PIECES

4,2,6 *contd.*
WIND OF CHANGE
WINS ON POINTS
WORD OF HONOUR

4,3,1,4
PLAY FOR A DRAW
RIDE FOR A FALL
RODE FOR A FALL
TAKE FOR A RIDE
TOOK FOR A RIDE

4,3,2,3
FROM DAY TO DAY
FROM TOP TO TOE

4,3,3,2
COME AND GET IT
MIND HOW YOU GO

4,3,5
BACK AND FORTH
BEAT THE CLOCK
BUYS AND SELLS
CALL THE SHOTS
CASE THE JOINT
CASH AND CARRY
COOK THE BOOKS
COSI FAN TUTTE
COST THE EARTH
CUTS THE CARDS
DEEP SEA DIVER
DIED THE DEATH
DOES THE TRICK
DOES THE TWIST
DOWN AND OUTER
DOWN THE DRAIN
DOWN THE HATCH
EBBS AND FLOWS
FACE THE MUSIC
FAST AND LOOSE
FEEL THE PINCH
FELT THE PINCH
FINE AND DANDY
FIRE AND SWORD
FISH AND CHIPS
FORE AND AFTER
FROM THE HEART
GATE LEG TABLE
GOES FOR BROKE
GUYS AND DOLLS
HELD THE FLOOR
HELP THE CAUSE
HERE AND THERE
HOLD THE FLOOR
HUGS THE COAST
JUMP THE QUEUE
KEEP FIT CLASS
KEEP THE PEACE
KEPT THE PEACE
KNEW THE ROPES
KNEW THE SCORE

KNOW THE ROPES
KNOW THE SCORE
KNUR AND SPELL
LAID THE TABLE
LAYS THE TABLE
LETS OFF STEAM
LIFE AND DEATH
LOST FOR WORDS
LOUD AND CLEAR
MADE OLD BONES
MADE THE GRADE
MAKE OLD BONES
MAKE THE GRADE
MEAT AND DRINK
MILK AND HONEY
NECK TIE PARTY
NICE ONE CYRIL
NONE THE WISER
NUTS AND BOLTS
OVER AND ABOVE
OVER AND UNDER
PAID THE PIPER
PAID THE PRICE
PAYS THE PIPER
PAYS THE PRICE
PIPE AND TABOR
PLAY THE DEVIL
PLAY THE FIELD
QUIT THE SCENE
READ AND WRITE
READ THE SIGNS
RIDE THE WAVES
RISE AND SHINE
RODE THE WAVES
ROSE HIP SYRUP
RULE THE ROAST
RULE THE ROOST
SAFE AND SOUND
SAGE AND ONION
SAND FLY FEVER
SEES THE LIGHT
SELL THE DUMMY
SETS THE SCENE
SHOT THE WORKS
SICK AND TIRED
SLIP THE CABLE
SOLD THE DUMMY
TAKE THE BLAME
TAKE THE FIELD
TAKE THE FLOOR
TAKE THE REINS
TELL THE TRUTH
THEN AND THERE
TIME AND AGAIN
TIPS THE SCALE
TOLD THE TRUTH
TOOK THE BLAME
TOOK THE FIELD
TOOK THE FLOOR
TOOK THE REINS

TURN THE SCREW
WAIF AND STRAY
WALK THE PLANK
WAYS AND MEANS
WELL AND TRULY
WENT FOR BROKE
WHIP AND DERRY
WINS THE POOLS
WITH ONE VOICE

4,4,1,3
HELD DOWN A JOB
HOLD DOWN A JOB
TAKE DOWN A PEG
TOOK DOWN A PEG

4,4,4
AULD LANG SYNE
BACK ROOM BOYS
BLEW ONES MIND
BLOW ONES MIND
CAME INTO PLAY
COME INTO PLAY
CUTS BOTH WAYS
DEAD GIVE AWAY
DRAG ONES FEET
FALL INTO LINE
FEED ONES FACE
FELL INTO LINE
FIND ONES FEET
FOLD ONES ARMS
FOUR EYED FISH
GETS ONES GOAT
GOOD TIME GIRL
HALF SEAS OVER
HAND OVER FIST
HANG ONES HEAD
HIDE ONES HEAD
HOME FROM HOME
HUNG ONES HEAD
JUST LIKE THAT
KEEP GOOD TIME
KEEP ONES COOL
KEEP ONES HEAD
KEEP ONES WORD
KEPT GOOD TIME
KEPT ONES HEAD
KEPT ONES WORD
KNEW FULL WELL
KNOW FULL WELL
LADY JANE GREY
LEFT HAND SIDE
LICK ONES LIPS
LOSE ONES COOL
LOSE ONES HAIR
LOSE ONES HEAD
LOST ONES COOL
LOST ONES HAIR
MADE ENDS MEET
MADE GOOD TIME
MADE ONES MARK

MAKE ENDS MEET
MAKE GOOD TIME
MAKE ONES MARK
MEND ONES WAYS
MIND YOUR HEAD
MIND YOUR STEP
OVER ONES HEAD
PACK ONES BAGS
PASS ONES WORD
PAST ONES BEST
PICK ONES SPOT
PING PONG BALL
PLAY WITH FIRE
POUR WITH RAIN
PUSH ONES LUCK
PUTS ONES CASE
RISK ONES LIFE
ROLL ONES EYES
RUNS INTO DEBT
SAVE ONES FACE
SAVE ONES NECK
SAVE ONES SKIN
SELL ONES SOUL
SHOW ONES FACE
SHOW ONES HAND
SLIP ONES MIND
SOLD ONES SOUL
SUIT ONES BOOK
SURE FIRE CERT
TAKE ONES SEAT
TAKE ONES TIME
TAKE ONES TURN
TEAR ONES HAIR
TEST TUBE BABY
THIN BLUE LINE
TOOK ONES TIME
TOOK ONES TURN
TORE ONES HAIR
TRUE LOVE KNOT
TURN ONES HEAD
USED ONES LOAF
USES ONES LOAF
VENI VIDI VICI
WHIP POOR WILL
WILD WEST SHOW
WITH OPEN ARMS
WORK ONES WILL

4,5,3
BALL POINT PEN
LONG DRAWN OUT
PIGS MIGHT FLY
SHOE SHINE BOY

4,6,2
HIGH TAILED IT

4,8
AFRO AMERICAN
ALLA CAPPELLA
ANTE MERIDIEM

4,8 *contd.*
ANTI AIRCRAFT
ANTI SEMITISM
ASTI SPUMANTE
AUTO IMMUNITY
BABY BATTERER
BABY CARRIAGE
BABY SNATCHER
BACK PEDALLED
BACK SLAPPING
BACK STABBING
BALL BEARINGS
BASS CLARINET
BEAM TRAWLING
BELL BOTTOMED
BEND SINISTER
BIRD WATCHING
BLOW MOULDING
BODY BUILDING
BODY CHECKING
BODY LANGUAGE
BODY SNATCHER
BODY STOCKING
BOMB DISPOSAL
BOOK LEARNING
BULK DISCOUNT
BULL ELEPHANT
BUMP STARTING
CAMP FOLLOWER
CAMP PREACHER
CAMP SHEETING
CANE BOTTOMED
CAPE COLOURED
CAPE HYACINTH
CARD CARRYING
CASE HARDENED
CASH REGISTER
CATS WHISKERS
CAVE PAINTING
CELL DIVISION
CLIP FASTENER
CLUB SANDWICH
CLUB TOGETHER
COAL MERCHANT
COCK FIGHTING
CODE BREAKING
COIN OPERATED
COLD SHOULDER
COOL CUSTOMER
CORK LINOLEUM
CORN EXCHANGE
CORN MERCHANT
CROP SPRAYING
DEAD LANGUAGE
DEMI MONDAINE
DEUS VOBISCUM
DOCK LABOURER
DOOM MERCHANT
DUAL MONARCHY
DUCK SHOOTING

EARL PALATINE
EAST INDIAMAN
ECHO LOCATION
ECHO SOUNDING
EURO AMERICAN
EURO SCEPTICS
EVEN TEMPERED
EVIL SPEAKING
EVIL TEMPERED
FAIT ACCOMPLI
FARM LABOURER
FILM DIRECTOR
FILM FESTIVAL
FILM INDUSTRY
FILM PREMIERE
FIRE FIGHTING
FIRE WATCHING
FISH HATCHERY
FIVE ARTICLES
FOLK MEDICINE
FOOT DRAGGING
FOOT REGIMENT
FOOT SLOGGING
FOOT SOLDIERS
FORK LUNCHEON
FORM MISTRESS
FOUL LANGUAGE
FREE DELIVERY
FREE STANDING
FREE SWIMMING
FREE THINKING
FREE WHEELING
FROG MARCHING
FUEL INJECTED
FULL BOTTOMED
FULL THROATED
FUME CUPBOARD
GAIN STRENGTH
GAME PRESERVE
GETS CRACKING
GETS TOGETHER
GLUE SNIFFING
GOAT ANTELOPE
GOES DOWNHILL
GOES STRAIGHT
GOLD RESERVES
GOLD STANDARD
GONE DOWNHILL
GOOD BREEDING
GOOD GRACIOUS
GOOD HUMOURED
GOOD RIDDANCE
GOOD TEMPERED
GOOD THINKING
GRAM MOLECULE
GRAM NEGATIVE
GRAM POSITIVE
GREW TOGETHER
GREX VENALIUM
GREY SQUIRREL

GRIT BLASTING
GROW TOGETHER
HAIR RESTORER
HAIR SPLITTER
HALF MARATHON
HALF MEASURES
HALF TIMBERED
HANG TOGETHER
HARD CURRENCY
HARD STANDING
HEAD FOREMOST
HEAD GARDENER
HEAD REGISTER
HEIR APPARENT
HELD TOGETHER
HELP YOURSELF
HEMP AGRIMONY
HERD INSTINCT
HIGH COLOURED
HIGH FALUTING
HIGH FIDELITY
HIGH HOLIDAYS
HIGH PRESSURE
HIGH PRIESTLY
HIGH REACHING
HIGH SOUNDING
HIGH SPIRITED
HIGH STEPPING
HIGH VELOCITY
HIRE PURCHASE
HOLD TOGETHER
HOLY ALLIANCE
HOLY MACKEREL
HOME COUNTIES
HOME CROFTING
HOME PRODUCED
HOME STRAIGHT
HORS DOEUVRES
HUNG TOGETHER
INDO EUROPEAN
INDO GERMANIC
JOHN CHINAMAN
JUMP STARTING
KERB CRAWLING
KERB MERCHANT
KICK UPSTAIRS
KNEE BREECHES
KNEE CROOKING
LACE CURTAINS
LAKE DISTRICT
LAKE DWELLING
LAKE MICHIGAN
LAKE SUPERIOR
LAMP STANDARD
LAND GRABBING
LAND SURVEYOR
LAND YACHTING
LAST FRONTIER
LAST JUDGMENT
LATH SPLITTER

LEAP FROGGING
LEFT HANDEDLY
LEFT STANDING
LICK TRENCHER
LIFE SCIENCES
LIFE SENTENCE
LIKE WILDFIRE
LINE ENGRAVER
LIVE TOGETHER
LOAD SHEDDING
LOAN SHARKING
LONG DISTANCE
LONG DIVISION
LONG STANDING
LONG TROUSERS
LONG VACATION
LORD ADVOCATE
LORD ORDINARY
LOSS ADJUSTER
LOST PROPERTY
MAIL CARRIAGE
MANY COLOURED
MASS HYSTERIA
MASS MURDERER
MASS PRODUCED
MEAN SPIRITED
MILK PORRIDGE
MIND BOGGLING
MINE DETECTOR
MINE SWEEPING
MINI COMPUTER
MINI MOTORWAY
MISS UNIVERSE
MOCK HEROICAL
MONO COMPOUND
MOSS TROOPING
MOST REVEREND
NAIL SCISSORS
NAME DROPPING
NECK MOULDING
NEON LIGHTING
NEWS BULLETIN
NINE WORTHIES
NOSE BLEEDING
NOSE PAINTING
NUNC DIMITTIS
OATH BREAKING
OPEN MARRIAGE
OPEN QUESTION
OPEN SANDWICH
OPEN SENTENCE
PART EXCHANGE
PASS JUDGMENT
PASS SENTENCE
PEAK DISTRICT
PEER PRESSURE
PIGS TROTTERS
PINK ELEPHANT
PLUM COLOURED
POET LAUREATE

4,8 *contd.*
POLE POSITION
POLE VAULTING
PONS ASINORUM
PONY CARRIAGE
PONY TREKKING
POOR RELATION
POOR SPIRITED
PORK SAUSAGES
POST DILUVIAL
POST DILUVIAN
POST EXCHANGE
POST GRADUATE
POST HYPNOTIC
POST MERIDIAN
POST MERIDIEM
POST PRANDIAL
POST TERTIARY
PULL TOGETHER
PULP NOVELIST
PUSH STARTING
PUTS STRAIGHT
RAIL SPLITTER
REAL PRESENCE
REED PHEASANT
RING COMPOUND
RING DOTTEREL
ROAD SURVEYOR
ROCK CLIMBING
ROCK SCORPION
ROOT PRESSURE
ROSE COLOURED
ROSH HASHANAH
ROSY COLOURED
ROSY FINGERED
RUBY COLOURED
RUNS SMOOTHLY
RUSH HEADLONG
RUST COLOURED
SAFE BREAKING
SAFE CRACKING
SAGE THRASHER
SAND BLASTING
SAND PAINTING
SEED MERCHANT
SEES DAYLIGHT
SELF ABSORBED
SELF ACTIVITY
SELF ADHESIVE
SELF AFFECTED
SELF BETRAYAL
SELF CATERING
SELF CLEANING
SELF CONTEMPT
SELF CREATION
SELF CRITICAL
SELF DECEIVED
SELF DECEIVER
SELF DESTRUCT
SELF DEVOTION

SELF DIRECTED
SELF DIRECTOR
SELF EDUCATED
SELF EFFACING
SELF EMPLOYED
SELF EXERTION
SELF FOCUSING
SELF GLORIOUS
SELF HYPNOSIS
SELF IDENTITY
SELF INTEREST
SELF JUDGMENT
SELF ORDAINED
SELF PORTRAIT
SELF RELIANCE
SELF REPROACH
SELF THINKING
SEMI ANNUALLY
SEMI DETACHED
SEMI OFFICIAL
SEMI PRECIOUS
SEMI TROPICAL
SHIP CHANDLER
SHOT BLASTING
SHOW BUSINESS
SICK HEADACHE
SIDE ENTRANCE
SIDE TRACKING
SIDE WHISKERS
SIGN LANGUAGE
SIGN PAINTING
SILK STOCKING
SINO AMERICAN
SKIN GRAFTING
SLIP CARRIAGE
SLOW HANDCLAP
SLOW PUNCTURE
SLUM DWELLING
SNAP DECISION
SNAP FASTENER
SODA FOUNTAIN
SOFT CURRENCY
SOFT PEDALLED
SOUL STIRRING
STAR BLASTING
STAR SPANGLED
STEP DAUGHTER
STEP PATRENTS
SUIT YOURSELF
TAKE MEASURES
TAKE PRISONER
TAPE RECORDED
TAPE RECORDER
TENT PREACHER
THES DANSANTS
TILL DOOMSDAY
TIME EXPOSURE
TIME HONOURED
TOLL GATHERER
TONE LANGUAGE

TOOK MEASURES
TOOK PRISONER
TOUR DHORIZON
TOUR OPERATOR
TOWN PLANNING
TRAP SHOOTING
TREE KANGAROO
TYPE CYLINDER
TYPE FOUNDING
TYPE SPECIMEN
TYRE PRESSURE
UGLY CUSTOMER
UGLY DUCKLING
USER FRIENDLY
VASE PAINTING
VERY REVEREND
VICE CHAIRMAN
VICE GOVERNOR
WALL PAINTING
WALL STREETER
WEAK SPIRITED
WELL BALANCED
WELL DIRECTED
WELL DISPOSED
WELL DRESSING
WELL EDUCATED
WELL FAVOURED
WELL GROUNDED
WELL INFORMED
WELL MANNERED
WELL PLEASING
WELL TEMPERED
WELL TIMBERED
WENT DOWNHILL
WENT STRAIGHT
WEST MIDLANDS
WHIP SCORPION
WILD HUNTSMAN
WILD HYACINTH
WIND CHANGING
WINE COLOURED
WINE MERCHANT
WING SHOOTING
WOOD ENGRAVER
WOOD HYACINTH
WORD BUILDING
WORD PAINTING
YOUR EMINENCE
YOUR HIGHNESS
YOUR LADYSHIP
YOUR LORDSHIP
ZINC OINTMENT

5,1,4,2
MAKES A FUSS OF
MAKES A PASS AT

5,1,6
BREAK A RECORD
BREAK A STRIKE
BRING A CHARGE

BROKE A RECORD
BROKE A STRIKE
CASTS A GLANCE
COINS A PHRASE
KEEPS A SECRET
LIFTS A FINGER
PLOTS A COURSE
SPILL A BIBFUL
SPILT A BIBFUL
TABLE A MOTION
TAKES A TUMBLE
TAKES A WICKET
THREW A WOBBLY
THROW A WOBBLY

5,2,1,4
BRING TO A HEAD
CLEAR AS A BELL
COMES TO A HEAD
DRUNK AS A LORD
GRIND TO A HALT
KICKS UP A FUSS
MERRY AS A GRIG
SOUND AS A BELL

5,2,2,3
MEANS TO AN END
PLAYS IT BY EAR
WHITE OF AN EGG

5,2,3,2
KEEPS AN EYE ON
TAKES IT OUT ON

5,2,5
ANGEL OF MERCY
ASHES TO ASHES
BEANS ON TOAST
BLACK AS PITCH
BLANC DE CHINE
BLAZE OF GLORY
BOARD OF TRADE
BRING TO LIGHT
BUNCH OF FIVES
CALLS TO ORDER
CHEEK TO CHEEK
CHIEF OF STAFF
CLERK OF WORKS
CLOTH OF STATE
CLOUD OF SMOKE
CLUBS TO DEATH
COAST TO COAST
COMES TO BLOWS
COMES TO GRIEF
COMES TO LIGHT
CREME DE CACAO
CREPE DE CHINE
DANCE OF DEATH
DEPTH OF FIELD
DEPTH OF FOCUS
DOING TO DEATH
DRIVE IN MOVIE

5,2,5 *contd.*
ENDED IN TEARS
EVERY SO OFTEN
FEAST OF ASSES
FEAST OF FOOLS
FEMME DU MONDE
FLEET OF TAXIS
FLOCK OF GEESE
FLOCK OF SHEEP
FORCE OF HABIT
FRESH AS PAINT
FRONT OF HOUSE
GLASS OF WATER
GOING IT ALONE
GOING TO COURT
GOING TO EARTH
GOING TO GRASS
GOING TO PRESS
GOING TO SLEEP
GOING TO WASTE
GRAIN OF TRUTH
HANGS IN THERE
HAPPY AS LARRY
HAPPY GO LUCKY
HASTA LA VISTA
HEADS OR TAILS
HEART OF STONE
HEART TO HEART
HOLDS IN CHECK
HOMME DU MONDE
HOTEL DE VILLE
HOUSE OF CARDS
HOUSE OF LORDS
HOUSE OF PEERS
HOUSE TO HOUSE
KEEPS IN CHECK
KEEPS IN TOUCH
LAUGH TO SCORN
LYING IN STATE
MERRY GO ROUND
MIGHT IS RIGHT
MOUTH TO MOUTH
MOVED TO TEARS
MOVES TO TEARS
OEILS DE BOEUF
ORDER OF MERIT
PICKS UP SPEED
PIECE OF BREAD
PIECE OF EIGHT
PIECE OF GOODS
PIECE OF PAPER
POINT OF ORDER
POINT TO POINT
POUND OF FLESH
PRICE OF MONEY
PRIDE OF PLACE
RHYME TO DEATH
RIGHT OF ENTRY
SHAFT OF LIGHT
SHEET OF GLASS

SHEET OF PAPER
SHORE TO SHORE
SHORT OF MONEY
SHORT OF SPACE
STAND UP COMIC
STATE OF SIEGE
STOCK IN TRADE
TAKEN BY STORM
TAKEN ON BOARD
TAKEN ON TRUST
TAKEN TO COURT
TAKES BY STORM
TAKES ON BOARD
TAKES ON TRUST
TAKES TO COURT
TAKES TO HEART
TERMS OF TRADE
TOWER OF BABEL
TRICK OR TREAT
VALET DE PLACE
VIOLA DA GAMBA
WAITS AT TABLE
WHICH IS WHICH
YOUNG AT HEART

5,3,1,3
QUEEN FOR A DAY

5,3,2,2
WANTS JAM ON IT

5,3,4
ABOVE THE LINE
ACTED THE FOOL
ACTED THE GOAT
AFTER THE FACT
ARGUE THE TOSS
BEATS THE BAND
BEATS THE DRUM
BELOW THE BELT
BELOW THE LINE
BELOW THE SALT
BIRDS EYE VIEW
BITES THE DUST
BLACK AND BLUE
BLOWS THE GAFF
BREAK THE BANK
BREAK THE NEWS
BROKE THE BANK
BROKE THE NEWS
CALLS THE TUNE
CARRY THE FLAG
CHALK AND TALK
CLEAN AND JERK
COACH AND FOUR
COACH AND PAIR
COMES AND GOES
CRACK THE WHIP
CROSS PLY TYRE
CURDS AND WHEY
DARBY AND JOAN

DEVIL MAY CARE
DRAWS THE LINE
EVERY MAN JACK
FIFTY PER CENT
FILLS THE BILL
FIRST AND LAST
FIRST SEA LORD
FLIES THE FLAG
FOOTS THE BILL
FORCE AND FEAR
FORCE THE PACE
GILDS THE LILY
GILDS THE PILL
GIVEN THE PUSH
GIVEN THE SACK
GIVEN THE SLIP
GOING FOR GOLD
HAPPY NEW YEAR
HEART AND HAND
HEART AND SOUL
HEAVE THE LEAD
HOLDS THE FORT
HOLDS THE LINE
HOLDS THE ROAD
HOOKS AND EYES
HORSE AND CART
INFRA RED LAMP
KNIFE AND FORK
LAGER AND LIME
LAUGH OUT LOUD
LEAVE FOR DEAD
LEAVE ONE COLD
LEAVE THE ROOM
LOOPS THE LOOP
MAKES THE PACE
MIGHT AND MAIN
MILES PER HOUR
MORES THE PITY
NEVER YOU MIND
PAINT THE LILY
PITCH AND TOSS
PLAYS FOR TIME
PLAYS THE FOOL
PLAYS THE GAME
PLAYS THE LEAD
PORGY AND BESS
PRAYS FOR RAIN
PUNCH AND JUDY
RAISE THE ROOF
RAISE THE WIND
RIGHT AND LEFT
RIGHT THE HELM
RINGS THE BELL
ROCKS THE BOAT
ROUND THE BEND
SCOOP THE POOL
SHIPS THE OARS
SHOUT THE ODDS
SHOWN THE DOOR
SHOWS THE FLAG

SMASH AND GRAB
SOWED THE SEED
SPEAK TOO SOON
SPICK AND SPAN
SPLIT THE VOTE
SPOKE TOO SOON
STAND THE PACE
STAYS THE PACE
STEAL THE SHOW
STEMS THE TIDE
STICK THE PACE
STOLE THE SHOW
STOOD THE PACE
STOPS THE SHOW
STUCK THE PACE
SUGAR THE PILL
SWEET AND SOUR
SWING THE LEAD
SWUNG THE LEAD
TAKES POT LUCK
TAKES THE BAIT
TAKES THE CAKE
TAKES THE LEAD
TAKES THE MICK
TAKES THE VEIL
THERE AND THEN
THICK AND FAST
THICK AND THIN
THINK OUT LOUD
THREE ACT PLAY
THREE PIN PLUG
TOOTH AND NAIL
TURKS CAP LILY
TURNS THE TIDE
TYING THE KNOT
UNDER AND OVER
UNDER THE HEEL
VENUS FLY TRAP
VODKA AND LIME
WATCH AND WARD
WHATS HER NAME
WHATS HIS NAME
WHATS ITS NAME
WHATS THE ODDS
WHEEL AND DEAL
WORMS EYE VIEW
WRACK AND RUIN

5,4,3
BITES ONES LIP
BLOWS ONES TOP
CARRY ONES BAT
DOING ONES BIT
DOING ONES NUT
FLIPS ONES LID
GOING ONES WAY
HOLDS ONES OWN
JOLLY JACK TAR
LOSES ONES RAG
LOSES ONES WAY

5,4,3 *contd.*
MAKES ONES DAY
MAKES ONES WAY
NEATS FOOT OIL
PICKS ONES WAY
PLAYS ONES ACE
PRESS HAND OUT
RAISE ONES HAT
RAPID FIRE GUN
RIGHT HAND MAN
SHOWS ONES AGE
SLUNG ONES BAT
SPORT ONES OAK
STUBS ONES TOE
TAKES ONES CUE
TAKES TIME OFF
THREE WISE MEN
TRUTH WILL OUT
UNDER ONES HAT
WENDS ONES WAY
WINGS ONES WAY

5,5,2
MAKES LIGHT OF
POURS SCORN ON
SHEDS LIGHT ON
THREW LIGHT ON
THROW LIGHT ON

5,7
ABOVE ONESELF
ACTOR MANAGER
ADDLE BRAINED
AGENT GENERAL
ALPHA BLOCKER
APPLE BLOSSOM
APPLE BOBBING
APRIL SHOWERS
APRON STRINGS
ARCUS SENILIS
BARMY BRAINED
BARON OFFICER
BASIC ENGLISH
BASIC PROCESS
BASSO RILIEVO
BEAUX ESPRITS
BELLY DANCING
BELLY LANDING
BENCH WARRANT
BIBLE POUNDER
BIBLE THUMPER
BIRDS NESTING
BIRTH CONTROL
BLACK COUNTRY
BLACK DIAMOND
BLACK ECONOMY
BLACK FISHING
BLACK HEARTED
BLACK MUSTARD
BLACK PUDDING
BLACK SALSIFY

BLAST FURNACE
BLOCK BOOKING
BLOCK CAPITAL
BLOCK RELEASE
BLOOD BLISTER
BLOOD BROTHER
BLOOD PUDDING
BOARD MEETING
BOBBY DAZZLER
BONNE VIVANTE
BRAIN SURGEON
BRAND LOYALTY
BRASS BOUNDER
BRASS RUBBING
BREAD PUDDING
BREAK THROUGH
BRIDE CHAMBER
BRING FORWARD
BUNKO STEERER
BURNT ALMONDS
CABIN CRUISER
CABLE RAILWAY
CABLE TRAMWAY
CAIRN TERRIER
CANDY STRIPED
CANON REGULAR
CANON SECULAR
CARRY FORWARD
CARRY THROUGH
CARTE BLANCHE
CAUSE CELEBRE
CAUSE TROUBLE
CHAIN GEARING
CHAIN REACTOR
CHAIN SMOKING
CHART BUSTING
CHECK WEIGHER
CHEFS DOEUVRE
CHESS PROBLEM
CHEST FREEZER
CHIEF JUSTICE
CHIEF MOURNER
CHIEF WITNESS
CHILD BENEFIT
CHILD PRODIGY
CHILD WELFARE
CIRRO CUMULUS
CIRRO STRATUS
CIVIL DEFENCE
CIVIL LIBERTY
CIVIL SERVANT
CIVIL SERVICE
CLAIM DAMAGES
CLEAR SIGHTED
CLOCK WATCHER
CLOSE COMPANY
CLOSE CROPPED
CLOSE FITTING
CLOSE GRAINED
CLOSE HARMONY

CLOSE MOUTHED
CLOUD CEILING
CLOUD CHAMBER
COACH STATION
COMES BETWEEN
COMES FORWARD
COMES UNSTUCK
CONIC SECTION
COUGH LOZENGE
COUGH MIXTURE
COUNT DRACULA
COURT DRESSER
COURT MARTIAL
COURT PLASTER
COVER VERSION
CRASH BARRIER
CRASH LANDING
CREAM CRACKER
CREME CARAMEL
CREPE SUZETTE
CROSS BUTTOCK
CROSS COUNTRY
CROSS CURRENT
CROSS EXAMINE
CROSS GRAINED
CROSS PURPOSE
CROSS SECTION
CROWN WITNESS
CRUEL HEARTED
CRUSH BARRIER
DAILY SERVICE
DAIRY FARMING
DANCE ROUTINE
DANSE MACABRE
DEATH DEALING
DEATH PENALTY
DEATH WARRANT
DELLA CRUSCAN
DEVIL WORSHIP
DRAFT DODGING
DRESS UNIFORM
DRINK DRIVING
DUTCH AUCTION
DUTCH COMFORT
DUTCH COURAGE
EARLY CLOSING
EARLY ENGLISH
EARLY WARNING
EARTH CREATED
EARTH SCIENCE
ELGIN MARBLES
ENJOY ONESELF
ETHYL ALCOHOL
EXACT SCIENCE
EXTRA SENSORY
EXTRA SPECIAL
FAINT HEARTED
FAITH HEALING
FALLS THROUGH
FALSE COLOURS

FALSE MODESTY
FANCY ONESELF
FAULT FINDING
FENCE MENDING
FIELD BATTERY
FIELD COLOURS
FIELD GLASSES
FIELD KITCHEN
FIELD MARSHAL
FIELD MEETING
FIELD OFFICER
FIERY FURNACE
FIRST FOOTING
FIRST INNINGS
FIRST NIGHTER
FIRST READING
FIRST REFUSAL
FIRST RESERVE
FIXED CAPITAL
FIXED CHARGES
FIXED PENALTY
FLAME THROWER
FLICK THROUGH
FLINT HEARTED
FLINT KNAPPER
FOOLS PARSLEY
FORCE FEEDING
FORCE MAJEURE
FOUND WANTING
FRONT BENCHER
FRONT LOADING
FRUIT MACHINE
FULLY FLEDGED
GAINS CONTROL
GAMES TEACHER
GIANT KILLING
GIRDS ONESELF
GIVES OFFENCE
GLASS BLOWING
GLASS CUTTING
GLASS SLIPPER
GLOBE THISTLE
GLOBE TROTTER
GOING AGAINST
GOING CONCERN
GOING FORWARD
GOING MISSING
GOING THROUGH
GOING WITHOUT
GOOSE PIMPLES
GRAND GUIGNOL
GRAND LARCENY
GRAND MARNIER
GRAND TOURING
GRASS WIDOWER
GRAVE CLOTHES
GREAT BELLIED
GREAT BRITAIN
GREAT EASTERN
GREAT HEARTED

5,7 contd.
GREAT WESTERN
GREEK GODDESS
GREEN FINGERS
GREEN GODDESS
GROSS TONNAGE
GROUP CAPTAIN
GROUP THERAPY
GUEST CHAMBER
GUILD BROTHER
GUILT COMPLEX
HABIT FORMING
HAIRS BREADTH
HANDS BREADTH
HAPPY LANDING
HASTY PUDDING
HAUTE COUTURE
HAUTE CUISINE
HEART DISEASE
HEART FAILURE
HEART RENDING
HEART STRINGS
HEAVY HEARTED
HEAVY SLEEPER
HEAVY WEATHER
HEDGE CREEPER
HEDGE HOPPING
HEDGE MUSTARD
HEDGE PARSLEY
HEDGE SPARROW
HELPS ONESELF
HOMME DESPRIT
HONEY BUZZARD
HONEY MOUTHED
HONEY TONGUED
HORSE BREAKER
HORSE DEALING
HORSE SOLDIER
HORSE TRADING
HORSE TRAINER
HOUSE BREAKER
HOUSE HUNTING
HOUSE HUSBAND
HOUSE PAINTER
HOUSE STEWARD
HOUSE SURGEON
HOUSE TRAINED
HOUSE WARMING
IMAGE BREAKER
IMAGE WORSHIP
INDEX LINKING
INNER CABINET
INNER SANCTUM
INTER SCIENCE
IONIC DIALECT
IRISH TERRIER
IRISH WHISKEY
JAPAN CURRENT
JAPAN LACQUER
JERRY BUILDER

JOINT ACCOUNT
JOINT TENANCY
KEEPS COUNSEL
KICKS ONESELF
KINGS COUNSEL
KINGS ENGLISH
KNIFE GRINDER
KYRIE ELEISON
LADYS CUSHION
LADYS FINGERS
LADYS SLIPPER
LADYS THISTLE
LARGE HEARTED
LASER PRINTER
LATIN AMERICA
LATIN QUARTER
LEGAL PROCESS
LEVEL PEGGING
LIGHT BRIGADE
LIGHT HEARTED
LIGHT RAILWAY
LIGHT SLEEPER
LIVER SAUSAGE
LOGIC CIRCUIT
LOGIC DIAGRAM
LOGIC PROBLEM
LOOKS ASKANCE
LOOKS DAGGERS
LOOKS FORWARD
LOOSE FORWARD
LOOSE HOUSING
LORRY HOPPING
LOSES CONTROL
LOSES ONESELF
LOWER BRACKET
LOWER CHAMBER
LOWER REGIONS
LUNAR CAUSTIC
MADAM SPEAKER
MAGIC CIRCLES
MAGIC LANTERN
MAGIC SPHERES
MAGIC SQUARES
MAJOR GENERAL
MAJOR PROPHET
MAKES BELIEVE
MAKES CERTAIN
MAKES CHANGES
MAKES FRIENDS
MAKES HISTORY
MAKES INROADS
MAKES WHOOPEE
MANGO CHUTNEY
MARSH HARRIER
MARSH WARBLER
MEALY MOUTHED
MERCY KILLING
MERRY DANCERS
MERRY ENGLAND
MEZZO RELIEVO

MEZZO RILIEVO
MEZZO SOPRANO
MILLS GRENADE
MINOR PLANETS
MINOR PREMISE
MINOR PROPHET
MIXED ABILITY
MIXED BATHING
MIXED CRYSTAL
MIXED DOUBLES
MIXED ECONOMY
MIXED FARMING
MODEL RAILWAY
MODUS VIVENDI
MOLLY MAGUIRE
MONEY CHANGER
MONEY GRUBBER
MONEY LENDING
MONEY MATTERS
MONEY SPINNER
MORAL COURAGE
MORAL SUPPORT
MORAL VICTORY
MOTOR BICYCLE
MOTOR CARAVAN
MOTOR CYCLING
MOTOR CYCLIST
MOTOR SCOOTER
MOTOR TRACTOR
MOUND BUILDER
MOUNT EVEREST
MOUTH FILLING
MUSIC TEACHER
NARCO THERAPY
NAVAL BRIGADE
NAVAL OFFICER
NERVE IMPULSE
NERVE RACKING
NEVER FAILING
NIGHT CLOTHES
NIGHT FISHING
NIGHT PROWLER
NIGHT TERRORS
NORTH AMERICA
NORTH COUNTRY
NORTH EASTERN
NORTH WESTERN
OPERA COMIQUE
OPERA GLASSES
ORGAN GALLERY
ORGAN GRINDER
OTTER HUNTING
PANEL BEATING
PANEL HEATING
PANEL WORKING
PAPER HANGING
PAPER MARBLER
PAPER PROFITS
PAPER STAINER
PAPER WASHING

PARTY MACHINE
PARTY VERDICT
PASSE PARTOUT
PEACE BREAKER
PEACE KEEPING
PEACE OFFICER
PEARL DISEASE
PEARL ESSENCE
PEARL FISHERY
PEARL FISHING
PEARL SHELLER
PEARL TAPIOCA
PEASE BLOSSOM
PEDAL PUSHERS
PENNY WEDDING
PENNY WHISTLE
PETTY LARCENY
PETTY OFFICER
PHOTO ETCHING
PHOTO PROCESS
PIANO RECITAL
PILOT BALLOON
PILOT OFFICER
PINCH HITTING
PIOUS OPINION
PLACE SETTING
PLAIN CLOTHES
PLAIN DARNING
PLAIN DEALING
PLAIN HEARTED
PLAIN SAILING
PLANE SAILING
PLANO CONCAVE
PLANO CONICAL
PLATE LEATHER
PLATT DEUTSCH
PLAYS FOOTSIE
POPES KNIGHTS
PORTE BONHEUR
PORTE MONNAIE
POTTS DISEASE
POUND FOOLISH
POWER STATION
PRAWN CRACKER
PREEN ONESELF
PRESS CUTTING
PRESS FORWARD
PRESS GALLERY
PRESS GANGING
PRESS OFFICER
PRESS RELEASE
PRICE CONTROL
PRICE CUTTING
PRIME NUMBERS
PRINT THROUGH
PRIVY CHAMBER
PRIVY COUNCIL
PRIZE FIGHTER
PROOF CORRECT
PROOF READING

5,7 *contd.*

PROTO HISTORY
PROUD HEARTED
PULLS STRINGS
PULLS THROUGH
PUPIL TEACHER
PURSE STRINGS
QUEEN CONSORT
QUEEN DOWAGER
QUEEN REGNANT
QUEUE JUMPING
QUICK SCENTED
QUICK SELLING
QUICK SIGHTED
QUILL DRIVING
QUILL FEATHER
RADIO AMATEUR
RADIO COMPASS
RADIO ELEMENT
RADIO ISOTOPE
RADIO STATION
RANGE ONESELF
REIGN SUPREME
RHUMB SAILING
RIFLE GRENADE
RIVER STEAMER
RIVER TERRACE
RIVER TRAFFIC
ROAST CHICKEN
ROMAN EMPEROR
ROMPS THROUGH
ROTOR STATION
ROUGH DIAMOND
ROUGH GRAINED
ROUGH GRAZING
ROUGH JUSTICE
ROUGH PASSAGE
ROUGH PERFECT
ROUGH WROUGHT
ROUND MOUTHED
ROYAL ACADEMY
ROYAL MARINES
ROYAL WARRANT
ROYAL WEDDING
SABIN VACCINE
SAINT MATTHEW
SAINT PATRICK
SALES MANAGER
SAVOY CABBAGE
SCARE HEADING
SCENE PAINTER
SCENE SHIFTER
SCREW STEAMER
SEDGE WARBLER
SEINE FISHING
SENDS PACKING
SERUM THERAPY
SERVO CONTROL
SHARE CAPITAL
SHARP LOOKING

SHARP SIGHTED
SHARP TONGUED
SHARP TOOTHED
SHAWL PATTERN
SHEEP FARMING
SHEEP SHEARER
SHEEP STATION
SHEEP STEALER
SHIFT ONESELF
SHIFT WORKING
SHIPS COMPANY
SHIPS HUSBAND
SHOCK TACTICS
SHOCK THERAPY
SHORT CHANGED
SHORT CHANGES
SHORT CIRCUIT
SHORT COMMONS
SHORT LISTING
SHORT MEASURE
SHORT SIGHTED
SHORT TERMISM
SHOWS PROMISE
SHOWS WILLING
SIGHT PLAYING
SIGHT READING
SIGHT SINGING
SKUNK CABBAGE
SLANG WHANGER
SLATE WRITING
SLAVE HOLDING
SLAVE TRAFFIC
SLEEP WALKING
SLINK BUTCHER
SMALL CAPITAL
SMALL CLOTHES
SMALL LETTERS
SMEAR TACTICS
SNAKE CHARMER
SNEAK PREVIEW
SNUFF DIPPING
SOLAR BATTERY
SOLAR ECLIPSE
SONIC BARRIER
SOUND BARRIER
SOUND EFFECTS
SOUND RANGING
SOUTH AMERICA
SOUTH COUNTRY
SOUTH EASTERN
SOUTH WESTERN
SPACE HEATING
SPACE SHUTTLE
SPACE STATION
SPACE VEHICLE
SPARK CHAMBER
SPEAK VOLUMES
SPEAR RUNNING
SPEAR THISTLE
SPEAR THROWER

SPEED BOATING
SPEED READING
SPINE CHILLER
SPIRE STEEPLE
SPLAY MOUTHED
SPLIT LEATHER
SPOKE VOLUMES
SPOON FEEDING
STACK AGAINST
STAFF CANTEEN
STAFF COLLEGE
STAFF OFFICER
STAFF SURGEON
STAGE MANAGED
STAGE MANAGER
STAGE MANAGES
STAGE THUNDER
STAGE WHISPER
STALL FEEDING
STAMP MACHINE
STAND ACCUSED
STAND AGAINST
STATE FUNERAL
STATE LOTTERY
STATE PENSION
STEAM CHAMBER
STEAM TURBINE
STEAM WHISTLE
STEEL ERECTOR
STIFF HEARTED
STILT WALKING
STOCK BREEDER
STOCK COMPANY
STOCK FARMING
STOCK JOBBERY
STOCK JOBBING
STONE BREAKER
STONE CUTTING
STONE DRESSER
STONE PARSLEY
STONY HEARTED
STOOD ACCUSED
STOOD AGAINST
STORM LANTERN
STORM SHUTTER
STORM TROOPER
STORM WARNING
STORY TELLING
STOUT HEARTED
STRAP HANGING
STRIP CARTOON
STUMP ORATORY
SUGAR REFINER
SUITS ONESELF
SWAMP CYPRESS
SWASH LETTERS
SWEET ALYSSUM
SWEET SCENTED
SWEET TALKING
SWEET TOOTHED

SWEET WILLIAM
SWINE KEEPING
SWORD BAYONET
TABLE LICENCE
TABLE MANNERS
TABLE TURNING
TAKES COMMAND
TAKES OFFENCE
TAKES UMBRAGE
THICK SKINNED
THICK SKULLED
THIEF CATCHER
THINK THROUGH
THIRD READING
TIGER COUNTRY
TIGHT FITTING
TOOTH DRAWING
TOTAL THEATRE
TRACE ELEMENT
TRADE JOURNAL
TRAGI COMICAL
TRAIL BLAZING
TRAIN SPOTTER
TRIAL BALANCE
TRIAL BALLOON
TRICK CYCLIST
TROOP CARRIER
TRUCE BREAKER
TRUST ACCOUNT
TRUST COMPANY
TRUTH TELLING
TURNS AGAINST
UNDER LICENCE
UNDER PRODUCE
UNDER PROTEST
UNDER SHERIFF
UPPER BRACKET
UPPER CLASSES
URBAN RENEWAL
VICAR GENERAL
VIRUS DISEASE
WASTE PRODUCT
WATCH CRYSTAL
WATCH OFFICER
WATER BAILIFF
WATER BALLAST
WATER BATTERY
WATER BISCUIT
WATER BLISTER
WATER BOATMAN
WATER BUFFALO
WATER CARRIER
WATER COOLING
WATER CULTURE
WATER DIVINER
WATER FLOWING
WATER HEMLOCK
WATER MEASURE
WATER MILFOIL
WATER OPOSSUM

5,7 *contd.*
WATER PARSNIP
WATER REACTOR
WATER SPANIEL
WATER TORTURE
WATER WAGTAIL
WAXED LEATHER
WEILS DISEASE
WELSH DRESSER
WELSH RAREBIT
WHALE FISHERY
WHALE FISHING
WHATS COOKING
WHEEL CLAMPED
WHITE ADMIRAL
WHITE BEARDED
WHITE CRESTED
WHITE CROWNED
WHITE FEATHER
WHITE LEATHER
WHITE LIVERED
WHITE PUDDING
WHITE RUSSIAN
WHOLE HEARTED
WHOLE SKINNED
WORKS AGAINST
WORKS COUNCIL
WORLD BEATING
WRONG FOOTING
YOUNG FOGYISH
YOURE WELCOME
YOUTH CUSTODY
ZONAL DEFENCE

6,1,5
BLAZED A TRAIL
BLAZES A TRAIL
COCKED A SNOOK
HAZARD A GUESS
MAKING A POINT
MAKING A STAND
MENAGE A TROIS
PACKED A PUNCH
PAYING A VISIT
PICKED A FIGHT
RAISED A SIEGE
RAISED A STINK
RAISES A SIEGE
RAISES A STINK
SPENDS A PENNY
STAKED A CLAIM
STAKES A CLAIM
STRAIN A POINT
STRIKE A CHORD
STRIKE A LIGHT
STRIKE A MATCH
STRUCK A CHORD
STRUCK A MATCH
TAKING A BRIEF
TAKING A CLASS

TAKING A DEKKO
THROWS A PARTY
THROWS A PUNCH

6,2,1,3
CALLED IT A DAY

6,2,2,2
FACING UP TO IT

6,2,4
BALSAM OF PERU
BALSAM OF TOLU
BRINGS TO BOOK
BRINGS TO HEEL
BRINGS TO LIFE
CALLED TO MIND
CHANGE OF LIFE
CHAPEL OF EASE
CHAPEL OF REST
COMING TO LIFE
COMING TO PASS
COMING TO REST
ELIXIR OF LIFE
GARDEN OF EDEN
HAVING NO IDEA
HEIGHT OF LAND
KNOCKS ON WOOD
LABOUR OF LOVE
LAYING TO REST
MARVEL OF PERU
MASTER AT ARMS
MATTER OF FACT
MATTER OF FORM
PAYING IN BOOK
PAYING IN FULL
PAYING IN KIND
PLAYED IT COOL
SADDLE OF LAMB
SECOND TO NONE
STANDS TO GAIN
STANDS TO LOSE
STRIKE IT RICH
STROKE OF LUCK
STRUCK IT RICH
TAKING AN OATH
TAKING AS READ
TAKING IN HAND
TAKING IN VAIN
TAKING IT EASY
TAKING TO TASK
TAKING UP ARMS
TALKED IT OVER
TEAMED UP WITH
TENANT AT WILL
THREAD OF LIFE
WALKED TO HEEL
WORKED TO RULE

6,3,3
BELLED THE CAT
BEYOND OUR KEN

BREAKS THE ICE
BRIDGE THE GAP
CAUGHT THE SUN
CHEWED THE CUD
CHEWED THE FAT
CLEARS THE AIR
CLEARS THE WAY
CLOSED THE GAP
CLOSES THE GAP
FINGER AND TOE
JUMPED FOR JOY
JUMPED THE GUN
KNOCKS FOR SIX
MISSED THE BUS
MISSES THE BUS
PAVING THE WAY
PILLAR BOX RED
SHAGGY INK CAP
SLINGS THE BAT
TAKING THE AIR
TAKING THE RAP
TAKING THE SUN
WALKED THE DOG
WIDENS THE GAP

6,4,2
LAYING EYES ON
MAKING EYES AT

6,6
ABSENT MINDED
ACTION REPLAY
ACTION TAKING
ADDERS TONGUE
AESOPS FABLES
ALKALI METALS
ANCIEN REGIME
ANGORA RABBIT
ANIMAL RIGHTS
ARCTIC CIRCLE
ARMOUR BEARER
ARMOUR PLATED
ATOMIC ENERGY
ATOMIC NUMBER
ATOMIC SECOND
ATOMIC THEORY
ATOMIC WEIGHT
AUSTIN FRIARS
AUTUMN CROCUS
BAILEY BRIDGE
BAKING POWDER
BALLET DANCER
BALLET MASTER
BALSAM POPLAR
BAMBOO SHOOTS
BANTAM WEIGHT
BASKET MAKING
BASKET STITCH
BEETLE BROWED
BEFORE CHRIST
BEYOND NUMBER

BIBBLE BABBLE
BINARY NUMBER
BINARY SYSTEM
BINARY WEAPON
BITTER ORANGE
BLOODY MINDED
BODICE RIPPER
BOMBER JACKET
BONNET MONKEY
BOOGIE WOOGIE
BORDER COLLIE
BOTTLE HOLDER
BOTTLE OPENER
BOTTLE WASHER
BOTTOM DRAWER
BOTTOM SAWYER
BOXING GLOVES
BRANDY BOTTLE
BRANDY BUTTER
BRANDY PAWNEE
BREAKS GROUND
BREAST CANCER
BREAST GIRDLE
BREECH LOADER
BROKEN BACKED
BROKEN WINDED
BROKER DEALER
BRONCO BUSTER
BUBBLE HEADED
BUENAS NOCHES
BUENAS TARDES
BULLET HEADED
BUNGEE JUMPER
BUNSEN BURNER
BURIAL GROUND
BUTTER COOLER
BUTTER MUSLIN
BUTTON SCURVY
BUYERS MARKET
CALICO FLOWER
CANADA BALSAM
CANARY YELLOW
CANDID CAMERA
CANDLE HOLDER
CANNON FODDER
CARBON DATING
CARBON FIBRES
CARPET BEETLE
CARTON PIERRE
CASUAL LABOUR
CATTLE MARKET
CAVEAT EMPTOR
CENTRE SPREAD
CETANE NUMBER
CHAISE LONGUE
CHANCE MEDLEY
CHANCE REMARK
CHANGE COLOUR
CHANGE PLACES
CHAPEL MASTER

6,6 *contd.*
CHASSE CROISE
CHEEKY MONKEY
CHEESE CUTTER
CHEESE HOPPER
CHEESE MONGER
CHEESE PARING
CHEESE STRAWS
CHEESE TASTER
CHERRY BOUNCE
CHERRY BRANDY
CHERRY LAUREL
CHERRY PICKER
CHERRY TOMATO
CHEVAL MIRROR
CHORUS MASTER
CHROME YELLOW
CHURCH BAZAAR
CHURCH PARADE
CHURCH WARDEN
CINEMA SCREEN
CINEMA VERITE
CIRCLE RIDING
CITRUS FRUITS
CLEVER CLEVER
CLICHE RIDDEN
CLOVEN FOOTED
CLOVEN HOOVED
COBBLE STONES
COLOUR FILTER
COLOUR SCHEME
COMBAT JACKET
COMING ACROSS
COMING ASHORE
COMING UNDONE
COMMON DEBTOR
COMMON GENDER
COMMON GROUND
COMMON MARKET
COMMON PRAYER
COMMON RIDING
COMMON SCHOOL
COMPOS MENTIS
CONTRA MUNDUM
COPPER BOTTOM
COPPER GLANCE
COPPER NICKEL
COTTON PICKER
COUNTY FAMILY
COUNTY SCHOOL
COUSIN GERMAN
COVENT GARDEN
CREDIT RATING
CREDIT TITLES
CREEPY CRAWLY
CUCKOO FLOWER
CUMULO CIRRUS
CUMULO NIMBUS
DANGER SIGNAL
DANISH PASTRY

DESERT ISLAND
DEVILS ISLAND
DEVILS TATTOO
DIESEL ENGINE
DINGLE DANGLE
DINNER JACKET
DIRECT ACCESS
DIRECT ACTION
DIRECT LABOUR
DIRECT METHOD
DIRECT MOTION
DIRECT OBJECT
DIRECT SPEECH
DOLMAN SLEEVE
DOMINO EFFECT
DOMINO THEORY
DONKEY ENGINE
DONKEY JACKET
DORMER WINDOW
DORSAL SUTURE
DOTTED AROUND
DOUBLE BANKED
DOUBLE CHARGE
DOUBLE DAGGER
DOUBLE DEALER
DOUBLE DECKER
DOUBLE GLAZED
DOUBLE HANDED
DOUBLE HEADED
DOUBLE LOCKED
DOUBLE OBELUS
DOUBLE PARKED
DOUBLE STOREY
DOUBLE VISION
DOVERS POWDER
DRAGON LIZARD
DRONGO CUCKOO
DUNMOW FLITCH
EASTER BONNET
EASTER CACTUS
EASTER ISLAND
EASTER PARADE
ELEVEN OCLOCK
ENGINE DRIVER
ENGINE FITTER
ERMINE STREET
ESCAPE CLAUSE
ESCORT AGENCY
EXPORT MARKET
EXPORT REJECT
FALCON GENTLE
FALLEN ARCHES
FAMILY CIRCLE
FAMILY DOCTOR
FAMILY FRIEND
FATHER FIGURE
FEEBLE MINDED
FELLOW MEMBER
FENNEL FLOWER
FEUDAL SYSTEM

FIDDLE FADDLE
FIDDLE STRING
FIGURE CASTER
FIGURE SKATER
FILING SYSTEM
FINGER BUFFET
FIRMER CHISEL
FITTED CARPET
FLOWER GARDEN
FLOWER PEOPLE
FLYING BRIDGE
FLYING CARPET
FLYING COLUMN
FLYING DOCTOR
FLYING JACKET
FLYING LIZARD
FLYING SAUCER
FOOLED AROUND
FORCED LABOUR
FOREST RANGER
FOSTER FATHER
FOSTER MOTHER
FOSTER PARENT
FOSTER SISTER
FOURTH ESTATE
FRANCO GERMAN
FREEZE DRYING
FRENCH POLISH
FRENCH WINDOW
FRIARS BALSAM
FROZEN ASSETS
FROZEN MITTEN
FULLER FIGURE
GAELIC COFFEE
GAINED GROUND
GANDER MOONER
GARDEN CENTRE
GARDEN SUBURB
GARRET MASTER
GARTER STITCH
GATHER BREATH
GATHER GROUND
GENTLE BREEZE
GERMAN SILVER
GIANTS KETTLE
GIANTS STRIDE
GIBBLE GABBLE
GIRDER BRIDGE
GIVING GROUND
GIVING NOTICE
GOLDEN FLEECE
GOLDEN LEGEND
GOLDEN NUMBER
GOLDEN PLOVER
GOLDEN SALMON
GOSPEL SINGER
GOSSIP COLUMN
GOSSIP MONGER
GOSSIP WRITER
GRANDE MARQUE

GRANNY ANNEXE
GRATED CHEESE
GRAVEL VOICED
GREASE MONKEY
GROUND ANNUAL
GROUND BEETLE
GROUND FEEDER
GROUND STOREY
GROUND STROKE
HABEAS CORPUS
HALTER NECKED
HAMMER HEADED
HARLEY STREET
HEALTH CENTRE
HEALTH RESORT
HEATER SHIELD
HEAVEN FORBID
HELIUM SPEECH
HERBAL REMEDY
HIATUS HERNIA
HIDDEN AGENDA
HIDDEN DEPTHS
HIGHLY STRUNG
HOLLOW GROUND
HONEST BROKER
HONOUR BRIGHT
HORROR STRUCK
HORSED AROUND
HORSES AROUND
HORTUS SICCUS
HOUSEY HOUSEY
HUBBLE BUBBLE
HUCKLE BACKED
HUGGER MUGGER
HUMPTY DUMPTY
HUNGER STRIKE
HUNTER KILLER
HURDLE RACING
IMMUNE SYSTEM
INDIAN MILLET
INDIAN MUTINY
INDIAN RUNNER
INDIAN SUMMER
INFANT SCHOOL
INKING ROLLER
INSECT POWDER
INSIDE CENTRE
INSTEP RAISER
ITALIC SCRIPT
JACKET POTATO
JACOBS LADDER
JIGSAW PUZZLE
JINGLE JANGLE
JOINED FORCES
JUNIOR OPTIME
KETTLE HOLDER
KICKED AROUND
KIDNEY POTATO
KIMONO SLEEVE
KNIGHT ERRANT

6,6 *contd.*
KNOCKS AROUND
KOMODO DRAGON
LABOUR MARKET
LABOUR SAVING
LAGGED BEHIND
LANCET WINDOW
LANDED GENTRY
LATENT ENERGY
LEAVES BEHIND
LEAVES UNSAID
LEGACY HUNTER
LETTER OPENER
LETTER WRITER
LINGUA FRANCA
LIQUID ASSETS
LIQUID HELIUM
LITTER BASKET
LITTLE ENDIAN
LITTLE FINGER
LITTLE HITLER
LITTLE OFFICE
LITTLE PEOPLE
LITTLE WONDER
LIVELY DEBATE
LIVERY STABLE
LIVING FOSSIL
LIVING MEMORY
LIZARD HIPPED
LONDON BRIDGE
LONELY HEARTS
LOOKED AGHAST
LOSING COLOUR
LOSING GROUND
LOSING WEIGHT
LOUNGE LIZARD
LOUVRE WINDOW
LUMBER JACKET
MAIDEN ASSIZE
MAIDEN BATTLE
MAIDEN CASTLE
MAIDEN FLIGHT
MAIDEN SPEECH
MAIDEN STAKES
MAIDEN VOYAGE
MAITRE DHOTEL
MAKING AMENDS
MAKING TRACKS
MANGEL WURZEL
MANUAL LABOUR
MANUAL WORKER
MARBLE CUTTER
MARINE BOILER
MARINE ENGINE
MARINE STORES
MARKER BEACON
MARKET GARDEN
MARKET LEADER
MARKET SQUARE
MASTER CUTLER

MASTER SWITCH
MASTER TAILOR
MEDIUM SHERRY
MENTAL ASYLUM
MERSEY TUNNEL
METEOR CRATER
METHOD ACTING
METHYL VIOLET
METRIC SYSTEM
MICKEY TAKING
MIDDLE GROUND
MIDDLE INCOME
MIDDLE SCHOOL
MIDDLE STATES
MIMINY PIMINY
MINGLE MANGLE
MIRROR WRITER
MISSEL THRUSH
MISTLE THRUSH
MOBILE POLICE
MONKEY ENGINE
MONKEY FLOWER
MONKEY HAMMER
MONKEY JACKET
MONKEY PUZZLE
MONKEY WRENCH
MORRIS DANCER
MOTHER CHURCH
MOTHER FIGURE
MOTHER LIQUOR
MOTHER TONGUE
MUDDLE HEADED
MURINE TYPHUS
MUTTON CUTLET
MUTTON HEADED
MUTUAL FRIEND
MUZZLE LOADER
NAPLES YELLOW
NARROW ESCAPE
NARROW MINDED
NARROW SQUEAK
NICKEL SILVER
NIDDLE NODDLE
NIMBLE FOOTED
NIMBLE WITTED
NIMINY PIMINY
NOLENS VOLENS
NORDIC SKIING
NORMAL SCHOOL
NORMAN FRENCH
NORWAY SPRUCE
NOTARY PUBLIC
NUDIST COLONY
OBJECT FINDER
OBJECT LESSON
OBTUSE ANGLED
OCTANE NUMBER
OCTANE RATING
OFFICE BEARER
OFFICE HOLDER

OFFICE JUNIOR
OFFICE SEEKER
ORANGE SQUASH
ORDERS AROUND
OXFORD STREET
PAGODA SLEEVE
PARADE GROUND
PARING CHISEL
PARISH CHURCH
PARISH PRIEST
PARROT WRASSE
PARTIE CARREE
PASSED MUSTER
PASSES MUSTER
PATENT OFFICE
PATENT REMEDY
PAVING STONES
PAYING HOMAGE
PEANUT BUTTER
PEBBLE POWDER
PELVIC GIRDLE
PENANG LAWYER
PENCIL SKETCH
PERSON FRIDAY
PETTER ENGINE
PHYSIC GARDEN
PICNIC BASKET
PICNIC HAMPER
PIGEON FLYING
PITTER PATTER
PLAINS INDIAN
PLAYED AROUND
PLAYED HOOKEY
PLAYED POSSUM
PLAYED TRICKS
PLAYED TRUANT
PLENUM SYSTEM
PLOUGH MONDAY
POCKET GOPHER
POCKET PISTOL
POLICE ESCORT
POLICY HOLDER
POLLEN BASKET
POMMES FRITES
POROUS ALLOYS
POROUS SEPTUM
PORTAL SYSTEM
POSTAL BALLOT
POSTER PAINTS
POTATO BLIGHT
POTATO CRISPS
POTATO FAMINE
POWDER CLOSET
POWDER MONKEY
PRETTY NEARLY
PRETTY PRETTY
PRETTY SPOKEN
PRINCE BISHOP
PRISON WARDER
PROCES VERBAL

PROFIT MARGIN
PROFIT TAKING
PROPER MOTION
PSEUDO GOTHIC
PUBLIC HEALTH
PUBLIC ORATOR
PUBLIC OUTCRY
PUBLIC SCHOOL
PUBLIC SECTOR
PURPLE AIRWAY
PUSHED AROUND
PUSHES AROUND
PUZZLE HEADED
PYJAMA JACKET
QUAKER COLOUR
QUARTZ SCHIST
QUEENS BOUNTY
QUEENS SPEECH
RABBIT WARREN
RABBLE ROUSER
RACING DRIVER
RACKET GROUND
RACKET TAILED
RADIAL ARTERY
RADIAL ENGINE
RADIUS VECTOR
RAFFLE TICKET
RAGGLE TAGGLE
RAGLAN SLEEVE
RAISED PASTRY
RANDOM ACCESS
RATTLE HEADED
RAZZLE DAZZLE
RECORD OFFICE
RECORD PLAYER
RECORD SLEEVE
REFLEX ACTION
REFLEX CAMERA
REFORM SCHOOL
REGENT STREET
REMAIN SILENT
REMAND CENTRE
REPAIR OUTFIT
RESCUE WORKER
RETINA CAMERA
RETURN CREASE
RETURN TICKET
RHESUS FACTOR
RIBBLE RABBLE
RIDING GLOVES
RIDING MASTER
RIDING SCHOOL
RIGHTS WRONGS
RIPPLE EFFECT
RIPPLE MARKED
RITUAL MURDER
ROBBER BARONS
ROCKER SWITCH
ROLLER SKATER
ROLLER SKATES

6,6 *contd.*

ROTARY ENGINE	SILVER SALVER	STREET SMARTS	VULGAR TONGUE
ROVING REPORT	SILVER SCREEN	STREET WALKER	WAITED AWHILE
RUBBER BULLET	SILVER VOICED	STRIKE BOTTOM	WALKIE TALKIE
RUBBER CHEQUE	SIMPLE MINDED	STRONG MINDED	WANKEL ENGINE
RUBBER GLOVES	SINGLE DECKER	STRUCK BOTTOM	WANTED COLUMN
RUBBER NECKED	SINGLE FIGURE	SUMMER SCHOOL	WANTED POSTER
RUBBER STAMPS	SINGLE HANDED	SUNDAY DRIVER	WASTED EFFORT
RUMBLE TUMBLE	SINGLE MINDED	SUNDAY SCHOOL	WEAKER VESSEL
SACRED BEETLE	SINGLE PARENT	SUNTAN LOTION	WEIGHS ANCHOR
SADDLE SHAPED	SINGLE SEATER	SYSTEM MONGER	WEIGHT LIFTER
SADDLE SPRING	SKINNY DIPPER	TAKING CHARGE	WELTER STAKES
SADDLE STITCH	SLEEPY HOLLOW	TAKING EFFECT	WELTER WEIGHT
SAFETY FACTOR	SLEEVE BUTTON	TAKING FLIGHT	WHISKY FRISKY
SAHARA DESERT	SLOANE RANGER	TAKING FRIGHT	WICKET KEEPER
SALMON FISHER	SLOUCH HATTED	TAKING NOTICE	WIGGLE WAGGLE
SALMON LADDER	SMOOTH BROWED	TAKING ORDERS	WILLOW GROUSE
SALMON TACKLE	SMOOTH COATED	TALCUM POWDER	WILTON CARPET
SALOON KEEPER	SMOOTH LEAVED	TALKED TURKEY	WINDOW SCREEN
SALOON PISTOL	SMOOTH MUSCLE	TALKEE TALKEE	WINKLE PICKER
SAMIAN LETTER	SMOOTH SPOKEN	TALLOW CANDLE	WINTER BARLEY
SAVING CLAUSE	SOCIAL CREDIT	TENANT FARMER	WINTER CHERRY
SCHOOL DOCTOR	SOCIAL WORKER	TENNIS PLAYER	WINTER CLOVER
SCHOOL FRIEND	SOCKET CHISEL	TENNIS RACKET	WINTER GARDEN
SCHOOL LEAVER	SOCKET WRENCH	TICKET AGENCY	WINTER SPORTS
SCOTCH BARLEY	SOFTLY SOFTLY	TICKET HOLDER	WITHIN LIMITS
SCOTCH BONNET	SPEECH MAKING	TICKET OFFICE	WITHIN REASON
SCOTCH DRAPER	SPIDER LEGGED	TICKET PORTER	WOMENS RIGHTS
SCOUTS HONOUR	SPIDER MONKEY	TICKET WRITER	WONDER MONGER
SCREEN WRITER	SPIDER STITCH	TIRLIE WIRLIE	WONDER STRUCK
SCRIPT WRITER	SPINAL COLUMN	TISSUE TYPING	WONDER WORKER
SEALED ORDERS	SPINAL MARROW	TITTLE TATTLE	WOODEN HEADED
SEASON TICKET	SPIRAL GALAXY	TOGGLE SWITCH	WOOLLY HAIRED
SECOND ADVENT	SPIRIT RAPPER	TOILET TISSUE	WOOLLY HEADED
SECOND BALLOT	SPLINT ARMOUR	TOOTSY WOOTSY	WOULFE BOTTLE
SECOND COMING	SPONGE DIVING	TRACER BULLET	YANKEE DOODLE
SECOND COUSIN	SPONGE FINGER	TRADED OPTION	YELLOW HAMMER
SECOND DEGREE	SPONGE FISHER	TRADES PEOPLE	YELLOW PEPPER
SECOND FIDDLE	SPONGE RUBBER	TRAVEL AGENCY	YELLOW RIBBON
SECOND NATURE	SPORTS JACKET	TRAVEL SOILED	YELLOW STREAK
SECOND STOREY	SPRING BEAUTY	TREBLE CHANCE	ZENITH SECTOR
SECOND STRIKE	SPRING BEETLE	TRENCH MORTAR	
SECOND STRING	SPRING HEADED	TRENCH PLOUGH	**7,1,4**
SECRET BALLOT	SPRING HEELED	TRIPLE HEADED	BLOWING A FUSE
SECRET POLICE	SPRING LOADED	TUNING HAMMER	CALLING A HALT
SEEING THINGS	SPRUNG RHYTHM	TUNNEL VISION	CASTING A VOTE
SENIOR OPTIME	SPURGE LAUREL	TURNED AROUND	CATCHES A COLD
SERIAL KILLER	SQUARE HEADED	TURNED TURTLE	CATCHES A CRAB
SERIAL NUMBER	SQUARE NUMBER	TURTLE NECKED	CAUSING A STIR
SHADOW BOXING	SQUARE RIGGED	TWELVE OCLOCK	CRACKED A CRIB
SHERRY TRIFLE	SQUARE RIGGER	TWENTY TWENTY	CRACKED A JOKE
SHIELD BEARER	STATUS SYMBOL	UNITED STATES	CUTTING A DASH
SHIELD MAIDEN	STEWED PRUNES	VACUUM PACKED	DEALING A BLOW
SHIELD SHAPED	STICKS AROUND	VEILED THREAT	DROPPED A LINE
SHILLY SHALLY	STICKY WICKET	VELVET SCOTER	FEELING A FOOL
SHRILL VOICED	STOOGE AROUND	VENUSS GIRDLE	HAILING A TAXI
SICKLE SHAPED	STORMY PETREL	VERMIN KILLER	LENDING A HAND
SILVER BEATER	STRAIT JACKET	VIOLIN STRING	LOOKING A FOOL
SILVER PLATED	STRAIT LACING	VISUAL PURPLE	PICKING A LOCK
SILVER SALMON	STREAM ANCHOR	VORTEX THEORY	PITCHED A TENT
	STREET KEEPER	VOTIVE TABLET	PITCHES A TENT

7,1,4 *contd.*
PLAYING A PART
PULLING A FACE
RINGING A BELL
RUNNING A RISK
SCORING A GOAL
SETTING A TRAP
SPRINGS A LEAK
STARTED A HARE
STRIKES A POSE
THUMBED A LIFT
THUMBED A RIDE

7,2,3
BROTHER IN LAW
CARRIED IT OFF
CARRIES IT OFF
CASTING AN EYE
COUNCIL OF WAR
CUSHION OF AIR
FATHERS IN LAW
FIGURED IT OUT
FIGURES IT OUT
FLOATED ON AIR
HITTING IT OFF
HONOURS OF WAR
KEEPING AT BAY
LAUGHED IT OFF
LENDING AN EAR
LETTING IT RIP
MOTHERS IN LAW
PLAYING TO WIN
PUTTING ON ICE
PUTTING TO BED
PUTTING TO SEA
SISTERS IN LAW
SURFACE TO AIR
SWEATED IT OUT
THEATRE OF WAR
WALKING ON AIR
WHETHER OR NOT
WORKING IT OUT

7,3,2
CROSSED THE TS
CROSSES THE TS
DOTTING THE IS
RUNNING OUT ON
WALKING OUT ON

7,5
ACADEMY AWARD
ADRENAL GLAND
ANISEED BALLS
APOSTLE SPOON
ARABIAN CAMEL
ARTISTS MODEL
ARTISTS PROOF
AUCTION ROOMS
AWKWARD SQUAD
BACKING STORE

BAGGAGE TRAIN
BALANCE SHEET
BALANCE WHEEL
BANBURY CROSS
BANDIED WORDS
BANDIES WORDS
BANKERS ORDER
BARBARY COAST
BARBARY SHEEP
BARBERS BLOCK
BARRIER CREAM
BASKING SHARK
BASTARD TITLE
BASTARD TYPES
BATHERS CRAMP
BATHING BELLE
BATHING DRESS
BATTING ORDER
BAYONET JOINT
BEARING CLOTH
BECHERS BROOK
BEDSIDE TABLE
BELGIAN FRANC
BENEFIT MATCH
BENEFIT NIGHT
BERMUDA GRASS
BETWEEN DECKS
BETWEEN TIMES
BEVERLY HILLS
BICYCLE CHAIN
BISHOPS COURT
BLADDER WRACK
BLARNEY STONE
BLISTER STEEL
BOILING POINT
BOLOGNA PHIAL
BONFIRE NIGHT
BOOKING CLERK
BOROUGH COURT
BOROUGH REEVE
BOUQUET GARNI
BOWHEAD WHALE
BOWLING ALLEY
BOWLING GREEN
BRACKET CLOCK
BRAISED STEAK
BRAMBLE BERRY
BRAMBLE FINCH
BREATHE AGAIN
BREWERS YEAST
BRIGADE MAJOR
BRISTOL BOARD
BRISTOL BRICK
BRITISH ISLES
BRITISH PLATE
BRITTLE BONES
BROMIDE PAPER
BROUGHT ABOUT
BROUGHT FORTH
BROUGHT ROUND

BROWNIE GUIDE
BROWNIE POINT
BRUSHED ASIDE
BRUSHES ASIDE
BUCKLED UNDER
BUCKLES UNDER
BUFFALO BERRY
BUFFALO GRASS
BURGLAR ALARM
BURMESE GLASS
BURNING GLASS
BURNING HOUSE
BURNING ISSUE
BURNING POINT
BURYING PLACE
BUTTERY HATCH
CABBAGE PATCH
CALCIUM OXIDE
CALLING NAMES
CALVARY CROSS
CANTING WHEEL
CAPITAL GAINS
CAPITAL GOODS
CAPSTAN LATHE
CAPSTAN TABLE
CARAWAY SEEDS
CARVING KNIFE
CASTING ASIDE
CASTING COUCH
CASTING LOOSE
CAVALRY TWILL
CENTURY PLANT
CHAMBER MUSIC
CHAMBER ORGAN
CHANGED HANDS
CHANGES HANDS
CHANNEL STONE
CHAPTER HOUSE
CHARNEL HOUSE
CHARTER MAYOR
CHARTER PARTY
CHECKER BOARD
CHEDDAR GORGE
CHEVRON BOARD
CHIMNEY BOARD
CHIMNEY PIECE
CHIMNEY SHAFT
CHIMNEY STACK
CHIMNEY STALK
CHIMNEY SWEEP
CHINESE BOXES
CHINESE PAPER
CHINESE WHITE
CHOPPED LOGIC
CHUCKIE STONE
CIRCUIT BOARD
CIRCUIT JUDGE
CIRCUIT RIDER
CLASSIC RACES
CLINKER BLOCK

CLINKER BUILT
CLOSING PRICE
CLOSING RANKS
CLOTHES BRUSH
CLOTHES HORSE
CLOTHES PRESS
CLOTHES SENSE
CLOTTED CREAM
COAXIAL CABLE
COLOGNE WATER
COLONEL BLIMP
COLONEL BOGEY
COMMAND PAPER
COMMUNE BONUM
COMPARE NOTES
COMPASS PLANE
COMPASS PLANT
CONCERT GRAND
CONCERT PARTY
CONCERT PITCH
CONCERT WALTZ
CONNATE WATER
CONNING TOWER
CONSOLE TABLE
CONTACT POINT
CONTROL BOARD
CONTROL GROUP
CONTROL PANEL
CONTROL TOWER
COOKING APPLE
COOKING RANGE
COOLING TOWER
COPYING PRESS
CORNISH PASTY
COSSACK BOOTS
COSTUME DRAMA
COSTUME PIECE
COUNCIL BOARD
COUNCIL HOUSE
COUNTED SHEEP
COUNTER BRACE
COUNTER CLAIM
COUNTER FORCE
COUNTER TENOR
COUNTER WEIGH
COUNTER WHEEL
COUNTRY DANCE
COUNTRY HOUSE
COUNTRY MUSIC
COUNTRY PARTY
COVERED WAGON
CRANIAL INDEX
CRICKET MATCH
CRICKET PITCH
CROOKES GLASS
CROSSED WIRES
CRYSTAL CLEAR
CRYSTAL GAZER
CULTURE SHOCK
CURLING IRONS

7,5 *contd.*
CURLING STONE
CURLING TONGS
CURRANT BREAD
CURRANT JELLY
CUSTARD APPLE
CUTTING LOOSE
CUTTING SHORT
DECIMAL PLACE
DECIMAL POINT
DIAMOND DRILL
DIAMOND FIELD
DIAMOND WHEEL
DIETARY FIBRE
DIGITAL CLOCK
DIVIDED SKIRT
DIVORCE COURT
DONKEYS YEARS
DOPPLER SHIFT
DOWNING TOOLS
DRAGONS BLOOD
DRAUGHT HORSE
DRAUGHT PROOF
DRAWING BLOOD
DRAWING BOARD
DRAWING FRAME
DRAWING PAPER
DRAWING TABLE
DRAWING TEETH
DRESDEN CHINA
DRIFTED APART
DRIVING WHEEL
DROPPED SCONE
DUCKING STOOL
EMERALD GREEN
ENDLESS CHAIN
ENDLESS SCREW
ENGLISH FLUTE
ENTERIC FEVER
EVENING CLASS
EVENING DRESS
EXHAUST STEAM
EXHAUST VALVE
EXPRESS TRAIN
FALLING ABOUT
FALLING APART
FALLING SHORT
FAMILLE JAUNE
FAMILLE NOIRE
FAMILLE VERTE
FASHION HOUSE
FATIGUE DRESS
FATIGUE PARTY
FEATHER BRAIN
FEATHER GRASS
FEDERAL AGENT
FEDERAL STATE
FEELING CHEAP
FEELING FAINT
FEELING SMALL

FERROUS OXIDE
FESTOON BLIND
FIGHTER PILOT
FIGHTER PLANE
FINANCE HOUSE
FINDING FAULT
FISHING SMACK
FLITTER MOUSE
FLOWING LOCKS
FOLDING MONEY
FOLDING STOOL
FOLDING STUFF
FOLIAGE PLANT
FOOLISH WITTY
FORCING HOUSE
FOREIGN DRAFT
FOREIGN PARTS
FORMULA THREE
FORWARD PRICE
FOWLING PIECE
FREIGHT TRAIN
FROSTED GLASS
FULLERS EARTH
FUNERAL MARCH
FUNERAL RITES
FUSIBLE METAL
GADDING ABOUT
GALLOWS MAKER
GASTRIC FEVER
GASTRIC JUICE
GATHERS ROUND
GATHERS SPEED
GENERAL ISSUE
GENERAL STAFF
GENERAL SYNOD
GETTING ABOUT
GETTING AHEAD
GETTING ALONG
GETTING IDEAS
GETTING READY
GETTING ROUND
GETTING THERE
GETTING TOUGH
GLARING ERROR
GOODWIN SANDS
GROWING APART
GROWING PAINS
GUIDING LIGHT
GUNTERS CHAIN
GUNTERS SCALE
HACKNEY COACH
HALFWAY HOUSE
HALLEYS COMET
HAMMOND ORGAN
HANGING ABOUT
HANGING JUDGE
HANGING LOOSE
HARBOUR LIGHT
HARNESS MAKER
HARVEST FIELD

HARVEST GOOSE
HARVEST MOUSE
HARVEST QUEEN
HATCHET FACED
HAULING ROUND
HAUNTED HOUSE
HEAVENS ABOVE
HESSIAN PAPER
HOLDING COURT
HOLDING FORTH
HOLDING HANDS
HOLDING WATER
HOODMAN BLIND
HUNTING FIELD
HUNTING KNIFE
HUNTING LODGE
ICELAND POPPY
IMPULSE BUYER
INJURED PRIDE
INSULIN SHOCK
INVERSE RATIO
INVOICE CLERK
IRONING BOARD
ISSUING FORTH
JAMAICA CEDAR
JAMAICA EBONY
JANUARY SALES
JAVELIN THROW
JAVELLE WATER
JESUITS DROPS
JOGGING ALONG
JOINING HANDS
JOLLIED ALONG
JOLLIES ALONG
JUMPING BEANS
JUMPING MOUSE
KEEPING CLEAR
KEEPING FAITH
KEEPING HOUSE
KEEPING QUIET
KEEPING STILL
KEEPING TRACK
KEEPING WATCH
KICKING ABOUT
KITCHEN DUTCH
KITCHEN RANGE
KITCHEN WENCH
KNOCKED ABOUT
KNUCKLE JOINT
KNUCKLE UNDER
LAISSEZ FAIRE
LALIQUE GLASS
LANDING CRAFT
LANDING FIELD
LANDING PLACE
LANDING SPEED
LANDING STAGE
LANDING STRIP
LANTERN JAWED
LANTERN SLIDE

LARKING ABOUT
LAUNDRY WOMAN
LEADING ACTOR
LEADING LIGHT
LEASING MAKER
LEATHER CLOTH
LEATHER GOODS
LEATHER KNIFE
LEATHER STRAP
LEAVING ALONE
LETTING ALONE
LETTING BLOOD
LETTING DRIVE
LETTING LOOSE
LETTING SLIDE
LIBERAL PARTY
LIBERTY HORSE
LICENCE PLATE
LICKETY SPLIT
LINCOLN GREEN
LIQUEUR GLASS
LOADING GAUGE
LOCKING HORNS
LODGING HOUSE
LOOKING AFTER
LOOKING GLASS
LOOKING SMALL
LOOMING LARGE
LOUNGED ABOUT
LOUNGES ABOUT
LURKING PLACE
MACHINE RULER
MALTESE CROSS
MANSION HOUSE
MARBLED WHITE
MARKING GAUGE
MARTINI HENRY
MASONIC LODGE
MEETING HOUSE
MEISSEN CHINA
MELODIC MINOR
MELTING POINT
MESSING ABOUT
MILKING STOOL
MILLERS THUMB
MINCING WORDS
MINERAL JELLY
MINERAL PITCH
MINERAL WATER
MINERVA PRESS
MOABITE STONE
MONSTRE SACRE
MORNING DRESS
MORNING GLORY
MORNING WATCH
MOTHERS UNION
MOUNTED GUARD
MOVABLE FEAST
NAPIERS BONES
NATURAL DEATH

7,5 *contd.*

NATURAL MAGIC	PERFECT TENSE	PULLING APART	RUNNING FIGHT
NATURAL ORDER	PERSIAN BERRY	PULLING ROUND	RUNNING FLUSH
NATURAL SCALE	PERSIAN WHEEL	PURBECK STONE	RUNNING SHORT
NECKING PARTY	PERSONA GRATA	PURPOSE BUILT	RUNNING TITLE
NESTING PLACE	PICKING HOLES	PURSUIT PLANE	RUNNING WATER
NEWGATE FRILL	PICKLED ONION	PUSHING ALONG	RUPERTS DROPS
NIAGARA FALLS	PICTURE FRAME	PUSHING ASIDE	RUSSIAN BOOTS
NITROUS OXIDE	PICTURE HOUSE	PUTTING ABOUT	SAILING ALONG
NOMINAL VALUE	PICTURE RATIO	PUTTING CLEEK	SALIENT POINT
NORFOLK CAPON	PIGEONS BLOOD	PUTTING GREEN	SALVAGE CORPS
NOTHING DOING	PILLION RIDER	PUTTING STONE	SCALLOP SHELL
NOUVEAU RICHE	PIONEER CORPS	PYTHIAN GAMES	SCANDAL SHEET
NOUVEAU ROMAN	PITCHER PLANT	PYTHIAN VERSE	SCARLET FEVER
NUBBING CHEAT	PLANNED AHEAD	QUAKING GRASS	SCARLET WOMAN
NUCLEAR POWER	PLASTER SAINT	QUARTER AFTER	SCATTER BRAIN
NUCLEAR WASTE	PLASTIC MONEY	QUARTER BOUND	SCISSOR BLADE
NURSERY RHYME	PLAYING ABOUT	QUARTER FINAL	SCISSOR TOOTH
NURSING CHAIR	PLAYING ALONG	QUARTER GUARD	SCOUTED ROUND
OBLIQUE ANGLE	PLAYING CARDS	QUARTER HORSE	SCRAPER BOARD
OLYMPIC GAMES	PLAYING FALSE	QUARTER LIGHT	SCRATCH BRUSH
OLYMPIC MEDAL	PLAYING FIELD	QUARTER MILER	SECULAR GAMES
OLYMPIC TORCH	PLAYING HAVOC	QUARTER PLATE	SEEKING AFTER
OMNIBUS TRAIN	PLEATED SKIRT	QUARTER ROUND	SELLING PLATE
OPENING NIGHT	PLUMMER BLOCK	QUARTER STAFF	SELLING PRICE
OPTICAL FIBRE	POLLING BOOTH	QUELQUE CHOSE	SELLING SHORT
ORCHARD GRASS	POPULAR FRONT	QUININE WATER	SERPENT STONE
ORCHARD HOUSE	POPULAR MUSIC	RACCOON BERRY	SERVICE COURT
ORDERED ABOUT	PORTERS LODGE	RAINBOW TROUT	SERVICE HATCH
OUTDOOR GAMES	POSTAGE STAMP	RAISING ALOFT	SERVING HATCH
OUTSIDE RIGHT	POSTURE MAKER	RAISING MONEY	SESSION CLERK
OUTWARD BOUND	POTTERS WHEEL	RALLIED ROUND	SESSION HOUSE
PACIFIC OCEAN	POUCHED MOUSE	RALLIES ROUND	SETTING ABOUT
PACKING PAPER	POURING FORTH	RATABLE VALUE	SETTING APART
PACKING PRESS	PRAIRIE VALUE	RATCHET WHEEL	SETTING ASIDE
PACKING SHEET	PRANCED ABOUT	READING ALOUD	SETTING FORTH
PADDOCK STOOL	PRANCES ABOUT	REMOVAL LORRY	SHAKING HANDS
PAINTED CLOTH	PREMIUM BONDS	REPUTED OWNER	SHALLOW GRAVE
PAINTED SNIPE	PRESSED AHEAD	RESERVE PRICE	SHATTER PROOF
PAISLEY SHAWL	PRESSED GLASS	RESTING PLACE	SHAVING BRUSH
PALETTE KNIFE	PRESSES AHEAD	RESTING SPORE	SHAVING STICK
PANDEAN PIPES	PRIMARY PHASE	RESTING STAGE	SHERIFF CLERK
PARKING METER	PRINCES METAL	RHYMING SLANG	SHERIFF COURT
PARKING PLACE	PRIVATE BEACH	RICHTER SCALE	SHIFTED ABOUT
PARQUET FLOOR	PRIVATE COACH	ROARING DRUNK	SHIPPED WATER
PARSLEY PIERT	PRIVATE HOTEL	ROCKING CHAIR	SHIRLEY POPPY
PARSLEY SAUCE	PRIVATE LIVES	ROCKING HORSE	SHOEING SMITH
PASSAGE MONEY	PRIVATE MEANS	ROCKING STONE	SHOWING FIGHT
PASSION FRUIT	PRIVATE WRONG	ROLLING ALONG	SHOWING FORTH
PASSION MUSIC	PROBATE COURT	ROLLING STOCK	SHUFFLE BOARD
PATTERN MAKER	PROBLEM CHILD	ROLLING STONE	SIAMESE TWINS
PATTERN WHEEL	PROBLEM NOVEL	ROOMING HOUSE	SILICON CHIPS
PAUPERS GRAVE	PROCESS BLOCK	ROSETTA STONE	SINGING ALONG
PECKING ORDER	PROTEST MARCH	RUBBING ALONG	SINGING HINNY
PENALTY BENCH	PRUNING KNIFE	RUBBING STONE	SITTING STILL
PEOPLES FRONT	PSYCHIC FORCE	RUNAWAY TRAIN	SITTING TIGHT
PEOPLES PARTY	PUDDING BASIN	RUNNING AFTER	SKATING ROUND
PEPPERS GHOST	PUDDING FACED	RUNNING ALONG	SKIFFLE GROUP
PERFECT FIFTH	PUDDING PLATE	RUNNING BOARD	SKINNED ALIVE
PERFECT PITCH	PUFFING BILLY	RUNNING CLOSE	SKIRTED ROUND
	PULLING AHEAD	RUNNING COSTS	SKITTLE ALLEY

7,5 *contd.*
SLIDING SCALE
SLIPPER SATIN
SLIPPER SOCKS
SNAGGLE TEETH
SNAGGLE TOOTH
SOLVENT ABUSE
SPANISH BROOM
SPANISH CRESS
SPANISH GRASS
SPANISH ONION
SPANISH SHEEP
SPARROW GRASS
SPECIAL AGENT
SPECIAL OFFER
SPECIAL TRUST
SPECTRE LEMUR
SPINDLE SHELL
SPLENIC FEVER
SPROUTS WINGS
SQUEAKY CLEAN
STADDLE STONE
STAINED GLASS
STATION HOUSE
STATION WAGON
STAYING POWER
STAYING STILL
STEEPLE CROWN
STEERED CLEAR
STENCIL PLATE
STEPPED ASIDE
STIRRUP STRAP
STOPPED SHORT
STREAKY BACON
STREETS AHEAD
STREETS APART
STRINGS ALONG
STUBBLE FIELD
STUBBLE GOOSE
STUFFED SHIRT
SUCCESS STORY
SUFFOLK PUNCH
SUMPTER HORSE
SUPPORT LEVEL
SUPREME COURT
SURFACE CRAFT
SURFACE NOISE
SURFACE WATER
SURFING BOARD
SWINDLE SHEET
SWIZZLE STICK
SYNODIC MONTH
TAGGING ALONG
TAILORS DUMMY
TAILORS GOOSE
TALKING HEADS
TALKING POINT
TALKING ROUND
TARTARE SAUCE
TELLING TALES

THEATRE ORGAN
THERMAL SHOCK
THERMIC LANCE
THIEVES LATIN
THOUGHT AGAIN
THOUGHT ALIKE
THOUGHT ALOUD
THOUGHT TWICE
THROUGH TRAIN
THUNDER CLOUD
THUNDER FLASH
THUNDER SHEET
THUNDER STORM
THYROID GLAND
TIFFANY GLASS
TIMOTHY GRASS
TOBACCO PLANT
TOBACCO POUCH
TORCHON PAPER
TOURIST CLASS
TRACING PAPER
TRADING STAMP
TRANSIT TRADE
TRESTLE TABLE
TRIBUNE GROUP
TRIBUTE MONEY
TRIGGER HAPPY
TRINITY HOUSE
TRIPLEX GLASS
TROLLEY TABLE
TROLLEY WHEEL
TROUSER PRESS
TRUMPET MAJOR
TRUMPET SHELL
TRUSTEE STOCK
TUBULAR BELLS
TUMBLER DRIER
TURNING ABOUT
TURNING ASIDE
TURNING LATHE
TURNING LOOSE
TURNING NASTY
TURNING POINT
TURNING ROUND
TWELFTH NIGHT
TWINING PLANT
TYPHOID FEVER
UNIFIED FIELD
UNIFIED SCALE
UPRIGHT PIANO
VANDYKE BEARD
VANDYKE BROWN
VANTAGE POINT
VARSITY MATCH
VELOUTE SAUCE
VENTURE SCOUT
VILLAGE GREEN
VILLAGE IDIOT
VINEGAR PLANT
VIRGINS BOWER

VIRTUAL IMAGE
VISIBLE MEANS
VITAMIN PILLS
WAITING ABOUT
WALKING STAFF
WALKING STICK
WASTING ASSET
WEATHER ALONG
WEATHER BOARD
WEATHER BOUND
WEATHER CHART
WEATHER GAUGE
WEATHER GLASS
WEATHER HOUSE
WEATHER PROOF
WEATHER STRIP
WEAVERS HITCH
WEDDING CARDS
WEDDING DOWER
WEDDING DRESS
WEDDING MARCH
WEEDING TONGS
WEEPING BIRCH
WELFARE STATE
WHATMAN PAPER
WILLING HORSE
WINDING SHEET
WINDING STAIR
WITHOUT DOUBT
WITHOUT PRICE
WORKING CLASS
WORKING HOURS
WORKING HOUSE
WORKING LUNCH
WORKING MODEL
WORKING ORDER
WORKING PAPER
WORKING PARTY
WORKING WOMAN
WREAKED HAVOC
WRITERS CRAMP
WRITING PAPER
WRITING TABLE

8,1,3
SMELLING A RAT
THROWING A FIT

8,2,2
CHUCKING IT IN
STICKING AT IT
WHOOPING IT UP

8,4
ABNORMAL LOAD
ABSOLUTE ZERO
ABSTRACT NOUN
ACHILLES HEEL
ADJUTANT BIRD
ALADDINS CAVE
ALADDINS LAMP

ALPHABET SOUP
ALVEOLAR ARCH
AMERICAN PLAN
ANSWERED BACK
ANYTHING GOES
APPARENT TIME
APPROACH ROAD
APPROACH SHOT
AQUILINE NOSE
ARRESTER GEAR
ARRESTER HOOK
ARTERIAL ROAD
ARTESIAN WELL
ASCORBIC ACID
ASSEMBLY HALL
ASSEMBLY LINE
ASSEMBLY ROOM
ATHLETES FOOT
ATLANTIC TIME
BACHELOR FLAT
BACHELOR GIRL
BACKWARD STEP
BAKERLOO LINE
BAKEWELL TART
BARNYARD FOWL
BATTERED BABY
BEAVERED AWAY
BENJAMIN TREE
BESSEMER IRON
BEVERAGE ROOM
BILLIARD BALL
BILLIARD HALL
BIRTHDAY BOOK
BIRTHDAY CAKE
BIRTHDAY CARD
BIRTHDAY SUIT
BOARDING CARD
BOARDING PASS
BOARDING PIKE
BOHEMIAN RUBY
BORROWED TIME
BOUNCING BACK
BRANDING IRON
BREAKING AWAY
BREAKING CAMP
BREAKING DOWN
BREAKING EVEN
BREECHES BUOY
BRIDGING LOAN
BRIGHTON ROCK
BRINGING DOWN
BRINGING HOME
BRINGING OVER
BRUSSELS LACE
BUBBLING OVER
BUCKLING DOWN
BUDDHIST MONK
BUGGINSS TURN
BUILDING SITE
BUSINESS CARD

8,4 *contd.*
BUSINESS LIKE
BUSINESS PARK
BUSINESS SUIT
BUTCHERS HOOK
BUTCHERS MEAT
BUTTERED EGGS
CALABASH TREE
CALAMITY JANE
CALENDAR LINE
CALENDAR YEAR
CANISTER SHOT
CARBOLIC ACID
CARDINAL BIRD
CARDINAL SINS
CARNIVAL WEEK
CARRIAGE FREE
CARRIAGE PAID
CARRYING AWAY
CARRYING BACK
CARRYING OVER
CASUALTY WARD
CATCHING FIRE
CAULKING IRON
CHANGING DOWN
CHANGING ENDS
CHANGING GEAR
CHANGING ROOM
CHARGING DOWN
CHARLESS WAIN
CHASTITY BELT
CHECKING ROOM
CHLOROUS ACID
CIRCULAR FILE
CIRCULAR NOTE
CITIZENS BAND
CLAIMING RACE
CLAMPING DOWN
CLEANING LADY
CLEARING BANK
CLERICAL GREY
CLIMBING DOWN
CLOUDING OVER
COLLARED DOVE
COMPOUND LEAF
COMPOUND TIME
COMPUTER GAME
CONVEYOR BELT
CORDUROY ROAD
COVENTRY BLUE
CRACKING DOWN
CRESCENT MOON
CRIMPING IRON
CRITICAL MASS
CROSSING OVER
CUPBOARD LOVE
CURRENCY NOTE
CYLINDER HEAD
CYLINDER LOCK
DELIVERY PIPE

DELIVERY TUBE
DIALLING CODE
DIALLING TONE
DISASTER AREA
DISCOUNT RATE
DISPATCH BOAT
DISPATCH CASE
DISTRICT LINE
DIVINITY HALL
DIVISION BELL
DOGTOOTH SPAR
DOMESDAY BOOK
DOOMSDAY BOOK
DOUBLING BACK
DRAINAGE TUBE
DRAINING AWAY
DRESSING CASE
DRESSING DOWN
DRESSING GOWN
DRESSING ROOM
DRINKING BOUT
DRINKING HORN
DRINKING SONG
DROPPING AWAY
DROPPING DOWN
DUCHESSE LACE
EIGHTEEN HOLE
ELECTRIC BLUE
ELECTRIC FIRE
ELECTRIC HARE
ELECTRON LENS
ELECTRON TUBE
ELECTRON VOLT
ELEPHANT SEAL
ELEVENTH HOUR
ENABLING BILL
ENTRANCE HALL
ETERNITY RING
EUROPEAN PLAN
EXCHANGE RATE
EXERCISE BIKE
EXERCISE BOOK
EXPLAINS AWAY
EXTENDED PLAY
FAMILIAR FACE
FAMILIAR RING
FIGHTING BACK
FIGHTING COCK
FIGHTING FISH
FIREMANS LIFT
FLAGGING DOWN
FLANDERS MARE
FLEXIBLE DISC
FLINGING DOWN
FLINGING OPEN
FLOATING DEBT
FLOATING DOCK
FLOATING MINE
FLOATING VOTE
FOLLOWED HOME

FOLLOWED SUIT
FOUNTAIN HEAD
FREEZING DOWN
FREEZING OVER
FREUDIAN SLIP
FRIGHTEN AWAY
FRITTERS AWAY
FULMINIC ACID
GALVANIC CELL
GAMBLING HALL
GARRISON TOWN
GEISSLER TUBE
GEODESIC DOME
GLAUBERS SALT
GOLDFISH BOWL
GRINDING DOWN
GUERNSEY LILY
HADRIANS WALL
HAMMERED HOME
HAPPENED UPON
HARMONIC MEAN
HEAVENLY BODY
HEAVENLY CITY
HEAVENLY HOST
HITCHING POST
HOSPITAL SHIP
HYDROGEN BOMB
IDENTITY CARD
IDENTITY DISC
IMPERIAL CITY
IMPERIAL YARD
INCIDENT ROOM
INCOMING TIDE
INVERTED ARCH
INVERTED SNOB
JACOBEAN LILY
JACQUARD LOOM
JOINTING RULE
JUDGMENT DEBT
JUDGMENT HALL
JUDGMENT SEAT
JUVENILE LEAD
KEYSTONE COPS
KILKENNY CATS
KILOWATT HOUR
KNACKERS YARD
KNOCKING BACK
KNOCKING COLD
KNOCKING COPY
KNOCKING DOWN
KNUCKLED DOWN
KNUCKLES DOWN
LABELLED ATOM
LEOPARDS BANE
LOLLIPOP LADY
LONSDALE BELT
LUMINOUS FLUX
LUNCHEON MEAT
LYSERGIC ACID
MAGAZINE RACK

MAGNETIC CORE
MAGNETIC DISC
MAGNETIC DRUM
MAGNETIC FLUX
MAGNETIC MINE
MAGNETIC TAPE
MAJORITY RULE
MANDARIN DUCK
MARATHON RACE
MARCHING SONG
MARGINAL LAND
MARGINAL SEAT
MARGINAL WARD
MARRIAGE RING
MARRIAGE VOWS
MATCHING PAIR
MEDICINE BALL
MERCHANT BANK
MERCHANT NAVY
MERCHANT SHIP
MIDNIGHT BLUE
MIDNIGHT MASS
MILITARY BAND
MISTRESS SHIP
MONETARY UNIT
MOSQUITO FISH
MOSQUITO HAWK
MOTORWAY EXIT
MOTORWAY SIGN
MOUNTAIN BIKE
MOUNTAIN BLUE
MOUNTAIN GOAT
MOUNTAIN HARE
MOUNTAIN LION
MOUNTAIN PASS
MOUNTAIN SIDE
MOURNING DOVE
MOURNING RING
MULBERRY BUSH
MULTIPLE SHOP
MULTIPLE STAR
MUSHROOM SOUP
MUTATION RATE
NATIONAL CALL
NATIONAL DEBT
NATIONAL DISH
NATIONAL GRID
NATIONAL HUNT
NATIONAL PARK
NATIVITY PLAY
NAUTICAL MILE
NEGATIVE POLE
NEGATIVE SIGN
NORTHERN LINE
OBSTACLE RACE
OFFICERS MESS
OFFICIAL LIST
ORIENTAL RUBY
PADDLING POOL
PANORAMA HEAD

8,4 *contd.*
PAPERING OVER
PARADISE FISH
PARAFFIN LAMP
PARALLEL BARS
PARIETAL BONE
PAVILION ROOF
PECTORAL FINS
PEDESTAL DESK
PENDENTE LITE
PENITENT FORM
PERIODIC WIND
PHRYGIAN MODE
PILGRIMS SIGN
PITCHING TOOL
PLANTAIN LILY
PLATANNA FROG
PLATFORM SOLE
PLATINUM LAMP
PLATONIC YEAR
PLEASURE BOAT
PLEASURE TRIP
PLIMSOLL LINE
PLOUGHED BACK
PLUGGING AWAY
PLUMBERS MATE
PLYMOUTH ROCK
POSITIVE POLE
POSITIVE RAYS
POSITIVE SIGN
PREACHED DOWN
PREACHES DOWN
PRESSING HOME
PRESSURE COOK
PRESSURE SUIT
PRIMEVAL ATOM
PRIMROSE PATH
PRINTERS MARK
PRINTERS REAM
PROMISED LAND
PROPERTY ROOM
QUARTERN LOAF
QUESTION MARK
QUESTION TIME
RAMBLING ROSE
RAYLEIGH DISC
REACTION TIME
RECESSED ARCH
RECITING NOTE
REFERRED PAIN
REINDEER MOSS
REPORTED BACK
RESERVED LIST
RINGSIDE SEAT
ROASTING JACK
ROASTING SPIT
ROCHELLE SALT
ROGATION DAYS
ROGATION WEEK
ROUNDING DOWN

SAPPHIRE WING
SCABBARD FISH
SCALPING TUFT
SCAPHOID BONE
SCHOLARS MATE
SCORPION FISH
SCOTLAND YARD
SCULLERY MAID
SCULLING BOAT
SCYTHIAN LAMB
SECURITY LEAK
SECURITY RISK
SELENIUM CELL
SENTINEL CRAB
SERGEANT FISH
SERVANTS HALL
SETTLING DOWN
SHETLAND PONY
SHETLAND WOOL
SHILLING MARK
SHIPPING LINE
SHOCKING PINK
SHOOTING DOWN
SHOOTING HOME
SHOOTING IRON
SHOOTING STAR
SHOPPING LIST
SHOPPING MALL
SHORTENS SAIL
SHOULDER BELT
SHOULDER BONE
SHOULDER HIGH
SHOULDER KNOT
SHOULDER PADS
SHOULDER SLIP
SHOUTING DOWN
SHUTTING AWAY
SHUTTING DOWN
SIDEREAL TIME
SIDEREAL YEAR
SIMMERED DOWN
SKELETON CREW
SKIPJACK TUNA
SKIPPING ROPE
SLEEPING PILL
SLIPPING AWAY
SMALLEST ROOM
SNARLING IRON
SNARLING TOOL
SNOWBALL TREE
SNOWDROP TREE
SNUBBING POST
SOLOMONS SEAL
SOUNDING LEAD
SOUNDING LINE
SOUNDING POST
SPARKING PLUG
SPEAKING TUBE
SPECIFIC HEAT
SPECIFIC NAME

SPELLING BOOK
SPILLING LINE
SPILLING OVER
SPINNING MILL
SPINNING MULE
SPLINTER BONE
SPONGING DOWN
SQUEEZED HOME
SQUEEZES HOME
SQUIRREL TAIL
STAGHORN MOSS
STAMPING MILL
STANDARD LAMP
STANDARD ROSE
STANDARD TIME
STANDING DOWN
STANDING FAST
STANDING FIRE
STANDING JOKE
STANDING OVER
STANDING ROOM
STANDING WAVE
STARTING GATE
STARTING POST
STEAMING OPEN
STEERING GEAR
STEPPING DOWN
STERLING AREA
STILETTO HEEL
STOCKING FOOT
STOCKING MASK
STOCKING SOLE
STOPPING DEAD
STOPPING OVER
STRAIGHT AWAY
STRAIGHT FACE
STRAIGHT GEAR
STRAIGHT PLAY
STRAIGHT TALK
STRIKING BACK
STRIKING DOWN
STRIKING DUMB
STRIKING HOME
STRIPPED ATOM
STRIPPED DOWN
STUDDING SAIL
SUNSHINE ROOF
SURGEONS KNOT
SURGICAL BOOT
SURGICAL SHOE
SWIMMING BATH
SWIMMING BELL
SWIMMING POND
SWIMMING POOL
SWINGING BOOM
SWINGING POST
SWITCHED OVER
SWITCHES OVER
TANTALUM LAMP
TEETHING RING

TELLURIC ACID
TEMPORAL LOBE
TEMPORAL PEER
TEMPTING FATE
TERMINAL UNIT
THINKING BACK
THINKING OVER
THORACIC DUCT
THROTTLE DOWN
THROTTLE PIPE
THROWING AWAY
THROWING DOWN
THROWING OPEN
THROWING OVER
TICKLING PINK
TOASTING FORK
TOASTING IRON
TOPPLING OVER
TOUCHING DOWN
TOUCHING WOOD
TOWERING OVER
TRACKING DOWN
TRAILING AWAY
TRAILING EDGE
TRAINING SHIP
TRANSFER BOOK
TRANSFER LIST
TRAPPIST MONK
TRAVESTY ROLE
TREASURE HUNT
TREASURY BILL
TREASURY NOTE
TROLLING BAIT
TROPICAL YEAR
TUBELESS TYRE
TUBEROUS ROOT
TUMBLING OVER
TURNPIKE ROAD
TWILIGHT ZONE
UMBRELLA TREE
VARIABLE GEAR
VENETIAN MAST
VICTORIA LINE
VICTORIA PLUM
VIRGINIA REEL
VISITING BOOK
VISITING CARD
VISITORS BOOK
VOLCANIC DUST
VOLCANIC ROCK
VOLCANIC SAND
WATCHING OVER
WATERING DOWN
WATERING HOLE
WEDGWOOD BLUE
WEDGWOOD WARE
WEIGHING DOWN
WHIPPING POST
WHISKING AWAY
WHISTLED AWAY

8,4 *contd.*
WHISTLES AWAY
WHITTLED AWAY
WHITTLES AWAY
WHOOPING SWAN

9,3
AFTERNOON NAP
APOSTOLIC SEE
ARMISTICE DAY
ARTILLERY MAN
ASCENSION DAY
AUSTRALIA DAY
AVOGADROS LAW
BALACLAVA CAP
BATTERING RAM
BOTTOMING OUT
BREAKFAST SET
BURROWING OWL
BUTTERFLY BOW
BUTTERFLY NET
BUTTERFLY NUT
CANCELLED OUT
CARDBOARD BOX
CARPENTER ANT
CARPENTER BEE
CARTRIDGE PEN
CHALLENGE CUP
CHEMISTRY SET
CHICKENED OUT
CHOCOLATE BOX
CHOCOLATE EGG
CHRISTIAN ERA
CHRISTMAS BOX
CHRISTMAS DAY
CHRISTMAS EVE
CIGARETTE END
COMMUNION CUP
COMPANION SET
COMPANION WAY
CONTRACTS OUT
CORDONING OFF
DALMATIAN DOG
DECLARING WAR
DISSECTED MAP
DORMITORY CAR
EXTRACTOR FAN
FINISHING OFF
FLATTENED OUT
FLOWERPOT MEN
FOLLOWING OUT
FOURPENNY ONE
FRIGHTENS OFF
FURNITURE VAN
GALLOPING OFF
GATHERING CRY
GATHERING WAY
GLADSTONE BAG
GRAPESEED OIL
GUERRILLA WAR

HARDENING OFF
HOLLOWING OUT
HYDRAULIC RAM
ICHNEUMON FLY
INNOCENTS DAY
INVISIBLE INK
KNOWLEDGE BOX
LACHRYMAL URN
LAUNCHING PAD
LEVELLING OFF
LEVELLING ROD
LIGHTNING BUG
LIGHTNING ROD
MARIOTTES LAW
MARMALADE CAT
MEASURING ROD
MEDULLARY RAY
MELLOWING OUT
MIDSUMMER DAY
MODELLING KIT
MOUSTACHE CUP
NEWSPAPER MAN
OFFERTORY BOX
ORCHESTRA PIT
ORGANISER BAG
OVERNIGHT BAG
PENSIONED OFF
PERMANENT WAY
PHEASANTS EYE
PISTACHIO NUT
POLISHING OFF
POLITICAL MAP
POLYTHENE BAG
POWDERING TUB
PRINCIPAL BOY
RABBETING SAW
RASPBERRY JAM
RECEIVING SET
REMAINDER MAN
RESONANCE BOX
RETAINING FEE
RHODESIAN MAN
SACRIFICE BID
SACRIFICE HIT
SAFFLOWER OIL
SASSAFRAS NUT
SASSAFRAS OIL
SATURATED FAT
SCREENING OFF
SEASONING TUB
SEVERANCE PAY
SHEPHERDS PIE
SHEPHERDS ROD
SHRUGGING OFF
SHUFFLING OFF
SKETCHING OUT
SKITTLING OUT
SLACKENED OFF
SMUGGLING DEN
SNAFFLING LAY

SPLASHING OUT
STOVEPIPE HAT
STRETCHED OUT
STRETCHES OUT
STRINGING OUT
STRIPPING OFF
STRIPPING OUT
SUBMARINE PEN
SWITCHING OFF
TELEPHONE BOX
THRASHING OUT
TRIGGERED OFF
UNWRITTEN LAW
VEGETABLE DYE
VEGETABLE OIL
VENTURING OUT
WANDERING JEW
WANDERING OFF
WEASELING OUT
WEASELLED OUT
WEATHERED OUT
WHISTLING OFF
WINNOWING FAN
WRIGGLING OUT
YORKSHIRE FOG

10,2
CONTRACTED IN
FRESHENING UP
LIGHTENING UP
QUICKENING UP
SHRIVELLED UP
SLACKENING UP
SOLDIERING ON
STRUGGLING ON
SWALLOWING UP
TOUGHENING UP

13 LETTERS

1,3,2,3,4
A FLY ON THE WALL

1,3,3,2,4
A FAT LOT OF GOOD

1,3,9
A NEW DEPARTURE
X RAY ASTRONOMY
X RAY TELESCOPE

1,4,2,3,3
A SHOT IN THE ARM

1,5,2,1,4
A WHALE OF A TIME

1,5,3,4
X MARKS THE SPOT

1,5,7
A SMALL FORTUNE

1,6,2,4
A TISSUE OF LIES

1,7,5
A QUARTER AFTER

1,8,4
A PARTHIAN SHOT

2,1,5,5
IN A CLEFT STICK
IN A SORRY STATE
ON A LARGE SCALE
ON A SMALL SCALE

2,1,10
ON A SHOESTRING

2,2,2,3,2,2
TO BE OR NOT TO BE

2,2,3,6
GO AS YOU PLEASE
GO TO ANY LENGTH
UP TO THE ELBOWS
UP TO THE MINUTE

2,2,4,2,3
IN NO TIME AT ALL

2,2,4,5
IN SO MANY WORDS

2,3,2,3,3
GO OUT OF THE WAY

2,3,3,2,3
AN EYE FOR AN EYE

2,3,3,5
TO SAY THE LEAST

2,3,4,2,2
ON THE FACE OF IT

2,3,4,4
AT THE SAME TIME
IF YOU DONT MIND
IN THE SAME BOAT
ON THE HIGH SEAS

2,3,5,3
GO THE WHOLE HOG
IN THE SHORT RUN

2,3,8
BY ALL ACCOUNTS
GO THE DISTANCE
IN ALL FAIRNESS
IN THE ABSTRACT
IN THE DOLDRUMS
IN THE MEANTIME
IN THE PIPELINE
NO OIL PAINTING
ON THE CONTRARY
ON THE PAVEMENT
ON THE SCROUNGE

2,4,1,6
TO COIN A PHRASE

2,4,2,1,4
AS THIN AS A RAKE

2,4,2,5
AS BOLD AS BRASS
AS HARD AS NAILS
AS WARM AS TOAST
BY WORD OF MOUTH
ON PAIN OF DEATH

2,4,3,4
GO OVER THE EDGE
GO OVER THE WALL
IN ONES OWN TIME
UP WITH THE LARK

2,4,4,3
AT ONES WITS END

2,4,7
AT ONES LEISURE
AT YOUR SERVICE
IN DIRE STRAITS
IN ONES ELEMENT
IN SOME MEASURE

2,5,2,1,3
AS BLIND AS A BAT
AS SWEET AS A NUT

2,5,2,4
AS LARGE AS LIFE
AS RIGHT AS RAIN
IN POINT OF FACT

2,5,6
AT RIGHT ANGLES
AT SHORT NOTICE
IN GREAT DEMAND
IN SHORT SUPPLY
LA BELLE EPOQUE
LE GRAND SIECLE
NO GREAT SHAKES
NO HOLDS BARRED
ST LUKES SUMMER

2,6,5
IN HONOUR BOUND
LA GRANDE ARMEE
NO CLAIMS BONUS
NO HIDING PLACE
ON TENTER HOOKS
ST VITUSS DANCE

2,7,4
ON SHANKSS PONY
ST MARTINS EVIL

2,8,3
ST BERNARDS DOG
ST CRISPINS DAY
ST PATRICKS DAY
ST SWITHINS DAY

2,11
AT LOGGERHEADS
BY APPOINTMENT
GO UNDERGROUND
IN CIRCULATION

IN COMPETITION
IN PERPSECTIVE

3,1,4,5
CAT O NINE TAILS

3,1,5,4
RAN A TIGHT SHIP
RUN A TIGHT SHIP

3,2,1,7
ONE IN A MILLION

3,2,2,3,3
GET IN ON THE ACT
GOT IN ON THE ACT

3,2,3,5
CUT TO THE QUICK
GUM UP THE WORKS
HOT ON THE TRAIL
LAG OF THE TIDES
LED TO THE ALTAR
MAN OF THE MATCH
MAN OF THE WORLD
OLD AS THE HILLS
OUT OF THE WOODS
PUT IN THE SHADE
PUT IN THE WRONG
PUT TO THE SWORD
RAN IN THE BLOOD
RUB OF THE GREEN
RUN IN THE BLOOD
SAT ON THE FENCE
SIT ON THE FENCE
TOP OF THE CLASS
WAR TO THE KNIFE
WAY OF THE CROSS

3,2,4,4
ALL IN GOOD TIME
GET TO ONES FEET
GOT TO ONES FEET
HAD IT BOTH WAYS
HAS IT BOTH WAYS
NOT ON YOUR LIFE
OUT OF ONES HEAD
OUT OF ONES MIND

3,2,5,3
OUT OF HARMS WAY

3,2,8
ALL IN WRESTLER
ARC DE TRIOMPHE
DAY OF JUDGMENT
DEN OF INIQUITY
GET IT TOGETHER
GOT IT TOGETHER
LAW OF AVERAGES
MAN OF BUSINESS
OIL OF LAVENDER
OUT OF PRACTICE
PAR OF EXCHANGE
RAY OF SUNSHINE

SAT IN JUDGMENT
SIT IN JUDGMENT

3,3,2,1,4
RED RAG TO A BULL

3,3,2,5
PUT OUT TO GRAZE
RAN OUT OF STEAM
RUN OUT OF STEAM

3,3,3,2,2
PUT THE LID ON IT

3,3,3,4
ONE FOR THE ROAD

3,3,4,3
RAG AND BONE MAN

3,3,5,2
PUT THE BRAKE ON
PUT THE SKIDS ON

3,3,7
ASK FOR TROUBLE
BAG AND BAGGAGE
BOX THE COMPASS
DID THE HONOURS
DIG FOR VICTORY
FOR THE PRESENT
GAS AND GAITERS
GET THE MESSAGE
GET THE PICTURE
GOT THE MESSAGE
GOT THE PICTURE
HIT THE CEILING
HIT THE JACKPOT
HOT AIR BALLOON
MAD COW DISEASE
OLD AGE PENSION
OLD BOY NETWORK
ORB AND SCEPTRE
PAY AND DISPLAY
PAY LIP SERVICE
PIG AND WHISTLE
PRE TAX PROFITS
RAM AIR TURBINE
TAR AND FEATHER
TIP THE BALANCE

3,4,1,5
ATE LIKE A HORSE
EAT LIKE A HORSE
FIT LIKE A GLOVE
OUT LIKE A LIGHT

3,4,2,4
CUT DOWN TO SIZE

3,4,3,3
FOR EVER AND AYE
FOR GOOD AND ALL
LAY DOWN THE LAW
OFF ONES OWN BAT

3,4,4,2
GET AWAY WITH IT
GET ONES HAND IN
GOT AWAY WITH IT
GOT ONES HAND IN
HAD DONE WITH IT
HAS DONE WITH IT
PUT ONES FACE ON
PUT ONES FEET UP
PUT ONES MIND TO
SET ONES MIND TO
SET ONES SEAL ON

3,4,6
AIR RAID WARDEN
ALL TIME RECORD
BIG GAME HUNTER
CRY BLUE MURDER
CUT ONES LOSSES
CUT ONES THROAT
DAY CARE CENTRE
FOR THAT MATTER
HIT ONES STRIDE
HIT ROCK BOTTOM
MAN MADE FIBRES
MID LIFE CRISIS
NOT GOOD ENOUGH
ODD COME SHORTS
OFF ONES ROCKER
OFF ONES STROKE
SUB POST OFFICE
THE BLUE YONDER
THE FLAT SEASON
THE GRIM REAPER
THE LAST SUPPER
THE MAIN CHANCE
THE REAL MACKAY

3,5,1,4
NOT WORTH A DAMN

3,5,2,3
THE DEVIL TO PAY

3,5,5
BIG WHITE CHIEF
DOW JONES INDEX
EYE LEVEL GRILL
ICE CREAM WAFER
OLD WIVES TALES
ONE NIGHT STAND
OUT HEROD HEROD
RAN RINGS ROUND
RUN RINGS ROUND
SUN DRIED BRICK
TEN PENNY PIECE
THE FIRST THING
THE LORDS TABLE
THE MIDAS TOUCH
THE OTHER WORLD
THE PENNY DROPS
THE SMALL PRINT

3,5,5 *contd.*
THE WHOLE SHOOT
THE WHOLE WORLD
TWO PENCE PIECE
TWO PENNY PIECE

3,6,2,2
HER NUMBER IS UP
HIS NUMBER IS UP

3,6,4
FOR MERCYS SAKE
LES GRANDS VINS
NOT BEFORE TIME
OLD CROCKS RACE
RED RIDING HOOD
RED SPIDER MITE
TAX RETURN FORM
TEN MINUTE RULE
THE CLOVEN HOOF
THE COMMON GOOD
THE COMMON WEAL
THE PARTYS OVER
THE VIRGIN MARY

3,7,3
ALL HALLOWS DAY
GAY LUSSACS LAW
PRE EMPTIVE BID

3,10
AIR COMPRESSOR
AIR LIEUTENANT
AIR LOADMASTER
ALL HALLOWMASS
ALL HALLOWTIDE
BIG BROTHERISM
GAY LIBERATION
HAD EVERYTHING
HAS EVERYTHING
HIS EXCELLENCY
HOT GOSPELLING
ILL CONSIDERED
JET PROPULSION
KIT INSPECTION
MAN MANAGEMENT
MAP PROJECTION
NON ACCEPTANCE
NON AGGRESSION
NON APPEARANCE
NON ATTENDANCE
NON COMPLIANCE
NON CONDUCTING
NON OBSERVANCE
NON PRODUCTION
NON PRODUCTIVE
NON RETURNABLE
PAN AFRICANISM
PAR EXCELLENCE
PRE QUALIFYING
PRE RAPHAELISM
PRE RAPHAELITE

PRO CHANCELLOR
RED SANDALWOOD
SEA GOOSEBERRY
SUN WORSHIPPER
TAX COLLECTING
TAX COLLECTION
TAX CONCESSION
TAX DEDUCTIBLE
TEA PLANTATION
THE FOOTLIGHTS
THE OPPOSITION
THE PARANORMAL
THE REVOLUTION
THE UNDERWORLD
TIC DOULOUREUX
TWO PENNYWORTH
WAR DEPARTMENT

4,1,3,5
HITS A BAD PATCH
WITH A BAD GRACE

4,1,4,2,2
HAVE A TIME OF IT
MADE A MEAL OF IT
MAKE A MEAL OF IT

4,1,4,4
DRAW A VEIL OVER
DREW A VEIL OVER
HAVE A GOOD TIME
MADE A FAST BUCK
MAKE A FAST BUCK
TAKE A BACK SEAT
TOOK A BACK SEAT

4,1,5,3
TEAR A STRIP OFF
TORE A STRIP OFF
TURN A BLIND EYE

4,1,6,2
GOES A BUNDLE ON

4,1,8
HAVE A BASINFUL
MADE A COMEBACK
MAKE A COMEBACK

4,2,1,6
HANG BY A THREAD
HUNG BY A THREAD
KICK UP A RUMPUS
KICK UP A SHINDY
SHIP IN A BOTTLE
SICK AS A PARROT
WEAK AS A KITTEN
WINS IN A CANTER

4,2,2,5
GOES UP IN SMOKE
HERE WE GO AGAIN
LAID IT ON THICK
LAYS IT ON THICK
TIED UP IN KNOTS

TIES UP IN KNOTS
WENT UP IN SMOKE

4,2,3,4
CALL OF THE WILD
CAME TO THE BOIL
COCK OF THE LOFT
COCK OF THE ROCK
COCK OF THE WALK
COIN IN THE SLOT
COLD IN THE HEAD
COME TO THE BOIL
DYED IN THE WOOL
FLAT OF THE HAND
FULL TO THE BRIM
GIVE TO THE DOGS
GOES BY THE BOOK
GOES TO THE DOGS
GOES TO THE WALL
GOES TO THE WARS
GONE TO THE DOGS
GONE TO THE WALL
HOLE IN THE WALL
KING OF THE ROAD
KISS IN THE RING
LADY OF THE LAKE
LADY OF THE LAMP
LAID ON THE LINE
LAYS ON THE LINE
LEAD BY THE NOSE
LEAP IN THE DARK
LIES ON THE OARS
LILY OF THE NILE
LIVE IN THE PAST
LOOK IN THE FACE
LUCK OF THE DRAW
MAID OF ALL WORK
NEXT ON THE LIST
PACE UP AND DOWN
PAIN IN THE NECK
PUTS ON ONE SIDE
PUTS ON THE LINE
RISE TO THE BAIT
ROSE TO THE BAIT
RULE OF THE ROAD
SAVE AS YOU EARN
SETS BY THE EARS
SHIP OF THE LINE
SHOT IN THE DARK
SLAP IN THE FACE
SLAP ON THE BACK
SOFT IN THE HEAD
STAB IN THE BACK
TAKE TO THE ROAD
TOAD IN THE HOLE
TOOK TO THE ROAD
TURN OF THE YEAR
TURN ON THE HEAT
WALK UP AND DOWN
WENT BY THE BOOK

WENT TO THE DOGS
WENT TO THE WALL
WENT TO THE WARS
WHAT DO YOU KNOW
WIDE OF THE MARK

4,2,4,3
HANG UP ONES HAT
HUNG UP ONES HAT
ROLL ON ROLL OFF
TAKE TO ONES BED
TOOK TO ONES BED
WEEK IN WEEK OUT
YEAR IN YEAR OUT

4,2,7
BANK OF ENGLAND
BIRD OF PASSAGE
CALL TO ACCOUNT
CHEF DE CUISINE
CODE OF CONDUCT
COLD AS CHARITY
COUP DE THEATRE
CUTS TO RIBBONS
DEAN OF FACULTY
DEUS EX MACHINA
EASY AS WINKING
FULL OF ONESELF
GATE OF JUSTICE
GENS DE LETTRES
GIFT OF TONGUES
HALL OF JUSTICE
HALL OF MIRRORS
HARD OF HEARING
HELD TO ACCOUNT
HOLD TO ACCOUNT
KEEN AS MUSTARD
LADY IN WAITING
LADY OF LEISURE
LINE OF THOUGHT
LOAD OF RUBBISH
LORD OF MISRULE
LORD OF SESSION
LOSS OF DIGNITY
MADE IN BRITAIN
MADE TO MEASURE
MESS OF POTTAGE
MILK OF SULPHUR
NECK OR NOTHING
NEXT TO NOTHING
NOLI ME TANGERE
PAID IN ADVANCE
PAIR OF BELLOWS
PAIR OF PYJAMAS
PAYS IN ADVANCE
RITE OF PASSAGE
ROBE DE CHAMBRE
ROSE OF JERICHO
SALT OF VITRIOL
SETS AN EXAMPLE
STOP AT NOTHING

4,2,7 *contd.*
TAKE IN LODGERS
TALK IN RIDDLES
TELL ME ANOTHER
TOOK IN LODGERS
UNIT OF ACCOUNT
VERS DE SOCIETE
WRIT OF INQUIRY

4,3,1,5
GAME FOR A LAUGH
GOOD FOR A LAUGH

4,3,2,4
STEP OUT OF LINE
TIME OUT OF MIND

4,3,3,3
BLEW THE LID OFF
BLOW THE LID OFF
LIFT THE LID OFF
MEAT AND TWO VEG
ONCE AND FOR ALL
PUTS THE CAT OUT
TAKE THE LID OFF
TOOK THE LID OFF

4,3,4,2
FROM THE WORD GO
GETS THE WIND UP
GRIN AND BEAR IT
KISS AND MAKE UP
PULL THE PLUG ON
PUTS THE BOOT IN

4,3,6
AIRS AND GRACES
BALL AND SOCKET
BEAT THE BOUNDS
BELT AND BRACES
BITE THE BULLET
BITS AND PIECES
CHOP AND CHANGE
CUTS THE CACKLE
DEEP SEA DIVING
EACH WAY DOUBLE
EACH WAY TREBLE
FAIR AND SQUARE
FITS AND STARTS
FROM THE OUTSET
GETS THE NEEDLE
GOES ONE BETTER
GOES THE ROUNDS
HALE AND HEARTY
HALF THE BATTLE
HARE AND HOUNDS
HELD THE RECORD
HIGH AND MIGHTY
HITS THE BOTTLE
HOLD THE RECORD
HOLE AND CORNER
JACK THE RIPPER
JUST THE TICKET

KEEP THE CHANGE
KICK THE BUCKET
LORD AND MASTER
MADE THE ROUNDS
MAKE THE ROUNDS
MILD AND BITTER
OILS THE WHEELS
OPEN AIR MARKET
OVER THE STICKS
OVER THE WICKET
PART AND PARCEL
PICK AND CHOOSE
PICK AND SHOVEL
PLAY THE MARKET
PLAY THE WANTON
POST WAR CREDIT
PRIM AND PROPER
PUSH THE BOTTLE
RACK AND PINION
RAID THE MARKET
RANZ DES VACHES
ROOT AND BRANCH
SALE AND RETURN
SALT AND PEPPER
SEES THE SIGHTS
SIGN THE PLEDGE
SLAP AND TICKLE
SLOT CAR RACING
SOAP BOX ORATOR
SPIT AND POLISH
STAY THE COURSE
TAKE THE MICKEY
TAKE THE PLUNGE
TIME AND MOTION
TIPS THE SCALES
TOOK THE MICKEY
TOOK THE PLUNGE
TROD THE BOARDS
TURN THE CORNER
TURN THE TABLES
WENT THE ROUNDS
WILD AND WOOLLY
WINE AND CHEESE
WITH ONE ACCORD
WORK THE ORACLE

4,4,1,4
EYES LIKE A HAWK
GOES LIKE A BOMB
GOES WITH A BANG
LIVE LIKE A LORD
ONCE UPON A TIME
READ LIKE A BOOK
ROOM WITH A VIEW
SANG LIKE A BIRD
SING LIKE A BIRD
WENT LIKE A BOMB
WENT WITH A BANG

4,4,2,3
AWAY FROM IT ALL

LONG TIME NO SEE
PLAY HARD TO GET
SOME LIKE IT HOT

4,4,3,2
GETS ONES EYE IN
KEEP ONES END UP
KEPT ONES END UP
PUTS ONES OAR IN
SETS ONES CAP AT
WORM ONES WAY IN

4,4,5
BARE BACK RIDER
BETS ONES BOOTS
BITE ONES THUMB
BOBS YOUR UNCLE
BURN ONES BOATS
COOK ONES GOOSE
COOL ONES HEELS
DEAD MENS SHOES
DICE WITH DEATH
DOES ONES STUFF
DOES ONES WORST
DOGS TAIL GRASS
EATS ONES WORDS
FALL FROM GRACE
FALL INTO PLACE
FELL FROM GRACE
FELL INTO PLACE
FIND ONES LEVEL
FORK LIFT TRUCK
GETS ONES CARDS
GOOD KING HENRY
GRIT ONES TEETH
HALF TIME SCORE
HANG SENG INDEX
HARD LUCK STORY
HEAD OVER HEELS
HOME MADE BREAD
HOME MADE CAKES
KEEP GOOD HOURS
KEEP OPEN HOUSE
KEPT GOOD HOURS
KEPT OPEN HOUSE
KICK INTO TOUCH
KICK ONES HEELS
KNEW ONES PLACE
KNEW ONES STUFF
KNIT ONES BROWS
KNOW ONES PLACE
KNOW ONES STUFF
LEFT HAND DRIVE
LEFT WELL ALONE
LETS WELL ALONE
LICK INTO SHAPE
LICK ONES CHOPS
LIKE GRIM DEATH
LOSE ONES NERVE
LOSE ONES SHIRT
LOST ONES NERVE

LOST ONES SHIRT
MIND THAT CHILD
NAME YOUR PRICE
OPEN ONES HEART
OPEN PLAN HOUSE
PAST ONES PRIME
PLAY ONES HUNCH
PLAY UPON WORDS
POPS ONES CLOGS
PUSH PULL TRAIN
PUTS INTO WORDS
RUBS ONES HANDS
SAVE ONES BACON
SHOW ONES PACES
SUCK ONES THUMB
TAKE ONES LEAVE
TOOK ONES LEAVE
TRIM ONES SAILS
WASH ONES HANDS
WHIP INTO SHAPE
WINS ONES SPURS
WOOD WOOL SLABS

4,5,2,2
JUST THINK OF IT

4,5,4
EAST NORTH EAST
EAST SOUTH EAST
FIVE POUND NOTE
FREE RANGE EGGS
HIGH WATER MARK
KNEW WHATS WHAT
KNOW WHATS WHAT
LORD PRIVY SEAL
LOSE HANDS DOWN
LOST HANDS DOWN
MADE FIRST BASE
MAKE FIRST BASE
PAGE THREE GIRL
READ WRITE HEAD
RIDE ROUGH SHOD
RODE ROUGH SHOD
STAR NOSED MOLE
TIME AFTER TIME
WIDE ANGLE LENS
WINS HANDS DOWN

4,6,3
EATS HUMBLE PIE
FELT TIPPED PEN
FOUR POSTER BED
HARD BOILED EGG
KNEW INSIDE OUT
KNOW INSIDE OUT
POST OFFICE BOX
PUSH BUTTON WAR
RING TAILED CAT
SOFT BOILED EGG
TURN INSIDE OUT
WELL WORKED OUT

4,7,2
HIGH TAILING IT
LETS ONESELF GO
TIME MARCHES ON
WELL THOUGHT OF

4,9
AFRO CARIBBEAN
ANTI MARKETEER
BABY SNATCHING
BACK FORMATION
BACK PEDALLING
BALL CARTRIDGE
BALL LIGHTNING
BANK STATEMENT
BIRD SANCTUARY
BODY SNATCHING
BUFF ORPINGTON
BUSH TELEGRAPH
CAMP FOLLOWERS
CANE FURNITURE
CARD CATALOGUE
CASE HARDENING
CASH DISPENSER
CAVE PAINTINGS
CINE PROJECTOR
CLUB SECRETARY
COST EFFECTIVE
DARK CONTINENT
DATA PROCESSOR
DEAD RECKONING
DEBT COLLECTOR
DECK PASSENGER
DOGS BREAKFAST
DRAG PARACHUTE
DRAW ATTENTION
DREW ATTENTION
DRUG ADDICTION
DRUM MAJORETTE
DUMB INSOLENCE
EASY LISTENING
FETE CHAMPETRE
FINE CHAMPAGNE
FINE GENTLEMAN
FIRE INSURANCE
FIRE RESISTANT
FOLK ETYMOLOGY
FOOD POISONING
FOOD PROCESSOR
FOOT PASSENGER
FORK LIGHTNING
FORM CRITICISM
FREE COMPANION
FUEL INJECTION
FULL FASHIONED
GAIN ADMISSION
GAME PRESERVER
GETS UNDRESSED
GOES OVERBOARD
GOLD MEDALLIST

GOOD AFTERNOON
GOOD GROUNDING
GOOD NATUREDLY
GOOD SAMARITAN
HAIR SPLITTING
HALF HEARTEDLY
HALF SOVEREIGN
HARD HEARTEDLY
HAVE HYSTERICS
HEAD RESTRAINT
HEAT EXCHANGER
HEAT RESISTANT
HIGH CHURCHISM
HIGH CHURCHMAN
HIGH CONSTABLE
HIGH EXPLOSIVE
HIGH FREQUENCY
HIGH PRIESTESS
HOLY COMMUNION
HOME ECONOMICS
HOME ECONOMIST
HOME SECRETARY
IRIS DIAPHRAGM
JOBS COMFORTER
JUMP OVERBOARD
KNEW BACKWARDS
KNOW BACKWARDS
LADY BOUNTIFUL
LAND MEASURING
LAND OWNERSHIP
LAND SURVEYING
LAWN SPRINKLER
LEAD POISONING
LIFE ASSURANCE
LIFE INSURANCE
LIFE PRESERVER
LIFT ATTENDANT
LIKE CLOCKWORK
LINE ENGRAVING
LINE FISHERMAN
LIVE CARTRIDGE
LONG DESCENDED
LONG SUFFERING
LORD PRESIDENT
LORD PROTECTOR
MILK CHOCOLATE
MILK DENTITION
MINE DETECTION
MINI SUBMARINE
MINT CONDITION
PAID ATTENTION
PALE IMITATION
PAYS ATTENTION
PINK ELEPHANTS
POST COMMUNION
POST MODERNISM
POST MODERNIST
POST OPERATIVE
RACE RELATIONS
RENT COLLECTOR

ROAD METALLING
ROAD TRANSPORT
ROOT VEGETABLE
RUBS SHOULDERS
RUDE AWAKENING
RULE BRITANNIA
RUST RESISTANT
SADO MASOCHISM
SADO MASOCHIST
SALE CATALOGUE
SEED CATALOGUE
SELF ABASEMENT
SELF ADDRESSED
SELF ADJUSTING
SELF APPOINTED
SELF APPROVING
SELF ASSERTION
SELF ASSURANCE
SELF AWARENESS
SELF COMMUNION
SELF CONCEITED
SELF CONDEMNED
SELF CONFESSED
SELF CONFIDENT
SELF CONSCIOUS
SELF CONTAINED
SELF CRITICISM
SELF DEFEATING
SELF DEPENDENT
SELF DIRECTING
SELF DIRECTION
SELF FINANCING
SELF GOVERNING
SELF IMPORTANT
SELF INDULGENT
SELF INFLICTED
SELF MOTIVATED
SELF OPERATING
SELF POSSESSED
SELF PROFESSED
SELF PROPELLED
SELF PUBLICIST
SELF RESTRAINT
SELF RIGHTEOUS
SELF SACRIFICE
SELF SATISFIED
SELF SUPPORTED
SEMI AUTOMATIC
SEMI BARBARIAN
SEMI BARBARISM
SEMI PERMEABLE
SHIP CHANDLERY
SHOP ASSISTANT
SIDE SPLITTING
SILK STOCKINGS
SNOW BLINDNESS
SOCK SUSPENDER
SOFT PEDALLING
SOIL MECHANICS
SOUL SEARCHING

STAR CATALOGUE
STAR TREATMENT
STAY STITCHING
STEP PARENTING
TAKE EXCEPTION
TAKE LIBERTIES
TAPE RECORDING
TENT PREACHING
TEST CRICKETER
TIME CONSUMING
TIME SIGNATURE
TOGA PRAETEXTA
TOOK EXCEPTION
TOOK LIBERTIES
TRAM CONDUCTOR
UNIT FURNITURE
UNIT PACKAGING
VICE ADMIRALTY
VICE CONSULATE
VICE PRESIDENT
VICE PRINCIPAL
WAIT PATIENTLY
WAVE MECHANICS
WELL APPOINTED
WELL CONDUCTED
WELL CONNECTED
WELL DEVELOPED
WELL PRESERVED
WELL REGULATED
WELL RESPECTED
WENT OVERBOARD
WING COMMANDER
WOOD ENGRAVING
WOOD SANDPIPER
WOOL GATHERING
WORD BLINDNESS
WORD PROCESSOR
WORD SPLITTING
YOUR REVERENCE

5,1,4,3
PULLS A FAST ONE
TURNS A DEAF EAR

5,1,5,2
STEAL A MARCH ON
STOLE A MARCH ON
TAKES A PRIDE IN
TAKES A SHINE TO

5,1,7
AFTER A FASHION
BEATS A RETREAT
COMES A CROPPER
DROPS A CLANGER
MAKES A BEELINE
MAKES A KILLING
POSED A PROBLEM
POSES A PROBLEM
PULLS A FLANKER
SERVE A PURPOSE

5,1,7 contd.
STAGE A PROTEST
TAKES A BEATING
TREAD A MEASURE

5,2,1,5
DRAWS TO A CLOSE
FRESH AS A DAISY
GIVEN ON A PLATE
GIVES ON A PLATE
KICKS UP A STINK
QUICK AS A FLASH
QUIET AS A MOUSE
SHARP AS A RAZOR
SOBER AS A JUDGE
STIFF AS A BOARD
WHITE AS A SHEET

5,2,2,4
LEAVE IT AT THAT

5,2,3,3
APPLE OF THE EYE
CHAMP AT THE BIT
FLASH IN THE PAN
LYING IN THE WAY
ORDER OF THE DAY
PICKS UP THE TAB
POKED IN THE EYE
POKES IN THE EYE
QUEEN OF THE MAY
SKIRL IN THE PAN
STATE OF THE ART
STICK IN THE MUD
TRIAL OF THE PYX
WHITE OF THE EYE

5,2,6
AGREE TO DIFFER
BEAST OF BURDEN
BUNCH OF GRAPES
CARTE DE VISITE
CHIEF OF POLICE
COMES UP TRUMPS
CORPS DE BALLET
COURT OF APPEAL
COURT OF HONOUR
CREME DE MENTHE
CROIX DE GUERRE
EAGER TO PLEASE
FIELD OF VISION
FLEET OF TRUCKS
GOING TO GROUND
GOING TO MARKET
GOING TO PIECES
GUARD OF HONOUR
GUEST OF HONOUR
HEART OF HEARTS
HOLDS TO RANSOM
HOUSE OF PRAYER
HOUSE OF REFUGE
KNOCK ON EFFECT

LYING AT ANCHOR
MEALS ON WHEELS
ORDER OF BATTLE
PASTE UP ARTIST
PICKS TO PIECES
PIECE OF ADVICE
PIECE OF STRING
PLACE ON RECORD
POINT OF HONOUR
PRICK ME DAINTY
PULLS TO PIECES
QUEEN OF HEAVEN
REIGN OF TERROR
RIDES TO HOUNDS
RIGHT OF COMMON
RIGHT OF SEARCH
SHORT OF BREATH
STAFF OF OFFICE
STAND ON TIPTOE
STAND TO REASON
STATE OF EVENTS
STATE OF UNREST
STICK OF CELERY
STOOD ON TIPTOE
STOOD TO REASON
TAKEN TO PIECES
TAKES TO PIECES
TRIAL BY RECORD
TURNS UP TRUMPS
VICAR OF CHRIST
WALKS ON TIPTOE
WINDS OF CHANGE

5,3,1,4
GOING FOR A SONG
PLAYS FOR A DRAW
RIDES FOR A FALL
STICK OUT A MILE
STUCK OUT A MILE
TAKEN FOR A RIDE
TAKES FOR A RIDE

5,3,2,3
THATS BIG OF HER
THATS BIG OF HIM

5,3,5
AGAIN AND AGAIN
ALPHA AND OMEGA
APPLE PIE ORDER
BEATS THE CLOCK
BLACK AND WHITE
BRAVE NEW WORLD
CALLS THE SHOTS
CHEAP AND NASTY
CLEAR THE COURT
CLEAR THE DECKS
CLEAR THE TABLE
CLOAK AND SWORD
CLOSE RUN THING
COOKS THE BOOKS

COSTS THE EARTH
CROSS THE FLOOR
DOING THE TRICK
DOING THE TWIST
DRIBS AND DRABS
EIGHT DAY CLOCK
FACED THE MUSIC
FACES THE MUSIC
FEELS THE PINCH
FETCH AND CARRY
FIRST DAY COVER
FLESH AND BLOOD
FLORA AND FAUNA
FORCE THE ISSUE
GOING FOR BROKE
GOODY TWO SHOES
HELPS THE CAUSE
HOLDS THE FLOOR
HONEY DEW MELON
HORSE AND BUGGY
JUMPS THE QUEUE
KEEPS THE PEACE
KNOWS THE ROPES
KNOWS THE SCORE
MAKES OLD BONES
MAKES THE GRADE
PAPER THE HOUSE
PEACE AND QUIET
PLAYS THE DEVIL
PLAYS THE FIELD
POINT FOR POINT
QUEER THE PITCH
QUITS THE SCENE
RAISE THE ALARM
RANTS AND RAVES
READS THE SIGNS
RIDES THE WAVES
ROUGH AND READY
ROUND THE BLOCK
ROUND THE CLOCK
ROUND THE TWIST
ROYAL AIR FORCE
RULED THE ROAST
RULED THE ROOST
RULES THE ROAST
RULES THE ROOST
SELLS THE DUMMY
SHOOT THE WORKS
SHORT AND SWEET
SLIPS THE CABLE
SMALL AND EARLY
SOUND THE ALARM
SPILL THE BEANS
SPILT THE BEANS
STEAK AND CHIPS
STONE THE CROWS
STURM UND DRANG
SWEEP THE BOARD
SWELL THE RANKS
SWEPT THE BOARD

TAKES THE BLAME
TAKES THE FIELD
TAKES THE FLOOR
TAKES THE REINS
TELLS THE TRUTH
THATS THE STUFF
THERE SHE BLOWS
THINK THE WORST
THREE DAY EVENT
THREE PER CENTS
TRIAL AND ERROR
TURNS THE SCREW
UNDER THE KNIFE
UNDER THE TABLE
WALKS THE PLANK
WATCH THE CLOCK
WINED AND DINED
WINES AND DINES

5,4,1,3
CRAZY LIKE A FOX
HOLDS DOWN A JOB
SLEEP LIKE A LOG
SLEEP LIKE A TOP
SLEPT LIKE A LOG
SLEPT LIKE A TOP
TAKEN DOWN A PEG
TAKES DOWN A PEG

5,4,4
BIRDS NEST SOUP
BLOWS ONES MIND
BREAK ONES DUCK
BREAK ONES WORD
BRING INTO LINE
BRING INTO PLAY
BROKE ONES DUCK
BROKE ONES WORD
CAMEL HAIR COAT
CLASS WILL TELL
CLOSE ONES EYES
COMES INTO PLAY
CRICK ONES NECK
DADDY LONG LEGS
DIXIE LAND JAZZ
DRAGS ONES FEET
FALLS INTO LINE
FEEDS ONES FACE
FINDS ONES FEET
FOLDS ONES ARMS
FORTY HOUR WEEK
FOUND ONES FEET
HANGS ONES HEAD
HEADS WILL ROLL
HEDGE ONES BETS
HIDES ONES HEAD
KEEPS GOOD TIME
KEEPS ONES COOL
KEEPS ONES HEAD
KEEPS ONES WORD
KNOWS FULL WELL

5,4,4 contd.

LICKS ONES LIPS
LOSES ONES COOL
LOSES ONES HAIR
LOSES ONES HEAD
MAKES ENDS MEET
MAKES GOOD TIME
MAKES ONES MARK
MENDS ONES WAYS
MIGHT HAVE BEEN
PACKS ONES BAGS
PICKS ONES SPOT
PLAYS WITH FIRE
POURS WITH RAIN
QUEEN ANNE LEGS
RIGHT HAND SIDE
RISKS ONES LIFE
ROLLS ONES EYES
SAVED ONES FACE
SAVED ONES NECK
SAVED ONES SKIN
SAVES ONES FACE
SAVES ONES NECK
SAVES ONES SKIN
SELLS ONES SOUL
SEVEN YEAR ITCH
SHAKE ONES FIST
SHAKE ONES HEAD
SHOOK ONES FIST
SHOOK ONES HEAD
SHOWS ONES FACE
SHOWS ONES HAND
SLING ONES HOOK
SLIPS ONES MIND
SLUNG ONES HOOK
SMACK ONES LIPS
SPEAK ONES MIND
SPOKE ONES MIND
STAKE ONES LIFE
STAND ONES HAND
STOOD ONES HAND
SUITS ONES BOOK
TAKES ONES SEAT
TAKES ONES TIME
TAKES ONES TURN
TEARS ONES HAIR
THICK WITH DUST
THREE LINE WHIP
THROW AWAY LINE
THUMB ONES NOSE
TIGHT HEAD PROP
TREAT LIKE DIRT
TRIED ONES LUCK
TRIES ONES LUCK
TURNS ONES HEAD
TWICE TOLD TALE
UNDER ONES BELT
UNDER ONES NOSE
USING ONES LOAF
WALLS HAVE EARS

WATCH ONES STEP
WORKS ONES WILL
WORTH ONES SALT

5,5,3

ANGRY YOUNG MAN
APRIL FOOLS DAY
EVERY WHICH WAY
FISRT WORLD WAR
GREAT WHITE WAY
KNOCK SPOTS OFF
LARGE SCALE MAP
MOUSE EARED BAT
SEVEN YEARS WAR
STIFF UPPER LIP
VALUE ADDED TAX
YLANG YLANG OIL

5,6,2

QUEER GOINGS ON
READY STEADY GO

5,8

ABOVE REPROACH
ALPHA PARTICLE
ANGLO AMERICAN
ANGLO CATHOLIC
ARGUS PHEASANT
ASSET STRIPPER
AUDIO CASSETTE
AUDIO ENGINEER
AUDIO LOCATION
BAGGY TROUSERS
BASSO PROFONDO
BIBLE POUNDING
BIBLE THUMPING
BLACK DIAMONDS
BLOCK CAPITALS
BLOCK PRINTING
BLOOD BROTHERS
BLOOD PRESSURE
BLOOD RELATION
BRASS FARTHING
BRENT BARNACLE
BROAD DAYLIGHT
BROAD SPECTRUM
BROWN SEAWEEDS
BRUSH KANGAROO
BURNT OFFERING
CABLE DRILLING
CABLE MOULDING
CASSE NOISETTE
CHAIN MOULDING
CHAIN REACTION
CHASE RAINBOWS
CHECK WEIGHMAN
CHEST EXPANDER
CHOIR PRACTICE
CHUCK FARTHING
CIVIL AVIATION
CIVIL ENGINEER

CLASS STRUGGLE
CLOCK WATCHING
CLOSE QUARTERS
CLOSE RELATIVE
COACH BUILDING
COUNT PALATINE
COURT CIRCULAR
COURT REPORTER
CREAM COLOURED
CROSS DRESSING
CROSS EXAMINED
CROSS EXAMINES
CROSS HATCHING
CROSS PURPOSES
CROSS QUESTION
CROSS REFERRED
CROSS THREADED
CROSS VAULTING
CROWN IMPERIAL
CROWN PRINCESS
CUBIC CAPACITY
DAIRY PRODUCTS
DEATH SENTENCE
DOLLS HOSPITAL
DOLLY MIXTURES
DOWNS SYNDROME
DRESS DESIGNER
DRESS IMPROVER
DRILL SERGEANT
EARTH MOVEMENT
EXACT SCIENCES
FERRO CONCRETE
FIDEI DEFENSOR
FIELD DRESSING
FIELD HOSPITAL
FIELD PREACHER
FILLE DHONNEUR
FINAL SOLUTION
FIRST OFFENDER
FIXED INTEREST
FLAME COLOURED
FLAME THROWING
FLASH FLOODING
FLESH COLOURED
FLINT KNAPPING
FOOLS PARADISE
FRUIT COCKTAIL
FUNNY BUSINESS
FUNNY PECULIAR
GAINS STRENGTH
GAMES MISTRESS
GLASS GRINDING
GLASS PAINTING
GLOBE TROTTING
GOING DOWNHILL
GOING STRAIGHT
GOOSE BARNACLE
GRAND NATIONAL
GRAND SEIGNEUR
GRAPE HYACINTH

GRASS STAGGERS
GREAT GRANDSON
GREEN MANURING
GREEN SICKNESS
GRIEF STRICKEN
GROUP DYNAMICS
GROUP MARRIAGE
GROUP PRACTICE
HANGS TOGETHER
HAPPY BIRTHDAY
HAPPY FAMILIES
HEART SICKNESS
HEART STIRRING
HEART STRICKEN
HEATH ROBINSON
HEAVY BREATHER
HEAVY HYDROGEN
HEAVY INDUSTRY
HEAVY PARTICLE
HEDGE ACCENTOR
HEDGE MARRIAGE
HOLDS TOGETHER
HORSE CHESTNUT
HORSE MACKEREL
HORSE SICKNESS
HOUSE BREAKING
HUMAN INTEREST
HYPNO ANALYSIS
INNER HEBRIDES
JERRY BUILDING
JUDGE ADVOCATE
KICKS UPSTAIRS
KINGS EVIDENCE
KINGS SHILLING
KNICK KNACKERY
KNIFE GRINDING
KNOCK SIDEWAYS
KNOCK TOGETHER
LANCE CORPORAL
LANCE SERGEANT
LATIN AMERICAN
LEGAL CAPACITY
LEGAL GUARDIAN
LEMON COLOURED
LEMON SQUEEZER
LEVEL CROSSING
LIGHT FINGERED
LIGHT HORSEMAN
LIGHT INDUSTRY
LIGHT INFANTRY
LIGHT SPIRITED
LIONS PROVIDER
LIVED TOGETHER
LIVER COLOURED
LOCAL PREACHER
LORDS ORDINARY
LORDS TEMPORAL
LOTUS POSITION
LOUIS QUATORZE
MAGIC MUSHROOM

5,8 *contd.*
MAJOR PROPHETS
MARSH MARIGOLD
MARSH SAMPHIRE
MEZZO SOPRANOS
MICRO ORGANISM
MINOR COUNTIES
MINOR PROPHETS
MISSA SOLEMNIS
MIXED BLESSING
MIXED FOURSOME
MIXED LANGUAGE
MIXED MARRIAGE
MIXED METAPHOR
MODUS OPERANDI
MONEY CHANGING
MONEY GRUBBING
MONEY TROUBLES
MOTOR TRACTION
MURAL PAINTING
MUSIC FESTIVAL
MUSIC MISTRESS
NAIVE PAINTING
NARCO ANALYSIS
NASTY ACCIDENT
NASTY BUSINESS
NAVAL HOSPITAL
NERVE WRACKING
NIGHT CLUBBING
NIGHT WATCHMAN
NITRO COMPOUND
NORTH EASTERLY
NORTH EASTWARD
NORTH WESTERLY
NORTH WESTWARD
OPTIC THALAMUS
ORBIS TERRARUM
OUTER HEBRIDES
OWNER OCCUPIED
OWNER OCCUPIER
OZONE FRIENDLY
PANIC STRICKEN
PAPER FASTENER
PAPER HANGINGS
PARIS FASHIONS
PARTI COLOURED
PARTY POLITICS
PARTY SPIRITED
PEACE DIVIDEND
PEACE OFFERING
PEACH COLOURED
PEARL NECKLACE
PEARL SHELLING
PENNY DREADFUL
PENNY FARTHING
PENNY PINCHING
PETIT DEJEUNER
PETTY SESSIONS
PHOTO EMISSION
PIANO CONCERTO

PIECE TOGETHER
PLAIN LANGUAGE
PLAIN SPEAKING
PLATE PRINTING
POETS LAUREATE
POLAR DISTANCE
POLAR EQUATION
POLAR EXPLORER
POSTE RESTANTE
POTTS FRACTURE
POTTY TRAINING
POWER ASSISTED
POWER POLITICS
POWER STEERING
PRAWN COCKTAIL
PRESS FASTENER
PRIME MERIDIAN
PRIME MINISTER
PRIZE FIGHTING
PROBE SCISSORS
PROOF CORRECTS
PROTO HISTORIC
PULLS TOGETHER
PURSE SNATCHER
PUTTY COLOURED
QUEEN VICTORIA
QUICK ANSWERED
QUICK TEMPERED
RADIO ACTINIUM
RADIO OPERATOR
RADIO SPECTRUM
READY RECKONER
REYES SYNDROME
RIGHT REVEREND
RIGHT THINKING
ROAST CHESTNUT
ROGUE ELEPHANT
ROMAN CATHOLIC
ROMAN NUMERALS
ROUGH SHOOTING
ROYAL MARRIAGE
ROYAL PECULIAR
ROYAL STANDARD
RUGBY FOOTBALL
RURAL DISTRICT
RUSTY COLOURED
SABLE ANTELOPE
SABLE COLOURED
SABRE RATTLING
SAINT SIMONIAN
SAINT SIMONISM
SAINT SIMONIST
SALAD DRESSING
SATIN SHEETING
SAUTE POTATOES
SERBO CROATIAN
SEVEN SLEEPERS
SHARE SECURITY
SHARP PRACTICE
SHEEP SHEARING

SHEEP STEALING
SHELL ORNAMENT
SHELL PARAKEET
SHIFT REGISTER
SHIPS REGISTER
SHOCK ABSORBER
SHORT CHANGING
SHORT DIVISION
SHORT TEMPERED
SHORT TROUSERS
SLATE COLOURED
SLEEP LEARNING
SLIDE TROMBONE
SMALL CAPITALS
SMEAR CAMPAIGN
SMOKE DETECTOR
SNUFF COLOURED
SOUND BOARDING
SOUTH EASTERLY
SOUTH EASTWARD
SOUTH WESTERLY
SOUTH WESTWARD
SPACE INVADERS
SPACE MEDICINE
SPACE PLATFORM
SPEED MERCHANT
SPELL BACKWARD
SPELT BACKWARD
SPINE CHILLING
SPRAY PAINTING
STAFF SERGEANT
STAGE MANAGING
STATE PRISONER
STATE RELIGION
STEAM CARRIAGE
STEAM GOVERNOR
STERN FOREMOST
STICK TOGETHER
STOCK BREEDING
STOCK EXCHANGE
STONE COLOURED
STONE DRESSING
STRAW COLOURED
STRIP LIGHTING
STUCK TOGETHER
SUGAR DIABETES
SUGAR REFINERY
SUGAR REFINING
SWEET CHESTNUT
SWEET NOTHINGS
SWEET SAVOURED
SWEET TEMPERED
TABLE FOOTBALL
TABLE SKITTLES
TABLE SPOONFUL
TAKEN PRISONER
TAKES MEASURES
TAKES PRISONER
THANK GOODNESS
THREE CORNERED

THREE QUARTERS
THREW TOGETHER
THROW TOGETHER
TITHE GATHERER
TRADE DISCOUNT
TRADE UNIONISM
TRADE UNIONIST
TRADE WEIGHTED
TRAIN SPOTTING
TRIAL MARRIAGE
TRUCE BREAKING
TRUNK DIALLING
TURBO ELECTRIC
UNDER CONTRACT
UNDER PRODUCED
UNDER PRODUCES
URBAN DISTRICT
VALUE JUDGMENT
VEXED QUESTION
VIDEO RECORDER
VINYL PLASTICS
VOWEL MUTATION
WATER CARRIAGE
WATER CHESTNUT
WATER DIVINING
WATER HYACINTH
WATER PLANTAIN
WATER PURSLANE
WATER SOFTENER
WHEEL CARRIAGE
WHEEL CLAMPING
WHITE ELEPHANT
WORLD LANGUAGE
WORLD PREMIERE
WRONG HEADEDLY
YOUNG FOGEYISH
YOUNG OFFENDER
ZEBRA CROSSING

6,1,4,2
MAKING A FUSS OF
MAKING A PASS AT

6,1,6
BREAKS A RECORD
BREAKS A STRIKE
BRINGS A CHARGE
COINED A PHRASE
LAYING A COURSE
LIFTED A FINGER
MISSED A SITTER
MISSES A SITTER
SAYING A PRAYER
SPILLS A BIBFUL
TABLED A MOTION
TABLES A MOTION
TAKING A TUMBLE
TAKING A WICKET
THROWS A WOBBLY

6,2,1,4
BRINGS TO A HEAD
COMING TO A HEAD
GRINDS TO A HALT
GROUND TO A HALT
KICKED UP A FUSS
STEADY AS A ROCK

6,2,2,3
PLAYED IT BY EAR

6,2,3,2
TAKING IT OUT ON

6,2,5
BREACH OF TRUST
BRIDGE OF BOATS
BRINGS TO LIGHT
BURDEN OF PROOF
CALLED IT QUITS
CALLED TO ORDER
CHANGE OF HEART
CHANGE OF VENUE
CHEVAL DE FRISE
COMING TO BLOWS
COMING TO GRIEF
COMING TO LIGHT
DOUBLE OR QUITS
EDITOR IN CHIEF
ENDING IN TEARS
ESPRIT DE CORPS
EXCUSE ME DANCE
FIGURE OF EIGHT
FLIGHT OF FANCY
GAGGLE OF GEESE
GIRDLE OF VENUS
LAUGHS TO SCORN
MAISON DE VILLE
MARGIN OF ERROR
MOMENT OF TRUTH
MOTHER OF PEARL
MOVING TO TEARS
PACKET OF SEEDS
PALAIS DE DANSE
PERIOD OF GRACE
PICKED UP SPEED
PIECES OF EIGHT
PRINCE OF PEACE
PRINCE OF WALES
REDUCE TO TEARS
RHYMED TO DEATH
RHYMES TO DEATH
SHADOW OF DEATH
SHIELD OF BRAWN
SOONER OR LATER
SQUIRE OF DAMES
STRIKE IT LUCKY
STRING OF BEADS
STRUCK IN YEARS
TAKING BY STORM
TAKING ON BOARD

TAKING ON TRUST
TAKING TO COURT
TAKING TO HEART
TICKLE TO DEATH
TONGUE IN CHEEK
WAITED AT TABLE

6,3,2,2
WANTED JAM ON IT

6,3,4
ACTING THE FOOL
ACTING THE GOAT
BEFORE THE BEAM
BEFORE THE MAST
BEFORE THE WIND
BESIDE THE MARK
BEYOND THE PALE
BITING THE DUST
BOSTON TWO STEP
BOUGHT AND SOLD
BREAKS THE BANK
BREAKS THE NEWS
BREAST THE TAPE
CALLED THE TUNE
COMMON LAW WIFE
CRACKS THE WHIP
DIPPED THE FLAG
DISHED THE DIRT
DISHES THE DIRT
DIVIDE AND RULE
FAITES VOS JEUX
FILLED THE BILL
FLYING THE FLAG
FOOTED THE BILL
FORCED THE PACE
FORCES THE PACE
GILDED THE LILY
GILDED THE PILL
HEAVES THE LEAD
HOPPED THE TWIG
JEKYLL AND HYDE
KILROY WAS HERE
KISSED THE BOOK
KISSES THE BOOK
LAUGHS OUT LOUD
LEAVES FOR DEAD
LEAVES ONE COLD
LEAVES THE ROOM
LITTLE BOY BLUE
LOOPED THE LOOP
MAKING THE PACE
MISSED THE BOAT
MISSED THE MARK
MISSED THE POST
MISSES THE BOAT
MISSES THE MARK
MISSES THE POST
OCCUPY THE MIND
PADDED THE HOOF
PAINTS THE LILY

PASSED THE BUCK
PASSED THE TIME
PASSES THE BUCK
PASSES THE TIME
PEPPER AND SALT
PLAYED FOR TIME
PLAYED THE FOOL
PLAYED THE GAME
PLAYED THE LEAD
PRAYED FOR RAIN
PROFIT AND LOSS
RADIAL PLY TYRE
RAISED THE ROOF
RAISED THE WIND
RAISES THE ROOF
RAISES THE WIND
RIDING THE FAIR
RIGHTS THE HELM
ROCKED THE BOAT
RUPERT THE BEAR
SCOOPS THE POOL
SHARPS THE WORD
SHOUTS THE ODDS
SHOWED THE FLAG
SOWING THE SEED
SPEAKS TOO SOON
SPLITS THE VOTE
STANDS THE PACE
STAYED THE PACE
STEALS THE SHOW
STICKS THE PACE
SUGARS THE PILL
SWINGS THE LEAD
TAKING POT LUCK
TAKING THE BAIT
TAKING THE CAKE
TAKING THE LEAD
TAKING THE MICK
TAKING THE VEIL
THINKS OUT LOUD
TIPPED THE WINK
TOEING THE LINE
TOPPED THE BILL
TURNED THE TIDE
VENUSS FLY TRAP
WATTLE AND DAUB
WINNIE THE POOH

6,4,3
BEYOND ONES KEN
BITING ONES LIP
BUTTON YOUR LIP
CHANCE ONES ARM
COGITO ERGO SUM
HAVING ONES WAY
LOSING ONES RAG
LOSING ONES WAY
MAKING ONES DAY
MAKING ONES WAY
MURDER WILL OUT

PAYING ONES WAY
PICKED ONES WAY
PLAYED ONES ACE
RAISED ONES HAT
RAISES ONES HAT
ROLLED INTO ONE
SECOND HAND CAR
SHOWED ONES AGE
SPORTS ONES OAK
TAKING ONES CUE
TAKING TIME OFF
TIPPED ONES HAT
WENDED ONES WAY
WINGED ONES WAY

6,5,2
LAYING HANDS ON
MAKING LIGHT OF
POURED SCORN ON
THROWS LIGHT ON

6,7
ABJECT POVERTY
ACTIVE SERVICE
ACTIVE VOLCANO
ADDING MACHINE
AERIAL RAILWAY
AGENTS GENERAL
ALMOND BLOSSOM
ANIMAL KINGDOM
ANIMAL SPIRITS
ANIMAL WORSHIP
ANNUAL HOLIDAY
ARDENT SPIRITS
ARMOUR PLATING
ASSERT ONESELF
ASTRAL SPIRITS
ATOMIC WARFARE
BADGER BAITING
BADGER DRAWING
BALLET DANCING
BALLOT RIGGING
BAMBOO CURTAIN
BARBER SURGEON
BARREL CHESTED
BARREL VAULTED
BASKET WEAVING
BASSET HORNIST
BATTLE CRUISER
BATTLE FATIGUE
BATTLE SCARRED
BEAUTY CONTEST
BEAUTY PARLOUR
BEETLE CRUSHER
BELLES LETTRES
BESIDE ONESELF
BEYOND COMPARE
BEYOND MEASURE
BOMBER COMMAND
BORDER TERRIER
BOSTON TERRIER

6,7 *contd.*

BOTTLE FEEDING	COTTON PICKING	FLYING MACHINE	INLAND REVENUE
BRANCH OFFICER	COTTON SPINNER	FLYING OFFICER	ISLAND HOPPING
BREAKS THROUGH	COUNTY BOROUGH	FLYING PICKETS	JUNIOR SERVICE
BREAST FEEDING	COUNTY COUNCIL	FLYING TRAPEZE	KICKED ONESELF
BREECH LOADING	COUNTY CRICKET	FOLLOW THROUGH	KIDDED ONESELF
BRIDGE BUILDER	COURTS MARTIAL	FORCED LANDING	KIDNEY MACHINE
BRINGS FORWARD	CREDIT SQUEEZE	FORGET ONESELF	KNIGHT MARSHAL
BROKEN HEARTED	CROHNS DISEASE	FORGOT ONESELF	KNIGHT SERVICE
BUBBLE CHAMBER	CRUISE MISSILE	FOSTER BROTHER	KNIGHT TEMPLAR
BUDGET ACCOUNT	DANDIE DINMONT	FRENCH CRICKET	KNOTTY PROBLEM
BUNGEE JUMPING	DANTES INFERNO	FRENCH MUSTARD	LADIES FINGERS
BUTTER FINGERS	DEARLY BELOVED	FRENCH WINDOWS	LADIES GALLERY
BUTTON THROUGH	DENIED ONESELF	FRIARS LANTERN	LAPSUS LINGUAE
CALICO PRINTER	DENIES ONESELF	FRIDGE FREEZER	LAUNCH VEHICLE
CAMERA OBSCURA	DENTAL SURGEON	FRINGE BENEFIT	LETTER CARRIER
CANDLE DIPPING	DINNER SERVICE	FRINGE DWELLER	LETTER FOUNDER
CANDLE LIGHTER	DIRECT CURRENT	FRYING TONIGHT	LETTER MISSIVE
CANDLE SNUFFER	DOUBLE BASSOON	FUSION REACTOR	LETTER PERFECT
CANVAS CLIMBER	DOUBLE CROSSED	FUTURE PERFECT	LINSEY WOOLSEY
CARBON DIOXIDE	DOUBLE CROSSER	GAINED CONTROL	LIQUID CRYSTAL
CARBON PROCESS	DOUBLE CROSSES	GARDEN VILLAGE	LISTED COMPANY
CARPET BEATING	DOUBLE DEALING	GARLIC MUSTARD	LITTLE THEATRE
CARPET BOMBING	DOUBLE DENSITY	GEIGER COUNTER	LIVERY COMPANY
CARPET SLIPPER	DOUBLE FEATURE	GENTLE HEARTED	LIVERY SERVANT
CARPET SWEEPER	DOUBLE FIGURES	GERMAN MEASLES	LOOKED ASKANCE
CASUAL CLOTHES	DOUBLE FRONTED	GHETTO BLASTER	LOOKED DAGGERS
CAUGHT NAPPING	DOUBLE GLAZING	GILDED CHAMBER	LOOKED FORWARD
CAUSED TROUBLE	DOUBLE JOINTED	GIRDED ONESELF	LOSING CONTROL
CAUSES TROUBLE	DOUBLE MEANING	GIVING OFFENCE	LOSING ONESELF
CENTRE FORWARD	DOUBLE PARKING	GLOBAL VILLAGE	MAKING BELIEVE
CHAMPS ELYSEES	DOUBLE SHUFFLE	GLOBAL WARMING	MAKING CERTAIN
CHANGE RINGING	DOUBLE WEDDING	GOLDEN CRESTED	MAKING CHANGES
CHARGE ACCOUNT	EMPIRE BUILDER	GOLDEN HAMSTER	MAKING FRIENDS
CHARGE CAPPING	ENJOYS ONESELF	GOLDEN JUBILEE	MAKING HISTORY
CHERRY BLOSSOM	ESCORT CARRIER	GOLDEN SECTION	MAKING INROADS
CHORAL SOCIETY	ESTATE BOTTLED	GOLDEN WEDDING	MAKING WHOOPEE
CHROME PLATING	EXCESS BAGGAGE	GORDON BENNETT	MARBLE HEARTED
CHURCH OFFICER	EXCESS LUGGAGE	GOSPEL SINGING	MARINE TRUMPET
CHURCH SERVICE	EXCESS POSTAGE	GOTHIC REVIVAL	MASHIE NIBLICK
CLOSED CIRCUIT	EXCUSE ONESELF	GRANDE VEDETTE	MASTER BUILDER
COARSE FISHING	EXPORT LICENCE	GRAVES DISEASE	MASTER MARINER
COARSE GRAINED	EXPOSE ONESELF	GROUND ANGLING	MEADOW SAFFRON
COCKER SPANIEL	FABIAN SOCIETY	GROUND CONTROL	MENTAL CRUELTY
COFFEE GROUNDS	FAMILY BUTCHER	GROUND OFFICER	MENTAL PATIENT
COFFEE MORNING	FAMILY REUNION	GUIDED MISSILE	MENTAL PICTURE
COFFEE SERVICE	FARMER GENERAL	HAMMER THROWER	METEOR SHOWERS
COMBAT FATIGUE	FELLOW CITIZEN	HAVING KITTENS	METEOR STREAMS
COMING BETWEEN	FELLOW FEELING	HEALTH VISITOR	MIDDLE AMERICA
COMING FORWARD	FIDDLE FADDLER	HEEBIE JEEBIES	MIDDLE BRACKET
COMING UNSTUCK	FIGURE CASTING	HELPED ONESELF	MIDDLE EASTERN
COMMIT ONESELF	FIGURE SKATING	HELTER SKELTER	MIDDLE ENGLISH
COMMIT SUICIDE	FILING CABINET	HEROIC COUPLET	MIDDLE KINGDOM
COMMON CARRIER	FILTER THROUGH	HIDDEN ECONOMY	MIDDLE PASSAGE
COMMON MEASURE	FINGER POINTER	HOLLOW HEARTED	MINERS ANAEMIA
CONSUL GENERAL	FINNAN HADDOCK	HUGGED ONESELF	MIRROR WRITING
COPPER CAPTAIN	FLICKS THROUGH	HUMANE SOCIETY	MOBILE LIBRARY
COPPER PYRITES	FLIGHT FEATHER	HUNGER MARCHER	MODERN ENGLISH
CORPUS CHRISTI	FLORAL DIAGRAM	HUNGER STRIKER	MORRIS DANCING
CORPUS DELICTI	FLOWER SERVICE	INDIAN TOBACCO	MOTHER COUNTRY
	FLYING COLOURS	INFILL HOUSING	MOTHER HUBBARD

6,7 *contd.*
MOTION PICTURE
MOWING MACHINE
MUDDLE THROUGH
NATIVE SPEAKER
NATURE RESERVE
NATURE WORSHIP
NEEDLE POINTED
NICKEL PLATING
NODDED THROUGH
NORWAY HADDOCK
NORWAY LOBSTER
NUCLEO PROTEIN
OBJETS TROUVES
OBTUSE ANGULAR
ORANGE BLOSSOM
ORIENT EXPRESS
ORKNEY ISLANDS
OXFORD ENGLISH
OYSTER CATCHER
OYSTER FISHERY
PADDLE STEAMER
PADDYS LANTERN
PARENT COMPANY
PARISH COUNCIL
PARROT DISEASE
PARROT FASHION
PARTED COMPANY
PASSED CURRENT
PASSED THROUGH
PASSES CURRENT
PASSES THROUGH
PATENT LEATHER
PENCIL COMPASS
PERIOD COSTUME
PETROL LIGHTER
PETROL STATION
PIDGIN ENGLISH
PIGEON CHESTED
PIGEON FANCIER
PIGEON HEARTED
PILOTS LICENCE
PISTOL WHIPPED
PLAYED FOOTSIE
PLOUGH THROUGH
PLURAL SOCIETY
POCKET BOROUGH
POCKET PICKING
POETIC JUSTICE
POETIC LICENCE
POLICE OFFICER
POLICE STATION
POOPER SCOOPER
POROUS PLASTER
POSTAL ADDRESS
POSTER COLOURS
POTATO DISEASE
POTTED SHRIMPS
POWDER COMPACT
PRAYER MEETING

PREENS ONESELF
PRINCE CONSORT
PRISON BREAKER
PRISON OFFICER
PROFIT SHARING
PROPER CHARLIE
PSEUDO ARCHAIC
PUBLIC COMPANY
PUBLIC HANGING
PUBLIC HOLIDAY
PUBLIC INQUIRY
PUBLIC LECTURE
PUBLIC LIBRARY
PUBLIC OPINION
PUBLIC RECORDS
PUBLIC SERVANT
PUBLIC SPEAKER
PUBLIC TRUSTEE
PUBLIC UTILITY
PUBLIC WARNING
PULLED STRINGS
PULLED THROUGH
PURPLE EMPEROR
PUSHED THROUGH
PUSHES THROUGH
QUAKER BUTTONS
QUARTZ CRYSTAL
QUEENS COUNSEL
QUEENS ENGLISH
QUEENS PROCTOR
QUEENS PUDDING
QUOTED COMPANY
RABBLE ROUSING
RACING TIPSTER
RANGED ONESELF
RANGES ONESELF
RATTLE BRAINED
RECORD BREAKER
REIGNS SUPREME
REMOTE CONTROL
REMOTE SENSING
RENTAL LIBRARY
REPEAT ONESELF
RETURN JOURNEY
RHAETO ROMANIC
RHODES SCHOLAR
RHYTHM SECTION
RIDING CLOTHES
RITUAL KILLING
RODENT OFFICER
ROGUES GALLERY
ROLLER BANDAGE
ROLLER BEARING
ROLLER COASTER
ROLLER SKATING
ROMANO BRITISH
ROMPED THROUGH
ROTTEN BOROUGH
RUBBER NECKING
RUBBER STAMPED

RUSSIA LEATHER
SACRED COLLEGE
SADDLE BLANKET
SAFETY BICYCLE
SAFETY CURTAIN
SALAMI TACTICS
SALMON FISHERY
SALMON FISHING
SALTED PEANUTS
SCENIC RAILWAY
SCHOOL LEAVING
SCHOOL MARMISH
SCHOOL TEACHER
SCHOOL UNIFORM
SCOTCH CURLIES
SCOTCH TERRIER
SCOTCH THISTLE
SCOTCH VERDICT
SCREEN PROCESS
SEANAD EIREANN
SEARCH WARRANT
SECOND CHAMBER
SECOND INNINGS
SECOND READING
SECRET PASSAGE
SECRET SERVICE
SEMPER FIDELIS
SEMPER PARATUS
SENIOR CITIZEN
SENIOR PARTNER
SENIOR SERVICE
SEWING MACHINE
SHABBY GENTEEL
SHADOW CABINET
SHAMMY LEATHER
SHARKS MANNERS
SHERRY COBBLER
SHIFTS ONESELF
SHOWED PROMISE
SHOWED WILLING
SHRILL TONGUED
SHROVE TUESDAY
SILVER JUBILEE
SILVER MOUNTED
SILVER TONGUED
SILVER WEDDING
SIMPLE HEARTED
SIMPLE LARCENY
SINGLE FIGURES
SINGLE SOLDIER
SKIING HOLIDAY
SKINNY DIPPING
SMOKED HADDOCK
SMOOTH CHINNED
SOCIAL CLIMBER
SOCIAL SCIENCE
SOCIAL SERVICE
SOCKET SPANNER
SOWING MACHINE
SPEAKS VOLUMES

SPEECH THERAPY
SPIRIT RAPPING
SPONGE FISHING
SPRING BALANCE
SPRING CHICKEN
SPRING CLEANER
SQUARE BASHING
SQUARE DANCING
SQUARE MEASURE
SQUEAK THROUGH
STACKS AGAINST
STANDS ACCUSED
STANDS AGAINST
STARCH REDUCED
STATES GENERAL
STILLS DISEASE
STRATO CRUISER
STRATO CUMULUS
STREET SWEEPER
STREET WALKING
STRIKE BREAKER
STRIKE THROUGH
STRING QUARTET
STRONG STOMACH
STRONG SWIMMER
STRUCK THROUGH
STUDIO POTTERY
SUITED ONESELF
SUMMER HOLIDAY
SUMMER PUDDING
SUSSEX SPANIEL
SWITCH SELLING
TAKING COMMAND
TAKING OFFENCE
TAKING UMBRAGE
TALENT SPOTTER
TENDER HEARTED
TENPIN BOWLING
THINKS THROUGH
TICKET MACHINE
TICKET WRITING
TISSUE CULTURE
TITTLE TATTLER
TOILET SERVICE
TOMATO KETCHUP
TONGUE LASHING
TONGUE TWISTER
TRACER ELEMENT
TRAVEL STAINED
TRENCH WARFARE
TRIPLE CROWNED
TRIPLE ENTENTE
TURING MACHINE
TURKEY BUZZARD
TURKEY VULTURE
TURNED AGAINST
TURNIP LANTERN
UNITED KINGDOM
UNITED NATIONS
VACUUM CLEANER

6,7 *contd.*
VENICE TREACLE
VERNAL EQUINOX
VICTOR LUDORUM
VIPERS BUGLOSS
VOTING MACHINE
VOTIVE PICTURE
WEIGHT LIFTING
WEIGHT WATCHER
WICKET KEEPING
WILLOW PATTERN
WILLOW WARBLER
WINDOW CLEANER
WINDOW CURTAIN
WINDOW SHOPPED
WINDOW SHOPPER
WINKLE PICKERS
WINTER GARDENS
WINTER SESSION
WITHIN EARSHOT
WONDER WORKING
WORKED AGAINST
YELLOW BELLIED
YELLOW BUNTING
YOUNGS MODULUS
ZENANA MISSION

7,1,5
BLAZING A TRAIL
CASTING A SPELL
COCKING A SNOOK
CUTTING A CAPER
CUTTING A TOOTH
DRAWING A BLANK
DROPPED A BRICK
HAZARDS A GUESS
PACKING A PUNCH
PICKING A FIGHT
RAISING A SIEGE
RAISING A STINK
RESERVE A TABLE
STAKING A CLAIM
STRAINS A POINT
STRETCH A POINT
STRIKES A CHORD
STRIKES A MATCH

7,2,1,3
CALLING IT A DAY

7,2,4
ABSENCE OF MIND
BALANCE OF MIND
BAPTISM OF FIRE
BEARING IN MIND
BELLOWS TO MEND
BONHEUR DU JOUR
BROUGHT TO BOOK
BROUGHT TO HEEL
BROUGHT TO LIFE
CALLING TO MIND

COLLEGE OF ARMS
CUTTING IT FINE
DRESSED TO KILL
EDITION DE LUXE
FALLING IN LOVE
FEELING AT HOME
KEEPING IN MIND
KEEPING IT DARK
KNOCKED ON WOOD
LETTING IT RIDE
OFFICER OF ARMS
PASSAGE OF ARMS
PLAYING IT COOL
PROPHET OF DOOM
PUTTING ON AIRS
PUTTING UP WITH
QUALITY OF LIFE
RUNNING TO SEED
SELLING IN BULK
SETTING IN HAND
SETTING ON EDGE
SETTING ON FIRE
SETTING TO WORK
SETTING UP SHOP
SLEIGHT OF HAND
STRIKES IT RICH
TALKING IT OVER
TEAMING UP WITH
WALKING TO HEEL
WORKING TO RULE

7,3,3
BEATING THE AIR
BEATING THE GUN
BELLING THE CAT
BRIDGED THE GAP
BRIDGES THE GAP
CARRIED THE CAN
CARRIED THE DAY
CARRIED TOO FAR
CARRIES THE CAN
CARRIES THE DAY
CARRIES TOO FAR
CATCHES THE SUN
CHEWING THE CUD
CHEWING THE FAT
CHIMNEY POT HAT
CLEARED THE AIR
CLEARED THE WAY
CLOSING THE GAP
HITTING FOR SIX
HITTING THE HAY
JUMPING FOR JOY
JUMPING THE GUN
KNOCKED FOR SIX
LEADING THE WAY
MISSING THE BUS
PRIVATE PAY BED
REYNARD THE FOX
SHAMPOO AND SET

SHOWING THE WAY
STOPPED THE ROT
THROUGH THE DAY
WALKING THE DOG
WHIPPED THE CAT
WIDENED THE GAP
WINNING THE CUP
WINNING THE DAY

7,4,2
CLAPPED EYES ON
KEEPING TABS ON
PANCAKE MAKE UP
PUTTING PAID TO
SETTING EYES ON
SETTING FIRE TO

7,6
ACRYLIC RESINS
ADIPOSE TISSUE
ADRENAL GLANDS
AFFAIRE DAMOUR
AFRICAN VIOLET
ALTERUM TANTUM
ANCIENT LIGHTS
APOSTLE SPOONS
APRICOT BRANDY
AQUEOUS HUMOUR
ASSAULT COURSE
AUCTION BRIDGE
BAGGAGE ANIMAL
BARGAIN HUNTER
BARNABY BRIGHT
BASCULE BRIDGE
BATHING BEAUTY
BATWING SLEEVE
BEDSIDE MANNER
BEGGING LETTER
BELISHA BEACON
BERMUDA SHORTS
BIDDING PRAYER
BISCUIT BARREL
BLANKET FINISH
BLANKET STITCH
BLISTER BEETLE
BOOKING OFFICE
BORSTAL SYSTEM
BOWLING CREASE
BREATHE FREELY
BRITISH EMPIRE
BRITISH LEGION
BROTHER GERMAN
BROWNIE GUIDER
BROWNIE POINTS
BUBONIC PLAGUE
BUDDING AUTHOR
BUDDING GENIUS
BURNETT SALMON
BURNING DESIRE
BURNING MIRROR
BURYING BEETLE

BURYING GROUND
BUTLERS PANTRY
CADMIUM YELLOW
CAPITAL ASSETS
CAPITAL LETTER
CAPITAL MURDER
CARDIAC ARREST
CAREERS MASTER
CARRIER PIGEON
CARRIER ROCKET
CARRION FLOWER
CASTING ANCHOR
CASTING WEIGHT
CAUSTIC POTASH
CAVALRY CHARGE
CAYENNE PEPPER
CENTRAL FORCES
CENTRAL POWERS
CHAMBER FELLOW
CHANGED COLOUR
CHANGED PLACES
CHANGES COLOUR
CHANGES PLACES
CHANNEL TUNNEL
CHARTER FLIGHT
CHARTER MEMBER
CHECKED SQUARE
CHEDDAR CHEESE
CHICKEN FARMER
CHIMNEY BREAST
CHINESE LEAVES
CHINESE PUZZLE
CHUCKIE STONES
CHUCKLE HEADED
CLIPPED SPEECH
CLOSING SPEECH
CLOSING STAGES
CLOTHES BASKET
COCONUT BUTTER
COMMAND MODULE
COMPANY DOCTOR
COMPASS NEEDLE
COMPASS SIGNAL
COMPASS WINDOW
COMPLEX NUMBER
CONCAVO CONVEX
CONCERT MASTER
CONTACT FLIGHT
CONTACT LENSES
CONTROL COLUMN
CONVEXO CONVEX
COPYING PENCIL
COTTAGE CHEESE
COUNCIL ESTATE
COUNCIL SCHOOL
COUNSEL KEEPER
COUNTER ATTACK
COUNTER BIDDER
COUNTER MOTION
COUNTER POISON

7,6 *contd.*
COUNTER SIGNAL
COUNTER SPYING
COUNTER WEIGHT
COUNTRY COUSIN
COVERED MARKET
COWPERS GLANDS
CRACKER BARREL
CROQUET MALLET
CROSSED CHEQUE
CROSSED SWORDS
CROSSES SWORDS
CRUISER WEIGHT
CRYSTAL GAZING
CRYSTAL PALACE
CULVERS PHYSIC
CURRIED FAVOUR
CURRIES FAVOUR
CURSORY GLANCE
CURTAIN RAISER
CUSTARD POWDER
CUTTING ACROSS
CUTTING REMARK
DANCING MASTER
DARNING NEEDLE
DEBTORS PRISON
DECIMAL PLACES
DECIMAL SYSTEM
DELAYED ACTION
DELTOID MUSCLE
DIAMOND BEETLE
DIAMOND POWDER
DISTANT COUSIN
DOCTORS ORDERS
DOPPLER EFFECT
DOWNING STREET
DRAUGHT ANIMAL
DRAUGHT ENGINE
DRAUGHT SCREEN
DRAWING MASTER
DRAWING PENCIL
DRAWING STUMPS
DRIVING LESSON
DRIVING MIRROR
DROPPED ANCHOR
DRUNKEN STUPOR
DUSTING POWDER
EASTERN CHURCH
EMERALD COPPER
ENGLISH SETTER
ETCHING NEEDLE
EXEMPLI GRATIA
EXHAUST SYSTEM
EXPRESS LETTER
EXPRESS PACKET
EXPRESS PARCEL
EYEBROW PENCIL
FACTORY WORKER
FALLING BEHIND
FEATHER BONNET

FEATHER DUSTER
FEATHER PILLOW
FEATHER STITCH
FEATURE LENGTH
FEEDING BOTTLE
FEMORAL ARTERY
FENCING MASTER
FERTILE GROUND
FISHING GROUND
FISHING TACKLE
FLEMISH SCHOOL
FLEMISH STITCH
FOOLING AROUND
FOREIGN LEGION
FOREIGN OFFICE
FORTUNE COOKIE
FORTUNE HUNTER
FORTUNE TELLER
FORWARD MARKET
FOUNDER MEMBER
FRILLED LIZARD
FROEBEL SYSTEM
GAINING GROUND
GASTRIC JUICES
GATHERS BREATH
GATHERS GROUND
GENERAL EFFECT
GENERAL LEGACY
GENERAL PARDON
GENETIC SPIRAL
GENTIAN VIOLET
GETTING ACROSS
GETTING AROUND
GLACIAL PERIOD
GLOWING REPORT
GLYPTAL RESINS
GOLIATH BEETLE
GRAMMAR SCHOOL
HACKING JACKET
HANDSEL MONDAY
HANGING AROUND
HANGING GARDEN
HANGING MATTER
HANGING VALLEY
HARBOUR LIGHTS
HARBOUR MASTER
HARNESS RACING
HARVEST SPIDER
HARVEST SUPPER
HEARING THINGS
HOBSONS CHOICE
HORSING AROUND
HOUSING ESTATE
HOUSING SCHEME
HUNTING GROUND
HUNTING SPIDER
ICELAND FALCON
IMPULSE BUYING
INCENSE BURNER
INCOMES POLICY

INFANTS SCHOOL
INSTANT COFFEE
ITALIAN GARDEN
ITCHING POWDER
JAMAICA PEPPER
JIGGERY POKERY
JOINING FORCES
JOINTED CACTUS
JOURNAL INTIME
KEEPING WICKET
KICKING AROUND
KINDRED SPIRIT
KINETIC ENERGY
KISSING COMFIT
KISSING COUSIN
KITCHEN GARDEN
KITCHEN KAFFIR
KNIGHTS ERRANT
KNOCKED AROUND
KNOWING BETTER
KNUCKLE HEADED
LAGGING BEHIND
LANDING GROUND
LATERAN TREATY
LATTICE BRIDGE
LATTICE GIRDER
LATTICE WINDOW
LAUNDRY BASKET
LEADING ASTRAY
LEADING SEAMAN
LEARNER DRIVER
LEASING MAKING
LEATHER JACKET
LEATHER WINGED
LEAVING BEHIND
LEAVING UNSAID
LETTERS PATENT
LIBERTY BODICE
LIBRARY TICKET
LICENCE HOLDER
LOMBARD STREET
LOOKING AGHAST
LOTTERY TICKET
LOZENGE SHAPED
LUNATIC ASYLUM
LUNATIC FRINGE
MACHINE GUNNER
MACHINE MINDER
MAGINOT MINDED
MANGOLD WURZEL
MARRONS GLACES
MATINEE JACKET
MIGRANT WORKER
MINERAL SPRING
MIRACLE MONGER
MIRACLE WORKER
MOANING MINNIE
MONTHLY REPORT
MORNING COFFEE
MORNING PRAYER

MUSICAL CHAIRS
MUSICAL COMEDY
NATURAL SYSTEM
NELSONS COLUMN
NERVOUS SYSTEM
NEWGATE FRINGE
NEWTONS CRADLE
NODDING DONKEY
NORFOLK JACKET
NUCLEAR ENERGY
NUCLEAR FUSION
NUCLEAR WEAPON
NURSERY CANNON
NURSERY SCHOOL
NURSERY SLOPES
OBLIQUE MOTION
OPENING SPEECH
OPTICAL FIBRES
ORBITAL ENGINE
ORDERED AROUND
ORDINAL NUMBER
OUTSIDE CHANCE
PAISLEY DESIGN
PARKING TICKET
PARLOUR TRICKS
PARQUET CIRCLE
PASCHAL CANDLE
PASCHAL FLOWER
PASSING MUSTER
PASSION FLOWER
PASSION SUNDAY
PAYROLL GIVING
PEACOCK FLOWER
PEACOCK THRONE
PELTIER EFFECT
PENALTY CORNER
PENSION SCHEME
PERFECT FOURTH
PERFECT INSECT
PERFECT METALS
PERFECT NUMBER
PERFECT TIMING
PERSIAN BLINDS
PERSIAN CARPET
PERSIAN POWDER
PICKLED ONIONS
PICKLED WALNUT
PICTURE PALACE
PICTURE WINDOW
PILGRIM BOTTLE
PINHOLE CAMERA
PINKING SHEARS
PITCHED BATTLE
PLASTIC BULLET
PLAYING AROUND
PLAYING HOOKEY
PLAYING POSSUM
PLAYING TRICKS
PLAYING TRUANT
PLENARY POWERS

7,6 *contd.*
POISSON DAVRIL
POLECAT FERRET
POMPIER LADDER
PONTOON BRIDGE
POPPING CREASE
PRAIRIE OYSTER
PRAYING INSECT
PRAYING MANTIS
PRESSED FLOWER
PRIMARY COLOUR
PRIMARY PLANET
PRIMARY SCHOOL
PRIMING POWDER
PRIVATE INCOME
PRIVATE SCHOOL
PRIVATE SECTOR
PRIVATE TREATY
PROCESS SERVER
PROMISE BREACH
PROVING GROUND
PRUNING SHEARS
PSYCHIC POWERS
PUDDING HEADED
PUDDING SLEEVE
PUNCTUM CAECUM
PURBECK MARBLE
PUSHING AROUND
PUTTING ACROSS
QUALITY STREET
QUANTUM NUMBER
QUANTUM THEORY
QUARTER DECKER
QUARTER GUNNER
QUARTER HOURLY
RADIANT ENERGY
RAILWAY BRIDGE
RAILWAY STITCH
RAILWAY TUNNEL
RAINBOW CHASER
RAINBOW TINTED
READERS DIGEST
READING MATTER
REDDING STRAIK
REEFING JACKET
REMAINS SILENT
RHODIAN SCHOOL
RIBSTON PIPPIN
RIGHTED WRONGS
RUNNING ACROSS
RUNNING BATTLE
RUNNING BUFFET
RUNNING LIGHTS
RUNNING SCARED
RUNNING STITCH
SABBATH BREACH
SABBATH SCHOOL
SAILING MASTER
SAILING ORDERS
SATANIC SCHOOL

SATSUMA ORANGE
SAVANNA FLOWER
SAVANNA FOREST
SCALING LADDER
SCANDAL BEARER
SCARLET RUNNER
SCREECH MARTIN
SCREECH THRUSH
SEASIDE RESORT
SECTION CUTTER
SEEMING SIMPLE
SELLERS MARKET
SERPENT LIZARD
SERVICE CHARGE
SESSION SINGER
SETTING ALIGHT
SEVENTH HEAVEN
SEVILLE ORANGE
SHADOWY FIGURE
SHERIFF DEPUTE
SHINGLE ROOFED
SHOPPED AROUND
SINGING MASTER
SISTINE CHAPEL
SITTING PRETTY
SITTING TARGET
SITTING TENANT
SKILLED LABOUR
SLIPPER LIMPET
SMOKING JACKET
SNAFFLE BRIDLE
SNOOKER PLAYER
SPANISH DAGGER
SPECIAL BRANCH
SPECIAL SCHOOL
SPECTRE SHRIMP
SPINDLE LEGGED
SPINDLE SHANKS
STATION MASTER
STIRRED ABROAD
STOOGED AROUND
STOOGES AROUND
STORAGE HEATER
STRIKES BOTTOM
STUFFED OLIVES
STUNTED GROWTH
STYPTIC PENCIL
SUBJECT MATTER
SUBJECT OBJECT
SUCKING BOTTLE
SULPHUR YELLOW
SUPPORT TIGHTS
SUPREME SOVIET
SURFACE VESSEL
SURFACE WORKER
SWALLOW TAILED
SWEATED LABOUR
SWOLLEN HEADED
SYNODIC PERIOD
TABLEAU VIVANT

TALKING TURKEY
THIMBLE RIGGED
THIMBLE RIGGER
THOUGHT READER
THROUGH TICKET
THUNDER SHOWER
THUNDER STRUCK
TICKETS PLEASE
TITULAR BISHOP
TOUCHED BOTTOM
TOUCHES BOTTOM
TRACTOR DRIVER
TRADING ESTATE
TRADING STAMPS
TRAFFIC CIRCLE
TRAFFIC ISLAND
TRAFFIC LIGHTS
TRAFFIC WARDEN
TRANSIT LOUNGE
TREACLE TOFFEE
TREASON FELONY
TRELLIS WINDOW
TRESTLE BRIDGE
TRIGGER FINGER
TRINITY SUNDAY
TROUSER BUTTON
TROUSER POCKET
TRUCIAL STATES
TRUMPET SHAPED
TUMBLER SWITCH
TURNING AROUND
TURNING CIRCLE
TURNING TURTLE
TURNKEY SYSTEM
UNARMED COMBAT
UTILITY PLAYER
VANTAGE GROUND
VICIOUS CIRCLE
VICTORY PARADE
VILLAGE SCHOOL
WAITING AWHILE
WALKING ORDERS
WALKING PAPERS
WALKING TICKET
WASHING POWDER
WATLING STREET
WEATHER ANCHOR
WEATHER BEATEN
WEATHER DRIVEN
WEATHER REPORT
WEATHER SYMBOL
WEATHER WINDOW
WEDDING FAVOUR
WEEDING CHISEL
WEEPING WILLOW
WEIGHED ANCHOR
WELCOME ABOARD
WESTERN CHURCH
WESTERN EMPIRE
WESTERN SCHISM

WHALING MASTER
WHEELER DEALER
WHISTLE BLOWER
WILDCAT STRIKE
WINDING ENGINE
WINDSOR CASTLE
WITHOUT FRILLS
WOOLLEN DRAPER

8,1,4
CATCHING A COLD
CATCHING A CRAB
CRACKING A CRIB
CRACKING A JOKE
DROPPING A LINE
PITCHING A TENT
SHEDDING A TEAR
SHOOTING A LINE
SPINNING A YARN
STARTING A HARE
STEALING A KISS
STRIKING A POSE
THUMBING A LIFT
THUMBING A RIDE

8,2,3
ARTICLES OF WAR
ATTORNEY AT LAW
BACHELOR OF LAW
BROTHERS IN LAW
CARRYING IT OFF
DAUGHTER IN LAW
FIGHTING IT OUT
FIGURING IT OUT
FLOATING ON AIR
LAUGHING IT OFF
PRISONER OF WAR
QUESTION OF LAW
SERJEANT AT LAW
SHOOTING IT OUT
SPELLING IT OUT
STANDING AT BAY
STANDING TO WIN
STICKING IT OUT
SWEATING IT OUT

8,3,2
CROSSING THE TS

8,5
ABERDEEN ANGUS
ABSOLUTE PITCH
ACCIDENT PRONE
ACCOUNTS CLERK
ACQUIRED TASTE
ADVANCED GUARD
ADVANCED LEVEL
ALKALINE EARTH
AMERICAN BOWLS
AMERICAN DREAM
AMNIOTIC FLUID
ANYBODYS GUESS

8,5 *contd.*
APOSTLES CREED
APPLETON LAYER
ARMOURED TRAIN
ATLANTIC OCEAN
ATTITUDE ANGLE
BANDYING WORDS
BANKRUPT STOCK
BARNACLE GOOSE
BATTERED WIVES
BEAUFORT SCALE
BECHAMEL SAUCE
BILLIARD CLOTH
BILLIARD TABLE
BIRTHDAY PARTY
BLANKETY BLANK
BLEEDING HEART
BLOTTING PAPER
BOARDING HOUSE
BOARDING PARTY
BOHEMIAN TOPAZ
BOULTING CLOTH
BOULTING HUTCH
BOUNDARY RIDER
BREAKING COVER
BREAKING FORTH
BREAKING LOOSE
BREAKING POINT
BREAKING RANKS
BREATHED AGAIN
BREATHES AGAIN
BREECHES BIBLE
BRINGING ABOUT
BRINGING FORTH
BRINGING ROUND
BRUSHING ASIDE
BUCKLING UNDER
BUDDHIST CROSS
BUILDING BLOCK
BUILDING BOARD
BULLETIN BOARD
BULLOCKS HEART
BURGUNDY PITCH
BUSINESS CYCLE
BUTCHERS BROOM
CALENDAR MONTH
CANNABIS RESIN
CAPTAINS CHAIR
CAPTAINS TABLE
CAPUCHIN CROSS
CARNIVAL QUEEN
CARRIAGE CLOCK
CARRIAGE DRIVE
CARRIAGE HORSE
CARRIAGE TRADE
CASEMENT CLOTH
CATERING CORPS
CELLULAR RADIO
CEREBRAL DEATH
CEREBRAL PALSY

CHANGING HANDS
CHLORINE WATER
CHOPPING BLOCK
CHOPPING BOARD
CHOPPING KNIFE
CHOPPING LOGIC
CLEANING WOMAN
CLEARING HOUSE
CLENCHED TEETH
CLERICAL ERROR
CLICKETY CLACK
CLICKETY CLICK
CLIMBING FRAME
CLIMBING PLANT
CLINICAL DEATH
CLINICAL TRIAL
COBBLERS PUNCH
COCKSPUR GRASS
COCKTAIL DRESS
COCKTAIL MIXER
COCKTAIL STICK
COMPARED NOTES
COMPOUND RATIO
COMPUTER CRIME
COMPUTER FRAUD
COMPUTER VIRUS
CONCRETE MIXER
CONCRETE MUSIC
CONCRETE STEEL
CONFETTI MONEY
CONSUMER GOODS
CORONERS COURT
CORRIDOR TRAIN
COTSWOLD STONE
COUNTING HOUSE
COUNTING SHEEP
COURTESY LIGHT
COURTESY TITLE
CREEPING JENNY
CREEPING JESUS
CRIBBAGE BOARD
CRITICAL ANGLE
CROWNING GLORY
CRUISING SPEED
CULTURED PEARL
CYLINDER BLOCK
DECISION TABLE
DENTISTS CHAIR
DENTISTS DRILL
DIHEDRAL ANGLE
DISASTER MOVIE
DISCOUNT STORE
DISPATCH RIDER
DISTRICT COURT
DISTRICT NURSE
DIVISION LOBBY
DOWNCAST SHAFT
DRAINAGE BASIN
DRAINING BOARD
DRAMATIC IRONY

DRESSING TABLE
DRIFTING APART
DRINKING STRAW
DRIPPING ROAST
DROPHEAD COUPE
DRUMMOND LIGHT
DUODENAL ULCER
DWELLING HOUSE
DWELLING PLACE
ELECTRIC CHAIR
ELECTRIC FENCE
ELECTRIC FIELD
ELECTRIC MOTOR
ELECTRIC ORGAN
ELECTRIC RAZOR
ELECTRIC SHOCK
ELECTRIC STORM
ELEPHANT FOLIO
ELEPHANT GRASS
ELEPHANT SHREW
EMINENCE GRISE
EMULSION PAINT
ENCLOSED ORDER
EXCHANGE BLOWS
EXCHANGE WORDS
EXPOSURE METER
EXTERIOR ANGLE
FEMININE RHYME
FIDDLERS MONEY
FIGHTING COCKS
FIGHTING DRUNK
FLANDERS POPPY
FLOATING CRANE
FLOATING GRASS
FLOATING LIGHT
FLOATING VOTER
FLORENCE FLASK
FOCUSING CLOTH
FOOTBALL MATCH
FOOTBALL PITCH
FOOTBALL POOLS
FREEZING POINT
GAMBLING HOUSE
GATHERED ROUND
GATHERED SPEED
GAUNTLET GUARD
GOODNESS KNOWS
GRABBING CRANE
GUARDIAN ANGEL
HANGMANS NOOSE
HARDWARE STORE
HARMONIC MINOR
HARMONIC RANGE
HAWAIIAN GOOSE
HEAVENLY TWINS
HERTZIAN WAVES
HIGHLAND DRESS
HIGHLAND FLING
HIGHLAND GAMES
HOMEWARD BOUND

HOTHOUSE PLANT
IMPACTED TOOTH
IMPERIAL POUND
IMPOSING STONE
INCLINED PLANE
INTEREST GROUP
INTERIOR ANGLE
INTERNAL RHYME
ISTHMIAN GAMES
JANIZARY MUSIC
JAPANESE CEDAR
JAPANESE PAPER
JEUNESSE DOREE
JOLLYING ALONG
JUDICIAL COURT
JUVENILE COURT
KANGAROO COURT
KANGAROO GRASS
KANGAROO THORN
KENTUCKY DERBY
KNOCKING ABOUT
KNOCKOUT DROPS
KNUCKLED UNDER
KNUCKLES UNDER
LATCHKEY CHILD
LAUGHING HYENA
LAUGHING STOCK
LAVATORY PAPER
LAVENDER WATER
LEARNING CURVE
LITERARY AGENT
LITERARY LUNCH
LITERARY WORLD
LOLLIPOP WOMAN
LONGCASE CLOCK
LORRAINE CROSS
LOUNGING ABOUT
LUMINOUS PAINT
MACKEREL GUIDE
MACKEREL MIDGE
MACKEREL SHARK
MAGAZINE RIFLE
MAGNETIC FIELD
MAGNETIC NORTH
MAGNETIC POLES
MAGNETIC STORM
MANIFOLD PAPER
MARRIAGE BANNS
MARRIAGE LINES
MARTELLO TOWER
MAZARINE BIBLE
MEDICINE CHEST
MERCALLI SCALE
MERMAIDS GLOVE
MERMAIDS PURSE
MIDNIGHT FEAST
MILITARY CROSS
MILITARY MEDAL
MINORITY GROUP
MISCHIEF MAKER

8,5 *contd.*

MONASTIC ORDER	PRANCING ABOUT	SKITTLES MATCH	THINKING ALOUD
MONOPOLY MONEY	PRECIOUS METAL	SKULKING PLACE	THINKING TWICE
MOUNTAIN CHAIN	PRECIOUS STONE	SLANGING MATCH	THOROUGH GOING
MOUNTAIN RANGE	PRESSING AHEAD	SLEEPING BERTH	THOROUGH PACED
MOUNTAIN SHEEP	PRESSURE CABIN	SLEEPING COACH	THRESHER WHALE
MOUNTING BLOCK	PRESSURE COOKS	SLEEPING ROUGH	THROTTLE LEVER
MOUNTING GUARD	PRESSURE GROUP	SMELLING SALTS	THROTTLE VALVE
MOURNING BRIDE	PRESSURE POINT	SMELTING HOUSE	THROWING STICK
MOURNING CLOAK	PRESSURE RIDGE	SMELTING WORKS	THROWING TABLE
MOURNING COACH	PRINCESS ROYAL	SOLDIERS HEART	TIPPLING HOUSE
MOURNING PIECE	PRINTERS DEVIL	SOUNDING BOARD	TITANIUM WHITE
MULTIPLE FRUIT	PRINTING HOUSE	SOUTHERN CROSS	TOREADOR PANTS
MULTIPLE STORE	PRINTING PAPER	SPACIOUS TIMES	TORTOISE SHELL
MUSHROOM CLOUD	PRINTING PRESS	SPARKING PLUGS	TRANSFER PAPER
NATIONAL FRONT	PROSPECT GLASS	SPEAKING CLOCK	TREADING WATER
NATIONAL GUARD	PULITZER PRIZE	SPEAKING VOICE	TREASURE CHEST
NATIONAL PRIDE	QUILTING FRAME	SPENDING MONEY	TREASURE HOUSE
NATIONAL TRUST	QUIZZING GLASS	SPINNING JENNY	TREASURE TROVE
NEGATIVE ANGLE	RALLYING POINT	SPITTING IMAGE	TREASURY BENCH
NONSENSE VERSE	RALLYING ROUND	SPLINTER GROUP	TROLLING SPOON
NOUVELLE VAGUE	RATEABLE VALUE	SPLINTER PARTY	TROPICAL MONTH
OCCLUDED FRONT	REDUCING AGENT	SPLINTER PROOF	TROPICAL STORM
ORDERING ABOUT	REDUCING FLAME	SPROCKET WHEEL	TURMERIC PAPER
ORDINARY GRADE	REGISTER HOUSE	SPROUTED WINGS	TWILIGHT SLEEP
ORDINARY LEVEL	REGISTER PLATE	SQUIRREL SHREW	UILLEANN PIPES
ORDNANCE DATUM	ROULETTE TABLE	STALKING HORSE	UMBRELLA GROUP
ORIENTAL TOPAZ	ROULETTE WHEEL	STANDING ALONE	UMBRELLA STAND
OUTBOARD MOTOR	ROUNDING ERROR	STANDING GUARD	UNSOLVED CRIME
OVERHEAD CABLE	SARATOGA TRUNK	STANDING ORDER	VARIABLE COSTS
PAINTERS COLIC	SCALPING KNIFE	STANDING PLACE	VARICOSE VEINS
PARAFFIN STOVE	SCORCHED EARTH	STANDING STONE	VAULTING HORSE
PARALLEL RULER	SCORPION GRASS	STANDING TREAT	VENETIAN BLIND
PARIETAL CELLS	SCOURING STICK	STANDING TRIAL	VICTORIA CROSS
PAVEMENT LIGHT	SCOUTING ROUND	STANHOPE PRESS	VICTORIA FALLS
PECTORAL CROSS	SCRUBBED ROUND	STARTING BLOCK	VIENNESE WALTZ
PEMBROKE TABLE	SERAPHIC ORDER	STARTING POINT	VIENNESE WHIRL
PENDULUM CLOCK	SERGEANT MAJOR	STARTING PRICE	VIRGINIA STOCK
PERCHING BIRDS	SHETLAND SHEEP	STARTING STALL	VISITING HOURS
PERIODIC TABLE	SHIFTING ABOUT	STEERING CLEAR	VOLCANIC GLASS
PHYSICAL FORCE	SHIFTING SANDS	STEERING WHEEL	VOLCANIC ROCKS
PHYSICAL JERKS	SHIPPING AGENT	STEPPING ASIDE	WALTZING MOUSE
PIECRUST TABLE	SHIPPING CLERK	STEPPING STONE	WARDROBE TRUNK
PILGRIMS SHELL	SHIPPING WATER	STICKING PLACE	WATCHING BRIEF
PINAFORE DRESS	SHOOTING BRAKE	STICKING POINT	WATERING HOUSE
PINAFORE SKIRT	SHOOTING CRAPS	STOCKING FRAME	WATERING PLACE
PIPELESS ORGAN	SHOOTING LODGE	STOPPING PLACE	WEATHERS ALONG
PLANNING AHEAD	SHOOTING PAINS	STOPPING SHORT	WHIPPING CREAM
PLATINUM BLACK	SHOOTING RANGE	STORMING PARTY	WHOOPING COUGH
PLATONIC SOLID	SHOOTING STARS	STRAIGHT ACTOR	WHOOPING CRANE
PLEASURE HOUSE	SHOOTING STICK	STRAIGHT ANGLE	WINGBACK CHAIR
PLOTTING PAPER	SHOPPING SPREE	STRAIGHT FACED	WOODCHIP BOARD
POISONED ARROW	SHOULDER BLADE	STRAIGHT FIGHT	WOODCHIP PAPER
PORRIDGE STICK	SHOULDER JOINT	STRAIGHT FLUSH	WREAKING HAVOC
PORTLAND SHEEP	SHOULDER STRAP	STRIKING PRICE	ZODIACAL LIGHT
PORTLAND STONE	SHOUTING MATCH	SURROUND SOUND	ZOLLNERS LINES
POSITIVE ANGLE	SHREDDED WHEAT	SYMBOLIC LOGIC	
POSITIVE ORGAN	SKELETON STAFF	TEACHING STAFF	**9,2,2**
POSTMANS KNOCK	SKINNING ALIVE	TERRACED HOUSE	SOMETHING IS UP
POWDERED SUGAR	SKIRTING BOARD	THINKING AGAIN	**9,4**
	SKIRTING ROUND	THINKING ALIKE	ADVANTAGE RULE

9,4 *contd.*
ALLIGATOR PEAR
AMUSEMENT PARK
ANCESTRAL HOME
ANSWERING BACK
ATTENTION SPAN
AUXILIARY VERB
AVOGADROS RULE
BACHELORS HALL
BAPTISMAL NAME
BAPTISMAL VOWS
BEAVERING AWAY
BEGINNERS LUCK
BLINDMANS BUFF
BOATSWAIN BIRD
BORROWING DAYS
BOWSTRING HEMP
BREAKDOWN GANG
BREAKFAST ROOM
BURLESQUE SHOW
BUTTERFLY FISH
CAMBRIDGE BLUE
CARTRIDGE BELT
CATCHMENT AREA
CATHEDRAL CITY
CATHERINE PEAR
CERTIFIED MILK
CHAMELEON LIKE
CHANTILLY LACE
CHAPARRAL COCK
CHARACTER PART
CHEQUERED FLAG
CHRISTIAN NAME
CHRISTMAS CAKE
CHRISTMAS CARD
CHRISTMAS ROSE
CHRISTMAS TIDE
CHRISTMAS TIME
CHRISTMAS TREE
CHURCHILL TANK
CIGARETTE CARD
CLEARANCE SALE
COMMUNION CARD
COMMUNION RAIL
COMMUNITY HOME
COMMUNITY WORK
COMPANION STAR
CONDENSED MILK
CONDENSED TYPE
CONDUCTED TOUR
CONDUCTOR RAIL
CONTAINER SHIP
CORIANDER SEED
CRANBERRY BUSH
CRANBERRY TREE
CROCODILE CLIP
CUTHBERTS DUCK
DANDELION WINE
DANGEROUS DRUG
DEPRESSED AREA

DIAPHRAGM PUMP
DIFFUSION TUBE
DISCHARGE TUBE
DORMITORY TOWN
DUNSTABLE ROAD
EDINBURGH ROCK
EIGHTSOME REEL
ELECTORAL VOTE
ELEPHANTS EARS
ELEPHANTS FOOT
EMERGENCY EXIT
ENDURANCE TEST
ESSENTIAL OILS
EXCHEQUER BILL
EXCLUSION ZONE
EXPANSION BOLT
EXPANSION CARD
EXPANSION PLAN
EXPANSION SLOT
EXPLAINED AWAY
EXPLODING STAR
EXPLOSIVE BOLT
FALLOPIAN TUBE
FERTILITY DRUG
FINANCIAL YEAR
FINISHING POST
FLOWERING RUSH
FOLLOWING HOME
FOLLOWING SUIT
FORTIFIED WINE
FRIGHTENS AWAY
FRITTERED AWAY
FURNISHED FLAT
GARDENING CLUB
GATHERING COAL
GATHERING PEAT
GEOMETRIC MEAN
GOVERNESS CART
GOVERNING BODY
GRAPPLING HOOK
GRAPPLING IRON
GREENLAND SEAL
GREENWICH TIME
GREETINGS CARD
GUNPOWDER PLOT
HAMMERING HOME
HAPPENING UPON
HARLEQUIN DUCK
HERCULEAN TASK
HOLLERITH CODE
HONEYCOMB MOTH
HOUSEHOLD GODS
HOUSEHOLD WORD
HURRICANE DECK
HURRICANE LAMP
HYDRAULIC BELT
HYDRAULIC JACK
IMAGINARY LINE
INDUCTION COIL
INDUCTION PORT

IRREGULAR VERB
JEQUIRITY BEAN
JERUSALEM PONY
JERUSALEM SAGE
KNOWLEDGE BASE
KNUCKLING DOWN
LACHRYMAL DUCT
LAUNCHING SITE
LICENSING LAWS
LIGHTNING TUBE
LISTENING POST
LOOSEHEAD PROP
MEASURING TAPE
MESSENGER WIRE
MICROWAVE OVEN
MILLSTONE GRIT
MODELLING CLAY
MONASTRAL BLUE
MOONLIGHT FLIT
NORWEGIAN OVEN
OVERNIGHT CASE
PALESTINE SOUP
PANTOMIME DAME
PARACHUTE JUMP
PARTITION WALL
PASSENGER LIST
PASSENGER MILE
PATERNITY SUIT
PERMANENT WAVE
PLOUGHING BACK
PNEUMATIC TYRE
PORCELAIN CLAY
POWDERING GOWN
PRACTICAL JOKE
PREACHING DOWN
PRECISION TOOL
PROMENADE DECK
PROPIONIC ACID
PROXIMITY FUSE
PTERYGOID BONE
QUADRATIC MEAN
QUADRUPLE TIME
QUOTATION MARK
RADIATION BELT
RASPBERRY BUSH
RECEIVING ROOM
RECEIVING SHIP
RECEPTION DESK
RECEPTION ROOM
REFERENCE BOOK
REFERENCE MARK
RELIEVING ARCH
REPORTING BACK
RESERVOIR ROCK
RETAINING WALL
REVOLVING DOOR
RORSCHACH TEST
SALICYLIC ACID
SALVATION ARMY
SAPODILLA PLUM

SATELLITE TOWN
SCRAMBLED EGGS
SECONDARY CELL
SECONDARY COIL
SECRETARY BIRD
SECRETARY TYPE
SEDENTARY SOIL
SEGMENTAL ARCH
SHEEPSKIN COAT
SHORTENED SAIL
SIGNATURE TUNE
SIMMERING DOWN
SMOKELESS FUEL
SMOKELESS ZONE
SMOOTHING IRON
SMOTHERED MATE
SMUGGLERS COVE
SOLDERING BOLT
SOLDERING IRON
SPARKLING WINE
SPIRITUAL PEER
SPONSORED WALK
SQUEEZING HOME
STRETCHER BOND
STRETCHER CASE
STRIPPING DOWN
SUBMARINE BASE
SUFFERING CATS
SULPHURIC ACID
SUSPENDER BELT
SWADDLING BAND
SWITCHING OVER
SYMPHONIC POEM
SYNTHETIC DRUG
TASMANIAN WOLF
TECHNICAL FOUL
TELEGRAPH POLE
TELEGRAPH WIRE
TELEPHONE BILL
TELEPHONE BOOK
TELEPHOTO LENS
THRESHING MILL
THROTTLED DOWN
THROTTLES DOWN
TOLERANCE DOSE
TRANSPORT CAFE
TRANSPORT SHIP
TRIUMPHAL ARCH
TRUMPETER SWAN
TURNBULLS BLUE
TURQUOISE BLUE
UMBILICAL CORD
UNADOPTED ROAD
UNCROWNED KING
UNIVERSAL TIME
VALENTINE CARD
VEGETABLE SOUP
VOLUNTARY WORK
WHIRLPOOL BATH
WHISTLING AWAY

9,4 *contd.*
WHISTLING SWAN
WHITTLING AWAY
YORKSHIRE GRIT

10,3
ABYSSINIAN CAT
ARTIFICIAL FLY
ARTIFICIAL LEG
BOTTOMLESS PIT
CANCELLING OUT
CHICKENING OUT
COLLECTING BOX
COMPRESSED AIR
CONCEPTUAL ART
CONNECTING ROD
CONTINUITY MAN
CONTRACTED OUT
DECORATION DAY
DIPLOMATIC BAG
FLATTENING OUT
FRIGHTENED OFF
GENERATION GAP
GREENHOUSE GAS
HORIZONTAL BAR
IMPUTATION TAX
INITIATION FEE
MERCANTILE LAW
NEAPOLITAN ICE
NUTCRACKER MAN
PARKINSONS LAW
PARLIAMENT MAN
PENINSULAR WAR
PENSIONING OFF
PERCUSSION CAP
PRESERVING PAN
QUEENSLAND NUT
REMITTANCE MAN
REPUBLICAN ERA
RESISTANCE BOX
RESTAURANT CAR
SCRIBBLING PAD
SLACKENING OFF
STRAIGHTEN OUT
STRAWBERRY JAM
STRETCHING OUT
SUBMACHINE GUN
TELEVISION SET
THREEPENNY BIT
TRAVELLERS JOY
TRIGGERING OFF
TYRRHENIAN SEA
VALENTINES DAY
VARNISHING DAY
WEASELLING OUT
WEATHERING OUT
YESTERDAYS MEN

11,2
CONTRACTING IN
SHRIVELLING UP

14 LETTERS
1,3,2,3,5
A BIT OF ALL RIGHT

1,3,2,8
A SOP TO CERBERUS

1,3,4,6
I BEG YOUR PARDON

1,4,2,3,4
A FOOT IN THE DOOR
A RIFT IN THE LUTE
A SHOT IN THE DARK

1,4,2,4,3
A FLEA IN ONES EAR
A WILL OF ONES OWN
A WORD IN ONES EAR

1,4,2,7
A LOAD OF RUBBISH
A MESS OF POTTAGE

1,4,9
A WARM RECEPTION

1,5,2,3,3
A PLACE IN THE SUN
A TOUCH OF THE SUN

1,5,5,3
A STIFF UPPER LIP

1,6,7
A STRONG STOMACH

2,1,4,2,5
AT A RATE OF KNOTS

2,1,5,2,4
IN A STATE OF FLUX

2,1,6,5
IN A LITTLE WHILE

2,2,3,4,3
IN AT THE DEEP END

2,2,3,7
GO TO ANY LENGTHS
GO TO THE COUNTRY

2,2,4,6
UP TO ONES TRICKS

2,2,5,5
OF NO FIXED ABODE

2,2,10
DO IT YOURSELFER

2,3,2,1,6
AS FIT AS A FIDDLE
AS MAD AS A HATTER

2,3,2,3,4
AN ACE IN THE HOLE

2,3,2,4,3
GO OUT OF ONES WAY

2,3,3,3,3
BE ALL AND END ALL

2,3,3,6
IN THE BIG LEAGUE
IN THE TOP FLIGHT
ON THE OFF CHANCE
TO THE NTH DEGREE

2,3,4,5
AS THE CROW FLIES
AT ONE FELL SWOOP
BY THE SAME TOKEN
IN ONE FELL SWOOP
ON THE SHOP FLOOR

2,3,5,2,2
IN THE THICK OF IT

2,3,5,4
ON THE RIGHT TACK
ON THE WINDY SIDE

2,3,6,3
IN THE FAMILY WAY
IN THE PUBLIC EYE

2,3,9
IN THE ASCENDANT
IN THE LIMELIGHT
NO WIN SITUATION
ON THE BANDWAGON
ON THE BREADLINE
ON THE DEFENSIVE
ON THE OUTSKIRTS
ON THE THRESHOLD

2,4,2,6
AS NEAR AS DAMMIT

2,4,3,5
DO ONES OWN THING
GO DOWN THE DRAIN
IN ONES OWN RIGHT

2,4,4,2,2
ON ONES HEAD BE IT

2,4,4,4
ON ONES BEAM ENDS
ON ONES LAST LEGS

2,4,8
AT FULL THROTTLE
DO ONES HOMEWORK
IN LOCO PARENTIS
ON ONES DOORSTEP

2,5,2,1,4
AS DRUNK AS A LORD

2,5,2,5
AS HAPPY AS LARRY

2,5,3,4
GO ROUND THE BEND

2,5,7
IN PLAIN ENGLISH

2,5,7 *contd.*
IN ROUND FIGURES

2,6,2,4
BY RETURN OF POST

2,6,6
IN LIVING MEMORY

2,7,5
AT DAGGERS DRAWN
ST ANDREWS CROSS
ST GEORGES CROSS

2,8,4
ST ANTHONYS FIRE

2,12
ON SUBSCRIPTION

3,1,5,5
ITS A SMALL WORLD

3,2,2,3,4
GET IT IN THE NECK
GOT IT IN THE NECK
LAY IT ON THE LINE

3,2,3,6
DOG IN THE MANGER
LAW OF THE JUNGLE
MAN IN THE STREET
MAN OF THE MOMENT
PIG IN THE MIDDLE
RAN IN THE FAMILY
RUN IN THE FAMILY
TOP OF THE LEAGUE

3,2,4,5
DIE IN ONES BOOTS
LIE IN ONES TEETH
NOT ON YOUR NELLY
OUT OF ONES DEPTH
OUT OF THIS WORLD
SAT ON ONES HANDS
SIT ON ONES HANDS

3,2,5,4
GET TO FIRST BASE
GOT TO FIRST BASE
ONE OF THESE DAYS

3,2,6,3
MAY IT PLEASE YOU

3,2,9
ALL IN WRESTLING
DAY OF ATONEMENT
MOP UP OPERATION
OUT OF CHARACTER
OUT OF CONDITION
PUT IN MOTHBALLS
WAR OF SECESSION

3,3,2,3,3
OLD MAN OF THE SEA

3,3,2,6
RAN OUT OF PETROL
RUN OUT OF PETROL
THE LAP OF LUXURY

3,3,3,3,2
PUT THE TIN HAT ON

3,3,3,5
FOR ALL THE WORLD
HOT OFF THE PRESS
OUT FOR THE COUNT
TWO FOR HIS HEELS
WET AND DRY PAPER

3,3,4,2,2
FOR THE HELL OF IT
FOR THE LOVE OF IT
GET THE HANG OF IT
GOT THE HANG OF IT

3,3,4,4
FOR THE HIGH JUMP
FOR THE MOST PART
HAD TWO LEFT FEET
HAS TWO LEFT FEET
LET THE SIDE DOWN
PAY FOR ONES SINS
RAN THE RULE OVER
RUN FOR DEAR LIFE
RUN THE RULE OVER

3,3,5,3
DOT AND CARRY ONE
HOW NOW BROWN COW

3,3,6,2
GET THE BREEZE UP
GOT THE BREEZE UP
PUT THE KIBOSH ON
PUT THE SCREWS ON

3,3,8
BEG THE QUESTION
FOR THE DURATION
HEN AND CHICKENS
HOT AND BOTHERED
OFF THE SHOULDER
POP THE QUESTION
RAN THE GAUNTLET
RUN THE GAUNTLET
THE SIX COUNTIES

3,4,2,5
FOR LOVE OR MONEY
HAD WHAT IT TAKES
HAS WHAT IT TAKES
ROD POLE OR PERCH
THE LIFE OF RILEY

3,4,3,1,3
FOR EVER AND A DAY

3,4,3,4
ALL OVER THE SHOP
ALL WELL AND GOOD

GET ONES OWN BACK
GOD REST HIS SOUL
GOD SAVE THE KING
GOT ONES OWN BACK
HOP SKIP AND JUMP
OFF WITH HER HEAD
OFF WITH HIS HEAD
THE GOOD OLD DAYS
THE LIFE AND SOUL

3,4,4,3
CRY ONES EYES OUT

3,4,5,2
DIG ONES HEELS IN
DUG ONES HEELS IN
SET ONES HEART ON

3,4,7
AIR RAID SHELTER
AIR RAID WARNING
AIR VICE MARSHAL
BIG GAME HUNTING
FOR GOOD MEASURE
ODD COME SHORTLY
OFF ONES TROLLEY
OLD TIME DANCING
PIT BULL TERRIER
PRO BONO PUBLICO
RAN INTO TROUBLE
RUN INTO TROUBLE
THE CATS PYJAMAS
THE MIND BOGGLES
THE UGLY SISTERS
WET ONES WHISTLE

3,5,6
ALL ROUND CAMERA
DRY ROAST PEANUT
HOT WATER BOTTLE
ICE CREAM CORNET
ONE ARMED BANDIT
THE GREAT BEYOND
THE SEVEN DWARFS

3,6,3,2
THE BUTLER DID IT

3,6,5
CUT THROAT RAZOR
GUY FAWKES NIGHT
HOB NAILED BOOTS
ILL GOTTEN GAINS
THE BEATEN TRACK
THE VELVET GLOVE
THE VIRGIN QUEEN
YOU SHOULD WORRY

3,7,4
BED SITTING ROOM
EGG CUSTARD TART
OLD PEOPLES HOME
PIN STRIPED SUIT
THE ETERNAL CITY

3,7,4 *contd.*
THE HIGHWAY CODE
THE HUNDRED DAYS
THE ROARING GAME

3,11
AIR CONDITIONED
AIR SUPERIORITY
AUF WIEDERSEHEN
BOA CONSTRICTOR
HIP REPLACEMENT
ILL NATUREDNESS
JOB DESCRIPTION
NIL DESPERANDUM
NON COMMUNICANT
NON DESTRUCTIVE
NON INVOLVEMENT
OLD ESTABLISHED
OLD GENTLEMANLY
PAN AMERICANISM
PRE ESTABLISHED
PRE ESTABLISHES
PRE RAPHAELITES
PRE REFORMATION
THE UNDERGROUND
TWO DIMENSIONAL

4,1,4,2,3
KNEW A MOVE OR TWO
KNOW A MOVE OR TWO

4,1,4,5
FLOG A DEAD HORSE
KEEP A GOOD HOUSE
KEPT A GOOD HOUSE

4,1,5,2,2
MADE A NIGHT OF IT
MAKE A NIGHT OF IT

4,1,5,4
KEEP A PLACE WARM
KEEP A TIGHT REIN
KEPT A PLACE WARM
KEPT A TIGHT REIN
RUNS A TIGHT SHIP
WALK A TIGHT ROPE

4,1,6,3
COCK A DOODLE DOO

4,1,9
CAST A HOROSCOPE
TAKE A RAINCHECK
TOOK A RAINCHECK
WITH A VENGEANCE

4,2,1,7
FLAT AS A PANCAKE
TALK IN A WHISPER
WORN TO A FRAZZLE

4,2,2,3,3
GETS IN ON THE ACT
GOES UP IN THE AIR
WENT UP IN THE AIR

4,2,3,5
BALL OF THE THUMB
COIN OF THE REALM
CUTS TO THE QUICK
DEAD TO THE WORLD
DIEU ET MON DROIT
DOWN IN THE DUMPS
DOWN IN THE MOUTH
FOAM AT THE MOUTH
GAVE UP THE GHOST
GIVE UP THE GHOST
GOES BY THE BOARD
GOES ON ALL FOURS
GUMS UP THE WORKS
HOLE IN THE HEART
JACK IN THE GREEN
LADY OF THE HOUSE
LEAD TO THE ALTAR
LEFT IN THE LURCH
LEFT ON THE SHELF
LONG IN THE TOOTH
LOST TO THE WORLD
LUCK OF THE DEVIL
LUCK OF THE IRISH
MARK OF THE BEAST
MELT IN THE MOUTH
NECK OF THE WOODS
PEER OF THE REALM
PICK OF THE BUNCH
PILE ON THE AGONY
PLAY TO THE CROWD
PUTS IN THE SHADE
PUTS IN THE WRONG
PUTS TO THE SWORD
ROOF OF THE MOUTH
ROOF OF THE WORLD
RUNS IN THE BLOOD
SALT OF THE EARTH
SEAT OF THE PANTS
SIGN OF THE CROSS
SIGN OF THE TIMES
SITS ON THE FENCE
SLAP ON THE WRIST
STAR OF THE EARTH
STAR OF THE NIGHT
STEP ON THE JUICE
TAKE UP THE SLACK
TALK OF THE DEVIL
TOOK UP THE SLACK
WARS OF THE ROSES
WEAK AT THE KNEES
WENT BY THE BOARD
WENT ON ALL FOURS
WITH AN ILL GRACE

4,2,4,4
CAPE OF GOOD HOPE
DOWN ON ONES LUCK
FALL ON DEAF EARS
FALL ON ONES FEET

FELL ON DEAF EARS
FELL ON ONES FEET
FLAT ON ONES BACK
FLAT ON ONES FACE
GETS TO ONES FEET
GOES TO ONES HEAD
HAVE IT BOTH WAYS
HELD UP ONES HEAD
HOLD UP ONES HEAD
KEEP AN OPEN MIND
KEPT AN OPEN MIND
LEND ME YOUR EARS
LIVE BY ONES WITS
MAKE UP ONES MIND
OVER MY DEAD BODY
PATE DE FOIE GRAS
REST ON ONES OARS
TURN ON ONES HEEL
TURN UP ONES NOSE
WENT TO ONES HEAD

4,2,8
BILL OF EXCHANGE
BIRD OF PARADISE
CASH ON DELIVERY
CODE OF PRACTICE
DEED OF COVENANT
FAIR TO MIDDLING
FLAG OF DISTRESS
FULL OF MISCHIEF
GETS IT TOGETHER
GOES TO EXTREMES
INNS OF CHANCERY
LINE OF BUSINESS
LOVE IN IDLENESS
MILK OF MAGNESIA
PAIR OF SCISSORS
PAIR OF TROUSERS
PAIR OF TWEEZERS
PICK AN ARGUMENT
RATE OF EXCHANGE
SACK OF POTATOES
SALT OF WORMWOOD
SEND TO COVENTRY
SENT TO COVENTRY
SITS IN JUDGMENT
WARD IN CHANCERY
WENT TO EXTREMES

4,3,1,6
GONE FOR A BURTON

4,3,2,5
FROM BAD TO WORSE
HARD NUT TO CRACK
PUTS OUT TO GRAZE
RUNS OUT OF STEAM

4,3,3,2,2
PUTS THE LID ON IT

4,3,3,4
BLOW HOT AND COLD

4,3,3,4 *contd.*
FORE AND AFT SAIL
GOOD FOR THE SOUL
JOBS FOR THE BOYS
LIVE AND LET LIVE
LIVE OFF THE LAND

4,3,4,3
PULL THE LONG BOW
PUSH THE BOAT OUT
READ THE RIOT ACT

4,3,5,2
PUTS THE BRAKE ON
PUTS THE SKIDS ON
WASH AND BRUSH UP

4,3,7
BEAT THE RETREAT
BLEW THE WHISTLE
BLOW THE WHISTLE
BOWS AND SCRAPES
BURY THE HATCHET
COPS AND ROBBERS
DEAN AND CHAPTER
DOES THE HONOURS
DRAW THE LONGBOW
DROP THE SUBJECT
FAST AND FURIOUS
FEND FOR ONESELF
FOOD FOR THOUGHT
GETS THE MESSAGE
GETS THE PICTURE
GODS OWN COUNTRY
GOES FOR NOTHING
GOOD FOR NOTHING
HALF DAY HOLIDAY
HELL FOR LEATHER
HITS THE CEILING
HITS THE JACKPOT
HUNT THE SLIPPER
HUNT THE THIMBLE
KING AND COUNTRY
LOOK FOR TROUBLE
MADE THE RUNNING
MAKE THE RUNNING
MODS AND ROCKERS
NAME AND ADDRESS
NEAR THE KNUCKLE
OPEN THE INNINGS
OPEN THE SCORING
OVER THE COUNTER
PAGE BOY HAIRCUT
PAID LIP SERVICE
PAYS LIP SERVICE
PINS AND NEEDLES
PULL THE STRINGS
RANG THE CHANGES
RING THE CHANGES
SAWN OFF SHOTGUN
SHOT GUN WEDDING

SPIT AND SAWDUST
TAIL END CHARLIE
TAKE FOR GRANTED
TAKE THE BISCUIT
TIPS THE BALANCE
TOOK FOR GRANTED
TOOK THE BISCUIT
TURN THE STOMACH
WALK THE STREETS
WENT FOR NOTHING

4,4,1,5
EATS LIKE A HORSE
GOES LIKE A DREAM
WENT LIKE A DREAM
WORK LIKE A CHARM

4,4,2,4
BOYS WILL BE BOYS
CUTS DOWN TO SIZE
FROM BANK TO BANK
FROM TIME TO TIME
LYON KING AT ARMS
LYON KING OF ARMS

4,4,3,3
GOES ONES OWN WAY
GOES OVER THE TOP
HUNT HIGH AND LOW
LAID DOWN THE LAW
LAYS DOWN THE LAW
SHOT FROM THE HIP
WENT ONES OWN WAY
WENT OVER THE TOP

4,4,4,2
EASY COME EASY GO
GETS AWAY WITH IT
GETS ONES HAND IN
HAVE DONE WITH IT
KEEP ONES CHIN UP
KEEP ONES HAIR ON
KEEP ONES HAND IN
KEPT ONES CHIN UP
KEPT ONES HAIR ON
KEPT ONES HAND IN
POKE ONES NOSE IN
PUTS ONES FACE ON
PUTS ONES FEET UP
PUTS ONES MIND TO
SETS ONES MIND TO
SETS ONES SEAL ON
TURN ONES HAND TO
WIND YOUR NECK IN

4,4,6
BACK SEAT DRIVER
BALL PARK FIGURE
BEAT ONES BRAINS
BEAT ONES BREAST
CAME FULL CIRCLE
COME FULL CIRCLE
CUTS ONES LOSSES

CUTS ONES THROAT
DEAD MANS HANDLE
DEAR JOHN LETTER
DING DONG BATTLE
GOES INTO DETAIL
GOES INTO HIDING
HELD ONES BREATH
HELD ONES TONGUE
HIGH RISK POLICY
HITS ONES STRIDE
HITS ROCK BOTTOM
HOLD ONES BREATH
HOLD ONES TONGUE
HOLD YOUR HORSES
HOWS YOUR FATHER
HYDE PARK CORNER
KEEP ONES TEMPER
KEPT ONES TEMPER
KNEW ONES ONIONS
KNOW ONES ONIONS
LEAD FREE PETROL
LICK ONES WOUNDS
LOSE ONES TEMPER
LOST ONES TEMPER
MANS BEST FRIEND
MEND ONES FENCES
MIND OVER MATTER
NINE DAYS WONDER
NINE HOLE COURSE
NINE MENS MORRIS
OPEN CAST MINING
OPEN DOOR POLICY
POLO NECK JUMPER
PULL ONES WEIGHT
RACK ONES BRAINS
REAR VIEW MIRROR
ROLL NECK JUMPER
RUSH ONES FENCES
SLAP BANG WALLOP
SNOW SHOE RABBIT
STIR ONES STUMPS
TAKE ONES CHANCE
TAKE ONES CHOICE
TALK DOWN SYSTEM
TOOK ONES CHANCE
TOOK ONES CHOICE
TRAP DOOR SPIDER
VENT ONES SPLEEN
WENT INTO DETAIL
WENT INTO HIDING

4,5,5
ACID HOUSE MUSIC
DOGS TOOTH GRASS
EAST COAST FEVER
FIVE PENNY PIECE
FOUR WHEEL DRIVE
FULL SPEED AHEAD
FULL STEAM AHEAD
GREY GOOSE QUILL

4,5,5 contd.
HIGH COURT JUDGE
HIGH SPEED STEEL
HIGH SPEED TRAIN
KEEP UNDER WRAPS
KEPT UNDER WRAPS
KING JAMES BIBLE
LATE NIGHT FINAL
MALE VOICE CHOIR
ROAD WORKS AHEAD
ROPE SOLED SHOES
RUNS RINGS ROUND
SOLE BONNE FEMME
WILD GOOSE CHASE
WRAP ROUND SKIRT

4,6,4
BEST BEFORE DATE
CLAW HAMMER COAT
DOWN MEMORY LANE
FIVE BARRED GATE
FOUR LETTER WORD
FOUR MINUTE MILE
HIGH HEELED SHOE
LORD MAYORS SHOW
MOCK TURTLE SOUP

4,7,3
SAFE DEPOSIT BOX
WELL THOUGHT OUT

4,10
ANTI FEDERALISM
ANTI FEDERALIST
ANTI JACOBINISM
AUTO INTOXICANT
AUTO SUGGESTION
BACK PROJECTION
BEAT GENERATION
BELT TIGHTENING
BILL DISCOUNTER
BULL HEADEDNESS
CACK HANDEDNESS
CAMP COMMANDANT
CAPE GOOSEBERRY
CAST ASPERSIONS
COLD SHOULDERED
COST ACCOUNTANT
COST ACCOUNTING
DATA PROCESSING
DEMI SEMIQUAVER
EVEN HANDEDNESS
FIRE WORSHIPPER
FLAG LIEUTENANT
FLAT FOOTEDNESS
FOOD CONTROLLER
FREE ENTERPRISE
FREE HANDEDNESS
FREE SPOKENNESS
GOOD COMPANIONS
GOOD FELLOWSHIP

GOOD HUMOUREDLY
GOOD NEIGHBOURS
GRAM EQUIVALENT
HAVE EVERYTHING
HIGH COMMISSION
HIGH HANDEDNESS
HIGH MINDEDNESS
HIGH PRIESTHOOD
HIGH PRINCIPLED
HIGH TECHNOLOGY
HOME DEPARTMENT
JOHN BARLEYCORN
LAKE WINDERMERE
LEFT HANDEDNESS
LEFT SPEECHLESS
LIFE EXPECTANCY
LIFE MEMBERSHIP
LOAN COLLECTION
LONG WINDEDNESS
LORD CHANCELLOR
LORD LIEUTENANT
MALE CHAUVINIST
MASS PRODUCTION
MOCK HEROICALLY
NEWS CONFERENCE
OPEN HANDEDNESS
OPEN MINDEDNESS
OPEN TOURNAMENT
OPEN UNIVERSITY
PAST PARTICIPLE
PLEA BARGAINING
POST MILLENNIAL
REED INSTRUMENT
SELF ABSORPTION
SELF ADMIRATION
SELF ASSUMPTION
SELF COMMITMENT
SELF COMPLACENT
SELF CONFIDENCE
SELF CONVICTION
SELF CORRECTING
SELF DEPENDENCE
SELF DETERMINED
SELF DEVELOPING
SELF DISCIPLINE
SELF EFFACEMENT
SELF EMPLOYMENT
SELF FLATTERING
SELF FULFILLING
SELF FULFILMENT
SELF GOVERNMENT
SELF IMMOLATION
SELF IMPORTANCE
SELF INDULGENCE
SELF INTERESTED
SELF JUSTIFYING
SELF MANAGEMENT
SELF POSSESSION
SELF PROCLAIMED
SELF PROPELLING

SELF PROPULSION
SELF PROTECTING
SELF PROTECTION
SELF PROTECTIVE
SELF REGULATING
SELF REGULATION
SELF REGULATORY
SELF RESPECTFUL
SELF RESPECTING
SELF SATISFYING
SELF SUFFICIENT
SELF SUPPORTING
SEMI CENTENNIAL
SEMI ELLIPTICAL
SEMI OFFICIALLY
SNOW SPECTACLES
SOFT UNDERBELLY
SOUL DESTROYING
TOWN COUNCILLOR
TREE WORSHIPPER
TURF ACCOUNTANT
VICE CHANCELLOR
VICE CONSULSHIP
VICE PRESIDENCY
WEAK MINDEDNESS
WILD ACCUSATION
WIND INSTRUMENT
WISH FULFILMENT
WORD PROCESSING
YOUR EXCELLENCY

5,1,4,2,2
MAKES A MEAL OF IT

5,1,4,4
DRAWS A VEIL OVER
MAKES A FAST BUCK
TAKES A BACK SEAT

5,1,5,3
TEARS A STRIP OFF
TURNS A BLIND EYE

5,1,6,2
GOING A BUNDLE ON

5,1,8
MAKES A COMEBACK
REACH A DECISION
STEAL A MARRIAGE
STOLE A MARRIAGE

5,2,1,3,3
CLEAN AS A NEW PIN

5,2,1,6
BURNT TO A CINDER
GHOST OF A CHANCE
HANGS BY A THREAD
KICKS UP A RUMPUS
KICKS UP A SHINDY

5,2,2,5
CREME DE LA CREME
GOING UP IN SMOKE

5,2,2,5 *contd.*
TYING UP IN KNOTS

5,2,3,4
BACKS TO THE WALL
BLACK IN THE FACE
BRING UP THE REAR
BROKE TO THE WIDE
CANON OF THE MASS
COMES TO THE BOIL
CURLS UP AND DIES
DRIVE TO THE WALL
DROVE TO THE WALL
GENIE OF THE LAMP
GIVEN TO THE DOGS
GOING BY THE BOOK
GOING TO THE DOGS
GOING TO THE WALL
GOING TO THE WARS
GRIST TO THE MILL
HOUSE OF ILL FAME
ICING ON THE CAKE
KNOCK ON THE HEAD
LEADS BY THE NOSE
LIVED IN THE PAST
LIVES IN THE PAST
LOOKS IN THE FACE
LYING ON THE OARS
ORDER OF THE BATH
ORDER OF THE BOOT
PACED UP AND DOWN
PACES UP AND DOWN
PENNY IN THE SLOT
POWER OF THE KEYS
PUNCH ON THE NOSE
QUICK ON THE DRAW
RISES TO THE BAIT
SAVED BY THE BELL
SCORE AN OWN GOAL
SMALL OF THE BACK
SMELL OF THE LAMP
SMELT OF THE LAMP
STABS IN THE BACK
STRAW IN THE WIND
TAKES TO THE ROAD
TAXED TO THE HILT
THORN IN THE SIDE
THROW OF THE DICE
WALKS UP AND DOWN
WATER ON THE KNEE

5,2,4,3
HANGS UP ONES HAT
SKATE ON THIN ICE
TAKES TO ONES BED
THREW IN ONES LOT
THREW UP ONES CAP
THROW IN ONES LOT
THROW UP ONES CAP
WHATS UP WITH YOU

5,2,7
APPLE OF DISCORD
BELLS OF IRELAND
BRING TO ACCOUNT
CALLS TO ACCOUNT
CEDAR OF LEBANON
CHAIN OF COMMAND
CHEST OF DRAWERS
CLASH OF CYMBALS
CLEAR AS CRYSTAL
COURT OF SESSION
CRIME OF PASSION
CRUMB OF COMFORT
FEMME DE CHAMBRE
FILLE DE CHAMBRE
HOLDS TO ACCOUNT
HOMME DE LETTRES
HOUSE OF COMMONS
LARES ET PENATES
LEAVE OF ABSENCE
MONEY OF ACCOUNT
OFFER AN OPINION
ORDER IN COUNCIL
PLACE OF WORSHIP
PLUCK UP COURAGE
RAISE AN EYEBROW
RITES OF PASSAGE
SPARE MY BLUSHES
STATE OF AFFAIRS
STICK AT NOTHING
STOPS AT NOTHING
STUCK AT NOTHING
SWARM OF LOCUSTS
TAKES IN LODGERS
TALKS IN RIDDLES
TRAIN OF THOUGHT
VALET DE CHAMBRE
WHEEL OF FORTUNE

5,3,2,4
STEPS OUT OF LINE

5,3,3,3
BLOWS THE LID OFF
LIFTS THE LID OFF
PENNY FOR THE GUY
ROSES ALL THE WAY
TAKES THE LID OFF

5,3,4,2
PULLS THE PLUG ON
THREW THE BOOK AT
THROW THE BOOK AT

5,3,6
BEATS THE BOUNDS
BITES THE BULLET
BLOCK AND TACKLE
BREAD AND BUTTER
BREAK NEW GROUND
BROKE NEW GROUND
CAUSE AND EFFECT

CHALK AND CHEESE
CHASE THE DRAGON
CLOAK AND DAGGER
COACH AND HORSES
CROWN AND ANCHOR
CYCLE PER SECOND
DODGE THE COLUMN
DUCKS AND DRAKES
EARLY DAY MOTION
EBBED AND FLOWED
FRONT END LOADED
FRONT END SYSTEM
GOING ONE BETTER
GOING THE ROUNDS
GRACE AND FAVOUR
GRASP THE NETTLE
HOLDS THE RECORD
KICKS THE BUCKET
LIGHT AND BITTER
LONGS AND SHORTS
LORDS AND LADIES
MAKES THE ROUNDS
MOTTE AND BAILEY
OILED THE WHEELS
PAPUA NEW GUINEA
PETER PAN COLLAR
PLAIN AND SIMPLE
PLAYS THE MARKET
PLAYS THE WANTON
PLEAD NOT GUILTY
PLUMB THE DEPTHS
PRESS THE BUTTON
PRICK THE GARTER
QUART AND TIERCE
RAIDS THE MARKET
RAISE THE MARKET
ROMEO AND JULIET
ROUGH AND TUMBLE
ROUND THE HOUSES
ROUND THE WICKET
SIGNS THE PLEDGE
STAYS THE COURSE
STOCK CAR RACING
TAKES THE MICKEY
TAKES THE PLUNGE
TOING AND FROING
TREAD THE BOARDS
TROOP THE COLOUR
TURNS THE CORNER
TURNS THE TABLES
UNDER THE HAMMER
WAIFS AND STRAYS
WATCH THE BIRDIE
WHEAT EAR STITCH
WORKS THE ORACLE

5,4,1,4
DRANK LIKE A FISH
DRINK LIKE A FISH
GOING LIKE A BOMB

5,4,1,4 *contd.*
GOING WITH A BANG
LIVED LIKE A LORD
LIVES LIKE A LORD
READS LIKE A BOOK
SERVE WITH A WRIT
SINGS LIKE A BIRD

5,4,2,3
OTHER FISH TO FRY
PLAYS HARD TO GET

5,4,3,2
KEEPS ONES END UP
STICK ONES OAR IN
STUCK ONES OAR IN
WORMS ONES WAY IN

5,4,5
BITES ONES THUMB
BLACK EYED SUSAN
BLESS THIS HOUSE
BREAK ONES HEART
BROKE ONES HEART
BURNS ONES BOATS
BURNT ONES BOATS
CALFS FOOT JELLY
COOKS ONES GOOSE
CRAMP ONES STYLE
CROSS ONES HEART
DICED WITH DEATH
DICES WITH DEATH
DOING ONES WORST
FALLS FROM GRACE
FALLS INTO PLACE
FINDS ONES LEVEL
FIRST TIME BUYER
FOUND ONES LEVEL
GNASH ONES TEETH
GOING AWAY DRESS
GRITS ONES TEETH
KEEPS GOOD HOURS
KEEPS OPEN HOUSE
KICKS INTO TOUCH
KICKS ONES HEELS
KNITS ONES BROWS
KNOCK DOWN PRICE
KNOCK INTO SHAPE
KNOWS ONES PLACE
KNOWS ONES STUFF
LEAVE WELL ALONE
LICKS INTO SHAPE
LICKS ONES CHOPS
LOSES ONES NERVE
LOSES ONES SHIRT
MAJOR ROAD AHEAD
OPENS ONES HEART
PAPER TAPE PUNCH
PLAYS ONES HUNCH
QUEEN ANNE STYLE
RAISE ONES GLASS

RAISE ONES VOICE
RIGHT HAND DRIVE
ROYAL TANK CORPS
SAVED ONES BACON
SAVES ONES BACON
SHOWS ONES PACES
SPLIT ONES SIDES
STONE COLD SOBER
STRUT ONES STUFF
SUCKS ONES THUMB
SUGAR PLUM FAIRY
TAKES ONES LEAVE
THIRD TIME LUCKY
THREE CARD MONTE
THREE CARD TRICK
THREE MILE LIMIT
TRIMS ONES SAILS
UNDER ONES THUMB
WATCH THIS SPACE
WHIPS INTO SHAPE

5,5,4
BRAIN FEVER BIRD
FANCY DRESS BALL
FIRST CLASS MAIL
FIRST CLASS POST
GOING GOING GONE
GOING GREAT GUNS
GREEN CROSS CODE
JOINT STOCK BANK
KNOWS WHATS WHAT
LOSES HANDS DOWN
MAKES FIRST BASE
MASON DIXON LINE
NEVER NEVER LAND
NORTH NORTH EAST
NORTH NORTH WEST
QUEEN ANNES DEAD
RIDES ROUGH SHOD
SOUTH SOUTH EAST
THREE POINT TURN
THREE SPEED GEAR
WHITE BLOOD CELL

5,6,3
CRIME DOESNT PAY
KNOWS INSIDE OUT
RHODE ISLAND RED
THREE BOTTLE MAN
TURNS INSIDE OUT
WHITE HEADED BOY

5,7,2
YOURE TELLING ME

5,9
ABOVE MENTIONED
ABOVE SUSPICION
ANNUS MIRABILIS
APPLE CHARLOTTE
ASSET STRIPPING
AUDIO FREQUENCY

BASHI BAZOUKERY
BLACK MARKETEER
BLANK CARTRIDGE
BLOOD POISONING
BLOOD SACRIFICE
CABIN PASSENGER
CASSE NOISETTES
CHAIN LIGHTNING
CHEST PROTECTOR
CHIEF CONSTABLE
CHIEF INSPECTOR
CHILD ALLOWANCE
CHILD RESISTANT
CHILE SALTPETRE
CIVIL LIBERTIES
CLASS CONSCIOUS
CLOSE ENCOUNTER
CLOUD FORMATION
COMMA BUTTERFLY
CRIME PASSIONEL
CROSS EXAMINING
CROSS INFECTION
CROSS QUESTIONS
CROSS REFERENCE
CROSS REFERRING
DAVIS APPARATUS
DEVIL INCARNATE
DRAWS ATTENTION
DRESS REHEARSAL
DRILL HUSBANDRY
DYERS GREENWEED
EARLY VICTORIAN
EARTH SATELLITE
ELDER STATESMAN
ELDER STATESMEN
FAINT HEARTEDLY
FAIRY GODMOTHER
FALSE EYELASHES
FALSE PRETENCES
FIELD ALLOWANCE
FIELD AMBULANCE
FIELD ARTILLERY
FIELD PREACHING
FIFTH AMENDMENT
FIFTH COLUMNIST
FIRST VIOLINIST
FIXED SATELLITE
FLASH BLINDNESS
FLOCK WALLPAPER
FULLY FASHIONED
GAINS ADMISSION
GLOBE ARTICHOKE
GLOVE STRETCHER
GOING OVERBOARD
GROSS INDECENCY
GROUP INSURANCE
HAPPY CHRISTMAS
HAUTE POLITIQUE
HEART SEARCHING
HEAVY BREATHING

5,9 *contd.*
HOMME DAFFAIRES
HORSE ARTILLERY
HORSE LATITUDES
HYDRO AEROPLANE
IMAGE CONVERTER
IRISH WOLFHOUND
IVORY PORCELAIN
JUICE EXTRACTOR
JUMPS OVERBOARD
KNOWS BACKWARDS
LIGHT HEARTEDLY
LOBAR PNEUMONIA
LORDS SPIRITUAL
LUCID INTERVALS
LUNAR DISTANCES
MAJOR GENERALCY
MERRY CHRISTMAS
MICRO ORGANISMS
MODEL AEROPLANE
MONEY SCRIVENER
MORAL TURPITUDE
MOTOR GENERATOR
MULTI OWNERSHIP
NIGHT BLINDNESS
NIGHT FLOWERING
NIGHT FOSSICKER
NORTH EASTWARDS
NORTH WESTWARDS
NYLON STOCKINGS
OCEAN GREYHOUND
ORGAN HARMONIUM
OSTEO ARTHRITIS
PENAL SERVITUDE
PETER PRINCIPLE
PETIT BATTEMENT
PETIT BOURGEOIS
PETTY CONSTABLE
PHOTO ENGRAVING
PIANO ACCORDION
PLAIN CHOCOLATE
PLATE TECTONICS
PLEAD IGNORANCE
PLUTO DEMOCRACY
POSSE COMITATUS
POWER BREAKFAST
PRIMA BALLERINA
PROOF CORRECTED
PURSE SNATCHING
QUEEN ELIZABETH
QUITE SOMETHING
RADAR ALTIMETER
RADIO ALTIMETER
RADIO ASTRONOMY
RADIO FREQUENCY
RADIO STRONTIUM
RADIO TELESCOPE
RAPID PROMOTION
RIVER BLINDNESS
ROYAL ARTILLERY

ROYAL ENGINEERS
ROYAL FUSILIERS
ROYAL HOUSEHOLD
RUSSO BYZANTINE
SALES ASSISTANT
SATEM LANGUAGES
SAUCE ESPAGNOLE
SCREW PROPELLER
SERUM HEPATITIS
SERVO MECHANISM
SHAWL WAISTCOAT
SHEET LIGHTNING
SHELF CATALOGUE
SHIPS CARPENTER
SHOCK TREATMENT
SHORT SIGHTEDLY
SHOVE HALFPENNY
SIEGE ARTILLERY
SOUTH EASTWARDS
SOUTH WESTWARDS
SPACE TRAVELLER
SPADE HUSBANDRY
STAGE DIRECTION
STAMP COLLECTOR
STAND CORRECTED
STEEL ENGRAVING
STOOD CORRECTED
STOUT HEARTEDLY
SUPER FLYWEIGHT
SWORD SWALLOWER
TABLE SPOONFULS
TAKES EXCEPTION
TAKES LIBERTIES
TERRA INCOGNITA
THIRD DIMENSION
THIRD PROGRAMME
THREE FARTHINGS
THREE HALFPENCE
THREE HALFPENNY
THREW OVERBOARD
THROW OVERBOARD
TOTAL ABSTAINER
TOTAL DEPRAVITY
TRUST TERRITORY
TUNER AMPLIFIER
TURBO GENERATOR
UNDER CONSTABLE
UNDER NOURISHED
UNDER PRODUCING
UNDER SECRETARY
UNDER SUSPICION
UNDUE INFLUENCE
URBAN GUERRILLA
UTTER BARRISTER
VERSE MONGERING
VICAR APOSTOLIC
VITAL FUNCTIONS
VITAL PRINCIPLE
VOWEL GRADATION
WAITS PATIENTLY

WATCH COMMITTEE
WATER BAROMETER
WATER BREATHING
WATER COLOURIST
WATER PIMPERNEL
WATER REPELLENT
WHITE CHRISTMAS
WHITE CORPUSCLE
WHOLE HEARTEDLY
WIDOW BEWITCHED
WORKS COMMITTEE
YOUNG PRETENDER
YOURS SINCERELY
YOUTH HOSTELLER

6,1,4,3
PULLED A FAST ONE
TURNED A DEAF EAR

6,1,5,2
STEALS A MARCH ON
TAKING A PRIDE IN
TAKING A SHINE TO

6,1,7
COMING A CROPPER
DEMAND A RECOUNT
MAKING A BEELINE
MAKING A KILLING
POSING A PROBLEM
PULLED A FLANKER
SERVED A PURPOSE
SERVES A PURPOSE
STAGED A PROTEST
STAGES A PROTEST
STRIKE A BARGAIN
STRUCK A BARGAIN
TAKING A BEATING
THANKS A MILLION
TREADS A MEASURE

6,2,1,5
KICKED UP A STINK

6,2,2,4
LEAVES IT AT THAT

6,2,3,3
BEWARE OF THE DOG
CALLED TO THE BAR
CAUGHT IN THE ACT
CAUGHT ON THE HOP
CHAMPS AT THE BIT
NIPPED IN THE BUD
PICKED UP THE TAB
POKING IN THE EYE
THATLL BE THE DAY

6,2,6
AFFAIR OF HONOUR
BUNDLE OF NERVES
BUREAU DE CHANGE
CLUTCH AT STRAWS
COMING UP TRUMPS

6,2,6 *contd.*

COMMIT TO MEMORY
COMMON OR GARDEN
COURSE OF EVENTS
EXCUSE MY FRENCH
FIGURE OF SPEECH
FLIGHT OF STAIRS
FOLLOW MY LEADER
HAVING IT COMING
KILLED IN ACTION
LEGION OF HONOUR
LETTER OF CREDIT
LETTER OF MARQUE
LISTEN TO REASON
LITTLE BY LITTLE
MAITRE DE BALLET
MASTER OF HOUNDS
MATRON OF HONOUR
MATTER OF COURSE
MATTER OF HONOUR
OBJECT OF VIRTUE
PACKET OF CRISPS
PARDON MY FRENCH
PAYING BY CHEQUE
PEARLS OF WISDOM
PERSON TO PERSON
PICKED TO PIECES
PLACED ON RECORD
PLACES ON RECORD
PLAGUE OF LONDON
POCKET AN INSULT
POETRY IN MOTION
PULLED TO PIECES
RIDING TO HOUNDS
SADDLE OF MUTTON
STANDS ON TIPTOE
STANDS TO REASON
STRING OF ONIONS
STRING OF PEARLS
STROKE OF GENIUS
TAKING TO PIECES
TURNED UP TRUMPS
WALKED ON TIPTOE

6,3,1,4

PLAYED FOR A DRAW
RIDING FOR A FALL
STICKS OUT A MILE
TAKING FOR A RIDE

6,3,2,3

SEEING EYE TO EYE

6,3,5

ACROSS THE BOARD
APPLES AND PEARS
BEFORE AND AFTER
BEHIND THE TIMES
BESIDE THE POINT
BOSTON TEA PARTY
BRIGHT AND EARLY

BUCKET AND SPADE
CALLED THE SHOTS
CARROT AND STICK
CHILLI CON CARNE
CLEARS THE DECKS
COMING AND GOING
COOKED THE BOOKS
FACING THE MUSIC
FORCED THE ISSUE
FORCES THE ISSUE
HAMMER AND TONGS
HELPED THE CAUSE
HUGGED THE COAST
JUMPED THE QUEUE
KNIVES AND FORKS
LATTER DAY SAINT
LAYING THE TABLE
MAKING OLD BONES
MAKING THE GRADE
MOPPED AND MOWED
PAPERS THE HOUSE
PAYING THE PIPER
PAYING THE PRICE
PICKED AND CHOSE
PLAYED THE DEVIL
PLAYED THE FIELD
PLOUGH THE SANDS
QUEERS THE PITCH
RAISED THE ALARM
RAISES THE ALARM
RANTED AND RAVED
RHYTHM AND BLUES
RIDING THE STANG
RIDING THE WAVES
RULING THE ROAST
RULING THE ROOST
SEEING THE LIGHT
SHAGGY DOG STORY
SHARPS AND FLATS
SHOOTS THE WORKS
SOUNDS THE ALARM
SPILLS THE BEANS
STEADY THE BUFFS
SWEEPS THE BOARD
SWELLS THE RANKS
TAKING THE BLAME
TAKING THE FIELD
TAKING THE FLOOR
TAKING THE REINS
THINKS THE WORST
TIPPED THE SCALE
TURNED THE SCREW
WALKED THE PLANK
WHEELS AND DEALS

6,4,1,3

SLEEPS LIKE A LOG
SLEEPS LIKE A TOP
TAKING DOWN A PEG

6,4,4

BEFORE ONES TIME
BREAKS ONES DUCK
BREAKS ONES WORD
BRINGS INTO LINE
BRINGS INTO PLAY
CENTRE HALF BACK
CHANGE ONES MIND
CHANGE ONES TUNE
CLOSED ONES EYES
CLOSES ONES EYES
COMING INTO PLAY
CRICKS ONES NECK
DEATHS HEAD MOTH
FOLDED ONES ARMS
FOLLOW ONES NOSE
HEDGED ONES BETS
HEDGES ONES BETS
HIDING ONES HEAD
HOLIER THAN THOU
INDIAN TAKE AWAY
LARGER THAN LIFE
LICKED ONES LIPS
LOSING ONES COOL
LOSING ONES HAIR
LOSING ONES HEAD
MAKING ENDS MEET
MAKING GOOD TIME
MAKING ONES MARK
MENDED ONES WAYS
MURDER MOST FOUL
PACKED ONES BAGS
PASSED ONES WORD
PASSES ONES WORD
PICKED ONES SPOT
PLAYED WITH FIRE
PLEASE TURN OVER
POURED WITH RAIN
POWDER ONES NOSE
PUSHED ONES LUCK
PUSHES ONES LUCK
RACKED WITH PAIN
RISKED ONES LIFE
ROLLED ONES EYES
SAVING ONES FACE
SAVING ONES NECK
SAVING ONES SKIN
SECOND HAND SHOP
SHAKES ONES FIST
SHAKES ONES HEAD
SHOWED ONES FACE
SHOWED ONES HAND
SLINGS ONES HOOK
SMACKS ONES LIPS
SPEAKS ONES MIND
STAKED ONES LIFE
STAKES ONES LIFE
STANDS ONES HAND
SUITED ONES BOOK
TAKING ONES SEAT

6,4,4 *contd.*
TAKING ONES TIME
TAKING ONES TURN
THUMBS ONES NOSE
TREATS LIKE DIRT
TRYING ONES LUCK
TURNED ONES HEAD
WORKED ONES WILL

6,5,3
DEVILS SNUFF BOX
KNOCKS SPOTS OFF
LITTLE GREEN MEN
SECOND WORLD WAR
THATLL TEACH HER
THATLL TEACH HIM
THATLL TEACH YOU

6,8
ABSENT MINDEDLY
ACTION PAINTING
ACTION STATIONS
ANGINA PECTORIS
ATOMIC RADIATOR
AURORA BOREALIS
BANANA REPUBLIC
BANNER HEADLINE
BAYEUX TAPESTRY
BEHIND SCHEDULE
BEYOND REPROACH
BODILY FUNCTION
BREECH DELIVERY
BRIDGE BUILDING
BUTTER FINGERED
BUTTON MUSHROOM
CARBON MONOXIDE
CAREER DIPLOMAT
CARPET SLIPPERS
CASTLE BUILDING
CASUAL LABOURER
CAUGHT UNAWARES
CHASED RAINBOWS
CHASES RAINBOWS
CHURCH MILITANT
CLAIMS ASSESSOR
CLOSED SYLLABLE
COFFEE WHITENER
COLLES FRACTURE
COLOUR SERGEANT
COMMON COURTESY
COMMON ENTRANCE
COMMON MULTIPLE
COMMON PARLANCE
COPPER BOTTOMED
COPPER FASTENED
COUNTY PALATINE
CRADLE SNATCHER
CREDIT TRANSFER
CREPES SUZETTES
CROQUE MONSIEUR
CYCLIC COMPOUND

CYSTIC FIBROSIS
DAZZLE PAINTING
DECREE ABSOLUTE
DESIGN ENGINEER
DEVILS ADVOCATE
DIESEL ELECTRIC
DIRECT DEBITING
DIRECT DRILLING
DIRECT TAXATION
DOUBLE BREASTED
DOUBLE CROSSING
DOUBLE DECLUTCH
DOUBLE ENTENDRE
DOUBLE EXPOSURE
DOUBLE JEOPARDY
DOUBLE NEGATIVE
DOUBLE STOPPING
DRAGON STANDARD
EDITIO PRINCEPS
EMPIRE BUILDING
ENFANT TERRIBLE
ESCAPE VELOCITY
FAMILY GROUPING
FAMILY PLANNING
FEEBLE MINDEDLY
FELLOW CREATURE
FIDDLE FADDLING
FINGER ALPHABET
FINGER PAINTING
FINGER POINTING
FLIGHT RECORDER
FLYING BEDSTEAD
FLYING BUTTRESS
FLYING DUTCHMAN
FLYING SCOTSMAN
FLYING SQUIRREL
FOSTER DAUGHTER
FRENCH CANADIAN
FRENCH DRESSING
FRENCH KNICKERS
FRENCH MARIGOLD
FRENCH POLISHER
FRINGE BENEFITS
FROZEN SHOULDER
GAELIC FOOTBALL
GAINED STRENGTH
GIANTS CAUSEWAY
GLOSSY MAGAZINE
GOLDEN PHEASANT
GRAHAM CRACKERS
GROUND SQUIRREL
GROUSE SHOOTING
GROWTH INDUSTRY
GUTTER MERCHANT
HORROR STRICKEN
HUDDLE TOGETHER
HYBRID COMPUTER
IMMUNE RESPONSE
INDIAN ELEPHANT
ISLAND UNIVERSE

JULIAN CALENDAR
KICKED UPSTAIRS
KNIGHT BACHELOR
KNIGHT BANNERET
KNIGHT ERRANTRY
KNOCKS SIDEWAYS
KNOCKS TOGETHER
LABOUR EXCHANGE
LABOUR MOVEMENT
LAMBDA PARTICLE
LANDED INTEREST
LAPSUS MEMORIAE
LAPTOP COMPUTER
LEAGUE FOOTBALL
LINEAR EQUATION
LIQUID PARAFFIN
LISTED BUILDING
LIVING QUARTERS
LIVING TOGETHER
LOADED QUESTION
LOVING KINDNESS
LUMBAR PUNCTURE
MAIDEN FORTRESS
MANILA ENVELOPE
MANUAL ALPHABET
MANUAL EXERCISE
MARKET GARDENER
MARKET RESEARCH
MASHED POTATOES
MAUNDY THURSDAY
MENTAL HOSPITAL
METHYL CHLORIDE
MIDDLE AMERICAN
MIDDLE DISTANCE
MINERS PHTHISIS
MIRROR SYMMETRY
MONKEY BUSINESS
MONROE DOCTRINE
MOTHER SUPERIOR
MOTION SICKNESS
MOVING PICTURES
MUCOUS MEMBRANE
MUZZLE VELOCITY
NATIVE LANGUAGE
NIMBLE FINGERED
NORMAN CONQUEST
NUMBER CRUNCHER
OCCULT SCIENCES
OFFSET PRINTING
ORANGE COLOURED
ORANGE SQUEEZER
OXFORD MOVEMENT
PANZER DIVISION
PARISH MAGAZINE
PARISH MINISTER
PARISH REGISTER
PASSED JUDGMENT
PASSED SENTENCE
PASSES JUDGMENT
PASSES SENTENCE

6,8 *contd.*
PATENT MEDICINE
PIECED TOGETHER
PIECES TOGETHER
PIGEON FANCYING
PILLOW FIGHTING
PINCER MOVEMENT
PISTOL WHIPPING
PLAGUE STRICKEN
PLEASE YOURSELF
POLICE SERGEANT
POLLEN ANALYSIS
POSTAL DISTRICT
POWDER MAGAZINE
PRINCE CHARMING
PRINCE IMPERIAL
PRISON BREAKING
PROPER FRACTION
PUBLIC DEFENDER
PUBLIC NUISANCE
PUBLIC SPEAKING
PUBLIC SPENDING
PUBLIC SPIRITED
PULLED TOGETHER
PURPLE COLOURED
PYJAMA TROUSERS
QUARTZ PORPHYRY
QUEENS EVIDENCE
QUICHE LORRAINE
QWERTY KEYBOARD
RABBIT SQUIRREL
RADIAL SYMMETRY
RADIAL VELOCITY
RECORD BREAKING
RIBBON BUILDING
RIDING BREECHES
ROCKET LAUNCHER
ROVING REPORTER
RUBBER SOLUTION
RUBBER STAMPING
RUSHED HEADLONG
RUSHES HEADLONG
SALMON COLOURED
SALOON CARRIAGE
SCHOOL HOLIDAYS
SCHOOL TEACHING
SCOTCH ATTORNEY
SCOTCH BLUEBELL
SCOTCH WOODCOCK
SCREEN PRINTING
SECOND MORTGAGE
SECOND THOUGHTS
SEEING DAYLIGHT
SENILE DEMENTIA
SENIOR WRANGLER
SEROUS MEMBRANE
SHALOM ALEICHEM
SHILLY SHALLIER
SILENT MAJORITY
SILVER PHEASANT

SIMPLE FRACTION
SIMPLE FRACTURE
SIMPLE INTEREST
SIMPLE SENTENCE
SINGLE BREASTED
SLEEPY SICKNESS
SOCIAL CONTRACT
SOCIAL DEMOCRAT
SOCIAL SECURITY
SOCIAL SERVICES
SODIUM CHLORIDE
SPEECH TRAINING
SPEEDY RECOVERY
SPELLS BACKWARD
SPRING CARRIAGE
SPRING CLEANING
SPRING LIGAMENT
SPRING MATTRESS
STICKS TOGETHER
STICKY FINGERED
STRIKE BREAKING
STRONG LANGUAGE
STUDIO AUDIENCE
SUMMER OLYMPICS
SUMMER SOLSTICE
SYSTEM BUILDING
SYSTEM SOFTWARE
TAKING MEASURES
TAKING PRISONER
TALLOW CHANDLER
TARGET LANGUAGE
TARGET PRACTICE
TERROR STRICKEN
THERMO ELECTRIC
THROWN TOGETHER
THROWS TOGETHER
TITTLE TATTLING
TRAVEL SICKNESS
TRIPLE ALLIANCE
TURKEY MERCHANT
TURTLE GRAPHICS
UNITED BRETHREN
UPHILL STRUGGLE
UPWARD MOBILITY
VESTED INTEREST
VOTIVE OFFERING
VULGAR FRACTION
WEIGHT WATCHING
WEIMAR REPUBLIC
WINDOW DRESSING
WINDOW ENVELOPE
WINDOW SHOPPING
WINTER OLYMPICS
WINTER QUARTERS
WINTER SOLSTICE
WOMENS MOVEMENT
WONDER STRICKEN
WOODEN OVERCOAT
YELLOW JAUNDICE
ZENITH DISTANCE

7,1,4,2
GETTING A LINE ON
PUTTING A STOP TO

7,1,6
BROUGHT A CHARGE
CASTING A GLANCE
COINING A PHRASE
GETTING A WICKET
KEEPING A SECRET
LIFTING A FINGER
MISSING A SITTER
PLOTTED A COURSE
TABLING A MOTION

7,2,1,4
BROUGHT TO A HEAD
KICKING UP A FUSS
WINNING BY A HEAD
WINNING BY A NECK

7,2,2,3
BELIEVE IT OR NOT
PLAYING IT BY EAR
PUTTING ON AN ACT
SUFFICE IT TO SAY

7,2,3,2
KEEPING AN EYE ON
PUTTING AN END TO

7,2,5
AFFAIRE DE COEUR
BALANCE OF POWER
BALANCE OF TRADE
BAPTISM OF BLOOD
BATTERY OF TESTS
BROUGHT TO LIGHT
CALLING IT QUITS
CALLING TO ORDER
CHEVAUX DE FRISE
CLUBBED TO DEATH
COLONEL IN CHIEF
CORRIDA DE TOROS
CUTTING UP ROUGH
GETTING TO GRIPS
GETTING TO SLEEP
GETTING UP STEAM
HANGING IN THERE
HOLDING IN CHECK
KEEPING IN CHECK
KEEPING IN TOUCH
KNIGHTS OF MALTA
LAUGHED TO SCORN
PICKING UP SPEED
PILLARS OF ISLAM
PLASTER OF PARIS
PLEASED AS PUNCH
PUTTING ON TRIAL
PUTTING TO DEATH
PUTTING TO SHAME
PUTTING TO SLEEP
REDUCED TO TEARS

7,2,5 *contd.*
REDUCES TO TEARS
REVENGE IS SWEET
RHYMING TO DEATH
RUNNING TO EARTH
SETTING IN ORDER
SETTING TO MUSIC
SETTING UP HOUSE
SILENCE IN COURT
SISTERS OF MERCY
SOMEONE OR OTHER
TICKLED TO DEATH
TICKLES TO DEATH
WAITING AT TABLE

7,3,2,2
WANTING JAM ON IT

7,3,4
BANGERS AND MASH
BEATING THE BAND
BEATING THE DRUM
BLOWING THE GAFF
CALLING ALL CARS
CALLING THE TUNE
CARRIED THE FLAG
CARRIES THE FLAG
CATHODE RAY TUBE
CRACKED THE WHIP
DECLINE AND FALL
DIPPING THE FLAG
DISHING THE DIRT
DRAWING THE LINE
FILLING THE BILL
FOOTING THE BILL
FORCING THE PACE
GETTING THE BIRD
GETTING THE BOOT
GETTING THE CHOP
GETTING THE PUSH
GETTING THE SACK
GILDING THE LILY
GILDING THE PILL
HEAVING THE LEAD
HITTING THE DECK
HITTING THE ROAD
HITTING THE ROOF
HITTING THE SACK
HOLDING THE FORT
HOLDING THE LINE
HOLDING THE ROAD
HOPPING THE TWIG
HUNDRED PER CENT
KISSING THE BOOK
LAUGHED OUT LOUD
LEAVING FOR DEAD
LEAVING ONE COLD
LEAVING THE ROOM
LOOPING THE LOOP
MISSING THE BOAT
MISSING THE MARK

MISSING THE POST
NAUGHTY BUT NICE
PADDING THE HOOF
PAINTED THE LILY
PASSING THE BUCK
PASSING THE TIME
PLAYING FOR TIME
PLAYING THE FOOL
PLAYING THE GAME
PLAYING THE LEAD
PRAYING FOR RAIN
PRESSED FOR TIME
PUTTING THE SHOT
RAISING THE ROOF
RAISING THE WIND
RIGHTED THE HELM
RINGING THE BELL
ROCKING THE BOAT
RUNNING THE SHOW
SAUSAGE AND MASH
SCOOPED THE POOL
SETTING THE PACE
SHIPPED THE OARS
SHOUTED THE ODDS
SHOWING THE FLAG
STAYING THE PACE
STEMMED THE TIDE
STOPPED THE SHOW
SUGARED THE PILL
THOUGHT OUT LOUD
THROUGH THE NOSE
TIPPING THE WINK
TOPPING THE BILL
TURNING THE TIDE
WILLING AND ABLE

7,4,3
BLOWING ONES TOP
CARRIED ONES BAT
CARRIES ONES BAT
CHANCED ONES ARM
CHANCES ONES ARM
FLIPPED ONES LID
GETTING ONES WAY
HEAVIER THAN AIR
HOLDING ONES OWN
LIGHTER THAN AIR
PICKING ONES WAY
PLAYING ONES ACE
RAISING ONES HAT
SAFFRON MILK CAP
SHOWING ONES AGE
SPORTED ONES OAK
STUBBED ONES TOE
TIPPING ONES HAT
WENDING ONES WAY
WINGING ONES WAY

7,5,2
POURING SCORN ON
SETTING LIGHT TO

7,7
ANCIENT HISTORY
ANNULAR ECLIPSE
APPLIED SCIENCE
ASSERTS ONESELF
BAGGAGE RECLAIM
BALLOON BARRAGE
BARGAIN COUNTER
BARRAGE BALLOON
BASTARD SAFFRON
BATHING COSTUME
BATHING MACHINE
BAYONET FITTING
BEGGING LETTERS
BENEFIT SOCIETY
BLISTER PLASTER
BOOLEAN ALGEBRA
BOROUGH ENGLISH
BOURBON BISCUIT
BOURBON WHISKEY
BREEDER REACTOR
BRIGHTS DISEASE
BRISTOL DIAMOND
BRISTOL FASHION
BRITISH DISEASE
BRONCHO DILATOR
BROTHEL CREEPER
BROUGHT FORWARD
BULIMIA NERVOSA
BURLING MACHINE
BUSMANS HOLIDAY
CABBAGE LETTUCE
CABINET EDITION
CABINET MEETING
CABINET PUDDING
CADMEAN VICTORY
CAISSON DISEASE
CALCIUM CARBIDE
CAPITAL LETTERS
CAPTAIN GENERAL
CARDIAC FAILURE
CARDIAC MASSAGE
CARRIED FORWARD
CARRIED THROUGH
CARRIES FORWARD
CARRIES THROUGH
CAUSING TROUBLE
CAUSTIC AMMONIA
CAVALRY OFFICER
CENTRAL HEATING
CENTRAL LOCKING
CHAMBER CONCERT
CHAMBER COUNCIL
CHAMBER COUNSEL
CHANNEL ISLANDS
CHANNEL SEAMING
CHANNEL STEAMER
CHANNEL SWIMMER
CHAPTER HEADING
CHARITY CONCERT

7,7 *contd.*

CHATEAU BOTTLED
CHICKEN FARMING
CHICKEN HEARTED
CHICKEN LIVERED
CHICKEN MARENGO
CHINESE CABBAGE
CHINESE LANTERN
CHINESE LAUNDRY
CIRCUIT BREAKER
CLITTER CLATTER
CLOUDED LEOPARD
CLUMBER SPANIEL
COALING STATION
COCONUT MATTING
COLLEGE PUDDING
COMFORT STATION
COMMITS ONESELF
COMMITS SUICIDE
CONCAVO CONCAVE
CONCERT PIANIST
CONSULS GENERAL
CONVEXO CONCAVE
COUNCIL CHAMBER
COUNSEL KEEPING
COUNTER BATTERY
COUNTER CURRENT
COUNTER TRADING
COUNTRY DANCING
CULTURE VULTURE
CURRENT ACCOUNT
CURRENT AFFAIRS
CURTAIN WALLING
CUTTING CORNERS
DANCING ACADEMY
DANCING PARTNER
DENYING ONESELF
DEPOSIT ACCOUNT
DESSERT SERVICE
DIAMOND JUBILEE
DIAMOND WEDDING
DIVIDED HIGHWAY
DOCTORS COMMONS
DRIVING LICENCE
ELECTRA COMPLEX
EMPEROR PENGUIN
ENDLESS GEARING
ENGLISH CHANNEL
ENGLISH DISEASE
ENGLISH GRAMMAR
ENGLISH MUSTARD
ENJOYED ONESELF
EXCUSED ONESELF
EXCUSES ONESELF
EXPOSED ONESELF
EXPOSES ONESELF
EXPRESS ONESELF
EXTINCT VOLCANO
EXTREME UNCTION
FACTORY FARMING

FALLING THROUGH
FANCIED ONESELF
FANCIES ONESELF
FEATHER BRAINED
FIGHTER COMMAND
FILLING STATION
FILTERS THROUGH
FINANCE COMPANY
FINDERS KEEPERS
FINGERS BREADTH
FISSION REACTOR
FLATTER ONESELF
FLICKED THROUGH
FOLDING MACHINE
FOLLOWS THROUGH
FOREIGN AFFAIRS
FORGETS ONESELF
FORTUNE HUNTING
FORTUNE TELLING
FORWARD LOOKING
FREEDOM FIGHTER
FUNERAL PARLOUR
FURTHER OUTLOOK
FUTTOCK SHROUDS
GAINING CONTROL
GATWICK AIRPORT
GENERAL AMNESTY
GENERAL COUNCIL
GENERAL OFFICER
GENERAL PURPOSE
GENERAL SERVANT
GENERAL WARRANT
GENUINE ARTICLE
GETTING DRESSED
GETTING HITCHED
GETTING THROUGH
GIRDING ONESELF
GRIFFON VULTURE
HANGING GARDENS
HELPING ONESELF
HERALDS COLLEGE
HERRING FISHERY
HIPPETY HOPPETY
HISTORY TEACHER
HOLDING COMPANY
HOSTILE WITNESS
HUGGING ONESELF
HUNTING LEOPARD
ICEBERG LETTUCE
INDUCED CURRENT
INERTIA SELLING
INSIDER DEALING
INSIDER TRADING
JAVELIN THROWER
JEDDART JUSTICE
KARAOKE MACHINE
KEEPING COUNSEL
KEYHOLE SURGERY
KICKING ONESELF
KIDDING ONESELF

KISSING STRINGS
KITCHEN CABINET
LEADING ACTRESS
LEADING COUNSEL
LENDING LIBRARY
LEXICAL MEANING
LIAISON OFFICER
LIBRARY EDITION
LIMITED COMPANY
LIMITED EDITION
LOOKING ASKANCE
LOOKING DAGGERS
LOOKING FORWARD
LUGGAGE CARRIER
MARBURG DISEASE
MEDICAL COLLEGE
MEDICAL OFFICER
MEDICAL STUDENT
MEETING HALFWAY
MILKING MACHINE
MILKING PARLOUR
MILLING MACHINE
MOROCCO LEATHER
MOTHERS MEETING
MUDDLED THROUGH
MUDDLES THROUGH
MUSTARD PLASTER
NATURAL HISTORY
NATURAL NUMBERS
NATURAL SCIENCE
NATURAL WASTAGE
NERVOUS IMPULSE
NODDING THROUGH
NUCLEAR FISSION
NUCLEAR PHYSICS
NUCLEAR REACTOR
NUCLEAR WARFARE
NUCLEAR WARHEAD
NURSING OFFICER
OCEANIC ISLANDS
OEDIPUS COMPLEX
OMNIBUS EDITION
OPENING BATSMAN
OPENING BATSMEN
ORDERLY OFFICER
ORDINAL NUMBERS
OSTRICH FEATHER
PACKAGE HOLIDAY
PACKING STATION
PAISLEY PATTERN
PANCAKE TUESDAY
PARLOUR BOARDER
PARTIAL ECLIPSE
PARTING COMPANY
PASSING CURRENT
PASSING THROUGH
PASSIVE SMOKING
PERFECT BINDING
PERFECT CADENCE
PHAEDRA COMPLEX

7,7 *contd.*
PHANTOM CIRCUIT
PICKLED CABBAGE
PICKLED HERRING
PICKLED WALNUTS
PICTURE GALLERY
PICTURE WRITING
PILGRIM FATHERS
PINBALL MACHINE
PLANING MACHINE
PLANNED ECONOMY
PLASTIC SURGEON
PLASTIC SURGERY
PLAYING FOOTSIE
PLOUGHS THROUGH
POLLING STATION
PRAIRIE CHICKEN
PREENED ONESELF
PRESSED FLOWERS
PRESSED FORWARD
PRESSES FORWARD
PRIMARY BATTERY
PRIMARY COLOURS
PRINCES FEATHER
PRINTED CIRCUIT
PRITTLE PRATTLE
PRIVATE BAPTISM
PRIVATE COMPANY
PROCESS CONTROL
PROMISE BREAKER
PROMISE KEEPING
PROVOST MARSHAL
PULLING STRINGS
PULLING THROUGH
PUMPING STATION
PUSHING THROUGH
PUTTING FORWARD
PUTTING THROUGH
PYRAMID SELLING
PYRRHIC VICTORY
QUALITY CONTROL
QUARTER GALLERY
QUARTER SECTION
RAILWAY CUTTING
RANGING ONESELF
READING GLASSES
READING MACHINE
REAPING MACHINE
REIGNED SUPREME
REPEATS ONESELF
REVISED EDITION
REVISED VERSION
RHUBARB RHUBARB
RHYMING COUPLET
ROARING FORTIES
ROMPING THROUGH
RUNNING BANQUET
RUNNING ERRANDS
RUNNING FOOTMAN
RUNNING REPAIRS

RUNNING RIGGING
RUNNING THROUGH
SABBATH BREAKER
SAVINGS ACCOUNT
SCATTER BRAINED
SCIENCE FICTION
SENDING PACKING
SERPENT GODDESS
SERPENT WORSHIP
SERVICE STATION
SHERIFF OFFICER
SHIFTED ONESELF
SHOWING PROMISE
SHOWING WILLING
SHUTTLE SERVICE
SINGING GALLERY
SISTINE MADONNA
SKIMBLE SKAMBLE
SMOKING CONCERT
SNAGGLE TOOTHED
SPECIAL LICENCE
SPECIAL VERDICT
SPINDLE SHANKED
SQUEAKS THROUGH
STACKED AGAINST
STATION MANAGER
STEEPLE CROWNED
STIRRUP LEATHER
STORAGE BATTERY
STORAGE HEATING
STRIKES THROUGH
SUBJECT HEADING
SUITING ONESELF
SULPHUR DIOXIDE
SUMMARY OFFENCE
SURFACE TENSION
SURGEON GENERAL
SUSPEND PAYMENT
SYSTEMS ANALYST
TALKING MACHINE
TERTIUS GAUDENS
THERMAL BARRIER
THERMAL IMAGING
THERMAL REACTOR
THERMAL SPRINGS
THIEVES KITCHEN
THIMBLE RIGGING
THOUGHT PROCESS
THOUGHT READING
THOUGHT THROUGH
THROUGH TRAFFIC
TOBACCO STOPPER
TORSION BALANCE
TORTURE CHAMBER
TRAFFIC SIGNALS
TRIVIAL PURSUIT
TRUMPET TONGUED
TRUSTEE ACCOUNT
TURBINE STEAMER
TURKISH DELIGHT

TURNING AGAINST
TURNKEY PACKAGE
VATICAN COUNCIL
VENDING MACHINE
VENTURE CAPITAL
VIRTUAL REALITY
VISIBLE EXPORTS
VISIBLE HORIZON
VISIBLE IMPORTS
VULPINE OPOSSUM
WALKING WOUNDED
WARRANT OFFICER
WASHING MACHINE
WEARING APPAREL
WEATHER STATION
WEEDING FORCEPS
WELFARE OFFICER
WEMBLEY STADIUM
WHEELER DEALING
WHISTLE BLOWING
WHITLEY COUNCIL
WILLING HEARTED
WILSONS DISEASE
WINNING GALLERY
WINNING THROUGH
WITCHES SABBATH
WOOLLEN DRAPERY
WORKING AGAINST
WORKING CAPITAL
WORKING CLOTHES
YEOMANS SERVICE

8,1,5
DROPPING A BRICK
HAZARDED A GUESS
RESERVED A TABLE
RESERVES A TABLE
SPENDING A PENNY
STRAINED A POINT
STRIKING A CHORD
STRIKING A MATCH
THROWING A PARTY
THROWING A PUNCH

8,2,1,3
STRAIGHT AS A DIE

8,2,4
BACHELOR OF ARTS
BRINGING TO BOOK
BRINGING TO HEEL
BRINGING TO LIFE
DRINKING UP TIME
KNOCKING ON WOOD
LIGHTING UP TIME
PRESENCE OF MIND
QUESTION OF FACT
RELEASED ON BAIL
SHOULDER OF LAMB
SHOULDER OF VEAL
SHUTTING UP SHOP

8,2,4 *contd.*
STANDING TO GAIN
STANDING TO LOSE
STRIKING IT RICH
THRILLED TO BITS

8,3,3
BREAKING THE ICE
BRIDGING THE GAP
CARRYING THE CAN
CARRYING THE DAY
CARRYING TOO FAR
CATCHING THE SUN
CLEARING THE AIR
CLEARING THE WAY
KNOCKING FOR SIX
SLINGING THE BAT
STOPPING THE ROT
WHIPPING THE CAT
WIDENING THE GAP

8,6
ACHILLES TENDON
AMERICAN INDIAN
APPROVED SCHOOL
AVIATION SPIRIT
BARBADOS CHERRY
BATHROOM SCALES
BEATIFIC VISION
BILLIARD MARKER
BINAURAL EFFECT
BLENHEIM ORANGE
BLENHEIM PALACE
BLOCKADE RUNNER
BLOCKING MOTION
BLUECOAT SCHOOL
BOARDING SCHOOL
BREAKING GROUND
BREATHED FREELY
BREEDING GROUND
BRUSSELS CARPET
BRUSSELS SPROUT
BUCKLEYS CHANCE
CALAMINE LOTION
CALLIPER SPLINT
CAPUCHIN MONKEY
CARDINAL BISHOP
CARDINAL FLOWER
CARDINAL NUMBER
CARDINAL POINTS
CARDINAL VIRTUE
CARDINAL WOLSEY
CASEMENT WINDOW
CASSETTE PLAYER
CATENARY SYSTEM
CATHOLIC CHURCH
CHAMPION JOCKEY
CHANCERY OFFICE
CHANGING COLOUR
CHANGING PLACES
CHARCOAL BURNER

CHESHIRE CHEESE
CIRCULAR LETTER
CITIZENS ARREST
CLERICAL COLLAR
COCKTAIL LOUNGE
COCKTAIL SHAKER
COLONIAL OFFICE
COLONIAL SYSTEM
COLORADO BEETLE
COLOURED PENCIL
COMPOUND ENGINE
COMPUTER DATING
CONCRETE JUNGLE
CONCRETE POETRY
CONJUGAL RIGHTS
CONTRACT BRIDGE
CONTRARY MOTION
COURTING COUPLE
COVERING LETTER
CRIMINAL RECORD
CROSSING SWORDS
CROSSING WARDEN
CRUTCHED FRIARS
CURRYING FAVOUR
DAYLIGHT SAVING
DEFERRED SHARES
DEUXIEME BUREAU
DISCOUNT BROKER
DISTRESS SIGNAL
DIVIDING ENGINE
DOUBTING THOMAS
DRESSING JACKET
DRINKING VESSEL
DROPPING ANCHOR
DUCTLESS GLANDS
ELECTRIC COOKER
ELECTRIC GUITAR
ELECTRIC HEATER
ELECTRIC SHAVER
ELECTRON CAMERA
ELECTRON OPTICS
ESPRESSO COFFEE
ETHYLENE GLYCOL
EXTENDED FAMILY
EXTERNAL DEGREE
FEATURES EDITOR
FEMININE ENDING
FIGHTING CHANCE
FIREMANS HELMET
FLEETING MOMENT
FLOATING BEACON
FLOATING BRIDGE
FLOATING CHARGE
FLOATING ISLAND
FLOATING KIDNEY
FLOATING POLICY
FOUNDERS SHARES
FOUNDING FATHER
GABRIELS HOUNDS
GATHERED BREATH

GATHERED GROUND
GEORGIAN PLANET
GRACIOUS LIVING
HAWAIIAN GUITAR
HEAVENLY BODIES
HERCULES BEETLE
HIGHLAND CATTLE
HONORARY MEMBER
HUMPBACK BRIDGE
IDENTITY CRISIS
IDENTITY PARADE
IMPERIAL GALLON
IMPERIAL OCTAVO
IMPERIAL WEIGHT
INCIDENT CENTRE
INCIDENT OFFICE
INDIRECT OBJECT
INDIRECT SPEECH
INNOCENT ABROAD
INTERIOR DESIGN
INTERIOR SPRUNG
INVERTED COMMAS
JAPANESE MEDLAR
JINGLING JOHNNY
JUDICIAL COMBAT
KNAPPING HAMMER
KNEADING TROUGH
KNITTING NEEDLE
KNOCKING AROUND
LEMONADE POWDER
LITERARY CRITIC
LITERARY EDITOR
LOMBARDY POPLAR
LUMINOUS ENERGY
LUNCHEON BASKET
MACARONI CHEESE
MACKEREL BREEZE
MAGNETIC BOTTLE
MAGNETIC NEEDLE
MANAGING EDITOR
MANDARIN COLLAR
MANDARIN ORANGE
MANIFOLD WRITER
MARATHON RUNNER
MARCHING ORDERS
MARRIAGE BROKER
MARTELLO TOWERS
MEDICINE BOTTLE
MERCHANT BANKER
MERCHANT PRINCE
MERCHANT TAILOR
MERIDIAN CIRCLE
METEORIC STONES
MILITARY POLICE
MILITARY SCHOOL
MISCHIEF MAKING
MOSQUITO CANOPY
MOUNTAIN BEAVER
MOUNTAIN LAUREL
MULTIPLE CHOICE

8,6 *contd.*
MULTIPLE CINEMA
MUNITION WORKER
NAPOLEON BRANDY
NATIONAL ANTHEM
NATIONAL CHURCH
NATIONAL SCHOOL
NEGATIVE PROTON
NOBLESSE OBLIGE
NORTHERN LIGHTS
NOUVEAUX RICHES
OBITUARY NOTICE
OPPOSITE NUMBER
ORDERING AROUND
ORDINARY SEAMAN
ORDINARY SHARES
ORDNANCE SURVEY
PARALLEL MOTION
PARALLEL SLALOM
PARMESAN CHEESE
PASTORAL CHARGE
PATELLAR REFLEX
PAVEMENT ARTIST
PEASANTS REVOLT
PECTORAL GIRDLE
PERIODIC SYSTEM
PERSONAL COLUMN
PERSONAL ESTATE
PERSONAL RIGHTS
PERSONAL STEREO
PHOSPHOR BRONZE
PLANNING BLIGHT
PLATFORM TICKET
PLATINUM BLONDE
PLEASURE GIVING
PLEASURE GROUND
PLEASURE SEEKER
PORTLAND CEMENT
POSITIVE ACTION
PRECIOUS LITTLE
PRECIOUS METALS
PRECIOUS STONES
PREPARED SPEECH
PRESSURE COOKED
PRESSURE COOKER
PRESSURE HELMET
PRIMROSE LEAGUE
PRINTING OFFICE
PROPERTY MASTER
PROVIDED SCHOOL
QUESTION MASTER
QUILTING COTTON
RATIONAL NUMBER
REGISTER OFFICE
REGISTRY OFFICE
REMAINED SILENT
REPORTED SPEECH
REPORTED VERSES
REVEREND MOTHER
REYNOLDS NUMBER

RIGHTING WRONGS
ROBINSON CRUSOE
ROCHELLE POWDER
ROGATION FLOWER
ROGATION SUNDAY
SANDWICH COURSE
SAPPHIRE QUARTZ
SCHOONER RIGGED
SCORPION SPIDER
SEIDLITZ POWDER
SHEEPDOG TRIALS
SHERLOCK HOLMES
SHERWOOD FOREST
SHIFTING BOARDS
SHOOTING JACKET
SHOPPING ARCADE
SHOPPING AROUND
SHOPPING BASKET
SHOPPING CENTRE
SHOULDER GIRDLE
SHOULDER HEIGHT
SLEEPING BEAUTY
SMELLING BOTTLE
SNAPPING TURTLE
SPAWNING GROUND
SPEAKERS CORNER
SPECIFIC LEGACY
SPORTING CHANCE
SQUADRON LEADER
SQUIRREL MONKEY
STAMPING GROUND
STANDARD BEARER
STANDING GROUND
STANDING ORDERS
STANNARY COURTS
STARTING BLOCKS
STARTING HANDLE
STARTING PISTOL
STEERING COLUMN
STICKING AROUND
STILETTO HEELED
STILLSON WRENCH
STINKING BADGER
STIRLING ENGINE
STIRRING ABROAD
STOCKING FILLER
STOCKING STITCH
STOMPING GROUND
STOOGING AROUND
STRADDLE LEGGED
STRAIGHT TICKET
STRIATED MUSCLE
STRIKING BOTTOM
STRIKING CIRCLE
SURGICAL SPIRIT
SWIMMING TRUNKS
TACTICAL VOTING
TACTICAL WEAPON
TAKEOVER BIDDER
TOUCHING BOTTOM

TRACTION ENGINE
TRANSFER TICKET
TREASURE ISLAND
ULTERIOR MOTIVE
UNEARNED INCOME
UPWARDLY MOBILE
VASCULAR BUNDLE
VASCULAR PLANTS
VENETIAN MOSAIC
VERTICAL ANGLES
VERTICAL CIRCLE
VIENNESE FINGER
VITREOUS HUMOUR
WATERING TROUGH
WEIGHING ANCHOR
WELCOMED ABOARD
WELCOMES ABOARD
WHIPLASH INJURY
WORMWOOD SCRUBS
WRONGFUL ARREST

9,1,4
SPRINGING A LEAK

9,2,3
BARRISTER AT LAW
BREAKFAST IN BED
DAUGHTERS IN LAW
PRISONERS OF WAR

9,5
ADMIRALTY CHART
ADMIRALTY HOUSE
ADVENTURE STORY
ALLIGATOR APPLE
ANOMALOUS WATER
ANTARCTIC OCEAN
APOSTOLIC VICAR
AUTOGRAPH ALBUM
AUTOMATIC DRIVE
AUTOMATIC PILOT
BADMINTON COURT
BEARNAISE SAUCE
BLACKPOOL TOWER
BREAKDOWN TRUCK
BREAKFAST TABLE
BREATHING AGAIN
BREATHING SPACE
BRITANNIA METAL
BUTTERFLY SCREW
BUTTERFLY VALVE
CALORIFIC VALUE
CANONICAL HOURS
CANTALOUP MELON
CARTESIAN DEVIL
CARTESIAN DIVER
CARTRIDGE PAPER
CATHEDRAL CLOSE
CATHERINE WHEEL
CHARACTER ACTOR
CHARACTER ESSAY

9,5 *contd.*
CHARLOTTE RUSSE
CHRISTMAS CAROL
CHRISTMAS DAISY
CHROMATIC SCALE
CIGARETTE PAPER
CLASSICAL LATIN
CLASSICAL MUSIC
CLEANSING CREAM
COMMITTEE STAGE
COMMUNION CLOTH
COMMUNION TABLE
COMMUNION WAFER
COMMUNITY CHEST
COMMUNITY NURSE
COMMUNITY RADIO
COMPANION HATCH
COMPARING NOTES
COMPOSING STICK
CONJURING TRICK
CONSUMERS GOODS
CONTAINER CRANE
CORIANDER SEEDS
CORPORATE STATE
CROCODILE TEARS
DANGEROUS DRUGS
DAVENPORT TRICK
DECORATED STYLE
DETECTIVE STORY
DEUTERIUM OXIDE
DIGESTIVE TRACT
DIRECTORS CHAIR
DISTILLED WATER
ELEPHANTS TRUNK
ENGINEERS CHAIN
ESPAGNOLE SAUCE
EXCHANGED BLOWS
EXCHANGED WORDS
EXCHANGES BLOWS
EXCHANGES WORDS
EXCLUSION ORDER
EXCURSION TRAIN
EXPANSION BOARD
EXPANSION JOINT
EXPLOSIVE RIVET
FALLOPIAN TUBES
FINISHING TOUCH
FLOWERING PLANT
FLOWERING SHRUB
FORBIDDEN FRUIT
GALLOPING MAJOR
GATHERING ROUND
GATHERING SPEED
GATHERING STORM
GENTLEMAN CADET
GENTLEMAN USHER
GLANDULAR FEVER
GREENLAND WHALE
GREGORIAN MODES
GRENADIER GUARD

HALLOWEEN PARTY
HEAVISIDE LAYER
HEXAGONAL CHESS
HOUSEHOLD GOODS
HYDRAULIC BRAKE
HYDRAULIC PRESS
IDENTICAL RHYME
IDENTICAL TWINS
IMAGINARY POINT
IMPERFECT TENSE
INDUCTION MOTOR
INDUCTION VALVE
INFLATION PROOF
INSURANCE CLAIM
IPSISSIMA VERBA
IRREGULAR VERBS
JERUSALEM BIBLE
JERUSALEM CROSS
JEWELLERS ROUGE
KNUCKLING UNDER
LACHRYMAL GLAND
LAMINATED GLASS
LANTHANUM GLASS
LEVELLING STAFF
LIBERATED WOMAN
MASCULINE RHYME
MATERNITY GRANT
MATERNITY LEAVE
MEZZANINE FLOOR
MONASTRAL GREEN
NEWSPAPER WOMAN
OPERATING TABLE
PANORAMIC SIGHT
PARAMOUNT CHIEF
PARCHMENT PAPER
PAROCHIAL BOARD
PARTRIDGE BERRY
PASSENGER TRAIN
PATCHWORK QUILT
PATERNITY LEAVE
PERMANENT PRESS
PERMANENT TEETH
PERPETUAL CHECK
PETROLEUM JELLY
PETTICOAT TAILS
PINEAPPLE JUICE
PITUITARY GLAND
PLOUGHING MATCH
PNEUMATIC DRILL
POLISHING PASTE
POLISHING SLATE
POLITICAL PARTY
PORCUPINE GRASS
PRACTICAL JOKER
PREACHING CROSS
PREACHING FRIAR
PREACHING HOUSE
PRESIDENT ELECT
PRINCIPAL FOCUS
PRINCIPAL PARTS

PROGRAMME MUSIC
PROPELLER BLADE
PROPELLER SHAFT
PROTECTED STATE
PROXIMATE CAUSE
PTERYGOID PLATE
PUERPERAL FEVER
QUOTATION MARKS
RABBETING PLANE
RADIATION BELTS
RECEIVING HOUSE
RECEIVING ORDER
RECEPTION CLASS
RECEPTION ORDER
RECORDING ANGEL
REDUCTION WORKS
REFECTORY TABLE
RELAPSING FEVER
REMITTENT FEVER
RESOLVING POWER
REVERSING LAYER
REVERSING LIGHT
REVOLVING DOORS
RHEUMATIC FEVER
SACRAMENT HOUSE
SALTPETRE PAPER
SATELLITE STATE
SCREAMING FARCE
SCRUBBING BOARD
SCRUBBING BRUSH
SCRUBBING ROUND
SECONDARY RADAR
SENSATION NOVEL
SENSITIVE FLAME
SENSITIVE PLANT
SHEFFIELD PLATE
SHEFFIELD STEEL
SHEPHERDS CHECK
SHEPHERDS CROOK
SHEPHERDS GLASS
SHEPHERDS PLAID
SHEPHERDS PURSE
SIMULATED PEARL
SMOOTHING PLANE
SOLITAIRE BOARD
SOVEREIGN STATE
SPECTATOR SPORT
SPLITTING HAIRS
SPROUTING WINGS
STAINLESS STEEL
STRINGING ALONG
STUMBLING BLOCK
STUMBLING STONE
SURRENDER VALUE
TASMANIAN DEVIL
TECHNICAL HITCH
TELEGRAPH BOARD
TELEGRAPH CABLE
TELEPHONE BOOTH
TELEPHONE KIOSK

9,5 *contd.*
TEMPERATE ZONES
THRESHING FLOOR
TRIFACIAL NERVE
TROCHLEAR NERVE
TURQUOISE GREEN
UNCROWNED QUEEN
UNIVERSAL DONOR
UNIVERSAL JOINT
VANISHING CREAM
VANISHING POINT
VEGETABLE MOULD
VITRIFIED FORTS
VITRIFIED WALLS
WALPURGIS NIGHT
WANDERING NERVE
WATCHMANS CLOCK
WEATHERED ALONG
WHOLEMEAL BREAD
WILLESDEN PAPER
WITHERING FLOOR
WORCESTER CHINA
WORCESTER SAUCE

10,4
ARTIFICIAL SILK
BANQUETING HALL
BATTENBERG CAKE
BELLADONNA LILY
BITUMINOUS COAL
BOATSWAINS MATE
BOATSWAINS PIPE
CALCULATED RISK
CANNONBALL TREE
CANTERBURY BELL
CAUTIONARY TALE
COLLECTIVE FARM
COLLECTIVE NOUN
COLLECTORS ITEM
COMMERCIAL ROOM
CONFERENCE ROOM
CONSULTING ROOM
CONTINUITY GIRL
COROMANDEL WORK
CORRUGATED IRON
CUMULATIVE VOTE
DERAILLEUR GEAR
DISSECTING ROOM
DISTRESSED AREA
ELDERBERRY WINE
ELECTRONIC MAIL
ENGAGEMENT RING
ENTERPRISE ZONE
EUCALYPTUS TREE
EUSTACHIAN TUBE
EVAPORATED MILK
EXPLAINING AWAY
EXPRESSION MARK
EXPRESSION STOP
FISHERMANS LUCK

FISHERMANS RING
FLORENTINE IRIS
FOUNDATION STOP
FRESHWATER FISH
FRIGHTENED AWAY
FRITTERING AWAY
GALVANISED IRON
GEOLOGICAL TIME
GOOSEBERRY BUSH
GOOSEBERRY FOOL
GOVERNMENT WHIP
GRANADILLA TREE
GREENFIELD SITE
HOUSEMAIDS KNEE
IMPERATIVE MOOD
INCENDIARY BOMB
INNOMINATE BONE
INNOMINATE VEIN
INSULATING TAPE
INTERNMENT CAMP
KILMARNOCK COWL
MAIDENHAIR TREE
MEERSCHAUM PIPE
MEMBERSHIP CARD
MEMORANDUM BOOK
MICHAELMAS TERM
MISSIONARY WORK
NINETEENTH HOLE
PADDINGTON BEAR
PARLIAMENT CAKE
PEDESTRIAN DECK
PEPPERCORN RENT
PEPPERMINT DROP
PERCUSSION FUSE
PERCUSSION LOCK
PERFORMING ARTS
PERFORMING FLEA
PERFORMING SEAL
PHOSPHORIC ACID
PHOTOFLOOD LAMP
PICCADILLY LINE
PLANTATION SONG
PONTEFRACT CAKE
PONTIFICAL MASS
POSSESSIVE CASE
PRAETORIAN GATE
PREVAILING WIND
PRIMORDIAL SOUP
PRODUCTION LINE
PROMISSORY NOTE
PROSCENIUM ARCH
PROVINCIAL ROSE
QUARANTINE FLAG
RECITATION ROOM
REGISTERED POST
RESISTANCE COIL
RESTRICTED AREA
RHINOCEROS BIRD
SABBATICAL YEAR
SCRATCHING POST

SCRIBBLING BOOK
SHORTENING SAIL
STATIONERS HALL
STRAWBERRY LEAF
STRAWBERRY MARK
STRAWBERRY ROAN
STRETCHING IRON
SUCCESSION DUTY
SULPHUROUS ACID
SUPPORTERS CLUB
SUPPORTING FILM
THROTTLING DOWN
TRANSVERSE WAVE
TRAVELLERS TALE
TRAVELLING FOLK
VEGETARIAN DIET
VEGETARIAN DISH
WHISPERING DOME
WINCHESTER DISC
WINCHESTER DISK
ZOOLOGICAL PARK

11,3
ACCUMULATOR BET
CAULIFLOWER EAR
CONDITIONAL FEE
CONTRACTING OUT
CORPORATION TAX
CREDIBILITY GAP
DANGEROUSLY ILL
EDUCATIONAL TOY
FRIGHTENING OFF
GINGERBREAD MAN
MAINTENANCE MAN
NEANDERTHAL MAN
OBSERVATION CAR
PERFORMANCE ART
REMEMBRANCE DAY
RENAISSANCE MAN
STRAIGHTENS OUT
SYMPATHETIC INK
UNACCOUNTED FOR
WITHHOLDING TAX

15 LETTERS

1,3,2,3,6
A CAT ON HOT BRICKS

1,4,2,3,5
A DROP IN THE OCEAN
A SLAP ON THE WRIST

1,4,2,8
A WORD IN EDGEWAYS

1,4,3,2,5
A FISH OUT OF WATER
A HARD NUT TO CRACK

1,5,2,1,6
A STORM IN A TEACUP

1,5,2,3,4
A STING IN THE TAIL

1,5,2,7
A MONTH OF SUNDAYS

1,5,3,2,4
A NASTY BIT OF WORK

1,6,2,6
A BUNDLE OF NERVES

1,9,5
A CHRISTMAS CAROL

2,1,6,2,4
AS A MATTER OF FACT

2,2,11
OF NO CONSEQUENCE

2,3,2,3,5
AS OLD AS THE HILLS
ON TOP OF THE WORLD

2,3,2,4,4
GO OFF AT HALF COCK

2,3,2,8
GO OUT OF BUSINESS

2,3,3,4,3
GO OFF THE DEEP END

2,3,3,7
GO FOR THE JUGULAR

2,3,4,1,5
GO OUT LIKE A LIGHT

2,3,4,2,1,3
AT THE DROP OF A HAT

2,3,4,2,4
ON THE ROAD TO RUIN

2,3,4,6
IN THE LAST RESORT

2,3,5,5
IN THE FIRST FLUSH
IN THE FIRST PLACE
IN THE SMALL HOURS
OF THE FIRST WATER
ON THE RIGHT TRACK
ON THE WRONG TRACK

2,3,6,4
ON THE DANGER LIST
TO THE MANNER BORN

2,3,10
IN ALL CONSCIENCE
IN THE ALTOGETHER
IN THE BACKGROUND
IN THE WILDERNESS

2,4,2,1,6
AS WEAK AS A KITTEN

2,4,2,2,5
BY HOOK OR BY CROOK

2,4,2,7
AS KEEN AS MUSTARD

2,4,3,2,4
NO SKIN OFF MY NOSE

2,4,3,3,3
IN THIS DAY AND AGE

2,4,3,6
ON WITH THE MOTLEY

2,5,2,1,5
AS SOUND AS A ROACH
AS THICK AS A PLANK
AS WHITE AS A SHEET

2,5,3,5
BY TRIAL AND ERROR
IN APPLE PIE ORDER
IN BLACK AND WHITE
IT TAKES ALL SORTS

2,5,8
AT CLOSE QUARTERS

2,6,2,1,4
AS STEADY AS A ROCK

2,7,4,2
GO THROUGH WITH IT

2,7,6
MY LEARNED FRIEND

2,8,5
ON SPEAKING TERMS

3,1,5,4,2
PUT A BRAVE FACE ON

3,1,11
RAN A TEMPERATURE
RUN A TEMPERATURE

3,2,1,5,4
MAD AS A MARCH HARE
WIN BY A SHORT HEAD
WON BY A SHORT HEAD

3,2,3,4,3
LET IT ALL HANG OUT

3,2,3,7
DIP OF THE HORIZON
FIT OF THE VAPOURS
OUT OF THE RUNNING
PIT OF THE STOMACH
TIP OF THE ICEBERG
TOP OF THE MORNING

3,2,4,6
NOT ON YOUR NELLIE

3,2,10
ACT OF PARLIAMENT
ACT OF SETTLEMENT
AGE OF DISCRETION
OUT OF COMMISSION
OUT OF PROPORTION

3,3,2,3,4
LOB LIE BY THE FIRE

THE END OF THE ROAD

3,3,3,3,3
THE HOW AND THE WHY

3,3,3,6
FLY OFF THE HANDLE
PAR FOR THE COURSE
PAY OFF OLD SCORES

3,3,4,2,3
FOR THE LIFE OF HER
FOR THE LIFE OF HIM

3,3,4,3,2
NOT THE WORD FOR IT

3,3,4,5
FOR THE TIME BEING
HIT THE HIGH SPOTS

3,3,5,2,2
GET THE WORST OF IT
GOT THE WORST OF IT

3,3,5,4
ALL THE WORLD OVER
EGG AND SPOON RACE
FOR OLD TIMES SAKE
PUT THE CLOCK BACK
SAW THE FUNNY SIDE
SEE THE FUNNY SIDE
WET THE BABYS HEAD

3,3,7,2
PUT THE MOCKERS ON

3,3,9
BED AND BREAKFAST
GET THE RUNAROUND
GOT THE RUNAROUND
HIT THE HEADLINES
LOW TAR CIGARETTE
OLD AGE PENSIONER
OLD RED SANDSTONE
RAN FOR PRESIDENT
RUN FOR PRESIDENT
SUM AND SUBSTANCE
THE LOW COUNTRIES

3,4,2,1,5
ANY PORT IN A STORM
RUB SALT IN A WOUND

3,4,2,2,4
TOO GOOD TO BE TRUE

3,4,2,4,2
NOT MUCH TO LOOK AT

3,4,2,6
THE BACK OF BEYOND

3,4,3,2,3
YOU CANT WIN EM ALL

3,4,3,5
ALL OVER THE PLACE
FOR LOVE NOR MONEY

3,4,3,5 *contd.*
GET INTO HOT WATER
GOD SAVE THE QUEEN
GOT INTO HOT WATER
ONE OVER THE EIGHT
PUT BACK THE CLOCK
THE SAME OLD STORY
THE SKYS THE LIMIT
TOM DICK AND HARRY

3,4,4,4
GET ONES HEAD DOWN
GOT ONES HEAD DOWN
LAY DOWN ONES ARMS
LAY DOWN ONES LIFE
LET ONES HAIR DOWN

3,4,5,3
EAT YOUR HEART OUT

3,4,8
RES IPSA LOQUITUR
THE FOUR FREEDOMS
THE GOOD SHEPHERD
THE PLOT THICKENS
TRY ONES PATIENCE

3,5,2,5
LET THERE BE LIGHT
PER ARDUA AD ASTRA
THE COAST IS CLEAR
THE SPORT OF KINGS

3,5,3,4
ALL ALONG THE LINE
HIT BELOW THE BELT
THE CHIPS ARE DOWN
THE WORSE FOR WEAR
YOU NEVER CAN TELL

3,5,7
AIR CHIEF MARSHAL
ALL NIGHT SITTING
DOW JONES AVERAGE
DRY ROAST PEANUTS
DRY STONE WALLING
HIP JOINT DISEASE
ICE CREAM PARLOUR
THE GREEK CALENDS
THE MERRY MONARCH
THE WEIRD SISTERS

3,6,2,4
TOO CLEVER BY HALF

3,6,3,3
SEE NAPLES AND DIE
THE GLOVES ARE OFF

3,6,4,2
THE POWERS THAT BE

3,6,6
AGE BEFORE BEAUTY
BOW STREET RUNNER
DEO OPTIMO MAXIMO

FAN TAILED PIGEON
LEG BEFORE WICKET
NON COMPOS MENTIS
NON PROFIT MAKING
ONE PARENT FAMILY
OUR MUTUAL FRIEND
THE BRIGHT LIGHTS
THE CHOSEN PEOPLE
THE COMMON PEOPLE
THE FOURTH ESTATE
THE WEAKER VESSEL

3,7,5
PRE EMPTION RIGHT
THE MORNING AFTER
THE SUPREME BEING

3,8,4
FOR GOODNESS SAKE
NEW SCOTLAND YARD
THE PROMISED LAND

3,12
AIR CONDITIONING
LAY IMPROPRIATOR
NON COMMISSIONED
NON CONTRIBUTORY
NON INTERVENTION
NON PROFESSIONAL
PAN PRESBYTERIAN
PRE ESTABLISHING
TEN COMMANDMENTS
THE COMMONWEALTH

4,1,4,2,4
TAKE A NAME IN VAIN
TOOK A NAME IN VAIN

4,1,4,6
TAKE A DEEP BREATH
TOOK A DEEP BREATH

4,1,5,2,3
KNEW A THING OR TWO
KNOW A THING OR TWO

4,1,5,5
MADE A CLEAN BREAK
MADE A CLEAN SWEEP
MADE A FRESH START
MAKE A CLEAN BREAK
MAKE A CLEAN SWEEP
MAKE A FRESH START

4,1,6,4
PLAY A LOSING GAME

4,1,10
WITH A DIFFERENCE

4,2,1,4,4
CALM AS A MILL POND
ONCE IN A BLUE MOON

4,2,1,8
COOL AS A CUCUMBER

DEAD AS A DOORNAIL
MUCH OF A MUCHNESS
ONCE IN A LIFETIME
TURN ON A SIXPENCE

4,2,2,3,4
GETS IT IN THE NECK
LAID IT ON THE LINE
LAYS IT ON THE LINE
TAKE IT ON THE CHIN
TOOK IT ON THE CHIN

4,2,2,5,2
TAKE IT OR LEAVE IT

4,2,2,7
CAME UP TO SCRATCH
COME UP TO SCRATCH
TURN IN ON ONESELF

4,2,3,3,3
STOP ME AND BUY ONE

4,2,3,6
BATS IN THE BELFRY
BORN IN THE PURPLE
BURR IN THE THROAT
CAME TO THE RESCUE
COME TO THE RESCUE
CRUX OF THE MATTER
DOWN TO THE GROUND
FALL TO THE GROUND
FELL TO THE GROUND
GOES TO ANY LENGTH
HARP ON ONE STRING
HEAD OF THE FAMILY
HEIR TO THE THRONE
JACK IN THE PULPIT
JACK OF ALL TRADES
JUMP AT THE CHANCE
KING OF THE CASTLE
KING OF THE JUNGLE
LILY OF THE VALLEY
LUMP IN THE THROAT
PICK UP THE PIECES
PICK UP THE THREAD
PUSS IN THE CORNER
RAZE TO THE GROUND
RUNS IN THE FAMILY
SHIP OF THE DESERT
SIGN OF THE ZODIAC
SLIP OF THE TONGUE
SLOW ON THE UPTAKE
SPUR OF THE MOMENT
THIN ON THE GROUND

4,2,4,2,3
LOVE ME LOVE MY DOG

4,2,4,5
ANTS IN ONES PANTS
DIED IN ONES BOOTS
DIES IN ONES BOOTS
DRAW IN ONES HORNS

4,2,4,5 *contd.*
DREW IN ONES HORNS
GIRD UP ONES LOINS
HANG UP ONES BOOTS
HUNG UP ONES BOOTS
LIED IN ONES TEETH
LIES IN ONES TEETH
SANK TO ONES KNEES
SINK TO ONES KNEES
SITS ON ONES HANDS
SKIN OF ONES TEETH
SURE OF ONES FACTS

4,2,5,1,3
ROOM TO SWING A CAT

4,2,5,4
GETS TO FIRST BASE
TAKE IT LYING DOWN
TOOK IT LYING DOWN

4,2,6,3
BACK TO SQUARE ONE

4,2,9
AXIS OF INCIDENCE
BILL OF ADVENTURE
DEED OF ACCESSION
EGGS IN MOONSHINE
HEAD ON COLLISION
NEAR AS NINEPENCE
ODDS ON FAVOURITE
PAIR OF CALLIPERS
PAIR OF COMPASSES
PAIR OF STOCKINGS
PUTS IN MOTHBALLS
ROCK OF GIBRALTAR
STAR OF BETHLEHEM
STAY OF EXECUTION
TAKE NO PRISONERS
TILT AT WINDMILLS
TOOK NO PRISONERS
TREE OF KNOWLEDGE
WRIT OF PRIVILEGE

4,3,2,3,3
LONG ARM OF THE LAW

4,3,2,6
RUNS OUT OF PETROL

4,3,3,3,2
PUTS THE TIN HAT ON

4,3,3,5
KEEP OFF THE GRASS
PLAY CAT AND MOUSE
PULL FOR THE SHORE
RIDE OUT THE STORM

4,3,4,2,2
GETS THE HANG OF IT
MADE THE BEST OF IT
MADE THE MOST OF IT
MAKE THE BEST OF IT

MAKE THE MOST OF IT

4,3,4,4
GAVE THE GAME AWAY
GIVE THE GAME AWAY
HAVE TWO LEFT FEET
LETS THE SIDE DOWN
OPEN AND SHUT CASE
OVER AND DONE WITH
PAID FOR ONES SINS
PAYS FOR ONES SINS
RUNS THE RULE OVER
WISH YOU WERE HERE

4,3,5,3
GOES THE WHOLE HOG
LOOK THE OTHER WAY
SONG AND DANCE MAN
TAKE THE CHILL OFF
TAKE THE WRAPS OFF
TOOK THE CHILL OFF
TOOK THE WRAPS OFF

4,3,6,2
GETS THE BREEZE UP
PUTS THE KIBOSH ON
PUTS THE SCREWS ON

4,3,8
BEER AND SKITTLES
BEGS THE QUESTION
DRAW THE CURTAINS
DREW THE CURTAINS
FROM THE SHOULDER
GOES THE DISTANCE
LIKE THE CLAPPERS
POPS THE QUESTION
RUNS THE GAUNTLET
WEAR THE BREECHES
WEAR THE TROUSERS
WORE THE BREECHES
WORE THE TROUSERS

4,4,1,6
WORK LIKE A TROJAN

4,4,2,5
CAME HOME TO ROOST
COME HOME TO ROOST
COME RAIN OR SHINE
FROM HAND TO MOUTH
FROM STEM TO STERN
HAVE WHAT IT TAKES
LOOK BACK IN ANGER

4,4,3,4
BOLT FROM THE BLUE
DONT ROCK THE BOAT
GETS ONES OWN BACK
GOES OVER THE EDGE
GOES OVER THE WALL
GONE WITH THE WIND
LONG LIVE THE KING
RAIN CATS AND DOGS

RISE WITH THE LARK
SWAM WITH THE TIDE
SWIM WITH THE TIDE
WENT OVER THE EDGE
WENT OVER THE WALL

4,4,5,2
DIGS ONES HEELS IN
POUR COLD WATER ON
PULL ONES SOCKS UP
SETS ONES HEART ON

4,4,7
ANTE POST BETTING
BALL ROOM DANCING
BODY LINE BOWLING
FALL OVER ONESELF
FELL OVER ONESELF
HALF TERM HOLIDAY
JUST GOOD FRIENDS
LINE ONES POCKETS
LOCH NESS MONSTER
LORD HIGH ADMIRAL
LORD HIGH STEWARD
LOSE ONES BALANCE
LOSE ONES FOOTING
LOST ONES BALANCE
LOST ONES FOOTING
PALM TREE JUSTICE
PULL ONES PUNCHES
ROAD FUND LICENCE
ROLL NECK SWEATER
ROLY POLY PUDDING
RUNS INTO TROUBLE
SOFT SHOE SHUFFLE
TAKE INTO ACCOUNT
TAKE SOME BEATING
TAKE UPON ONESELF
TIME ZONE DISEASE
TIME ZONE FATIGUE
TOOK INTO ACCOUNT
TOOK SOME BEATING
TOOK UPON ONESELF
WETS ONES WHISTLE
WORK ONES PASSAGE

4,5,3,3
PASS ROUND THE HAT
REDS UNDER THE BED

4,5,4,2
MADE SHORT WORK OF
MAKE SHORT WORK OF

4,5,6
DAMP PROOF COURSE
FULL DRESS DEBATE
HOLY ROMAN EMPIRE
POST DATED CHEQUE
READ WRITE MEMORY
STOP FRAME CAMERA
WIND CHILL FACTOR
WITH BATED BREATH

4,6,5
FOUR STROKE CYCLE
MANY HEADED BEAST
RIFT VALLEY FEVER
TAKE FRENCH LEAVE
TOOK FRENCH LEAVE
WALL STREET CRASH

4,7,4
FINE TOOTHED COMB
GAVE ONESELF AIRS
GAVE ONESELF AWAY
GIVE ONESELF AIRS
GIVE ONESELF AWAY
HOPE AGAINST HOPE
KEEP BRITAIN TIDY
PEAK VIEWING TIME
RACE AGAINST TIME
SING ANOTHER SONG
SING ANOTHER TUNE
WEAR SEVERAL HATS
WORE SEVERAL HATS

4,8,3
ANTI AIRCRAFT GUN
DAVY CROCKETT HAT

4,9,2
MADE MINCEMEAT OF
MAKE MINCEMEAT OF

4,11
BOMB CALORIMETER
CAPE NIGHTINGALE
DICK WHITTINGTON
DUAL CARRIAGEWAY
DUAL PERSONALITY
FIRE WORSHIPPING
FOUL MOUTHEDNESS
FOUR DIMENSIONAL
FREE ASSOCIATION
FREE HEARTEDNESS
GOES UNDERGROUND
GOOD NATUREDNESS
HALF HEARTEDNESS
HALF WELLINGTONS
HARD HEARTEDNESS
HEIR PRESUMPTIVE
HERB CHRISTOPHER
KIND HEARTEDNESS
LIVE PERFORMANCE
LONG SIGHTEDNESS
LORD CHAMBERLAIN
MASS OBSERVATION
MASS RADIOGRAPHY
MOOG SYNTHESIZER
NEAR SIGHTEDNESS
OPEN HEARTEDNESS
OPEN HOSTILITIES
OPEN SCHOLARSHIP
POST MILLENARIAN
PURE MATHEMATICS

RENT RESTRICTION
ROOM TEMPERATURE
SADO MASOCHISTIC
SAVE APPEARANCES
SELF ADVANCEMENT
SELF COMPLACENCE
SELF CONFIDENTLY
SELF DESTRUCTION
SELF DESTRUCTIVE
SELF DETERMINING
SELF DEVELOPMENT
SELF EXAMINATION
SELF EXPLANATORY
SELF HUMILIATION
SELF IMPORTANTLY
SELF IMPROVEMENT
SELF POLLINATION
SELF PORTRAITURE
SELF PROPAGATING
SELF REALISATION
SELF REALIZATION
SELF SACRIFICING
SELF SUFFICIENCY
SEMI INDEPENDENT
SOFT COMMODITIES
SOFT FURNISHINGS
SPOT ADVERTISING
TRUE HEARTEDNESS
VICE CHAMBERLAIN
WARM HEARTEDNESS
WELL CONDITIONED
WELL INTENTIONED
WELL UPHOLSTERED
WENT UNDERGROUND
WITH COMPLIMENTS
XMAS DECORATIONS

5,1,4,2,3
KNOWS A MOVE OR TWO

5,1,4,5
FLOGS A DEAD HORSE
KEEPS A GOOD HOUSE

5,1,5,2,2
MAKES A NIGHT OF IT

5,1,5,4
KEEPS A PLACE WARM
KEEPS A TIGHT REIN
NEVER A CROSS WORD
WALKS A TIGHT ROPE

5,1,9
NURSE A GRIEVANCE
TAKES A RAINCHECK

5,2,1,4,3
HAPPY AS A SAND BOY

5,2,1,7
BIRDS OF A FEATHER
CLEAN AS A WHISTLE
HORNS OF A DILEMMA

LIGHT AS A FEATHER
PROUD AS A PEACOCK
TALKS IN A WHISPER

5,2,2,3,3
GOING UP IN THE AIR

5,2,2,6
POINT OF NO RETURN

5,2,3,5
ARMED TO THE TEETH
BURNT AT THE STAKE
CARDS ON THE TABLE
CLERK OF THE COURT
FIGHT TO THE DEATH
FLICK OF THE WRIST
FLING TO THE WINDS
FLUNG TO THE WINDS
FOAMS AT THE MOUTH
FRONT OF THE HOUSE
GIVES UP THE GHOST
GOING BY THE BOARD
GOING ON ALL FOURS
HOVER ON THE BRINK
JEWEL IN THE CROWN
LEADS TO THE ALTAR
MELTS IN THE MOUTH
PILED ON THE AGONY
PILES ON THE AGONY
PLAYS TO THE CROWD
RAISE TO THE BENCH
SCENE OF THE CRIME
SNAKE IN THE GRASS
TAKES UP THE SLACK
THORN IN THE FLESH
THREW IN THE CARDS
THREW IN THE TOWEL
THREW TO THE WINDS
THROW IN THE CARDS
THROW IN THE TOWEL
THROW TO THE WINDS
TOUGH AS OLD BOOTS
TRICK OF THE TRADE
WATER ON THE BRAIN
WOMAN OF THE WORLD

5,2,4,4
FALLS ON DEAF EARS
FALLS ON ONES FEET
GOING TO ONES HEAD
HOLDS UP ONES HEAD
KEEPS AN OPEN MIND
LIVED BY ONES WITS
LIVES BY ONES WITS
MAKES UP ONES MIND
PRICK UP ONES EARS
RESTS ON ONES OARS
STICK TO ONES GUNS
STUCK TO ONES GUNS
TURNS ON ONES HEEL
TURNS UP ONES NOSE

5,2,5,3
CATCH AS CATCH CAN

5,2,8
CORNO DI BASSETTO
ERROR OF JUDGMENT
ERROR OF OMISSION
GOING TO EXTREMES
LYING IN HOSPITAL
PICKS AN ARGUMENT
PIECE OF NONSENSE
PLACE OF BUSINESS
POWER OF ATTORNEY
QUEEN OF PUDDINGS
ROGER DE COVERLEY
SENDS TO COVENTRY
STAMP OF APPROVAL
STAND ON CEREMONY
STAND UP COMEDIAN
STOOD ON CEREMONY
SWORD OF DAMOCLES
TEARS OF LAUGHTER
TOWER OF STRENGTH
TRIAL OF STRENGTH

5,3,2,5
LAUGH OUT OF COURT

5,3,3,4
EVERY NOW AND THEN
LIVED OFF THE LAND
LIVES OFF THE LAND
MONEY FOR OLD ROPE
REACH FOR THE MOON
RIGHT OFF THE REEL

5,3,4,3
PAINT THE TOWN RED
PULLS THE LONG BOW
READS THE RIOT ACT
SINCE THE YEAR DOT
WASTE NOT WANT NOT

5,3,7
ABOVE THE WEATHER
AIDED AND ABETTED
ALIVE AND KICKING
BEATS THE RETREAT
BLOOD AND THUNDER
BLOWS THE WHISTLE
BOWED AND SCRAPED
BOXED THE COMPASS
BOXES THE COMPASS
CHEAT THE GALLOWS
CHOPS AND CHANGES
CROSS THE CHANNEL
CROSS THE RUBICON
DAVID AND GOLIATH
DOING THE HONOURS
DRAWS THE LONGBOW
DROPS THE SUBJECT
DUTCH ELM DISEASE
FENDS FOR ONESELF

FRONT END LOADING
GOING FOR NOTHING
LOOKS FOR TROUBLE
MAKES THE RUNNING
OPENS THE INNINGS
OPENS THE SCORING
PICKS AND CHOOSES
PULLS THE STRINGS
RINGS THE CHANGES
SHEET FED PRINTER
STARS AND STRIPES
SWEEP THE CHIMNEY
SWEPT THE CHIMNEY
SWORD AND BUCKLER
TAKEN FOR GRANTED
TAKES FOR GRANTED
TAKES THE BISCUIT
THREE DAY EVENTER
TURNS THE STOMACH
UNDER THE COUNTER
UNDER THE WEATHER
WALKS THE STREETS
WIELD THE SCEPTRE
WINES AND SPIRITS
WORTH THE WHISTLE

5,4,1,5
GOING LIKE A DREAM
LAUGH LIKE A DRAIN
SHAKE LIKE A JELLY
SHOOK LIKE A JELLY
WORKS LIKE A CHARM

5,4,3,3
GOING ONES OWN WAY
GOING OVER THE TOP
HUNTS HIGH AND LOW
SHOOT FROM THE HIP
UNDER LOCK AND KEY

5,4,4,2
KEEPS ONES CHIN UP
KEEPS ONES HAIR ON
KEEPS ONES HAND IN
POKED ONES NOSE IN
POKES ONES NOSE IN
TURNS ONES HAND TO

5,4,6
BEATS ONES BRAINS
BEATS ONES BREAST
CATCH ONES BREATH
COMES FULL CIRCLE
GOING INTO DETAIL
GOING INTO HIDING
HOLDS ONES BREATH
HOLDS ONES TONGUE
HORSE SHOE MAGNET
KEEPS ONES TEMPER
KNOWS ONES ONIONS
LICKS ONES WOUNDS
LOOSE LEAF BINDER

LOSES ONES TEMPER
MENDS ONES FENCES
MORAL HIGH GROUND
PAPER TAPE READER
PULLS ONES WEIGHT
RACKS ONES BRAINS
RAISE ONES SIGHTS
SHORT TERM MEMORY
SHOUT BLUE MURDER
STAGE DOOR JOHNNY
STAND ONES GROUND
STIRS ONES STUMPS
STOOD ONES GROUND
TAKES ONES CHANCE
TAKES ONES CHOICE
THREE RING CIRCUS
TIGHT ROPE WALKER
VENTS ONES SPLEEN
WHATS YOUR POISON

5,5,5
CROWN GREEN BOWLS
FIFTY PENCE PIECE
FORTY EIGHT HOURS
FRONT WHEEL DRIVE
KEEPS UNDER WRAPS
MONTE CARLO RALLY
NIGHT AFTER NIGHT
POINT BLANK RANGE
SOLID STATE LIGHT
SPLIT LEVEL HOUSE
THREE PIECE SUITE

5,6,2,2
THINK BETTER OF IT
THINK LITTLE OF IT

5,6,4
AUDIO VISUAL AIDS
CLOUD CUCKOO LAND
FIRST DEGREE BURN
LAPIS LAZULI BLUE
LAPIS LAZULI WARE
ROYAL ALBERT HALL
SEVEN DEADLY SINS
SLING BACKED SHOE
THIRD DEGREE BURN
THREE LEGGED RACE

5,7,3
EARLY CLOSING DAY
LIGHT MACHINE GUN
PLAIN CLOTHES MAN
STARK STARING MAD
WORLD WITHOUT END
WRITE ONESELF OFF
WROTE ONESELF OFF

5,10
ANNUS HORRIBILIS
BATCH PROCESSING
BLAST FURNACEMAN
BRAKE HORSEPOWER

5,10 *contd.*
CABLE TELEVISION
CARRY CONVICTION
CASTS ASPERSIONS
CLOUD COMPELLING
COURT MARTIALLED
CROSS QUESTIONED
DAILY OCCURRENCE
DEVIL WORSHIPPER
DRILL INSTRUCTOR
EXTRA CURRICULAR
FATAL ATTRACTION
FIRST LIEUTENANT
FIRST PRINCIPLES
FRESH VEGETABLES
GRAND INQUISITOR
GREAT GRANDCHILD
GREEN REVOLUTION
GREEN WOODPECKER
INFRA DIGNITATEM
IRISH SWEEPSTAKE
LEGAL SEPARATION
LIGHT HEADEDNESS
LIGHT LITERATURE
LIGHT MINDEDNESS
LOCAL GOVERNMENT
LORDS LIEUTENANT
MANIC DEPRESSIVE
MORAL PHILOSOPHY
MORAL REARMAMENT
NOBLE MINDEDNESS
NORTH COUNTRYMAN
NORTH EASTWARDLY
NORTH WESTWARDLY
OWNER OCCUPATION
PARTY GOVERNMENT
PEACE CONFERENCE
PENAL SETTLEMENT
PHOTO MECHANICAL
POLAR EXPEDITION
PRESS CONFERENCE
PRICE COMMISSION
PRIVY COUNCILLOR
PROOF CORRECTING
PROOF CORRECTION
QUASI HISTORICAL
QUICK WITTEDNESS
RADIO GRAMOPHONE
RAISE OBJECTIONS
RIGHT HANDEDNESS
RIGHT HONOURABLE
RIGHT MINDEDNESS
RISUS SARDONICUS
ROBIN GOODFELLOW
ROUND SHOULDERED
ROYAL COMMISSION
ROYAL TOURNAMENT
RUDDY COMPLEXION
SALES RESISTANCE
SENSE PERCEPTION

SLAVE TRAFFICKER
SOBER MINDEDNESS
SOUTH EASTWARDLY
SOUTH WESTWARDLY
SPACE TRAVELLING
SPLIT INFINITIVE
STAMP COLLECTION
STAND OFFISHNESS
STATE DEPARTMENT
STEAM NAVIGATION
SUGAR PLANTATION
TABLE DECORATION
TOTAL ABSTINENCE
UNDER PRIVILEGED
UNDER PRODUCTION
UPPER ATMOSPHERE
VITAL STATISTICS
WHITE RHINOCEROS
WOODY NIGHTSHADE
WRONG HEADEDNESS
YOURS FAITHFULLY
YOUTH HOSTELLING

6,1,3,5
STRIKE A BAD PATCH
STRUCK A BAD PATCH

6,1,4,2,2
HAVING A TIME OF IT
MAKING A MEAL OF IT

6,1,4,4
HAVING A GOOD TIME
MAKING A FAST BUCK
TAKING A BACK SEAT

6,1,5,3
TURNED A BLIND EYE

6,1,8
HAVING A BASINFUL
MAKING A COMEBACK
STEALS A MARRIAGE

6,2,1,6
HUNGRY AS A HUNTER
KICKED UP A RUMPUS
KICKED UP A SHINDY

6,2,2,5
LAYING IT ON THICK
LAYING ON OF HANDS

6,2,3,4
BEWARE OF THE BULL
BRIDGE OF THE NOSE
COMING TO THE BOIL
CURLED UP AND DIED
DRIVES TO THE WALL
KITTEN ON THE KEYS
KNIGHT OF THE ROAD
KNIGHT OF THE WHIP
LAYING ON THE LINE
LEADER OF THE BAND
LIVING IN THE PAST

LOOKED IN THE FACE
MIDDLE OF THE ROAD
NECTAR OF THE GODS
PACING UP AND DOWN
PIPPED AT THE POST
RISING TO THE BAIT
ROOTED TO THE SPOT
ROTTEN TO THE CORE
SCORED AN OWN GOAL
SCORES AN OWN GOAL
SCRUFF OF THE NECK
SILENT AS THE TOMB
SMELLS OF THE LAMP
SOAKED TO THE SKIN
TAKING TO THE ROAD
WALKED UP AND DOWN
WHITES OF THE EYES

6,2,4,3
SKATED ON THIN ICE
SKATES ON THIN ICE
TAKING TO ONES BED
THROWS IN ONES LOT
THROWS UP ONES CAP

6,2,7
BATTLE OF BRITAIN
BREACH OF PROMISE
BRINGS TO ACCOUNT
CALLED TO ACCOUNT
CENTRE OF GRAVITY
CENTRE OF INERTIA
CHANGE OF SCENERY
CHURCH OF ENGLAND
COMEDY OF HUMOURS
COMEDY OF MANNERS
COMITY OF NATIONS
HAUNCH OF VENISON
JOINED UP WRITING
LEAGUE OF NATIONS
LITTLE OR NOTHING
MATTER OF OPINION
OFFERS AN OPINION
PAYING IN ADVANCE
PILLAR OF SOCIETY
PLUCKS UP COURAGE
POCKET AN AFFRONT
PURPLE OF CASSIUS
RAISED AN EYEBROW
RAISES AN EYEBROW
SAFETY IN NUMBERS
SCALES OF JUSTICE
SECOND IN COMMAND
SHIVER ME TIMBERS
SHIVER MY TIMBERS
STATUE OF LIBERTY
STICKS AT NOTHING
TAKING IN LODGERS
TALKED IN RIDDLES

6,3,3,3
LIFTED THE LID OFF

6,3,3,3 *contd.*
TAKING THE LID OFF

6,3,4,2
PULLED THE PLUG ON
THROWS THE BOOK AT

6,3,6
ANYONE FOR TENNIS
ASCEND THE THRONE
BEHIND THE SCENES
BEYOND THE FRINGE
BITING THE BULLET
BREAKS NEW GROUND
BUBBLE AND SQUEAK
CASTOR AND POLLUX
CAUGHT AND BOWLED
CAUGHT RED HANDED
CHASED THE DRAGON
CHASES THE DRAGON
CORNER THE MARKET
DODGED THE COLUMN
DODGES THE COLUMN
FUNNEL WEB SPIDER
GRASPS THE NETTLE
GREASE THE WHEELS
GROUND NUT SCHEME
HAMMER AND SICKLE
HANSEL AND GRETEL
INCOME TAX DEMAND
KICKED THE BUCKET
LATTER DAY SAINTS
LOAVES AND FISHES
MAKING THE ROUNDS
MIDDLE AGE SPREAD
OILING THE WHEELS
PESTLE AND MORTAR
PLAYED THE MARKET
PLAYED THE WANTON
PLUMBS THE DEPTHS
POISON PEN LETTER
POPEYE THE SAILOR
PRUNES AND PRISMS
PUSHED THE BOTTLE
PUSHES THE BOTTLE
RAIDED THE MARKET
RAISED THE MARKET
RAISES THE MARKET
SEEING THE SIGHTS
SETTLE OLD SCORES
SIGNED THE PLEDGE
SINBAD THE SAILOR
SPOILT FOR CHOICE
STAYED THE COURSE
STOCKS AND SHARES
TABLES AND CHAIRS
TAKING THE MICKEY
TAKING THE PLUNGE
TIPPED THE SCALES
TREADS THE BOARDS
TURNED THE CORNER

TURNED THE TABLES
WINING AND DINING
WORKED THE ORACLE

6,4,1,4
DRINKS LIKE A FISH
LIVING LIKE A LORD
SERVED WITH A WRIT
SERVES WITH A WRIT

6,4,2,3
PLAYED HARD TO GET

6,4,3,2
STICKS ONES OAR IN
WORMED ONES WAY IN

6,4,5
BITING ONES THUMB
BREAKS ONES HEART
COOKED ONES GOOSE
CRAMPS ONES STYLE
DICING WITH DEATH
DINING ROOM TABLE
DOUBLE YOUR MONEY
EATING ONES WORDS
FAMOUS LAST WORDS
GINGER BEER PLANT
INDIAN ROPE TRICK
KICKED INTO TOUCH
KICKED ONES HEELS
KNOCKS INTO SHAPE
LADDER BACK CHAIR
LEAVES WELL ALONE
LICKED INTO SHAPE
LICKED ONES CHOPS
LOSING ONES NERVE
LOSING ONES SHIRT
OPENED ONES HEART
PLAYED ONES HUNCH
PLIGHT ONES TROTH
POPPED ONES CLOGS
RAISED ONES GLASS
RAISED ONES VOICE
RAISES ONES GLASS
RAISES ONES VOICE
RUBBED ONES HANDS
SAVING ONES BACON
SHOWED ONES PACES
SPLITS ONES SIDES
SPREAD ONES WINGS
STRUTS ONES STUFF
SUCKED ONES THUMB
TAKING ONES LEAVE
TWENTY FOUR HOURS
WASHED ONES HANDS
WHITER THAN WHITE

6,5,4
BULLET PROOF VEST
COFFEE TABLE BOOK
DOUBLE WHITE LINE
LOSING HANDS DOWN

MAKING FIRST BASE
RIDING ROUGH SHOD
SECOND CLASS MAIL
SECOND CLASS POST
YELLOW BRICK ROAD

6,6,3
EATING HUMBLE PIE
TURNED INSIDE OUT

6,9
ACTION COMMITTEE
ANIMAL MAGNETISM
AURORA AUSTRALIS
BEFORE MENTIONED
BEYOND SUSPICION
BINARY OPERATION
BLONDE BOMBSHELL
BONDED WAREHOUSE
BRONZE MEDALLIST
BUNKER MENTALITY
CANVAS STRETCHER
CARNAL KNOWLEDGE
CHARGE DAFFAIRES
COLOUR BLINDNESS
COMMON KNOWLEDGE
COOKED BREAKFAST
CRADLE SNATCHING
CREASE RESISTANT
CRYPTO COMMUNIST
DIESEL HYDRAULIC
DOLLAR DIPLOMACY
DOUBLE BARRELLED
DOUBLE PNEUMONIA
DOUBLE STANDARDS
DUPLEX APARTMENT
EASTER OFFERINGS
ESCAPE MECHANISM
FAMILY ALLOWANCE
FATHER CHRISTMAS
FELLOW TRAVELLER
FLOWER ARRANGING
FLYING PHALANGER
FOURTH DIMENSION
FRENCH POLISHING
GAINED ADMISSION
GOLDEN DELICIOUS
GOLDEN HANDSHAKE
GOLDEN RECTANGLE
GOLDEN RETRIEVER
GOLDEN SAXIFRAGE
GOSSIP COLUMNIST
HAVING HYSTERICS
HEALTH INSURANCE
HIGHER EDUCATION
INDIAN LIQUORICE
INDIAN WRESTLING
INDOOR FIREWORKS
INFANT MORTALITY
JUMPED OVERBOARD
LABOUR INTENSIVE

6,9 *contd.*
LESSER CELANDINE
LIEBIG CONDENSER
LITTLE ENGLANDER
LONDON TRANSPORT
MARINE INSURANCE
MARKET GARDENING
MASTER CARPENTER
MASTER CRAFTSMAN
MEADOW SAXIFRAGE
MENTAL BREAKDOWN
MIDDLE EASTERNER
MOVING STAIRCASE
MUTUAL INSURANCE
NUMBER CRUNCHING
PAYING ATTENTION
PENCIL SHARPENER
PERIOD FURNITURE
PLEURO PNEUMONIA
POLICE CONSTABLE
POLICE INSPECTOR
PUBLIC OWNERSHIP
PUBLIC RELATIONS
PUBLIC TRANSPORT
PUBLIC UTILITIES
RACING CERTAINTY
RADIUM EMANATION
REFUSE COLLECTOR
REGIUS PROFESSOR
RIDING COMMITTEE
RUBBED SHOULDERS
SALAMI TECHNIQUE
SALOON PASSENGER
SCHOOL INSPECTOR
SECOND ADVENTIST
SECOND CHILDHOOD
SELECT COMMITTEE
SERIAL TECHNIQUE
SHABBY GENTILITY
SHADOW PANTOMIME
SHRINK RESISTANT
SILVER MEDALLIST
SOCIAL DEMOCRACY
SOCIAL INSURANCE
SOCIAL SECRETARY
SPIRAL STAIRCASE
STABLE COMPANION
STANDS CORRECTED
STRAIT WAISTCOAT
STREET FURNITURE
TAKING EXCEPTION
TAKING LIBERTIES
TENDER HEARTEDLY
THROWN OVERBOARD
THROWS OVERBOARD
TICKET COLLECTOR
TICKET INSPECTOR
TIPPED CIGARETTE
TORQUE CONVERTER
UNFAIR ADVANTAGE

UNITED PROVINCES
VIRGIN PARCHMENT
WAITED PATIENTLY
WALRUS MOUSTACHE
WASHED OVERBOARD
WHITED SEPULCHRE
WIENER SCHNITZEL
WILLOW PATTERNED
WINDOW GARDENING
WOMANS INTUITION
WONDER MONGERING
YELLOW PIMPERNEL

7,1,4,3
PULLING A FAST ONE
TURNING A DEAF EAR

7,1,7
BEATING A RETREAT
DROPPED A CLANGER
PULLING A FLANKER
SERVING A PURPOSE
STAGING A PROTEST
STRIKES A BARGAIN
VITAMIN B COMPLEX

7,2,1,5
DRAWING TO A CLOSE
KICKING UP A STINK
PUTTING UP A FIGHT

7,2,2,4
LEAVING IT AT THAT
QUARTER OF AN HOUR

7,2,3,3
CASTLES IN THE AIR
CHAMPED AT THE BIT
ECLIPSE OF THE SUN
GETTING IN THE WAY
NIPPING IN THE BUD
PICKING UP THE TAB
PUTTING ON THE MAP

7,2,6
BENEFIT OF CLERGY
COMMITS TO MEMORY
COUNCIL OF EUROPE
COUNCIL OF STATES
FREEDOM OF SPEECH
HARBOUR OF REFUGE
HOLDING TO RANSOM
PICKING TO PIECES
PILLARS OF WISDOM
PLACING ON RECORD
POCKETS AN INSULT
PREFECT OF POLICE
PULLING TO PIECES
PUTTING IT MILDLY
PUTTING ON RECORD
PUTTING TO RIGHTS
RUNNING TO GROUND
SETTING AT NOUGHT

SETTING TO RIGHTS
SILENCE IS GOLDEN
STRANGE TO RELATE
TURNING UP TRUMPS
WALKING ON TIPTOE
WASHING UP LIQUID
WINNING ON POINTS

7,3,1,4
PLAYING FOR A DRAW

7,3,2,3
ANOTHER CUP OF TEA

7,3,3,2
BETWEEN YOU AND ME

7,3,5
AGAINST THE CLOCK
AGAINST THE GRAIN
BEATING THE CLOCK
CALLING THE SHOTS
CHAPTER AND VERSE
CLEARED THE DECKS
CONFUSE THE ISSUE
COOKING THE BOOKS
COSTING THE EARTH
CROSSED THE FLOOR
CROSSES THE FLOOR
CUTTING THE CARDS
DELIVER THE GOODS
FEELING THE PINCH
FORCING THE ISSUE
HELPING THE CAUSE
HOLDING THE FLOOR
HUGGING THE COAST
JUMPING OFF PLACE
JUMPING THE QUEUE
KEEPING THE PEACE
KNOWING THE ROPES
KNOWING THE SCORE
LETTING OFF STEAM
MEXICAN HAT DANCE
MUSTARD AND CRESS
PAPERED THE HOUSE
PEACHES AND CREAM
PERSONA NON GRATA
PLAYING THE DEVIL
PLAYING THE FIELD
PLOUGHS THE SANDS
PUTTING THE STONE
QUEERED THE PITCH
QUITTED THE SCENE
RAISING THE ALARM
READING THE SIGNS
ROMULUS AND REMUS
SELLING THE DUMMY
SETTING THE SCENE
SHEATHE THE SWORD
SLIPPED THE CABLE
SOUNDED THE ALARM
SWELLED THE RANKS

7,3,5 *contd.*
TELLING THE TRUTH
THOUGHT THE WORST
THROUGH THE NIGHT
TIPPING THE SCALE
TOSSING THE CABER
TURNING THE SCREW
VANILLA ICE CREAM
WALKING THE PLANK
WATCHED THE CLOCK
WATCHES THE CLOCK
WEATHER THE STORM
WHISTLE AND FLUTE
WINNING THE POOLS

7,4,1,3
HOLDING DOWN A JOB

7,4,4
BLOWING ONES MIND
BROUGHT INTO LINE
BROUGHT INTO PLAY
CHANGED ONES MIND
CHANGED ONES TUNE
CHANGES ONES MIND
CHANGES ONES TUNE
CHINESE TAKE AWAY
CLOSING DOWN SALE
CLOSING ONES EYES
CRICKED ONES NECK
CUTTING BOTH WAYS
DRAGGED ONES FEET
FALLING INTO LINE
FEATHER ONES NEST
FEEDING ONES FACE
FINDING ONES FEET
FOLDING ONES ARMS
FOLLOWS ONES NOSE
GETTING ONES GOAT
HANGING ONES HEAD
HEDGING ONES BETS
KEEPING GOOD TIME
KEEPING ONES COOL
KEEPING ONES HEAD
KEEPING ONES WORD
KNOWING FULL WELL
MENDING ONES WAYS
NUCLEAR FREE ZONE
PACKING ONES BAGS
PASSING ONES WORD
PICKING ONES SPOT
PLAYING WITH FIRE
POURING WITH RAIN
POWDERS ONES NOSE
PUSHING ONES LUCK
PUTTING ONES CASE
QUICKEN ONES PACE
RISKING ONES LIFE
ROLLING ONES EYES
RUNNING INTO DEBT
SELLING ONES SOUL

SHAKING ONES FIST
SHAKING ONES HEAD
SHOWING ONES FACE
SHOWING ONES HAND
SLIPPED ONES MIND
SMACKED ONES LIPS
STAKING ONES LIFE
STRETCH ONES LEGS
SUITING ONES BOOK
TEARING ONES HAIR
THUMBED ONES NOSE
TIGHTEN ONES BELT
TREATED LIKE DIRT
TURNING ONES HEAD
WATCHED ONES STEP
WATCHES ONES STEP
WHISTLE STOP TOUR
WORKING ONES WILL

7,5,3
KNOCKED SPOTS OFF

7,8
AERATED CONCRETE
AFRICAN ELEPHANT
AFRICAN MARIGOLD
AMATEUR CHAMPION
ANCIENT MONUMENT
BARGAIN BASEMENT
BERMUDA TRIANGLE
BRITISH RAILWAYS
BROTHEL CREEPERS
BURNING MOUNTAIN
BURNING QUESTION
CABINET MINISTER
CAREERS MISTRESS
CASTING DIRECTOR
CHAMBER PRACTICE
CHANNEL CROSSING
CHASING RAINBOWS
CHICKEN CHASSEUR
CHICKEN MARYLAND
CHINESE CHECKERS
CHINESE PAVILION
CHINESE WHISPERS
CHRISTY MINSTREL
CIRCUIT TRAINING
CLUBBED TOGETHER
COMPANY CHAIRMAN
COMPANY DIRECTOR
COMPANY PROMOTER
COMPLEX SENTENCE
CONCERT OVERTURE
COTTAGE HOSPITAL
COTTAGE INDUSTRY
COUNTER IRRITANT
COUNTER MOVEMENT
COUNTER PROPOSAL
CRICKET PAVILION
CUSTOMS OFFICIAL
DECIMAL CURRENCY

DECIMAL FRACTION
DECIMAL NOTATION
DEFENCE MINISTER
DIGITAL COMPUTER
DRAUGHT PROOFING
ENGLISH LANGUAGE
ENTENTE CORDIALE
ETERNAL TRIANGLE
EVENING PRIMROSE
EXPRESS DELIVERY
FALLING SICKNESS
FLANNEL TROUSERS
FOREIGN EXCHANGE
FORWARD DELIVERY
FUNERAL DIRECTOR
GAINING STRENGTH
GENERAL ASSEMBLY
GENERAL DELIVERY
GENERAL ELECTION
GENERAL EPISTLES
GENERAL FACTOTUM
GENERAL PRACTICE
GETTING CRACKING
GETTING TOGETHER
GRAVITY PLATFORM
GROWING TOGETHER
HACKNEY CARRIAGE
HACKNEY COACHMAN
HANGING BUTTRESS
HANGING TOGETHER
HARVEST FESTIVAL
HOLDING TOGETHER
HOUSING MINISTER
HUDDLED TOGETHER
INSIGHT LEARNING
INSULIN REACTION
INVITED AUDIENCE
ITALIAN VERMOUTH
JEEPERS CREEPERS
KICKING UPSTAIRS
KITCHEN GARDENER
KNIGHTS TEMPLARS
KNOCKED SIDEWAYS
KNOCKED TOGETHER
KNUCKLE SANDWICH
LANDING CARRIAGE
LAPSANG SOUCHONG
LATERAL THINKING
LATERAN COUNCILS
LEADING BUSINESS
LEADING QUESTION
LETTERS ROGATORY
LIMITED MONARCHY
LOGICAL ANALYSIS
LOGICAL DESIGNER
LOGICAL ELEMENTS
MACHINE LANGUAGE
MACHINE READABLE
MOLOTOV COCKTAIL
MORNING SICKNESS

7,8 *contd.*
MUSICAL DIRECTOR
MUSIQUE CONCRETE
MUTATIS MUTANDIS
NATURAL RELIGION
NATURAL THEOLOGY
NAUGHTY NINETIES
NEWGATE CALENDAR
NORFOLK DUMPLING
NUCLEAR REACTION
ORBITAL MOTORWAY
OUTSIDE INTEREST
PARASOL MUSHROOM
PARTIAL FRACTION
PARTIAL PRESSURE
PASSING JUDGMENT
PASSING SENTENCE
PASSIVE IMMUNITY
PASSIVE RESISTER
PEACOCK PHEASANT
PELICAN CROSSING
PERFECT INTERVAL
PERFECT STRANGER
PICTURE MOULDING
PICTURE POSTCARD
PICTURE RESTORER
PIECING TOGETHER
POVERTY STRICKEN
PRAIRIE SCHOONER
PRIVATE HOSPITAL
PRIVATE JUDGMENT
PROVOST SERGEANT
PULLING TOGETHER
PUTTING STRAIGHT
QUARTER SESSIONS
RAILWAY CARRIAGE
RAILWAY CROSSING
RAILWAY TERMINUS
RAINBOW COLOURED
RAINBOW DRESSING
RESERVE CURRENCY
RUFFLED FEATHERS
RUNNING SMOOTHLY
RUSHING HEADLONG
RUSSIAN DRESSING
RUSSIAN ROULETTE
SABBATH BREAKING
SAILORS HORNPIPE
SCATTER CUSHIONS
SECONDS PENDULUM
SERVICE INDUSTRY
SESSION MUSICIAN
SMOKING CARRIAGE
SPANISH CHESTNUT
SPANISH WINDLASS
SPECIAL DELIVERY
SPECIAL PLEADING
SPECIAL WARRANTY
STORAGE CAPACITY
SUBJECT SUPERIOR

SUNRISE INDUSTRY
SUSTAIN INJURIES
SYSTEMS ANALYSIS
TENSILE STRENGTH
UNKNOWN QUANTITY
UNLUCKY THIRTEEN
WEATHER BOARDING
WEATHER FORECAST
WEDDING CEREMONY
WISHFUL THINKING
WITCHES CAULDRON
WITHOUT CEREMONY
WITHOUT THINKING
WORKING MAJORITY

8,1,6
BREAKING A RECORD
BREAKING A STRIKE
BRINGING A CHARGE
PLOTTING A COURSE
SPILLING A BIBFUL
THROWING A WOBBLY

8,2,1,4
BRINGING TO A HEAD
GRINDING TO A HALT
STUBBORN AS A MULE

8,2,5
ARTICLES OF FAITH
BACHELOR OF MUSIC
BRINGING TO LIGHT
BUSINESS AS USUAL
CHERCHEZ LA FEMME
CLUBBING TO DEATH
CONTEMPT OF COURT
CREATURE OF HABIT
EMBARRAS DE CHOIX
FOUNTAIN OF YOUTH
LAUGHING TO SCORN
MINISTER OF STATE
MINISTRY OF WORKS
PARTNERS IN CRIME
PETITION OF RIGHT
REDUCING TO TEARS
SENTENCE TO DEATH
TICKLING TO DEATH

8,3,4
BREAKING THE BANK
BREAKING THE NEWS
CARRIAGE AND PAIR
CARRYING THE FLAG
CRACKING THE WHIP
LAUGHING OUT LOUD
MEDITATE THE MUSE
MILITARY TWO STEP
OCCUPIED THE MIND
OCCUPIES THE MIND
OVERSTEP THE MARK
PAINTING THE LILY
RIGHTING THE HELM

SCOOPING THE POOL
SHIPPING THE OARS
SHOUTING THE ODDS
SPEAKING TOO SOON
STANDING THE PACE
STEALING THE SHOW
STEMMING THE TIDE
STICKING THE PACE
STOPPING THE SHOW
STRAPPED FOR CASH
SUGARING THE PILL
SWINGING THE LEAD
THINKING OUT LOUD

8,4,3
CARRYING ONES BAT
FLIPPING ONES LID
SPORTING ONES OAK
STUBBING ONES TOE
VERTICAL TAKE OFF

8,5,2
SHEDDING LIGHT ON
THROWING LIGHT ON

8,7
ABERDEEN TERRIER
ADJUTANT GENERAL
AFFLUENT SOCIETY
AIRCRAFT CARRIER
AIREDALE TERRIER
AMERICAN EXPRESS
ANDERSON SHELTER
ANIMATED CARTOON
ANOREXIA NERVOSA
ARMOURED CRUISER
ASSERTED ONESELF
ATLANTIC CHARTER
ATTORNEY GENERAL
AUTUMNAL EQUINOX
AVERSION THERAPY
BAKEWELL PUDDING
BALLROOM DANCING
BESSEMER PROCESS
BINOMIAL THEOREM
BIRTHDAY HONOURS
BIRTHDAY PRESENT
BLENHEIM SPANIEL
BORDEAUX MIXTURE
BORNHOLM DISEASE
BREAKING THROUGH
BRINGING FORWARD
BRUSSELS SPROUTS
BUILDING SOCIETY
BURGUNDY MIXTURE
BUSINESS VENTURE
CARDINAL NUMBERS
CARDINAL VIRTUES
CARELESS DRIVING
CARRIAGE DRIVING
CARRIAGE FORWARD

8,7 *contd.*
CARRYING FORWARD
CARRYING THROUGH
CASEMENT CURTAIN
CHAPELLE ARDENTE
CHEMICAL WARFARE
CIRCULAR MEASURE
CITIZENS CHARTER
COCKTAIL CABINET
COMPLETE ANNUITY
COMPOUND ANIMALS
COMPUTER SCIENCE
COSMETIC SURGERY
CREATIVE WRITING
CRIMINAL CLASSES
CRIMPING MACHINE
CROSSING SWEEPER
DAYLIGHT ROBBERY
DEFERRED ANNUITY
DEFERRED PAYMENT
DEFINITE ARTICLE
DELAYING TACTICS
DELIRIUM TREMENS
DEMENTIA PRAECOX
DESIGNER STUBBLE
DEVILLED KIDNEYS
DIRECTOR GENERAL
DISTRESS WARRANT
DISTRICT COUNCIL
DISTRICT VISITOR
DIVIDEND WARRANT
DOMESTIC ECONOMY
DOMESTIC PROBLEM
DOMESTIC SCIENCE
DOORSTEP SELLING
DRESSING STATION
DRILLING MACHINE
DUELLING PISTOLS
ELECTRIC BATTERY
ELECTRIC BLANKET
ELECTRIC CURRENT
ELECTRIC FURNACE
ENJOYING ONESELF
EUROPEAN COUNCIL
EXCHANGE CONTROL
EXCHANGE STUDENT
EXCHANGE TEACHER
EXCUSING ONESELF
EXPANDED PLASTIC
EXPENSES ACCOUNT
EXPOSING ONESELF
EXTERNAL STUDENT
FALKLAND ISLANDS
FANCYING ONESELF
FEMININE PRONOUN
FENESTRA ROTUNDA
FILTERED THROUGH
FLAGGING SPIRITS
FLATTERS ONESELF
FLEETING GLIMPSE

FLICKING THROUGH
FLOATING BATTERY
FLOATING CAPITAL
FOLLOWED THROUGH
FOUCAULT CURRENT
FRANKING MACHINE
FREEZING MIXTURE
FRICTION WELDING
FRIENDLY SOCIETY
GALVANIC BATTERY
GAZETTED OFFICER
GLORIOUS TWELFTH
GOVERNOR GENERAL
GREENERY YALLERY
HEATHROW AIRPORT
IMPERIAL MEASURE
INDECENT ASSAULT
INFERIOR PLANETS
INFERNAL MACHINE
INTERNAL STUDENT
JAPANNED LEATHER
JEHOVAHS WITNESS
JUDICIAL TRUSTEE
KANGAROO JUSTICE
KILOGRAM CALORIE
KNITTING MACHINE
KNITTING NEEDLES
KNITTING PATTERN
KNOCKOUT AUCTION
LABRADOR CURRENT
LACHRYMA CHRISTI
LANGUAGE BARRIER
LAUGHING JACKASS
LIFEBOAT STATION
LUNCHEON VOUCHER
MAGNETIC BATTERY
MAJORITY VERDICT
MARRIAGE LICENCE
MARRIAGE PARTNER
MARRIAGE PORTION
MEDICINE DROPPER
MERCHANT SERVICE
MERIDIAN PASSAGE
METEORIC SHOWERS
MILITARY ACADEMY
MILITARY HONOURS
MONTAGUS HARRIER
MORRISON SHELTER
MOSQUITO CURTAIN
MOTORWAY MADNESS
MOUNTAIN BICYCLE
MOUNTAIN BRAMBLE
MOUNTAIN RAILWAY
MOURNING CLOTHES
MUDDLING THROUGH
MULBERRY HARBOUR
NATIONAL COSTUME
NATIONAL GALLERY
NATIONAL HOLIDAY
NATIONAL SERVICE

NAUTICAL ALMANAC
NORTHERN IRELAND
NOUVELLE CUISINE
ORIENTAL EMERALD
OVERFLOW MEETING
PASTORAL ADDRESS
PATHETIC FALLACY
PEASECOD BELLIED
PEASECOD CUIRASS
PERSONAL EFFECTS
PERSONAL PRONOUN
PERSONAL SERVICE
PLANNING OFFICER
PLEASURE GARDENS
PLEASURE SEEKING
PLOUGHED THROUGH
PLYMOUTH BROTHER
PORTRAIT GALLERY
PORTRAIT PAINTER
POSITIVE VETTING
PREENING ONESELF
PRESSING FORWARD
PRESSURE COOKING
PRINTING MACHINE
QUESTION BEGGING
RECEIVED ENGLISH
RECEIVER GENERAL
REGIONAL COUNCIL
REICHIAN THERAPY
REIGNING MONARCH
REIGNING SUPREME
RELATIVE DENSITY
RELATIVE PRONOUN
REPEATED ONESELF
RESEARCH CHEMIST
ROMANTIC REVIVAL
SEALYHAM TERRIER
SEAPLANE CARRIER
SECURITY BLANKET
SECURITY COUNCIL
SERGEANT DRUMMER
SHIFTING ONESELF
SHILLING SHOCKER
SHOOTING GALLERY
SICKNESS BENEFIT
SLEEPING DRAUGHT
SLEEPING PARTNER
SMELTING FURNACE
SOUTHERN IRELAND
SPARRING PARTNER
SPEAKING TRUMPET
SPEAKING VOLUMES
SPECIFIC GRAVITY
SPECIFIC IMPULSE
SQUEAKED THROUGH
STACKING AGAINST
STAMPING MACHINE
STANDARD ENGLISH
STANDING ACCUSED
STANDING AGAINST

8,7 *contd.*
STANDING OVATION
STANDING RIGGING
STAPLING MACHINE
STICKING PLASTER
STOCKING FILLERS
STRADDLE CARRIER
STRAIGHT ACTRESS
STRAIGHT TALKING
STRIKING THROUGH
SUPERIOR PLANETS
SUSPENSE ACCOUNT
SWIMMING COSTUME
SWINGING SIXTIES
SYNOPTIC GOSPELS
TABLEAUX VIVANTS
TEACHING MACHINE
TERMINAL ILLNESS
TERTIARY COLLEGE
TEUTONIC KNIGHTS
THATCHED COTTAGE
THINKING THROUGH
TICKLISH PROBLEM
TRAINING COLLEGE
VIRGINIA CREEPER
WALTZING MATILDA
WEIGHING MACHINE
WHIRLING DERVISH
WIRELESS STATION

9,1,5
HAZARDING A GUESS
RESERVING A TABLE
STRAINING A POINT
STRETCHED A POINT
STRETCHES A POINT

9,2,4
DELIVERED BY HAND
GENTLEMAN AT ARMS
MESSENGER AT ARMS

9,6
ADVANTAGE SERVER
ALUMINIUM BRONZE
AMBULANCE CHASER
AMBULANCE DRIVER
AMUSEMENT ARCADE
ANTARCTIC CIRCLE
ANTENATAL CLINIC
AUTOGRAPH HUNTER
AXMINSTER CARPET
BALACLAVA HELMET
BLEACHING POWDER
BREAKFAST CEREAL
BREATHING FREELY
BUTTERFLY FLOWER
BUTTERFLY ORCHID
BUTTERFLY ORCHIS
BUTTERFLY STROKE
BYZANTINE CHURCH

BYZANTINE EMPIRE
CHAMPAGNE BOTTLE
CHARACTER SKETCH
CHEQUERED CAREER
CHOCOLATE ECLAIR
CHRISTMAS ANNUAL
CHRISTMAS CACTUS
CHRISTMAS ISLAND
CHRISTMAS SPIRIT
CIGARETTE HOLDER
CLUSTERED COLUMN
COLLEGIAL CHURCH
COLLISION COURSE
COMMUNITY CENTRE
COMMUNITY SCHOOL
COMMUNITY SPIRIT
COMMUNITY WORKER
COMPANION LADDER
CROSSWORD PUZZLE
DEPARTURE LOUNGE
DEPENDENT CLAUSE
DETENTION CENTRE
DIRECTION FINDER
DISPLACED PERSON
DOMINICAL LETTER
DRUIDICAL CIRCLE
DUPLICATE BRIDGE
ELECTORAL SYSTEM
ENDOWMENT POLICY
ESSENTIAL ORGANS
EXCLUSION CLAUSE
EXCURSION TICKET
FIBONACCI SERIES
FINANCIAL WIZARD
FINISHING SCHOOL
FURNITURE POLISH
GATHERING BREATH
GATHERING GROUND
GENTLEMAN FARMER
GLADSTONE SHERRY
GRENADIER GUARDS
GREYHOUND RACING
GUERRILLA STRIKE
HOUSEHOLD GUARDS
HOUSEHOLD TROOPS
HYDRAULIC MINING
ILCHESTER CHEESE
IMMERSION HEATER
INDELIBLE PENCIL
INNOCENTS ABROAD
INSURANCE BROKER
INSURANCE POLICY
LANDSCAPE ARTIST
LIGHTNING STRIKE
LIMBURGER CHEESE
LOGISTICS VESSEL
LYMPHATIC SYSTEM
MANGANESE BRONZE
MASCULINE ENDING
MEDULLARY SHEATH

MOLECULAR WEIGHT
MOSSBAUER EFFECT
NEWSPAPER SELLER
ORCHESTRA STALLS
ORGANISED LABOUR
PANORAMIC CAMERA
PARACHUTE TROOPS
PASSENGER PIGEON
PEREGRINE FALCON
PERIPHERY CAMERA
PERMANENT MAGNET
PERPETUAL CURATE
PERPETUAL MOTION
PETRIFIED FOREST
PINEAPPLE CHUNKS
PLANETARY NEBULA
PNEUMATIC TROUGH
PNEUMONIA BLOUSE
POLISHING POWDER
POLITICAL ANIMAL
POLITICAL ASYLUM
POLITICAL STATUS
PORCELAIN CEMENT
POSIGRADE ROCKET
POTENTIAL ENERGY
PRINCIPAL CLAUSE
PRISMATIC POWDER
PROBOSCIS MONKEY
PROGRAMME SELLER
PROXIMATE OBJECT
RECEIVING OFFICE
RECEPTION CENTRE
RECORDING STUDIO
REFECTION SUNDAY
REMAINING SILENT
REVOLVING CREDIT
SCHEDULED FLIGHT
SCHOOLBOY HOWLER
SCREAMING ABDABS
SCRIPTURE READER
SECESSION CHURCH
SECONDARY ACTION
SECONDARY CAUSES
SECONDARY GROWTH
SECONDARY MODERN
SECONDARY PICKET
SECONDARY SCHOOL
SENSATION MONGER
SHORTHAND TYPIST
SHRINKING VIOLET
SITUATION COMEDY
SLAPSTICK COMEDY
SPRINKLER SYSTEM
SQUATTERS RIGHTS
STRATEGIC METALS
STRETCHER BEARER
STROLLING PLAYER
SURROGATE MOTHER
TELEPHONE NUMBER
THRESHOLD LIGHTS

9,6 *contd.*
THUMBNAIL SKETCH
TREMBLING POPLAR
UNSKILLED LABOUR
VEGETABLE GARDEN
VEGETABLE MARROW
VERTEBRAL COLUMN
VOLUNTARY MUSCLE
VOLUNTARY SCHOOL
WAISTCOAT POCKET
WELCOMING ABOARD

10,5
ALIMENTARY CANAL
ASTRONOMER ROYAL
AUSTRALIAN RULES
BANKRUPTCY COURT
BANQUETING HOUSE
BIMETALLIC STRIP
BIOLOGICAL CLOCK
BLACKWATER FEVER
BLOOMSBURY GROUP
CALIFORNIA POPPY
CANTERBURY BELLS
CAPITATION GRANT
COLLECTION PLATE
COLLECTIVE NOUNS
COMMERCIAL BREAK
COMMISSARY COURT
COMMISSION AGENT
CONFIDENCE TRICK
CONSCIENCE MONEY
CORRUGATED PAPER
CURRICULUM VITAE
DEMOLITION SQUAD
DEPARTMENT STORE
DEVONSHIRE CREAM
DIPLOMATIC CORPS
DISORDERLY HOUSE
DISSECTING TABLE
ELECTRONIC BRAIN
ELECTRONIC MUSIC
ELECTRONIC ORGAN
ELECTRONIC PIANO
EUSTACHIAN VALVE
EXCHANGING BLOWS
EXCHANGING WORDS
FORWARDING AGENT
FOUNDATION CREAM
FOUNDATION STONE
GRANULATED SUGAR
GRAPEFRUIT JUICE
HEREDITARY TITLE
HESITATION WALTZ
HISTORICAL NOVEL

INCIDENTAL MUSIC
INSTRUMENT PANEL
INSULATING BOARD
INVESTMENT TRUST
LEGITIMATE DRAMA
MAGNIFYING GLASS
MICHAELMAS DAISY
MICROMETER GAUGE
MINIMISING GLASS
MONUMENTAL MASON
MOUSSELINE SAUCE
NUTCRACKER SUITE
OCCASIONAL TABLE
OCCUPATION LEVEL
OPPOSITION BENCH
OPPOSITION PARTY
PANCREATIC JUICE
PARABIOTIC TWINS
PARLIAMENT CLOCK
PARLIAMENT HINGE
PARLIAMENT HOUSE
PEPPERMINT CREAM
PERFORMING RIGHT
PERIPHERAL UNITS
PHOTOGRAPH ALBUM
PRAETORIAN GUARD
PREVAILING WINDS
PROTECTION MONEY
PURCHASING POWER
QUALIFYING ROUND
REFRACTIVE INDEX
RINGELMANN CHART
SATURATION POINT
SCRIBBLING PAPER
SERPENTINE VERSE
SHORTENING BREAD
STAGNATION POINT
STRETCHING FRAME
STRUCTURAL STEEL
SUCCESSION HOUSE
TATTERSALL CHECK
TELESCOPIC SIGHT
TEMPERANCE HOTEL
TRANSISTOR RADIO
TRANSVERSE FLUTE
TRAVELLERS TALES
TRAVELLING CLOCK
TRIANGULAR PRISM
TRIGEMINAL NERVE
WEATHERING ALONG
WINCHESTER RIFLE
WINDSCREEN WIPER

11,4
ALTERNATIVE VOTE
BARTHOLOMEW TIDE

BIQUADRATIC ROOT
BRISTLECONE PINE
CANDELABRUM TREE
COMBINATION LOCK
CONDITIONAL MOOD
CONJUNCTIVE MOOD
CONSIGNMENT NOTE
CONSOLATION RACE
CONVENIENCE FOOD
DEVELOPMENT AREA
DISCHARGING ARCH
ELECTRICITY BILL
EQUINOCTIAL LINE
EQUINOCTIAL YEAR
EXCLAMATION MARK
FRIGHTENING AWAY
FULMINATING GOLD
GEOMETRICAL MEAN
GRASSHOPPER MIND
HIPPOCRATIC OATH
ILLUSTRIOUS PAST
LOGARITHMIC SINE
MARSHALLING YARD
OBSERVATION POST
PERFORMANCE TEST
PERSONALITY CULT
PHOSPHOROUS ACID
PUNCTUATION MARK
REFRESHMENT ROOM
RELIABILITY TEST
RESTORATION PLAY
SCARBOROUGH FAIR
STOCKBROKER BELT
SUBSISTANCE WAGE
TERRITORIAL ARMY
TRADITIONAL JAZZ
ULTRAVIOLET RAYS
ULTRAVIOLET STAR
UNFURNISHED FLAT
VICTUALLING BILL
VICTUALLING SHIP
VICTUALLING YARD
WHITECHAPEL CART
WITHDRAWING ROOM

12,3
ANNUNCIATION DAY
COMMONWEALTH DAY
DISAPPEARING ACT
INDEPENDENCE DAY
PANTECHNICON VAN
REGISTRATION FEE
RESURRECTION MAN
RESURRECTION PIE
STRAIGHTENED OUT
THANKSGIVING DAY

PHRASES BY
TOTAL LENGTH

3

I DO
O ME
O MY

4

AT IT
BIG C
C IN C
C OF E
D DAY
DO IN
DO UP
ET AL
G MAN
GO AT
GO GO
GO IN
GO ON
GO UP
HA HA
HE HE
HI FI
I SAY
I SPY
IN IT
IN ON
J PEN
JU JU
M WAY
NO GO
NO NO
NON U
NOT I
ON TO
OR SO
RO RO
SO SO
T BAR
TA TA
TO BE
TO DO
X RAY
YO YO

5

A BOMB
A DEUX
A GO GO
A ROAD
ACT UP
AD HOC
AD LIB
AD MAN
AD MEN
ADD ON
ADD UP
ALL IN
ALL UP

AS WAS
AS YET
AT ALL
AT ONE
AT SEA
ATE IN
ATE UP
B SIDE
BAGS I
BE OFF
BID IN
BID UP
BOB UP
BOW IN
BUY IN
BUY UP
BY FAR
BY LAW
CAN DO
CAN IT
COP IT
CRY UP
CS GAS
CUT IN
CUT UP
D MARK
DIG IN
DIG UP
DIP IN
DO OUT
DRY UP
DUG IN
DUG UP
E BOAT
EAT IN
EAT UP
END ON
END UP
EYE UP
FED UP
FIT IN
FIT UP
FIX IT
FIX ON
FIX UP
FLY BY
FLY IN
FRY UP
G CLEF
G SUIT
GEE UP
GEN UP
GET AT
GET BY
GET IN
GET ON
GET UP
GO APE
GO BAD
GO DRY

GO FAR
GO FOR
GO MAD
GO OFF
GO OUT
GOOD O
GOT AT
GOT BY
GOT IN
GOT ON
GOT UP
GUM UP
H BOMB
HAD IT
HAD ON
HAD TO
HAD UP
HAS IT
HAS ON
HAS TO
HAS UP
HE MAN
HEM IN
HEN DO
HET UP
HIT IT
HIT ON
HO HUM
HOG IT
HOO HA
HOP IT
HOT UP
HOW SO
I AND I
ID EST
IN ALL
IN BUD
IN CAR
IN FUN
IN LAW
IN OFF
IN ONE
IN TWO
IN USE
INK IN
KEY IN
KUO YU
LAY BY
LAY IN
LAY ON
LAY TO
LAY UP
LED IN
LED ON
LED UP
LET BE
LET GO
LET IN
LET ON
LET UP

LIE BY
LIE IN
LIE ON
LIE TO
LIE UP
LIT UP
LOG IN
LUG IN
M ROOF
ME TOO
MET UP
MID ON
MIX IN
MIX IT
MIX UP
MOP UP
MR BIG
MUG UP
MY EYE
MY GOD
MY HAT
NIP IN
NO END
NO JOY
NO ONE
NO USE
NO WAY
NOT SO
NOT UP
OF OLD
OF USE
OH BOY
ON AIR
ON CUE
ON DIT
ON END
ON ICE
ON OFF
ON TAP
ON TOW
OP ART
OWN UP
OX BOW
OX EYE
PAY IN
PAY UP
PER SE
PI JAW
PIG IT
PIN UP
POP IN
POP UP
PRO AM
PUT BY
PUT IN
PUT ON
PUT UP
Q BOAT
RAN IN
RAN ON

RAN TO
RAN UP
RAT ON
REV UP
RIG UP
RUB ON
RUB UP
RUN IN
RUN ON
RUN TO
RUN UP
SAT BY
SAT IN
SAT ON
SAT UP
SAY SO
SAYS I
SCI FI
SET BY
SET IN
SET ON
SET TO
SET UP
SEW UP
SIT BY
SIT IN
SIT ON
SIT UP
SO FAR
SOL FA
SUM UP
SUN UP
T BONE
TEE UP
TIE IN
TIE UP
TIP UP
TO LET
TO WIT
TOG UP
TON UP
TOP UP
TOT UP
TRY ON
TWO UP
U BEND
U BOAT
U BOLT
U TURN
UH HUH
UP END
UP TOP
USE UP
V BOMB
V NECK
V SIGN
VE DAY
VJ DAY
WHY SO
WU SHU

5 and 6 **LETTERS**

5 *contd.*
X RAYS
ZAP UP
ZIP IN
ZIP ON
ZIP UP

6
A LEG UP
A LEVEL
A RUM DO
ACK ACK
ACT ONE
ACT OUT
ACT TWO
ACTS UP
AD MASS
ADD ONS
ADDS UP
AGE OLD
AIR ARM
AIR BAG
AIR BED
AIR BUS
AIR GAS
AIR GUN
AIR SAC
ALL BUT
ALL DAY
ALL OUT
AND HOW
AS SUCH
AS WELL
ASH BIN
ASH CAN
ASH KEY
ASH PAN
ASH PIT
AT BEST
AT EASE
AT HAND
AT HOME
AT LAST
AT MOST
AT ODDS
AT ONCE
AT REST
AT RISK
AT STUD
AT WILL
ATE OUT
AU FAIT
AU FOND
AU PAIR
AYE AYE
B MOVIE
BACK UP
BAD LOT
BAG NET
BANG ON

BANG UP
BAY RUM
BEAR UP
BEAT IT
BEAT UP
BED OUT
BED PAN
BEEF UP
BEER UP
BEG OFF
BEL AIR
BEL AMI
BELT UP
BEN OIL
BIDS IN
BIDS UP
BIG BEN
BIG BUG
BIG CAT
BIG END
BIG POT
BIG TOE
BIG TOP
BIN BAG
BLEW IN
BLEW UP
BLOW IN
BLOW UP
BO PEEP
BO TREE
BOB FLY
BON AMI
BON MOT
BON TON
BONE UP
BOO HOO
BOOK IN
BOOK UP
BORE UP
BOW LEG
BOW OUT
BOW SAW
BOW TIE
BOWS IN
BOX BED
BOX VAN
BREW UP
BUCK UP
BUMP UP
BURN IN
BURN UP
BUS BAR
BUST UP
BUTT IN
BUY OFF
BUY OUT
BUYS IN
BUYS UP
BY HAND
BY JOVE

BY LANE
BYE BYE
BYE LAW
CAGE IN
CALL BY
CALL IN
CALL ON
CALL UP
CAME AT
CAME BY
CAME IN
CAME TO
CAME UP
CASH IN
CASH UP
CAST ON
CAST UP
CAVE IN
CHA CHA
CHI CHI
CHIN UP
CHIP IN
CHOP UP
CLAM UP
CLIP ON
CLUE IN
COCK UP
COIN IT
COME AT
COME BY
COME IN
COME ON
COME TO
COME UP
CON MAN
CON ROD
COOL IT
COP OUT
COPS IT
CROP UP
CRY OFF
CRY OUT
CUP TIE
CURL UP
CUS CUS
CUT OFF
CUT OUT
CUTS IN
CUTS UP
DAY BED
DAY GLO
DAY OFF
DAY OLD
DE LUXE
DE NOVO
DE TROP
DEAD ON
DEE JAY
DEJA VU
DER TAG

DES RES
DIE OFF
DIE OUT
DIG OUT
DIGS IN
DIGS UP
DIK DIK
DIM SUM
DIP OUT
DIPS IN
DISH UP
DO BIRD
DO DOWN
DO OVER
DO TIME
DO WELL
DOES IN
DOES UP
DOG EAR
DOG END
DOG LEG
DOG TAG
DONE IN
DONE UP
DOSI DO
DRAG ON
DRAG UP
DRAW IN
DRAW ON
DRAW UP
DREW IN
DREW ON
DREW UP
DROP BY
DROP IN
DROP ON
DRY BOB
DRY FLY
DRY ICE
DRY OUT
DRY ROT
DRY RUN
DRY SKI
DUFF UP
DUG OUT
DUMP ON
DUN COW
DUST UP
E LAYER
EAT OUT
EATS IN
EATS UP
EEL SET
EGG BOX
EN BLOC
END USE
ENDS UP
ET ALIA
EURO MP
EVEN SO

EVEN UP
EVER SO
EYED UP
EYES UP
FA LA LA
FADE IN
FAG END
FALL IN
FALL ON
FAN JET
FAN OUT
FAN TAN
FAR CRY
FAR OFF
FAR OUT
FAT CAT
FELL IN
FELL ON
FILL IN
FILL UP
FIN RAY
FIRE UP
FIRM UP
FIT OUT
FITS IN
FITS UP
FLEW BY
FLEW IN
FLY MAN
FLY OUT
FLY ROD
FOB OFF
FOLD IN
FOOT IT
FOR ALL
FOR AYE
FOR WHY
FORK UP
FOUL UP
FOX BAT
FU YUNG
FULL UP
FUN RUN
G AGENT
GANG UP
GAS BAG
GAS CAP
GAS GUN
GAS JAR
GAS JET
GAS OIL
GAS TAP
GAVE IN
GAVE UP
GEAR UP
GEE GEE
GENS UP
GET OFF
GET OUT
GETS AT

6 *contd.*

GETS BY	HIT MAN	IN NEED	LEAD IN	MAY DEW
GETS IN	HIT OFF	IN PART	LEAD ON	MEET UP
GETS ON	HIT OUT	IN PLAY	LEAD UP	MESS UP
GETS UP	HITS ON	IN SITU	LEAN ON	MET MAN
GIVE IN	HOG PEN	IN STEP	LEAN TO	MID AIR
GIVE UP	HOG RAT	IN TIME	LED OFF	MID OFF
GO AWAY	HOGS IT	IN TOTO	LED OUT	MID SEA
GO BACK	HOLD IN	IN TRAY	LEFT BE	MID SKY
GO BUST	HOLD IT	IN TUNE	LEG BYE	MIST UP
GO DOWN	HOLD ON	IN TURN	LEG MAN	MOB CAP
GO EASY	HOLD UP	IN VAIN	LET FLY	MOB LAW
GO INTO	HOLE UP	IN VIEW	LET OFF	MOCK UP
GO KART	HOOK UP	IN WORD	LET OUT	MOD CON
GO LIVE	HOOP LA	INK BAG	LET RIP	MOO COW
GO OVER	HOP OFF	INK CAP	LETS BE	MOPS UP
GO PHUT	HOPS IT	INK SAC	LETS GO	MOVE IN
GO SLOW	HORN IN	INKS IN	LETS IN	MR CHAD
GO SOFT	HOT AIR	JA WOHL	LETS ON	MUCK IN
GO WEST	HOT DOG	JET LAG	LETS UP	MUD PIE
GOES AT	HOT ROD	JET SKI	LIE LOW	MUGS UP
GOES IN	HOTS UP	JOB LOT	LIES BY	MUSK OX
GOES ON	HOVE TO	JOIN IN	LIES IN	MUU MUU
GOES UP	HOW NOW	JOIN UP	LIES ON	MY FOOT
GOT OFF	HUB CAP	JUMP ON	LIES TO	MY LADY
GOT OUT	HUNG IN	JUST SO	LIES UP	MY LORD
GREW UP	HUNG ON	KEEP IN	LIFT UP	MY WORD
GROW UP	HUNG UP	KEEP ON	LINE UP	NEAR BY
GRU GRU	HUSH UP	KEEP UP	LINK IN	NEED BE
GUMS UP	HYPE UP	KEPT IN	LINK UP	NEM CON
GUN DOG	I CHING	KEPT ON	LIVE IN	NEW AGE
GUN SHY	ICE AGE	KEPT UP	LIVE ON	NEW MAN
GUNG HO	ICE AXE	KEY MAN	LOCK IN	NID NOD
HAD A GO	ICE BAG	KEY PAD	LOCK ON	NIGH ON
HAIR DO	ICE CAP	KEY PIN	LOCK UP	NIP OUT
HAND IN	ICE PAN	KEY WAY	LOFT UP	NIPS IN
HANG IN	ICE RUN	KEYS IN	LOG HUT	NO BALL
HANG ON	IF ONLY	KIA ORA	LOG MAN	NO DICE
HANG UP	ILL BET	KICK IN	LOG OUT	NO FEAR
HARD BY	ILL GOT	KISS ME	LOG SAW	NO GOOD
HARD UP	ILL OFF	KIT BAG	LOGS IN	NO HOPE
HARP ON	ILL SAY	KIT CAR	LONG ON	NO JOKE
HAS A GO	ILL USE	KIT CAT	LOOK AT	NO LESS
HAUL IN	IN A ROW	KUNG FU	LOOK IN	NO MORE
HAUL UP	IN A RUT	L PLATE	LOOK ON	NO SIDE
HAVE IT	IN A WAY	LA DI DA	LOOK UP	NOD OFF
HAVE ON	IN CALF	LAC DYE	LOW KEY	NON EGO
HAVE TO	IN CARE	LAID BY	LOW TAR	NOSH UP
HAVE UP	IN CASE	LAID IN	LUGS IN	NOT OUT
HAW HAW	IN CASH	LAID ON	MADE DO	NUT OIL
HEAD ON	IN DEBT	LAID UP	MADE IT	O LEVEL
HELD IN	IN FACT	LASH UP	MADE UP	OAK NUT
HELD ON	IN FOAL	LAW DAY	MAKE DO	OBI MAN
HELD UP	IN FULL	LAY BYS	MAKE IT	ODD JOB
HEMS IN	IN HAND	LAY LOW	MAKE UP	ODDS ON
HEN BIT	IN HOCK	LAY OFF	MAN DAY	OF LATE
HEN RUN	IN JOKE	LAY OUT	MAP OUT	OF NOTE
HEP CAT	IN KIND	LAYS BY	MARK UP	OFF AIR
HIGH UP	IN LAWS	LAYS IN	MASH UP	OFF DAY
HINT AT	IN LINE	LAYS ON	MAU MAU	OFF KEY
	IN LOVE	LAYS UP	MAY BUG	OH DEAR

6 contd.	PENT UP	RAKE IN	SAIL BY	SINK IN
OIL GAS	PERK UP	RAKE UP	SANK IN	SIT OUT
OIL MAN	PET SIT	RAM JET	SAP ROT	SITS BY
OIL PAN	PICK AT	RAN DRY	SAT OUT	SITS IN
OIL RIG	PICK ON	RAN LOW	SAVE UP	SITS ON
OLD AGE	PICK UP	RAN OFF	SAW FIT	SITS UP
OLD BOY	PIG BED	RAN OUT	SAW OFF	SIX DAY
OLD HAT	PIG MAN	RANG IN	SAW OUT	SIX GUN
OLD MAN	PIG NUT	RANG UP	SAW RED	SIZE UP
OLD TOM	PIG RAT	RAT PIT	SAYS HE	SKI BOB
ON A PAR	PIGS IT	RAT TAT	SEA AIR	SKI DOO
ON CALL	PILE UP	RATS ON	SEA APE	SKI RUN
ON DUTY	PIN LEG	RAVE ON	SEA BOY	SKI TOW
ON EDGE	PIN MAN	RAVE UP	SEA CAT	SKIP IT
ON FILE	PIPE UP	READ UP	SEA COB	SLIP ON
ON FIRE	PIT PAT	RED ANT	SEA COW	SLIP UP
ON FOOT	PIT SAW	RED BOX	SEA DOG	SLOW UP
ON HAND	PLAY AT	RED BUD	SEA EAR	SNAP UP
ON HIGH	PLAY ON	RED CAP	SEA EEL	SO LONG
ON HIRE	PLAY UP	RED DOG	SEA FOG	SO MANY
ON HOLD	PLUG IN	RED GUM	SEA FOX	SO MUCH
ON LINE	POO POO	RED HAT	SEA GOD	SO THEN
ON OATH	POP ART	RED HOT	SEA ICE	SO WHAT
ON SPEC	POP EYE	RED MAN	SEA LAW	SOLD ON
ON TICK	POP GUN	RED OUT	SEA MEW	SOLD UP
ON TIME	POP OFF	RED RAG	SEA OWL	SOUP UP
ON VIEW	POP OUT	RED ROT	SEA PAY	SOW BUG
ONE DAY	POPS IN	REIN IN	SEA PEN	SPOT ON
ONE OFF	POPS UP	RELY ON	SEA WAY	STAG DO
ONE WAY	POST OP	REVS UP	SEE FIT	STAY IN
OO LA LA	POT ALE	REX CAT	SEE OFF	STAY ON
OPEN UP	POT BOY	RIDE UP	SEE OUT	STAY UP
OPT OUT	POT HAT	RIG OUT	SEE RED	STEP IN
OR ELSE	POT LID	RIGS UP	SEE YOU	STEP UP
OWNS UP	POT MAN	RING IN	SELL ON	STIR UP
OX BIRD	PRE TAX	RING UP	SELL UP	STOP GO
OX EYED	PRE WAR	RIP OFF	SEND IN	STOP IN
PACK UP	PREY ON	RIP RAP	SEND ON	SUB SEA
PAD OUT	PRO TEM	RIP SAW	SEND UP	SUCH AS
PAD SAW	PROP UP	RISE UP	SENT IN	SUCK IN
PAID IN	PRY OUT	RISK IT	SENT ON	SUMS UP
PAID UP	PUG DOG	ROAD UP	SET OFF	SUN DEW
PASS BY	PULL IN	RODE UP	SET OUT	SUN GOD
PASS ON	PULL ON	ROLL IN	SET TOS	SWAN IN
PASS UP	PULL UP	ROLL ON	SETS BY	SWAN UP
PAST IT	PUMP IN	ROLL UP	SETS IN	SWOT UP
PAY BED	PUMP UP	ROPE IN	SETS ON	T PLATE
PAY BOX	PUT OFF	ROSE UP	SETS UP	T SHIRT
PAY DAY	PUT OUT	ROW DOW	SEWN UP	TACK ON
PAY OFF	PUT PUT	RUB OUT	SEWS UP	TAG END
PAY OUT	PUTS BY	RUBS UP	SHE ASS	TAI CHI
PAYS IN	PUTS IN	RUN DRY	SHOT UP	TAKE IN
PAYS UP	PUTS ON	RUN LOW	SHOW UP	TAKE IT
PEA HEN	PUTS UP	RUN OFF	SHUT IN	TAKE ON
PEG BOX	PYE DOG	RUN OUT	SHUT UP	TAKE TO
PEG LEG	Q FEVER	RUNS IN	SIDE ON	TAKE UP
PEG OUT	RACK UP	RUNS ON	SIGN IN	TALK AT
PEG TOP	RAG BAG	RUNS TO	SIGN ON	TALK IN
PEN NIB	RAG DAY	RUNS UP	SIGN UP	TALK TO
PEN PAL	RAG TAG	SAG BAG	SIN BIN	TALK UP

6 *contd.*

TAN PIT
TAN VAT
TART UP
TE DEUM
TEA BAG
TEA SET
TEA URN
TEAR UP
TEE OFF
TEED UP
TEES UP
TELE AD
TELL ON
TEX MEX
THE BOX
THE END
THE FEW
THE LAW
THE LOT
THE MOB
THE WAY
TIB CAT
TIC TAC
TIE PIN
TIE ROD
TIE WIG
TIED IN
TIED UP
TIES IN
TIES UP
TIN CAN
TIN GOD
TIN HAT
TIP CAT
TIP OFF
TO A MAN
TO A TEE
TO BOOT
TO DATE
TO HAND
TOE RAG
TOGS UP
TOLD ON
TOM CAT
TOM TOM
TONE UP
TOO BAD
TOO TOO
TOOK IN
TOOK IT
TOOK ON
TOOK TO
TOOK UP
TOOL UP
TOP DOG
TOP HAT
TOP OUT
TOPS UP
TORE UP

TORN UP
TOSS UP
TOTS UP
TOW NET
TOY BOY
TOY DOG
TREK OX
TRY OUT
TUCK IN
TUM TUM
TUNE IN
TUNE UP
TURN IN
TURN ON
TURN TO
TURN UP
TUT TUT
TV GAME
TWIG IT
TWO BIT
TWO PLY
TWO WAY
UP BEAT
UP ENDS
UP LINE
UP TOWN
USED UP
USES UP
VOTE IN
VOX POP
WADE IN
WAIT ON
WAIT UP
WAKE UP
WALK IN
WALK IT
WALK ON
WALL UP
WANT AD
WANT IN
WAR CRY
WAR GOD
WARM UP
WASH UP
WAY OUT
WELL IN
WENT BY
WENT IN
WENT ON
WENT UP
WET BOB
WET FLY
WET ROT
WHAT HO
WHAT IF
WHET ON
WHIP IN
WHY NOT
WIN OUT
WIND UP

WIPE UP
WIRE IN
WISE UP
WITH IT
WOKE UP
WON OUT
WORK IN
WORK ON
WORK UP
WOW WOW
WRAP UP
X RAYED
YES MAN
YO HO HO
YOM TOB
YOO HOO
YOU ALL
YOU BET
YUM YUM
ZAPS UP
ZERO IN
ZIP OFF
ZIPS UP

7

A BAD HAT
A BAD JOB
A DROITE
A FAR CRY
A GAUCHE
A LA MODE
A PRIORI
ACK EMMA
ACT FOUR
ACTED UP
ACTS OUT
ADDED UP
AGA KHAN
AIR BASE
AIR CELL
AIR COOL
AIR CREW
AIR DROP
AIR LANE
AIR LOCK
AIR MISS
AIR PLAY
AIR PUMP
AIR RAID
AIR TRAP
ALI BABA
ALL DONE
ALL HAIL
ALL OVER
ALL STAR
ALL TIME
ALL TOLD
ALMS FEE
ALMS MAN
ALSO RAN

AMBS ACE
AND SO ON
ANT BIRD
ANT HILL
ANT LION
ANY MORE
ARC LAMP
ARM REST
ARMY ANT
ART DECO
ART FORM
ART SONG
AS A RULE
AS OF NOW
AS USUAL
ASH TRAY
AT A BLOW
AT A LOSS
AT A PUSH
AT A WORD
AT AN END
AT FAULT
AT FIRST
AT ISSUE
AT LARGE
AT LEAST
AT ONE GO
AT PEACE
AT STAKE
AT TABLE
AT TIMES
ATE AWAY
AXLE BOX
BABY SIT
BACK END
BACK OFF
BACK OUT
BACKS UP
BAD DEBT
BAD FORM
BAD LUCK
BAD NEWS
BAD SHOT
BAD SHOW
BAD TRIP
BAG LADY
BAIL OUT
BALE OUT
BALL BOY
BAND AID
BAND BOX
BAND SAW
BANG OFF
BANG OUT
BANGS UP
BAR BELL
BAR CODE
BAR IRON
BAR NONE
BAR ROOM

BARGE IN
BARN OWL
BASE FEE
BASS BAR
BATH BUN
BAWL OUT
BAY LEAF
BAY SALT
BEAM SEA
BEAN BAG
BEAR CAT
BEAR OUT
BEARS UP
BEAT OFF
BEAT OUT
BEATS IT
BEATS UP
BED DOWN
BED REST
BED ROLL
BED WORK
BEDS OUT
BEE GLUE
BEE HIVE
BEE KITE
BEE MOTH
BEE SKEP
BEEF TEA
BEEFS UP
BEER MAT
BEET FLY
BEGS OFF
BELL BOY
BELL JAR
BELT OUT
BELTS UP
BEST BOY
BEST END
BEST MAN
BETH DIN
BID FAIR
BIG BAND
BIG BANG
BIG CATS
BIG DEAL
BIG FISH
BIG GAME
BIG GUNS
BIG HEAD
BIG NAME
BIG SHOT
BIG TIME
BIRD DOG
BIT PART
BLAZE UP
BLEW OUT
BLOT OUT
BLOW DRY
BLOW OUT
BLOWS IN

7 LETTERS

7 *contd.*

BLOWS UP
BLUE FOX
BLUE JAY
BLUE SKY
BLUE TIT
BOAT FLY
BOER WAR
BOG DOWN
BOG MOSS
BOGY MAN
BONE ASH
BONE BED
BONE DRY
BONE OIL
BONED UP
BONES UP
BOOK END
BOOK OUT
BOOKS IN
BOOKS UP
BOOT BOY
BOOZE UP
BORE OUT
BOW HAND
BOWED IN
BOWL OUT
BOWS OUT
BOX CALF
BOX COAT
BOX KITE
BOX ROOM
BOX SEAT
BRAN TUB
BREAK IN
BREAK UP
BREN GUN
BREWS UP
BRING IN
BRING ON
BRING UP
BROKE IN
BRUSH UP
BUCK EYE
BUCKS UP
BUG EYED
BUILD IN
BUILD UP
BUILT IN
BUILT UP
BULL ANT
BULL PEN
BULL PUP
BUM BOAT
BUMP OFF
BUMPS UP
BUNK BED
BURN OUT
BURNS IN
BURNT IN

BURNT UP
BUS FARE
BUS LANE
BUS PASS
BUS STOP
BUSH CAT
BUSH FLY
BUTT END
BUTTS IN
BUY A PUP
BUY OVER
BUYS OFF
BUYS OUT
BUZZ OFF
BUZZ SAW
BUZZ WIG
BY A NOSE
BY AND BY
BY THE BY
CAB RANK
CAGED IN
CAGES IN
CALL BOX
CALL BOY
CALL OFF
CALL OUT
CALLS BY
CALLS IN
CALLS ON
CAME OFF
CAME OUT
CAMI TOP
CAMP BED
CAMP OUT
CAP A PIE
CAR COAT
CAR PARK
CAR POOL
CAR SICK
CAR WASH
CARRY ON
CART OFF
CARVE UP
CASE LAW
CASH COW
CAST OFF
CAST OUT
CASTS UP
CAT DOOR
CAT FLAP
CAT LIKE
CAT SHOW
CAT WALK
CATCH IT
CATCH ON
CATCH UP
CATS EAR
CATS EYE
CATS PAW
CAVED IN

CAVES IN
CB RADIO
CHAIN UP
CHALK UP
CHEAT ON
CHECK IN
CHECK UP
CHEER UP
CHIME IN
CHIP HAT
CHIP OFF
CHIPS IN
CHOC BAR
CHOC ICE
CHOKE UP
CHOPS UP
CHUCK UP
CHURN UP
CITY MAN
CLAMS UP
CLAY PIT
CLEAN UP
CLEAR UP
CLOCK IN
CLOCK ON
CLOCK UP
CLOSE IN
CLOSE ON
CLOSE UP
CLUED IN
CLUED UP
CLUES IN
COAL BOX
COAL GAS
COAL PIT
COAL TAR
COAL TIT
COB LOAF
COB PIPE
COIN BOX
COINS IT
COLD WAR
COMB OUT
COME NOW
COME OFF
COME OUT
COMES AT
COMES BY
COMES IN
COMES TO
COMES UP
CON BRIO
CONE OFF
COOL BAG
COOL BOX
COOL OFF
COON CAN
COP SHOP
COPS OUT
COPY CAT

CORK LEG
CORK MAT
CORK OAK
CORN BIN
CORN FED
CORN LAW
CORN OIL
CORN PIT
COUGH UP
COVER IN
COVER UP
COW CALF
CRAB NUT
CRAB OIL
CRACK UP
CREW CUT
CRIED UP
CRIES UP
CROPS UP
CROW BAR
CRY BABY
CRY DOWN
CRY WOLF
CUE BALL
CUI BONO
CUP CAKE
CUP GAME
CUP TIED
CURE ALL
CURLS UP
CUT BACK
CUT DEAD
CUT DOWN
CUTS OFF
CUTS OUT
D NOTICE
DAMN ALL
DASH OFF
DASH OUT
DASH POT
DAY BOOK
DAY CARE
DAY ROOM
DAY TRIP
DAY WORK
DE FACTO
DEAD END
DEAD EYE
DEAD SEA
DEAD SET
DEAF AID
DEAL OUT
DEAR SIR
DEARY ME
DECK OUT
DEEP FRY
DEEP SEA
DESK TOP
DEW DROP
DEW FALL

DEW POND
DICE BOX
DID TIME
DIE AWAY
DIE CAST
DIE DOWN
DIE HARD
DIE WORK
DIED OFF
DIED OUT
DIES OFF
DIES OUT
DIGS OUT
DIKA OIL
DINE OUT
DIPS OUT
DIRT BED
DISH OUT
DISH RAG
DO A TURN
DO IT NOW
DO OR DIE
DOE EYED
DOE SKIN
DOES OUT
DOG ROSE
DOG SHOW
DOG SLED
DOGS EAR
DOING IN
DOING UP
DON JUAN
DONE FOR
DONE OUT
DOS A DOS
DRAFT OX
DRAG BAR
DRAG NET
DRAG OUT
DRAGS ON
DRAGS UP
DRANK IN
DRANK UP
DRAW BAR
DRAW NET
DRAW OFF
DRAW OUT
DRAWS IN
DRAWS ON
DRAWS UP
DREAM UP
DRESS UP
DREW OFF
DRIED UP
DRIES UP
DRINK IN
DRINK UP
DRIP DRY
DRIVE IN
DROP NET

7 *contd.*	EYE BATH	FIXED IT	FULL FED	GO DUTCH
DROP OFF	EYE DROP	FIXED ON	FUN FAIR	GO FOR IT
DROP OUT	EYE HOLE	FIXED UP	FUN PARK	GO FORTH
DROPS BY	EYE SPOT	FIXES IT	FUR BALL	GO MAN GO
DROPS IN	EYE WASH	FIXES ON	FUR COAT	GO ROUND
DROPS ON	EYING UP	FIXES UP	FUR SEAL	GO SPARE
DRY CELL	FACE OFF	FLAG DAY	FUSE BOX	GO TO BED
DRY CURE	FACE OUT	FLARE UP	FUSS POT	GO TO POT
DRY DOCK	FADE OUT	FLAT CAP	G AGENTS	GO TO SEA
DRY EYED	FADED IN	FLAT HAT	G STRING	GO TO WAR
DRY HOLE	FADES IN	FLAT OUT	GALA PIE	GO UNDER
DRY ICED	FAIR DAY	FLEA BAG	GALL FLY	GO WRONG
DRY LAND	FAIR DOS	FLEA PIT	GALL NUT	GOA BEAN
DRY SHOD	FALL GUY	FLEW OUT	GAME BAG	GOD SLOT
DRY WASH	FALL OFF	FLIES BY	GANG SAW	GOES BAD
DUCK OUT	FALL OUT	FLIES IN	GANGS UP	GOES DRY
DUE EAST	FALLS IN	FLIP TOP	GAS BILL	GOES FAR
DUE WEST	FALLS ON	FLY FISH	GAS COAL	GOES FOR
DUFFS UP	FAN CLUB	FLY FLAP	GAS COKE	GOES MAD
DUMPS ON	FAN MAIL	FLY HALF	GAS FIRE	GOES OFF
DUN BIRD	FAN PALM	FLY HIGH	GAS LAMP	GOES OUT
DUST BAG	FANS OUT	FLY KICK	GAS MAIN	GOING AT
DUST PAN	FAR EAST	FLY LINE	GAS MASK	GOING IN
DYE WORK	FAR WEST	FLY OPEN	GAS OVEN	GOING ON
E NUMBER	FARM OUT	FLY PAST	GAS PIPE	GOING UP
E REGION	FAST DAY	FLY RAIL	GAS RING	GOLD BUG
EACH WAY	FAT FACE	FLY SOLO	GAS TANK	GOLF BAG
EAR BONE	FAT HEAD	FLY SWAT	GAS TRAP	GONE BAD
EAR HOLE	FAUX PAS	FOBS OFF	GAS WELL	GONE FOR
EAR PLUG	FELL OFF	FOG BANK	GATE LEG	GONE MAD
EAR SHOT	FELL OUT	FOG BELL	GATE MAN	GONE OFF
EARLY ON	FELT HAT	FOG LAMP	GAVE EAR	GONE OUT
EASE OFF	FEN FIRE	FOLD OUT	GAVE OFF	GOOD AND
EAST END	FERN OWL	FOLDS IN	GAVE OUT	GOOD BYE
EAT AWAY	FETCH UP	FOLK ART	GAVE WAY	GOOD DAY
EATS OUT	FIG LEAF	FOO YUNG	GEAR BOX	GOOD EGG
EDGE OUT	FIG TREE	FOOT TON	GEARS UP	GOT BACK
EDIT OUT	FILE OFF	FOOTS IT	GEE WHIZ	GOT DOWN
EGG CASE	FILL OUT	FOR EVER	GET BACK	GOT EVEN
EGG COSY	FILLS IN	FOR FREE	GET DOWN	GOT OVER
EGG FLIP	FILLS UP	FOR GOOD	GET EVEN	GREAT GO
EGO TRIP	FILM FAN	FOR LIFE	GET LOST	GREY HEN
ELF SHOT	FILM SET	FOR ONCE	GET OVER	GREY LAG
EN EFFET	FIND OUT	FOR REAL	GET REAL	GREY OWL
EN GARDE	FINE LEG	FOR RENT	GETS OFF	GROSS UP
EN MASSE	FIR CONE	FOR SALE	GETS OUT	GROW BAG
EN PRISE	FIR TREE	FOR SHOW	GILL NET	GROWN UP
EN ROUTE	FIR WOOD	FOR SURE	GIN FIZZ	GROWS UP
EN SUITE	FIRE BAR	FORK OUT	GIN TRAP	GUM TREE
END USER	FIRE BOX	FORKS UP	GIVE EAR	GUN DECK
ENDED UP	FIRE OFF	FOULS UP	GIVE OFF	GUN LOCK
EVEN NOW	FIRED UP	FOUR ALE	GIVE OUT	GUY ROPE
EVEN OUT	FIRES UP	FOX EVIL	GIVE WAY	GYM SHOE
EVENS UP	FIRMS UP	FOX HUNT	GIVES IN	GYM SLIP
EVIL EYE	FISH DAY	FOX TAIL	GIVES UP	HACK LOG
EWE LAMB	FISH NET	FOX TRAP	GLAD EYE	HACK SAW
EWE MILK	FISH OIL	FOX TROT	GLORY BE	HAG RIDE
EWE NECK	FISH OUT	FRAME UP	GLUE EAR	HAG SEED
EX CURIA	FITS OUT	FROWN ON	GLUE POT	HAG WEED
EX PARTE	FIVE BAR	FT INDEX	GO AHEAD	HAIR DOS

7 *contd.*

HAIR NET	HINTS AT	I ASK YOU	INK HORN	KNOCK ON
HAIR OIL	HIP BATH	I HAVE IT	INKED IN	KNOCK UP
HALF A MO	HIP BELT	ICE BLUE	INN SIGN	KNOW ALL
HALF APE	HIP BONE	ICE BOAT	IRON AGE	KNOW HOW
HALF DAY	HIP LOCK	ICE COLD	IRON MAN	L PLATES
HALF PAY	HIRE CAR	ICE CUBE	IRON ORE	LACE UPS
HALF WIT	HIRE OUT	ICE FALL	IRON OUT	LADY DAY
HAND GUN	HIS NIBS	ICE FERN	IRON PAN	LAID OFF
HAND OUT	HIT LIST	ICE FLOE	IVY BUSH	LAID OUT
HANDS UP	HITCH UP	ICE FREE	IVY CLAD	LAND RAT
HANG OFF	HITS OFF	ICE HILL	JACK TAR	LAND TAX
HANG OUT	HITS OUT	ICE OVER	JAI ALAI	LASH OUT
HANGS IN	HIVE BEE	ICE PICK	JAM TART	LAST OUT
HANGS ON	HIVE OFF	ICE RINK	JAVA MAN	LATCH ON
HANGS UP	HOB A NOB	ICE SHOW	JAZZ AGE	LAW BOOK
HARD HAT	HOCK DAY	ICE SPAR	JET DEAU	LAW LIST
HARD HIT	HOG DEER	ICH DIEN	JIB BOOM	LAW LORD
HARD MAN	HOG FISH	ILL BRED	JIB DOOR	LAY BACK
HARD PAD	HOG MANE	ILL FAME	JOE SOAP	LAY BARE
HARD ROE	HOG NOSE	ILL LUCK	JOHN DOE	LAY DOWN
HARD RUN	HOG SKIN	ILL USED	JOINS IN	LAY INTO
HARD SET	HOLD ALL	ILL WILL	JOINS UP	LAY OPEN
HARD WON	HOLD OFF	IN A DAZE	JOY RIDE	LAY OVER
HARE LIP	HOLD OUT	IN A RUSH	JU JITSU	LAYS OFF
HARPS ON	HOLDS IN	IN A SPOT	JUG BAND	LAYS OUT
HAS BEEN	HOLDS ON	IN A STEW	JUKE BOX	LAZY EYE
HAULS IN	HOLDS UP	IN A WORD	JUMP JET	LEAD OFF
HAULS UP	HOLE OUT	IN AND IN	JUMP OFF	LEAD OUT
HAUT TON	HOLED UP	IN BLOOD	JUMPS ON	LEADS IN
HAVE A GO	HOLES UP	IN BRIEF	JUNK MAN	LEADS ON
HAVE NOT	HOLM OAK	IN BUILT	JURY BOX	LEADS UP
HAWK EYE	HOLY DAY	IN CROWD	JUST NOW	LEAK OUT
HEAD BOY	HOLY JOE	IN DEPTH	KEEP FIT	LEAN TOS
HEAD OFF	HOLY ONE	IN DOUBT	KEEP MUM	LEANS ON
HEAD OUT	HOLY SEE	IN FOCUS	KEEP OFF	LEANT ON
HEAD SEA	HOLY WAR	IN FOR IT	KEEPS IN	LEAP DAY
HEAL ALL	HOME RUN	IN FORCE	KEEPS ON	LEAVE BE
HEAR OUT	HOOK PIN	IN FRONT	KEEPS UP	LEAVE GO
HEAVE HO	HOP HEAD	IN HOLES	KEG BEER	LEE SIDE
HEAVE TO	HOP POLE	IN HOUSE	KEPT FIT	LEE TIDE
HEEL TAP	HOP SACK	IN LIMBO	KEPT MUM	LEFT OFF
HEIGH HO	HOP TREE	IN NO WAY	KEPT OFF	LEFT OUT
HELD OFF	HOP VINE	IN ORDER	KEY RING	LEG BAIL
HELD OUT	HOP YARD	IN PLACE	KEY WORD	LEG IRON
HELL CAT	HOPS OFF	IN POWER	KEYED IN	LEG PULL
HELP OUT	HORN MAD	IN PRINT	KEYED UP	LEG REST
HEM LINE	HORN OWL	IN SHAPE	KICK OFF	LEG SHOW
HEN COOP	HORNS IN	IN SHORT	KICK OUT	LEG SIDE
HEN TOED	HOT LINE	IN SPATE	KICKS IN	LEG SLIP
HEN WIFE	HOT SEAT	IN STOCK	KID SKIN	LEG SPIN
HER NIBS	HOT SPOT	IN STORE	KILL OFF	LET DOWN
HERB TEA	HOT WELL	IN STYLE	KILN DRY	LET DROP
HIGH DAY	HOW COME	IN TEARS	KING PIN	LET FALL
HIGH HAT	HOWDY DO	IN THING	KING ROD	LET IN ON
HIGH KEY	HUNG OFF	IN TOUCH	KIP DOWN	LET SLIP
HIGH SET	HUNG OUT	IN TRAIN	KIT BOAT	LETS FLY
HIGH TEA	HUNT OUT	IN TRUST	KNEE CAP	LETS OFF
HIGH TOP	HURRY UP	IN TRUTH	KNEE PAD	LETS OUT
HIND GUT	HYPED UP	IN VOICE	KNEE PAN	LETS RIP
	HYPES UP	INK FEED	KNEES UP	LIE ABED

7 *contd.*

LIE BACK
LIE DOWN
LIE HARD
LIE OVER
LIES LOW
LIFT BOY
LIFT MAN
LIFT OFF
LIFTS UP
LIGHT UP
LIKE MAD
LILY PAD
LINE OUT
LINEAR A
LINEAR B
LINED UP
LINES UP
LINK MAN
LINKS IN
LINKS UP
LION CUB
LIP READ
LIVE OAK
LIVE OUT
LIVED IN
LIVED ON
LIVES IN
LIVES ON
LOCK JAW
LOCK NUT
LOCK OUT
LOCKS IN
LOCKS ON
LOCKS UP
LOFTS UP
LOG BOOK
LOG FIRE
LOG ROLL
LOGS OUT
LONG AGO
LONG ARM
LONG HOP
LONG LEG
LONG OFF
LONG PIG
LONG TOM
LONG TON
LOOK FOR
LOOK OUT
LOOK SEE
LOOK YOU
LOOKS AT
LOOKS IN
LOOKS ON
LOOKS UP
LOSE OUT
LOST OUT
LOW BORN
LOW BRED

LOW BROW
LOW COST
LOW DOWN
LOW GEAR
LOW LIFE
LOW PAID
LOW RISE
LOW TIDE
LOW TOBY
LUMP SUM
LYING BY
LYING IN
LYING ON
LYING TO
LYING UP
MADE FOR
MADE HAY
MADE OFF
MADE OUT
MADE WAR
MADE WAY
MAE WEST
MAIL BAG
MAIL BOX
MAIL CAR
MAIL GIG
MAIL VAN
MAKE FOR
MAKE HAY
MAKE OFF
MAKE OUT
MAKE WAR
MAKE WAY
MAKES DO
MAKES IT
MAKES UP
MALT TEA
MAN DAYS
MAN HOUR
MAN JACK
MAN LIKE
MAN MADE
MAN O WAR
MAN SIZE
MAN WEEK
MAN YEAR
MANX CAT
MAO SUIT
MAP BOOK
MAPS OUT
MARK OFF
MARK OUT
MARKS UP
MARL PIT
MASH TUB
MASH TUN
MASH VAT
MAY BIRD
MAY LADY
MAY LILY

MAY LORD
MAY TIME
MAY TREE
MEAT FLY
MEAT MAN
MEAT PIE
MEAT TEA
MEAT TUB
MEETS UP
MEN O WAR
MENS REA
MESS TIN
MID HOUR
MID TERM
MID WEEK
MID YEAR
MIDDLE C
MILD ALE
MILK BAR
MILK CAP
MILK COW
MILK JUG
MILK RUN
MILK SOP
MILL RUN
MIND OUT
MIND YOU
MINI BUS
MINI CAB
MINI CAR
MINI SUB
MISS OUT
MISTS UP
MIXED IN
MIXED IT
MIXED UP
MIXES IN
MIXES IT
MIXES UP
MOCK SUN
MOD CONS
MOLE OUT
MONO SKI
MOON GOD
MOT TEST
MOVE OUT
MOVED IN
MOVES IN
MR RIGHT
MRS MOPP
MUCKS IN
MUD BATH
MUD FLAP
MUD FLAT
MUG SHOT
MUSK RAT
NAIL BED
NAIL GUN
NAME DAY
NEO NAZI

NEST EGG
NET CORD
NET GAME
NET PLAY
NEW DEAL
NEW LAID
NEW LOOK
NEW MADE
NEW MOON
NEW MOWN
NEW TOWN
NEW WAVE
NEW YEAR
NEW YORK
NINE PIN
NIPS OUT
NIT PICK
NO CAN DO
NO DOUBT
NO ENTRY
NO HOPER
NO SWEAT
NO TRUMP
NODS OFF
NON DRIP
NON HERO
NON SKID
NON SLIP
NON STOP
NON USER
NOR EAST
NOR WEST
NOSE JOB
NOSE OUT
NOT HALF
NOTE PAD
NOW THEN
NUT GALL
NUT HOOK
NUT TREE
OAK FERN
OAK GALL
OAK LUMP
OAK MAST
OAK TREE
OAK WOOD
OAR FISH
OAR LOCK
ODD FISH
ODD JOBS
OF A SORT
OF NO USE
OF SORTS
OFF BASE
OFF DUTY
OFF LINE
OFF SITE
OFF SPIN
OFFER UP
OHMS LAW

OIL BELT
OIL CAKE
OIL DRUM
OIL MILL
OIL PALM
OIL RICH
OIL SEED
OIL WELL
OLD BEAN
OLD BILL
OLD BIRD
OLD DEAR
OLD FACE
OLD GANG
OLD GIRL
OLD GOLD
OLD HAND
OLD LADY
OLD MAID
OLD NICK
OLD ROSE
OLD SALT
OLD SONG
OLD TIME
OLD WIFE
ON A ROLL
ON AND ON
ON APPRO
ON BOARD
ON DRIVE
ON GOING
ON OFFER
ON ORDER
ON PAPER
ON SHORE
ON SIGHT
ON STAGE
ON TERMS
ON THE GO
ON THE UP
ON TOAST
ON TRIAL
ON TRUST
ONE EYED
ONE SHOT
ONE STEP
ONE TIME
OPEN AIR
OPEN DAY
OPEN END
OPEN OUT
OPEN SEA
OPEN TOP
OPENS UP
OPTS OUT
OPUS DEI
OUR LADY
OUT OF IT
OUT TAKE
OUT TRAY

7 contd.

OVER AGE	PH VALUE	POP EYED	PUTT OUT	RED ROOT
OVER ALL	PHASE IN	POP SHOP	QUEUE UP	RED ROSE
OWL EYED	PHONE IN	POP SONG	QUI VIVE	RED SEED
OWL MOTH	PI MESON	POPS OFF	QUIDS IN	RED SNOW
OWN GOAL	PICK OFF	POPS OUT	QUITE SO	RED TAPE
OWNED UP	PICK OUT	PORK PIE	QUO JURE	RED WINE
OX FENCE	PICKS AT	POST BAG	R MONTHS	REDS OUT
PACK ICE	PICKS ON	POST BOX	RACE CUP	REED BED
PACKS UP	PICKS UP	POST BOY	RACKS UP	REEL OFF
PAD TREE	PIE EYED	POST BUS	RADIUM A	REIN ARM
PADS OUT	PIE SHOP	POST DAY	RADIUM B	REINS IN
PAGE BOY	PIECE UP	POST WAR	RAG BABY	RENT DAY
PAID OFF	PIG DEER	POT BANK	RAG BOOK	REST DAY
PAID OUT	PIG EYED	POT HEAD	RAG BUSH	RIB BONE
PAIR OAR	PIG HERD	POT HERB	RAG DOLL	RIDE OUT
PAIR OFF	PIG IRON	POT LUCK	RAG FAIR	RIDES UP
PALE ALE	PIGS EAR	POT SHOP	RAG WEEK	RIGHT ON
PALM CAT	PILE CAP	POT SHOT	RAG WOOL	RIGS OUT
PALM OIL	PILED UP	POUR OUT	RAIL CAR	RING OFF
PAN LOAF	PILES UP	POY BIRD	RAKE OFF	RING OUT
PARA NUT	PILL BOX	PRE EMPT	RAKED IN	RINGS IN
PART OFF	PIN CURL	PRE SELL	RAKED UP	RINGS UP
PAS SEUL	PIN DOWN	PRE SOLD	RAKES IN	RIOT ACT
PASS OFF	PIN EYED	PRE WASH	RAKES UP	RIP CORD
PASS OUT	PIN TUCK	PRESS ON	RAN AMOK	RIPS OFF
PASTE UP	PINE TAR	PRESS UP	RAN AWAY	RISES UP
PATCH UP	PINK EYE	PREYS ON	RAN DOWN	RISKS IT
PAY BACK	PINK GIN	PRO RATA	RAN HARD	ROAD BED
PAY BILL	PINT POT	PROP JET	RAN INTO	ROAD HOG
PAY CASH	PIP EMMA	PROPS UP	RAN OVER	ROAD MAP
PAY DESK	PIPE KEY	PSYCH UP	RAN RIOT	ROCK COD
PAY DIRT	PIPED UP	PUFF BOX	RAN WILD	ROCK OIL
PAY LIST	PIPES UP	PUG MILL	RANG OFF	ROCK TAR
PAY LOAD	PIT A PAT	PUG MOTH	RAPE OIL	RODE OUT
PAY ROLL	PIT BROW	PUG NOSE	RARE GAS	ROE DEER
PAY SLIP	PIT BULL	PULL OFF	RAT A TAT	ROLL BAR
PAYS OFF	PIT COAL	PULL OUT	RAT HOLE	ROLL OUT
PAYS OUT	PIT PONY	PULLS IN	RAT RACE	ROLL TOP
PEA FOWL	PIT PROP	PULLS UP	RAT TRAP	ROLLS IN
PEA SOUP	PIT STOP	PUMP GUN	RATE CAP	ROLLS UP
PEAT BED	PITCH IN	PUMP OUT	RAW DEAL	ROOD DAY
PEAT BOG	PITH HAT	PUMPS IN	RAW SILK	ROOF TOP
PEEL OFF	PLAY ACT	PUMPS UP	READ OFF	ROOT CAP
PEEP OUT	PLAY BOX	PUNCH UP	READ OUT	ROOT OUT
PEEP TOE	PLAY DAY	PUNT GUN	READS UP	ROPED IN
PEG AWAY	PLAY OFF	PUP TENT	REAL ALE	ROPES IN
PEG BACK	PLAY OUT	PUSH OFF	RED BOOK	ROSE BAY
PEG DOWN	PLAY PEN	PUSH OUT	RED CARD	ROSE BUD
PEG TOPS	PLAYS AT	PUSH PIN	RED CENT	ROSE BUG
PEGS OUT	PLAYS ON	PUSH TUG	RED CLAY	ROSE HIP
PEN CASE	PLAYS UP	PUT AWAY	RED DEER	ROSE RED
PEN NAME	PLUGS IN	PUT BACK	RED FACE	ROUGH IN
PEP PILL	PO FACED	PUT DOWN	RED FLAG	ROUGH IT
PEP TALK	POE BIRD	PUT IT ON	RED GAME	ROUND ON
PER CENT	POINT UP	PUT ON TO	RED HAND	ROUND UP
PERKS UP	POLE AXE	PUT OVER	RED HEAD	ROW PORT
PET HATE	POLL TAX	PUT TO IT	RED HEAT	ROYAL WE
PET NAME	POOH BAH	PUT UPON	RED LANE	RUB DOWN
PEW RENT	POOR BOX	PUTS OFF	RED LEAD	RUB IT IN
	POOR LAW	PUTS OUT	RED MEAT	RUBS OUT

7 contd.	SEA BASS	SEE HERE	SICK DAY	SOUR SOP
RUBY RED	SEA BIRD	SEE LIFE	SIDE BOX	SOW SKIN
RULE OUT	SEA BLUE	SEE OVER	SIGN OFF	SPA WELL
RUM BABA	SEA BOAT	SEE TO IT	SIGN OUT	SPEAK UP
RUM SHOP	SEA CALF	SEED OIL	SIGNS IN	SPEED UP
RUMP END	SEA COAL	SEEK OUT	SIGNS UP	SPIN DRY
RUN AMOK	SEA COOK	SEES FIT	SILK HAT	SPIN OFF
RUN AWAY	SEA CROW	SEES OFF	SINE DIE	SPIN OUT
RUN DOWN	SEA DACE	SEES OUT	SING OUT	SPOKE UP
RUN HARD	SEA DOVE	SEES RED	SINKS IN	SPRAY ON
RUN INTO	SEA DUCK	SEIZE UP	SIT BACK	SPUN OUT
RUN OVER	SEA FIRE	SELL OFF	SIT DOWN	SPY HOLE
RUN RIOT	SEA FISH	SELL OUT	SIT UPON	ST LEGER
RUN TIME	SEA FOAM	SELLS ON	SITS OUT	STACK UP
RUN WILD	SEA FOLK	SELLS UP	SIX BITS	STAND BY
RUNS DRY	SEA FOWL	SEND OFF	SIX FOOT	STAND IN
RUNS LOW	SEA FRET	SEND OUT	SIX PACK	STAND ON
RUNS OFF	SEA GATE	SENDS IN	SIZED UP	STAND TO
RUNS OUT	SEA GIRT	SENDS ON	SIZES UP	STAND UP
RUSH MAT	SEA HAAR	SENDS UP	SKI LIFT	STAR LED
RYE ROLL	SEA HAWK	SENT OFF	SKID LID	STAR MAP
RYE WOLF	SEA KALE	SENT OUT	SKID PAD	START IN
SAD EYED	SEA KING	SERVE UP	SKID PAN	START UP
SAD IRON	SEA LANE	SET BACK	SKID ROW	STAVE IN
SAGE TEA	SEA LARK	SET DOWN	SKIPS IT	STAY OUT
SAIL ARM	SEA LEGS	SET FAIR	SKY BLUE	STAY PUT
SAILS BY	SEA LIKE	SET FOOT	SKY HIGH	STAYS IN
SALT BOX	SEA LILY	SET FREE	SKY SIGN	STAYS ON
SALT EEL	SEA LINE	SET LINE	SKY WAVE	STAYS UP
SALT FAT	SEA LION	SET SAIL	SLEEP IN	STEAM UP
SALT PAN	SEA LOCH	SET UPON	SLEEP ON	STEN GUN
SALT PIT	SEA LORD	SETS OFF	SLEPT IN	STEP CUT
SAND BAR	SEA MAID	SETS OUT	SLEPT ON	STEP OUT
SAND BED	SEA MILE	SEX BOMB	SLICE UP	STEP SON
SAND BOX	SEA MOSS	SHAKE UP	SLIP OFF	STEPS IN
SAND BOY	SEA PASS	SHAPE UP	SLIP ONS	STEPS UP
SAND EEL	SEA PATH	SHE BEAR	SLIPS ON	STEW CAN
SAND FLY	SEA PIKE	SHIH TZU	SLIPS UP	STICK BY
SAND PIT	SEA PINK	SHIP BOY	SLOE GIN	STICK IN
SANG OUT	SEA ROAD	SHIP WAY	SLOP OUT	STICK TO
SAT BACK	SEA ROOM	SHOE TIE	SLOWS UP	STICK UP
SAT DOWN	SEA SALT	SHOOK UP	SMASH UP	STIR FRY
SAVE ALL	SEA SAND	SHOOT UP	SNAPS UP	STIRS UP
SAVED UP	SEA SLUG	SHOP BOY	SNARL UP	STOCK UP
SAVES UP	SEA STAR	SHOT GUN	SNEAK UP	STOKE UP
SAW BILL	SEA TANG	SHOT OFF	SNOW BOX	STONE ME
SAW BUCK	SEA TERM	SHOT PUT	SNOW FLY	STOOD IN
SAW EDGE	SEA TURN	SHOW BIZ	SNOW ICE	STOOD ON
SAW FISH	SEA VIEW	SHOW BOX	SNUFF IT	STOOD TO
SAW LIFE	SEA WALL	SHOW OFF	SO AND SO	STOOD UP
SAW MILL	SEA WARE	SHOWS UP	SO THERE	STOP GAP
SAW OVER	SEA WAVE	SHUT EYE	SOAP BOX	STOP OFF
SAW TO IT	SEA WIFE	SHUT OFF	SOBER UP	STOPS IN
SAWN OFF	SEA WIND	SHUT OUT	SODA POP	STOVE IN
SAY WHEN	SEA WING	SHUTS IN	SOFA BED	STUCK BY
SAYS SHE	SEA WOLF	SHUTS UP	SOFT ROE	STUCK IN
SAYS YOU	SEA WORM	SHY COCK	SOLD OFF	STUCK ON
SCARE UP	SEA WORN	SI UNITS	SOLD OUT	STUCK TO
SCRUB UP	SEAL OFF	SICK BAY	SORT OUT	STUCK UP
SEA BANK	SEAL WAX	SICK BED	SOUPS UP	STUMP UP

7 LETTERS

7 contd.

STUN GUN	TEA TRAY	TO A TURN	TWO TONE	WEE FREE
SUB HEAD	TEACH IN	TO ORDER	TYING IN	WEEK END
SUCKS IN	TEAR GAS	TO SCALE	TYING UP	WEIGH IN
SUN BIRD	TEAR OFF	TO SPARE	TYPE BAR	WEIGH UP
SUN CULT	TEAR PIT	TOBY JUG	U SHAPED	WELL FED
SUN DECK	TEARS UP	TOC EMMA	UP A TREE	WELL MET
SUN DISC	TEED OFF	TOE HOLD	UP ENDED	WELL NOW
SUN LAMP	TEES OFF	TOE JUMP	UP FRONT	WELL OFF
SUN ROOF	TELE ADS	TOE LOOP	UP TEMPO	WELL SET
SUSS OUT	TELL OFF	TOLD OFF	UP TRAIN	WELL WON
SWEAR IN	TELLS ON	TOLL BAR	USING UP	WENT BAD
SWEEP UP	TENT BED	TONED UP	UVA URSI	WENT DRY
SWEPT UP	TENT FLY	TONES UP	V NECKED	WENT FAR
SWORN IN	TENT GUY	TOO MUCH	V SHAPED	WENT MAD
SWOTS UP	TENT PEG	TOOK AIM	VENT PEG	WENT OFF
T SHAPED	TEST BAN	TOOK OFF	VIN ROSE	WENT OUT
T SQUARE	TEST BED	TOOK OUT	VINE ROD	WEST END
TACKS ON	THAW OUT	TOOLS UP	VIS A VIS	WET CELL
TAG LINE	THE BARD	TOP BOOT	VOTED IN	WET DOCK
TAIL END	THE CAPE	TOP HOLE	VOTES IN	WET FISH
TAIL FLY	THE EAST	TOP LINE	WADED IN	WET LOOK
TAIL OFF	THE FLAT	TOP SOIL	WADES IN	WET SHOD
TAKE AIM	THE LUMP	TOPS OUT	WAGE WAR	WET SUIT
TAKE OFF	THE OAKS	TORE OFF	WAITS ON	WHAT FOR
TAKE OUT	THE PILL	TOTE BAG	WAITS UP	WHAT NOT
TAKEN IN	THE PITS	TOUCH UP	WALK OFF	WHATS UP
TAKEN ON	THE ROCK	TOW PATH	WALK OUT	WHEY TUB
TAKEN UP	THE ROPE	TOW ROPE	WALKS IT	WHIP SAW
TAKES IN	THE RUMP	TOWN END	WALKS ON	WHIPS IN
TAKES IT	THE SAME	TRADE IN	WALL EYE	WHIZ KID
TAKES ON	THE TOPS	TRADE UP	WALLS UP	WHOS WHO
TAKES TO	THE WEST	TRAM CAR	WANT OUT	WIDE BOY
TAKES UP	THE WORD	TRIED ON	WANT WIT	WILD ASS
TALK BIG	THE YARD	TRIES ON	WANTS IN	WILD CAT
TALK OUT	THE YIPS	TROT OUT	WAR BABY	WILD DOG
TALKS AT	THIN OUT	TRUE RIB	WAR DRUM	WILD MAN
TALKS TO	THINK UP	TRY IT ON	WAR GAME	WIN OVER
TALL HAT	THREW IN	TUCK BOX	WAR HAWK	WIND BAG
TALLY HO	THREW ON	TUCKS IN	WAR HEAD	WINDS UP
TAN BARK	THREW UP	TUG BOAT	WAR HERO	WINE BAG
TANK CAR	THROW IN	TUNED IN	WAR LOAN	WINE BAR
TANK TOP	THROW ON	TUNED UP	WAR SONG	WINE SAP
TANT PIS	THROW UP	TUNES IN	WARD OFF	WINE VAT
TAP ROOM	THUS FAR	TUNES UP	WARMS UP	WING NUT
TAP SHOE	TICK OFF	TURF OUT	WART HOG	WINS OUT
TAR SAND	TIDE RIP	TURN OFF	WASH DAY	WIPE OUT
TARTS UP	TIDE WAY	TURN OUT	WASH OUT	WIPED UP
TAX DISC	TIDY SUM	TURNS IN	WASH POT	WIPES UP
TAX FREE	TIE BEAM	TURNS ON	WASH TUB	WIRE BAR
TEA BAGS	TIE CLIP	TURNS TO	WATCH IT	WIRE MAN
TEA CAKE	TIE DOWN	TURNS UP	WAX DOLL	WIRE WAY
TEA COSY	TILE HAT	TWIGS IT	WAX MOTH	WIRED IN
TEA DISH	TILE RED	TWIN BED	WAX TREE	WIRES IN
TEA LADY	TIME GUN	TWIN SET	WAY BILL	WISE GUY
TEA LEAF	TIME LAG	TWIN TUB	WAY POST	WOE IS ME
TEA ROOM	TIME OUT	TWO BITS	WEAK TEA	WOLF CUB
TEA ROSE	TIN MINE	TWO DEEP	WEAR OFF	WOLF DOG
TEA SHOP	TIN TACK	TWO PART	WEAR OUT	WON OVER
TEA TIME	TIPS OFF	TWO STEP	WEB FOOT	WOOD OIL
	TIRE OUT	TWO TIME	WEB TOED	WOOD OWL

7 contd.

WOOD TAR
WOOL OIL
WORE OFF
WORK BAG
WORK BOX
WORK DAY
WORK FOR
WORK OFF
WORK OUT
WORK SHY
WORKS IN
WORKS ON
WORKS UP
WORN OUT
WORTH IT
WOULD BE
WOUND UP
WRAPS UP
WRITE UP
WRONG UN
WROTE UP
WRY NECK
WYCH ELM
X RAYING
YARD ARM
YEAR END
YEW TREE
YOLK SAC
YULE LOG
ZAP IT UP
ZEROS IN
ZIP CODE
ZIP NECK

8

A BIENTOT
A BIT MUCH
A DAB HAND
A DIM VIEW
A FAIR COP
A GOOD JOB
A GOOD RUN
A LA CARTE
A RAW DEAL
ABOVE ALL
ABOVE PAR
ACES HIGH
ACES WILD
ACID BATH
ACID DROP
ACID HEAD
ACID RAIN
ACID TEST
ACORN CUP
ACT OF GOD
ACT OF WAR
ACT THREE
ACTED OUT
ACTING UP

AD LIBBED
AD LIBBER
ADAMS ALE
ADAMS RIB
ADDING UP
AFTER ALL
AGAR AGAR
AGE GROUP
AGNUS DEI
AIR BENDS
AIR BRAKE
AIR BRICK
AIR BRUSH
AIR COOLS
AIR COVER
AIR FORCE
AIR POWER
AIR RIFLE
AIR SCOUT
AIR TO AIR
ALE HOUSE
ALL ALONE
ALL ALONG
ALL AT SEA
ALL CLEAR
ALL FOUND
ALL FOURS
ALL IN ALL
ALL IN ONE
ALL MY EYE
ALL RIGHT
ALL ROUND
ALL STARS
ALL THE GO
ALL THERE
ALLEN KEY
ALLEY CAT
ALMS FOLK
ALOE VERA
ALTER EGO
ANT EATER
ANTE POST
ANTI HERO
ANTS EGGS
ANTS NEST
ANZAC DAY
APPLE PIE
APRES SKI
ARBOR DAY
ARC LIGHT
AREA CODE
ARECA NUT
ARK ROYAL
ARM IN ARM
ARMS RACE
ARMY CAMP
ARMY LIST
ART CLASS
ART PAPER
ART UNION

ARUM LILY
AS IT WERE
AS ONE MAN
ASH BLOND
ASH LEACH
ASH PLANT
ASH STAND
ASK AFTER
ASK FOR IT
AT A PINCH
AT A PRICE
AT ANCHOR
AT BOTTOM
AT DINNER
AT LENGTH
AT THE BAR
ATOM BOMB
ATTIC WIT
AU GRATIN
AU REVOIR
AUGER BIT
AUTO DA FE
AVE MARIA
AWAY GAME
BABY BOOM
BABY DOLL
BABY SITS
BABY TALK
BACK AXLE
BACK COMB
BACK DATE
BACK DOOR
BACK DOWN
BACK HEEL
BACK LANE
BACKED UP
BACKS OFF
BAD BLOOD
BAD DREAM
BAD FAITH
BAD LOSER
BAD PATCH
BADLY OFF
BAIL BALL
BAIL DOCK
BAILS OUT
BAKER DAY
BALD COOT
BALD HEAD
BALE DOCK
BALE FIRE
BALED OUT
BALES OUT
BALL BOYS
BALL GAME
BALL GIRL
BALL GOWN
BALL PARK
BALL ROOM
BAND FISH

BANG TAIL
BANGED UP
BANGS OUT
BANK BILL
BANK BOOK
BANK LOAN
BANK NOTE
BANK RATE
BAR CHART
BAR CODED
BAR GRAPH
BAR LUNCH
BAR STOOL
BARGED IN
BARGES IN
BARN DOOR
BASE BORN
BASE COIN
BASE LINE
BASE RATE
BASE RING
BASS CLEF
BASS DRUM
BASS HORN
BASS TUBA
BASS VIOL
BATON GUN
BATTLE ON
BAWLS OUT
BAY HORSE
BE A SPORT
BE MOTHER
BEACH HUT
BEAD ROLL
BEAM ENDS
BEAM TREE
BEAN KING
BEAN TREE
BEAR ARMS
BEAR AWAY
BEAR DOWN
BEARS EAR
BEARS OUT
BEAT DOWN
BEAT TIME
BEAT TO IT
BEATEN UP
BEATS OFF
BEATS OUT
BEAU JOUR
BEAU PERE
BED LINEN
BED PLATE
BEDDY BYE
BEDS DOWN
BEE BREAD
BEE EATER
BEE HOUSE
BEEFED UP
BEER PUMP

BEL CANTO
BEL PAESE
BELL BIRD
BELL BUOY
BELL PULL
BELL ROPE
BELL TENT
BELLE VUE
BELOW PAR
BELTED UP
BELTS OUT
BEN NEVIS
BEND OVER
BENT OVER
BERG WIND
BERRY BUG
BEST GIRL
BEST MAID
BEST PART
BETA RAYS
BETEL NUT
BEVIN BOY
BI WEEKLY
BI YEARLY
BIG APPLE
BIG BREAK
BIG CHIEF
BIG DADDY
BIG HOUSE
BIG MONEY
BIG MOUTH
BIG NOISE
BIG STICK
BIG WHEEL
BILE DUCT
BILLY CAN
BIN LINER
BIND OVER
BIRCH FLY
BIRCH ROD
BIRD CALL
BIRD EYED
BIRD LIME
BIT BY BIT
BLACK ART
BLACK BOX
BLACK CAP
BLACK CAT
BLACK EYE
BLACK FLY
BLACK FOX
BLACK ICE
BLACK OUT
BLACK RAT
BLACK ROD
BLACK SEA
BLACK TEA
BLACK TIE
BLAST OFF
BLESS YOU

8 *contd.*

BLEW AWAY	BORE DOWN	BULLS EYE	CAME AWAY	CAUGHT UP
BLEW OVER	BORN FOOL	BULLY BOY	CAME BACK	CAVE BEAR
BLIND GUT	BORNE OUT	BULLY OFF	CAME DOWN	CAVING IN
BLOOD RED	BOSS EYED	BUMP INTO	CAME HOME	CEDAR NUT
BLOTS OUT	BOTTLE UP	BUMPED UP	CAME OVER	CELL MATE
BLOW AWAY	BOUGHT IN	BUMPS OFF	CAMP FIRE	CHAINS UP
BLOW LAMP	BOUGHT UP	BUN FIGHT	CAMP IT UP	CHAIR BED
BLOW OVER	BOW BELLS	BUNG HOLE	CAMP SITE	CHALK OUT
BLOWS OUT	BOWED OUT	BUNG VENT	CAMPS OUT	CHALKS UP
BLUE BABY	BOWING IN	BUNGED UP	CANE MILL	CHANCE IT
BLUE BOOK	BOWL OVER	BUNK BEDS	CANON LAW	CHANGE UP
BLUE CHIP	BOWLS OUT	BUNNY HOP	CANT HOOK	CHAT SHOW
BLUE FILM	BOX CLOTH	BUNNY HUG	CANT RAIL	CHEATS ON
BLUE FUNK	BOX FRAME	BUOYED UP	CAP IT ALL	CHECK KEY
BLUE GREY	BOX PLEAT	BURN DOWN	CAPE CART	CHECK OFF
BLUE HARE	BOX WAGON	BURNED UP	CAPE HORN	CHECK OUT
BLUE MOON	BOY SCOUT	BURNT OUT	CAPE TOWN	CHECKS IN
BLUE NOTE	BOYS CLUB	BUSH BABY	CAPER TEA	CHECKS UP
BLURT OUT	BRAIN FAG	BUSH BUCK	CAR CRASH	CHEE CHEE
BOARD OUT	BRAKE PAD	BUTTED IN	CAR FERRY	CHEERS UP
BOAT DECK	BRAKE VAN	BUTTER UP	CAR PHONE	CHESS SET
BOAT HOOK	BRAN MASH	BUTTON UP	CARD CASE	CHEW OVER
BOAT LOAD	BRAND NEW	BUYING IN	CARD FILE	CHEZ NOUS
BOAT SONG	BRASS HAT	BUYING UP	CARD GAME	CHICK PEA
BOB MAJOR	BRAT PACK	BUYS A PUP	CARD PLAY	CHILL OUT
BOB MINOR	BREAD BIN	BUYS OVER	CARD VOTE	CHIMED IN
BOB ROYAL	BREAK JAW	BUZZ BOMB	CARE WORN	CHIMES IN
BOBBY PIN	BREAK OFF	BUZZ WORD	CARRY ALL	CHIN CHIN
BODES LAW	BREAK OUT	BY CHANCE	CARRY OFF	CHINA INK
BODY BLOW	BREAK VOW	BY CHOICE	CARRY OUT	CHINA TEA
BODY SHOP	BREAKS IN	BY DESIGN	CARTS OFF	CHIP SHOP
BOG LATIN	BREAKS UP	BY ITSELF	CARVE OUT	CHIP SHOT
BOGEY MAN	BREWED UP	BY RETURN	CARVED UP	CHIPS OFF
BOGS DOWN	BRICK RED	BY RIGHTS	CARVES UP	CHOKE OFF
BOIL OVER	BRIDE BED	BY THE BYE	CASE BOOK	CHOKED UP
BOMB SITE	BRIEF BAG	BY THE WAY	CASE LOAD	CHOKES UP
BONA FIDE	BRIM FULL	CAB STAND	CASE WORK	CHOO CHOO
BONE ACHE	BRING OFF	CABIN BOY	CASH BOOK	CHOP CHOP
BONE DUST	BRING OUT	CABLE CAR	CASH CARD	CHOP SUEY
BONE IDLE	BRINGS IN	CACHE POT	CASH CROP	CHOTA PEG
BONE LACE	BRINGS ON	CAFE NOIR	CASH DESK	CHOUX BUN
BONE MEAL	BRINGS UP	CAGING IN	CASH DOWN	CHOW CHOW
BONE MILL	BROKE OFF	CAKE HOLE	CASH FLOW	CHOW MEIN
BONING UP	BROKE OUT	CALF LOVE	CASH SALE	CHUCK OUT
BONY PIKE	BROKEN IN	CALF TIME	CASHED IN	CHUCKS UP
BOOB TUBE	BROOD SAC	CALL AWAY	CASHED UP	CHURN OUT
BOOK CLUB	BROWN ALE	CALL BACK	CASHES IN	CHURN OWL
BOOK ENDS	BROWN OWL	CALL BIRD	CASHES UP	CHURNS UP
BOOK MATE	BROWN RAT	CALL GIRL	CAST A NET	CI DEVANT
BOOKED IN	BRUSH OFF	CALL NOTE	CAST AWAY	CIDER CUP
BOOKED UP	BUBBLE UP	CALL OVER	CAST IRON	CIGAR BOX
BOOKS OUT	BUCKED UP	CALL SIGN	CAST LOTS	CINE FILM
BOOM IRON	BUFF COAT	CALLED BY	CASTS OFF	CITY DESK
BOOM TOWN	BUILDS IN	CALLED IN	CASTS OUT	CITY HALL
BOOT HOOK	BUILDS UP	CALLED ON	CATCH ALL	CIVIL DAY
BOOT JACK	BULL BEEF	CALLS OFF	CATCH OUT	CIVIL LAW
BOOT SALE	BULL CALF	CALLS OUT	CATS FOOT	CIVIL WAR
BORE ARMS	BULL HOOF	CALM DOWN	CATS MEAT	CLASS WAR
BORE AWAY	BULL HORN	CALOR GAS	CATS TAIL	CLAW BACK
	BULL RING	CAM WHEEL	CAUGHT ON	CLAY MILL

8 *contd.*

CLAY PIPE
CLEAN CUT
CLEAN OUT
CLEANS UP
CLEAR CUT
CLEAR OFF
CLEAR OUT
CLEARS UP
CLIP CLOP
CLIP HOOK
CLOCK OFF
CLOCK OUT
CLOCKS IN
CLOCKS UP
CLOSED IN
CLOSED UP
CLOSES IN
CLOSES UP
CLOTH CAP
CLUB FACE
CLUB FOOT
CLUB HEAD
CLUB SODA
CLUING IN
CLY FAKER
COACH BOX
COACH WAY
COAL DUST
COAL FACE
COAL FLAP
COAL HOLE
COAL MINE
COAL SACK
COCA COLA
COCK CROW
COCK EYED
COCO WOOD
COCOA FAT
COD PIECE
CODE BOOK
CODE NAME
COG WHEEL
COINED IT
COLD FEET
COLD FISH
COLD SNAP
COLD SORE
COLE SLAW
COLOUR IN
COLOUR UP
COMBS OUT
COME AWAY
COME BACK
COME COME
COME DOWN
COME HOME
COME OVER
COMES OFF
COMES OUT

COMING AT
COMING BY
COMING IN
COMING TO
COMING UP
CON AMORE
CON TRICK
CONED OFF
CONES OFF
CONY WOOL
COOLS OFF
COOPED UP
COPPED IT
COQ AU VIN
CORE TIME
CORK HEEL
CORK SOLE
CORK TREE
CORN BALL
CORN CURE
CORN FLAG
CORN LAWS
CORN MILL
CORN MOTH
CORN RENT
COT DEATH
COTTON ON
COUGHS UP
COUNT OUT
COURT DAY
COVERS IN
COVERS UP
COW WHALE
COWS LICK
CRAB TREE
CRACKS UP
CRAM FULL
CRANE FLY
CRASH OUT
CREAM BUN
CREAM NUT
CREAM TEA
CREW NECK
CRIED OFF
CRIED OUT
CRIES OFF
CRIES OUT
CROSS EYE
CROSS PLY
CROSS RIB
CROWN CAP
CROWN SAW
CRUDE OIL
CRUSH BAR
CRUSH HAT
CRYING UP
CUB SCOUT
CUBE ROOT
CUFF LINK
CUL DE SAC

CUP FINAL
CUP MATCH
CUP OF TEA
CUSS WORD
CUT A DASH
CUT GLASS
CUT IT OUT
CUT LOOSE
CUT NO ICE
CUT PRICE
CUT SHORT
CUTS BACK
CUTS DEAD
CUTS DOWN
CYCLE CAR
DAMP DOWN
DARK AGES
DARK ROOM
DASH AWAY
DATE LINE
DATE PALM
DATE TREE
DAVIS CUP
DAVY LAMP
DAWN RAID
DAY BY DAY
DAY SHIFT
DAY SIGHT
DAY TO DAY
DAY WOMAN
DEAD BEAT
DEAD CART
DEAD CERT
DEAD DUCK
DEAD HAND
DEAD HEAD
DEAD HEAT
DEAD LOCK
DEAD LOSS
DEAD SHOT
DEAD SPIT
DEAD WOOD
DEAF MUTE
DEALS OUT
DEALT OUT
DEATH BED
DEATH CAP
DEATH RAY
DEATH ROW
DECK GAME
DECK HAND
DECK LOAD
DECKS OUT
DEED POLL
DEEP DOWN
DEEP DYED
DEER HORN
DEER PARK
DEMI JOUR
DEMI LUNE

DEMI VOLT
DEMI WOLF
DENE HOLE
DERBY DAY
DERBY HAT
DESK WORK
DEW BERRY
DEWY EYED
DICE GAME
DICE PLAY
DID A TURN
DIE HAPPY
DIE STOCK
DIED AWAY
DIED DOWN
DIED HARD
DIES AWAY
DIES DOWN
DIES HARD
DIES IRAE
DILLY BAG
DINED OUT
DINER OUT
DINES OUT
DING DONG
DIP STICK
DIPPED IN
DIRT ROAD
DIRTY DOG
DISC FILE
DISHED UP
DISHES UP
DITTY BAG
DIVAN BED
DIVE BOMB
DO BATTLE
DO GOODER
DOCK DUES
DOES DOWN
DOES OVER
DOES TIME
DOES WELL
DOG DAISY
DOG EARED
DOG HOUSE
DOG LATIN
DOG TIRED
DOG TRICK
DOG WATCH
DOG WEARY
DOG WHEAT
DOGGY BAG
DOGS BODY
DOGS HOME
DOGS LIFE
DOGS MEAT
DOGS NOSE
DOING OUT
DOLLY TUB
DONE DOWN

DONE OVER
DONE WELL
DONT KNOW
DOOR BELL
DOOR CASE
DOOR KNOB
DOOR SILL
DOSS DOWN
DOT THE IS
DOUBLE UP
DOUGH BOY
DOUM PALM
DOVE COTE
DOVE EYED
DOVE LIKE
DOWEL PIN
DOWEL ROD
DOWN HOME
DOWN LINE
DOWN TOWN
DOWN TROD
DRAG RACE
DRAGS OUT
DRAM SHOP
DRAW BACK
DRAW GEAR
DRAW LOTS
DRAW NEAR
DRAWS OFF
DRAWS OUT
DREAMS UP
DREAMT UP
DREW BACK
DREW LOTS
DREW NEAR
DRIED OUT
DRIES OUT
DRIFT ICE
DRIFT NET
DRIFT WAY
DRINKS IN
DRINKS UP
DRIP FEED
DRIVE OUT
DROP AWAY
DROP DEAD
DROP DOWN
DROP GOAL
DROP KICK
DROP SHOT
DROPS OFF
DROPS OUT
DROVE OUT
DROWN OUT
DRY CLEAN
DRY STEAM
DRY STONE
DRYING UP
DUCK DOWN
DUCK HAWK

8 LETTERS

8 contd.
DUCK POND
DUCK SHOT
DUCK SOUP
DUCK TAIL
DUCKS EGG
DUCKS OUT
DUE NORTH
DUE SOUTH
DUFFED UP
DULL EYED
DULL THUD
DUMB BELL
DUMB SHOW
DUMMY RUN
DUMPED ON
DUNG HEAP
DUNG HILL
DUST BALL
DUST BATH
DUST BOWL
DUST CART
DUST COAT
DUST HOLE
DUST TRAP
DUTCH HOE
DUTY FREE
DUTY PAID
DYE HOUSE
DYE WORKS
DYING OFF
DYING OUT
E NUMBERS
EAGLE OWL
EAGLE RAY
EAR PLUGS
EAR SHELL
EARTH FED
EARTH HOG
EARTH NUT
EASED OFF
EASES OFF
EAST SIDE
EATING IN
EATING UP
EATS AWAY
EAU DE NIL
EAU DE VIE
ECCE HOMO
EDGE RAIL
EDGE TOOL
EDGED OUT
EDGES OUT
EDITS OUT
EGG BOUND
EGG FRUIT
EGG PLANT
EGG SLICE
EGG SPOON
EGG TIMER

EGG WHISK
EL DORADO
ELF CHILD
EN CROUTE
END PAPER
END TO END
ENDING UP
ENTRY FEE
EPIC POEM
ESSEX MAN
ET CETERA
ETON CROP
ETON SUIT
EVENED UP
EVENS OUT
EVIL DEED
EVIL DOER
EX GRATIA
EX LIBRIS
EXCUSE ME
EXIT POLL
EYE DROPS
EYE LEVEL
EYE PIECE
EYE SALVE
EYE TEETH
EYE TOOTH
EYE WATER
EYES DOWN
FACE ACHE
FACE DOWN
FACE LIFT
FACE MASK
FACE PACK
FACED OUT
FACES OUT
FADE AWAY
FADED OUT
FADES OUT
FADING IN
FAIL SAFE
FAIR COPY
FAIR DEAL
FAIR GAME
FAIR ISLE
FAIR PLAY
FALL AWAY
FALL BACK
FALL DOWN
FALL OVER
FALLS OFF
FALLS OUT
FALSE GOD
FALSE HEM
FALSE LEG
FALSE RIB
FAN DANCE
FAN WHEEL
FANCY MAN
FAR FLUNG

FAR NORTH
FAR SOUTH
FARCY BUD
FARM HAND
FARMS OUT
FAST FOOD
FAST TALK
FASTEN ON
FAT FACED
FAT STOCK
FATTEN UP
FEAST DAY
FEED LINE
FEED PIPE
FEED PUMP
FEEL FREE
FELL BACK
FELL DOWN
FELL OVER
FELO DE SE
FEME SOLE
FEN BERRY
FERN SEED
FETCH OUT
FETE DIEU
FIELD BED
FIELD DAY
FIELD GUN
FIGHT OFF
FILE COPY
FILE PAST
FILED OFF
FILES OFF
FILLED IN
FILLED UP
FILLS OUT
FILM NOIR
FILM STAR
FIN WHALE
FINDS OUT
FINE ARTS
FINE GAEL
FINE LADY
FINE SPUN
FINE TUNE
FINISH UP
FIRE AWAY
FIRE BACK
FIRE BIRD
FIRE BOMB
FIRE DOOR
FIRE FLAG
FIRE HOSE
FIRE OPAL
FIRE RISK
FIRE TRAP
FIRE TUBE
FIRE WALK
FIRED OFF
FIRES OFF

FIRING UP
FIRM DOWN
FIRMED UP
FIRST AID
FIRST DAY
FISH BONE
FISH CAKE
FISH FARM
FISH GLUE
FISH GUTS
FISH HOOK
FISH MEAL
FISH POND
FISH STEW
FISH TAIL
FISH TANK
FISH WEIR
FITTED IN
FITTED UP
FIXING IT
FIXING ON
FIXING UP
FLAG DOWN
FLAKE OUT
FLARED UP
FLARES UP
FLASH GUN
FLAT FOOT
FLAT RACE
FLAT RATE
FLAT SPIN
FLAT TYRE
FLAX BUSH
FLAX COMB
FLAX LILY
FLAX MILL
FLAX SEED
FLEA BANE
FLEA BITE
FLESH FLY
FLESH OUT
FLESH POT
FLEW HIGH
FLEW OPEN
FLEW SOLO
FLIES OUT
FLIM FLAM
FLING OUT
FLIP FLAP
FLIP FLOP
FLIP SIDE
FLOCK BED
FLUE PIPE
FLUNG OUT
FLUSH BOX
FLY A KITE
FLY BLOWN
FLY PAPER
FLY SHEET
FLY SPRAY

FLY TYING
FLYING BY
FLYING IN
FOAM BATH
FOB WATCH
FOG LIGHT
FOIE GRAS
FOLDED IN
FOLDS OUT
FOLK HERO
FOLK SONG
FOLK TALE
FOLK TUNE
FOLLOW ON
FOLLOW UP
FOOD CARD
FOOD FISH
FOOLS CAP
FOOT BATH
FOOT PUMP
FOOT RACE
FOOT ROPE
FOOTED IT
FOR A TIME
FOR KEEPS
FOR KICKS
FOR MERCY
FOR SHAME
FOR SHORT
FORCE FED
FORE BODY
FORE RANK
FORGET IT
FORK OVER
FORKED UP
FORKS OUT
FORM ROOM
FORT KNOX
FOSSE WAY
FOUL FISH
FOUL PLAY
FOULED UP
FOUND OUT
FOUR BALL
FOUR BITS
FOUR EYES
FOUR PACK
FOUR PART
FOWL PEST
FOX BRUSH
FOX EARTH
FOX GRAPE
FRAME SAW
FRANK FEE
FREAK OUT
FREE ATOM
FREE CITY
FREE FALL
FREE GIFT
FREE HAND

8 contd.

FREE KICK	GANGED UP	GLOVE BOX	GONE SOFT	HAIR WAVE
FREE LIST	GAOL BIRD	GLOW WORM	GONE WEST	HAIR WORK
FREE LOVE	GAS BLACK	GNAW AWAY	GOOD FORM	HAIR WORM
FREE PORT	GAS BOARD	GO ABROAD	GOOD LADY	HALF BACK
FREE SHOT	GAS FIRED	GO GETTER	GOOD SHOW	HALF BRED
FREE VOTE	GAS GLOBE	GO GO GIRL	GOOD TURN	HALF COCK
FREE WILL	GAS METER	GO HALVES	GOOD WORK	HALF DEAD
FREEZE UP	GAS MOTOR	GO HUNGRY	GOON SHOW	HALF DONE
FRESH AIR	GAS PLANT	GO METRIC	GOOSE EGG	HALF FACE
FRESH RUN	GAS POKER	GO NATIVE	GOT ABOUT	HALF HOUR
FRIED EGG	GAS STOVE	GO PLACES	GOT AHEAD	HALF INCH
FROG FISH	GAS TIGHT	GO PUBLIC	GOT ALONG	HALF LIFE
FROM A TO B	GAS WORKS	GO STEADY	GOT IDEAS	HALF LOAF
FROM A TO Z	GATE FINE	GO TO SEED	GOT READY	HALF MAST
FRONT MAN	GATE POST	GO TO TOWN	GOT ROUND	HALF MOON
FROTH FLY	GATHER UP	GO TOO FAR	GOT THERE	HALF NOTE
FROU FROU	GAUDY DAY	GOAL KICK	GOT TOUGH	HALF PINT
FROWNS ON	GAVE AWAY	GOAL LINE	GOUGE OUT	HALF TERM
FRUIT BAT	GAVE ODDS	GOAT MOTH	GRACE CUP	HALF TIDE
FRUIT BUD	GAVE REIN	GOBBLE UP	GRAND CRU	HALF TIME
FRUIT FLY	GEAR CASE	GOD AWFUL	GRAND MAL	HALF TINT
FRUIT PIE	GEAR DOWN	GOD BLESS	GRASS BOX	HALF TONE
FUEL CELL	GEARED UP	GOD GIVEN	GREAT APE	HALF YEAR
FUEL PIPE	GENNED UP	GOD KNOWS	GREAT AUK	HALL DOOR
FUEL TANK	GERM CELL	GODS ACRE	GREAT GUN	HALL MOOT
FULL BACK	GET ABOUT	GOES AWAY	GREAT MAN	HAND BALL
FULL BORE	GET AHEAD	GOES BACK	GREAT TIT	HAND CART
FULL COCK	GET ALONG	GOES BUST	GREAT TOE	HAND DOWN
FULL EYED	GET IDEAS	GOES DOWN	GREAT WAR	HAND KNIT
FULL FACE	GET READY	GOES INTO	GREEK GOD	HAND LINE
FULL HAND	GET ROUND	GOES LIVE	GREEN BAG	HAND LOOM
FULL MOON	GET THERE	GOES OVER	GREEN EYE	HAND MILL
FULL PAGE	GET TOUGH	GOES SOFT	GREEN TEA	HAND OVER
FULL PELT	GETS BACK	GOES WEST	GREY AREA	HAND PICK
FULL SAIL	GETS DOWN	GOING BAD	GREY COAT	HAND POST
FULL STOP	GETS EVEN	GOING DRY	GREY EYED	HANDS OFF
FULL TILT	GETS OVER	GOING FAR	GREY FISH	HANDS OUT
FULL TIME	GIFT BOOK	GOING FOR	GREY MARE	HANG BACK
FULL TOSS	GIFT SHOP	GOING MAD	GREY WOLF	HANG FIRE
FUMED OAK	GIFT WRAP	GOING OFF	GROG SHOP	HANG OVER
FUNNY MAN	GIG LAMPS	GOING OUT	GROO GROO	HANGER ON
FUR TRADE	GIN AND IT	GOINGS ON	GRUB SHOP	HANGS OFF
FUSE WIRE	GIN RUMMY	GOLD COIN	GUARD DOG	HANGS OUT
FUZZ BALL	GIN SLING	GOLD DISC	GUIDE DOG	HARA KIRI
GABLE END	GIVE AWAY	GOLD DUST	GULL WING	HARD AT IT
GAD ABOUT	GIVE ODDS	GOLD FOIL	GUM RESIN	HARD CASE
GAFF SAIL	GIVE OVER	GOLD LACE	GUMMED UP	HARD CASH
GAIN TIME	GIVE REIN	GOLD LEAF	GYM TUNIC	HARD COPY
GALL DUCT	GIVES EAR	GOLD MINE	HACK WORK	HARD CORE
GAME BALL	GIVES OFF	GOLD RING	HAD A BALL	HARD DISC
GAME BIRD	GIVES OUT	GOLD RUSH	HAD A BASH	HARD DISK
GAME CALL	GIVES WAY	GOLD WIRE	HAD A STAB	HARD EDGE
GAME COCK	GIVING IN	GOLF BALL	HAD IDEAS	HARD LUCK
GAME FISH	GIVING UP	GOLF CLUB	HAD IT OUT	HARD ROCK
GAME LAWS	GLAD HAND	GONE AWAY	HAD WORDS	HARD SELL
GAME PLAN	GLAD RAGS	GONE BACK	HAIL MARY	HARD WORK
GAMMY LEG	GLAM ROCK	GONE BUST	HAIR BALL	HARE FOOT
GANG MILL	GLASS EYE	GONE DOWN	HAIR BAND	HARES EAR
GANG SHOW	GLASS JAW	GONE INTO	HAIR GRIP	HARK BACK
	GLEE CLUB	GONE OVER	HAIR TAIL	HARP SEAL

8 LETTERS

8 *contd.*

HARPED ON
HAS A BALL
HAS A BASH
HAS A STAB
HAS BEENS
HAS IDEAS
HAS IT OUT
HAS WORDS
HAT TRICK
HAULED IN
HAULED UP
HAVE NOTS
HAVING IT
HAVING ON
HAVING TO
HAVING UP
HAWK EYED
HAWK MOTH
HAY FEVER
HAZEL NUT
HEAD BOOM
HEAD COLD
HEAD GIRL
HEAD RENT
HEAD WIND
HEADS OFF
HEADS OUT
HEAR HEAR
HEAR TELL
HEARD OUT
HEARS OUT
HEAT PUMP
HEAT SINK
HEAT UNIT
HEAT WAVE
HEATH HEN
HEAVES TO
HEAVY SEA
HEAVY WET
HEDGE HOP
HEEL BALL
HELD BACK
HELD DOWN
HELD GOOD
HELD OVER
HELD SWAY
HELL BENT
HELL FIRE
HELL GATE
HELL HOLE
HELPS OUT
HEMMED IN
HEMP PALM
HEMP SEED
HEN COURT
HEN FLESH
HEN HOUSE
HEN NIGHT
HEN PARTY

HEN ROOST
HERB BEER
HERE GOES
HIC JACET
HIDE AWAY
HIDY HOLE
HIGH BORN
HIGH BRED
HIGH CAMP
HIGH GEAR
HIGH HAND
HIGH JUMP
HIGH KICK
HIGH LIFE
HIGH MASS
HIGH NOON
HIGH RISE
HIGH RISK
HIGH ROAD
HIGH SEAS
HIGH SPOT
HIGH TECH
HIGH TIDE
HIGH TIME
HIGH TOBY
HIGH WIRE
HIGHER UP
HILL FORT
HIND WING
HINTED AT
HIP FLASK
HIP JOINT
HIRED OUT
HIRES OUT
HIT IT OFF
HIVE NEST
HIVED OFF
HIVES OFF
HOCK CART
HOCK TIDE
HOG MANED
HOGGED IT
HOGS BACK
HOKY POKY
HOLD BACK
HOLD DOWN
HOLD GOOD
HOLD HARD
HOLD OVER
HOLD SWAY
HOLDS OFF
HOLDS OUT
HOLED OUT
HOLES OUT
HOLING UP
HOLLY OAK
HOLY CITY
HOLY LAND
HOLY ROOD
HOLY WEEK

HOLY WRIT
HOLY YEAR
HOME BASE
HOME BIRD
HOME FARM
HOME FIRE
HOME GAME
HOME HELP
HOME LIFE
HOME LOAN
HOME MADE
HOME PORT
HOME RULE
HOME TOWN
HONEY ANT
HONEY BEE
HONEY DEW
HONEY SAC
HONG KONG
HOOF MARK
HOOK WORM
HOPPED IT
HORN RIMS
HORNED IN
HORSE BOX
HORSE BOY
HORSE HOE
HOSE REEL
HOT METAL
HOT MONEY
HOT PANTS
HOT PLATE
HOT STUFF
HOT TODDY
HOT WATER
HOTTED UP
HOUR HAND
HOUSE DOG
HOUSE TAX
HOVER BED
HOVER BUS
HOVER FLY
HOWL DOWN
HOWS THAT
HUB BRAKE
HULA HOOP
HULA HULA
HUMP BACK
HUNG BACK
HUNG BEEF
HUNG FIRE
HUNG JURY
HUNG MEAT
HUNG OVER
HUNT BALL
HUNT DOWN
HUNTS OUT
HUSH HUSH
HUSHED UP
HUSHES UP

HYDE PARK
HYENA DOG
HYMN BOOK
HYPING UP
I DARE SAY
I DECLARE
ICE BOUND
ICE CRAFT
ICE CREAM
ICE CUBES
ICE DANCE
ICE FIELD
ICE HOUSE
ICE LOLLY
ICE SHEET
ICE SKATE
ICE WATER
ICE YACHT
ICED OVER
ICES OVER
IDEAS MAN
IDEE FIXE
IDIOT BOX
IDLE TIME
ILL BEING
ILL BLOOD
ILL FATED
ILL SPENT
ILL TIMED
ILL TREAT
ILL USAGE
IN A FLASH
IN A HURRY
IN A JIFFY
IN A PADDY
IN A SENSE
IN A TRICE
IN A WHILE
IN AND OUT
IN CAMERA
IN CHARGE
IN CLOVER
IN COMMON
IN CREDIT
IN DANGER
IN DEMAND
IN DETAIL
IN EFFECT
IN FAVOUR
IN FLIGHT
IN FUTURE
IN MID AIR
IN PERSON
IN PIECES
IN POCKET
IN PRISON
IN PUBLIC
IN QUOTES
IN SEASON
IN SECRET

IN SHTOOK
IN SPADES
IN TANDEM
IN THE AIR
IN THE BAG
IN THE CAN
IN THE END
IN THE RAW
IN THE RED
IN THE WAY
IN UNISON
INCH TAPE
INCH WORM
INERT GAS
INFRA DIG
INFRA RED
INKING IN
INNER BAR
INNER MAN
INTER NOS
IRISH CAR
IRISH ELK
IRISH SEA
IRON CLAD
IRON GREY
IRON HAND
IRON LUNG
IRON MINE
IRONS OUT
IT IS SAID
ITCH MITE
IVORY NUT
JACK BOOT
JACK FOOL
JACK HIGH
JACK PLUG
JAIL BAIT
JAIL BIRD
JAPAN WAX
JAW LEVER
JAZZ BAND
JELLY BAG
JET BLACK
JET PLANE
JET SKIER
JEWS HARP
JIB CRANE
JIG BORER
JOG ALONG
JOHN BULL
JOHN DORY
JOINED IN
JOINED UP
JOKE BOOK
JOY RIDER
JOY STICK
JUMBO JET
JUMP BAIL
JUMP SHIP
JUMP SUIT

8 *contd.*

JUMP TO IT	KNOT HOLE	LEAD MINE	LIFT PUMP	LONG SHOT
JUMPED ON	LABOR DAY	LEAD TIME	LIFTED UP	LONG SLIP
JUMPED UP	LACE BOOT	LEADS OFF	LIFTS OFF	LONG SPUN
JUMPS OFF	LACE WING	LEADS OUT	LIGHT ALE	LONG STAY
JUNK BOND	LADLE OUT	LEAF BASE	LIGHT PEN	LONG STOP
JUNK FOOD	LADY FERN	LEAF CURL	LIGHTS UP	LONG SUIT
JUNK MAIL	LADY LOVE	LEAF FALL	LIKE FURY	LONG TERM
JUNK SHOP	LADY LUCK	LEAF SCAR	LILY POND	LONG TIME
JUNK YARD	LAID BACK	LEAKS OUT	LIMA WOOD	LONG TOGS
JURY LIST	LAID BARE	LEANED ON	LIMBER UP	LONG VIEW
JURY MAST	LAID DOWN	LEAP FROG	LIME TREE	LONG WAIT
KAKA BEAK	LAID INTO	LEAP YEAR	LIME TWIG	LONG WAVE
KAKA BILL	LAID OPEN	LEAVE OFF	LIME WOOD	LOOK AWRY
KALA AZAR	LAID WORK	LEAVE OUT	LINE FISH	LOOK BACK
KEEL OVER	LAKE ERIE	LEAVES BE	LINING UP	LOOK DOWN
KEEP AT IT	LAMB LIKE	LED HORSE	LINKED IN	LOOK HERE
KEEP BACK	LAME DUCK	LEE BOARD	LINKED UP	LOOK INTO
KEEP BUSY	LAND AHOY	LEE GAUGE	LINO TILE	LOOK LIKE
KEEP DOWN	LAND ARMY	LEE SHORE	LION LIKE	LOOK OVER
KEEP IT UP	LAND BANK	LEFT BANK	LIP SALVE	LOOK UP TO
KEEP TIME	LAND CRAB	LEFT HAND	LISTEN IN	LOOKED AT
KEEPS FIT	LAND FISH	LEFT HOOK	LITTLE GO	LOOKED IN
KEEPS MUM	LAND GIRL	LEFT OVER	LIVE A LIE	LOOKED ON
KEEPS OFF	LAND HAUL	LEFT SIDE	LIVE BAIT	LOOKED UP
KEPT AT IT	LAND LINE	LEFT WING	LIVE BORN	LOOKER ON
KEPT BACK	LAND MINE	LEG BREAK	LIVE DOWN	LOOKS FOR
KEPT BUSY	LAND ROLL	LEG GUARD	LIVE IT UP	LOOKS OUT
KEPT DOWN	LANDS END	LEG WOMAN	LIVE LOAD	LOONY BIN
KEPT TIME	LAP BOARD	LEGAL AID	LIVE RAIL	LOOP LINE
KEY FRUIT	LAST GASP	LEMON DAB	LIVE WELL	LOOSE BOX
KEY PLATE	LAST HEIR	LENT LILY	LIVE WIRE	LOOSE CUT
KEY PUNCH	LAST POST	LET ALONE	LIVED OUT	LOOSE END
KEYING IN	LAST WORD	LET BLOOD	LIVES OUT	LOOSEN UP
KICKED IN	LATE CALL	LET DRIVE	LIVING IN	LOP EARED
KICKS OFF	LAUGH OFF	LET IT RIP	LIVING ON	LOP SIDED
KICKS OUT	LAW AGENT	LET LOOSE	LOAD LINE	LORDS DAY
KID GLOVE	LAW COURT	LET ME SEE	LOAF CAKE	LORRY HOP
KILL TIME	LAW GIVER	LET SLIDE	LOAN WORD	LOSE FACE
KILLS OFF	LAW MAKER	LETS DOWN	LOCH NESS	LOSE TIME
KING BIRD	LAY AN EGG	LETS DROP	LOCK AWAY	LOSES OUT
KING CRAB	LAY ASIDE	LETS FALL	LOCK GATE	LOST FACE
KING CROW	LAY AWAKE	LETS IN ON	LOCKED IN	LOST SOUL
KING JOHN	LAY CLAIM	LETS SLIP	LOCKED ON	LOST TIME
KING LIKE	LAY SHAFT	LEVEL OFF	LOCKED UP	LOUIS DOR
KING SIZE	LAY UNDER	LEWIS GUN	LOCKS OUT	LOVE DRUG
KINGS MAN	LAY VICAR	LIAR DICE	LOFTED UP	LOVE GAME
KIPS DOWN	LAY WASTE	LIE AWAKE	LOG CABIN	LOVE KNOT
KIRK TOWN	LAYING BY	LIE DOGGO	LOG CANOE	LOVE NEST
KISS CURL	LAYING IN	LIE UNDER	LOG HOUSE	LOVE SEAT
KITE MARK	LAYING ON	LIES BACK	LOGGED IN	LOVE SONG
KNEE DEEP	LAYING UP	LIES DOWN	LOK SABHA	LOVE SUIT
KNEE HIGH	LAYS BARE	LIES OVER	LONE WOLF	LOW DUTCH
KNEE JERK	LAYS DOWN	LIFE BUOY	LONG FACE	LOW LATIN
KNEE SOCK	LAYS INTO	LIFE LINE	LONG HAIR	LOW LIVED
KNIFE BOX	LAYS OPEN	LIFE PEER	LONG HAUL	LOW SLUNG
KNOCK OFF	LAZY DAYS	LIFE RAFT	LONG JUMP	LOW WATER
KNOCK OUT	LAZY JACK	LIFE RENT	LONG LIFE	LUCKY BAG
KNOCKS ON	LEACH TUB	LIFE SIZE	LONG MARK	LUCKY DIP
KNOCKS UP	LEAD FREE	LIFE WORK	LONG ODDS	LUCKY JIM
	LEAD LINE	LIFT GIRL	LONG ROBE	LUGGED IN

8 LETTERS

8 contd.

LUMPY JAW	MAN HOURS	MINE HOST	NAIL BOMB	NORTH SEA
LUNCH BOX	MAN OF GOD	MINI SKIS	NAIL DOWN	NOSE BAND
LUNG FISH	MAN OF LAW	MINOR KEY	NAIL FILE	NOSE CONE
LYING LOW	MAN OF WAR	MIST OVER	NAIL HEAD	NOSE DIVE
LYNCH LAW	MAN POWER	MISTED UP	NAIL HOLE	NOSE RING
LYNCH MOB	MAN SIZED	MIXED BAG	NAKED EYE	NOSED OUT
LYNX EYED	MAN TO MAN	MIXER TAP	NAME DROP	NOSES OUT
LYRE BIRD	MAN WEEKS	MIXING IN	NAME PART	NOT A HOPE
MAD APPLE	MAN YEARS	MIXING IT	NAVY BLUE	NOT A PEEP
MADE A BED	MANY EYED	MIXING UP	NAVY LIST	NOTA BENE
MADE AWAY	MANY ROOT	MOBY DICK	NAVY YARD	NOTE CASE
MADE GOOD	MAORI HEN	MOCK MOON	NEAP TIDE	NUT BROWN
MADE IT UP	MARK DOWN	MOLE EYED	NEAR BEER	OAK APPLE
MADE LOVE	MARK TIME	MOLED OUT	NEAR EAST	OAK CHEST
MADE OVER	MARKED UP	MOLES OUT	NEAR HAND	OAT GRASS
MADE PLAY	MARKS OFF	MONA LISA	NEAR MISS	OBI WOMAN
MADE ROAD	MARKS OUT	MONEY BAG	NEAT HERD	OCEAN BED
MADE ROOM	MARRY OFF	MONEY BOX	NECK BAND	OF COURSE
MADE SAIL	MARSH GAS	MOON BOOT	NECK BONE	OFF AND ON
MADE SURE	MARSH TIT	MOON EYED	NEED FIRE	OFF BOARD
MADE TIME	MASHED UP	MOON FISH	NEON LAMP	OFF BREAK
MAGIC BOX	MASHES UP	MOON POOL	NERVE END	OFF DRIVE
MAGIC EYE	MASS BELL	MOOT CASE	NERVE GAS	OFF SALES
MAH JONGG	MASS BOOK	MOOT HALL	NEVER WAS	OFF STAGE
MAIL BOAT	MAXI COAT	MOPPED UP	NEW BLOOD	OFF WHITE
MAIL CART	MAY APPLE	MORAL LAW	NEW BLOWN	OFFERS UP
MAIL SHOT	MAY BLOOM	MORAY EEL	NEW BROOM	OIL FIELD
MAIN DECK	MAY QUEEN	MOSS ROSE	NEW FOUND	OIL FIRED
MAIN DRAG	MEA CULPA	MOT JUSTE	NEW LIGHT	OIL GAUGE
MAIN LINE	MEAL TIME	MOTH BALL	NEW MATHS	OIL PAINT
MAIN ROAD	MEAN BORN	MOTOR BUS	NEW RISEN	OIL PAPER
MAJOR KEY	MEAN WELL	MOTOR CAR	NEW STYLE	OIL PRESS
MAKE A BED	MEAT BALL	MOTOR JET	NEW WOMAN	OIL SHALE
MAKE AWAY	MEAT LOAF	MOUSE DUN	NEW WORLD	OIL SLICK
MAKE GOOD	MEAT RACK	MOUSE EAR	NEWLY WED	OLD FOGEY
MAKE IT UP	MEAT SAFE	MOVE AWAY	NEWS ROOM	OLD GLORY
MAKE LOVE	MELT AWAY	MOVE BACK	NEXT BEST	OLD GUARD
MAKE OVER	MELT DOWN	MOVE OVER	NEXT DOOR	OLD HARRY
MAKE PLAY	MEM SAHIB	MOVED OUT	NICE WORK	OLD STORY
MAKE ROOM	MEN OF WAR	MOVES OUT	NIGHT AIR	OLD STYLE
MAKE SAIL	MERRY MEN	MOVING IN	NIGHT APE	OLD TIMER
MAKE SURE	MESH WORK	MOWN DOWN	NIGHT FLY	OLD WOMAN
MAKE TIME	MESS DECK	MUCH LESS	NIGHT OUT	OLD WORLD
MAKES FOR	MESS ROOM	MUCK HEAP	NIGHT OWL	OLIVE OIL
MAKES HAY	MESSED UP	MUCK RAKE	NINE PINS	OLIVE OYL
MAKES OFF	MESSES UP	MUCKED IN	NIPPED IN	ON AND OFF
MAKES OUT	METER MAN	MUD FLATS	NIT PICKS	ON CAMERA
MAKES WAR	MID OCEAN	MUD GUARD	NO GO AREA	ON CREDIT
MAKES WAY	MID POINT	MUDDLE UP	NO LONGER	ON DEMAND
MAKING DO	MILCH COW	MUGGED UP	NO MATTER	ON PARADE
MAKING IT	MILK LOAF	MULE DEER	NO THANKS	ON PATROL
MAKING UP	MILK WARM	MULTI PLY	NO TRUMPS	ON RECORD
MAL DE MER	MILK WEED	MUSCLE IN	NO WONDER	ON REMAND
MALA FIDE	MILKY WAY	MUSIC BOX	NOAHS ARK	ON SAFARI
MALT KILN	MILL GIRL	MUSIC PEN	NOBLE ART	ON STREAM
MALT MILL	MILL HAND	MUSK BALL	NOBLE GAS	ON STRIKE
MAN ALIVE	MILL WORK	MUSK DEER	NON EVENT	ON TARGET
MAN CHILD	MINCE PIE	MUSK PEAR	NON METAL	ON THE AIR
MAN EATER	MIND CURE	MUSK ROSE	NON STICK	ON THE DOT
	MINDS EYE	MUTE SWAN	NON UNION	ON THE HOP

8 *contd.*

ON THE JOB	PAID CASH	PEEPS OUT	PIPE DOWN	POP GROUP
ON THE MAP	PAINT BOX	PEGS AWAY	PIPE LINE	POPE JOAN
ON THE MAT	PAIR BOND	PEGS BACK	PIPE RACK	POPES EYE
ON THE NOD	PAIR CASE	PEGS DOWN	PIPE ROLL	POPPED IN
ON THE RUN	PALE EYED	PELL MELL	PIPE STEM	POPPED UP
ON THE SLY	PALL MALL	PEN WIPER	PIPING UP	POPPY DAY
ON THE WAY	PALM TREE	PEP PILLS	PIRI PIRI	POPPY OIL
ON TIPTOE	PALM WINE	PER ANNUM	PIS ALLER	PORK CHOP
ON VELVET	PAN PIPES	PERKED UP	PIT VIPER	PORT WINE
ONCE OVER	PANDA CAR	PETER MAN	PITH TREE	POST CODE
ONE BY ONE	PANEL PIN	PETER PAN	PIVOT MAN	POST DATE
ONE HORSE	PANEL SAW	PETIT MAL	PIXY RING	POST FREE
ONE LINER	PAPER BAG	PEW CHAIR	PLACE MAT	POST GIRL
ONE OR TWO	PAPER BOY	PHASE OUT	PLAIN BOB	POST HOLE
ONE PIECE	PAPER DAY	PHASED IN	PLANK BED	POST HORN
ONE SIDED	PAR AVION	PHASES IN	PLANT OUT	POST MILL
ONE TO ONE	PAR VALUE	PHONER IN	PLANT POT	POST PAID
OPEN BOOK	PARDON ME	PHOTO FIT	PLAY ACTS	POST ROAD
OPEN CAST	PARMA HAM	PIA MATER	PLAY BACK	POST TIME
OPEN DOOR	PART SONG	PIANO KEY	PLAY BALL	POST TOWN
OPEN FIRE	PART TIME	PICK ME UP	PLAY DOWN	POT AU FEU
OPEN MIND	PARTY HAT	PICK N MIX	PLAY FAIR	POT BELLY
OPEN PLAN	PARTY MAN	PICK OVER	PLAY GOER	POT BOUND
OPEN ROAD	PASS AWAY	PICKED AT	PLAY HOST	POT METAL
OPEN SHOP	PASS BAND	PICKED UP	PLAY SAFE	POT PLANT
OPEN TOWN	PASS BOOK	PICKER UP	PLAYED AT	POT ROAST
OPEN WORK	PASS LAWS	PICKS OFF	PLAYED ON	POT SHARD
OPENED UP	PASS OVER	PICKS OUT	PLAYED UP	POT STICK
OPENS OUT	PASSED BY	PIE CHART	PLAYS OFF	POT STILL
OPERA HAT	PASSED ON	PIE GRAPH	PLAYS OUT	POUNCE ON
OPIUM DEN	PASSED UP	PIECE OUT	PLEIN AIR	POUND DAY
OPTED OUT	PASSER BY	PIECED UP	PLOUGH IN	POURS OUT
ORAL EXAM	PASSES BY	PIECES UP	PLUG AWAY	POWER CUT
OSIER BED	PASSES ON	PIED NOIR	PLUG UGLY	PRE ELECT
OUT HEROD	PASSES UP	PIER HEAD	PLUM CAKE	PRE EMPTS
OUT OF BED	PATCH BOX	PIG FACED	PLUM DUFF	PRE EXIST
OUT OF USE	PATTY PAN	PIG SWILL	PLUMB BOB	PRE PRINT
OUTER BAR	PAY A CALL	PIG WOMAN	PLUS SIGN	PRE SELLS
OVEN BIRD	PAY PHONE	PIGGED IT	POINT OUT	PREACH AT
OVEN DOOR	PAY ROUND	PIKE HEAD	POINT SET	PREACH UP
OVER SHOE	PAY SHEET	PILE IT ON	POINTS UP	PRESS BED
OVERDO IT	PAYING IN	PILING UP	POLE AXED	PRESS BOX
OVERT ACT	PAYING UP	PILOT JET	POLE AXES	PRESS UPS
OWL GLASS	PAYS BACK	PIN MAKER	POLE STAR	PREYED ON
OWL LIGHT	PAYS CASH	PIN MONEY	POLISH UP	PRICE TAG
OWN BRAND	PEA CHICK	PIN POINT	POLKA DOT	PRICE WAR
OWN LABEL	PEA GREEN	PIN PRICK	POLO NECK	PRIE DIEU
OWNING UP	PEA VINER	PIN WHEEL	POND LIFE	PRIED OUT
OX PECKER	PEAK LOAD	PINCE NEZ	POND LILY	PRIES OUT
OX TONGUE	PEAK TIME	PINCH HIT	PONY CLUB	PRINT OUT
OX WARBLE	PEAR DROP	PINE CONE	PONY SKIN	PRINT RUN
PACK IT IN	PEAR TREE	PINE TREE	PONY TAIL	PRIX FIXE
PACK IT UP	PEARL EYE	PINE WOOD	POOH POOH	PRIZE MAN
PACK LOAD	PEASE COD	PINE WOOL	POOL ROOM	PRO FORMA
PACK MULE	PEAT BANK	PING PONG	POOR HAND	PRONG HOE
PACKED UP	PEAT MOOR	PINK EYED	POOR JACK	PROSE MAN
PAD CLOTH	PEAT MOSS	PINK LADY	POOR LAWS	PSYCHE UP
PAD HORSE	PEELS OFF	PINT SIZE	POOR RATE	PUB CRAWL
PAID BACK	PEEP HOLE	PIOU PIOU	POOR SHOW	PUCKER UP
	PEEP SHOW	PIPE CASE	POOR SOUL	PUFF BIRD

8 LETTERS

8 *contd.*
PUFF PUFF
PUFFED UP
PUG FACED
PUG NOSED
PULL AWAY
PULL BACK
PULL DOWN
PULL OVER
PULL RANK
PULLED IN
PULLED UP
PULLS OFF
PULLS OUT
PULZA OIL
PUMP HEAD
PUMP HOOD
PUMP IRON
PUMP ROOM
PUMP WELL
PUMPED IN
PUMPED UP
PUMPS OUT
PUNCH BAG
PUNK ROCK
PUNT POLE
PUPA CASE
PUPIL AGE
PUPPY DOG
PUPPY FAT
PURE GOLD
PURSE NET
PUSH BALL
PUSH BIKE
PUSH CART
PUSH OVER
PUSH PAST
PUSH PULL
PUSS MOTH
PUSSY CAT
PUT ABOUT
PUT ON ICE
PUT TO BED
PUT TO SEA
PUT UP JOB
PUTS AWAY
PUTS BACK
PUTS DOWN
PUTS IT ON
PUTS ON TO
PUTS OVER
PUTS TO IT
PUTS UPON
PUTTER ON
PUTTS OUT
QUAE VIDE
QUART POT
QUEEN BEE
QUEUED UP
QUEUES UP

QUILL NIB
QUILL PEN
QUIT RENT
QUIZ BOOK
QUIZ GAME
QUIZ SHOW
QUO VADIS
RACE CARD
RACE PATH
RACE RIOT
RACK RAIL
RACK RENT
RACKED UP
RADAR GUN
RADIO HAM
RAFT PORT
RAFT ROPE
RAG PAPER
RAG TRADE
RAG WOMAN
RAIL HEAD
RAIN BIRD
RAKING IN
RAKING UP
RAMS HORN
RAN A RISK
RAN AFTER
RAN ALONG
RAN CLOSE
RAN OUT ON
RAN SHORT
RANG BACK
RANG DOWN
RANG TRUE
RAPE SEED
RARA AVIS
RARE BIRD
RATE CAPS
RATS TAIL
RATTED ON
RATTLE ON
RAW STEAK
RAW UMBER
RAZOR CUT
REACH OUT
READS OFF
READS OUT
READY WIT
REAL BEER
REAL LIFE
REAL TIME
REAR ARCH
REAR LAMP
REAR RANK
RECKON ON
RECKON UP
RED ALERT
RED ALGAE
RED BELLY
RED BIDDY

RED BRICK
RED CEDAR
RED CROSS
RED DWARF
RED FACED
RED GIANT
RED GUARD
RED LIGHT
RED SHANK
RED SHIFT
RED SHIRT
REED BAND
REED BIRD
REED MACE
REED PIPE
REEF BAND
REEF KNOT
REELS OFF
REIN HAND
REINED IN
RELIED ON
RELIES ON
RENT A MOB
RENT FREE
RENT ROLL
REST CURE
REST HOME
REST ROOM
REVVED UP
RH FACTOR
RIB ROAST
RICE BEER
RICE GLUE
RICE MILK
RICE SOUP
RICK RACK
RIDE DOWN
RIDES OUT
RIDING UP
RIFF RAFF
RIFLE PIT
RIGGED UP
RIGHT ARM
RIGHT OFF
RING BACK
RING BARK
RING BOLT
RING DIAL
RING DOVE
RING DOWN
RING DYKE
RING FORT
RING MAIN
RING PULL
RING ROAD
RING TAIL
RING TIME
RING TRUE
RING WALK
RING WALL

RINGS OFF
RINSE OUT
RISING UP
RISKED IT
RIVER BED
RIVER RAT
ROAD BOOK
ROAD HUMP
ROAD SHOW
ROAD SIGN
ROAD TEST
ROCK BAND
ROCK BIRD
ROCK CAKE
ROCK DOVE
ROCK FALL
ROCK FISH
ROCK HEWN
ROCK SALT
ROCK WOOD
ROCK WOOL
RODE DOWN
ROLE PLAY
ROLL CALL
ROLL NECK
ROLL OVER
ROLLED IN
ROLLED UP
ROLY POLY
ROMAN LAW
ROMP HOME
ROOD BEAM
ROOD LOFT
ROOF RACK
ROOM MATE
ROOT BEER
ROOT CROP
ROOTS OUT
ROPE WALK
ROPE YARN
ROPES END
ROPING IN
ROSE BOWL
ROSE BUSH
ROSE COMB
ROSE DROP
ROSE HUED
ROSE KNOT
ROSE LEAF
ROSE PINK
ROSE ROOT
ROSE TREE
ROSIN OIL
ROUGH CUT
ROUGH DRY
ROUGH HEW
ROUGH OUT
ROUGHS IN
ROUGHS IT
ROUND ARM

ROUND OFF
ROUND OUT
ROUND TOP
ROUNDS ON
ROUNDS UP
ROW BARGE
ROW HOUSE
ROWDY DOW
ROYAL BOX
RUB ALONG
RUB OFF ON
RUBS DOWN
RUBS IT ON
RULED OUT
RULES OUT
RUM PUNCH
RUM SHRUB
RUM TI TUM
RUMP BONE
RUN A RISK
RUN AFTER
RUN ALONG
RUN CLOSE
RUN FOR IT
RUN OUT ON
RUN SHORT
RUNNER UP
RUNS AMOK
RUNS AWAY
RUNS DOWN
RUNS HARD
RUNS INTO
RUNS OVER
RUNS RIOT
RUNS WILD
RUSH HOUR
RUSH LIKE
RUSH RING
RUSTLE UP
RYDER CUP
RYE BREAD
RYE FLOUR
RYE GRASS
RYE STRAW
SABRE CUT
SACK COAT
SACK RACE
SACK TREE
SAD FACED
SADDLE UP
SAFE SEAT
SAGE COCK
SAGO PALM
SAIL BOAT
SAIL FISH
SAIL LOFT
SAIL ROOM
SAIL YARD
SAILED BY
SALAD OIL

8 *contd.*

SALE ROOM	SCORE OFF	SEE STARS	SETTLE UP	SICK ROOM
SALES TAX	SCOT FREE	SEED CAKE	SEWER GAS	SIDE DISH
SALIC LAW	SCOUT CAR	SEED CORN	SEWER RAT	SIDE DOOR
SALT AWAY	SCOUT LAW	SEED FISH	SEWING UP	SIDE DRUM
SALT BEEF	SCRAG END	SEED LEAF	SHAKE OFF	SIDE FACE
SALT CAKE	SCRAP MAN	SEED LIKE	SHAKE OUT	SIDE KICK
SALT DOME	SCREW CAP	SEED PLOT	SHAKES UP	SIDE LAMP
SALT DOWN	SCRUBS UP	SEED SHOP	SHALE OIL	SIDE LINE
SALT FLAT	SE TENANT	SEED TIME	SHAPED UP	SIDE PATH
SALT LAKE	SEA BEACH	SEEDY TOE	SHAPES UP	SIDE POST
SALT LICK	SEA BEAST	SEEKS OUT	SHARE OUT	SIDE ROAD
SALT MINE	SEA BOOTS	SEES LIFE	SHARK OIL	SIDE SHOW
SALT PLUG	SEA BORNE	SEES OVER	SHARP SET	SIDE SLIP
SAME HERE	SEA BREAM	SEES TO IT	SHE DEVIL	SIDE STEP
SAND BATH	SEA CHART	SEINE NET	SHEEP DIP	SIDE VIEW
SAND DART	SEA CLIFF	SEIZED UP	SHEEP KED	SIDE WIND
SAND DUNE	SEA DEVIL	SEIZES UP	SHEEP PEN	SIEGE GUN
SAND FLAG	SEA EAGLE	SELF HEAL	SHEEP POX	SIGN AWAY
SAND HEAP	SEA FIGHT	SELF HELP	SHEEP RUN	SIGNED IN
SAND HILL	SEA FLOOR	SELF LOVE	SHEER OFF	SIGNED ON
SAND HOLE	SEA FRONT	SELF MADE	SHEET FED	SIGNED UP
SAND LARK	SEA FROTH	SELF PITY	SHEET TIN	SIGNS OFF
SAND MOLE	SEA GOING	SELF RULE	SHELL OUT	SIGNS OUT
SAND SHOE	SEA GRAPE	SELF SAME	SHIFT KEY	SILLY ASS
SAND STAR	SEA GRASS	SELF WILL	SHIN BONE	SIN EATER
SAND TRAP	SEA GREEN	SELL A PUP	SHIP LOAD	SINE WAVE
SAND WASP	SEA HORSE	SELLS OFF	SHIP WORM	SING SONG
SAND WORM	SEA HOUND	SELLS OUT	SHIPS LOG	SINGS OUT
SAP GREEN	SEA JELLY	SEMI AXIS	SHIRT PIN	SINK HOLE
SAPI UTAN	SEA LEMON	SEMI DOME	SHOE LACE	SINK UNIT
SASH CORD	SEA LEVEL	SEMI MUTE	SHOE SHOP	SINN FEIN
SASH DOOR	SEA LOACH	SEMI NUDE	SHOE TREE	SIT STILL
SAT STILL	SEA LUNGS	SEND DOWN	SHOOK OFF	SIT TIGHT
SAT TIGHT	SEA MOUNT	SEND WORD	SHOOK OUT	SITS BACK
SAUCE BOX	SEA NYMPH	SENDS OFF	SHOOT OFF	SITS DOWN
SAVE FACE	SEA ONION	SENDS OUT	SHOOT OUT	SITTER IN
SAVE TIME	SEA ORACH	SENNA POD	SHOOTS UP	SITZ BATH
SAVING UP	SEA OTTER	SENNA TEA	SHOP BELL	SIZING UP
SAW A WOLF	SEA PERCH	SENT DOWN	SHOP DOOR	SKENE DHU
SAW BLADE	SEA POWER	SENT WORD	SHOP GIRL	SKI SLOPE
SAW BONES	SEA ROBIN	SENTRY GO	SHOP SIGN	SKI STICK
SAW EDGED	SEA ROVER	SERVE OUT	SHORT CUT	SKIN DEEP
SAW FRAME	SEA SCOUT	SERVED UP	SHORT LEG	SKIN GAME
SAW ROUND	SEA SHRUB	SERVES UP	SHORT SEA	SKIN TEST
SAW STARS	SEA SNAIL	SET A TRAP	SHOT DOWN	SKUA GULL
SAW TOOTH	SEA SNAKE	SET ABOUT	SHOT HOLE	SKY DIVER
SAXE BLUE	SEA SNIPE	SET APART	SHOVE OFF	SKY PILOT
SCALY LEG	SEA STORM	SET ASIDE	SHOW A LEG	SLACK JAW
SCARED UP	SEA TROUT	SET FORTH	SHOW BILL	SLAG HEAP
SCARES UP	SEA WATER	SET PIECE	SHOW BOAT	SLAP BANG
SCARF PIN	SEA WOMAN	SET SCREW	SHOW DOWN	SLAP DASH
SCENE BAY	SEA WRACK	SET TERMS	SHOWED UP	SLATE AXE
SCENE MAN	SEAL PIPE	SETS BACK	SHOWS OFF	SLEEP OFF
SCENE ONE	SEAL RING	SETS DOWN	SHRUG OFF	SLEEPS IN
SCENE TWO	SEALS OFF	SETS FOOT	SHUT AWAY	SLEEPS ON
SCENT BAG	SEARCH ME	SETS FREE	SHUT DOWN	SLEPT OFF
SCENT BOX	SEAT BELT	SETS SAIL	SHUTS OFF	SLICED UP
SCOOP NET	SEDGE FLY	SETS UPON	SHUTS OUT	SLICES UP
SCOOP OUT	SEE A WOLF	SETTER UP	SICK JOKE	SLIME PIT
	SEE ROUND	SETTLE IN	SICK LIST	SLING INK

8 *contd.*

SLINK OFF	SOFT MEAT	SPUR GEAR	STITCH UP	SWAMP OAK
SLIP AWAY	SOFT ROCK	SPY MONEY	STOCK POT	SWAN LAKE
SLIP CASE	SOFT SELL	SPY PLANE	STOCKS UP	SWAN MARK
SLIP DOCK	SOFT SHOE	SQUAB PIE	STOKED UP	SWAN NECK
SLIP KNOT	SOFT SOAP	SQUAD CAR	STOKES UP	SWAN SONG
SLIP ROAD	SOFT SPOT	SQUARE UP	STONE AGE	SWAP LINE
SLIP SHOE	SOFTEN UP	SRI LANKA	STONE AXE	SWAP SHOP
SLIPS OFF	SOIL PIPE	ST JULIEN	STONE FLY	SWEARS IN
SLOP BOWL	SOLAR DAY	STACKS UP	STONE OIL	SWEEP NET
SLOP PAIL	SOLD A PUP	STAFF CAR	STONE PIT	SWEEP SAW
SLOP SHOP	SOLO STOP	STAG HUNT	STONE SAW	SWEEPS UP
SLOPE OFF	SOME HOPE	STAGE BOX	STOOD OFF	SWEET BAY
SLOPS OUT	SON IN LAW	STAIR ROD	STOOD OUT	SWELL BOX
SLOW BURN	SON OF MAN	STAKE NET	STOOD PAT	SWILL TUB
SLOW DOWN	SONG FORM	STAKE OUT	STOP COCK	SWITCH ON
SLOW WORM	SONG LIKE	STALL FED	STOP DEAD	SWORD ARM
SLOWED UP	SORTS OUT	STAMP ACT	STOP OVER	SWORD CUT
SLUNG INK	SOUL FOOD	STAMP OUT	STOPS OFF	TABBY CAT
SLUNK OFF	SOUL MATE	STAND OFF	STRAW HAT	TABLE MAT
SMALL ADS	SOUND BAR	STAND OUT	STRAW MAN	TABLE TOP
SMALL ALE	SOUND BOX	STAND PAT	STRAY CAT	TAC AU TAC
SMALL ARM	SOUND OFF	STANDS BY	STRAY DOG	TACKED ON
SMALL FRY	SOUND OUT	STANDS IN	STRIKE UP	TAG ALONG
SMASH HIT	SOUPED UP	STANDS ON	STRING UP	TAIL COAT
SMELL OUT	SOUR EYED	STANDS TO	STRIP MAP	TAIL GATE
SMELT OUT	SOUR MASH	STANDS UP	STRIP OFF	TAIL PIPE
SMOKE BOX	SOUSE TUB	STANK OUT	STRIP OUT	TAIL ROPE
SMOKE DRY	SOUTH SEA	STAR DUST	STROLL ON	TAIL SPIN
SMOKE OUT	SOW BREAD	STAR GAZE	STRUCK ON	TAIL WIND
SNACK BAR	SOYA BEAN	STAR SIGN	STRUCK UP	TAILS OFF
SNAKE OIL	SPACE AGE	STAR TRAP	STRUNG UP	TAJ MAHAL
SNAKE PIT	SPACE BAR	STAR TURN	STUCK OUT	TAKE A BOW
SNAP LINK	SPACE OUT	STAR WARS	STUD BOLT	TAKE ARMS
SNEAKS UP	SPAN ROOF	START OUT	STUD BOOK	TAKE AWAY
SNIFF OUT	SPAR DECK	STARTS IN	STUD FARM	TAKE BACK
SNIP SNAP	SPARE RIB	STARTS UP	STUMPS UP	TAKE BETS
SNOW BOOT	SPARK GAP	STAVES IN	STUNT MAN	TAKE CARE
SNOW EYES	SPARK OFF	STAY BOLT	SUCH LIKE	TAKE DOWN
SNOW HOLE	SPARK OUT	STAY LACE	SUCKED IN	TAKE FIVE
SNOW SHOE	SPEAK OUT	STAY OVER	SUGAR GUM	TAKE HEED
SNOWED IN	SPEAKS UP	STAY TAPE	SUI JURIS	TAKE NOTE
SNOWED UP	SPEAR GUN	STAYED IN	SUIT CASE	TAKE OVER
SNOWY OWL	SPEED COP	STAYED ON	SUM TOTAL	TAKE PART
SNUB NOSE	SPEEDS UP	STAYED UP	SUMMED UP	TAKE ROOT
SNUFF OUT	SPELL OUT	STAYS OUT	SUMMON UP	TAKE SILK
SNUFFS IT	SPELT OUT	STAYS PUT	SUN BAKED	TAKE WING
SO CALLED	SPICE BOX	STEADY ON	SUN BLIND	TAKEN OUT
SO HELP ME	SPIKE OIL	STEAM CAR	SUN BLINK	TAKES AIM
SO MUCH SO	SPINS OUT	STEAMS UP	SUN CURED	TAKES OFF
SOAP DISH	SPIT CURL	STEEL PEN	SUN DRESS	TAKES OUT
SOAP SUDS	SPLIT PEA	STEP DOWN	SUN DRIED	TAKING IN
SOB STORY	SPLIT PIN	STEP ON IT	SUN DROPS	TAKING IT
SOB STUFF	SPOKE OUT	STEPS OUT	SUN SHADE	TAKING ON
SOBERS UP	SPOON FED	STICK LAC	SUN VISOR	TAKING TO
SODA JERK	SPOT CASH	STICK OUT	SUNNY JIM	TAKING UP
SODA LIME	SPOT KICK	STICKS BY	SUPER EGO	TALK BACK
SOFT LINE	SPOT WELD	STICKS IN	SUPER JET	TALK DOWN
SOFT LOAN	SPRAY GUN	STICKS TO	SURE CARD	TALK INTO
SOFT MARK	SPUN SILK	STING RAY	SURE FIRE	TALK OVER
	SPUN YARN	STINK OUT	SURF BOAT	TALK SHOP

8 *contd.*

TALK SHOW	TENT COAT	THROWS UP	TOOK A BOW	TRIC TRAC
TALKED AT	TENT POLE	THRUM CAP	TOOK ARMS	TRIED OUT
TALKED TO	TENT ROPE	THUMBS UP	TOOK BACK	TRIES OUT
TALKS BIG	TENT WORK	TICK AWAY	TOOK BETS	TRIP WIRE
TALKS OUT	TERM TIME	TICK OVER	TOOK CARE	TROTS OUT
TALL COPY	TEST ACTS	TICK SHOP	TOOK DOWN	TROUT ROD
TALL SHIP	TEST CASE	TICK TACK	TOOK FIVE	TRUE BILL
TALL TALE	TEST TUBE	TICK TICK	TOOK HEED	TRUE BLUE
TALLY HOS	TEXT BOOK	TICK TOCK	TOOK NOTE	TRUE BORN
TAN BALLS	THANK YOU	TICKS OFF	TOOK OVER	TRUE BRED
TANK TRAP	THANKS BE	TIDE GATE	TOOK PART	TRUE LOVE
TAP DANCE	THAWS OUT	TIDE OVER	TOOK ROOT	TRUE TIME
TAP HOUSE	THE ASHES	TIDE RACE	TOOK SILK	TRYING ON
TAP SHOES	THE BENDS	TIE BREAK	TOOK WING	TUB THUMP
TAP WATER	THE BLITZ	TIED DOWN	TOOL SHED	TUBE WORM
TAPE DECK	THE BLUES	TIES DOWN	TOOLED UP	TUCK SHOP
TAPER OFF	THE BRINY	TIGER CAT	TOP BRASS	TUCKED IN
TAR BRUSH	THE BUFFS	TIGER NUT	TOP DRESS	TUG OF WAR
TAR PAPER	THE CHAIR	TIGHT FIT	TOP HEAVY	TUNING IN
TARTED UP	THE CLOTH	TILE HUNG	TOP LEVEL	TUNING UP
TASK WORK	THE DERBY	TILT BOAT	TOP LINER	TURBO CAR
TASTE BUD	THE DEVIL	TIME BOMB	TOP NOTCH	TURBO JET
TAU CROSS	THE DOWNS	TIME CARD	TOP STONE	TURFS OUT
TAU STAFF	THE DRINK	TIME CODE	TOP TABLE	TURKS CAP
TAWNY OWL	THE ENEMY	TIME FUSE	TOPPED UP	TURN AWAY
TAX EXILE	THE FANCY	TIME SLOT	TORE AWAY	TURN BACK
TAX HAVEN	THE FLOOD	TIME UNIT	TORE DOWN	TURN DOWN
TAX PAYER	THE GOODS	TIME WARP	TORE INTO	TURN INTO
TAX POINT	THE GREYS	TIME WORN	TORE OPEN	TURN IT IN
TAXI RANK	THE HALLS	TIME ZONE	TORN DOWN	TURN IT UP
TE IGITUR	THE HOUSE	TIN MINER	TOSSED UP	TURN OVER
TEA BREAK	THE LIONS	TIN PLATE	TOSSES UP	TURN TAIL
TEA CADDY	THE MAFIA	TINT TOOL	TOTAL WAR	TURN TURK
TEA CHEST	THE PRESS	TINY TOTS	TOTTED UP	TURN UPON
TEA CLOTH	THE SKIDS	TIPSY KEY	TOUCH OFF	TURNED IN
TEA DANCE	THE SMOKE	TIRED OUT	TOW PLANE	TURNED ON
TEA HOUSE	THE THING	TIRES OUT	TOWN HALL	TURNED TO
TEA PARTY	THE TWIST	TO A FAULT	TRAD JAZZ	TURNED UP
TEA PLANT	THE UNION	TO AND FRO	TRADE GAP	TURNS OFF
TEA TABLE	THE USUAL	TO BE SURE	TRADE OFF	TURNS OUT
TEA TOWEL	THE WEALD	TODDY CAT	TRADE WAR	TV DINNER
TEAM MATE	THE WORKS	TOE PIECE	TRADED IN	TWIN BEDS
TEAM WORK	THICK EAR	TOE TO TOE	TRADED UP	TWIN BORN
TEAR AWAY	THINK OUT	TOG VALUE	TRADES IN	TWIN TOWN
TEAR DOWN	THINKS UP	TOGGED UP	TRADES UP	TWO EDGED
TEAR DROP	THINS OUT	TOIL WORN	TRAIL NET	TWO FACED
TEAR DUCT	THIRD MAN	TOLL CALL	TRAIL OFF	TWO PIECE
TEAR INTO	THOLE PIN	TOLL FREE	TRAM LINE	TWO SCORE
TEAR OPEN	THREE MAN	TOLL GATE	TRAM ROAD	TWO SIDED
TEARS OFF	THREE PLY	TOM NODDY	TRAM STOP	TWO TICKS
TEDDY BOY	THREE WAY	TOM THUMB	TRAP DOOR	TWO TIMED
TEE SHIRT	THREW OFF	TOMMY BAR	TRAP FALL	TWO TIMER
TEEING UP	THREW OUT	TOMMY GUN	TRASH CAN	TWO TIMES
TELL A LIE	THROW OFF	TOMMY ROT	TRAWL NET	TYPE BODY
TELL TALE	THROW OUT	TONE DEAF	TREE FERN	TYPE CASE
TELLS OFF	THROWN IN	TONE DOWN	TREE FROG	TYPE FACE
TEN PENCE	THROWN ON	TONE POEM	TREE LILY	TYPE HIGH
TEN SCORE	THROWN UP	TONING UP	TREE MOSS	UNCLE SAM
TENON SAW	THROWS IN	TOO RIGHT	TRIAL DAY	UNCLE TOM
	THROWS ON	TOODLE OO	TRIAL RUN	UNDER AGE

8 *contd.*

UNDER WAY	WANTED IN	WEAR THIN	WIG BLOCK	WOOD WREN
UP ANCHOR	WANTS OUT	WEARS OFF	WIG MAKER	WOOL BALL
UP ENDING	WAR BRIDE	WEARS OUT	WILD BIRD	WOOL CARD
UP IN ARMS	WAR CLOUD	WEE FREES	WILD BOAR	WOOL COMB
UP MARKET	WAR CRIME	WEIGH OUT	WILD BORN	WOOL DYED
UP TO DATE	WAR DANCE	WEIGHS IN	WILD CARD	WOOL MILL
UPAS TREE	WAR GAMER	WEIGHS UP	WILD DUCK	WOOL PACK
UPON OATH	WAR HORSE	WELL AWAY	WILD FOWL	WORD PLAY
UPPER CUT	WAR PAINT	WELL BORN	WILD HUNT	WORE AWAY
USE FORCE	WAR TRIAL	WELL BRED	WILD LAND	WORE DOWN
USED CARS	WAR WEARY	WELL DECK	WILD MARE	WORE THIN
VEE JOINT	WAR WHOOP	WELL DOER	WILD OATS	WORK AT IT
VENA CAVA	WAR WIDOW	WELL DONE	WILD RICE	WORK MATE
VENT HOLE	WARD ROOM	WELL HEAD	WILD SILK	WORK OVER
VENT PIPE	WARDS OFF	WELL HOLE	WILD WEST	WORK UPON
VENT PLUG	WARMED UP	WELL MADE	WILD WOOD	WORKED IN
VERY WELL	WASH AWAY	WELL NIGH	WIND BAND	WORKED ON
VICE DEAN	WASH BOWL	WELL READ	WIND CONE	WORKED UP
VIN BLANC	WASH DOWN	WELL ROOM	WIND DOWN	WORKS FOR
VIN ROUGE	WASHED UP	WELL SEEN	WIND SAIL	WORKS OFF
VINE CLAD	WATCH BOX	WELL THEN	WIND SIDE	WORKS OUT
VINE GALL	WATCH CAP	WELL TO DO	WIND SOCK	WORLD WAR
VITAMIN A	WATCH DOG	WELL WELL	WIND SURF	WORM CAST
VITAMIN B	WATCH KEY	WELL WISH	WINE CASK	WORM GEAR
VITAMIN C	WATCH OUT	WELL WORN	WINE GUMS	WORM HOLE
VITAMIN D	WATER BAG	WENT AWAY	WINE LAKE	WORN AWAY
VITAMIN E	WATER BED	WENT BUST	WINE LIST	WORN DOWN
VITAMIN H	WATER BOX	WENT DOWN	WINE SHOP	WORRY OUT
VITAMIN K	WATER BUG	WENT INTO	WINE SKIN	WORSE OFF
VITAMIN L	WATER BUS	WENT LIVE	WING CASE	WRING OUT
VIVA VOCE	WATER DOG	WENT SOFT	WING HALF	WRIST PIN
VOICE BOX	WATER FLY	WEST BANK	WING SHOT	WRITE OFF
VOTE DOWN	WATER GOD	WET NURSE	WINS OVER	WRITE OUT
VOTING IN	WATER ICE	WET PAINT	WIPED OUT	WRITES UP
WADING IN	WATER JET	WHALE OIL	WIPES OUT	WROTE OFF
WAGON BED	WATER JUG	WHARF RAT	WIPING UP	WROTE OUT
WAGON BOX	WATER KEY	WHAT ELSE	WIRE HAIR	WRUNG OUT
WAGON LIT	WATER RAM	WHAT NEXT	WIRE MESH	WRY SMILE
WAIT UPON	WATER RAT	WHAT OF IT	WIRE NAIL	X RAY TUBE
WAITED ON	WATER SKI	WHAT THEN	WIRE ROPE	XMAS TREE
WAITED UP	WATER TAP	WHATS NEW	WIRE WOOL	YALE LOCK
WAKE UP TO	WATER YAM	WHEAT EAR	WIRING IN	YEAR BOOK
WALK AWAY	WATT HOUR	WHEY FACE	WITCH ELM	YET AGAIN
WALK AWRY	WAVE DOWN	WHIM WHAM	WITH CALF	YOGI BEAR
WALK INTO	WAVY HAIR	WHIP HAND	WITH FOAL	YOKE MATE
WALK OVER	WAX CLOTH	WHIP TAIL	WITH THAT	YOUNG MAN
WALK TALL	WAX LIGHT	WHIT WEEK	WOKE UP TO	ZAPPED UP
WALKED IT	WAX MATCH	WHITE ANT	WOLF PACK	ZAPS IT UP
WALKED ON	WAX PAPER	WHITE EYE	WOOD CHAT	ZERO HOUR
WALKER ON	WAY BOARD	WHITE HOT	WOOD COAL	ZERO IN ON
WALKS OFF	WAY GOING	WHITE LIE	WOOD IBIS	ZERO RATE
WALKS OUT	WAY MAKER	WHITE MAN	WOOD LARK	ZEROED IN
WALL BARS	WAY POINT	WHITE OUT	WOOD MITE	ZEROES IN
WALL EYED	WAY TRAIN	WHITE RAT	WOOD PILE	ZIP FRONT
WALL GAME	WEAK EYED	WHITE TIE	WOOD PULP	ZIPPED UP
WALL PASS	WEAK LINK	WHIZZ KID	WOOD RUSH	ZONE AXIS
WALL UNIT	WEAK SPOT	WHO DUN IT	WOOD SAGE	ZOOM LENS
WALLED UP	WEAR AWAY	WHOLE HOG	WOOD TICK	ZOOT SUIT
WANTED AD	WEAR DOWN	WIDE EYED	WOOD WASP	
	WEAR IRON	WIDE OPEN	WOOD WOOL	

9

A BIG NOISE
A BIT THICK
A CAPPELLA
A CUT ABOVE
A DOGS LIFE
A FAST BUCK
A GOOD SORT
A GOOD TURN
A GOOD WORD
A MUGS GAME
A QUICK ONE
A RAINY DAY
A THICK EAR
A THIN TIME
A VAST MANY
AARONS ROD
ABOUT FACE
ABOUT TURN
ACID DROPS
ACID HOUSE
ACTING OUT
AD LIBBING
AD NAUSEAM
AD VALOREM
ADI GRANTH
AFRO ASIAN
AFTER CROP
AFTER LIFE
AGONY AUNT
AIR BRAKES
AIR BUBBLE
AIR COOLED
AIR ENGINE
AIR JACKET
AIR LETTER
AIR MINDED
AIR PIRACY
AIR POCKET
AIR STRIKE
AIR TRAVEL
AIRY FAIRY
AITCH BONE
ALARM BELL
ALARM CALL
ALDIS LAMP
ALE CONNER
ALICE BAND
ALL ABOARD
ALL AT ONCE
ALL BLACKS
ALL COMERS
ALL ENDS UP
ALL IS LOST
ALL RULING
ALL SEEING
ALL SQUARE
ALL THE WAY
ALLA BREVE

ALLEZ VOUS
ALMA MATER
ALMOND OIL
ALMS HOUSE
ALMS WOMAN
ALPHA PLUS
ALPHA RAYS
ALTER EGOS
AMBER FISH
AMINO ACID
AN EVEN BET
ANCHOR LEG
ANCHOR MAN
ANDY PANDY
ANGEL CAKE
ANGEL DUST
ANGEL FISH
ANGEL FOOD
ANGLE IRON
ANGLE SHOT
ANGLE WORM
ANGORA CAT
ANKLE BOOT
ANKLE SOCK
ANTI NOVEL
ANY AMOUNT
ANY DAY NOW
ANY OFFERS
ANY OLD HOW
APPIAN WAY
APPLE CART
APPLE JACK
APPLE JOHN
APPLE TART
APPLE TREE
APPLE WIFE
APRES GOUT
APRIL FOOL
AQUA REGIA
AQUA VITAE
ARCH ENEMY
ARCTIC FOX
ARGUS EYED
ARGY BARGY
ARMY CORPS
ARROW HEAD
ARROW SHOT
ART DEALER
ART MASTER
AS REGARDS
AS YOU WERE
ASH BLONDE
ASH BUCKET
ASHEN GREY
AT A GLANCE
AT A LOW EBB
AT ANY RATE
AT COMMAND
AT FULL SEA
AT LEISURE

AT LIBERTY
AT ONE TIME
AT PRESENT
AT THE HELM
AT THE MOST
AT THE TIME
ATTIC SALT
AU COURANT
AU FROMAGE
AU NATUREL
AU SECOURS
AUGER HOLE
AUGER WORM
AUGUR WELL
AUNT SALLY
AURIC ACID
AUTOS DA FE
AWAY MATCH
AWE STRUCK
BABY BUGGY
BABY GRAND
BABY HOUSE
BACK BENCH
BACK BLOCK
BACK BOARD
BACK CHAIN
BACK CLOTH
BACK COMBS
BACK CRAWL
BACK CROSS
BACK DATED
BACK DATES
BACK HEELS
BACK PEDAL
BACK PLATE
BACK SHIFT
BACK SLANG
BACK WATER
BACKED OFF
BACKING UP
BACKS DOWN
BAD TEMPER
BAILED OUT
BAIN MARIE
BAL MASQUE
BALD EAGLE
BALD FACED
BALD TRUTH
BALDI COOT
BALING OUT
BALL DRESS
BALL GIRLS
BALL POINT
BALLOT BOX
BALSA WOOD
BALSAM FIR
BANANA OIL
BAND WHEEL
BANGED OUT

BANGING UP
BANK AGENT
BANK CLERK
BANK PAPER
BANK STOCK
BAR CODING
BAR MAGNET
BAR OF SOAP
BARD CRAFT
BARE BONES
BARGING IN
BARM CLOTH
BARN DANCE
BARRET CAP
BARROW BOY
BAS RELIEF
BASE METAL
BASIC SALT
BATH BRICK
BATH CHAIR
BATH SALTS
BATH STONE
BATH TOWEL
BATTLE AXE
BATTLE CRY
BATTLED ON
BATTLES ON
BAWLED OUT
BAY WINDOW
BE MY GUEST
BE ONESELF
BEACH BALL
BEAD HOUSE
BEAM TRAWL
BEAN CAPER
BEAR BERRY
BEARING UP
BEARS ARMS
BEARS AWAY
BEARS DOWN
BEARS FOOT
BEAT MUSIC
BEATING IT
BEATING UP
BEATS DOWN
BEATS TIME
BEATS TO IT
BEAU GESTE
BEAU IDEAL
BEAU MONDE
BEAUX ARTS
BEAVER RAT
BED CLOSET
BED JACKET
BEDDED OUT
BEDDY BYES
BEE FLOWER
BEE KEEPER
BEECH FERN
BEECH MAST

BEECH WOOD
BEEF CURRY
BEEFING UP
BEER HOUSE
BEER MONEY
BEET SUGAR
BEETLE OFF
BEGGAR MAN
BEGGED OFF
BEL ESPRIT
BELL CRANK
BELL GLASS
BELL METAL
BELL PUNCH
BELL TOWER
BELLE AMIE
BELLE MERE
BELLY ACHE
BELLY BAND
BELLY FLOP
BELTED OUT
BELTING UP
BEN VENUTO
BENCH HOLE
BENCH MARK
BENDS OVER
BERG ADDER
BERG CEDAR
BESOM HEAD
BETE NOIRE
BETTER OFF
BEVIN BOYS
BIBLE BELT
BIDDING IN
BIDDING UP
BIG BERTHA
BIG CHEESE
BIG DIPPER
BIG ENDIAN
BIG HEADED
BILE DUCTS
BILGE KEEL
BILGE PUMP
BILLY GOAT
BILLY LIAR
BINDS OVER
BINGO HALL
BIRD BRAIN
BIRD TABLE
BIRDS FOOT
BIRDS NEST
BIRTH MARK
BIRTH PILL
BIRTH RATE
BIRTH SIGN
BIT PLAYER
BLACK ARTS
BLACK BASS
BLACK BEAR
BLACK BELT

9 LETTERS

9 *contd.*
BLACK BESS
BLACK BOOK
BLACK FLAG
BLACK GOLD
BLACK HAND
BLACK HOLE
BLACK LOOK
BLACK MARK
BLACK MASS
BLACK MONK
BLACK POPE
BLACK SPOT
BLACK SWAN
BLACKS OUT
BLADE BONE
BLANK DOOR
BLANK PAGE
BLAST HOLE
BLAST PIPE
BLASTS OFF
BLAZE AWAY
BLEW A FUSE
BLIND DATE
BLIND ROAD
BLIND SIDE
BLIND SPOT
BLOCK BOOK
BLOCK SHIP
BLOCK TYPE
BLOCK VOTE
BLOOD BANK
BLOOD BATH
BLOOD CLOT
BLOOD FEUD
BLOOD LINE
BLOOD TEST
BLOOD TYPE
BLOOD WORM
BLOW A FUSE
BLOW DRIED
BLOW DRIES
BLOW TORCH
BLOW VALVE
BLOWING IN
BLOWING UP
BLOWS AWAY
BLOWS OVER
BLUE BLOOD
BLUE GREEN
BLUE MOULD
BLUE MOVIE
BLUE PETER
BLUE RINSE
BLUE SKIES
BLUE WATER
BLUE WHALE
BLURTS OUT
BLUSH ROSE
BOAR HOUND

BOAR SPEAR
BOARD GAME
BOARD ROOM
BOARDS OUT
BOARS HEAD
BOAT TRAIN
BOB CHERRY
BOBBLE HAT
BODY CHECK
BODY CLOCK
BOFORS GUN
BOG MYRTLE
BOILED EGG
BOILS OVER
BOLD FACED
BOMB ALLEY
BOMB HAPPY
BOMB PROOF
BON MARCHE
BON VIVANT
BON VIVEUR
BON VOYAGE
BONA FIDES
BOND PAPER
BOND SLAVE
BOND WOMAN
BONE BLACK
BONE CHINA
BONE EARTH
BONE WEARY
BONGO DRUM
BOOBY TRAP
BOOK TALLY
BOOK TOKEN
BOOK TRADE
BOOK VALUE
BOOKED OUT
BOOKING IN
BOOKING UP
BORN AGAIN
BORN MIMIC
BORNE AWAY
BOSSA NOVA
BOTANY BAY
BOTTLE GAS
BOTTLE OFF
BOTTLE OUT
BOTTLED UP
BOTTLES UP
BOTTOM END
BOTTOM OUT
BOTTOMS UP
BOUGHT OFF
BOUGHT OUT
BOUND OVER
BOVVER BOY
BOW BACKED
BOW LEGGED
BOW WINDOW
BOWER BIRD

BOWING OUT
BOWLED OUT
BOWLER HAT
BOWLS OVER
BOX AND COX
BOX CAMERA
BOX CLEVER
BOX GIRDER
BOX NUMBER
BOX OFFICE
BOXING DAY
BOY BISHOP
BOYLES LAW
BRAIN DEAD
BRAIN WAVE
BRAKE DRUM
BRAKE PADS
BRAKE SHOE
BRAND IRON
BRAND NAME
BRASS BAND
BRASS NECK
BRAZIL NUT
BREAD CORN
BREAD LINE
BREAD ROLL
BREAD TREE
BREAK A LEG
BREAK AWAY
BREAK CAMP
BREAK DOWN
BREAK EVEN
BREAK IT UP
BREAK WIND
BREAKS OFF
BREAKS OUT
BREAST FED
BREWING UP
BRIC A BRAC
BRICK DUST
BRICK KILN
BRICK WALL
BRIDES MAN
BRIEF CASE
BRIER ROOT
BRIER WOOD
BRING DOWN
BRING HOME
BRING OVER
BRINGS OFF
BRINGS OUT
BROAD BEAN
BROAD BRIM
BROAD LEAF
BROKE AWAY
BROKE CAMP
BROKE DOWN
BROKE EVEN
BROKEN MAN
BRONZE AGE

BROUGHT IN
BROUGHT ON
BROUGHT UP
BROWN BEAR
BROWN BESS
BROWN COAL
BROWN RICE
BRUSH FIRE
BRUSHED UP
BRUSHES UP
BUBBLE CAR
BUBBLE GUM
BUBBLED UP
BUBBLES UP
BUCK TEETH
BUCKING UP
BUCKS FIZZ
BUCKS HORN
BUDGET DAY
BUFF STICK
BUFF WHEEL
BUFFET CAR
BUG HUNTER
BUGLE BAND
BUGLE CALL
BULL NOSED
BULL TROUT
BULL WHALE
BULLY BEEF
BULLY ROOK
BUMBLE BEE
BUMP START
BUMPED OFF
BUMPING UP
BUMPS INTO
BUNNY GIRL
BUONA SERA
BURMA ROAD
BURMA STAR
BURNED OUT
BURNING IN
BURNING UP
BURNS DOWN
BURNT CORK
BURNT DOWN
BURNT SACK
BUS DRIVER
BUSH METAL
BUSH PILOT
BUT AND BEN
BUTT SHAFT
BUTTER BOX
BUTTER FAT
BUTTER OIL
BUTTER PAT
BUTTERS UP
BUTTING IN
BUTTONS UP
BUYING OFF
BUYING OUT

BY DEGREES
BY NO MEANS
BY NUMBERS
BY ONESELF
BY PRODUCT
CAB DRIVER
CABIN CREW
CABIN SHIP
CADDIE CAR
CALF BOUND
CALFS FOOT
CALL A HALT
CALL NAMES
CALLED OFF
CALLED OUT
CALLING BY
CALLING IN
CALLING ON
CALLS AWAY
CALLS BACK
CALLS OVER
CALMS DOWN
CAME ABOUT
CAME CLEAN
CAME ROUND
CAMEO PART
CAMEO ROLE
CAMEO WARE
CAMERA SHY
CAMP CHAIR
CAMP FEVER
CAMP STOOL
CAMPED OUT
CAMPER VAN
CAMPS IT UP
CAN OPENER
CANADA DAY
CANAL BANK
CANAL BOAT
CANCEL OUT
CANDLE END
CANDLE NUT
CANDLE WAX
CANE BRAKE
CANE CHAIR
CANE SUGAR
CANNON BIT
CANT BOARD
CAP IN HAND
CAP PISTOL
CAPE DUTCH
CAPER BUSH
CAPSID BUG
CARD INDEX
CARD SHARP
CARD TABLE
CARD TRICK
CARE LABEL
CARE ORDER
CARPET BAG

9 contd.

CARPET ROD	CHAIN GEAR	CHURN MILK	COACH LINE	CONGER EEL
CARRIED ON	CHAIN MAIL	CHURNED UP	COACH ROAD	CONING OFF
CARRIES ON	CHAIN PIER	CHURNS OUT	COACH TOUR	CONJURE UP
CARRY AWAY	CHAIN PUMP	CIGAR TREE	COACH TRIP	CONY CATCH
CARRY BACK	CHAINED UP	CIPHER KEY	COAL BOARD	COOL HOUSE
CARRY OVER	CHALKED UP	CITY STATE	COAL FIELD	COOLED OFF
CART HORSE	CHALKS OUT	CIVIL LIST	COAL FIRED	COPE STONE
CART TRACK	CHANCED IT	CIVIL TIME	COAL HOUSE	COPING SAW
CARTED OFF	CHANCES IT	CIVIL YEAR	COAL MINER	COPPED OUT
CARVED OUT	CHANGED UP	CLAM SHELL	COAL OWNER	COPPER AGE
CARVES OUT	CHANGES UP	CLAMMED UP	COAST ROAD	COPPING IT
CARVING UP	CHAR A BANC	CLAMP DOWN	COAT FROCK	COR BLIMEY
CASE BOUND	CHARGE MAN	CLAP HANDS	COAT TAILS	CORAL FISH
CASE KNIFE	CHART ROOM	CLARET CUP	COCK A HOOP	CORAL REEF
CASE STUDY	CHASE PORT	CLARET JUG	COCK HORSE	CORAL ROCK
CASH LIMIT	CHAW BACON	CLASS BOOK	COCK ROBIN	CORAL ROOT
CASH POINT	CHEAP JACK	CLAWS BACK	COCKED HAT	CORAL WORT
CASH PRIZE	CHEATED ON	CLAY COURT	COCKS COMB	CORDON OFF
CASHEW NUT	CHECK BOOK	CLAY SLATE	COCO DE MER	CORK SCREW
CASHING IN	CHECK REIN	CLEANED UP	COCOA WOOD	CORN BORER
CASHING UP	CHECK TILL	CLEANS OUT	COD FISHER	CORN BRAKE
CASK STAND	CHECKED IN	CLEAR EYED	CODE NAMED	CORN BREAD
CAST A VOTE	CHECKED UP	CLEAR SOUP	COFFEE BAR	CORN DOLLY
CAST AN EYE	CHECKS OFF	CLEARED UP	COFFEE BUG	CORNER BOY
CAST ASIDE	CHECKS OUT	CLEARS OUT	COFFEE CUP	COST PRICE
CAST DOUBT	CHEEK BONE	CLERK LIKE	COFFEE POT	COSTA RICA
CAST LOOSE	CHEERED UP	CLEW LINES	COFFEE SET	COTE DAZUR
CAST STEEL	CHEESE VAT	CLIFF FACE	COFFER DAM	COTTER PIN
CASTE MARK	CHEONG SAM	CLIMB DOWN	COINING IT	COTTON GIN
CASTING UP	CHERRY BOB	CLING FILM	COLD CREAM	COTTONS ON
CASTOR OIL	CHERRY PIE	CLIP JOINT	COLD DRAWN	COUGH DROP
CASTS A NET	CHERRY PIT	CLOCHE HAT	COLD FRAME	COUGHED UP
CASTS AWAY	CHESS CLUB	CLOCK CARD	COLD FRONT	COUNT DOWN
CASTS LOTS	CHEWS OVER	CLOCK GOLF	COLD HOUSE	COUNTS OUT
CAT FAMILY	CHIEF WHIP	CLOCKED IN	COLD STEEL	COUP DETAT
CAT LITTER	CHILD CARE	CLOCKED UP	COLD WATER	COURT CARD
CAT RIGGED	CHILD STAR	CLOCKS OFF	COLLIE DOG	COURT FOOL
CAT WITTED	CHILD WIFE	CLOCKS OUT	COLOUR BAR	COURT HAND
CATCH COLD	CHILLS OUT	CLOG DANCE	COLOURS IN	COURT ROLL
CATCH CROP	CHIMING IN	CLOSE CALL	COLOURS UP	COURT SHOE
CATCH FIRE	CHINA CLAY	CLOSE DOWN	COMBED OUT	COVER GIRL
CATCHES ON	CHINA JUTE	CLOSE KNIT	COME ABOUT	COVER NOTE
CATCHES UP	CHINA ROSE	CLOSING IN	COME AGAIN	COVERED IN
CAUDLE CUP	CHINA WARE	CLOSING UP	COME AND GO	COVERED UP
CAUGHT OUT	CHIPPED IN	CLOTH EARS	COME CLEAN	COWES WEEK
CAVE CANEM	CHOIR GIRL	CLOTH HALL	COME OF AGE	CRAB APPLE
CEASE FIRE	CHOKE BACK	CLOTH YARD	COME OFF IT	CRAB EATER
CEASE TO BE	CHOKE COIL	CLOUD BASE	COME ROUND	CRAB FACED
CEDAR TREE	CHOKED OFF	CLOUD OVER	COMES AWAY	CRAB SALAD
CEE SPRING	CHOKES OFF	CLOUT NAIL	COMES BACK	CRABS EYES
CELL BLOCK	CHOKING UP	CLOUT SHOE	COMES DOWN	CRACK DOWN
CELTIC SEA	CHOP HOUSE	CLOVE HOOK	COMES HOME	CRACKED UP
CENTRE BIT	CHOP LOGIC	CLOVE PINK	COMES OVER	CRADLE CAP
CERE CLOTH	CHOP STICK	CLUB CLASS	COMING OFF	CRAFT SHOP
CEST A DIRE	CHOPPED UP	CLUB MONEY	COMING OUT	CRAMP IRON
CEST LA VIE	CHUBB LOCK	CLUTCH BAG	COMMON ERA	CRAMP RING
CHA CHA CHA	CHUCK IT IN	CLY FAKING	COMMON LAW	CRASH DIVE
CHAIN BOLT	CHUCKED UP	COACH BOLT	CON DOLORE	CRASH LAND
CHAIN GANG	CHUCKS OUT	COACH HIRE	CONE SHELL	CRAZY GOLF
	CHUMP CHOP	COACH HORN	CONGA DRUM	CREAM CAKE

9 LETTERS

9 *contd.*

CREAM HORN
CREAM PUFF
CREAM SODA
CRESTA RUN
CRIED DOWN
CRIED WOLF
CRIES DOWN
CRIES WOLF
CRIME WAVE
CRO MAGNON
CROPPED UP
CROSS EYED
CROSS KICK
CROSS OVER
CROSS TALK
CROW BERRY
CROWN BARK
CROWN LAND
CROWS BILL
CROWS FEET
CROWS FOOT
CROWS NEST
CRUEL BLOW
CRYING OFF
CRYING OUT
CT SCANNER
CUBAN HEEL
CUBBY HOLE
CUBIC FOOT
CUBIC INCH
CUBIC YARD
CUFF LINKS
CUP WINNER
CUPIDS BOW
CURLING UP
CURLY KALE
CURRY COMB
CURTAIN UP
CUT A CAPER
CUT A TOOTH
CUT ACROSS
CUT AND RUN
CUT IT FINE
CUT THROAT
CUTS A DASH
CUTS LOOSE
CUTS SHORT
CUTTING IN
CUTTING UP
CUTTY SARK
DAIRY FARM
DAISY BELL
DALAI LAMA
DAMP PATCH
DAMP PROOF
DAMP SQUIB
DAMPS DOWN
DAMSON JAM
DANCE BAND

DANCE HALL
DANCE STEP
DANCE TUNE
DANDY CART
DANDY ROLL
DAPPLE BAY
DARE DEVIL
DARK DEEDS
DARK HORSE
DART BOARD
DASHED OFF
DASHED OUT
DASHES OFF
DASHES OUT
DATE STAMP
DATUM LINE
DAVY JONES
DAY CENTRE
DAY LABOUR
DAY OF REST
DAY RETURN
DAY SCHOOL
DE RIGUEUR
DEAD DRUNK
DEAD HEADS
DEAD LEVEL
DEAD MARCH
DEADLY SIN
DEAL A BLOW
DEAR MADAM
DEATH BELL
DEATH CELL
DEATH DUTY
DEATH MASK
DEATH RATE
DEATH ROLL
DEATH TRAP
DEATH WISH
DEBIT CARD
DECK CARGO
DECK CHAIR
DECK HOUSE
DECKED OUT
DECOY DUCK
DEEP DRAWN
DEEP FRIED
DEEP FRIES
DEEP SOUTH
DEEP TONED
DEEP VOICE
DEEP WATER
DEER HOUND
DEER MOUSE
DEGREE DAY
DEI GRATIA
DELTA WING
DEMI DEVIL
DEMI GORGE
DEMI LANCE
DEMI MONDE

DEMON KING
DEN OF VICE
DEPTH BOMB
DERRING DO
DESERT PEA
DESERT RAT
DESK BOUND
DESK DIARY
DEVIL CRAB
DEVIL FISH
DEVILS OWN
DIAL A RIDE
DIB STONES
DICKY BIRD
DIE SINKER
DIED HAPPY
DIES HAPPY
DIESEL OIL
DIET BREAD
DIET SHEET
DIGGING IN
DIGGING UP
DIKA BREAD
DILL WATER
DIME NOVEL
DIME STORE
DINING CAR
DINING OUT
DINNER SET
DIP SWITCH
DIPPED OUT
DIPPING IN
DIRECT HIT
DIRECT TAX
DIRT CHEAP
DIRT TRACK
DIRTY LOOK
DIRTY WORD
DIRTY WORK
DISC BRAKE
DISC DRIVE
DISC STORE
DISC WHEEL
DISH CLOTH
DISH WATER
DISHED OUT
DISHES OUT
DISHING UP
DIXIE LAND
DO ONES BIT
DO ONES NUT
DO TO DEATH
DO YOU MIND
DOC MARTEN
DOCTOR WHO
DOES A TURN
DOG COLLAR
DOG EAT DOG
DOG KENNEL
DOG RACING

DOG SALMON
DOG VIOLET
DOGS OF WAR
DOGS TOOTH
DOING DOWN
DOING OVER
DOING TIME
DOING WELL
DOLCE VITA
DOLLAR GAP
DOLLY BIRD
DOLLY SHOP
DOLLY SHOT
DONOR CARD
DOOR CHEEK
DOOR PLATE
DOPE FIEND
DOSS HOUSE
DOT MATRIX
DOTS THE IS
DOUBLE ACT
DOUBLE BAR
DOUBLE BED
DOUBLE TOP
DOUBLED UP
DOUBLES UP
DOVE HOUSE
DOVER SOLE
DOVES FOOT
DOWN LYING
DOWN QUILT
DOWN SOUTH
DOWN TOOLS
DOWN TRAIN
DOWN UNDER
DRAG QUEEN
DRAGGED ON
DRAGGED UP
DRAIN AWAY
DRAIN PIPE
DRAIN TILE
DRAIN TRAP
DRAUGHT OX
DRAW BLOOD
DRAW SHEET
DRAW TABLE
DRAW TEETH
DRAWING IN
DRAWING UP
DRAWS BACK
DRAWS LOTS
DRAWS NEAR
DRAY HORSE
DREAM LAND
DREAMED UP
DREDGE BOX
DRESS COAT
DRESS DOWN
DRESS SUIT
DRESSED UP

DRESSES UP
DREW BLOOD
DREW TEETH
DRIED EGGS
DRIED MILK
DRIFT LAND
DRIFT SAIL
DRIFT WEED
DRIFT WOOD
DRILL HALL
DRILL HOLE
DRIP STONE
DRIVE HOME
DRIVES OUT
DROP A LINE
DROP DRILL
DROP SCONE
DROPPED BY
DROPPED IN
DROPPED ON
DROPS AWAY
DROPS DOWN
DROVE HOME
DROVE ROAD
DROWNS OUT
DRUG FIEND
DRUG STORE
DRUM BRAKE
DRUM MAJOR
DRURY LANE
DRY CLEANS
DRY SHERRY
DRY SKIING
DRY WALLER
DRYING OUT
DUCK BOARD
DUCKED OUT
DUCKS DOWN
DUCKS FOOT
DUDE RANCH
DUFFEL BAG
DUFFING UP
DUMB CLUCK
DUMB PIANO
DUMPING ON
DUNCES CAP
DURA MATER
DUST BRUSH
DUST COVER
DUST DEVIL
DUST SHEET
DUST STORM
DUTCH BARN
DUTCH DOLL
DUTCH LEAF
DUTCH OVEN
DUTCH WIFE
DUTY BOUND
DYERS WOAD
DYING AWAY

9 *contd.*

DYING DOWN
DYING HARD
DYING SWAN
EACH OTHER
EAGLE EYED
EAGLE HAWK
EAR COCKLE
EARLIER ON
EARLY BIRD
EARLY DAYS
EASILY LED
EASING OFF
EAST ENDER
EASTER DAY
EASTER EGG
EASY CHAIR
EASY GOING
EASY MONEY
EASY RIDER
EASY TERMS
EASY TOUCH
EATING OUT
EDGED TOOL
EDGING OUT
EDITED OUT
EEL BASKET
EGG BEATER
EGG POWDER
ELBOW ROOM
EMBER DAYS
EMBER WEEK
EMBRYO SAC
EMPIRE DAY
EN FAMILLE
EN PASSANT
EN TOUT CAS
END READER
ENERGY GAP
ENTRE NOUS
ENTRY FORM
ERRAND BOY
ESKIMO DOG
ESSEX GIRL
ESTATE CAR
ET TU BRUTE
EVEN MONEY
EVENED OUT
EVENING UP
EVERY INCH
EWE CHEESE
EWE NECKED
EX LIBRISM
EX LIBRIST
EX OFFICIO
EX SERVICE
EXCISE LAW
EXTRA TIME
EYE LOTION
EYE MUSCLE

EYE OPENER
EYE SHADOW
EYE SOCKET
EYE STRAIN
FACE CLOTH
FACE CREAM
FACE FACTS
FACE GUARD
FACE PLATE
FACE SAVER
FACE VALUE
FACING OUT
FACT SHEET
FADING OUT
FAGGED OUT
FAIR FACED
FAIR TRIAL
FAIRS FAIR
FAIRY KING
FAIRY RING
FAIRY TALE
FALL ABOUT
FALL APART
FALL SHORT
FALLING IN
FALLING ON
FALLS BACK
FALLS DOWN
FALLS OVER
FALSE DAWN
FALSE GODS
FALSE NOSE
FAMILY MAN
FAN SHAPED
FANCY CAKE
FANCY FAIR
FANCY FREE
FANNED OUT
FAR AFIELD
FAR SEEING
FARDEL BAG
FARM PLACE
FARM STEAD
FARMED OUT
FAST FOODS
FASTENS ON
FAT CHANCE
FAT HEADED
FATTENS UP
FEAST RITE
FEE FAW FUM
FEE SIMPLE
FEEL A FOOL
FEEL CHEAP
FEEL FAINT
FEEL SMALL
FELL ABOUT
FELL APART
FELL SHORT
FELLOW MAN

FELT A FOOL
FELT CHEAP
FELT FAINT
FELT SMALL
FERRY BOAT
FETCHED UP
FETCHES UP
FEVER HEAT
FIDDLE BOW
FIELD BOOK
FIELD GREY
FIELD LARK
FIELD TRIP
FIEND LIKE
FIFE MAJOR
FIG LEAVES
FIGHT BACK
FIGHTS OFF
FILED PAST
FILING OFF
FILLED OUT
FILLER CAP
FILLING IN
FILLING UP
FILM ACTOR
FILM EXTRA
FILM STRIP
FILTER BED
FILTER TIP
FIND FAULT
FINE DRAWN
FINE SPRAY
FINE TUNED
FINGER TIP
FINING POT
FINISH OFF
FIRE ALARM
FIRE ARROW
FIRE BLAST
FIRE BREAK
FIRE DRILL
FIRE EATER
FIRE GRATE
FIRE IRONS
FIRE POWER
FIRE STICK
FIRE STORM
FIRE WATER
FIRED AWAY
FIRED BACK
FIRES AWAY
FIRES BACK
FIRING OFF
FIRING PIN
FIRMING UP
FIRMS DOWN
FIRST BASE
FIRST BORN
FIRST FOOT
FIRST GEAR

FIRST HAND
FIRST LADY
FIRST MATE
FIRST NAME
FIRST RATE
FIRST SLIP
FISH CREEL
FISH EATER
FISH JOINT
FISH KNIFE
FISH PLATE
FISH SAUCE
FISH SLICE
FISH SPEAR
FISHED OUT
FISHES OUT
FIT TO BUST
FITTED OUT
FITTING IN
FITTING UP
FIVE A SIDE
FIVE PENCE
FIXED IDEA
FIXED ODDS
FIXED STAR
FLAG WAVER
FLAGS DOWN
FLAKED OUT
FLAKES OUT
FLAME LEAF
FLAME TREE
FLAP EARED
FLARE PATH
FLARE STAR
FLARING UP
FLASH BACK
FLASH BULB
FLASH BURN
FLASH CARD
FLASH FIRE
FLASH OVER
FLAT BROKE
FLESH MEAT
FLESH TINT
FLEW A KITE
FLIES HIGH
FLIES OPEN
FLIES SOLO
FLING DOWN
FLING OPEN
FLINGS OUT
FLOAT TANK
FLOOD LAMP
FLOOR PLAN
FLOOR SHOW
FLOSS SILK
FLOUR MILL
FLOW CHART
FLOW SHEET
FLOWER BED

FLOWER BUD
FLUNG DOWN
FLUNG OPEN
FLUTE A BEC
FLUTE BIRD
FLY BITTEN
FLY FISHER
FLY ORCHIS
FLY POWDER
FLYING FOX
FLYING JIB
FLYING OUT
FOAM GLASS
FOBBED OFF
FOG SIGNAL
FOLDED OUT
FOLDING IN
FOLIC ACID
FOLK CRAFT
FOLK DANCE
FOLK MUSIC
FOLK RIGHT
FOLK WEAVE
FOLLOW OUT
FOLLOWS ON
FOLLOWS UP
FONDUE SET
FOOD CANAL
FOOD CHAIN
FOOL HAPPY
FOOLS GOLD
FOOLS MATE
FOOT BRAKE
FOOT FAULT
FOOT POUND
FOOT STALL
FOOTING IT
FOR A START
FOR CHOICE
FOR EFFECT
FOR MY PART
FORAGE CAP
FORCE FEED
FORCE LAND
FORCE PUMP
FORE BRACE
FORE BRAIN
FORE CITED
FORE WHEEL
FOREST FLY
FOREST LAW
FOREST OAK
FORK CHUCK
FORK LUNCH
FORKED OUT
FORKING UP
FORKS OVER
FORM CLASS
FORM GENUS
FORM HORSE

9 LETTERS

9 contd.
FOSTER SON
FOUGHT OFF
FOULING UP
FOUR BY TWO
FOUR FLUSH
FOUR HORSE
FOUR WHEEL
FOX HUNTER
FREAKS OUT
FREE AGENT
FREE BOARD
FREE DIVER
FREE FIGHT
FREE HOUSE
FREE LANCE
FREE LIVER
FREE LOVER
FREE LUNCH
FREE RANGE
FREE RIDER
FREE SPACE
FREE TRADE
FREE VERSE
FREE WHEEL
FREE WORLD
FREEZE DRY
FREEZE OUT
FRENCH FRY
FRESHEN UP
FRIAR TUCK
FRIARS CAP
FRIED EGGS
FRIED RICE
FROCK COAT
FROG EATER
FROG MARCH
FRONT AXLE
FRONT DOOR
FRONT LINE
FRONT PAGE
FRONT RANK
FRONT ROOM
FROST BITE
FROWNED ON
FROZEN OUT
FRUIT CAKE
FRUIT TREE
FRYING PAN
FUEL GAUGE
FULL BLAST
FULL BLOOD
FULL BLOWN
FULL CREAM
FULL DRESS
FULL FACED
FULL FLING
FULL GROWN
FULL HOUSE
FULL MARKS

FULL OF WOE
FULL ORGAN
FOUGHT OFF
FULL PITCH
FULL QUOTA
FULL SCALE
FULL SCORE
FULL SPLIT
FUNNEL NET
FUNNEL WEB
FUNNY BONE
FUNNY FARM
FUNNY HA HA
FUR COLLAR
FUR LINING
FURTHER ON
GADS ABOUT
GAINS TIME
GALL MIDGE
GALL STONE
GALLOP OFF
GALWAY BAY
GAME CHIPS
GAME POINT
GAMES ROOM
GAMMA RAYS
GANGING UP
GAOL BREAK
GAOL FEVER
GAS BOTTLE
GAS BURNER
GAS COOKER
GAS COOLED
GAS ENGINE
GAS ESCAPE
GAS FILLED
GAS FITTER
GAS HEATER
GAS HELMET
GAS HOLDER
GAS MANTLE
GATE HOUSE
GATE MONEY
GATE TOWER
GATHER WAY
GATHERS UP
GAVE BIRTH
GAVE CHASE
GAVE FORTH
GAVE IT A GO
GAVE VOICE
GAZE HOUND
GEAR LEVER
GEAR RATIO
GEAR SHIFT
GEAR STICK
GEAR WHEEL
GEARING UP
GEARS DOWN
GENNING UP
GENOA CAKE

GENS DE LOI
GERM LAYER
GERM PLASM
GET ACROSS
GET AROUND
GET AT ABLE
GETS ABOUT
GETS AHEAD
GETS ALONG
GETS IDEAS
GETS READY
GETS ROUND
GETS THERE
GETS TOUGH
GETTING AT
GETTING BY
GETTING IN
GETTING ON
GETTING UP
GHOST LIKE
GHOST MOTH
GHOST TOWN
GIANT STAR
GIFT HORSE
GIFT TOKEN
GILL HOUSE
GILT EDGED
GILT SPURS
GIN PALACE
GINGER ALE
GINGER NUT
GINGER POP
GINGER TOM
GIPSY MOTH
GIRL GUIDE
GIRL SCOUT
GIVE BIRTH
GIVE CHASE
GIVE FORTH
GIVE IT A GO
GIVE VOICE
GIVEN AWAY
GIVEN NAME
GIVES AWAY
GIVES ODDS
GIVES REIN
GIVING EAR
GIVING OFF
GIVING OUT
GIVING WAY
GLASS CHIN
GLASS SOAP
GLASS WOOL
GLIDE PATH
GLOBE FISH
GLORY HOLE
GLOSS OVER
GNAWS AWAY
GO AGAINST
GO BANANAS

GO BERSERK
GO BETWEEN
GO FOR GOLD
GO FORWARD
GO GETTING
GO HAYWIRE
GO IT ALONE
GO MISSING
GO ONES WAY
GO THROUGH
GO TO COURT
GO TO EARTH
GO TO GRASS
GO TO PRESS
GO TO SLEEP
GO TO WASTE
GO WHISTLE
GO WITHOUT
GOA BUTTER
GOA POWDER
GOATS HAIR
GOBBLED UP
GOBBLES UP
GOD FORBID
GOD HELP US
GODS TRUTH
GOES AHEAD
GOES DUTCH
GOES FORTH
GOES ROUND
GOES TO BED
GOES TO POT
GOES TO SEA
GOES TO WAR
GOES UNDER
GOES WRONG
GOGGLE BOX
GOING AWAY
GOING BACK
GOING BUST
GOING DOWN
GOING INTO
GOING OVER
GOING SLOW
GOING SOFT
GOING WEST
GOLD BRICK
GOLD CHAIN
GOLD CLOTH
GOLD COAST
GOLD CREST
GOLD FEVER
GOLD LACED
GOLD MEDAL
GOLD MINER
GOLD PAINT
GOLD PLATE
GOLD POINT
GOLDEN AGE
GOLDEN BOY

GOLDEN EYE
GOLF LINKS
GOLF WIDOW
GONE AHEAD
GONE GOOSE
GONE TO BED
GONE TO POT
GONE TO SEA
GONE UNDER
GONE WRONG
GONG STICK
GOOD CAUSE
GOOD GOING
GOOD GRIEF
GOOD HANDS
GOOD LOOKS
GOOD ORDER
GOOD SENSE
GOOD SIZED
GOOD SPORT
GOOD STUFF
GOOD TASTE
GOOD TO SEE
GOOD VALUE
GOOD WORKS
GOOSE FAIR
GOOSE FISH
GOOSE GIRL
GOOSE NECK
GOOSE SKIN
GOOSE STEP
GOOSE WING
GOT ACROSS
GOT AROUND
GOUGED OUT
GOUGES OUT
GRACE NOTE
GRADE RISE
GRAND AUNT
GRAND DUKE
GRAND PRIX
GRAND SLAM
GRAND TOUR
GRASS PLOT
GRAVEL PIT
GRAVY BOAT
GRAVY SOUP
GREASE GUN
GREAT AUNT
GREAT DANE
GREAT HALL
GREAT SEAL
GREEK FIRE
GREEK GIFT
GREEK GODS
GREEK NOSE
GREEN BELT
GREEN CARD
GREEN CORN
GREEN CROP

9 contd.

GREEN EYED	HALF FACED	HAVE A STAB	HIGH LEVEL	HONEY BEAR
GREEN ROOM	HALF LIGHT	HAVE AT HIM	HIGH POINT	HONEY BIRD
GREW APART	HALF MILER	HAVE IDEAS	HIGH SPEED	HONEY CART
GREY FRIAR	HALF POUND	HAVE IT OUT	HIGH TABLE	HONKY TONK
GREY GOOSE	HALF PRICE	HAVE WORDS	HIGH TONED	HOOF PRINT
GRILL ROOM	HALF SWORD	HAVING A GO	HIGH WATER	HOOK NOSED
GRIMMS LAW	HALF TITLE	HAWK NOSED	HILL BILLY	HOP GARDEN
GRIND DOWN	HALF TRUTH	HEAD COUNT	HIND BRAIN	HOP PICKER
GRIST MILL	HALL TABLE	HEAD DRESS	HIND WHEEL	HOP PILLOW
GROS POINT	HAM FISTED	HEAD FIRST	HINDER END	HOP SCOTCH
GROSSED UP	HAMMER TOE	HEAD MONEY	HINTING AT	HOPPED OFF
GROSSES UP	HAND BRAKE	HEAD RHYME	HIP GIRDLE	HOPPING IT
GROUND ASH	HAND GLASS	HEAD START	HIP POCKET	HORN MAKER
GROUND HOG	HAND OF GOD	HEAD WATER	HIRED HELP	HORN SPOON
GROUND ICE	HAND ORGAN	HEADED OFF	HIRING OUT	HORNED OWL
GROUND NUT	HAND PAPER	HEADED OUT	HIT AND RUN	HORNING IN
GROUND OAK	HAND PRESS	HEARD TELL	HIT FOR SIX	HORS SERIE
GROW APART	HAND PUNCH	HEARS TELL	HIT OR MISS	HORS TEXTE
GROWING UP	HAND SCREW	HEART BEAT	HIT PARADE	HORSE FAIR
GRUB SCREW	HAND TOWEL	HEART SICK	HIT THE HAY	HORSE FOOT
GUARD RAIL	HANDED OUT	HEARTH RUG	HIT WICKET	HORSE RACE
GUARD ROOM	HANDS DOWN	HEARTH TAX	HITCH HIKE	HORSE SHOE
GUARD SHIP	HANDS OVER	HEATH FOWL	HITCHED UP	HOT AND HOT
GUARDS VAN	HANDS TURN	HEAVING TO	HITCHES UP	HOT POTATO
GUESS WORK	HANG ABOUT	HEAVY DUTY	HITS IT OFF	HOT RODDER
GUEST ROOM	HANG LOOSE	HEAVY ROCK	HITTING ON	HOTEL DIEU
GUIDE BOOK	HANGING IN	HEAVY SPAR	HIVE HONEY	HOTTING UP
GUIDE POST	HANGING ON	HEDGE HOPS	HIVING OFF	HOUND FISH
GUIDE RAIL	HANGS BACK	HEEL PIECE	HOAR FROST	HOUR GLASS
GUIDE ROPE	HANGS FIRE	HEIR AT LAW	HOGGING IT	HOUSE BOAT
GUINEA HEN	HANSOM CAB	HELD COURT	HOI POLLOI	HOUSE CALL
GUINEA PIG	HAPPY DAYS	HELD FORTH	HOLD COURT	HOUSE COAT
GULLY HOLE	HAPPY HOUR	HELD HANDS	HOLD FORTH	HOUSE DUTY
GUM ARABIC	HARD APORT	HELD WATER	HOLD HANDS	HOUSE HUNT
GUMMING UP	HARD COURT	HELL TO PAY	HOLD WATER	HOUSE MATE
GUN BARREL	HARD CURED	HELPED OUT	HOLDING IN	HOUSE ROOM
GUN TURRET	HARD DRAWN	HEM STITCH	HOLDING ON	HOW ARE YOU
GUY FAWKES	HARD FACTS	HEMMING IN	HOLDING UP	HOWLS DOWN
GYPSY MOTH	HARD LINES	HEN WITTED	HOLDS BACK	HUE AND CRY
HAD A LAUGH	HARD METAL	HERB PETER	HOLDS DOWN	HUM AND HAW
HAD NO IDEA	HARD PASTE	HERBAL TEA	HOLDS GOOD	HUMBLE PIE
HAG RIDDEN	HARD STUFF	HERE WE ARE	HOLDS OVER	HUNG ABOUT
HAIL A TAXI	HARD TIMES	HEROIC AGE	HOLDS SWAY	HUNG LOOSE
HAIL STORM	HARD WORDS	HEY PRESTO	HOLE IN ONE	HUNG TILES
HAIR BRUSH	HARDEN OFF	HIDE BOUND	HOLING OUT	HUNKY DORY
HAIR DRIER	HARES FOOT	HIDEY HOLE	HOLLOW OUT	HUNTED OUT
HAIR DRYER	HARKS BACK	HIGH ALTAR	HOLLY FERN	HUNTS DOWN
HAIR PIECE	HARPING ON	HIGH BLOWN	HOLY BIBLE	HURRIED UP
HAIR SHIRT	HAS A LAUGH	HIGH CHAIR	HOLY GHOST	HURRIES UP
HAIR SLIDE	HAS NO IDEA	HIGH CLASS	HOLY GRAIL	HUSH MONEY
HAIR SPRAY	HASH BROWN	HIGH COURT	HOLY WATER	HUSH PUPPY
HAIR WAVER	HATHA YOGA	HIGH CROSS	HOME COMER	HUSHING UP
HALF A TICK	HAUL ROUND	HIGH DUTCH	HOME CROFT	HUT CIRCLE
HALF BAKED	HAULING IN	HIGH FLIER	HOME GROWN	ICE ANCHOR
HALF BOARD	HAULING UP	HIGH FLOWN	HOME GUARD	ICE BUCKET
HALF BREED	HAUT MONDE	HIGH FLYER	HOME MATCH	ICE HOCKEY
HALF CASTE	HAVE A BALL	HIGH GRADE	HOME MOVIE	ICE SKATED
HALF CROWN	HAVE A BASH	HIGH GROWN	HOME NURSE	ICE SKATER
HALF DOZEN	HAVE A CARE	HIGH HORSE	HOME RULER	ICE SKATES
		HIGH JINKS	HOME TRUTH	ICED WATER

9 *contd.*

ICING OVER	IN THE WARS	JET DRIVEN	KEEPS BACK	LADLED OUT
IDEAL HOME	IN THE WIND	JET LAGGED	KEEPS BUSY	LADLES OUT
IDEE RECUE	IN TOP FORM	JET SETTER	KEEPS DOWN	LADY SMOCK
IDIOT CARD	IN TRANSIT	JET SKIING	KEEPS TIME	LADYS MAID
IDLE WHEEL	IN TROUBLE	JET STREAM	KEG BITTER	LAG BEHIND
ILL AT EASE	INCOME TAX	JEU DE MOTS	KENNEL MAN	LAGER BEER
ILL BODING	INDEX LINK	JEWEL CASE	KEPT AT BAY	LAGER LOUT
ILL GOTTEN	INDIAN FIG	JOB CENTRE	KEPT CLEAR	LAID AN EGG
ILL HEALTH	INDIAN INK	JOB MASTER	KEPT FAITH	LAID ASIDE
ILL HUMOUR	INDIAN RED	JOB OF WORK	KEPT HOUSE	LAID CLAIM
ILL JUDGED	INGLE NOOK	JOBS TEARS	KEPT QUIET	LAID PAPER
ILL NATURE	INGLE SIDE	JOCK SCOTT	KEPT STILL	LAID WASTE
ILL OMENED	INK BOTTLE	JOCK STRAP	KEPT TRACK	LAKE BASIN
ILL SEE YOU	INK ERASER	JOE BLOGGS	KEPT WATCH	LAKE HURON
ILL TEMPER	INK PENCIL	JOE MILLER	KEPT WOMAN	LAKE POETS
ILL VERSED	INNER CITY	JOE PUBLIC	KERB DRILL	LAMB OF GOD
ILL WISHER	INNER PART	JOGS ALONG	KICK ABOUT	LAMBS EARS
IN A BAD WAY	INNER TUBE	JOIN HANDS	KICK PLEAT	LAMBS WOOL
IN A BIG WAY	INNER WARD	JOINING IN	KICK START	LAMP BLACK
IN A CORNER	INSECT NET	JOINING UP	KICKED OFF	LAMP GLASS
IN A PICKLE	INSIDE JOB	JOINT HEIR	KICKED OUT	LAMP SHADE
IN ANY CASE	INSIDE OUT	JOINT WILL	KICKING IN	LANCE JACK
IN ARREARS	INTER ALIA	JOINT WORM	KID SISTER	LANCE WOOD
IN BETWEEN	INTER ARTS	JOLLY GOOD	KIDS STUFF	LAND AGENT
IN CAHOOTS	IPSE DIXIT	JOSS HOUSE	KILLED OFF	LAND FLOOD
IN COMPANY	IPSO FACTO	JOSS STICK	KILLS TIME	LAND GRANT
IN CONCERT	IRISH MOSS	JOY RIDING	KILN DRIED	LAND OF NOD
IN CONTROL	IRISH STEW	JUDAS HOLE	KILNER JAR	LAND ROVER
IN COUNCIL	IRON CROSS	JUDAS KISS	KING APPLE	LAND VALUE
IN DEFAULT	IRON CROWN	JUDAS TREE	KING COBRA	LAND YACHT
IN DISGUST	IRON HORSE	JUG OF MILK	KING HENRY	LANGUE DOC
IN EARNEST	IRON MINER	JUKE JOINT	KING JAMES	LAP ROLLER
IN ESSENCE	IRONED OUT	JULIET CAP	KING MIDAS	LAPSE RATE
IN FASHION	ISLE OF ELY	JUMP LEADS	KING PRAWN	LARDY CAKE
IN FULL CRY	ISLE OF MAN	JUMP START	KING SIZED	LARK ABOUT
IN GENERAL	IT IS ALL UP	JUMPED OFF	KINGS EVIL	LARKS HEEL
IN HARNESS	ITSY BITSY	JUMPING ON	KIRBY GRIP	LASER BEAM
IN KEEPING	IVORY GATE	JUMPS BAIL	KIWI FRUIT	LASER DISC
IN PASSING	IVORY PALM	JUMPS SHIP	KLIEG EYES	LASHED OUT
IN PATIENT	IVY LEAGUE	JUNE BRIDE	KNEE CORDS	LASHES OUT
IN PRIVATE	IVY LEAVED	JUST A TICK	KNEE JOINT	LAST DITCH
IN RESERVE	JACK BLOCK	JUST ABOUT	KNIFE EDGE	LAST MAN IN
IN SERVICE	JACK BOOTS	JUST CAUSE	KNIFE REST	LAST RITES
IN TATTERS	JACK FROST	JUST FANCY	KNOB STICK	LAST STRAW
IN THE BATH	JACK KETCH	JUST RIGHT	KNOCK BACK	LAST THING
IN THE BUFF	JACK KNIFE	KAURI PINE	KNOCK COLD	LAST WALTZ
IN THE CART	JACK NASTY	KEELS OVER	KNOCK DOWN	LATCHED ON
IN THE CLUB	JACK SNIPE	KEEP AT BAY	KNOCK KNEE	LATCHES ON
IN THE DARK	JACK SPRAT	KEEP CLEAR	KNOCKED ON	LATE COMER
IN THE DOCK	JACK STRAW	KEEP COUNT	KNOCKED UP	LATE SHIFT
IN THE KNOW	JADE GREEN	KEEP FAITH	KNOCKER UP	LATE START
IN THE MAIN	JAIL BREAK	KEEP HOUSE	KNOCKS OFF	LATTER DAY
IN THE NEWS	JAIL FEVER	KEEP QUIET	KNOCKS OUT	LATTER END
IN THE NICK	JAM PACKED	KEEP STILL	KNOT HOLES	LAUGHS OFF
IN THE NUDE	JAY WALKER	KEEP TRACK	KOALA BEAR	LAUNCH PAD
IN THE PINK	JELLY BABY	KEEP WATCH	LABOUR DAY	LAW CENTRE
IN THE ROAD	JENA GLASS	KEEPING IN	LACE FRAME	LAW GIVING
IN THE SOUP	JENNY WREN	KEEPING ON	LACE PAPER	LAW WRITER
IN THE SWIM	JERRY SHOP	KEEPING UP	LACK BRAIN	LAWN MOWER
	JERSEY COW	KEEPS AT IT	LADIES MAN	LAWN PARTY

9 contd.

LAY EYES ON	LETS IT RIP	LIVE IN SIN	LOOKING IN	LYME HOUND
LAY FALLOW	LETS LOOSE	LIVE ON AIR	LOOKING ON	LYMPH NODE
LAY FIGURE	LETS SLIDE	LIVE SHELL	LOOKING UP	LYON COURT
LAY IN WAIT	LETTER BOX	LIVED A LIE	LOOKS AWRY	MAD DOCTOR
LAY READER	LETTING BE	LIVED DOWN	LOOKS BACK	MAD HATTER
LAY RECTOR	LETTING GO	LIVED IT UP	LOOKS DOWN	MADE A BOMB
LAY SISTER	LETTING IN	LIVED WELL	LOOKS INTO	MADE A FACE
LAY TO REST	LETTING ON	LIVER SPOT	LOOKS OVER	MADE A MOVE
LAYER CAKE	LETTING UP	LIVES A LIE	LOOKS UP TO	MADE AFTER
LAYING OFF	LEVEL BEST	LIVES DOWN	LOOM LARGE	MADE FUN OF
LAYING OUT	LEVEL COIL	LIVES IT UP	LOON PANTS	MADE HASTE
LAYS AN EGG	LEVELS OFF	LIVES WELL	LOOSE LEAF	MADE MERRY
LAYS ASIDE	LEYDEN JAR	LIVING OUT	LOOSENS UP	MADE MONEY
LAYS CLAIM	LHASA APSO	LOAF BREAD	LORD KNOWS	MADE PEACE
LAYS WASTE	LIBEL SUIT	LOAF SUGAR	LORD MAYOR	MADE READY
LAZY BONES	LIE FALLOW	LOAN SHARK	LOSE COUNT	MADE SENSE
LAZY SUSAN	LIE IN WAIT	LOCAL CALL	LOSE HEART	MADE USE OF
LAZY TONGS	LIES AWAKE	LOCAL TIME	LOSE TOUCH	MADE WAVES
LEAD COLIC	LIES UNDER	LOCK CHAIN	LOSE TRACK	MAGIC CUBE
LEAD OXIDE	LIFE BLOOD	LOCK GATES	LOSES FACE	MAGIC WAND
LEAD PAINT	LIFE CLASS	LOCK HORNS	LOSES TIME	MAIL COACH
LEADING IN	LIFE CYCLE	LOCKED OUT	LOSING OUT	MAIL ORDER
LEADING ON	LIFE FORCE	LOCKING IN	LOST CAUSE	MAIL PLANE
LEADING UP	LIFE SAVER	LOCKING ON	LOST CHORD	MAIL TRAIN
LEAF GREEN	LIFE SIZED	LOCKING UO	LOST COUNT	MAIN STORE
LEAF METAL	LIFE STYLE	LOCKS AWAY	LOST HEART	MAJOR AXIS
LEAF MOULD	LIFE WEARY	LODGE GATE	LOST TOUCH	MAJOR DOMO
LEAF STALK	LIFTED OFF	LOFTING UP	LOST TRACK	MAJOR MODE
LEAKED OUT	LIFTING UP	LOG ROLLER	LOUD MOUTH	MAJOR SUIT
LEAN FACED	LIGHT BULB	LOG TABLES	LOUNGE BAR	MAJOR TERM
LEANING ON	LIGHT FOOT	LOGGED OUT	LOUSE WORT	MAJOR TONE
LEASE LEND	LIGHT WORK	LOGGING IN	LOVE APPLE	MAKE A BOMB
LEAVES OFF	LIGHT YEAR	LOIN CLOTH	LOVE ARROW	MAKE A FACE
LEAVES OUT	LIGHTEN UP	LONDON IVY	LOVE CHARM	MAKE A MOVE
LEAVING BE	LIGHTS OUT	LONG CHAIN	LOVE CHILD	MAKE AFTER
LED ASTRAY	LIKE A BIRD	LONG DATED	LOVE MATCH	MAKE FUN OF
LED THE WAY	LIKE A SHOT	LONG DOZEN	LOVE STORY	MAKE HASTE
LEFT ALONE	LIKE AS NOT	LONG DRAWN	LOVE TOKEN	MAKE MERRY
LEFT OVERS	LIKE STINK	LONG DRINK	LOVING CUP	MAKE MONEY
LEFT WHEEL	LILY WHITE	LONG EARED	LOW CHURCH	MAKE MY DAY
LEG OF LAMB	LIMBERS UP	LONG FACED	LOW COMEDY	MAKE OR MAR
LEG OF PORK	LIME GREEN	LONG JOHNS	LOW DOWNER	MAKE PEACE
LEG PULLER	LIME JUICE	LONG LIVED	LOW GERMAN	MAKE READY
LEG THEORY	LINE BLOCK	LONG MARCH	LOW LOADER	MAKE SENSE
LEGAL MIND	LINE FENCE	LONG METRE	LOW MINDED	MAKE USE OF
LEGAL YEAR	LINEN FOLD	LONG RANGE	LOW NECKED	MAKE WAVES
LEMON CURD	LINKING IN	LONG SHEEP	LOW RELIEF	MAKES A BED
LEMON DROP	LINKING UP	LONG SKIRT	LOW SUNDAY	MAKES AWAY
LEMON PEEL	LION HEART	LONG WHIST	LOWER CASE	MAKES GOOD
LEMON SOLE	LION TAMER	LOOK A FOOL	LOWER DECK	MAKES IT UP
LEND A HAND	LIP READER	LOOK AFTER	LUCK PENNY	MAKES LOVE
LEND AN EAR	LIST PRICE	LOOK ALIKE	LUGGING IN	MAKES OVER
LEND LEASE	LISTENS IN	LOOK ROUND	LUMP SUGAR	MAKES PLAY
LENT A HAND	LITTER BIN	LOOK SHARP	LUNAR YEAR	MAKES ROOM
LENT AN EAR	LITTER BUG	LOOK SMALL	LUNCH HOUR	MAKES SAIL
LET IT RIDE	LITTLE AUK	LOOK SMART	LUNCH TIME	MAKES SURE
LETS ALONE	LITTLE END	LOOKED FOR	LYAM HOUND	MAKES TIME
LETS BLOOD	LITTLE MAN	LOOKED OUT	LYING BACK	MAKING FOR
LETS DRIVE	LITTLE TOE	LOOKERS ON	LYING DOWN	MAKING HAY
	LIVE BIRTH	LOOKING AT	LYING OVER	MAKING OFF

9 LETTERS

9 *contd.*

MAKING OUT	METER MAID	MONKEY JAR	MUSCLED IN	NIT PICKER
MAKING WAR	METRIC TON	MONKEY NUT	MUSCLES IN	NO COMMENT
MAKING WAY	MEZZA VOCE	MONKEY RUN	MUSIC CASE	NO KIDDING
MAL DU PAYS	MID SEASON	MONKS HOOD	MUSIC HALL	NO PROBLEM
MALLEE HEN	MID WICKET	MONO SKIER	MUSIC RACK	NO SMOKING
MALT FLOOR	MID WINTER	MONT BLANC	MUSIC ROLL	NODDED OFF
MALT HORSE	MIDDLE AGE	MOON BOOTS	MUSIC ROOM	NOISES OFF
MALT HOUSE	MIDDLE EAR	MOON DAISY	MUSK MELON	NON MEMBER
MAN AT ARMS	MILD STEEL	MOON FACED	MUSK PLANT	NON PERSON
MAN FRIDAY	MILK CHURN	MOOT COURT	MUSK SHREW	NON SMOKER
MANOR SEAT	MILK FEVER	MOOT HOUSE	MYRTLE WAX	NONCE WORD
MANY SIDED	MILK FLOAT	MOOT POINT	NAIL BRUSH	NONE OTHER
MAO JACKET	MILK GLAND	MOP AND MOW	NAILS DOWN	NOR EASTER
MAPLE LEAF	MILK HOUSE	MOP HEADED	NAME BRAND	NOR WESTER
MAPPED OUT	MILK ROUND	MOPPING UP	NAME CHILD	NORTH EAST
MARCH HARE	MILK SHAKE	MORAL CODE	NAME NAMES	NORTH POLE
MARCH PAST	MILK STOUT	MORTAL SIN	NAME PLATE	NORTH STAR
MARDI GRAS	MILK SUGAR	MOSAIC LAW	NANDI BEAR	NORTH WEST
MARES NEST	MILK TEETH	MOSAIC MAP	NANNY GOAT	NOSE BLEED
MARES TAIL	MILK TOOTH	MOSS AGATE	NEAT STALL	NOSE FLUTE
MARKED MAN	MILL HORSE	MOSS GREEN	NECK CLOTH	NOSE PIECE
MARKED OFF	MILL OWNER	MOST NOBLE	NECK PIECE	NOSE WHEEL
MARKED OUT	MILL TOOTH	MOTH BALLS	NEEDLE GUN	NOSING OUT
MARKET DAY	MILL WHEEL	MOTH EATEN	NEEDS MUST	NOT A THING
MARKET MAN	MILLS BOMB	MOTH PROOF	NEO GOTHIC	NOT AT HOME
MARKING UP	MIND CURER	MOTHER WIT	NEO NAZISM	NOT GUILTY
MARKS DOWN	MINE FIELD	MOTOR BIKE	NEON LIGHT	NOT LIKELY
MARKS TIME	MINE LAYER	MOTOR BOAT	NERVE CELL	NOT PROVEN
MARSH HAWK	MINE OWNER	MOTOR SHOW	NERVE ENDS	NOTHING ON
MASHING UP	MINE SHAFT	MOUND BIRD	NET PLAYER	NOTRE DAME
MASS GRAVE	MINI DRESS	MOUNT ETNA	NEVER MIND	NOVUS HOMO
MASS MEDIA	MINI SKIRT	MOUSE DEER	NEW GUINEA	NUMBER ONE
MASTER KEY	MINOR AXIS	MOUSE HOLE	NEW JERSEY	NUMBER TEN
MATCH PLAY	MINOR MODE	MOUSE HUNT	NEW MEXICO	NUMBER TWO
MAXI DRESS	MINOR POET	MOUSE TAIL	NEWS FLASH	NUNS FLESH
MAXI SKIRT	MINOR SUIT	MOUSE TRAP	NEWS PRINT	NURSE MAID
MAY BEETLE	MINOR TERM	MOUTH HARP	NEWS SHEET	NUT BUTTER
MEADOW RUE	MINOR TONE	MOVE HOUSE	NEWS STAND	NUT CUTLET
MEANS TEST	MINT JULEP	MOVED AWAY	NEWS VALUE	NUT WRENCH
MEANS WELL	MINT SAUCE	MOVED BACK	NEXT OF KIN	NUX VOMICA
MEANT WELL	MINT STATE	MOVED OVER	NEXT WORLD	NYMPH LIKE
MEASURE UP	MINUS SIGN	MOVES AWAY	NIGHT BELL	OAST HOUSE
MEAT EATER	MINUTE GUN	MOVES BACK	NIGHT BIRD	OBJET DART
MEAT JELLY	MIRE SNIPE	MOVES OVER	NIGHT CLUB	ODD JOBBER
MEAT PASTE	MISS WORLD	MOVING OUT	NIGHT DUTY	ODD JOBMAN
MEAT WAGON	MISSED OUT	MR SPEAKER	NIGHT GOWN	ODD MAN OUT
MEDAL PLAY	MISSES OUT	MRS GRUNDY	NIGHT LIFE	ODD ONE OUT
MEETING UP	MISTING UP	MUCK RAKER	NIGHT REST	OF THAT ILK
MELLOW OUT	MISTS OVER	MUCK SWEAT	NIGHT ROBE	OFF CENTRE
MELTS AWAY	MOB HANDED	MUCKING IN	NIGHT SPOT	OFF CHANCE
MELTS DOWN	MODERN ART	MUDDLED UP	NIGHT TIDE	OFF COLOUR
MEN AT ARMS	MOHS SCALE	MUDDLES UP	NIGHT TIME	OFF LIMITS
MEN AT WORK	MOLE DRAIN	MUFFIN CAP	NIGHT WORK	OFF PUTTER
MENTAL AGE	MOLE SPADE	MUFFIN MAN	NILE GREEN	OFF STREAM
MERRY MAKE	MOLING OUT	MUG HUNTER	NINE LIVES	OFF STREET
MESS ABOUT	MONEY BAGS	MUGGING UP	NIP CHEESE	OFF THE AIR
MESSING UP	MONEY BELT	MULTI WALL	NIPPED OUT	OFF THE MAP
MET OFFICE	MONEY BILL	MUMMY CASE	NIPPING IN	OFF THE PEG
METAL WORK	MONEY DOWN	MUMMYS BOY	NISSEN HUT	OFFERED UP
	MONKEY BAG	MUSCLE MAN	NIT PICKED	OFFICE BOY

9 contd.

OIL BURNER	OPEN SKIES	PAINT TRAY	PATROL CAR	PER SALTUM
OIL COLOUR	OPEN SPACE	PAIR HORSE	PAUL JONES	PERKING UP
OIL ENGINE	OPENED OUT	PAIR ROYAL	PAY A VISIT	PET SITTER
OIL FILTER	OPENING UP	PAIRED OFF	PAY HOMAGE	PET THEORY
OIL TANKER	OPTIC LOBE	PALACE CAR	PAY IN FULL	PETER BOAT
OKEY DOKEY	OPTIC TUBE	PALM BEACH	PAY IN KIND	PETIT FOUR
OLD BAILEY	OPTING OUT	PALM CIVET	PAY OFFICE	PETIT PAIN
OLD FOSSIL	ORANG UTAN	PALM COURT	PAY PACKET	PETRI DISH
OLD MASTER	ORANGE TIP	PALM SUGAR	PAYING OFF	PETROL CAN
OLD SCHOOL	ORDER BOOK	PAN ARABIC	PAYING OUT	PETTY CASH
OLD STAGER	ORDER FORM	PAN SLAVIC	PAYS A CALL	PEW FELLOW
OLIVE BACK	ORGAN LOFT	PANAMA HAT	PEA JACKET	PEW HOLDER
ON A STRING	ORGAN PIPE	PANEL GAME	PEA SOUPER	PEW OPENER
ON ACCOUNT	ORGAN STOP	PANS PIPES	PEACE DRUG	PEWTER POT
ON BALANCE	ORLOP DECK	PANTS SUIT	PEACE PILL	PHASED OUT
ON COMMAND	ORRIS ROOT	PAPAL BULL	PEACE PIPE	PHASES OUT
ON DRAUGHT	OUR FATHER	PAPER CLIP	PEACH PALM	PHASING IN
ON HOLIDAY	OUT AND OUT	PAPER FILE	PEACH TREE	PHONE CALL
ON IMPULSE	OUT AT HEEL	PAPER GIRL	PEACH WOOD	PHOTO CALL
ON LICENCE	OUT OF CASH	PAPER MILL	PEAK HOURS	PHYSIC NUT
ON ONES OWN	OUT OF DATE	PAPER OVER	PEAKED CAP	PIANO KEYS
ON ONES TOD	OUT OF FORM	PAPER PULP	PEANUT OIL	PIANO ROLL
ON ONES WAY	OUT OF HAND	PAPER REED	PEARL EDGE	PIANO WIRE
ON REQUEST	OUT OF MIND	PAPER TAPE	PEARL EYED	PICK A LOCK
ON STAND BY	OUT OF PLAY	PARA GRASS	PEARL GREY	PICK HOLES
ON THE BALL	OUT OF STEP	PARGE WORK	PEASE MEAL	PICK PURSE
ON THE BOIL	OUT OF SYNC	PARIAH DOG	PEAT CREEL	PICK THANK
ON THE CLUB	OUT OF TIME	PARISH TOP	PEAT SMOKE	PICK TOOTH
ON THE DOLE	OUT OF TOWN	PARITY LAW	PEAT SPADE	PICKED OFF
ON THE HOOF	OUT OF TRUE	PARK BENCH	PEAT STACK	PICKED OUT
ON THE HOUR	OUT OF TUNE	PARKED CAR	PEDAL BONE	PICKET OUT
ON THE LINE	OUT OF WORK	PARROT CRY	PEEL HOUSE	PICKING AT
ON THE MAKE	OUT PARISH	PARROT JAW	PEEL TOWER	PICKING ON
ON THE MEND	OUT PORTER	PART OWNER	PEELED OFF	PICKING UP
ON THE MOVE	OUT SENTRY	PART TIMER	PEEP OF DAY	PICKS OVER
ON THE NAIL	OUT TO STUD	PARTY CALL	PEEP SIGHT	PIECE RATE
ON THE NOSE	OUT WITH IT	PARTY GOER	PEEPED OUT	PIECE WORK
ON THE RACK	OUTER TUBE	PARTY JURY	PEER GROUP	PIECED OUT
ON THE RISE	OUTSIDE IN	PARTY LINE	PEGGED OUT	PIECES OUT
ON THE ROAD	OVEN GLOVE	PARTY WALL	PEKING MAN	PIECING UP
ON THE SIDE	OVEN READY	PAS DARMES	PELE HOUSE	PIED PIPER
ON THE SPOT	OVER AGAIN	PAS DE CHAT	PELE TOWER	PIER GLASS
ON THE TOWN	OVER SHOES	PAS DE DEUX	PELVIC FIN	PIER TABLE
ON THE TROT	OVER THERE	PASO DOBLE	PEN AND INK	PIGGING IT
ON THE TURN	OVERDID IT	PASS CHECK	PEN DRIVER	PIGGY BANK
ON THE WING	OX BOW LAKE	PASSED OFF	PEN FRIEND	PIKE PERCH
ON THIN ICE	OYSTER BED	PASSED OUT	PEN PUSHER	PILAU RICE
ONE ACROSS	PACK CLOTH	PASSERS BY	PENAL CODE	PILED IT ON
ONE AND ALL	PACK DRILL	PASSES OFF	PENAL LAWS	PILES IT ON
ONE HANDED	PACK HORSE	PASSES OUT	PENCIL ORE	PILLAR BOX
ONE LEGGED	PACK TRAIN	PASSING BY	PENNY GAFF	PILOT BOAT
ONE OCLOCK	PACKED OUT	PASSING ON	PENNY MAIL	PILOT FISH
ONION EYED	PACKING UP	PASSING UP	PENNY POST	PILOT LAMP
ONION SKIN	PACKS IT IN	PAST GLORY	PENNY RENT	PIN MAKING
OPEN ARMED	PACKS IT UP	PAST TENSE	PENNY WISE	PIN STRIPE
OPEN COURT	PAD SADDLE	PASTE DOWN	PENNY WORT	PIN UP GIRL
OPEN ENDED	PADDED OUT	PATCH TEST	PEPPER BOX	PINCH HITS
OPEN HOUSE	PADDLE BOX	PATCHED UP	PEPPER POT	PINE FINCH
OPEN ORDER	PAGE PROOF	PATCHES UP	PER CAPITA	PINE RESIN
	PAID A CALL	PATNA RICE	PER CONTRA	PINEAL EYE

9 LETTERS

9 contd.
PINT SIZED
PINT STOUP
PIPE DREAM
PIPE LAYER
PIPE LIGHT
PIPE MAJOR
PIPE ORGAN
PIPED DOWN
PIPES DOWN
PIPING HOT
PIQUE WORK
PISTON ROD
PIT SAWYER
PITCH DARK
PITCHED IN
PITCHES IN
PIXIE RING
PIXY STOOL
PLACE A BET
PLACE CARD
PLACE KICK
PLACE NAME
PLAGUE PIT
PLAIN COOK
PLAIN DARN
PLAIN JANE
PLAN AHEAD
PLANE TREE
PLANT LICE
PLANT LIKE
PLANT LORE
PLANTS OUT
PLATE RACK
PLATE RAIL
PLATE ROOM
PLAY A PART
PLAY ABOUT
PLAY ACTED
PLAY ACTOR
PLAY ALONG
PLAY FALSE
PLAY GOING
PLAY HAVOC
PLAY TO WIN
PLAY WORLD
PLAYED OFF
PLAYED OUT
PLAYING AT
PLAYING ON
PLAYING UP
PLAYS BACK
PLAYS BALL
PLAYS DOWN
PLAYS FAIR
PLAYS HOST
PLAYS SAFE
PLOUGHS IN
PLUGGED IN
PLUGS AWAY

PLUM STONE
PLUMB LINE
PLUMB RULE
PLUME BIRD
PLUME MOTH
PLUS FOURS
POGO STICK
POINT DUTY
POINT LACE
POINTED UP
POINTS OUT
POISON GAS
POISON IVY
POISON PEN
POKE FUN AT
POKER DICE
POKER FACE
POKER WORK
POLAR AXIS
POLAR BEAR
POLAR BODY
POLE AXING
POLE VAULT
POLICE BOX
POLICE DOG
POLISH OFF
POLL MONEY
POLLEN SAC
POMACE FLY
POND SNAIL
POODLE DOG
POOP SCOOP
POOR CLARE
POP ARTIST
POP RECORD
POP SINGER
POPES NOSE
POPPED OFF
POPPED OUT
POPPING IN
POPPING UP
POPPY HEAD
POPPY SEED
PORN SQUAD
PORT SALUT
POSSET CUP
POST DATED
POST ENTRY
POST NATAL
POT BARLEY
POT BOILER
POT HANGER
POT HUNTER
POT LIQUOR
POT POURRI
POTATO ROT
POUNCE BAG
POUNCE BOX
POUNCED ON
POUNCES ON

POUND CAKE
POUR FORTH
POURED OUT
POWDER BOX
POWDER KEG
POWER DIVE
POWER LOOM
POWER PACK
POWER UNIT
PRAYER MAT
PRAYER RUG
PRE ELECTS
PRE EMPTED
PRE EMPTOR
PRE EXISTS
PRE SHRANK
PRE SHRINK
PRE SHRUNK
PRE VERNAL
PRE WASHED
PRE WASHES
PRESS BOOK
PRESS CLUB
PRESS GANG
PRESS HOME
PRESS MARK
PRESS ROOM
PRESS STUD
PRESS WORK
PRESSED ON
PRESSES ON
PREYING ON
PRICE CODE
PRICE LIST
PRICE RING
PRIME COST
PRIME TIME
PRINT SHOP
PRINTS OUT
PRISON VAN
PRIVY SEAL
PRIZE BULL
PRIZE CREW
PRIZE LIST
PRIZE RING
PRO AND CON
PRO PATRIA
PRO RE NATA
PROMPT BOX
PROOF MARK
PROOF READ
PROOF TEXT
PROP SHAFT
PROPPED UP
PROSE POEM
PRYING OUT
PSALM BOOK
PSALM TUNE
PSYCHED UP
PSYCHES UP

PUBLIC ACT
PUBLIC BAR
PUBLIC KEY
PUBLIC LAW
PUCKERS UP
PUFF ADDER
PUFF PASTE
PUFFED OUT
PUG ENGINE
PULL A FACE
PULL AHEAD
PULL APART
PULL ROUND
PULLED OFF
PULLED OUT
PULLING IN
PULLING UP
PULLS AWAY
PULLS BACK
PULLS DOWN
PULLS OVER
PULLS RANK
PULP NOVEL
PULSE RATE
PULSE WAVE
PUMP WATER
PUMPED OUT
PUMPING IN
PUMPING UP
PUMPS IRON
PUNCH BALL
PUNCH BOWL
PUNCH CARD
PUNCH LINE
PUPPY LOVE
PURE BLOOD
PUSH ALONG
PUSH ASIDE
PUSH CHAIR
PUSH START
PUSHED OFF
PUSHED OUT
PUSHES OFF
PUSHES OUT
PUT ACROSS
PUT ON AIRS
PUT PAID TO
PUT UP WITH
PUTS ABOUT
PUTS ON ICE
PUTS TO BED
PUTS TO SEA
PUTTED OUT
PUTTER OUT
PUTTING BY
PUTTING IN
PUTTING ON
PUTTING UP
PUZZLE PEG
QUAIL PIPE

QUARTER TO
QUEEN ANNE
QUEEN CAKE
QUEEN JANE
QUEEN LIKE
QUEEN MARY
QUEEN POST
QUEEN SIZE
QUEER COVE
QUEER FISH
QUEUE JUMP
QUEUING UP
QUICK BORN
QUICK EYED
QUICK FIRE
QUICK TIME
QUICKEN UP
QUIT CLAIM
QUITE A FEW
RA RA SKIRT
RABBIT PIE
RACE TRACK
RACING CAR
RACKING UP
RADAR TRAP
RADIO MAST
RADIO PILL
RADIO STAR
RADIO WAVE
RAG PICKER
RAIL BORNE
RAIL FENCE
RAIL MOTOR
RAIN BOUND
RAIN CLOUD
RAIN GAUGE
RAIN MAKER
RAIN WATER
RAINED OFF
RAISE CAIN
RAISE HELL
RAISED PIE
RAN ACROSS
RAN SCARED
RAN TO SEED
RANG A BELL
RANK RIDER
RAPID FIRE
RARAE AVES
RARE EARTH
RAREE SHOW
RAT POISON
RATTING ON
RATTLED ON
RATTLES ON
RAVING MAD
RAY OF HOPE
RAZOR BACK
RAZOR BILL
RAZOR CLAM

9 contd.

RAZOR EDGE	RICE PAPER	ROAD TRAIN	ROUND EYED	SADDLED UP
RAZOR FISH	RICE WATER	ROAD WORKS	ROUND FISH	SADDLES UP
READ ALOUD	RICH RHYME	ROAST BEEF	ROUND GAME	SAFE HOUSE
READING UP	RIDES DOWN	ROAST DUCK	ROUND TRIP	SAFETY NET
READY MADE	RIDGE BONE	ROAST LAMB	ROUND WORM	SAFETY PIN
REAL IMAGE	RIDGE POLE	ROAST PORK	ROUNDED ON	SAGA NOVEL
REAR GUARD	RIDGE ROPE	ROBBER FLY	ROUNDED UP	SAGE APPLE
REAR LIGHT	RIDGE TILE	ROBE MAKER	ROUNDS OFF	SAGE DERBY
RECKONS ON	RIDING OUT	ROBIN HOOD	ROUNDS OUT	SAGE GREEN
RECKONS UP	RIDING ROD	ROCK BASIN	ROUTE STEP	SAIL ALONG
RED BERETS	RIFLE BIRD	ROCK BORER	ROWAN TREE	SAIL BORNE
RED CARPET	RIFLE SHOT	ROCK CANDY	ROWEL HEAD	SAIL CLOTH
RED DEVILS	RIGGED OUT	ROCK DRILL	ROWEL SPUR	SAIL FLUKE
RED DRAGON	RIGGING UP	ROCK GROUP	ROYAL BLUE	SAIL MAKER
RED ENSIGN	RIGHT AWAY	ROCK MUSIC	ROYAL LINE	SAILING BY
RED HAIRED	RIGHT BANK	ROCK N ROLL	ROYAL MAIL	SAILOR HAT
RED HEADED	RIGHT HAND	ROCK PERCH	ROYAL MAST	SAILOR MAN
RED HEELED	RIGHT HOOK	ROCK PIPIT	ROYAL MILE	SAINT JOHN
RED INDIAN	RIGHT SIDE	ROCK PLANT	ROYAL ROAD	SAINT LUKE
RED LEGGED	RIGHT WING	ROCK SNAKE	RUBBED OUT	SAINT MARK
RED LETTER	RING A BELL	ROCK SOLID	RUBBING UP	SAINT PAUL
RED MULLET	RING CANAL	ROD PUPPET	RUBS ALONG	SAINTS DAY
RED PEPPER	RING CROSS	ROLL ALONG	RUE THE DAY	SALAD BOWL
RED PLAGUE	RING DANCE	ROLLING IN	RUGBY BALL	SALAD DAYS
RED PLANET	RING FENCE	ROLLING UP	RUIN AGATE	SALAD HERB
RED POLLED	RING GAUGE	ROLLS OVER	RULING OUT	SALE PRICE
RED RIBAND	RING MONEY	ROMAN A CLE	RUM BUTTER	SALES TALK
RED RIBBON	RING OUSEL	ROMAN NOSE	RUM RUNNER	SALLEE MAN
RED SALMON	RING OUZEL	ROMAN ROAD	RUMP STEAK	SALLY ARMY
RED SPIDER	RING SNAKE	ROMANY RYE	RUN ACROSS	SALLY LUNN
RED SQUARE	RINGING IN	ROMPS HOME	RUN OF LUCK	SALMON FLY
RED TAPISM	RINGING UP	ROOF BOARD	RUN RESIST	SALMON FRY
RED TAPIST	RINGS BACK	ROOF GUARD	RUN SCARED	SALOON BAR
REDDING UP	RINGS DOWN	ROOF PLATE	RUN TO SEED	SALOON CAR
REED GRASS	RINGS TRUE	ROOT CANAL	RUNE CRAFT	SALT GLAZE
REED KNIFE	RINKY DINK	ROOT CAUSE	RUNE STAVE	SALT MARSH
REED ORGAN	RINSED OUT	ROOT HOUSE	RUNNERS UP	SALT MONEY
REEF POINT	RINSES OUT	ROOT PRUNE	RUNNING IN	SALT SPOON
REELED OFF	RIOT AGENT	ROOTED OUT	RUNNING ON	SALT WATER
REFLEX ARC	RIOT SQUAD	ROPE DANCE	RUNNING TO	SALT WORKS
REINING IN	RIPPED OFF	ROPE HOUSE	RUNNING UP	SALTS AWAY
REJOICE IN	RISING SUN	ROPE MAKER	RUNS A RISK	SALTS DOWN
RELAY RACE	RISK MONEY	ROPE SOLED	RUNS AFTER	SAM BROWNE
RELIEF MAP	RISKING IT	ROPE TRICK	RUNS ALONG	SAME AGAIN
RELYING ON	RIVER BANK	ROSE APPLE	RUNS CLOSE	SAND BLAST
RENNET BAG	RIVER BOAT	ROSE ELDER	RUNS OUT ON	SAND BLIND
RES GESTAE	RIVER HEAD	ROSE NOBLE	RUNS SHORT	SAND BREAK
RESCUE BID	RIVER SAND	ROSE TOPAZ	RURAL DEAN	SAND DANCE
REST HOUSE	RIVER TIDE	ROSE WATER	RUSH LIGHT	SAND DEVIL
REVEL ROUT	RIVER WALL	ROSY CROSS	RUST PROOF	SAND GLASS
REVVING UP	RIVET HEAD	ROTOR SHIP	RUSTLED UP	SAND GRAIN
REX RABBIT	RIVET HOLE	ROTTEN EGG	RUSTLES UP	SAND GRASS
RHINE WINE	RIX DOLLAR	ROTTEN ROW	RYE WHISKY	SAND MASON
RHUMB LINE	ROAD BLOCK	ROUGH DRAW	SABRE WING	SAND PRIDE
RHYME WORD	ROAD BORNE	ROUGH HEWN	SACRED APE	SAND SNAKE
RICE FIELD	ROAD CRAFT	ROUGH SHOD	SACRED CAT	SAND SPOUT
RICE FLOUR	ROAD MAKER	ROUGHED IN	SACRED COW	SAND STORM
RICE GRAIN	ROAD METAL	ROUGHED IT	SADDLE BAG	SAND TABLE
RICE GRASS	ROAD SENSE	ROUGHS OUT	SADDLE BAR	SAND WEDGE
	ROAD TESTS	ROUND DOWN	SADDLE BOW	SAND YACHT

9 contd.

SANG ALONG
SANS SOUCI
SASH FRAME
SAUCE BOAT
SAUCER EYE
SAVED FACE
SAVED TIME
SAVES FACE
SAVES TIME
SAVILE ROW
SAW THINGS
SAY CHEESE
SCALE BEAM
SCALE FERN
SCALE FISH
SCALE LEAF
SCALE MOSS
SCALE WORK
SCALY BARK
SCAMP WORK
SCARE LINE
SCARF RING
SCARING UP
SCENE DOCK
SCENE FOUR
SCHOOL AGE
SCHOOL DAY
SCHOOL TIE
SCOOP NECK
SCOOPS OUT
SCORE CARD
SCORE DRAW
SCORED OFF
SCORES OFF
SCOTCH EGG
SCOTCH ELM
SCOTCH FIR
SCOTS PINE
SCOTTY DOG
SCRAP BOOK
SCRAP HEAP
SCRAP IRON
SCRAP YARD
SCRAPE GUT
SCRAPE OFF
SCREEN OFF
SCREW BOLT
SCREW DOWN
SCREW JACK
SCREW NAIL
SCREW PILE
SCREW PINE
SCREW WORM
SCROLL SAW
SCRUB BIRD
SCRUB FOWL
SCRUM HALF
SE BAPTIST
SEA ANCHOR

SEA BATHER
SEA BOTTOM
SEA BREACH
SEA BREEZE
SEA CHANGE
SEA DRAGON
SEA FISHER
SEA GINGER
SEA GIRDLE
SEA ISLAND
SEA LAWYER
SEA NETTLE
SEA ORANGE
SEA RANGER
SEA ROBBER
SEA ROCKET
SEA ROVING
SEA SALMON
SEA SHANTY
SEA STRAND
SEA TURTLE
SEA URCHIN
SEA WALLED
SEAL POINT
SEALED OFF
SEAMY SIDE
SEARCH FEE
SEAT STICK
SECOND MAN
SEE NO EVIL
SEE THINGS
SEED DRILL
SEED FIELD
SEED MONEY
SEED PEARL
SEED PLANT
SEED STALK
SEEING FIT
SEEING OFF
SEEING OUT
SEEING RED
SEEK AFTER
SEES A WOLF
SEES ROUND
SEES STARS
SEINE BOAT
SEIZING UP
SELF AWARE
SELF BUILD
SELF DOUBT
SELF DRIVE
SELF IMAGE
SELF PRIDE
SELL SHORT
SELLING ON
SELLING UP
SELLS A PUP
SEMI GRAND
SEMI LUNAR
SEMI METAL

SEMI RIGID
SENDING IN
SENDING ON
SENDS DOWN
SENDS WORD
SENECA OIL
SENNA PODS
SENTRY BOX
SERVE TIME
SERVED OUT
SERVES OUT
SERVING UP
SET ALIGHT
SET EYES ON
SET FIRE TO
SET IN HAND
SET ON EDGE
SET ON FIRE
SET SPEECH
SET SQUARE
SET TO WORK
SET UP SHOP
SETS A TRAP
SETS ABOUT
SETS APART
SETS ASIDE
SETS FORTH
SETTER OFF
SETTER OUT
SETTING BY
SETTING IN
SETTING ON
SETTING UP
SETTLE BED
SETTLED IN
SETTLED UP
SETTLES IN
SETTLES UP
SEVEN SEAS
SEX APPEAL
SEX KITTEN
SEX SYMBOL
SHADE TREE
SHADOW BOX
SHAGGY CAP
SHAGGY DOG
SHAKE A LEG
SHAKE DOWN
SHAKES OFF
SHAKES OUT
SHAKING UP
SHALE MINE
SHANGRI LA
SHANK BONE
SHAPING UP
SHARED OUT
SHARES OUT
SHARP EYED
SHED A TEAR
SHEEP HOOK

SHEEP LICE
SHEEP SCAB
SHEEP TICK
SHEEP WASH
SHEEPS EYE
SHEERS OFF
SHEET FILM
SHEET IRON
SHEET LEAD
SHELF LIFE
SHELF MARK
SHELL HOLE
SHELL LIKE
SHELL PINK
SHELL SAND
SHELL SUIT
SHELLS OUT
SHIFT WORK
SHIP CANAL
SHIP FEVER
SHIP MONEY
SHIP OWNER
SHIP WATER
SHIRE MOOT
SHIRT BAND
SHIRT STUD
SHIRT TAIL
SHOCK HEAD
SHOCK WAVE
SHOE BRUSH
SHOE LACES
SHOOK A LEG
SHOOK DOWN
SHOOT DOWN
SHOOT HOME
SHOOTS OFF
SHOP FLOOR
SHOP FRONT
SHORE BOAT
SHORE CRAB
SHORE SIDE
SHORT COAT
SHORT GAME
SHORT HAUL
SHORT HORN
SHORT LIFE
SHORT LIST
SHORT ODDS
SHORT SALE
SHORT SLIP
SHORT STOP
SHORT TERM
SHORT TIME
SHORT WAVE
SHOT A LINE
SHOT CRAPS
SHOT IT OUT
SHOT TOWER
SHOUT DOWN
SHOVED OFF

SHOVEL HAT
SHOVES OFF
SHOW FIGHT
SHOW FORTH
SHOW HOUSE
SHOW TRIAL
SHOWED OFF
SHOWING UP
SHOWS A LEG
SHRIMP NET
SHRIVEL UP
SHRUGS OFF
SHUTS AWAY
SHUTS DOWN
SICK HOUSE
SICK LEAVE
SIDE ISSUE
SIDE LIGHT
SIDE TABLE
SIDE TRACK
SIDE WHEEL
SIGHT HOLE
SIGHT LINE
SIGHT READ
SIGHT SING
SIGNAL BOX
SIGNED OFF
SIGNED OUT
SIGNING IN
SIGNING ON
SIGNING UP
SIGNS AWAY
SILK GLAND
SILK GRASS
SILVER AGE
SILVER FIR
SILVER FOX
SIMON PURE
SIMPLE VOW
SIN EATING
SINE CURVE
SING ALONG
SINGED CAT
SINGLE TAX
SINKING IN
SIREN SUIT
SISAL HEMP
SITS STILL
SITS TIGHT
SITTING BY
SITTING IN
SITTING ON
SITTING UP
SIX DAY WAR
SIX FOOTER
SIX OCLOCK
SIXTH FORM
SKATE OVER
SKETCH OUT
SKEW WHIFF

9 contd.

SKI FLYING	SMELL A RAT	SOFT SHELL	SPEAKS OUT	STAGE HAND
SKI JORING	SMELLS OUT	SOFT SOAPS	SPEECH DAY	STAGE LEFT
SKI KITING	SMELT A RAT	SOFT TOUCH	SPEED BOAT	STAGE NAME
SKI SCHOOL	SMOCK MILL	SOFTENS UP	SPEED TRAP	STAGE PLAY
SKIN ALIVE	SMOKE BALL	SOI DISANT	SPEEDED UP	STAIR WELL
SKIN DIVER	SMOKE BOMB	SOLAR CELL	SPELLS OUT	STAKE BOAT
SKIN GRAFT	SMOKE HOLE	SOLAR TIME	SPICE BUSH	STAKED OUT
SKIN TIGHT	SMOKE RING	SOLAR WIND	SPICE CAKE	STAKES OUT
SKINNY DIP	SMOKED HAM	SOLAR YEAR	SPIDER LEG	STALK EYED
SKIPPED IT	SMOKED OUT	SOLD SHORT	SPIDER MAN	STALL FEED
SKUNK BIRD	SMOKES OUT	SOLDIER ON	SPIDER WEB	STAMP DUTY
SKY DIVING	SMOOTH DAB	SOLEMN VOW	SPIKE FISH	STAMPS OUT
SKY TROOPS	SMUG FACED	SOLID FUEL	SPILL OVER	STAND DOWN
SLACK ROPE	SNAIL FISH	SOLO WHIST	SPILT OVER	STAND EASY
SLACKEN UP	SNAIL LIKE	SOME HOPES	SPIN A YARN	STAND FAST
SLANT EYED	SNAKE BELT	SON OF A GUN	SPIN DRIED	STAND FIRE
SLAP HAPPY	SNAKE BITE	SONG CYCLE	SPIN DRIER	STAND OVER
SLATE CLUB	SNAKE CULT	SONG TITLE	SPIN DRIES	STAND PIPE
SLATE GREY	SNAPPED UP	SONIC BANG	SPIN DRYER	STANDER BY
SLAVE SHIP	SNARE DRUM	SONIC BOOM	SPIRAL ARM	STANDS OFF
SLEEPS OFF	SNEAK RAID	SONS IN LAW	SPIRIT GUM	STANDS OUT
SLEEVE NUT	SNEAKED UP	SORE POINT	SPIT IT OUT	STANDS PAT
SLICING UP	SNEEZE BOX	SORTED OUT	SPLASH OUT	STAR BURST
SLIDE RULE	SNELLS LAW	SOTTO VOCE	SPLAY FOOT	STAR DRIFT
SLING BACK	SNIFFS OUT	SOU WESTER	SPLIT MIND	STAR GAZED
SLINGS INK	SNIPE FISH	SOUGHT OUT	SPLIT PEAS	STAR GAZER
SLINKS OFF	SNOW BERRY	SOUL MUSIC	SPLIT RING	STAR GAZES
SLIP ANGLE	SNOW BLIND	SOUND FILM	SPOIL BARK	STAR GRASS
SLIP BOARD	SNOW BOOTS	SOUND HOLE	SPOKEN FOR	STAR JELLY
SLIPPED ON	SNOW BOUND	SOUND POEM	SPONGE BAG	STAR PUPIL
SLIPPED UP	SNOW BREAK	SOUND POET	SPOON FEED	STAR SHELL
SLIPS AWAY	SNOW FIELD	SOUND WAVE	SPORTS CAR	STAR SIGNS
SLOP BASIN	SNOW GOOSE	SOUNDS OFF	SPOT CHECK	STAR STONE
SLOPE ARMS	SNOW GUARD	SOUNDS OUT	SPOT DANCE	STAR WHEEL
SLOPED OFF	SNOW PLANT	SOUP PLATE	SPOT WELDS	STARTED IN
SLOPES OFF	SNOW SHOES	SOUP SPOON	SPOUT HOLE	STARTED UP
SLOPPY JOE	SNOW WATER	SOUPING UP	SPRING BED	STARTS OUT
SLOTH BEAR	SNOW WHITE	SOUR GOURD	SPRING GUN	STARVE OUT
SLOUCH HAT	SNUB NOSED	SOUTH BANK	SPRUCE FIR	STATE BANK
SLOW HOUND	SNUFF FILM	SOUTH EAST	SPUN A YARN	STATUS QUO
SLOW MARCH	SNUFF MILL	SOUTH POLE	SPUN SUGAR	STAVING IN
SLOW MATCH	SNUFFED IT	SOUTH SEAS	SPUR ROWEL	STAY MAKER
SLOW PACED	SNUFFS OUT	SOUTH WEST	SPUR WHEEL	STAY STILL
SLOWING UP	SNUGGLE UP	SOYA SAUCE	SQUARE LEG	STAYED OUT
SLOWS DOWN	SO TO SPEAK	SPACE RACE	SQUARED UP	STAYED PUT
SLUSH FUND	SOAP OPERA	SPACE SUIT	SQUARES UP	STAYING IN
SLY AS A FOX	SOAP WORKS	SPACE TIME	SQUINT EYE	STAYING ON
SMALL ARMS	SOAR EAGLE	SPACE WALK	SRI LANKAN	STAYING UP
SMALL BEER	SOAY SHEEP	SPACED OUT	ST BERNARD	STAYS OVER
SMALL BORE	SOB SISTER	SPACES OUT	ST TRINIAN	STEAM BATH
SMALL COAL	SOBERED UP	SPADE BONE	STABLE BOY	STEAM IRON
SMALL HAND	SOCIAL WAR	SPARE PART	STABLE MAN	STEAM OPEN
SMALL PICA	SODA WATER	SPARE ROOM	STACK ROOM	STEAM PIPE
SMALL TALK	SOFA TABLE	SPARE TIME	STACKED UP	STEAMED UP
SMALL TIME	SOFT DRINK	SPARE TYRE	STAFF DUTY	STEEL BAND
SMALL TOWN	SOFT FRUIT	SPARK COIL	STAFF ROOM	STEEL BLUE
SMART ALEC	SOFT GOODS	SPARK PLUG	STAG DANCE	STEEL CLAD
SMART CARD	SOFT GRASS	SPARKS OFF	STAG NIGHT	STEEL DRUM
SMEAR TEST	SOFT PEDAL	SPARKS OUT	STAG PARTY	STEEL GREY
		SPEAK EASY	STAGE DOOR	STEEL WARE

9 contd.

STEEL WOOL	STORY BOOK	SUN SPURGE	TAKE APART	TASTE BUDS
STEP ASIDE	STORY LINE	SUNNY SIDE	TAKE COVER	TAX EXEMPT
STEP CHILD	STRAP HANG	SURE THING	TAKE HEART	TAX PAYING
STEP DANCE	STRAW WORK	SURF CANOE	TAKE IN TOW	TAX REBATE
STEP STONE	STRAW POLL	SURF RIDER	TAKE ISSUE	TAX RELIEF
STEPPED IN	STRAW ROPE	SUSSED OUT	TAKE LEAVE	TAX RETURN
STEPPED UP	STRAW STEM	SUSSES OUT	TAKE PAINS	TEA DEALER
STEPS DOWN	STRAW WORK	SWALLOW UP	TAKE PLACE	TEA GARDEN
STICK AT IT	STREAM ICE	SWAMP BOAT	TAKE SHAPE	TEA KETTLE
STICK EM UP	STREET CAR	SWAN ABOUT	TAKE SIDES	TEA LEAVES
STICKS OUT	STREET MAP	SWAN GOOSE	TAKE STEPS	TEA TASTER
STICKY END	STRIKE OFF	SWANS DOWN	TAKE STOCK	TEA THINGS
STIFF NECK	STRIKE OIL	SWARM CELL	TAKE TURNS	TEAR DROPS
STILL BORN	STRIKE OUT	SWART BACK	TAKEN BACK	TEAR GLAND
STILL LIFE	STRIKE PAY	SWEAR WORD	TAKEN DOWN	TEAR SHEET
STILL ROOM	STRIKES UP	SWEAT BAND	TAKEN OVER	TEARING UP
STINK BOMB	STRING BAG	SWEAT SHOP	TAKES A BOW	TEARS AWAY
STINK WOOD	STRING OUT	SWEAT SUIT	TAKES ARMS	TEARS DOWN
STINKS OUT	STRING PEA	SWEET CORN	TAKES BACK	TEARS INTO
STIR CRAZY	STRING TIE	SWEET FLAG	TAKES BETS	TEARS OPEN
STIRRED UP	STRINGS UP	SWEET SHOP	TAKES CARE	TEDDY BEAR
STOCK CUBE	STRIP CLUB	SWEET TALK	TAKES DOWN	TEDDY GIRL
STOCK FARM	STRIP DOWN	SWINE FISH	TAKES FIVE	TEDDY SUIT
STOCK LIST	STRIP LEAF	SWING BACK	TAKES HEED	TEE SQUARE
STOCK ROOM	STRIP MILL	SWING DOOR	TAKES NOTE	TEEING OFF
STOCK WHIP	STRIP MINE	SWING WING	TAKES OVER	TELL TALES
STOCKED UP	STRIPS OFF	SWISS ROLL	TAKES PART	TELLING ON
STOKE HOLE	STRIPS OUT	SWITCH OFF	TAKES ROOT	TEMPT FATE
STOKES LAW	STROKE OAR	SWIVEL EYE	TAKES SILK	TEN A PENNY
STOKING UP	STRONG BOX	SWIVEL GUN	TAKES WING	TEN OCLOCK
STONE BASS	STRONG TEA	SWORD BELT	TAKING AIM	TENOR CLEF
STONE CAST	STRUCK OFF	SWORD BILL	TAKING OFF	TENT CLOTH
STONE COAL	STRUCK OIL	SWORD CANE	TAKING OUT	TENT DRESS
STONE COLD	STRUCK OUT	SWORD HAND	TALK ROUND	TENT MAKER
STONE DEAF	STRUNG OUT	SWORD KNOT	TALKED BIG	TESLA COIL
STONE HARD	STUCK AT IT	SWORD LIKE	TALKED OUT	TEST DRIVE
STONE HAWK	STUD GROOM	SWORD RACK	TALKING AT	TEST MATCH
STONE LILY	STUD HORSE	SWORD TAIL	TALKING TO	TEST PAPER
STONE MILL	STUD POKER	SWOTTED UP	TALKS BACK	TEST PILOT
STONE PINE	STUMPED UP	SYLPH LIKE	TALKS DOWN	TETE A TETE
STOOD DOWN	STYLE BOOK	T JUNCTION	TALKS INTO	THATS FLAT
STOOD FAST	SUB JUDICE	TABLE BOOK	TALKS OVER	THATS THAT
STOOD FIRE	SUCKING IN	TABLE GAME	TALKS SHOP	THAWED OUT
STOOD OVER	SUEZ CANAL	TABLE LEAF	TALL ORDER	THE ABDABS
STOP PRESS	SUGAR BEAN	TABLE MAID	TALL STORY	THE ARMADA
STOP SHORT	SUGAR BEET	TABLE SALT	TANK WAGON	THE BIG TOP
STOP THIEF	SUGAR BOWL	TABLE TALK	TANT MIEUX	THE BOWERY
STOP WATCH	SUGAR CANE	TABLE WARE	TAP DANCED	THE CREEPS
STOPPED IN	SUGAR CUBE	TABLE WINE	TAP DANCER	THE DAMNED
STOPS DEAD	SUGAR LOAF	TACKING ON	TAP DANCES	THE EIGHTS
STOPS OVER	SUGAR LUMP	TAGS ALONG	TAPE DRIVE	THE JET SET
STORE ROOM	SUGAR MILL	TAIL BOARD	TAPE PUNCH	THE OCCULT
STORE SHIP	SUGAR PALM	TAIL ENDER	TAPERS OFF	THE POLICE
STORM BIRD	SUGAR PLUM	TAIL LIGHT	TAPPET ROD	THE PURPLE
STORM COCK	SUGAR SOAP	TAIL RHYME	TAPPIT HEN	THE ROYALS
STORM CONE	SUMMING UP	TAILED OFF	TARGET MAN	THE SCRUBS
STORM DRUM	SUMMONS UP	TAKE A SEAT	TAROT CARD	THE SHIRES
STORM SAIL	SUN BONNET	TAKE A TURN	TARTING UP	THE SPHINX
STORM WIND	SUN DOWNER	TAKE AFTER	TASK FORCE	THE STATES
	SUN LOUNGE	TAKE AMISS	TASK GROUP	THE STICKS

9 *contd.*

THE UNIONS	TIGER WOLF	TOOK PLACE	TREE RINGS	TURNS BACK
THEM AND US	TIGER WOOD	TOOK SHAPE	TREE SHREW	TURNS DOWN
THEME PARK	TIGHT KNIT	TOOK SIDES	TREE SNAKE	TURNS INTO
THEME SONG	TIGHT ROPE	TOOK STEPS	TREE STUMP	TURNS OVER
THEME TUNE	TIGHT SPOT	TOOK STOCK	TREE TRUNK	TURNS TAIL
THEYRE OFF	TILE STONE	TOOK TURNS	TRI WEEKLY	TURNS TURK
THIGH BONE	TIM WHISKY	TOOLING UP	TRIED IT ON	TURNS UPON
THIGH BOOT	TIME CLOCK	TOOTH PICK	TRIES IT ON	TURRET GUN
THIN FACED	TIME FLIES	TOP BOOTED	TRILBY HAT	TWICE OVER
THIN ON TOP	TIME LAPSE	TOP DRAWER	TRIPE SHOP	TWIGGED IT
THINK BACK	TIME LIMIT	TOP FLIGHT	TROD WATER	TWIN BIRTH
THINK OVER	TIME OF DAY	TOP SAWYER	TROOP SHIP	TWO A PENNY
THINK TANK	TIME SHARE	TOP SECRET	TROTH RING	TWO BY FOUR
THINKS OUT	TIME SHEET	TOPPED OUT	TROUT FARM	TWO DECKER
THIRD HAND	TIME TRIAL	TOPPING UP	TRUCK LOAD	TWO FISTED
THIRD RATE	TIN LIZZIE	TORCH LILY	TRUCK SHOP	TWO FOOTED
THIS WAY UP	TIN MINING	TORCH RACE	TRUMP CARD	TWO HANDED
THORN BUSH	TIN OPENER	TORCH SONG	TRUMP SUIT	TWO HANDER
THOUGHT UP	TINDER BOX	TOSSING UP	TRUMPED UP	TWO HEADED
THRASH OUT	TING A LING	TOTEM POLE	TRUNK CALL	TWO LEGGED
THREE CARD	TINT BLOCK	TOTTING UP	TRUNK LINE	TWO MASTED
THREE DECK	TIP AND RUN	TOUCH DOWN	TRUNK MAIL	TWO MASTER
THREE FOOT	TIPPED OFF	TOUCH LINE	TRUNK ROAD	TWO OCLOCK
THREE FOUR	TIPSY CAKE	TOUCH MARK	TRUSS BEAM	TWO ROOMED
THREW A FIT	TIRING OUT	TOUCH TYPE	TRUST DEED	TWO SHAKES
THREW AWAY	TIT FOR TAT	TOUCH WOOD	TRUST FUND	TWO TIMING
THREW DOWN	TITHE BARN	TOUCHED UP	TRUTH DRUG	TYING DOWN
THREW OPEN	TITHE FREE	TOUCHES UP	TRYING OUT	TYPE METAL
THREW OVER	TITLE DEED	TOUGH LUCK	TSETSE FLY	TYRE CHAIN
THROW A FIT	TITLE LEAF	TOUGHEN UP	TUB THUMPS	TYRE GAUGE
THROW AWAY	TITLE PAGE	TOWEL RACK	TUBE SKIRT	UGLY AS SIN
THROW BACK	TITLE ROLE	TOWEL RAIL	TUCKING IN	UNDER ARMS
THROW DOWN	TO A DEGREE	TOWER MILL	TUDOR ROSE	UNDER FIRE
THROW OPEN	TO THE BONE	TOWER OVER	TUG OF LOVE	UNDER OATH
THROW OVER	TO THE CORE	TOWING NET	TULIP ROOT	UNDER RIPE
THROWN OFF	TO THE FORE	TOWN CLERK	TULIP TREE	UNDER SAIL
THROWN OUT	TO THE FULL	TOWN CRIER	TULIP WOOD	UNHEARD OF
THROWS OFF	TO THE LAST	TOWN HOUSE	TUMBLE CAR	UNHOLY ROW
THROWS OUT	TOAD EATER	TOY POODLE	TUNING KEY	UNION FLAG
THRUST HOE	TOAST RACK	TRACK DOWN	TUNING PEG	UNION JACK
THUMB HOLE	TOG RATING	TRACK SHOE	TUNING PIN	UNIT PRICE
THUMB MARK	TOGGING UP	TRACK SUIT	TURF SPADE	UNIT TRUST
THUMB TACK	TOILET SET	TRADE DOWN	TURFED OUT	UNLIVED IN
TIC TAC TOE	TOLD TALES	TRADE MARK	TURKEY HEN	UP AND DOWN
TICKED OFF	TOLL HOUSE	TRADE NAME	TURKEY OAK	UP AND OVER
TICKET DAY	TONED DOWN	TRADE SALE	TURKEY RED	UP COUNTRY
TICKS AWAY	TONES DOWN	TRADE WIND	TURKS HEAD	UP CURRENT
TICKS OVER	TONKA BEAN	TRADED OFF	TURN ABOUT	UP DRAUGHT
TIDAL WAVE	TOODLE PIP	TRADES OFF	TURN ASIDE	UP THE POLE
TIDE GAUGE	TOOK A SEAT	TRADING IN	TURN LOOSE	UP THE WALL
TIDE TABLE	TOOK A TURN	TRADING UP	TURN NASTY	UP TO SNUFF
TIDE WATER	TOOK AFTER	TRAIL AWAY	TURN ROUND	UPPER CASE
TIDED OVER	TOOK AMISS	TRAILS OFF	TURNED OFF	UPPER DECK
TIDES OVER	TOOK APART	TRAIN BAND	TURNED OUT	UPPER HAND
TIE DYEING	TOOK COVER	TRAIN MILE	TURNING IN	UPS A DAISY
TIED HOUSE	TOOK HEART	TRANS SHIP	TURNING ON	URN SHAPED
TIGER LILY	TOOK IN TOW	TRAWL FISH	TURNING TO	URSA MAJOR
TIGER MOTH	TOOK ISSUE	TRAWL LINE	TURNING UP	URSA MINOR
TIGER TAIL	TOOK LEAVE	TRAY CLOTH	TURNIP TOP	USED FORCE
	TOOK PAINS	TREE LINED	TURNS AWAY	USES FORCE

9 LETTERS

9 contd.

VACANT LOT
VADE MECUM
VANITY BAG
VANITY BOX
VEE GUTTER
VENIAL SIN
VERS LIBRE
VERY LIGHT
VIA CRUCIS
VIA LACTEA
VICE CHAIR
VICE REGAL
VICE SQUAD
VICE VERSA
VIDE INFRA
VIDE SUPRA
VIDEO GAME
VIDEO TUBE
VIN DU PAYS
VINE FRUIT
VINE STOCK
VINGT ET UN
VIOLIN BOW
VISION MIX
VISOR MASK
VISUAL AID
VITA GLASS
VOGUE WORD
VOICE OVER
VOICE VOTE
VOL AU VENT
VOLTE FACE
VOTED DOWN
VOTES DOWN
VOX POPULI
WAFER CAKE
WAGE SLAVE
WAGES SLIP
WAGON LOAD
WAIST DEEP
WAIST HIGH
WAIT ABOUT
WAIT FOR IT
WAITING ON
WAITING UP
WAITS UPON
WAKE ROBIN
WAKES WEEK
WALK ABOUT
WALK ON AIR
WALK OUT ON
WALKED OFF
WALKED OUT
WALKING IT
WALKING ON
WALKS AWAY
WALKS INTO
WALKS TALL
WALL BOARD

WALL PLATE
WALL SPACE
WALLING UP
WANDER OFF
WANTED OUT
WANTING IN
WAR BONNET
WAR CRIMES
WAR GAMING
WAR MUSEUM
WAR OFFICE
WARDED OFF
WARDEN PIE
WARM FRONT
WARMING UP
WASH BASIN
WASH BOARD
WASH CLOTH
WASH HOUSE
WASH STAND
WASHED OUT
WASHING UP
WASP STING
WASP STUNG
WASPS NEST
WASTE AWAY
WASTE PIPE
WATCH BILL
WATCH FIRE
WATCH OVER
WATER BATH
WATER BUCK
WATER BULL
WATER BUTT
WATER CART
WATER CASK
WATER COCK
WATER COOL
WATER CURE
WATER DECK
WATER DOWN
WATER FERN
WATER FLOW
WATER FOWL
WATER GATE
WATER HEAD
WATER HOLE
WATER JUMP
WATER LINE
WATER MAIN
WATER MILL
WATER PIPE
WATER POLO
WATER PUMP
WATER RAIL
WATER RATE
WATER RICE
WATER SEAL
WATER VOLE
WATER WORN

WAVE A WAND
WAVE ASIDE
WAVE POWER
WAVED DOWN
WAVES DOWN
WAX JACKET
WAY WARDEN
WEAK KNEED
WEAK POINT
WEAKER SEX
WEALTH TAX
WEARS AWAY
WEARS DOWN
WEARS THIN
WEASEL CAT
WEASEL OUT
WEB FOOTED
WEB OFFSET
WEEK ABOUT
WEEK ENDER
WEIGH DOWN
WEIGHED IN
WEIGHED UP
WEIGHS OUT
WELL BEING
WELL BORER
WELL BUILT
WELL DOING
WELL HOUSE
WELL KNOWN
WELL LINED
WELL MEANT
WELL OILED
WELL SET UP
WELL SPENT
WELL TIMED
WELSH HARP
WENT AHEAD
WENT DUTCH
WENT FORTH
WENT ROUND
WENT TO BED
WENT TO POT
WENT TO SEA
WENT TO WAR
WENT UNDER
WENT WRONG
WEST NORTH
WHALE BACK
WHALE BOAT
WHALE BONE
WHALE CALF
WHALE LINE
WHAT A HOPE
WHAT GIVES
WHAT PRICE
WHATS TO DO
WHATS WHAT
WHEAT CORN
WHEAT CROP

WHEAT GERM
WHEAT MEAL
WHEAT MOTH
WHEEL LOCK
WHEEL RACE
WHEEL SPIN
WHEY FACED
WHIP ROUND
WHIP SNAKE
WHIP STOCK
WHIPPED IN
WHIPPER IN
WHISK AWAY
WHISKY MAC
WHITE BEAR
WHITE FLAG
WHITE GOLD
WHITE HART
WHITE HEAT
WHITE HOLE
WHITE HOPE
WHITE LADY
WHITE LEAD
WHITE LIME
WHITE LINE
WHITE ROSE
WHITE SALE
WHITE SALT
WHITE TEAK
WHITE WINE
WHITED OUT
WHITES OUT
WHIZZ BANG
WHOLE NOTE
WHOLE TONE
WHOOP IT UP
WIDE ANGLE
WIDE AWAKE
WIDOW BIRD
WILD BIRDS
WILD GEESE
WILD GOOSE
WILD GRAPE
WILD HONEY
WILD MANGO
WILD PARTY
WILD THYME
WILD WATER
WILL POWER
WIN THE CUP
WIN THE DAY
WIND BREAK
WIND CHART
WIND GAUGE
WIND HOVER
WIND POWER
WIND SURFS
WINDING UP
WINDOW BAR
WINDOW BOX

WINDOW TAX
WINDS DOWN
WINE GLASS
WINE PARTY
WINE PRESS
WINE VAULT
WING SHELL
WING SNAIL
WINKLE OUT
WIPING OUT
WIRE BRUSH
WIRE GAUGE
WIRE GAUZE
WIRE GRASS
WIRE WHEEL
WISE WOMAN
WITCH HUNT
WITCH WIFE
WITH A BUMP
WITH A WILL
WITH CHILD
WITH YOUNG
WOLF HOUND
WOLFS BANE
WOLFS CLAW
WOLFS FOOT
WON THE CUP
WON THE DAY
WOOD BORER
WOOD HOUSE
WOOD NYMPH
WOOD PAPER
WOOD SCREW
WOOD SUGAR
WOODEN LEG
WORD BLIND
WORD SALAD
WORK BENCH
WORK ETHIC
WORK IT OUT
WORK OF ART
WORK STUDY
WORK TABLE
WORKED FOR
WORKED OFF
WORKED OUT
WORKING IN
WORKING ON
WORKING UP
WORKS AT IT
WORKS OVER
WORKS UPON
WORLD BANK
WORM EATEN
WORM FENCE
WORM WHEEL
WORSE LUCK
WOUND DOWN
WRAP ROUND
WRAPPED UP

9 contd.

WRINGS OUT	ACCESS ROAD	AND SO FORTH	BABY WALKER	BASTARD BAR
WRIST SHOT	ACCESS TIME	AND SO TO BED	BACK BLOCKS	BATH OLIVER
WRITE DOWN	ACCOUNT DAY	ANGEL FALLS	BACK BURNER	BATHING BOX
WRITE HOME	ACOL SYSTEM	ANGEL WATER	BACK COMBED	BATHING HUT
WRITES OFF	ACT OF UNION	ANGLO IRISH	BACK DATING	BATTERY HEN
WRITES OUT	ACT THE FOOL	ANGLO SAXON	BACK GARDEN	BATTLING ON
WRITING UP	ACT THE GOAT	ANILINE DYE	BACK HANDED	BAWDY HOUSE
WRITTEN UP	ACT YOUR AGE	ANKLE CHAIN	BACK HANDER	BAWLING OUT
WRONG DOER	ACTION PLAN	ANKLE STRAP	BACK HEELED	BE PREPARED
WRONG FOOT	ACTIVE LIFE	ANNO DOMINI	BACK MARKER	BEACH BUGGY
WRONG SIDE	ACTIVE LIST	ANSWER BACK	BACK NUMBER	BEAKER FOLK
WROTE DOWN	ACUTE ANGLE	ANTE BELLUM	BACK PEDALS	BEAM ENGINE
WROTE HOME	AD ABSURDUM	ANTI RACIST	BACK STREET	BEAM SYSTEM
WROUGHT UP	ADAM AND EVE	ANTI SEMITE	BACK STROKE	BEAM WEAPON
WRY NECKED	ADAMS APPLE	ANY OLD IRON	BACK TO BACK	BEAN SPROUT
WYCH HAZEL	ADDLE PATED	ANYONE ELSE	BACKED DOWN	BEAR GARDEN
X PARTICLE	ADVICE NOTE	APPLE SAUCE	BACKING OFF	BEAR IN MIND
XENON LAMP	AERIAL VIEW	APPLE WOMAN	BAD COMPANY	BEAR LEADER
YACHT CLUB	AERO ENGINE	APRON STAGE	BAD FEELING	BEARD GRASS
YACHT RACE	AFTER GUARD	AQUA FORTIS	BAD GRAMMAR	BEARER BOND
YAKETY YAK	AFTER IMAGE	ARC WELDING	BAG OF BONES	BEARING OUT
YANKEE BET	AFTER LIGHT	ARCH PRIEST	BAGGAGE CAR	BEAST FABLE
YARD OF ALE	AGE BRACKET	ARCHER FISH	BAILING OUT	BEAT THE AIR
YEAR ROUND	AGENCY SHOP	ARMOUR CLAD	BAKED APPLE	BEAT THE GUN
YELLOW DOG	AGONY UNCLE	ARMS LENGTH	BAKED BEANS	BEATEN DOWN
YES PLEASE	AID AND ABET	ARROW GRASS	BAKING SODA	BEATEN TO IT
YO HEAVE HO	AIDE DE CAMP	ART GALLERY	BALD HEADED	BEATING OFF
YOM KIPPUR	AIR BLADDER	ART NOUVEAU	BALL FLOWER	BEATING OUT
YOU NAME IT	AIR BRUSHED	ART STUDENT	BALL OF FIRE	BEAU GARCON
YOUNG FOGY	AIR COOLING	ARTY CRAFTY	BALL PLAYER	BEAUTY SPOT
YOUNG LADY	AIR CURTAIN	AS PER USUAL	BALLET GIRL	BEAVER AWAY
YOUNG TURK	AIR CUSHION	AS THEY COME	BALLET SHOE	BEAVER TREE
YOUTH CLUB	AIR FREIGHT	ASSAY PIECE	BAN THE BOMB	BEAVER WOOD
ZAPPING UP	AIR HOSTESS	ASTRAL BODY	BANANA BOAT	BECHE DE MER
ZERO RATED	AIR MARSHAL	AT A PREMIUM	BANANA SKIN	BED OF NAILS
ZERO RATES	AIR OFFICER	AT A STRETCH	BAND OF HOPE	BED OF ROSES
ZEROING IN	AIR PASSAGE	AT A TANGENT	BAND STRING	BED SWERVER
ZINC COLIC	AIR SUPPORT	AT A VENTURE	BANDY WORDS	BED WETTING
ZINC OXIDE	ALARM CLOCK	AT ALL COSTS	BANGING OUT	BEDDED DOWN
ZINC WHITE	ALARM RADIO	AT ALL HOURS	BANK CHEQUE	BEDDING OUT
ZIPPING UP	ALL HALLOWS	AT FULL PELT	BAR COUNCIL	BEE KEEPING
ZONAL AXIS	ALL MOD CONS	AT GUNPOINT	BAR MITZVAH	BEER BARREL
	ALL PURPOSE	AT HALF COCK	BAR PARLOUR	BEER BOTTLE
10	ALL ROUNDER	AT LONG LAST	BARBARY APE	BEER ENGINE
	ALL THE BEST	AT THE READY	BARBED WIRE	BEER GARDEN
A BETTER BET	ALL THE RAGE	AT THE WHEEL	BARBIE DOLL	BEER PARLOR
A FAT CHANCE	ALL THE SAME	AT VARIANCE	BARGE BOARD	BEETLE EYED
A GOOD THING	ALL WEATHER	ATOMIC BOMB	BARIUM MEAL	BEETLED OFF
A NEAR THING	ALLEN SCREW	ATOMIC PILE	BARK BEETLE	BEETLES OFF
A QUARTER TO	ALMOND CAKE	ATOMIC TIME	BARKING MAD	BEFORE LONG
A SOFT TOUCH	ALMOND EYED	AUGER SHELL	BARLEY WINE	BEGGING OFF
A SORE THUMB	ALMOND TREE	AULD REEKIE	BARNABY DAY	BEHIND BARS
A TIGHT SPOT	ALPINE RACE	AVANT GARDE	BARREL ROLL	BEHIND HAND
ABLE BODIED	ALTAR CLOTH	AXLE GREASE	BARRIER ACT	BEHIND TIME
ABLE SEAMAN	ALTAR RAILS	BABA AU RHUM	BARROW TRAM	BELL BEAKER
ABOVE BOARD	ALTAR STONE	BABE IN ARMS	BASE MINDED	BELL FLOWER
ABOVE NAMED	AMINO ACIDS	BABY BOOMER	BASIL THYME	BELL RINGER
ABOVE PRICE	AMINO GROUP	BABY JUMPER	BASS FIDDLE	BELL SHAPED
ABOVE WATER	ANCHOR HOLD	BABY MINDER	BASS GUITAR	BELL THE CAT
ACCESS CARD	AND ALL THAT	BABY SITTER	BASSET HORN	BELL TURRET

10 *contd.*

BELL WETHER	BLACKED OUT	BOOM CARPET	BREAKS DOWN	BRUSHING UP
BELLY DANCE	BLANK VERSE	BOOT CLOSER	BREAKS EVEN	BRUTE FORCE
BELLY LAUGH	BLASTED OAK	BOOT POLISH	BREAST FEED	BUBBLE BATH
BELTED EARL	BLASTED OFF	BORE IN MIND	BREAST HIGH	BUBBLE OVER
BELTING OUT	BLEARY EYED	BORED STIFF	BREAST KNOT	BUBBLE PACK
BENGAL FIRE	BLIND ALLEY	BOSOM BUDDY	BREAST WALL	BUBBLING UP
BERLIN BLUE	BLIND DRUNK	BOTTLE BANK	BREATH TEST	BUBBLY JOCK
BERLIN WALL	BLOCK GRANT	BOTTLE FEED	BRENT GOOSE	BUCK RABBIT
BERLIN WOOL	BLOOD COUNT	BOTTLE FISH	BRICK EARTH	BUCKET SEAT
BERMUDA RIG	BLOOD DONOR	BOTTLE HEAD	BRIDES CAKE	BUCKET SHOP
BESOM RIDER	BLOOD GROUP	BOTTLE NECK	BRIDES MAID	BUCKLE DOWN
BEST SELLER	BLOOD MONEY	BOTTLE NOSE	BRIDGE CLUB	BUCKS PARTY
BETTER HALF	BLOOD PLATE	BOTTLE TREE	BRIDGE ROLL	BUENOS DIAS
BETTING MAN	BLOOD PURGE	BOTTLED OFF	BRIDGE WORK	BUFF JERKIN
BIBLE CLASS	BLOOD ROYAL	BOTTLED OUT	BRIDLE HAND	BUFFALO NUT
BIG BAD WOLF	BLOOD WAGON	BOTTLES OFF	BRIDLE PATH	BUFFER ZONE
BIG BROTHER	BLOODY EYED	BOTTLES OUT	BRIDLE REIN	BUILDING IN
BIG MOUTHED	BLOODY MARY	BOTTLING UP	BRIDLE ROAD	BUILDING UP
BILGE WATER	BLOTTED OUT	BOTTOM LINE	BRING ABOUT	BULK BUYING
BILL AND COO	BLOW BY BLOW	BOTTOMS OUT	BRING FORTH	BULL HEADED
BILL BROKER	BLOW DRYING	BOUGHT A PUP	BRING ROUND	BULL NECKED
BILL OF FARE	BLOW ME DOWN	BOUGHT OVER	BRINGING IN	BULL ROARER
BILL OF SALE	BLOWING OUT	BOUNCE BACK	BRINGING ON	BULLDOG ANT
BILLET DOUX	BLOWS A FUSE	BOUTS RIMES	BRINGING UP	BULLET HEAD
BINARY STAR	BLUE BONNET	BOW FRONTED	BRINGS DOWN	BULLET TREE
BIRD OF PREY	BLUE CHEESE	BOWIE KNIFE	BRINGS HOME	BULLIED OFF
BIRD PEPPER	BLUE COLLAR	BOWLED OVER	BRINGS OVER	BULLIES OFF
BIRD SKIING	BLUE ENSIGN	BOWLING OUT	BROAD ARROW	BUMBLE FOOT
BIRD SPIDER	BLUE MURDER	BOXING RING	BROAD BASED	BUMP STARTS
BIRD STRIKE	BLUE PENCIL	BOYS IN BLUE	BROAD BEANS	BUMPED INTO
BIRD WITTED	BLUE RIBAND	BRAIN DEATH	BROAD GAUGE	BUMPING OFF
BISCUIT TIN	BLUE RIBBON	BRAIN DRAIN	BROAD SCOTS	BUNCH GRASS
BISHOP BIRD	BLURTED OUT	BRAKE BLOCK	BROKE COVER	BUNGEE JUMP
BISHOPS CAP	BOARD WAGES	BRAKE LIGHT	BROKE FORTH	BUON GIORNO
BIT OF STUFF	BOARDED OUT	BRAKE WHEEL	BROKE LOOSE	BURMESE CAT
BIT ONES LIP	BOAT PEOPLE	BRANCH LINE	BROKE RANKS	BURNET MOTH
BIT THE DUST	BOAT RACING	BRANCH WORK	BROKEN DOWN	BURNING OUT
BITTER ROOT	BOB MAXIMUS	BRAND IMAGE	BROKEN HOME	BURNT CREAM
BLACK BREAD	BOBBIN LACE	BRANDY BALL	BROKEN REED	BURNT UMBER
BLACK CLOUD	BODY CAVITY	BRANDY SNAP	BROME GRASS	BURROW DUCK
BLACK DEATH	BODY COLOUR	BRASS FACED	BROMIC ACID	BUS SHELTER
BLACK EARTH	BODY POPPER	BRASS PLATE	BRONX CHEER	BUS STATION
BLACK FACED	BODY WARMER	BRASS TACKS	BRONZE WING	BUSH JACKET
BLACK FRIAR	BOG TROTTER	BRASSED OFF	BROOD POUCH	BUSH SHRIKE
BLACK FROST	BOGGED DOWN	BRAZEN FACE	BROUGHT OFF	BUSY AS A BEE
BLACK LIGHT	BOILED OVER	BREAD BOARD	BROUGHT OUT	BUSY LIZZIE
BLACK LOOKS	BOILER SUIT	BREAD FRUIT	BROWN ALGAE	BUTTER BALL
BLACK MAGIC	BOLL WEEVIL	BREAD KNIFE	BROWN BREAD	BUTTER BEAN
BLACK MARIA	BOMBAY DUCK	BREAD SAUCE	BROWN DWARF	BUTTER BIRD
BLACK MONEY	BON APPETIT	BREAD STICK	BROWN PAPER	BUTTER DISH
BLACK PAPER	BOND HOLDER	BREAK COVER	BROWN SAUCE	BUTTER FISH
BLACK PATCH	BONDED DEBT	BREAK FORTH	BROWN SHIRT	BUTTER MILK
BLACK POWER	BONDI BEACH	BREAK LOOSE	BROWN STOUT	BUTTER WIFE
BLACK SHEEP	BONGO DRUMS	BREAK OF DAY	BROWN STUDY	BUTTERED UP
BLACK SHIRT	BONUS ISSUE	BREAK POINT	BROWN SUGAR	BUTTERY BAR
BLACK SNAKE	BONY FISHES	BREAK RANKS	BROWN TROUT	BUTTON BUSH
BLACK STONE	BOOBY PRIZE	BREAKING IN	BROWNED OFF	BUTTON HOLE
BLACK WATCH	BOOK HOLDER	BREAKING UP	BRUSH ASIDE	BUTTON HOOK
BLACK WIDOW	BOOK HUNTER	BREAKS AWAY	BRUSHED OFF	BUTTON WOOD
	BOOKING OUT	BREAKS CAMP	BRUSHES OFF	BUTTONED UP

10 contd.

BUY AND SELL	CANVAS WORK	CHAIN CABLE	CHIPPING IN	CLEW GARNET
BUYING A PUP	CAP AND GOWN	CHAIN DRIVE	CHOIR ORGAN	CLICK CLACK
BUYING OVER	CAPE DOCTOR	CHAIN SMOKE	CHOKE CHAIN	CLIMBS DOWN
BY ALL MEANS	CAPE PIGEON	CHAIN STORE	CHOKED BACK	CLISH CLASH
BY AND LARGE	CAPER SAUCE	CHAINING UP	CHOKES BACK	CLOCK RADIO
BY ANY MEANS	CAPITAL SIN	CHAISE CART	CHOKING OFF	CLOCK TOWER
BY CONTRAST	CAPITAL SUM	CHALKED OUT	CHOPPING UP	CLOCKED OFF
BY ELECTION	CARBON COPY	CHALKING UP	CHOPS LOGIC	CLOCKED OUT
CABBAGE FLY	CARD HOLDER	CHANCING IT	CHORUS GIRL	CLOCKING IN
CABIN CLASS	CARD PLAYER	CHANGE DOWN	CHORUS LINE	CLOCKING UP
CACK HANDED	CARD READER	CHANGE ENDS	CHOTA HAZRI	CLOG DANCER
CADET CORPS	CAREER GIRL	CHANGE GEAR	CHUCK WAGON	CLOSE ORDER
CADET FORCE	CAREER PATH	CHANGE OVER	CHUCKED OUT	CLOSE RANKS
CAFE AU LAIT	CARPET MOTH	CHANGING UP	CHUCKER OUT	CLOSE SHAVE
CALICO BUSH	CARRIED OFF	CHANK SHELL	CHUCKS IT IN	CLOSE THING
CALICO TREE	CARRIED OUT	CHAPEL CART	CHURCH ARMY	CLOSED BOOK
CALICO WOOD	CARRIER BAG	CHAR A BANCS	CHURCH GOER	CLOSED DOOR
CALL IT A DAY	CARRIES OFF	CHARGE DOWN	CHURN DRILL	CLOSED DOWN
CALL OPTION	CARRIES OUT	CHARGE HAND	CHURN STAFF	CLOSED MIND
CALL TO MIND	CARRY IT OFF	CHARITY BOY	CHURNED OUT	CLOSED SHOP
CALL TRUMPS	CARRYING ON	CHAUD FROID	CHURNING UP	CLOSES DOWN
CALLED AWAY	CARTING OFF	CHEATING ON	CIDER PRESS	CLOSET PLAY
CALLED BACK	CARVING OUT	CHECK CLERK	CINDER CONE	CLOTH EARED
CALLED OVER	CASE BOTTLE	CHECKED OFF	CINDER PATH	CLOTHES PEG
CALLING OFF	CASE HARDEN	CHECKED OUT	CINE CAMERA	CLOTHES PIN
CALLING OUT	CASE WORKER	CHECKING IN	CINE VERITE	CLOUDS OVER
CALLS A HALT	CASH CREDIT	CHECKING UP	CINEMA GOER	CLOVE HITCH
CALLS NAMES	CASH IN HAND	CHEEK PIECE	CINQUE FOIL	CLOVEN HOOF
CALMED DOWN	CASPIAN SEA	CHEEK POUCH	CINQUE PORT	CLUB FOOTED
CAMBRIC TEA	CAST A SPELL	CHEERING UP	CIRCLE LINE	CLUSTER CUP
CAME ACROSS	CAST ANCHOR	CHEESE MITE	CIRCUS RING	COACH BUILT
CAME ASHORE	CASTING NET	CHEESED OFF	CITRIC ACID	COACH HORSE
CAME TO LIFE	CASTING OFF	CHELSEA BUN	CITRON TREE	COACH HOUSE
CAME TO PASS	CASTING OUT	CHEQUE BOOK	CITRON WOOD	COACH STAND
CAME TO REST	CASTS A VOTE	CHEQUE CARD	CITRUS WOOD	COACH WHEEL
CAME UNDONE	CASTS AN EYE	CHERRY BEAN	CITY CENTRE	COAL BUNKER
CAMEL CORPS	CASTS ASIDE	CHERRY PLUM	CITY EDITOR	COAL CELLAR
CAMELS HAIR	CASTS LOOSE	CHERRY TREE	CITY LIGHTS	COAL CUTTER
CAMEO SHELL	CASUS BELLI	CHEW THE CUD	CITY LIMITS	COAL MINING
CAMINO REAL	CAT BURGLAR	CHEW THE FAT	CIVIC CROWN	COAL PORTER
CAMPED IT UP	CAT SCANNER	CHEWED OVER	CIVIL DEATH	COARSE FISH
CAMPING OUT	CATCH A CRAB	CHEWING GUM	CLAMMING UP	COAT ARMOUR
CAMPO SANTO	CATCH BASIN	CHICKEN OUT	CLAMPS DOWN	COAT HANGER
CAN OF WORMS	CATCHES OUT	CHICKEN POX	CLAP EYES ON	COAT OF ARMS
CANARY BIRD	CATCHING ON	CHICKEN RUN	CLAPPED OUT	COAT OF MAIL
CANARY WOOD	CATCHING UP	CHIEF BARON	CLASP KNIFE	COBALT BLUE
CANCELS OUT	CATS CRADLE	CHIFF CHAFF	CLASSIC CAR	COCK A SNOOK
CANDLE COAL	CATTLE CAKE	CHILD BRIDE	CLAW HAMMER	COCOA BEANS
CANDLE FISH	CATTLE GRID	CHILD PROOF	CLAWED BACK	COCONUT OIL
CANDLE TREE	CATTLE SHOW	CHILDS PLAY	CLAY PIGEON	COCONUT SHY
CANDLE WOOD	CAUGHT FIRE	CHILLED OUT	CLEAN BREAK	COD FISHERY
CANDY FLOSS	CAUSE A STIR	CHIMNEY POT	CLEAN HANDS	COD FISHING
CANIS MAJOR	CAUSTIC WIT	CHIMNEY TOP	CLEAN SLATE	CODE NUMBER
CANIS MINOR	CAVITY WALL	CHINA ASTER	CLEAN SWEEP	CODLIN MOTH
CANNED BEER	CAXTON HALL	CHINA GOOSE	CLEANED OUT	CODS WALLOP
CANNON BONE	CEASED TO BE	CHINA GRASS	CLEANING UP	COFFEE BEAN
CANNON GAME	CELLAR BOOK	CHINA STONE	CLEAR AS MUD	COFFEE MILL
CANNON SHOT	CELLAR FLAP	CHINA WHITE	CLEARED OUT	COFFEE ROOM
CANVAS BACK	CENTRE HALF	CHIP BASKET	CLEARING UP	COFFEE SHOP
	CENTRE RAIL	CHIPPED OFF	CLEVER DICK	COFFEE TREE

10 LETTERS

10 *contd.*

COFFER FISH
COFFIN BONE
COFFIN NAIL
COKING COAL
COLD CHISEL
COLD SHOWER
COLD TURKEY
COLLAR BONE
COLLAR STUD
COLLEGE CAP
COLOUR CODE
COLOUR FAST
COLOUR FILM
COLOUR WASH
COLOURED IN
COLOURED UP
COLTS TOOTH
COMBING OUT
COME ACROSS
COME ASHORE
COME AT ABLE
COME HITHER
COME ON DOWN
COME TO LIFE
COME TO PASS
COME TO REST
COME UNDONE
COMES ABOUT
COMES CLEAN
COMES ROUND
COMIC OPERA
COMIC STRIP
COMING AWAY
COMING BACK
COMING DOWN
COMING HOME
COMING OVER
COMMON COLD
COMMON NOUN
COMMON ROOM
COMMON TIME
COMPANY CAR
COMPASS SAW
CON SPIRITO
CONJURED UP
CONJURES UP
CONTACT MAN
CONTOUR MAP
CONTRACT IN
CONY BURROW
COOKER HOOD
COOLING OFF
COPPER NOSE
COPPER WIRE
COPPER WORK
COPPING OUT
COPY TYPING
COPY TYPIST
COPYING INK

COR ANGLAIS
CORAL BERRY
CORDON BLEU
CORDONS OFF
CORK CARPET
CORK CUTTER
CORK HEELED
CORK TIPPED
CORKING PIN
CORN CIRCLE
CORN CUTTER
CORN DEALER
CORN DOLLIE
CORN FACTOR
CORN MILLER
CORN WEEVIL
CORNED BEEF
CORNER FLAG
CORNER SHOP
COSA NOSTRA
COSMIC RAYS
COSSACK HAT
COST CENTRE
COSTA BRAVA
COTTAGE PIE
COTTON BELT
COTTON BOLL
COTTON MILL
COTTON REEL
COTTON WOOL
COTTON WORM
COTTONED ON
COUCH GRASS
COUGHING UP
COUNCIL TAX
COUNT SHEEP
COUNT WHEEL
COUNTED OUT
COUNTER BID
COUNTER SPY
COUNTRY BOX
COUNTRY PUB
COUNTY TOWN
COUP DE MAIN
COUP DESSAI
COURT DRESS
COURT HOUSE
COURT ORDER
COVER DRIVE
COVER POINT
COVERED WAY
COVERING IN
COVERING UP
COW PARSLEY
CRAB NEBULA
CRACK A CRIB
CRACK A JOKE
CRACKING UP
CRACKS DOWN
CRADLE SONG

CRAFT GUILD
CRAKE BERRY
CRANES BILL
CRASH PROOF
CRASHED OUT
CRASHES OUT
CRATER LAKE
CRAZY QUILT
CREAM SLICE
CREDIT CARD
CREPE PAPER
CREPE SOLED
CRI DE COEUR
CRICKET BAT
CRIME SHEET
CRIMEAN WAR
CRISS CROSS
CROP CIRCLE
CROP DUSTER
CROPPING UP
CROSS CHECK
CROSS CLAIM
CROSS GUARD
CROSS PARTY
CROSS REFER
CROSS THE TS
CROW SHRIKE
CROWN AGENT
CROWN COURT
CROWN DERBY
CROWN GREEN
CROWN WHEEL
CRUET STAND
CRYING DOWN
CRYING WOLF
CRYSTAL SET
CUB HUNTING
CUCKOO PINT
CUCKOO SPIT
CUP AND BALL
CUP AND RING
CUP OF COCOA
CUP WINNERS
CURATES EGG
CURD CHEESE
CURFEW BELL
CURRANT BUN
CUSTARD PIE
CUT A FIGURE
CUT CORNERS
CUT FLOWERS
CUT UP ROUGH
CUTS A CAPER
CUTS A TOOTH
CUTS ACROSS
CUTS IT FINE
CUTTING OFF
CUTTING OUT
CUTTLE BONE
CYANIC ACID

CYCLO CROSS
DAILY BREAD
DAILY DOZEN
DAILY PAPER
DAIRY CREAM
DAISY CHAIN
DAISY WHEEL
DAMASK PLUM
DAMASK ROSE
DAMP COURSE
DAMPEN DOWN
DAMPING OFF
DANCE MUSIC
DANDY BRUSH
DANGER LINE
DANISH BLUE
DANKE SCHON
DAPPLE GREY
DARK SECRET
DART PLAYER
DASHED AWAY
DASHES AWAY
DASHING OFF
DASHING OUT
DATA LOGGER
DATE CODING
DAWN CHORUS
DAWN PATROL
DAY BOARDER
DAY NURSERY
DAY RELEASE
DAY SCHOLAR
DAY TRIPPER
DAYS OF YORE
DEAD CENTRE
DEAD GROUND
DEAD HEADED
DEAD LETTER
DEAD RINGER
DEAD WEIGHT
DEADLY SINS
DEAF MUTISM
DEALING OUT
DEALS A BLOW
DEALT A BLOW
DEATH KNELL
DEATH SQUAD
DEATH WATCH
DEATHS HEAD
DECK BRIDGE
DECK QUOITS
DECK TENNIS
DECKING OUT
DECKLE EDGE
DECLARE WAR
DECREE NISI
DEEP FREEZE
DEEP FRYING
DEEP PURPLE
DEEP ROOTED

DEEP SEATED
DEER FOREST
DELFT CHINA
DENVER BOOT
DEO GRATIAS
DEO VOLENTE
DERNIER CRI
DESERT BOOT
DEWAR FLASK
DICE PLAYER
DID ONES BIT
DIE CASTING
DIE SINKING
DIGGING OUT
DIKA BUTTER
DILL PICKLE
DILLY DALLY
DINING HALL
DINING ROOM
DINNER GOWN
DINNER HOUR
DINNER LADY
DINNER TIME
DIP THE FLAG
DIPPING OUT
DIRECT LINE
DIRTY MONEY
DIRTY TRICK
DISC BRAKES
DISC JOCKEY
DISC PLAYER
DISH WASHER
DISHING OUT
DITCH WATER
DIVE BOMBER
DIVING BELL
DIVING BIRD
DIVING SUIT
DIZZY SPELL
DO PORRIDGE
DO THE TRICK
DO THE TWIST
DOC MARTENS
DOCK MASTER
DOCK STRIKE
DOG BISCUIT
DOG FANCIER
DOG HANDLER
DOG LICENCE
DOG PARSLEY
DOGGER BANK
DOGS CHANCE
DOGS DINNER
DOGS FENNEL
DOGS TONGUE
DOING A TURN
DOLLAR AREA
DOLLS HOUSE
DONALD DUCK
DONER KEBAB

10 contd.

DONKEY PUMP	DREW A BLANK	EAST INDIAN	FAIR HEADED	FER DE LANCE
DONKEY WORK	DREW STUMPS	EAST INDIES	FAIR MINDED	FERRIC ACID
DOOR HANDLE	DRIFT APART	EASTER LILY	FAIRY LIGHT	FERRO ALLOY
DOOR KEEPER	DRINK MONEY	EASY DOES IT	FAIRY QUEEN	FERRY HOUSE
DOOR TO DOOR	DRINKING IN	EASY STREET	FAIRY STORY	FETCHED OUT
DORIAN MODE	DRINKING UP	EATING AWAY	FALCON EYED	FETCHES OUT
DOROTHY BAG	DRIVE SHAFT	EBB AND FLOW	FALL BEHIND	FETCHING UP
DORSAL FINS	DRIVES HOME	ECCLES CAKE	FALL IN LOVE	FEVER PITCH
DOSSED DOWN	DRIVING OUT	EDITING OUT	FALLEN ARCH	FIANNA FAIL
DOSSES DOWN	DROP A BRICK	EGG AND DART	FALLEN STAR	FIBRE GLASS
DOTTED LINE	DROP ANCHOR	EGG CUSTARD	FALLING OFF	FIELD EVENT
DOTTED NOTE	DROP HAMMER	EGG ON TOAST	FALLING OUT	FIELD GLASS
DOUBLE AXEL	DROPPED OFF	EGO TRIPPER	FALLOW DEER	FIELD NOTES
DOUBLE BACK	DROPPED OUT	EIGHTH ARMY	FALLS ABOUT	FIELD TRAIN
DOUBLE BASS	DROPPING BY	ELEVEN PLUS	FALLS APART	FIFTY FIFTY
DOUBLE BILL	DROPPING IN	EMBER GOOSE	FALLS SHORT	FIFTY PENCE
DOUBLE CHIN	DROPPING ON	EMERALD CUT	FALSE ALARM	FIGHT IT OUT
DOUBLE DOOR	DROPS A LINE	EMERY BOARD	FALSE SHAME	FIGHTS BACK
DOUBLE DYED	DROWNED OUT	EMERY CLOTH	FALSE START	FILE CUTTER
DOUBLE FLAT	DROWNED RAT	EMERY PAPER	FALSE TEETH	FILE LEADER
DOUBLE PARK	DRUG ADDICT	EMERY WHEEL	FAMILY NAME	FILING PAST
DOUBLE SALT	DRUG PUSHER	EMI SCANNER	FAMILY TREE	FILLING OUT
DOUBLE STAR	DRUM BRAKES	EMPIRE GOWN	FAN TRACERY	FILM CENSOR
DOUBLE TAKE	DRY BATTERY	END IN TEARS	FANCY DRESS	FILM CRITIC
DOUBLE TALK	DRY CANTEEN	END PRODUCT	FANCY GOODS	FILM REVIEW
DOUBLE TIME	DRY CLEANED	ENGINE ROOM	FANCY WOMAN	FILM STUDIO
DOUBLING UP	DRY FARMING	ENTREE DISH	FANNING OUT	FINAL SCORE
DOUGH BAKED	DRY MEASURE	EPSOM DOWNS	FAR AND AWAY	FINDING OUT
DOUGLAS FIR	DUAL SCHOOL	EPSOM SALTS	FAR AND NEAR	FINDS FAULT
DOWEL JOINT	DUCHY COURT	EQUALS SIGN	FAR AND WIDE	FINE TUNING
DOWER HOUSE	DUCK BILLED	ERRAND GIRL	FAR FETCHED	FINGERS END
DOWN AND OUT	DUCK LEGGED	ESCAPE ROAD	FAR SIGHTED	FINISHED UP
DOWN AT HEEL	DUCKED DOWN	ESKIMO ROLL	FARMING OUT	FINISHES UP
DOWN MARKET	DUCKING OUT	ESTATE DUTY	FAST ASLEEP	FINITE VERB
DOWNS TOOLS	DUFFEL COAT	ETON COLLAR	FAST BOWLER	FINNO UGRIC
DRAFT HORSE	DULL WITTED	ETON JACKET	FAST TALKER	FIRE BLIGHT
DRAG RACING	DUMB BLONDE	EVEN CHANCE	FAST WORKER	FIRE BUCKET
DRAGGED OUT	DUMB WAITER	EVEN HANDED	FASTENED ON	FIRE EATING
DRAGGING ON	DUMMY WHIST	EVENING OUT	FATHERS DAY	FIRE ENGINE
DRAGGING UP	DUMPY LEVEL	EVIL MINDED	FATHOM LINE	FIRE ESCAPE
DRAGON FISH	DUNDEE CAKE	EVIL WORKER	FATTED CALF	FIRE HAZARD
DRAGON TREE	DUNG BEETLE	EX CATHEDRA	FATTENED UP	FIRE OFFICE
DRAINS AWAY	DUST JACKET	EXCESS FARE	FATTY ACIDS	FIRE POLICY
DRAUGHT BAR	DUTCH CLOCK	EXHAUST GAS	FATTY HEART	FIRE RAISER
DRAW A BLANK	DUTCH TREAT	EXTRA COVER	FAULT PLANE	FIRE SHOVEL
DRAW STRING	DUTCH UNCLE	EXTRA SOLAR	FEATHER BED	FIRE WALKER
DRAW STUMPS	DYING HAPPY	EYE CONTACT	FEE FI FO FUM	FIRE WARDEN
DRAWING OFF	DYING WORDS	EYE WITNESS	FEEL AT HOME	FIRING AWAY
DRAWING OUT	EACH WAY BET	FACE FUNGUS	FEELS A FOOL	FIRING BACK
DRAWING PEN	EAGLES NEST	FACE POWDER	FEELS CHEAP	FIRING LINE
DRAWING PIN	EAR BASHING	FACE SAVING	FEELS FAINT	FIRMED DOWN
DRAWS BLOOD	EAR TRUMPET	FACE TO FACE	FEELS SMALL	FIRST AIDER
DRAWS TEETH	EAR WITNESS	FACE UP TO IT	FEET OF CLAY	FIRST CLASS
DREAD LOCKS	EARLS COURT	FACED FACTS	FELL BEHIND	FIRST FLOOR
DREAM WORLD	EARLY START	FACES FACTS	FELL IN LOVE	FIRST FRUIT
DREAMING UP	EARTH HOUSE	FAINT HEART	FELL WALKER	FIRST LIGHT
DRESS SENSE	EARTH LIGHT	FAIR DINKUM	FELLOW HEIR	FIRST NIGHT
DRESS SHIRT	EARTH SHINE	FAIR ENOUGH	FELT AT HOME	FIRST PRIZE
DRESSING UP	EARTH TABLE	FAIR GROUND	FEME COVERT	FIRST THING
	EAST ANGLIA	FAIR HAIRED	FEN CRICKET	FISCAL YEAR

10 *contd.*

FISH CARVER
FISH DINNER
FISH EATERS
FISH FARMER
FISH FINGER
FISH GUTTER
FISH KETTLE
FISHING OUT
FISHING ROD
FITTING OUT
FIVE FINGER
FIVE OCLOCK
FIVE POINTS
FIVE SENSES
FIVE STONES
FIXED COSTS
FIXED LIGHT
FIXED STARS
FLAG WAVING
FLAK JACKET
FLAKE WHITE
FLAKING OUT
FLASH BOARD
FLASH FLOOD
FLASH POINT
FLAT FOOTED
FLAT RACING
FLATTEN OUT
FLEA BEETLE
FLEA BITTEN
FLEA CIRCUS
FLEA MARKET
FLESH BROTH
FLESH BRUSH
FLESH EATER
FLESH WOUND
FLESHED OUT
FLESHES OUT
FLEUR DE LIS
FLEUR DE LYS
FLICK KNIFE
FLIES A KITE
FLIGHT CREW
FLIGHT DECK
FLIGHT PATH
FLIGHT PLAN
FLINGS DOWN
FLINGS OPEN
FLINT GLASS
FLINT HEART
FLOAT BOARD
FLOAT GLASS
FLOAT ON AIR
FLOAT PLANE
FLOAT STONE
FLOCK PAPER
FLOOD GATES
FLOOD LEVEL
FLOOD PLAIN

FLOOR SPACE
FLOPPY DISC
FLOPPY DISK
FLOWER BELL
FLOWER GIRL
FLOWER HEAD
FLOWER SHOW
FLOWN COVER
FLUID DRIVE
FLUID OUNCE
FLY BY NIGHT
FLY FISHING
FLY FLAPPER
FLY THE FLAG
FLYING BOAT
FLYING BOMB
FLYING FISH
FLYING HIGH
FLYING LEAP
FLYING OPEN
FLYING SHOT
FLYING SOLO
FLYING SUIT
FLYING WING
FOAM RUBBER
FOBBING OFF
FOCAL POINT
FOLDING OUT
FOLK MEMORY
FOLK SINGER
FOLK SPEECH
FOLLOW HOME
FOLLOW SUIT
FOLLOWED ON
FOLLOWED UP
FOLLOWS OUT
FOOD VALUES
FOOL AROUND
FOOT CANDLE
FOOT LICKER
FOOT RACING
FOOT WARMER
FOR ALL THAT
FOR CERTAIN
FOR EXAMPLE
FOR MY MONEY
FOR NOTHING
FOR THE BEST
FOR THE CHOP
FOR THE REST
FOR TWO PINS
FORCED SALE
FORCING PIT
FORE AND AFT
FORE DAMNED
FORE HAMMER
FORE NOTICE
FORE QUOTED
FOREIGN AID
FOREST TREE

FORK TAILED
FORKED OVER
FORKING OUT
FORM CRITIC
FORM LETTER
FORM MASTER
FORMIC ACID
FORMULA ONE
FORMULA TWO
FORTY NINER
FORTY WINKS
FOSSIL FUEL
FOSTER HOME
FOUGHT BACK
FOUL SPOKEN
FOUND FAULT
FOUND MONEY
FOUR COLOUR
FOUR FIGURE
FOUR FOOTED
FOUR HANDED
FOUR IN HAND
FOUR LEAFED
FOUR LEAVED
FOUR LEGGED
FOUR OCLOCK
FOUR POSTER
FOUR SEATER
FOUR SQUARE
FOURTH RATE
FOURTH WALL
FOWLING NET
FOX HUNTING
FOX TERRIER
FRAME HOUSE
FRAME MAKER
FREAKED OUT
FREE AGENCY
FREE CHURCH
FREE DIVING
FREE FISHER
FREE FLIGHT
FREE FOODER
FREE FOOTED
FREE FOR ALL
FREE HANDED
FREE LABOUR
FREE MARKET
FREE MINDED
FREE PARDON
FREE SAMPLE
FREE SCHOOL
FREE SKATER
FREE SPEECH
FREE SPIRIT
FREE SPOKEN
FREE STATES
FREE STROKE
FREE TRADER
FREE VERSER

FREE WHEELS
FREEZE DOWN
FREEZE OVER
FREEZES OUT
FREIGHT CAR
FRENCH ALPS
FRENCH BEAN
FRENCH HEEL
FRENCH HORN
FRENCH KISS
FRENCH LOAF
FRENCH ROLL
FRENCH SASH
FRENCH SEAM
FRESH BLOWN
FRESH FRUIT
FRESHENS UP
FRIARS COWL
FRIED BREAD
FRINGE TREE
FROG HOPPER
FROGS MOUTH
FROM CHOICE
FROM ON HIGH
FRONT BENCH
FRONT TEETH
FRONT TOOTH
FROWNING ON
FROZEN DOWN
FROZEN OVER
FRUIT JUICE
FRUIT KNIFE
FRUIT SALAD
FUDDY DUDDY
FULL BODIED
FULL BOTTOM
FULL CIRCLE
FULL COCKED
FULL COUSIN
FULL HANDED
FULL LENGTH
FULL NELSON
FULL OF LIFE
FULL ORDERS
FULL RIGGED
FULL SAILED
FULL SISTER
FULL VOICED
FUND HOLDER
FUND RAISER
FUNGUS GALL
FUNNY MONEY
FUNNY PAPER
FUNNY STUFF
FUSION BOMB
FUZZY WUZZY
GAFF RIGGED
GAIN GROUND
GAINED TIME
GALL STONES

GALLIC ACID
GALLOPS OFF
GALLUP POLL
GAMBIT PAWN
GAME DEALER
GAME WARDEN
GAMING LAWS
GANDER MOON
GANG OF FOUR
GAP TOOTHED
GARAGE SALE
GARBAGE CAN
GARDEN CITY
GARDEN GATE
GARDEN PATH
GARDEN PEAS
GARDEN WALL
GAS BRACKET
GAS CHAMBER
GAS FURNACE
GAS GUZZLER
GAS TURBINE
GATE KEEPER
GATE LEGGED
GATHERED UP
GATHERS WAY
GATLING GUN
GAUDY NIGHT
GAUGE GLASS
GAUGING ROD
GAVE GROUND
GAVE NOTICE
GAY GORDONS
GEAR CHANGE
GEARED DOWN
GEISHA GIRL
GELDER ROSE
GEM CUTTING
GENEVA GOWN
GERM THEORY
GET A LINE ON
GET A MOVE ON
GET A WICKET
GET DRESSED
GET HITCHED
GET KNOTTED
GET ONES WAY
GET STUCK IN
GET STUFFED
GET THE BIRD
GET THE BOOT
GET THE CHOP
GET THE PUSH
GET THE SACK
GET THROUGH
GET TO GRIPS
GET TO SLEEP
GET UP AND GO
GET UP STEAM
GET WEAVING

10 contd.

GETS ACROSS	GOES TO TOWN	GOT TO GRIPS	GREY HAIRED	HAND BARROW
GETS AROUND	GOES TOO FAR	GOT TO SLEEP	GREY HEADED	HAND BASKET
GETTING OFF	GOGGLE EYED	GOT UP STEAM	GREY MARKET	HAND GALLOP
GETTING OUT	GOING AHEAD	GOTHIC ARCH	GREY MATTER	HAND IN HAND
GHOST STORY	GOING DUTCH	GOUGING OUT	GREY PARROT	HAND LOTION
GHOST WRITE	GOING FORTH	GRACE A DIEU	GRIDDLE CAR	HAND ME DOWN
GIANT PANDA	GOING ROUND	GRACIOUS ME	GRINDS DOWN	HAND PICKED
GIDDY PACED	GOING TO BED	GRAND HOTEL	GRIPE WATER	HAND SIGNAL
GIMBAL RING	GOING TO POT	GRAND JESUS	GROSSING UP	HAND TO HAND
GIMLET EYED	GOING TO SEA	GRAND JUROR	GROUND BASS	HANDED DOWN
GINGER BEER	GOING TO WAR	GRAND MARCH	GROUND CREW	HANDED OVER
GINGER WINE	GOING UNDER	GRAND NIECE	GROUND DOWN	HANDING OUT
GIRL FRIDAY	GOING WRONG	GRAND OPERA	GROUND GAME	HANDY DANDY
GIRL FRIEND	GOLD BEATER	GRAND PIANO	GROUND MAIL	HANG AROUND
GIVE GROUND	GOLD DIGGER	GRAND STYLE	GROUND PLAN	HANG GLIDER
GIVE NOTICE	GOLD MINING	GRAND TOTAL	GROUND RENT	HANGING OFF
GIVES BIRTH	GOLD NUGGET	GRAND UNCLE	GROUND RULE	HANGING OUT
GIVES CHASE	GOLD PLATED	GRANDE DAME	GROUSE MOOR	HANGS ABOUT
GIVES FORTH	GOLD RECORD	GRANDS PRIX	GROWING BAG	HANGS LOOSE
GIVES IT A GO	GOLD THREAD	GRANNY FLAT	GRUB STREET	HANKY PANKY
GIVES VOICE	GOLD WASHER	GRANNY KNOT	GRUFF VOICE	HAPPEN UPON
GIVING AWAY	GOLDEN BULL	GRANT IN AID	GUARD HOUSE	HAPPY EVENT
GIVING ODDS	GOLDEN CALF	GRAPE LOUSE	GUEST HOUSE	HARBOUR BAR
GIVING REIN	GOLDEN DISC	GRAPE SUGAR	GUEST NIGHT	HARD BITTEN
GLAMOUR BOY	GOLDEN GATE	GRAPH PAPER	GUINEA CORN	HARD BOILED
GLANCE COAL	GOLDEN GIRL	GRASS COURT	GUINEA FOWL	HARD CHEESE
GLASS CLOTH	GOLDEN MEAN	GRASS GREEN	GUINEA WORM	HARD DONE BY
GLASS COACH	GOLDEN ROSE	GRASS GROWN	GULF STATES	HARD EARNED
GLASS FACED	GOLDEN RULE	GRASS ROOTS	GULF STREAM	HARD FOUGHT
GLASS FIBRE	GOLDEN SEAL	GRASS SKIRT	GUT SCRAPER	HARD HEADED
GLASS PAPER	GOLF COURSE	GRASS SNAKE	HACKNEY CAB	HARD LABOUR
GLASSY EYED	GOMBEEN MAN	GRASS VERGE	HAD KITTENS	HARD PUSHED
GLEBE HOUSE	GONE METRIC	GRASS WIDOW	HAD ONES WAY	HARD RIDING
GLIDE SLOPE	GONE TO SEED	GRAVE MAKER	HAIL FELLOW	HARD WORKER
GLOSS PAINT	GOOD FOR YOU	GRAVEL WALK	HAILS A TAXI	HARDENS OFF
GLOVE FIGHT	GOOD FRIDAY	GRAVELY ILL	HAIR PENCIL	HARE LIPPED
GLOVE MONEY	GOOD HEALTH	GRAVY TRAIN	HAIR POWDER	HAREM SKIRT
GNAMMA HOLE	GOOD LOOKER	GREASY POLE	HAIR RAISER	HARKED BACK
GNAWED AWAY	GOOD PEOPLE	GREAT GROSS	HAIR STROKE	HARMAN BECK
GO DOWNHILL	GOOD TEMPER	GREAT LAKES	HAIR WAVING	HARPOON GUN
GO FOR BROKE	GOOD TIMING	GREAT NIECE	HALF A CROWN	HARVEST BUG
GO GO DANCER	GOODNESS ME	GREAT SCOTT	HALF A DOZEN	HARVEST FLY
GO STRAIGHT	GOODS TRAIN	GREAT UNCLE	HALF AN HOUR	HAS KITTENS
GO TO BLAZES	GOODS WAGON	GRECIAN URN	HALF COCKED	HAS ONES WAY
GO TO GROUND	GOODY GOODY	GRECO ROMAN	HALF DOLLAR	HASH BROWNS
GO TO MARKET	GOONEY BIRD	GREEDY GUTS	HALF HOURLY	HASTA LUEGO
GO TO PIECES	GOOSE BUMPS	GREEK CROSS	HALF HUNTER	HATCHET JOB
GO TO THE BAD	GOOSE GRASS	GREEK MODES	HALF INCHED	HATCHET MAN
GOAL TENDER	GOOSE QUILL	GREEK MYTHS	HALF LENGTH	HAULS ROUND
GOATS BEARD	GOSPEL SIDE	GREEN ALGAE	HALF NELSON	HAUNCH BONE
GOB STOPPER	GOT A LINE ON	GREEN BERET	HALF SISTER	HAUTE ECOLE
GOBBLING UP	GOT A WICKET	GREEN EARTH	HALF VOLLEY	HAVE A DEKKO
GOBI DESERT	GOT DRESSED	GREEN GOOSE	HALF WITTED	HAVE A HEART
GOD FEARING	GOT HITCHED	GREEN LIGHT	HALF YEARLY	HAVE A LAUGH
GOD WILLING	GOT ONES WAY	GREEN PAPER	HALL PORTER	HAVE NO IDEA
GOES ABROAD	GOT THE BIRD	GREEN PARTY	HALO EFFECT	HAWK BEAKED
GOES METRIC	GOT THE BOOT	GREEN POUND	HALTER NECK	HAWK BILLED
GOES NATIVE	GOT THE CHOP	GREEN SALAD	HAMMER BEAM	HAWSER LAID
GOES TO SEED	GOT THE PUSH	GREEN SNAKE	HAMMER HOME	HEAD BANGER
	GOT THROUGH	GREY COATED	HAMMER TOED	HEAD HUGGER

10 LETTERS

10 contd.

HEAD OFFICE	HIGH PLACES	HOME MOVIES	HYBRID BILL	IN THE CHAIR
HEAD STREAM	HIGH PRICED	HONEY CROCK	I BELIEVE SO	IN THE CLEAR
HEAD WAITER	HIGH PRIEST	HONEY EATER	I KID YOU NOT	IN THE DRINK
HEADING OFF	HIGH RANKER	HONEY GUIDE	IAMBIC FOOT	IN THE EVENT
HEADING OUT	HIGH RELIEF	HONEY STALK	ICE BREAKER	IN THE FLESH
HEALTH CAMP	HIGH ROLLER	HONEY SWEET	ICE DANCING	IN THE MONEY
HEALTH FARM	HIGH SCHOOL	HONEY WAGON	ICE HILLING	IN THE RIGHT
HEALTH FOOD	HIGH SEASON	HONOURS MAN	ICE MACHINE	IN THE ROUGH
HEAR NO EVIL	HIGH STREET	HOOK AND EYE	ICE SKATING	IN THE ROUND
HEAR THINGS	HIGH TAIL IT	HOP BITTERS	ICELAND DOG	IN THE SHADE
HEARING AID	HILL DIGGER	HOP PICKING	ICING SUGAR	IN THE WINGS
HEARING OUT	HINGE JOINT	HOP SACKING	IDAEAN VINE	IN THE WRONG
HEART BLOCK	HIP HUGGERS	HOP THE TWIG	IDIOT BOARD	IN TRACTION
HEART GRIEF	HIPPETY HOP	HOPPING MAD	IDIOT PROOF	IN TRAINING
HEART OF OAK	HIRDY GIRDY	HOPPING OFF	IDLE HEADED	IN TWO MINDS
HEART SHELL	HIS MAJESTY	HORN RIMMED	IDLE PULLEY	IN TWO TICKS
HEART SPOON	HIS WORSHIP	HORN SILVER	IFS AND BUTS	INCH BY INCH
HEART THROB	HIT AND MISS	HORNED TOAD	IGNES FATUI	INDIA PAPER
HEARTS EASE	HIT THE DECK	HORROR FILM	ILL ADVISED	INDIAN CLUB
HEAT SHIELD	HIT THE ROAD	HORSE BRASS	ILL BEHAVED	INDIAN CORN
HEAT STROKE	HIT THE ROOF	HORSE CLOTH	ILL BUY THAT	INDIAN FILE
HEATHER ALE	HIT THE SACK	HORSE COPER	ILL DEFINED	INDIAN FIRE
HEAVEN SENT	HITCH HIKED	HORSE FACED	ILL FEELING	INDIAN HEMP
HEAVY ARMED	HITCH HIKER	HORSE RIDER	ILL FORTUNE	INDIAN MEAL
HEAVY GOING	HITCH HIKES	HORSE SENSE	ILL FOUNDED	INDIAN PIPE
HEAVY METAL	HITCHING UP	HORSE TAMER	ILL LOOKING	INDIAN RICE
HEAVY SUGAR	HITS FOR SIX	HORSE THIEF	ILL MATCHED	INDIGO BIRD
HEAVY WATER	HITS THE HAY	HOT BLOODED	ILL NATURED	INDOOR GAME
HEBREW YEAR	HITTING OFF	HOUNDS FOOT	ILL STARRED	INERT GASES
HEEL AND TOE	HITTING OUT	HOUSE AGENT	IMMUNE BODY	INGLE CHEEK
HELLO DOLLY	HITTY MISSY	HOUSE GUEST	IN A BAD MOOD	INJURY TIME
HELLS ANGEL	HOBBY HORSE	HOUSE OF GOD	IN ABSENTIA	INK SLINGER
HELLS BELLS	HOCK MONDAY	HOUSE PARTY	IN ADDITION	INK STAINED
HELLS TEETH	HOCKEY LINE	HOUSE PLANT	IN ANY EVENT	INLAND BILL
HELPING OUT	HOCUS POCUS	HOUSE PROUD	IN BAD ODOUR	INLET VALVE
HEMP NETTLE	HOD CARRIER	HOUSE RULES	IN BUSINESS	INNER HOUSE
HEN HARRIER	HODGE PODGE	HOVER MOWER	IN CHANCERY	INNER LIGHT
HER MAJESTY	HOITY TOITY	HOVER TRAIN	IN CONFLICT	INNER SPACE
HERB BENNET	HOKEY COKEY	HOW DARE YOU	IN DISARRAY	INNER VOICE
HERB GARDEN	HOLDING OFF	HOW DO YOU DO	IN DISGRACE	INS AND OUTS
HERB ROBERT	HOLDING OUT	HOWLED DOWN	IN DISGUISE	INSIDE EDGE
HERE YOU ARE	HOLDS COURT	HOWS TRICKS	IN DISTRESS	INSIDE LEFT
HERES TO YOU	HOLDS FORTH	HUBBA HUBBA	IN EXCELSIS	IRISH LINEN
HERMIT CRAB	HOLDS WATER	HUBBLES LAW	IN EXTREMIS	IRON FISTED
HEROIC POEM	HOLLOW EYED	HUCKLE BONE	IN FIGHTING	IRON HANDED
HIGH AND DRY	HOLLOW WARE	HUG ME TIGHT	IN GOOD NICK	IRON MAIDEN
HIGH AND LOW	HOLLOWS OUT	HUG ONESELF	IN GOOD PART	IRON MINING
HIGH CHURCH	HOLUS BOLUS	HUMAN BEING	IN GOOD TIME	IRON RATION
HIGH COLOUR	HOLY FATHER	HUMAN ERROR	IN HOT WATER	IRON WILLED
HIGH COMEDY	HOLY ISLAND	HUMMING TOP	IN JEOPARDY	IRONING OUT
HIGH FLYING	HOLY OFFICE	HUMP BACKED	IN MEMORIAM	ISLE OF DOGS
HIGH GERMAN	HOLY ORDERS	HUNG AROUND	IN MOURNING	ISLE OF SKYE
HIGH HANDED	HOLY SPIRIT	HUNTED DOWN	IN NAME ONLY	ISSUE FORTH
HIGH HEELED	HOLY TERROR	HUNTING BOX	IN ONES CUPS	ITALIC TYPE
HIGH LIVING	HOMBURG HAT	HUNTING CAP	IN ONES TURN	IVORY BLACK
HIGH MINDED	HOME AND DRY	HUNTING OUT	IN POSITION	IVORY COAST
HIGH NECKED	HOME BREWED	HURDLE RACE	IN PROGRESS	IVORY TOWER
HIGH OCTANE	HOME COMING	HURDY GURDY	IN SEQUENCE	IVY MANTLED
HIGH PLACED	HOME GROUND	HURLY BURLY	IN STITCHES	JACK A DANDY
	HOME MARKET	HURRYING UP	IN THE BLACK	JACK KNIFED

10 *contd.*

JACK KNIFES	KEEPS HOUSE	KNOCK KNEED	LAUGHED OFF	LENTIL SOUP
JACK PRIEST	KEEPS QUIET	KNOCKED OFF	LAUNDRY MAN	LEOPARD CAT
JACK RABBIT	KEEPS STILL	KNOCKED OUT	LAURIC ACID	LETS FACE IT
JACK STRAWS	KEEPS TRACK	KNOCKING ON	LAVER BREAD	LETS IT RIDE
JACK THE LAD	KEEPS WATCH	KNOCKING UP	LAW ABIDING	LETTER BOMB
JAM SESSION	KENNEL CLUB	KNOCKS BACK	LAW BREAKER	LETTER BOOK
JAMAICA RUM	KENNEL MAID	KNOCKS COLD	LAW OFFICER	LETTER CARD
JANUS FACED	KENTISH COB	KNOCKS DOWN	LAWN TENNIS	LETTER CLIP
JAPAN EARTH	KENTISH MAN	KNOW BETTER	LAY A COURSE	LETTER FILE
JAR OF HONEY	KENTISH RAG	KNUCKLE BOW	LAY BAPTISM	LETTING FLY
JAW BREAKER	KEPT IN MIND	KODIAK BEAR	LAY BROTHER	LETTING OFF
JAY WALKING	KEPT IT DARK	KU KLUX KLAN	LAY HANDS ON	LETTING OUT
JERRY BUILT	KEPT TABS ON	LABOUR CAMP	LAY IN STATE	LETTING RIP
JET SETTING	KEPT WICKET	LABOUR CLUB	LAYING BARE	LEVER WATCH
JEU DE PAUME	KERB MARKET	LACE PILLOW	LAYING DOWN	LEY FARMING
JEU DESPRIT	KERB TRADER	LACK LUSTRE	LAYING INTO	LIBERTY CAP
JEUNE FILLE	KERB VENDOR	LACTIC ACID	LAYING OPEN	LIE IN STATE
JEWEL HOUSE	KETTLE PINS	LADDER BACK	LAYS EYES ON	LIES FALLOW
JEWS HOUSES	KEW GARDENS	LADLING OUT	LAYS TO REST	LIES IN WAIT
JOCKEY CLUB	KEWPIE DOLL	LADY CHAPEL	LAZAR HOUSE	LIFE GIVING
JOCKEYS CAP	KEYHOLE SAW	LADY GODIVA	LE MOT JUSTE	LIFE GUARDS
JOIN FORCES	KHMER ROUGE	LADY KILLER	LEAD ASTRAY	LIFE JACKET
JOINT STOCK	KICK AROUND	LADYS SMOCK	LEAD GLANCE	LIFE MEMBER
JOLIE LAIDE	KICKING OFF	LAGS BEHIND	LEAD PENCIL	LIFE ROCKET
JOLLY ALONG	KICKING OUT	LAID EYES ON	LEAD PIPING	LIFE SAVING
JOLLY ROGER	KICKS ABOUT	LAID TO REST	LEAD THE WAY	LIFE SCHOOL
JOUR DE FETE	KID BROTHER	LAKE SCHOOL	LEADING MAN	LIFE TENANT
JOURNAL BOX	KID ONESELF	LAMBS TAILS	LEADING OFF	LIFTING OFF
JUGGED HARE	KIDNEY BEAN	LAMMAS TIDE	LEADING OUT	LIGHT ARMED
JULIAN YEAR	KILL OR CURE	LAMP BURNER	LEAF CUTTER	LIGHT HORSE
JUMBLE SALE	KILLED TIME	LANCET ARCH	LEAF HOPPER	LIGHT METER
JUMP FOR JOY	KILLING OFF	LAND BREEZE	LEAF INSECT	LIGHT MUSIC
JUMP STARTS	KINCHIN LAY	LAND BRIDGE	LEAF MOSAIC	LIGHT OPERA
JUMP THE GUN	KINETIC ART	LAND JOBBER	LEAGUE GAME	LIGHT ORGAN
JUMPED BAIL	KING ALFRED	LAND LOCKED	LEAKING OUT	LIGHT PROOF
JUMPED SHIP	KING ARTHUR	LAND LUBBER	LEAN WITTED	LIGHT TABLE
JUMPING OFF	KING CANUTE	LAND MINING	LEAP SECOND	LIGHT TOWER
JUNGLE FOWL	KING EDWARD	LAND OFFICE	LEAVE ALONE	LIGHT WATER
JUNIOR MISS	KING GEORGE	LAND OWNING	LEAVING OFF	LIGHTENS UP
JUNK DEALER	KING HAROLD	LAND PIRATE	LEAVING OUT	LIGHTING UP
JURY RIGGED	KING OF ARMS	LANGUE DOIL	LED CAPTAIN	LIKE BILLY O
JURY RUDDER	KING SALMON	LANTERN JAW	LEDGER BAIT	LIKE MINDED
JURY SYSTEM	KINGS BENCH	LAP JOINTED	LEDGER LINE	LIMBER NECK
JUST THE JOB	KINGS CHAIR	LAPPET MOTH	LEE ENFIELD	LIMBERED UP
KACK HANDED	KINGS SCOUT	LARGE ORDER	LEFT BEHIND	LIMPET MINE
KAFFIR CORN	KIPPED DOWN	LARGE SCALE	LEFT FOOTED	LINE FISHER
KARATE CHOP	KISS OF LIFE	LARKS ABOUT	LEFT HANDED	LINE OF LIFE
KEELED OVER	KITE FLYING	LASHING OUT	LEFT HANDER	LINEN PAPER
KEEN PRICES	KITH AND KIN	LASSA FEVER	LEFT UNSAID	LINK MOTION
KEEP IN MIND	KITTEN MOTH	LAST CHANCE	LEFT WINGER	LINSEED OIL
KEEP IT DARK	KLIEG LIGHT	LAST MAN OUT	LEG PULLING	LION HUNTER
KEEP TABS ON	KNEE LENGTH	LAST MINUTE	LEG SPINNER	LIONS MOUTH
KEEP WICKET	KNEW BETTER	LAST ORDERS	LEG WARMERS	LIONS SHARE
KEEPING FIT	KNICK KNACK	LAST RESORT	LEGACY DUTY	LIP READING
KEEPING MUM	KNIFE BOARD	LAST SUPPER	LEGAL EAGLE	LIP SERVICE
KEEPING OFF	KNIFE PLEAT	LATCHING ON	LEMON DROPS	LIQUOR LAWS
KEEPS AT BAY	KNIFE POINT	LATENT HEAT	LEMON JUICE	LISTENED IN
KEEPS CLEAR	KNIGHTS FEE	LATIN CROSS	LEMON THYME	LISTENER IN
KEEPS FAITH	KNOCK ABOUT	LATTER BORN	LENDS A HAND	LITANY DESK
	KNOCK IT OFF	LAUGH IT OFF	LENDS AN EAR	LITMUS TEST

10 LETTERS

10 *contd.*

LITTER LOUT
LITTLE BEAR
LITTLE JOHN
LIVED IN SIN
LIVED ON AIR
LIVER SALTS
LIVES IN SIN
LIVES ON AIR
LIVING A LIE
LIVING DOWN
LIVING IT UP
LIVING ROOM
LIVING WAGE
LIVING WELL
LIVING WILL
LOADED DICE
LOADING BAY
LOAN HOLDER
LOAN OFFICE
LOBSTER POT
LOCAL RADIO
LOCH LOMOND
LOCK KEEPER
LOCKED AWAY
LOCKER ROOM
LOCKING NUT
LOCKING OUT
LOCUST BEAN
LOG ROLLING
LOGAN STONE
LOGGING OUT
LONG HAIRED
LONG HEADED
LONG ISLAND
LONG LEGGED
LONG PLAYER
LONG TAILED
LONG WINDED
LOOK AGHAST
LOOK LIVELY
LOOK OUT MAN
LOOKED AWRY
LOOKED BACK
LOOKED DOWN
LOOKED INTO
LOOKED OVER
LOOKED UP TO
LOOKING FOR
LOOKING OUT
LOOKS A FOOL
LOOKS AFTER
LOOKS SMALL
LOOMS LARGE
LOOSE COVER
LOOSENED UP
LORD HELP US
LOSE COLOUR
LOSE GROUND
LOSE WEIGHT

LOSES COUNT
LOSES HEART
LOSES TOUCH
LOSES TRACK
LOSING FACE
LOSING GAME
LOSING TIME
LOSS LEADER
LOSS OF FACE
LOSS OF LIFE
LOST COLOUR
LOST GROUND
LOST TRIBES
LOST WEIGHT
LOTUS EATER
LOUD VOICED
LOUIS SEIZE
LOUNGE SUIT
LOUVRE DOOR
LOVE AFFAIR
LOVE BROKER
LOVE LETTER
LOVE POTION
LOVERS KNOT
LOVERS LANE
LOVERS LEAP
LOVEY DOVEY
LOVING CARE
LOW CEILING
LOW COUNTRY
LOW PITCHED
LOW PROFILE
LOW TENSION
LOWER CLASS
LOWER HOUSE
LUCKY BREAK
LUCKY CHARM
LUCKY PIECE
LUCKY STARS
LUCKY STONE
LUCY STONER
LUGGAGE VAN
LUMBER MILL
LUMBER ROOM
LUMBER YARD
LUNAR CYCLE
LUNAR MONTH
LUNCH BREAK
LUTINE BELL
LYDFORD LAW
LYDIAN MODE
LYING AWAKE
LYING UNDER
LYMPH GLAND
MACE BEARER
MACH NUMBER
MACHINE GUN
MADDER LAKE
MADE A POINT
MADE A STAND

MADE AMENDS
MADE EYES AT
MADE GROUND
MADE TRACKS
MAGIC CUBES
MAGIC SPELL
MAGNA CARTA
MAGNUM OPUS
MAID MARIAN
MAIDEN AUNT
MAIDEN NAME
MAIDEN OVER
MAIDEN PINK
MAIDEN RACE
MAILED FIST
MAIN ARTERY
MAIN CHANCE
MAIN CLAUSE
MAIN COURSE
MAIN STREAM
MAIN STREET
MAJOR SCALE
MAJOR THIRD
MAKE A POINT
MAKE A STAND
MAKE AMENDS
MAKE EYES AT
MAKE TRACKS
MAKE WEIGHT
MAKES A BOMB
MAKES A FACE
MAKES A MOVE
MAKES AFTER
MAKES FUN OF
MAKES HASTE
MAKES MERRY
MAKES MONEY
MAKES PEACE
MAKES READY
MAKES SENSE
MAKES USE OF
MAKES WAVES
MAKING A BED
MAKING AWAY
MAKING GOOD
MAKING IT UP
MAKING LOVE
MAKING OVER
MAKING PLAY
MAKING ROOM
MAKING SAIL
MAKING SURE
MAKING TIME
MALE RHYMES
MALLEE BIRD
MALLEE FOWL
MALT LIQUOR
MALT WHISKY
MALTA FEVER
MALTESE DOG

MAMMY WAGON
MAN AND WIFE
MAN OF STRAW
MAN SERVANT
MANILA HEMP
MANNA GRASS
MANOR HOUSE
MANY HEADED
MANY THANKS
MAP MOUNTER
MAP READING
MAPLE SUGAR
MAPLE SYRUP
MAPPING OUT
MARBLE ARCH
MARC BRANDY
MARCEL WAVE
MARCH WINDS
MARINE GLUE
MARINE SOAP
MARKED DOWN
MARKED TIME
MARKER BOMB
MARKER FLAG
MARKET BELL
MARKET HALL
MARKET TOWN
MARKING INK
MARKING OFF
MARKING OUT
MARRIED OFF
MARRIES OFF
MARROW BONE
MARSH FEVER
MARSH ROBIN
MARTIAL ART
MARTIAL LAW
MASKED BALL
MASS MEDIUM
MASS MURDER
MASS NUMBER
MASTER CARD
MASTER HAND
MASTER RACE
MASTER WORK
MATCH MAKER
MATCH POINT
MATRON LIKE
MAY BLOSSOM
MEADOW LARK
MEAL TICKET
MEAN STREAK
MEASURED UP
MEASURES UP
MEAT MARKET
MEDIUM TERM
MEDIUM WAVE
MELBA SAUCE
MELBA TOAST
MELLOWS OUT

MELTED AWAY
MELTED DOWN
MELTING POT
MEMORY BANK
MENTAL HOME
MENU DRIVEN
MERRY WIDOW
MERSEY BEAT
MESSAGE BOY
MET HALFWAY
MEXICAN TEA
MEZZO FORTE
MEZZO PIANO
MICKEY FINN
MID MORNING
MIDAS TOUCH
MIDDLE AGED
MIDDLE AGES
MIDDLE EAST
MIDDLE GAME
MIDDLE NAME
MIDDLE TERM
MIDDLE WEST
MILD SPOKEN
MILK BOTTLE
MILK OF LIME
MILKY WHITE
MILL STREAM
MILLET SEED
MIME ARTIST
MINCE WORDS
MIND BENDER
MIND HEALER
MIND READER
MINE HUNTER
MINE LAYING
MINE WORKER
MINERAL OIL
MINERS LAMP
MINI BUDGET
MINI BUFFET
MINI SERIES
MINIMAL ART
MINOR CANON
MINOR SCALE
MINOR THIRD
MINUTE BELL
MINUTE HAND
MISS THE BUS
MISSEL TREE
MISSING OUT
MISTED OVER
MITRE SHELL
MIXED GRILL
MIXED TRAIN
MIZZEN MAST
MIZZEN SAIL
MOBILE HOME
MOBILE SHOP
MOCHA STONE

10 *contd.*

MOCK HEROIC	MUSIC STAND	NEXT IN LINE	OBOE DAMORE	ON THE VERGE
MOCK MODEST	MUSIC STOOL	NIGHT CLOUD	OCEAN BASIN	ON THE WAGON
MOCK ORANGE	MUSICAL BOX	NIGHT GLASS	OCEAN GOING	ON THE WATCH
MOCK PRIVET	MUSK BEETLE	NIGHT LIGHT	OCEAN PERCH	ON THE WAY UP
MOCK TURTLE	MUSK ORCHID	NIGHT NURSE	ODD LOOKING	ON THE WHOLE
MODERN JAZZ	MUSK TURTLE	NIGHT RIDER	OFF BALANCE	ON YOUR BIKE
MONDAY CLUB	MUSKET SHOT	NIGHT SHIFT	OFF LICENCE	ONE ACT PLAY
MONEY MAKER	MUSSEL PLUM	NIGHT SIGHT	OFF ONES NUT	ONE ANOTHER
MONEY ORDER	MUSTARD GAS	NIGHT TRAIN	OFF PUTTING	ONE MAN BAND
MONEY TAKER	MUSTER BOOK	NIGHT WATCH	OFF SPINNER	ONE MAN SHOW
MONEY TALKS	MUSTER FILE	NIHIL AD REM	OFF THE CUFF	ONE NIGHTER
MONKEY BOAT	MUTTON CHOP	NINE OCLOCK	OFF THE FACE	ONE SIDEDLY
MONKEY NUTS	MUTTON FIST	NIP AND TUCK	OFF THE HOOK	ONE YEAR OLD
MONKEY PUMP	MUTTON HEAD	NIPPING OUT	OFF THE MARK	ONYX MARBLE
MONKEY ROPE	MUTUAL WALL	NIT PICKING	OFF THE REEL	OPEN ACCESS
MONKEY SUIT	MY FAIR LADY	NITRIC ACID	OFF THE WALL	OPEN HANDED
MONKEY TAIL	MY OLD DUTCH	NO MANS LAND	OFFERING UP	OPEN LETTER
MONKS CLOTH	MYSTERY MAN	NO NONSENSE	OFFICE GIRL	OPEN MARKET
MONTE CARLO	NAIL BITING	NO SUCH LUCK	OIL COLOURS	OPEN MINDED
MONTERO CAP	NAIL POLISH	NO THANK YOU	OIL OF THYME	OPEN PRISON
MOON FLOWER	NAILED DOWN	NOBEL PRIZE	OIL PAINTER	OPEN SEASON
MORAL SENSE	NAKED FLAME	NOBLE GASES	OLD COUNTRY	OPEN SECRET
MORE OR LESS	NAKED TRUTH	NOBLE HOUSE	OLD ENGLISH	OPEN SESAME
MORTAL COIL	NAMBY PAMBY	NOBLE METAL	OLD HUNDRED	OPEN SPACES
MOSS STITCH	NAME THE DAY	NOD THROUGH	OLD MASTERS	OPEN STITCH
MOTH FLOWER	NAMED NAMES	NODDING OFF	OLD SOLDIER	OPEN TOPPED
MOTHER CELL	NAMES NAMES	NOM DE PLUME	OLDE WORLDE	OPENING OUT
MOTHER CITY	NAPKIN RING	NOMINAL PAR	OLIVE GREEN	OPERA BUFFA
MOTHER LAND	NARROW BOAT	NOMINAL SUM	OMNIBUS BOX	OPERA CLOAK
MOTHER SHIP	NARROW SEAS	NON ALIGNED	ON ALL FOURS	OPERA GLASS
MOTHER TO BE	NATIVE BORN	NON CONTENT	ON APPROVAL	OPERA HOUSE
MOTHERS DAY	NATIVE LAND	NON FERROUS	ON FURLOUGH	OPERA SERIA
MOTOR COACH	NATURAL GAS	NON FICTION	ON LOCATION	OPIUM EATER
MOTOR CYCLE	NATURAL LAW	NON MEMBERS	ON OCCASION	OPIUM POPPY
MOTOR LORRY	NATURE CURE	NON PAYMENT	ON ONES MIND	OPTIC NERVE
MOUNT GUARD	NATURE MYTH	NON PLAYING	ON ONES TOES	ORANGE LILY
MOUNT OLIVE	NAUTCH GIRL	NON SMOKING	ON SCHEDULE	ORANGE PEEL
MOUNT SINAI	NAVAL CROWN	NON STARTER	ON THE BENCH	ORANGE ROOT
MOUTH ORGAN	NECK OF LAMB	NON SWIMMER	ON THE BLINK	ORANGE TREE
MOVED HOUSE	NECK OF LAND	NON VIOLENT	ON THE BLOCK	ORANGE WOOD
MOVES HOUSE	NEEDLE CASE	NORTH BOUND	ON THE BRAIN	ORDER ABOUT
MOVING AWAY	NEEDLE FISH	NORTH POLAR	ON THE BRINK	ORDER PAPER
MOVING BACK	NEER DO WELL	NORWAY PINE	ON THE CARDS	ORIONS BELT
MOVING OVER	NERVE AGENT	NOSE TO TAIL	ON THE CHEAP	OSTRICH EGG
MR UNIVERSE	NERVE FIBRE	NOT EXACTLY	ON THE CROSS	OTHER RANKS
MUCK RAKING	NESTING BOX	NOT FOR SALE	ON THE FENCE	OTTER HOUND
MUD SLINGER	NET FISHING	NOT TO WORRY	ON THE FRITZ	OTTER SHREW
MUD VOLCANO	NETTLE FISH	NOTE OF HAND	ON THE HOUSE	OUIJA BOARD
MUDDLING UP	NETTLE RASH	NOTHING BUT	ON THE LATCH	OUT AT ELBOW
MUFFIN BELL	NEVER NEVER	NOUN CLAUSE	ON THE LEVEL	OUT DWELLER
MULTI STAGE	NEW EDITION	NOW AND THEN	ON THE LOOSE	OUT OF COURT
MULTI TRACK	NEW ENGLAND	NUCLEAR WAR	ON THE MARCH	OUT OF DOORS
MUMBO JUMBO	NEW MOWN HAY	NUDGE NUDGE	ON THE PROWL	OUT OF FOCUS
MUMMY CLOTH	NEW ORLEANS	NUDIST CAMP	ON THE QUIET	OUT OF JOINT
MUNTZ METAL	NEW ZEALAND	NUMBER NINE	ON THE ROCKS	OUT OF ORDER
MURPHYS LAW	NEWS AGENCY	NURSE CHILD	ON THE ROPES	OUT OF PLACE
MUSCLING IN	NEWS VENDOR	NURSE SHARK	ON THE SHELF	OUT OF PRINT
MUSIC HOUSE	NEWS WRITER	OATH TAKING	ON THE SLATE	OUT OF REACH
MUSIC PAPER	NEXT FRIEND	OBJECT BALL	ON THE STUMP	OUT OF SHAPE
		OBJETS DART	ON THE TILES	OUT OF SIGHT

10 *contd.*

OUT OF SORTS
OUT OF STOCK
OUT OF SYNCH
OUT OF TOUCH
OUT ON A LIMB
OUT PATIENT
OUT PENSION
OUTER SPACE
OVEN GLOVES
OVER AND OUT
OVER THE TOP
OVERDOES IT
OWNERS RISK
OX ANTELOPE
OX EYE DAISY
OXFORD BAGS
OXFORD BLUE
OXFORD SHOE
OXTAIL SOUP
OXYGEN MAST
OXYGEN TENT
OYSTER BANK
OZONE LAYER
PACE BOWLER
PACE SETTER
PACIFIC RIM
PACK A PUNCH
PACK ANIMAL
PACK SADDLE
PACKED IT IN
PACKED IT UP
PACKET BOAT
PACKET SHIP
PACKING BOX
PAD THE HOOF
PADDED CELL
PADDING OUT
PADDLE BOAT
PADDLE WOOD
PADDY FIELD
PADDY WHACK
PAGE PROOFS
PAGE TURNER
PAGODA TREE
PAID A VISIT
PAID HOMAGE
PAID IN FULL
PAID IN KIND
PAIN KILLER
PAINT BRUSH
PAIRING OFF
PALL BEARER
PALM BRANCH
PALM BUTTER
PALM GREASE
PALM KERNEL
PALM SUNDAY
PALSY WALSY
PAN AFRICAN

PAN ARABISM
PAN SLAVISM
PANCAKE DAY
PANEL TRUCK
PANTON SHOE
PAPAL BRIEF
PAPAL CROSS
PAPER CHAIN
PAPER CHASE
PAPER CLIPS
PAPER CLOTH
PAPER GAUGE
PAPER KNIFE
PAPER MAKER
PAPER MONEY
PAPER ROUND
PAPER TIGER
PAPERS OVER
PAR EXEMPLE
PARA RUBBER
PARANA PINE
PARCEL BOMB
PARCEL POST
PARENTS DAY
PARI MUTUEL
PARIS GREEN
PARISH PUMP
PARK KEEPER
PARKING BAY
PARKING LOT
PARLOUR CAR
PARPEN WALL
PARROT BEAK
PARROT BILL
PARROT FISH
PARSON BIRD
PARTING CUP
PARTY FUNDS
PARTY GOING
PARTY TRICK
PARVO VIRUS
PAS DE TROIS
PASS MUSTER
PASSED AWAY
PASSED OVER
PASSED PAWN
PASSES AWAY
PASSES OVER
PASSING OFF
PASSING OUT
PAST MASTER
PASTE GRAIN
PASTRY COOK
PASTY FACED
PATCHING UP
PATTER SONG
PAVE THE WAY
PAY ONES WAY
PAY STATION
PAYING BACK

PAYING CASH
PAYS A VISIT
PAYS HOMAGE
PAYS IN FULL
PAYS IN KIND
PEA TRAINER
PEACE CORPS
PEACE ENVOY
PEACE OF GOD
PEACE PARTY
PEACH BLOOM
PEACH MELBA
PEACH STONE
PEACH WATER
PEAK PERIOD
PEAR SHAPED
PEARL DIVER
PEARL SHELL
PEARL STONE
PEARL WHITE
PEARLY KING
PEASE BROSE
PEAT CASTER
PEAU DE SOIE
PEBBLE DASH
PEBBLE WARE
PECTIC ACID
PEDAL BOARD
PEDAL CYCLE
PEDAL ORGAN
PEDAL POINT
PEEL AND EAT
PEELING OFF
PEEPING OUT
PEEPING TOM
PEG TANKARD
PEGGED AWAY
PEGGED BACK
PEGGED DOWN
PEGGING OUT
PEN FEATHER
PEN PUSHING
PENALTY BOX
PENCIL CASE
PENCIL LEAD
PENNY A LINE
PENNY BLACK
PENNY PIECE
PENNY PINCH
PENNY PLAIN
PENNY SHARE
PENNY STONE
PENSION OFF
PEPPER CAKE
PEPPER TREE
PERIOD PLAY
PERSIAN CAT
PET SITTING
PETER SEE ME
PETIT POINT

PETITS POIS
PETRI PLATE
PETROL BLUE
PETROL BOMB
PETROL PUMP
PETROL TANK
PEWTER MILL
PHASING OUT
PHRASE BOOK
PIANO ORGAN
PIANO STOOL
PICK A FIGHT
PICK AND MIX
PICK CHEESE
PICK POCKET
PICKED OVER
PICKET DUTY
PICKET LINE
PICKING OFF
PICKING OUT
PICKLED EGG
PICKS A LOCK
PICKS HOLES
PICTURE ROD
PIE COUNTER
PIE DIAGRAM
PIECE GOODS
PIECING OUT
PIED A TERRE
PIEDS NOIRS
PIETRA DURA
PIG IN A POKE
PIG STICKER
PIGEON HOLE
PIGEON PAIR
PIGEON POST
PIGEON TOED
PIGEON WING
PILE DRIVER
PILING IT ON
PILLAR ROOT
PILLOW BERE
PILLOW LACE
PILLOW TALK
PILOT CLOTH
PILOT HOUSE
PILOT LIGHT
PILOT WHALE
PIN CUSHION
PIN FEATHER
PIN STRIPED
PINA COLADA
PINCE NEZED
PINE BARREN
PINE BEAUTY
PINE BEETLE
PINE FOREST
PINE KERNEL
PINE MARTEN
PINE NEEDLE

PINEAL BODY
PINT OF BEER
PINT OF MILK
PIOUS FRAUD
PIPE FITTER
PIPE LAYING
PIPE OPENER
PIPE WRENCH
PIPED MUSIC
PIPING CROW
PIPING DOWN
PIPING HARE
PIRATE SHIP
PISTOL SHOT
PISTOL WHIP
PISTON RING
PIT VILLAGE
PITCH A TENT
PITCH BLACK
PITCH WHEEL
PITCHING IN
PITH HELMET
PITTA BREAD
PIXIE STOOL
PLACED A BET
PLACES A BET
PLAGUE SORE
PLAGUE SPOT
PLAID CYMRU
PLAIN CHANT
PLAIN TRUTH
PLANE CHART
PLANE CRASH
PLANE TABLE
PLANS AHEAD
PLANT HOUSE
PLANT LOUSE
PLANTED OUT
PLASTIC ART
PLASTIC BAG
PLASTIC MAC
PLAT DU JOUR
PLATE GLASS
PLATE LAYER
PLATE PROOF
PLAY ACTING
PLAY AROUND
PLAY HOOKEY
PLAY IT COOL
PLAY POSSUM
PLAY TRICKS
PLAY TRUANT
PLAY WRITER
PLAYED BACK
PLAYED BALL
PLAYED DOWN
PLAYED FAIR
PLAYED HOST
PLAYED SAFE
PLAYING OFF

10 *contd.*

PLAYING OUT	POSTAL CARD	PRETTY MUCH	PULLS A FACE	QUEEN SIZED
PLAYS A PART	POSTAL CODE	PRETTY PASS	PULLS AHEAD	QUEENS WARE
PLAYS ABOUT	POSTAL NOTE	PRETTY WELL	PULLS APART	QUEUE JUMPS
PLAYS FALSE	POSTAL TUBE	PRICE INDEX	PULP CAVITY	QUICK FIRER
PLAYS HAVOC	POSTAL VOTE	PRICE LEVEL	PULP ENGINE	QUICK MARCH
PLAYS TO WIN	POT BELLIED	PRICK EARED	PUMP ACTION	QUICK MATCH
PLOUGH BACK	POT BOILING	PRICK LOUSE	PUMP HANDLE	QUICK STICK
PLOUGH IRON	POT HUNTING	PRIEST HOLE	PUMPED IRON	QUICK TRICK
PLOUGH TAIL	POT OF MONEY	PRIEST KING	PUMPING OUT	QUICKENS UP
PLOUGH TEAM	POTATO PEEL	PRIEST LIKE	PUNCH DRUNK	QUID PRO QUO
PLOUGH TREE	POTATO RING	PRIMA DONNA	PUNCH LADLE	QUINIC ACID
PLOUGHED IN	POTTY CHAIR	PRIMA FACIE	PUNK ROCKER	QUINK GOOSE
PLOVERS EGG	POUCHED RAT	PRIME MOVER	PUNTO BANCO	QUINSY WORT
PLUG SOCKET	POUNCET BOX	PRINT WORKS	PUPPET PLAY	QUINT MAJOR
PLUGGING IN	POUNCING ON	PRINTED OUT	PUPPET SHOW	QUINT MINOR
PLUME GRASS	POUND FORCE	PRISON BARS	PURE REASON	QUITE RIGHT
PLUNGE BATH	POURING OUT	PRISON CAMP	PURE SILVER	QUIZ MASTER
PLURAL VOTE	POURS FORTH	PRISON CELL	PURPLE BORN	QUONSET HUT
PLUS STRAIN	POUSSE CAFE	PRISON DOOR	PURPLE FISH	RABBIT HOLE
POACHED EGG	POWDER BLUE	PRISON SHIP	PURPLE HUED	RABBIT SKIN
POCKET BOOK	POWDER DOWN	PRISON YARD	PURSE SEINE	RACCOON DOG
POCKET COMB	POWDER MILL	PRIVATE ACT	PUSH AROUND	RACE COURSE
POCKET HOLE	POWDER PUFF	PRIVATE BUS	PUSH BUTTON	RACE MEMORY
POINT BLANK	POWDER ROOM	PRIVATE EYE	PUSH STARTS	RACE WALKER
POINT FACED	POWER BLOCK	PRIVATE LAW	PUSH STROKE	RACK RENTER
POINT TAKEN	POWER DRILL	PRIVATE WAR	PUSHED PAST	RACKET TAIL
POINTED OUT	POWER HOUSE	PRIVY PURSE	PUSHES PAST	RADIAL TYRE
POINTING UP	POWER LATHE	PRIZE COURT	PUSHING OFF	RADIO TIMES
POISON FANG	POWER PLANT	PRIZE FIGHT	PUSHING OUT	RADIO WAVES
POISON PILL	POWER POINT	PRIZE MONEY	PUT A STOP TO	RADIUM BOMB
POKE BONNET	PRAIRIE DOG	PRO TEMPORE	PUT AN END TO	RAFT BRIDGE
POKED FUN AT	PRAYER BEAD	PROMPT BOOK	PUT AND TAKE	RAFTER BIRD
POKER FACED	PRAYER BOOK	PROMPT COPY	PUT FORWARD	RAGGED LADY
POKES FUN AT	PRE ELECTED	PROMPT NOTE	PUT ON AN ACT	RAIN DOCTOR
POLES APART	PRE EMINENT	PROMPT SIDE	PUT ON TRIAL	RAIN FOREST
POLISHED UP	PRE EMPTING	PROOF HOUSE	PUT PUTTING	RAIN MAKING
POLISHES UP	PRE EMPTION	PROOF READS	PUT THE SHOT	RAIN SHOWER
POLL PARROT	PRE EMPTIVE	PROOF SHEET	PUT THROUGH	RAISE ALOFT
POLLEN TUBE	PRE EXISTED	PROPER NAME	PUT TO DEATH	RAISE MONEY
POLLING DAY	PRE GLACIAL	PROPER NOUN	PUT TO SHAME	RAISED CAIN
POLO PLAYER	PRE QUALIFY	PROPPING UP	PUT TO SLEEP	RAISED HELL
POME CITRON	PRE SELLING	PROTON BEAM	PUTS ACROSS	RAISES CAIN
POMPOUS ASS	PRE SHRINKS	PROUD FLESH	PUTS ON AIRS	RAISES HELL
PONY ENGINE	PRE TENSION	PSYCHIC BID	PUTS PAID TO	RAJYA SABHA
POOR RELIEF	PRE WASHING	PSYCHING UP	PUTS UP WITH	RALLY CROSS
POP CONCERT	PREACH DOWN	PUBLIC BILL	PUTTING OFF	RALLY ROUND
POPLAR TREE	PREACHED AT	PUBLIC SALE	PUTTING OUT	RAN ERRANDS
POPPING OFF	PREACHED UP	PUCKA SAHIB	PUTTY FACED	RAN THE SHOW
POPPING OUT	PREACHES AT	PUCKERED UP	PUTTY KNIFE	RAN THROUGH
POPPY WATER	PREACHES UP	PUDDING BAG	PUZZLE BOOK	RAN TO EARTH
PORK BARREL	PREEN GLAND	PUDDING PIE	PUZZLE HEAD	RANGING ROD
PORK PIE HAT	PREMIER CRU	PUFF PASTRY	QUAI DORSAY	RANK RIDING
PORT DE BRAS	PREP SCHOOL	PULLED AWAY	QUAKER BIRD	RAP SESSION
PORT OF CALL	PRESENT DAY	PULLED BACK	QUAKING ASH	RARING TO GO
PORTAL VEIN	PRESS AGENT	PULLED DOWN	QUARRY TILE	RASCAL LIKE
POST BELLUM	PRESS AHEAD	PULLED OVER	QUARTER BOY	RAT CATCHER
POST CHAISE	PRESS GANGS	PULLED RANK	QUARTER DAY	RAT HUNTING
POST MODERN	PRESS MONEY	PULLING OFF	QUARTER ILL	RATE CAPPED
POST MORTEM	PRESS PROOF	PULLING OUT	QUARTZ MILL	RATION BOOK
POST OFFICE	PRESSING ON	PULLMAN CAR	QUARTZ ROCK	

10 *contd.*

RATION CARD	RHYME ROYAL	ROBING ROOM	ROUGH HOUSE	RUNNER BEAN
RATTLE HEAD	RIB ROASTER	ROCK BADGER	ROUGH RIDER	RUNNING DOG
RATTLE PATE	RIB TICKLER	ROCK BOTTOM	ROUGH STUFF	RUNNING DRY
RATTLING ON	RIBBON FISH	ROCK GARDEN	ROUGH TRADE	RUNNING GAG
RAVENS BONE	RIBBON SEAL	ROCK HOPPER	ROUGHED OUT	RUNNING LOW
RAVENS DUCK	RICK BARTON	ROCK LIZARD	ROUGHING IN	RUNNING OFF
RAW RECRUIT	RICK LIFTER	ROCK OF AGES	ROUGHING IT	RUNNING OUT
RAZOR BLADE	RIDE A HOBBY	ROCK PIGEON	ROUND ABOUT	RUNS ACROSS
RAZOR SHARP	RIDE AND TIE	ROCK SALMON	ROUND DANCE	RUNS SCARED
RAZOR SHELL	RIDGE PIECE	ROCK STEADY	ROUND DOZEN	RUNS TO SEED
RAZOR STROP	RIDING BOOT	ROCK TURBOT	ROUND EARED	RUSH CANDLE
REACHED OUT	RIDING COAT	ROCK VIOLET	ROUND FACED	RUSH HOLDER
REACHES OUT	RIDING CROP	ROGUE MONEY	ROUND HOUSE	RUSSIAN TEA
READ MY LIPS	RIDING DOWN	ROLLED GOLD	ROUND NOSED	RUST BUCKET
READING AGE	RIDING HIGH	ROLLED OVER	ROUND ROBIN	RUST FUNGUS
READING OFF	RIDING HOOD	ROLLING PIN	ROUND TABLE	RUSTIC SEAT
READING OUT	RIDING ROBE	ROLLS ALONG	ROUND TOWER	RUSTIC WARE
READS ALOUD	RIDING SUIT	ROLLS OF FAT	ROUNDED OFF	RUSTIC WORK
READY MONEY	RIDING WHIP	ROLLS ROYCE	ROUNDED OUT	RUSTLING UP
READY TO EAT	RIFLE CORPS	ROMAN A CLEF	ROUNDING ON	SABBATH DAY
READY TO SEW	RIFLE GREEN	ROMAN BATHS	ROUNDING UP	SABRE TOOTH
REAL ESTATE	RIFLE RANGE	ROMAN SNAIL	ROUNDS DOWN	SACK OF COAL
REAL NUMBER	RIFT VALLEY	ROMAN VILLA	ROUTE MARCH	SACRED FISH
REAL SCHOOL	RIGGING OUT	ROMPED HOME	ROVER SCOUT	SAD HEARTED
REAL TENNIS	RIGHT ABOUT	ROMPER SUIT	ROWAN BERRY	SADDLE ROOF
REAMING BIT	RIGHT DRAWN	ROOD SCREEN	ROWDY DOWDY	SADDLE ROOM
RECKONED ON	RIGHT OF WAY	ROOF GARDEN	ROWING BOAT	SADDLE SOAP
RECKONED UP	RIGHT WHALE	ROOM FELLOW	ROWING CLUB	SADDLE SORE
RED ADMIRAL	RIGHT WHEEL	ROOT PRUNED	ROYAL ASCOT	SADDLE TREE
RED BLOODED	RING BINDER	ROOT PRUNES	ROYAL BARGE	SADDLING UP
RED BRIGADE	RING FINGER	ROOT RUBBER	ROYAL BURGH	SAFARI PARK
RED CABBAGE	RING MASTER	ROOT SYSTEM	ROYAL FLUSH	SAFARI SUIT
RED FIGURED	RING NECKED	ROOTING OUT	ROYAL HOUSE	SAFE BLOWER
RED HERRING	RING PLOVER	ROPE DANCER	ROYAL ICING	SAFETY BELT
RED JASMINE	RING ROLLER	ROPE LADDER	ROYAL JELLY	SAFETY BOLT
RED MURRAIN	RING TAILED	ROPE MAKING	ROYAL VISIT	SAFETY CAGE
RED SANDERS	RINGING OFF	ROPE STITCH	ROYAL YACHT	SAFETY FILM
RED SEAWEED	RINGS A BELL	ROPE WALKER	RUB A DUB DUB	SAFETY FUSE
RED SNAPPER	RINSING OUT	ROSE BEETLE	RUB OFF ON TO	SAFETY LAMP
REDDING OUT	RIOT POLICE	ROSE COMBED	RUBBED DOWN	SAFETY LOCK
REED THRUSH	RIP ROARING	ROSE GARDEN	RUBBED IT IN	SAFETY PLUG
REELING OFF	RIPPING OFF	ROSE LAUREL	RUBBER BAND	SAFETY WEAR
REFORM BILL	RIPPING SAW	ROSE LIPPED	RUBBER NECK	SAGE CHEESE
REGENT BIRD	RIPPLE MARK	ROSE MALLOW	RUBBER SOLE	SAGE GROUSE
REJOICED IN	RISING TIDE	ROSE QUARTZ	RUBBER SUIT	SAGE RABBIT
REJOICES IN	RIVER BASIN	ROSE TINTED	RUBBER TREE	SAIL FLYING
REMAND HOME	RIVER CRAFT	ROSE WINDOW	RUBBING OUT	SAIL MAKING
REMOVAL VAN	RIVER DRIFT	ROSIN PLANT	RUBBLE WORK	SAILOR LIKE
RENT A CROWD	RIVER HORSE	ROTARY CLUB	RUBIKS CUBE	SAILOR SUIT
RENT AN ARMY	RIVER MOUTH	ROTOR PLANE	RUBY SILVER	SAILS ALONG
REPAIR SHOP	RIVER WATER	ROUEN CROSS	RUDDER FISH	SAINT DAVID
REPORT BACK	ROAD BRIDGE	ROUGE CROIX	RUE BARGAIN	SAINT PETER
REPRO PROOF	ROAD MAKING	ROUGH CIDER	RUGBY UNION	SAL ATTICUM
REST CENTRE	ROAD MENDER	ROUGH DRAFT	RUIN MARBLE	SALAD CREAM
RETIRED PAY	ROAD ROLLER	ROUGH DRIED	RUM RUNNING	SALAD PLANT
REVIEW BODY	ROAD RUNNER	ROUGH DRIES	RUMPUS ROOM	SALAD PLATE
REVIEW COPY	ROAD SAFETY	ROUGH GUESS	RUN ERRANDS	SALE OF WORK
RH NEGATIVE	ROAD TESTED	ROUGH GUIDE	RUN THE SHOW	SALES CLERK
RH POSITIVE	ROAD TO RUIN	ROUGH HEWER	RUN THROUGH	SALES DRIVE
	ROBBER CRAB	ROUGH HOUND	RUN TO EARTH	SALMON LEAP

10 contd.
SALMON PINK
SALOON DECK
SALT BUTTER
SALT CELLAR
SALTED AWAY
SALTED DOWN
SAMIAN WARE
SAND BINDER
SAND BUNKER
SAND CASTLE
SAND GROUSE
SAND HOPPER
SAND LIZARD
SAND MARTIN
SAND PLOUGH
SAND SUCKER
SANTA CLAUS
SASH WINDOW
SATIN PAPER
SAUCER EYED
SAUSAGE DOG
SAVAGE BLOW
SAVING FACE
SAVING GAME
SAVING TIME
SAW TOOTHED
SAXON SHORE
SAXONY BLUE
SAY A PRAYER
SCALDED CAT
SCALE BOARD
SCALE MODEL
SCARF JOINT
SCARLET HAT
SCATTER GUN
SCENE THREE
SCENT GLAND
SCENT ORGAN
SCENT SPRAY
SCHICK TEST
SCHISM SHOP
SCHOOL BELL
SCHOOL BOOK
SCHOOL DAME
SCHOOL FEES
SCHOOL MAAM
SCHOOL MARM
SCHOOL MATE
SCHOOL MISS
SCHOOL SONG
SCHOOL TERM
SCHOOL TIME
SCHOOL WORK
SCHOOL YEAR
SCISSOR CUT
SCISSOR LEG
SCOOPED OUT
SCORE A GOAL
SCORE BOARD

SCORING OFF
SCOT AND LOT
SCOTCH HAND
SCOTCH KALE
SCOTCH MIST
SCOTCH PINE
SCOTCH ROSE
SCOTCH SNAP
SCOTCH TAPE
SCOTS GREYS
SCOTTIE DOG
SCOUT ROUND
SCOUTS PACE
SCRAP METAL
SCRAPED OFF
SCRAPES OFF
SCRATCH PAD
SCRATCH WIG
SCREECH OWL
SCREEN TEST
SCREENS OFF
SCREW PLATE
SCREW PRESS
SCRIP ISSUE
SCRUB ROUND
SCRUBBED UP
SCUBA DIVER
SEA ANEMONE
SEA BATHING
SEA BISCUIT
SEA CABBAGE
SEA CAPTAIN
SEA FISHING
SEA GODDESS
SEA KEEPING
SEA LEOPARD
SEA MONSTER
SEA PASSAGE
SEA POACHER
SEA SERPENT
SEA SERVICE
SEA SOLDIER
SEA SURGEON
SEA UNICORN
SEA WHISTLE
SEAL FISHER
SEALED BEAM
SEALED BOOK
SEALING DAY
SEALING OFF
SEALING WAX
SEAM BOWLER
SECOND BEST
SECOND HAND
SECOND HOME
SECOND MARK
SECOND RATE
SECOND SELF
SECOND WIND
SECONDS OUT

SECULAR ARM
SECURE UNIT
SEDAN CHAIR
SEE THROUGH
SEED OYSTER
SEED POTATO
SEED VESSEL
SEEING LIFE
SEEING OVER
SEEING TO IT
SEEKING OUT
SEEKS AFTER
SEES THINGS
SELF ACTION
SELF DECEIT
SELF DENIAL
SELF DRIVEN
SELF ESTEEM
SELF HATRED
SELF PARODY
SELF PRAISE
SELF REGARD
SELF ROLLED
SELF RULING
SELF SEEKER
SELF STYLED
SELF TAUGHT
SELF WILLED
SELL BY DATE
SELL IN BULK
SELLING OFF
SELLING OUT
SELLS SHORT
SEMI ANNUAL
SEMI DIVINE
SEMI LIQUID
SEMI LUNATE
SEMI OPAQUE
SEMI WEEKLY
SEMPER IDEM
SENDING OFF
SENDING OUT
SENSE DATUM
SENSE ORGAN
SEPTIC TANK
SERBO CROAT
SERIAL TIME
SERPENT GOD
SERVANT MAN
SERVED TIME
SERVES TIME
SERVING OUT
SERVO MOTOR
SESAME SEED
SET AGAINST
SET IN ORDER
SET LIGHT TO
SET THE PACE
SET TO MUSIC
SET UP HOUSE

SETS ALIGHT
SETS EYES ON
SETS FIRE TO
SETS IN HAND
SETS ON EDGE
SETS ON FIRE
SETS TO WORK
SETS UP SHOP
SETTING OFF
SETTING OUT
SETTLE DOWN
SETTLING IN
SETTLING UP
SEVEN A SIDE
SEVEN SAGES
SEVEN STARS
SEVENTH DAY
SEWAGE FARM
SHADE PLANT
SHADOW MARK
SHADOW PLAY
SHAFT HORSE
SHAGGY MANE
SHAKE HANDS
SHAKES A LEG
SHAKES DOWN
SHAKING OFF
SHAKING OUT
SHALE MINER
SHAME ON YOU
SHANTY TOWN
SHARE PRICE
SHARING OUT
SHARP EDGED
SHARP NOSED
SHEAR STEEL
SHEATH BILL
SHEATH FISH
SHEDS A TEAR
SHEEP FACED
SHEEP LOUSE
SHEEP TRACK
SHEEPS HEAD
SHEERED OFF
SHEET GLASS
SHEET METAL
SHEET MUSIC
SHEET OF ICE
SHELL MONEY
SHELLED OUT
SHIELD HAND
SHIELD MAID
SHIFT ABOUT
SHIN BARKER
SHIN OF BEEF
SHIP LETTER
SHIP MASTER
SHIP RIGGED
SHIPS WATER
SHIRE HORSE

SHIRE REEVE
SHIRT FRILL
SHIRT FRONT
SHISH KEBAB
SHOCK PROOF
SHOCK STALL
SHOE BUCKLE
SHOE POLISH
SHOOK HANDS
SHOOT A LINE
SHOOT CRAPS
SHOOT IT OUT
SHOOTING UP
SHOOTS DOWN
SHOOTS HOME
SHOP AROUND
SHOP LIFTER
SHOP SOILED
SHOP WALKER
SHOP WINDOW
SHORE GOING
SHORE LEAVE
SHORT COATS
SHORT LISTS
SHORT LIVED
SHORT METRE
SHORT RANGE
SHORT TRACK
SHORT WHIST
SHOT PUTTER
SHOUTS DOWN
SHOVEL HEAD
SHOVING OFF
SHOW THE WAY
SHOWED A LEG
SHOWER BATH
SHOWING OFF
SHOWS FIGHT
SHOWS FORTH
SHRIMP GIRL
SHRIVELS UP
SHUFFLE CAP
SHUFFLE OFF
SHUT UP SHOP
SHUTTING IN
SHUTTING UP
SIAMESE CAT
SICK AS A DOG
SICK LISTED
SICK MAKING
SIDE BY SIDE
SIDE EFFECT
SIDE OF BEEF
SIDE SADDLE
SIDE STREET
SIDE STROKE
SIDE TRACKS
SIEGE PIECE
SIEGE TRAIN
SIEGE WORKS

10 *contd.*

SIGHT READS	SLEEP TIGHT	SNIFFED OUT	SOURCE BOOK	SPRING HARE
SIGHT SINGS	SLEEPING IN	SNIFFER DOG	SOUTH BOUND	SPRING LOCK
SIGN MANUAL	SLEEPING ON	SNOW CAPPED	SOUTH POLAR	SPRING ROLL
SIGN WRITER	SLEEPY HEAD	SNOW PLOUGH	SOW THE SEED	SPRING TIDE
SIGNED AWAY	SLEEVE LINK	SNUFF BROWN	SOW THISTLE	SPRUCE PINE
SIGNED COPY	SLEIGH BELL	SNUFF MOVIE	SPACE PROBE	SPUR HEELED
SIGNET RING	SLEIGH RIDE	SNUFF SPOON	SPACING OUT	SQUARE DEAL
SIGNING OFF	SLEPT ROUGH	SNUFF TAKER	SPADE BEARD	SQUARE FOOT
SIGNING OUT	SLIDE VALVE	SNUFFED OUT	SPANISH FLY	SQUARE INCH
SILK COTTON	SLIME MOULD	SNUFFING IT	SPARE PARTS	SQUARE KNOT
SILK SCREEN	SLING BACKS	SNUGGLED UP	SPARK PLUGS	SQUARE MEAL
SILLY BILLY	SLING FRUIT	SNUGGLES UP	SPARKED OFF	SQUARE MILE
SILLY GOOSE	SLIP STITCH	SOAKING WET	SPARKED OUT	SQUARE ROOT
SILLY MID ON	SLIP STREAM	SOAP BOILER	SPEAKING UP	SQUARE SAIL
SILLY POINT	SLIP STRING	SOAP BUBBLE	SPEAR POINT	SQUARE TOED
SILVER COIN	SLIPPED OFF	SOAP FLAKES	SPEAR SHAFT	SQUARE TOES
SILVER FISH	SLIPPING ON	SOAP POWDER	SPECTRE BAT	SQUARE YARD
SILVER FOIL	SLIPPING UP	SOBERING UP	SPEED LIMIT	SQUARING UP
SILVER LEAF	SLIT POCKET	SOCIAL EVIL	SPEEDING UP	SQUEEZE BOX
SILVER TRAY	SLIT TRENCH	SOCIAL WORK	SPELL IT OUT	SQUINT EYED
SILVER TREE	SLOOP OF WAR	SOCK IT TO ME	SPELT IT OUT	SQUINT EYES
SIMMER DOWN	SLOPED ARMS	SODA JERKER	SPENT FORCE	SQUIRE LIKE
SIMNEL CAKE	SLOPES ARMS	SODA SIPHON	SPERM WHALE	ST JOHNS DAY
SINE QUA NON	SLOPING OFF	SODIUM LAMP	SPHINX MOTH	ST STEPHENS
SINGING OUT	SLOPPED OUT	SOFT BOILED	SPIDER CRAB	ST TIBBS EVE
SINGLE EYED	SLOW FOOTED	SOFT FRUITS	SPIDERS WEB	ST TRINIANS
SINGLE FILE	SLOW MOTION	SOFT HEADED	SPIKE GRASS	STABLE GIRL
SINGLES BAR	SLOW MOVING	SOFT OPTION	SPILLS OVER	STABLE ROOM
SINGS ALONG	SLOW WINGED	SOFT PALATE	SPIN BOWLER	STACKING UP
SINK OR SWIM	SLOWED DOWN	SOFT PEDALS	SPIN DRYING	STAFF CORPS
SINN FEINER	SLUICE GATE	SOFT SOAPED	SPINAL CORD	STAFF NURSE
SISAL GRASS	SLUSH MONEY	SOFT SPOKEN	SPINDLE OIL	STAG BEETLE
SITTING OUT	SMALL CRAFT	SOFTENED UP	SPINEL RUBY	STAGE CRAFT
SIX SHOOTER	SMALL HOURS	SOKA GAKKAI	SPINS A YARN	STAGE FEVER
SIXTH SENSE	SMALL PRINT	SOLAR FLARE	SPIRIT BLUE	STAGE HORSE
SKATE ROUND	SMALL SWORD	SOLAR MONTH	SPIRIT LAMP	STAGE RIGHT
SKATED OVER	SMALL WARES	SOLAR PANEL	SPLASH BACK	STAGE WAGON
SKATES OVER	SMART ALICK	SOLAR POWER	SPLASH DOWN	STAIR TOWER
SKENE OCCLE	SMART MONEY	SOLD IN BULK	SPLINT BONE	STAKE MONEY
SKETCH BOOK	SMELLS A RAT	SOLDIERS ON	SPLINT COAL	STAKING OUT
SKI BOBBING	SMOCK FROCK	SOLEMN MASS	SPLIT HAIRS	STALL FEEDS
SKI JUMPING	SMOKE ALARM	SOLID STATE	SPLIT IMAGE	STAMP ALBUM
SKI RUNNING	SMOKE BOARD	SON AND HEIR	SPLIT LEVEL	STAMP HINGE
SKIN DIVING	SMOKE DRIED	SONATA FORM	SPLIT SHIFT	STAMP PAPER
SKINS ALIVE	SMOKE DRIES	SONG THRUSH	SPODE CHINA	STAMPED OUT
SKIPPING IT	SMOKE STACK	SORBIC ACID	SPOIL SPORT	STAND ALONE
SKIRT ROUND	SMOKING CAP	SORE THROAT	SPONGE BATH	STAND AT BAY
SKITTLE OUT	SMOKING OUT	SORTING OUT	SPONGE CAKE	STAND GUARD
SKY JUMPING	SMOOTH BORE	SOUL SISTER	SPONGE DOWN	STAND TO WIN
SKY MARSHAL	SNAFFLE BIT	SOUND BOARD	SPOON FEEDS	STAND TREAT
SKY WRITING	SNAIL PACED	SOUND MIXER	SPOT HEIGHT	STAND TRIAL
SLACK WATER	SNAIL SHELL	SOUND RADIO	SPOT WELDED	STANDERS BY
SLACKEN OFF	SNAIL WHEEL	SOUND SHIFT	SPOT WELDER	STANDING BY
SLACKENS UP	SNAILS PACE	SOUND TRACK	SPOTTED DOG	STANDING IN
SLANG WHANG	SNAKE DANCE	SOUNDED OFF	SPRAY DRIED	STANDING ON
SLAP UP MEAL	SNAKE HOUSE	SOUNDED OUT	SPRAY DRIFT	STANDING TO
SLAVE OWNER	SNAKES HEAD	SOUP TICKET	SPRAY PAINT	STANDING UP
SLAVE TRADE	SNAPPING UP	SOUP TUREEN	SPREAD OVER	STANDS DOWN
SLEEP ROUGH	SNEAK THIEF	SOUR GRAPES	SPRING CART	STANDS FAST
	SNEAKING UP	SOUR ORANGE	SPRING CLIP	STANDS FIRE

10 contd.

STANDS OVER	STIFLE BONE	STRIP TEASE	SWEETIE PIE	TAKES AMISS
STAPLE DIET	STILL BIRTH	STRIPS DOWN	SWELL ORGAN	TAKES APART
STAR BRIGHT	STILL HOUSE	STROKE PLAY	SWINE FEVER	TAKES COVER
STAR GAZING	STILL STAND	STRONG HEAD	SWING MUSIC	TAKES HEART
STAR SHAPED	STINK BRAND	STRONG MEAT	SWING SHELF	TAKES IN TOW
STARK NAKED	STIR ABROAD	STRONG SUIT	SWING STOCK	TAKES ISSUE
STARRY EYED	STIRRING UP	STRUCK BACK	SWING SWANG	TAKES LEAVE
START A HARE	STIRRUP CUP	STRUCK DOWN	SWING WHEEL	TAKES PAINS
STARTED OUT	STITCHED UP	STRUCK DUMB	SWISS FRANC	TAKES PLACE
STARTING IN	STITCHES UP	STRUCK HOME	SWISS GUARD	TAKES SHAPE
STARTING UP	STOCK AGENT	STRUGGLE ON	SWISS WATCH	TAKES SIDES
STARVED OUT	STOCK STILL	STUBBLE FED	SWITCH OVER	TAKES STEPS
STARVES OUT	STOCKING UP	STUCK IT OUT	SWITCHED ON	TAKES STOCK
STATE COACH	STOLE A KISS	STUDIO FLAT	SWITCHES ON	TAKES TURNS
STATE HOUSE	STONE BORER	STUDY GROUP	SWIVEL HOOK	TAKING A BOW
STATE OF WAR	STONE BREAK	STUMPING UP	SWORD BLADE	TAKING ARMS
STATE PAPER	STONE FRUIT	SUB HEADING	SWORD DANCE	TAKING BACK
STATE TRIAL	STONE MASON	SUCH AS IT IS	SWORD GRASS	TAKING BETS
STATIC LINE	STONE SNIPE	SUCH IS LIFE	SWORD STICK	TAKING CARE
STATUTE LAW	STONE STILL	SUCKING CUP	SWOTTING UP	TAKING DOWN
STAY AT HOME	STONY BROKE	SUCKING PIG	T BONE STEAK	TAKING FIVE
STAYED OVER	STOOD ALONE	SUCKS TO YOU	TABLE CLOTH	TAKING HEED
STAYING OUT	STOOD AT BAY	SUGAR APPLE	TABLE COVER	TAKING NOTE
STAYING PUT	STOOD GUARD	SUGAR BASIN	TABLE DHOTE	TAKING OVER
STAYS STILL	STOOD TO WIN	SUGAR CANDY	TABLE KNIFE	TAKING PART
STEAK HOUSE	STOOD TREAT	SUGAR DADDY	TABLE LINEN	TAKING ROOT
STEAL A KISS	STOOD TRIAL	SUGAR GRASS	TABLE MONEY	TAKING SILK
STEAM CRANE	STOP THE ROT	SUGAR MAPLE	TABLE SPOON	TAKING WING
STEAM GAUGE	STOPPED OFF	SUGAR TONGS	TABLE WATER	TALE TELLER
STEAM NAVVY	STOPPING IN	SUI GENERIS	TABULA RASA	TALK IT OVER
STEAM POWER	STOPS SHORT	SUMMER CAMP	TACK HAMMER	TALK TURKEY
STEAM RADIO	STORKS BILL	SUMMER TERM	TAGGED ATOM	TALKED BACK
STEAM TRAIN	STORM CLOUD	SUMMER TIME	TAILING OFF	TALKED DOWN
STEAM YACHT	STORM GLASS	SUMMONED UP	TAILOR BIRD	TALKED INTO
STEAMING UP	STORM TRACK	SUN LOUNGER	TAILOR MADE	TALKED OVER
STEAMS OPEN	STORM WATER	SUN WORSHIP	TAKE A BRIEF	TALKED SHOP
STEEL PLATE	STRAIGHT UP	SUNDAY BEST	TAKE A CLASS	TALKING BIG
STEEPLE HAT	STRAW PLAIT	SUPER DUPER	TAKE A DEKKO	TALKING OUT
STEER CLEAR	STREAM GOLD	SUPER ROYAL	TAKE AN OATH	TALKS ROUND
STEM STITCH	STREET ARAB	SUPPLY SIDE	TAKE AS READ	TALLY CLERK
STEP BY STEP	STREET CRED	SURE ENOUGH	TAKE CHARGE	TALLY TRADE
STEP DANCER	STREET DOOR	SURF BATHER	TAKE EFFECT	TANK ENGINE
STEP LADDER	STREET WARD	SURF RIDING	TAKE FLIGHT	TAP DANCING
STEP PARENT	STRETCH OUT	SUSSING OUT	TAKE FRIGHT	TAPE READER
STEP ROCKET	STRICT DIET	SWALLOWS UP	TAKE IN HAND	TAPE RECORD
STEPPED OUT	STRIFE TORN	SWAMP FEVER	TAKE IN VAIN	TAPERED OFF
STEPPING IN	STRIKE BACK	SWAN AROUND	TAKE IT EASY	TAPPET RING
STEPPING UP	STRIKE DOWN	SWAN MAIDEN	TAKE NOTICE	TARGET AREA
STEPS ASIDE	STRIKE DUMB	SWAN NECKED	TAKE ORDERS	TARIFF WALL
STERN CHASE	STRIKE HOME	SWAN UPPING	TAKE THE AIR	TAROT CARDS
STERN FRAME	STRIKES OFF	SWEARING IN	TAKE THE RAP	TAWNY EAGLE
STERN SHEET	STRIKES OIL	SWEAT BLOOD	TAKE THE SUN	TAX BRACKET
STICK IT OUT	STRIKES OUT	SWEAT GLAND	TAKE TO TASK	TAX EVASION
STICKING BY	STRIKING UP	SWEAT IT OUT	TAKE UP ARMS	TAX SHELTER
STICKING IN	STRING BAND	SWEAT SHIRT	TAKEN ABACK	TAXI DANCER
STICKING TO	STRING BASS	SWEEP SEINE	TAKEN APART	TAXI DRIVER
STICKING UP	STRING BEAN	SWEEPING UP	TAKEN IN TOW	TEA BISCUIT
STICKS AT IT	STRING VEST	SWEET BRIAR	TAKES A SEAT	TEA CLIPPER
STICKY BACK	STRINGS OUT	SWEET BRIER	TAKES A TURN	TEA DRINKER
	STRIP POKER	SWEET TALKS	TAKES AFTER	TEA PLANTER

10 *contd.*
TEA SERVICE
TEA TASTING
TEA TROLLEY
TEAM SPIRIT
TEAM UP WITH
TEAR JERKER
TEARING OFF
TEENY WEENY
TELLING OFF
TELLS TALES
TEMPTS FATE
TENDER LOIN
TENNIS BALL
TENNIS CLUB
TENNIS SHOE
TENT STITCH
TENTER HOOK
TERRA FIRMA
TEST FLIGHT
TEXAS TOWER
THAI BOXING
THAWING OUT
THE ARCHERS
THE CHANNEL
THE COMMONS
THE COUNTRY
THE CREATOR
THE DANSANT
THE EVIL ONE
THE FAIR SEX
THE HARD WAY
THE HEAVIES
THE HORRORS
THE NEEDLES
THE RED ARMY
THE ROCKIES
THE SHIVERS
THE THREE RS
THE TWELFTH
THE UNKNOWN
THE UP AND UP
THE WISE MEN
THE YEAR DOT
THERE THERE
THIEVES DEN
THIGH BOOTS
THILL HORSE
THIMBLE RIG
THINK AGAIN
THINK ALIKE
THINK ALOUD
THINK TWICE
THINKING UP
THINKS BACK
THINKS OVER
THINNED OUT
THIRD CLASS
THIRD FORCE
THIRD PARTY

THIRD REICH
THIRD WORLD
THORN APPLE
THORN HEDGE
THOUGHT OUT
THREAD LACE
THREAD WORM
THREE BALLS
THREE PARTS
THREE PIECE
THREE SIDED
THRIFT SHOP
THROAT BAND
THRONE ROOM
THROUGH PUT
THROW STICK
THROWING IN
THROWING ON
THROWING UP
THROWN AWAY
THROWN DOWN
THROWN OPEN
THROWN OVER
THROWN SILK
THROWS A FIT
THROWS AWAY
THROWS DOWN
THROWS OPEN
THROWS OVER
THUMB A LIFT
THUMB A RIDE
THUMB INDEX
THUMB STALL
THUMBS DOWN
THUNDER BOX
THUNDER GOD
TICKED AWAY
TICKED OVER
TICKER TAPE
TICKETY BOO
TICKING OFF
TICKLE PINK
TIDING OVER
TIE BREAKER
TIE THE KNOT
TIGER BADGE
TIGER SHARK
TIGER SNAKE
TIGHT LACED
TILT HAMMER
TIM WHISKEY
TIMBER LINE
TIMBER TOES
TIMBER TREE
TIMBER WOLF
TIMBER YARD
TIME KEEPER
TIME KILLER
TIME SAVING
TIME SERVER

TIME SHARER
TIME SIGNAL
TIME SWITCH
TIN SOLDIER
TIN WHISTLE
TIP ONES HAT
TIP THE WINK
TIP UP TRUCK
TIPPING OFF
TITLE FIGHT
TITLE SHEET
TO CAP IT ALL
TO ONES FACE
TO THE DEATH
TO THE POINT
TOAD EATING
TODDY LADLE
TODDY STICK
TOE THE LINE
TOGGLE IRON
TOILET ROLL
TOILET SOAP
TOKEN MONEY
TOM COLLINS
TOM O BEDLAM
TOMATO SOUP
TONGUE TIED
TONGUE WORK
TONIC SOL FA
TONIC WATER
TOOK A BRIEF
TOOK A CLASS
TOOK A DEKKO
TOOK AN OATH
TOOK CHARGE
TOOK EFFECT
TOOK FLIGHT
TOOK FRIGHT
TOOK IN HAND
TOOK IN VAIN
TOOK IT EASY
TOOK NOTICE
TOOK ORDERS
TOOK THE AIR
TOOK THE RAP
TOOK THE SUN
TOOK TO TASK
TOOK UP ARMS
TOOTH PASTE
TOP BILLING
TOP DRESSED
TOP DRESSES
TOP GALLANT
TOP SOILING
TOP THE BILL
TOPI WALLAH
TOPPING OUT
TOPPLE OVER
TORCH DANCE
TORPEDO NET

TORRID ZONE
TORSION BAR
TOTAL WRECK
TOUCH AND GO
TOUCH JUDGE
TOUCH ME NOT
TOUCH PAPER
TOUCH TYPED
TOUCH TYPES
TOUCHED OFF
TOUCHES OFF
TOUCHING UP
TOUGHENS UP
TOUR OF DUTY
TOURING CAR
TOUT DE MEME
TOWER BLOCK
TOWERS OVER
TOWING PATH
TOWN CENTRE
TOXIC WASTE
TOY SPANIEL
TRACE HORSE
TRACK EVENT
TRACK SCOUT
TRACK SHOES
TRACKER DOG
TRACKS DOWN
TRADE BOARD
TRADE CYCLE
TRADE PLATE
TRADE PRICE
TRADE ROUTE
TRADE UNION
TRADE WINDS
TRADED DOWN
TRADES DOWN
TRADES FOLK
TRADING OFF
TRAFFIC COP
TRAFFIC JAM
TRAGI COMIC
TRAILED OFF
TRAILS AWAY
TRAIN CRASH
TRAIN FERRY
TRAMMEL NET
TRAMWAY CAR
TRANS SONIC
TRAVEL SICK
TREAD WATER
TREAD WHEEL
TREATY PORT
TREBLE CLEF
TREE HOPPER
TREE MALLOW
TREE OF LIFE
TRENCH COAT
TRENCH FEET
TRENCH FOOT

TRICK TRACK
TRIGGER OFF
TRIP HAMMER
TRIPLE BILL
TRIPLE JUMP
TRIPLE TIME
TROLLEY BUS
TROLLEY CAR
TROLLEY MAN
TROOP HORSE
TROTTED OUT
TROU DE LOUP
TROUSER LEG
TROUT SPOON
TROY WEIGHT
TRUCKLE BED
TRUE TO LIFE
TRUFFLE DOG
TRUFFLE PIG
TRUNDLE BED
TRUNK MAKER
TRUST HOUSE
TRUST STOCK
TRUTH SERUM
TRUTH TABLE
TRUTH VALUE
TRYING IT ON
TUB THUMPED
TUB THUMPER
TULIP EARED
TUMBLE CART
TUMBLE OVER
TUMBLE WEED
TUNING FORK
TURFING OUT
TURKEY COCK
TURKEY TROT
TURN AROUND
TURN TURTLE
TURNED AWAY
TURNED BACK
TURNED DOWN
TURNED INTO
TURNED OVER
TURNED TAIL
TURNED TURK
TURNED UPON
TURNING OFF
TURNING OUT
TURNING SAW
TURNS ABOUT
TURNS ASIDE
TURNS LOOSE
TURNS NASTY
TURNS ROUND
TURRET SHIP
TURTLE DOVE
TURTLE NECK
TURTLE SOUP
TWEET TWEET

10 *contd.*

TWELFTH MAN
TWIGGING IT
TWIN SISTER
TWIST DRILL
TWO ACT PLAY
TWO OF A KIND
TWO PIN PLUG
TWO WHEELED
TWO WHEELER
TWO YEAR OLD
TYBURN TREE
TYPE CUTTER
TYPE HOLDER
TYPING POOL
UGRO FINNIC
ULTRA VIRES
UNCARED FOR
UNDER CLERK
UNDER COVER
UNDER TRICK
UNDER WATER
UNDUE HASTE
UNHOPED FOR
UP A GUM TREE
UP AND ABOUT
UP AND DOING
UP AND UNDER
UP FOR GRABS
UP IN THE AIR
UP THE CREEK
UP TO A POINT
UP TO NO GOOD
UP TO TRICKS
UPHILL TASK
UPON MY SOUL
UPON MY WORD
UPPER CLASS
UPPER CRUST
UPPER HOUSE
UPSIDE DOWN
USING FORCE
UTILITY MAN
VACUUM PUMP
VACUUM TUBE
VALUE ADDED
VAMPIRE BAT
VANITY CASE
VANITY FAIR
VAPOUR BATH
VELVET CRAB
VELVET DUCK
VELVET PILE
VENTURE OUT
VENUS SHELL
VENUSS COMB
VERBAL NOTE
VERBAL NOUN
VEREY LIGHT
VERNERS LAW

VERSE MAKER
VERSE SMITH
VESPER BELL
VESTRY ROOM
VETERAN CAR
VICE CONSUL
VICHY WATER
VIDEO NASTY
VIETNAM WAR
VINE BRANCH
VINHO VERDE
VINTAGE CAR
VIRGIN GOLD
VIRGIN KNOT
VIRGIN SOIL
VISUAL AIDS
VISUAL ARTS
VISUAL AXIS
VITAL FLAME
VITAL FORCE
VITAL SIGNS
VITAL SPARK
VOCAL CORDS
VOCAL MUSIC
VOCAL SCORE
VOICE PRINT
VOL AU VENTS
VOLENTE DEO
VOLLEY BALL
VOTING DOWN
VOWEL POINT
VOWEL RHYME
WAGE EARNER
WAGE FREEZE
WAGE PACKET
WAGON TRAIN
WAGON WHEEL
WAIT AND SEE
WAIT AWHILE
WAITED UPON
WAITS ABOUT
WAKEY WAKEY
WALK AROUND
WALK OF LIFE
WALK ON PART
WALK THE DOG
WALK TO HEEL
WALKED AWAY
WALKED INTO
WALKED TALL
WALKING OFF
WALKING OUT
WALKS ON AIR
WALKS OUT ON
WALKY TALKY
WALL FACING
WALL LIZARD
WALL STREET
WALL TO WALL
WALNUT TREE

WAMPUM BELT
WANDER PLUG
WANDERS OFF
WANTING OUT
WAR GODDESS
WAR MACHINE
WARD SISTER
WARDING OFF
WARMING PAN
WARSAW PACT
WASH BOTTLE
WASHED AWAY
WASHED DOWN
WASHING OUT
WASSAIL CUP
WASTE PAPER
WASTED AWAY
WASTES AWAY
WATCH CHAIN
WATCH GLASS
WATCH GUARD
WATCH HOUSE
WATCH LIGHT
WATCH NIGHT
WATCH STRAP
WATCH TOWER
WATER BLOOM
WATER BORNE
WATER BOUND
WATER BREAK
WATER CHUTE
WATER CLOCK
WATER COOLS
WATER CRAFT
WATER CRANE
WATER CYCLE
WATER FRAME
WATER GAUGE
WATER GLASS
WATER GUARD
WATER HORSE
WATER JOINT
WATER LEMON
WATER LEVEL
WATER MAIZE
WATER MELON
WATER METER
WATER MOUSE
WATER MUSIC
WATER NYMPH
WATER OUZEL
WATER PIPES
WATER PLANT
WATER PLATE
WATER POWER
WATER SKIED
WATER SKIER
WATER SKIES
WATER SNAKE
WATER SPOUT

WATER TABLE
WATER THYME
WATER TOWER
WATER WHEEL
WATER WINGS
WATERS DOWN
WATTLE BIRD
WAVE ENERGY
WAVE MOTION
WAVED A WAND
WAVED ASIDE
WAVES A WAND
WAVES ASIDE
WAVING DOWN
WAX LYRICAL
WAY BAGGAGE
WAY FREIGHT
WAY STATION
WAY TRAFFIC
WAYSIDE INN
WEAK HEADED
WEAK MINDED
WEAK MOMENT
WEAK WILLED
WEARING OFF
WEARING OUT
WEASEL COOT
WEASEL WORD
WEASELS OUT
WEATHER BOX
WEATHER EYE
WEATHER MAP
WEATHER OUT
WEAVER BIRD
WEDDING BED
WEDDING DAY
WEED KILLER
WEEDING HOE
WEEK ENDING
WEEPING ASH
WEEPING ELM
WEIGH HOUSE
WEIGHED OUT
WEIGHING IN
WEIGHING UP
WEIGHS DOWN
WELCOME MAT
WELL BORING
WELL CHOSEN
WELL EARNED
WELL ENOUGH
WELL FORMED
WELL HEELED
WELL I NEVER
WELL JUDGED
WELL MINDED
WELL PLACED
WELL SINKER
WELL SPOKEN
WELL SPRING

WELL WISHED
WELL WISHER
WELLS FARGO
WELSH ONION
WELTER RACE
WENDY HOUSE
WENT ABROAD
WENT HALVES
WENT HUNGRY
WENT NATIVE
WENT PLACES
WENT TO SEED
WENT TO TOWN
WENT TOO FAR
WEST INDIAN
WEST INDIES
WESTWARD HO
WET BLANKET
WET THROUGH
WHALE SHARK
WHALING GUN
WHATS UP DOC
WHEAT FIELD
WHEAT MIDGE
WHEEL CHAIR
WHEEL CLAMP
WHEEL HOUSE
WHEN IN ROME
WHERE ITS AT
WHIP TAILED
WHIP THE CAT
WHIPPING IN
WHIRL ABOUT
WHISKS AWAY
WHISKY SOUR
WHIST DRIVE
WHISTLE OFF
WHIT MONDAY
WHITE BEARD
WHITE BRASS
WHITE BREAD
WHITE DWARF
WHITE FACED
WHITE FLOUR
WHITE FRIAR
WHITE FROST
WHITE GOODS
WHITE HORSE
WHITE HOUSE
WHITE LIGHT
WHITE MAGIC
WHITE METAL
WHITE NIGHT
WHITE NOISE
WHITE PAPER
WHITE SAUCE
WHITE SUGAR
WHITE WATER
WHITE WHALE
WHITE WITCH

10 *contd.*

WHITING OUT
WHITSUN ALE
WHOLE WHEAT
WHOOPS IT UP
WHYDAH BIRD
WICKET DOOR
WICKET GATE
WIDE BODIED
WIDE SCREEN
WIDOWS MITE
WIDOWS PEAK
WILD ANIMAL
WILD CHERRY
WILD FLOWER
WILD FOWLER
WILD GARLIC
WILLOW HERB
WILLOW WREN
WILLY NILLY
WIN BY A HEAD
WIN BY A NECK
WIN THROUGH
WIND CHANGE
WIND FLOWER
WIND SLEEVE
WIND SURFED
WIND SURFER
WIND TUNNEL
WINDOW PANE
WINDOW SASH
WINDOW SEAT
WINDOW SHOP
WINDOW SILL
WINE BIBBER
WINE BOTTLE
WINE CELLAR
WINE COOLER
WINE FUNNEL
WINE GROWER
WINE REGION
WINE TASTER
WINE WAITER
WING COLLAR
WING FOOTED
WING MIRROR
WING SPREAD
WING WALKER
WINKLED OUT
WINKLES OUT
WINNING OUT
WINS THE CUP
WINS THE DAY
WINTER CLAD
WINTER CROP
WIRE BRIDGE
WIRE DANCER
WIRE HAIRED
WIRE PULLER
WIRE WALKER

WIRED GLASS
WISE OLD OWL
WISHING CAP
WISHY WASHY
WITCH ALDER
WITCH HAZEL
WITH WEIGHT
WITNESS BOX
WIZEN FACED
WOLF SPIDER
WOMAN HATER
WON BY A HEAD
WON BY A NECK
WON THROUGH
WONDER DRUG
WONDER WORK
WONGA WONGA
WOOD BORING
WOOD CARVER
WOOD CUTTER
WOOD GROUSE
WOOD PIGEON
WOOD SORREL
WOOD SPIRIT
WOODEN HEAD
WOODEN SHOE
WOODEN TYPE
WOOL CARDER
WOOL CHURCH
WOOL COMBER
WOOL DRIVER
WOOL GROWER
WOOL PACKER
WOOL PICKER
WOOL SHEARS
WOOL STAPLE
WOOL WINDER
WOOLLY BEAR
WORD FINDER
WORD MEMORY
WORD SQUARE
WORK BASKET
WORK FELLOW
WORK PEOPLE
WORK TO RULE
WORKED AT IT
WORKED OVER
WORKED UPON
WORKING DAY
WORKING FOR
WORKING MAN
WORKING OUT
WORKS IT OUT
WORLD POWER
WORLD WEARY
WORM POWDER
WORRIED OUT
WORRIES OUT
WORRY BEADS
WRAPPING UP

WREAK HAVOC
WRIGGLE OUT
WRIST WATCH
WRITES DOWN
WRITES HOME
WRITING INK
WRITING OFF
WRITING OUT
WRITTEN LAW
WRITTEN OFF
WRONG DOING
WRONG FOOTS
WRONG TIMED
WRY MOUTHED
YARD MASTER
YARD OF LAND
YEAR ON YEAR
YELLOW CARD
YELLOW FLAG
YELLOW JACK
YELLOW LINE
YELLOW SNOW
YELLOW SOAP
YELLOW SPOT
YELLOW WOOD
YIELD POINT
YLANG YLANG
YOKE FELLOW
YOU DONT SAY
YOU KNOW WHO
YOUNG BLOOD
YOUNG FOGEY
YOUR HONOUR
YOURS TRULY
ZAPPED IT UP
ZEBRA FINCH
ZEND AVESTA
ZENER CARDS
ZENER DIODE
ZERO OPTION
ZERO RATING
ZERO VALENT
ZEROED IN ON
ZEROES IN ON
ZINC WORKER
ZODIAC SIGN
ZONAL INDEX
ZONE TICKET

11

A BAG OF BONES
A BIT OF FLUFF
A BONE TO PICK
A CLEAN SHEET
A CLEAN SLATE
A CLEAN SWEEP
A DIME A DOZEN
A LONE FIGURE
A PIG IN A POKE
A RIPE OLD AGE

A SCREW LOOSE
A SLATE LOOSE
A SWEET TOOTH
A VOTRE SANTE
ABANDON SHIP
ABIDE WITH ME
ABOVE GROUND
ABSTRACT ART
ACCOUNT BOOK
ACETATE FILM
ACTS THE FOOL
ACTS THE GOAT
ACUTE ACCENT
AD INFINITUM
ADDLE HEADED
ADDRESS BOOK
ADVANCE COPY
AEOLIAN HARP
AFGHAN HOUND
AFRICAN TEAK
AFTER DINNER
AFTER EFFECT
AGAINST TIME
AGE OF REASON
AGENT ORANGE
AGONY COLUMN
AHEAD OF TIME
AIDE MEMOIRE
AIDES DE CAMP
AIR CORRIDOR
AIR LAYERING
AIR MECHANIC
AIR MINISTRY
AIR SICKNESS
AIR TERMINAL
AIR UMBRELLA
ALBUM SLEEVE
ALL AMERICAN
ALL CHEERING
ALL ELECTRIC
ALL FOOLS DAY
ALL POWERFUL
ALL SOULS DAY
ALL STANDING
ALL THE WHILE
ALL TIME HIGH
ALL VERY WELL
ALMIGHTY GOD
ALTO RELIEVO
ALTO RILIEVO
AMOUR PROPRE
AN EASY TOUCH
AND THEN SOME
ANGLO FRENCH
ANGLO INDIAN
ANGLO NORMAN
ANGST RIDDEN
ANISEED BALL
ANNUAL RINGS
ANSWERS BACK

11 *contd.*

ANTI FEDERAL
ANTI HEROINE
ANTI JACOBIN
ANTI SEMITIC
ANTI VITAMIN
ANY OLD THING
ANYTHING BUT
APPEAL COURT
APPLE BLIGHT
APRON STRING
ARCH PRELATE
ARCH VILLAIN
ARCTIC OCEAN
ARGIE BARGIE
ARMED COMBAT
ARMED ESCORT
ARMED FORCES
ARMOUR PLATE
ARMOURED CAR
ARROW HEADED
ARROW POISON
ART MISTRESS
ARTS COUNCIL
ARTS STUDENT
AS DRY AS DUST
AS GOOD AS NEW
AS UGLY AS SIN
ASKING PRICE
ASSAULT BOAT
ASSAY MASTER
ASSAY OFFICE
ASSES BRIDGE
ASTRAL PLANE
AT A DISCOUNT
AT A LOOSE END
AT ALL EVENTS
AT ALL POINTS
AT EVERY TURN
AT FIRST HAND
AT FULL BLAST
AT ONES ELBOW
AT THE DOUBLE
AT THE LATEST
AT THE MOMENT
ATOM SMASHER
ATOMIC CLOCK
ATOMIC POWER
ATTACHE CASE
AU CONTRAIRE
AUBREY HOLES
AUCTION ROOM
AUDIO VISUAL
AVEC PLAISIR
AVOCADO PEAR
AWE STRICKEN
BABY BOUNCER
BABY SITTING
BACK BENCHER
BACK BENCHES

BACK BLOCKER
BACK COMBING
BACK COUNTRY
BACK DRAUGHT
BACK HEELING
BACK STREETS
BACK TO EARTH
BACK TO FRONT
BACKING DOWN
BAD LANGUAGE
BAD TEMPERED
BAG OF CRISPS
BAG OF NERVES
BAG OF TRICKS
BAGGING HOOK
BAILYS BEADS
BAKED ALASKA
BAKERS DOZEN
BALD AS A COOT
BALL AND CLAW
BALL BEARING
BALLAD OPERA
BALLET SHOES
BALLOON BACK
BALLOON TYRE
BALLOT PAPER
BANANA SPLIT
BANBURY CAKE
BANDY LEGGED
BANG THE DRUM
BANK ACCOUNT
BANK BALANCE
BANK HOLIDAY
BANK MANAGER
BANK OF ISSUE
BANKERS CARD
BANNER CLOUD
BAR SINISTER
BARBADOS LEG
BARBERS POLE
BARBERS SHOP
BARBOLA WORK
BARE KNUCKLE
BARGE COUPLE
BARGE STONES
BARKERS MILL
BARKING DEER
BARLEY BRAKE
BARLEY BROTH
BARLEY SUGAR
BARLEY WATER
BARN STORMER
BARON BAILIE
BARON OF BEEF
BARRACK ROOM
BARRAGE FIRE
BARREL HOUSE
BARREL ORGAN
BARREL VAULT
BARRIER REEF

BARYTA PAPER
BASHI BAZOUK
BASKET CHAIR
BASKET MAKER
BASKET WEAVE
BASSET HOUND
BASTARD FILE
BASTARD TEAK
BASTEL HOUSE
BASTILLE DAY
BAT PRINTING
BATH MITZVAH
BATHING SUIT
BATON CHARGE
BATON ROUNDS
BATTALIA PIE
BATTLE PIECE
BATTLE ROYAL
BAY WINDOWED
BEACH MASTER
BEACH RESCUE
BEAM TRAWLER
BEAR BAITING
BEAR WITNESS
BEARDED LADY
BEARING ARMS
BEARING AWAY
BEARING DOWN
BEARING REIN
BEARS BREECH
BEARS IN MIND
BEAST OF PREY
BEAT THE BAND
BEAT THE DRUM
BEATING DOWN
BEATING TIME
BEATING TO IT
BEATS THE AIR
BEATS THE GUN
BEAUTY QUEEN
BEAUTY SLEEP
BEAVERS AWAY
BED AND BOARD
BED OF HONOUR
BEDDING DOWN
BEDSIDE BOOK
BEDSIDE LAMP
BEECH MARTEN
BEEF BRAINED
BEER PARLOUR
BEER SHAMPOO
BEETLE DRIVE
BEETLING OFF
BEGGING BOWL
BELAYING PIN
BELGIAN HARE
BELL FOUNDER
BELL FOUNDRY
BELL HOUSING
BELL RINGING

BELLE DE NUIT
BELLOWS FISH
BELLS THE CAT
BELLY BUTTON
BELLY DANCER
BELOW STAIRS
BENDING OVER
BENGAL LIGHT
BENGAL TIGER
BERTHON BOAT
BESSEMER PIG
BETA BLOCKER
BETTING SHOP
BETTING SLIP
BETTY MARTIN
BETWEEN MAID
BEWICKS SWAN
BEYOND A JOKE
BEYOND DOUBT
BEYOND PRICE
BIAS BINDING
BIAS DRAWING
BICYCLE BELL
BICYCLE CLIP
BICYCLE POLO
BICYCLE PUMP
BIEN ENTENDU
BIG BUSINESS
BILL CHAMBER
BILL OF COSTS
BILLETS DOUX
BILLIARD CUE
BILLY BUNTER
BILLY THE KID
BINARY SCALE
BINDING OVER
BIRD BRAINED
BIRD CATCHER
BIRD FANCIER
BIRD WATCHER
BITE ONES LIP
BITE THE DUST
BITS AND BOBS
BITTER APPLE
BITTER LEMON
BITTER SWEET
BLACK AND TAN
BLACK BEAUTY
BLACK BEETLE
BLACK BOTTOM
BLACK BROWED
BLACK BRYONY
BLACK CATTLE
BLACK COATED
BLACK COFFEE
BLACK COMEDY
BLACK FISHER
BLACK FOREST
BLACK FRIARS
BLACK FRIDAY

11 contd.

BLACK HUMOUR
BLACK LETTER
BLACK MARKET
BLACK MONDAY
BLACK VELVET
BLACKING OUT
BLADDER WORM
BLANK CHEQUE
BLANK WINDOW
BLANKET BATH
BLASTING OFF
BLAZE A TRAIL
BLESS MY SOUL
BLEW ONES TOP
BLEW THE GAFF
BLIND AS A BAT
BLIND STOREY
BLISTER CARD
BLISTER PACK
BLOCK LETTER
BLOCK SYSTEM
BLOOD FLOWER
BLOOD ORANGE
BLOOD SPORTS
BLOOD STREAM
BLOOD VESSEL
BLOODY SWEAT
BLOTTING OUT
BLOTTING PAD
BLOW ONES TOP
BLOW THE GAFF
BLOWING AWAY
BLOWING OVER
BLUE EYED BOY
BLUE POINTER
BLUE WHITING
BLUNT WITTED
BLURTING OUT
BOARD SCHOOL
BOARDING OUT
BOAT BUILDER
BODY AND SOUL
BODY BUILDER
BODY POLITIC
BODY POPPING
BOG ASPHODEL
BOG TROTTERS
BOGGING DOWN
BOILED SHIRT
BOILED SWEET
BOILER MAKER
BOILING OVER
BOLD AS BRASS
BOLT UPRIGHT
BOND SERVICE
BONNE CHANCE
BOOK ACCOUNT
BOOK LEARNED
BOOK OF HOURS

BOOK OF WORDS
BOOK THROUGH
BOOKER PRIZE
BOOKING HALL
BOOM AND BUST
BOOT TOPPING
BOOTLACE TIE
BORNE IN MIND
BOSOM FRIEND
BOTHY BALLAD
BOTTLE BRUSH
BOTTLE GLASS
BOTTLE GREEN
BOTTLE NOSED
BOTTLE PARTY
BOTTLING OFF
BOTTLING OUT
BOTTOM HEAVY
BOTTOMED OUT
BOULDER CLAY
BOUNCED BACK
BOUNCES BACK
BOVVER BOOTS
BOW WINDOWED
BOWLINE KNOT
BOWLING OVER
BOX JUNCTION
BOXER SHORTS
BOXING GLOVE
BOYS BRIGADE
BRACE AND BIT
BRAIN DAMAGE
BRAIN TEASER
BRAINS TRUST
BRAKE LINING
BRAMAH PRESS
BRAMBLE BUSH
BRANCH PILOT
BRAND LEADER
BRANDY GLASS
BRASS RUBBER
BRAZEN FACED
BREAD BASKET
BREAK GROUND
BREAK THE ICE
BREAKFAST TV
BREAKING OFF
BREAKING OUT
BREAKS COVER
BREAKS FORTH
BREAKS LOOSE
BREAKS RANKS
BREECH BIRTH
BREEZE BLOCK
BRIDAL SUITE
BRIDGE HOUSE
BRING TO BEAR
BRING TO BOOK
BRING TO HEEL
BRING TO LIFE

BRINGING OFF
BRINGING OUT
BRINGS ABOUT
BRINGS FORTH
BRINGS ROUND
BRISTLE FERN
BRISTLE TAIL
BRISTOL MILK
BRITISH RAIL
BRITISH WARM
BRITTLE STAR
BROAD CHURCH
BROAD LEAVED
BROAD MINDED
BROKE GROUND
BROKE THE ICE
BRONZE MEDAL
BRONZED SKIN
BROUGHT DOWN
BROUGHT HOME
BROUGHT OVER
BRUSH TURKEY
BRUSHING OFF
BUBBLED OVER
BUBBLES OVER
BUCK PASSING
BUCKET WHEEL
BUCKLE UNDER
BUCKLED DOWN
BUCKLES DOWN
BUFF LEATHER
BUFFALO BILL
BUFFALO BIRD
BUFFER STATE
BUFFER STOCK
BULK CARRIER
BULL BAITING
BULL MASTIFF
BULL TERRIER
BULLDOG CLIP
BULLET PROOF
BULLY FOR HER
BULLY FOR HIM
BULLY FOR YOU
BULLYING OFF
BUMBLE PUPPY
BUMP STARTED
BUMPING INTO
BUMPING RACE
BUNDLE OF FUN
BUNNY RABBIT
BURIAL PLACE
BURIDANS ASS
BURLING IRON
BURNING BUSH
BURNING DOWN
BURNT SIENNA
BUSTED FLUSH
BUTCHER BIRD
BUTT WELDING

BUTTED JOINT
BUTTER BEANS
BUTTER CLOTH
BUTTER KNIFE
BUTTER PAPER
BUTTER PLATE
BUTTERING UP
BUTTONING UP
CAAING WHALE
CABBAGE MOTH
CABBAGE PALM
CABBAGE ROSE
CABLE LENGTH
CABLE STITCH
CAFE SOCIETY
CAKES AND ALE
CALABAR BEAN
CALL IT QUITS
CALL THE TUNE
CALL TO ORDER
CALLED A HALT
CALLED NAMES
CALLING AWAY
CALLING BACK
CALLING CARD
CALLING OVER
CALLOW YOUTH
CALLS IT A DAY
CALLS TO MIND
CALMING DOWN
CAME AND WENT
CAME BETWEEN
CAME FORWARD
CAME TO A HEAD
CAME TO BLOWS
CAME TO GRIEF
CAME TO LIGHT
CAME UNSTUCK
CAMEL BACKED
CAMELS THORN
CAMOMILE TEA
CAMP MEETING
CAMPING IT UP
CANADA GOOSE
CANARY GRASS
CANDIED PEEL
CANDLE LIGHT
CANDLE POWER
CANDY STRIPE
CANINE TOOTH
CANNED MUSIC
CANNON METAL
CANNON PROOF
CANTING COIN
CAP AND BELLS
CAPE SPARROW
CAPER SPURGE
CAPITAL LEVY
CAPITAL SHIP
CAR BOOT SALE

11 *contd.*

CAR SICKNESS
CARAVAN PARK
CARAVAN SITE
CARAWAY SEED
CARBON PAPER
CARBON STEEL
CARD OF ENTRY
CARD SHARPER
CARDINAL SIN
CARDING WOOL
CAREER WOMAN
CAREY STREET
CARNOT CYCLE
CARPET SNAKE
CARPET TILES
CARRIAGE DOG
CARRICK BEND
CARRIED AWAY
CARRIED BACK
CARRIED OVER
CARRIES AWAY
CARRIES BACK
CARRIES OVER
CARRION CROW
CARRY THE CAN
CARRY THE DAY
CARRY TOO FAR
CARRY WEIGHT
CARRYING OFF
CARRYING OUT
CARTE DU JOUR
CARVEL BUILT
CASE HISTORY
CASE IN POINT
CASH ACCOUNT
CASH MACHINE
CASH PAYMENT
CASH RAILWAY
CAST A GLANCE
CASTER SUGAR
CASTILE SOAP
CASTING A NET
CASTING AWAY
CASTING LOTS
CASTING VOTE
CASTLE GUARD
CASTOR SUGAR
CASTS A SPELL
CASTS ANCHOR
CAT AND MOUSE
CATCH PHRASE
CATCH THE SUN
CATCH THE TEN
CATCHES FIRE
CATCHING OUT
CATHODE RAYS
CATS WHISKER
CATTLE THIEF
CAUGHT A COLD

CAUGHT A CRAB
CAUGHT SHORT
CAUSED A STIR
CAUSES A STIR
CAUSTIC LIME
CAUSTIC SODA
CAVE DWELLER
CAVEAT ACTOR
CAVO RILIEVO
CELTIC CROSS
CEMENT MIXER
CEMENT STONE
CEMENT WATER
CENTRAL BANK
CENTRAL FIRE
CENTRAL LINE
CENTRAL PARK
CENTRE BOARD
CENTRE COURT
CENTRE PARTY
CENTRE PIECE
CHAFF CUTTER
CHAIN ARMOUR
CHAIN BRIDGE
CHAIN DRIVEN
CHAIN LETTER
CHAIN PLATES
CHAIN SMOKER
CHALKING OUT
CHANCE COMER
CHANGE HANDS
CHANGE HOUSE
CHANGED DOWN
CHANGED ENDS
CHANGED GEAR
CHANGES DOWN
CHANGES ENDS
CHANGES GEAR
CHANNEL SEAM
CHAOS THEORY
CHAPEL ROYAL
CHARGE HOUSE
CHARGE NURSE
CHARGE SHEET
CHARGED DOWN
CHARGES DOWN
CHARITY GIRL
CHARITY WALK
CHARLESS LAW
CHARM SCHOOL
CHART BUSTER
CHEAP LABOUR
CHECK ACTION
CHECK STRING
CHECKING OFF
CHECKING OUT
CHEDDAR PINK
CHEEK BY JOWL
CHEER LEADER
CHEESE BOARD

CHEESE PRESS
CHEESE STRAW
CHEESE WRING
CHEF DOEUVRE
CHELSEA WARE
CHEMIN DE FER
CHEQUER WORK
CHERRY STONE
CHESHIRE CAT
CHESS PLAYER
CHEVAL GLASS
CHEWING OVER
CHEWS THE CUD
CHEWS THE FAT
CHICK A BIDDY
CHICKEN COOP
CHICKEN FEED
CHICKEN WIRE
CHICKENS OUT
CHIEF BARKER
CHILEAN PINE
CHILL FACTOR
CHILLING OUT
CHIMNEY NOOK
CHINESE BURN
CHIP CARVING
CHIPPING OFF
CHLORIC ACID
CHOCK A BLOCK
CHOIR MASTER
CHOIR SCHOOL
CHOIR SCREEN
CHOIR STALLS
CHOKING BACK
CHOKING COIL
CHOLERA BELT
CHOOSE SIDES
CHOUX PASTRY
CHROMIC ACID
CHUCKED IT IN
CHUCKLE HEAD
CHURCH BELLS
CHURCH BENCH
CHURCH COURT
CHURCH GOING
CHURCH MOUSE
CHURCH ORGAN
CHURCH TOWER
CHURNING OUT
CIGAR SHAPED
CINDER TRACK
CINE BIOLOGY
CINEMA ORGAN
CINQUE PORTS
CIRCLE RIDER
CIRCULAR SAW
CITIZEN KANE
CITRUS FRUIT
CITY COMPANY
CITY FATHERS

CITY MISSION
CITY SLICKER
CIVIC CENTRE
CIVIL RIGHTS
CIVVY STREET
CLAM CHOWDER
CLAMPED DOWN
CLARION CALL
CLASS ACTION
CLASS FELLOW
CLASS LEADER
CLAW AND BALL
CLAWING BACK
CLEAN BOWLED
CLEAN LIMBED
CLEAN LIVING
CLEAN SHAVEN
CLEANING OUT
CLEAR HEADED
CLEAR THE AIR
CLEAR THE WAY
CLEARING OUT
CLEFT PALATE
CLICK BEETLE
CLIENT STATE
CLIFF HANGER
CLIMBED DOWN
CLOCKING OFF
CLOCKING OUT
CLOG DANCING
CLOSE AT HAND
CLOSE FINISH
CLOSE FISTED
CLOSE LIPPED
CLOSE SEASON
CLOSE SECOND
CLOSE TENNIS
CLOSE THE GAP
CLOSED CHAIN
CLOSED RANKS
CLOSET DRAMA
CLOSING DOWN
CLOSING TIME
CLOTH OF GOLD
CLOTHES LINE
CLOTHES MOTH
CLOTHES POLE
CLOTHES PROP
CLOUD OF DUST
CLOUDED OVER
CLOVER GRASS
CLUB STEWARD
CLUB TO DEATH
CLUSTER BOMB
COACH OFFICE
COACHING INN
COAL SCUTTLE
COAL TAR SOAP
COAL WHIPPER
COAT OF PAINT

11 *contd.*

COBBLE STONE
COCK A LEEKIE
COCK AND BULL
COCK SPARROW
COCKS A SNOOK
COCKTAIL BAR
COCOA BUTTER
COCONUT PALM
COD LIVER OIL
CODE BREAKER
COFFEE BERRY
COFFEE BREAK
COFFEE HOUSE
COFFEE MAKER
COFFEE STALL
COFFEE TABLE
COIN A PHRASE
COLD BLOODED
COLD CALLING
COLD CASTING
COLD COMFORT
COLD FORGING
COLD HARBOUR
COLD HEARTED
COLD STORAGE
COLD WELDING
COLOUR BLIND
COLOUR CODED
COLOURING IN
COLOURING UP
COME BETWEEN
COME FORWARD
COME TO A HEAD
COME TO BLOWS
COME TO GRIEF
COME TO LIGHT
COME UNSTUCK
COME UPPANCE
COMES ACROSS
COMES ASHORE
COMES TO LIFE
COMES TO PASS
COMES TO REST
COMES UNDONE
COMET FINDER
COMIC RELIEF
COMING ABOUT
COMING CLEAN
COMING OF AGE
COMING ROUND
COMMAND POST
COMME IL FAUT
COMMON CHORD
COMMON FORMS
COMMON METRE
COMMON SENSE
COMMON THIEF
COMMON TOUCH
COMPACT DISC

COMPASS CARD
COMPASS ROSE
COMPOST HEAP
COMPOUND EYE
CONCERT GOER
CONCERT HALL
CONFOUND YOU
CONJURING UP
CONTACT LENS
CONTANGO DAY
CONTOUR LINE
CONTRA DANCE
CONTRA TENOR
CONTRACT OUT
CONTRACTS IN
CONTROL ROOM
CONTROL UNIT
CONY CATCHER
COOK GENERAL
COOKERY BOOK
COPING STONE
COPPER BEECH
COPPER FACED
COPPERS NARK
CORAL ISLAND
CORDONED OFF
CORN IN EGYPT
CORN PLASTER
CORNEAL LENS
CORNER STONE
CORNICE HOOK
CORNICE POLE
CORNICE RAIL
CORNICE RING
CORNISH CLAY
CORPS DELITE
CORS ANGLAIS
COSTA BLANCA
COSTA DEL SOL
COSTUME PLAY
COTTAGE LOAF
COTTON CANDY
COTTON PLANT
COTTON PRESS
COTTONING ON
COUCH POTATO
COUNTER BORE
COUNTER MOVE
COUNTER PLOT
COUNTER ROLL
COUNTER TURN
COUNTER VIEW
COUNTER VOTE
COUNTER WORK
COUNTING OUT
COUNTRY CLUB
COUNTRY FOLK
COUNTRY LANE
COUNTRY ROCK
COUNTRY SEAT

COUNTS SHEEP
COUNTY COURT
COUP DE GRACE
COUPLING BOX
COURT TENNIS
COURTLY LOVE
COVER CHARGE
COWBOY BOOTS
CRACK OF DAWN
CRACK OF DOOM
CRACK TROOPS
CRACKED DOWN
CRACKS A CRIB
CRACKS A JOKE
CRANE NECKED
CRASH COURSE
CRASH HELMET
CRASHING OUT
CRAWLER LANE
CRAZY PAVING
CREAM CHEESE
CREME BRULEE
CREPE RUBBER
CRICKET BALL
CRIMEN FALSI
CROCK OF GOLD
CROOKES TUBE
CROP SPRAYER
CROQUET LAWN
CROSS LEGGED
CROSS REFERS
CROSS STITCH
CROSS SWORDS
CROSSED LINE
CROSSED OVER
CROSSES OVER
CROWD PULLER
CROWN ANTLER
CROWN COLONY
CROWN COURTS
CROWN JEWELS
CROWN LAWYER
CROWN LIVING
CROWN OCTAVO
CROWN OFFICE
CROWN PRINCE
CROWNED HEAD
CRYPTIC CLUE
CRYSTAL BALL
CUB REPORTER
CUCKOO CLOCK
CULINARY ART
CULVERS ROOT
CUP FINALIST
CUP OF COFFEE
CUPRO NICKEL
CURLING POND
CURLY GREENS
CURLY HEADED
CURRANT CAKE

CURRANT WINE
CURRY FAVOUR
CURRY POWDER
CURTAIN CALL
CURTAIN WALL
CUSTARD TART
CUSTOM BUILT
CUSTOM HOUSE
CUT AND DRIED
CUT BOTH WAYS
CUT OFF POINT
CUT THE CARDS
CUTS AND RUNS
CUTS CORNERS
CUTS UP ROUGH
CUTTING BACK
CUTTING DEAD
CUTTING DOWN
CUTTING EDGE
CYCLING CLUB
CYPRESS TREE
DAIL EIREANN
DAIRY CATTLE
DAISY CUTTER
DAK BUNGALOW
DAMASK STEEL
DAMPING DOWN
DANCING BEAR
DANCING GIRL
DANGER MONEY
DANGER POINT
DANISH BACON
DARE DEVILRY
DARK GLASSES
DASHING AWAY
DATE OF BIRTH
DAWN CYPRESS
DAY IN DAY OUT
DAY LABOURER
DAYS OF GRACE
DE PROFUNDIS
DEAD AS A DODO
DEAD HEADING
DEAD OF NIGHT
DEAF AND DUMB
DEAF AS A POST
DEATH RATTLE
DEATH THROES
DECK OF CARDS
DECK OFFICER
DECK PASSAGE
DECKLE EDGED
DECLARED WAR
DECLARES WAR
DEFERRED PAY
DELAYED DROP
DELIVERY MAN
DELIVERY VAN
DELLA ROBBIA
DELTA WINGED

11 *contd.*
DEMON BARBER
DEMON BOWLER
DENTAL FLOSS
DENY ONESELF
DEPTH CHARGE
DERBY WINNER
DESERT BOOTS
DEVILS BONES
DEVILS BOOKS
DIAMOND BACK
DIAMOND DUST
DIAMOND MINE
DIAMOND RING
DIANA MONKEY
DICE PLAYING
DICKIN MEDAL
DID THE TRICK
DID THE TWIST
DIE THE DEATH
DIESEL TRAIN
DIGITAL FACE
DINING TABLE
DINNER DANCE
DINNER PARTY
DINNER TABLE
DINNER WAGON
DIPS THE FLAG
DIRE STRAITS
DIRECT DEBIT
DIRTY OLD MAN
DISC PARKING
DISH THE DIRT
DISMAL JIMMY
DISPATCH BOX
DISTAFF SIDE
DIVE BOMBING
DIVINE RIGHT
DIVING BOARD
DIVING DRESS
DIVINING ROD
DIVORCE SUIT
DO ME A FAVOUR
DO ONES STUFF
DO ONES WORST
DOCK WARRANT
DOES ONES BIT
DOES TO DEATH
DOGGY PADDLE
DOGS MERCURY
DOLLY CAMERA
DOLLY SWITCH
DOLLY VARDEN
DOMESTIC PET
DOMINION DAY
DONE TO A TURN
DONE TO DEATH
DONKEY DERBY
DOOR KNOCKER
DOS AND DONTS

DOSSING DOWN
DOT AND CARRY
DOTTED THE IS
DOUBLE AGENT
DOUBLE BLANK
DOUBLE BLIND
DOUBLE BLUFF
DOUBLE CHECK
DOUBLE CREAM
DOUBLE CROSS
DOUBLE DOORS
DOUBLE DUTCH
DOUBLE EAGLE
DOUBLE EDGED
DOUBLE ENTRY
DOUBLE FAULT
DOUBLE FIRST
DOUBLE HELIX
DOUBLE PARKS
DOUBLE QUICK
DOUBLE SHARP
DOUBLE SPACE
DOUBLE SPEAK
DOUBLE THINK
DOUBLED BACK
DOUBLES BACK
DOWN DRAUGHT
DOWN HEARTED
DOWN PAYMENT
DOWN THE LINE
DOWN THE WIND
DOWN TO EARTH
DOWN TRODDEN
DOWNED TOOLS
DRAFT DODGER
DRAGGING OUT
DRAGOON BIRD
DRAINED AWAY
DRAM DRINKER
DRAMA SCHOOL
DRAW THE LINE
DRAWING BACK
DRAWING LOTS
DRAWING NEAR
DRAWING ROOM
DRAWS A BLANK
DRAWS STUMPS
DREAM TICKET
DREDGING BOX
DRESDEN WARE
DRESS CIRCLE
DRESS LENGTH
DRESS SHIELD
DRESSED CRAB
DRESSED DOWN
DRESSES DOWN
DREW THE LINE
DRIFT ANCHOR
DRIFT MINING
DRILL HARROW

DRILL MASTER
DRILL PLOUGH
DRINK DRIVER
DRIPPING PAN
DRIVING GEAR
DRIVING HOME
DRIVING RAIN
DRIVING TEST
DROP FORGING
DROPPED AWAY
DROPPED DOWN
DROPPING OFF
DROPPING OUT
DROPS A BRICK
DROPS ANCHOR
DROWNING OUT
DRY CLEANERS
DRY CLEANING
DUAL CONTROL
DUAL PURPOSE
DUCHESSE SET
DUCKING DOWN
DUCKING POND
DULL BRAINED
DUMDUM FEVER
DUMPER TRUCK
DUPLEX HOUSE
DUSTY MILLER
DUTCH CHEESE
DUTY OFFICER
DWARFED TREE
DYERS ROCKET
D IL EIREANN
EAGER BEAVER
EAR PIERCING
EARL MARSHAL
EARTH MOTHER
EARTH TREMOR
EARTHS CRUST
EAST BY NORTH
EATING APPLE
EATING HOUSE
EATING IRONS
ECHO CHAMBER
ECHO SOUNDER
ECONOMY SIZE
EIFFEL TOWER
EIGHT OCLOCK
EJECTOR SEAT
ELASTIC BAND
ELBOW GREASE
ELECTRIC ARC
ELECTRIC EEL
ELECTRIC EYE
ELECTRIC RAY
ELECTRON GUN
ELEPHANT BOY
ELEPHANT GUN
ELKHORN FERN
EMERALD ISLE

EMERALD TYPE
EMERY POWDER
EMPEROR MOTH
EMPTY HANDED
EMPTY HEADED
ENABLING ACT
ENDLESS WORM
ENDS IN TEARS
ENGLISH HORN
ENLISTED MAN
ENTRANCE FEE
EPOCH MAKING
EQUAL RIGHTS
ESCAPE HATCH
ESCAPE ROUTE
ESCAPE VALVE
ESCAPE WHEEL
ESTATE AGENT
ETERNAL CITY
ETHMOID BONE
ETON COLLEGE
EURO DOLLARS
EURO SCEPTIC
EVENING MEAL
EVENING STAR
EVER AND ANON
EVEREST PACK
EVIL STARRED
EX DIRECTORY
EXEUNT OMNES
EXHAUST PIPE
EXPLAIN AWAY
EXPORT DRIVE
EYE CATCHING
EYE OF A STORM
FACE FLANNEL
FACE LIFTING
FACED UP TO IT
FACES UP TO IT
FACING FACTS
FACT FINDING
FACTORY ACTS
FACTORY FARM
FACTORY SHIP
FACTS OF LIFE
FADING LIGHT
FAIR DEALING
FAIR WEATHER
FAITH HEALER
FALL THROUGH
FALLING BACK
FALLING DOWN
FALLING OVER
FALLING STAR
FALLS BEHIND
FALLS IN LOVE
FALSE ACACIA
FALSE BOTTOM
FALSI CRIMEN
FAMILLE ROSE

11 *contd.*

FAMILY BAKER
FAMILY BIBLE
FAMILY CREST
FAN VAULTING
FANCY STITCH
FAR REACHING
FARES PLEASE
FARM OFFICES
FARMER GILES
FARMERS LUNG
FASCIA BOARD
FASHION SHOW
FAST BOWLING
FAST FORWARD
FAST NEUTRON
FAST REACTOR
FASTENING ON
FATA MORGANA
FATHER IN LAW
FATIGUE DUTY
FATTENING UP
FATUOUS FIRE
FAULT FINDER
FEAST OF LOTS
FEATHER PALM
FEATURE FILM
FED ONES FACE
FEELS AT HOME
FELIX THE CAT
FELL THROUGH
FELL WALKING
FELT FELT PEN
FEMME FATALE
FERRIS WHEEL
FETCHING OUT
FETE GALANTE
FIBRE OPTICS
FIDDLE DE DEE
FIDDLER CRAB
FIELD MADDER
FIELD OF VIEW
FIELD SPORTS
FIFTH AVENUE
FIFTH COLUMN
FIGHTING FIT
FIGHTING OFF
FIGHTS IT OUT
FIGURE IT OUT
FILET MIGNON
FILING CLERK
FILL THE BILL
FILLET STEAK
FILM ACTRESS
FILTER PAPER
FILTHY LUCRE
FIN DE SIECLE
FINAL DEMAND
FIND THE LADY
FINE WRITING

FINES HERBES
FINGER FOODS
FINISHED OFF
FINISHES OFF
FINISHING UP
FINNO UGRIAN
FIPPLE FLUTE
FIRE BLANKET
FIRE BOMBING
FIRE BRIGADE
FIRE CONTROL
FIRE CRACKER
FIRE CURTAIN
FIRE FIGHTER
FIRE MARSHAL
FIRE OFFICER
FIRE RAISING
FIRE STATION
FIRE WALKING
FIRE WATCHER
FIRE WORSHIP
FIRING ORDER
FIRING PARTY
FIRING POINT
FIRING SQUAD
FIRMING DOWN
FIRST COUSIN
FIRST ELEVEN
FIRST FOOTER
FIRST FRUITS
FIRST SCHOOL
FIRST STOREY
FIRST STRIKE
FISH BELLIED
FISH EYE LENS
FISH FARMING
FISH FINGERS
FISH GUTTING
FISH PACKING
FISH TORPEDO
FISHING BOAT
FISHING LINE
FISSION BOMB
FITTING ROOM
FITTING SHOP
FIVE DAY WEEK
FIVE EIGHTHS
FIXED ASSETS
FIXED INCOME
FLAG CAPTAIN
FLAG OF TRUCE
FLAG OFFICER
FLAG WAGGING
FLAGGED DOWN
FLAKY PASTRY
FLAP MOUTHED
FLAT EARTHER
FLATTENS OUT
FLAX DRESSER
FLEET AIR ARM

FLEET FOOTED
FLEET OF CARS
FLEET OF FOOT
FLEET PRISON
FLEET STREET
FLEMISH BOND
FLESH COLOUR
FLESH MARKET
FLESHING OUT
FLEURS DE LIS
FLEURS DE LYS
FLEW THE FLAG
FLINGING OUT
FLIP ONES LID
FLIP TOP PACK
FLOATING RIB
FLOATS ON AIR
FLOCK MASTER
FLOOR TIMBER
FLOORING SAW
FLORAL DANCE
FLOWER CHILD
FLOWER CLOCK
FLOWER POWER
FLOWER STALK
FLUX DENSITY
FLY DRESSING
FLYING A KITE
FLYING CORPS
FLYING LEMUR
FLYING PARTY
FLYING SQUAD
FLYING START
FLYING VISIT
FOILED AGAIN
FOLDING DOOR
FOLIAGE LEAF
FOLK DANCING
FOLK SINGING
FOLLOWED OUT
FOLLOWING ON
FOLLOWING UP
FOLLOWS HOME
FOLLOWS SUIT
FOOLS AROUND
FOOLS ERRAND
FOOLS RUSH IN
FOOT FAULTED
FOOT SLOGGER
FOOT SOLDIER
FOOT THE BILL
FOR ALL I CARE
FOR GODS SAKE
FOR INSTANCE
FOR STARTERS
FOR THE BIRDS
FORCED MARCH
FORE RECITED
FOREIGN BILL
FOREIGN BODY

FORGET ME NOT
FORKING OVER
FORLORN HOPE
FORM TEACHER
FORMAL CAUSE
FORMAL LOGIC
FORT WILLIAM
FORTH BRIDGE
FORTUNE BOOK
FORWARD PASS
FOSBURY FLOP
FOSSIL FIRED
FOSTER CHILD
FOSTER NURSE
FOUGHT IT OUT
FOUL MOUTHED
FOUNDERS DAY
FOUNTAIN PEN
FOUR ACT PLAY
FOUR FLUSHER
FOUR POUNDER
FOUR WHEELED
FOUR WHEELER
FOURTH WORLD
FOX AND GEESE
FRAME OF MIND
FRANC TIREUR
FRANK PLEDGE
FREAKING OUT
FREE AND EASY
FREE AS A BIRD
FREE COUNTRY
FREE FALLING
FREE HEARTED
FREE PARKING
FREE RADICAL
FREE SKATING
FREE THOUGHT
FREE WHEELED
FREEZE DRIED
FREEZE DRIES
FREEZE FRAME
FREEZES DOWN
FREEZES OVER
FREEZING OUT
FRENCH BERRY
FRENCH BREAD
FRENCH CHALK
FRENCH FRANC
FRENCH FRIES
FRENCH LEAVE
FRENCH PLEAT
FRENCH STICK
FRENCH TOAST
FRENCH WHITE
FRESH FIELDS
FRESHENED UP
FRIEND OR FOE
FRIGATE BIRD
FRIGHTEN OFF

11 *contd.*
FRIGID ZONES
FRITTER AWAY
FROG MARCHED
FROG MARCHES
FROM SCRATCH
FROM WAY BACK
FRONT LOADER
FRONT RANKER
FRONT RUNNER
FROST BITTEN
FROTH BLOWER
FROZEN NORTH
FROZEN PIPES
FROZEN STIFF
FULL BLOODED
FULL BROTHER
FULL CHARGED
FULL FRONTAL
FULL HEARTED
FULL MOUTHED
FULL OF BEANS
FULL TIME JOB
FULLERS HERB
FULLING MILL
FUME CHAMBER
FUND RAISING
FUNERAL HOME
FUNERAL PYRE
FUSIDIC ACID
FUTURE TENSE
FUZZY HAIRED
GABLE WINDOW
GADDED ABOUT
GAFF TOPSAIL
GAIN CONTROL
GAINING TIME
GAINS GROUND
GALAM BUTTER
GALL BLADDER
GALLEY PROOF
GALLEY SLAVE
GALLOPED OFF
GALLOWS BIRD
GALLOWS FREE
GALLOWS TREE
GAMBIT PIECE
GAMBLING DEN
GAMBREL ROOF
GAME FISHING
GAME LICENCE
GAME OF SKILL
GAMES MASTER
GAMES THEORY
GAMING HOUSE
GAMING TABLE
GAMMON STEAK
GANDER MONTH
GANG WARFARE
GANTRY CRANE

GARAM MASALA
GARAND RIFLE
GARDEN GLASS
GARDEN HOUSE
GARDEN PARTY
GARDEN PATCH
GAS FITTINGS
GAS GUZZLING
GASTRIC MILL
GATHER ROUND
GATHER SPEED
GATHERED WAY
GATHERING UP
GAUZE WINGED
GAVE OFFENCE
GAY DECEIVER
GAY LOTHARIO
GAZING STOCK
GEARING DOWN
GEFILTE FISH
GENERAL LINE
GENERAL POST
GENERIC NAME
GENETIC CODE
GENEVA BANDS
GENEVA BIBLE
GENEVA CROSS
GENS DEGLISE
GENS DU MONDE
GENTLE CRAFT
GENTLE GIANT
GENTLE TOUCH
GEORGE CROSS
GEORGE MEDAL
GERM WARFARE
GERMAN FLUTE
GET CRACKING
GET IN THE WAY
GET ONES GOAT
GET TOGETHER
GET WELL SOON
GETS A LINE ON
GETS A WICKET
GETS DRESSED
GETS HITCHED
GETS ONES WAY
GETS THE BIRD
GETS THE BOOT
GETS THE CHOP
GETS THE PUSH
GETS THE SACK
GETS THROUGH
GETS TO GRIPS
GETS TO SLEEP
GETS UP STEAM
GETTING BACK
GETTING DOWN
GETTING EVEN
GETTING OVER
GHOST WRITER

GIANT FENNEL
GIANT KILLER
GIDDY HEADED
GIDEON BIBLE
GIFT VOUCHER
GIFT WRAPPED
GILA MONSTER
GILD THE LILY
GILD THE PILL
GILDED SPURS
GILDED YOUTH
GIN AND TONIC
GINGER GROUP
GIRD ONESELF
GIVE AND TAKE
GIVE OFFENCE
GIVES GROUND
GIVES NOTICE
GIVING BIRTH
GIVING CHASE
GIVING FORTH
GIVING IT A GO
GIVING VOICE
GLAD TIDINGS
GLAMOUR GIRL
GLASS BLOWER
GLASS CUTTER
GLASS GAZING
GLASS OF BEER
GLASS OF MILK
GLASS OF WINE
GLEE SINGERS
GLIDER PILOT
GLORIA PATRI
GLOTTAL STOP
GLOVE PUPPET
GLOVE SHIELD
GLUE SNIFFER
GNAWING AWAY
GO A BUNDLE ON
GO BY THE BOOK
GO LIKE A BOMB
GO ONE BETTER
GO OVERBOARD
GO THE ROUNDS
GO TO THE DOGS
GO TO THE WALL
GO TO THE WARS
GO UP IN SMOKE
GO WITH A BANG
GOAL TENDING
GOD BLESS YOU
GOD BOTHERER
GOD FORSAKEN
GODS COUNTRY
GOES AGAINST
GOES FOR GOLD
GOES FORWARD
GOES IT ALONE
GOES MISSING

GOES ONES WAY
GOES THROUGH
GOES TO COURT
GOES TO EARTH
GOES TO PRESS
GOES TO SLEEP
GOES TO WASTE
GOES WITHOUT
GOG AND MAGOG
GOING ABROAD
GOING HALVES
GOING HUNGRY
GOING METRIC
GOING NATIVE
GOING PLACES
GOING STEADY
GOING STRONG
GOING TO SEED
GOING TO TOWN
GOING TOO FAR
GOLD BEATING
GOLD BULLION
GOLD CRESTED
GOLD DIGGING
GOLD RESERVE
GOLDEN ARROW
GOLDEN BOUGH
GOLDEN CHAIN
GOLDEN EAGLE
GOLDEN GOOSE
GOLDEN HELLO
GOLDEN HORDE
GOLDEN OLDIE
GOLDEN SYRUP
GOLGI BODIES
GOLIATH FROG
GONE FISHING
GONE GOSLING
GONE MISSING
GONE THROUGH
GONE TO EARTH
GONE TO GRASS
GONE TO LUNCH
GONE TO SLEEP
GONE TO WASTE
GOOD COMPANY
GOOD EVENING
GOOD FORTUNE
GOOD HEAVENS
GOOD HUNTING
GOOD LOOKING
GOOD MORNING
GOOD NATURED
GOOD OFFICES
GOODS ENGINE
GOOSE FLOWER
GOOSE WINGED
GORDIAN KNOT
GOSPEL TRUTH
GOT CRACKING

11 *contd.*

GOT IN THE WAY
GOT ONES GOAT
GOT TOGETHER
GRADE SCHOOL
GRAECO ROMAN
GRAHAM BREAD
GRAHAM FLOUR
GRAIN OF SAND
GRAN TURISMO
GRAND CANYON
GRAND FINALE
GRAND MASTER
GRAND NEPHEW
GRAND OLD MAN
GRAND SIECLE
GRANDE ARMEE
GRANDE ECOLE
GRANNY BONDS
GRANNY SMITH
GRANT OF ARMS
GRANTH SAHIB
GRAPHIC ARTS
GRASS CUTTER
GRAVE ACCENT
GRAVE DIGGER
GRAVEN IMAGE
GRAVITY WAVE
GREASE PAINT
GREASE PROOF
GREASY SPOON
GREAT CIRCLE
GREAT NEPHEW
GREAT OCTAVE
GREAT PLAGUE
GREAT SCHISM
GRECIAN BEND
GRECIAN NOSE
GREEK CHURCH
GREEN BERETS
GREEN CHEESE
GREEN DRAGON
GREEN KEEPER
GREEN LINNET
GREEN MONKEY
GREEN PEPPER
GREEN PLOVER
GREEN TURTLE
GRESHAMS LAW
GRETNA GREEN
GRIZZLY BEAR
GROSS INCOME
GROUND COVER
GROUND FLOOR
GROUND FROST
GROUND GLASS
GROUND RULES
GROUND SLOTH
GROUND SPEED
GROUND STAFF

GROUND SWELL
GROUND TO AIR
GROUP THEORY
GRUFF VOICED
GUELDER ROSE
GUIDING STAR
GUILTY PARTY
GUINEA GRASS
GUN CARRIAGE
GUTTA PERCHA
GUTTER PRESS
GUTTER SNIPE
GYPSUM BLOCK
HACKING COAT
HAD IT COMING
HAGIA SOPHIA
HAILED A TAXI
HAIR BRAINED
HAIR RAISING
HAIR TRIGGER
HAIRPIN BEND
HALCYON DAYS
HALF AND HALF
HALF BROTHER
HALF HEARTED
HALF HOLIDAY
HALF MEASURE
HALF POUNDER
HALF STARVED
HALF THE TIME
HALL BEDROOM
HAMMER BRACE
HAMMER DRILL
HAMMER THROW
HAMMERS HOME
HAND AND FOOT
HAND FEEDING
HAND GRENADE
HAND KNITTED
HAND ME DOWNS
HAND OF GLORY
HAND ON HEART
HAND SIGNALS
HAND TO MOUTH
HANDING DOWN
HANDING OVER
HANG GLIDING
HANG IN THERE
HANGDOG LOOK
HANGING BACK
HANGING FIRE
HANGS AROUND
HAPPENS UPON
HAPPY ENDING
HAPPY MEDIUM
HARBOUR DUES
HARD AND FAST
HARD AS NAILS
HARD DRINKER
HARD GRAINED

HARD HEARTED
HARD HITTING
HARD PRESSED
HARD PUT TO IT
HARD WEARING
HARDENED OFF
HARDY ANNUAL
HARE BRAINED
HARE KRISHNA
HARICOT BEAN
HARKING BACK
HARNESS ROOM
HARRIS TWEED
HARTS TONGUE
HARUM SCARUM
HARVEST HOME
HARVEST LADY
HARVEST LORD
HARVEST MITE
HARVEST MOON
HARVEST TICK
HARVEY SMITH
HAS IT COMING
HASTA MANANA
HAULED ROUND
HAVE KITTENS
HAVE ONES WAY
HAVE YOU DONE
HAVING A BALL
HAVING A BASH
HAVING A STAB
HAVING IDEAS
HAVING IT OUT
HAVING WORDS
HEAD BANGING
HEAD TEACHER
HEALTH STAMP
HEARD THINGS
HEARING TELL
HEARS THINGS
HEARSE CLOTH
HEART ATTACK
HEART EASING
HEART MURMUR
HEART SHAPED
HEART STRING
HEARTH BRUSH
HEARTH STONE
HEARTS BLOOD
HEAT BARRIER
HEATHER BELL
HEAVEN KNOWS
HEAVY HANDED
HEAVY HEADED
HEAVY SMOKER
HECTIC FEVER
HEDGE HOPPED
HEDGE HOPPER
HEDGE PARSON
HEDGE SCHOOL

HELD IN CHECK
HELD ONES OWN
HELD THE FORT
HELD THE LINE
HELD THE ROAD
HELL ON EARTH
HELLO SAILOR
HELMET SHELL
HELP ONESELF
HELPING HAND
HELVE HAMMER
HEMPEN WIDOW
HER LADYSHIP
HERB TRINITY
HERO WORSHIP
HEROIC VERSE
HERRING BONE
HERRING GULL
HERRING POND
HESSIAN BOOT
HIC ET UBIQUE
HID ONES HEAD
HIDE AND SEEK
HIDING PLACE
HIGH ADMIRAL
HIGH AS A KITE
HIGH BAILIFF
HIGH COMMAND
HIGH DENSITY
HIGH FALUTIN
HIGH FINANCE
HIGH HEARTED
HIGH OLD TIME
HIGH PITCHED
HIGH POWERED
HIGH PROFILE
HIGH RANKING
HIGH ROLLING
HIGH SHERIFF
HIGH SIGHTED
HIGH SOCIETY
HIGH SPIRITS
HIGH STEPPER
HIGH TAILS IT
HIGH TENSION
HIGH TREASON
HIGH VOLTAGE
HIGH WIRE ACT
HIGHER GRADE
HIGHWAY CODE
HILL PASTURE
HILL STATION
HIS HOLINESS
HIS LORDSHIP
HISTORY BOOK
HITCH HIKING
HITS THE DECK
HITS THE ROAD
HITS THE ROOF
HITS THE SACK

11 *contd.*

HOBBLE SKIRT
HOCKEY PITCH
HOCKEY STICK
HOLD IN CHECK
HOLD ONES OWN
HOLD THE FORT
HOLD THE LINE
HOLD THE ROAD
HOLDING BACK
HOLDING DOWN
HOLDING GOOD
HOLDING OVER
HOLDING SWAY
HOLIDAY CAMP
HOLLOW TOOTH
HOLLOWED OUT
HOME AND AWAY
HOME CIRCUIT
HOME COOKING
HOME CROFTER
HOME DEFENCE
HOME KEEPING
HOME MADE JAM
HOME STRETCH
HOMO ERECTUS
HOMO HABILIS
HOMO SAPIENS
HONEST INJUN
HONEST TO GOD
HONEY BADGER
HONEY LOCUST
HONEY SUCKLE
HONITON LACE
HONOUR BOUND
HONOURS EASY
HONOURS LIST
HOORAH HENRY
HOP O MY THUMB
HOPS THE TWIG
HORN MADNESS
HORN MERCURY
HORNED POPPY
HORNED VIPER
HORNETS NEST
HORROR STORY
HORS DOEUVRE
HORSE AROUND
HORSE COLLAR
HORSE DEALER
HORSE DOCTOR
HORSE DRENCH
HORSE GUARDS
HORSE MARINE
HORSE PISTOL
HORSE RACING
HORSE RIDING
HOSPITAL BED
HOT CROSS BUN
HOT SPIRITED

HOT TEMPERED
HOTEL KEEPER
HOUNDS TOOTH
HOUSE ARREST
HOUSE FATHER
HOUSE HUNTER
HOUSE LIGHTS
HOUSE MARTIN
HOUSE MOTHER
HOUSE OF KEYS
HOVE THE LEAD
HOWLING DOWN
HUG THE COAST
HUGS ONESELF
HUMAN DYNAMO
HUMAN NATURE
HUMAN RIGHTS
HUMMING BIRD
HUNG IN THERE
HUNGER MARCH
HUNGER PANGS
HUNTERS MOON
HUNTING CROP
HUNTING DOWN
HUNTING HORN
HUNTING SEAT
HUNTING SONG
HUNTING WHIP
HURDLE RACER
HURRY SCURRY
HUSH PUPPIES
HYDRA HEADED
HYDROGEN ION
ICE YACHTING
ICELAND MOSS
IF YOU PLEASE
IGNEOUS ROCK
IGNIS FATUUS
IGNITION KEY
ILL AFFECTED
ILL ASSORTED
ILL BREEDING
ILL DISPOSED
ILL FAVOURED
ILL HUMOURED
ILL INFORMED
ILL MANNERED
ILL TEMPERED
IN A BAD LIGHT
IN A FLAT SPIN
IN A GOOD MOOD
IN A LARGE WAY
IN A MINORITY
IN A NUTSHELL
IN A QUANDARY
IN A SMALL WAY
IN ABSTRACTO
IN AN INSTANT
IN ARMS REACH
IN CHARACTER

IN COLD BLOOD
IN COMMITTEE
IN DEEP WATER
IN DREAMLAND
IN DUE COURSE
IN DUPLICATE
IN FULL BLAST
IN FULL SWING
IN GOOD FAITH
IN GOOD HEART
IN GOOD ODOUR
IN GOOD SHAPE
IN HYSTERICS
IN MICROCOSM
IN MINIATURE
IN MOTHBALLS
IN ONES POWER
IN ONES SLEEP
IN PRINCIPLE
IN SUBSTANCE
IN THE CHORUS
IN THE MAKING
IN THE MIDDLE
IN THE OFFING
IN THE SADDLE
IN THE THROES
IN TWO SHAKES
INCENSE BOAT
INDEX FINGER
INDEX LINKED
INDEX NUMBER
INDIA RUBBER
INDIAN BREAD
INDIAN CRESS
INDIAN CURRY
INDIAN OCEAN
INDIRECT TAX
INDO CHINESE
INDOOR GAMES
INERTIA REEL
INITIAL CELL
INK BLOT TEST
INKING TABLE
INNS OF COURT
INSIDE RIGHT
INSIDE STORY
INSIDE TRACK
INTER PARTES
ION EXCHANGE
IONIC SCHOOL
IRISH COFFEE
IRISH GUARDS
IRISH SETTER
IRON CURTAIN
IRON FILINGS
IRON FOUNDER
IRON FOUNDRY
IRON HEARTED
IRON PYRITES
ISLE OF WIGHT

ISSUED FORTH
ISSUES FORTH
ITCHY PALMED
JACK AND JILL
JACK KNIFING
JACK RUSSELL
JACOBS SHEEP
JACOBS STAFF
JAFFA ORANGE
JAM DOUGHNUT
JAM TOMORROW
JAMAICA BARK
JAMAICA PLUM
JAPAN LAUREL
JAPAN TALLOW
JAUNTING CAR
JELLIED EELS
JELLY BABIES
JENNY DONKEY
JESSE WINDOW
JESUITS BARK
JESUS CHRIST
JINGLE BELLS
JOGGED ALONG
JOHN COLLINS
JOIE DE VIVRE
JOIN THE CLUB
JOINED HANDS
JOINT TENANT
JOKING APART
JOURNEY WORK
JUBILEE CLIP
JUBILEE LINE
JUDGMENT DAY
JUMP STARTED
JUMPING BAIL
JUMPING BEAN
JUMPING DEER
JUMPING HARE
JUMPING JACK
JUMPING SHIP
JUMPS FOR JOY
JUMPS THE GUN
JUNCTION BOX
JUNGLE FEVER
JUNGLE JUICE
JUNIPER TREE
JURY PROCESS
JURY SERVICE
JUST A MINUTE
JUST DESERTS
JUST MARRIED
KAFFIR BREAD
KANGAROO RAT
KEELING OVER
KEEP A SECRET
KEEP AN EYE ON
KEEP COUNSEL
KEEP IN CHECK
KEEP IN TOUCH

11 contd.

KEEP SMILING
KEEPING AT IT
KEEPING BACK
KEEPING BUSY
KEEPING DOWN
KEEPING ROOM
KEEPING TIME
KEEPS IN MIND
KEEPS IT DARK
KEEPS TABS ON
KEEPS WICKET
KENDAL GREEN
KENTISH FIRE
KEPLERS LAWS
KEPT A SECRET
KEPT AN EYE ON
KEPT COUNSEL
KEPT IN CHECK
KEPT IN TOUCH
KERB CRAWLER
KEY INDUSTRY
KHAKI SHORTS
KICK ONESELF
KICK UP A FUSS
KICKED ABOUT
KICKS AROUND
KIDNEY STONE
KIDS ONESELF
KILLER WHALE
KILLING TIME
KIND HEARTED
KIND NATURED
KIND REGARDS
KING CHARLES
KING OF BIRDS
KING OF KINGS
KING PENGUIN
KING RICHARD
KING STEPHEN
KING WILLIAM
KINGDOM COME
KINGS BOUNTY
KINGS SPEECH
KINGS YELLOW
KIPPING DOWN
KIRK SESSION
KISS AND TELL
KISS ME QUICK
KISS OF DEATH
KISS THE BOOK
KISSING GATE
KITCHEN MAID
KITCHEN SINK
KITCHEN UNIT
KITE BALLOON
KLEIN BOTTLE
KNEE CAPPING
KNEE TRIBUTE
KNIFE SWITCH

KNOCK AROUND
KNOCK FOR SIX
KNOCK ON WOOD
KNOCK RATING
KNOCKED BACK
KNOCKED COLD
KNOCKED DOWN
KNOCKING OFF
KNOCKING OUT
KNOCKS ABOUT
KNOW NOTHING
KNOW THYSELF
KNOWS BETTER
KNUCKLE BONE
KNUCKLE DOWN
KNUCKLE HEAD
KOKUM BUTTER
LABOUR FORCE
LABOUR PARTY
LABOUR UNION
LABRADOR DOG
LABRADOR TEA
LACQUER TREE
LADY PROVOST
LADYS FINGER
LADYS MANTLE
LAID A COURSE
LAID HANDS ON
LAKE DWELLER
LAKE ONTARIO
LAMBETH WALK
LAMBS TONGUE
LANCE KNIGHT
LAND GRABBER
LAND JOBBING
LAND MEASURE
LAND STEWARD
LANDING GEAR
LANDING SHIP
LAP OF HONOUR
LAP OF LUXURY
LAPIS LAZULI
LARGE HANDED
LARGE MINDED
LARKED ABOUT
LAST HONOURS
LAST OFFICES
LATCH STRING
LATENT IMAGE
LATTICE LEAF
LAUGHING GAS
LAUGHING OFF
LAUGHS IT OFF
LAUNDRY LIST
LAUNDRY MAID
LAUREL WATER
LAW AND ORDER
LAW BREAKING
LAW MERCHANT
LAW OF NATURE

LAY AT ANCHOR
LAY IN THE WAY
LAY THE TABLE
LAYING AN EGG
LAYING ASIDE
LAYING CLAIM
LAYING WASTE
LAYS A COURSE
LAYS HANDS ON
LEACH TROUGH
LEADER CABLE
LEADING CARD
LEADING CASE
LEADING EDGE
LEADING LADY
LEADS ASTRAY
LEADS THE WAY
LEAF CUTTING
LEAGUE MATCH
LEAGUE TABLE
LEATHER BACK
LEATHER BELT
LEATHER COAT
LEATHER HEAD
LEATHER NECK
LEAVE BEHIND
LEAVE TAKING
LEAVE UNSAID
LEAVES ALONE
LEAVING SHOP
LECHER WIRES
LECTURE HALL
LECTURE TOUR
LEFT FOR DEAD
LEFT ONE COLD
LEFT THE ROOM
LEG OF MUTTON
LEGAL TENDER
LEISURE SUIT
LEISURE WEAR
LEMON BARLEY
LEMON CHEESE
LEMON SQUASH
LEMON YELLOW
LEOPARD MOTH
LEOPARD SKIN
LESE MAJESTY
LET OFF STEAM
LETTER BOARD
LETTER STAMP
LETTING DOWN
LETTING DROP
LETTING FALL
LETTING IN ON
LETTING SLIP
LEVEL HEADED
LEVELLED OFF
LIBEL ACTION
LIBERAL ARTS
LIBERTY BOAT

LIBERTY HALL
LIBERTY SHIP
LIBRARY BOOK
LIBRARY LIST
LICK OF PAINT
LICK PLATTER
LICK SPITTLE
LIE AT ANCHOR
LIE DETECTOR
LIE IN THE WAY
LIES IN STATE
LIFE ANNUITY
LIFE HISTORY
LIFE IS SWEET
LIFE PEERAGE
LIFE PEERESS
LIFE SAVINGS
LIFT A FINGER
LIGHT ENGINE
LIGHT FOOTED
LIGHT HANDED
LIGHT HEADED
LIGHT MINDED
LIGHT WINGED
LIGHTENED UP
LIGHTER FUEL
LIGNUM SCRUB
LIGNUM SWAMP
LIKE FOR LIKE
LIKE THE WIND
LILY LIVERED
LIMBERING UP
LINE DRAWING
LINE FISHING
LINE OF SIGHT
LINE PRINTER
LINE SHOOTER
LINEAR MOTOR
LINEN DRAPER
LINKED VERSE
LION HEARTED
LIP ROUNDING
LIP SMACKING
LISTENING IN
LITANY STOOL
LITMUS PAPER
LITTLE DEVIL
LITTLE WOMAN
LIVE CIRCUIT
LIVE CONCERT
LIVING DEATH
LIVING IN SIN
LIVING ON AIR
LO AND BEHOLD
LOAD BEARING
LOAF OF BREAD
LOAN SOCIETY
LOBBY SYSTEM
LOCAL ACTION
LOCAL COLOUR

11 contd.

LOCAL OPTION
LOCHABER AXE
LOCKED HORNS
LOCKING AWAY
LOCUM TENENS
LODGE KEEPER
LOLLIPOP MAN
LONDON PRIDE
LONELY HEART
LONG CLOTHES
LONG HUNDRED
LONG MEASURE
LONG PLAYING
LONG SIGHTED
LONG WAISTED
LOOK ASKANCE
LOOK DAGGERS
LOOK FORWARD
LOOKED A FOOL
LOOKED AFTER
LOOKED SMALL
LOOKING AWRY
LOOKING BACK
LOOKING DOWN
LOOKING INTO
LOOKING OVER
LOOKING UP TO
LOOKS AGHAST
LOOMED LARGE
LOOP THE LOOP
LOOSE BODIED
LOOSE CHANGE
LOOSE LIMBED
LOOSENING UP
LORD PROVOST
LORDS PRAYER
LORRY DRIVER
LOSE CONTROL
LOSE ONES RAG
LOSE ONES WAY
LOSE ONESELF
LOSES COLOUR
LOSES GROUND
LOSES WEIGHT
LOSING COUNT
LOSING HEART
LOSING TOUCH
LOSING TRACK
LOST CONTROL
LOST HORIZON
LOST ONES RAG
LOST ONES WAY
LOST ONESELF
LOTUS EATERS
LOUD MOUTHED
LOUIS QUINZE
LOUIS TREIZE
LOUNGE ABOUT
LOUNGE CHAIR

LOUVRE BOARD
LOVE IN A MIST
LOVE IS BLIND
LOVE LETTERS
LOW PRESSURE
LOW SPIRITED
LUCKY NUMBER
LUCKY STRIKE
LUGGAGE RACK
LUING CATTLE
LUNAR THEORY
LUNCHEON BAR
LUXURY GOODS
LYING FALLOW
LYING IN WAIT
MACASSAR OIL
MACHINE CODE
MACHINE MADE
MACHINE SHOP
MACHINE TOOL
MACHINE WORK
MACKEREL SKY
MAD SCRAMBLE
MAD STAGGERS
MADE A FUSS OF
MADE A PASS AT
MADE BELIEVE
MADE CERTAIN
MADE CHANGES
MADE FRIENDS
MADE HISTORY
MADE INROADS
MADE LIGHT OF
MADE ONES DAY
MADE ONES WAY
MADE THE PACE
MADE TO ORDER
MADE WHOOPEE
MADEIRA CAKE
MADEIRA WINE
MADONNA LILY
MAGAZINE GUN
MAGIC BULLET
MAGIC CARPET
MAGIC CIRCLE
MAGIC MARKER
MAGIC SPHERE
MAGIC SQUARE
MAGINOT LINE
MAGNUM BONUM
MAID SERVANT
MAIL CARRIER
MAIL CATCHER
MAILING LIST
MAKE A FUSS OF
MAKE A PASS AT
MAKE BELIEVE
MAKE CERTAIN
MAKE CHANGES
MAKE FRIENDS

MAKE HISTORY
MAKE INROADS
MAKE LIGHT OF
MAKE ONES DAY
MAKE ONES WAY
MAKE OR BREAK
MAKE THE PACE
MAKE WHOOPEE
MAKES A POINT
MAKES A STAND
MAKES AMENDS
MAKES EYES AT
MAKES TRACKS
MAKING A BOMB
MAKING A FACE
MAKING A MOVE
MAKING AFTER
MAKING FUN OF
MAKING HASTE
MAKING MERRY
MAKING MONEY
MAKING PEACE
MAKING READY
MAKING SENSE
MAKING USE OF
MAKING WAVES
MALACCA CANE
MALIBU BOARD
MALT EXTRACT
MALT VINEGAR
MAN WATCHING
MANILA PAPER
MANY TONGUED
MAP MEASURER
MARBLE EDGED
MARBLE PAPER
MARINE STORE
MARK MY WORDS
MARKED CARDS
MARKET CROSS
MARKET PLACE
MARKET PRICE
MARKET SHARE
MARKET WOMAN
MARKING DOWN
MARKING TIME
MARLIN SPIKE
MARRIAGE BED
MARRYING OFF
MARSH MALLOW
MARTIAL ARTS
MASONIC HALL
MASS MEETING
MASS PRODUCE
MASTER CLASS
MASTER CLOCK
MASTER MASON
MASTER WHEEL
MATINEE COAT
MATINEE IDOL

MAUNDY MONEY
MEADOW BROWN
MEADOW GRASS
MEADOW SWEET
MEANING WELL
MEASURING UP
MECHLIN LACE
MEDICINE MAN
MEDIUM WAVES
MEDLEY RELAY
MEEK AND MILD
MEET HALFWAY
MEGATON BOMB
MEISSEN WARE
MELLOWED OUT
MELTING AWAY
MELTING DOWN
MEMBERS ONLY
MEMENTO MORI
MEMORIAL DAY
MEMORY TRACE
MEN SERVANTS
MERRY ANDREW
MERRY MAKERS
MERRY MAKING
MERSEY SOUND
MESONIC ATOM
MESSAGE GIRL
MESSED ABOUT
MESSES ABOUT
METHOD ACTOR
MEXICAN WAVE
MICKEY MOUSE
MID ATLANTIC
MIDDLE CLASS
MIDDLE EARTH
MIDDLE EIGHT
MIDDLE SIZED
MIDDLE STUMP
MIDDLE WATCH
MIDDLE WORLD
MIDNIGHT SUN
MIDWIFE TOAD
MILK PUDDING
MILKING TIME
MILLE FLEURS
MILLET GRASS
MINCED WORDS
MINCES WORDS
MIND BENDING
MIND BLOWING
MIND HEALING
MIND READING
MINE SWEEPER
MINE THROWER
MINERAL WELL
MINIMUM WAGE
MINOD DETAIL
MINOR ORDERS
MINOR PLANET

11 *contd.*

MINUTE GLASS
MINUTE STEAK
MINUTE WALTZ
MINUTE WATCH
MIRACLE DRUG
MIRACLE PLAY
MIRROR IMAGE
MISE EN SCENE
MISS A SITTER
MISS THE BOAT
MISS THE MARK
MISS THE POST
MISSING LINK
MISTING OVER
MITRAL VALVE
MIXED NUMBER
MIXING VALVE
MOBIUS STRIP
MOCK MODESTY
MOCKING BIRD
MODERN DANCE
MOLE DRAINER
MOLUCCA BEAN
MONEY BROKER
MONEY FOR JAM
MONEY LENDER
MONEY MAKING
MONEY MARKET
MONEY SPIDER
MONEY SUPPLY
MONEY TO BURN
MONEYS WORTH
MONKEY BLOCK
MONKEY BOARD
MONKEY BREAD
MONKEY GLAND
MONKEY SHINE
MONKEY WHEEL
MOON GODDESS
MOON MADNESS
MOPS AND MOWS
MORAL DEFEAT
MORE AND MORE
MORE FOOL YOU
MORNAY SAUCE
MORNING CALL
MORNING COAT
MORNING GOWN
MORNING ROOM
MORNING STAR
MORNING TIDE
MORRIS CHAIR
MORRIS DANCE
MORTAR BOARD
MORTISE LOCK
MORTONS FORK
MOSES BASKET
MOSQUITO NET
MOSS TROOPER

MOTHER GOOSE
MOTHER IN LAW
MOTHERS HELP
MOTHERS RUIN
MOTIVE POWER
MOTOR DRIVEN
MOTOR LAUNCH
MOTTLE FACED
MOULIN ROUGE
MOUNT ARARAT
MOUNTAIN AIR
MOUNTAIN ASH
MOUNTAIN CAT
MOUNTAIN DEW
MOUNTAIN TOP
MOUNTS GUARD
MOUSE COLOUR
MOVE TO TEARS
MOVING HOUSE
MRS MALAPROP
MUCH OBLIGED
MUD SLINGING
MUD WRESTLER
MUFFIN FIGHT
MULBERRY FIG
MULTI ACCESS
MUMS THE WORD
MURDER PARTY
MURPHYS GAME
MUSCLE BOUND
MUSCOVY DUCK
MUSEUM PIECE
MUSIC CENTRE
MUSIC HOLDER
MUSIC MASTER
MUSIC SELLER
MUSICAL SAND
MUSSEL SCALP
MUSSEL SCAUP
MUSSEL SHELL
MUSTARD BATH
MUTT AND JEFF
MUTTON CLOTH
MUTUAL FUNDS
MYSTERY SHIP
MYSTERY TOUR
NAIL VARNISH
NAILING DOWN
NAME CALLING
NAME DROPPER
NAMING NAMES
NAPIERS RODS
NARROW GAUGE
NATTIER BLUE
NATURAL BORN
NATURE TRAIL
NAVEL ORANGE
NE PLUS ULTRA
NEAR SIGHTED
NEAR THE BONE

NECK AND NECK
NECTAR GUIDE
NEEDLE CRAFT
NEEDLE PAPER
NEEDLE POINT
NERVE CENTRE
NERVE ENDING
NET CURTAINS
NET PRACTICE
NETBALL TEAM
NEUTRON BOMB
NEUTRON STAR
NEVER ENDING
NEVER FADING
NEVER SAY DIE
NEW BORN BABE
NEW POTATOES
NEW YEARS DAY
NEW YEARS EVE
NICE AND EASY
NICENE CREED
NICKEL STEEL
NIGHT ATTIRE
NIGHT FLIGHT
NIGHT FLOWER
NIGHT FLYING
NIGHT HUNTER
NIGHT PORTER
NIGHT SCHOOL
NIGHT WAKING
NIGHT WORKER
NIKKEI INDEX
NINNY HAMMER
NIP IN THE AIR
NIP IN THE BUD
NITRIC OXIDE
NITROUS ACID
NITTY GRITTY
NO ADMISSION
NO SUCH THING
NO TIME AT ALL
NO VACANCIES
NOBLE MINDED
NOBLE SAVAGE
NOBODYS FOOL
NODS THROUGH
NOM DE GUERRE
NON BELIEVER
NON DELIVERY
NON ELECTRIC
NON EXISTENT
NON METALLIC
NON PARTISAN
NON RESIDENT
NON SEQUITUR
NON SPECIFIC
NON UNIONIST
NON VIOLENCE
NONE THE LESS
NORMAN CROSS

NORTH EASTER
NOSE NIPPERS
NOSEY PARKER
NOT A BIT OF IT
NOT A PATCH ON
NOT A SAUSAGE
NOT UP TO MUCH
NOTHING IN IT
NOTHING LESS
NOTHING TO IT
NOTICE BOARD
NOW AND AGAIN
NOWHERE NEAR
NUBBING COVE
NUCLEIC ACID
NUEE ARDENTE
NULL AND VOID
NUMBER PLATE
NUNS VEILING
NURSING HOME
OAK APPLE DAY
OBJECT GLASS
OBJET TROUVE
OBLIQUE CASE
OBTUSE ANGLE
OCCAMS RAZOR
OCEAN STREAM
OCTAVE FLUTE
ODDS AND ENDS
OEIL DE BOEUF
OF NECESSITY
OFF COLOURED
OFF ONES FEED
OFF ONES FOOD
OFF ONES GAME
OFF ONES HEAD
OFF ONES OATS
OFF THE LEASE
OFF THE RAILS
OFF THE TRACK
OFF THE WAGON
OFFICE BLOCK
OFFICE HOURS
OFFICE PARTY
OFFSIDE RULE
OIL OF CLOVES
OIL PAINTING
OIL PLATFORM
OIL REFINERY
OLD BACHELOR
OLD DOMINION
OLD FOGEYISH
OLD KING COLE
OLD TRAFFORD
OLIVE BRANCH
OLIVER TWIST
OMNIBUS BOOK
ON A PEDESTAL
ON CLOUD NINE
ON EASY TERMS

11 *contd.*

ON HORSEBACK
ON NO ACCOUNT
ON ONES GUARD
ON ONES PLATE
ON PRINCIPLE
ON THAT SCORE
ON THE CARPET
ON THE FIDDLE
ON THE MARKET
ON THE RAZZLE
ON THE STREET
ON THE WAY OUT
ON YOUR MARKS
ONCE OR TWICE
ONE IN THE EYE
ONE WAY GLASS
OPEN CIRCUIT
OPEN HARMONY
OPEN HEARTED
OPEN MOUTHED
OPEN THE DOOR
OPEN VERDICT
OPENING TIME
OPERA DANCER
OPERA SINGER
OPINION POLL
OPIUM SMOKER
ORAL HISTORY
ORANGE JUICE
ORANGE STICK
ORBITAL ROAD
ORCHID HOUSE
ORDER AROUND
ORDERLY ROOM
ORDERS ABOUT
OREGON TRAIL
ORGAN SCREEN
ORIEL WINDOW
ORIGINAL SIN
OSTRICH FARM
OSTRICH LIKE
OUT AND ABOUT
OUT AND OUTER
OUT FOR A DUCK
OUT FOR BLOOD
OUT OF ACTION
OUT OF BOUNDS
OUT OF BREATH
OUT OF COURSE
OUT OF FAVOUR
OUT OF HUMOUR
OUT OF KILTER
OUT OF POCKET
OUT OF SEASON
OUT OF THE ARK
OUT OF THE WAY
OUT ON STRIKE
OUT PATIENTS
OUTSIDE EDGE

OUTSIDE HALF
OUTSIDE LEFT
OVER AND OVER
OVER THE HILL
OVER THE HUMP
OVER THE MOON
OVER THE ODDS
OVERDOING IT
OWNER DRIVER
OXFORD UNION
OYSTER KNIFE
OYSTER PATTY
OYSTER PLANT
OYSTER SHELL
OYSTER TONGS
PACE BOWLING
PACK OF CARDS
PACKAGE DEAL
PACKAGE TOUR
PACKED LUNCH
PACKING CASE
PACKING IT IN
PACKING IT UP
PACKS A PUNCH
PADDLE BOARD
PADDLE SHAFT
PADDLE WHEEL
PADS THE HOOF
PAID ONES WAY
PAIN BARRIER
PAINT BRIDGE
PAINT ROLLER
PAINTED LADY
PAINTED VEIL
PAIR BONDING
PAIR OF BOOTS
PAIR OF SHOES
PAIR OF SOCKS
PAIR OF STAYS
PAIR OF STEPS
PAIRING TIME
PALACE GUARD
PALAIS GLIDE
PALM CABBAGE
PALMYRA WOOD
PAMPAS GRASS
PAN AMERICAN
PAN SLAVONIC
PANAMA CANAL
PANCAKE BELL
PANCAKE RACE
PANCHEN LAMA
PANDORAS BOX
PANEL BEATER
PANEL DOCTOR
PANEL SYSTEM
PANIC ATTACK
PANIC BUYING
PANIC MONGER
PANIC STRUCK

PANTY GIRDLE
PAPAL STATES
PAPER CUTTER
PAPER FEEDER
PAPER FOLDER
PAPER HANGER
PAPER MAKING
PAPER OFFICE
PAPER WEIGHT
PAPERED OVER
PAPIER COLLE
PAPIER MACHE
PARAFFIN OIL
PARAFFIN WAX
PARAGUAY TEA
PARENT CRAFT
PARISH CLERK
PARITY CHECK
PARK AND RIDE
PARK OFFICER
PARLOUR GAME
PARLOUR MAID
PARLOUR PINK
PARMA VIOLET
PARPEN STONE
PARSLEY FERN
PARSONS NOSE
PART COMPANY
PART PAYMENT
PART SINGING
PART TIME JOB
PART WRITING
PARTI COATED
PARTY POOPER
PARTY POPPER
PARTY SPIRIT
PAS DE QUATRE
PAS REDOUBLE
PASCHAL LAMB
PASCHAL MOON
PASS CURRENT
PASS THE BUCK
PASS THE TIME
PASS THROUGH
PASSAGE BOAT
PASSAGE RITE
PASSING AWAY
PASSING BELL
PASSING NOTE
PASSING OVER
PASSING RICH
PASSING SHOT
PASSION PLAY
PASSION TIDE
PASSION WEEK
PASTURE LAND
PAT OF BUTTER
PATCH POCKET
PATENT RIGHT
PATENT ROLLS

PATENT STILL
PATROL WAGON
PATRON SAINT
PATTERN RACE
PATTERN SHOP
PAVED THE WAY
PAVES THE WAY
PAVING STONE
PAX VOBISCUM
PAY BY CHEQUE
PAY THE PIPER
PAY THE PRICE
PAYING A CALL
PAYING GUEST
PAYS ONES WAY
PEACE KEEPER
PEACE MONGER
PEACE OF MIND
PEACH BRANDY
PEACOCK BLUE
PEACOCK FISH
PEACOCK LIKE
PEAK VIEWING
PEAL OF BELLS
PEARL BARLEY
PEARL BUTTON
PEARL DIVING
PEARL FISHER
PEARL HARBOR
PEARL MILLET
PEARL MUSSEL
PEARL OYSTER
PEARL POWDER
PEARLY GATES
PEARLY QUEEN
PEASANTS WAR
PEAT CASTING
PEBBLE STONE
PEDAL ACTION
PEEP THROUGH
PEGGING AWAY
PEGGING BACK
PEGGING DOWN
PELTON WHEEL
PENAL COLONY
PENAL REFORM
PENAL SYSTEM
PENALTY AREA
PENALTY GOAL
PENALTY KICK
PENALTY LINE
PENALTY SHOT
PENALTY SPOT
PENCIL CEDAR
PENCIL SKIRT
PENCIL STONE
PENDANT POST
PENNY A LINER
PENNY ARCADE
PENSIONS OFF

11 *contd.*

PEOPLE MOVER
PEPPER GRASS
PEPTIC ULCER
PEREIRA BARK
PERIGORD PIE
PERIOD DRESS
PERIOD PIECE
PERSIAN GULF
PERSIAN LAMB
PERSONA MUTA
PET AVERSION
PETERS PENCE
PETITS FOURS
PHANTOM LIMB
PHANTOM PAIN
PHARAOHS ANT
PHONE NUMBER
PHOTO FINISH
PHOTO RELIEF
PHRASAL VERB
PHRYGIAN CAP
PIANO NOBILE
PIANO PLAYER
PIANO SCHOOL
PICK ONES WAY
PICK UP SPEED
PICK UP TRUCK
PICK YOUR OWN
PICKED A LOCK
PICKED HOLES
PICKET FENCE
PICKET GUARD
PICKING OVER
PICKLED EGGS
PICKS A FIGHT
PICTURE BOOK
PICTURE CARD
PICTURE CORD
PICTURE GOER
PICTURE PLAY
PICTURE RAIL
PICTURE WIRE
PIE IN THE SKY
PIECE OF CAKE
PIECE OF LUCK
PIECE OF WORK
PIEDS A TERRE
PIERCED EARS
PIG IGNORANT
PIG STICKING
PIGEON FLIER
PIGEON FLYER
PIGEON HOUSE
PIGEONS MILK
PIGS WHISPER
PILE DRIVING
PILLAR SAINT
PILLION SEAT
PILLOW FIGHT

PILOT BURNER
PILOT ENGINE
PILOT JACKET
PILOT SCHEME
PILTDOWN MAN
PINCH HITTER
PINCH OF SALT
PINKING IRON
PINT OF LAGER
PIPE CLEANER
PIPE DREAMER
PIPE FITTING
PIPE LIGHTER
PIPE OF PEACE
PIPE STOPPLE
PIPE TOBACCO
PIRATE RADIO
PISTOL WHIPS
PIT DWELLING
PITCH ROOFED
PITCHED ROOF
PIVOT BRIDGE
PLACE HUNTER
PLACE OF WORK
PLACING A BET
PLACKET HOLE
PLAIN DEALER
PLAIN SPOKEN
PLANAR DIODE
PLANO CONVEX
PLANTING OUT
PLASTER CAST
PLASTER WORK
PLASTIC BOMB
PLASTIC CLAY
PLATE ARMOUR
PLATE BASKET
PLATE LAYING
PLATE WARMER
PLAY ACTRESS
PLAY FOOTSIE
PLAY FOR TIME
PLAY IT BY EAR
PLAY ON WORDS
PLAY ONES ACE
PLAY THE FOOL
PLAY THE GAME
PLAY THE LEAD
PLAYED A PART
PLAYED ABOUT
PLAYED FALSE
PLAYED HAVOC
PLAYED TO WIN
PLAYER PIANO
PLAYING BACK
PLAYING BALL
PLAYING CARD
PLAYING DOWN
PLAYING FAIR
PLAYING HOST

PLAYING SAFE
PLAYS AROUND
PLAYS HOOKEY
PLAYS IT COOL
PLAYS POSSUM
PLAYS TRICKS
PLAYS TRUANT
PLEA BARGAIN
PLEAD GUILTY
PLEIN AIRIST
PLOT A COURSE
PLOUGH STAFF
PLOUGH STILT
PLOUGHING IN
PLOUGHS BACK
PLUGGED AWAY
PLUM BLOSSOM
PLUM PUDDING
PLUMBIC ACID
PLYMOUTH HOE
POCKET GLASS
POCKET GUIDE
POCKET HANKY
POCKET KNIFE
POCKET MONEY
POCKET MOUSE
POCKET PIECE
POCKET SIZED
POCKET VENUS
POINT DAPPUI
POINT OF SALE
POINT OF VIEW
POINT SOURCE
POINTING OUT
POISON GLAND
POKING FUN AT
POKING STICK
POLAR CIRCLE
POLAR FORCES
POLAR LIGHTS
POLE VAULTER
POLICE COURT
POLICE FORCE
POLICE STATE
POLISHED OFF
POLISHES OFF
POLISHING UP
POLLEN COUNT
POLLEN GRAIN
POMPEIAN RED
PONT LEVEQUE
PONY AND TRAP
PONY EXPRESS
POODLE FAKER
POOLS COUPON
POOR LOOKOUT
POP FASTENER
POP FESTIVAL
POPULAR SONG
PORK BUTCHER

PORT ADMIRAL
PORT CHARGES
PORT OF ENTRY
PORTER HOUSE
POST AND PAIR
POST CAPTAIN
POST GLACIAL
POST NUPTIAL
POST VILLAGE
POSTAL ORDER
POSTAL UNION
POSTERN GATE
POTASH WATER
POTATO APPLE
POTATO CHIPS
POTATO CRISP
POTATO SALAD
POTS AND PANS
POTS OF MONEY
POTTING SHED
POULTRY FARM
POULTRY YARD
POUND KEEPER
POUND WEIGHT
POUR SCORN ON
POURED FORTH
POURING RAIN
POVERTY LINE
POVERTY TRAP
POWDER FLASK
POWER DIVING
POWER DRIVEN
PRAIRIE WOLF
PRANCE ABOUT
PRAY FOR RAIN
PRAYER BEADS
PRAYER WHEEL
PRE CAMBRIAN
PRE CONQUEST
PRE ELECTING
PRE ELECTION
PRE EMINENCE
PRE EMPTIBLE
PRE EXISTENT
PRE EXISTING
PRE IGNITION
PRE STRESSED
PREACHING AT
PREACHING UP
PRECIOUS FEW
PREMIUM BOND
PRESENT ARMS
PRESS BUTTON
PRESS GANGED
PRESS OFFICE
PRESSED HOME
PRESSES HOME
PRESTER JOHN
PRETTY PENNY
PRICE FIXING

11 *contd.*

PRICKLE BACK
PRICKLY HEAT
PRICKLY PEAR
PRIESTS HOLE
PRIMARY CELL
PRIMARY COIL
PRIME NUMBER
PRIMING IRON
PRIMING WIRE
PRIMROSE WAY
PRIMUS STOVE
PRINT SELLER
PRINTERS INK
PRINTING INK
PRINTING OUT
PRISON HOUSE
PRIVATE BANK
PRIVATE BILL
PRIVATE LIFE
PRIVATE VIEW
PRIVATE WARD
PRIZE WINNER
PROBATE DUTY
PROBLEM PAGE
PROBLEM PLAY
PROCHAIN AMI
PRODIGAL SON
PRODUCER GAS
PROJET DE LOI
PRONG HORNED
PROOF CHARGE
PROOF PULLER
PROOF READER
PROOF SPIRIT
PROP FORWARD
PROPERTY MAN
PROPERTY TAX
PROS AND CONS
PROSE WRITER
PROUD MINDED
PROXY WEDDED
PRUNING BILL
PRUNING HOOK
PRUSSIC ACID
PSI PARTICLE
PUBLIC BATHS
PUBLIC ENEMY
PUBLIC FUNDS
PUBLIC HOUSE
PUBLIC IMAGE
PUBLIC LANDS
PUBLIC PURSE
PUBLIC WORKS
PUCKERING UP
PUDDING PIPE
PULL STRINGS
PULL THROUGH
PULLED A FACE
PULLED AHEAD

PULLED APART
PULLED ROUND
PULLING AWAY
PULLING BACK
PULLING DOWN
PULLING OVER
PULLING RANK
PUMICE STONE
PUMP PRIMING
PUMPING IRON
PUNCHED TAPE
PUNT FISHING
PUPPY WALKER
PURCHASE TAX
PURE BLOODED
PURE CULTURE
PURE SCIENCE
PURPLE FINCH
PURPLE HEART
PURPLE PATCH
PURSE BEARER
PURSE SEINER
PURSE TAKING
PUSH BICYCLE
PUSH STARTED
PUSH THROUGH
PUSHED ALONG
PUSHED ASIDE
PUSHES ALONG
PUSHES ASIDE
PUSHING PAST
PUSS IN BOOTS
PUSSY WILLOW
PUT IT MILDLY
PUT ON RECORD
PUT ON THE MAP
PUT ONES CASE
PUT STRAIGHT
PUT TO RIGHTS
PUT UP A FIGHT
PUTRID FEVER
PUTS A STOP TO
PUTS AN END TO
PUTS FORWARD
PUTS ON AN ACT
PUTS ON TRIAL
PUTS THE SHOT
PUTS THROUGH
PUTS TO DEATH
PUTS TO SHAME
PUTS TO SLEEP
PUTTING AWAY
PUTTING BACK
PUTTING DOWN
PUTTING IT ON
PUTTING ON TO
PUTTING OVER
PUTTING TO IT
PUTTING UPON
PUTTY POWDER

QUANTUM JUMP
QUANTUM LEAP
QUARREL PANE
QUARTER BACK
QUARTER DECK
QUARTER HOUR
QUARTER JACK
QUARTER NOTE
QUARTER PAST
QUARTER RAIL
QUARTER SEAL
QUARTER TONE
QUARTER WIND
QUARTZ GLASS
QUEEN MOTHER
QUEEN REGENT
QUEEN STITCH
QUEENS BENCH
QUEENS GUIDE
QUEER STREET
QUEUE JUMPED
QUEUE JUMPER
QUICK CHANGE
QUICK FIRING
QUICK FREEZE
QUICK FROZEN
QUICK STICKS
QUICK WITTED
QUICKENED UP
QUIET PLEASE
QUILL DRIVER
QUILTING BEE
QUINSY BERRY
QUITCH GRASS
QUITE A CATCH
QUO WARRANTO
QUOTA SYSTEM
RABBET JOINT
RABBIT HUTCH
RABBIT PUNCH
RABBLE ROUSE
RACE MEETING
RACE WALKING
RACK AND RUIN
RACK RAILWAY
RACKET COURT
RACKET PRESS
RACQUET BALL
RADAR BEACON
RADIANT HEAT
RADICAL AXIS
RADICAL SIGN
RADIO BEACON
RADIO GALAXY
RAGGED ROBIN
RAGTIME BAND
RAILROAD CAR
RAILWAY LINE
RAIN CHAMBER
RAISE A SIEGE

RAISE A STINK
RAISED ALOFT
RAISED BEACH
RAISED MONEY
RAISES ALOFT
RAISES MONEY
RAISING CAIN
RAISING HELL
RAISON DETRE
RALLYING CRY
RAMAN EFFECT
RAN INTO DEBT
RAN SMOOTHLY
RAN TO GROUND
RANG THE BELL
RANGING POLE
RANK AND FILE
RANT AND RAVE
RAS TAFARIAN
RAT CATCHING
RAT KANGAROO
RATE CAPPING
RATE CUTTING
RATION MONEY
RATTLE BRAIN
RATTLE PATED
RATTLE SNAKE
RAW MATERIAL
REACH ME DOWN
REACHING OUT
READING BOOK
READING DESK
READING LAMP
READING ROOM
READY TO WEAR
READY WITTED
REAPING HOOK
REAR ADMIRAL
RECKONING ON
RECKONING UP
RECORD TOKEN
RED CRESCENT
RED HOT POKER
RED SQUIRREL
REDDING COMB
REED BUNTING
REED DRAWING
REED SPARROW
REED WARBLER
REEF BUILDER
REFLEX LIGHT
REFUGEE CAMP
REGENCY BUCK
REILS ISLAND
REJOICING IN
REPORT STAGE
REPORTS BACK
REQUEST NOTE
REQUEST STOP
REQUIEM MASS

11 LETTERS

11 *contd.*
RES JUDICATA
RESCUE GRASS
RESCUE PARTY
RESERVE BANK
RESERVE FUND
REST ASSURED
REST IN PEACE
RETIRED LIST
RETRO ROCKET
RETURN MATCH
RETURN SHOCK
REVERSE GEAR
REVERSE PASS
RHENISH WINE
RHODE ISLAND
RHODIAN LAWS
RHUMB COURSE
RHYME LETTER
RHYME SCHEME
RIB ROASTING
RIB TICKLING
RIB VAULTING
RIBBON GRASS
RICE BISCUIT
RICE PUDDING
RIDDLE ME REE
RIDING CLOAK
RIDING GLOVE
RIDING HABIT
RIDING HORSE
RIDING SKIRT
RIGGING LOFT
RIGGING TREE
RIGHT ANGLED
RIGHT AS RAIN
RIGHT HANDED
RIGHT HANDER
RIGHT MINDED
RIGHT OF WAYS
RIGHT WINGER
RIGHT WRONGS
RIGHTS ISSUE
RIGOR MORTIS
RING CIRCUIT
RING PULL CAN
RING STOPPER
RING THE BELL
RINGING BACK
RINGING DOWN
RINGING TRUE
RISK CAPITAL
RITUAL CHOIR
RIVER BOTTOM
ROAD HAULAGE
ROAD MANAGER
ROAD MENDING
ROAD SWEEPER
ROAD TESTING
ROAD TRAFFIC

ROCK AND ROLL
ROCK CLIMBER
ROCK CRYSTAL
ROCK FORMING
ROCK SPARROW
ROCK THE BOAT
ROCKER PANEL
ROCKET MOTOR
ROCKET PLANE
ROCKET RANGE
ROCKING TOOL
ROGUES LATIN
ROGUES MARCH
ROI FAINEANT
ROLE PLAYING
ROLL TOP DESK
ROLLED ALONG
ROLLER BLIND
ROLLER SKATE
ROLLER TOWEL
ROLLING MILL
ROLLING OVER
ROMAN A THESE
ROMAN CANDLE
ROMAN EMPIRE
ROMAN FLEUVE
ROMP THROUGH
ROMPING HOME
RONTGEN UNIT
ROOM DIVIDER
ROOM SERVICE
ROOT CLIMBER
ROOT PRUNING
ROSE CAMPION
ROSEWOOD OIL
ROSY CHEEKED
ROTTEN APPLE
ROUGE DRAGON
ROUGE ET NOIR
ROUGH COATED
ROUGH DRYING
ROUGH LEGGED
ROUGH SPOKEN
ROUGHING OUT
ROUND BACKED
ROUND HEADED
ROUND OF GOLF
ROUNDED DOWN
ROUNDING OFF
ROUNDING OUT
ROUPING WIFE
ROYAL ASSENT
ROYAL FAMILY
ROYAL OCTAVO
ROYAL PARDON
ROYAL TENNIS
ROYSTON CROW
RUBBED ALONG
RUBBER CORED
RUBBER NECKS

RUBBER PLANT
RUBBER SOLED
RUBBER STAMP
RUBBING DOWN
RUBBING IT IN
RUBBING POST
RUBBISH HEAP
RUBBLE STONE
RUBY WEDDING
RUGBY LEAGUE
RULE OF FAITH
RULE OF THREE
RULE OF THUMB
RUMBLE STRIP
RUMMAGE SALE
RUMOUR HAS IT
RUN INTO DEBT
RUN SMOOTHLY
RUN TO GROUND
RUNNING AMOK
RUNNING AWAY
RUNNING COST
RUNNING DOWN
RUNNING FIRE
RUNNING GEAR
RUNNING HARD
RUNNING HEAD
RUNNING INTO
RUNNING KNOT
RUNNING MATE
RUNNING OVER
RUNNING RIOT
RUNNING SORE
RUNNING WILD
RUNS ERRANDS
RUNS THE SHOW
RUNS THROUGH
RUNS TO EARTH
RUPERTS DROP
RUSH BEARING
SABRE RATTLE
SACRED HEART
SADDLE CLOTH
SADDLE GIRTH
SADDLE HORSE
SAFE BLOWING
SAFE BREAKER
SAFE CONDUCT
SAFE CRACKER
SAFE DEPOSIT
SAFE KEEPING
SAFETY CATCH
SAFETY FIRST
SAFETY GLASS
SAFETY LIGHT
SAFETY MATCH
SAFETY PAPER
SAFETY RAZOR
SAFETY VALVE
SAFFRON CAKE

SAID A PRAYER
SAILED ALONG
SAILING BOAT
SAILING CLUB
SAILING SHIP
SAINT ANDREW
SAINT GEORGE
SAL AMMONIAC
SAL VOLATILE
SALK VACCINE
SALLEE ROVER
SALMON BERRY
SALMON COBLE
SALMON SPEAR
SALMON TROUT
SALOON RIFLE
SALT GLAZING
SALTING AWAY
SALTING DOWN
SALVAGE CREW
SAMIAN EARTH
SAMIAN STONE
SAMPLER WORK
SANCHO PEDRO
SANCTUS BELL
SAND SKIPPER
SANDS OF TIME
SANDWICH MAN
SANG DE BOEUF
SARGASSO SEA
SAT SAPIENTI
SATAN MONKEY
SATIN FINISH
SATIN STITCH
SATSUMA WARE
SAUCE BOTTLE
SAUCEPAN LID
SAUSAGE MEAT
SAUSAGE ROLL
SAVING GRACE
SAVINGS BANK
SAVOIR FAIRE
SAW DAYLIGHT
SAW EYE TO EYE
SAW THE LIGHT
SAYS A PRAYER
SCALE ARMOUR
SCALE INSECT
SCARED STIFF
SCARLET BEAN
SCATTER RUGS
SCENE A FAIRE
SCENT BOTTLE
SCHICKS TEST
SCHISM HOUSE
SCHOLAR LIKE
SCHOOL BOARD
SCHOOL CHILD
SCHOOL HOUSE
SCHOOL NURSE

11 *contd.*

SCIENCE PARK
SCISSOR BILL
SCISSOR CASE
SCISSOR TAIL
SCOOPING OUT
SCORE POINTS
SCORED A GOAL
SCORES A GOAL
SCORPION FLY
SCOTCH BROTH
SCOTCH CATCH
SCOTCH IRISH
SCOTS GUARDS
SCOUT MASTER
SCOUTS ROUND
SCRAPE PENNY
SCRAPING OFF
SCRATCH COAT
SCRATCH TEST
SCRATCH WORK
SCREECH HAWK
SCREEN WIPER
SCREENED OFF
SCREW THREAD
SCREW WRENCH
SCRIVE BOARD
SCRUB TURKEY
SCRUB TYPHUS
SCRUBBING UP
SCRUBS ROUND
SCUBA DIVING
SCURVY GRASS
SCUTCH BLADE
SCUTTLE BUTT
SCYTHE STONE
SEA CRAYFISH
SEA CUCUMBER
SEA DOTTEREL
SEA ELEPHANT
SEA LAVENDER
SEA PURSLANE
SEA ROSEMARY
SEA SCORPION
SEA SCOUTING
SEAL FISHING
SEAL ROOKERY
SEAM BOWLING
SEAM WELDING
SEAMING LACE
SEARCH PARTY
SEASIDE TOWN
SECOND CLASS
SECOND FLOOR
SECOND GUESS
SECOND JOINT
SECOND RATER
SECOND REICH
SECOND SIGHT
SECOND TEETH

SECONDS HAND
SECRET AGENT
SECTION MARK
SECULAR HYMN
SEE DAYLIGHT
SEE EYE TO EYE
SEE THE LIGHT
SEE YOU LATER
SEEING A WOLF
SEEING ROUND
SEEING STARS
SEEING STONE
SELDOM TIMES
SELENIC ACID
SELF ASSUMED
SELF ASSURED
SELF CENTRED
SELF CONCEIT
SELF CONCERN
SELF CONTROL
SELF CREATED
SELF DEFENCE
SELF DESPAIR
SELF DEVOTED
SELF EVIDENT
SELF EXAMPLE
SELF HEALING
SELF IMPOSED
SELF INDUCED
SELF LOADING
SELF LOCKING
SELF MADE MAN
SELF NEGLECT
SELF RAISING
SELF RELIANT
SELF RESPECT
SELF SEEKING
SELF SERVICE
SELF SERVING
SELF STARTER
SELF SUPPORT
SELF TORTURE
SELF TRAINED
SELF WORSHIP
SELLING A PUP
SELLING RACE
SELLS IN BULK
SEMBLING BOX
SEMI DIURNAL
SEMI ELLIPSE
SEMI MONTHLY
SEMI SKILLED
SENATE HOUSE
SEND PACKING
SENDING DOWN
SENDING WORD
SENT PACKING
SERPENT STAR
SERVANT GIRL
SERVICE BOOK

SERVICE FLAT
SERVICE LINE
SERVICE ROAD
SERVICE ROOM
SERVICE TREE
SERVING TIME
SESAME GRASS
SESAME SEEDS
SET AT NOUGHT
SET THE SCENE
SET TO RIGHTS
SETS IN ORDER
SETS LIGHT TO
SETS THE PACE
SETS TO MUSIC
SETS UP HOUSE
SETTING BACK
SETTING DOWN
SETTING FOOT
SETTING FREE
SETTING SAIL
SETTING UPON
SETTLED DOWN
SETTLES DOWN
SETTLING DAY
SEVEN OCLOCK
SEWAGE WORKS
SHACKLE BOLT
SHACKLE BONE
SHADOW BOXED
SHADOW BOXES
SHADOW FIGHT
SHAKES HANDS
SHAKING A LEG
SHAKING DOWN
SHAM ABRAHAM
SHARD BEETLE
SHARE PUSHER
SHARP WITTED
SHAVING FOAM
SHAVING SOAP
SHAWL COLLAR
SHEATH KNIFE
SHED LIGHT ON
SHEEP FARMER
SHEERING OFF
SHEET ANCHOR
SHEET COPPER
SHEET RUBBER
SHELL CRATER
SHELL JACKET
SHELL PARROT
SHELLING OUT
SHERRY PARTY
SHIFT WORKER
SHIFTS ABOUT
SHINTY STICK
SHIP BISCUIT
SHIP CAPTAIN
SHIP RAILWAY

SHIP THE OARS
SHIPS PAPERS
SHIRT BUTTON
SHIRT SLEEVE
SHOCK HEADED
SHOCK HORROR
SHOCK TROOPS
SHODDY GOODS
SHOE LEATHER
SHOEING HORN
SHOOTING BOX
SHOOTING OFF
SHOOTING WAR
SHOOTS A LINE
SHOOTS CRAPS
SHOOTS IT OUT
SHOP LIFTING
SHOP STEWARD
SHOPPING BAG
SHOPS AROUND
SHORT CHANGE
SHORT HANDED
SHORT LISTED
SHORT PRICED
SHORT SHRIFT
SHORT SPOKEN
SHORT TENNIS
SHORT TERMER
SHORT WINDED
SHORTEN SAIL
SHOT PUTTING
SHOULDER BAG
SHOULDER PAD
SHOUTED DOWN
SHOVEL BOARD
SHOW OF HANDS
SHOW ONES AGE
SHOW PROMISE
SHOW STOPPER
SHOW THE FLAG
SHOW WILLING
SHOWED FIGHT
SHOWED FORTH
SHOWING A LEG
SHOWN THE WAY
SHOWS THE WAY
SHRINK PROOF
SHRUGGED OFF
SHUFFLED OFF
SHUFFLES OFF
SHUTS UP SHOP
SHUTTING OFF
SHUTTING OUT
SICK BENEFIT
SICK TO DEATH
SIDE EFFECTS
SIDE OF BACON
SIDE TRACKED
SIDEREAL DAY
SIEGE BASKET

11 *contd.*

SIERRA LEONE
SIGHT PLAYER
SIGHT READER
SIGHT SCREEN
SIGHT SINGER
SIGHT UNSEEN
SIGN PAINTER
SIGN WRITING
SIGNS OF LIFE
SILENT NIGHT
SILICON CHIP
SILK THROWER
SILLY MID OFF
SILLY OLD MOO
SILLY SEASON
SILVER BIRCH
SILVER MEDAL
SILVER PAPER
SILVER PLATE
SILVER POINT
SILVER SPOON
SILVER WHITE
SIMMERS DOWN
SIMPLE SIMON
SIN OFFERING
SINEWS OF WAR
SINGING AWAY
SINGING SAND
SINGLE CREAM
SINGLE ENTRY
SINGLE HOUSE
SINGLE TRACK
SINGLES CLUB
SINKING FUND
SINN FEINISM
SISTER IN LAW
SIT DOWN MEAL
SITTING BACK
SITTING DOWN
SITTING DUCK
SITTING ROOM
SKATED ROUND
SKATES ROUND
SKATING OVER
SKATING RINK
SKELETON KEY
SKETCHED OUT
SKETCHES OUT
SKIMMED MILK
SKIN AND BONE
SKIRTS ROUND
SKITTLE BALL
SKITTLED OUT
SKITTLES OUT
SKY COLOURED
SKYE TERRIER
SLACK HANDED
SLACKENED UP
SLACKENS OFF

SLATE PENCIL
SLATE WRITER
SLAVE DRIVER
SLAVE HOLDER
SLAVE LABOUR
SLAVE STATES
SLAVE TRADER
SLEDGE CHAIR
SLEEP WALKER
SLEEPING BAG
SLEEPING CAR
SLEEPING OFF
SLEEPS ROUGH
SLEEVE BOARD
SLEEVE NOTES
SLEIGH BELLS
SLEUTH HOUND
SLICE OF LIFE
SLICE OF LUCK
SLIDING KEEL
SLIDING SEAT
SLIME FUNGUS
SLING THE BAT
SLINGING INK
SLINKING OFF
SLIPPED AWAY
SLIPPED DISC
SLIPPER BATH
SLIPPERY ELM
SLIPPING OFF
SLOPING ARMS
SLOPPING OUT
SLOT MACHINE
SLOW BUT SURE
SLOW RELEASE
SLOW SIGHTED
SLOWING DOWN
SLUM DWELLER
SMALL CHANGE
SMALL LETTER
SMALL MINDED
SMALL OCTAVE
SMALL QUARTO
SMALL SCREEN
SMALL WONDER
SMART TICKET
SMARTY BOOTS
SMARTY PANTS
SMELLING OUT
SMILE PLEASE
SMOKE DRYING
SMOKE HELMET
SMOKE SCREEN
SMOKE SIGNAL
SMOKE TUNNEL
SMOKED GLASS
SMOKED TROUT
SMOKING ROOM
SMOKY QUARTZ
SMOOTH FACED

SMOOTH PACED
SNAFFLE REIN
SNAIL DARTER
SNAKES ALIVE
SNAP OUT OF IT
SNATCH PURSE
SNATCH SQUAD
SNATCH THIEF
SNIFFING OUT
SNOW GOGGLES
SNOW LEOPARD
SNOWED UNDER
SNUFF DIPPER
SNUFF TAKING
SNUFFING OUT
SNUGGLING UP
SO FAR SO GOOD
SO HELP ME GOD
SOAP BOILING
SOBER MINDED
SOBER SUITED
SOCIAL WHALE
SOFT CENTRED
SOFT HEARTED
SOFT SHELLED
SOFT SOAPING
SOFTENING UP
SOIL SCIENCE
SOLAR ENERGY
SOLAR PLEXUS
SOLAR SYSTEM
SOLDIER CRAB
SOLDIER LIKE
SOLDIERED ON
SOLID COLOUR
SOLID MATTER
SOMEONE ELSE
SON OF A BITCH
SONG SPARROW
SORBO RUBBER
SOUGHT AFTER
SOUL BROTHER
SOUND ADVICE
SOUND SYSTEM
SOUNDING OFF
SOUNDING OUT
SOUNDING ROD
SOUP KITCHEN
SOUTH BY EAST
SOUTH BY WEST
SOUTH EASTER
SOWS THE SEED
SPACE HEATER
SPACE TRAVEL
SPACE WRITER
SPACER PLATE
SPADE GUINEA
SPANG COCKLE
SPANISH FOWL
SPANISH MAIN

SPANISH MOSS
SPANISH SOAP
SPANISH WALK
SPARKING OFF
SPARKING OUT
SPARROW BILL
SPARROW HAWK
SPATTER WORK
SPAWNING BED
SPEAK NO EVIL
SPEAKING OUT
SPECK OF DUST
SPECTRE CRAB
SPEECH MAKER
SPELLING BEE
SPELLING OUT
SPELLS IT OUT
SPEND A PENNY
SPENT A PENNY
SPIDER PLANT
SPIDER WHEEL
SPILL STREAM
SPIN BOWLING
SPINA BIFIDA
SPINACH BEET
SPINAL CANAL
SPINAL CHORD
SPINDLE LEGS
SPINDLE TREE
SPINNING OUT
SPINNING TOP
SPIRIT LEVEL
SPIRIT WORLD
SPLASH BOARD
SPLASHED OUT
SPLASHES OUT
SPLAY FOOTED
SPLINTER BAR
SPLIT SCREEN
SPLIT SECOND
SPLITS HAIRS
SPOILT PAPER
SPONGE CLOTH
SPONGE DIVER
SPONGED DOWN
SPONGES DOWN
SPORTS SHIRT
SPOT THE BALL
SPOT WELDING
SPOTTED DICK
SPRANG A LEAK
SPRAY DRYING
SPREAD EAGLE
SPREAD SHEET
SPRING A LEAK
SPRING CLEAN
SPRING FEVER
SPRING ONION
SPRING WATER
SPRING WHEAT

11 *contd.*

SPROUT WINGS
SPUD BASHING
SPUR GEARING
SPUR LEATHER
SQUARE DANCE
SQUARE FACED
SQUASH COURT
SQUEEZE HOME
SQUEEZE PLAY
ST AGNESS EVE
ST DAVIDS DAY
ST ELMOS FIRE
ST JOHNS WORT
STAFF OF LIFE
STAFF SYSTEM
STAGE DRIVER
STAGE EFFECT
STAGE FRIGHT
STAGE MANAGE
STAGE PLAYER
STAGE STRUCK
STAGING AREA
STAGING BASE
STAGING POST
STAIR CARPET
STAIR TURRET
STAKE A CLAIM
STALL READER
STAMP OFFICE
STAMPING OUT
STAND AT EASE
STAND OFFISH
STAND TO GAIN
STAND TO LOSE
STANDING OFF
STANDING OUT
STANDING PAT
STANDS ALONE
STANDS AT BAY
STANDS GUARD
STANDS TO WIN
STANDS TREAT
STANDS TRIAL
STANNIC ACID
STAR BILLING
STAR CHAMBER
STAR CROSSED
STAR OF DAVID
STAR QUALITY
STAR STUDDED
STAR THISTLE
STARCH PAPER
STARTER HOME
STARTERS GUN
STARTING OUT
STARTS A HARE
STARVING OUT
STATE OF FLUX
STATE OF PLAY

STATE PRISON
STATE SCHOOL
STATE SECRET
STATELY HOME
STATUTE BOOK
STATUTE MILE
STAVE CHURCH
STAY THE PACE
STAYED STILL
STAYING OVER
STEADY GOING
STEADY STATE
STEALS A KISS
STEAM BOILER
STEAM DIGGER
STEAM DRIVEN
STEAM ENGINE
STEAM HAMMER
STEAM JACKET
STEAM PACKET
STEAM ROLLER
STEAM SHOVEL
STEAM VESSEL
STEAMED OPEN
STEEL HEADED
STEEL PLATED
STEERAGE WAY
STEERS CLEAR
STEM THE TIDE
STEM TO STERN
STEP DANCING
STEPPED DOWN
STEPPING OUT
STERN CHASER
STEWED FRUIT
STICK AROUND
STICK INSECT
STICK OF ROCK
STICKING OUT
STICKS IT OUT
STIFF NECKED
STIFLE JOINT
STILT WALKER
STINKING OUT
STIRRUP BONE
STIRRUP IRON
STIRRUP PUMP
STIRS ABROAD
STITCHING UP
STOCK FARMER
STOCK FEEDER
STOCK JOBBER
STOCK MARKET
STOCK PHRASE
STOCK SADDLE
STOMACH ACHE
STOMACH PUMP
STONE CIRCLE
STONE CURLEW
STONE CUTTER

STONE FALCON
STONE HAMMER
STONE PLOVER
STONES THROW
STOOD TO GAIN
STOOD TO LOSE
STOOL PIGEON
STOP THE SHOW
STOPPED DEAD
STOPPED OVER
STOPPING OFF
STOPS THE ROT
STORM BEATEN
STORM CELLAR
STORM CENTRE
STORM PETREL
STORM SIGNAL
STORM TOSSED
STORM TROOPS
STORM WINDOW
STORY TELLER
STOUT FELLOW
STOVE ENAMEL
STRAIGHT ARM
STRAIGHT CUT
STRAIGHT MAN
STRAIGHT OFF
STRAIGHT OUT
STRAIT LACED
STRAIT LACER
STRAP HANGER
STRAW CUTTER
STREET CRIES
STREET LEVEL
STREET SMART
STREET VALUE
STRIDE PIANO
STRIKE A POSE
STRIKE BOUND
STRIKE FORCE
STRIKE HANDS
STRIKES BACK
STRIKES DOWN
STRIKES DUMB
STRIKES HOME
STRIKING OFF
STRIKING OIL
STRIKING OUT
STRING ALONG
STRINGING UP
STRINGY BARK
STRIP SEARCH
STRIPPED OFF
STRIPPED OUT
STRONG DRINK
STRONG POINT
STRUCK A POSE
STRUGGLED ON
STRUGGLES ON
STRUNG ALONG

STUB ONES TOE
STUBBLE RAKE
STUCK AROUND
STUDIO COUCH
STUMP ORATOR
STUN GRENADE
SUCH AND SUCH
SUCKING FISH
SUCTION PUMP
SUDDEN DEATH
SUET PUDDING
SUGAR COATED
SUGAR OF LEAD
SUGAR SIFTER
SUICIDE PACT
SUIT ONESELF
SULPHUR ROOT
SUM OF THINGS
SUMMER HOUSE
SUMMER STOCK
SUMMIT LEVEL
SUMMIT TALKS
SUMMONING UP
SUMMUM BONUM
SUNNY SIDE UP
SUPPER CLOTH
SUPPLY SIDER
SUPPORT AREA
SUPPORT HOSE
SURF BATHING
SURFACE MAIL
SURGEON FISH
SURINAM TOAD
SWAGGER CANE
SWAGGER COAT
SWALLOW DIVE
SWALLOW TAIL
SWALLOWED UP
SWARM OF BEES
SWEATER GIRL
SWEATS IT OUT
SWEENEY TODD
SWEEP WASHER
SWEET AS A NUT
SWEET CICELY
SWEET FENNEL
SWEET POTATO
SWEET SHERRY
SWEET TALKED
SWEET WILLOW
SWELLED HEAD
SWIFT FOOTED
SWIFT WINGED
SWING BRIDGE
SWING HANDLE
SWING PLOUGH
SWISS CHEESE
SWISS GUARDS
SWITCHED OFF
SWITCHES OFF

11 *contd.*

SWITCHING ON
SWIVEL CHAIR
SWIVEL JOINT
SWORD BEARER
SWORD SHAPED
SYRUP OF FIGS
SYSTEM BUILT
SYSTEM MAKER
TABLE FOR TWO
TABLE NAPKIN
TABLE TENNIS
TAGGED ALONG
TAI CHI CHUAN
TAIL FEATHER
TAILED RHYME
TAKE A TUMBLE
TAKE A WICKET
TAKE BY STORM
TAKE COMMAND
TAKE HOME PAY
TAKE IT OUT ON
TAKE OFFENCE
TAKE ON BOARD
TAKE ON TRUST
TAKE ONES CUE
TAKE POT LUCK
TAKE THE BAIT
TAKE THE CAKE
TAKE THE LEAD
TAKE THE MICK
TAKE THE VEIL
TAKE TIME OFF
TAKE TO COURT
TAKE TO HEART
TAKE UMBRAGE
TAKEN AS READ
TAKEN IN HAND
TAKEN IN VAIN
TAKEN TO TASK
TAKEOVER BID
TAKES A BRIEF
TAKES A CLASS
TAKES A DEKKO
TAKES AN OATH
TAKES AS READ
TAKES CHARGE
TAKES EFFECT
TAKES FLIGHT
TAKES FRIGHT
TAKES IN HAND
TAKES IN VAIN
TAKES IT EASY
TAKES NOTICE
TAKES ORDERS
TAKES THE AIR
TAKES THE RAP
TAKES THE SUN
TAKES TO TASK
TAKES UP ARMS

TAKING A SEAT
TAKING A TURN
TAKING AFTER
TAKING AMISS
TAKING APART
TAKING COVER
TAKING HEART
TAKING IN TOW
TAKING ISSUE
TAKING LEAVE
TAKING PAINS
TAKING PLACE
TAKING SHAPE
TAKING SIDES
TAKING STEPS
TAKING STOCK
TAKING TURNS
TALENT SCOUT
TALK YOU DOWN
TALKED ROUND
TALKING BACK
TALKING BOOK
TALKING DOWN
TALKING HEAD
TALKING INTO
TALKING OVER
TALKING SHOP
TALKS IT OVER
TALKS TURKEY
TALLY SYSTEM
TAM O SHANTER
TAMMANY HALL
TAMMIE NORIE
TAN COLOURED
TANTALUS CUP
TAP DRESSING
TAPE MACHINE
TAPE RECORDS
TAPERING OFF
TARTAR SAUCE
TATTIE BOGLE
TEA CANISTER
TEA CEREMONY
TEA STRAINER
TEACHERS PET
TEACHING AID
TEAMS UP WITH
TEAR JERKING
TEAR STAINED
TEARING AWAY
TEARING DOWN
TEARING INTO
TEARING OPEN
TEENY BOPPER
TEETER BOARD
TELPHER LINE
TEMPTED FATE
TEMPUS FUGIT
TENNIS COURT
TENNIS ELBOW

TENNIS MATCH
TENT PEGGING
TENTER HOOKS
TERM OF YEARS
TERTIUM QUID
TEST CRICKET
THAT FIGURES
THAT IS TO SAY
THATCH BOARD
THATS DONE IT
THATS TORN IT
THE ALMIGHTY
THE BIG APPLE
THE BIG SMOKE
THE BITER BIT
THE CENOTAPH
THE CONQUEST
THE CRUSADES
THE DEPARTED
THE DUKERIES
THE FAITHFUL
THE FINE ARTS
THE GAME IS UP
THE GOOD BOOK
THE GREATEST
THE LAST GASP
THE LAST WORD
THE NAKED EYE
THE NEW WORLD
THE NOBLE ART
THE OLD ENEMY
THE OLD WORLD
THE OTHER DAY
THE PROPHETS
THE PYRAMIDS
THE RED CROSS
THE REDEEMER
THE SIZE OF IT
THE WHOLE HOG
THEATRE GOER
THERE YOU ARE
THESIS NOVEL
THICK HEADED
THICK LIPPED
THICK WITTED
THIMBLE CASE
THIMBLE RIGS
THIN AS A RAKE
THIN RED LINE
THIN SKINNED
THINKING OUT
THINKS AGAIN
THINKS ALOUD
THINKS TWICE
THINNING OUT
THIRD DEGREE
THIRD ESTATE
THIRSTY WORK
THIS AND THAT
THIS INSTANT

THISTLE DOWN
THOMPSON GUN
THOUGHT BACK
THOUGHT OVER
THOUGHT WAVE
THRASHED OUT
THRASHES OUT
THREE CHEERS
THREE COLOUR
THREE DECKER
THREE HANDED
THREE LEAVED
THREE LEGGED
THREE MASTED
THREE MASTER
THREE OCLOCK
THREW A PARTY
THREW A PUNCH
THROAT STRAP
THROUGH BALL
THROUGH BOLT
THROUGH PASS
THROW A PARTY
THROW A PUNCH
THROWING OFF
THROWING OUT
THRUST STAGE
THUMBS A LIFT
THUMBS A RIDE
THUNDER CLAP
THUNDER DART
THUNDER PEAL
TIBETAN APSO
TICK TACK MAN
TICKET AGENT
TICKET PUNCH
TICKING AWAY
TICKING OVER
TICKLED PINK
TICKLES PINK
TIED COTTAGE
TIED THE KNOT
TIES THE KNOT
TIFFANY LAMP
TIGHT FISTED
TIGHT LACING
TIGHT LIPPED
TIMBER HITCH
TIME CAPSULE
TIME DEPOSIT
TIME KEEPING
TIME KILLING
TIME MACHINE
TIME SERVING
TIME SHARING
TIN PAN ALLEY
TIN SOLDIERS
TIN STREAMER
TIP IT AND RUN
TIP THE SCALE

11 *contd.*

TIPS ONES HAT
TIPS THE WINK
TISSUE PAPER
TITHE PAYING
TITLE HOLDER
TO ADVANTAGE
TO ONES TASTE
TO THE LETTER
TOBACCO PIPE
TOED THE LINE
TOES THE LINE
TOFFEE APPLE
TOFFEE NOSED
TOGGLE JOINT
TOILET CLOTH
TOILET COVER
TOILET GLASS
TOILET PAPER
TOILET TABLE
TOILET WATER
TOM AND JERRY
TOMMY ATKINS
TONE CONTROL
TONE PICTURE
TOOK A TUMBLE
TOOK A WICKET
TOOK BY STORM
TOOK COMMAND
TOOK IT OUT ON
TOOK OFFENCE
TOOK ON BOARD
TOOK ONES CUE
TOOK POT LUCK
TOOK THE BAIT
TOOK THE CAKE
TOOK THE LEAD
TOOK THE MICK
TOOK THE VEIL
TOOK TIME OFF
TOOK TO COURT
TOOK TO HEART
TOOK UMBRAGE
TOOTH DRAWER
TOOTH PICKER
TOOTH POWDER
TOP DRESSING
TOP PRIORITY
TOP TO BOTTOM
TOPPLED OVER
TOPPLES OVER
TOPS THE BILL
TORCH BEARER
TORCH SINGER
TORCHON LACE
TORPEDO BOAT
TORPEDO BOOM
TORPEDO TUBE
TORQUE METER
TOTAL RECALL

TOUCH BOTTOM
TOUCH IN GOAL
TOUCH SCREEN
TOUCH TYPING
TOUCH TYPIST
TOUCHED DOWN
TOUCHED WOOD
TOUCHES DOWN
TOUCHES WOOD
TOUCHING OFF
TOUGH MINDED
TOUGHENED UP
TOUR DE FORCE
TOUT DE SUITE
TOUT LE MONDE
TOWER BRIDGE
TOWERED OVER
TOWING BITTS
TOWN AND GOWN
TOWN COUNCIL
TOWN DWELLER
TRACER SHELL
TRACK LAYING
TRACK RECORD
TRACKED DOWN
TRADE SECRET
TRADES UNION
TRADING DOWN
TRADING POST
TRAGI COMEDY
TRAIL BLAZER
TRAILED AWAY
TRAILING OFF
TRAIN BEARER
TRANS SONICS
TRANSFER DAY
TRANSFER FEE
TRANSIT CAMP
TRANSIT DUTY
TRAVEL AGENT
TREADS WATER
TREE BICYCLE
TREE CREEPER
TREE SURGEON
TREE SURGERY
TREE WORSHIP
TRELLIS WORK
TRENCH FEVER
TRENCHER CAP
TRENCHER FED
TRENCHER MAN
TRIAL BY JURY
TRIATIC STAY
TRIGGERS OFF
TRINITY TERM
TRIPLE CROWN
TRIPLE EVENT
TRIPLE POINT
TROJAN HORSE
TROMPE LOEIL

TROTH PLIGHT
TROTTING OUT
TROUBLE SPOT
TROUSER CLIP
TROUSER SUIT
TROUT BASKET
TROUT STREAM
TRUCK DRIVER
TRUCK SYSTEM
TRUE HEARTED
TRUE SEEMING
TRUMPET CALL
TRUMPET TONE
TRUST ESTATE
TRUTH TELLER
TRUTH TO TELL
TRY ONES LUCK
TUB THUMPING
TUBE STATION
TUCKING MILL
TUDOR FLOWER
TUMBLE DRIER
TUMBLED OVER
TUMBLES OVER
TUMMY BUTTON
TURBINE PUMP
TURBO RAM JET
TURKISH BATH
TURN AGAINST
TURN OF SPEED
TURN THE TIDE
TURNED ABOUT
TURNED ASIDE
TURNED LOOSE
TURNED NASTY
TURNED ROUND
TURNING AWAY
TURNING BACK
TURNING DOWN
TURNING INTO
TURNING OVER
TURNING TAIL
TURNING TURK
TURNING UPON
TURNOVER TAX
TURNPIKE MAN
TURNS AROUND
TURNS TURTLE
TURRET CLOCK
TURRET LATHE
TURTLE SHELL
TUSSOCK MOTH
TUTTI FRUTTI
TWEEZER CASE
TWENTY PENCE
TWIN BROTHER
TWO LINE WHIP
TWO PENNORTH
TWO STOREYED
TWOS COMPANY

TYPE FOUNDER
TYPE FOUNDRY
ULTIMA THULE
UNCALLED FOR
UNDER A CLOUD
UNDER ARREST
UNDER CANVAS
UNDER DRIVEN
UNDER DURESS
UNDER REVIEW
UNDER SCHOOL
UNDER STRESS
UNDER THE SUN
UNION LEADER
UNIT PRICING
UNLOOKED FOR
UNTHOUGHT OF
UNWISHED FOR
UP AGAINST IT
UP AND COMING
UP FOR THE CUP
UP ON A CHARGE
UP ON THE SHOT
UP TO SCRATCH
UP TO THE EYES
UP TO THE HILT
UP TO THE MARK
UPCAST SHAFT
UPPER STOREY
UPS AND DOWNS
USE ONES LOAF
UTILITY ROOM
V FOR VICTORY
VACUUM BRAKE
VACUUM FLASK
VAGRANCY ACT
VAPOUR TRAIL
VARIETY SHOW
VATICAN CITY
VEDETTE BOAT
VELVET PAPER
VENETIAN RED
VENICE GLASS
VENN DIAGRAM
VENTRAL FINS
VENTURED OUT
VENTURES OUT
VENTURI TUBE
VENUS DE MILO
VERNAL GRASS
VERSE MAKING
VERSE MONGER
VESTRY CLERK
VIA DOLOROSA
VICAR CHORAL
VICAR FORANE
VICAR OF BRAY
VICE ADMIRAL
VICE MARSHAL
VICTORIA DAY

11 *contd.*

VICTORY SHIP
VIDEO CAMERA
VIDEO SIGNAL
VIENNA STEAK
VILLAGE CART
VILLAGE HALL
VILLAGE POND
VILLAGE PUMP
VINE DISEASE
VINE DRESSER
VINTAGE PORT
VINTAGE YEAR
VINYL RESINS
VIOLA DAMORE
VIPERS GRASS
VIRGIN BIRTH
VISION MIXER
VISITING DAY
VITAMIN PILL
VOCAL CHORDS
VOIX CELESTE
VOLCANIC ASH
VOLCANIC MUD
VOLTAIC CELL
VOTING PAPER
VULGAR LATIN
WAGE EARNING
WAILING WALL
WAIT AT TABLE
WAITED ABOUT
WAITING LIST
WAITING MAID
WAITING ROOM
WAITING UPON
WAITS AWHILE
WAKING HOURS
WALKED ON AIR
WALKED OUT ON
WALKING AWAY
WALKING CANE
WALKING CASE
WALKING INTO
WALKING PART
WALKING RACE
WALKING TALL
WALKING TOAD
WALKS THE DOG
WALKS TO HEEL
WALTER MITTY
WANDERED OFF
WANT JAM ON IT
WAR CRIMINAL
WAR MEMORIAL
WAR NEUROSIS
WAR OF NERVES
WARD OF COURT
WARM AS TOAST
WARM BLOODED
WARM HEARTED

WARP AND WEFT
WARTS AND ALL
WASH AND WEAR
WASHING AWAY
WASHING DOWN
WASHING LINE
WASHING SODA
WASP TONGUED
WASP WAISTED
WASSAIL BOUT
WASTE BASKET
WASTING AWAY
WATCH POCKET
WATCH SPRING
WATCHED OVER
WATCHES OVER
WATER BARREL
WATER BEARER
WATER BEETLE
WATER BOTTLE
WATER CANNON
WATER CEMENT
WATER CLOSET
WATER COLOUR
WATER COOLED
WATER COOLER
WATER DOCTOR
WATER ENGINE
WATER FINDER
WATER HAMMER
WATER JACKET
WATER MEADOW
WATER MONKEY
WATER PISTOL
WATER SKIING
WATER SPIDER
WATER SPIRIT
WATER SPRING
WATER SPRITE
WATER SUPPLY
WATER THRUSH
WATER VAPOUR
WATER VIOLET
WATERED DOWN
WATERING CAN
WATERY GRAVE
WAVING A WAND
WAVING ASIDE
WAX CHANDLER
WAX PAINTING
WEAK HEARTED
WEAK SIGHTED
WEAR AND TEAR
WEARING AWAY
WEARING DOWN
WEARING THIN
WEARY WILLIE
WEASEL FACED
WEASELED OUT
WEATHER ROLL

WEATHER SHIP
WEATHER SIGN
WEATHER VANE
WEATHER WISE
WEATHER WORN
WEATHERS OUT
WEAVER FINCH
WEAVERS KNOT
WEB FINGERED
WEDDING CAKE
WEDDING RING
WEDDING VOWS
WEDGE SHAPED
WEEDING FORK
WEEDING HOOK
WEEPING ROCK
WEEPING TREE
WEIGH ANCHOR
WEIGHED DOWN
WEIGHING OUT
WELL AND GOOD
WELL BEHAVED
WELL BELOVED
WELL DEFINED
WELL DRESSED
WELL ENTERED
WELL FOUNDED
WELL GROOMED
WELL MEANING
WELL ORDERED
WELL ROUNDED
WELL SINKING
WELL THUMBED
WELL TRODDEN
WELL WISHING
WELSH COLLIE
WELSH GUARDS
WELSH RABBIT
WEND ONES WAY
WENT AGAINST
WENT FOR GOLD
WENT FORWARD
WENT MISSING
WENT ONES WAY
WENT THROUGH
WENT TO COURT
WENT TO EARTH
WENT TO PRESS
WENT TO SLEEP
WENT TO WASTE
WENT WITHOUT
WEST BY NORTH
WEST COUNTRY
WESTERN ROLL
WESTERN WALL
WHALE FISHER
WHALING PORT
WHAT AILS HER
WHAT AILS HIM
WHAT AILS YOU

WHAT HAVE YOU
WHAT THE HELL
WHEEL CLAMPS
WHEEL OF LIFE
WHEEL PLOUGH
WHEN PIGS FLY
WHETHER OR NO
WHIPPING BOY
WHIPPING TOP
WHIPS THE CAT
WHISKED AWAY
WHISKEY SOUR
WHISKY TODDY
WHIST PLAYER
WHISTLE AWAY
WHISTLE STOP
WHISTLED OFF
WHISTLES OFF
WHITE BOTTLE
WHITE COFFEE
WHITE COLLAR
WHITE ENSIGN
WHITE FRIARS
WHITE HEADED
WHITE KNIGHT
WHITE LISTED
WHITE RABBIT
WHITE SPIRIT
WHITE WINGED
WHITING POUT
WHITSUN WEEK
WHITTLE AWAY
WHOLE HOGGER
WHOLE NUMBER
WHOLE STITCH
WHOLLY OWNED
WHOOPED IT UP
WIDE RANGING
WIDEN THE GAP
WIDOWS WEEDS
WILD ANIMALS
WILD FLOWERS
WILD FOWLING
WILD MUSTARD
WIN ON POINTS
WIN THE POOLS
WIND FURNACE
WIND MACHINE
WIND SURFING
WINDFALL TAX
WINDING DOWN
WINDOW BLIND
WINDOW FRAME
WINDOW GLASS
WINDOW LEDGE
WINDOW SHOPS
WINDSOR KNOT
WINDSOR SOAP
WINE AND DINE
WINE BIBBING

11 *contd.*

WINE GROWING
WINE HARVEST
WINE TASTING
WING FORWARD
WING ONES WAY
WING WALKING
WINKLING OUT
WINNING OVER
WINNING POST
WINS BY A HEAD
WINS BY A NECK
WINS THROUGH
WINTER APPLE
WINTER SWEET
WINTER WHEAT
WIRE DANCING
WIRE NETTING
WIRE PULLING
WIRE WALKING
WIRE WHEELED
WISDOM TOOTH
WISHING BONE
WISHING WELL
WITCH DOCTOR
WITCH RIDDEN
WITCHES BREW
WITCHS BROOM
WITH KNOBS ON
WITHIN REACH
WITHOUT FAIL
WOBBLE BOARD
WOLF WHISTLE
WON ON POINTS
WON THE POOLS
WOOD ANEMONE
WOOD CARVING
WOOD CUTTING
WOOD SWALLOW
WOOD WARBLER
WOODEN HORSE
WOODEN SPOON
WOOL CARDING
WOOL COMBING
WOOL GROWING
WOOL PACKING
WOOL STAPLER
WOOLLEN MILL
WORD FOR WORD
WORD OF MOUTH
WORD PAINTER
WORD PERFECT
WORD PICTURE
WORD PUZZLER
WORDS FAIL ME
WORK AGAINST
WORK STATION
WORKING AT IT
WORKING BEAM
WORKING EDGE

WORKING GIRL
WORKING OVER
WORKING UPON
WORKING WEEK
WORKMAN LIKE
WORKS TO RULE
WORLD BEATER
WORLD CRUISE
WORLD SERIES
WORLD WAR ONE
WORLD WAR TWO
WORLDLY WISE
WORM GEARING
WORRYING OUT
WREAKS HAVOC
WRECK MASTER
WRIGGLED OUT
WRIGGLES OUT
WRINGING OUT
WRINGING WET
WRITING BOOK
WRITING CASE
WRITING DESK
WRITING DOWN
WRITING HOME
WRITTEN DOWN
WRONG FOOTED
WRONG HEADED
WRONG NUMBER
WROUGHT IRON
X CHROMOSOME
X RAY THERAPY
Y CHROMOSOME
YEAST POWDER
YELLOW BELLY
YELLOW FEVER
YELLOW METAL
YELLOW PAGES
YELLOW PERIL
YELLOW PRESS
YOU AND YOURS
YOU DIRTY RAT
YOU KNOW WHAT
YOUNG PERSON
YOUR FUNERAL
YOUR MAJESTY
YOUR WORSHIP
YOUTH HOSTEL
YOUTH LEADER
ZAPPING IT UP
ZEROING IN ON
ZIP FASTENER

12

A BAG OF NERVES
A CRYING SHAME
A FINE ROMANCE
A FOOLS ERRAND
A GOOD INNINGS
A KINGS RANSOM

A LIKELY STORY
A PIECE OF CAKE
A PRETTY PENNY
A QUARTER PAST
A TIGHT CORNER
ABNORMAL LOAD
ABOVE ONESELF
ABOVE THE LINE
ABSENT MINDED
ABSOLUTE ZERO
ABSTRACT NOUN
ACADEMY AWARD
ACHILLES HEEL
ACTED THE FOOL
ACTED THE GOAT
ACTION REPLAY
ACTION TAKING
ACTOR MANAGER
AD REFERENDUM
ADDERS TONGUE
ADDLE BRAINED
ADJUTANT BIRD
ADRENAL GLAND
AESOPS FABLES
AFRO AMERICAN
AFTER THE FACT
AFTERNOON NAP
AGE OF CONSENT
AGENT GENERAL
AIR AMBULANCE
AIR COMMODORE
AIR CONDITION
AIR FORCE BLUE
AIR SEA RESCUE
ALADDINS CAVE
ALADDINS LAMP
ALKALI METALS
ALL AND SUNDRY
ALL IMPORTANT
ALL INCLUSIVE
ALL OF A DITHER
ALL OF A DOODAH
ALL OF A SUDDEN
ALL OF THE TIME
ALL OR NOTHING
ALL SAINTS DAY
ALL SYSTEMS GO
ALLA CAPPELLA
ALPHA BLOCKER
ALPHABET SOUP
ALVEOLAR ARCH
AMERICAN PLAN
AN ALL TIME LOW
AN AXE TO GRIND
ANCIEN REGIME
AND NO MISTAKE
AND THATS THAT
ANGEL OF MERCY
ANGORA RABBIT
ANIMAL RIGHTS

ANISEED BALLS
ANSWERED BACK
ANTE MERIDIEM
ANTI AIRCRAFT
ANTI SEMITISM
ANY QUESTIONS
ANYTHING GOES
APOSTLE SPOON
APOSTOLIC SEE
APPARENT TIME
APPLE BLOSSOM
APPLE BOBBING
APPROACH ROAD
APPROACH SHOT
APRIL SHOWERS
APRON STRINGS
AQUILINE NOSE
ARABIAN CAMEL
ARCTIC CIRCLE
ARCUS SENILIS
ARGUE THE TOSS
ARMISTICE DAY
ARMOUR BEARER
ARMOUR PLATED
ARRESTER GEAR
ARRESTER HOOK
ARTERIAL ROAD
ARTESIAN WELL
ARTILLERY MAN
ARTISTS MODEL
ARTISTS PROOF
AS BLACK AS INK
AS CLEAR AS MUD
AS GOOD AS GOLD
AS OFTEN AS NOT
AS SURE AS A GUN
ASCENSION DAY
ASCORBIC ACID
ASH WEDNESDAY
ASHES TO ASHES
ASK ME ANOTHER
ASSEMBLY HALL
ASSEMBLY LINE
ASSEMBLY ROOM
ASTI SPUMANTE
AT ARMS LENGTH
AT DEATHS DOOR
AT FIRST BLUSH
AT FIRST LIGHT
AT KNIFE POINT
ATE HUMBLE PIE
ATE ONES WORDS
ATHLETES FOOT
ATLANTIC TIME
ATOMIC ENERGY
ATOMIC NUMBER
ATOMIC SECOND
ATOMIC THEORY
ATOMIC WEIGHT
AUCTION ROOMS

12 contd.

AULD LANG SYNE	BASSO RILIEVO	BIRDS EYE VIEW	BOMB DISPOSAL
AUSTIN FRIARS	BASTARD TITLE	BIRDS NESTING	BOMBER JACKET
AUSTRALIA DAY	BASTARD TYPES	BIRTH CONTROL	BONFIRE NIGHT
AUTO IMMUNITY	BATHERS CRAMP	BIRTHDAY BOOK	BONNE VIVANTE
AUTUMN CROCUS	BATHING BELLE	BIRTHDAY CAKE	BONNET MONKEY
AVOGADROS LAW	BATHING DRESS	BIRTHDAY CARD	BOOGIE WOOGIE
AWE INSPIRING	BATTERED BABY	BIRTHDAY SUIT	BOOK LEARNING
AWKWARD SQUAD	BATTERING RAM	BISHOPS COURT	BOOKING CLERK
BABY BATTERER	BATTING ORDER	BIT ONES THUMB	BORDER COLLIE
BABY CARRIAGE	BAY AT THE MOON	BIT THE BULLET	BOROUGH COURT
BABY SNATCHER	BAYONET JOINT	BITES ONES LIP	BOROUGH REEVE
BACHELOR FLAT	BE OFF WITH YOU	BITES THE DUST	BORROWED TIME
BACHELOR GIRL	BEAM TRAWLING	BITTER ORANGE	BOTTLE HOLDER
BACK AND FORTH	BEANS ON TOAST	BLACK AND BLUE	BOTTLE OPENER
BACK OF BEYOND	BEARING CLOTH	BLACK AS PITCH	BOTTLE WASHER
BACK PEDALLED	BEAT A RETREAT	BLACK COUNTRY	BOTTOM DRAWER
BACK ROOM BOYS	BEAT THE CLOCK	BLACK DIAMOND	BOTTOM SAWYER
BACK SLAPPING	BEATS THE BAND	BLACK ECONOMY	BOTTOMING OUT
BACK STABBING	BEATS THE DRUM	BLACK FISHING	BOUNCING BACK
BACKING STORE	BEAUX ESPRITS	BLACK HEARTED	BOUQUET GARNI
BACKWARD STEP	BEAVERED AWAY	BLACK MUSTARD	BOW AND SCRAPE
BAGGAGE TRAIN	BECHERS BROOK	BLACK PUDDING	BOW COMPASSES
BAILEY BRIDGE	BEDSIDE TABLE	BLACK SALSIFY	BOWHEAD WHALE
BAKERLOO LINE	BEETLE BROWED	BLADDER WRACK	BOWLING ALLEY
BAKEWELL TART	BEFORE CHRIST	BLANC DE CHINE	BOWLING GREEN
BAKING POWDER	BELGIAN FRANC	BLARNEY STONE	BOX OF MATCHES
BALACLAVA CAP	BELL BOTTOMED	BLAST FURNACE	BOXING GLOVES
BALANCE SHEET	BELLED THE CAT	BLAZE OF GLORY	BOY MEETS GIRL
BALANCE WHEEL	BELLY DANCING	BLAZED A TRAIL	BRACKET CLOCK
BALL BEARINGS	BELLY LANDING	BLAZES A TRAIL	BRAIN SURGEON
BALL OF STRING	BELOW THE BELT	BLEW ONES MIND	BRAISED STEAK
BALL POINT PEN	BELOW THE LINE	BLISTER STEEL	BRAMBLE BERRY
BALLET DANCER	BELOW THE SALT	BLOCK BOOKING	BRAMBLE FINCH
BALLET MASTER	BENCH WARRANT	BLOCK CAPITAL	BRAND LOYALTY
BALSAM OF PERU	BEND SINISTER	BLOCK RELEASE	BRANDING IRON
BALSAM OF TOLU	BENEFIT MATCH	BLOOD BLISTER	BRANDY BOTTLE
BALSAM POPLAR	BENEFIT NIGHT	BLOOD BROTHER	BRANDY BUTTER
BAMBOO SHOOTS	BENJAMIN TREE	BLOOD PUDDING	BRANDY PAWNEE
BANBURY CROSS	BERMUDA GRASS	BLOODY MINDED	BRASS BOUNDER
BANDIED WORDS	BESSEMER IRON	BLOW MOULDING	BRASS RUBBING
BANDIES WORDS	BET ONES BOOTS	BLOW ONES MIND	BREAD PUDDING
BANG TO RIGHTS	BETWEEN DECKS	BLOWING A FUSE	BREAK A RECORD
BANG UP TO DATE	BETWEEN TIMES	BLOWS ONES TOP	BREAK A STRIKE
BANKERS ORDER	BEVERAGE ROOM	BLOWS THE GAFF	BREAK THE BANK
BANTAM WEIGHT	BEVERLY HILLS	BOARD MEETING	BREAK THE NEWS
BAR BILLIARDS	BEYOND NUMBER	BOARD OF TRADE	BREAK THROUGH
BARBARY COAST	BEYOND OUR KEN	BOARDING CARD	BREAKFAST SET
BARBARY SHEEP	BIBBLE BABBLE	BOARDING PASS	BREAKING AWAY
BARBERS BLOCK	BIBLE POUNDER	BOARDING PIKE	BREAKING CAMP
BARMY BRAINED	BIBLE THUMPER	BOBBY DAZZLER	BREAKING DOWN
BARNYARD FOWL	BICYCLE CHAIN	BODICE RIPPER	BREAKING EVEN
BARON OFFICER	BILL OF LADING	BODY BUILDING	BREAKS GROUND
BARRIER CREAM	BILL OF RIGHTS	BODY CHECKING	BREAKS THE ICE
BASIC ENGLISH	BILLIARD BALL	BODY LANGUAGE	BREAST CANCER
BASIC PROCESS	BILLIARD HALL	BODY SNATCHER	BREAST GIRDLE
BASKET MAKING	BINARY NUMBER	BODY STOCKING	BREATHE AGAIN
BASKET STITCH	BINARY SYSTEM	BOG PIMPERNEL	BREECH LOADER
BASKING SHARK	BINARY WEAPON	BOHEMIAN RUBY	BREECHES BUOY
BASS CLARINET	BIRD OF WONDER	BOILING POINT	BREWERS YEAST
	BIRD WATCHING	BOLOGNA PHIAL	BRIDE CHAMBER

12 contd.

BRIDGE THE GAP
BRIDGING LOAN
BRIGADE MAJOR
BRIGHTON ROCK
BRING A CHARGE
BRING FORWARD
BRING TO A HEAD
BRING TO LIGHT
BRINGING DOWN
BRINGING HOME
BRINGING OVER
BRINGS TO BOOK
BRINGS TO HEEL
BRINGS TO LIFE
BRISTOL BOARD
BRISTOL BRICK
BRITISH ISLES
BRITISH PLATE
BRITTLE BONES
BROKE A RECORD
BROKE A STRIKE
BROKE THE BANK
BROKE THE NEWS
BROKEN BACKED
BROKEN WINDED
BROKER DEALER
BROMIDE PAPER
BRONCO BUSTER
BROTHER IN LAW
BROUGHT ABOUT
BROUGHT FORTH
BROUGHT ROUND
BROWNIE GUIDE
BROWNIE POINT
BRUSHED ASIDE
BRUSHES ASIDE
BRUSSELS LACE
BUBBLE HEADED
BUBBLING OVER
BUCKLED UNDER
BUCKLES UNDER
BUCKLING DOWN
BUDDHIST MONK
BUENAS NOCHES
BUENAS TARDES
BUFFALO BERRY
BUFFALO GRASS
BUGGINSS TURN
BUILDING SITE
BULK DISCOUNT
BULL ELEPHANT
BULLET HEADED
BUMP STARTING
BUNCH OF FIVES
BUNGEE JUMPER
BUNKO STEERER
BUNSEN BURNER
BURGLAR ALARM
BURIAL GROUND

BURMESE GLASS
BURNING GLASS
BURNING HOUSE
BURNING ISSUE
BURNING POINT
BURNT ALMONDS
BURROWING OWL
BURYING PLACE
BUS CONDUCTOR
BUSINESS CARD
BUSINESS LIKE
BUSINESS PARK
BUSINESS SUIT
BUTCHERS HOOK
BUTCHERS MEAT
BUTTER COOLER
BUTTER MUSLIN
BUTTERED EGGS
BUTTERFLY BOW
BUTTERFLY NET
BUTTERFLY NUT
BUTTERY HATCH
BUTTON SCURVY
BUYERS MARKET
BUYS AND SELLS
BY A LONG CHALK
BY A SHORT HEAD
CABBAGE PATCH
CABIN CRUISER
CABLE RAILWAY
CABLE TRAMWAY
CAIRN TERRIER
CALABASH TREE
CALAMITY JANE
CALCIUM OXIDE
CALENDAR LINE
CALENDAR YEAR
CALICO FLOWER
CALL OF NATURE
CALL THE SHOTS
CALLED IT A DAY
CALLED TO MIND
CALLING A HALT
CALLING NAMES
CALLS THE TUNE
CALLS TO ORDER
CALVARY CROSS
CAME A CROPPER
CAME INTO PLAY
CAME UP TRUMPS
CAMP FOLLOWER
CAMP PREACHER
CAMP SHEETING
CANADA BALSAM
CANARY YELLOW
CANCELLED OUT
CANDID CAMERA
CANDLE HOLDER
CANDY STRIPED
CANE BOTTOMED

CANISTER SHOT
CANNON FODDER
CANON REGULAR
CANON SECULAR
CANTING WHEEL
CAP OF LIBERTY
CAPE COLOURED
CAPE HYACINTH
CAPITAL GAINS
CAPITAL GOODS
CAPSTAN LATHE
CAPSTAN TABLE
CARAWAY SEEDS
CARBOLIC ACID
CARBON DATING
CARBON FIBRES
CARD CARRYING
CARDBOARD BOX
CARDINAL BIRD
CARDINAL SINS
CARNIVAL WEEK
CARPENTER ANT
CARPENTER BEE
CARPET BEETLE
CARRIAGE FREE
CARRIAGE PAID
CARRIED IT OFF
CARRIES IT OFF
CARRY FORWARD
CARRY ONES BAT
CARRY THE FLAG
CARRY THROUGH
CARRYING AWAY
CARRYING BACK
CARRYING OVER
CARTE BLANCHE
CARTON PIERRE
CARTRIDGE PEN
CARVING KNIFE
CASE HARDENED
CASE THE JOINT
CASH AND CARRY
CASH REGISTER
CASTING A VOTE
CASTING AN EYE
CASTING ASIDE
CASTING COUCH
CASTING LOOSE
CASTS A GLANCE
CASUAL LABOUR
CASUALTY WARD
CAT AND FIDDLE
CAT O MOUNTAIN
CATCHES A COLD
CATCHES A CRAB
CATCHING FIRE
CATS WHISKERS
CATTLE MARKET
CAUGHT THE SUN
CAULKING IRON

CAUSE CELEBRE
CAUSE TROUBLE
CAUSING A STIR
CAVALRY TWILL
CAVE PAINTING
CAVEAT EMPTOR
CELL DIVISION
CENTRE SPREAD
CENTURY PLANT
CEST LA GUERRE
CETANE NUMBER
CHAIN GEARING
CHAIN REACTOR
CHAIN SMOKING
CHAISE LONGUE
CHALK AND TALK
CHALLENGE CUP
CHAMBER MUSIC
CHAMBER ORGAN
CHANCE MEDLEY
CHANCE REMARK
CHANGE COLOUR
CHANGE OF LIFE
CHANGE PLACES
CHANGED HANDS
CHANGES HANDS
CHANGING DOWN
CHANGING ENDS
CHANGING GEAR
CHANGING ROOM
CHANNEL STONE
CHAPEL MASTER
CHAPEL OF EASE
CHAPEL OF REST
CHAPTER HOUSE
CHARGING DOWN
CHARLESS WAIN
CHARNEL HOUSE
CHART BUSTING
CHARTER MAYOR
CHARTER PARTY
CHASSE CROISE
CHASTITY BELT
CHECK WEIGHER
CHECKER BOARD
CHECKING ROOM
CHEDDAR GORGE
CHEEK TO CHEEK
CHEEKY MONKEY
CHEESE CUTTER
CHEESE HOPPER
CHEESE MONGER
CHEESE PARING
CHEESE STRAWS
CHEESE TASTER
CHEFS DOEUVRE
CHEMISTRY SET
CHERRY BOUNCE
CHERRY BRANDY
CHERRY LAUREL

12 contd.

CHERRY PICKER
CHERRY TOMATO
CHESS PROBLEM
CHEST FREEZER
CHEVAL MIRROR
CHEVRON BOARD
CHEWED THE CUD
CHEWED THE FAT
CHICKENED OUT
CHIEF JUSTICE
CHIEF MOURNER
CHIEF OF STAFF
CHIEF WITNESS
CHILD BENEFIT
CHILD PRODIGY
CHILD WELFARE
CHIMNEY BOARD
CHIMNEY PIECE
CHIMNEY SHAFT
CHIMNEY STACK
CHIMNEY STALK
CHIMNEY SWEEP
CHINESE BOXES
CHINESE PAPER
CHINESE WHITE
CHLOROUS ACID
CHOCOLATE BOX
CHOCOLATE EGG
CHOPPED LOGIC
CHORUS MASTER
CHRISTIAN ERA
CHRISTMAS BOX
CHRISTMAS DAY
CHRISTMAS EVE
CHROME YELLOW
CHUCKIE STONE
CHUCKING IT IN
CHURCH BAZAAR
CHURCH PARADE
CHURCH WARDEN
CIGARETTE END
CINEMA SCREEN
CINEMA VERITE
CIRCLE RIDING
CIRCUIT BOARD
CIRCUIT JUDGE
CIRCUIT RIDER
CIRCULAR FILE
CIRCULAR NOTE
CIRRO CUMULUS
CIRRO STRATUS
CITIZENS BAND
CITRUS FRUITS
CIVIL DEFENCE
CIVIL LIBERTY
CIVIL SERVANT
CIVIL SERVICE
CLAIM DAMAGES
CLAIMING RACE

CLAMPING DOWN
CLASSIC RACES
CLEAN AND JERK
CLEANING LADY
CLEAR AS A BELL
CLEAR SIGHTED
CLEARING BANK
CLEARS THE AIR
CLEARS THE WAY
CLERICAL GREY
CLERK OF WORKS
CLEVER CLEVER
CLICHE RIDDEN
CLIMBING DOWN
CLINKER BLOCK
CLINKER BUILT
CLIP FASTENER
CLOCK WATCHER
CLOSE COMPANY
CLOSE CROPPED
CLOSE FITTING
CLOSE GRAINED
CLOSE HARMONY
CLOSE MOUTHED
CLOSED THE GAP
CLOSES THE GAP
CLOSING PRICE
CLOSING RANKS
CLOTH OF STATE
CLOTHES BRUSH
CLOTHES HORSE
CLOTHES PRESS
CLOTHES SENSE
CLOTTED CREAM
CLOUD CEILING
CLOUD CHAMBER
CLOUD OF SMOKE
CLOUDING OVER
CLOVEN FOOTED
CLOVEN HOOVED
CLUB SANDWICH
CLUB TOGETHER
CLUBS TO DEATH
COACH AND FOUR
COACH AND PAIR
COACH STATION
COAL MERCHANT
COAST TO COAST
COAXIAL CABLE
COBBLE STONES
COCK FIGHTING
COCKED A SNOOK
CODE BREAKING
CODE OF HONOUR
COIN OPERATED
COINS A PHRASE
COLD SHOULDER
COLLARED DOVE
COLOGNE WATER
COLONEL BLIMP

COLONEL BOGEY
COLOUR FILTER
COLOUR SCHEME
COMBAT JACKET
COME A CROPPER
COME AND GET IT
COME INTO PLAY
COME UP TRUMPS
COMES AND GOES
COMES BETWEEN
COMES FORWARD
COMES TO A HEAD
COMES TO BLOWS
COMES TO GRIEF
COMES TO LIGHT
COMES UNSTUCK
COMING ACROSS
COMING ASHORE
COMING TO LIFE
COMING TO PASS
COMING TO REST
COMING UNDONE
COMMAND PAPER
COMMON DEBTOR
COMMON GENDER
COMMON GROUND
COMMON MARKET
COMMON PRAYER
COMMON RIDING
COMMON SCHOOL
COMMUNE BONUM
COMMUNION CUP
COMPANION SET
COMPANION WAY
COMPARE NOTES
COMPASS PLANE
COMPASS PLANT
COMPOS MENTIS
COMPOUND LEAF
COMPOUND TIME
COMPUTER GAME
CONCERT GRAND
CONCERT PARTY
CONCERT PITCH
CONCERT WALTZ
CONIC SECTION
CONNATE WATER
CONNING TOWER
CONSOLE TABLE
CONTACT POINT
CONTRA MUNDUM
CONTRACTED IN
CONTRACTS OUT
CONTROL BOARD
CONTROL GROUP
CONTROL PANEL
CONTROL TOWER
CONVEYOR BELT
COOK THE BOOKS
COOKING APPLE

COOKING RANGE
COOL CUSTOMER
COOLING TOWER
COPPER BOTTOM
COPPER GLANCE
COPPER NICKEL
COPYING PRESS
CORDONING OFF
CORDUROY ROAD
CORK LINOLEUM
CORN EXCHANGE
CORN MERCHANT
CORN ON THE COB
CORNISH PASTY
COSI FAN TUTTE
COSSACK BOOTS
COST OF LIVING
COST THE EARTH
COSTUME DRAMA
COSTUME PIECE
COTTON PICKER
COUGH LOZENGE
COUGH MIXTURE
COUNCIL BOARD
COUNCIL HOUSE
COUNCIL OF WAR
COUNT DRACULA
COUNTED SHEEP
COUNTER BRACE
COUNTER CLAIM
COUNTER FORCE
COUNTER TENOR
COUNTER WEIGH
COUNTER WHEEL
COUNTRY DANCE
COUNTRY HOUSE
COUNTRY MUSIC
COUNTRY PARTY
COUNTY FAMILY
COUNTY SCHOOL
COUP DE FOUDRE
COUP DE MAITRE
COURT DRESSER
COURT MARTIAL
COURT PLASTER
COUSIN GERMAN
COVENT GARDEN
COVENTRY BLUE
COVER VERSION
COVERED WAGON
CRACK THE WHIP
CRACKED A CRIB
CRACKED A JOKE
CRACKING DOWN
CRANIAL INDEX
CRASH BARRIER
CRASH LANDING
CREAM CRACKER
CREDIT RATING
CREDIT TITLES

12 *contd.*

CREEPY CRAWLY
CREME CARAMEL
CREME DE CACAO
CREPE DE CHINE
CREPE SUZETTE
CRESCENT MOON
CRICKET MATCH
CRICKET PITCH
CRIMPING IRON
CRITICAL MASS
CROOKES GLASS
CROP SPRAYING
CROSS BUTTOCK
CROSS COUNTRY
CROSS CURRENT
CROSS EXAMINE
CROSS GRAINED
CROSS PLY TYRE
CROSS PURPOSE
CROSS SECTION
CROSSED THE TS
CROSSED WIRES
CROSSES THE TS
CROSSING OVER
CROWN WITNESS
CRUEL HEARTED
CRUSH BARRIER
CRYSTAL CLEAR
CRYSTAL GAZER
CUCKOO FLOWER
CULTURE SHOCK
CUMULO CIRRUS
CUMULO NIMBUS
CUP AND SAUCER
CUP FINALISTS
CUPBOARD LOVE
CURDS AND WHEY
CURL UP AND DIE
CURLING IRONS
CURLING STONE
CURLING TONGS
CURRANT BREAD
CURRANT JELLY
CURRENCY NOTE
CUSHION OF AIR
CUSTARD APPLE
CUT AND THRUST
CUT THE CACKLE
CUT TO RIBBONS
CUTS BOTH WAYS
CUTS THE CARDS
CUTTING A DASH
CUTTING LOOSE
CUTTING SHORT
CYLINDER HEAD
CYLINDER LOCK
CZAR OF RUSSIA
DAFT AS A BRUSH
DAILY SERVICE

DAIRY FARMING
DALMATIAN DOG
DANCE OF DEATH
DANCE ROUTINE
DANGER SIGNAL
DANISH PASTRY
DANSE MACABRE
DARBY AND JOAN
DAY BLINDNESS
DEAD AS MUTTON
DEAD GIVE AWAY
DEAD LANGUAGE
DEALING A BLOW
DEATH DEALING
DEATH PENALTY
DEATH WARRANT
DEBT OF HONOUR
DEBT OF NATURE
DECIMAL PLACE
DECIMAL POINT
DECLARING WAR
DEEP SEA DIVER
DELIVERY PIPE
DELIVERY TUBE
DELLA CRUSCAN
DEMI MONDAINE
DEN OF THIEVES
DEPTH OF FIELD
DEPTH OF FOCUS
DESERT SIGNAL
DEUS VOBISCUM
DEVIL MAY CARE
DEVIL WORSHIP
DEVILS ISLAND
DEVILS TATTOO
DIALLING CODE
DIALLING TONE
DIAMOND DRILL
DIAMOND FIELD
DIAMOND WHEEL
DID ONES STUFF
DID ONES WORST
DIED THE DEATH
DIESEL ENGINE
DIETARY FIBRE
DIGITAL CLOCK
DINGLE DANGLE
DINNER JACKET
DIRECT ACCESS
DIRECT ACTION
DIRECT LABOUR
DIRECT METHOD
DIRECT MOTION
DIRECT OBJECT
DIRECT SPEECH
DISASTER AREA
DISCOUNT RATE
DISPATCH BOAT
DISPATCH CASE
DISSECTED MAP

DISTRICT LINE
DIVIDED SKIRT
DIVINITY HALL
DIVISION BELL
DIVORCE COURT
DO IT YOURSELF
DO NOT DISTURB
DO THE HONOURS
DOCK LABOURER
DOES THE TRICK
DOES THE TWIST
DOGTOOTH SPAR
DOING ONES BIT
DOING ONES NUT
DOING TO DEATH
DOLMAN SLEEVE
DOMESDAY BOOK
DOMINO EFFECT
DOMINO THEORY
DONKEY ENGINE
DONKEY JACKET
DONKEYS YEARS
DOOM MERCHANT
DOOMSDAY BOOK
DOPPLER SHIFT
DORMER WINDOW
DORMITORY CAR
DORSAL SUTURE
DOTTED AROUND
DOTTING THE IS
DOUBLE BANKED
DOUBLE CHARGE
DOUBLE DAGGER
DOUBLE DEALER
DOUBLE DECKER
DOUBLE GLAZED
DOUBLE HANDED
DOUBLE HEADED
DOUBLE LOCKED
DOUBLE OBELUS
DOUBLE PARKED
DOUBLE STOREY
DOUBLE VISION
DOUBLING BACK
DOVERS POWDER
DOWN AND OUTER
DOWN THE DRAIN
DOWN THE HATCH
DOWNING TOOLS
DRAFT DODGING
DRAG ONES FEET
DRAGON LIZARD
DRAGONS BLOOD
DRAINAGE TUBE
DRAINING AWAY
DRAUGHT HORSE
DRAUGHT PROOF
DRAW TO A CLOSE
DRAWING BLOOD
DRAWING BOARD

DRAWING FRAME
DRAWING PAPER
DRAWING TABLE
DRAWING TEETH
DRAWS THE LINE
DRESDEN CHINA
DRESS UNIFORM
DRESSING CASE
DRESSING DOWN
DRESSING GOWN
DRESSING ROOM
DREW TO A CLOSE
DRIFTED APART
DRINK DRIVING
DRINKING BOUT
DRINKING HORN
DRINKING SONG
DRIVE IN MOVIE
DRIVING WHEEL
DRONGO CUCKOO
DROP A CLANGER
DROPPED A LINE
DROPPED SCONE
DROPPING AWAY
DROPPING DOWN
DRUNK AS A LORD
DUAL MONARCHY
DUCHESSE LACE
DUCK SHOOTING
DUCKING STOOL
DUNMOW FLITCH
DUTCH AUCTION
DUTCH COMFORT
DUTCH COURAGE
EACH TO HIS OWN
EAR SPLITTING
EARL PALATINE
EARLY CLOSING
EARLY ENGLISH
EARLY WARNING
EARTH CREATED
EARTH SCIENCE
EAST INDIAMAN
EASTER BONNET
EASTER CACTUS
EASTER ISLAND
EASTER PARADE
EASY ON THE EYE
EAT HUMBLE PIE
EAT ONES WORDS
EAU DE COLOGNE
EAU DE JAVELLE
EBBS AND FLOWS
ECHO LOCATION
ECHO SOUNDING
EGG AND ANCHOR
EIGHTEEN HOLE
ELECTRIC BLUE
ELECTRIC FIRE
ELECTRIC HARE

12 *contd.*

ELECTRON LENS
ELECTRON TUBE
ELECTRON VOLT
ELEPHANT SEAL
ELEVEN OCLOCK
ELEVENTH HOUR
ELGIN MARBLES
ELIXIR OF LIFE
EMERALD GREEN
ENABLING BILL
END OF THE LINE
ENDED IN TEARS
ENDLESS CHAIN
ENDLESS SCREW
ENGINE DRIVER
ENGINE FITTER
ENGLISH FLUTE
ENJOY ONESELF
ENTERIC FEVER
ENTRANCE HALL
ERMINE STREET
ESCAPE CLAUSE
ESCORT AGENCY
ETERNITY RING
ETHYL ALCOHOL
EURO AMERICAN
EURO SCEPTICS
EUROPEAN PLAN
EVEN TEMPERED
EVENING CLASS
EVENING DRESS
EVERY MAN JACK
EVERY SO OFTEN
EVIL SPEAKING
EVIL TEMPERED
EX SERVICEMAN
EX SERVICEMEN
EXACT SCIENCE
EXCHANGE RATE
EXERCISE BIKE
EXERCISE BOOK
EXHAUST STEAM
EXHAUST VALVE
EXPLAINS AWAY
EXPORT MARKET
EXPORT REJECT
EXPRESS TRAIN
EXTENDED PLAY
EXTRA SENSORY
EXTRA SPECIAL
EXTRACTOR FAN
EYE OF A NEEDLE
FACE THE MUSIC
FACING UP TO IT
FAINT HEARTED
FAIT ACCOMPLI
FAITH HEALING
FALCON GENTLE
FALL INTO LINE

FALLEN ARCHES
FALLING ABOUT
FALLING APART
FALLING SHORT
FALLS THROUGH
FALSE COLOURS
FALSE MODESTY
FAMILIAR FACE
FAMILIAR RING
FAMILLE JAUNE
FAMILLE NOIRE
FAMILLE VERTE
FAMILY CIRCLE
FAMILY DOCTOR
FAMILY FRIEND
FANCY ONESELF
FARM LABOURER
FASHION HOUSE
FAST AND LOOSE
FATHER FIGURE
FATHERS IN LAW
FATIGUE DRESS
FATIGUE PARTY
FAULT FINDING
FEAST OF ASSES
FEAST OF FOOLS
FEATHER BRAIN
FEATHER GRASS
FEDERAL AGENT
FEDERAL STATE
FEEBLE MINDED
FEED ONES FACE
FEEL THE PINCH
FEELING A FOOL
FEELING CHEAP
FEELING FAINT
FEELING SMALL
FELL INTO LINE
FELLOW MEMBER
FELT THE PINCH
FEMME DU MONDE
FENCE MENDING
FENNEL FLOWER
FERROUS OXIDE
FESTOON BLIND
FEUDAL SYSTEM
FIDDLE FADDLE
FIDDLE STRING
FIELD BATTERY
FIELD COLOURS
FIELD GLASSES
FIELD KITCHEN
FIELD MARSHAL
FIELD MEETING
FIELD OFFICER
FIERY FURNACE
FIFTY PER CENT
FIGHTER PILOT
FIGHTER PLANE
FIGHTING BACK

FIGHTING COCK
FIGHTING FISH
FIGURE CASTER
FIGURE SKATER
FIGURED IT OUT
FIGURES IT OUT
FILING SYSTEM
FILLS THE BILL
FILM DIRECTOR
FILM FESTIVAL
FILM INDUSTRY
FILM PREMIERE
FINANCE HOUSE
FIND ONES FEET
FINDING FAULT
FINE AND DANDY
FINGER AND TOE
FINGER BUFFET
FINISHING OFF
FIRE AND SWORD
FIRE FIGHTING
FIRE OF LONDON
FIRE WATCHING
FIREMANS LIFT
FIRMER CHISEL
FIRST AND LAST
FIRST FOOTING
FIRST INNINGS
FIRST NIGHTER
FIRST READING
FIRST REFUSAL
FIRST RESERVE
FIRST SEA LORD
FISH AND CHIPS
FISH HATCHERY
FISHING SMACK
FIT AS A FIDDLE
FITTED CARPET
FIVE ARTICLES
FIXED CAPITAL
FIXED CHARGES
FIXED PENALTY
FLAGGING DOWN
FLAME THROWER
FLANDERS MARE
FLATTENED OUT
FLEET OF TAXIS
FLEXIBLE DISC
FLICK THROUGH
FLIES THE FLAG
FLINGING DOWN
FLINGING OPEN
FLINT HEARTED
FLINT KNAPPER
FLIPS ONES LID
FLITTER MOUSE
FLOATED ON AIR
FLOATING DEBT
FLOATING DOCK
FLOATING MINE

FLOATING VOTE
FLOCK OF GEESE
FLOCK OF SHEEP
FLOWER GARDEN
FLOWER PEOPLE
FLOWERPOT MEN
FLOWING LOCKS
FLYING BRIDGE
FLYING CARPET
FLYING COLUMN
FLYING DOCTOR
FLYING JACKET
FLYING LIZARD
FLYING SAUCER
FOLD ONES ARMS
FOLDING MONEY
FOLDING STOOL
FOLDING STUFF
FOLIAGE PLANT
FOLK MEDICINE
FOLLOWED HOME
FOLLOWED SUIT
FOLLOWING OUT
FOOLED AROUND
FOOLISH WITTY
FOOLS PARSLEY
FOOT DRAGGING
FOOT REGIMENT
FOOT SLOGGING
FOOT SOLDIERS
FOOTS THE BILL
FOR PETES SAKE
FOR PITYS SAKE
FOR THE RECORD
FORCE AND FEAR
FORCE FEEDING
FORCE MAJEURE
FORCE OF HABIT
FORCE THE PACE
FORCED LABOUR
FORCING HOUSE
FORE AND AFTER
FOREIGN DRAFT
FOREIGN PARTS
FOREST RANGER
FORK LUNCHEON
FORM MISTRESS
FORMULA THREE
FORWARD PRICE
FOSTER FATHER
FOSTER MOTHER
FOSTER PARENT
FOSTER SISTER
FOUL LANGUAGE
FOUND WANTING
FOUNTAIN HEAD
FOUR EYED FISH
FOURPENNY ONE
FOURTH ESTATE
FOWLING PIECE

12 *contd.*

FOX AND HOUNDS
FRANCO GERMAN
FREE AS THE AIR
FREE DELIVERY
FREE OF CHARGE
FREE STANDING
FREE SWIMMING
FREE THINKING
FREE WHEELING
FREEZE DRYING
FREEZING DOWN
FREEZING OVER
FREIGHT TRAIN
FRENCH POLISH
FRENCH WINDOW
FRESH AS PAINT
FRESHENING UP
FREUDIAN SLIP
FRIARS BALSAM
FRIGHTEN AWAY
FRIGHTENS OFF
FRITTERS AWAY
FROG MARCHING
FROM DAY TO DAY
FROM THE HEART
FROM TOP TO TOE
FRONT BENCHER
FRONT LOADING
FRONT OF HOUSE
FROSTED GLASS
FROZEN ASSETS
FROZEN MITTEN
FRUIT MACHINE
FUEL INJECTED
FULL BOTTOMED
FULL THROATED
FULLER FIGURE
FULLERS EARTH
FULLY FLEDGED
FULMINIC ACID
FUME CUPBOARD
FUNERAL MARCH
FUNERAL RITES
FURNITURE VAN
FUSIBLE METAL
GADDING ABOUT
GAELIC COFFEE
GAIN STRENGTH
GAINED GROUND
GAINS CONTROL
GALLOPING OFF
GALLOWS MAKER
GALVANIC CELL
GAMBLING HALL
GAME PRESERVE
GAMES TEACHER
GANDER MOONER
GARDEN CENTRE
GARDEN OF EDEN

GARDEN SUBURB
GARRET MASTER
GARRISON TOWN
GARTER STITCH
GAS CONDENSER
GASTRIC FEVER
GASTRIC JUICE
GATE LEG TABLE
GATHER BREATH
GATHER GROUND
GATHERING CRY
GATHERING WAY
GATHERS ROUND
GATHERS SPEED
GEISSLER TUBE
GEM ENGRAVING
GENERAL ISSUE
GENERAL STAFF
GENERAL SYNOD
GENS DE GUERRE
GENTLE BREEZE
GEODESIC DOME
GERMAN SILVER
GET ONES CARDS
GET ONES EYE IN
GET RICH QUICK
GET THE NEEDLE
GET THE WIND UP
GET UNDRESSED
GETS CRACKING
GETS IN THE WAY
GETS ONES GOAT
GETS TOGETHER
GETTING ABOUT
GETTING AHEAD
GETTING ALONG
GETTING IDEAS
GETTING READY
GETTING ROUND
GETTING THERE
GETTING TOUGH
GIANT KILLING
GIANTS KETTLE
GIANTS STRIDE
GIBBLE GABBLE
GIFT OF THE GAB
GILDS THE LILY
GILDS THE PILL
GIRDER BRIDGE
GIRDS ONESELF
GIVE ON A PLATE
GIVEN THE PUSH
GIVEN THE SACK
GIVEN THE SLIP
GIVES OFFENCE
GIVING GROUND
GIVING NOTICE
GLADSTONE BAG
GLARING ERROR
GLASS BLOWING

GLASS CUTTING
GLASS OF WATER
GLASS SLIPPER
GLAUBERS SALT
GLOBE THISTLE
GLOBE TROTTER
GLUE SNIFFING
GO BY THE BOARD
GO FOR NOTHING
GO INTO DETAIL
GO INTO HIDING
GO LIKE A DREAM
GO ON ALL FOURS
GO ONES OWN WAY
GO OVER THE TOP
GO TO EXTREMES
GO TO ONES HEAD
GO UP IN THE AIR
GOAT ANTELOPE
GOD BE WITH YOU
GOES DOWNHILL
GOES FOR BROKE
GOES STRAIGHT
GOES TO GROUND
GOES TO PIECES
GOING AGAINST
GOING CONCERN
GOING FOR GOLD
GOING FORWARD
GOING IT ALONE
GOING MISSING
GOING ONES WAY
GOING THROUGH
GOING TO COURT
GOING TO EARTH
GOING TO GRASS
GOING TO PRESS
GOING TO SLEEP
GOING TO WASTE
GOING WITHOUT
GOLD RESERVES
GOLD STANDARD
GOLDEN FLEECE
GOLDEN LEGEND
GOLDEN NUMBER
GOLDEN PLOVER
GOLDEN SALMON
GOLDFISH BOWL
GONE DOWNHILL
GONE TO PIECES
GOOD BREEDING
GOOD GRACIOUS
GOOD HUMOURED
GOOD RIDDANCE
GOOD TEMPERED
GOOD THINKING
GOOD TIME GIRL
GOODWIN SANDS
GOOSE PIMPLES
GOSPEL SINGER

GOSSIP COLUMN
GOSSIP MONGER
GOSSIP WRITER
GOT ONES CARDS
GOT ONES EYE IN
GOT THE NEEDLE
GOT THE WIND UP
GOT UNDRESSED
GRAIN OF TRUTH
GRAM MOLECULE
GRAM NEGATIVE
GRAM POSITIVE
GRAND GUIGNOL
GRAND LARCENY
GRAND MARNIER
GRAND TOURING
GRANDE MARQUE
GRANNY ANNEXE
GRAPESEED OIL
GRASS WIDOWER
GRATED CHEESE
GRAVE CLOTHES
GRAVEL VOICED
GREASE MONKEY
GREAT BELLIED
GREAT BRITAIN
GREAT EASTERN
GREAT HEARTED
GREAT WESTERN
GREEK GODDESS
GREEN FINGERS
GREEN GODDESS
GREW TOGETHER
GREX VENALIUM
GREY SQUIRREL
GRIND TO A HALT
GRINDING DOWN
GRIT BLASTING
GROSS TONNAGE
GROUND ANNUAL
GROUND BEETLE
GROUND FEEDER
GROUND STOREY
GROUND STROKE
GROUP CAPTAIN
GROUP THERAPY
GROW TOGETHER
GROWING APART
GROWING PAINS
GUERNSEY LILY
GUERRILLA WAR
GUEST CHAMBER
GUIDING LIGHT
GUILD BROTHER
GUILT COMPLEX
GUNTERS CHAIN
GUNTERS SCALE
GUYS AND DOLLS
HABEAS CORPUS
HABIT FORMING

12 *contd.*

HACKNEY COACH
HAD A BASINFUL
HAD A GOOD TIME
HAD A TIME OF IT
HAD HYSTERICS
HADRIANS WALL
HAILING A TAXI
HAIR RESTORER
HAIR SPLITTER
HAIRS BREADTH
HALF MARATHON
HALF MEASURES
HALF SEAS OVER
HALF TIMBERED
HALFWAY HOUSE
HALLEYS COMET
HALTER NECKED
HAMMER HEADED
HAMMERED HOME
HAMMOND ORGAN
HAND OVER FIST
HANDS BREADTH
HANG ONES HEAD
HANG TOGETHER
HANGING ABOUT
HANGING JUDGE
HANGING LOOSE
HANGS IN THERE
HAPPENED UPON
HAPPY AS LARRY
HAPPY GO LUCKY
HAPPY LANDING
HAPPY NEW YEAR
HARBOUR LIGHT
HARD CURRENCY
HARD STANDING
HARDENING OFF
HARLEY STREET
HARMONIC MEAN
HARNESS MAKER
HARVEST FIELD
HARVEST GOOSE
HARVEST MOUSE
HARVEST QUEEN
HAS A BASINFUL
HAS A GOOD TIME
HAS A TIME OF IT
HAS HYSTERICS
HASTA LA VISTA
HASTY PUDDING
HATCHET FACED
HAULING ROUND
HAUNTED HOUSE
HAUTE COUTURE
HAUTE CUISINE
HAVE A NICE DAY
HAVE IT COMING
HAVING NO IDEA
HAZARD A GUESS

HEAD FOREMOST
HEAD GARDENER
HEAD REGISTER
HEADS OR TAILS
HEALTH CENTRE
HEALTH RESORT
HEART AND HAND
HEART AND SOUL
HEART DISEASE
HEART FAILURE
HEART OF STONE
HEART RENDING
HEART STRINGS
HEART TO HEART
HEATER SHIELD
HEAVE THE LEAD
HEAVEN FORBID
HEAVENLY BODY
HEAVENLY CITY
HEAVENLY HOST
HEAVENS ABOVE
HEAVY HEARTED
HEAVY SLEEPER
HEAVY WEATHER
HEDGE CREEPER
HEDGE HOPPING
HEDGE MUSTARD
HEDGE PARSLEY
HEDGE SPARROW
HEIGHT OF LAND
HEIR APPARENT
HEIR BY CUSTOM
HELD DOWN A JOB
HELD THE FLOOR
HELD TO RANSOM
HELD TOGETHER
HELIUM SPEECH
HELP THE CAUSE
HELP YOURSELF
HELPS ONESELF
HEMP AGRIMONY
HER NAME IS MUD
HERBAL REMEDY
HERD INSTINCT
HERE AND THERE
HESSIAN PAPER
HIATUS HERNIA
HIDDEN AGENDA
HIDDEN DEPTHS
HIDE ONES HEAD
HIGH COLOURED
HIGH FALUTING
HIGH FIDELITY
HIGH HOLIDAYS
HIGH PRESSURE
HIGH PRIESTLY
HIGH REACHING
HIGH SOUNDING
HIGH SPIRITED
HIGH STEPPING

HIGH TAILED IT
HIGH VELOCITY
HIGHLY STRUNG
HIP HIP HOORAY
HIP HIP HURRAH
HIRE PURCHASE
HIS NAME IS MUD
HIS REVERENCE
HIT A BAD PATCH
HIT THE BOTTLE
HITCHING POST
HITTING IT OFF
HOLD DOWN A JOB
HOLD THE FLOOR
HOLD TO RANSOM
HOLD TOGETHER
HOLDING COURT
HOLDING FORTH
HOLDING HANDS
HOLDING WATER
HOLDS IN CHECK
HOLDS ONES OWN
HOLDS THE FORT
HOLDS THE LINE
HOLDS THE ROAD
HOLLOW GROUND
HOLLOWING OUT
HOLY ALLIANCE
HOLY MACKEREL
HOLY OF HOLIES
HOME COUNTIES
HOME CROFTING
HOME FROM HOME
HOME PRODUCED
HOME STRAIGHT
HOMME DESPRIT
HOMME DU MONDE
HONEST BROKER
HONEY BUZZARD
HONEY MOUTHED
HONEY TONGUED
HONOUR BRIGHT
HONOURS OF WAR
HOODMAN BLIND
HOOKS AND EYES
HORN OF PLENTY
HORROR STRUCK
HORS DE COMBAT
HORS DE SAISON
HORS DOEUVRES
HORSE AND CART
HORSE BREAKER
HORSE DEALING
HORSE SOLDIER
HORSE TRADING
HORSE TRAINER
HORSED AROUND
HORSES AROUND
HORTUS SICCUS
HOSPITAL SHIP

HOT CHESTNUTS
HOT FAVOURITE
HOT GOSPELLER
HOTEL DE VILLE
HOUSE BREAKER
HOUSE HUNTING
HOUSE HUSBAND
HOUSE OF CARDS
HOUSE OF LORDS
HOUSE OF PEERS
HOUSE PAINTER
HOUSE STEWARD
HOUSE SURGEON
HOUSE TO HOUSE
HOUSE TRAINED
HOUSE WARMING
HOUSEY HOUSEY
HUBBLE BUBBLE
HUCKLE BACKED
HUGGER MUGGER
HUGS THE COAST
HUMPTY DUMPTY
HUNG ONES HEAD
HUNG TOGETHER
HUNGER STRIKE
HUNTER KILLER
HUNTING FIELD
HUNTING KNIFE
HUNTING LODGE
HURDLE RACING
HYDRAULIC RAM
HYDROGEN BOMB
HYMN OF PRAISE
I DONT THINK SO
I SHOULD WORRY
I WOULDNT KNOW
ICE CREAM SODA
ICELAND POPPY
ICHNEUMON FLY
IDENTITY CARD
IDENTITY DISC
IF THE CAP FITS
ILL TREATMENT
IMAGE BREAKER
IMAGE WORSHIP
IMMUNE SYSTEM
IMPERIAL CITY
IMPERIAL YARD
IMPULSE BUYER
IN A COLD SWEAT
IN A GOOD LIGHT
IN ALL HONESTY
IN AT THE DEATH
IN CONCLUSION
IN CONFERENCE
IN FINE FETTLE
IN GOOD HEALTH
IN HOT PURSUIT
IN ONES POCKET
IN OTHER WORDS

12 *contd.*
IN PARTICULAR
IN POOR HEALTH
IN PROPORTION
IN QUARANTINE
IN SHORT ORDER
IN SUCCESSION
IN THE BALANCE
IN THE BOX SEAT
IN THE EXTREME
IN THE FASHION
IN THE LONG RUN
IN THE PICTURE
IN THE RUNNING
IN THIS REGARD
INCIDENT ROOM
INCOMING TIDE
INDEX LINKING
INDIAN MILLET
INDIAN MUTINY
INDIAN RUNNER
INDIAN SUMMER
INDO EUROPEAN
INDO GERMANIC
INFANT SCHOOL
INFRA RED LAMP
INJURED PRIDE
INKING ROLLER
INNER CABINET
INNER SANCTUM
INNOCENTS DAY
INSECT POWDER
INSIDE CENTRE
INSTEP RAISER
INSULIN SHOCK
INTER SCIENCE
INVERSE RATIO
INVERTED ARCH
INVERTED SNOB
INVISIBLE INK
INVOICE CLERK
IONIC DIALECT
IRISH TERRIER
IRISH WHISKEY
IRONING BOARD
ISSUING FORTH
ITALIC SCRIPT
ITS AN ILL WIND
JACK A LANTERN
JACK IN OFFICE
JACK IN THE BOX
JACK O LANTERN
JACKET POTATO
JACOBEAN LILY
JACOBS LADDER
JACQUARD LOOM
JAMAICA CEDAR
JAMAICA EBONY
JANUARY SALES
JAPAN CURRENT

JAPAN LACQUER
JAVELIN THROW
JAVELLE WATER
JE NE SAIS QUOI
JERRY BUILDER
JESUITS DROPS
JET PROPELLED
JIGSAW PUZZLE
JINGLE JANGLE
JOGGING ALONG
JOHN CHINAMAN
JOINED FORCES
JOINING HANDS
JOINT ACCOUNT
JOINT TENANCY
JOINTING RULE
JOLLIED ALONG
JOLLIES ALONG
JOLLY JACK TAR
JUDGMENT DEBT
JUDGMENT HALL
JUDGMENT SEAT
JUMP STARTING
JUMP THE QUEUE
JUMPED FOR JOY
JUMPED THE GUN
JUMPING BEANS
JUMPING MOUSE
JUNIOR OPTIME
JUST LIKE THAT
JUVENILE LEAD
KEEP FIT CLASS
KEEP GOOD TIME
KEEP ONES COOL
KEEP ONES HEAD
KEEP ONES WORD
KEEP THE PEACE
KEEPING AT BAY
KEEPING CLEAR
KEEPING FAITH
KEEPING HOUSE
KEEPING QUIET
KEEPING STILL
KEEPING TRACK
KEEPING WATCH
KEEPS A SECRET
KEEPS AN EYE ON
KEEPS COUNSEL
KEEPS IN CHECK
KEEPS IN TOUCH
KEPT GOOD TIME
KEPT ONES HEAD
KEPT ONES WORD
KEPT THE PEACE
KERB CRAWLING
KERB MERCHANT
KETTLE HOLDER
KEY OF THE DOOR
KEY SIGNATURE
KEYSTONE COPS

KICK UP A STINK
KICK UPSTAIRS
KICKED AROUND
KICKING ABOUT
KICKS ONESELF
KICKS UP A FUSS
KIDNEY POTATO
KILKENNY CATS
KILOWATT HOUR
KIMONO SLEEVE
KING OF BEASTS
KINGS COUNSEL
KINGS ENGLISH
KITCHEN DUTCH
KITCHEN RANGE
KITCHEN WENCH
KNACKERS YARD
KNEE BREECHES
KNEE CROOKING
KNEW FULL WELL
KNEW THE ROPES
KNEW THE SCORE
KNIFE AND FORK
KNIFE GRINDER
KNIGHT ERRANT
KNOCKED ABOUT
KNOCKING BACK
KNOCKING COLD
KNOCKING COPY
KNOCKING DOWN
KNOCKS AROUND
KNOCKS FOR SIX
KNOCKS ON WOOD
KNOW FULL WELL
KNOW THE ROPES
KNOW THE SCORE
KNOWLEDGE BOX
KNUCKLE JOINT
KNUCKLE UNDER
KNUCKLED DOWN
KNUCKLES DOWN
KNUR AND SPELL
KOMODO DRAGON
KYRIE ELEISON
LABELLED ATOM
LABOUR MARKET
LABOUR OF LOVE
LABOUR SAVING
LACE CURTAINS
LACHRYMAL URN
LADY JANE GREY
LADYS CUSHION
LADYS FINGERS
LADYS SLIPPER
LADYS THISTLE
LAGER AND LIME
LAGGED BEHIND
LAID THE TABLE
LAISSEZ FAIRE
LAKE DISTRICT

LAKE DWELLING
LAKE MICHIGAN
LAKE SUPERIOR
LALIQUE GLASS
LAMP STANDARD
LANCET WINDOW
LAND GRABBING
LAND O THE LEAL
LAND SURVEYOR
LAND YACHTING
LANDED GENTRY
LANDING CRAFT
LANDING FIELD
LANDING PLACE
LANDING SPEED
LANDING STAGE
LANDING STRIP
LANTERN JAWED
LANTERN SLIDE
LARGE HEARTED
LARKING ABOUT
LASER PRINTER
LAST FRONTIER
LAST JUDGMENT
LATE IN THE DAY
LATENT ENERGY
LATH SPLITTER
LATIN AMERICA
LATIN QUARTER
LAUGH OUT LOUD
LAUGH TO SCORN
LAUGHED IT OFF
LAUNCHING PAD
LAUNDRY WOMAN
LAW OF NATIONS
LAW OF OCTAVES
LAW OF THE LAND
LAW STATIONER
LAWS OF HONOUR
LAWS OF MOTION
LAY COMMUNION
LAY IT ON THICK
LAY ON THE LINE
LAY ON THE OARS
LAYING EYES ON
LAYING TO REST
LAYS THE TABLE
LEADING ACTOR
LEADING LIGHT
LEAP FROGGING
LEASING MAKER
LEATHER CLOTH
LEATHER GOODS
LEATHER KNIFE
LEATHER STRAP
LEAVE FOR DEAD
LEAVE ONE COLD
LEAVE THE ROOM
LEAVES BEHIND
LEAVES UNSAID

12 contd.

LEAVING ALONE
LED BY THE NOSE
LEFT HAND SIDE
LEFT HANDEDLY
LEFT IN THE AIR
LEFT IT AT THAT
LEFT STANDING
LEGACY HUNTER
LEGAL PROCESS
LENDING A HAND
LENDING AN EAR
LEOPARDS BANE
LET ONESELF GO
LET WELL ALONE
LETS OFF STEAM
LETTER OPENER
LETTER WRITER
LETTING ALONE
LETTING BLOOD
LETTING DRIVE
LETTING IT RIP
LETTING LOOSE
LETTING SLIDE
LEVEL PEGGING
LEVELLING OFF
LEVELLING ROD
LIBERAL PARTY
LIBERTY HORSE
LICENCE PLATE
LICK ONES LIPS
LICK TRENCHER
LICKETY SPLIT
LIE OF THE LAND
LIE ON THE OARS
LIES AT ANCHOR
LIES IN THE WAY
LIFE AND DEATH
LIFE SCIENCES
LIFE SENTENCE
LIFTS A FINGER
LIGHT BRIGADE
LIGHT HEARTED
LIGHT RAILWAY
LIGHT SLEEPER
LIGHTENING UP
LIGHTNING BUG
LIGHTNING ROD
LIKE WILDFIRE
LINCOLN GREEN
LINE ENGRAVER
LINE OF BATTLE
LINE OF BEAUTY
LINE OF VISION
LINGUA FRANCA
LIQUEUR GLASS
LIQUID ASSETS
LIQUID HELIUM
LITTER BASKET
LITTLE ENDIAN

LITTLE FINGER
LITTLE HITLER
LITTLE OFFICE
LITTLE PEOPLE
LITTLE WONDER
LIVE TOGETHER
LIVELY DEBATE
LIVER SAUSAGE
LIVERY STABLE
LIVING FOSSIL
LIVING MEMORY
LIZARD HIPPED
LOAD SHEDDING
LOADING GAUGE
LOAN SHARKING
LOCK UP GARAGE
LOCKING HORNS
LODGING HOUSE
LOGIC CIRCUIT
LOGIC DIAGRAM
LOGIC PROBLEM
LOLLIPOP LADY
LONDON BRIDGE
LONELY HEARTS
LONG DISTANCE
LONG DIVISION
LONG DRAWN OUT
LONG STANDING
LONG TROUSERS
LONG VACATION
LONSDALE BELT
LOOKED AGHAST
LOOKING A FOOL
LOOKING AFTER
LOOKING GLASS
LOOKING SMALL
LOOKS ASKANCE
LOOKS DAGGERS
LOOKS FORWARD
LOOMING LARGE
LOOPS THE LOOP
LOOSE FORWARD
LOOSE HOUSING
LORD ADVOCATE
LORD ORDINARY
LORRY HOPPING
LOSE ONES COOL
LOSE ONES HAIR
LOSE ONES HEAD
LOSES CONTROL
LOSES ONES RAG
LOSES ONES WAY
LOSES ONESELF
LOSING COLOUR
LOSING GROUND
LOSING WEIGHT
LOSS ADJUSTER
LOSS OF MEMORY
LOST FOR WORDS
LOST ONES COOL

LOST ONES HAIR
LOST PROPERTY
LOUD AND CLEAR
LOUNGE LIZARD
LOUNGED ABOUT
LOUNGES ABOUT
LOUVRE WINDOW
LOW CHURCHISM
LOW CHURCHMAN
LOW FREQUENCY
LOW WATERMARK
LOWER BRACKET
LOWER CHAMBER
LOWER REGIONS
LUMBER JACKET
LUMINOUS FLUX
LUNAR CAUSTIC
LUNCHEON MEAT
LURKING PLACE
LYING IN STATE
LYSERGIC ACID
MACHINE RULER
MAD AS A HATTER
MADAM SPEAKER
MADE A BEELINE
MADE A KILLING
MADE ENDS MEET
MADE GOOD TIME
MADE OLD BONES
MADE ONES MARK
MADE THE GRADE
MAGAZINE RACK
MAGIC CIRCLES
MAGIC LANTERN
MAGIC SPHERES
MAGIC SQUARES
MAGNETIC CORE
MAGNETIC DISC
MAGNETIC DRUM
MAGNETIC FLUX
MAGNETIC MINE
MAGNETIC TAPE
MAID OF HONOUR
MAIDEN ASSIZE
MAIDEN BATTLE
MAIDEN CASTLE
MAIDEN FLIGHT
MAIDEN SPEECH
MAIDEN STAKES
MAIDEN VOYAGE
MAIL CARRIAGE
MAITRE DHOTEL
MAJOR GENERAL
MAJOR PROPHET
MAJORITY RULE
MAKE A BEELINE
MAKE A KILLING
MAKE ENDS MEET
MAKE GOOD TIME
MAKE IT SNAPPY

MAKE OLD BONES
MAKE ONES MARK
MAKE THE GRADE
MAKE UP ARTIST
MAKES A FUSS OF
MAKES A PASS AT
MAKES BELIEVE
MAKES CERTAIN
MAKES CHANGES
MAKES FRIENDS
MAKES HISTORY
MAKES INROADS
MAKES LIGHT OF
MAKES ONES DAY
MAKES ONES WAY
MAKES THE PACE
MAKES WHOOPEE
MAKING A POINT
MAKING A STAND
MAKING AMENDS
MAKING EYES AT
MAKING TRACKS
MALTESE CROSS
MAN ABOUT TOWN
MAN IN THE MOON
MAN OF DESTINY
MAN OF LETTERS
MAN OVERBOARD
MANDARIN DUCK
MANGEL WURZEL
MANGO CHUTNEY
MANSION HOUSE
MANUAL LABOUR
MANUAL WORKER
MANY COLOURED
MARATHON RACE
MARBLE CUTTER
MARBLED WHITE
MARCHING SONG
MARGINAL LAND
MARGINAL SEAT
MARGINAL WARD
MARINE BOILER
MARINE ENGINE
MARINE STORES
MARIOTTES LAW
MARKER BEACON
MARKET GARDEN
MARKET LEADER
MARKET SQUARE
MARKING GAUGE
MARMALADE CAT
MARRIAGE RING
MARRIAGE VOWS
MARSH HARRIER
MARSH WARBLER
MARTINI HENRY
MARVEL OF PERU
MASONIC LODGE
MASS HYSTERIA

12 *contd.*

MASS MURDERER
MASS PRODUCED
MASTER AT ARMS
MASTER CUTLER
MASTER SWITCH
MASTER TAILOR
MATCHING PAIR
MATTER OF FACT
MATTER OF FORM
MEALY MOUTHED
MEAN SPIRITED
MEANS TO AN END
MEASURING ROD
MEAT AND DRINK
MEDICINE BALL
MEDIUM SHERRY
MEDULLARY RAY
MEETING HOUSE
MEISSEN CHINA
MELLOWING OUT
MELODIC MINOR
MELTING POINT
MENAGE A TROIS
MEND ONES WAYS
MENTAL ASYLUM
MERCHANT BANK
MERCHANT NAVY
MERCHANT SHIP
MERCY KILLING
MERRY AS A GRIG
MERRY DANCERS
MERRY ENGLAND
MERRY GO ROUND
MERSEY TUNNEL
MESSING ABOUT
METEOR CRATER
METHOD ACTING
METHYL VIOLET
METRIC SYSTEM
MEZZO RELIEVO
MEZZO RILIEVO
MEZZO SOPRANO
MICKEY TAKING
MID VICTORIAN
MIDDLE GROUND
MIDDLE INCOME
MIDDLE SCHOOL
MIDDLE STATES
MIDNIGHT BLUE
MIDNIGHT MASS
MIDSUMMER DAY
MIGHT AND MAIN
MIGHT IS RIGHT
MILES PER HOUR
MILITARY BAND
MILK AND HONEY
MILK PORRIDGE
MILKING STOOL
MILLERS THUMB

MILLS GRENADE
MIMINY PIMINY
MINCING WORDS
MIND BOGGLING
MIND HOW YOU GO
MIND YOUR HEAD
MIND YOUR STEP
MINE DETECTOR
MINE SWEEPING
MINERAL JELLY
MINERAL PITCH
MINERAL WATER
MINERVA PRESS
MINGLE MANGLE
MINI COMPUTER
MINI MOTORWAY
MINOR PLANETS
MINOR PREMISE
MINOR PROPHET
MIRROR WRITER
MISS UNIVERSE
MISSED THE BUS
MISSEL THRUSH
MISSES THE BUS
MISTLE THRUSH
MISTRESS SHIP
MIXED ABILITY
MIXED BATHING
MIXED CRYSTAL
MIXED DOUBLES
MIXED ECONOMY
MIXED FARMING
MOABITE STONE
MOBILE POLICE
MOCK HEROICAL
MODEL RAILWAY
MODELLING KIT
MODUS VIVENDI
MOLLY MAGUIRE
MONETARY UNIT
MONEY CHANGER
MONEY GRUBBER
MONEY LENDING
MONEY MATTERS
MONEY SPINNER
MONKEY ENGINE
MONKEY FLOWER
MONKEY HAMMER
MONKEY JACKET
MONKEY PUZZLE
MONKEY WRENCH
MONO COMPOUND
MONSTRE SACRE
MORAL COURAGE
MORAL SUPPORT
MORAL VICTORY
MORES THE PITY
MORNING DRESS
MORNING GLORY
MORNING WATCH

MORRIS DANCER
MOSQUITO FISH
MOSQUITO HAWK
MOSS TROOPING
MOST REVEREND
MOTHER CHURCH
MOTHER FIGURE
MOTHER LIQUOR
MOTHER TONGUE
MOTHERS IN LAW
MOTHERS UNION
MOTOR BICYCLE
MOTOR CARAVAN
MOTOR CYCLING
MOTOR CYCLIST
MOTOR SCOOTER
MOTOR TRACTOR
MOTORWAY EXIT
MOTORWAY SIGN
MOUND BUILDER
MOUNT EVEREST
MOUNTAIN BIKE
MOUNTAIN BLUE
MOUNTAIN GOAT
MOUNTAIN HARE
MOUNTAIN LION
MOUNTAIN PASS
MOUNTAIN SIDE
MOUNTED GUARD
MOURNING DOVE
MOURNING RING
MOUSTACHE CUP
MOUTH FILLING
MOUTH TO MOUTH
MOVABLE FEAST
MOVED TO TEARS
MOVES TO TEARS
MUD IN YOUR EYE
MUD WRESTLING
MUDDLE HEADED
MULBERRY BUSH
MULTIPLE SHOP
MULTIPLE STAR
MURINE TYPHUS
MUSHROOM SOUP
MUSIC TEACHER
MUTATION RATE
MUTTON CUTLET
MUTTON HEADED
MUTUAL FRIEND
MUZZLE LOADER
NAIL SCISSORS
NAME DROPPING
NAPIERS BONES
NAPLES YELLOW
NARCO THERAPY
NARROW ESCAPE
NARROW MINDED
NARROW SQUEAK
NATIONAL CALL

NATIONAL DEBT
NATIONAL DISH
NATIONAL GRID
NATIONAL HUNT
NATIONAL PARK
NATIVITY PLAY
NATURAL DEATH
NATURAL MAGIC
NATURAL ORDER
NATURAL SCALE
NAUTICAL MILE
NAVAL BRIGADE
NAVAL OFFICER
NEAR AS DAMMIT
NEATS FOOT OIL
NECK MOULDING
NECK OF MUTTON
NECK TIE PARTY
NECKING PARTY
NEGATIVE POLE
NEGATIVE SIGN
NEO DARWINIAN
NEO DARWINISM
NEO DARWINIST
NEON LIGHTING
NERVE IMPULSE
NERVE RACKING
NEST OF TABLES
NESTING PLACE
NEVER FAILING
NEVER YOU MIND
NEW DIMENSION
NEW ENGLANDER
NEW FASHIONED
NEW JERSEY TEA
NEW MODEL ARMY
NEW TESTAMENT
NEWGATE FRILL
NEWS BULLETIN
NEWSPAPER MAN
NIAGARA FALLS
NICE ONE CYRIL
NICKEL SILVER
NIDDLE NODDLE
NIGHT CLOTHES
NIGHT FISHING
NIGHT PROWLER
NIGHT TERRORS
NIMBLE FOOTED
NIMBLE WITTED
NIMINY PIMINY
NINE WORTHIES
NIPS IN THE BUD
NITROUS OXIDE
NO BED OF ROSES
NO FIXED ABODE
NO FLIES ON HER
NO FLIES ON HIM
NOLENS VOLENS
NOMINAL VALUE

12 contd.

NON ADMISSION
NON ALCOHOLIC
NON ALIGNMENT
NON ATTENTION
NON CHRISTIAN
NON COMBATANT
NON COMMITTAL
NON COMMUNION
NON CONDUCTOR
NON EFFECTIVE
NON EFFICIENT
NON ESSENTIAL
NON EXECUTIVE
NON EXISTENCE
NON FICTIONAL
NON FLAMMABLE
NON RESIDENCE
NON RESIDENTS
NONE SO PRETTY
NONE THE WISER
NORDIC SKIING
NORFOLK CAPON
NORMAL SCHOOL
NORMAN FRENCH
NORTH AMERICA
NORTH COUNTRY
NORTH EASTERN
NORTH WESTERN
NORTHERN LINE
NORWAY SPRUCE
NOSE BLEEDING
NOSE PAINTING
NOT CALLED FOR
NOTARY PUBLIC
NOTHING DOING
NOUVEAU RICHE
NOUVEAU ROMAN
NUBBING CHEAT
NUCLEAR POWER
NUCLEAR WASTE
NUDIST COLONY
NUNC DIMITTIS
NURSERY RHYME
NURSING CHAIR
NUTS AND BOLTS
OATH BREAKING
OBJECT FINDER
OBJECT LESSON
OBLIQUE ANGLE
OBOE DI CACCIA
OBSTACLE RACE
OBTUSE ANGLED
OCTANE NUMBER
OCTANE RATING
ODD COME SHORT
OEILS DE BOEUF
OF MICE AND MEN
OF THE ESSENCE
OFF ONES CHEST

OFF ONES CHUMP
OFF ONES GUARD
OFF ONES HANDS
OFF THE GROUND
OFF THE HINGES
OFF THE RECORD
OFFERTORY BOX
OFFICE BEARER
OFFICE HOLDER
OFFICE JUNIOR
OFFICE SEEKER
OFFICERS MESS
OFFICIAL LIST
OIL OF VITRIOL
OIL THE WHEELS
OLD FASHIONED
OLD FOLKS HOME
OLD MANS BEARD
OLD PRETENDER
OLD SCHOOL TIE
OLD TESTAMENT
OLD WIVES TALE
OLYMPIC GAMES
OLYMPIC MEDAL
OLYMPIC TORCH
OMNIBUS TRAIN
ON A KNIFE EDGE
ON AN EVEN KEEL
ON AND ON AND ON
ON BENDED KNEE
ON ONES UPPERS
ON THE DECLINE
ON THE HORIZON
ON THE INSTANT
ON THE PAYROLL
ON THE QUI VIVE
ON THE RAMPAGE
ON THE REBOUND
ON THE STREETS
ON THE UP AND UP
ON THE WARPATH
ON THE WAY DOWN
ONCE IN A WHILE
ONE FELL SWOOP
ONE FOR HIS NOB
ONE HORSE RACE
ONE HORSE TOWN
ONE JUMP AHEAD
ONE OF THE LADS
ONE SIDEDNESS
ONE TRACK MIND
ONE UPMANSHIP
ONE WAY MIRROR
ONE WAY STREET
OPEN MARRIAGE
OPEN QUESTION
OPEN SANDWICH
OPEN SENTENCE
OPENING NIGHT
OPERA COMIQUE

OPERA GLASSES
OPTICAL FIBRE
ORANGE SQUASH
ORCHARD GRASS
ORCHARD HOUSE
ORCHESTRA PIT
ORDER OF MERIT
ORDERED ABOUT
ORDERS AROUND
ORGAN GALLERY
ORGAN GRINDER
ORGANISER BAG
ORIENTAL RUBY
OTTER HUNTING
OUT IN THE OPEN
OUT OF CONTEXT
OUT OF CONTROL
OUT OF FASHION
OUT OF SPIRITS
OUT OF THE BLUE
OUT OF THE BODY
OUT OF THE ROAD
OUT OF THE WOOD
OUT OF THIN AIR
OUT OF TROUBLE
OUT ON ONES EAR
OUT PENSIONER
OUTDOOR GAMES
OUTSIDE RIGHT
OUTWARD BOUND
OVER AND ABOVE
OVER AND UNDER
OVER ONES HEAD
OVERNIGHT BAG
OXFORD STREET
OXY ACETYLENE
PACIFIC OCEAN
PACK OF HOUNDS
PACK OF WOLVES
PACK ONES BAGS
PACKED A PUNCH
PACKING PAPER
PACKING PRESS
PACKING SHEET
PADDLING POOL
PADDOCK STOOL
PAGODA SLEEVE
PAID BY CHEQUE
PAID THE PIPER
PAID THE PRICE
PAID UP MEMBER
PAINT THE LILY
PAINTED CLOTH
PAINTED SNIPE
PAIR OF GLOVES
PAIR OF PLIERS
PAIR OF SHORTS
PAIR OF TIGHTS
PAISLEY SHAWL
PALETTE KNIFE

PANDEAN PIPES
PANEL BEATING
PANEL HEATING
PANEL WORKING
PANORAMA HEAD
PAPER HANGING
PAPER MARBLER
PAPER PROFITS
PAPER STAINER
PAPER WASHING
PAPERING OVER
PARADE GROUND
PARADISE FISH
PARAFFIN LAMP
PARALLEL BARS
PARIETAL BONE
PARING CHISEL
PARISH CHURCH
PARISH PRIEST
PARKING METER
PARKING PLACE
PARQUET FLOOR
PARROT WRASSE
PARSLEY PIERT
PARSLEY SAUCE
PART EXCHANGE
PART OF SPEECH
PARTIE CARREE
PARTY MACHINE
PARTY VERDICT
PAS DE BOURREE
PASS JUDGMENT
PASS ONES WORD
PASS SENTENCE
PASSAGE MONEY
PASSE PARTOUT
PASSED MUSTER
PASSES MUSTER
PASSION FRUIT
PASSION MUSIC
PAST ONES BEST
PAT ON THE BACK
PATENT OFFICE
PATENT REMEDY
PATTERN MAKER
PATTERN WHEEL
PAUPERS GRAVE
PAVILION ROOF
PAVING STONES
PAVING THE WAY
PAY AS YOU EARN
PAY ATTENTION
PAY IN ADVANCE
PAYING A VISIT
PAYING HOMAGE
PAYING IN BOOK
PAYING IN FULL
PAYING IN KIND
PAYS BY CHEQUE
PAYS THE PIPER

12 *contd.*

PAYS THE PRICE
PEACE BREAKER
PEACE KEEPING
PEACE OFFICER
PEAK DISTRICT
PEANUT BUTTER
PEARL DISEASE
PEARL ESSENCE
PEARL FISHERY
PEARL FISHING
PEARL SHELLER
PEARL TAPIOCA
PEASE BLOSSOM
PEBBLE POWDER
PECKING ORDER
PECTORAL FINS
PEDAL PUSHERS
PEDESTAL DESK
PEER PRESSURE
PELVIC GIRDLE
PEN FEATHERED
PENALTY BENCH
PENANG LAWYER
PENCIL SKETCH
PENDENTE LITE
PENITENT FORM
PENNY WEDDING
PENNY WHISTLE
PENSIONED OFF
PEOPLES FRONT
PEOPLES PARTY
PEPPERS GHOST
PERFECT FIFTH
PERFECT PITCH
PERFECT TENSE
PERIODIC WIND
PERMANENT WAY
PERSIAN BERRY
PERSIAN WHEEL
PERSON FRIDAY
PERSONA GRATA
PETTER ENGINE
PETTY LARCENY
PETTY OFFICER
PHEASANTS EYE
PHI BETA KAPPA
PHOTO ETCHING
PHOTO PROCESS
PHRYGIAN MODE
PHYSIC GARDEN
PIANO RECITAL
PICK ONES SPOT
PICK TO PIECES
PICK UP THE TAB
PICKED A FIGHT
PICKING A LOCK
PICKING HOLES
PICKLED ONION
PICKS ONES WAY

PICKS UP SPEED
PICNIC BASKET
PICNIC HAMPER
PICTURE FRAME
PICTURE HOUSE
PICTURE RATIO
PIECE OF BREAD
PIECE OF EIGHT
PIECE OF GOODS
PIECE OF PAPER
PIGEON FLYING
PIGEONS BLOOD
PIGS MIGHT FLY
PIGS TROTTERS
PILGRIMS SIGN
PILLAR BOX RED
PILLION RIDER
PILOT BALLOON
PILOT OFFICER
PIN FEATHERED
PINCH HITTING
PING PONG BALL
PINK ELEPHANT
PINT OF BITTER
PIONEER CORPS
PIOUS OPINION
PIPE AND TABOR
PISTACHIO NUT
PITCH AND TOSS
PITCHED A TENT
PITCHER PLANT
PITCHES A TENT
PITCHING TOOL
PITTER PATTER
PLACE SETTING
PLAIN CLOTHES
PLAIN DARNING
PLAIN DEALING
PLAIN HEARTED
PLAIN SAILING
PLAINS INDIAN
PLANE SAILING
PLANNED AHEAD
PLANO CONCAVE
PLANO CONICAL
PLANTAIN LILY
PLASTER SAINT
PLASTIC MONEY
PLATANNA FROG
PLATE LEATHER
PLATFORM SOLE
PLATINUM LAMP
PLATONIC YEAR
PLATT DEUTSCH
PLAY FOR A DRAW
PLAY THE DEVIL
PLAY THE FIELD
PLAY WITH FIRE
PLAYED AROUND
PLAYED HOOKEY

PLAYED IT COOL
PLAYED POSSUM
PLAYED TRICKS
PLAYED TRUANT
PLAYING A PART
PLAYING ABOUT
PLAYING ALONG
PLAYING CARDS
PLAYING FALSE
PLAYING FIELD
PLAYING HAVOC
PLAYING TO WIN
PLAYS FOOTSIE
PLAYS FOR TIME
PLAYS IT BY EAR
PLAYS ONES ACE
PLAYS THE FOOL
PLAYS THE GAME
PLAYS THE LEAD
PLEASURE BOAT
PLEASURE TRIP
PLEATED SKIRT
PLENUM SYSTEM
PLIMSOLL LINE
PLOTS A COURSE
PLOUGH MONDAY
PLOUGHED BACK
PLUGGING AWAY
PLUM COLOURED
PLUMBERS MATE
PLUMMER BLOCK
PLYMOUTH ROCK
POCKET GOPHER
POCKET PISTOL
POET LAUREATE
POINT OF ORDER
POINT TO POINT
POKE IN THE EYE
POLE POSITION
POLE VAULTING
POLICE ESCORT
POLICY HOLDER
POLISHING OFF
POLITICAL MAP
POLLEN BASKET
POLLING BOOTH
POLYTHENE BAG
POMMES FRITES
PONS ASINORUM
PONY CARRIAGE
PONY TREKKING
POOR RELATION
POOR SPIRITED
POP ONES CLOGS
POP UP TOASTER
POPES KNIGHTS
POPULAR FRONT
POPULAR MUSIC
PORGY AND BESS
PORK SAUSAGES

POROUS ALLOYS
POROUS SEPTUM
PORTAL SYSTEM
PORTE BONHEUR
PORTE MONNAIE
PORTERS LODGE
POSE A PROBLEM
POSITIVE POLE
POSITIVE RAYS
POSITIVE SIGN
POST DILUVIAL
POST DILUVIAN
POST EXCHANGE
POST GRADUATE
POST HYPNOTIC
POST MERIDIAN
POST MERIDIEM
POST PRANDIAL
POST TERTIARY
POSTAGE STAMP
POSTAL BALLOT
POSTER PAINTS
POSTURE MAKER
POT COMPANION
POTATO BLIGHT
POTATO CRISPS
POTATO FAMINE
POTTERS WHEEL
POTTS DISEASE
POUCHED MOUSE
POUND FOOLISH
POUND OF FLESH
POUR WITH RAIN
POURING FORTH
POURS SCORN ON
POWDER CLOSET
POWDER MONKEY
POWDERING TUB
POWER STATION
PRAIRIE VALUE
PRANCED ABOUT
PRANCES ABOUT
PRAWN CRACKER
PRAYS FOR RAIN
PRE DRAVIDIAN
PRE ECLAMPSIA
PRE EMINENTLY
PRE ESTABLISH
PRE EXISTENCE
PRE QUALIFIED
PRE QUALIFIES
PRE SHRINKING
PRE TENSIONED
PREACHED DOWN
PREACHES DOWN
PREEN ONESELF
PREMIUM BONDS
PRESS CUTTING
PRESS FORWARD
PRESS GALLERY

12 *contd.*

PRESS GANGING
PRESS HAND OUT
PRESS OFFICER
PRESS RELEASE
PRESSED AHEAD
PRESSED GLASS
PRESSES AHEAD
PRESSING HOME
PRESSURE COOK
PRESSURE SUIT
PRETTY NEARLY
PRETTY PRETTY
PRETTY SPOKEN
PRICE CONTROL
PRICE CUTTING
PRICE OF MONEY
PRIDE OF PLACE
PRIMARY PHASE
PRIME NUMBERS
PRIMEVAL ATOM
PRIMROSE PATH
PRINCE BISHOP
PRINCES METAL
PRINCIPAL BOY
PRINT THROUGH
PRINTERS MARK
PRINTERS REAM
PRISON WARDER
PRIVATE BEACH
PRIVATE COACH
PRIVATE HOTEL
PRIVATE LIVES
PRIVATE MEANS
PRIVATE WRONG
PRIVY CHAMBER
PRIVY COUNCIL
PRIZE FIGHTER
PROBATE COURT
PROBLEM CHILD
PROBLEM NOVEL
PROCES VERBAL
PROCESS BLOCK
PROFIT MARGIN
PROFIT TAKING
PROMISED LAND
PROOF CORRECT
PROOF READING
PROPER MOTION
PROPERTY ROOM
PROTEST MARCH
PROTO HISTORY
PROUD HEARTED
PRUNING KNIFE
PSEUDO GOTHIC
PSI PHENOMENA
PSYCHIC FORCE
PUBLIC HEALTH
PUBLIC ORATOR
PUBLIC OUTCRY

PUBLIC SCHOOL
PUBLIC SECTOR
PUDDING BASIN
PUDDING FACED
PUDDING PLATE
PUFFING BILLY
PULL A FAST ONE
PULL A FLANKER
PULL TO PIECES
PULL TOGETHER
PULLING A FACE
PULLING AHEAD
PULLING APART
PULLING ROUND
PULLS STRINGS
PULLS THROUGH
PULP NOVELIST
PUNCH AND JUDY
PUPIL TEACHER
PURBECK STONE
PURPLE AIRWAY
PURPOSE BUILT
PURSE STRINGS
PURSUIT PLANE
PUSH ONES LUCK
PUSH STARTING
PUSHED AROUND
PUSHES AROUND
PUSHING ALONG
PUSHING ASIDE
PUT A SOCK IN IT
PUT INTO WORDS
PUT ON ONE SIDE
PUT ON THE LINE
PUT ONES OAR IN
PUT THE BOOT IN
PUT THE CAT OUT
PUTS IT MILDLY
PUTS ON RECORD
PUTS ON THE MAP
PUTS ONES CASE
PUTS STRAIGHT
PUTS TO RIGHTS
PUTS UP A FIGHT
PUTTING ABOUT
PUTTING CLEEK
PUTTING GREEN
PUTTING ON ICE
PUTTING STONE
PUTTING TO BED
PUTTING TO SEA
PUZZLE HEADED
PYJAMA JACKET
PYTHIAN GAMES
PYTHIAN VERSE
QUAKER COLOUR
QUAKING GRASS
QUARTER AFTER
QUARTER BOUND
QUARTER FINAL

QUARTER GUARD
QUARTER HORSE
QUARTER LIGHT
QUARTER MILER
QUARTER PLATE
QUARTER ROUND
QUARTER STAFF
QUARTERN LOAF
QUARTZ SCHIST
QUEEN CONSORT
QUEEN DOWAGER
QUEEN FOR A DAY
QUEEN REGNANT
QUEENS BOUNTY
QUEENS SPEECH
QUELQUE CHOSE
QUESTION MARK
QUESTION TIME
QUEUE JUMPING
QUICK SCENTED
QUICK SELLING
QUICK SIGHTED
QUICKENING UP
QUILL DRIVING
QUILL FEATHER
QUININE WATER
QUIT THE SCENE
RABBETING SAW
RABBIT WARREN
RABBLE ROUSER
RACCOON BERRY
RACING DRIVER
RACKET GROUND
RACKET TAILED
RADIAL ARTERY
RADIAL ENGINE
RADIO AMATEUR
RADIO COMPASS
RADIO ELEMENT
RADIO ISOTOPE
RADIO STATION
RADIUS VECTOR
RAFFLE TICKET
RAGGLE TAGGLE
RAGLAN SLEEVE
RAGS TO RICHES
RAIL SPLITTER
RAINBOW TROUT
RAISE ONES HAT
RAISE THE ROOF
RAISE THE WIND
RAISED A SIEGE
RAISED A STINK
RAISED PASTRY
RAISES A SIEGE
RAISES A STINK
RAISING ALOFT
RAISING MONEY
RALLIED ROUND
RALLIES ROUND

RAMBLING ROSE
RANDOM ACCESS
RANGE ONESELF
RAPID FIRE GUN
RASPBERRY JAM
RATABLE VALUE
RATCHET WHEEL
RATTLE HEADED
RAW MATERIALS
RAYLEIGH DISC
RAZZLE DAZZLE
REACTION TIME
READ AND WRITE
READ THE SIGNS
READING ALOUD
REAL PRESENCE
RECEIVING SET
RECESSED ARCH
RECITING NOTE
RECORD OFFICE
RECORD PLAYER
RECORD SLEEVE
RED BLOOD CELL
RED CORPUSCLE
RED LETTER DAY
REED PHEASANT
REFERRED PAIN
REFLEX ACTION
REFLEX CAMERA
REFORM SCHOOL
REGENT STREET
REIGN SUPREME
REINDEER MOSS
REMAIN SILENT
REMAINDER MAN
REMAND CENTRE
REMOVAL LORRY
REPAIR OUTFIT
REPORTED BACK
REPUTED OWNER
RESCUE WORKER
RESERVE PRICE
RESERVED LIST
RESONANCE BOX
RESTING PLACE
RESTING SPORE
RESTING STAGE
RETAINING FEE
RETINA CAMERA
RETURN CREASE
RETURN TICKET
RHESUS FACTOR
RHODESIAN MAN
RHUMB SAILING
RHYME TO DEATH
RHYMING SLANG
RIBBLE RABBLE
RICHTER SCALE
RIDE FOR A FALL
RIDE THE WAVES

12 contd.

RIDE TO HOUNDS
RIDING GLOVES
RIDING MASTER
RIDING SCHOOL
RIFLE GRENADE
RIGHT AND LEFT
RIGHT HAND MAN
RIGHT OF ENTRY
RIGHT THE HELM
RIGHTS WRONGS
RING COMPOUND
RING DOTTEREL
RINGING A BELL
RINGS THE BELL
RINGSIDE SEAT
RIOT OF COLOUR
RIP VAN WINKLE
RIPPLE EFFECT
RIPPLE MARKED
RISE AND SHINE
RISK ONES LIFE
RITUAL MURDER
RIVER STEAMER
RIVER TERRACE
RIVER TRAFFIC
ROAD SURVEYOR
ROARING DRUNK
ROAST CHICKEN
ROASTING JACK
ROASTING SPIT
ROBBER BARONS
ROCHELLE SALT
ROCK CLIMBING
ROCK SCORPION
ROCKER SWITCH
ROCKING CHAIR
ROCKING HORSE
ROCKING STONE
ROCKS THE BOAT
RODE FOR A FALL
RODE THE WAVES
RODE TO HOUNDS
ROGATION DAYS
ROGATION WEEK
ROLL OF HONOUR
ROLL ONES EYES
ROLLER SKATER
ROLLER SKATES
ROLLING ALONG
ROLLING STOCK
ROLLING STONE
ROMAN EMPEROR
ROMPS THROUGH
ROOM AT THE TOP
ROOMING HOUSE
ROOT PRESSURE
ROSE COLOURED
ROSE HIP SYRUP
ROSE OF SHARON

ROSETTA STONE
ROSH HASHANAH
ROSY COLOURED
ROSY FINGERED
ROTARY ENGINE
ROTOR STATION
ROUGH DIAMOND
ROUGH GRAINED
ROUGH GRAZING
ROUGH JUSTICE
ROUGH PASSAGE
ROUGH PERFECT
ROUGH WROUGHT
ROUND MOUTHED
ROUND THE BEND
ROUNDING DOWN
ROVING REPORT
ROYAL ACADEMY
ROYAL MARINES
ROYAL WARRANT
ROYAL WEDDING
RUB ONES HANDS
RUB SHOULDERS
RUBBER BULLET
RUBBER CHEQUE
RUBBER GLOVES
RUBBER NECKED
RUBBER STAMPS
RUBBING ALONG
RUBBING STONE
RUBY COLOURED
RULE THE ROAST
RULE THE ROOST
RUMBLE TUMBLE
RUN OF THE MILL
RUNAWAY TRAIN
RUNNING A RISK
RUNNING AFTER
RUNNING ALONG
RUNNING BOARD
RUNNING CLOSE
RUNNING COSTS
RUNNING FIGHT
RUNNING FLUSH
RUNNING OUT ON
RUNNING SHORT
RUNNING TITLE
RUNNING WATER
RUNS INTO DEBT
RUNS SMOOTHLY
RUNS TO GROUND
RUPERTS DROPS
RUSH HEADLONG
RUSSIAN BOOTS
RUST COLOURED
SABIN VACCINE
SACRED BEETLE
SACRIFICE BID
SACRIFICE HIT
SADDLE OF LAMB

SADDLE SHAPED
SADDLE SPRING
SADDLE STITCH
SAFE AND SOUND
SAFE AS HOUSES
SAFE BREAKING
SAFE CRACKING
SAFETY FACTOR
SAFFLOWER OIL
SAGE AND ONION
SAGE THRASHER
SAHARA DESERT
SAILING ALONG
SAINT MATTHEW
SAINT PATRICK
SALE OR RETURN
SALES MANAGER
SALIENT POINT
SALMON FISHER
SALMON LADDER
SALMON TACKLE
SALOON KEEPER
SALOON PISTOL
SALT OF SORREL
SALT OF TARTAR
SALTED PEANUT
SALVAGE CORPS
SAMIAN LETTER
SAND BLASTING
SAND FLY FEVER
SAND PAINTING
SAPPHIRE WING
SASSAFRAS NUT
SASSAFRAS OIL
SATURATED FAT
SAVE ONES FACE
SAVE ONES NECK
SAVE ONES SKIN
SAVING CLAUSE
SAVOY CABBAGE
SAW THE SIGHTS
SCABBARD FISH
SCALLOP SHELL
SCALPING TUFT
SCANDAL SHEET
SCAPHOID BONE
SCARE HEADING
SCARLET FEVER
SCARLET WOMAN
SCATTER BRAIN
SCENE PAINTER
SCENE SHIFTER
SCHOLARS MATE
SCHOOL DOCTOR
SCHOOL FRIEND
SCHOOL LEAVER
SCISSOR BLADE
SCISSOR TOOTH
SCOOP THE POOL
SCORING A GOAL

SCORPION FISH
SCOTCH BARLEY
SCOTCH BONNET
SCOTCH DRAPER
SCOTLAND YARD
SCOUTED ROUND
SCOUTS HONOUR
SCRAPER BOARD
SCRATCH BRUSH
SCREEN WRITER
SCREENING OFF
SCREW STEAMER
SCRIPT WRITER
SCULLERY MAID
SCULLING BOAT
SCYTHIAN LAMB
SEA PORCUPINE
SEALED ORDERS
SEASON TICKET
SEASONING TUB
SECOND ADVENT
SECOND BALLOT
SECOND COMING
SECOND COUSIN
SECOND DEGREE
SECOND FIDDLE
SECOND NATURE
SECOND STOREY
SECOND STRIKE
SECOND STRING
SECOND TO NONE
SECRET BALLOT
SECRET POLICE
SECULAR GAMES
SECURITY LEAK
SECURITY RISK
SEDGE WARBLER
SEE THE SIGHTS
SEED MERCHANT
SEEING THINGS
SEEKING AFTER
SEES DAYLIGHT
SEES THE LIGHT
SEINE FISHING
SELENIUM CELL
SELF ABSORBED
SELF ACTIVITY
SELF ADHESIVE
SELF AFFECTED
SELF BETRAYAL
SELF CATERING
SELF CLEANING
SELF CONTEMPT
SELF CREATION
SELF CRITICAL
SELF DECEIVED
SELF DECEIVER
SELF DESTRUCT
SELF DEVOTION
SELF DIRECTED

12 *contd.*

SELF DIRECTOR
SELF EDUCATED
SELF EFFACING
SELF EMPLOYED
SELF EXERTION
SELF FOCUSING
SELF GLORIOUS
SELF HYPNOSIS
SELF IDENTITY
SELF INTEREST
SELF JUDGMENT
SELF ORDAINED
SELF PORTRAIT
SELF RELIANCE
SELF REPROACH
SELF THINKING
SELL ONES SOUL
SELL THE DUMMY
SELLING PLATE
SELLING PRICE
SELLING SHORT
SEMI ANNUALLY
SEMI DETACHED
SEMI OFFICIAL
SEMI PRECIOUS
SEMI TROPICAL
SENDS PACKING
SENIOR OPTIME
SENTINEL CRAB
SERGEANT FISH
SERIAL KILLER
SERIAL NUMBER
SERPENT STONE
SERUM THERAPY
SERVANTS HALL
SERVICE COURT
SERVICE HATCH
SERVING HATCH
SERVO CONTROL
SESSION CLERK
SESSION HOUSE
SET AN EXAMPLE
SET BY THE EARS
SET ONES CAP AT
SETS AT NOUGHT
SETS THE SCENE
SETS TO RIGHTS
SETTING A TRAP
SETTING ABOUT
SETTING APART
SETTING ASIDE
SETTING FORTH
SETTLING DOWN
SEVERANCE PAY
SHADOW BOXING
SHAFT OF LIGHT
SHAGGY INK CAP
SHAKING HANDS
SHALLOW GRAVE

SHARE CAPITAL
SHARP LOOKING
SHARP SIGHTED
SHARP TONGUED
SHARP TOOTHED
SHATTER PROOF
SHAVING BRUSH
SHAVING STICK
SHAWL PATTERN
SHEDS LIGHT ON
SHEEP FARMING
SHEEP SHEARER
SHEEP STATION
SHEEP STEALER
SHEET OF GLASS
SHEET OF PAPER
SHEPHERDS PIE
SHEPHERDS ROD
SHERIFF CLERK
SHERIFF COURT
SHERRY TRIFLE
SHETLAND PONY
SHETLAND WOOL
SHIELD BEARER
SHIELD MAIDEN
SHIELD SHAPED
SHIFT ONESELF
SHIFT WORKING
SHIFTED ABOUT
SHILLING MARK
SHILLY SHALLY
SHIP CHANDLER
SHIPPED WATER
SHIPPING LINE
SHIPS COMPANY
SHIPS HUSBAND
SHIPS THE OARS
SHIRLEY POPPY
SHOCK TACTICS
SHOCK THERAPY
SHOCKING PINK
SHOE SHINE BOY
SHOEING SMITH
SHOOTING DOWN
SHOOTING HOME
SHOOTING IRON
SHOOTING STAR
SHOPPING LIST
SHOPPING MALL
SHORE TO SHORE
SHORT CHANGED
SHORT CHANGES
SHORT CIRCUIT
SHORT COMMONS
SHORT LISTING
SHORT MEASURE
SHORT OF MONEY
SHORT OF SPACE
SHORT SIGHTED
SHORT TERMISM

SHORTENS SAIL
SHOT BLASTING
SHOT IN THE ARM
SHOT THE WORKS
SHOULDER BELT
SHOULDER BONE
SHOULDER HIGH
SHOULDER KNOT
SHOULDER PADS
SHOULDER SLIP
SHOUT THE ODDS
SHOUTING DOWN
SHOW BUSINESS
SHOW ONES FACE
SHOW ONES HAND
SHOWING FIGHT
SHOWING FORTH
SHOWN THE DOOR
SHOWS ONES AGE
SHOWS PROMISE
SHOWS THE FLAG
SHOWS WILLING
SHRILL VOICED
SHRIVELLED UP
SHRUGGING OFF
SHUFFLE BOARD
SHUFFLING OFF
SHUTTING AWAY
SHUTTING DOWN
SIAMESE TWINS
SICK AND TIRED
SICK HEADACHE
SICKLE SHAPED
SIDE ENTRANCE
SIDE OF MUTTON
SIDE TRACKING
SIDE WHISKERS
SIDEREAL TIME
SIDEREAL YEAR
SIGHT PLAYING
SIGHT READING
SIGHT SINGING
SIGN LANGUAGE
SIGN PAINTING
SILICON CHIPS
SILK STOCKING
SILVER BEATER
SILVER PLATED
SILVER SALMON
SILVER SALVER
SILVER SCREEN
SILVER VOICED
SIMMERED DOWN
SIMPLE MINDED
SINGING ALONG
SINGING HINNY
SINGLE DECKER
SINGLE FIGURE
SINGLE HANDED
SINGLE MINDED

SINGLE PARENT
SINGLE SEATER
SINO AMERICAN
SISTERS IN LAW
SITTING STILL
SITTING TIGHT
SIX FEET UNDER
SIX OF THE BEST
SKATING ROUND
SKELETON CREW
SKETCHING OUT
SKIFFLE GROUP
SKIN GRAFTING
SKINNED ALIVE
SKINNY DIPPER
SKIPJACK TUNA
SKIPPING ROPE
SKIRTED ROUND
SKITTLE ALLEY
SKITTLING OUT
SKUNK CABBAGE
SLACKENED OFF
SLACKENING UP
SLANG WHANGER
SLATE WRITING
SLAVE HOLDING
SLAVE TRAFFIC
SLEEP WALKING
SLEEPING PILL
SLEEPY HOLLOW
SLEEVE BUTTON
SLIDING SCALE
SLINGS THE BAT
SLINK BUTCHER
SLIP CARRIAGE
SLIP ONES MIND
SLIP THE CABLE
SLIPPER SATIN
SLIPPER SOCKS
SLIPPING AWAY
SLOANE RANGER
SLOUCH HATTED
SLOW HANDCLAP
SLOW PUNCTURE
SLUM DWELLING
SLUNG ONES BAT
SMALL CAPITAL
SMALL CLOTHES
SMALL LETTERS
SMALLEST ROOM
SMASH AND GRAB
SMEAR TACTICS
SMELLING A RAT
SMOOTH BROWED
SMOOTH COATED
SMOOTH LEAVED
SMOOTH MUSCLE
SMOOTH SPOKEN
SMUGGLING DEN
SNAFFLING LAY

12 *contd.*

SNAGGLE TEETH
SNAGGLE TOOTH
SNAKE CHARMER
SNAP DECISION
SNAP FASTENER
SNARLING IRON
SNARLING TOOL
SNEAK PREVIEW
SNOW IN SUMMER
SNOWBALL TREE
SNOWDROP TREE
SNUBBING POST
SNUFF DIPPING
SOCIAL CREDIT
SOCIAL WORKER
SOCKET CHISEL
SOCKET WRENCH
SODA FOUNTAIN
SOFT CURRENCY
SOFT PEDALLED
SOFTLY SOFTLY
SOLAR BATTERY
SOLAR ECLIPSE
SOLD ONES SOUL
SOLD THE DUMMY
SOLDIERING ON
SOLOMONS SEAL
SOLVENT ABUSE
SON ET LUMIERE
SONIC BARRIER
SOUL STIRRING
SOUND AS A BELL
SOUND BARRIER
SOUND EFFECTS
SOUND RANGING
SOUNDING LEAD
SOUNDING LINE
SOUNDING POST
SOUTH AMERICA
SOUTH COUNTRY
SOUTH EASTERN
SOUTH WESTERN
SOWED THE SEED
SPACE HEATING
SPACE SHUTTLE
SPACE STATION
SPACE VEHICLE
SPANISH BROOM
SPANISH CRESS
SPANISH GRASS
SPANISH ONION
SPANISH SHEEP
SPARK CHAMBER
SPARKING PLUG
SPARROW GRASS
SPEAK TOO SOON
SPEAK VOLUMES
SPEAKING TUBE
SPEAR RUNNING

SPEAR THISTLE
SPEAR THROWER
SPECIAL AGENT
SPECIAL OFFER
SPECIAL TRUST
SPECIFIC HEAT
SPECIFIC NAME
SPECTRE LEMUR
SPEECH MAKING
SPEED BOATING
SPEED READING
SPELLING BOOK
SPENDS A PENNY
SPICK AND SPAN
SPIDER LEGGED
SPIDER MONKEY
SPIDER STITCH
SPILL A BIBFUL
SPILLING LINE
SPILLING OVER
SPILT A BIBFUL
SPINAL COLUMN
SPINAL MARROW
SPINDLE SHELL
SPINE CHILLER
SPINNING MILL
SPINNING MULE
SPIRAL GALAXY
SPIRE STEEPLE
SPIRIT RAPPER
SPLASHING OUT
SPLAY MOUTHED
SPLENIC FEVER
SPLINT ARMOUR
SPLINTER BONE
SPLIT LEATHER
SPLIT THE VOTE
SPOKE TOO SOON
SPOKE VOLUMES
SPONGE DIVING
SPONGE FINGER
SPONGE FISHER
SPONGE RUBBER
SPONGING DOWN
SPOON FEEDING
SPORT ONES OAK
SPORTS JACKET
SPOT OF BOTHER
SPRING BEAUTY
SPRING BEETLE
SPRING HEADED
SPRING HEELED
SPRING LOADED
SPRINGS A LEAK
SPROUTS WINGS
SPRUNG RHYTHM
SPURGE LAUREL
SQUARE HEADED
SQUARE NUMBER
SQUARE RIGGED

SQUARE RIGGER
SQUEAKY CLEAN
SQUEEZED HOME
SQUEEZES HOME
SQUIRREL TAIL
ST ANDREWS DAY
ST GEORGES DAY
ST PETERS FISH
ST PETERS WORT
STACK AGAINST
STADDLE STONE
STAFF CANTEEN
STAFF COLLEGE
STAFF OFFICER
STAFF SURGEON
STAGE MANAGED
STAGE MANAGER
STAGE MANAGES
STAGE THUNDER
STAGE WHISPER
STAGHORN MOSS
STAINED GLASS
STAKED A CLAIM
STAKES A CLAIM
STALL FEEDING
STAMP MACHINE
STAMPING MILL
STAND ACCUSED
STAND AGAINST
STAND THE PACE
STAND UP COMIC
STANDARD LAMP
STANDARD ROSE
STANDARD TIME
STANDING DOWN
STANDING FAST
STANDING FIRE
STANDING JOKE
STANDING OVER
STANDING ROOM
STANDING WAVE
STANDS TO GAIN
STANDS TO LOSE
STAR BLASTING
STAR SPANGLED
STARTED A HARE
STARTING GATE
STARTING POST
STATE FUNERAL
STATE LOTTERY
STATE OF SIEGE
STATE PENSION
STATION HOUSE
STATION WAGON
STATUS SYMBOL
STAYING POWER
STAYING STILL
STAYS THE PACE
STEAL THE SHOW
STEAM CHAMBER

STEAM TURBINE
STEAM WHISTLE
STEAMING OPEN
STEEL ERECTOR
STEEPLE CROWN
STEERED CLEAR
STEERING GEAR
STEMS THE TIDE
STENCIL PLATE
STEP DAUGHTER
STEP ON THE GAS
STEP PATRENTS
STEPPED ASIDE
STEPPING DOWN
STERLING AREA
STEWED PRUNES
STICK THE PACE
STICKING AT IT
STICKS AROUND
STICKY WICKET
STIFF HEARTED
STILETTO HEEL
STILT WALKING
STIRRUP STRAP
STOCK BREEDER
STOCK COMPANY
STOCK FARMING
STOCK IN TRADE
STOCK JOBBERY
STOCK JOBBING
STOCKING FOOT
STOCKING MASK
STOCKING SOLE
STOLE THE SHOW
STONE BREAKER
STONE CUTTING
STONE DRESSER
STONE PARSLEY
STONY HEARTED
STOOD ACCUSED
STOOD AGAINST
STOOD THE PACE
STOOGE AROUND
STOP GO POLICY
STOPPED SHORT
STOPPING DEAD
STOPPING OVER
STOPS THE SHOW
STORM LANTERN
STORM SHUTTER
STORM TROOPER
STORM WARNING
STORMY PETREL
STORY TELLING
STOUT HEARTED
STOVEPIPE HAT
STRAIGHT AWAY
STRAIGHT FACE
STRAIGHT GEAR
STRAIGHT PLAY

12 contd.

STRAIGHT TALK	SUNTAN LOTION	TAKE TO PIECES	TEAMED UP WITH
STRAIN A POINT	SUPPORT LEVEL	TAKEN BY STORM	TEAR ONES HAIR
STRAIT JACKET	SUPREME COURT	TAKEN ON BOARD	TEETHING RING
STRAIT LACING	SURE FIRE CERT	TAKEN ON TRUST	TELEPHONE BOX
STRAP HANGING	SURFACE CRAFT	TAKEN TO COURT	TELL THE TRUTH
STREAKY BACON	SURFACE NOISE	TAKES A TUMBLE	TELLING TALES
STREAM ANCHOR	SURFACE TO AIR	TAKES A WICKET	TELLURIC ACID
STREET KEEPER	SURFACE WATER	TAKES BY STORM	TEMPORAL LOBE
STREET SMARTS	SURFING BOARD	TAKES COMMAND	TEMPORAL PEER
STREET WALKER	SURGEONS KNOT	TAKES IT OUT ON	TEMPTING FATE
STREETS AHEAD	SURGICAL BOOT	TAKES OFFENCE	TEN GALLON HAT
STREETS APART	SURGICAL SHOE	TAKES ON BOARD	TEN POUND NOTE
STRETCHED OUT	SWALLOWING UP	TAKES ON TRUST	TENANT AT WILL
STRETCHES OUT	SWAMP CYPRESS	TAKES ONES CUE	TENANT FARMER
STRIKE A CHORD	SWASH LETTERS	TAKES POT LUCK	TENNIS PLAYER
STRIKE A LIGHT	SWEATED IT OUT	TAKES THE BAIT	TENNIS RACKET
STRIKE A MATCH	SWEET ALYSSUM	TAKES THE CAKE	TENT PREACHER
STRIKE BOTTOM	SWEET AND SOUR	TAKES THE LEAD	TERMINAL UNIT
STRIKE IT RICH	SWEET SCENTED	TAKES THE MICK	TERMS OF TRADE
STRIKES A POSE	SWEET TALKING	TAKES THE VEIL	TEST TUBE BABY
STRIKING BACK	SWEET TOOTHED	TAKES TIME OFF	THE ACROPOLIS
STRIKING DOWN	SWEET WILLIAM	TAKES TO COURT	THE BEES KNEES
STRIKING DUMB	SWIMMING BATH	TAKES TO HEART	THE BITTER END
STRIKING HOME	SWIMMING BELL	TAKES UMBRAGE	THE DIE IS CAST
STRINGING OUT	SWIMMING POND	TAKING A BRIEF	THE DONE THING
STRINGS ALONG	SWIMMING POOL	TAKING A CLASS	THE HARD STUFF
STRIP CARTOON	SWINDLE SHEET	TAKING A DEKKO	THE LAMB OF GOD
STRIPPED ATOM	SWINE KEEPING	TAKING AN OATH	THE LAST ENEMY
STRIPPED DOWN	SWING THE LEAD	TAKING AS READ	THE LAST STRAW
STRIPPING OFF	SWINGING BOOM	TAKING CHARGE	THE OLD BAILEY
STRIPPING OUT	SWINGING POST	TAKING EFFECT	THE OTHER SIDE
STROKE OF LUCK	SWITCHED OVER	TAKING FLIGHT	THE REAL MCCOY
STRONG MINDED	SWITCHES OVER	TAKING FRIGHT	THE REAL THING
STRUCK A CHORD	SWITCHING OFF	TAKING IN HAND	THE RED PLANET
STRUCK A MATCH	SWIZZLE STICK	TAKING IN VAIN	THE STORY GOES
STRUCK BOTTOM	SWORD BAYONET	TAKING IT EASY	THE TIME OF DAY
STRUCK IT RICH	SWUNG THE LEAD	TAKING NOTICE	THE TREATMENT
STRUGGLING ON	SYNODIC MONTH	TAKING ORDERS	THE UPPER HAND
STUBBLE FIELD	SYSTEM MONGER	TAKING THE AIR	THE VERY THING
STUBBLE GOOSE	TABLE A MOTION	TAKING THE RAP	THE WICKED ONE
STUBS ONES TOE	TABLE LICENCE	TAKING THE SUN	THE WORLDS END
STUCK THE PACE	TABLE MANNERS	TAKING TO TASK	THE WORM TURNS
STUDDING SAIL	TABLE TURNING	TAKING UP ARMS	THEATRE OF WAR
STUFFED SHIRT	TAGGING ALONG	TALCUM POWDER	THEATRE ORGAN
STUMP ORATORY	TAILORS DUMMY	TALKED IT OVER	THEN AND THERE
SUBMARINE PEN	TAILORS GOOSE	TALKED TURKEY	THERE AND THEN
SUCCESS STORY	TAKE A BEATING	TALKEE TALKEE	THERMAL SHOCK
SUCK IT AND SEE	TAKE A PRIDE IN	TALKING HEADS	THERMIC LANCE
SUFFOLK PUNCH	TAKE A SHINE TO	TALKING POINT	THES DANSANTS
SUGAR REFINER	TAKE DOWN A PEG	TALKING ROUND	THICK AND FAST
SUGAR THE PILL	TAKE FOR A RIDE	TALLOW CANDLE	THICK AND THIN
SUIT ONES BOOK	TAKE MEASURES	TANTALUM LAMP	THICK SKINNED
SUIT YOURSELF	TAKE ONES SEAT	TAP ON THE HEAD	THICK SKULLED
SUITS ONESELF	TAKE ONES TIME	TAPE RECORDED	THIEF CATCHER
SUMMER SCHOOL	TAKE ONES TURN	TAPE RECORDER	THIEVES LATIN
SUMPTER HORSE	TAKE PRISONER	TARTARE SAUCE	THIN BLUE LINE
SUNDAY DRIVER	TAKE THE BLAME	TAX ALLOWANCE	THINK OUT LOUD
SUNDAY SCHOOL	TAKE THE FIELD	TAX AVOIDANCE	THINK THROUGH
SUNSHINE ROOF	TAKE THE FLOOR	TAX COLLECTOR	THINKING BACK
	TAKE THE REINS	TAX THRESHOLD	THINKING OVER

12 contd.

THIRD READING	TOBACCO PLANT	TRAVEL SOILED	TURNING ROUND
THORACIC DUCT	TOBACCO POUCH	TRAVESTY ROLE	TURNPIKE ROAD
THOUGHT AGAIN	TOGGLE SWITCH	TREASURE HUNT	TURNS AGAINST
THOUGHT ALIKE	TOILET TISSUE	TREASURY BILL	TURNS THE TIDE
THOUGHT ALOUD	TOLD THE TRUTH	TREASURY NOTE	TURTLE NECKED
THOUGHT TWICE	TOLL GATHERER	TREBLE CHANCE	TWELFTH NIGHT
THRASHING OUT	TONE LANGUAGE	TREE KANGAROO	TWELVE OCLOCK
THREAD OF LIFE	TOOK A BEATING	TRENCH MORTAR	TWENTY TWENTY
THREE ACT PLAY	TOOK A PRIDE IN	TRENCH PLOUGH	TWILIGHT ZONE
THREE PIN PLUG	TOOK A SHINE TO	TRESTLE TABLE	TWINING PLANT
THREE WISE MEN	TOOK DOWN A PEG	TRIAL BALANCE	TWO HORSE RACE
THREW A WOBBLY	TOOK FOR A RIDE	TRIAL BALLOON	TWO SPEED GEAR
THREW LIGHT ON	TOOK MEASURES	TRIBUNE GROUP	TWO UP TWO DOWN
THROTTLE DOWN	TOOK ONES TIME	TRIBUTE MONEY	TYING THE KNOT
THROTTLE PIPE	TOOK ONES TURN	TRICK CYCLIST	TYPE CYLINDER
THROUGH TRAIN	TOOK PRISONER	TRICK OR TREAT	TYPE FOUNDING
THROW A WOBBLY	TOOK THE BLAME	TRIGGER HAPPY	TYPE SPECIMEN
THROW LIGHT ON	TOOK THE FIELD	TRIGGERED OFF	TYPHOID FEVER
THROWING A FIT	TOOK THE FLOOR	TRINITY HOUSE	TYRE PRESSURE
THROWING AWAY	TOOK THE REINS	TRIPLE HEADED	UGLY CUSTOMER
THROWING DOWN	TOOK TO PIECES	TRIPLEX GLASS	UGLY DUCKLING
THROWING OPEN	TOOTH AND NAIL	TROD A MEASURE	UMBRELLA TREE
THROWING OVER	TOOTH DRAWING	TROLLEY TABLE	UNDER AND OVER
THROWS A PARTY	TOOTSY WOOTSY	TROLLEY WHEEL	UNDER LICENCE
THROWS A PUNCH	TOP OF THE FORM	TROLLING BAIT	UNDER ONES HAT
THUMBED A LIFT	TOP OF THE POPS	TROOP CARRIER	UNDER PRODUCE
THUMBED A RIDE	TOPPLING OVER	TROPICAL YEAR	UNDER PROTEST
THUNDER CLOUD	TORCHON PAPER	TROUSER PRESS	UNDER SHERIFF
THUNDER FLASH	TORE ONES HAIR	TRUCE BREAKER	UNDER THE HEEL
THUNDER SHEET	TOTAL THEATRE	TRUE LOVE KNOT	UNIFIED FIELD
THUNDER STORM	TOUCHING DOWN	TRUMPET MAJOR	UNIFIED SCALE
THYROID GLAND	TOUCHING WOOD	TRUMPET SHELL	UNITED STATES
TICKET AGENCY	TOUGHENING UP	TRUST ACCOUNT	UNWRITTEN LAW
TICKET HOLDER	TOUR DE FRANCE	TRUST COMPANY	UP ONES STREET
TICKET OFFICE	TOUR DHORIZON	TRUSTEE STOCK	UP TO ONES NECK
TICKET PORTER	TOUR OPERATOR	TRUTH TELLING	UPON MY HONOUR
TICKET WRITER	TOURIST CLASS	TRUTH WILL OUT	UPPER BRACKET
TICKLING PINK	TOWER OF BABEL	TSAR OF RUSSIA	UPPER CLASSES
TIE UP IN KNOTS	TOWERING OVER	TU WHIT TU WHOO	UPRIGHT PIANO
TIFFANY GLASS	TOWN PLANNING	TUBELESS TYRE	URBAN RENEWAL
TIGER COUNTRY	TRACE ELEMENT	TUBEROUS ROOT	USED ONES LOAF
TIGHT FITTING	TRACER BULLET	TUBULAR BELLS	USER FRIENDLY
TILL DOOMSDAY	TRACING PAPER	TUMBLER DRIER	USES ONES LOAF
TIME AND AGAIN	TRACKING DOWN	TUMBLING OVER	VACUUM PACKED
TIME EXPOSURE	TRADE JOURNAL	TUNING HAMMER	VALET DE PLACE
TIME HONOURED	TRADED OPTION	TUNNEL VISION	VANDYKE BEARD
TIMOTHY GRASS	TRADES PEOPLE	TURKS CAP LILY	VANDYKE BROWN
TIN STREAMING	TRADING STAMP	TURN A DEAF EAR	VANTAGE POINT
TIP THE SCALES	TRAGI COMICAL	TURN OF PHRASE	VARIABLE GEAR
TIPS THE SCALE	TRAIL BLAZING	TURN ONES HEAD	VARSITY MATCH
TIRLIE WIRLIE	TRAILING AWAY	TURN THE SCREW	VASE PAINTING
TISSUE TYPING	TRAILING EDGE	TURN UP TRUMPS	VEGETABLE DYE
TITTLE TATTLE	TRAIN SPOTTER	TURNED AROUND	VEGETABLE OIL
TO ALL INTENTS	TRAINING SHIP	TURNED TURTLE	VEILED THREAT
TO ERR IS HUMAN	TRANSFER BOOK	TURNING ABOUT	VELOUTE SAUCE
TO HELL WITH IT	TRANSFER LIST	TURNING ASIDE	VELVET SCOTER
TO PERFECTION	TRANSIT TRADE	TURNING LATHE	VENETIAN MAST
TOASTING FORK	TRAP SHOOTING	TURNING LOOSE	VENI VIDI VICI
TOASTING IRON	TRAPPIST MONK	TURNING NASTY	VENTURE SCOUT
	TRAVEL AGENCY	TURNING POINT	VENTURING OUT

12 *contd.*

VENUS FLY TRAP
VENUSS GIRDLE
VERMIN KILLER
VERY REVEREND
VICAR GENERAL
VICE CHAIRMAN
VICE GOVERNOR
VICTORIA LINE
VICTORIA PLUM
VILLAGE GREEN
VILLAGE IDIOT
VIM AND VIGOUR
VIN ORDINAIRE
VINEGAR PLANT
VIOLA DA GAMBA
VIOLIN STRING
VIRGINIA REEL
VIRGINS BOWER
VIRTUAL IMAGE
VIRUS DISEASE
VISIBLE MEANS
VISITING BOOK
VISITING CARD
VISITORS BOOK
VISUAL PURPLE
VITAMIN PILLS
VODKA AND LIME
VOLCANIC DUST
VOLCANIC ROCK
VOLCANIC SAND
VORTEX THEORY
VOTIVE TABLET
VULGAR TONGUE
WAG AT THE WALL
WAG BY THE WALL
WAIF AND STRAY
WAITED AWHILE
WAITING ABOUT
WAITS AT TABLE
WALK ON TIPTOE
WALK THE PLANK
WALKED THE DOG
WALKED TO HEEL
WALKIE TALKIE
WALKING ON AIR
WALKING OUT ON
WALKING STAFF
WALKING STICK
WALL PAINTING
WALL STREETER
WANDERING JEW
WANDERING OFF
WANKEL ENGINE
WANTED COLUMN
WANTED POSTER
WANTS JAM ON IT
WASTE PRODUCT
WASTED EFFORT
WASTING ASSET

WATCH AND WARD
WATCH CRYSTAL
WATCH OFFICER
WATCHING OVER
WATER BAILIFF
WATER BALLAST
WATER BATTERY
WATER BISCUIT
WATER BLISTER
WATER BOATMAN
WATER BUFFALO
WATER CARRIER
WATER COOLING
WATER CULTURE
WATER DIVINER
WATER FLOWING
WATER HEMLOCK
WATER MEASURE
WATER MILFOIL
WATER OPOSSUM
WATER PARSNIP
WATER REACTOR
WATER SPANIEL
WATER TORTURE
WATER WAGTAIL
WATERING DOWN
WATERING HOLE
WAXED LEATHER
WAY PASSENGER
WAYS AND MEANS
WEAK SPIRITED
WEAKER VESSEL
WEASELING OUT
WEASELLED OUT
WEATHER ALONG
WEATHER BOARD
WEATHER BOUND
WEATHER CHART
WEATHER GAUGE
WEATHER GLASS
WEATHER HOUSE
WEATHER PROOF
WEATHER STRIP
WEATHERED OUT
WEAVERS HITCH
WEDDING CARDS
WEDDING DOWER
WEDDING DRESS
WEDDING MARCH
WEDGWOOD BLUE
WEDGWOOD WARE
WEEDING TONGS
WEEPING BIRCH
WEIGHING DOWN
WEIGHS ANCHOR
WEIGHT LIFTER
WEILS DISEASE
WELFARE STATE
WELL AND TRULY
WELL BALANCED

WELL DIRECTED
WELL DISPOSED
WELL DRESSING
WELL EDUCATED
WELL FAVOURED
WELL GROUNDED
WELL I DECLARE
WELL INFORMED
WELL MANNERED
WELL PLEASING
WELL TEMPERED
WELL TIMBERED
WELSH DRESSER
WELSH RAREBIT
WELTER STAKES
WELTER WEIGHT
WENDS ONES WAY
WENT DOWNHILL
WENT FOR BROKE
WENT STRAIGHT
WENT TO GROUND
WENT TO MARKET
WENT TO PIECES
WEST MIDLANDS
WHALE FISHERY
WHALE FISHING
WHATMAN PAPER
WHATS COOKING
WHATS HER NAME
WHATS HIS NAME
WHATS ITS NAME
WHATS THE ODDS
WHEEL AND DEAL
WHEEL CLAMPED
WHETHER OR NOT
WHICH IS WHICH
WHIP AND DERRY
WHIP POOR WILL
WHIP SCORPION
WHIPPING POST
WHISKING AWAY
WHISKY FRISKY
WHISTLED AWAY
WHISTLES AWAY
WHISTLING OFF
WHITE ADMIRAL
WHITE BEARDED
WHITE CRESTED
WHITE CROWNED
WHITE FEATHER
WHITE LEATHER
WHITE LIVERED
WHITE OF AN EGG
WHITE PUDDING
WHITE RUSSIAN
WHITTLED AWAY
WHITTLES AWAY
WHO DARES WINS
WHOLE HEARTED
WHOLE SKINNED

WHOOPING IT UP
WHOOPING SWAN
WICKET KEEPER
WIDENS THE GAP
WIGGLE WAGGLE
WILD HUNTSMAN
WILD HYACINTH
WILD WEST SHOW
WILL O THE WISP
WILLING HORSE
WILLOW GROUSE
WILTON CARPET
WIN HANDS DOWN
WIN IN A CANTER
WIN ONES SPURS
WIND CHANGING
WIND OF CHANGE
WINDING SHEET
WINDING STAIR
WINDOW SCREEN
WINE COLOURED
WINE MERCHANT
WING SHOOTING
WINGS ONES WAY
WINKLE PICKER
WINNOWING FAN
WINS ON POINTS
WINS THE POOLS
WINTER BARLEY
WINTER CHERRY
WINTER CLOVER
WINTER GARDEN
WINTER SPORTS
WITH ONE VOICE
WITH OPEN ARMS
WITHIN LIMITS
WITHIN REASON
WITHOUT DOUBT
WITHOUT PRICE
WOE BETIDE HER
WOE BETIDE HIM
WOE BETIDE YOU
WOMENS RIGHTS
WON HANDS DOWN
WON IN A CANTER
WON ONES SPURS
WONDER MONGER
WONDER STRUCK
WONDER WORKER
WOOD ENGRAVER
WOOD HYACINTH
WOODEN HEADED
WOOLLY HAIRED
WOOLLY HEADED
WORD BUILDING
WORD OF HONOUR
WORD PAINTING
WORK ONES WILL
WORKED TO RULE
WORKING CLASS

12 contd.

WORKING HOURS
WORKING HOUSE
WORKING IT OUT
WORKING LUNCH
WORKING MODEL
WORKING ORDER
WORKING PAPER
WORKING PARTY
WORKING WOMAN
WORKS AGAINST
WORKS COUNCIL
WORLD BEATING
WORMS EYE VIEW
WOULFE BOTTLE
WRACK AND RUIN
WREAKED HAVOC
WRIGGLING OUT
WRITERS CRAMP
WRITING PAPER
WRITING TABLE
WRONG FOOTING
X RAY SPECTRUM
YANKEE DOODLE
YELLOW HAMMER
YELLOW PEPPER
YELLOW RIBBON
YELLOW STREAK
YORKSHIRE FOG
YOU NEVER KNOW
YOUNG AT HEART
YOUNG FOGYISH
YOUR EMINENCE
YOUR HIGHNESS
YOUR LADYSHIP
YOUR LORDSHIP
YOURE WELCOME
YOUTH CUSTODY
ZENITH SECTOR
ZINC OINTMENT
ZONAL DEFENCE

13

A FAT LOT OF GOOD
A FLY ON THE WALL
A NEW DEPARTURE
A PARTHIAN SHOT
A QUARTER AFTER
A SHOT IN THE ARM
A SMALL FORTUNE
A TISSUE OF LIES
A WHALE OF A TIME
ABERDEEN ANGUS
ABJECT POVERTY
ABOVE REPROACH
ABSENCE OF MIND
ABSOLUTE PITCH
ABYSSINIAN CAT
ACCIDENT PRONE
ACCOUNTS CLERK

ACQUIRED TASTE
ACRYLIC RESINS
ACTING THE FOOL
ACTING THE GOAT
ACTIVE SERVICE
ACTIVE VOLCANO
ADDING MACHINE
ADIPOSE TISSUE
ADRENAL GLANDS
ADVANCED GUARD
ADVANCED LEVEL
ADVANTAGE RULE
AERIAL RAILWAY
AFFAIRE DAMOUR
AFRICAN VIOLET
AFRO CARIBBEAN
AFTER A FASHION
AGAIN AND AGAIN
AGENTS GENERAL
AGREE TO DIFFER
AIR COMPRESSOR
AIR LIEUTENANT
AIR LOADMASTER
AIR RAID WARDEN
AIRS AND GRACES
ALKALINE EARTH
ALL HALLOWMASS
ALL HALLOWS DAY
ALL HALLOWTIDE
ALL IN GOOD TIME
ALL IN WRESTLER
ALL TIME RECORD
ALLIGATOR PEAR
ALMOND BLOSSOM
ALPHA AND OMEGA
ALPHA PARTICLE
ALTERUM TANTUM
AMERICAN BOWLS
AMERICAN DREAM
AMNIOTIC FLUID
AMUSEMENT PARK
AN EYE FOR AN EYE
ANCESTRAL HOME
ANCIENT LIGHTS
ANGLO AMERICAN
ANGLO CATHOLIC
ANGRY YOUNG MAN
ANIMAL KINGDOM
ANIMAL SPIRITS
ANIMAL WORSHIP
ANNUAL HOLIDAY
ANSWERING BACK
ANTI MARKETEER
ANYBODYS GUESS
APOSTLE SPOONS
APOSTLES CREED
APPLE OF THE EYE
APPLE PIE ORDER
APPLETON LAYER
APRICOT BRANDY

APRIL FOOLS DAY
AQUEOUS HUMOUR
ARC DE TRIOMPHE
ARDENT SPIRITS
ARGUS PHEASANT
ARMOUR PLATING
ARMOURED TRAIN
ARTICLES OF WAR
ARTIFICIAL FLY
ARTIFICIAL LEG
AS BLIND AS A BAT
AS BOLD AS BRASS
AS HARD AS NAILS
AS LARGE AS LIFE
AS RIGHT AS RAIN
AS SWEET AS A NUT
AS THIN AS A RAKE
AS WARM AS TOAST
ASK FOR TROUBLE
ASSAULT COURSE
ASSERT ONESELF
ASSET STRIPPER
ASTRAL SPIRITS
AT LOGGERHEADS
AT ONES LEISURE
AT ONES WITS END
AT RIGHT ANGLES
AT SHORT NOTICE
AT THE SAME TIME
AT YOUR SERVICE
ATE LIKE A HORSE
ATLANTIC OCEAN
ATOMIC WARFARE
ATTENTION SPAN
ATTITUDE ANGLE
ATTORNEY AT LAW
AUCTION BRIDGE
AUDIO CASSETTE
AUDIO ENGINEER
AUDIO LOCATION
AUXILIARY VERB
AVOGADROS RULE
AWAY FROM IT ALL
BABY SNATCHING
BACHELOR OF LAW
BACHELORS HALL
BACK FORMATION
BACK PEDALLING
BADGER BAITING
BADGER DRAWING
BAG AND BAGGAGE
BAGGAGE ANIMAL
BAGGY TROUSERS
BALANCE OF MIND
BALL AND SOCKET
BALL CARTRIDGE
BALL LIGHTNING
BALLET DANCING
BALLOT RIGGING
BAMBOO CURTAIN

BANDYING WORDS
BANK OF ENGLAND
BANK STATEMENT
BANKRUPT STOCK
BAPTISM OF FIRE
BAPTISMAL NAME
BAPTISMAL VOWS
BARBER SURGEON
BARE BACK RIDER
BARGAIN HUNTER
BARNABY BRIGHT
BARNACLE GOOSE
BARREL CHESTED
BARREL VAULTED
BASCULE BRIDGE
BASKET WEAVING
BASSET HORNIST
BASSO PROFONDO
BATHING BEAUTY
BATTERED WIVES
BATTLE CRUISER
BATTLE FATIGUE
BATTLE SCARRED
BATWING SLEEVE
BEARING IN MIND
BEAST OF BURDEN
BEAT THE BOUNDS
BEATING THE AIR
BEATING THE GUN
BEATS A RETREAT
BEATS THE CLOCK
BEAUFORT SCALE
BEAUTY CONTEST
BEAUTY PARLOUR
BEAVERING AWAY
BECHAMEL SAUCE
BEDSIDE MANNER
BEETLE CRUSHER
BEFORE THE BEAM
BEFORE THE MAST
BEFORE THE WIND
BEGGING LETTER
BEGINNERS LUCK
BELISHA BEACON
BELLES LETTRES
BELLING THE CAT
BELLOWS TO MEND
BELT AND BRACES
BERMUDA SHORTS
BESIDE ONESELF
BESIDE THE MARK
BETS ONES BOOTS
BEYOND COMPARE
BEYOND MEASURE
BEYOND ONES KEN
BEYOND THE PALE
BIBLE POUNDING
BIBLE THUMPING
BIDDING PRAYER
BIG BROTHERISM

13 *contd.*

BIG GAME HUNTER
BIG WHITE CHIEF
BILLIARD CLOTH
BILLIARD TABLE
BIRD OF PASSAGE
BIRD SANCTUARY
BIRDS NEST SOUP
BIRTHDAY PARTY
BISCUIT BARREL
BITE ONES THUMB
BITE THE BULLET
BITING ONES LIP
BITING THE DUST
BITS AND PIECES
BLACK AND WHITE
BLACK DIAMONDS
BLANKET FINISH
BLANKET STITCH
BLANKETY BLANK
BLAZING A TRAIL
BLEEDING HEART
BLEW THE LID OFF
BLINDMANS BUFF
BLISTER BEETLE
BLOCK CAPITALS
BLOCK PRINTING
BLOOD BROTHERS
BLOOD PRESSURE
BLOOD RELATION
BLOTTING PAPER
BLOW THE LID OFF
BLOWS ONES MIND
BOARDING HOUSE
BOARDING PARTY
BOATSWAIN BIRD
BOBS YOUR UNCLE
BODY SNATCHING
BOHEMIAN TOPAZ
BOMBER COMMAND
BONHEUR DU JOUR
BOOKING OFFICE
BORDER TERRIER
BORROWING DAYS
BORSTAL SYSTEM
BOSTON TERRIER
BOSTON TWO STEP
BOTTLE FEEDING
BOTTOMLESS PIT
BOUGHT AND SOLD
BOULTING CLOTH
BOULTING HUTCH
BOUNDARY RIDER
BOWLING CREASE
BOWSTRING HEMP
BOX THE COMPASS
BRANCH OFFICER
BRASS FARTHING
BRAVE NEW WORLD
BREACH OF TRUST

BREAK ONES DUCK
BREAK ONES WORD
BREAKDOWN GANG
BREAKFAST ROOM
BREAKING COVER
BREAKING FORTH
BREAKING LOOSE
BREAKING POINT
BREAKING RANKS
BREAKS A RECORD
BREAKS A STRIKE
BREAKS THE BANK
BREAKS THE NEWS
BREAKS THROUGH
BREAST FEEDING
BREAST THE TAPE
BREATHE FREELY
BREATHED AGAIN
BREATHES AGAIN
BREECH LOADING
BREECHES BIBLE
BRENT BARNACLE
BRIDGE BUILDER
BRIDGE OF BOATS
BRIDGED THE GAP
BRIDGES THE GAP
BRING INTO LINE
BRING INTO PLAY
BRINGING ABOUT
BRINGING FORTH
BRINGING ROUND
BRINGS A CHARGE
BRINGS FORWARD
BRINGS TO A HEAD
BRINGS TO LIGHT
BRITISH EMPIRE
BRITISH LEGION
BROAD DAYLIGHT
BROAD SPECTRUM
BROKE ONES DUCK
BROKE ONES WORD
BROKEN HEARTED
BROTHER GERMAN
BROTHERS IN LAW
BROUGHT TO BOOK
BROUGHT TO HEEL
BROUGHT TO LIFE
BROWN SEAWEEDS
BROWNIE GUIDER
BROWNIE POINTS
BRUSH KANGAROO
BRUSHING ASIDE
BUBBLE CHAMBER
BUBONIC PLAGUE
BUCKLING UNDER
BUDDHIST CROSS
BUDDING AUTHOR
BUDDING GENIUS
BUDGET ACCOUNT
BUFF ORPINGTON

BUILDING BLOCK
BUILDING BOARD
BULLETIN BOARD
BULLOCKS HEART
BUNCH OF GRAPES
BUNGEE JUMPING
BURDEN OF PROOF
BURGUNDY PITCH
BURLESQUE SHOW
BURN ONES BOATS
BURNETT SALMON
BURNING DESIRE
BURNING MIRROR
BURNT OFFERING
BURYING BEETLE
BURYING GROUND
BUSH TELEGRAPH
BUSINESS CYCLE
BUTCHERS BROOM
BUTLERS PANTRY
BUTTER FINGERS
BUTTERFLY FISH
BUTTON THROUGH
BUTTON YOUR LIP
BY ALL ACCOUNTS
BY APPOINTMENT
BY WORD OF MOUTH
CABLE DRILLING
CABLE MOULDING
CADMIUM YELLOW
CALENDAR MONTH
CALICO PRINTER
CALL OF THE WILD
CALL TO ACCOUNT
CALLED IT QUITS
CALLED THE TUNE
CALLED TO ORDER
CALLING IT A DAY
CALLING TO MIND
CALLS THE SHOTS
CAMBRIDGE BLUE
CAME TO THE BOIL
CAMEL HAIR COAT
CAMERA OBSCURA
CAMP FOLLOWERS
CANCELLING OUT
CANDLE DIPPING
CANDLE LIGHTER
CANDLE SNUFFER
CANE FURNITURE
CANNABIS RESIN
CANVAS CLIMBER
CAPITAL ASSETS
CAPITAL LETTER
CAPITAL MURDER
CAPTAINS CHAIR
CAPTAINS TABLE
CAPUCHIN CROSS
CARBON DIOXIDE
CARBON PROCESS

CARD CATALOGUE
CARDIAC ARREST
CAREERS MASTER
CARNIVAL QUEEN
CARPET BEATING
CARPET BOMBING
CARPET SLIPPER
CARPET SWEEPER
CARRIAGE CLOCK
CARRIAGE DRIVE
CARRIAGE HORSE
CARRIAGE TRADE
CARRIED THE CAN
CARRIED THE DAY
CARRIED TOO FAR
CARRIER PIGEON
CARRIER ROCKET
CARRIES THE CAN
CARRIES THE DAY
CARRIES TOO FAR
CARRION FLOWER
CARRYING IT OFF
CARTE DE VISITE
CARTRIDGE BELT
CASE HARDENING
CASEMENT CLOTH
CASH DISPENSER
CASSE NOISETTE
CASTING A SPELL
CASTING ANCHOR
CASTING WEIGHT
CASUAL CLOTHES
CAT O NINE TAILS
CATCHES THE SUN
CATCHING A COLD
CATCHING A CRAB
CATCHMENT AREA
CATERING CORPS
CATHEDRAL CITY
CATHERINE PEAR
CAUGHT NAPPING
CAUSED TROUBLE
CAUSES TROUBLE
CAUSTIC POTASH
CAVALRY CHARGE
CAVE PAINTINGS
CAYENNE PEPPER
CELLULAR RADIO
CENTRAL FORCES
CENTRAL POWERS
CENTRE FORWARD
CEREBRAL DEATH
CEREBRAL PALSY
CERTIFIED MILK
CHAIN MOULDING
CHAIN REACTION
CHAMBER FELLOW
CHAMELEON LIKE
CHAMP AT THE BIT
CHAMPS ELYSEES

13 *contd.*

CHANCE ONES ARM
CHANGE OF HEART
CHANGE OF VENUE
CHANGE RINGING
CHANGED COLOUR
CHANGED PLACES
CHANGES COLOUR
CHANGES PLACES
CHANGING HANDS
CHANNEL TUNNEL
CHANTILLY LACE
CHAPARRAL COCK
CHARACTER PART
CHARGE ACCOUNT
CHARGE CAPPING
CHARTER FLIGHT
CHARTER MEMBER
CHASE RAINBOWS
CHEAP AND NASTY
CHECK WEIGHMAN
CHECKED SQUARE
CHEDDAR CHEESE
CHEF DE CUISINE
CHEQUERED FLAG
CHERRY BLOSSOM
CHEST EXPANDER
CHEVAL DE FRISE
CHEWING THE CUD
CHEWING THE FAT
CHICKEN FARMER
CHICKENING OUT
CHIEF OF POLICE
CHIMNEY BREAST
CHIMNEY POT HAT
CHINESE LEAVES
CHINESE PUZZLE
CHLORINE WATER
CHOIR PRACTICE
CHOP AND CHANGE
CHOPPING BLOCK
CHOPPING BOARD
CHOPPING KNIFE
CHOPPING LOGIC
CHORAL SOCIETY
CHRISTIAN NAME
CHRISTMAS CAKE
CHRISTMAS CARD
CHRISTMAS ROSE
CHRISTMAS TIDE
CHRISTMAS TIME
CHRISTMAS TREE
CHROME PLATING
CHUCK FARTHING
CHUCKIE STONES
CHUCKLE HEADED
CHURCH OFFICER
CHURCH SERVICE
CHURCHILL TANK
CIGARETTE CARD

CINE PROJECTOR
CIVIL AVIATION
CIVIL ENGINEER
CLAPPED EYES ON
CLASS STRUGGLE
CLASS WILL TELL
CLEANING WOMAN
CLEAR THE COURT
CLEAR THE DECKS
CLEAR THE TABLE
CLEARANCE SALE
CLEARED THE AIR
CLEARED THE WAY
CLEARING HOUSE
CLENCHED TEETH
CLERICAL ERROR
CLICKETY CLACK
CLICKETY CLICK
CLIMBING FRAME
CLIMBING PLANT
CLINICAL DEATH
CLINICAL TRIAL
CLIPPED SPEECH
CLOAK AND SWORD
CLOCK WATCHING
CLOSE ONES EYES
CLOSE QUARTERS
CLOSE RELATIVE
CLOSE RUN THING
CLOSED CIRCUIT
CLOSING SPEECH
CLOSING STAGES
CLOSING THE GAP
CLOTHES BASKET
CLUB SECRETARY
COACH BUILDING
COARSE FISHING
COARSE GRAINED
COBBLERS PUNCH
COCK OF THE LOFT
COCK OF THE ROCK
COCK OF THE WALK
COCKER SPANIEL
COCKING A SNOOK
COCKSPUR GRASS
COCKTAIL DRESS
COCKTAIL MIXER
COCKTAIL STICK
COCONUT BUTTER
CODE OF CONDUCT
COFFEE GROUNDS
COFFEE MORNING
COFFEE SERVICE
COGITO ERGO SUM
COIN IN THE SLOT
COINED A PHRASE
COLD AS CHARITY
COLD IN THE HEAD
COLLECTING BOX
COLLEGE OF ARMS

COMBAT FATIGUE
COME TO THE BOIL
COMES A CROPPER
COMES INTO PLAY
COMES UP TRUMPS
COMING BETWEEN
COMING FORWARD
COMING TO A HEAD
COMING TO BLOWS
COMING TO GRIEF
COMING TO LIGHT
COMING UNSTUCK
COMMAND MODULE
COMMIT ONESELF
COMMIT SUICIDE
COMMON CARRIER
COMMON LAW WIFE
COMMON MEASURE
COMMUNION CARD
COMMUNION RAIL
COMMUNITY HOME
COMMUNITY WORK
COMPANION STAR
COMPANY DOCTOR
COMPARED NOTES
COMPASS NEEDLE
COMPASS SIGNAL
COMPASS WINDOW
COMPLEX NUMBER
COMPOUND RATIO
COMPRESSED AIR
COMPUTER CRIME
COMPUTER FRAUD
COMPUTER VIRUS
CONCAVO CONVEX
CONCEPTUAL ART
CONCERT MASTER
CONCRETE MIXER
CONCRETE MUSIC
CONCRETE STEEL
CONDENSED MILK
CONDENSED TYPE
CONDUCTED TOUR
CONDUCTOR RAIL
CONFETTI MONEY
CONNECTING ROD
CONSUL GENERAL
CONSUMER GOODS
CONTACT FLIGHT
CONTACT LENSES
CONTAINER SHIP
CONTINUITY MAN
CONTRACTED OUT
CONTRACTING IN
CONTROL COLUMN
CONVEXO CONVEX
COOK ONES GOOSE
COOKS THE BOOKS
COOL ONES HEELS
COPPER CAPTAIN

COPPER PYRITES
COPYING PENCIL
CORIANDER SEED
CORONERS COURT
CORPS DE BALLET
CORPUS CHRISTI
CORPUS DELICTI
CORRIDOR TRAIN
COST EFFECTIVE
COSTS THE EARTH
COTSWOLD STONE
COTTAGE CHEESE
COTTON PICKING
COTTON SPINNER
COUNCIL ESTATE
COUNCIL SCHOOL
COUNSEL KEEPER
COUNT PALATINE
COUNTER ATTACK
COUNTER BIDDER
COUNTER MOTION
COUNTER POISON
COUNTER SIGNAL
COUNTER SPYING
COUNTER WEIGHT
COUNTING HOUSE
COUNTING SHEEP
COUNTRY COUSIN
COUNTY BOROUGH
COUNTY COUNCIL
COUNTY CRICKET
COUP DE THEATRE
COURT CIRCULAR
COURT OF APPEAL
COURT OF HONOUR
COURT REPORTER
COURTESY LIGHT
COURTESY TITLE
COURTS MARTIAL
COVERED MARKET
COWPERS GLANDS
CRACKER BARREL
CRACKING A CRIB
CRACKING A JOKE
CRACKS THE WHIP
CRANBERRY BUSH
CRANBERRY TREE
CRAZY LIKE A FOX
CREAM COLOURED
CREDIT SQUEEZE
CREEPING JENNY
CREEPING JESUS
CREME DE MENTHE
CRIBBAGE BOARD
CRICK ONES NECK
CRITICAL ANGLE
CROCODILE CLIP
CROHNS DISEASE
CROIX DE GUERRE
CROQUET MALLET

13 *contd.*

CROSS DRESSING
CROSS EXAMINED
CROSS EXAMINES
CROSS HATCHING
CROSS PURPOSES
CROSS QUESTION
CROSS REFERRED
CROSS THE FLOOR
CROSS THREADED
CROSS VAULTING
CROSSED CHEQUE
CROSSED SWORDS
CROSSES SWORDS
CROSSING THE TS
CROWN IMPERIAL
CROWN PRINCESS
CROWNING GLORY
CRUISE MISSILE
CRUISER WEIGHT
CRUISING SPEED
CRY BLUE MURDER
CRYSTAL GAZING
CRYSTAL PALACE
CUBIC CAPACITY
CULTURED PEARL
CULVERS PHYSIC
CURRIED FAVOUR
CURRIES FAVOUR
CURSORY GLANCE
CURTAIN RAISER
CUSTARD POWDER
CUT DOWN TO SIZE
CUT ONES LOSSES
CUT ONES THROAT
CUT TO THE QUICK
CUTHBERTS DUCK
CUTS THE CACKLE
CUTS TO RIBBONS
CUTTING A CAPER
CUTTING A TOOTH
CUTTING ACROSS
CUTTING IT FINE
CUTTING REMARK
CYLINDER BLOCK
DADDY LONG LEGS
DAIRY PRODUCTS
DANCING MASTER
DANDELION WINE
DANDIE DINMONT
DANGEROUS DRUG
DANTES INFERNO
DARK CONTINENT
DARNING NEEDLE
DATA PROCESSOR
DAUGHTER IN LAW
DAY CARE CENTRE
DAY OF JUDGMENT
DEAD MENS SHOES
DEAD RECKONING

DEAN OF FACULTY
DEARLY BELOVED
DEATH SENTENCE
DEBT COLLECTOR
DEBTORS PRISON
DECIMAL PLACES
DECIMAL SYSTEM
DECISION TABLE
DECK PASSENGER
DECORATION DAY
DEEP SEA DIVING
DELAYED ACTION
DELTOID MUSCLE
DEN OF INIQUITY
DENIED ONESELF
DENIES ONESELF
DENTAL SURGEON
DENTISTS CHAIR
DENTISTS DRILL
DEPRESSED AREA
DEUS EX MACHINA
DIAMOND BEETLE
DIAMOND POWDER
DIAPHRAGM PUMP
DICE WITH DEATH
DID THE HONOURS
DIFFUSION TUBE
DIG FOR VICTORY
DIHEDRAL ANGLE
DINNER SERVICE
DIPLOMATIC BAG
DIPPED THE FLAG
DIRECT CURRENT
DISASTER MOVIE
DISCHARGE TUBE
DISCOUNT STORE
DISHED THE DIRT
DISHES THE DIRT
DISPATCH RIDER
DISTANT COUSIN
DISTRICT COURT
DISTRICT NURSE
DIVIDE AND RULE
DIVISION LOBBY
DIXIE LAND JAZZ
DOCTORS ORDERS
DOES ONES STUFF
DOES ONES WORST
DOGS BREAKFAST
DOGS TAIL GRASS
DOING THE TRICK
DOING THE TWIST
DOLLS HOSPITAL
DOLLY MIXTURES
DOPPLER EFFECT
DORMITORY TOWN
DOUBLE BASSOON
DOUBLE CROSSED
DOUBLE CROSSER
DOUBLE CROSSES

DOUBLE DEALING
DOUBLE DENSITY
DOUBLE FEATURE
DOUBLE FIGURES
DOUBLE FRONTED
DOUBLE GLAZING
DOUBLE JOINTED
DOUBLE MEANING
DOUBLE OR QUITS
DOUBLE PARKING
DOUBLE SHUFFLE
DOUBLE WEDDING
DOW JONES INDEX
DOWNCAST SHAFT
DOWNING STREET
DOWNS SYNDROME
DRAG PARACHUTE
DRAGS ONES FEET
DRAINAGE BASIN
DRAINING BOARD
DRAMATIC IRONY
DRAUGHT ANIMAL
DRAUGHT ENGINE
DRAUGHT SCREEN
DRAW A VEIL OVER
DRAW ATTENTION
DRAWING A BLANK
DRAWING MASTER
DRAWING PENCIL
DRAWING STUMPS
DRAWS TO A CLOSE
DRESS DESIGNER
DRESS IMPROVER
DRESSED TO KILL
DRESSING TABLE
DREW A VEIL OVER
DREW ATTENTION
DRIBS AND DRABS
DRIFTING APART
DRILL SERGEANT
DRINKING STRAW
DRIPPING ROAST
DRIVING LESSON
DRIVING MIRROR
DROPHEAD COUPE
DROPPED A BRICK
DROPPED ANCHOR
DROPPING A LINE
DROPS A CLANGER
DRUG ADDICTION
DRUM MAJORETTE
DRUMMOND LIGHT
DRUNKEN STUPOR
DUMB INSOLENCE
DUNSTABLE ROAD
DUODENAL ULCER
DUSTING POWDER
DWELLING HOUSE
DWELLING PLACE
DYED IN THE WOOL

EACH WAY DOUBLE
EACH WAY TREBLE
EAGER TO PLEASE
EARTH MOVEMENT
EAST NORTH EAST
EAST SOUTH EAST
EASTERN CHURCH
EASY AS WINKING
EASY LISTENING
EAT LIKE A HORSE
EATS HUMBLE PIE
EATS ONES WORDS
EDINBURGH ROCK
EDITION DE LUXE
EDITOR IN CHIEF
EIGHT DAY CLOCK
EIGHTSOME REEL
ELECTORAL VOTE
ELECTRIC CHAIR
ELECTRIC FENCE
ELECTRIC FIELD
ELECTRIC MOTOR
ELECTRIC ORGAN
ELECTRIC RAZOR
ELECTRIC SHOCK
ELECTRIC STORM
ELEPHANT FOLIO
ELEPHANT GRASS
ELEPHANT SHREW
ELEPHANTS EARS
ELEPHANTS FOOT
EMERALD COPPER
EMERGENCY EXIT
EMINENCE GRISE
EMPIRE BUILDER
EMULSION PAINT
ENCLOSED ORDER
ENDING IN TEARS
ENDURANCE TEST
ENGLISH SETTER
ENJOYS ONESELF
ESCORT CARRIER
ESPRIT DE CORPS
ESSENTIAL OILS
ESTATE BOTTLED
ETCHING NEEDLE
EVERY WHICH WAY
EXACT SCIENCES
EXCESS BAGGAGE
EXCESS LUGGAGE
EXCESS POSTAGE
EXCHANGE BLOWS
EXCHANGE WORDS
EXCHEQUER BILL
EXCLUSION ZONE
EXCUSE ME DANCE
EXCUSE ONESELF
EXEMPLI GRATIA
EXHAUST SYSTEM
EXPANSION BOLT

13 *contd.*

EXPANSION CARD
EXPANSION PLAN
EXPANSION SLOT
EXPLAINED AWAY
EXPLODING STAR
EXPLOSIVE BOLT
EXPORT LICENCE
EXPOSE ONESELF
EXPOSURE METER
EXPRESS LETTER
EXPRESS PACKET
EXPRESS PARCEL
EXTERIOR ANGLE
EYE LEVEL GRILL
EYEBROW PENCIL
EYES LIKE A HAWK
FABIAN SOCIETY
FACED THE MUSIC
FACES THE MUSIC
FACTORY WORKER
FAIR AND SQUARE
FAITES VOS JEUX
FALL FROM GRACE
FALL INTO PLACE
FALLING BEHIND
FALLING IN LOVE
FALLOPIAN TUBE
FALLS INTO LINE
FAMILY BUTCHER
FAMILY REUNION
FARMER GENERAL
FEATHER BONNET
FEATHER DUSTER
FEATHER PILLOW
FEATHER STITCH
FEATURE LENGTH
FEEDING BOTTLE
FEEDS ONES FACE
FEELING AT HOME
FEELS THE PINCH
FELL FROM GRACE
FELL INTO PLACE
FELLOW CITIZEN
FELLOW FEELING
FELT TIPPED PEN
FEMININE RHYME
FEMORAL ARTERY
FENCING MASTER
FERRO CONCRETE
FERTILE GROUND
FERTILITY DRUG
FETCH AND CARRY
FETE CHAMPETRE
FIDDLE FADDLER
FIDDLERS MONEY
FIDEI DEFENSOR
FIELD DRESSING
FIELD HOSPITAL
FIELD OF VISION

FIELD PREACHER
FIGHTING COCKS
FIGHTING DRUNK
FIGHTING IT OUT
FIGURE CASTING
FIGURE OF EIGHT
FIGURE SKATING
FIGURING IT OUT
FILING CABINET
FILLE DHONNEUR
FILLED THE BILL
FILTER THROUGH
FINAL SOLUTION
FINANCIAL YEAR
FIND ONES LEVEL
FINDS ONES FEET
FINE CHAMPAGNE
FINE GENTLEMAN
FINGER POINTER
FINISHING POST
FINNAN HADDOCK
FIRE INSURANCE
FIRE RESISTANT
FIRST DAY COVER
FIRST OFFENDER
FISHING GROUND
FISHING TACKLE
FISRT WORLD WAR
FIT LIKE A GLOVE
FITS AND STARTS
FIVE POUND NOTE
FIXED INTEREST
FLAME COLOURED
FLAME THROWING
FLANDERS POPPY
FLASH FLOODING
FLASH IN THE PAN
FLAT OF THE HAND
FLATTENING OUT
FLEET OF TRUCKS
FLEMISH SCHOOL
FLEMISH STITCH
FLESH AND BLOOD
FLESH COLOURED
FLICKS THROUGH
FLIGHT FEATHER
FLIGHT OF FANCY
FLINT KNAPPING
FLOATING CRANE
FLOATING GRASS
FLOATING LIGHT
FLOATING ON AIR
FLOATING VOTER
FLORA AND FAUNA
FLORAL DIAGRAM
FLORENCE FLASK
FLOWER SERVICE
FLOWERING RUSH
FLYING COLOURS
FLYING MACHINE

FLYING OFFICER
FLYING PICKETS
FLYING THE FLAG
FLYING TRAPEZE
FOCUSING CLOTH
FOLDS ONES ARMS
FOLK ETYMOLOGY
FOLLOW THROUGH
FOLLOWING HOME
FOLLOWING SUIT
FOOD POISONING
FOOD PROCESSOR
FOOLING AROUND
FOOLS PARADISE
FOOT PASSENGER
FOOTBALL MATCH
FOOTBALL PITCH
FOOTBALL POOLS
FOOTED THE BILL
FOR EVER AND AYE
FOR GOOD AND ALL
FOR MERCYS SAKE
FOR THAT MATTER
FOR THE PRESENT
FORCE THE ISSUE
FORCED LANDING
FORCED THE PACE
FORCES THE PACE
FOREIGN LEGION
FOREIGN OFFICE
FORGET ONESELF
FORGOT ONESELF
FORK LIFT TRUCK
FORK LIGHTNING
FORM CRITICISM
FORTIFIED WINE
FORTUNE COOKIE
FORTUNE HUNTER
FORTUNE TELLER
FORTY HOUR WEEK
FORWARD MARKET
FOSTER BROTHER
FOUND ONES FEET
FOUNDER MEMBER
FOUR POSTER BED
FREE COMPANION
FREE RANGE EGGS
FREEZING POINT
FRENCH CRICKET
FRENCH MUSTARD
FRENCH WINDOWS
FRESH AS A DAISY
FRIARS LANTERN
FRIDGE FREEZER
FRIGHTENED OFF
FRIGHTENS AWAY
FRILLED LIZARD
FRINGE BENEFIT
FRINGE DWELLER
FRITTERED AWAY

FROEBEL SYSTEM
FROM THE OUTSET
FROM THE WORD GO
FRUIT COCKTAIL
FRYING TONIGHT
FUEL INJECTION
FULL FASHIONED
FULL OF ONESELF
FULL TO THE BRIM
FUNNY BUSINESS
FUNNY PECULIAR
FURNISHED FLAT
FUSION REACTOR
FUTURE PERFECT
GAGGLE OF GEESE
GAIN ADMISSION
GAINED CONTROL
GAINING GROUND
GAINS STRENGTH
GAMBLING HOUSE
GAME FOR A LAUGH
GAME PRESERVER
GAMES MISTRESS
GARDEN VILLAGE
GARDENING CLUB
GARLIC MUSTARD
GAS AND GAITERS
GASTRIC JUICES
GATE OF JUSTICE
GATHERED ROUND
GATHERED SPEED
GATHERING COAL
GATHERING PEAT
GATHERS BREATH
GATHERS GROUND
GAUNTLET GUARD
GAY LIBERATION
GAY LUSSACS LAW
GEIGER COUNTER
GENERAL EFFECT
GENERAL LEGACY
GENERAL PARDON
GENERATION GAP
GENETIC SPIRAL
GENS DE LETTRES
GENTIAN VIOLET
GENTLE HEARTED
GEOMETRIC MEAN
GERMAN MEASLES
GET AWAY WITH IT
GET IN ON THE ACT
GET IT TOGETHER
GET ONES HAND IN
GET THE MESSAGE
GET THE PICTURE
GET TO ONES FEET
GETS ONES CARDS
GETS ONES EYE IN
GETS THE NEEDLE
GETS THE WIND UP

13 *contd.*

GETS UNDRESSED
GETTING ACROSS
GETTING AROUND
GHETTO BLASTER
GIFT OF TONGUES
GILDED CHAMBER
GILDED THE LILY
GILDED THE PILL
GIRDED ONESELF
GIRDLE OF VENUS
GIVE TO THE DOGS
GIVEN ON A PLATE
GIVES ON A PLATE
GIVING OFFENCE
GLACIAL PERIOD
GLASS GRINDING
GLASS PAINTING
GLOBAL VILLAGE
GLOBAL WARMING
GLOBE TROTTING
GLOWING REPORT
GLYPTAL RESINS
GO AS YOU PLEASE
GO OUT OF THE WAY
GO OVER THE EDGE
GO OVER THE WALL
GO THE DISTANCE
GO THE WHOLE HOG
GO TO ANY LENGTH
GO UNDERGROUND
GOES A BUNDLE ON
GOES BY THE BOOK
GOES LIKE A BOMB
GOES ONE BETTER
GOES OVERBOARD
GOES THE ROUNDS
GOES TO THE DOGS
GOES TO THE WALL
GOES TO THE WARS
GOES UP IN SMOKE
GOES WITH A BANG
GOING DOWNHILL
GOING FOR A SONG
GOING FOR BROKE
GOING STRAIGHT
GOING TO GROUND
GOING TO MARKET
GOING TO PIECES
GOLD MEDALLIST
GOLDEN CRESTED
GOLDEN HAMSTER
GOLDEN JUBILEE
GOLDEN SECTION
GOLDEN WEDDING
GOLIATH BEETLE
GONE TO THE DOGS
GONE TO THE WALL
GOOD AFTERNOON
GOOD FOR A LAUGH

GOOD GROUNDING
GOOD KING HENRY
GOOD NATUREDLY
GOOD SAMARITAN
GOODNESS KNOWS
GOODY TWO SHOES
GOOSE BARNACLE
GORDON BENNETT
GOSPEL SINGING
GOT AWAY WITH IT
GOT IN ON THE ACT
GOT IT TOGETHER
GOT ONES HAND IN
GOT THE MESSAGE
GOT THE PICTURE
GOT TO ONES FEET
GOTHIC REVIVAL
GOVERNESS CART
GOVERNING BODY
GRABBING CRANE
GRAMMAR SCHOOL
GRAND NATIONAL
GRAND SEIGNEUR
GRANDE VEDETTE
GRAPE HYACINTH
GRAPPLING HOOK
GRAPPLING IRON
GRASS STAGGERS
GRAVES DISEASE
GREAT GRANDSON
GREAT WHITE WAY
GREEN MANURING
GREEN SICKNESS
GREENHOUSE GAS
GREENLAND SEAL
GREENWICH TIME
GREETINGS CARD
GRIEF STRICKEN
GRIN AND BEAR IT
GRINDS TO A HALT
GRIT ONES TEETH
GROUND ANGLING
GROUND CONTROL
GROUND OFFICER
GROUND TO A HALT
GROUP DYNAMICS
GROUP MARRIAGE
GROUP PRACTICE
GUARD OF HONOUR
GUARDIAN ANGEL
GUEST OF HONOUR
GUIDED MISSILE
GUM UP THE WORKS
GUNPOWDER PLOT
HACKING JACKET
HAD DONE WITH IT
HAD EVERYTHING
HAD IT BOTH WAYS
HAIR SPLITTING
HALE AND HEARTY

HALF HEARTEDLY
HALF SOVEREIGN
HALF THE BATTLE
HALF TIME SCORE
HALL OF JUSTICE
HALL OF MIRRORS
HAMMER THROWER
HAMMERING HOME
HANDSEL MONDAY
HANG BY A THREAD
HANG SENG INDEX
HANG UP ONES HAT
HANGING AROUND
HANGING GARDEN
HANGING MATTER
HANGING VALLEY
HANGMANS NOOSE
HANGS ONES HEAD
HANGS TOGETHER
HAPPENING UPON
HAPPY BIRTHDAY
HAPPY FAMILIES
HARBOUR LIGHTS
HARBOUR MASTER
HARD BOILED EGG
HARD HEARTEDLY
HARD LUCK STORY
HARD OF HEARING
HARDWARE STORE
HARE AND HOUNDS
HARLEQUIN DUCK
HARMONIC MINOR
HARMONIC RANGE
HARNESS RACING
HARVEST SPIDER
HARVEST SUPPER
HAS DONE WITH IT
HAS EVERYTHING
HAS IT BOTH WAYS
HAVE A BASINFUL
HAVE A GOOD TIME
HAVE A TIME OF IT
HAVE HYSTERICS
HAVING KITTENS
HAVING ONES WAY
HAWAIIAN GOOSE
HAZARDS A GUESS
HEAD OVER HEELS
HEAD RESTRAINT
HEADS WILL ROLL
HEALTH VISITOR
HEARING THINGS
HEART OF HEARTS
HEART SICKNESS
HEART STIRRING
HEART STRICKEN
HEAT EXCHANGER
HEAT RESISTANT
HEATH ROBINSON
HEAVENLY TWINS

HEAVES THE LEAD
HEAVY BREATHER
HEAVY HYDROGEN
HEAVY INDUSTRY
HEAVY PARTICLE
HEDGE ACCENTOR
HEDGE MARRIAGE
HEDGE ONES BETS
HEEBIE JEEBIES
HELD THE RECORD
HELD TO ACCOUNT
HELPED ONESELF
HELPS THE CAUSE
HELTER SKELTER
HER NUMBER IS UP
HERCULEAN TASK
HERE WE GO AGAIN
HEROIC COUPLET
HERTZIAN WAVES
HIDDEN ECONOMY
HIDES ONES HEAD
HIGH AND MIGHTY
HIGH CHURCHISM
HIGH CHURCHMAN
HIGH CONSTABLE
HIGH EXPLOSIVE
HIGH FREQUENCY
HIGH PRIESTESS
HIGH TAILING IT
HIGH WATER MARK
HIGHLAND DRESS
HIGHLAND FLING
HIGHLAND GAMES
HIS EXCELLENCY
HIS NUMBER IS UP
HIT ONES STRIDE
HIT ROCK BOTTOM
HIT THE CEILING
HIT THE JACKPOT
HITS A BAD PATCH
HITS THE BOTTLE
HITTING FOR SIX
HITTING THE HAY
HOBSONS CHOICE
HOLD THE RECORD
HOLD TO ACCOUNT
HOLDS DOWN A JOB
HOLDS THE FLOOR
HOLDS TO RANSOM
HOLDS TOGETHER
HOLE AND CORNER
HOLE IN THE WALL
HOLLERITH CODE
HOLLOW HEARTED
HOLY COMMUNION
HOME ECONOMICS
HOME ECONOMIST
HOME MADE BREAD
HOME MADE CAKES
HOME SECRETARY

13 *contd.*

HOMEWARD BOUND
HONEY DEW MELON
HONEYCOMB MOTH
HOPPED THE TWIG
HORIZONTAL BAR
HORSE AND BUGGY
HORSE CHESTNUT
HORSE MACKEREL
HORSE SICKNESS
HORSING AROUND
HOT AIR BALLOON
HOT GOSPELLING
HOT ON THE TRAIL
HOTHOUSE PLANT
HOUSE BREAKING
HOUSE OF PRAYER
HOUSE OF REFUGE
HOUSEHOLD GODS
HOUSEHOLD WORD
HOUSING ESTATE
HOUSING SCHEME
HUGGED ONESELF
HUMAN INTEREST
HUMANE SOCIETY
HUNG BY A THREAD
HUNG UP ONES HAT
HUNGER MARCHER
HUNGER STRIKER
HUNTING GROUND
HUNTING SPIDER
HURRICANE DECK
HURRICANE LAMP
HYDRAULIC BELT
HYDRAULIC JACK
HYPNO ANALYSIS
ICE CREAM WAFER
ICELAND FALCON
IF YOU DONT MIND
ILL CONSIDERED
IMAGINARY LINE
IMPACTED TOOTH
IMPERIAL POUND
IMPOSING STONE
IMPULSE BUYING
IMPUTATION TAX
IN A CLEFT STICK
IN A SORRY STATE
IN ALL FAIRNESS
IN CIRCULATION
IN COMPETITION
IN DIRE STRAITS
IN GREAT DEMAND
IN HONOUR BOUND
IN NO TIME AT ALL
IN ONES ELEMENT
IN ONES OWN TIME
IN PERPSECTIVE
IN POINT OF FACT
IN SHORT SUPPLY

IN SO MANY WORDS
IN SOME MEASURE
IN THE ABSTRACT
IN THE DOLDRUMS
IN THE MEANTIME
IN THE PIPELINE
IN THE SAME BOAT
IN THE SHORT RUN
INCENSE BURNER
INCLINED PLANE
INCOMES POLICY
INDIAN TOBACCO
INDUCTION COIL
INDUCTION PORT
INFANTS SCHOOL
INFILL HOUSING
INITIATION FEE
INLAND REVENUE
INNER HEBRIDES
INSTANT COFFEE
INTEREST GROUP
INTERIOR ANGLE
INTERNAL RHYME
IRIS DIAPHRAGM
IRREGULAR VERB
ISLAND HOPPING
ISTHMIAN GAMES
ITALIAN GARDEN
ITCHING POWDER
JACK THE RIPPER
JAMAICA PEPPER
JANIZARY MUSIC
JAPANESE CEDAR
JAPANESE PAPER
JEKYLL AND HYDE
JEQUIRITY BEAN
JERRY BUILDING
JERUSALEM PONY
JERUSALEM SAGE
JET PROPULSION
JEUNESSE DOREE
JIGGERY POKERY
JOBS COMFORTER
JOINING FORCES
JOINTED CACTUS
JOLLYING ALONG
JOURNAL INTIME
JUDGE ADVOCATE
JUDICIAL COURT
JUMP OVERBOARD
JUMPING FOR JOY
JUMPING THE GUN
JUMPS THE QUEUE
JUNIOR SERVICE
JUST THE TICKET
JUST THINK OF IT
JUVENILE COURT
KANGAROO COURT
KANGAROO GRASS
KANGAROO THORN

KEEN AS MUSTARD
KEEP GOOD HOURS
KEEP ONES END UP
KEEP OPEN HOUSE
KEEP THE CHANGE
KEEPING IN MIND
KEEPING IT DARK
KEEPING TABS ON
KEEPING WICKET
KEEPS GOOD TIME
KEEPS ONES COOL
KEEPS ONES HEAD
KEEPS ONES WORD
KEEPS THE PEACE
KENTUCKY DERBY
KEPT GOOD HOURS
KEPT ONES END UP
KEPT OPEN HOUSE
KICK INTO TOUCH
KICK ONES HEELS
KICK THE BUCKET
KICK UP A RUMPUS
KICK UP A SHINDY
KICKED ONESELF
KICKED UP A FUSS
KICKING AROUND
KICKS UP A STINK
KICKS UPSTAIRS
KIDDED ONESELF
KIDNEY MACHINE
KILROY WAS HERE
KINDRED SPIRIT
KINETIC ENERGY
KING OF THE ROAD
KINGS EVIDENCE
KINGS SHILLING
KISS AND MAKE UP
KISS IN THE RING
KISSED THE BOOK
KISSES THE BOOK
KISSING COMFIT
KISSING COUSIN
KIT INSPECTION
KITCHEN GARDEN
KITCHEN KAFFIR
KNEW BACKWARDS
KNEW INSIDE OUT
KNEW ONES PLACE
KNEW ONES STUFF
KNEW WHATS WHAT
KNICK KNACKERY
KNIFE GRINDING
KNIGHT MARSHAL
KNIGHT SERVICE
KNIGHT TEMPLAR
KNIGHTS ERRANT
KNIT ONES BROWS
KNOCK ON EFFECT
KNOCK SIDEWAYS
KNOCK SPOTS OFF

KNOCK TOGETHER
KNOCKED AROUND
KNOCKED FOR SIX
KNOCKED ON WOOD
KNOCKING ABOUT
KNOCKOUT DROPS
KNOTTY PROBLEM
KNOW BACKWARDS
KNOW INSIDE OUT
KNOW ONES PLACE
KNOW ONES STUFF
KNOW WHATS WHAT
KNOWING BETTER
KNOWLEDGE BASE
KNOWS FULL WELL
KNOWS THE ROPES
KNOWS THE SCORE
KNUCKLE HEADED
KNUCKLED UNDER
KNUCKLES UNDER
KNUCKLING DOWN
LA BELLE EPOQUE
LA GRANDE ARMEE
LACHRYMAL DUCT
LADIES FINGERS
LADIES GALLERY
LADY BOUNTIFUL
LADY IN WAITING
LADY OF LEISURE
LADY OF THE LAKE
LADY OF THE LAMP
LAG OF THE TIDES
LAGGING BEHIND
LAID IT ON THICK
LAID ON THE LINE
LANCE CORPORAL
LANCE SERGEANT
LAND MEASURING
LAND OWNERSHIP
LAND SURVEYING
LANDING GROUND
LAPSUS LINGUAE
LARGE SCALE MAP
LATCHKEY CHILD
LATERAN TREATY
LATIN AMERICAN
LATTICE BRIDGE
LATTICE GIRDER
LATTICE WINDOW
LAUGHING HYENA
LAUGHING IT OFF
LAUGHING STOCK
LAUGHS OUT LOUD
LAUGHS TO SCORN
LAUNCH VEHICLE
LAUNCHING SITE
LAUNDRY BASKET
LAVATORY PAPER
LAVENDER WATER
LAW OF AVERAGES

13 *contd.*

LAWN SPRINKLER
LAY DOWN THE LAW
LAYING A COURSE
LAYING HANDS ON
LAYS IT ON THICK
LAYS ON THE LINE
LE GRAND SIECLE
LEAD BY THE NOSE
LEAD POISONING
LEADING ASTRAY
LEADING SEAMAN
LEADING THE WAY
LEAP IN THE DARK
LEARNER DRIVER
LEARNING CURVE
LEASING MAKING
LEATHER JACKET
LEATHER WINGED
LEAVE IT AT THAT
LEAVES FOR DEAD
LEAVES ONE COLD
LEAVES THE ROOM
LEAVING BEHIND
LEAVING UNSAID
LED TO THE ALTAR
LEFT HAND DRIVE
LEFT WELL ALONE
LEGAL CAPACITY
LEGAL GUARDIAN
LEMON COLOURED
LEMON SQUEEZER
LES GRANDS VINS
LETS ONESELF GO
LETS WELL ALONE
LETTER CARRIER
LETTER FOUNDER
LETTER MISSIVE
LETTER PERFECT
LETTERS PATENT
LETTING IT RIDE
LEVEL CROSSING
LIBERTY BODICE
LIBRARY TICKET
LICENCE HOLDER
LICENSING LAWS
LICK INTO SHAPE
LICK ONES CHOPS
LICKS ONES LIPS
LIES ON THE OARS
LIFE ASSURANCE
LIFE INSURANCE
LIFE PRESERVER
LIFT ATTENDANT
LIFT THE LID OFF
LIFTED A FINGER
LIGHT FINGERED
LIGHT HORSEMAN
LIGHT INDUSTRY
LIGHT INFANTRY

LIGHT SPIRITED
LIGHTNING TUBE
LIKE CLOCKWORK
LIKE GRIM DEATH
LILY OF THE NILE
LINE ENGRAVING
LINE FISHERMAN
LINE OF THOUGHT
LINSEY WOOLSEY
LIONS PROVIDER
LIQUID CRYSTAL
LISTED COMPANY
LISTENING POST
LITERARY AGENT
LITERARY LUNCH
LITERARY WORLD
LITTLE BOY BLUE
LITTLE THEATRE
LIVE CARTRIDGE
LIVE IN THE PAST
LIVE LIKE A LORD
LIVED TOGETHER
LIVER COLOURED
LIVERY COMPANY
LIVERY SERVANT
LOAD OF RUBBISH
LOCAL PREACHER
LOLLIPOP WOMAN
LOMBARD STREET
LONG DESCENDED
LONG SUFFERING
LONG TIME NO SEE
LONGCASE CLOCK
LOOK IN THE FACE
LOOKED ASKANCE
LOOKED DAGGERS
LOOKED FORWARD
LOOKING AGHAST
LOOPED THE LOOP
LOOSEHEAD PROP
LORD AND MASTER
LORD OF MISRULE
LORD OF SESSION
LORD PRESIDENT
LORD PRIVY SEAL
LORD PROTECTOR
LORDS ORDINARY
LORDS TEMPORAL
LORRAINE CROSS
LOSE HANDS DOWN
LOSE ONES NERVE
LOSE ONES SHIRT
LOSES ONES COOL
LOSES ONES HAIR
LOSES ONES HEAD
LOSING CONTROL
LOSING ONES RAG
LOSING ONES WAY
LOSING ONESELF
LOSS OF DIGNITY

LOST HANDS DOWN
LOST ONES NERVE
LOST ONES SHIRT
LOTTERY TICKET
LOTUS POSITION
LOUIS QUATORZE
LOUNGING ABOUT
LOZENGE SHAPED
LUCK OF THE DRAW
LUMINOUS PAINT
LUNATIC ASYLUM
LUNATIC FRINGE
LYING AT ANCHOR
LYING IN THE WAY
MACHINE GUNNER
MACHINE MINDER
MACKEREL GUIDE
MACKEREL MIDGE
MACKEREL SHARK
MAD COW DISEASE
MADE A COMEBACK
MADE A FAST BUCK
MADE A MEAL OF IT
MADE FIRST BASE
MADE IN BRITAIN
MADE THE ROUNDS
MADE TO MEASURE
MAGAZINE RIFLE
MAGIC MUSHROOM
MAGINOT MINDED
MAGNETIC FIELD
MAGNETIC NORTH
MAGNETIC POLES
MAGNETIC STORM
MAID OF ALL WORK
MAISON DE VILLE
MAJOR PROPHETS
MAKE A COMEBACK
MAKE A FAST BUCK
MAKE A MEAL OF IT
MAKE FIRST BASE
MAKE THE ROUNDS
MAKES A BEELINE
MAKES A KILLING
MAKES ENDS MEET
MAKES GOOD TIME
MAKES OLD BONES
MAKES ONES MARK
MAKES THE GRADE
MAKING A FUSS OF
MAKING A PASS AT
MAKING BELIEVE
MAKING CERTAIN
MAKING CHANGES
MAKING FRIENDS
MAKING HISTORY
MAKING INROADS
MAKING LIGHT OF
MAKING ONES DAY
MAKING ONES WAY

MAKING THE PACE
MAKING WHOOPEE
MAN MADE FIBRES
MAN MANAGEMENT
MAN OF BUSINESS
MAN OF THE MATCH
MAN OF THE WORLD
MANGOLD WURZEL
MANIFOLD PAPER
MAP PROJECTION
MARBLE HEARTED
MARGIN OF ERROR
MARINE TRUMPET
MARRIAGE BANNS
MARRIAGE LINES
MARRONS GLACES
MARSH MARIGOLD
MARSH SAMPHIRE
MARTELLO TOWER
MASHIE NIBLICK
MASTER BUILDER
MASTER MARINER
MATINEE JACKET
MAZARINE BIBLE
MEADOW SAFFRON
MEALS ON WHEELS
MEASURING TAPE
MEAT AND TWO VEG
MEDICINE CHEST
MENDS ONES WAYS
MENTAL CRUELTY
MENTAL PATIENT
MENTAL PICTURE
MERCALLI SCALE
MERCANTILE LAW
MERMAIDS GLOVE
MERMAIDS PURSE
MESS OF POTTAGE
MESSENGER WIRE
METEOR SHOWERS
METEOR STREAMS
MEZZO SOPRANOS
MICRO ORGANISM
MICROWAVE OVEN
MID LIFE CRISIS
MIDDLE AMERICA
MIDDLE BRACKET
MIDDLE EASTERN
MIDDLE ENGLISH
MIDDLE KINGDOM
MIDDLE PASSAGE
MIDNIGHT FEAST
MIGHT HAVE BEEN
MIGRANT WORKER
MILD AND BITTER
MILITARY CROSS
MILITARY MEDAL
MILK CHOCOLATE
MILK DENTITION
MILK OF SULPHUR

13 *contd.*

MILLSTONE GRIT
MIND THAT CHILD
MINE DETECTION
MINERAL SPRING
MINERS ANAEMIA
MINI SUBMARINE
MINOR COUNTIES
MINOR PROPHETS
MINORITY GROUP
MINT CONDITION
MIRACLE MONGER
MIRACLE WORKER
MIRROR WRITING
MISCHIEF MAKER
MISSA SOLEMNIS
MISSED A SITTER
MISSED THE BOAT
MISSED THE MARK
MISSED THE POST
MISSES A SITTER
MISSES THE BOAT
MISSES THE MARK
MISSES THE POST
MISSING THE BUS
MIXED BLESSING
MIXED FOURSOME
MIXED LANGUAGE
MIXED MARRIAGE
MIXED METAPHOR
MOANING MINNIE
MOBILE LIBRARY
MODELLING CLAY
MODERN ENGLISH
MODUS OPERANDI
MOMENT OF TRUTH
MONASTIC ORDER
MONASTRAL BLUE
MONEY CHANGING
MONEY GRUBBING
MONEY TROUBLES
MONOPOLY MONEY
MONTHLY REPORT
MOONLIGHT FLIT
MORNING COFFEE
MORNING PRAYER
MORRIS DANCING
MOTHER COUNTRY
MOTHER HUBBARD
MOTHER OF PEARL
MOTION PICTURE
MOTOR TRACTION
MOUNTAIN CHAIN
MOUNTAIN RANGE
MOUNTAIN SHEEP
MOUNTING BLOCK
MOUNTING GUARD
MOURNING BRIDE
MOURNING CLOAK
MOURNING COACH

MOURNING PIECE
MOUSE EARED BAT
MOVING TO TEARS
MOWING MACHINE
MUDDLE THROUGH
MULTIPLE FRUIT
MULTIPLE STORE
MURAL PAINTING
MURDER WILL OUT
MUSHROOM CLOUD
MUSIC FESTIVAL
MUSIC MISTRESS
MUSICAL CHAIRS
MUSICAL COMEDY
NAIVE PAINTING
NAME YOUR PRICE
NARCO ANALYSIS
NASTY ACCIDENT
NASTY BUSINESS
NATIONAL FRONT
NATIONAL GUARD
NATIONAL PRIDE
NATIONAL TRUST
NATIVE SPEAKER
NATURAL SYSTEM
NATURE RESERVE
NATURE WORSHIP
NAVAL HOSPITAL
NEAPOLITAN ICE
NECK OR NOTHING
NEEDLE POINTED
NEGATIVE ANGLE
NELSONS COLUMN
NERVE WRACKING
NERVOUS SYSTEM
NEWGATE FRINGE
NEWTONS CRADLE
NEXT ON THE LIST
NEXT TO NOTHING
NICKEL PLATING
NIGHT CLUBBING
NIGHT WATCHMAN
NITRO COMPOUND
NO CLAIMS BONUS
NO GREAT SHAKES
NO HIDING PLACE
NO HOLDS BARRED
NO OIL PAINTING
NODDED THROUGH
NODDING DONKEY
NOLI ME TANGERE
NON ACCEPTANCE
NON AGGRESSION
NON APPEARANCE
NON ATTENDANCE
NON COMPLIANCE
NON CONDUCTING
NON OBSERVANCE
NON PRODUCTION
NON PRODUCTIVE

NON RETURNABLE
NONSENSE VERSE
NORFOLK JACKET
NORTH EASTERLY
NORTH EASTWARD
NORTH WESTERLY
NORTH WESTWARD
NORWAY HADDOCK
NORWAY LOBSTER
NORWEGIAN OVEN
NOT BEFORE TIME
NOT GOOD ENOUGH
NOT ON YOUR LIFE
NOT WORTH A DAMN
NOUVELLE VAGUE
NUCLEAR ENERGY
NUCLEAR FUSION
NUCLEAR WEAPON
NUCLEO PROTEIN
NURSERY CANNON
NURSERY SCHOOL
NURSERY SLOPES
NUTCRACKER MAN
OBJETS TROUVES
OBLIQUE MOTION
OBTUSE ANGULAR
OCCLUDED FRONT
OCCUPY THE MIND
ODD COME SHORTS
OFF ONES OWN BAT
OFF ONES ROCKER
OFF ONES STROKE
OFFICER OF ARMS
OIL OF LAVENDER
OILS THE WHEELS
OLD AGE PENSION
OLD AS THE HILLS
OLD BOY NETWORK
OLD CROCKS RACE
OLD WIVES TALES
ON A LARGE SCALE
ON A SHOESTRING
ON A SMALL SCALE
ON PAIN OF DEATH
ON SHANKSS PONY
ON TENTER HOOKS
ON THE CONTRARY
ON THE FACE OF IT
ON THE HIGH SEAS
ON THE PAVEMENT
ON THE SCROUNGE
ONCE AND FOR ALL
ONCE UPON A TIME
ONE FOR THE ROAD
ONE IN A MILLION
ONE NIGHT STAND
OPEN AIR MARKET
OPEN ONES HEART
OPEN PLAN HOUSE
OPENING SPEECH

OPTIC THALAMUS
OPTICAL FIBRES
ORANGE BLOSSOM
ORB AND SCEPTRE
ORBIS TERRARUM
ORBITAL ENGINE
ORDER OF BATTLE
ORDER OF THE DAY
ORDERED AROUND
ORDERING ABOUT
ORDINAL NUMBER
ORDINARY GRADE
ORDINARY LEVEL
ORDNANCE DATUM
ORIENT EXPRESS
ORIENTAL TOPAZ
ORKNEY ISLANDS
OUT HEROD HEROD
OUT LIKE A LIGHT
OUT OF HARMS WAY
OUT OF ONES HEAD
OUT OF ONES MIND
OUT OF PRACTICE
OUT OF THE WOODS
OUTBOARD MOTOR
OUTER HEBRIDES
OUTSIDE CHANCE
OVER THE STICKS
OVER THE WICKET
OVERHEAD CABLE
OVERNIGHT CASE
OWNER OCCUPIED
OWNER OCCUPIER
OXFORD ENGLISH
OYSTER CATCHER
OYSTER FISHERY
OZONE FRIENDLY
PACE UP AND DOWN
PACKET OF SEEDS
PACKING A PUNCH
PACKS ONES BAGS
PADDED THE HOOF
PADDLE STEAMER
PADDYS LANTERN
PAGE THREE GIRL
PAID ATTENTION
PAID IN ADVANCE
PAIN IN THE NECK
PAINTERS COLIC
PAINTS THE LILY
PAIR OF BELLOWS
PAIR OF PYJAMAS
PAISLEY DESIGN
PALAIS DE DANSE
PALE IMITATION
PALESTINE SOUP
PAN AFRICANISM
PANCAKE MAKE UP
PANIC STRICKEN
PANTOMIME DAME

13 LETTERS

13 contd.

PAPER FASTENER
PAPER HANGINGS
PAPER THE HOUSE
PAR EXCELLENCE
PAR OF EXCHANGE
PARACHUTE JUMP
PARAFFIN STOVE
PARALLEL RULER
PARENT COMPANY
PARIETAL CELLS
PARIS FASHIONS
PARISH COUNCIL
PARKING TICKET
PARKINSONS LAW
PARLIAMENT MAN
PARLOUR TRICKS
PARQUET CIRCLE
PARROT DISEASE
PARROT FASHION
PART AND PARCEL
PARTED COMPANY
PARTI COLOURED
PARTITION WALL
PARTY POLITICS
PARTY SPIRITED
PASCHAL CANDLE
PASCHAL FLOWER
PASSAGE OF ARMS
PASSED CURRENT
PASSED THE BUCK
PASSED THE TIME
PASSED THROUGH
PASSENGER LIST
PASSENGER MILE
PASSES CURRENT
PASSES THE BUCK
PASSES THE TIME
PASSES THROUGH
PASSING MUSTER
PASSION FLOWER
PASSION SUNDAY
PAST ONES PRIME
PASTE UP ARTIST
PATENT LEATHER
PATERNITY SUIT
PAVEMENT LIGHT
PAY AND DISPLAY
PAY LIP SERVICE
PAYING ONES WAY
PAYROLL GIVING
PAYS ATTENTION
PAYS IN ADVANCE
PEACE AND QUIET
PEACE DIVIDEND
PEACE OFFERING
PEACH COLOURED
PEACOCK FLOWER
PEACOCK THRONE
PEARL NECKLACE

PEARL SHELLING
PECTORAL CROSS
PELTIER EFFECT
PEMBROKE TABLE
PENALTY CORNER
PENCIL COMPASS
PENDULUM CLOCK
PENINSULAR WAR
PENNY DREADFUL
PENNY FARTHING
PENNY PINCHING
PENSION SCHEME
PENSIONING OFF
PEPPER AND SALT
PERCHING BIRDS
PERCUSSION CAP
PERFECT FOURTH
PERFECT INSECT
PERFECT METALS
PERFECT NUMBER
PERFECT TIMING
PERIOD COSTUME
PERIOD OF GRACE
PERIODIC TABLE
PERMANENT WAVE
PERSIAN BLINDS
PERSIAN CARPET
PERSIAN POWDER
PETIT DEJEUNER
PETROL LIGHTER
PETROL STATION
PETTY SESSIONS
PHOTO EMISSION
PHYSICAL FORCE
PHYSICAL JERKS
PIANO CONCERTO
PICK AND CHOOSE
PICK AND SHOVEL
PICKED ONES WAY
PICKED UP SPEED
PICKING A FIGHT
PICKLED ONIONS
PICKLED WALNUT
PICKS ONES SPOT
PICKS TO PIECES
PICKS UP THE TAB
PICTURE PALACE
PICTURE WINDOW
PIDGIN ENGLISH
PIECE OF ADVICE
PIECE OF STRING
PIECE TOGETHER
PIECES OF EIGHT
PIECRUST TABLE
PIG AND WHISTLE
PIGEON CHESTED
PIGEON FANCIER
PIGEON HEARTED
PILGRIM BOTTLE
PILGRIMS SHELL

PILOTS LICENCE
PINAFORE DRESS
PINAFORE SKIRT
PINHOLE CAMERA
PINK ELEPHANTS
PINKING SHEARS
PIPELESS ORGAN
PISTOL WHIPPED
PITCHED BATTLE
PITCHING A TENT
PLACE ON RECORD
PLAIN LANGUAGE
PLAIN SPEAKING
PLANNING AHEAD
PLASTIC BULLET
PLATE PRINTING
PLATINUM BLACK
PLATONIC SOLID
PLAY HARD TO GET
PLAY ONES HUNCH
PLAY THE MARKET
PLAY THE WANTON
PLAY UPON WORDS
PLAYED FOOTSIE
PLAYED FOR TIME
PLAYED IT BY EAR
PLAYED ONES ACE
PLAYED THE FOOL
PLAYED THE GAME
PLAYED THE LEAD
PLAYING AROUND
PLAYING HOOKEY
PLAYING IT COOL
PLAYING POSSUM
PLAYING TRICKS
PLAYING TRUANT
PLAYS FOR A DRAW
PLAYS THE DEVIL
PLAYS THE FIELD
PLAYS WITH FIRE
PLEASURE HOUSE
PLENARY POWERS
PLOTTING PAPER
PLOUGH THROUGH
PLOUGHING BACK
PLURAL SOCIETY
PNEUMATIC TYRE
POCKET BOROUGH
POCKET PICKING
POETIC JUSTICE
POETIC LICENCE
POETS LAUREATE
POINT FOR POINT
POINT OF HONOUR
POISONED ARROW
POISSON DAVRIL
POKED IN THE EYE
POKES IN THE EYE
POLAR DISTANCE
POLAR EQUATION

POLAR EXPLORER
POLECAT FERRET
POLICE OFFICER
POLICE STATION
POMPIER LADDER
PONTOON BRIDGE
POOPER SCOOPER
POPPING CREASE
POPS ONES CLOGS
PORCELAIN CLAY
POROUS PLASTER
PORRIDGE STICK
PORTLAND SHEEP
PORTLAND STONE
POSED A PROBLEM
POSES A PROBLEM
POSITIVE ANGLE
POSITIVE ORGAN
POST COMMUNION
POST MODERNISM
POST MODERNIST
POST OFFICE BOX
POST OPERATIVE
POST WAR CREDIT
POSTAL ADDRESS
POSTE RESTANTE
POSTER COLOURS
POSTMANS KNOCK
POTATO DISEASE
POTTED SHRIMPS
POTTS FRACTURE
POTTY TRAINING
POURED SCORN ON
POURS WITH RAIN
POWDER COMPACT
POWDERED SUGAR
POWDERING GOWN
POWER ASSISTED
POWER POLITICS
POWER STEERING
PRACTICAL JOKE
PRAIRIE OYSTER
PRANCING ABOUT
PRAWN COCKTAIL
PRAYED FOR RAIN
PRAYER MEETING
PRAYING INSECT
PRAYING MANTIS
PRE EMPTIVE BID
PRE QUALIFYING
PRE RAPHAELISM
PRE RAPHAELITE
PRE TAX PROFITS
PREACHING DOWN
PRECIOUS METAL
PRECIOUS STONE
PRECISION TOOL
PREENS ONESELF
PRESERVING PAN
PRESS FASTENER

13 contd.

PRESSED FLOWER
PRESSING AHEAD
PRESSURE CABIN
PRESSURE COOKS
PRESSURE GROUP
PRESSURE POINT
PRESSURE RIDGE
PRICK ME DAINTY
PRIM AND PROPER
PRIMARY COLOUR
PRIMARY PLANET
PRIMARY SCHOOL
PRIME MERIDIAN
PRIME MINISTER
PRIMING POWDER
PRINCE CONSORT
PRINCE OF PEACE
PRINCE OF WALES
PRINCESS ROYAL
PRINTERS DEVIL
PRINTING HOUSE
PRINTING PAPER
PRINTING PRESS
PRISON BREAKER
PRISON OFFICER
PRISONER OF WAR
PRIVATE INCOME
PRIVATE PAY BED
PRIVATE SCHOOL
PRIVATE SECTOR
PRIVATE TREATY
PRIZE FIGHTING
PRO CHANCELLOR
PROBE SCISSORS
PROCESS SERVER
PROFIT AND LOSS
PROFIT SHARING
PROMENADE DECK
PROMISE BREACH
PROOF CORRECTS
PROPER CHARLIE
PROPHET OF DOOM
PROPIONIC ACID
PROSPECT GLASS
PROTO HISTORIC
PROVING GROUND
PROXIMITY FUSE
PRUNING SHEARS
PSEUDO ARCHAIC
PSYCHIC POWERS
PTERYGOID BONE
PUBLIC COMPANY
PUBLIC HANGING
PUBLIC HOLIDAY
PUBLIC INQUIRY
PUBLIC LECTURE
PUBLIC LIBRARY
PUBLIC OPINION
PUBLIC RECORDS

PUBLIC SERVANT
PUBLIC SPEAKER
PUBLIC TRUSTEE
PUBLIC UTILITY
PUBLIC WARNING
PUDDING HEADED
PUDDING SLEEVE
PULITZER PRIZE
PULL THE PLUG ON
PULLED STRINGS
PULLED THROUGH
PULLS A FAST ONE
PULLS A FLANKER
PULLS TO PIECES
PULLS TOGETHER
PUNCTUM CAECUM
PURBECK MARBLE
PURPLE EMPEROR
PURSE SNATCHER
PUSH BUTTON WAR
PUSH PULL TRAIN
PUSH THE BOTTLE
PUSHED THROUGH
PUSHES THROUGH
PUSHING AROUND
PUT IN THE SHADE
PUT IN THE WRONG
PUT ONES FACE ON
PUT ONES FEET UP
PUT ONES MIND TO
PUT OUT TO GRAZE
PUT THE BRAKE ON
PUT THE LID ON IT
PUT THE SKIDS ON
PUT TO THE SWORD
PUTS INTO WORDS
PUTS ON ONE SIDE
PUTS ON THE LINE
PUTS ONES OAR IN
PUTS THE BOOT IN
PUTS THE CAT OUT
PUTTING ACROSS
PUTTING ON AIRS
PUTTING PAID TO
PUTTING UP WITH
PUTTY COLOURED
QUADRATIC MEAN
QUADRUPLE TIME
QUAKER BUTTONS
QUALITY OF LIFE
QUALITY STREET
QUANTUM NUMBER
QUANTUM THEORY
QUARTER DECKER
QUARTER GUNNER
QUARTER HOURLY
QUARTZ CRYSTAL
QUEEN ANNE LEGS
QUEEN OF HEAVEN
QUEEN OF THE MAY

QUEEN VICTORIA
QUEENS COUNSEL
QUEENS ENGLISH
QUEENS PROCTOR
QUEENS PUDDING
QUEENSLAND NUT
QUEER GOINGS ON
QUEER THE PITCH
QUESTION OF LAW
QUICK ANSWERED
QUICK AS A FLASH
QUICK TEMPERED
QUIET AS A MOUSE
QUILTING FRAME
QUITS THE SCENE
QUIZZING GLASS
QUOTATION MARK
QUOTED COMPANY
RABBLE ROUSING
RACE RELATIONS
RACING TIPSTER
RACK AND PINION
RADIAL PLY TYRE
RADIANT ENERGY
RADIATION BELT
RADIO ACTINIUM
RADIO OPERATOR
RADIO SPECTRUM
RAG AND BONE MAN
RAID THE MARKET
RAILWAY BRIDGE
RAILWAY STITCH
RAILWAY TUNNEL
RAINBOW CHASER
RAINBOW TINTED
RAISE THE ALARM
RAISED ONES HAT
RAISED THE ROOF
RAISED THE WIND
RAISES ONES HAT
RAISES THE ROOF
RAISES THE WIND
RAISING A SIEGE
RAISING A STINK
RALLYING POINT
RALLYING ROUND
RAM AIR TURBINE
RAN A TIGHT SHIP
RAN IN THE BLOOD
RAN OUT OF STEAM
RAN RINGS ROUND
RANGED ONESELF
RANGES ONESELF
RANTS AND RAVES
RANZ DES VACHES
RASPBERRY BUSH
RATEABLE VALUE
RATTLE BRAINED
RAY OF SUNSHINE
READ LIKE A BOOK

READ WRITE HEAD
READERS DIGEST
READING MATTER
READS THE SIGNS
READY RECKONER
READY STEADY GO
RECEIVING ROOM
RECEIVING SHIP
RECEPTION DESK
RECEPTION ROOM
RECORD BREAKER
RED RAG TO A BULL
RED RIDING HOOD
RED SANDALWOOD
RED SPIDER MITE
REDDING STRAIK
REDUCE TO TEARS
REDUCING AGENT
REDUCING FLAME
REEFING JACKET
REFERENCE BOOK
REFERENCE MARK
REGISTER HOUSE
REGISTER PLATE
REIGN OF TERROR
REIGNS SUPREME
RELIEVING ARCH
REMAINS SILENT
REMITTANCE MAN
REMOTE CONTROL
REMOTE SENSING
RENT COLLECTOR
RENTAL LIBRARY
REPEAT ONESELF
REPORTING BACK
REPUBLICAN ERA
RESERVE A TABLE
RESERVOIR ROCK
RESISTANCE BOX
RESTAURANT CAR
RETAINING WALL
RETURN JOURNEY
REVOLVING DOOR
REYES SYNDROME
REYNARD THE FOX
RHAETO ROMANIC
RHODES SCHOLAR
RHODIAN SCHOOL
RHYMED TO DEATH
RHYMES TO DEATH
RHYTHM SECTION
RIBSTON PIPPIN
RIDE ROUGH SHOD
RIDES FOR A FALL
RIDES THE WAVES
RIDES TO HOUNDS
RIDING CLOTHES
RIDING THE FAIR
RIGHT HAND SIDE
RIGHT OF COMMON

13 *contd.*

RIGHT OF SEARCH
RIGHT REVEREND
RIGHT THINKING
RIGHTED WRONGS
RIGHTS THE HELM
RING TAILED CAT
RISE TO THE BAIT
RISKS ONES LIFE
RITE OF PASSAGE
RITUAL KILLING
ROAD METALLING
ROAD TRANSPORT
ROAST CHESTNUT
ROBE DE CHAMBRE
ROCKED THE BOAT
RODE ROUGH SHOD
RODENT OFFICER
ROGUE ELEPHANT
ROGUES GALLERY
ROLL ON ROLL OFF
ROLLED INTO ONE
ROLLER BANDAGE
ROLLER BEARING
ROLLER COASTER
ROLLER SKATING
ROLLS ONES EYES
ROMAN CATHOLIC
ROMAN NUMERALS
ROMANO BRITISH
ROMPED THROUGH
ROOM WITH A VIEW
ROOT AND BRANCH
ROOT VEGETABLE
RORSCHACH TEST
ROSE OF JERICHO
ROSE TO THE BAIT
ROTTEN BOROUGH
ROUGH AND READY
ROUGH SHOOTING
ROULETTE TABLE
ROULETTE WHEEL
ROUND THE BLOCK
ROUND THE CLOCK
ROUND THE TWIST
ROUNDING ERROR
ROYAL AIR FORCE
ROYAL MARRIAGE
ROYAL PECULIAR
ROYAL STANDARD
RUB OF THE GREEN
RUBBER NECKING
RUBBER STAMPED
RUBS ONES HANDS
RUBS SHOULDERS
RUDE AWAKENING
RUGBY FOOTBALL
RULE BRITANNIA
RULE OF THE ROAD
RULED THE ROAST

RULED THE ROOST
RULES THE ROAST
RULES THE ROOST
RUN A TIGHT SHIP
RUN IN THE BLOOD
RUN OUT OF STEAM
RUN RINGS ROUND
RUNNING ACROSS
RUNNING BATTLE
RUNNING BUFFET
RUNNING LIGHTS
RUNNING SCARED
RUNNING STITCH
RUNNING TO SEED
RUPERT THE BEAR
RURAL DISTRICT
RUSSIA LEATHER
RUST RESISTANT
RUSTY COLOURED
SABBATH BREACH
SABBATH SCHOOL
SABLE ANTELOPE
SABLE COLOURED
SABRE RATTLING
SACRED COLLEGE
SADDLE BLANKET
SADO MASOCHISM
SADO MASOCHIST
SAFETY BICYCLE
SAFETY CURTAIN
SAILING MASTER
SAILING ORDERS
SAINT SIMONIAN
SAINT SIMONISM
SAINT SIMONIST
SALAD DRESSING
SALAMI TACTICS
SALE AND RETURN
SALE CATALOGUE
SALICYLIC ACID
SALMON FISHERY
SALMON FISHING
SALT AND PEPPER
SALT OF VITRIOL
SALTED PEANUTS
SALVATION ARMY
SANG LIKE A BIRD
SAPODILLA PLUM
SARATOGA TRUNK
SAT IN JUDGMENT
SAT ON THE FENCE
SATANIC SCHOOL
SATELLITE TOWN
SATIN SHEETING
SATSUMA ORANGE
SAUTE POTATOES
SAVANNA FLOWER
SAVANNA FOREST
SAVE AS YOU EARN
SAVE ONES BACON

SAVED ONES FACE
SAVED ONES NECK
SAVED ONES SKIN
SAVES ONES FACE
SAVES ONES NECK
SAVES ONES SKIN
SAYING A PRAYER
SCALING LADDER
SCALPING KNIFE
SCANDAL BEARER
SCARLET RUNNER
SCENIC RAILWAY
SCHOOL LEAVING
SCHOOL MARMISH
SCHOOL TEACHER
SCHOOL UNIFORM
SCOOPS THE POOL
SCORCHED EARTH
SCORPION GRASS
SCOTCH CURLIES
SCOTCH TERRIER
SCOTCH THISTLE
SCOTCH VERDICT
SCOURING STICK
SCOUTING ROUND
SCRAMBLED EGGS
SCREECH MARTIN
SCREECH THRUSH
SCREEN PROCESS
SCRIBBLING PAD
SCRUBBED ROUND
SEA GOOSEBERRY
SEANAD EIREANN
SEARCH WARRANT
SEASIDE RESORT
SECOND CHAMBER
SECOND HAND CAR
SECOND INNINGS
SECOND READING
SECONDARY CELL
SECONDARY COIL
SECRET PASSAGE
SECRET SERVICE
SECRETARY BIRD
SECRETARY TYPE
SECTION CUTTER
SEDENTARY SOIL
SEED CATALOGUE
SEEMING SIMPLE
SEES THE SIGHTS
SEGMENTAL ARCH
SELF ABASEMENT
SELF ADDRESSED
SELF ADJUSTING
SELF APPOINTED
SELF APPROVING
SELF ASSERTION
SELF ASSURANCE
SELF AWARENESS
SELF COMMUNION

SELF CONCEITED
SELF CONDEMNED
SELF CONFESSED
SELF CONFIDENT
SELF CONSCIOUS
SELF CONTAINED
SELF CRITICISM
SELF DEFEATING
SELF DEPENDENT
SELF DIRECTING
SELF DIRECTION
SELF FINANCING
SELF GOVERNING
SELF IMPORTANT
SELF INDULGENT
SELF INFLICTED
SELF MOTIVATED
SELF OPERATING
SELF POSSESSED
SELF PROFESSED
SELF PROPELLED
SELF PUBLICIST
SELF RESTRAINT
SELF RIGHTEOUS
SELF SACRIFICE
SELF SATISFIED
SELF SUPPORTED
SELLERS MARKET
SELLING IN BULK
SELLS ONES SOUL
SELLS THE DUMMY
SEMI AUTOMATIC
SEMI BARBARIAN
SEMI BARBARISM
SEMI PERMEABLE
SEMPER FIDELIS
SEMPER PARATUS
SENIOR CITIZEN
SENIOR PARTNER
SENIOR SERVICE
SERAPHIC ORDER
SERBO CROATIAN
SERGEANT MAJOR
SERJEANT AT LAW
SERPENT LIZARD
SERVE A PURPOSE
SERVICE CHARGE
SESSION SINGER
SET ONES MIND TO
SET ONES SEAL ON
SETS AN EXAMPLE
SETS BY THE EARS
SETS ONES CAP AT
SETTING ALIGHT
SETTING EYES ON
SETTING FIRE TO
SETTING IN HAND
SETTING ON EDGE
SETTING ON FIRE
SETTING TO WORK

13 *contd.*

SETTING UP SHOP
SEVEN SLEEPERS
SEVEN YEAR ITCH
SEVEN YEARS WAR
SEVENTH HEAVEN
SEVILLE ORANGE
SEWING MACHINE
SHABBY GENTEEL
SHADOW CABINET
SHADOW OF DEATH
SHADOWY FIGURE
SHAKE ONES FIST
SHAKE ONES HEAD
SHAMMY LEATHER
SHAMPOO AND SET
SHARE SECURITY
SHARKS MANNERS
SHARP AS A RAZOR
SHARP PRACTICE
SHARPS THE WORD
SHEDDING A TEAR
SHEEP SHEARING
SHEEP STEALING
SHEEPSKIN COAT
SHELL ORNAMENT
SHELL PARAKEET
SHERIFF DEPUTE
SHERRY COBBLER
SHETLAND SHEEP
SHIELD OF BRAWN
SHIFT REGISTER
SHIFTING ABOUT
SHIFTING SANDS
SHIFTS ONESELF
SHINGLE ROOFED
SHIP CHANDLERY
SHIP IN A BOTTLE
SHIP OF THE LINE
SHIPPING AGENT
SHIPPING CLERK
SHIPPING WATER
SHIPS REGISTER
SHOCK ABSORBER
SHOOK ONES FIST
SHOOK ONES HEAD
SHOOT THE WORKS
SHOOTING A LINE
SHOOTING BRAKE
SHOOTING CRAPS
SHOOTING IT OUT
SHOOTING LODGE
SHOOTING PAINS
SHOOTING RANGE
SHOOTING STARS
SHOOTING STICK
SHOP ASSISTANT
SHOPPED AROUND
SHOPPING SPREE
SHORT AND SWEET

SHORT CHANGING
SHORT DIVISION
SHORT OF BREATH
SHORT TEMPERED
SHORT TROUSERS
SHORTENED SAIL
SHOT IN THE DARK
SHOULDER BLADE
SHOULDER JOINT
SHOULDER STRAP
SHOUTING MATCH
SHOUTS THE ODDS
SHOW ONES PACES
SHOWED ONES AGE
SHOWED PROMISE
SHOWED THE FLAG
SHOWED WILLING
SHOWING THE WAY
SHOWS ONES FACE
SHOWS ONES HAND
SHREDDED WHEAT
SHRILL TONGUED
SHRIVELLING UP
SHROVE TUESDAY
SICK AS A PARROT
SIDE SPLITTING
SIGN THE PLEDGE
SIGNATURE TUNE
SILK STOCKINGS
SILVER JUBILEE
SILVER MOUNTED
SILVER TONGUED
SILVER WEDDING
SIMMERING DOWN
SIMPLE HEARTED
SIMPLE LARCENY
SING LIKE A BIRD
SINGING MASTER
SINGLE FIGURES
SINGLE SOLDIER
SISTINE CHAPEL
SIT IN JUDGMENT
SIT ON THE FENCE
SITTING PRETTY
SITTING TARGET
SITTING TENANT
SKELETON STAFF
SKIING HOLIDAY
SKILLED LABOUR
SKINNING ALIVE
SKINNY DIPPING
SKIRL IN THE PAN
SKIRTING BOARD
SKIRTING ROUND
SKITTLES MATCH
SKULKING PLACE
SLACKENING OFF
SLANGING MATCH
SLAP AND TICKLE
SLAP IN THE FACE

SLAP ON THE BACK
SLATE COLOURED
SLEEP LEARNING
SLEEP LIKE A LOG
SLEEP LIKE A TOP
SLEEPING BERTH
SLEEPING COACH
SLEEPING ROUGH
SLEIGHT OF HAND
SLEPT LIKE A LOG
SLEPT LIKE A TOP
SLIDE TROMBONE
SLING ONES HOOK
SLIPPER LIMPET
SLIPS ONES MIND
SLIPS THE CABLE
SLOT CAR RACING
SLUNG ONES HOOK
SMACK ONES LIPS
SMALL AND EARLY
SMALL CAPITALS
SMEAR CAMPAIGN
SMELLING SALTS
SMELTING HOUSE
SMELTING WORKS
SMOKE DETECTOR
SMOKED HADDOCK
SMOKELESS FUEL
SMOKELESS ZONE
SMOKING JACKET
SMOOTH CHINNED
SMOOTHING IRON
SMOTHERED MATE
SMUGGLERS COVE
SNAFFLE BRIDLE
SNOOKER PLAYER
SNOW BLINDNESS
SNUFF COLOURED
SOAP BOX ORATOR
SOBER AS A JUDGE
SOCIAL CLIMBER
SOCIAL SCIENCE
SOCIAL SERVICE
SOCK SUSPENDER
SOCKET SPANNER
SOFT BOILED EGG
SOFT IN THE HEAD
SOFT PEDALLING
SOIL MECHANICS
SOLDERING BOLT
SOLDERING IRON
SOLDIERS HEART
SOME LIKE IT HOT
SOMETHING IS UP
SOONER OR LATER
SOUL SEARCHING
SOUND BOARDING
SOUND THE ALARM
SOUNDING BOARD
SOUTH EASTERLY

SOUTH EASTWARD
SOUTH WESTERLY
SOUTH WESTWARD
SOUTHERN CROSS
SOWING MACHINE
SOWING THE SEED
SPACE INVADERS
SPACE MEDICINE
SPACE PLATFORM
SPACIOUS TIMES
SPANISH DAGGER
SPARKING PLUGS
SPARKLING WINE
SPEAK ONES MIND
SPEAKING CLOCK
SPEAKING VOICE
SPEAKS TOO SOON
SPEAKS VOLUMES
SPECIAL BRANCH
SPECIAL SCHOOL
SPECTRE SHRIMP
SPEECH THERAPY
SPEED MERCHANT
SPELL BACKWARD
SPELLING IT OUT
SPELT BACKWARD
SPENDING MONEY
SPILL THE BEANS
SPILLS A BIBFUL
SPILT THE BEANS
SPINDLE LEGGED
SPINDLE SHANKS
SPINE CHILLING
SPINNING A YARN
SPINNING JENNY
SPIRIT RAPPING
SPIRITUAL PEER
SPIT AND POLISH
SPITTING IMAGE
SPLINTER GROUP
SPLINTER PARTY
SPLINTER PROOF
SPLITS THE VOTE
SPOKE ONES MIND
SPONGE FISHING
SPONSORED WALK
SPORTS ONES OAK
SPRAY PAINTING
SPRING BALANCE
SPRING CHICKEN
SPRING CLEANER
SPROCKET WHEEL
SPROUTED WINGS
SQUARE BASHING
SQUARE DANCING
SQUARE MEASURE
SQUEAK THROUGH
SQUEEZING HOME
SQUIRE OF DAMES
SQUIRREL SHREW

13 *contd.*

ST BERNARDS DOG
ST CRISPINS DAY
ST LUKES SUMMER
ST MARTINS EVIL
ST PATRICKS DAY
ST SWITHINS DAY
ST VITUSS DANCE
STAB IN THE BACK
STACKS AGAINST
STAFF OF OFFICE
STAFF SERGEANT
STAGE A PROTEST
STAGE MANAGING
STAKE ONES LIFE
STAKING A CLAIM
STALKING HORSE
STAND ON TIPTOE
STAND ONES HAND
STAND TO REASON
STANDING ALONE
STANDING AT BAY
STANDING GUARD
STANDING ORDER
STANDING PLACE
STANDING STONE
STANDING TO WIN
STANDING TREAT
STANDING TRIAL
STANDS ACCUSED
STANDS AGAINST
STANDS THE PACE
STANHOPE PRESS
STAR CATALOGUE
STAR NOSED MOLE
STAR TREATMENT
STARCH REDUCED
STARTING A HARE
STARTING BLOCK
STARTING POINT
STARTING PRICE
STARTING STALL
STATE OF EVENTS
STATE OF THE ART
STATE OF UNREST
STATE PRISONER
STATE RELIGION
STATES GENERAL
STATION MASTER
STAY STITCHING
STAY THE COURSE
STAYED THE PACE
STEADY AS A ROCK
STEAK AND CHIPS
STEAL A MARCH ON
STEALING A KISS
STEALS THE SHOW
STEAM CARRIAGE
STEAM GOVERNOR
STEERING CLEAR

STEERING WHEEL
STEP OUT OF LINE
STEP PARENTING
STEPPING ASIDE
STEPPING STONE
STERN FOREMOST
STICK IN THE MUD
STICK OF CELERY
STICK OUT A MILE
STICK TOGETHER
STICKING IT OUT
STICKING PLACE
STICKING POINT
STICKS THE PACE
STIFF AS A BOARD
STIFF UPPER LIP
STILLS DISEASE
STIRRED ABROAD
STOCK BREEDING
STOCK EXCHANGE
STOCKING FRAME
STOLE A MARCH ON
STONE COLOURED
STONE DRESSING
STONE THE CROWS
STOOD ON TIPTOE
STOOD ONES HAND
STOOD TO REASON
STOOGED AROUND
STOOGES AROUND
STOP AT NOTHING
STOPPED THE ROT
STOPPING PLACE
STOPPING SHORT
STORAGE HEATER
STORMING PARTY
STRAIGHT ACTOR
STRAIGHT ANGLE
STRAIGHT FACED
STRAIGHT FIGHT
STRAIGHT FLUSH
STRAIGHTEN OUT
STRAINS A POINT
STRATO CRUISER
STRATO CUMULUS
STRAW COLOURED
STRAWBERRY JAM
STREET SWEEPER
STREET WALKING
STRETCH A POINT
STRETCHER BOND
STRETCHER CASE
STRETCHING OUT
STRIKE BREAKER
STRIKE IT LUCKY
STRIKE THROUGH
STRIKES A CHORD
STRIKES A MATCH
STRIKES BOTTOM
STRIKES IT RICH

STRIKING A POSE
STRIKING PRICE
STRING OF BEADS
STRING QUARTET
STRIP LIGHTING
STRIPPING DOWN
STRONG STOMACH
STRONG SWIMMER
STRUCK IN YEARS
STRUCK THROUGH
STUCK OUT A MILE
STUCK TOGETHER
STUDIO POTTERY
STUFFED OLIVES
STUNTED GROWTH
STURM UND DRANG
STYPTIC PENCIL
SUB POST OFFICE
SUBJECT MATTER
SUBJECT OBJECT
SUBMACHINE GUN
SUBMARINE BASE
SUCK ONES THUMB
SUCKING BOTTLE
SUFFERING CATS
SUGAR DIABETES
SUGAR REFINERY
SUGAR REFINING
SUGARS THE PILL
SUITED ONESELF
SUITS ONES BOOK
SULPHUR YELLOW
SULPHURIC ACID
SUMMER HOLIDAY
SUMMER PUDDING
SUN DRIED BRICK
SUN WORSHIPPER
SUPPORT TIGHTS
SUPREME SOVIET
SURFACE VESSEL
SURFACE WORKER
SURROUND SOUND
SUSPENDER BELT
SUSSEX SPANIEL
SWADDLING BAND
SWALLOW TAILED
SWEATED LABOUR
SWEATING IT OUT
SWEEP THE BOARD
SWEET CHESTNUT
SWEET NOTHINGS
SWEET SAVOURED
SWEET TEMPERED
SWELL THE RANKS
SWEPT THE BOARD
SWINGS THE LEAD
SWITCH SELLING
SWITCHING OVER
SWOLLEN HEADED
SYMBOLIC LOGIC

SYMPHONIC POEM
SYNODIC PERIOD
SYNTHETIC DRUG
TABLE FOOTBALL
TABLE SKITTLES
TABLE SPOONFUL
TABLEAU VIVANT
TABLED A MOTION
TABLES A MOTION
TAKE A BACK SEAT
TAKE EXCEPTION
TAKE IN LODGERS
TAKE LIBERTIES
TAKE ONES LEAVE
TAKE THE LID OFF
TAKE THE MICKEY
TAKE THE PLUNGE
TAKE TO ONES BED
TAKE TO THE ROAD
TAKEN DOWN A PEG
TAKEN FOR A RIDE
TAKEN PRISONER
TAKEN TO PIECES
TAKES A BEATING
TAKES A PRIDE IN
TAKES A SHINE TO
TAKES DOWN A PEG
TAKES FOR A RIDE
TAKES MEASURES
TAKES ONES SEAT
TAKES ONES TIME
TAKES ONES TURN
TAKES PRISONER
TAKES THE BLAME
TAKES THE FIELD
TAKES THE FLOOR
TAKES THE REINS
TAKES TO PIECES
TAKING A TUMBLE
TAKING A WICKET
TAKING BY STORM
TAKING COMMAND
TAKING IT OUT ON
TAKING OFFENCE
TAKING ON BOARD
TAKING ON TRUST
TAKING ONES CUE
TAKING POT LUCK
TAKING THE BAIT
TAKING THE CAKE
TAKING THE LEAD
TAKING THE MICK
TAKING THE VEIL
TAKING TIME OFF
TAKING TO COURT
TAKING TO HEART
TAKING UMBRAGE
TALENT SPOTTER
TALK IN RIDDLES
TALKING IT OVER

13 *contd.*

TALKING TURKEY	THERE SHE BLOWS	TITANIUM WHITE	TREASURY BENCH
TAPE RECORDING	THICK WITH DUST	TITHE GATHERER	TREAT LIKE DIRT
TAR AND FEATHER	THIMBLE RIGGED	TITTLE TATTLER	TRELLIS WINDOW
TASMANIAN WOLF	THIMBLE RIGGER	TITULAR BISHOP	TRENCH WARFARE
TAX COLLECTING	THINK THE WORST	TO BE OR NOT TO BE	TRESTLE BRIDGE
TAX COLLECTION	THINKING AGAIN	TO COIN A PHRASE	TRIAL AND ERROR
TAX CONCESSION	THINKING ALIKE	TO SAY THE LEAST	TRIAL BY RECORD
TAX DEDUCTIBLE	THINKING ALOUD	TOAD IN THE HOLE	TRIAL MARRIAGE
TAX RETURN FORM	THINKING TWICE	TOEING THE LINE	TRIAL OF THE PYX
TEA PLANTATION	THINKS OUT LOUD	TOGA PRAETEXTA	TRIED ONES LUCK
TEACHING STAFF	THINKS THROUGH	TOILET SERVICE	TRIES ONES LUCK
TEAMING UP WITH	THOROUGH GOING	TOLERANCE DOSE	TRIGGER FINGER
TEAR A STRIP OFF	THOROUGH PACED	TOMATO KETCHUP	TRIGGERING OFF
TEARS ONES HAIR	THOUGHT READER	TONGUE IN CHEEK	TRIM ONES SAILS
TECHNICAL FOUL	THREE CORNERED	TONGUE LASHING	TRINITY SUNDAY
TELEGRAPH POLE	THREE DAY EVENT	TONGUE TWISTER	TRIPLE CROWNED
TELEGRAPH WIRE	THREE LINE WHIP	TOOK A BACK SEAT	TRIPLE ENTENTE
TELEPHONE BILL	THREE PER CENTS	TOOK EXCEPTION	TRIUMPHAL ARCH
TELEPHONE BOOK	THREE QUARTERS	TOOK IN LODGERS	TROD THE BOARDS
TELEPHOTO LENS	THREEPENNY BIT	TOOK LIBERTIES	TROLLING SPOON
TELEVISION SET	THRESHER WHALE	TOOK ONES LEAVE	TROPICAL MONTH
TELL ME ANOTHER	THRESHING MILL	TOOK THE LID OFF	TROPICAL STORM
TELLS THE TRUTH	THREW TOGETHER	TOOK THE MICKEY	TROUSER BUTTON
TEN MINUTE RULE	THROTTLE LEVER	TOOK THE PLUNGE	TROUSER POCKET
TEN PENNY PIECE	THROTTLE VALVE	TOOK TO ONES BED	TRUCE BREAKING
TENDER HEARTED	THROTTLED DOWN	TOOK TO THE ROAD	TRUCIAL STATES
TENPIN BOWLING	THROTTLES DOWN	TOP OF THE CLASS	TRUMPET SHAPED
TENT PREACHING	THROUGH THE DAY	TOPPED THE BILL	TRUMPETER SWAN
TERRACED HOUSE	THROUGH TICKET	TORE A STRIP OFF	TRUNK DIALLING
TEST CRICKETER	THROW AWAY LINE	TOREADOR PANTS	TUMBLER SWITCH
THANK GOODNESS	THROW TOGETHER	TORTOISE SHELL	TURBO ELECTRIC
THATS BIG OF HER	THROWING STICK	TOUCHED BOTTOM	TURING MACHINE
THATS BIG OF HIM	THROWING TABLE	TOUCHES BOTTOM	TURKEY BUZZARD
THATS THE STUFF	THROWS A WOBBLY	TRACER ELEMENT	TURKEY VULTURE
THE BLUE YONDER	THROWS LIGHT ON	TRACTOR DRIVER	TURMERIC PAPER
THE CLOVEN HOOF	THUMB ONES NOSE	TRADE DISCOUNT	TURN A BLIND EYE
THE COMMON GOOD	THUMBING A LIFT	TRADE UNIONISM	TURN INSIDE OUT
THE COMMON WEAL	THUMBING A RIDE	TRADE UNIONIST	TURN OF THE YEAR
THE DEVIL TO PAY	THUNDER SHOWER	TRADE WEIGHTED	TURN ON THE HEAT
THE FIRST THING	THUNDER STRUCK	TRADING ESTATE	TURN THE CORNER
THE FLAT SEASON	TIC DOULOUREUX	TRADING STAMPS	TURN THE TABLES
THE FOOTLIGHTS	TICKET MACHINE	TRAFFIC CIRCLE	TURNBULLS BLUE
THE GRIM REAPER	TICKET WRITING	TRAFFIC ISLAND	TURNED AGAINST
THE LAST SUPPER	TICKETS PLEASE	TRAFFIC LIGHTS	TURNED THE TIDE
THE LORDS TABLE	TICKLE TO DEATH	TRAFFIC WARDEN	TURNING AROUND
THE MAIN CHANCE	TIED UP IN KNOTS	TRAIN SPOTTING	TURNING CIRCLE
THE MIDAS TOUCH	TIES UP IN KNOTS	TRAM CONDUCTOR	TURNING TURTLE
THE OPPOSITION	TIGHT HEAD PROP	TRANSFER PAPER	TURNIP LANTERN
THE OTHER WORLD	TIME AFTER TIME	TRANSIT LOUNGE	TURNKEY SYSTEM
THE PARANORMAL	TIME AND MOTION	TRANSPORT CAFE	TURNS A DEAF EAR
THE PARTYS OVER	TIME CONSUMING	TRANSPORT SHIP	TURNS ONES HEAD
THE PENNY DROPS	TIME MARCHES ON	TRAVEL STAINED	TURNS THE SCREW
THE REAL MACKAY	TIME OUT OF MIND	TRAVELLERS JOY	TURNS UP TRUMPS
THE REVOLUTION	TIME SIGNATURE	TREACLE TOFFEE	TURQUOISE BLUE
THE SMALL PRINT	TIP THE BALANCE	TREAD A MEASURE	TWICE TOLD TALE
THE UNDERWORLD	TIPPED ONES HAT	TREADING WATER	TWILIGHT SLEEP
THE VIRGIN MARY	TIPPED THE WINK	TREASON FELONY	TWO PENCE PIECE
THE WHOLE SHOOT	TIPPLING HOUSE	TREASURE CHEST	TWO PENNY PIECE
THE WHOLE WORLD	TIPS THE SCALES	TREASURE HOUSE	TWO PENNYWORTH
	TISSUE CULTURE	TREASURE TROVE	TYRRHENIAN SEA

13 and 14 LETTERS

UILLEANN PIPES
UMBILICAL CORD
UMBRELLA GROUP
UMBRELLA STAND
UNADOPTED ROAD
UNARMED COMBAT
UNCROWNED KING
UNDER CONTRACT
UNDER ONES BELT
UNDER ONES NOSE
UNDER PRODUCED
UNDER PRODUCES
UNDER THE KNIFE
UNDER THE TABLE
UNIT FURNITURE
UNIT OF ACCOUNT
UNIT PACKAGING
UNITED KINGDOM
UNITED NATIONS
UNIVERSAL TIME
UNSOLVED CRIME
UP TO THE ELBOWS
UP TO THE MINUTE
UP WITH THE LARK
URBAN DISTRICT
USING ONES LOAF
UTILITY PLAYER
VACUUM CLEANER
VALENTINE CARD
VALENTINES DAY
VALUE ADDED TAX
VALUE JUDGMENT
VANTAGE GROUND
VARIABLE COSTS
VARICOSE VEINS
VARNISHING DAY
VAULTING HORSE
VEGETABLE SOUP
VENETIAN BLIND
VENICE TREACLE
VENUSS FLY TRAP
VERNAL EQUINOX
VERS DE SOCIETE
VEXED QUESTION
VICAR OF CHRIST
VICE ADMIRALTY
VICE CONSULATE
VICE PRESIDENT
VICE PRINCIPAL
VICIOUS CIRCLE
VICTOR LUDORUM
VICTORIA CROSS
VICTORIA FALLS
VICTORY PARADE
VIDEO RECORDER
VIENNESE WALTZ
VIENNESE WHIRL
VILLAGE SCHOOL
VINYL PLASTICS

VIPERS BUGLOSS
VIRGINIA STOCK
VISITING HOURS
VOLCANIC GLASS
VOLCANIC ROCKS
VOLUNTARY WORK
VOTING MACHINE
VOTIVE PICTURE
VOWEL MUTATION
WAIT PATIENTLY
WAITED AT TABLE
WAITING AWHILE
WALK UP AND DOWN
WALKING ORDERS
WALKING PAPERS
WALKING THE DOG
WALKING TICKET
WALKING TO HEEL
WALKS ON TIPTOE
WALKS THE PLANK
WALLS HAVE EARS
WALTZING MOUSE
WANTED JAM ON IT
WAR DEPARTMENT
WAR TO THE KNIFE
WARDROBE TRUNK
WASH ONES HANDS
WASHING POWDER
WATCH ONES STEP
WATCH THE CLOCK
WATCHING BRIEF
WATER CARRIAGE
WATER CHESTNUT
WATER DIVINING
WATER HYACINTH
WATER PLANTAIN
WATER PURSLANE
WATER SOFTENER
WATERING HOUSE
WATERING PLACE
WATLING STREET
WATTLE AND DAUB
WAVE MECHANICS
WAY OF THE CROSS
WEAK AS A KITTEN
WEASELLING OUT
WEATHER ANCHOR
WEATHER BEATEN
WEATHER DRIVEN
WEATHER REPORT
WEATHER SYMBOL
WEATHER WINDOW
WEATHERING OUT
WEATHERS ALONG
WEDDING FAVOUR
WEEDING CHISEL
WEEK IN WEEK OUT
WEEPING WILLOW
WEIGHED ANCHOR
WEIGHT LIFTING

WEIGHT WATCHER
WELCOME ABOARD
WELL APPOINTED
WELL CONDUCTED
WELL CONNECTED
WELL DEVELOPED
WELL PRESERVED
WELL REGULATED
WELL RESPECTED
WELL THOUGHT OF
WELL WORKED OUT
WENDED ONES WAY
WENT BY THE BOOK
WENT LIKE A BOMB
WENT OVERBOARD
WENT THE ROUNDS
WENT TO THE DOGS
WENT TO THE WALL
WENT TO THE WARS
WENT UP IN SMOKE
WENT WITH A BANG
WESTERN CHURCH
WESTERN EMPIRE
WESTERN SCHISM
WHALING MASTER
WHAT DO YOU KNOW
WHEEL CARRIAGE
WHEEL CLAMPING
WHEELER DEALER
WHIP INTO SHAPE
WHIPPED THE CAT
WHIPPING CREAM
WHIRLPOOL BATH
WHISTLE BLOWER
WHISTLING AWAY
WHISTLING SWAN
WHITE AS A SHEET
WHITE ELEPHANT
WHITE OF THE EYE
WHITTLING AWAY
WHOOPING COUGH
WHOOPING CRANE
WICKET KEEPING
WIDE ANGLE LENS
WIDE OF THE MARK
WIDENED THE GAP
WILD AND WOOLLY
WILDCAT STRIKE
WILLOW PATTERN
WILLOW WARBLER
WINDING ENGINE
WINDOW CLEANER
WINDOW CURTAIN
WINDOW SHOPPED
WINDOW SHOPPER
WINDS OF CHANGE
WINDSOR CASTLE
WINE AND CHEESE
WINED AND DINED
WINES AND DINES

WING COMMANDER
WINGBACK CHAIR
WINGED ONES WAY
WINKLE PICKERS
WINNIE THE POOH
WINNING THE CUP
WINNING THE DAY
WINS HANDS DOWN
WINS IN A CANTER
WINS ONES SPURS
WINTER GARDENS
WINTER SESSION
WITH A BAD GRACE
WITH ONE ACCORD
WITHIN EARSHOT
WITHOUT FRILLS
WONDER WORKING
WOOD ENGRAVING
WOOD SANDPIPER
WOOD WOOL SLABS
WOODCHIP BOARD
WOODCHIP PAPER
WOOL GATHERING
WOOLLEN DRAPER
WORD BLINDNESS
WORD PROCESSOR
WORD SPLITTING
WORK THE ORACLE
WORKED AGAINST
WORKING TO RULE
WORKS ONES WILL
WORLD LANGUAGE
WORLD PREMIERE
WORM ONES WAY IN
WORTH ONES SALT
WREAKING HAVOC
WRIT OF INQUIRY
WRONG HEADEDLY
X MARKS THE SPOT
X RAY ASTRONOMY
X RAY TELESCOPE
YEAR IN YEAR OUT
YELLOW BELLIED
YELLOW BUNTING
YESTERDAYS MEN
YLANG YLANG OIL
YORKSHIRE GRIT
YOUNG FOGEYISH
YOUNG OFFENDER
YOUNGS MODULUS
YOUR REVERENCE
ZEBRA CROSSING
ZENANA MISSION
ZODIACAL LIGHT
ZOLLNERS LINES

14

A BIT OF ALL RIGHT
A FLEA IN ONES EAR
A FOOT IN THE DOOR

14 contd.
A LOAD OF RUBBISH
A MESS OF POTTAGE
A PLACE IN THE SUN
A RIFT IN THE LUTE
A SHOT IN THE DARK
A SOP TO CERBERUS
A STIFF UPPER LIP
A STRONG STOMACH
A TOUCH OF THE SUN
A WARM RECEPTION
A WILL OF ONES OWN
A WORD IN ONES EAR
ABOVE MENTIONED
ABOVE SUSPICION
ABSENT MINDEDLY
ACCUMULATOR BET
ACHILLES TENDON
ACID HOUSE MUSIC
ACROSS THE BOARD
ACTION PAINTING
ACTION STATIONS
ADMIRALTY CHART
ADMIRALTY HOUSE
ADVENTURE STORY
AFFAIR OF HONOUR
AFFAIRE DE COEUR
AIR CONDITIONED
AIR RAID SHELTER
AIR RAID WARNING
AIR SUPERIORITY
AIR VICE MARSHAL
ALL IN WRESTLING
ALL OVER THE SHOP
ALL ROUND CAMERA
ALL WELL AND GOOD
ALLIGATOR APPLE
AMERICAN INDIAN
AN ACE IN THE HOLE
ANCIENT HISTORY
ANGINA PECTORIS
ANNULAR ECLIPSE
ANNUS MIRABILIS
ANOMALOUS WATER
ANTARCTIC OCEAN
ANTI FEDERALISM
ANTI FEDERALIST
ANTI JACOBINISM
APOSTOLIC VICAR
APPLE CHARLOTTE
APPLE OF DISCORD
APPLES AND PEARS
APPLIED SCIENCE
APPROVED SCHOOL
ARTIFICIAL SILK
AS DRUNK AS A LORD
AS FIT AS A FIDDLE
AS HAPPY AS LARRY
AS MAD AS A HATTER
AS NEAR AS DAMMIT

AS THE CROW FLIES
ASSERTS ONESELF
ASSET STRIPPING
AT A RATE OF KNOTS
AT DAGGERS DRAWN
AT FULL THROTTLE
AT ONE FELL SWOOP
ATOMIC RADIATOR
AUDIO FREQUENCY
AUF WIEDERSEHEN
AURORA BOREALIS
AUTO INTOXICANT
AUTO SUGGESTION
AUTOGRAPH ALBUM
AUTOMATIC DRIVE
AUTOMATIC PILOT
AVIATION SPIRIT
BACHELOR OF ARTS
BACK PROJECTION
BACK SEAT DRIVER
BACKS TO THE WALL
BADMINTON COURT
BAGGAGE RECLAIM
BALANCE OF POWER
BALANCE OF TRADE
BALL OF THE THUMB
BALL PARK FIGURE
BALLOON BARRAGE
BANANA REPUBLIC
BANGERS AND MASH
BANNER HEADLINE
BANQUETING HALL
BAPTISM OF BLOOD
BARBADOS CHERRY
BARGAIN COUNTER
BARRAGE BALLOON
BARRISTER AT LAW
BASHI BAZOUKERY
BASTARD SAFFRON
BATHING COSTUME
BATHING MACHINE
BATHROOM SCALES
BATTENBERG CAKE
BATTERY OF TESTS
BAYEUX TAPESTRY
BAYONET FITTING
BE ALL AND END ALL
BEARNAISE SAUCE
BEAT GENERATION
BEAT ONES BRAINS
BEAT ONES BREAST
BEAT THE RETREAT
BEATIFIC VISION
BEATING THE BAND
BEATING THE DRUM
BEATS THE BOUNDS
BED SITTING ROOM
BEFORE AND AFTER
BEFORE ONES TIME
BEG THE QUESTION

BEGGING LETTERS
BEHIND SCHEDULE
BEHIND THE TIMES
BELIEVE IT OR NOT
BELLADONNA LILY
BELLS OF IRELAND
BELT TIGHTENING
BENEFIT SOCIETY
BESIDE THE POINT
BEST BEFORE DATE
BEWARE OF THE DOG
BEYOND REPROACH
BIG GAME HUNTING
BILL DISCOUNTER
BILL OF EXCHANGE
BILLIARD MARKER
BINAURAL EFFECT
BIRD OF PARADISE
BITES ONES THUMB
BITES THE BULLET
BITUMINOUS COAL
BLACK EYED SUSAN
BLACK IN THE FACE
BLACK MARKETEER
BLACKPOOL TOWER
BLANK CARTRIDGE
BLENHEIM ORANGE
BLENHEIM PALACE
BLESS THIS HOUSE
BLEW THE WHISTLE
BLISTER PLASTER
BLOCK AND TACKLE
BLOCKADE RUNNER
BLOCKING MOTION
BLOOD POISONING
BLOOD SACRIFICE
BLOW HOT AND COLD
BLOW THE WHISTLE
BLOWING ONES TOP
BLOWING THE GAFF
BLOWS THE LID OFF
BLUECOAT SCHOOL
BOA CONSTRICTOR
BOARDING SCHOOL
BOATSWAINS MATE
BOATSWAINS PIPE
BODILY FUNCTION
BOOLEAN ALGEBRA
BOROUGH ENGLISH
BOSTON TEA PARTY
BOURBON BISCUIT
BOURBON WHISKEY
BOWS AND SCRAPES
BOYS WILL BE BOYS
BRAIN FEVER BIRD
BREAD AND BUTTER
BREAK NEW GROUND
BREAK ONES HEART
BREAKDOWN TRUCK
BREAKFAST IN BED

14 *contd.*

BREAKFAST TABLE
BREAKING GROUND
BREAKING THE ICE
BREAKS ONES DUCK
BREAKS ONES WORD
BREATHED FREELY
BREATHING AGAIN
BREATHING SPACE
BREECH DELIVERY
BREEDER REACTOR
BREEDING GROUND
BRIDGE BUILDING
BRIDGING THE GAP
BRIGHT AND EARLY
BRIGHTS DISEASE
BRING TO ACCOUNT
BRING UP THE REAR
BRINGING TO BOOK
BRINGING TO HEEL
BRINGING TO LIFE
BRINGS INTO LINE
BRINGS INTO PLAY
BRISTOL DIAMOND
BRISTOL FASHION
BRITANNIA METAL
BRITISH DISEASE
BROKE NEW GROUND
BROKE ONES HEART
BROKE TO THE WIDE
BRONCHO DILATOR
BROTHEL CREEPER
BROUGHT A CHARGE
BROUGHT FORWARD
BROUGHT TO A HEAD
BROUGHT TO LIGHT
BRUSSELS CARPET
BRUSSELS SPROUT
BUCKET AND SPADE
BUCKLEYS CHANCE
BULIMIA NERVOSA
BULL HEADEDNESS
BUNDLE OF NERVES
BUREAU DE CHANGE
BURLING MACHINE
BURNS ONES BOATS
BURNT ONES BOATS
BURNT TO A CINDER
BURY THE HATCHET
BUSMANS HOLIDAY
BUTTER FINGERED
BUTTERFLY SCREW
BUTTERFLY VALVE
BUTTON MUSHROOM
BY RETURN OF POST
BY THE SAME TOKEN
CABBAGE LETTUCE
CABIN PASSENGER
CABINET EDITION
CABINET MEETING

CABINET PUDDING
CACK HANDEDNESS
CADMEAN VICTORY
CAISSON DISEASE
CALAMINE LOTION
CALCIUM CARBIDE
CALCULATED RISK
CALFS FOOT JELLY
CALLED THE SHOTS
CALLED TO THE BAR
CALLING ALL CARS
CALLING IT QUITS
CALLING THE TUNE
CALLING TO ORDER
CALLIPER SPLINT
CALLS TO ACCOUNT
CALORIFIC VALUE
CAME FULL CIRCLE
CAMP COMMANDANT
CANNONBALL TREE
CANON OF THE MASS
CANONICAL HOURS
CANTALOUP MELON
CANTERBURY BELL
CAPE GOOSEBERRY
CAPE OF GOOD HOPE
CAPITAL LETTERS
CAPTAIN GENERAL
CAPUCHIN MONKEY
CARBON MONOXIDE
CARDIAC FAILURE
CARDIAC MASSAGE
CARDINAL BISHOP
CARDINAL FLOWER
CARDINAL NUMBER
CARDINAL POINTS
CARDINAL VIRTUE
CARDINAL WOLSEY
CAREER DIPLOMAT
CARPET SLIPPERS
CARRIED FORWARD
CARRIED ONES BAT
CARRIED THE FLAG
CARRIED THROUGH
CARRIES FORWARD
CARRIES ONES BAT
CARRIES THE FLAG
CARRIES THROUGH
CARROT AND STICK
CARRYING THE CAN
CARRYING THE DAY
CARRYING TOO FAR
CARTESIAN DEVIL
CARTESIAN DIVER
CARTRIDGE PAPER
CASEMENT WINDOW
CASH ON DELIVERY
CASSE NOISETTES
CASSETTE PLAYER
CAST A HOROSCOPE

CAST ASPERSIONS
CASTING A GLANCE
CASTLE BUILDING
CASUAL LABOURER
CATCHING THE SUN
CATENARY SYSTEM
CATHEDRAL CLOSE
CATHERINE WHEEL
CATHODE RAY TUBE
CATHOLIC CHURCH
CAUGHT IN THE ACT
CAUGHT ON THE HOP
CAUGHT UNAWARES
CAULIFLOWER EAR
CAUSE AND EFFECT
CAUSING TROUBLE
CAUSTIC AMMONIA
CAUTIONARY TALE
CAVALRY OFFICER
CEDAR OF LEBANON
CENTRAL HEATING
CENTRAL LOCKING
CENTRE HALF BACK
CHAIN LIGHTNING
CHAIN OF COMMAND
CHALK AND CHEESE
CHAMBER CONCERT
CHAMBER COUNCIL
CHAMBER COUNSEL
CHAMPION JOCKEY
CHAMPS AT THE BIT
CHANCED ONES ARM
CHANCERY OFFICE
CHANCES ONES ARM
CHANGE ONES MIND
CHANGE ONES TUNE
CHANGING COLOUR
CHANGING PLACES
CHANNEL ISLANDS
CHANNEL SEAMING
CHANNEL STEAMER
CHANNEL SWIMMER
CHAPTER HEADING
CHARACTER ACTOR
CHARACTER ESSAY
CHARCOAL BURNER
CHARITY CONCERT
CHARLOTTE RUSSE
CHASE THE DRAGON
CHASED RAINBOWS
CHASES RAINBOWS
CHATEAU BOTTLED
CHESHIRE CHEESE
CHEST OF DRAWERS
CHEST PROTECTOR
CHEVAUX DE FRISE
CHICKEN FARMING
CHICKEN HEARTED
CHICKEN LIVERED
CHICKEN MARENGO

14 *contd.*

CHIEF CONSTABLE
CHIEF INSPECTOR
CHILD ALLOWANCE
CHILD RESISTANT
CHILE SALTPETRE
CHILLI CON CARNE
CHINESE CABBAGE
CHINESE LANTERN
CHINESE LAUNDRY
CHRISTMAS CAROL
CHRISTMAS DAISY
CHROMATIC SCALE
CHURCH MILITANT
CIGARETTE PAPER
CIRCUIT BREAKER
CIRCULAR LETTER
CITIZENS ARREST
CIVIL LIBERTIES
CLAIMS ASSESSOR
CLASH OF CYMBALS
CLASS CONSCIOUS
CLASSICAL LATIN
CLASSICAL MUSIC
CLAW HAMMER COAT
CLEAN AS A NEW PIN
CLEANSING CREAM
CLEAR AS CRYSTAL
CLEARING THE AIR
CLEARING THE WAY
CLEARS THE DECKS
CLERICAL COLLAR
CLITTER CLATTER
CLOAK AND DAGGER
CLOSE ENCOUNTER
CLOSED ONES EYES
CLOSED SYLLABLE
CLOSES ONES EYES
CLOUD FORMATION
CLOUDED LEOPARD
CLUBBED TO DEATH
CLUMBER SPANIEL
CLUTCH AT STRAWS
COACH AND HORSES
COALING STATION
COCK A DOODLE DOO
COCKTAIL LOUNGE
COCKTAIL SHAKER
COCONUT MATTING
CODE OF PRACTICE
COFFEE WHITENER
COIN OF THE REALM
COINING A PHRASE
COLD SHOULDERED
COLLECTIVE FARM
COLLECTIVE NOUN
COLLECTORS ITEM
COLLEGE PUDDING
COLLES FRACTURE
COLONEL IN CHIEF

COLONIAL OFFICE
COLONIAL SYSTEM
COLORADO BEETLE
COLOUR SERGEANT
COLOURED PENCIL
COME FULL CIRCLE
COMES TO THE BOIL
COMFORT STATION
COMING A CROPPER
COMING AND GOING
COMING INTO PLAY
COMING UP TRUMPS
COMMA BUTTERFLY
COMMERCIAL ROOM
COMMIT TO MEMORY
COMMITS ONESELF
COMMITS SUICIDE
COMMITTEE STAGE
COMMON COURTESY
COMMON ENTRANCE
COMMON MULTIPLE
COMMON OR GARDEN
COMMON PARLANCE
COMMUNION CLOTH
COMMUNION TABLE
COMMUNION WAFER
COMMUNITY CHEST
COMMUNITY NURSE
COMMUNITY RADIO
COMPANION HATCH
COMPARING NOTES
COMPOSING STICK
COMPOUND ENGINE
COMPUTER DATING
CONCAVO CONCAVE
CONCERT PIANIST
CONCRETE JUNGLE
CONCRETE POETRY
CONDITIONAL FEE
CONFERENCE ROOM
CONJUGAL RIGHTS
CONJURING TRICK
CONSULS GENERAL
CONSULTING ROOM
CONSUMERS GOODS
CONTAINER CRANE
CONTINUITY GIRL
CONTRACT BRIDGE
CONTRACTING OUT
CONTRARY MOTION
CONVEXO CONCAVE
COOKED THE BOOKS
COOKS ONES GOOSE
COPPER BOTTOMED
COPPER FASTENED
COPS AND ROBBERS
CORIANDER SEEDS
COROMANDEL WORK
CORPORATE STATE
CORPORATION TAX

CORRIDA DE TOROS
CORRUGATED IRON
COST ACCOUNTANT
COST ACCOUNTING
COUNCIL CHAMBER
COUNSEL KEEPING
COUNTER BATTERY
COUNTER CURRENT
COUNTER TRADING
COUNTRY DANCING
COUNTY PALATINE
COURSE OF EVENTS
COURT OF SESSION
COURTING COUPLE
COVERING LETTER
CRACKED THE WHIP
CRADLE SNATCHER
CRAMP ONES STYLE
CREDIBILITY GAP
CREDIT TRANSFER
CREME DE LA CREME
CREPES SUZETTES
CRICKS ONES NECK
CRIME DOESNT PAY
CRIME OF PASSION
CRIME PASSIONEL
CRIMINAL RECORD
CROCODILE TEARS
CROQUE MONSIEUR
CROSS EXAMINING
CROSS INFECTION
CROSS ONES HEART
CROSS QUESTIONS
CROSS REFERENCE
CROSS REFERRING
CROSSING SWORDS
CROSSING WARDEN
CROWN AND ANCHOR
CRUMB OF COMFORT
CRUTCHED FRIARS
CRY ONES EYES OUT
CULTURE VULTURE
CUMULATIVE VOTE
CURLS UP AND DIES
CURRENT ACCOUNT
CURRENT AFFAIRS
CURRYING FAVOUR
CURTAIN WALLING
CUT THROAT RAZOR
CUTS DOWN TO SIZE
CUTS ONES LOSSES
CUTS ONES THROAT
CUTS TO THE QUICK
CUTTING CORNERS
CUTTING UP ROUGH
CYCLE PER SECOND
CYCLIC COMPOUND
CYSTIC FIBROSIS
DANCING ACADEMY
DANCING PARTNER

DANGEROUS DRUGS
DANGEROUSLY ILL
DATA PROCESSING
DAUGHTERS IN LAW
DAVENPORT TRICK
DAVIS APPARATUS
DAY OF ATONEMENT
DAYLIGHT SAVING
DAZZLE PAINTING
DEAD MANS HANDLE
DEAD TO THE WORLD
DEAN AND CHAPTER
DEAR JOHN LETTER
DEATHS HEAD MOTH
DECLINE AND FALL
DECORATED STYLE
DECREE ABSOLUTE
DEED OF COVENANT
DEFERRED SHARES
DEMAND A RECOUNT
DEMI SEMIQUAVER
DENYING ONESELF
DEPOSIT ACCOUNT
DERAILLEUR GEAR
DESIGN ENGINEER
DESSERT SERVICE
DETECTIVE STORY
DEUTERIUM OXIDE
DEUXIEME BUREAU
DEVIL INCARNATE
DEVILS ADVOCATE
DEVILS SNUFF BOX
DIAMOND JUBILEE
DIAMOND WEDDING
DICED WITH DEATH
DICES WITH DEATH
DIE IN ONES BOOTS
DIESEL ELECTRIC
DIEU ET MON DROIT
DIG ONES HEELS IN
DIGESTIVE TRACT
DING DONG BATTLE
DIPPING THE FLAG
DIRECT DEBITING
DIRECT DRILLING
DIRECT TAXATION
DIRECTORS CHAIR
DISCOUNT BROKER
DISHING THE DIRT
DISSECTING ROOM
DISTILLED WATER
DISTRESS SIGNAL
DISTRESSED AREA
DIVIDED HIGHWAY
DIVIDING ENGINE
DO IT YOURSELFER
DO ONES HOMEWORK
DO ONES OWN THING
DOCTORS COMMONS

DODGE THE COLUMN
DOES THE HONOURS
DOG IN THE MANGER
DOGS TOOTH GRASS
DOING ONES WORST
DOT AND CARRY ONE
DOUBLE BREASTED
DOUBLE CROSSING
DOUBLE DECLUTCH
DOUBLE ENTENDRE
DOUBLE EXPOSURE
DOUBLE JEOPARDY
DOUBLE NEGATIVE
DOUBLE STOPPING
DOUBTING THOMAS
DOWN IN THE DUMPS
DOWN IN THE MOUTH
DOWN MEMORY LANE
DOWN ON ONES LUCK
DRAGON STANDARD
DRANK LIKE A FISH
DRAW THE LONGBOW
DRAWING THE LINE
DRAWS A VEIL OVER
DRAWS ATTENTION
DRESS REHEARSAL
DRESSING JACKET
DRILL HUSBANDRY
DRINK LIKE A FISH
DRINKING UP TIME
DRINKING VESSEL
DRIVE TO THE WALL
DRIVING LICENCE
DROP THE SUBJECT
DROPPING A BRICK
DROPPING ANCHOR
DROVE TO THE WALL
DRY ROAST PEANUT
DUCKS AND DRAKES
DUCTLESS GLANDS
DUG ONES HEELS IN
DYERS GREENWEED
EARLY DAY MOTION
EARLY VICTORIAN
EARTH SATELLITE
EAST COAST FEVER
EASY COME EASY GO
EATS LIKE A HORSE
EBBED AND FLOWED
EDITIO PRINCEPS
EDUCATIONAL TOY
EGG CUSTARD TART
ELDER STATESMAN
ELDER STATESMEN
ELDERBERRY WINE
ELECTRA COMPLEX
ELECTRIC COOKER
ELECTRIC GUITAR
ELECTRIC HEATER
ELECTRIC SHAVER

ELECTRON CAMERA
ELECTRON OPTICS
ELECTRONIC MAIL
ELEPHANTS TRUNK
EMPEROR PENGUIN
EMPIRE BUILDING
ENDLESS GEARING
ENFANT TERRIBLE
ENGAGEMENT RING
ENGINEERS CHAIN
ENGLISH CHANNEL
ENGLISH DISEASE
ENGLISH GRAMMAR
ENGLISH MUSTARD
ENJOYED ONESELF
ENTERPRISE ZONE
ESCAPE VELOCITY
ESPAGNOLE SAUCE
ESPRESSO COFFEE
ETHYLENE GLYCOL
EUCALYPTUS TREE
EUSTACHIAN TUBE
EVAPORATED MILK
EVEN HANDEDNESS
EXCHANGED BLOWS
EXCHANGED WORDS
EXCHANGES BLOWS
EXCHANGES WORDS
EXCLUSION ORDER
EXCURSION TRAIN
EXCUSE MY FRENCH
EXCUSED ONESELF
EXCUSES ONESELF
EXPANSION BOARD
EXPANSION JOINT
EXPLAINING AWAY
EXPLOSIVE RIVET
EXPOSED ONESELF
EXPOSES ONESELF
EXPRESS ONESELF
EXPRESSION MARK
EXPRESSION STOP
EXTENDED FAMILY
EXTERNAL DEGREE
EXTINCT VOLCANO
EXTREME UNCTION
FACING THE MUSIC
FACTORY FARMING
FAINT HEARTEDLY
FAIR TO MIDDLING
FAIRY GODMOTHER
FALL ON DEAF EARS
FALL ON ONES FEET
FALLING THROUGH
FALLOPIAN TUBES
FALLS FROM GRACE
FALLS INTO PLACE
FALSE EYELASHES
FALSE PRETENCES
FAMILY GROUPING

14 contd.

FAMILY PLANNING
FANCIED ONESELF
FANCIES ONESELF
FANCY DRESS BALL
FAST AND FURIOUS
FEATHER BRAINED
FEATURES EDITOR
FEEBLE MINDEDLY
FELL ON DEAF EARS
FELL ON ONES FEET
FELLOW CREATURE
FEMININE ENDING
FEMME DE CHAMBRE
FEND FOR ONESELF
FIDDLE FADDLING
FIELD ALLOWANCE
FIELD AMBULANCE
FIELD ARTILLERY
FIELD PREACHING
FIFTH AMENDMENT
FIFTH COLUMNIST
FIGHTER COMMAND
FIGHTING CHANCE
FIGURE OF SPEECH
FILLE DE CHAMBRE
FILLING STATION
FILLING THE BILL
FILTERS THROUGH
FINANCE COMPANY
FINDERS KEEPERS
FINDS ONES LEVEL
FINGER ALPHABET
FINGER PAINTING
FINGER POINTING
FINGERS BREADTH
FINISHING TOUCH
FIRE WORSHIPPER
FIREMANS HELMET
FIRST CLASS MAIL
FIRST CLASS POST
FIRST TIME BUYER
FIRST VIOLINIST
FISHERMANS LUCK
FISHERMANS RING
FISSION REACTOR
FIVE BARRED GATE
FIVE PENNY PIECE
FIXED SATELLITE
FLAG LIEUTENANT
FLAG OF DISTRESS
FLASH BLINDNESS
FLAT AS A PANCAKE
FLAT FOOTEDNESS
FLAT ON ONES BACK
FLAT ON ONES FACE
FLATTER ONESELF
FLEETING MOMENT
FLICKED THROUGH
FLIGHT OF STAIRS

FLIGHT RECORDER
FLIPPED ONES LID
FLOATING BEACON
FLOATING BRIDGE
FLOATING CHARGE
FLOATING ISLAND
FLOATING KIDNEY
FLOATING POLICY
FLOCK WALLPAPER
FLOG A DEAD HORSE
FLORENTINE IRIS
FLOWERING PLANT
FLOWERING SHRUB
FLYING BEDSTEAD
FLYING BUTTRESS
FLYING DUTCHMAN
FLYING SCOTSMAN
FLYING SQUIRREL
FOAM AT THE MOUTH
FOLDED ONES ARMS
FOLDING MACHINE
FOLLOW MY LEADER
FOLLOW ONES NOSE
FOLLOWS THROUGH
FOOD CONTROLLER
FOOD FOR THOUGHT
FOOTING THE BILL
FOR ALL THE WORLD
FOR EVER AND A DAY
FOR GOOD MEASURE
FOR LOVE OR MONEY
FOR THE DURATION
FOR THE HELL OF IT
FOR THE HIGH JUMP
FOR THE LOVE OF IT
FOR THE MOST PART
FORBIDDEN FRUIT
FORCED THE ISSUE
FORCES THE ISSUE
FORCING THE PACE
FORE AND AFT SAIL
FOREIGN AFFAIRS
FORGETS ONESELF
FORTUNE HUNTING
FORTUNE TELLING
FORWARD LOOKING
FOSTER DAUGHTER
FOUND ONES LEVEL
FOUNDATION STOP
FOUNDERS SHARES
FOUNDING FATHER
FOUR LETTER WORD
FOUR MINUTE MILE
FOUR WHEEL DRIVE
FREE ENTERPRISE
FREE HANDEDNESS
FREE SPOKENNESS
FREEDOM FIGHTER
FRENCH CANADIAN
FRENCH DRESSING

FRENCH KNICKERS
FRENCH MARIGOLD
FRENCH POLISHER
FRESHWATER FISH
FRIGHTENED AWAY
FRIGHTENING OFF
FRINGE BENEFITS
FRITTERING AWAY
FROM BAD TO WORSE
FROM BANK TO BANK
FROM TIME TO TIME
FRONT END LOADED
FRONT END SYSTEM
FROZEN SHOULDER
FULL OF MISCHIEF
FULL SPEED AHEAD
FULL STEAM AHEAD
FULLY FASHIONED
FUNERAL PARLOUR
FURTHER OUTLOOK
FUTTOCK SHROUDS
GABRIELS HOUNDS
GAELIC FOOTBALL
GAINED STRENGTH
GAINING CONTROL
GAINS ADMISSION
GALLOPING MAJOR
GALVANISED IRON
GATHERED BREATH
GATHERED GROUND
GATHERING ROUND
GATHERING SPEED
GATHERING STORM
GATWICK AIRPORT
GAVE UP THE GHOST
GENERAL AMNESTY
GENERAL COUNCIL
GENERAL OFFICER
GENERAL PURPOSE
GENERAL SERVANT
GENERAL WARRANT
GENIE OF THE LAMP
GENTLEMAN CADET
GENTLEMAN USHER
GENUINE ARTICLE
GEOLOGICAL TIME
GEORGIAN PLANET
GET IT IN THE NECK
GET ONES OWN BACK
GET THE BREEZE UP
GET THE HANG OF IT
GET TO FIRST BASE
GETS AWAY WITH IT
GETS IN ON THE ACT
GETS IT TOGETHER
GETS ONES HAND IN
GETS THE MESSAGE
GETS THE PICTURE
GETS TO ONES FEET
GETTING A LINE ON

14 *contd.*

GETTING A WICKET
GETTING DRESSED
GETTING HITCHED
GETTING ONES WAY
GETTING THE BIRD
GETTING THE BOOT
GETTING THE CHOP
GETTING THE PUSH
GETTING THE SACK
GETTING THROUGH
GETTING TO GRIPS
GETTING TO SLEEP
GETTING UP STEAM
GHOST OF A CHANCE
GIANTS CAUSEWAY
GILDING THE LILY
GILDING THE PILL
GINGERBREAD MAN
GIRDING ONESELF
GIVE UP THE GHOST
GIVEN TO THE DOGS
GLANDULAR FEVER
GLOBE ARTICHOKE
GLOSSY MAGAZINE
GLOVE STRETCHER
GNASH ONES TEETH
GO DOWN THE DRAIN
GO OUT OF ONES WAY
GO ROUND THE BEND
GO TO ANY LENGTHS
GO TO THE COUNTRY
GOD REST HIS SOUL
GOD SAVE THE KING
GODS OWN COUNTRY
GOES BY THE BOARD
GOES FOR NOTHING
GOES INTO DETAIL
GOES INTO HIDING
GOES LIKE A DREAM
GOES ON ALL FOURS
GOES ONES OWN WAY
GOES OVER THE TOP
GOES TO EXTREMES
GOES TO ONES HEAD
GOES UP IN THE AIR
GOING A BUNDLE ON
GOING AWAY DRESS
GOING BY THE BOOK
GOING GOING GONE
GOING GREAT GUNS
GOING LIKE A BOMB
GOING ONE BETTER
GOING OVERBOARD
GOING THE ROUNDS
GOING TO THE DOGS
GOING TO THE WALL
GOING TO THE WARS
GOING UP IN SMOKE
GOING WITH A BANG

GOLDEN PHEASANT
GONE FOR A BURTON
GOOD COMPANIONS
GOOD FELLOWSHIP
GOOD FOR NOTHING
GOOD FOR THE SOUL
GOOD HUMOUREDLY
GOOD NEIGHBOURS
GOOSEBERRY BUSH
GOOSEBERRY FOOL
GOT IT IN THE NECK
GOT ONES OWN BACK
GOT THE BREEZE UP
GOT THE HANG OF IT
GOT TO FIRST BASE
GOVERNMENT WHIP
GRACE AND FAVOUR
GRACIOUS LIVING
GRAHAM CRACKERS
GRAM EQUIVALENT
GRANADILLA TREE
GRASP THE NETTLE
GREEN CROSS CODE
GREENFIELD SITE
GREENLAND WHALE
GREGORIAN MODES
GRENADIER GUARD
GREY GOOSE QUILL
GRIFFON VULTURE
GRIST TO THE MILL
GRITS ONES TEETH
GROSS INDECENCY
GROUND SQUIRREL
GROUP INSURANCE
GROUSE SHOOTING
GROWTH INDUSTRY
GUMS UP THE WORKS
GUTTER MERCHANT
GUY FAWKES NIGHT
HAD TWO LEFT FEET
HAD WHAT IT TAKES
HALF DAY HOLIDAY
HALLOWEEN PARTY
HAMMER AND TONGS
HANGING GARDENS
HANGING IN THERE
HANGS BY A THREAD
HANGS UP ONES HAT
HAPPY CHRISTMAS
HARD NUT TO CRACK
HAS TWO LEFT FEET
HAS WHAT IT TAKES
HAUTE POLITIQUE
HAVE DONE WITH IT
HAVE EVERYTHING
HAVE IT BOTH WAYS
HAVING IT COMING
HAWAIIAN GUITAR
HAZARDED A GUESS
HEART SEARCHING

HEAVENLY BODIES
HEAVIER THAN AIR
HEAVING THE LEAD
HEAVISIDE LAYER
HEAVY BREATHING
HEDGED ONES BETS
HEDGES ONES BETS
HELD ONES BREATH
HELD ONES TONGUE
HELD UP ONES HEAD
HELL FOR LEATHER
HELPED THE CAUSE
HELPING ONESELF
HEN AND CHICKENS
HERALDS COLLEGE
HERCULES BEETLE
HERRING FISHERY
HEXAGONAL CHESS
HIDING ONES HEAD
HIGH COMMISSION
HIGH COURT JUDGE
HIGH HANDEDNESS
HIGH HEELED SHOE
HIGH MINDEDNESS
HIGH PRIESTHOOD
HIGH PRINCIPLED
HIGH RISK POLICY
HIGH SPEED STEEL
HIGH SPEED TRAIN
HIGH TECHNOLOGY
HIGHLAND CATTLE
HIP REPLACEMENT
HIPPETY HOPPETY
HISTORY TEACHER
HITS ONES STRIDE
HITS ROCK BOTTOM
HITS THE CEILING
HITS THE JACKPOT
HITTING THE DECK
HITTING THE ROAD
HITTING THE ROOF
HITTING THE SACK
HOB NAILED BOOTS
HOLD ONES BREATH
HOLD ONES TONGUE
HOLD UP ONES HEAD
HOLD YOUR HORSES
HOLDING COMPANY
HOLDING IN CHECK
HOLDING ONES OWN
HOLDING THE FORT
HOLDING THE LINE
HOLDING THE ROAD
HOLDS THE RECORD
HOLDS TO ACCOUNT
HOLE IN THE HEART
HOLIER THAN THOU
HOME DEPARTMENT
HOMME DAFFAIRES
HOMME DE LETTRES

14 contd.

HONORARY MEMBER
HOP SKIP AND JUMP
HOPPING THE TWIG
HORROR STRICKEN
HORSE ARTILLERY
HORSE LATITUDES
HOSTILE WITNESS
HOT AND BOTHERED
HOT OFF THE PRESS
HOT WATER BOTTLE
HOUSE OF COMMONS
HOUSE OF ILL FAME
HOUSEHOLD GOODS
HOUSEMAIDS KNEE
HOW NOW BROWN COW
HOWS YOUR FATHER
HUDDLE TOGETHER
HUGGED THE COAST
HUGGING ONESELF
HUMPBACK BRIDGE
HUNDRED PER CENT
HUNT HIGH AND LOW
HUNT THE SLIPPER
HUNT THE THIMBLE
HUNTING LEOPARD
HYBRID COMPUTER
HYDE PARK CORNER
HYDRAULIC BRAKE
HYDRAULIC PRESS
HYDRO AEROPLANE
I BEG YOUR PARDON
ICE CREAM CORNET
ICEBERG LETTUCE
ICING ON THE CAKE
IDENTICAL RHYME
IDENTICAL TWINS
IDENTITY CRISIS
IDENTITY PARADE
ILL GOTTEN GAINS
ILL NATUREDNESS
IMAGE CONVERTER
IMAGINARY POINT
IMMUNE RESPONSE
IMPERATIVE MOOD
IMPERFECT TENSE
IMPERIAL GALLON
IMPERIAL OCTAVO
IMPERIAL WEIGHT
IN A LITTLE WHILE
IN A STATE OF FLUX
IN AT THE DEEP END
IN LIVING MEMORY
IN LOCO PARENTIS
IN ONE FELL SWOOP
IN ONES OWN RIGHT
IN PLAIN ENGLISH
IN ROUND FIGURES
IN THE ASCENDANT
IN THE BIG LEAGUE

IN THE FAMILY WAY
IN THE LIMELIGHT
IN THE PUBLIC EYE
IN THE THICK OF IT
IN THE TOP FLIGHT
INCENDIARY BOMB
INCIDENT CENTRE
INCIDENT OFFICE
INDIAN ELEPHANT
INDIAN TAKE AWAY
INDIRECT OBJECT
INDIRECT SPEECH
INDUCED CURRENT
INDUCTION MOTOR
INDUCTION VALVE
INERTIA SELLING
INFLATION PROOF
INNOCENT ABROAD
INNOMINATE BONE
INNOMINATE VEIN
INNS OF CHANCERY
INSIDER DEALING
INSIDER TRADING
INSULATING TAPE
INSURANCE CLAIM
INTERIOR DESIGN
INTERIOR SPRUNG
INTERNMENT CAMP
INVERTED COMMAS
IPSISSIMA VERBA
IRISH WOLFHOUND
IRREGULAR VERBS
ISLAND UNIVERSE
ITS A SMALL WORLD
IVORY PORCELAIN
JACK IN THE GREEN
JAPANESE MEDLAR
JAVELIN THROWER
JEDDART JUSTICE
JERUSALEM BIBLE
JERUSALEM CROSS
JEWELLERS ROUGE
JINGLING JOHNNY
JOB DESCRIPTION
JOBS FOR THE BOYS
JOHN BARLEYCORN
JOINT STOCK BANK
JUDICIAL COMBAT
JUICE EXTRACTOR
JULIAN CALENDAR
JUMPED THE QUEUE
JUMPS OVERBOARD
KARAOKE MACHINE
KEEP A GOOD HOUSE
KEEP A PLACE WARM
KEEP A TIGHT REIN
KEEP AN OPEN MIND
KEEP ONES CHIN UP
KEEP ONES HAIR ON
KEEP ONES HAND IN

KEEP ONES TEMPER
KEEP UNDER WRAPS
KEEPING A SECRET
KEEPING AN EYE ON
KEEPING COUNSEL
KEEPING IN CHECK
KEEPING IN TOUCH
KEEPS GOOD HOURS
KEEPS ONES END UP
KEEPS OPEN HOUSE
KEPT A GOOD HOUSE
KEPT A PLACE WARM
KEPT A TIGHT REIN
KEPT AN OPEN MIND
KEPT ONES CHIN UP
KEPT ONES HAIR ON
KEPT ONES HAND IN
KEPT ONES TEMPER
KEPT UNDER WRAPS
KEYHOLE SURGERY
KICKED UP A STINK
KICKED UPSTAIRS
KICKING ONESELF
KICKING UP A FUSS
KICKS INTO TOUCH
KICKS ONES HEELS
KICKS THE BUCKET
KICKS UP A RUMPUS
KICKS UP A SHINDY
KIDDING ONESELF
KILLED IN ACTION
KILMARNOCK COWL
KING AND COUNTRY
KING JAMES BIBLE
KISSING STRINGS
KISSING THE BOOK
KITCHEN CABINET
KNAPPING HAMMER
KNEADING TROUGH
KNEW A MOVE OR TWO
KNEW ONES ONIONS
KNIGHT BACHELOR
KNIGHT BANNERET
KNIGHT ERRANTRY
KNIGHTS OF MALTA
KNITS ONES BROWS
KNITTING NEEDLE
KNIVES AND FORKS
KNOCK DOWN PRICE
KNOCK INTO SHAPE
KNOCK ON THE HEAD
KNOCKING AROUND
KNOCKING FOR SIX
KNOCKING ON WOOD
KNOCKS SIDEWAYS
KNOCKS SPOTS OFF
KNOCKS TOGETHER
KNOW A MOVE OR TWO
KNOW ONES ONIONS
KNOWS BACKWARDS

14 LETTERS

14 *contd.*

KNOWS INSIDE OUT
KNOWS ONES PLACE
KNOWS ONES STUFF
KNOWS WHATS WHAT
KNUCKLING UNDER
LABOUR EXCHANGE
LABOUR MOVEMENT
LACHRYMAL GLAND
LADY OF THE HOUSE
LAID DOWN THE LAW
LAKE WINDERMERE
LAMBDA PARTICLE
LAMINATED GLASS
LANDED INTEREST
LANTHANUM GLASS
LAPSUS MEMORIAE
LAPTOP COMPUTER
LARES ET PENATES
LARGER THAN LIFE
LATE NIGHT FINAL
LATTER DAY SAINT
LAUGHED OUT LOUD
LAUGHED TO SCORN
LAW OF THE JUNGLE
LAY IT ON THE LINE
LAYING THE TABLE
LAYS DOWN THE LAW
LEAD FREE PETROL
LEAD TO THE ALTAR
LEADING ACTRESS
LEADING COUNSEL
LEADS BY THE NOSE
LEAGUE FOOTBALL
LEAVE OF ABSENCE
LEAVE WELL ALONE
LEAVES IT AT THAT
LEAVING FOR DEAD
LEAVING ONE COLD
LEAVING THE ROOM
LEFT HANDEDNESS
LEFT IN THE LURCH
LEFT ON THE SHELF
LEFT SPEECHLESS
LEGION OF HONOUR
LEMONADE POWDER
LEND ME YOUR EARS
LENDING LIBRARY
LET THE SIDE DOWN
LETTER OF CREDIT
LETTER OF MARQUE
LEVELLING STAFF
LEXICAL MEANING
LIAISON OFFICER
LIBERATED WOMAN
LIBRARY EDITION
LICK ONES WOUNDS
LICKED ONES LIPS
LICKS INTO SHAPE
LICKS ONES CHOPS

LIE IN ONES TEETH
LIFE EXPECTANCY
LIFE MEMBERSHIP
LIFTING A FINGER
LIFTS THE LID OFF
LIGHT AND BITTER
LIGHT HEARTEDLY
LIGHTER THAN AIR
LIGHTING UP TIME
LIMITED COMPANY
LIMITED EDITION
LINE OF BUSINESS
LINEAR EQUATION
LIQUID PARAFFIN
LISTED BUILDING
LISTEN TO REASON
LITERARY CRITIC
LITERARY EDITOR
LITTLE BY LITTLE
LITTLE GREEN MEN
LIVE AND LET LIVE
LIVE BY ONES WITS
LIVE OFF THE LAND
LIVED IN THE PAST
LIVED LIKE A LORD
LIVES IN THE PAST
LIVES LIKE A LORD
LIVING QUARTERS
LIVING TOGETHER
LOADED QUESTION
LOAN COLLECTION
LOBAR PNEUMONIA
LOMBARDY POPLAR
LONG IN THE TOOTH
LONG WINDEDNESS
LONGS AND SHORTS
LOOK FOR TROUBLE
LOOKING ASKANCE
LOOKING DAGGERS
LOOKING FORWARD
LOOKS IN THE FACE
LOOPING THE LOOP
LORD CHANCELLOR
LORD LIEUTENANT
LORD MAYORS SHOW
LORDS AND LADIES
LORDS SPIRITUAL
LOSE ONES TEMPER
LOSES HANDS DOWN
LOSES ONES NERVE
LOSES ONES SHIRT
LOSING ONES COOL
LOSING ONES HAIR
LOSING ONES HEAD
LOST ONES TEMPER
LOST TO THE WORLD
LOVE IN IDLENESS
LOVING KINDNESS
LUCID INTERVALS
LUCK OF THE DEVIL

LUCK OF THE IRISH
LUGGAGE CARRIER
LUMBAR PUNCTURE
LUMINOUS ENERGY
LUNAR DISTANCES
LUNCHEON BASKET
LYING ON THE OARS
LYON KING AT ARMS
LYON KING OF ARMS
MACARONI CHEESE
MACKEREL BREEZE
MADE A NIGHT OF IT
MADE THE RUNNING
MAGNETIC BOTTLE
MAGNETIC NEEDLE
MAIDEN FORTRESS
MAIDENHAIR TREE
MAINTENANCE MAN
MAITRE DE BALLET
MAJOR GENERALCY
MAJOR ROAD AHEAD
MAKE A NIGHT OF IT
MAKE THE RUNNING
MAKE UP ONES MIND
MAKES A COMEBACK
MAKES A FAST BUCK
MAKES A MEAL OF IT
MAKES FIRST BASE
MAKES THE ROUNDS
MAKING A BEELINE
MAKING A KILLING
MAKING ENDS MEET
MAKING GOOD TIME
MAKING OLD BONES
MAKING ONES MARK
MAKING THE GRADE
MALE CHAUVINIST
MALE VOICE CHOIR
MAN IN THE STREET
MAN OF THE MOMENT
MANAGING EDITOR
MANDARIN COLLAR
MANDARIN ORANGE
MANIFOLD WRITER
MANILA ENVELOPE
MANS BEST FRIEND
MANUAL ALPHABET
MANUAL EXERCISE
MARATHON RUNNER
MARBURG DISEASE
MARCHING ORDERS
MARK OF THE BEAST
MARKET GARDENER
MARKET RESEARCH
MARRIAGE BROKER
MARTELLO TOWERS
MASCULINE RHYME
MASHED POTATOES
MASON DIXON LINE
MASS PRODUCTION

14 *contd.*

MASTER OF HOUNDS
MATERNITY GRANT
MATERNITY LEAVE
MATRON OF HONOUR
MATTER OF COURSE
MATTER OF HONOUR
MAUNDY THURSDAY
MAY IT PLEASE YOU
MEDICAL COLLEGE
MEDICAL OFFICER
MEDICAL STUDENT
MEDICINE BOTTLE
MEERSCHAUM PIPE
MEETING HALFWAY
MELT IN THE MOUTH
MEMBERSHIP CARD
MEMORANDUM BOOK
MEND ONES FENCES
MENDED ONES WAYS
MENTAL HOSPITAL
MERCHANT BANKER
MERCHANT PRINCE
MERCHANT TAILOR
MERIDIAN CIRCLE
MERRY CHRISTMAS
METEORIC STONES
METHYL CHLORIDE
MEZZANINE FLOOR
MICHAELMAS TERM
MICRO ORGANISMS
MIDDLE AMERICAN
MIDDLE DISTANCE
MILITARY POLICE
MILITARY SCHOOL
MILK OF MAGNESIA
MILKING MACHINE
MILKING PARLOUR
MILLING MACHINE
MIND OVER MATTER
MINERS PHTHISIS
MIRROR SYMMETRY
MISCHIEF MAKING
MISSING A SITTER
MISSING THE BOAT
MISSING THE MARK
MISSING THE POST
MISSIONARY WORK
MOCK HEROICALLY
MOCK TURTLE SOUP
MODEL AEROPLANE
MODS AND ROCKERS
MONASTRAL GREEN
MONEY OF ACCOUNT
MONEY SCRIVENER
MONKEY BUSINESS
MONROE DOCTRINE
MOP UP OPERATION
MOPPED AND MOWED
MORAL TURPITUDE

MOROCCO LEATHER
MOSQUITO CANOPY
MOTHER SUPERIOR
MOTHERS MEETING
MOTION SICKNESS
MOTOR GENERATOR
MOTTE AND BAILEY
MOUNTAIN BEAVER
MOUNTAIN LAUREL
MOVING PICTURES
MUCOUS MEMBRANE
MUDDLED THROUGH
MUDDLES THROUGH
MULTI OWNERSHIP
MULTIPLE CHOICE
MULTIPLE CINEMA
MUNITION WORKER
MURDER MOST FOUL
MUSTARD PLASTER
MUZZLE VELOCITY
NAME AND ADDRESS
NAPOLEON BRANDY
NATIONAL ANTHEM
NATIONAL CHURCH
NATIONAL SCHOOL
NATIVE LANGUAGE
NATURAL HISTORY
NATURAL NUMBERS
NATURAL SCIENCE
NATURAL WASTAGE
NAUGHTY BUT NICE
NEANDERTHAL MAN
NEAR THE KNUCKLE
NECK OF THE WOODS
NEGATIVE PROTON
NERVOUS IMPULSE
NEVER NEVER LAND
NEWS CONFERENCE
NEWSPAPER WOMAN
NIGHT BLINDNESS
NIGHT FLOWERING
NIGHT FOSSICKER
NIL DESPERANDUM
NIMBLE FINGERED
NINE DAYS WONDER
NINE HOLE COURSE
NINE MENS MORRIS
NINETEENTH HOLE
NIPPED IN THE BUD
NO WIN SITUATION
NOBLESSE OBLIGE
NODDING THROUGH
NON COMMUNICANT
NON DESTRUCTIVE
NON INVOLVEMENT
NORMAN CONQUEST
NORTH EASTWARDS
NORTH NORTH EAST
NORTH NORTH WEST
NORTH WESTWARDS

NORTHERN LIGHTS
NOT ON YOUR NELLY
NOUVEAUX RICHES
NUCLEAR FISSION
NUCLEAR PHYSICS
NUCLEAR REACTOR
NUCLEAR WARFARE
NUCLEAR WARHEAD
NUMBER CRUNCHER
NURSING OFFICER
NYLON STOCKINGS
OBITUARY NOTICE
OBJECT OF VIRTUE
OBSERVATION CAR
OCCULT SCIENCES
OCEAN GREYHOUND
OCEANIC ISLANDS
ODD COME SHORTLY
OEDIPUS COMPLEX
OF NO FIXED ABODE
OFF ONES TROLLEY
OFF THE SHOULDER
OFF WITH HER HEAD
OFF WITH HIS HEAD
OFFER AN OPINION
OFFSET PRINTING
OILED THE WHEELS
OLD ESTABLISHED
OLD GENTLEMANLY
OLD MAN OF THE SEA
OLD PEOPLES HOME
OLD TIME DANCING
OMNIBUS EDITION
ON ONES BEAM ENDS
ON ONES DOORSTEP
ON ONES HEAD BE IT
ON ONES LAST LEGS
ON SUBSCRIPTION
ON THE BANDWAGON
ON THE BREADLINE
ON THE DEFENSIVE
ON THE OFF CHANCE
ON THE OUTSKIRTS
ON THE RIGHT TACK
ON THE SHOP FLOOR
ON THE THRESHOLD
ON THE WINDY SIDE
ONE ARMED BANDIT
ONE OF THESE DAYS
OPEN CAST MINING
OPEN DOOR POLICY
OPEN HANDEDNESS
OPEN MINDEDNESS
OPEN THE INNINGS
OPEN THE SCORING
OPEN TOURNAMENT
OPEN UNIVERSITY
OPENING BATSMAN
OPENING BATSMEN
OPENS ONES HEART

14 *contd.*
OPERATING TABLE
OPPOSITE NUMBER
ORANGE COLOURED
ORANGE SQUEEZER
ORDER IN COUNCIL
ORDER OF THE BATH
ORDER OF THE BOOT
ORDERING AROUND
ORDERLY OFFICER
ORDINAL NUMBERS
ORDINARY SEAMAN
ORDINARY SHARES
ORDNANCE SURVEY
ORGAN HARMONIUM
OSTEO ARTHRITIS
OSTRICH FEATHER
OTHER FISH TO FRY
OUT FOR THE COUNT
OUT OF CHARACTER
OUT OF CONDITION
OUT OF ONES DEPTH
OUT OF THIS WORLD
OVER MY DEAD BODY
OVER THE COUNTER
OXFORD MOVEMENT
PACED UP AND DOWN
PACES UP AND DOWN
PACKAGE HOLIDAY
PACKED ONES BAGS
PACKET OF CRISPS
PACKING STATION
PADDING THE HOOF
PADDINGTON BEAR
PAGE BOY HAIRCUT
PAID LIP SERVICE
PAINTED THE LILY
PAIR OF SCISSORS
PAIR OF TROUSERS
PAIR OF TWEEZERS
PAISLEY PATTERN
PAN AMERICANISM
PANCAKE TUESDAY
PANORAMIC SIGHT
PANZER DIVISION
PAPER TAPE PUNCH
PAPERS THE HOUSE
PAPUA NEW GUINEA
PARALLEL MOTION
PARALLEL SLALOM
PARAMOUNT CHIEF
PARCHMENT PAPER
PARDON MY FRENCH
PARISH MAGAZINE
PARISH MINISTER
PARISH REGISTER
PARLIAMENT CAKE
PARLOUR BOARDER
PARMESAN CHEESE
PAROCHIAL BOARD

PARTIAL ECLIPSE
PARTING COMPANY
PARTRIDGE BERRY
PASSED JUDGMENT
PASSED ONES WORD
PASSED SENTENCE
PASSENGER TRAIN
PASSES JUDGMENT
PASSES ONES WORD
PASSES SENTENCE
PASSING CURRENT
PASSING THE BUCK
PASSING THE TIME
PASSING THROUGH
PASSIVE SMOKING
PAST PARTICIPLE
PASTORAL CHARGE
PATCHWORK QUILT
PATE DE FOIE GRAS
PATELLAR REFLEX
PATENT MEDICINE
PATERNITY LEAVE
PAVEMENT ARTIST
PAY FOR ONES SINS
PAYING BY CHEQUE
PAYING THE PIPER
PAYING THE PRICE
PAYS LIP SERVICE
PEARLS OF WISDOM
PEASANTS REVOLT
PECTORAL GIRDLE
PEDESTRIAN DECK
PEER OF THE REALM
PENAL SERVITUDE
PENNY FOR THE GUY
PENNY IN THE SLOT
PEPPERCORN RENT
PEPPERMINT DROP
PERCUSSION FUSE
PERCUSSION LOCK
PERFECT BINDING
PERFECT CADENCE
PERFORMANCE ART
PERFORMING ARTS
PERFORMING FLEA
PERFORMING SEAL
PERIODIC SYSTEM
PERMANENT PRESS
PERMANENT TEETH
PERPETUAL CHECK
PERSON TO PERSON
PERSONAL COLUMN
PERSONAL ESTATE
PERSONAL RIGHTS
PERSONAL STEREO
PETER PAN COLLAR
PETER PRINCIPLE
PETIT BATTEMENT
PETIT BOURGEOIS
PETROLEUM JELLY

PETTICOAT TAILS
PETTY CONSTABLE
PHAEDRA COMPLEX
PHANTOM CIRCUIT
PHOSPHOR BRONZE
PHOSPHORIC ACID
PHOTO ENGRAVING
PHOTOFLOOD LAMP
PIANO ACCORDION
PICCADILLY LINE
PICK AN ARGUMENT
PICK OF THE BUNCH
PICKED AND CHOSE
PICKED ONES SPOT
PICKED TO PIECES
PICKED UP THE TAB
PICKING ONES WAY
PICKING UP SPEED
PICKLED CABBAGE
PICKLED HERRING
PICKLED WALNUTS
PICTURE GALLERY
PICTURE WRITING
PIECED TOGETHER
PIECES TOGETHER
PIG IN THE MIDDLE
PIGEON FANCYING
PILE ON THE AGONY
PILGRIM FATHERS
PILLARS OF ISLAM
PILLOW FIGHTING
PIN STRIPED SUIT
PINBALL MACHINE
PINCER MOVEMENT
PINEAPPLE JUICE
PINS AND NEEDLES
PISTOL WHIPPING
PIT BULL TERRIER
PITUITARY GLAND
PLACE OF WORSHIP
PLACED ON RECORD
PLACES ON RECORD
PLAGUE OF LONDON
PLAGUE STRICKEN
PLAIN AND SIMPLE
PLAIN CHOCOLATE
PLANING MACHINE
PLANNED ECONOMY
PLANNING BLIGHT
PLANTATION SONG
PLASTER OF PARIS
PLASTIC SURGEON
PLASTIC SURGERY
PLATE TECTONICS
PLATFORM TICKET
PLATINUM BLONDE
PLAY TO THE CROWD
PLAYED FOR A DRAW
PLAYED THE DEVIL
PLAYED THE FIELD

14 *contd.*

PLAYED WITH FIRE
PLAYING FOOTSIE
PLAYING FOR TIME
PLAYING IT BY EAR
PLAYING ONES ACE
PLAYING THE FOOL
PLAYING THE GAME
PLAYING THE LEAD
PLAYS HARD TO GET
PLAYS ONES HUNCH
PLAYS THE MARKET
PLAYS THE WANTON
PLEA BARGAINING
PLEAD IGNORANCE
PLEAD NOT GUILTY
PLEASE TURN OVER
PLEASE YOURSELF
PLEASED AS PUNCH
PLEASURE GIVING
PLEASURE GROUND
PLEASURE SEEKER
PLOTTED A COURSE
PLOUGH THE SANDS
PLOUGHING MATCH
PLOUGHS THROUGH
PLUCK UP COURAGE
PLUMB THE DEPTHS
PLUTO DEMOCRACY
PNEUMATIC DRILL
POCKET AN INSULT
POETRY IN MOTION
POKE ONES NOSE IN
POKING IN THE EYE
POLICE SERGEANT
POLISHING PASTE
POLISHING SLATE
POLITICAL PARTY
POLLEN ANALYSIS
POLLING STATION
POLO NECK JUMPER
PONTEFRACT CAKE
PONTIFICAL MASS
POP THE QUESTION
PORCUPINE GRASS
PORTLAND CEMENT
POSING A PROBLEM
POSITIVE ACTION
POSSE COMITATUS
POSSESSIVE CASE
POST MILLENNIAL
POSTAL DISTRICT
POURED WITH RAIN
POURING SCORN ON
POWDER MAGAZINE
POWDER ONES NOSE
POWER BREAKFAST
POWER OF THE KEYS
PRACTICAL JOKER
PRAETORIAN GATE

PRAIRIE CHICKEN
PRAYING FOR RAIN
PRE ESTABLISHED
PRE ESTABLISHES
PRE RAPHAELITES
PRE REFORMATION
PREACHING CROSS
PREACHING FRIAR
PREACHING HOUSE
PRECIOUS LITTLE
PRECIOUS METALS
PRECIOUS STONES
PREENED ONESELF
PREPARED SPEECH
PRESENCE OF MIND
PRESIDENT ELECT
PRESS THE BUTTON
PRESSED FLOWERS
PRESSED FOR TIME
PRESSED FORWARD
PRESSES FORWARD
PRESSURE COOKED
PRESSURE COOKER
PRESSURE HELMET
PREVAILING WIND
PRICK THE GARTER
PRIMA BALLERINA
PRIMARY BATTERY
PRIMARY COLOURS
PRIMORDIAL SOUP
PRIMROSE LEAGUE
PRINCE CHARMING
PRINCE IMPERIAL
PRINCES FEATHER
PRINCIPAL FOCUS
PRINCIPAL PARTS
PRINTED CIRCUIT
PRINTING OFFICE
PRISON BREAKING
PRISONERS OF WAR
PRITTLE PRATTLE
PRIVATE BAPTISM
PRIVATE COMPANY
PRO BONO PUBLICO
PROCESS CONTROL
PRODUCTION LINE
PROGRAMME MUSIC
PROMISE BREAKER
PROMISE KEEPING
PROMISSORY NOTE
PROOF CORRECTED
PROPELLER BLADE
PROPELLER SHAFT
PROPER FRACTION
PROPERTY MASTER
PROSCENIUM ARCH
PROTECTED STATE
PROVIDED SCHOOL
PROVINCIAL ROSE
PROVOST MARSHAL

PROXIMATE CAUSE
PTERYGOID PLATE
PUBLIC DEFENDER
PUBLIC NUISANCE
PUBLIC SPEAKING
PUBLIC SPENDING
PUBLIC SPIRITED
PUERPERAL FEVER
PULL ONES WEIGHT
PULL THE LONG BOW
PULL THE STRINGS
PULLED A FAST ONE
PULLED A FLANKER
PULLED TO PIECES
PULLED TOGETHER
PULLING STRINGS
PULLING THROUGH
PULLS THE PLUG ON
PUMPING STATION
PUNCH ON THE NOSE
PURPLE COLOURED
PURSE SNATCHING
PUSH THE BOAT OUT
PUSHED ONES LUCK
PUSHES ONES LUCK
PUSHING THROUGH
PUT IN MOTHBALLS
PUT THE KIBOSH ON
PUT THE SCREWS ON
PUT THE TIN HAT ON
PUTS IN THE SHADE
PUTS IN THE WRONG
PUTS ONES FACE ON
PUTS ONES FEET UP
PUTS ONES MIND TO
PUTS OUT TO GRAZE
PUTS THE BRAKE ON
PUTS THE LID ON IT
PUTS THE SKIDS ON
PUTS TO THE SWORD
PUTTING A STOP TO
PUTTING AN END TO
PUTTING FORWARD
PUTTING ON AN ACT
PUTTING ON TRIAL
PUTTING THE SHOT
PUTTING THROUGH
PUTTING TO DEATH
PUTTING TO SHAME
PUTTING TO SLEEP
PYJAMA TROUSERS
PYRAMID SELLING
PYRRHIC VICTORY
QUALITY CONTROL
QUARANTINE FLAG
QUART AND TIERCE
QUARTER GALLERY
QUARTER SECTION
QUARTZ PORPHYRY
QUEEN ANNE STYLE

14 *contd.*

QUEEN ANNES DEAD
QUEEN ELIZABETH
QUEENS EVIDENCE
QUEERS THE PITCH
QUESTION MASTER
QUESTION OF FACT
QUICHE LORRAINE
QUICK ON THE DRAW
QUILTING COTTON
QUITE SOMETHING
QUOTATION MARKS
QWERTY KEYBOARD
RABBETING PLANE
RABBIT SQUIRREL
RACK ONES BRAINS
RACKED WITH PAIN
RADAR ALTIMETER
RADIAL SYMMETRY
RADIAL VELOCITY
RADIATION BELTS
RADIO ALTIMETER
RADIO ASTRONOMY
RADIO FREQUENCY
RADIO STRONTIUM
RADIO TELESCOPE
RAIDS THE MARKET
RAILWAY CUTTING
RAISE AN EYEBROW
RAISE ONES GLASS
RAISE ONES VOICE
RAISE THE MARKET
RAISED THE ALARM
RAISES THE ALARM
RAISING ONES HAT
RAISING THE ROOF
RAISING THE WIND
RAN IN THE FAMILY
RAN INTO TROUBLE
RAN OUT OF PETROL
RAN THE GAUNTLET
RAN THE RULE OVER
RANG THE CHANGES
RANGING ONESELF
RANTED AND RAVED
RAPID PROMOTION
RATE OF EXCHANGE
RATIONAL NUMBER
REACH A DECISION
READ THE RIOT ACT
READING GLASSES
READING MACHINE
READS LIKE A BOOK
REAPING MACHINE
REAR VIEW MIRROR
RECEIVING HOUSE
RECEIVING ORDER
RECEPTION CLASS
RECEPTION ORDER
RECITATION ROOM

RECORD BREAKING
RECORDING ANGEL
REDUCED TO TEARS
REDUCES TO TEARS
REDUCTION WORKS
REED INSTRUMENT
REFECTORY TABLE
REGISTER OFFICE
REGISTERED POST
REGISTRY OFFICE
REIGNED SUPREME
RELAPSING FEVER
RELEASED ON BAIL
REMAINED SILENT
REMEMBRANCE DAY
REMITTENT FEVER
RENAISSANCE MAN
REPEATS ONESELF
REPORTED SPEECH
REPORTED VERSES
RESERVED A TABLE
RESERVES A TABLE
RESISTANCE COIL
RESOLVING POWER
REST ON ONES OARS
RESTRICTED AREA
REVENGE IS SWEET
REVEREND MOTHER
REVERSING LAYER
REVERSING LIGHT
REVISED EDITION
REVISED VERSION
REVOLVING DOORS
REYNOLDS NUMBER
RHEUMATIC FEVER
RHINOCEROS BIRD
RHODE ISLAND RED
RHUBARB RHUBARB
RHYMING COUPLET
RHYMING TO DEATH
RHYTHM AND BLUES
RIBBON BUILDING
RIDES ROUGH SHOD
RIDING BREECHES
RIDING FOR A FALL
RIDING THE STANG
RIDING THE WAVES
RIDING TO HOUNDS
RIGHT HAND DRIVE
RIGHTED THE HELM
RIGHTING WRONGS
RING THE CHANGES
RINGING THE BELL
RISES TO THE BAIT
RISKED ONES LIFE
RITES OF PASSAGE
RIVER BLINDNESS
ROAD WORKS AHEAD
ROARING FORTIES
ROBINSON CRUSOE

ROCHELLE POWDER
ROCKET LAUNCHER
ROCKING THE BOAT
ROD POLE OR PERCH
ROGATION FLOWER
ROGATION SUNDAY
ROLL NECK JUMPER
ROLLED ONES EYES
ROMEO AND JULIET
ROMPING THROUGH
ROOF OF THE MOUTH
ROOF OF THE WORLD
ROPE SOLED SHOES
ROSES ALL THE WAY
ROUGH AND TUMBLE
ROUND THE HOUSES
ROUND THE WICKET
ROVING REPORTER
ROYAL ARTILLERY
ROYAL ENGINEERS
ROYAL FUSILIERS
ROYAL HOUSEHOLD
ROYAL TANK CORPS
RUBBER SOLUTION
RUBBER STAMPING
RULING THE ROAST
RULING THE ROOST
RUN FOR DEAR LIFE
RUN IN THE FAMILY
RUN INTO TROUBLE
RUN OUT OF PETROL
RUN THE GAUNTLET
RUN THE RULE OVER
RUNNING BANQUET
RUNNING ERRANDS
RUNNING FOOTMAN
RUNNING REPAIRS
RUNNING RIGGING
RUNNING THE SHOW
RUNNING THROUGH
RUNNING TO EARTH
RUNS A TIGHT SHIP
RUNS IN THE BLOOD
RUNS OUT OF STEAM
RUNS RINGS ROUND
RUSH ONES FENCES
RUSHED HEADLONG
RUSHES HEADLONG
RUSSO BYZANTINE
SABBATH BREAKER
SABBATICAL YEAR
SACK OF POTATOES
SACRAMENT HOUSE
SADDLE OF MUTTON
SAFE DEPOSIT BOX
SAFFRON MILK CAP
SALES ASSISTANT
SALMON COLOURED
SALOON CARRIAGE
SALT OF THE EARTH

14 *contd.*
SALT OF WORMWOOD
SALTPETRE PAPER
SANDWICH COURSE
SAPPHIRE QUARTZ
SAT ON ONES HANDS
SATELLITE STATE
SATEM LANGUAGES
SAUCE ESPAGNOLE
SAUSAGE AND MASH
SAVED BY THE BELL
SAVED ONES BACON
SAVES ONES BACON
SAVING ONES FACE
SAVING ONES NECK
SAVING ONES SKIN
SAVINGS ACCOUNT
SAWN OFF SHOTGUN
SCATTER BRAINED
SCHOOL HOLIDAYS
SCHOOL TEACHING
SCHOONER RIGGED
SCIENCE FICTION
SCOOPED THE POOL
SCORE AN OWN GOAL
SCORPION SPIDER
SCOTCH ATTORNEY
SCOTCH BLUEBELL
SCOTCH WOODCOCK
SCRATCHING POST
SCREAMING FARCE
SCREEN PRINTING
SCREW PROPELLER
SCRIBBLING BOOK
SCRUBBING BOARD
SCRUBBING BRUSH
SCRUBBING ROUND
SEAT OF THE PANTS
SECOND HAND SHOP
SECOND MORTGAGE
SECOND THOUGHTS
SECOND WORLD WAR
SECONDARY RADAR
SEEING DAYLIGHT
SEEING EYE TO EYE
SEEING THE LIGHT
SEIDLITZ POWDER
SELF ABSORPTION
SELF ADMIRATION
SELF ASSUMPTION
SELF COMMITMENT
SELF COMPLACENT
SELF CONFIDENCE
SELF CONVICTION
SELF CORRECTING
SELF DEPENDENCE
SELF DETERMINED
SELF DEVELOPING
SELF DISCIPLINE
SELF EFFACEMENT

SELF EMPLOYMENT
SELF FLATTERING
SELF FULFILLING
SELF FULFILMENT
SELF GOVERNMENT
SELF IMMOLATION
SELF IMPORTANCE
SELF INDULGENCE
SELF INTERESTED
SELF JUSTIFYING
SELF MANAGEMENT
SELF POSSESSION
SELF PROCLAIMED
SELF PROPELLING
SELF PROPULSION
SELF PROTECTING
SELF PROTECTION
SELF PROTECTIVE
SELF REGULATING
SELF REGULATION
SELF REGULATORY
SELF RESPECTFUL
SELF RESPECTING
SELF SATISFYING
SELF SUFFICIENT
SELF SUPPORTING
SEMI CENTENNIAL
SEMI ELLIPTICAL
SEMI OFFICIALLY
SEND TO COVENTRY
SENDING PACKING
SENILE DEMENTIA
SENIOR WRANGLER
SENSATION NOVEL
SENSITIVE FLAME
SENSITIVE PLANT
SENT TO COVENTRY
SEROUS MEMBRANE
SERPENT GODDESS
SERPENT WORSHIP
SERUM HEPATITIS
SERVE WITH A WRIT
SERVED A PURPOSE
SERVES A PURPOSE
SERVICE STATION
SERVO MECHANISM
SET ONES HEART ON
SETS ONES MIND TO
SETS ONES SEAL ON
SETTING IN ORDER
SETTING LIGHT TO
SETTING THE PACE
SETTING TO MUSIC
SETTING UP HOUSE
SHAGGY DOG STORY
SHAKES ONES FIST
SHAKES ONES HEAD
SHALOM ALEICHEM
SHARPS AND FLATS
SHAWL WAISTCOAT

SHEEPDOG TRIALS
SHEET LIGHTNING
SHEFFIELD PLATE
SHEFFIELD STEEL
SHELF CATALOGUE
SHEPHERDS CHECK
SHEPHERDS CROOK
SHEPHERDS GLASS
SHEPHERDS PLAID
SHEPHERDS PURSE
SHERIFF OFFICER
SHERLOCK HOLMES
SHERWOOD FOREST
SHIFTED ONESELF
SHIFTING BOARDS
SHILLY SHALLIER
SHIPPED THE OARS
SHIPS CARPENTER
SHOCK TREATMENT
SHOOTING JACKET
SHOOTS THE WORKS
SHOPPING ARCADE
SHOPPING AROUND
SHOPPING BASKET
SHOPPING CENTRE
SHORT SIGHTEDLY
SHORTENING SAIL
SHOT FROM THE HIP
SHOT GUN WEDDING
SHOULDER GIRDLE
SHOULDER HEIGHT
SHOULDER OF LAMB
SHOULDER OF VEAL
SHOUTED THE ODDS
SHOVE HALFPENNY
SHOWED ONES FACE
SHOWED ONES HAND
SHOWING ONES AGE
SHOWING PROMISE
SHOWING THE FLAG
SHOWING WILLING
SHOWS ONES PACES
SHUTTING UP SHOP
SHUTTLE SERVICE
SIEGE ARTILLERY
SIGN OF THE CROSS
SIGN OF THE TIMES
SIGNS THE PLEDGE
SILENCE IN COURT
SILENT MAJORITY
SILVER PHEASANT
SIMPLE FRACTION
SIMPLE FRACTURE
SIMPLE INTEREST
SIMPLE SENTENCE
SIMULATED PEARL
SINGING GALLERY
SINGLE BREASTED
SINGS LIKE A BIRD
SISTERS OF MERCY

14 *contd.*

SISTINE MADONNA
SIT ON ONES HANDS
SITS IN JUDGMENT
SITS ON THE FENCE
SKATE ON THIN ICE
SKIMBLE SKAMBLE
SLAP BANG WALLOP
SLAP ON THE WRIST
SLEEPING BEAUTY
SLEEPS LIKE A LOG
SLEEPS LIKE A TOP
SLEEPY SICKNESS
SLINGING THE BAT
SLINGS ONES HOOK
SMACKS ONES LIPS
SMALL OF THE BACK
SMELL OF THE LAMP
SMELLING BOTTLE
SMELT OF THE LAMP
SMOKING CONCERT
SMOOTHING PLANE
SNAGGLE TOOTHED
SNAPPING TURTLE
SNOW SHOE RABBIT
SNOW SPECTACLES
SOCIAL CONTRACT
SOCIAL DEMOCRAT
SOCIAL SECURITY
SOCIAL SERVICES
SODIUM CHLORIDE
SOFT UNDERBELLY
SOLE BONNE FEMME
SOLITAIRE BOARD
SOMEONE OR OTHER
SOUL DESTROYING
SOUNDS THE ALARM
SOUTH EASTWARDS
SOUTH SOUTH EAST
SOUTH WESTWARDS
SOVEREIGN STATE
SPACE TRAVELLER
SPADE HUSBANDRY
SPARE MY BLUSHES
SPAWNING GROUND
SPEAKERS CORNER
SPEAKS ONES MIND
SPECIAL LICENCE
SPECIAL VERDICT
SPECIFIC LEGACY
SPECTATOR SPORT
SPEECH TRAINING
SPEEDY RECOVERY
SPELLS BACKWARD
SPENDING A PENNY
SPILLS THE BEANS
SPINDLE SHANKED
SPIT AND SAWDUST
SPLIT ONES SIDES
SPLITTING HAIRS

SPORTED ONES OAK
SPORTING CHANCE
SPRING CARRIAGE
SPRING CLEANING
SPRING LIGAMENT
SPRING MATTRESS
SPRINGING A LEAK
SPROUTING WINGS
SQUADRON LEADER
SQUEAKS THROUGH
SQUIRREL MONKEY
ST ANDREWS CROSS
ST ANTHONYS FIRE
ST GEORGES CROSS
STABS IN THE BACK
STACKED AGAINST
STAGE DIRECTION
STAGED A PROTEST
STAGES A PROTEST
STAINLESS STEEL
STAKED ONES LIFE
STAKES ONES LIFE
STAMP COLLECTOR
STAMPING GROUND
STAND CORRECTED
STANDARD BEARER
STANDING GROUND
STANDING ORDERS
STANDING TO GAIN
STANDING TO LOSE
STANDS ON TIPTOE
STANDS ONES HAND
STANDS TO REASON
STANNARY COURTS
STAR OF THE EARTH
STAR OF THE NIGHT
STARTING BLOCKS
STARTING HANDLE
STARTING PISTOL
STATE OF AFFAIRS
STATION MANAGER
STATIONERS HALL
STAYING THE PACE
STAYS THE COURSE
STEADY THE BUFFS
STEAL A MARRIAGE
STEALS A MARCH ON
STEEL ENGRAVING
STEEPLE CROWNED
STEERING COLUMN
STEMMED THE TIDE
STEP ON THE JUICE
STEPS OUT OF LINE
STICK AT NOTHING
STICK ONES OAR IN
STICKING AROUND
STICKS OUT A MILE
STICKS TOGETHER
STICKY FINGERED
STILETTO HEELED

STILLSON WRENCH
STINKING BADGER
STIR ONES STUMPS
STIRLING ENGINE
STIRRING ABROAD
STIRRUP LEATHER
STOCK CAR RACING
STOCKING FILLER
STOCKING STITCH
STOLE A MARRIAGE
STOMPING GROUND
STONE COLD SOBER
STOOD CORRECTED
STOOGING AROUND
STOPPED THE SHOW
STOPPING THE ROT
STOPS AT NOTHING
STORAGE BATTERY
STORAGE HEATING
STOUT HEARTEDLY
STRADDLE LEGGED
STRAIGHT AS A DIE
STRAIGHT TICKET
STRAIGHTENS OUT
STRAINED A POINT
STRAW IN THE WIND
STRAWBERRY LEAF
STRAWBERRY MARK
STRAWBERRY ROAN
STRETCHING IRON
STRIATED MUSCLE
STRIKE A BARGAIN
STRIKE BREAKING
STRIKES THROUGH
STRIKING A CHORD
STRIKING A MATCH
STRIKING BOTTOM
STRIKING CIRCLE
STRIKING IT RICH
STRING OF ONIONS
STRING OF PEARLS
STRINGING ALONG
STROKE OF GENIUS
STRONG LANGUAGE
STRUCK A BARGAIN
STRUT ONES STUFF
STUBBED ONES TOE
STUCK AT NOTHING
STUCK ONES OAR IN
STUDIO AUDIENCE
STUMBLING BLOCK
STUMBLING STONE
SUBJECT HEADING
SUCCESSION DUTY
SUCKS ONES THUMB
SUFFICE IT TO SAY
SUGAR PLUM FAIRY
SUGARED THE PILL
SUITED ONES BOOK
SUITING ONESELF

14 contd.

SULPHUR DIOXIDE
SULPHUROUS ACID
SUMMARY OFFENCE
SUMMER OLYMPICS
SUMMER SOLSTICE
SUPER FLYWEIGHT
SUPPORTERS CLUB
SUPPORTING FILM
SURFACE TENSION
SURGEON GENERAL
SURGICAL SPIRIT
SURRENDER VALUE
SUSPEND PAYMENT
SWARM OF LOCUSTS
SWEEPS THE BOARD
SWELLS THE RANKS
SWIMMING TRUNKS
SWORD SWALLOWER
SYMPATHETIC INK
SYSTEM BUILDING
SYSTEM SOFTWARE
SYSTEMS ANALYST
TABLE SPOONFULS
TABLING A MOTION
TACTICAL VOTING
TACTICAL WEAPON
TAIL END CHARLIE
TAKE A RAINCHECK
TAKE FOR GRANTED
TAKE ONES CHANCE
TAKE ONES CHOICE
TAKE THE BISCUIT
TAKE UP THE SLACK
TAKEOVER BIDDER
TAKES A BACK SEAT
TAKES EXCEPTION
TAKES IN LODGERS
TAKES LIBERTIES
TAKES ONES LEAVE
TAKES THE LID OFF
TAKES THE MICKEY
TAKES THE PLUNGE
TAKES TO ONES BED
TAKES TO THE ROAD
TAKING A BEATING
TAKING A PRIDE IN
TAKING A SHINE TO
TAKING DOWN A PEG
TAKING FOR A RIDE
TAKING MEASURES
TAKING ONES SEAT
TAKING ONES TIME
TAKING ONES TURN
TAKING PRISONER
TAKING THE BLAME
TAKING THE FIELD
TAKING THE FLOOR
TAKING THE REINS
TAKING TO PIECES

TALK DOWN SYSTEM
TALK IN A WHISPER
TALK OF THE DEVIL
TALKING MACHINE
TALKS IN RIDDLES
TALLOW CHANDLER
TARGET LANGUAGE
TARGET PRACTICE
TASMANIAN DEVIL
TAXED TO THE HILT
TEARS A STRIP OFF
TECHNICAL HITCH
TELEGRAPH BOARD
TELEGRAPH CABLE
TELEPHONE BOOTH
TELEPHONE KIOSK
TEMPERATE ZONES
TERRA INCOGNITA
TERROR STRICKEN
TERTIUS GAUDENS
THANKS A MILLION
THATLL BE THE DAY
THATLL TEACH HER
THATLL TEACH HIM
THATLL TEACH YOU
THE BEATEN TRACK
THE BUTLER DID IT
THE CATS PYJAMAS
THE ETERNAL CITY
THE GOOD OLD DAYS
THE GREAT BEYOND
THE HIGHWAY CODE
THE HUNDRED DAYS
THE LAP OF LUXURY
THE LIFE AND SOUL
THE LIFE OF RILEY
THE MIND BOGGLES
THE ROARING GAME
THE SEVEN DWARFS
THE SIX COUNTIES
THE UGLY SISTERS
THE UNDERGROUND
THE VELVET GLOVE
THE VIRGIN QUEEN
THERMAL BARRIER
THERMAL IMAGING
THERMAL REACTOR
THERMAL SPRINGS
THERMO ELECTRIC
THIEVES KITCHEN
THIMBLE RIGGING
THINKS THE WORST
THIRD DIMENSION
THIRD PROGRAMME
THIRD TIME LUCKY
THORN IN THE SIDE
THOUGHT OUT LOUD
THOUGHT PROCESS
THOUGHT READING
THOUGHT THROUGH

THREE BOTTLE MAN
THREE CARD MONTE
THREE CARD TRICK
THREE FARTHINGS
THREE HALFPENCE
THREE HALFPENNY
THREE MILE LIMIT
THREE POINT TURN
THREE SPEED GEAR
THRESHING FLOOR
THREW IN ONES LOT
THREW OVERBOARD
THREW THE BOOK AT
THREW UP ONES CAP
THRILLED TO BITS
THROTTLING DOWN
THROUGH THE NOSE
THROUGH TRAFFIC
THROW IN ONES LOT
THROW OF THE DICE
THROW OVERBOARD
THROW THE BOOK AT
THROW UP ONES CAP
THROWING A PARTY
THROWING A PUNCH
THROWN TOGETHER
THROWS TOGETHER
THUMBS ONES NOSE
TICKLED TO DEATH
TICKLES TO DEATH
TIPPED THE SCALE
TIPPING ONES HAT
TIPPING THE WINK
TIPS THE BALANCE
TITTLE TATTLING
TO THE NTH DEGREE
TOBACCO STOPPER
TOING AND FROING
TOOK A RAINCHECK
TOOK FOR GRANTED
TOOK ONES CHANCE
TOOK ONES CHOICE
TOOK THE BISCUIT
TOOK UP THE SLACK
TOP OF THE LEAGUE
TOPPING THE BILL
TORSION BALANCE
TORTURE CHAMBER
TOTAL ABSTAINER
TOTAL DEPRAVITY
TOUCHING BOTTOM
TOWN COUNCILLOR
TRACTION ENGINE
TRAFFIC SIGNALS
TRAIN OF THOUGHT
TRANSFER TICKET
TRANSVERSE WAVE
TRAP DOOR SPIDER
TRAVEL SICKNESS
TRAVELLERS TALE

14 *contd.*

TRAVELLING FOLK	UPWARD MOBILITY	WATCHMANS CLOCK
TREAD THE BOARDS	UPWARDLY MOBILE	WATER BAROMETER
TREADS A MEASURE	URBAN GUERRILLA	WATER BREATHING
TREASURE ISLAND	UTTER BARRISTER	WATER COLOURIST
TREATS LIKE DIRT	VALET DE CHAMBRE	WATER ON THE KNEE
TREE WORSHIPPER	VANISHING CREAM	WATER PIMPERNEL
TRIFACIAL NERVE	VANISHING POINT	WATER REPELLENT
TRIMS ONES SAILS	VASCULAR BUNDLE	WATERING TROUGH
TRIPLE ALLIANCE	VASCULAR PLANTS	WEAK AT THE KNEES
TRIVIAL PURSUIT	VATICAN COUNCIL	WEAK MINDEDNESS
TROCHLEAR NERVE	VEGETABLE MOULD	WEARING APPAREL
TROOP THE COLOUR	VEGETARIAN DIET	WEATHER STATION
TRUMPET TONGUED	VEGETARIAN DISH	WEATHERED ALONG
TRUST TERRITORY	VENDING MACHINE	WEEDING FORCEPS
TRUSTEE ACCOUNT	VENETIAN MOSAIC	WEIGHING ANCHOR
TRYING ONES LUCK	VENT ONES SPLEEN	WEIGHT WATCHING
TUNER AMPLIFIER	VENTURE CAPITAL	WEIMAR REPUBLIC
TURBINE STEAMER	VERSE MONGERING	WELCOMED ABOARD
TURBO GENERATOR	VERTICAL ANGLES	WELCOMES ABOARD
TURF ACCOUNTANT	VERTICAL CIRCLE	WELFARE OFFICER
TURKEY MERCHANT	VESTED INTEREST	WELL THOUGHT OUT
TURKISH DELIGHT	VICAR APOSTOLIC	WEMBLEY STADIUM
TURN ON ONES HEEL	VICE CHANCELLOR	WENDING ONES WAY
TURN ONES HAND TO	VICE CONSULSHIP	WENT BY THE BOARD
TURN THE STOMACH	VICE PRESIDENCY	WENT FOR NOTHING
TURN UP ONES NOSE	VIENNESE FINGER	WENT INTO DETAIL
TURNED A DEAF EAR	VIRTUAL REALITY	WENT INTO HIDING
TURNED ONES HEAD	VISIBLE EXPORTS	WENT LIKE A DREAM
TURNED THE SCREW	VISIBLE HORIZON	WENT ON ALL FOURS
TURNED UP TRUMPS	VISIBLE IMPORTS	WENT ONES OWN WAY
TURNING AGAINST	VITAL FUNCTIONS	WENT OVER THE TOP
TURNING THE TIDE	VITAL PRINCIPLE	WENT TO EXTREMES
TURNKEY PACKAGE	VITREOUS HUMOUR	WENT TO ONES HEAD
TURNS A BLIND EYE	VITRIFIED FORTS '	WENT UP IN THE AIR
TURNS INSIDE OUT	VITRIFIED WALLS	WET AND DRY PAPER
TURNS THE CORNER	VOTIVE OFFERING	WET ONES WHISTLE
TURNS THE TABLES	VOWEL GRADATION	WHATS UP WITH YOU
TURQUOISE GREEN	VULGAR FRACTION	WHEAT EAR STITCH
TURTLE GRAPHICS	VULPINE OPOSSUM	WHEEL OF FORTUNE
TWO DIMENSIONAL	WAIFS AND STRAYS	WHEELER DEALING
TWO FOR HIS HEELS	WAITING AT TABLE	WHEELS AND DEALS
TYING UP IN KNOTS	WAITS PATIENTLY	WHIPLASH INJURY
ULTERIOR MOTIVE	WALK A TIGHT ROPE	WHIPPING THE CAT
UNACCOUNTED FOR	WALK THE STREETS	WHIPS INTO SHAPE
UNCROWNED QUEEN	WALKED ON TIPTOE	WHISPERING DOME
UNDER CONSTABLE	WALKED THE PLANK	WHISTLE BLOWING
UNDER NOURISHED	WALKING WOUNDED	WHITE BLOOD CELL
UNDER ONES THUMB	WALKS UP AND DOWN	WHITE CHRISTMAS
UNDER PRODUCING	WALPURGIS NIGHT	WHITE CORPUSCLE
UNDER SECRETARY	WANDERING NERVE	WHITE HEADED BOY
UNDER SUSPICION	WANTING JAM ON IT	WHITLEY COUNCIL
UNDER THE HAMMER	WAR OF SECESSION	WHOLE HEARTEDLY
UNDUE INFLUENCE	WARD IN CHANCERY	WHOLEMEAL BREAD
UNEARNED INCOME	WARRANT OFFICER	WIDENING THE GAP
UNITED BRETHREN	WARS OF THE ROSES	WIDOW BEWITCHED
UNIVERSAL DONOR	WASH AND BRUSH UP	WILD ACCUSATION
UNIVERSAL JOINT	WASHING MACHINE	WILD GOOSE CHASE
UP TO ONES TRICKS	WATCH COMMITTEE	WILLESDEN PAPER
UPHILL STRUGGLE	WATCH THE BIRDIE	WILLING AND ABLE
	WATCH THIS SPACE	WILLING HEARTED

14 contd.
WILSONS DISEASE
WINCHESTER DISC
WINCHESTER DISK
WIND INSTRUMENT
WIND YOUR NECK IN
WINDOW DRESSING
WINDOW ENVELOPE
WINDOW SHOPPING
WINGING ONES WAY
WINNING BY A HEAD
WINNING BY A NECK
WINNING GALLERY
WINNING THROUGH
WINTER OLYMPICS
WINTER QUARTERS
WINTER SOLSTICE
WISH FULFILMENT
WITCHES SABBATH
WITH A VENGEANCE
WITH AN ILL GRACE
WITHERING FLOOR
WITHHOLDING TAX
WOMENS MOVEMENT
WONDER STRICKEN
WOODEN OVERCOAT
WOOLLEN DRAPERY
WORCESTER CHINA
WORCESTER SAUCE
WORD PROCESSING
WORK LIKE A CHARM
WORKED ONES WILL
WORKING AGAINST
WORKING CAPITAL
WORKING CLOTHES
WORKS COMMITTEE
WORKS THE ORACLE
WORMS ONES WAY IN
WORMWOOD SCRUBS
WORN TO A FRAZZLE
WRAP ROUND SKIRT
WRONGFUL ARREST
YELLOW JAUNDICE
YEOMANS SERVICE
YOU SHOULD WORRY
YOUNG PRETENDER
YOUR EXCELLENCY
YOURE TELLING ME
YOURS SINCERELY
YOUTH HOSTELLER
ZENITH DISTANCE
ZOOLOGICAL PARK

15

A BUNDLE OF NERVES
A CAT ON HOT BRICKS
A CHRISTMAS CAROL
A DROP IN THE OCEAN
A FISH OUT OF WATER
A HARD NUT TO CRACK

A MONTH OF SUNDAYS
A NASTY BIT OF WORK
A SLAP ON THE WRIST
A STING IN THE TAIL
A STORM IN A TEACUP
A WORD IN EDGEWAYS
ABERDEEN TERRIER
ABOVE THE WEATHER
ACT OF PARLIAMENT
ACT OF SETTLEMENT
ACTION COMMITTEE
ADJUTANT GENERAL
ADVANTAGE SERVER
AERATED CONCRETE
AFFLUENT SOCIETY
AFRICAN ELEPHANT
AFRICAN MARIGOLD
AGAINST THE CLOCK
AGAINST THE GRAIN
AGE BEFORE BEAUTY
AGE OF DISCRETION
AIDED AND ABETTED
AIR CHIEF MARSHAL
AIR CONDITIONING
AIRCRAFT CARRIER
AIREDALE TERRIER
ALIMENTARY CANAL
ALIVE AND KICKING
ALL ALONG THE LINE
ALL NIGHT SITTING
ALL OVER THE PLACE
ALL THE WORLD OVER
ALTERNATIVE VOTE
ALUMINIUM BRONZE
AMATEUR CHAMPION
AMBULANCE CHASER
AMBULANCE DRIVER
AMERICAN EXPRESS
AMUSEMENT ARCADE
ANCIENT MONUMENT
ANDERSON SHELTER
ANIMAL MAGNETISM
ANIMATED CARTOON
ANNUNCIATION DAY
ANNUS HORRIBILIS
ANOREXIA NERVOSA
ANOTHER CUP OF TEA
ANTARCTIC CIRCLE
ANTE POST BETTING
ANTENATAL CLINIC
ANTI AIRCRAFT GUN
ANTS IN ONES PANTS
ANY PORT IN A STORM
ANYONE FOR TENNIS
ARMED TO THE TEETH
ARMOURED CRUISER
ARTICLES OF FAITH
AS A MATTER OF FACT
AS KEEN AS MUSTARD
AS OLD AS THE HILLS

AS SOUND AS A ROACH
AS STEADY AS A ROCK
AS THICK AS A PLANK
AS WEAK AS A KITTEN
AS WHITE AS A SHEET
ASCEND THE THRONE
ASSERTED ONESELF
ASTRONOMER ROYAL
AT CLOSE QUARTERS
AT THE DROP OF A HAT
ATLANTIC CHARTER
ATTORNEY GENERAL
AUDIO VISUAL AIDS
AURORA AUSTRALIS
AUSTRALIAN RULES
AUTOGRAPH HUNTER
AUTUMNAL EQUINOX
AVERSION THERAPY
AXIS OF INCIDENCE
AXMINSTER CARPET
BACHELOR OF MUSIC
BACK TO SQUARE ONE
BAKEWELL PUDDING
BALACLAVA HELMET
BALL ROOM DANCING
BALLROOM DANCING
BANKRUPTCY COURT
BANQUETING HOUSE
BARGAIN BASEMENT
BARTHOLOMEW TIDE
BATCH PROCESSING
BATS IN THE BELFRY
BATTLE OF BRITAIN
BEATING A RETREAT
BEATING THE CLOCK
BEATS ONES BRAINS
BEATS ONES BREAST
BEATS THE RETREAT
BED AND BREAKFAST
BEER AND SKITTLES
BEFORE MENTIONED
BEGS THE QUESTION
BEHIND THE SCENES
BENEFIT OF CLERGY
BERMUDA TRIANGLE
BESSEMER PROCESS
BETWEEN YOU AND ME
BEWARE OF THE BULL
BEYOND SUSPICION
BEYOND THE FRINGE
BILL OF ADVENTURE
BIMETALLIC STRIP
BINARY OPERATION
BINOMIAL THEOREM
BIOLOGICAL CLOCK
BIQUADRATIC ROOT
BIRDS OF A FEATHER
BIRTHDAY HONOURS
BIRTHDAY PRESENT
BITING ONES THUMB

15 *contd.*
BITING THE BULLET
BLACKWATER FEVER
BLAST FURNACEMAN
BLEACHING POWDER
BLENHEIM SPANIEL
BLONDE BOMBSHELL
BLOOD AND THUNDER
BLOOMSBURY GROUP
BLOWING ONES MIND
BLOWS THE WHISTLE
BODY LINE BOWLING
BOLT FROM THE BLUE
BOMB CALORIMETER
BONDED WAREHOUSE
BORDEAUX MIXTURE
BORN IN THE PURPLE
BORNHOLM DISEASE
BOW STREET RUNNER
BOWED AND SCRAPED
BOXED THE COMPASS
BOXES THE COMPASS
BRAKE HORSEPOWER
BREACH OF PROMISE
BREAKFAST CEREAL
BREAKING A RECORD
BREAKING A STRIKE
BREAKING THE BANK
BREAKING THE NEWS
BREAKING THROUGH
BREAKS NEW GROUND
BREAKS ONES HEART
BREATHING FREELY
BRIDGE OF THE NOSE
BRINGING A CHARGE
BRINGING FORWARD
BRINGING TO A HEAD
BRINGING TO LIGHT
BRINGS TO ACCOUNT
BRISTLECONE PINE
BRITISH RAILWAYS
BRONZE MEDALLIST
BROTHEL CREEPERS
BROUGHT INTO LINE
BROUGHT INTO PLAY
BRUSSELS SPROUTS
BUBBLE AND SQUEAK
BUILDING SOCIETY
BULLET PROOF VEST
BUNKER MENTALITY
BURGUNDY MIXTURE
BURNING MOUNTAIN
BURNING QUESTION
BURNT AT THE STAKE
BURR IN THE THROAT
BUSINESS AS USUAL
BUSINESS VENTURE
BUTTERFLY FLOWER
BUTTERFLY ORCHID
BUTTERFLY ORCHIS

BUTTERFLY STROKE
BY HOOK OR BY CROOK
BY TRIAL AND ERROR
BYZANTINE CHURCH
BYZANTINE EMPIRE
CABINET MINISTER
CABLE TELEVISION
CALIFORNIA POPPY
CALLED TO ACCOUNT
CALLING THE SHOTS
CALM AS A MILL POND
CAME HOME TO ROOST
CAME TO THE RESCUE
CAME UP TO SCRATCH
CANDELABRUM TREE
CANTERBURY BELLS
CANVAS STRETCHER
CAPE NIGHTINGALE
CAPITATION GRANT
CARDINAL NUMBERS
CARDINAL VIRTUES
CARDS ON THE TABLE
CAREERS MISTRESS
CARELESS DRIVING
CARNAL KNOWLEDGE
CARRIAGE AND PAIR
CARRIAGE DRIVING
CARRIAGE FORWARD
CARRY CONVICTION
CARRYING FORWARD
CARRYING ONES BAT
CARRYING THE FLAG
CARRYING THROUGH
CASEMENT CURTAIN
CASTING DIRECTOR
CASTLES IN THE AIR
CASTOR AND POLLUX
CASTS ASPERSIONS
CATCH AS CATCH CAN
CATCH ONES BREATH
CAUGHT AND BOWLED
CAUGHT RED HANDED
CENTRE OF GRAVITY
CENTRE OF INERTIA
CHAMBER PRACTICE
CHAMPAGNE BOTTLE
CHAMPED AT THE BIT
CHANGE OF SCENERY
CHANGED ONES MIND
CHANGED ONES TUNE
CHANGES ONES MIND
CHANGES ONES TUNE
CHANNEL CROSSING
CHAPELLE ARDENTE
CHAPTER AND VERSE
CHARACTER SKETCH
CHARGE DAFFAIRES
CHASED THE DRAGON
CHASES THE DRAGON
CHASING RAINBOWS

CHEAT THE GALLOWS
CHEMICAL WARFARE
CHEQUERED CAREER
CHERCHEZ LA FEMME
CHICKEN CHASSEUR
CHICKEN MARYLAND
CHINESE CHECKERS
CHINESE PAVILION
CHINESE TAKE AWAY
CHINESE WHISPERS
CHOCOLATE ECLAIR
CHOPS AND CHANGES
CHRISTMAS ANNUAL
CHRISTMAS CACTUS
CHRISTMAS ISLAND
CHRISTMAS SPIRIT
CHRISTY MINSTREL
CHURCH OF ENGLAND
CIGARETTE HOLDER
CIRCUIT TRAINING
CIRCULAR MEASURE
CITIZENS CHARTER
CLEAN AS A WHISTLE
CLEARED THE DECKS
CLERK OF THE COURT
CLOSING DOWN SALE
CLOSING ONES EYES
CLOUD COMPELLING
CLOUD CUCKOO LAND
CLUBBED TOGETHER
CLUBBING TO DEATH
CLUSTERED COLUMN
COCKTAIL CABINET
COFFEE TABLE BOOK
COLLECTION PLATE
COLLECTIVE NOUNS
COLLEGIAL CHURCH
COLLISION COURSE
COLOUR BLINDNESS
COMBINATION LOCK
COME HOME TO ROOST
COME RAIN OR SHINE
COME TO THE RESCUE
COME UP TO SCRATCH
COMEDY OF HUMOURS
COMEDY OF MANNERS
COMES FULL CIRCLE
COMING TO THE BOIL
COMITY OF NATIONS
COMMERCIAL BREAK
COMMISSARY COURT
COMMISSION AGENT
COMMITS TO MEMORY
COMMON KNOWLEDGE
COMMONWEALTH DAY
COMMUNITY CENTRE
COMMUNITY SCHOOL
COMMUNITY SPIRIT
COMMUNITY WORKER
COMPANION LADDER

15 *contd.*

COMPANY CHAIRMAN
COMPANY DIRECTOR
COMPANY PROMOTER
COMPLETE ANNUITY
COMPLEX SENTENCE
COMPOUND ANIMALS
COMPUTER SCIENCE
CONCERT OVERTURE
CONDITIONAL MOOD
CONFIDENCE TRICK
CONFUSE THE ISSUE
CONJUNCTIVE MOOD
CONSCIENCE MONEY
CONSIGNMENT NOTE
CONSOLATION RACE
CONTEMPT OF COURT
CONVENIENCE FOOD
COOKED BREAKFAST
COOKED ONES GOOSE
COOKING THE BOOKS
COOL AS A CUCUMBER
CORNER THE MARKET
CORNO DI BASSETTO
CORRUGATED PAPER
COSMETIC SURGERY
COSTING THE EARTH
COTTAGE HOSPITAL
COTTAGE INDUSTRY
COUNCIL OF EUROPE
COUNCIL OF STATES
COUNTER IRRITANT
COUNTER MOVEMENT
COUNTER PROPOSAL
COURT MARTIALLED
CRACKING THE WHIP
CRADLE SNATCHING
CRAMPS ONES STYLE
CREASE RESISTANT
CREATIVE WRITING
CREATURE OF HABIT
CRICKED ONES NECK
CRICKET PAVILION
CRIMINAL CLASSES
CRIMPING MACHINE
CROSS QUESTIONED
CROSS THE CHANNEL
CROSS THE RUBICON
CROSSED THE FLOOR
CROSSES THE FLOOR
CROSSING SWEEPER
CROSSWORD PUZZLE
CROWN GREEN BOWLS
CRUX OF THE MATTER
CRYPTO COMMUNIST
CURLED UP AND DIED
CURRICULUM VITAE
CUSTOMS OFFICIAL
CUTTING BOTH WAYS
CUTTING THE CARDS

DAILY OCCURRENCE
DAMP PROOF COURSE
DAVID AND GOLIATH
DAVY CROCKETT HAT
DAYLIGHT ROBBERY
DEAD AS A DOORNAIL
DECIMAL CURRENCY
DECIMAL FRACTION
DECIMAL NOTATION
DEED OF ACCESSION
DEFENCE MINISTER
DEFERRED ANNUITY
DEFERRED PAYMENT
DEFINITE ARTICLE
DELAYING TACTICS
DELIRIUM TREMENS
DELIVER THE GOODS
DELIVERED BY HAND
DEMENTIA PRAECOX
DEMOLITION SQUAD
DEO OPTIMO MAXIMO
DEPARTMENT STORE
DEPARTURE LOUNGE
DEPENDENT CLAUSE
DESIGNER STUBBLE
DETENTION CENTRE
DEVELOPMENT AREA
DEVIL WORSHIPPER
DEVILLED KIDNEYS
DEVONSHIRE CREAM
DICING WITH DEATH
DICK WHITTINGTON
DIED IN ONES BOOTS
DIES IN ONES BOOTS
DIESEL HYDRAULIC
DIGITAL COMPUTER
DIGS ONES HEELS IN
DINING ROOM TABLE
DIP OF THE HORIZON
DIPLOMATIC CORPS
DIRECTION FINDER
DIRECTOR GENERAL
DISAPPEARING ACT
DISCHARGING ARCH
DISORDERLY HOUSE
DISPLACED PERSON
DISSECTING TABLE
DISTRESS WARRANT
DISTRICT COUNCIL
DISTRICT VISITOR
DIVIDEND WARRANT
DODGED THE COLUMN
DODGES THE COLUMN
DOING THE HONOURS
DOLLAR DIPLOMACY
DOMESTIC ECONOMY
DOMESTIC PROBLEM
DOMESTIC SCIENCE
DOMINICAL LETTER
DONT ROCK THE BOAT

DOORSTEP SELLING
DOUBLE BARRELLED
DOUBLE PNEUMONIA
DOUBLE STANDARDS
DOUBLE WHITE LINE
DOUBLE YOUR MONEY
DOW JONES AVERAGE
DOWN TO THE GROUND
DRAGGED ONES FEET
DRAUGHT PROOFING
DRAW IN ONES HORNS
DRAW THE CURTAINS
DRAWING TO A CLOSE
DRAWS THE LONGBOW
DRESSING STATION
DREW IN ONES HORNS
DREW THE CURTAINS
DRILL INSTRUCTOR
DRILLING MACHINE
DRINKS LIKE A FISH
DRIVES TO THE WALL
DROPPED A CLANGER
DROPS THE SUBJECT
DRUIDICAL CIRCLE
DRY ROAST PEANUTS
DRY STONE WALLING
DUAL CARRIAGEWAY
DUAL PERSONALITY
DUELLING PISTOLS
DUPLEX APARTMENT
DUPLICATE BRIDGE
DUTCH ELM DISEASE
EARLY CLOSING DAY
EASTER OFFERINGS
EAT YOUR HEART OUT
EATING HUMBLE PIE
EATING ONES WORDS
ECLIPSE OF THE SUN
EGG AND SPOON RACE
EGGS IN MOONSHINE
ELECTORAL SYSTEM
ELECTRIC BATTERY
ELECTRIC BLANKET
ELECTRIC CURRENT
ELECTRIC FURNACE
ELECTRICITY BILL
ELECTRONIC BRAIN
ELECTRONIC MUSIC
ELECTRONIC ORGAN
ELECTRONIC PIANO
EMBARRAS DE CHOIX
ENDOWMENT POLICY
ENGLISH LANGUAGE
ENJOYING ONESELF
ENTENTE CORDIALE
EQUINOCTIAL LINE
EQUINOCTIAL YEAR
ERROR OF JUDGMENT
ERROR OF OMISSION
ESCAPE MECHANISM

15 *contd.*

ESSENTIAL ORGANS
ETERNAL TRIANGLE
EUROPEAN COUNCIL
EUSTACHIAN VALVE
EVENING PRIMROSE
EVERY NOW AND THEN
EXCHANGE CONTROL
EXCHANGE STUDENT
EXCHANGE TEACHER
EXCHANGING BLOWS
EXCHANGING WORDS
EXCLAMATION MARK
EXCLUSION CLAUSE
EXCURSION TICKET
EXCUSING ONESELF
EXPANDED PLASTIC
EXPENSES ACCOUNT
EXPOSING ONESELF
EXPRESS DELIVERY
EXTERNAL STUDENT
EXTRA CURRICULAR
FALKLAND ISLANDS
FALL OVER ONESELF
FALL TO THE GROUND
FALLING INTO LINE
FALLING SICKNESS
FALLS ON DEAF EARS
FALLS ON ONES FEET
FAMILY ALLOWANCE
FAMOUS LAST WORDS
FAN TAILED PIGEON
FANCYING ONESELF
FATAL ATTRACTION
FATHER CHRISTMAS
FEATHER ONES NEST
FEEDING ONES FACE
FEELING THE PINCH
FELL OVER ONESELF
FELL TO THE GROUND
FELLOW TRAVELLER
FEMININE PRONOUN
FENDS FOR ONESELF
FENESTRA ROTUNDA
FIBONACCI SERIES
FIFTY PENCE PIECE
FIGHT TO THE DEATH
FILTERED THROUGH
FINANCIAL WIZARD
FINDING ONES FEET
FINE TOOTHED COMB
FINISHING SCHOOL
FIRE WORSHIPPING
FIRST DEGREE BURN
FIRST LIEUTENANT
FIRST PRINCIPLES
FIT OF THE VAPOURS
FLAGGING SPIRITS
FLANNEL TROUSERS
FLATTERS ONESELF

FLEETING GLIMPSE
FLICK OF THE WRIST
FLICKING THROUGH
FLING TO THE WINDS
FLIPPING ONES LID
FLOATING BATTERY
FLOATING CAPITAL
FLOGS A DEAD HORSE
FLOWER ARRANGING
FLUNG TO THE WINDS
FLY OFF THE HANDLE
FLYING PHALANGER
FOAMS AT THE MOUTH
FOLDING ONES ARMS
FOLLOWED THROUGH
FOLLOWS ONES NOSE
FOR GOODNESS SAKE
FOR LOVE NOR MONEY
FOR OLD TIMES SAKE
FOR THE LIFE OF HER
FOR THE LIFE OF HIM
FOR THE TIME BEING
FORCING THE ISSUE
FOREIGN EXCHANGE
FORTY EIGHT HOURS
FORWARD DELIVERY
FORWARDING AGENT
FOUCAULT CURRENT
FOUL MOUTHEDNESS
FOUNDATION CREAM
FOUNDATION STONE
FOUNTAIN OF YOUTH
FOUR DIMENSIONAL
FOUR STROKE CYCLE
FOURTH DIMENSION
FRANKING MACHINE
FREE ASSOCIATION
FREE HEARTEDNESS
FREEDOM OF SPEECH
FREEZING MIXTURE
FRENCH POLISHING
FRESH VEGETABLES
FRICTION WELDING
FRIENDLY SOCIETY
FRIGHTENING AWAY
FROM HAND TO MOUTH
FROM STEM TO STERN
FROM THE SHOULDER
FRONT END LOADING
FRONT OF THE HOUSE
FRONT WHEEL DRIVE
FULL DRESS DEBATE
FULMINATING GOLD
FUNERAL DIRECTOR
FUNNEL WEB SPIDER
FURNITURE POLISH
GAINED ADMISSION
GAINING STRENGTH
GALVANIC BATTERY
GATHERING BREATH

GATHERING GROUND
GAVE ONESELF AIRS
GAVE ONESELF AWAY
GAVE THE GAME AWAY
GAZETTED OFFICER
GENERAL ASSEMBLY
GENERAL DELIVERY
GENERAL ELECTION
GENERAL EPISTLES
GENERAL FACTOTUM
GENERAL PRACTICE
GENTLEMAN AT ARMS
GENTLEMAN FARMER
GEOMETRICAL MEAN
GET INTO HOT WATER
GET ONES HEAD DOWN
GET THE RUNAROUND
GET THE WORST OF IT
GETS IT IN THE NECK
GETS ONES OWN BACK
GETS THE BREEZE UP
GETS THE HANG OF IT
GETS TO FIRST BASE
GETTING CRACKING
GETTING IN THE WAY
GETTING ONES GOAT
GETTING TOGETHER
GINGER BEER PLANT
GIRD UP ONES LOINS
GIVE ONESELF AIRS
GIVE ONESELF AWAY
GIVE THE GAME AWAY
GIVES UP THE GHOST
GLADSTONE SHERRY
GLORIOUS TWELFTH
GO FOR THE JUGULAR
GO OFF AT HALF COCK
GO OFF THE DEEP END
GO OUT LIKE A LIGHT
GO OUT OF BUSINESS
GO THROUGH WITH IT
GOD SAVE THE QUEEN
GOES OVER THE EDGE
GOES OVER THE WALL
GOES THE DISTANCE
GOES THE WHOLE HOG
GOES TO ANY LENGTH
GOES UNDERGROUND
GOING BY THE BOARD
GOING FOR NOTHING
GOING INTO DETAIL
GOING INTO HIDING
GOING LIKE A DREAM
GOING ON ALL FOURS
GOING ONES OWN WAY
GOING OVER THE TOP
GOING TO EXTREMES
GOING TO ONES HEAD
GOING UP IN THE AIR
GOLDEN DELICIOUS

15 *contd.*

GOLDEN HANDSHAKE
GOLDEN RECTANGLE
GOLDEN RETRIEVER
GOLDEN SAXIFRAGE
GONE WITH THE WIND
GOOD NATUREDNESS
GOSSIP COLUMNIST
GOT INTO HOT WATER
GOT ONES HEAD DOWN
GOT THE RUNAROUND
GOT THE WORST OF IT
GOVERNOR GENERAL
GRAND INQUISITOR
GRANULATED SUGAR
GRAPEFRUIT JUICE
GRASPS THE NETTLE
GRASSHOPPER MIND
GRAVITY PLATFORM
GREASE THE WHEELS
GREAT GRANDCHILD
GREEN REVOLUTION
GREEN WOODPECKER
GREENERY YALLERY
GRENADIER GUARDS
GREYHOUND RACING
GRINDING TO A HALT
GROUND NUT SCHEME
GROWING TOGETHER
GUERRILLA STRIKE
HACKNEY CARRIAGE
HACKNEY COACHMAN
HALF HEARTEDNESS
HALF TERM HOLIDAY
HALF WELLINGTONS
HAMMER AND SICKLE
HANG UP ONES BOOTS
HANGING BUTTRESS
HANGING ONES HEAD
HANGING TOGETHER
HANSEL AND GRETEL
HAPPY AS A SAND BOY
HARBOUR OF REFUGE
HARD HEARTEDNESS
HARP ON ONE STRING
HARVEST FESTIVAL
HAUNCH OF VENISON
HAVE TWO LEFT FEET
HAVE WHAT IT TAKES
HAVING A BASINFUL
HAVING A GOOD TIME
HAVING A TIME OF IT
HAVING HYSTERICS
HAZARDING A GUESS
HEAD OF THE FAMILY
HEAD ON COLLISION
HEALTH INSURANCE
HEATHROW AIRPORT
HEDGING ONES BETS
HEIR PRESUMPTIVE

HEIR TO THE THRONE
HELPING THE CAUSE
HERB CHRISTOPHER
HEREDITARY TITLE
HESITATION WALTZ
HIGHER EDUCATION
HIP JOINT DISEASE
HIPPOCRATIC OATH
HISTORICAL NOVEL
HIT BELOW THE BELT
HIT THE HEADLINES
HIT THE HIGH SPOTS
HOLDING DOWN A JOB
HOLDING THE FLOOR
HOLDING TO RANSOM
HOLDING TOGETHER
HOLDS ONES BREATH
HOLDS ONES TONGUE
HOLDS UP ONES HEAD
HOLY ROMAN EMPIRE
HOPE AGAINST HOPE
HORNS OF A DILEMMA
HORSE SHOE MAGNET
HOUSEHOLD GUARDS
HOUSEHOLD TROOPS
HOUSING MINISTER
HOVER ON THE BRINK
HUDDLED TOGETHER
HUGGING THE COAST
HUNG UP ONES BOOTS
HUNGRY AS A HUNTER
HUNTS HIGH AND LOW
HYDRAULIC MINING
ICE CREAM PARLOUR
ILCHESTER CHEESE
ILLUSTRIOUS PAST
IMMERSION HEATER
IMPERIAL MEASURE
IN ALL CONSCIENCE
IN APPLE PIE ORDER
IN BLACK AND WHITE
IN THE ALTOGETHER
IN THE BACKGROUND
IN THE FIRST FLUSH
IN THE FIRST PLACE
IN THE LAST RESORT
IN THE SMALL HOURS
IN THE WILDERNESS
IN THIS DAY AND AGE
INCIDENTAL MUSIC
INCOME TAX DEMAND
INDECENT ASSAULT
INDELIBLE PENCIL
INDEPENDENCE DAY
INDIAN LIQUORICE
INDIAN ROPE TRICK
INDIAN WRESTLING
INDOOR FIREWORKS
INFANT MORTALITY
INFERIOR PLANETS

INFERNAL MACHINE
INFRA DIGNITATEM
INNOCENTS ABROAD
INSIGHT LEARNING
INSTRUMENT PANEL
INSULATING BOARD
INSULIN REACTION
INSURANCE BROKER
INSURANCE POLICY
INTERNAL STUDENT
INVESTMENT TRUST
INVITED AUDIENCE
IRISH SWEEPSTAKE
IT TAKES ALL SORTS
ITALIAN VERMOUTH
JACK IN THE PULPIT
JACK OF ALL TRADES
JAPANNED LEATHER
JEEPERS CREEPERS
JEHOVAHS WITNESS
JEWEL IN THE CROWN
JOINED UP WRITING
JUDICIAL TRUSTEE
JUMP AT THE CHANCE
JUMPED OVERBOARD
JUMPING OFF PLACE
JUMPING THE QUEUE
JUST GOOD FRIENDS
KANGAROO JUSTICE
KEEP BRITAIN TIDY
KEEP OFF THE GRASS
KEEPING GOOD TIME
KEEPING ONES COOL
KEEPING ONES HEAD
KEEPING ONES WORD
KEEPING THE PEACE
KEEPS A GOOD HOUSE
KEEPS A PLACE WARM
KEEPS A TIGHT REIN
KEEPS AN OPEN MIND
KEEPS ONES CHIN UP
KEEPS ONES HAIR ON
KEEPS ONES HAND IN
KEEPS ONES TEMPER
KEEPS UNDER WRAPS
KICKED INTO TOUCH
KICKED ONES HEELS
KICKED THE BUCKET
KICKED UP A RUMPUS
KICKED UP A SHINDY
KICKING UP A STINK
KICKING UPSTAIRS
KILOGRAM CALORIE
KIND HEARTEDNESS
KING OF THE CASTLE
KING OF THE JUNGLE
KITCHEN GARDENER
KITTEN ON THE KEYS
KNEW A THING OR TWO
KNIGHT OF THE ROAD

15 *contd.*

KNIGHT OF THE WHIP
KNIGHTS TEMPLARS
KNITTING MACHINE
KNITTING NEEDLES
KNITTING PATTERN
KNOCKED SIDEWAYS
KNOCKED SPOTS OFF
KNOCKED TOGETHER
KNOCKOUT AUCTION
KNOCKS INTO SHAPE
KNOW A THING OR TWO
KNOWING FULL WELL
KNOWING THE ROPES
KNOWING THE SCORE
KNOWS A MOVE OR TWO
KNOWS ONES ONIONS
KNUCKLE SANDWICH
LABOUR INTENSIVE
LABRADOR CURRENT
LACHRYMA CHRISTI
LADDER BACK CHAIR
LAID IT ON THE LINE
LANDING CARRIAGE
LANDSCAPE ARTIST
LANGUAGE BARRIER
LAPIS LAZULI BLUE
LAPIS LAZULI WARE
LAPSANG SOUCHONG
LATERAL THINKING
LATERAN COUNCILS
LATTER DAY SAINTS
LAUGH LIKE A DRAIN
LAUGH OUT OF COURT
LAUGHING JACKASS
LAUGHING OUT LOUD
LAUGHING TO SCORN
LAY DOWN ONES ARMS
LAY DOWN ONES LIFE
LAY IMPROPRIATOR
LAYING IT ON THICK
LAYING ON OF HANDS
LAYING ON THE LINE
LAYS IT ON THE LINE
LEADER OF THE BAND
LEADING BUSINESS
LEADING QUESTION
LEADS TO THE ALTAR
LEAGUE OF NATIONS
LEAVES WELL ALONE
LEAVING IT AT THAT
LEG BEFORE WICKET
LEGAL SEPARATION
LEGITIMATE DRAMA
LESSER CELANDINE
LET IT ALL HANG OUT
LET ONES HAIR DOWN
LET THERE BE LIGHT
LETS THE SIDE DOWN
LETTERS ROGATORY

LETTING OFF STEAM
LICKED INTO SHAPE
LICKED ONES CHOPS
LICKS ONES WOUNDS
LIEBIG CONDENSER
LIED IN ONES TEETH
LIES IN ONES TEETH
LIFEBOAT STATION
LIFTED THE LID OFF
LIGHT AS A FEATHER
LIGHT HEADEDNESS
LIGHT LITERATURE
LIGHT MACHINE GUN
LIGHT MINDEDNESS
LIGHTNING STRIKE
LIKE THE CLAPPERS
LILY OF THE VALLEY
LIMBURGER CHEESE
LIMITED MONARCHY
LINE ONES POCKETS
LITTLE ENGLANDER
LITTLE OR NOTHING
LIVE PERFORMANCE
LIVED BY ONES WITS
LIVED OFF THE LAND
LIVES BY ONES WITS
LIVES OFF THE LAND
LIVING IN THE PAST
LIVING LIKE A LORD
LOAVES AND FISHES
LOB LIE BY THE FIRE
LOCAL GOVERNMENT
LOCH NESS MONSTER
LOGARITHMIC SINE
LOGICAL ANALYSIS
LOGICAL DESIGNER
LOGICAL ELEMENTS
LOGISTICS VESSEL
LONDON TRANSPORT
LONG ARM OF THE LAW
LONG LIVE THE KING
LONG SIGHTEDNESS
LOOK BACK IN ANGER
LOOK THE OTHER WAY
LOOKED IN THE FACE
LOOKS FOR TROUBLE
LOOSE LEAF BINDER
LORD CHAMBERLAIN
LORD HIGH ADMIRAL
LORD HIGH STEWARD
LORDS LIEUTENANT
LOSE ONES BALANCE
LOSE ONES FOOTING
LOSES ONES TEMPER
LOSING HANDS DOWN
LOSING ONES NERVE
LOSING ONES SHIRT
LOST ONES BALANCE
LOST ONES FOOTING
LOVE ME LOVE MY DOG

LOW TAR CIGARETTE
LUMP IN THE THROAT
LUNCHEON VOUCHER
LYING IN HOSPITAL
LYMPHATIC SYSTEM
MACHINE LANGUAGE
MACHINE READABLE
MAD AS A MARCH HARE
MADE A CLEAN BREAK
MADE A CLEAN SWEEP
MADE A FRESH START
MADE MINCEMEAT OF
MADE SHORT WORK OF
MADE THE BEST OF IT
MADE THE MOST OF IT
MAGNETIC BATTERY
MAGNIFYING GLASS
MAJORITY VERDICT
MAKE A CLEAN BREAK
MAKE A CLEAN SWEEP
MAKE A FRESH START
MAKE MINCEMEAT OF
MAKE SHORT WORK OF
MAKE THE BEST OF IT
MAKE THE MOST OF IT
MAKES A NIGHT OF IT
MAKES THE RUNNING
MAKES UP ONES MIND
MAKING A COMEBACK
MAKING A FAST BUCK
MAKING A MEAL OF IT
MAKING FIRST BASE
MAKING THE ROUNDS
MANGANESE BRONZE
MANIC DEPRESSIVE
MANY HEADED BEAST
MARINE INSURANCE
MARKET GARDENING
MARRIAGE LICENCE
MARRIAGE PARTNER
MARRIAGE PORTION
MARSHALLING YARD
MASCULINE ENDING
MASS OBSERVATION
MASS RADIOGRAPHY
MASTER CARPENTER
MASTER CRAFTSMAN
MATTER OF OPINION
MEADOW SAXIFRAGE
MEDICINE DROPPER
MEDITATE THE MUSE
MEDULLARY SHEATH
MELTS IN THE MOUTH
MENDING ONES WAYS
MENDS ONES FENCES
MENTAL BREAKDOWN
MERCHANT SERVICE
MERIDIAN PASSAGE
MESSENGER AT ARMS
METEORIC SHOWERS

15 *contd.*

MEXICAN HAT DANCE
MICHAELMAS DAISY
MICROMETER GAUGE
MIDDLE AGE SPREAD
MIDDLE EASTERNER
MIDDLE OF THE ROAD
MILITARY ACADEMY
MILITARY HONOURS
MILITARY TWO STEP
MINIMISING GLASS
MINISTER OF STATE
MINISTRY OF WORKS
MOLECULAR WEIGHT
MOLOTOV COCKTAIL
MONEY FOR OLD ROPE
MONTAGUS HARRIER
MONTE CARLO RALLY
MONUMENTAL MASON
MOOG SYNTHESIZER
MORAL HIGH GROUND
MORAL PHILOSOPHY
MORAL REARMAMENT
MORNING SICKNESS
MORRISON SHELTER
MOSQUITO CURTAIN
MOSSBAUER EFFECT
MOTORWAY MADNESS
MOUNTAIN BICYCLE
MOUNTAIN BRAMBLE
MOUNTAIN RAILWAY
MOURNING CLOTHES
MOUSSELINE SAUCE
MOVING STAIRCASE
MUCH OF A MUCHNESS
MUDDLING THROUGH
MULBERRY HARBOUR
MUSICAL DIRECTOR
MUSIQUE CONCRETE
MUSTARD AND CRESS
MUTATIS MUTANDIS
MUTUAL INSURANCE
MY LEARNED FRIEND
NATIONAL COSTUME
NATIONAL GALLERY
NATIONAL HOLIDAY
NATIONAL SERVICE
NATURAL RELIGION
NATURAL THEOLOGY
NAUGHTY NINETIES
NAUTICAL ALMANAC
NEAR AS NINEPENCE
NEAR SIGHTEDNESS
NECTAR OF THE GODS
NEVER A CROSS WORD
NEW SCOTLAND YARD
NEWGATE CALENDAR
NEWSPAPER SELLER
NIGHT AFTER NIGHT
NIPPING IN THE BUD

NO SKIN OFF MY NOSE
NOBLE MINDEDNESS
NON COMMISSIONED
NON COMPOS MENTIS
NON CONTRIBUTORY
NON INTERVENTION
NON PROFESSIONAL
NON PROFIT MAKING
NORFOLK DUMPLING
NORTH COUNTRYMAN
NORTH EASTWARDLY
NORTH WESTWARDLY
NORTHERN IRELAND
NOT MUCH TO LOOK AT
NOT ON YOUR NELLIE
NOT THE WORD FOR IT
NOUVELLE CUISINE
NUCLEAR FREE ZONE
NUCLEAR REACTION
NUMBER CRUNCHING
NURSE A GRIEVANCE
NUTCRACKER SUITE
OBSERVATION POST
OCCASIONAL TABLE
OCCUPATION LEVEL
OCCUPIED THE MIND
OCCUPIES THE MIND
ODDS ON FAVOURITE
OF NO CONSEQUENCE
OF THE FIRST WATER
OFFERS AN OPINION
OILING THE WHEELS
OLD AGE PENSIONER
OLD RED SANDSTONE
ON SPEAKING TERMS
ON THE DANGER LIST
ON THE RIGHT TRACK
ON THE ROAD TO RUIN
ON THE WRONG TRACK
ON TOP OF THE WORLD
ON WITH THE MOTLEY
ONCE IN A BLUE MOON
ONCE IN A LIFETIME
ONE OVER THE EIGHT
ONE PARENT FAMILY
OPEN AND SHUT CASE
OPEN HEARTEDNESS
OPEN HOSTILITIES
OPEN SCHOLARSHIP
OPENED ONES HEART
OPENS THE INNINGS
OPENS THE SCORING
OPPOSITION BENCH
OPPOSITION PARTY
ORBITAL MOTORWAY
ORCHESTRA STALLS
ORGANISED LABOUR
ORIENTAL EMERALD
OUR MUTUAL FRIEND
OUT OF COMMISSION

OUT OF PROPORTION
OUT OF THE RUNNING
OUTSIDE INTEREST
OVER AND DONE WITH
OVERFLOW MEETING
OVERSTEP THE MARK
OWNER OCCUPATION
PACING UP AND DOWN
PACKING ONES BAGS
PAID FOR ONES SINS
PAINT THE TOWN RED
PAINTING THE LILY
PAIR OF CALLIPERS
PAIR OF COMPASSES
PAIR OF STOCKINGS
PALM TREE JUSTICE
PAN PRESBYTERIAN
PANCREATIC JUICE
PANORAMIC CAMERA
PANTECHNICON VAN
PAPER TAPE READER
PAPERED THE HOUSE
PAR FOR THE COURSE
PARABIOTIC TWINS
PARACHUTE TROOPS
PARASOL MUSHROOM
PARLIAMENT CLOCK
PARLIAMENT HINGE
PARLIAMENT HOUSE
PARTIAL FRACTION
PARTIAL PRESSURE
PARTNERS IN CRIME
PARTY GOVERNMENT
PASS ROUND THE HAT
PASSENGER PIGEON
PASSING JUDGMENT
PASSING ONES WORD
PASSING SENTENCE
PASSIVE IMMUNITY
PASSIVE RESISTER
PASTORAL ADDRESS
PATHETIC FALLACY
PAY OFF OLD SCORES
PAYING ATTENTION
PAYING IN ADVANCE
PAYS FOR ONES SINS
PEACE CONFERENCE
PEACHES AND CREAM
PEACOCK PHEASANT
PEAK VIEWING TIME
PEASECOD BELLIED
PEASECOD CUIRASS
PELICAN CROSSING
PENAL SETTLEMENT
PENCIL SHARPENER
PEPPERMINT CREAM
PER ARDUA AD ASTRA
PEREGRINE FALCON
PERFECT INTERVAL
PERFECT STRANGER

15 *contd.*

PERFORMANCE TEST
PERFORMING RIGHT
PERIOD FURNITURE
PERIPHERAL UNITS
PERIPHERY CAMERA
PERMANENT MAGNET
PERPETUAL CURATE
PERPETUAL MOTION
PERSONA NON GRATA
PERSONAL EFFECTS
PERSONAL PRONOUN
PERSONAL SERVICE
PERSONALITY CULT
PESTLE AND MORTAR
PETITION OF RIGHT
PETRIFIED FOREST
PHOSPHOROUS ACID
PHOTO MECHANICAL
PHOTOGRAPH ALBUM
PICK UP THE PIECES
PICK UP THE THREAD
PICKING ONES SPOT
PICKING TO PIECES
PICKING UP THE TAB
PICKS AN ARGUMENT
PICKS AND CHOOSES
PICTURE MOULDING
PICTURE POSTCARD
PICTURE RESTORER
PIECE OF NONSENSE
PIECING TOGETHER
PILED ON THE AGONY
PILES ON THE AGONY
PILLAR OF SOCIETY
PILLARS OF WISDOM
PINEAPPLE CHUNKS
PIPPED AT THE POST
PIT OF THE STOMACH
PLACE OF BUSINESS
PLACING ON RECORD
PLAIN CLOTHES MAN
PLANETARY NEBULA
PLANNING OFFICER
PLAY A LOSING GAME
PLAY CAT AND MOUSE
PLAYED HARD TO GET
PLAYED ONES HUNCH
PLAYED THE MARKET
PLAYED THE WANTON
PLAYING FOR A DRAW
PLAYING THE DEVIL
PLAYING THE FIELD
PLAYING WITH FIRE
PLAYS TO THE CROWD
PLEASURE GARDENS
PLEASURE SEEKING
PLEURO PNEUMONIA
PLIGHT ONES TROTH
PLOTTING A COURSE

PLOUGHED THROUGH
PLOUGHS THE SANDS
PLUCKS UP COURAGE
PLUMBS THE DEPTHS
PLYMOUTH BROTHER
PNEUMATIC TROUGH
PNEUMONIA BLOUSE
POCKET AN AFFRONT
POCKETS AN INSULT
POINT BLANK RANGE
POINT OF NO RETURN
POISON PEN LETTER
POKED ONES NOSE IN
POKES ONES NOSE IN
POLAR EXPEDITION
POLICE CONSTABLE
POLICE INSPECTOR
POLISHING POWDER
POLITICAL ANIMAL
POLITICAL ASYLUM
POLITICAL STATUS
POPEYE THE SAILOR
POPPED ONES CLOGS
POPS THE QUESTION
PORCELAIN CEMENT
PORTRAIT GALLERY
PORTRAIT PAINTER
POSIGRADE ROCKET
POSITIVE VETTING
POST DATED CHEQUE
POST MILLENARIAN
POTENTIAL ENERGY
POUR COLD WATER ON
POURING WITH RAIN
POVERTY STRICKEN
POWDERS ONES NOSE
POWER OF ATTORNEY
PRAETORIAN GUARD
PRAIRIE SCHOONER
PRE EMPTION RIGHT
PRE ESTABLISHING
PREENING ONESELF
PREFECT OF POLICE
PRESS CONFERENCE
PRESSING FORWARD
PRESSURE COOKING
PREVAILING WINDS
PRICE COMMISSION
PRICK UP ONES EARS
PRINCIPAL CLAUSE
PRINTING MACHINE
PRISMATIC POWDER
PRIVATE HOSPITAL
PRIVATE JUDGMENT
PRIVY COUNCILLOR
PROBOSCIS MONKEY
PROGRAMME SELLER
PROOF CORRECTING
PROOF CORRECTION
PROTECTION MONEY

PROUD AS A PEACOCK
PROVOST SERGEANT
PROXIMATE OBJECT
PRUNES AND PRISMS
PUBLIC OWNERSHIP
PUBLIC RELATIONS
PUBLIC TRANSPORT
PUBLIC UTILITIES
PULL FOR THE SHORE
PULL ONES PUNCHES
PULL ONES SOCKS UP
PULLED THE PLUG ON
PULLING A FAST ONE
PULLING A FLANKER
PULLING TO PIECES
PULLING TOGETHER
PULLS ONES WEIGHT
PULLS THE LONG BOW
PULLS THE STRINGS
PUNCTUATION MARK
PURCHASING POWER
PURE MATHEMATICS
PURPLE OF CASSIUS
PUSHED THE BOTTLE
PUSHES THE BOTTLE
PUSHING ONES LUCK
PUSS IN THE CORNER
PUT A BRAVE FACE ON
PUT BACK THE CLOCK
PUT THE CLOCK BACK
PUT THE MOCKERS ON
PUTS IN MOTHBALLS
PUTS THE KIBOSH ON
PUTS THE SCREWS ON
PUTS THE TIN HAT ON
PUTTING IT MILDLY
PUTTING ON RECORD
PUTTING ON THE MAP
PUTTING ONES CASE
PUTTING STRAIGHT
PUTTING THE STONE
PUTTING TO RIGHTS
PUTTING UP A FIGHT
QUALIFYING ROUND
QUARTER OF AN HOUR
QUARTER SESSIONS
QUASI HISTORICAL
QUEEN OF PUDDINGS
QUEERED THE PITCH
QUESTION BEGGING
QUICK WITTEDNESS
QUICKEN ONES PACE
QUITTED THE SCENE
RACE AGAINST TIME
RACING CERTAINTY
RACKS ONES BRAINS
RADIO GRAMOPHONE
RADIUM EMANATION
RAIDED THE MARKET
RAILWAY CARRIAGE

15 contd.

RAILWAY CROSSING
RAILWAY TERMINUS
RAIN CATS AND DOGS
RAINBOW COLOURED
RAINBOW DRESSING
RAISE OBJECTIONS
RAISE ONES SIGHTS
RAISE TO THE BENCH
RAISED AN EYEBROW
RAISED ONES GLASS
RAISED ONES VOICE
RAISED THE MARKET
RAISES AN EYEBROW
RAISES ONES GLASS
RAISES ONES VOICE
RAISES THE MARKET
RAISING THE ALARM
RAN A TEMPERATURE
RAN FOR PRESIDENT
RAZE TO THE GROUND
REACH FOR THE MOON
READ WRITE MEMORY
READING THE SIGNS
READS THE RIOT ACT
RECEIVED ENGLISH
RECEIVER GENERAL
RECEIVING OFFICE
RECEPTION CENTRE
RECORDING STUDIO
REDS UNDER THE BED
REDUCING TO TEARS
REFECTION SUNDAY
REFRACTIVE INDEX
REFRESHMENT ROOM
REFUSE COLLECTOR
REGIONAL COUNCIL
REGISTRATION FEE
REGIUS PROFESSOR
REICHIAN THERAPY
REIGNING MONARCH
REIGNING SUPREME
RELATIVE DENSITY
RELATIVE PRONOUN
RELIABILITY TEST
REMAINING SILENT
RENT RESTRICTION
REPEATED ONESELF
RES IPSA LOQUITUR
RESEARCH CHEMIST
RESERVE CURRENCY
RESERVING A TABLE
RESTORATION PLAY
RESTS ON ONES OARS
RESURRECTION MAN
RESURRECTION PIE
REVOLVING CREDIT
RIDE OUT THE STORM
RIDING COMMITTEE
RIDING ROUGH SHOD

RIFT VALLEY FEVER
RIGHT HANDEDNESS
RIGHT HONOURABLE
RIGHT MINDEDNESS
RIGHT OFF THE REEL
RIGHTING THE HELM
RINGELMANN CHART
RINGS THE CHANGES
RISE WITH THE LARK
RISING TO THE BAIT
RISKING ONES LIFE
RISUS SARDONICUS
ROAD FUND LICENCE
ROBIN GOODFELLOW
ROCK OF GIBRALTAR
ROGER DE COVERLEY
ROLL NECK SWEATER
ROLLING ONES EYES
ROLY POLY PUDDING
ROMANTIC REVIVAL
ROMULUS AND REMUS
ROOM TEMPERATURE
ROOM TO SWING A CAT
ROOTED TO THE SPOT
ROTTEN TO THE CORE
ROUND SHOULDERED
ROYAL ALBERT HALL
ROYAL COMMISSION
ROYAL TOURNAMENT
RUB SALT IN A WOUND
RUBBED ONES HANDS
RUBBED SHOULDERS
RUDDY COMPLEXION
RUFFLED FEATHERS
RUN A TEMPERATURE
RUN FOR PRESIDENT
RUNNING INTO DEBT
RUNNING SMOOTHLY
RUNNING TO GROUND
RUNS IN THE FAMILY
RUNS INTO TROUBLE
RUNS OUT OF PETROL
RUNS THE GAUNTLET
RUNS THE RULE OVER
RUSHING HEADLONG
RUSSIAN DRESSING
RUSSIAN ROULETTE
SABBATH BREAKING
SADO MASOCHISTIC
SAFETY IN NUMBERS
SAILORS HORNPIPE
SALAMI TECHNIQUE
SALES RESISTANCE
SALOON PASSENGER
SANK TO ONES KNEES
SATURATION POINT
SAVE APPEARANCES
SAVING ONES BACON
SAW THE FUNNY SIDE
SCALES OF JUSTICE

SCARBOROUGH FAIR
SCATTER CUSHIONS
SCENE OF THE CRIME
SCHEDULED FLIGHT
SCHOOL INSPECTOR
SCHOOLBOY HOWLER
SCOOPING THE POOL
SCORED AN OWN GOAL
SCORES AN OWN GOAL
SCREAMING ABDABS
SCRIBBLING PAPER
SCRIPTURE READER
SCRUFF OF THE NECK
SEALYHAM TERRIER
SEAPLANE CARRIER
SECESSION CHURCH
SECOND ADVENTIST
SECOND CHILDHOOD
SECOND CLASS MAIL
SECOND CLASS POST
SECOND IN COMMAND
SECONDARY ACTION
SECONDARY CAUSES
SECONDARY GROWTH
SECONDARY MODERN
SECONDARY PICKET
SECONDARY SCHOOL
SECONDS PENDULUM
SECURITY BLANKET
SECURITY COUNCIL
SEE NAPLES AND DIE
SEE THE FUNNY SIDE
SEEING THE SIGHTS
SELECT COMMITTEE
SELF ADVANCEMENT
SELF COMPLACENCE
SELF CONFIDENTLY
SELF DESTRUCTION
SELF DESTRUCTIVE
SELF DETERMINING
SELF DEVELOPMENT
SELF EXAMINATION
SELF EXPLANATORY
SELF HUMILIATION
SELF IMPORTANTLY
SELF IMPROVEMENT
SELF POLLINATION
SELF PORTRAITURE
SELF PROPAGATING
SELF REALISATION
SELF REALIZATION
SELF SACRIFICING
SELF SUFFICIENCY
SELLING ONES SOUL
SELLING THE DUMMY
SEMI INDEPENDENT
SENDS TO COVENTRY
SENSATION MONGER
SENSE PERCEPTION
SENTENCE TO DEATH

15 *contd.*

SERGEANT DRUMMER
SERIAL TECHNIQUE
SERPENTINE VERSE
SERVED WITH A WRIT
SERVES WITH A WRIT
SERVICE INDUSTRY
SERVING A PURPOSE
SESSION MUSICIAN
SETS ONES HEART ON
SETTING AT NOUGHT
SETTING THE SCENE
SETTING TO RIGHTS
SETTLE OLD SCORES
SEVEN DEADLY SINS
SHABBY GENTILITY
SHADOW PANTOMIME
SHAKE LIKE A JELLY
SHAKING ONES FIST
SHAKING ONES HEAD
SHEATHE THE SWORD
SHEDDING LIGHT ON
SHEET FED PRINTER
SHIFTING ONESELF
SHILLING SHOCKER
SHIP OF THE DESERT
SHIPPING THE OARS
SHIVER ME TIMBERS
SHIVER MY TIMBERS
SHOOK LIKE A JELLY
SHOOT FROM THE HIP
SHOOTING GALLERY
SHORT TERM MEMORY
SHORTENING BREAD
SHORTHAND TYPIST
SHOUT BLUE MURDER
SHOUTING THE ODDS
SHOWED ONES PACES
SHOWING ONES FACE
SHOWING ONES HAND
SHRINK RESISTANT
SHRINKING VIOLET
SICKNESS BENEFIT
SIGN OF THE ZODIAC
SIGNED THE PLEDGE
SILENCE IS GOLDEN
SILENT AS THE TOMB
SILVER MEDALLIST
SINBAD THE SAILOR
SINCE THE YEAR DOT
SING ANOTHER SONG
SING ANOTHER TUNE
SINK TO ONES KNEES
SITS ON ONES HANDS
SITUATION COMEDY
SKATED ON THIN ICE
SKATES ON THIN ICE
SKIN OF ONES TEETH
SLAPSTICK COMEDY
SLAVE TRAFFICKER

SLEEPING DRAUGHT
SLEEPING PARTNER
SLING BACKED SHOE
SLIP OF THE TONGUE
SLIPPED ONES MIND
SLIPPED THE CABLE
SLOW ON THE UPTAKE
SMACKED ONES LIPS
SMELLS OF THE LAMP
SMELTING FURNACE
SMOKING CARRIAGE
SNAKE IN THE GRASS
SOAKED TO THE SKIN
SOBER MINDEDNESS
SOCIAL DEMOCRACY
SOCIAL INSURANCE
SOCIAL SECRETARY
SOFT COMMODITIES
SOFT FURNISHINGS
SOFT SHOE SHUFFLE
SOLID STATE LIGHT
SONG AND DANCE MAN
SOUNDED THE ALARM
SOUTH EASTWARDLY
SOUTH WESTWARDLY
SOUTHERN IRELAND
SPACE TRAVELLING
SPANISH CHESTNUT
SPANISH WINDLASS
SPARRING PARTNER
SPEAKING TOO SOON
SPEAKING TRUMPET
SPEAKING VOLUMES
SPECIAL DELIVERY
SPECIAL PLEADING
SPECIAL WARRANTY
SPECIFIC GRAVITY
SPECIFIC IMPULSE
SPILLING A BIBFUL
SPIRAL STAIRCASE
SPLIT INFINITIVE
SPLIT LEVEL HOUSE
SPLITS ONES SIDES
SPOILT FOR CHOICE
SPORTING ONES OAK
SPOT ADVERTISING
SPREAD ONES WINGS
SPRINKLER SYSTEM
SPUR OF THE MOMENT
SQUATTERS RIGHTS
SQUEAKED THROUGH
STABLE COMPANION
STACKING AGAINST
STAGE DOOR JOHNNY
STAGING A PROTEST
STAGNATION POINT
STAKING ONES LIFE
STAMP COLLECTION
STAMP OF APPROVAL
STAMPING MACHINE

STAND OFFISHNESS
STAND ON CEREMONY
STAND ONES GROUND
STAND UP COMEDIAN
STANDARD ENGLISH
STANDING ACCUSED
STANDING AGAINST
STANDING OVATION
STANDING RIGGING
STANDING THE PACE
STANDS CORRECTED
STAPLING MACHINE
STAR OF BETHLEHEM
STARK STARING MAD
STARS AND STRIPES
STATE DEPARTMENT
STATUE OF LIBERTY
STAY OF EXECUTION
STAYED THE COURSE
STEALING THE SHOW
STEALS A MARRIAGE
STEAM NAVIGATION
STEMMING THE TIDE
STICK TO ONES GUNS
STICKING PLASTER
STICKING THE PACE
STICKS AT NOTHING
STICKS ONES OAR IN
STIRS ONES STUMPS
STOCKBROKER BELT
STOCKING FILLERS
STOCKS AND SHARES
STOOD ON CEREMONY
STOOD ONES GROUND
STOP FRAME CAMERA
STOP ME AND BUY ONE
STOPPING THE SHOW
STORAGE CAPACITY
STRADDLE CARRIER
STRAIGHT ACTRESS
STRAIGHT TALKING
STRAIGHTENED OUT
STRAINING A POINT
STRAIT WAISTCOAT
STRANGE TO RELATE
STRAPPED FOR CASH
STRATEGIC METALS
STREET FURNITURE
STRETCH ONES LEGS
STRETCHED A POINT
STRETCHER BEARER
STRETCHES A POINT
STRETCHING FRAME
STRIKE A BAD PATCH
STRIKES A BARGAIN
STRIKING THROUGH
STROLLING PLAYER
STRUCK A BAD PATCH
STRUCTURAL STEEL
STRUTS ONES STUFF

15 contd.

STUBBING ONES TOE
STUBBORN AS A MULE
STUCK TO ONES GUNS
SUBJECT SUPERIOR
SUBSISTANCE WAGE
SUCCESSION HOUSE
SUCKED ONES THUMB
SUGAR PLANTATION
SUGARING THE PILL
SUITING ONES BOOK
SUM AND SUBSTANCE
SUNRISE INDUSTRY
SUPERIOR PLANETS
SURE OF ONES FACTS
SURROGATE MOTHER
SUSPENSE ACCOUNT
SUSTAIN INJURIES
SWAM WITH THE TIDE
SWEEP THE CHIMNEY
SWELLED THE RANKS
SWEPT THE CHIMNEY
SWIM WITH THE TIDE
SWIMMING COSTUME
SWINGING SIXTIES
SWINGING THE LEAD
SWORD AND BUCKLER
SWORD OF DAMOCLES
SYNOPTIC GOSPELS
SYSTEMS ANALYSIS
TABLE DECORATION
TABLEAUX VIVANTS
TABLES AND CHAIRS
TAKE A DEEP BREATH
TAKE A NAME IN VAIN
TAKE FRENCH LEAVE
TAKE INTO ACCOUNT
TAKE IT LYING DOWN
TAKE IT ON THE CHIN
TAKE IT OR LEAVE IT
TAKE NO PRISONERS
TAKE SOME BEATING
TAKE THE CHILL OFF
TAKE THE WRAPS OFF
TAKE UPON ONESELF
TAKEN FOR GRANTED
TAKES A RAINCHECK
TAKES FOR GRANTED
TAKES ONES CHANCE
TAKES ONES CHOICE
TAKES THE BISCUIT
TAKES UP THE SLACK
TAKING A BACK SEAT
TAKING EXCEPTION
TAKING IN LODGERS
TAKING LIBERTIES
TAKING ONES LEAVE
TAKING THE LID OFF
TAKING THE MICKEY
TAKING THE PLUNGE

TAKING TO ONES BED
TAKING TO THE ROAD
TALKED IN RIDDLES
TALKS IN A WHISPER
TATTERSALL CHECK
TEACHING MACHINE
TEARING ONES HAIR
TEARS OF LAUGHTER
TELEPHONE NUMBER
TELESCOPIC SIGHT
TELLING THE TRUTH
TEMPERANCE HOTEL
TEN COMMANDMENTS
TENDER HEARTEDLY
TENSILE STRENGTH
TERMINAL ILLNESS
TERRITORIAL ARMY
TERTIARY COLLEGE
TEUTONIC KNIGHTS
THANKSGIVING DAY
THATCHED COTTAGE
THE BACK OF BEYOND
THE BRIGHT LIGHTS
THE CHIPS ARE DOWN
THE CHOSEN PEOPLE
THE COAST IS CLEAR
THE COMMON PEOPLE
THE COMMONWEALTH
THE END OF THE ROAD
THE FOUR FREEDOMS
THE FOURTH ESTATE
THE GLOVES ARE OFF
THE GOOD SHEPHERD
THE GREEK CALENDS
THE HOW AND THE WHY
THE LOW COUNTRIES
THE MERRY MONARCH
THE MORNING AFTER
THE PLOT THICKENS
THE POWERS THAT BE
THE PROMISED LAND
THE SAME OLD STORY
THE SKYS THE LIMIT
THE SPORT OF KINGS
THE SUPREME BEING
THE WEAKER VESSEL
THE WEIRD SISTERS
THE WORSE FOR WEAR
THIN ON THE GROUND
THINK BETTER OF IT
THINK LITTLE OF IT
THINKING OUT LOUD
THINKING THROUGH
THIRD DEGREE BURN
THORN IN THE FLESH
THOUGHT THE WORST
THREE DAY EVENTER
THREE LEGGED RACE
THREE PIECE SUITE
THREE RING CIRCUS

THRESHOLD LIGHTS
THREW IN THE CARDS
THREW IN THE TOWEL
THREW TO THE WINDS
THROUGH THE NIGHT
THROW IN THE CARDS
THROW IN THE TOWEL
THROW TO THE WINDS
THROWING A WOBBLY
THROWING LIGHT ON
THROWN OVERBOARD
THROWS IN ONES LOT
THROWS OVERBOARD
THROWS THE BOOK AT
THROWS UP ONES CAP
THUMBED ONES NOSE
THUMBNAIL SKETCH
TICKET COLLECTOR
TICKET INSPECTOR
TICKLING TO DEATH
TICKLISH PROBLEM
TIGHT ROPE WALKER
TIGHTEN ONES BELT
TILT AT WINDMILLS
TIME ZONE DISEASE
TIME ZONE FATIGUE
TIP OF THE ICEBERG
TIPPED CIGARETTE
TIPPED THE SCALES
TIPPING THE SCALE
TO THE MANNER BORN
TOM DICK AND HARRY
TOO CLEVER BY HALF
TOO GOOD TO BE TRUE
TOOK A DEEP BREATH
TOOK A NAME IN VAIN
TOOK FRENCH LEAVE
TOOK INTO ACCOUNT
TOOK IT LYING DOWN
TOOK IT ON THE CHIN
TOOK NO PRISONERS
TOOK SOME BEATING
TOOK THE CHILL OFF
TOOK THE WRAPS OFF
TOOK UPON ONESELF
TOP OF THE MORNING
TORQUE CONVERTER
TOSSING THE CABER
TOTAL ABSTINENCE
TOUGH AS OLD BOOTS
TOWER OF STRENGTH
TRADITIONAL JAZZ
TRAINING COLLEGE
TRANSISTOR RADIO
TRANSVERSE FLUTE
TRAVELLERS TALES
TRAVELLING CLOCK
TREADS THE BOARDS
TREATED LIKE DIRT
TREE OF KNOWLEDGE

15 *contd.*

TREMBLING POPLAR
TRIAL OF STRENGTH
TRIANGULAR PRISM
TRICK OF THE TRADE
TRIGEMINAL NERVE
TRUE HEARTEDNESS
TRY ONES PATIENCE
TURN IN ON ONESELF
TURN ON A SIXPENCE
TURNED A BLIND EYE
TURNED INSIDE OUT
TURNED THE CORNER
TURNED THE TABLES
TURNING A DEAF EAR
TURNING ONES HEAD
TURNING THE SCREW
TURNING UP TRUMPS
TURNS ON ONES HEEL
TURNS ONES HAND TO
TURNS THE STOMACH
TURNS UP ONES NOSE
TWENTY FOUR HOURS
ULTRAVIOLET RAYS
ULTRAVIOLET STAR
UNDER LOCK AND KEY
UNDER PRIVILEGED
UNDER PRODUCTION
UNDER THE COUNTER
UNDER THE WEATHER
UNFAIR ADVANTAGE
UNFURNISHED FLAT
UNITED PROVINCES
UNKNOWN QUANTITY
UNLUCKY THIRTEEN
UNSKILLED LABOUR
UPPER ATMOSPHERE
VANILLA ICE CREAM
VEGETABLE GARDEN
VEGETABLE MARROW
VENTS ONES SPLEEN
VERTEBRAL COLUMN
VERTICAL TAKE OFF
VICE CHAMBERLAIN
VICTUALLING BILL
VICTUALLING SHIP
VICTUALLING YARD
VIRGIN PARCHMENT
VIRGINIA CREEPER
VITAL STATISTICS

VITAMIN B COMPLEX
VOLUNTARY MUSCLE
VOLUNTARY SCHOOL
WAISTCOAT POCKET
WAITED PATIENTLY
WALKED UP AND DOWN
WALKING ON TIPTOE
WALKING THE PLANK
WALKS A TIGHT ROPE
WALKS THE STREETS
WALL STREET CRASH
WALRUS MOUSTACHE
WALTZING MATILDA
WARM HEARTEDNESS
WASHED ONES HANDS
WASHED OVERBOARD
WASHING UP LIQUID
WASTE NOT WANT NOT
WATCHED ONES STEP
WATCHED THE CLOCK
WATCHES ONES STEP
WATCHES THE CLOCK
WATER ON THE BRAIN
WEAR SEVERAL HATS
WEAR THE BREECHES
WEAR THE TROUSERS
WEATHER BOARDING
WEATHER FORECAST
WEATHER THE STORM
WEATHERING ALONG
WEDDING CEREMONY
WEIGHING MACHINE
WELCOMING ABOARD
WELL CONDITIONED
WELL INTENTIONED
WELL UPHOLSTERED
WENT OVER THE EDGE
WENT OVER THE WALL
WENT UNDERGROUND
WET THE BABYS HEAD
WETS ONES WHISTLE
WHATS YOUR POISON
WHIRLING DERVISH
WHISTLE AND FLUTE
WHISTLE STOP TOUR
WHITE RHINOCEROS
WHITECHAPEL CART
WHITED SEPULCHRE
WHITER THAN WHITE
WHITES OF THE EYES

WIELD THE SCEPTRE
WIENER SCHNITZEL
WILLOW PATTERNED
WIN BY A SHORT HEAD
WINCHESTER RIFLE
WIND CHILL FACTOR
WINDOW GARDENING
WINDSCREEN WIPER
WINES AND SPIRITS
WINING AND DINING
WINNING ON POINTS
WINNING THE POOLS
WIRELESS STATION
WISH YOU WERE HERE
WISHFUL THINKING
WITCHES CAULDRON
WITH A DIFFERENCE
WITH BATED BREATH
WITH COMPLIMENTS
WITHDRAWING ROOM
WITHOUT CEREMONY
WITHOUT THINKING
WOMAN OF THE WORLD
WOMANS INTUITION
WON BY A SHORT HEAD
WONDER MONGERING
WOODY NIGHTSHADE
WORE SEVERAL HATS
WORE THE BREECHES
WORE THE TROUSERS
WORK LIKE A TROJAN
WORK ONES PASSAGE
WORKED THE ORACLE
WORKING MAJORITY
WORKING ONES WILL
WORKS LIKE A CHARM
WORLD WITHOUT END
WORMED ONES WAY IN
WORTH THE WHISTLE
WRIT OF PRIVILEGE
WRITE ONESELF OFF
WRONG HEADEDNESS
WROTE ONESELF OFF
XMAS DECORATIONS
YELLOW BRICK ROAD
YELLOW PIMPERNEL
YOU CANT WIN EM ALL
YOU NEVER CAN TELL
YOURS FAITHFULLY
YOUTH HOSTELLING